THE
PUBLIC GENERAL ACTS

AND CHURCH ASSEMBLY MEASURES

1969

with
Lists of the Public General Acts
and Local Acts
and a Table of the Effect of Legislation
and an Index

PART II

LONDON
HER MAJESTY'S STATIONERY OFFICE
1970
PRICE £10 10s. 0d. [£10·50] NET
(for both parts)

Printed by C. H. BAYLIS.
Controller of Her Majesty's Stationery Office and
Queen's Printer of Acts of Parliament

SBN 11 840044 4

c

The Public General Acts
and Church Assembly Measures
which received the Royal Assent in 1969
in which year ended the SEVENTEENTH
and began the EIGHTEENTH YEAR
of the Reign of HER MAJESTY
QUEEN ELIZABETH THE SECOND
and
ended the Third Session
and began the Fourth Session
of the Forty-Fourth Parliament of the
United Kingdom of Great Britain
and Northern Ireland

e

CONTENTS

PART II

CONTENTS

PART III

TABLE I

Alphabetical List of

the Public General Acts of 1969

TABLE II

Chronological List of

the Public General Acts of 1969

* Consolidation Act.

* Consolidation Act.

TABLE III

Alphabetical List of

the Local and Personal Acts of 1969

TABLE IV

Chronological List of

the Church Assembly Measures of 1969

Measures passed by the National Assembly of the Church of England
which received the Royal Assent during the year 1969

No. 1.   Clergy Pensions (Amendment) Measure 1969.
No. 2.   Synodical Government Measure 1969.

Nurses Act 1969

1969 CHAPTER 47

An Act to amend the Nurses Act 1957 and the Nurses
(Scotland) Act 1951.   [25th July 1969]

BE IT ENACTED by the Queen's most Excellent Majesty, by and
with the advice and consent of the Lords Spiritual and
Temporal, and Commons, in this present Parliament
assembled, and by the authority of the same, as follows:—

1.—(1) The following subsection shall be substituted for sub-section (1) of section 2 of the Nurses Act 1957 (duty of the Council to maintain the register and the roll of nurses):—   *Registration and enrolment of mental nurses and nurses for the mentally subnormal.*
1957 c. 15.
1919 c. 94.

" (1) It shall be the duty of the Council—

(*a*) to maintain, in accordance with rules in that behalf
made by them, the register of nurses established in
pursuance of the Nurses Registration Act, 1919,
which shall consist of—

(i) a general part containing the names of all
nurses who satisfy the conditions of admission
thereto ;

(ii) a part containing the names of nurses
trained in the nursing and care of persons
suffering from mental disorder other than severe
subnormality or subnormality ;

(iii) a part containing the names of nurses
trained in the nursing and care of persons
suffering from severe subnormality or subnormality ;

(iv) a part containing the names of nurses
trained in the nursing of sick children ; and

(v) such other parts as may be prescribed :

2 K

1943 c. 17.

(b) to maintain, in accordance with rules in that behalf made by them and by the name of the roll of nurses, the roll established in pursuance of Part I of the Nurses Act, 1943, which shall consist of

(i) a general part containing the names of all nurses who satisfy the conditions of admission thereto ;

(ii) a part containing the names of nurses trained in the nursing and care of persons suffering from mental disorder other than severe subnormality or subnormality ;

(iii) a part containing the names of nurses trained in the nursing and care of persons suffering from severe subnormality or subnormality ;

(iv) such other parts as may be prescribed."

1957 c. 15.

(2) In section 27 of the Nurses Act 1957 (penalties for false assumption of title of registered or enrolled nurse, etc.), the following paragraph shall be substituted for paragraph (b) of subsection (1) : —

" (b) being a person whose name is included in any part or parts of the register but not in another part, takes or uses any name, title, addition, description, uniform or badge, or otherwise does any act of any kind, implying that his name is included in that other part ; or "

and the following paragraph shall be inserted after paragraph (a) of subsection (2) : —

" (aa) being a person whose name is included in any part or parts of the roll but not in another part, takes or uses any name, title, addition, description, uniform or badge, or otherwise does any act of any kind implying that his name is included in that other part ; or "

Constitution of General Nursing Council for England and Wales.

2.—(1) Paragraph 1 of Schedule 1 to the Nurses Act 1957 (constitution of Council) shall be amended as follows : —

(a) in sub-paragraph (a) (elected members) for the word " eighteen " there shall be substituted the word " twenty-two " ;

(b) in sub-paragraph (b) (members appointed by Secretary of State) for the word " thirteen " there shall be substituted the word " fourteen " ;

(c) in sub-paragraph (c) (members appointed by Secretary of State for Education and Science) for the word " three " there shall be substituted the word " two " ;

(*d*) at the end of the paragraph there shall be added the following sub-paragraphs: —

" (*e*) one person, who shall be a certified midwife within the meaning of the Midwives Act 1951 en- 1951 c. 53. gaged in the teaching of obstetrics to persons undergoing the prescribed training for admission to the register, appointed by the Central Midwives Board after consultation with persons and bodies having special knowledge and experience of the work of midwives so engaged ; and

(*f*) one person, who shall be both a registered nurse and a health visitor engaged in or concerned with the teaching of persons undergoing the prescribed training for admission to the register or to the roll, appointed by the Council for the Training of Health Visitors after consultation with persons and bodies having special knowledge and experience of the work of registered nurses and health visitors so engaged."

(2) For paragraph 2(1) of that Schedule there shall be substituted the following: —

" (1) Of the elected members of the Council—

(*a*) fifteen, who shall be registered general nurses, shall be elected by persons (hereinafter referred to as ' the general electors ') who, on the prescribed date, are registered general nurses or nurses registered in any part of the register prescribed under section 2(1)(*a*)(v) of this Act ;

(*b*) three shall be registered mental nurses elected by persons who, on the prescribed date, are registered mental nurses ;

(*c*) one shall be a registered nurse for the mentally subnormal elected by persons who, on the prescribed date, are registered nurses for the mentally subnormal ;

(*d*) one shall be a registered sick children's nurse elected by persons who, on the prescribed date, are registered sick children's nurses ;

(*e*) one shall be an enrolled general nurse, who shall be elected by persons who, on the prescribed date, are enrolled general nurses or nurses enrolled in any part of the roll prescribed under section 2(1)(*b*)(iv) of this Act ; and

(*f*) one shall be an enrolled mental nurse or an enrolled nurse for the mentally subnormal, who shall

2 K 2

be elected by persons who, on the prescribed date, are enrolled mental nurses or enrolled nurses for the mentally subnormal."

(3) For paragraph 2(2) of that Schedule there shall be substituted the following:—

" (2)(*a*) For the purposes of the election of the fifteen nurses mentioned in head (*a*) of the foregoing sub-paragraph, England and Wales shall be divided into fifteen areas determined by the Secretary of State and one of those nurses shall be elected for each area.

(*b*) Each of the nurses elected under the foregoing sub-paragraph shall, on the date fixed for the purpose of the election as the last date for the receipt of nomination papers, be engaged in work for which the employment of a registered nurse or an enrolled nurse, as the case may be, is requisite or for which a registered nurse or an enrolled nurse, as the case may be, is commonly employed ; and, in the case of the fifteen nurses elected under head (*a*) of the foregoing sub-paragraph, shall on the said date be so engaged in the area for which he is elected."

(4) For paragraph 3 of that Schedule there shall be substituted the following:—

" 3. Of the members of the Council appointed under paragraph 1(*b*) of this Schedule—

(*a*) two shall be registered medical practitioners engaged from time to time in teaching persons undergoing training prescribed for admission to the general part of the register, appointed by the Secretary of State after consultation with persons and bodies having special knowledge and experience of the work of medical practitioners so engaged ;

(*b*) one shall be a registered medical practitioner engaged from time to time in teaching persons undergoing training prescribed for admission to a part of the register containing the names of nurses trained in the nursing and care of persons suffering from mental disorder, appointed by the Secretary of State after consultation with persons and bodies having special knowledge and experience of the work of medical practitioners so engaged ;

(*c*) two shall be registered nurses engaged in training persons undergoing training prescribed for admission to the general part of the roll, appointed by the Secretary of State after consultation with persons and bodies having special knowledge and experience of the work of nurses so engaged ;

(*d*) two shall be registered nurses engaged in training persons undergoing training prescribed for admission to a part of the roll containing the names of nurses trained in the nursing and care of persons suffering from mental disorder, appointed by the Secretary of State after consultation with persons and bodies having special knowledge and experience of the work of nurses so engaged ;

(*e*) one shall be a registered nurse employed in services provided under section 25 of the National Health 1946 c. 81. Service Act 1946 and engaged in teaching persons undergoing the prescribed training for admission to the register or to the roll, appointed by the Secretary of State after consultation with persons and bodies having special knowledge and experience in the work of nurses so employed ; and

(*f*) two shall be persons engaged in the control and management of hospitals, appointed by the Secretary of State after consultation with persons and bodies having special knowledge and experience of such control and management."

(5) In paragraph 6(1) of that Schedule for the words from " if the member was appointed " to " as the case may be " there shall be substituted the words " if he was an appointed member, be filled by a person appointed by the Secretary of State or body that appointed him ".

3.—(1) Paragraph 1 of Schedule 1 to the Nurses (Scotland) Constitution Act 1951 (constitution of the General Nursing Council for of General Scotland) shall be amended as follows :— Nursing Council for
        Scotland.

(*a*) in sub-paragraph (*a*) (elected members) for the word Scotland. " thirteen " there shall be substituted the word " four- 1951 c. 55. teen " ;

(*b*) in sub-paragraph (*b*) (members appointed by the Secretary of State) for the word " eleven " there shall be substituted the word " twelve ".

(2) For paragraph 2 of that Schedule there shall be substituted the following :—

" 2.—(1) Of the elected members of the Council—

(*a*) six, who shall be registered general nurses, shall be elected by registered general nurses or nurses registered in any part of the register prescribed under section 2(2)(*f*) of this Act ;

(b) two, who shall be registered mental nurses, shall be elected by nurses so registered, and one of the persons so elected shall be a man and one a woman ;

(c) one, who shall be a registered nurse for mental defectives, shall be elected by nurses so registered ;

(d) one, who shall be a registered sick children's nurse, shall be elected by nurses so registered ;

(e) two, who shall be persons holding certificates given by virtue of section 6(1)(f) of this Act (which provides for the giving of certificates to persons trained in the teaching of nursing), shall be elected by such persons ;

(f) two, who shall be enrolled nurses, shall be elected by enrolled nurses.

(2) Each of the nurses elected under the foregoing sub-paragraph shall, on the date fixed for the purpose of the election as the last date for the receipt of nomination papers, be engaged in Scotland in work for which the employment of a registered nurse or an enrolled nurse, as the case may be, is requisite or for which a registered nurse or an enrolled nurse, as the case may be, is commonly employed."

The Mental Nurses Committees.
1957 c. 15.

4.—(1) The following shall be substituted for subsections (1) and (2) of section 18 of the Nurses Act 1957 :—

" (1) The Council shall appoint a Mental Nurses Committee consisting of—

(a) such number of persons, being members of the Council, as may be prescribed ; and

(b) such persons other than members of the Council, not exceeding four in number, as may be nominated by the Secretary of State, after consultation with the Council, for appointment to the Committee ;

a majority of whom shall be nurses who are registered mental nurses or registered nurses for the mentally subnormal.

(2) The term of office of the members of the Mental Nurses Committee shall be such as may be prescribed, and rules made by the Council may provide for the selection of a chairman of the Committee, the summoning of meetings and any matter relating to its proceedings."

(2) In subsection (3) of that section (matters to be referred to the Committee) the following paragraphs shall be substituted for paragraphs (a) and (b)—

" (*a*) any matter which wholly or mainly concerns registered or enrolled mental nurses or registered or enrolled nurses for the mentally subnormal (other than a question whether a person shall be registered or enrolled or shall be removed from or restored to the register or the roll or a matter arising out of any such question) ; and

(*b*) any matter relating to the training of persons for admission to a part of the register or roll containing the names of nurses trained in the nursing and care of persons suffering from mental disorder ; ".

(3) The following shall be substituted for subsections (1) and (3) of section 5 of the Nurses (Scotland) Act 1951 : —   1951 c. 55

" (1) The Council shall appoint a Mental Nurses Committee consisting of—

(*a*) such number of persons, being members of the Council, as may be prescribed ; and

(*b*) such persons other than members of the Council, not exceeding four in number, as may be nominated by the Secretary of State, after consultation with the Council, for appointment to the Committee ;

a majority of whom shall be nurses who are either registered mental nurses or registered nurses for mental defectives.

(3) The term of office of the members of the Mental Nurses Committee shall be as may be prescribed."

5. The Enrolled Nurses Committee established by section 3 of the Nurses Act 1943 and the Enrolled Nurses Committee established by section 3 of the Nurses (Scotland) Act 1943 (which were so named by section 1(1) of the Nurses (Amendment) Act 1961) shall cease to exist on the coming into operation of section 2 and section 3 of this Act respectively.

Abolition of Enrolled Nurses Committees. 1943 c. 17. 1943 c. 33. 1961 c. 14.

6. An area nurse-training committee or (in Scotland) a regional nurse-training committee may (without an order under Schedule 2 to the Nurses Act 1957 or Schedule 4 to the Nurses (Scotland) Act 1951) make to its members and the members of any subcommittee of that committee such payments in respect of any loss of earnings they would otherwise have made or any additional expenses (including travelling and subsistence expenses) to which they would not otherwise have been subject, being loss or expenses necessarily suffered or incurred by them for the purpose of enabling them to perform duties as members of the committee or sub-committee, as the case may be, as the Secretary of State may, with the approval of the Minister for the Civil Service, from time to time determine.

Allowances to members of nurse-training committee or sub-committee thereof. 1957 c. 15.

2 K 4

Fees.
1957 c. 15.
1951 c. 55.

7.—(1) Rules made under section 3(1) of the Nurses Act 1957 or under section 6(1) of the Nurses (Scotland) Act 1951 may contain provisions requiring, as a condition of the recognition of any person as a person who has undergone the prescribed training, the payment by him to the Council, within such period after beginning the training as may be prescribed, of such fee as the Council may, with the approval of the Secretary of State, from time to time determine.

(2) A fee may be prescribed under section 4(1) of the Nurses Act 1957 or under section 7(1) of the Nurses (Scotland) Act 1951 (registration of nurses trained abroad) in respect of an application to be registered under that section as well as in respect of such a registration ; and accordingly in each of those subsections the words " on an application made in the prescribed manner and accompanied by such fee, if any, as may be prescribed " shall be inserted between the words " who " and " proves ", and the words " on making an application in the prescribed manner and " shall be omitted.

Abolition of
duty to publish
periodical lists
of changes in
register, etc.

8. Section 9(2) of the Nurses Act 1957 and section 8(2) of the Nurses (Scotland) Act 1951 (duty of Council to publish lists of changes in the register, the roll or the list) shall cease to have effect.

Interpretation.

9.—(1) Section 33 of the Nurses Act 1957 shall apply for the interpretation of this Act in its application to England and Wales, and section 34 of the Nurses (Scotland) Act 1951 shall apply for the interpretation of this Act in its application to Scotland.

(2) References in this Act to any enactment are references thereto as amended by any other enactment, including, except where the context otherwise requires, this Act.

Minor and
consequential
amendments
and repeals.

10.—(1) The enactments mentioned in Schedule 1 to this Act shall have effect subject to the minor and consequential amendments set out in that Schedule.

(2) The enactments specified in Schedule 2 to this Act are hereby repealed to the extent specified in the third column of that Schedule.

Commencement,
transitional
provisions,
citation and
extent.

11.—(1) The provisions of this Act other than sections 2 to 4 shall come into force one month after the passing of this Act.

(2) Section 2 and subsections (1) and (2) of section 4 of this Act shall not come into force until 22nd September 1970, but without prejudice to the validity of any scheme prescribed, election held or appointment made in pursuance of section 2 before that date.

(3) Sections 3 and 4(3) of this Act shall not come into force until 1st December 1970, but without prejudice to the validity of any scheme prescribed, election held or appointment made in pursuance of section 3 before that date.

(4) Notwithstanding anything in paragraphs 5 and 6 of Schedule 1 to the Nurses Act 1957, the appointed members of the Council shall cease to hold office on 21st September 1970 and— 1957 c. 15.

> (a) if a casual vacancy among the members of the Council occurs in the six months preceding 22nd September 1970 it need not be filled ; and
>
> (b) the members of the Council appointed to take office on 22nd September 1970 shall hold office for three years.

(5) The first additional member of the General Nursing Council for Scotland to be appointed by the Secretary of State by virtue of section 3(1)(b) of this Act shall take office on 1st December 1970 and shall hold office for three years.

(6) This Act may be cited as the Nurses Act 1969 ; and—

> (a) this Act and the Nurses Acts 1957 to 1967 may be cited together as the Nurses Acts 1957 to 1969 ; and
>
> (b) this Act and the Nurses (Scotland) Acts 1951 to 1967 may be cited together as the Nurses (Scotland) Acts 1951 to 1969.

(7) Sections 1 and 2 of this Act do not extend to Scotland and section 3 of this Act extends to Scotland only.

(8) This Act does not extend to Northern Ireland.

SCHEDULES

Section 10(1).

SCHEDULE 1

Minor and Consequential Amendments

1951 c. 55.

The Nurses (Scotland) Act 1951

1. In section 2(4) and section 3(2) of the Nurses (Scotland) Act 1951, for the word " evidence " there shall be substituted the words " sufficient evidence " in each case.

2. In section 11(3) of that Act, for the words " and Third Schedules " there shall be substituted the word " Schedule ".

3. In section 12 of that Act, the following paragraph shall be substituted for paragraph (*b*) of subsection (3):—

"(*b*) being a person whose name is included in any part or parts of the register but not in another part, takes or uses any name, title, addition, description, uniform or badge, or otherwise does any act of any kind, implying that his name is included in that other part ; ".

4. In section 15 of that Act for the words " either of the said Committees " there shall be substituted the words " of the said Committee ".

5. In section 34 of that Act the following definition shall be inserted at the appropriate place :—

" registered general nurse " means a nurse whose name is included in the general part of the register.

1957 c. 15.

The Nurses Act 1957

6. In section 2(2) of the Nurses Act 1957, after the words " a part of the register " there shall be inserted the words " or the roll ".

7. In section 7(4) of that Act for the words " the appropriate authority " there shall be substituted the words " the Council ".

8. In section 8 of that Act—

(*a*) in subsection (1), after the words " the register ", in each place where they occur, there shall be inserted the words " or roll " ;

(*b*) in subsection (2), for the words preceding " and no such request " there shall be substituted the words " No request under the foregoing subsection shall be made by the Council with respect to any part of the register or roll containing the names of nurses trained in the nursing and care of persons suffering from mental disorder of any description unless the Council are satisfied that means exist whereby members of the public can readily ascertain whether a registered or enrolled nurse has been so trained " and

(*c*) at the end of subsection (3) there shall be added the words " or the roll ".

9. In section 31 of that Act, for the words "the part of the register" in the first place where they occur there shall be substituted the words "any part of the register or the roll", after the words "mental disorder" there shall be inserted the words "of any description", and for the words "the First and the Third Schedules" there shall be substituted the words "the First Schedule".

10. In section 33(1) of that Act, in the definition of "registered mental nurse", after the word "disorder" there shall be added the words "other than severe subnormality or subnormality", and the following definitions shall be inserted at the appropriate points:—

"enrolled general nurse" means a nurse whose name is included in the general part of the roll;

"enrolled mental nurse" means a nurse whose name is included in the part of the roll containing the names of nurses trained in the nursing and care of persons suffering from mental disorder other than severe subnormality or subnormality;

"enrolled nurse for the mentally subnormal" means a nurse whose name is included in the part of the roll containing the names of nurses trained in the nursing and care of persons suffering from severe subnormality or subnormality;

"registered general nurse" means a nurse whose name is included in the general part of the register.

"registered nurse for the mentally subnormal" means a nurse whose name is included in the part of the register containing the names of nurses trained in the nursing and care of persons suffering from severe subnormality or subnormality;

"severe subnormality" and "subnormality" have the same meanings respectively as in the Mental Health Act 1959.

11. In section 33(3) of that Act, after the words "the register", in the first place where they occur, there shall be inserted the words "the roll", and after the words "a part of the register" there shall be inserted the words "a part of the roll".

The Nurses (Amendment) Act 1961

12. In section 4 of the Nurses (Amendment) Act 1961, for the words from the beginning to "occurs" there shall be substituted the words "In paragraph 4 of Schedule 1 to the Act of 1957 for the word 'fourteen'".

13. In section 6 of that Act—

(*a*) the words "by the Minister of Health or, as the case may be, the Secretary of State" shall be omitted;

(*b*) for the words "or of his being engaged in the teaching of any subject" there shall be substituted the words "or of his being engaged in or concerned with any kind of teaching or training"; and

(*c*) for the words "the Minister or, as the case may be, the Secretary of State" there shall be substituted the words "the Secretary of State or body that appointed him".

The Nurses Act 1964

14. In section 3 of the Nurses Act 1964, in the definition of " the roll ", there shall be added at the end the words " and includes, unless the context otherwise requires, a part of the roll."

Section 10(2).

SCHEDULE 2

Enactments Repealed

Chapter	Short Title	Extent of Repeal
14 & 15 Geo. 6. c. 55.	The Nurses (Scotland) Act 1951.	Section 4. In section 7(1) the words " on making an application in the prescribed manner and ". Section 8(2). In section 10 the words " or by the Enrolled Nurses Committee, as the case may be,". In section 15 the words " and to the members of the Enrolled Nurses Committee ". In section 33(2) the words " or paragraph 2 of the Third Schedule ". Schedules 2 and 3. In Schedule 4, paragraph 2(c).
5 & 6 Eliz. 2. c. 15.	The Nurses Act 1957.	In section 4(1) the words " on making an application in the prescribed manner and ". In section 7, paragraph (b) of subsection (5), and the word " and " preceding that paragraph. Section 9(2). Section 19. In Schedule 2, paragraph 2(c). Schedules 3 and 4.
7 & 8 Eliz. 2. c. 72.	The Mental Health Act 1959.	In Schedule 7, the entries relating to sections 2, 8 and 18 of and Schedules 1 and 3 to the Nurses Act 1957.
8 & 9 Eliz. 2. c. 61.	The Mental Health (Scotland) Act 1960.	In Schedule 4, the entry relating to Schedule 3 to the Nurses (Scotland) Act 1951.
9 & 10 Eliz. 2. c. 14.	The Nurses (Amendment) Act 1961.	In section 1, in subsection (1) the words from " and the Assistant Nurses Committee " to the end of the subsection, and in subsection (2) the words " the Assistant Nurses Committee " and the words " the Enrolled Nurses Committee ". In section 4, subsections (2) and (3).

Chapter	Short Title	Extent of Repeal
9 & 10 Eliz. 2. c. 14.—*cont.*	The Nurses (Amendment) Act 1961.—*cont.*	In section 6, the words " by the Minister of Health or, as the case may be, the Secretary of State ". Section 7(2)(*b*) and (*c*). In Schedule 1, paragraphs 1, 3, 4, 5, 6, 8, 9, 11, 14 and 16 and, in paragraph 13 and paragraph 15, the words from the beginning to " papers; and ".

Post Office Act 1969

1969 CHAPTER 48

An Act to abolish the office of master of the Post Office, distribute the business conducted by the holder thereof amongst authorities constituted for the purpose and make provision consequential on the abolition of that office and the distribution of the business so conducted; to amend, replace or repeal certain provisions of the enactments relating to posts, telegraphs and savings banks; to amend the law relating to stamp duty; and to empower the Treasury to dispose of their interest in the shares of Cable and Wireless Limited.

[25th July 1969]

BE IT ENACTED by the Queen's most Excellent Majesty, by and with the advice and consent of the Lords Spiritual and Temporal, and Commons, in this present Parliament assembled, and by the authority of the same, as follows:—

PART I

ABOLITION OF OFFICE OF MASTER OF THE POST OFFICE

1.—(1) On such day as Her Majesty may by Order in Council appoint for the purposes of this Act (in this Act referred to as the "appointed day"), the office of master of the Post Office shall cease to exist.

Abolition of office of master of the Post Office.

(2) The following provisions of this Act shall have effect for the purpose of distributing powers and duties, and rights and liabilities, of the person for the time being holder of the office of master of the Post Office and property used or appropriated for use for, or in connection with, the discharge of that person's functions, and of making other provision whereof the making is for the most part rendered necessary or expedient in consequence of the abolition of the office of master of the Post Office.

2 K* 4

Part II

The Minister of Posts and Telecommunications and his Functions

The Minister of Posts and Telecommunications.

2.—(1) It shall be lawful for Her Majesty to appoint (but so that the first appointment made shall not take effect before the appointed day) a Minister of Posts and Telecommunications who shall have—

(a) such of the functions of the Postmaster General as are transferred to him by, or by virtue of, the following provisions of this Act ; and

(b) such functions as are conferred on him by those provisions.

1964 c. 98.

(2) Schedule 1 to the Ministers of the Crown Act 1964 (provisions as to new Ministers and their departments) shall apply (except as provided in subsection (4) below) to the Minister of Posts and Telecommunications, and references in that Schedule to the Minister and the Ministry shall be construed accordingly.

(3) The offices of Minister of Posts and Telecommunications and of Parliamentary Secretary to the Ministry of Posts and Telecommunications shall be included—

1957 c. 20.

(a) among the ministerial offices referred to in section 2 of the House of Commons Disqualification Act 1957 (maximum number of Ministers in the House of Commons) ; and

(b) among the offices in respect of which salaries are payable, at the annual rates of £8,500 and £3,750 respectively, under section 1 of the Ministerial Salaries Consolidation Act 1965.

1965 c. 58.

(4) So much of Schedule 1 to the Ministers of the Crown Act 1964 as provides for the defraying of expenses out of moneys provided by Parliament shall not apply to expenses of the Minister of Posts and Telecommunications consisting in the making by him, in exercise of powers conferred by this Act, of a loan.

1967 c. 13.

(5) Schedule 2 to the Parliamentary Commissioner Act 1967 (which specifies departments and authorities subject to investigation under that Act) shall have effect as if, after the reference to the Ministry of Overseas Development, there were inserted a reference to the Ministry of Posts and Telecommunications.

(6) In the following provisions of this Act, " the Minister " means the Minister of Posts and Telecommunications, but anything done before the appointed day by the Postmaster General

in exercise of any power or duty conferred or imposed on the Minister by, or by virtue of, the following provisions of this Act shall be as valid and effective for all purposes as if it had been done by the Minister, and anything done before that day to the Postmaster General by any other person in exercise of a power so conferred on him shall be as valid and effective as if it had been done to the Minister.

(7) In consequence of subsection (3) above—

(a) in Schedule 2 to the House of Commons Disqualification Act 1957, immediately before the words " Minister of Power " there shall be inserted the words " Minister of Posts and Telecommunications " and immediately before the words " Parliamentary Secretary to the Ministry of Power " there shall be inserted the words " Parliamentary Secretary to the Ministry of Posts and Telecommunications " ; and

1957 c. 20.

(b) in Schedule 1 to the Ministerial Salaries Consolidation Act 1965, immediately before the entry relating to the Minister of Power there shall be inserted the following entry—

1965 c. 58.

> " Minister of Posts and Telecommunications ... £8,500 ",

and immediately before the entry (under the heading " Parliamentary Secretaries ") relating to the Ministry of Power there shall be inserted the following entry—

> " Ministry of Posts and Telecommunications ... £3,750 ".

3.—(1) The functions which, immediately before the appointed day, are vested in the Postmaster General by virtue of the following provisions, namely,—

Transfer to the Minister of the Postmaster General's functions with respect to wireless telegraphy, and provisions consequential thereon.

(a) those of the Wireless Telegraphy Act 1949 which remain in force on and after that day and those of the Wireless Telegraphy Act 1967 ; and

(b) those of the Television Act 1964 ;

shall, on that day, vest in the Minister ; and, accordingly, as from that day,—

1949 c. 54.
1967 c. 72.
1964 c. 21.

(i) references in those provisions to the Postmaster General (except those in section 5 of the Wireless Telegraphy Act 1967), and the first reference to him in section 24(4) of the Merchant Shipping (Safety and Load Line Conventions) Act 1932 (report of dangers to navigation) shall be construed as referring to the Minister, and references to the Postmaster General in the said section 5, the second and third references to him in the said section 24(4) and the references to him in section 9(3)

1932 c. 9.

Pᴀʀᴛ II
1952 c. 66.
1955 c. 11
(N.I.).

1949 c. 54.
1967 c. 72.

1961 c. 15.

of the Defamation Act 1952 (extension to broadcasting of certain defences) and of the Defamation Act (Northern Ireland) 1955 shall be construed as including references to the Minister ; and

(ii) any reference to the Postmaster General in a provision of regulations, rules or a licence under the Wireless Telegraphy Act 1949 or the Wireless Telegraphy Act 1967 which is in force at the beginning of that day shall (unless the context otherwise requires) be construed as referring to the Minister and any reference to an officer of the Post Office in any such provision shall (unless the context otherwise requires) be construed as referring to a person acting under the authority of the Minister.

(2) As from the appointed day,—

(*a*) section 2(1) of the Wireless Telegraphy Act 1949 (fees and charges for wireless telegraphy licences) shall, subject to the foregoing subsection, have effect as originally enacted, and not as amended by section 16(4) of the Post Office Act 1961 (which dispenses, in certain cases, with the requirement of the consent of the Treasury to the making of regulations under the first-mentioned section) ;

(*b*) Schedule 1 to the Wireless Telegraphy Act 1949 (procedure in relation to suspension and revocation of authorities to wireless personnel) shall have effect with the substitution, for paragraph 3 thereof, of the following paragraph : —

" 3.—(1) There shall be paid by the Minister of Posts and Telecommunications—

(*a*) the expenses, to such extent as he may determine, incurred by an advisory committee under this Schedule ; and

(*b*) such sums as he may determine in respect of the expenses of the members of the committee.

(2) The approval of the Treasury shall be requisite to a determination under head (*a*) of the foregoing sub-paragraph and that of the Minister for the Civil Service to a determination under head (*b*) of that sub-paragraph ".

(3) The Minister shall, as from the appointed day, have power to make, in such cases or classes of cases as the Treasury may determine, refunds of sums paid under section 2(1) of the Wireless Telegraphy Act 1949 (fees and charges for wireless telegraphy licences).

(4) A payment made in exercise of the power conferred by the last foregoing subsection shall be defrayed out of sums received under the Wireless Telegraphy Act 1949 by the Minister.

PART II

1949 c. 54.

(5) The surplus of sums received under the Wireless Telegraphy Act 1949 by the Minister over sums paid in exercise of the power conferred by subsection (3) above shall from time to time be paid into the Consolidated Fund of the United Kingdom (hereafter in this Act referred to as the " Consolidated Fund "), and any sums received under section 11(4) of the Wireless Telegraphy Act 1967 by the Minister shall be so paid.

1967 c. 72

(6) Section 20(3) of the Wireless Telegraphy Act 1949 (power of Her Majesty in Council to extend that Act to the Isle of Man and the Channel Islands) shall have effect as if the reference to that Act included a reference to the foregoing provisions of this section, and section 36 of the Merchant Shipping (Safety and Load Line Conventions) Act 1932 (application of Part I of that Act to British possessions) shall have effect as if any reference to that Part included a reference to the said provisions.

1932 c. 9.

4. The functions which are vested in the Postmaster General by virtue of section 6 of the Commonwealth Telegraphs Act 1949 (provisions as to pensions of employees of Cable and Wireless Limited and certain other persons) shall, on the appointed day, vest in the Minister ; and, accordingly, as from that day, references in that section to the Postmaster General shall be construed as referring to the Minister.

Transfer to the Minister of the Postmaster General's functions under section 6 of the Commonwealth Telegraphs Act 1949

1949 c. 39.

5. The power conferred by subsection (3) of section 1 of the Recorded Delivery Service Act 1962 on the Postmaster General by order to make such amendments of enactments contained in local or private Acts as appear to him to be necessary or expedient in consequence of subsection (1) of that section shall, on the appointed day, vest in the Minister ; and, accordingly, as from that day, the reference to the Postmaster General in the said subsection (3) and the reference to him in subsection (4) of that section (which lays on him a duty of consultation before making an order under subsection (3)) shall each be construed as referring to the Minister.

Transfer to the Minister of the Postmaster General's power to make orders under the Recorded Delivery Service Act 1962.

1962 c. 27.

PART III

THE NEW AUTHORITY FOR THE CONDUCT OF POSTAL AND TELEGRAPHIC BUSINESS

The Post Office

6.—(1) There shall be established a public authority, to be called the Post Office, which shall have such powers and duties as are conferred and imposed on it by, or by virtue of, the following provisions of this Act ; so, however, that, until the

The Post Office.

appointed day, the purpose for which its powers are exercised shall be restricted to the preparation for the assumption by it of functions theretofore discharged by the Postmaster General.

(2) The Post Office shall consist of a chairman and, to a number not exceeding twelve nor falling short of—

> (a) three, as regards the period beginning with the day on which this Act is passed and ending with the day immediately preceding the appointed day ; and

> (b) six, after the expiration of that period,

of other members, whether part-time or full-time.

(3) The chairman of the Post Office shall be appointed by the Minister, and the other members of the Post Office shall be appointed by the Minister after consultation with the chairman.

(4) Schedule 1 to this Act shall have effect as respects the Post Office and the members thereof.

(5) It is hereby declared that the Post Office is not to be regarded as the servant or agent of the Crown, or as enjoying any status, immunity or privilege of the Crown, or (subject to the express provisions of this Act relating to stamp duty) as exempt from any tax, duty, rate, levy or other charge whatsoever, whether general or local, and that its property is not to be regarded as property of, or property held on behalf of, the Crown.

Powers and Duties of the Post Office

Powers of the Post Office.

7.—(1) The Post Office shall have power—

> (a) to provide postal services (including cash on delivery services) and telecommunication services ;

> (b) to provide a banking service of the kind commonly known as a giro system and such other services by means of which money may be remitted (whether by means of money orders, postal orders or otherwise) as it thinks fit ;

> (c) to provide data processing services ; and

> (d) to perform services for Her Majesty's Government in the United Kingdom, Her Majesty's Government in Northern Ireland or the government of a country or territory outside the United Kingdom or for local or national health service authorities in the United Kingdom.

(2) The Post Office shall have power, for the purpose of securing the effective exercise of any of the powers conferred on it by the foregoing subsection, or in connection with or in consequence of an exercise thereof, to do anything that appears

to the Post Office to be requisite, advantageous or convenient for it to do, including in particular (but without prejudice to the generality of the foregoing words) power—

(a) to construct, manufacture, produce, purchase, take on hire or hire-purchase, install, maintain and repair anything required for the purposes of its business or of the business of a subsidiary of its;

(b) to construct, manufacture, produce or purchase for supply to others any articles of a kind similar to any so required and to install, maintain, repair and test for others articles of such a kind;

(c) to provide others with the services of persons employed by it for the purpose of undertaking for them tasks of a kind which, in the course of the provision or performance by it of any service falling within the foregoing subsection, are undertaken by persons so employed;

(d) to provide, for the benefit of others, consultancy and advisory services concerning anything that it does in exercise of its powers or has power to do and facilities for the training of persons for any purpose connected with anything that it so does or has power to do;

(e) to enter into and carry out agreements with any person for the carrying on by him, whether as its agent or otherwise, of any of the activities which itself may carry on or for the carrying on jointly by him and it of any of those activities;

(f) to acquire land which is required by it for, or in connection with, the exercise of its powers or as to which it can reasonably be foreseen that it will be so required;

(g) to dispose (whether absolutely or for a term of years) of any part of its undertaking or any property which in its opinion is not required by it for or in connection with the exercise of its powers, and, in particular, to dispose of an interest in, or right over, any property which, subject to the interest or right, is retained by it;

(h) for the purposes of its business, to subscribe for or acquire any securities of an incorporated company or other body corporate, to procure its admission to membership of an incorporated company limited by guarantee and not having a share capital, to promote the formation of an incorporated company or participate in the promotion of such a company or to acquire an undertaking or part of an undertaking;

(i) to give or lend money to, or give a guarantee for the benefit of, any person with whom it has entered into an agreement by virtue of paragraph (e) above for the purpose of enabling him to carry out the agreement and, for the purposes of its business, to give or lend money to, or give a guarantee for the benefit of, any other person for the purposes of an undertaking carried on by him or, where that person is a body corporate, an undertaking carried on by a subsidiary of its ;

(j) to do anything for the purpose of advancing the skill of persons employed by it or that of persons who, though not so employed, are engaging themselves, or have it in contemplation to engage themselves, in work of a kind in the case of which it has or may have a direct or indirect concern in the products thereof ;

(k) to promote (either by prosecuting it itself or by its promoting it by others) research into matters which affect, or arise out of, the carrying on of its business, or other matters which, though not such as aforesaid, are such as to which it appears to it that advantage will or may accrue to it as a consequence of research's being prosecuted into them ;

(l) to promote the doing of such work as is requisite to enable there to be turned to account—

(i) the results of research (whether promoted by it or not) into matters affecting, or arising out of, the carrying on of its business ;

(ii) the results of research promoted by it into other matters ;

(m) to provide assistance (including financial assistance) to any institution or body whose activities (or any of them) are such as, in its opinion, to be of benefit to it ;

(n) to carry for hire or reward passengers in vehicles used by it for the purposes of its business ;

(o) to enter into, and carry out, agreements with persons who carry on business as carriers of goods, for the carriage by it on their behalf of goods consigned to them for carriage by them ;

(p) to provide houses, hostels and other like accommodation for persons engaged in its business ;

(q) to make loans to persons employed by it (including, in particular, loans to assist them to acquire housing accommodation) and to guarantee loans made to persons so employed (including, in particular, loans made by building societies and other bodies for housing purposes) ;

(r) to promote recreational activities for, and activities conducing to the welfare of, persons who are, or have been, engaged in its business or have been officers, servants or agents of the Postmaster General and the families of such persons and to assist the promotion by others of such activities ;

and may turn its resources to account so far as not required for the purposes of its business.

(3) For the avoidance of doubt, it is hereby declared that the foregoing provisions of this section relate only to the capacity of the Post Office as a statutory corporation, and nothing in those provisions shall be construed as authorising the disregard by it of any enactment or rule of law.

(4) The Post Office shall not be regarded as a common carrier in respect of any of its activities.

(5) The provisions of this section shall not be construed as limiting any power of the Post Office conferred by or under any subsequent provision of this Act.

(6) Nothing in this section shall be taken to confine the exercise of the powers thereby conferred on the Post Office to the British Islands.

8. The Post Office shall have power—

(*a*) to furnish any authority or person outside the United Kingdom with assistance (whether financial, technical or of any other nature) if, in its opinion, the consequences of doing so will enure for its benefit ;

(*b*) to enter into, and carry out, agreements with the Minister of Overseas Development whereunder it acts, at the expense of that Minister, as the instrument by means whereof technical assistance is furnished by him in exercise of the power conferred on him by section 1(1) of the Overseas Aid Act 1966

9.—(1) It shall be the duty of the Post Office (consistently with any directions given to it under the following provisions of this Part of this Act) so to exercise its powers as to meet the social, industrial and commercial needs of the British Islands in regard to matters that are subserved by those powers and, in particular, to provide throughout those Islands (save in so far as the provision thereof is, in its opinion, impracticable or not reasonably practicable) such services for the conveyance of letters and such telephone services as satisfy all reasonable demands for them.

(2) In discharging the duty imposed on it by the foregoing subsection, the Post Office shall have regard—

(*a*) to the desirability of improving and developing its operating systems ;

(*b*) to developments in the field of communications ; and

(*c*) to efficiency and economy.

(3) Subsection (1) above shall not be taken to preclude the Post Office from interrupting, suspending or restricting, in case of emergency, any service provided by it.

(4) Nothing in this section shall be construed as imposing upon the Post Office, either directly or indirectly, any form of duty or liability enforceable by proceedings before any court.

Power to promote and oppose Bills, &c.

1936 c. 52.

10. The Post Office may, with the consent of the Minister, promote, and may, without any such consent, oppose, Bills in Parliament, Bills in the Parliament of Northern Ireland and orders under the Private Legislation Procedure (Scotland) Act 1936.

Powers of the Minister of Posts and Telecommunications over the Post Office

General ministerial control and supervision of the Post Office.

11.—(1) The Minister may, after consultation with the Post Office, give to it such directions of a general character as to the exercise by it of its powers as appear to the Minister to be requisite in the national interest.

(2) If it appears to the Minister that there is a defect in the general plans or arrangements of the Post Office for exercising any of its powers, he may, after consultation with it, give it directions of a general character for remedying the defect.

(3) Without prejudice to the foregoing provisions of this section, if it appears to the Minister to be requisite or expedient so to do—

   (*a*) in the interests of national security or relations with the government of a country or territory outside the British Islands ; or

   (*b*) in order—

      (i) to discharge, or facilitate the discharge of, an obligation binding on Her Majesty's Government in the United Kingdom by virtue of its being a member of an international organisation or a party to an international agreement ;

      (ii) to attain, or facilitate the attainment of, any other object the attainment of which is, in the Minister's opinion, requisite or expedient in view of Her Majesty's Government in the United Kingdom being a member of such an organisation or a party to such an agreement ; or

      (iii) to enable Her Majesty's Government in the United Kingdom to become a member of such an organisation or a party to such an agreement ;

he may, after consultation with the Post Office, give to it directions requiring it (according to the circumstances of the case) to secure that a particular thing that it or a subsidiary of its is doing is no longer done or that a particular thing that it has power to do, but is not being done either by it or by a subsidiary of its, is so done.

(4) If it appears to the Minister that the Post Office is showing undue preference to, or is exercising undue discrimination against, any person or persons of any class or description in the charges or other terms and conditions applicable to services provided by it, being services which, by virtue of the following provisions of this Part of this Act, it has the exclusive privilege of providing, he may, after consultation with the Post Office, give it such directions as appear to him requisite to secure that it ceases so to do.

(5) The Post Office shall comply with directions given to it under any of the foregoing provisions of this section.

(6) The Post Office shall not disclose any directions given to it under any of the foregoing provisions of this section if the Minister notifies it that he is of opinion that it is against the interests of national security to do so.

(7) In the case of a wholly owned subsidiary of the Post Office, it shall so exercise the rights conferred on it by the holding of its interest therein as to secure that no person is appointed to be a director of the subsidiary except after previous consultation with the Minister as to his suitability for appointment.

(8) The Post Office, in carrying out any such work of development as involves substantial outlay on capital account and, if it has subsidiaries, in securing the carrying out by them of any such work, shall act in accordance with a general programme settled from time to time with the approval of the Minister.

(9) The Post Office shall furnish the Minister with such returns, accounts and other information with respect to its property and activities, and, if it has subsidiaries, with respect to their property and activities, as he may from time to time require.

(10) Without prejudice to the provisions of the last foregoing subsection, the Post Office shall, as soon as possible after the end of each accounting year, make to the Minister a report on the exercise and performance by it of its functions during that year (which shall include such particulars as the Minister may, after consultation with the Post Office and with the approval of the Treasury, direct with respect to its activities and those of its subsidiaries so far as consisting in the construction, manufacture

PART III

or production of articles in that year), and the Minister shall lay a copy of every such report before each House of Parliament.

(11) The report made under the last foregoing subsection for any year shall set out any directions given under this section by the Minister to the Post Office during that year, except such (if any) as were the subject of notifications under subsection (6) above.

Power of the Minister to direct the Post Office to do work for government departments and local authorities.

12.—(1) Subject to the provisions of this section, the Minister may, after consultation with the Post Office, give to it a direction that it shall do, for Her Majesty's Government in the United Kingdom or Her Majesty's Government in Northern Ireland, work of such a description as may be specified in the direction, being work consisting in the effecting of transactions in normal business hours in such parts of post offices as are open to the public during those hours for the transaction of postal business.

(2) Subject to the provisions of this section, the Minister may, after consultation with the Post Office, give to it a direction that it shall, in normal business hours, issue, on behalf of a local authority in Great Britain specified in the direction, licences of the following kinds (or of such of them as may be so specified) namely:—

    (*a*) dog licences ;

    (*b*) licences for dealing in game ; and

    (*c*) licences for killing game ;

but so that no direction be given under this subsection with reference to a local authority except at its request.

(3) Subject to the provisions of this section, the Minister may, after consultation with the Post Office, give to it a direction that it shall, in normal business hours, issue licences under the Vehicles (Excise) Act (Northern Ireland) 1954 on behalf of a county council or county borough council in Northern Ireland specified in the direction, but so that no direction be given under this subsection with respect to such a council except at its request.

1954 c. 17 (N.I.).

(4) The Post Office shall comply with a direction given to it under subsection (1), (2) or (3) above.

(5) In the event of a dispute's arising as to the places at which, days on which or periods during which work is to be done in compliance with a direction given under subsection (1) above or licences are to be issued in compliance with a direction given under subsection (2) or (3) above, it shall be determined by the Minister.

(6) The Minister shall not give a direction under subsection (1), (2) or (3) above or proceed to a determination under the last foregoing subsection except after taking into consideration the administrative arrangements of the Post Office for the time being in force and the facilities available to it for the time being for doing the work in question or, as the case may be, issuing the licences in question and for exercising and performing its other functions.

(7) In consideration of its complying with a direction given under subsection (1) above, the Post Office shall be entitled to receive payment from the Crown (of an amount to be determined, in the event of a dispute's arising as to the amount thereof, by the Minister), and the direction may include provision as to the person by whom the payment is to be made and the manner in which it is to be defrayed.

(8) In consideration of its complying with a direction given under subsection (2) above with reference to a local authority in Scotland, the Post Office shall be entitled to receive payment from that authority (of an amount to be determined, in the event of a dispute's arising as to the amount thereof, by the Minister).

(9) In consideration of its complying with a direction given under subsection (3) above, the Post Office shall be entitled to receive payment from the Crown in right of Her Majesty's Government in Northern Ireland (of an amount to be determined, in the event of a dispute's arising as to the amount thereof, by the Minister).

(10) No direction shall be given under this section requiring the Post Office to do anything before the appointed day.

13.—(1) Consultation with the Minister by the Post Office shall be requisite before it or a subsidiary of its constructs, manufactures or produces, for the relevant purpose, things of any kind to an extent substantially greater than that to which the Postmaster General constructed, manufactured or produced, for the corresponding purpose, things of that kind during the period beginning with the 1st April 1961 and ending with the day immediately preceding the appointed day; and it shall similarly be requisite before the Post Office or a subsidiary of its constructs, manufactures or produces, to a substantial extent for the relevant purpose, things of a kind that the Postmaster General did not construct, manufacture or produce for the corresponding purpose during that period.

Restriction of carrying on by the Post Office and its subsidiaries of certain activities.

(2) The approval of the Minister shall be requisite to the carrying on by the Post Office or a subsidiary of its of activities

consisting in the construction, manufacture, production or purchase for supply to outside persons of things for use by such persons otherwise than in connection with services provided by the Post Office or a subsidiary of its; and—

　　(*a*) the approval of the Minister may be given for the purposes of this subsection subject to such conditions (if any) as he may deem fit; but

　　(*b*) notwithstanding the giving of approval, the Minister may at any time, after consultation with the Post Office, direct it to discontinue or, as the case may be, to exercise its control over a subsidiary of its so as to require the subsidiary to discontinue, any activity that the Post Office or, as the case may be, the subsidiary is carrying on with approval.

(3) The Minister shall publish, in such manner as he thinks fit, particulars of any approval given under the last foregoing subsection by him, and shall send them to the Confederation of British Industry and the Trades Union Congress.

(4) In carrying on any activities to which subsection (2) of this section applies the Post Office shall act as if it were a company engaged in a commercial enterprise, and it shall so exercise its control over a subsidiary of its that carries on any such activities as to ensure that the subsidiary so acts.

(5) In this section,—

　　(*a*) " outside persons " means persons other than the Post Office or its subsidiaries;

　　(*b*) " the relevant purpose " means the purpose of use by the Post Office or a subsidiary of its or of supply to outside persons for use by them in connection with services provided by the Post Office or a subsidiary of its; and

　　(*c*) " the corresponding purpose " means the purpose of use by the Postmaster General or of supply to others for use by them in connection with services provided by him;

and, for the purposes of this section, the assembly of an article in the course of its installation at the place where it is to be used shall not be taken to constitute its manufacture, construction or production.

The Post Office Users' Councils

The Post
Office Users'
Councils.
14.—(1) There shall be established, in accordance with the provisions of this section,—

　　(*a*) a users' council for the British Islands, to be called " the Post Office Users' National Council "; and (*b*) a users' council for Scotland, to be called " the Post Office Users' Council for Scotland ", a users' council for Wales and Monmouthshire, to be called " the Post Office Users' Council for Wales and Monmouthshire " and a users' council for Northern Ireland, to be called " the Post Office Users' Council for Northern Ireland " ;

and the Post Office Users' National Council is hereafter in this section referred to as " the National Council " and the councils mentioned in paragraph (*b*) above are so referred to as " Country Councils ".

(2) The National Council shall consist of—

(*a*) a chairman appointed by the Minister ;

(*b*) the chairmen of the Country Councils ;

(*c*) such other members, not exceeding twenty-six, as the Minister may appoint after consultation with such bodies as appear to him to be representative of the interests of persons likely to be concerned with matters within the competence of the Council ;

(*d*) such other members, not exceeding three, as the Minister may appoint without any such consultation ;

and, in appointing members in pursuance of paragraph (*c*) above, the Minister shall have regard to the desirability of having members who are familiar with the special requirements and circumstances of particular parts of the British Islands.

(3) Each of the Country Councils shall consist of a chairman appointed by the Minister and such other members, not exceeding twenty-four, as the Minister may appoint after consultation with the chairman and such bodies in the part of the United Kingdom for which the Council is to be or is established as appear to him to be representative of the interests of persons likely to be concerned with matters within the competence of the Council.

(4) A person appointed to be a member of a council established under this section shall hold and vacate office in accordance with the terms of his appointment ; but, notwithstanding anything in those terms, he may at any time resign his office by notice in writing to the Minister.

(5) A person who has held office as a member of a council established under this section shall be eligible for reappointment.

(6) The Minister and the Post Office may each refer to the National Council, for consideration and report, any matter relating to the services provided by the Post Office.

(7) In the case of each of the Country Councils, the Minister and the Post Office may each refer to it for consideration and report a matter relating to services provided by the Post Office

that affects persons in the part of the United Kingdom for which the Council is established (being persons for whom those services are provided), but does not affect others, but neither shall refer to it any other matter.

(8) It shall be the duty of each of the Country Councils—

    (*a*) to consider—

        (i) any matter relating to the services provided by the Post Office in the part of the United Kingdom for which the Council is established which is the subject of a representation (other than one appearing to the Council to be frivolous) made to the Council by, or on behalf of, a user in that part of the United Kingdom of those services ; and

        (ii) any matter relating to the services so provided in that part of the United Kingdom which appears to the Council to be one to which consideration ought to be given by it notwithstanding that no representation has been made to it with respect to it ;

and, if it is of opinion that action ought to be taken with respect to any such matter, to give to the Minister, the Post Office and the National Council notice of that fact (stating whether or not the matter was the subject of a representation made to the Council) and of the action which the Council thinks ought to be taken ;

    (*b*) to consider any matter which is referred to it under the last foregoing subsection and to report thereon to the Minister and the Post Office.

(9) It shall be the duty of the National Council—

    (*a*) to consider—

        (i) any matter relating to the services provided by the Post Office in the British Islands which is the subject of a representation (other than one appearing to the Council to be frivolous) made to the Council by or on behalf of a user of the services so provided in those Islands ; and

        (ii) any matter relating to the services so provided in those Islands which appears to the Council to be one to which consideration ought to be given by it notwithstanding that no representation has been made to it with respect to it ;

and, if it is of opinion that action ought to be taken with respect to any such matter, to give to the Minister and the Post Office notice of that fact (stating whether or not the matter was the subject of a representation made to the Council) and of the action which the Council thinks ought to be taken ;

(*b*) to consider the subject-matter of a notice given to it in pursuance of subsection (8)(*a*) above by a Country Council and to transmit to the Minister, the Post Office and that Council its observations thereon ;

(*c*) to consider any matter referred to it under subsection (6) above and to report thereon to the Minister and the Post Office.

(10) Where it falls to the National Council to consider a matter that affects persons in a part of the United Kingdom for which one of the Country Councils is established, being persons for whom services are provided by the Post Office, but does not affect persons elsewhere for whom services are so provided, it shall be the duty of the National Council to consult with that Country Council with respect to that matter.

(11) Every council established under this section shall meet when convened by the chairman thereof, but not less frequently than twice a year ; and, without prejudice to the discretion of the chairman to call a meeting whenever he thinks fit, he shall call a meeting when required to do so by any three members of the council.

(12) Minutes shall be kept of the proceedings at each meeting of each of the councils established under this section but, subject to that, each of those councils may determine its own quorum and procedure.

(13) It shall be the duty of each of the Country Councils to comply with a requisition made on it by the National Council for a copy of the minutes of a specified meeting of the Council.

(14) Each of the councils established under this section shall, as respects each accounting year, make to the Minister a report on the exercise and performance by the council of its functions during that year and the Minister shall lay a copy of each such report before each House of Parliament.

(15) Each of the councils established under this section shall be furnished by the Minister with such officers and staff as appear to him to be requisite for the proper discharge of its functions, and with such office accommodation and equipment, and such services, as appear to him to be so requisite.

(16) The Minister may pay such allowances and remuneration to the chairman of the National Council and the officers and staff of any of the councils established under this section as he may determine and such allowances to the members of any of those councils (other than the chairman of the National Council) as he may determine ; and may pay such expenses of any of those councils as he may determine.

(17) The Minister may pay such allowances as he may determine to members of any body recognised by him, after

PART III

consultation with the National Council, to be assisting the Council to ascertain the opinion of users of services provided by the Post Office in any part of the British Islands, and may pay such expenses of a body so recognised as he may determine ; but he shall not recognise a body to be assisting the National Council to ascertain the opinion of users of services so provided in any part of the United Kingdom for which one of the Country Councils is established except after consultation with that Council.

1961 c. 15.

(18) Notwithstanding section 1(3) of the Post Office Act 1961, any expenses incurred by the Postmaster General in the discharge, by virtue of section 2(6) of this Act, of the duty imposed by subsection (15) above or the exercise, by virtue of the said section 2(6), of the power conferred by subsection (16) or (17) above shall be defrayed out of moneys provided by Parliament, and moneys so provided for the payment by the Postmaster General of those expenses shall be excepted from the operation of section 1(2) of the Post Office Act 1961.

(19) The approval of the Minister for the Civil Service shall be requisite as regards the number of persons to be furnished under subsection (15) above and to a determination under subsection (16) or (17) above by the Minister relating to allowances or remuneration, and the approval of the Treasury shall be requisite to a determination under either of the last-mentioned subsections by the Minister relating to the expenses of a body.

1957 c. 20.

(20) Part III of Schedule 1 to the House of Commons Disqualification Act 1957 (which specifies offices whereof the holders are disqualified under that Act) shall, in its application to the House of Commons of the United Kingdom, be amended by inserting, at the appropriate point in alphabetical order, the words " Chairman of the Post Office Users' National Council ".

Duty of the Post Office to consult the Post Office Users' National Council about certain proposals.

15.—(1) Before the Post Office so puts into effect any major proposals relating to any of its main services as to affect the persons for whom they are provided, it shall be incumbent on it, subject to the next following subsection, to refer the proposals to, and consult thereon with, the Post Office Users' National Council.

(2) The foregoing subsection shall not apply to proposals containing no matter other than such as is requisite to comply with a direction given by the Minister under section 11(3) or (4) or 12 of this Act or matter ancillary to matter such as is so requisite.

(3) Any question arising whether or not any proposals are major proposals or relate to a main service shall be referred to the Minister, whose decision shall be final.

(4) The validity of any action taken by the Post Office shall not be impugned on the ground that it was taken otherwise than in pursuance of proposals that had been the subject of a reference under subsection (1) above, but ought not to have been so taken.

*General Provisions as to Transfer to the Post Office
of Property, Rights and Liabilities of the Postmaster General*

16.—(1) On the appointed day, there shall vest by virtue of this section in the Post Office—

> (a) all property which, immediately before that day, is vested in the Postmaster General and held in trust for Her Majesty;

> (b) all works and apparatus belonging to the Postmaster General to which the enactments relating to telegraphs apply;

> (c) the portions of the tube laid by the Pneumatic Despatch Company, Limited, that are vested in the Postmaster General under the Post Office (Pneumatic Tubes Acquisition) Act 1922;

> (d) all estates and interests in land in the Channel Islands which, immediately before that day, are vested in Her Majesty, being estates and interests in land then occupied or used, in whole or in part, by the Postmaster General or (for, or in connection with, the exercise and performance of any of the Postmaster General's functions) by an officer or servant of the Crown;

> (e) all property which, immediately before that day, is vested in the Crown and used, or appropriated for use, for, or in connection with, the exercise and performance of any of the Postmaster General's functions (being neither land nor property falling within paragraph (b) or (c) above);

> (f) all interests of the Minister of Public Building and Works in the land delineated (and coloured blue) on the plans deposited in connection with the Bill for this Act with that Minister and authenticated by the signature of the Postmaster General (being land in the City of Edinburgh which, though held by that Minister, is occupied by the Postmaster General);

> (g) all rights and liabilities enjoyed by, or incumbent on, the Crown immediately before that day with reference to the functions of the Postmaster General (including, in particular, but without prejudice to the generality of the foregoing words, all rights so enjoyed, and liabilities so incumbent, that subsist by virtue of a contract entered into by the Minister of Public Building and Works on behalf of the Crown for the erection or

Part III

Vesting in the Post Office of property, rights and liabilities generally.

1922 c. 43.

execution of buildings or works on land in whose case an estate or interest therein vests in the Post Office by virtue of paragraph (*a*) above, not being land which, immediately before that day, is the subject of an agreement to which the parties are the Postmaster General, the Minister of Public Building and Works and the Post Office for the conveyance, assignment or transfer by the Post Office to that Minister of the estate or interest that so vests).

(2) The following shall be excepted from the operation of the foregoing subsection, namely,—

(*a*) chattels or corporeal moveables used, or appropriated for use, exclusively for, or in connection with, the exercise and performance by the Postmaster General of his functions under the Government Annuities Act 1929, the Post Office Savings Bank Acts 1954 and 1966, the National Debt Act 1958 or the National Loans Act 1968, not being telegraphic apparatus ;

1929 c. 29.

1958 c. 6 (7 & 8 Eliz. 2).
1968 c. 13.
1958 c. 51.

(*b*) records within the meaning of the Public Records Act 1958 ;

(*c*) copyright (other than copyright in registered designs) ;

(*d*) property for whose vesting in the Post Office or the Minister of Public Building and Works provision is made by the following provisions of this Act ;

(*e*) rights and liabilities for whose vesting in the Post Office provision is so made ;

(*f*) rights and liabilities enjoyed by, or incumbent on, the Crown referable solely to the exercise and performance by the Postmaster General of his functions under the Wireless Telegraphy Acts 1949 to 1967 (other than rights and liabilities that subsist by virtue of a contract for the supply of chattels or corporeal moveables or by virtue of such a contract to which the Minister of Public Building and Works is a party as falls within subsection (1)(*g*) above) ;

(*g*) rights and liabilities enjoyed by, or incumbent on, the Crown referable solely to the exercise and performance by the Postmaster General of his functions under the Government Annuities Act 1929, the Post Office Savings Bank Acts 1954 and 1966, the National Debt Act 1958 or the National Loans Act 1968 (other than rights and liabilities that subsist by virtue of such a contract to which the Minister of Public Building and Works is a party as falls within subsection (1)(*g*) above) ;

(*h*) rights and liabilities that subsist by virtue of section 46 of the Patents Act 1949 or paragraph 1 of Schedule 1 to the Registered Designs Act 1949 (Crown use of patented inventions and registered designs); PART III 1949 c. 87. 1949 c. 88.

(*i*) rights and liabilities that subsist by virtue of a contract entered into by the Controller of Her Majesty's Stationery Office on behalf of the Crown; and

(*j*) rights and liabilities that subsist under such a contract entered into on behalf of the Crown as falls within subsection (1) of section 18 of this Act (it being assumed that subsection (2) thereof had been omitted).

17.—(1) If it appears to the Minister expedient so to do for the purpose of removing any difficulties or uncertainties arising out of the operation of the last foregoing section, he may by order— Power of the Minister to override section 16 in case of difficulty or uncertainty.

(*a*) direct that such property (other than land), rights or liabilities as may be specified in the order (being property, rights or liabilities which, apart from the order, would vest in the Post Office by virtue of that section or which have so vested) shall, notwithstanding that section, not so vest or, as the case may be, be deemed not to have so vested; or

(*b*) direct that such property (other than land), rights or liabilities as may be so specified (being property, rights or liabilities which, apart from the order, would not so vest or which have not so vested) shall, notwithstanding that section, so vest on the appointed day or, as the case may be, on such day as may be so specified.

(2) No order shall be made under this section by the Minister with respect to chattels or corporeal moveables after the expiration of the period of twelve months beginning with the appointed day.

(3) Where an order under this section operates to the advantage of the Post Office, the Minister may, with the consent of the Treasury, direct that the debt that will fall, or has fallen, by virtue of the following provisions of this Part of this Act, to be assumed by the Post Office to him shall be increased by a sum specified in the direction (being a sum appearing to him to represent the value of the advantage); and where an order under this section operates to the disadvantage of the Post Office, the Minister may, with the like consent, direct that that debt shall be reduced by a sum specified in the direction (being a sum sufficient, in his opinion, to compensate the Post Office for the disadvantage).

Part III

Vesting in
the Post Office
of rights and
liabilities
under certain
contracts
conferring on
the Crown
incidental
rights as to
patents, &c.

18.—(1) Where a contract entered into on behalf of the Crown by the Postmaster General contains provision conferring on the Crown (otherwise than by reference to the office of master of the Post Office and incidentally only to other matters with which the contract is principally concerned) rights in respect of a patent, invention or registered design, the rights of the Crown subsisting by virtue of the contract (other than such as subsist by virtue of that provision) and the liabilities of the Crown so subsisting (other than such, if any, as relate to payment in respect of an exercise of rights that so subsist) shall, on the appointed day, vest in the Post Office by virtue of this section but the Post Office shall—

(*a*) enjoy, concurrently with the Crown and subject to the like liability (if any) as is incumbent on the Crown to make payment in respect of an exercise thereof, the Crown's rights under the contract that so subsist and

(*b*) be liable to satisfy any unsatisfied liability of the Crown to make payment in respect of an exercise by the Postmaster General, on behalf of the Crown, of those rights.

(2) In so far as a contract provides for the terms upon which use of an invention may be made by virtue of section 46 of the Patents Act 1949 for the manufacture of articles by the department of the Postmaster General or the manufacture and supply to that department of articles by a person authorised by it or provides for the terms upon which use of a registered design may be made by virtue of paragraph 1 of Schedule 1 to the Registered Designs Act 1949 for either of these purposes, it shall be excepted from the operation of the foregoing subsection.

1949 c. 87.

1949 c. 88.

Transfer of
assets of the
Post Office
Fund and
general
reserve, of
certain other
moneys, and
of certain
investments.

1961 c. 15.

19.—(1) On the appointed day, the assets of the Post Office Fund and of the general reserve maintained by the Postmaster General in pursuance of section 7 of the Post Office Act 1961 shall, by virtue of this section, vest in the Post Office, and that fund and that reserve shall cease to exist.

(2) On the appointed day, there shall vest in the Post Office, by virtue of this section,—

(*a*) all moneys in the hands of the Postmaster General which, though not forming part of the assets of the Post Office Fund, would, if this Act had not passed, have fallen to be paid by him into that fund ;

(*b*) any right of the Postmaster General to repayment of Ways and Means advances made by him under section 11 (investment powers) of the Post Office Act 1961 :

(*c*) any bills or securities vested in him in consequence of an exercise of the power of investment conferred on him by that section ; and

(*d*) any shares acquired by him under Part VII of this Act.

*Transfer to the Post Office of the Postmaster General's
statutory Rights and Liabilities as to Mails and Telegraphs
and of Rights and Liabilities, &c., of his under certain
Acts authorising the Acquisition of Land or the
Execution of Works*

20.—(1) On the appointed day—

(a) the right which, by virtue of subsection (1) of section 29 of the Post Office Act 1953 (hereafter in this section referred to as the " principal Act "), the Postmaster General enjoys immediately before that day to require a person by whom a ship is owned or worked to carry parcels in the ship and the countervailing obligation which, by virtue of subsection (2) of that section, is, immediately before that day, incumbent on him to pay remuneration for services rendered under that section shall become those of the Post Office ;

(b) the rights which, by virtue of sections 33, 34, 36(1) and 42 of the principal Act (which contain provisions enabling him to compel railway undertakers to undertake the conveyance of mail-bags by train and by ships which are owned or worked by them or in the case of which they are parties to arrangements for the use, maintenance or working thereof) he enjoys immediately before that day and the countervailing obligations with respect to payment of remuneration for services performed which, immediately before that day, are, by virtue of sections 35 and 36(2) of the principal Act, incumbent on him shall become those of the Post Office ;

(c) the right which, by virtue of section 44(1)(b) and (c) of the principal Act, he enjoys immediately before that day to require the British Railways Board and certain other bodies which provide transport services to perform (subject to the restrictions imposed by section 45 of the principal Act) reasonable services with regard to the conveyance of mail-bags and the countervailing obligation which, by virtue of section 44(2) of the principal Act, is, immediately before that day, incumbent on him to pay remuneration for services performed shall become those of the Post Office ; and

(d) the obligation to him which, by virtue of subsection (1) of section 38 of the principal Act, is, immediately before that day, incumbent on railway undertakers to perform services with respect to the conveyance of mail-bags and the other matters mentioned in that subsection and the right which, by virtue of subsection (2) of that section, they enjoy, immediately before that

Rights and liabilities as to conveyance of mails.

1953 c. 36.

day, to receive from him remuneration for services performed shall respectively become an obligation to the Post Office and a right against it.

(2) Accordingly, as from the appointed day,—

> (*a*) sections 29, 33 to 36, 38, 44 and 45 of the principal Act shall have effect as if, for references to the Postmaster General, there were substituted references to the Post Office ; and

> (*b*) sections 39, 40 and 41 of that Act (which respectively prohibit railway undertakers from making byelaws, &c., which militate against the provisions of that Act relating to the conveyance of mails by railway, provide for the manner in which notices may be served under that Act on railway undertakers and penalize certain refusals and neglects by such undertakers in the matter of the conveyance of mails by railway) shall have similar effect.

Rights and liabilities as to telegraphs.

21.—(1) On the appointed day, the rights and liabilities which, by virtue of the provisions of the Telegraph Acts which are not repealed by this Act, are enjoyed by, and incumbent on, the Postmaster General immediately before that day shall become those of the Post Office, and it shall become subject to the restrictions imposed by those provisions to which the Postmaster General is subject immediately before that day ; and, accordingly,—

1868 c. 110.

1863 c. 112.

> (*a*) on that day, so much of section 2 of the Telegraph Act 1868 as provides that the term " the company " in the Telegraph Act 1863 shall, in addition to the meaning assigned to it in that Act, mean the Postmaster General shall cease to have effect ; and

1950 c. 39.

1878 c. 76.

1911 c. 39.

1916 c. 40.

> (*b*) as from that day, references in the said provisions and in section 20 of the Public Utilities Street Works Act 1950 (which extends the powers exercisable under section 21 of the Telegraph Act 1863) to the company and to the Postmaster General (except references in such of those provisions as are expressly dealt with by the following provisions of this Act and except the first two references to the company in section 30 of the Telegraph Act 1863, the first three such references in section 33 of that Act, the ninth reference to the Postmaster General in section 6 of the Telegraph Act 1878, the first reference to him in the Telegraph (Construction) Act 1911 and the first reference to him in the Telegraph (Construction) Act 1916) shall be construed as referring to the Post Office, except so far as the context excludes such a construction, and

the excepted references in the said sections 30, 33 and PART III
6 and those in the two last-mentioned Acts shall be
construed as including references to the Post Office.

(2) In this section " the Telegraph Acts " means the Tele- 1863 c. 112.
graph Act 1863, the Telegraph Act 1868, the Telegraph Act 1868 c. 110.
1870, the Telegraph Act 1878, the Telegraph (Isle of Man) 1878 c. 76.
Act 1889, the Telegraph Act 1892, the Telegraph (Construction) 1889 c. 34.
Act 1908, the Telegraph (Arbitration) Act 1909, the Telegraph 1892 c. 59.
(Construction) Act 1911 and the Telegraph (Construction) Act 1909 c. 20.
1916. 1911 c. 39.
1916 c. 40.

22.—(1) Any provision of the Sites Acts, the Post Office Rights and
Extension Act 1865, the Manchester Post Office Act 1876, the liabilities, &c.,
Post Office (London) Railway Act 1913, the Post Office (Site arising out of
and Railway) Act 1954, the Post Office Works Act 1959 or the authorising the
Post Office Subway Act 1966 which is in force immediately acquisition of
before the appointed day and contains references to the Post- land or the
master General shall, so far as necessary for preserving its effect execution
on and after that day, have effect as from that day as if those of works.
references were references to the Post Office. 1865 c. 87.
1876 c. iii.

(2) As from the appointed day, any rights or powers vested 1913 c. cxvi.
in, or exercisable by, the Post Office under the enactments 1954 c. xxix.
relating to telegraphs in respect of works of any kind whatsoever 1959 c. 43.
executed under those enactments shall extend to, and may be 1966 c. 25.
exercised by it in respect of, the portions of the tube constructed
by the Pneumatic Despatch Company, Limited, that vest in the
Post Office by virtue of section 16 of this Act.

(3) Section 20 of the Bristol Cattle Market Act 1930 (which 1930 c. clxxix.
empowers the Postmaster General, amongst others, to enter into
and carry out agreements with reference to any of the matters
referred to in that Act or the agreements mentioned in that
section) shall, as from the appointed day, have effect with the
substitution, for the reference to the Postmaster General, of a
reference to the Post Office.

(4) Section 16 of the City of London (Various Powers) Act 1950 c. v.
1950 (which provides for the continuance of the making, by
the Postmaster General, the Mayor and commonalty and citizens
of the city of London acting by the common council and the
Mercers' Company of certain periodic payments to the incumbents and clerks of certain benefices in the city, being payments
originally required to be made under enactments repealed by
that Act) shall, as from the appointed day, have effect as if, in
Schedule 1 to that Act, for references to the Postmaster General,
there were substituted references to the Post Office; and the
rights of indemnity in favour of the Postmaster General that are
saved by the proviso to section 18 of that Act shall, as from that
day, enure for the benefit of the Post Office and the charges

PART III on property to secure the payment of money payable to the Postmaster General in respect of indemnities so saved which are themselves also saved by that proviso shall, as from that day, have effect accordingly.

(5) The reference in subsection (1) above to the Sites Acts is a reference to the Acts passed during the years 1885 to 1938 (both inclusive) the short title of each of which consists of the words "The Post Office (Sites) Act" followed by the year in which it was passed.

Exclusive Privilege of the Post Office with respect to the Conveyance, &c., of Letters

Exclusive privilege of the Post Office with respect to the conveyance, &c., of letters.

1953 c. 36.

23.—(1) Subject to the restriction imposed by the following subsection, as from the appointed day, the privilege with respect to the conveyance of letters and the performance of services of receiving, collecting, despatching and delivering letters which, by virtue of section 3 of the Post Office Act 1953 is (subject to the exceptions provided for by that section) enjoyed by the Postmaster General at the passing of this Act, shall (subject to the like exceptions) become that of the Post Office ; and, accordingly, as from that day,—

> (a) that section shall have effect as if, for references to the Postmaster General, there were substituted references to the Post Office ; and
>
> (b) section 4 of that Act (which penalizes infringements of the privilege conferred by the said section 3) and sections 26 to 28 thereof (which make provision for securing the due transmission of postal packets carried in ships or aircraft inward bound) shall have similar effect.

(2) The said restriction is that the power to authorise letters to be sent, conveyed and delivered otherwise than by post and the collection of letters otherwise than by an officer of the Post Office which is conferred by the proviso to subsection (1) of the said section 3 and with which the Post Office becomes invested by virtue of the foregoing subsection shall not be exercisable except with the consent of, or in accordance with the terms of a general authority given by, the Minister.

Exclusive Privilege of the Post Office with respect to Telecommunication

Exclusive privilege of the Post Office with respect to telecommunication.

24.—(1) Subject to the following provisions of this Act, as from the appointed day, the Post Office shall have throughout the British Islands, the exclusive privilege of running systems for the conveyance, through the agency of electric, magnetic, electro-magnetic, electro-chemical or electro-mechanical energy of—

> (a) speech, music and other sounds ;

(*b*) visual images ;

(*c*) signals serving for the impartation (whether as between persons and persons, things and things or persons and things) of any matter otherwise than in the form of sound or visual images ; and

(*d*) signals serving for the actuation or control of machinery or apparatus.

(2) In the case of an infringement, in relation to a system not extending beyond the British Islands, of the privilege conferred by the foregoing subsection, the person running the system (or, if different people run different parts of it, each of them), shall be guilty of an offence and liable,—

(*a*) on summary conviction, to a fine not exceeding £400 ;

(*b*) on conviction on indictment, to a fine or to imprisonment for a term not exceeding two years, or to both,

and, in the case of an infringement, in relation to a system extending beyond those Islands, of that privilege, the person running the portion of the system within those Islands (or, if different people run different parts of it, each of them) shall be guilty of an offence and similarly liable.

(3) Where a body corporate is guilty of an offence under this section and that offence is proved to have been committed with the consent or connivance of, or to be attributable to any neglect on the part of, any director, manager, secretary or other similar officer of the body corporate or any person who was purporting to act in any such capacity, he, as well as the body corporate, shall be guilty of that offence and shall be liable to be proceeded against and punished accordingly.

In this subsection, the expression " director ", in relation to a body corporate established by or under any enactment for the purpose of carrying on under national ownership any industry or part of an industry or undertaking, being a body corporate whose affairs are managed by its members, means a member of that body corporate.

(4) In any proceedings in respect of an offence under this section consisting in the running of a system in the case of which, at the time of the commission of the offence, different parts were run by different persons, it shall be a defence for the defendant to prove that a part of the system had been included without his knowledge and that, had it not been, the running of the system would not have constituted an infringement of the privilege conferred by subsection (1) above.

2 L*

PART III
General
classes of acts
not infringing
the telecom-
munication
privilege.

25.—(1) The privilege conferred by subsection (1) of the last foregoing section is not infringed by—

(*a*) the running of a system in the case of which the only agency involved in the conveyance of things thereby conveyed is light and the things thereby conveyed are so conveyed as to be capable of being received or perceived by the eye and without more ;

(*b*) the running by a person of a system in the case of which all the apparatus comprised therein is situate either—

(i) on a single set of premises occupied by him ; or

(ii) in a vehicle, vessel, aircraft or hovercraft or in two or more vehicles, vessels, aircraft or hovercraft mechanically coupled together ; or

(*c*) the running by a single individual of a system in the case of which—

(i) all the apparatus comprised therein is under his control ; and

(ii) everything conveyed by it that falls within paragraphs (*a*) to (*d*) of the said subsection (1) is conveyed solely for domestic purposes of his.

(2) In the case of a business carried on by a person, the said privilege is not infringed by the running, for the purposes of that business, of a system with respect to which,—

(*a*) in a case in which all the apparatus therein comprised is situate in the British Islands, no person except him or the Post Office is concerned in the control of the apparatus ;

(*b*) in any other case, no person except him or the Post Office is concerned in the control of so much of the apparatus as is so situate ;

provided—

(i) that nothing falling within paragraphs (*a*) to (*d*) of subsection (1) of the last foregoing section is conveyed by the system by way of rendering a service to another ;

(ii) that, in so far as sounds or visual images are conveyed by the system, they are not conveyed for the purpose of their being heard or seen by persons other than the person carrying on that business or any servants of his engaged in the conduct thereof ;

(iii) that in so far as such signals as are mentioned in paragraph (*c*) of that subsection are conveyed by the system, they are not conveyed for the purpose of imparting matter otherwise than to the person carrying on that business, any servants of his engaged in the

conduct thereof or things used in the course of that   Part III
business and controlled by him ; and

(iv) that, in so far as such signals as are mentioned in paragraph (*d*) of that subsection are conveyed by the system,
they are not conveyed for the purpose of actuating or
controlling machinery or apparatus used otherwise than
in the course of that business.

(3) In the case of a system in the case of which all the
apparatus therein comprised is let on hire by the Post Office, the
said privilege is not infringed by the running of the system by
the person to whom the apparatus is let on hire ; and in the
case of a system in the case of which part of the apparatus comprised therein consists of apparatus let on hire by the Post Office
to a person, the said privilege is not infringed by the running
by him of so much of the system as comprises the last-mentioned
apparatus.

(4) In this section " business " includes a trade, profession or
employment and includes any activity carried on by a body of
persons, whether corporate or unincorporated, and " vessel "
means a vessel of any description used in navigation.

26.—(1) The privilege conferred by subsection (1) of section Acts relating
24 of this Act is not infringed by a broadcasting authority by to broadcasting
reason only of the transmission by it, by wireless telegraphy, of not infringing
sounds or visual images from a transmitting station for general the telecom-
reception direct from that station, nor is it infringed by the munication
reception of sounds or visual images transmitted, by wireless privilege.
telegraphy, from a transmitting station for general reception
direct from that station or through the medium of a relay service
licensed under the Wireless Telegraphy Act 1949.   1949 c. 54

(2) In this section, " broadcasting authority " means a person
licensed under the Wireless Telegraphy Act 1949 to broadcast
programmes for general reception and " wireless telegraphy "
has the same meaning as in that Act.

27.—(1) A licence may, with the consent of, or in accord- Saving for
ance with the terms of a general authority given by, the Minister, things done
be granted by the Post Office, either unconditionally or subject under licence.
to any conditions specified in the licence, and either irrevocably
or subject to revocation as therein specified, for the running
of any such system falling within subsection (1) of section 24
of this Act as is specified in the licence ; and nothing done under,
and in accordance with, a licence granted under this subsection
shall constitute an infringement of the privilege conferred by
that subsection.

(2) A licence granted under the foregoing subsection shall,
unless previously revoked in accordance with any terms in that
behalf contained in the licence, continue in force for such period
as may be specified therein.

(3) A licence granted under subsection (1) above may be granted either to all persons, to persons of a class or to a particular person, and may include (without prejudice to the power to impose conditions conferred by that subsection) conditions requiring the rendering to the Post Office of a payment on the grant of the licence or the rendering to it of periodic payments during the currency of the licence, or both.

(4) A payment required by virtue of this section to be rendered to the Post Office may be recovered by it in any court of competent jurisdiction as if it were a simple contract debt.

(5) A licence granted under subsection (1) above (not being one expressed to be granted to a specified person) shall be published in such manner as appears to the Post Office to be appropriate for bringing it to the attention of the persons for whose benefit it will enure, and a licence expressed to be so granted must be in writing.

(6) No person shall be concerned to inquire whether the grant of a licence under subsection (1) above was, or was not, effected with the consent of, or in accordance with the terms of a general authority given by, the Minister; and the validity of a licence granted under that subsection shall not be impugned on the ground that it was granted neither with the consent of, nor in accordance with the terms of a general authority given by, him.

(7) In the application of subsection (4) above to Scotland, the words " as if it were a simple contract debt " shall be omitted.

(8) Section 6(1) of this Act shall not operate so as to preclude the grant by the Post Office before the appointed day of licences under subsection (1) above.

(9) For the purposes of a licence granted under subsection (1) above, the definition of a class of persons may be framed by reference to any circumstances whatever.

Charges and other Terms and Conditions applicable to Services

Schemes for determining charges and other terms and conditions applicable to services.

28.—(1) The Post Office may make, as respects any of the services provided by it, a scheme for determining either or both of the following, namely,—

    (*a*) the charges which (save in so far as they are the subject of an agreement between it and a person availing himself of those services) are to be made by it; and

    (*b*) the other terms and conditions which (save as aforesaid) are to be applicable to those services;

but so that no provision be included in any such scheme for limiting liability of the Post Office for loss or damage or for amending the rules of law with respect to evidence.

(2) A scheme made under this section may, as respects the services to which it relates, adopt such system for the determination of the charges or other terms and conditions or (as the case may be) the charges and other terms and conditions that are to be applicable as may appear desirable and, in particular and without prejudice to the generality of the foregoing words, may, in all or any cases, leave the determination thereof to the Post Office subject to such (if any) conditions and limitations as may be provided for in the scheme.

(3) A scheme made under this section may, as respects the services to which it relates, specify the manner in which, time at which and person by whom the charges that are to be applicable are to be paid.

(4) A scheme made under this section may make different provision for different cases or classes of cases determined by, or in accordance with, the provisions of the scheme.

(5) A charge exigible by virtue of this section may be recovered by the Post Office in any court of competent jurisdiction as if it were a simple contract debt.

(6) A scheme made under this section may revoke or amend any previous scheme so made.

(7) A scheme made under this section shall come into operation on such day as is specified therein, not being earlier than the day after that on which publication of the scheme in the London, Edinburgh and Belfast Gazettes has been effected ; and conclusive evidence of a scheme so made may be given, in all courts of justice and in all legal proceedings whatsoever, by the production of a copy of any of those Gazettes purporting to contain it.

(8) In the application of subsection (5) above to Scotland, the words " as if it were a simple contract debt " shall be omitted.

Limitation of Liability

29.—(1) Save as provided by the next following section, no proceedings in tort shall lie against the Post Office in respect of any loss or damage suffered by any person by reason of—

Exclusion of liability of the Post Office, its officers and servants, in relation to posts and telecommunications.

  (*a*) anything done or omitted to be done in relation to anything in the post or omission to carry out arrangements for the collection of anything to be conveyed by post ;

  (*b*) failure to provide, or delay in providing, a telecommunication service, apparatus associated therewith or a service ancillary thereto ;

  (*c*) failure, interruption, suspension or restriction of a telecommunication service or a service ancillary thereto or delay of, or fault in, communication by means of a telecommunication service ; or (*d*) error in, or omission from, a directory for use in connection with a telecommunication service.

(2) No officer or servant of the Post Office or person who, not being such an officer or servant, is a sub-postmaster or telephone exchange attendant shall be subject, except at the suit of the Post Office, to any civil liability for any loss or damage in the case of which liability of the Post Office therefor is excluded by the foregoing subsection.

(3) No person engaged in or about the carriage of mail and no officer, servant, agent or sub-contractor of such person shall be subject except at the suit of the Post Office to any civil liability for any loss or damage in the case of which liability of the Post Office therefor is excluded by subsection (1) of this section.

(4) In the application of subsection (1) above to Scotland, the reference to proceedings in tort shall be construed in the same way as in section 43(*b*) of the Crown Proceedings Act 1947.

        30.—(1) Subject to the provisions of this section, proceedings shall lie against the Post Office under this section, but not otherwise, in respect of loss of, or damage to, a registered inland packet in so far as the loss or damage is due to any wrongful act done or any neglect or default committed by an officer, servant or agent of the Post Office while performing or purporting to perform his functions as such in relation to the receipt, carriage, delivery or other dealing with the packet; but no proceedings shall lie under this section in relation to a packet unless begun within the period of twelve months beginning with the day on which the packet was posted.

(2) For the purposes of any proceedings under this section in relation to a packet it shall be presumed, until the contrary is shown, that loss of, or damage to, the packet was due to a wrongful act done, or neglect or default committed by, an officer, servant or agent of the Post Office while performing or purporting to perform such functions of his as aforesaid.

(3) The amount recoverable in any proceedings under this section in relation to a packet shall not exceed—

        (*a*) the market value of the packet (excluding the market value of any message or information which it bears) at the time when the cause of action arises; or

        (*b*) the maximum amount available under a scheme made under section 28 of this Act for compensating the persons aggrieved having regard to the fee paid in respect of the registration of the packet.

(4) The Post Office shall not be liable under this section in respect of a packet unless any such conditions as are required

by a scheme under section 28 of this Act to be complied with in relation to registered inland packets have been complied with in the case of the packet.

(5) No relief shall be available under this section in relation to a packet except upon a claim by the sender or the addressee of the packet; and the sender or addressee of the packet shall be entitled to claim any relief available under this section in respect of the packet, whether or not he is the person damnified by the injury complained of, and to give a good discharge in respect of all claims in respect of the packet under this section: but where the court is satisfied, upon an application by a person who is not the sender or addressee of the packet, that the sender and the addressee are unable or unwilling to enforce their remedies in respect of the packet under this section, the court may, upon such terms as to security, caution, costs, expenses and otherwise as the court thinks just, allow that other person to bring proceedings under this section in the name of the sender or the addressee of the packet.

(6) Where, by virtue of the last foregoing subsection, a person recovers any money or property which, apart from that subsection, would have been recoverable by some other person, the money or property so recovered shall be held on trust for that other person.

(7) In this section—

" agent " includes an independent contractor;

" inland packet " means anything which is posted in the British Islands for delivery at a place in those Islands to the person to whom it is addressed;

" sender ", in relation to a packet, has such meaning as may be assigned to it by any provision of a scheme made under section 28 of this Act, being a provision relating to registered inland packets;

and any reference in this section to the sender or addressee of a packet includes a reference to his personal representatives.

Finance

31.—(1) As from the appointed day, it shall be the duty of the Post Office so to exercise its powers as to secure that its revenues are not less than sufficient to meet all charges properly chargeable to revenue account, taking one year with another.

General duty of the Post Office as to finance.

(2) The Post Office shall charge to revenue in every year all charges that are proper to be made to revenue, including, in particular, proper provision for the depreciation of assets and proper allocations to general reserve; and the reference in the foregoing subsection to charges properly chargeable to revenue account shall be construed accordingly.

2 L* 4

32.—(1) Without prejudice to its power to establish specific reserves, the Post Office shall establish and maintain a general reserve.

(2) The management by the Post Office of its general reserve, the sums to be carried from time to time to the credit thereof, and the application of the moneys comprised therein shall (subject to the following provisions of this section) be as the Post Office may determine.

(3) None of the moneys comprised in the Post Office's general reserve shall be applied otherwise than for the purposes of the Post Office.

(4) The Minister may, with the approval of the Treasury, give to the Post Office directions as to any matter relating to the establishment or management of the Post Office's general reserve or the carrying of sums to the credit thereof or the application of the moneys comprised therein, and the Post Office shall comply with the directions.

33.—(1) The Post Office shall, on the appointed day, assume a debt due to the Minister whereof the amount shall (subject to the effect of any direction given under section 17 of this Act) be the excess of the aggregate of the following amounts:—

    (*a*) so much of advances made under section 9 of the Post Office Act 1961 by the Treasury to the Postmaster General as remains outstanding immediately before that day; and

    (*b*) so much of the amount referred to in section 13(2) of that Act as remains outstanding immediately before that day;

over the aggregate of—

    (i) the net book value of all chattels and corporeal moveables which, immediately before the appointed day, are used, or appropriated for use, by the Postmaster General, being chattels and corporeal moveables that do not, by virtue of section 16 of this Act, vest in the Post Office and in the provision of which the Postmaster General has incurred expenditure treated by him as capital expenditure; and

    (ii) the aggregate of the sums of which, under the following provisions of this Act, the Post Office is entitled to credit for the purposes of this section.

(2) The rate of interest on the said debt and the date from which interest is to begin to accrue, the arrangements for paying off the principal of the said debt, and the other terms of the said debt shall be such as the Minister, with the approval of the Treasury, may from time to time determine; and different rates

and dates may be determined under this subsection with respect Part III to different portions of the said debt.

(3) Any sums received by the Minister by way of interest on, or repayment of, the said debt shall be paid into the National Loans Fund.

(4) In this section " net book value " means, in relation to chattels and corporeal moveables, the value thereof (after deducting depreciation) as shown in the books by reference to which the final statement of accounts under section 12 of the Post Office Act 1961 is prepared. 1961 c. 15.

34.—(1) As regards so much of any sum lent under section 8(1) of the Post Office Act 1961 by the Bank of England to the Postmaster General as is outstanding immediately before the appointed day, the liability to repay it, and to pay interest thereon, shall on that day be transferred to the Post Office. The Post Office to be liable in respect of loans and guarantees under section 8 of the Post Office Act 1961.

(2) If, on or after the appointed day, any sums are issued out of the Consolidated Fund in fulfilment of a guarantee given under the said section 8, the Post Office shall make to the Treasury, at such times and in such manner as the Treasury may from time to time direct, payments, of such amounts as they may so direct, in or towards repayment of the sums and payments of interest on what is outstanding for the time being in respect of the sums at such rate as they may direct.

(3) The last foregoing subsection shall, as from the appointed day, have effect in relation to sums issued as aforesaid before that day that have not been repaid before that day as it has effect in relation to sums so issued on or after that day.

35.—(1) The Post Office may borrow temporarily, by way of overdraft or otherwise, either from the Minister or, with the consent of the Minister and the approval of the Treasury, from any other person, such sums in sterling as it may require for meeting its obligations and performing its functions. The Post Office's borrowing powers.

(2) The Post Office may borrow from the Minister (otherwise than by way of temporary loan) such sums in sterling as it may require for all or any of the following purposes, namely,—

(a) provision of money for meeting any expenses incurred by it in connection with any works the cost of which is properly chargeable to capital account;

(b) provision of working capital required by it;

(c) subscription for, or acquisition of, securities of an incorporated company or other body corporate, promotion of the formation of an incorporated company or participation in the promotion of such a company or acquisition of an undertaking or part of an undertaking ;

(d) payment off of any part of the debt assumed by it under section 33 of this Act, repayment of any money borrowed by the Postmaster General the liability to repay which is transferred to it by the last foregoing section, payment of a sum in or towards repayment of a sum issued out of the Consolidated Fund in fulfilment of a guarantee given under section 8 of the Post Office Act 1961 and repayment of money borrowed by it ;

1961 c. 15.

(e) any other purpose for which capital moneys are properly applicable.

(3) The Post Office, with the consent of the Minister, may, from such person and on such terms as he may, with the approval of the Treasury specify, borrow, in a currency other than sterling, any sum which it has power to borrow in sterling from the Minister.

(4) References in this section to borrowing by the Post Office do not include—

(a) borrowing by it from a body corporate which is its subsidiary ;

(b) receiving money in its capacity as the provider of any services or using money received in that capacity.

(5) Nothing in this section shall be taken as exempting the Post Office from the provisions of any order under section 1 of the Borrowing (Control and Guarantees) Act 1946 or section 2 of the Loans Guarantee and Borrowing Regulation Act (Northern Ireland) 1946 or from the provisions of the Exchange Control Act 1947.

1946 c. 58.
1946 c. 18 (N.I.).
1947 c. 14.

(6) This section shall come into operation on the appointed day.

Limitation of indebtedness.

36.—(1) The Post Office shall not have power to borrow money except in accordance with the last foregoing section.

(2) The aggregate of—

(a) the amount outstanding in respect of the principal of any money borrowed under the last foregoing section by the Post Office ; and

(b) so much as is outstanding of the debt assumed by it by virtue of section 33 of this Act ;

shall not at any time exceed £2,300 million or such greater sum, not exceeding £2,800 million, as the Minister may from time to time by order specify.

(3) An order under the last foregoing subsection shall be made by statutory instrument, and no such order shall be made unless a draft thereof has been approved by a resolution of the Commons House of Parliament.

(4) Subsection (4) of the last foregoing section shall apply for the purposes of this section as it applies for the purposes of that.

37.—(1) The Minister may, with the approval of the Treasury, Loans by the lend to the Post Office any sums which it has power to borrow Minister to the under section 35(1) or (2) of this Act. Post Office.

(2) Any loans which the Minister makes under this section shall be repaid to him at such times and by such methods, and interest thereon shall be paid to him at such rates and at such times, as he may, with the approval of the Treasury, from time to time direct.

(3) The Treasury may issue out of the National Loans Fund to the Minister such sums as are necessary to enable him to make loans under this section.

(4) Any sums received under subsection (2) above by the Minister shall be paid into the National Loans Fund.

38.—(1) The Treasury may guarantee, in such manner and Treasury on such conditions as they may think fit, the repayment of guarantees. the principal of, and the payment of interest on, any sums which the Post Office borrows from a person other than the Minister.

(2) Immediately after a guarantee is given under this section, the Treasury shall lay a statement of the guarantee before each House of Parliament ; and where any sum is issued for fulfilling a guarantee so given the Treasury shall, as soon as possible after the end of each financial year, beginning with that in which the sum is issued and ending with that in which all liability in respect of the principal of the sum and in respect of interest thereon is finally discharged, lay before each House of Parliament a statement relating to that sum.

(3) Any sums required by the Treasury for fulfilling a guarantee under this section shall be charged on and issued out of the Consolidated Fund.

(4) If any sums are issued in fulfilment of a guarantee given under this section, the Post Office shall make to the Treasury, at such times and in such manner as the Treasury may from time to time direct, payments, of such amounts as the Treasury

PART III   may so direct, in or towards repayment of the sums so issued and payments of interest on what is outstanding for the time being in respect of sums so issued at such rate as the Treasury may so direct.

(5) Any sums received under the last foregoing subsection by the Treasury shall be paid into the Consolidated Fund.

Accounts of the Minister with reference to Post Office indebtedness to him.

39. The Minister shall, as respects each financial year, prepare in such form and manner as the Treasury may direct, an account of sums received by him as mentioned in section 33(3) of this Act, of sums received by him under subsection (2) of section 37 of this Act and of sums issued to him under subsection (3) of that section and of the disposal by him of those sums respectively, and send it to the Comptroller and Auditor General not later than the end of November following the year ; and the Comptroller and Auditor General shall examine, certify and report on the account and lay copies of it, together with his report, before each House of Parliament.

Banking

The Post Office as banker.

40. So far as regards the provision by it, in exercise of the power conferred on it by virtue of section 7(1)(*b*) of this Act, of a banking service, the Post Office shall be deemed for all purposes to be a bank and a banker and to be carrying on the business of banking and a banking undertaking, but shall not be required to furnish to the Commissioners of Inland Revenue any returns under the provisions of section 21 of the Bank Charter Act 1844 or section 13 of the Bank Notes (Scotland) Act 1845.

1844 c. 32.
1845 c. 38.

The Post Office's liabilities as banker to be matched by cash and liquid assets.

41. So long as the Post Office provides, in exercise of the power conferred on it by virtue of section 7(1)(*b*) of this Act, a banking service, it shall be its duty to secure that, at every point of time in any period,—

(*a*) such proportion of the aggregate of the sums owed at that point of time by it to persons in the capacity of customers of its with reference to that service as has previously been determined, in relation to that period, by it with the approval of the Treasury, is matched by assets of its of one or more of the classes specified in Part I of Schedule 2 to this Act ; and

(*b*) the residue of that aggregate is matched by assets of its of one or more of the classes specified in Part II of that Schedule.

The Post Office's Accounts, and Audit thereof

42.—(1) The Post Office shall keep proper accounts and other The Post records and shall prepare in respect of each accounting year a Office's statement of accounts in such form as the Minister, with the accounts, approval of the Treasury, may direct, being a form which shall thereof. conform to the best commercial standards.

(2) The accounts of the Post Office shall be audited by auditors appointed by the Minister after consultation with it, and a person shall not be qualified to be so appointed unless he is a member of one or more of the following bodies—

the Institute of Chartered Accountants in England and Wales;

the Institute of Chartered Accountants of Scotland;

the Association of Certified and Corporate Accountants;

the Institute of Chartered Accountants in Ireland;

any other body of accountants established in the United Kingdom and for the time being recognised for the purposes of section 161(1)(*a*) of the Companies Act 1948 c. 38. 1948 by the Board of Trade;

but a Scottish firm may be so appointed if each of the partners is qualified to be so appointed.

(3) So soon as the accounts of the Post Office have been audited, it shall send to the Minister a copy of the statement thereof together with a copy of any report made by the auditors on the statement, and the Minister shall lay them before each House of Parliament.

Pensions and other Benefits

43.—(1) The Post Office shall, in the case of such persons Staff pensions. engaged in its business as may be determined by it with the approval of the Minister (not being members of the Post Office), pay such pensions, allowances or gratuities to or in respect of them as may be so determined, make such payments towards the provision of such pensions, allowances or gratuities as may be so determined or provide and maintain such schemes (whether contributory or not) for the payment of such pensions, allowances or gratuities as may be so determined.

(2) Where a participant in such a scheme as aforesaid becomes a member of the Post Office, he may be treated for the purposes of the scheme as if his service as a member of the Post Office were service as a person engaged in its business otherwise than as such a member, and his rights under the scheme shall not be affected by paragraph 4(1)(*b*) of Schedule 1 to this Act.

Part III
The Post
Office to pay
pensions, &c.,
referable to
the service
of certain
former civil
servants.
1965 c. 74.
44.—(1) Subject to the provisions of this section, the following shall, instead of being paid out of moneys provided by Parliament, be paid by the Post Office, that is to say:—

> (a) any sum that falls to be paid in respect of a period beginning on or after the appointed day by way of allowance or pension under the Superannuation Act 1965 referable to the service of a person who—

>> (i) ceased to be a civil servant before that day; and

>> (ii) immediately before he so ceased, was employed in the department of the Postmaster General otherwise than wholly in connection with the discharge of the Postmaster General's functions under the following enactments (or any of them), that is to say, the Government Annuities Act 1929, the Post Office Savings Bank Act 1954, the National Debt Act 1958, the Post Office Savings Bank Act 1966 and the National Loans Act 1968;

1929 c. 29.
1954 c. 62.
1958 c. 6 (7 & 8
Eliz. 2).
1966 c. 12.
1968 c. 13.

> (b) any additional allowance or gratuity under the Superannuation Act 1965 that falls to be paid on or after the appointed day, being an allowance or gratuity referable to the service of any such person; and

> (c) any sum that falls to be so paid under that Act to any such person by way of return (with or without interest) of periodical contributions.

(2) Where, in the case of such a person as aforesaid, the following conditions are satisfied, namely,—

> (a) that, after he ceased to be a civil servant, but before the appointed day, he began to serve in a department other than that of the Postmaster General in an unestablished capacity; and

> (b) that his service in that department continued after the beginning of the appointed day;

the foregoing subsection shall not apply to so much of any payment by way of a superannuation or additional allowance granted under the Superannuation Act 1965 to him or of a pension granted under that Act in respect of his service (being a pension the annual rate of which is determined by reference to the rate of his superannuation allowance) as is attributable to—

> (i) a completed year of service which begins on or after the appointed day; or

(ii) a completed year of service which begins before, and
ends after, that day, being a year in the case of which
more than one hundred and eighty-two of the days
therein comprised fall after the day immediately
preceding that day.

45.—(1) Section 12 of the Superannuation Act 1965 (cessation
or reduction of superannuation allowance on re-employment) shall
apply in the case of any such person as is therein mentioned who
is appointed to fill an office in the Post Office immediately upon
his ceasing to serve in the department of the Postmaster General
as in the case of a person appointed to fill an office in a public
department.

(2) For the purposes of section 13 of the Superannuation Act
1965 (additions to allowances in certain cases of unestablished
employment after retirement), service in the Post Office that
immediately follows service in the department of the Postmaster
General shall be treated as service in the civil service in an
unestablished capacity.

46. Where, in the case of a person who has ceased to be a
civil servant, the following conditions are satisfied, namely,—

(a) that, immediately before he so ceased, he was employed
elsewhere than in the department of the Postmaster
General;

(b) that, after he so ceased, but before the appointed day,
he began to serve in that department in an unestablished capacity and continued to serve therein until
the appointed day; and

(c) that, on the appointed day, he began a period of service
in the Post Office;

so much of any payment by way of a superannuation or
additional allowance granted under the Superannuation Act
1965 to him or of a pension granted under that Act in respect
of his service (being a pension the annual rate of which is determined by reference to the rate of his superannuation allowance)
as is attributable to—

(i) a completed year of service which begins on or after
the appointed day; or

(ii) a completed year of service which begins before, and
ends after, that day, being a year in the case of which
more than one hundred and eighty-two of the days
therein comprised fall after the day immediately
preceding that day;

shall, instead of being paid out of moneys provided by Parliament, be paid by the Post Office.

PART III
Making, by
the Minister,
in considera-
tion of the
Exchequer's
being relieved
of certain
liabilities
with respect
to pensions,
of payments
to trustees
appointed by
the Post Office.

47.—(1) In consideration of the fact that, after the beginning of the appointed day, the Exchequer will, by virtue of the foregoing provisions of this Part of this Act, be relieved of liabilities in respect of the provision of pensions, gratuities and other like benefits to, and in respect of, certain persons, the following provisions of this section shall have effect.

(2) It shall be assumed that, on the appointed day, the Minister is the holder of an amount of $2\frac{1}{2}\%$ Consolidated Stock equal in nominal value to such sum (not being less than £1,000 million nor more than £1,500 million) as he may determine for the purposes of this section (which amount is hereafter in this section referred to as the " assumed amount of stock ") ; and trustees appointed by the Post Office for the purposes of this section (hereafter in this section referred to as " the trustees ")—

(a) shall, subject to the following provisions of this section, be entitled to receive from him, in accordance with those provisions, quarterly payments (hereafter in this section referred to as " capital payments ") which shall severally be taken to represent the proceeds of assumed sales of portions of the assumed amount of stock and shall continue to be made until, by the operation of this section, the assumed amount of stock has been exhausted, and

(b) shall also, subject as aforesaid, be entitled to receive from him, in accordance with the said provisions, quarterly payments (hereafter in this section referred to as " interest payments ") of which the first shall be taken to represent interest on the assumed amount of stock and each subsequent one shall be taken to represent interest on the residue of the assumed amount of stock remaining on the immediately preceding day on which an interest payment was payable.

(3) Capital and interest payments shall be payable on the same days as those on which dividends are payable in respect of $2\frac{1}{2}\%$ Consolidated Stock, that is to say, 5th January, 5th April, 5th July and 5th October (which days are hereafter in this section referred to as " pay-days "), the first of those payments being payable on the first pay-day following the appointed day.

(4) Subject to the next following subsection, the aggregate of the sums that the trustees are, by virtue of this section, entitled to receive on a pay-day shall be £11,250,000.

(5) Capital payments may be reduced or withheld by the Minister in not more than five financial years (but so that none be reduced or withheld unless, beforehand, the Post Office has

been notified by him of the intended reduction or withholding
and the reduction or withholding has been approved by resolution of the Commons House of Parliament), subject, however, to this qualification, that if the Minister avails himself of the benefit of this subsection in two successive financial years it shall not be open to him to avail himself of it in the financial year next following.

(6) For the purpose of computing the amount of the first interest payment, it shall be assumed that interest on the assumed amount of stock begins to accrue on the appointed day and accrues from day to day.

(7) Each interest payment subsequent to the first shall be equal to that which would be payable by way of dividend on an actual holding of $2\frac{1}{2}\%$ Consolidated Stock equal to so much of the assumed amount of stock as was outstanding on the day on which the immediately preceding interest payment was payable.

(8) If, in the case of a pay-day on which a capital payment is payable, the residue of the assumed amount of stock that remained on the immediately preceding pay-day is of an amount such that the proceeds of an assumed sale thereof for the purpose of computing the amount of that payment amount to a sum less than that which, apart from this subsection, the trustees are entitled to receive by way thereof, the requirements of this section shall be deemed to be complied with by the payment by the Minister to the trustees of an amount equal to those proceeds and of the interest payment payable on the first-mentioned pay-day.

(9) For the purposes of this section, an assumed sale of a portion of the assumed amount of stock shall be assumed to take place on the last day before the payment representing the proceeds of the sale is due on which bargains in $2\frac{1}{2}\%$ Consolidated Stock, other than bargains at special prices, were recorded on the London Stock Exchange, and at a price half way between the highest and lowest prices at which bargains in that stock, other than bargains at special prices, were recorded on that Exchange on that day.

(10) Trustees appointed by the Post Office for the purposes of this section shall hold moneys received by them thereunder, and any sums accruing by reason of the investment by them of any moneys so received, upon such trusts as may be declared by the Post Office for the purposes of this section, being trusts the objects of which consist in the payment, or the making of provision for the payment, of pensions, allowances and gratuities to, and in respect of, persons with respect to whom

determinations made under section 43 of this Act are in force and in the reimbursement of the Post Office sums paid under section 44 or 46 of this Act.

(11) Section 6(1) of this Act shall not operate so as to preclude the appointment of trustees or the declaration of trusts by the Post Office for the purposes of this section before the appointed day.

Amendment of section 6 of the Commonwealth Telegraphs Act 1949.

1949 c. 39.

48. Subsection (2) of section 6 of the Commonwealth Telegraphs Act 1949 (which provides for the making of regulations with respect to the payment of pensions to, or in respect of, employees of Cable and Wireless Limited) shall have effect as if, in paragraph (c) and sub-paragraphs (d)(iv), (v) and (vi), references which, by virtue of section 4 of this Act, are to be construed as referring to the Minister included references to the Post Office.

Provisions as to pensions of former employees of Cable and Wireless Limited and certain other persons.

49.—(1) The Minister may, by statutory instrument (which shall be subject to annulment in pursuance of a resolution of either House of Parliament) make, with the consent of the Minister for the Civil Service, such regulations with respect to the payment of pensions to, or in respect of, persons who, at the passing of this Act are serving in the department of the Postmaster General, being—

  (a) persons who have pension rights under any of the following schemes, that is to say, the existing pension schemes, the scheme for the payment of pensions commonly known as the Cable and Wireless Pension Fund (being a scheme subsisting by virtue of regulations made under section 6 of the Commonwealth Telegraphs Act 1949) and the scheme for the payment of pensions commonly known as the Cable and Wireless Staff Dependants' Fund (being a scheme so subsisting) ; or

  (b) persons, other than as aforesaid, who have been in the employment of Cable and Wireless Limited ;

as appear to him to be requisite for securing that they, and persons claiming in right of them, are not adversely affected in the matter of pension rights by reason only that, in consequence of this Act, they cease to serve in that department.

(2) Subsections (2) to (4), (7) and (8) of the said section 6 shall apply for the purposes of this section as if references to that section and subsection (1) thereof included references to the foregoing subsection, as if, for references to the existing pension schemes (except in subsection (8)), there were substituted references to the schemes mentioned in subsection (1)(a) above,

and as if, in subsection (7), for the reference to 1st January 1947
there were substituted a reference to the day on which this Act
passes ; and subsection (5) of that section shall, in its application
to subsection (2)(*a*), as applied by this section, have effect as if,
for the references to the purposes of any of the existing pension
schemes, there were substituted a reference to the purposes of
any of the schemes so mentioned.

(3) Regulations under this section may amend or revoke provisions of regulations under the said section 6.

50. If the sole remaining pension which, on 31st October   The Post Office to
1968, is in course of payment under the Injuries in War (Com-   continue payment of the remaining
pensation) Act 1915 at the expense of the Postmaster General   pension under the Injuries in War
is still in course of payment immediately before the appointed   (Compensation) Act 1915.
day, it shall, as from that day, be, by virtue of this section,   1915 c. 24.
payable by the Post Office at the annual rate at which it is
payable immediately before that day.

51.—(1) The Secretary of State, with the consent of the   Payments to
Treasury, may from time to time make to the Post Office, out   the Post Office
of the National Insurance Fund, such payments as are necessary   out of the National
to secure that, from year to year, it receives the aggregate of   Insurance
the sums that might, in the estimation of the Government   Fund and the
Actuary (after consultation with the Secretary of State and the   Industrial
Post Office), have been paid to members, officers and servants   Injuries Fund.
of the Post Office under the National Insurance Act 1965 by   1965 c. 51.
way of sickness benefit and maternity benefit consisting in
maternity allowance had they not, under agreements entered
into by them with the Post Office, undertaken to refrain from
claiming those benefits in consideration, while entitled to claim
them, of their drawing unabated sick pay.

(2) The Secretary of State, with the consent of the Treasury,
may from time to time make to the Post Office, out of the
Industrial Injuries Fund, such payments as are necessary to
secure that, from year to year, it receives the aggregate of the
sums that might, in the estimation of the Government Actuary
(after consultation with the Secretary of State and the Post
Office) have been paid to members, officers and servants of the
Post Office under the National Insurance (Industrial Injuries)   1965 c. 52.
Act 1965 by way of injury benefit had they not, under agreements entered into by them with the Post Office, undertaken to
refrain from claiming it in consideration, while entitled to claim
it, of their drawing unabated sick pay.

(3) In the application of this section to Northern Ireland—

    (*a*) for the references to the Secretary of State there shall
        be substituted references to the Ministry of Health and
        Social Services for Northern Ireland ;

(*b*) for the references to the Treasury there shall be substituted references to the Ministry of Finance for Northern Ireland;

(*c*) for the references to the National Insurance Fund and the Industrial Injuries Fund there shall be substituted respectively references to the Northern Ireland National Insurance Fund and the Northern Ireland Industrial Injuries Fund; and

1965 c. 51.
1965 c. 52.

1966 c. 6 (N.I.).
1966 c. 9 (N.I.).

(*d*) for the references to the National Insurance Act 1965 and the National Insurance (Industrial Injuries) Act 1965 there shall be substituted respectively references to the National Insurance Act (Northern Ireland) 1966 and the National Insurance (Industrial Injuries) Act (Northern Ireland) 1966.

Rating

Rating in
England and
Wales.
1967 c. 9.

52.—(1) For the purposes of valuation lists prepared under section 68 of the General Rate Act 1967 so as to come into force on any 1st April after the appointed day, the Minister of Housing and Local Government shall, after consultation with the Post Office and such associations of local authorities and such local authorities as he considers appropriate,—

(*a*) by order determine the aggregate amount of the rateable values of all hereditaments occupied by the Post Office by any such property as follows, namely, posts, wires, underground cables and ducts, telephone kiosks and other equipment not within a building, being property used for the purposes of telecommunication services; and

(*b*) by order determine the aggregate amount of the rateable values of the hereditaments occupied by the Post Office by the underground railway;

and such person as that Minister may by order specify shall, in such manner as that Minister may by order prescribe,—

(i) apportion the amount determined under paragraph (*a*) above among the rating districts in which the hereditaments mentioned in that paragraph are situate; and

(ii) apportion the amount determined under paragraph (*b*) above among the rating districts in which the hereditaments mentioned in that paragraph are situate;

and (subject to the provisions of this section) for the purposes of those lists, so much of the amount determined under paragraph (*a*) above as is apportioned to a rating district shall be the rateable value of such of the hereditaments mentioned in that paragraph as are in that district, and so much of the amount determined under paragraph (*b*) above as is apportioned to a rating district shall be the rateable value of such of the hereditaments mentioned in that paragraph as are in that district; and rateable values shall be shown accordingly in lists transmitted to rating authorities in pursuance of section 68(2) of the General Rate Act 1967.

(2) An order under paragraph (*a*) of the foregoing subsection may, if the Minister of Housing and Local Government thinks fit, provide, with respect to each of the years subsequent to the first with respect to which the order has effect or with respect to such of those years as may be specified in the order,—

    (*a*) for the aggregate amount referred to in that paragraph to be re-determined in manner prescribed by the order; or

    (*b*) for the apportioned parts of that amount to be varied in manner so prescribed;

and, where such an order includes such provision as is authorised by paragraph (*a*) of this subsection to be included therein, the aggregate amount, as re-determined in accordance with the order, shall be apportioned amongst the rating districts in which the hereditaments in question are situate in like manner as that amount, as determined by the order, was apportioned.

(3) Where an order under this section includes any such provision as is authorised by the last foregoing subsection to be included therein it may, further, include provision for effecting such alterations in rateable values shown in rating lists as are rendered requisite in consequence of an apportionment effected by virtue of the last foregoing subsection or a variation effected by virtue of the order and for any incidental, supplementary or consequential matters for which it appears to the Minister of Housing and Local Government requisite to provide for the purposes of the order.

(4) No proposal shall be made under section 69 of the General Rate Act 1967 for the alteration of a rateable value shown, by virtue of this section, in a list.

(5) For the purposes of the law relating to rating, the Post Office shall be treated as not being a public utility undertaking.

(6) An order under this section shall be made by statutory instrument which shall be subject to annulment in pursuance of a resolution of either House of Parliament.

PART III
1967 c. 9.

1913 c. cxvi.

1954 c. xxix.

(7) Expressions used in this section and in the General Rate Act 1967 have the same meanings in this section as in that Act, and the expression " the underground railway " means the railway constructed, and the works executed, by the Postmaster General in exercise of the powers conferred by the Post Office (London) Railway Act 1913, and the railway constructed, and the works associated therewith executed, by him in exercise of the powers conferred by the Post Office (Site and Railway) Act 1954.

(8) This section extends to England and Wales only.

Rating in
Scotland.

53.—(1) For the purposes of the valuation roll for the year 1971-72 and for each subsequent year of revaluation, the Secretary of State shall, after consultation with the Post Office and such associations of local authorities and such local authorities as he considers appropriate, by order determine the aggregate amount of the rateable values of all lands and heritages occupied by the Post Office by any such property as follows, namely, posts, wires, underground cables and ducts, telephone kiosks and other equipment not within a building, being property used for the purposes of telecommunication services.

(2) The aggregate amount determined under the foregoing subsection shall be entered by the Assessor of Public Undertakings (Scotland) in the valuation roll made up by him and shall be apportioned by him in that roll among rating areas in such manner as the Secretary of State may by order determine.

(3) An order under subsection (1) above may, if the Secretary of State thinks fit, provide, with respect to each of the years subsequent to the first with respect to which the order has effect or with respect to such of those years as may be specified in the order,—

(a) for the aggregate amount referred to in that subsection to be re-determined in manner prescribed by the order ; or

(b) for the apportioned parts of that amount to be varied in manner so prescribed ;

and, where such an order includes such provision as is authorised by paragraph (a) above to be included therein, the aggregate amount, as re-determined in accordance with the order, shall be apportioned among rating areas in like manner as that amount, as determined by the order, was apportioned.

(4) Where an order under this section includes any such provision as is authorised by the last foregoing subsection to be included therein it may, further, include provision for effecting such alterations in rateable values shown in the valuation roll as are rendered requisite in consequence of an apportionment effected by virtue of the last foregoing subsection or a variation effected by virtue of the order and for any incidental, supplementary or consequential matters for which it appears to the Secretary of State requisite to provide for the purposes of the order.

(5) The rate to be levied by a county council for the year 1971-72 and subsequent years on the rateable value apportioned to their area by virtue of subsection (2) above shall be the mean of the county rate and the highest aggregate rate levied in the separately rated areas of the landward area of the county.

(6) An order under this section shall be made by statutory instrument which shall be subject to annulment in pursuance of a resolution of either House of Parliament.

(7) In this section " county rate " has the same meaning as in section 224(1) of the Local Government (Scotland) Act 1947, and other expressions have the same meanings as in the Local Government (Scotland) Act 1966.

1947 c. 43.
1966 c. 51.

(8) This section extends to Scotland only.

54.—(1) For the purposes of any valuation lists coming into force for the year beginning 1st April in a relevant year the Secretary of State shall, after consultation with the Post Office and such associations of rating authorities and such rating authorities as he considers appropriate, by order determine the aggregate amount of the net annual value of the following hereditaments occupied by the Post Office for the purposes of telecommunication services, namely, posts, wires, underground cables and ducts, telephone kiosks and other equipment not within a building.

(2) The aggregate amount determined under subsection (1) above shall be apportioned by the Commissioner of Valuation for Northern Ireland in the valuation lists prepared by him among the areas of local authorities in such manner as the Secretary of State may by order prescribe.

(3) An order under subsection (1) above may, if the Secretary of State thinks fit, provide, with respect to each of the years subsequent to the first with respect to which the order has effect

or with respect to such of those years as may be specified in the order,—

> (*a*) for the aggregate amount referred to in that subsection to be re-determined in manner prescribed by the order ; or

> (*b*) for the apportioned parts of that amount to be varied in manner so prescribed ;

and, where such an order includes such provision as is authorised by paragraph (*a*) above to be included therein, the aggregate amount, as re-determined in accordance with the order, shall be apportioned among the areas of the local authorities in which the hereditaments in question are situate in like manner as that amount, as determined by the order, was apportioned.

(4) Where an order under this section includes any such provision as is authorised by the last foregoing subsection to be included therein it may, further, include provision for effecting such alterations in net annual values shown in valuation lists as are rendered requisite in consequence of an apportionment effected by virtue of that subsection or a variation effected by virtue of the order and for any incidental, supplementary or consequential matters for which it appears to the Secretary of State requisite to provide for the purposes of the order.

(5) Where the Secretary of State makes an order under subsection (1) above which includes any such provision as is authorised by subsection (3) above, any such hereditament as is mentioned in subsection (1) above shall, for the purposes of 1854 c. 8. sections 4 and 5 of the Valuation (Ireland) Act 1854, be deemed to have been included in any lists prepared under those sections for any year in which any re-determination or variation effected by virtue of the order has effect.

(6) The Commissioner of Valuation for Northern Ireland shall not—

> (*a*) make any interim revision of the net annual value of any such hereditament as is mentioned in subsection (1) above ; or

> (*b*) except as authorised by virtue of the foregoing provisions of this section, make any annual revision of any such hereditament as is so mentioned.

(7) The Post Office shall, for the purposes of section 4 of the 1928 c. 30 Rating and Valuation (Apportionment) Act (Northern Ireland) (N.I.). 1928, be deemed not to be a public supply undertaking.

(8) An order under this section shall be made by statutory instrument which shall be subject to annulment in pursuance of a resolution of either House of Parliament.

(9) In this section—

" annual revision " means a revision under section 5 of the Valuation (Ireland) Act 1854 ;   1854 c. 8.

" interim revision " means a revision under section 13 of the Local Government (Finance) Act (Northern Ireland) 1936 c. 10 1936 or section 4 of the Valuation Acts Amendment (N.I.). Act (Northern Ireland) 1953 ;   1953 c. 10 (N.I.).

" local authorities " means the councils of counties, county and other boroughs and of urban and rural districts ;

" relevant year " means—

(*a*) unless the third general revaluation comes into force before 1st April, 1973, the year 1973 ;

(*b*) until the third general revaluation comes into force, each successive fifth year after the year 1973 ;

(*c*) the calendar year in which the third, and any subsequent, general revaluation first comes into force.

(10) This section extends to Northern Ireland only.

Lands

55.—(1) The Minister may authorise the Post Office to Compulsory purchase compulsorily any land in Great Britain which is purchase of required by it for, or in connection with, the exercise of its powers land in Great or as to which it can reasonably be foreseen that it will be so Britain. required ; and the Acquisition of Land (Authorisation Procedure) 1946 c. 49. Act 1946 shall apply to the compulsory purchase of land in Great Britain by the Post Office as if the Post Office were a local authority within the meaning of that Act and as if this Act had been in force immediately before the commencement of that Act.

(2) The power of purchasing land compulsorily in this section shall include power to acquire, by the creation of a new right an easement or other right over land, other than land which would, for the purposes of the Acquisition of Land (Authorisation Procedure) Act 1946, form part of a common, open space or fuel or field garden allotment.

2 M

PART III

1946 c. 49.
1947 c. 42.

(3) In the application of this section to Scotland, there shall be substituted, for any reference to the Acquisition of Land (Authorisation Procedure) Act 1946, a reference to the Acquisition of Land (Authorisation Procedure) (Scotland) Act 1947 and, for any reference to an easement, a reference to a servitude ; and the reference in the last foregoing subsection to a fuel or field garden allotment shall be omitted.

Compulsory purchase of land in Northern Ireland.

56.—(1) Where the Post Office desires to acquire, otherwise than by agreement, any land in Northern Ireland required by it for, or in connection with, the exercise of its powers or as to which it can reasonably be foreseen that it will be so required, it may apply to the Minister for an order vesting that land in it, and the Minister shall have power to make such an order.

1948 c. 28
(N.I.).

(2) For the purposes of the acquisition of land by means of a vesting order under this section, Schedules 5 and 6 to the Roads Act (Northern Ireland) 1948 (as amended by any enactment of the Parliament of Northern Ireland passed before the passing of this Act) are hereby incorporated in this Act subject to the modifications specified in Schedule 3 to this Act.

1919 c. 57.

1964 c. 29
(N.I.).

(3) The Acquisition of Land (Assessment of Compensation) Act 1919 shall, in its application to any land vested in the Post Office by an order made under this section, have effect as amended by the Lands Tribunal and Compensation Act (Northern Ireland) 1964.

1954 c. 33
(N.I.).

(4) In this section, and in Schedule 3 to this Act and in the said Schedule 5 as incorporated in this Act, " land " has the meaning assigned to it by section 45(1)(a) of the Interpretation Act (Northern Ireland) 1954 and, in Schedule 3 to this Act and in the said Schedule 5 as so incorporated, " estate " has the meaning assigned to it by section 45(2) of that Act.

Entry, for exploratory purposes, on land in England or Wales.

57.—(1) A person duly authorised in writing by the Post Office may, at any reasonable time, enter upon and survey any land in England or Wales other than land covered by buildings or used as a garden or pleasure ground, for the purpose of ascertaining whether the land would be suitable for use for the purposes of its business.

1962 c. 38.

(2) Sections 211(6) and 212(1) to (3) and (6) of the Town and Country Planning Act 1962 (which contain supplementary provisions relating to the powers of entry conferred by section 211(1) to (5) thereof) shall have effect in relation to the power

conferred by this section as they have effect in relation to the PART III powers conferred by the said section 211, subject, however, to the following modifications, namely,—

(*a*) that section 211(6) (which relates to power to search and bore for the purpose of ascertaining the nature of the subsoil or the presence of minerals therein) shall so have effect as if the words " or the presence of minerals therein " were omitted ; and

(*b*) that section 212(1) (which requires twenty-four hours' notice to be given of an intended entry upon occupied land) shall so have effect as if, for the words " twenty-four hours ", there were substituted the words " twenty-eight days ".

(3) Where, in an exercise of the power conferred by this section, any damage is caused to land or to chattels, any person interested in the land or chattels may recover from the Post Office compensation in respect of the damage ; and where, in consequence of an exercise of that power, any person is disturbed in his enjoyment of any land or chattels, he may recover from the Post Office compensation in respect of the disturbance.

(4) Section 128 of the Town and Country Planning Act 1962 1962 c. 38. (which provides for the determination of disputes as to compensation under Part VII of that Act) shall apply to any question of disputed compensation under this section.

(5) This section shall come into operation on the appointed day.

58.—(1) A person duly authorised in writing by the Post Office Entry, for may, at any reasonable time, enter upon and survey any land in exploratory Scotland, other than land covered by buildings or used as a purposes, on garden or pleasure ground, for the purpose of ascertaining land in Scotland. whether the land would be suitable for use for the purposes of its business.

(2) Subsections (4) to (6) and subsection (9) of section 99 of the Town and Country Planning (Scotland) Act 1947 (sup- 1947 c. 53. plementary provisions as to powers of entry) shall have effect in relation to the power conferred by this section as they have effect in relation to the powers conferred by the said section 99 subject, however, to the following modifications, namely,—

(*a*) that section 99(4) (twenty-four hours' notice to be given of an intended entry upon occupied land) shall so have effect as if, for the words, " twenty-four hours ",

Pᴀʀᴛ III
there were substituted the words " twenty-eight days " ; and

(b) that section 99(9) (power to search and bore for minerals, &c.) shall so have effect as if the words " or the presence of minerals therein " were omitted.

(3) Where, in an exercise of the power conferred by this section, any damage is caused to land or to corporeal moveables, any person interested in the land or corporeal movables may recover from the Post Office compensation in respect of the damage ; and where, in consequence of an exercise of that power, any person is disturbed in his enjoyment of any land or corporeal moveables, he may recover from the Post Office compensation in respect of the disturbance.

(4) Any question arising under this section as to the effect of damage or as to the amount of compensation shall, in the case of dispute be determined by arbitration, and the reference in such an arbitration shall be to a single arbiter to be appointed by agreement between the parties or, in default of an agreement, by the Minister.

(5) This section shall come into operation on the appointed day.

Entry, for exploratory purposes, on land in Northern Ireland.

59.—(1) A person duly authorised in writing by the Post Office may, at any reasonable time, enter upon and survey any land in Northern Ireland, other than land covered by buildings or used as a garden or pleasure ground, for the purpose of ascertaining whether the land would be suitable for use for the purposes of its business.

1965 c. 23 (N.I.).

(2) Subsections (2) to (5) and (8) of section 40 of the Land Development Values (Compensation) Act (Northern Ireland) 1965 (which contain supplementary provisions relating to the power of entry conferred by subsection (1) of that section) shall have effect in relation to the power conferred by this section as they have effect in relation to the power conferred by the said subsection (1), subject, however, to the following modifications, namely,—

(a) that section 40(2) (which relates to power to search and bore for the purpose of ascertaining the nature of the subsoil or the presence of minerals therein) shall so have effect as if the words " or the presence of minerals therein " were omitted ; and

(*b*) that section 40(3)(*b*) (which requires three days' notice   PART III
to be given of an intended entry upon occupied land)
shall so have effect as if, for the word " three ", there
were substituted the word " twenty-eight ".

(3) Where, in an exercise of the power conferred by this
section, any damage is caused to land or to chattels, any person
interested in the land or chattels may recover from the Post
Office compensation in respect of the damage ; and where, in
consequence of an exercise of that power, any person is disturbed in his enjoyment of any land or chattels, he may recover
from the Post Office compensation in respect of the disturbance.

(4) Section 31 of the Land Development Values (Compensa- 1965 c. 23
tion) Act (Northern Ireland) 1965 (which provides for the deter- (N.I.).
mination of disputes as to compensation under Part III of that
Act) shall apply to any question of disputed compensation under
this section.

(5) This section shall come into operation on the appointed
day.

60.—(1) For the purpose of the acquisition by the Post Office Application, to
by agreement of land in England or Wales, the provisions of acquisitions of
Part I of the Compulsory Purchase Act 1965 (so far as land by the
applicable) other than sections 4 to 8, section 27 and section 31 agreement, of
shall apply. certain
                                                              statutory
(2) For the purpose of the acquisition by the Post Office by provisions
agreement of land in Scotland, section 37(2) of the Town and relating to
Country Planning (Scotland) Act 1947 (incorporation of Lands compulsory
Clauses Acts) shall, with any necessary modifications, apply for purchase.
the purposes of this Act as it applies for the purposes of that 1965 c. 56.
Act. 1947 c. 53.

(3) For the purpose of the acquisition by the Post Office by
agreement of land in Northern Ireland, the Lands Clauses Acts
shall be incorporated with this Act except for sections 127 to
133 (sale of superfluous land) and sections 150 and 151 (access
to the special Act) of the Lands Clauses Consolidation Act 1845. 1845 c. 18.

61. The Chancellor and Council of the Duchy of Lancaster Power to sell to
may, if they think fit, agree with the Post Office for the sale, the Post Office
and absolutely make sale, for such sum of money as appears to Her Majesty
to them to be sufficient consideration for the same, of any land in right of the
belonging to Her Majesty in right of the Duchy of Lancaster Duchy of Lan-
which the Post Office seeks to acquire in exercise of the power caster.
conferred on it by virtue of section 7(2)(*f*) of this Act.

2 M 3

PART III
Requisitions on
title as to
Treasury consent
to dealings with
land precluded.

62. A person dealing with the Post Office in respect of land shall not be bound or entitled to inquire whether the consent of the Treasury to any previous dealing with the land was requisite or whether, if it was, it was given.

Status of land
vested in the Post
Office by virtue of
Part III.

63. Land vested in the Post Office by virtue of this Part of this Act shall be deemed for all purposes to have been acquired by it for the purposes of its undertaking.

Miscellaneous Matters

Inviolability
of mails.

64.—(1) Subject to the provisions of this section, a packet in the post, anything contained in a packet in the post and a mail-bag containing a packet in the post shall (if it is not the property of the Crown) have the like immunity from examination under a power conferred by or under any enactment (whether passed before or after this Act), from seizure or detention under such a power, from seizure under distress or in execution and from retention by virtue of a lien, as it would have if it were the property of the Crown.

(2) The Post Office and a person who is engaged in its business shall be entitled to the like immunity from prosecution for possession of anything contained in a packet in the post, being a thing whose possession is prohibited by or under any enactment (whether passed before or after this Act), and for failure to comply, as respects anything contained in a packet in the post, with any condition or restriction imposed by or under any enactment (whether passed before or after this Act) with respect to its possession, carriage or delivery, as the Post Office and that person would be entitled to if the Post Office were a government department.

1953 c. 36.

(3) Subsection (1) above does not apply to a power conferred by an enactment for the time being in force relating to customs in its application, by virtue of section 16 of the Post Office Act 1953 or any regulations made under that section, to goods contained in postal packets, or to the powers conferred by sections 17 (detention of postal packets containing contraband) and 26(6) (search and seizure of postal packets by officers of customs and excise) of that Act.

Obligation
of secrecy.

65.—(1) Information obtained by a person in the course of the provision for another, by virtue of this Part of this Act, of data processing services or services connected therewith shall not, without the consent of that other, be disclosed by the first-mentioned person except for the purpose of performing his duties in relation to those services or in such cases as may be required by law.

(2) A person who discloses information in contravention of the foregoing subsection shall be liable—

(a) on conviction on indictment, to imprisonment for a term not exceeding two years or to a fine, or to both ;

(b) on summary conviction, to a fine not exceeding £400.

66.—(1) Any statutory provision made with respect to a harbour authority shall, on the appointed day, cease to have effect in so far as it exempts mail-bags or any description thereof from charges.

(2) No charge imposed by a harbour authority in respect of goods brought into, taken out of, or carried through a harbour which, in the exercise and performance of statutory powers and duties, they are engaged in improving, maintaining or managing shall apply to goods contained in—

(a) mail-bags carried by the Post Office or consigned by it to another for carriage (whether to a foreign administration or not) or by a foreign administration to it for carriage ; or

(b) mail-bags consigned by one foreign administration to another, being mail-bags which, when in the United Kingdom, are in the charge of the Post Office.

(3) Charges in respect of mail-bags and their contents exigible by a harbour authority at a harbour which, in the exercise and performance of statutory powers and duties, they are engaged in improving, maintaining or managing (being mail-bags carried or consigned as aforesaid) shall, notwithstanding anything in any statutory provision made with respect to the authority, not be payable before the expiration of the period of eight weeks beginning with the day on which the bags are brought within the limits of the harbour, and shall be recoverable by means of proceedings instituted in that behalf in any court of competent jurisdiction to the exclusion of any other means.

(4) In this section, except in its application to Northern Ireland or the Isle of Man, references to a harbour which, in the exercise and performance of statutory powers and duties, a harbour authority are engaged in improving, maintaining or managing shall be construed in like manner as if they were contained in the Harbours Act 1964.

(5) In the application of this section to Northern Ireland, references to a harbour which, in the exercise and performance

PART III   of statutory powers and duties, a harbour authority are engaged in improving, maintaining or managing shall be construed as references to a harbour which is being improved, maintained or managed by such an authority in the exercise of powers conferred by a statutory provision, in the performance of duties imposed by a statutory provision or in the exercise and performance of powers conferred and duties imposed by a statutory provision.

(6) In the application of this section to the Isle of Man, references to a harbour which, in the exercise and performance of statutory powers and duties, a harbour authority are engaged in improving, maintaining or managing shall be construed as referring to a harbour vested in the Isle of Man Harbour Board.

Mail-bags not to be subject to control by harbour authorities.

67. Nothing in a statutory provision made (whether before or after this Act) with respect to a harbour authority shall extend to regulate or subject to control—

(a) mail-bags carried by the Post Office or consigned by it to another for carriage (whether to a foreign administration or not) or by a foreign administration to it for carriage ; or

(b) mail-bags consigned by one foreign administration to another, being mail-bags which, when in the United Kingdom, are in the charge of the Post Office.

Abolition of exemptions from tolls.
1953 c. 36.

68. On the appointed day, the following shall cease to have effect, namely,—

(a) section 77 of the Post Office Act 1953 (exemption from toll) ; and

(b) any other statutory provision, in so far as (apart from this section) it would operate to exempt from a toll a person engaged in the business of the Post Office or an animal or vehicle used for the purposes of that business, or a mail-bag (within the meaning of the Post Office Act 1953) or person in charge thereof.

Documentary evidence as to sums due for services.

69.—(1) A certificate of the Post Office that a specified sum is due to it from a specified person under provisions of a scheme made under section 28 of this Act with respect to telecommunication services shall, in any proceedings instituted by it against him or his personal representatives or against it by him or his personal representatives, be evidence (and, in Scotland, sufficient evidence) of that fact.

(2) A certificate of the Post Office that a specified sum is due to it from a specified person under an agreement with respect to telecommunication services provided by it shall (subject to any term of the agreement to the contrary), in any proceedings instituted by it against him or his personal representatives or against it by him or his personal representatives, be evidence (and, in Scotland, sufficient evidence) of that fact.

(3) In any proceedings instituted by or against the Post Office to which the rate at which a charge was levied at any time, in respect of a service, by an authority outside the British Islands is material, a certificate of the Post Office that the charge was levied at that rate at that time in respect of that service by that authority shall be conclusive evidence of that fact.

70.—(1) Where, in the British Islands, a money or postal order issued by the Post Office is presented for payment by a banker to whom it has been delivered for collection, payment of it to him discharges it.

Provisions as to money and postal orders.

(2) Where, in the British Islands,—

(a) an uncrossed money or postal order issued by the Post Office, being an order expressed to be payable to a person specified or described therein and being, or purporting to be, signed by him or on his behalf ; or

(b) an uncrossed postal order so issued, being an order not expressed to be payable to such a person ;

is presented for payment otherwise than by a banker to whom it has been delivered for collection, payment of the order to the person by whom it is presented discharges it.

(3) A money or postal order issued by the Post Office is discharged by the payment thereof outside the British Islands in accordance with arrangements in that behalf made by the Post Office.

(4) Where a money or postal order issued by a foreign administration is paid by the Post Office to a banker to whom it has been delivered for collection on behalf of a person other than the true owner of the order, the Post Office shall not be liable to the true owner of the order by reason of having paid it to that banker.

(5) Where—

(a) an uncrossed money or postal order issued by a foreign administration, being an order expressed to be payable

2 M*

to a person specified or described therein and purporting to be signed by him or on his behalf ; or

(b) an uncrossed postal order so issued, being an order not expressed to be payable to such a person ;

is presented to the Post Office for payment otherwise than by a banker to whom it has been delivered for collection or the true owner of the order, payment of the order by the Post Office to the person presenting it shall not render the Post Office liable to the true owner of the order.

(6) No proceedings shall lie against the Post Office for loss or damage due to refusal by it to pay, or delay by it in paying, a money or postal order issued by it or a foreign administration.

(7) A scheme made under section 28 of this Act may provide that a money or postal order issued by the Post Office or a foreign administration will not, after the expiration of a specified period, be paid by the Post Office except on satisfaction of specified conditions.

(8) References in this section (except that in subsection (3)) to a money order issued by the Post Office shall be construed as including references to an order issued by it in pursuance of
1953 c. 36.   such an arrangement as is mentioned in section 24 of the Post Office Act 1953 (arrangements with other countries as to transmission of small sums through post offices), being an order which is for the payment of money in the British Islands and corresponds to a money order issued by the Post Office.

Recoupment of losses on money orders wrongly paid to bankers.   **71.**—(1) Where, after payment by the Post Office to a banker to whom it has been delivered for collection of a money order issued by the Post Office or a foreign administration, it is found that it ought not to have been paid, the sum paid may be deducted from sums subsequently falling to be paid by the Post Office to that banker by way of payment of money orders so issued that have been delivered to him for collection.

(2) References in this section to a money order issued by the Post Office shall be construed as including references to an order issued by it in pursuance of such an arrangement as is mentioned in section 24 of the Post Office Act 1953, being an order which is for the payment of money in the British Islands and corresponds to a money order issued by the Post Office.

Remuneration of the Post Office for services rendered in relation to parliamentary elections.
1949 c. 68.   **72.**—(1) In the case of a postal or telegraphic service rendered by the Post Office in pursuance of the Representation of the People Act 1949 without charge, the Post Office shall be entitled to be remunerated for having rendered it at the rate for the time being fixed in relation thereto by virtue of section 28 of this Act.

(2) A sum which, by virtue of the foregoing subsection, the PART III
Post Office is entitled to receive shall be charged on, and issued
out of, the Consolidated Fund.

73. The Post Office may reimburse the Minister the whole Reimburse-
or any part of a sum paid by him by way of contribution ment by the
towards the expenses of an international organisation of which Post Office of
Her Majesty's Government in the United Kingdom is a member, contributions
being an organisation concerned with activities which the Post to international
Office has power to carry on. organisations.

74.—(1) In the case of the Post Office, section 61 of the Taxation
Finance Act 1965 (company reconstructions without change of of the
ownership) shall, as from the appointed day, apply, so far as Post Office's
applicable, as if the Postmaster General had been a company capital gains.
and the condition mentioned in subsection (1)(*a*) were satisfied. 1965 c. 25.

(2) Part III of the Finance Act 1965 (capital gains) shall
apply in relation to a disposal by the Post Office of an asset
acquired by virtue of this Part of this Act as if the acquisition
or provision of the asset by the Crown had been the acquisition
or provision of it by the Post Office.

75.—(1) The Public Records Act 1958 shall, as from the Records.
appointed day, have effect as if the Post Office were included 1958 c. 51.
amongst the bodies and establishments set out in Part II of the
Table at the end of paragraph 3 of Schedule 1 to that Act.

(2) The Minister shall have power by order to vest in the Post
Office the property in such records of the department of the
Postmaster General as may be specified in or described by the
order, and to give to the Post Office, with respect to records in
the case of which the property therein has been vested in the
Post Office by an order under this subsection, such directions as
he thinks fit for securing that they are available to the Crown
for inspection and copying.

76. The provisions of Schedule 4 to this Act shall have effect Consequential
for adapting the provisions of the enactments and Orders in adaptations of
Council therein mentioned in consequence of the assumption by enactments.
the Post Office of functions which, before the appointed day, are
exercised and performed by the Postmaster General.

77. The provisions of Schedule 5 of this Act shall have effect Repair of
for repairing minor deficiencies in the Telegraph Act 1863, the minor statutory
Telegraph Act 1868, the Post Office (Protection) Act 1884 and 1863 c. 112
the Post Office Act 1953. 1868 c. 110.
1884 c. 76.
1953 c. 36.

PART III
Penalization
of improper
use of tele-
communication
services.

78. A person who—

(*a*) sends, by means of a public telecommunication service, a message or other matter that is grossly offensive or of an indecent, obscene or menacing character ; or

(*b*) for the purpose of causing annoyance, inconvenience or needless anxiety to another, sends by those means a message that he knows to be false or persistently makes use for that purpose of public telecommunication services ;

shall be guilty of an offence and liable, on summary conviction, to a fine not exceeding £50.

Amendment of
law as to
packets
addressed to a
poste restante.
1953 c. 36.

79. Section 87(2)(*c*) of the Post Office Act 1953 (which provides that delivery of a postal packet at the premises to which it is addressed or redirected, or to the addressee's servant or agent or to some other person considered to be authorised to receive the packet, shall be a delivery to the addressee) shall have effect as if, after the word " redirected ", there were inserted the words " (except they be a post office from which it is to be collected) ".

Provision of
information
to persons
holding office
under the
Crown.

80. A requirement to do what is necessary to inform designated persons holding office under the Crown concerning matters and things transmitted or in course of transmission by means of postal or telecommunication services provided by the Post Office may be laid on the Post Office for the like purposes and in the like manner as, at the passing of this Act, a requirement may be laid on the Postmaster General to do what is necessary to inform such persons concerning matters and things transmitted or in course of transmission by means of such services provided by him.

Modification of
enactments
relating to
wages councils.
1959 c. 69.
1938 c. 44.

1945 c. 21
(N.I.).

S.R. & O.
1952/193
(N.I.).

81.—(1) There shall be excluded from the workers in relation to whom the Road Haulage Wages Council and any wages council established under Part I of the Wages Councils Act 1959 may operate any persons employed by the Post Office on road haulage work within the meaning of the Road Haulage Wages Act 1938 ; and there shall be excluded from the workers in relation to whom the Road Haulage Wages Council (Northern Ireland) and any wages council established under the Wages Councils Act (Northern Ireland) 1945 may operate any persons employed by the Post Office on road haulage work within the meaning of paragraph 1 of the Schedule to the Road Haulage Wages Council (Northern Ireland) (Variation) Order 1952.

(2) Part II of the Road Haulage Wages Act 1938 (provisions with respect to the remuneration of workers employed by private

carriers in connection with the mechanical transport of goods by road) shall not apply to work done by a person employed by the Post Office.   Part III

(3) For the purposes of any wages regulation order in force under Part II of the Wages Councils Act 1959 on the appointed day, vehicles which are being used by the Post Office by persons employed by it, being vehicles which are specified in licences, shall be deemed to be vehicles not specified in any licence, and so much of section 94(10) of the Transport Act 1968 as requires vehicles not specified in an A licence or a B licence to be treated as so specified if used wholly or mainly for a purpose for which, but for section 93 of that Act, an A licence or a B licence would be required shall not apply to vehicles that are being used by the Post Office by persons employed by it.   1959 c. 69.   1968 c. 73.

82.—(1) The Minister may, at the request of a county council and after consultation with the Post Office, give to the Post Office a direction that, during such period as may be specified in the direction (which shall not begin before the appointed day nor end after the day immediately preceding the transfer date), it shall, in normal business hours, issue on behalf of the council licences under the Vehicles (Excise) Act 1962.   Power of the Minister, pending transfer to the Minister of Transport from county councils of functions connected with issue of vehicle excise licences, to direct the Post Office to issue such licences.

(2) Subsections (4), (5) and (6) of section 12 of this Act shall apply for the purposes of the foregoing subsection as if any reference in those subsections to subsection (2) of that section included a reference to the foregoing subsection.

(3) In consideration of its complying with a direction given under this section with reference to a county council, the Post Office shall be entitled to receive payment from that council (of an amount to be determined, in the event of a dispute's arising as to the amount thereof, by the Minister).   1962 c. 13.

(4) In this section the expression " county council " shall be construed in like manner as if it were contained in the Vehicles (Excise) Act 1962 and " the transfer date " means the date which, by virtue of subsection (2) of section 1 of the Vehicle and Driving Licences Act 1969, is appointed by the Minister of Transport for the purposes of subsection (1) of that section.   1969 c. 27.

83. The following provisions of the Telegraph Act 1868 shall cease to have effect on the appointed day, namely,—   Repeal of certain provisions of the Telegraph Act 1868.   1868 c. 110.

(*a*) section 9(6)(*g*) (the effect of which is to require the transmission, free of charge, of business telegrams sent by the successors to certain railway undertakers);

(*b*) section 9(7) (the effect of which is to enable the said successors to be required to transmit the telegrams of others by means of lines controlled by them);

2 M* 3

PART III
1869 c. 73.

(c) section 9(8) (the effect of which, as read with section 5 of the Telegraph Act 1869, is to enable the said successors to work, without infringement of the exclusive privilege conferred by section 4 of that Act, telegraphs erected under arrangements made by them with certain traders); and

(d) section 12 (the effect of which is to subject part of the British Waterways Board's canal system to a wayleave for telegraphs and to require the transmission, free of charge, of certain telegrams sent by that Board).

Exemption from postage of certain petitions and addresses, and limitation of amount of postage recoverable in respect of parliamentary proceedings.

84.—(1) Notwithstanding anything in a scheme made under section 28 of this Act,—

(a) petitions and addresses forwarded to Her Majesty or, in Northern Ireland, to the Governor of Northern Ireland, by post shall be exempt from postage chargeable by the Post Office; and

(b) petitions and addresses to Her Majesty, and petitions addressed to either House of Parliament, sent by post to a member of either House of Parliament shall be exempt from postage so chargeable if the petitions or addresses do not exceed thirty-two ounces in weight and are sent without covers or in covers open at the sides.

(2) Notwithstanding anything in a scheme made under section 28 of this Act, where the postage chargeable by the Post Office on a packet consisting of parliamentary proceedings has not been prepaid by the sender or has been insufficiently prepaid by him, there shall not be recoverable by the Post Office (whether from the sender or the addressee) a sum exceeding the amount, as the case may be, of the postage or of the deficiency.

(3) In the application of this section to Northern Ireland, " Parliament " includes the Parliament of Northern Ireland and " parliamentary " shall be construed accordingly.

Final accounts under the Post Office Act 1961.

1961 c. 15.

85.—(1) The following provisions shall have effect in relation to the financial year ending 31st March next before the appointed day:—

(a) the duties imposed by section 12 of the Post Office Act 1961 on the Postmaster General to prepare, in respect of each financial year, a statement of accounts and a report on the business of the Post Office, shall, if not discharged by him before the appointed day, be discharged instead by the Post Office;

(*b*) the duty imposed by that section on him to lay before
Parliament copies of that report having annexed thereto
copies of the statement of accounts and of the
Comptroller and Auditor General's report thereon
shall, if not discharged by the Postmaster General
before the appointed day, be discharged instead by
the Minister ;

(*c*) the statement of accounts in respect of that year and
the copy of the Comptroller and Auditor General's
report thereon shall, if not returned by him to the
Postmaster General before the appointed day, be
returned to the Post Office ; and

(*d*) the Post Office shall transmit to the Minister copies
of any document prepared by, or returned to, it in
pursuance of this subsection.

(2) If the appointed day is other than a 1st April, the said
section 12 and the last foregoing subsection shall have effect
in relation to the period beginning with the immediately preceding 1st April and ending with the day immediately preceding
the appointed day as they apply with respect to the financial
year mentioned in that subsection, subject, however,—

(*a*) in the case of that section, to the modification that
anything required to be done before the end of a
specified month shall be done as soon as possible ;
and

(*b*) in the case of that subsection, to the omission of any
such words as render conditional a duty thereby
imposed.

86.—(1) In this Part of this Act, unless the context otherwise Interpretation
requires, the following expressions have the meanings hereby of Part III.
assigned to them respectively, that is to say : —

" accounting year " means the period beginning with the
appointed day and ending with 31st March next following or any subsequent period of twelve months beginning with the end of a previous accounting year ;

" banker " includes a body of persons, whether incorporated
or not, who carry on the business of banking ;

" the British Islands " means the United Kingdom, the Isle
of Man and the Channel Islands ;

" cash on delivery service " means a service whereby the
Post Office or a foreign administration collects or
secures the collection of a sum of money on the
delivery of anything consigned for conveyance by post
and remits it to the sender thereof ;

" foreign administration " means a postal administration
other than the Post Office ;

2 M* 4

PART III

1964 c. 40.

"harbour", except in relation to Northern Ireland or the Isle of Man, has the same meaning as in the Harbours Act 1964, in relation to Northern Ireland, means any harbour, whether natural or artificial, and any port, haven or estuary, and includes a dock and a wharf, quay, pier, jetty or other place at which seagoing ships (including hovercraft) can ship or unship goods or embark or disembark passengers and, in relation to the Isle of Man, has the meaning assigned to it by section 1 of the Harbours (Isle of Man) Act 1961 (of Tynwald);

"harbour authority", except in relation to Northern Ireland or the Isle of Man, has the same meaning as in the Harbours Act 1964, in relation to Northern Ireland, means any person in whom are vested, by any statutory provision, the powers or duties of improving, maintaining or managing a harbour and, in relation to the Isle of Man, means the Isle of Man Harbour Board;

1968 c. 59.

"hovercraft" has the same meaning as in the Hovercraft Act 1968;

"land" includes any interest in land and any right over land;

"local authority",—

    (*a*) in relation to England and Wales, means the council of a county, county borough or county district, the Greater London Council, the council of a London borough or the Common Council of the City of London;

    (*b*) in relation to Scotland, means a county council or a town council;

    (*c*) in relation to Northern Ireland, means the council of a county, county borough or county district or a joint board constituted under the Public Health Acts (Northern Ireland) 1878 to 1966 or section 7(1) of the Water Supplies and Sewerage Act (Northern Ireland) 1945;

1945 c. 17
(N.I.).

"mail-bag" includes any container in which articles are enclosed by the Post Office or a foreign administration for the purpose of the conveyance thereof by post;

"national health service authority"—

    (*a*) in relation to England and Wales, means a regional hospital board, board of governors of a teaching hospital or hospital management committee established under Part II of the National Health Service Act 1946 or an executive council established under section 31 of that Act;

1946 c. 81.

(b) in relation to Scotland, means a regional PART III
hospital board or board of management established
under Part II of the National Health Service 1947 c. 27.
(Scotland) Act 1947 or an executive council established under section 32 of that Act ;

(c) in relation to Northern Ireland, means the
Northern Ireland General Health Services Board, the
Northern Ireland Hospitals Authority, a hospital
management committee established under Part III
of the Health Services Act (Northern Ireland) 1948 1948 c. 3
or a special care management committee established (N.I.).
under Part I of the Mental Health Act (Northern 1961 c. 15
Ireland) 1961 ; (N.I.).

" statutory provision ", except in relation to Northern Ireland or the Isle of Man, has the same meaning as
in section 57(1) of the Harbours Act 1964, in relation 1964 c. 40.
to Northern Ireland, has the same meaning as in
section 1(f) of the Interpretation Act (Northern Ireland) 1954 c. 33
1954 and, in relation to the Isle of Man, means an (N.I.).
Act of Tynwald.

(2) Any reference in this Part of this Act to a subsidiary shall
be construed in accordance with section 154 of the Companies 1948 c. 38.
Act 1948 and any reference therein to a wholly owned subsidiary shall be construed in accordance with section 150(4) of
that Act.

(3) Any reference in this Part of this Act to data processing
shall be construed as including a reference to the storage and
retrieval of information.

(4) Nothing in this Part of this Act shall be taken to restrict
the construction of references to the Post Office's business so as
to exclude the performance of services which, by virtue of
section 7(1)(d) of this Act, it has power to perform.

87.—(1) In the event of the conclusion of any such agreement Power of Her
as follows, namely,— Majesty in
(a) an agreement between the Minister and the Government Council to
of the Isle of Man providing for either or both of the provision if
following, namely,— the Post Office
(i) the surrender by the Post Office, as regards surrenders
that Isle, of the privilege conferred on the Post regards the
Office by section 3 of the Post Office Act 1953 and Isle of Man
the administration in that Isle of postal services by, or the Channel
or under the authority of, that government instead Islands.
of by the Post Office ; 1953 c. 36.
(ii) the surrender by the Post Office, as regards that
Isle, of the privilege conferred on the Post Office by

section 24 of this Act and the administration in that Isle of telecommunication services by, or under the authority of, that government instead of by the Post Office ;

(b) an agreement between the Minister and the States of Jersey providing for either or both of the following, namely,—

(i) the surrender by the Post Office, as regards the Bailiwick of Jersey, of the privilege conferred on the Post Office by the said section 3 and the administration in that Bailiwick of postal services by, or under the authority of, the States instead of by the Post Office ;

(ii) the surrender by the Post Office, as regards that Bailiwick, of the privilege conferred on the Post Office by the said section 24 and the administration in that Bailiwick by, or under the authority of, the States instead of by the Post Office of such telecommunication services as are being administered there by the Post Office ; or

(c) an agreement between the Minister and the States of Guernsey providing for either or both of the following, namely,—

(i) the surrender by the Post Office, as regards the Bailiwick of Guernsey, of the privilege conferred on the Post Office by the said section 3 and the administration in that Bailiwick of postal services by, or under the authority of, the States instead of by the Post Office ;

(ii) the surrender by the Post Office, as regards that Bailiwick, of the privilege conferred on the Post Office by the said section 24 and the administration in that Bailiwick by, or under the authority of, the States instead of by the Post Office of such telecommunication services as are being administered there by the Post Office ;

Her Majesty may by Order in Council make such provision as it appears to Her requisite or expedient to make in order to enable effect to be given to the agreement or in consequence of the conclusion thereof, including in particular, provision for the amendment or repeal of enactments (including enactments contained in this Act) or other instruments.

(2) The power conferred by the foregoing subsection on Her Majesty to make an Order in Council shall include power, exercisable in like manner, to vary or revoke an Order in Council made in exercise of that power.

Extent of Part III and related Schedules   PART III

88.—(1) The following shall extend to the Isle of Man and Extent of
the Channel Islands, namely,—

(*a*) this Part of this Act, except sections 76 and 77 and any
provision which, by its terms, is limited in its operation
to a part of the United Kingdom ; and

(*b*) Schedules 1 and 2 to this Act.

(2) Section 76 of, and Schedule 4 to, this Act shall—

(*a*) in their application to an enactment that is expressed
(either in the Act containing it or in another Act, and
either directly or indirectly) to extend to the Isle of
Man, extend to that Isle ; and

(*b*) in their application to an enactment that is so expressed
to extend to the Channel Islands, extend to those
Islands.

(3) Section 67(1) of the Civil Aviation Act 1949 (power of 1949 c. 67.
Her Majesty in Council by Order to direct that any of the
provisions of that Act shall extend to any of the Channel
Islands and to the Isle of Man) shall have effect as if the reference
to any of the provisions of that Act included a reference to
section 76 of, and Schedule 4 to, this Act so far as relating to
that Act.

(4) Section 77 of, and Schedule 5 to, this Act—

(*a*) shall, except so far as relating to the Post Office 1884 c. 76.
(Protection) Act 1884, extend to the Isle of Man ; and

(*b*) shall, except so far as relating to that Act and the
Telegraph Act 1863, extend to the Channel Islands.   1863 c. 112.

(5) Subsections (1), (2) and (4) above shall have effect subject
to the provisions of any Order in Council made under the last
foregoing section.

(6) Sections 24(2) and 65(2) of this Act shall, in their application to the Isle of Man, have effect with the substitution, for the
references to indictment, of references to information.

PART IV

CONTROL OF PROGRAMME DISTRIBUTION SYSTEMS

89.—(1) Subject to the provisions of this section and to any Licensing of
exceptions for which provision may be made by order of the distribution
Minister, it shall not, as from the appointed day, be lawful, systems.
except under, and in accordance with, a written licence in that
behalf granted by him, for a system to be run for—

(*a*) the distribution in the United Kingdom, through the
agency of energy of any of the kinds specified in subsection (2) below, of a programme of matter serving,

by means of sounds or visual images (or both), to inform persons of anything or to educate or entertain them ; or

(b) the conveyance, through the agency of energy of any of the said kinds, of any such programme as aforesaid to a place in the United Kingdom to which members of the public have access (whether on payment or not), for the purpose of its being presented there to members of the public.

(2) The said kinds of energy are electric, magnetic, electro-magnetic, electro-chemical and electro-mechanical.

(3) In the event of a contravention of this section in relation to a system, the person running it (or, if different parts of it are run by different persons, each of them) shall be guilty of an offence and liable, on summary conviction, to a fine not exceeding £400.

(4) This section shall not apply to the Post Office, the British Broadcasting Corporation or the Independent Television Authority.

(5) Where a body corporate is guilty of an offence under this section and that offence is proved to have been committed with the consent or connivance of, or to be attributable to any neglect on the part of, any director, manager, secretary or other similar officer of the body corporate or any person who was purporting to act in any such capacity, he, as well as the body corporate, shall be guilty of that offence and shall be liable to be proceeded against and punished accordingly.

In this section, the expression " director ", in relation to a body corporate established by or under an enactment for the purpose of carrying on under national ownership an industry or part of an industry or undertaking, being a body corporate whose affairs are managed by the members thereof, means a member of that body corporate.

(6) Without prejudice to subsection (3) of this section, compliance with subsection (1) thereof shall be enforceable by civil proceedings by the Crown for an injunction or for any other appropriate relief.

(7) The prohibition imposed by this section shall not extend to the doing of anything by the sole means of apparatus for wireless telegraphy (within the meaning of the Wireless Telegraphy Act 1949).

1949 c. 54.

(8) In the application of subsection (6) above to Scotland, for the words " civil proceedings by the Crown for an injunction ", there shall be substituted the words " civil proceedings by the Lord Advocate for an interdict ".

90.—(1) A licence granted under the last foregoing section may be issued subject to such terms, provisions and limitations as the Minister may think fit.

(2) A licence so granted shall, unless previously revoked by the Minister, continue in force for such period as may be specified in the licence.

(3) A licence so granted may be revoked, or the terms, provisions or limitations thereof varied, by a notice in writing of the Minister served on the holder of the licence or by a general notice applicable to licences of the class to which the licence in question belongs published in such manner as may be specified in the licence.

(4) On the issue or renewal of a licence so granted, and, where the regulations under this section so provide, at such times thereafter as may be prescribed by the regulations, there shall be paid to the Minister by the person to whom the licence is issued such sums as may be prescribed by regulations to be made by the Minister with the consent of the Treasury; but this provision shall be subject to the qualification that the regulations thereunder may contain provisions authorising, in such cases as are not otherwise dealt with under the regulations, the charge by the Minister of such sums, whether on the issue or renewal of the licence or subsequently, as may in the particular case appear to him to be proper.

(5) Different provision may be made by regulations under the last foregoing subsection in relation to different licences, according to the nature, terms, provisions, limitations and duration thereof.

(6) A payment required by virtue of this section to be rendered to the Minister may be recovered by him in any court of competent jurisdiction as if it were a simple contract debt.

(7) The Minister shall have power to make, in such cases or classes of cases as the Treasury may determine, refunds of sums received by him under subsection (4) above.

(8) A payment made in exercise of the power conferred by the last foregoing subsection shall be defrayed out of sums received by the Minister under subsection (4) above.

(9) The surplus of sums received under subsection (4) above over sums paid in exercise of the power conferred by subsection (7) above shall from time to time be paid into the Consolidated Fund.

(10) In the application of subsection (6) above to Scotland, the words " as if it were a simple contract debt " shall be omitted.

91.—(1) If, in England, Wales or Northern Ireland, a justice of the peace, or, in Scotland, the sheriff, is satisfied by information on oath that there is reasonable ground for suspecting that an offence under section 89 of this Act has been, or is being, committed, and that evidence of the commission of the offence is to be found on any premises specified in the information, he may grant a search warrant authorising any person or persons authorised in that behalf by the Minister and named in the warrant, with or without any constables, to enter, at any time within one month from the date of the warrant, the premises specified in the information and to search the premises and examine and test any apparatus found thereon.

(2) Where, under this section, a person has a right to examine any apparatus on any premises, it shall be the duty of any person who is on the premises to give him any such assistance as he may reasonably require in the examination or testing of the apparatus.

(3) A person who—

(a) obstructs a person in the exercise of powers conferred on him under this section ; or

(b) fails or refuses to give to a person any assistance which he is, under this section, under a duty to give to him ;

shall be guilty of an offence and liable, on summary conviction, to a fine not exceeding £400, and a person who discloses, otherwise than for the purposes of this Part of this Act or of a report of proceedings thereunder, any information obtained by means of an exercise of powers conferred by this section, being information relating to a manufacturing process or trade secret, shall be guilty of an offence and liable—

(i) on conviction on indictment, to imprisonment for a term not exceeding two years or to a fine, or to both ;

(ii) on summary conviction, to a fine not exceeding £400.

92.—(1) The power conferred by section 89 of this Act on the Minister to make an order and the power conferred on him by section 90 of this Act to make regulations shall be exercisable by statutory instrument.

(2) A statutory instrument by which either of the aforesaid powers is exercised shall be subject to annulment in pursuance of a resolution of either House of Parliament.

(3) The power conferred by section 89 of this Act on the Minister to make an order shall include power, exercisable in like manner, to vary or revoke an order made in exercise of that power.

PART V

PROVISIONS FOR SECURING THE CONTINUANCE OF
THE CARRYING ON, UNDER THE AUSPICES OF A
DIRECTOR OF SAVINGS IN PLACE OF THE
POSTMASTER GENERAL, OF CERTAIN FINANCIAL
BUSINESS

The Director of Savings

93.—(1) The Treasury may appoint (but so that the first Appointment, appointment made shall not take effect before the appointed and functions day) a person to be Director of Savings who shall have such and expenses, functions as are conferred on him by, or by virtue of, the &c., of the functions as are conferred on him by, or by virtue of, the Director of following provisions of this Act. Savings.

(2) The expenses of the Director of Savings shall, unless required by some provision of this Act to be borne in some other manner, be defrayed out of moneys provided by Parliament.

(3) Schedule 2 to the Parliamentary Commissioner Act 1967 1967 c. 13. shall have effect as if, after the reference to the National Debt Office, there were inserted a reference to the Department for National Savings.

(4) For the purposes of the Criminal Evidence Act 1965 and 1965 c. 20. the Criminal Evidence Act (Northern Ireland) 1965 (which make 1965 c. 15 certain trade or business records admissible as evidence in (N.I.). criminal proceedings) the expression " business " shall include the activities of the Director of Savings.

Replacement of the Postmaster General by the Director of Savings for the Purposes of the Post Office Savings Bank Acts 1954 and 1966, and Provisions consequential thereon

94.—(1) On the appointed day, section 1 of the Post Office The National Savings Bank Act 1954 (which empowers the Postmaster Savings Bank. General to authorise his officers, or others, to receive and repay 1954 c. 62. deposits) shall cease to have effect ; but, as from the beginning of that day, the establishment which exists in consequence of the enactment of that section shall, by the name of the National Savings Bank, continue in existence for the receipt and repayment of deposits, and its business shall be carried on by the Director of Savings.

(2) Accordingly, as from the appointed day, in the Post Office Savings Bank Acts 1954 and 1966 and in the following provisions of this Act the expression " deposit " (when used as a noun) shall be taken to refer to a deposit with the National Savings Bank and the expression " depositor " shall (save in so

PART V   far as the context otherwise requires) be construed accordingly, and—

1954 c. 62.   (*a*) the provisions of the Post Office Savings Bank Act 1954 specified in column 1 of Part 1 of Schedule 6 to this Act shall have effect subject to the amendments respectively specified in relation thereto in column 2 of that Part ;

1966 c. 12.   (*b*) the provisions of the Post Office Savings Bank Act 1966 specified in column 1 of Part II of that Schedule shall have effect subject to the amendments respectively specified in relation thereto in column 2 of that Part ;

(*c*) the enactments specified in column 1 of Part III of that Schedule shall have effect subject to the amendments respectively specified in relation thereto in column 2 of that Part ; and

(*d*) any reference to the Postmaster General in a nomination executed under regulations made, or having effect as if made, under section 2 of the Post Office Savings Bank Act 1954 shall be construed as referring to the Director of Savings.

1947 c. 44.   (3) The amendment of section 27 of the Crown Proceedings Act 1947 effected by virtue of subsection (2)(*c*) above is an amendment of that section as well in its application to the Crown in right of Her Majesty's Government in Northern Ireland as in its application to the Crown in right of Her Majesty's Government in the United Kingdom.

1889 c. 63.   (4) Without prejudice to the operation of section 37 of the Interpretation Act 1889 (which relates to the exercise of statutory powers between the passing and commencement of an Act), the power conferred by section 2 of the Post Office Savings Bank Act 1954, as amended by Schedule 6 to this Act, and that conferred by section 2 of the Post Office Savings Bank Act 1966, as so amended, may each be exercised at any time after the passing of this Act as if so much of that Schedule as amends those sections had come into operation on the passing of this Act, but so that regulations made in exercise of the power conferred by the one section or the other, as so amended, shall not come into operation before the appointed day.

Application of ordinary deposits.   **95.**—(1) For section 16 of the Post Office Savings Bank Act 1954 (repayment of sums withdrawn by depositors, payment of expenses and investment of funds), there shall be substituted the following section :—

" (1) There shall be paid out of ordinary deposits—

(*a*) all sums referable to such deposits that are withdrawn by or on behalf of depositors ;

(*b*) such sums as the Treasury may from time to time   Part V
determine to be equal to those expended by the
Director of Savings in the execution of this Act;
and

(*c*) the expenses incurred by the Commissioners in
the execution of this Act.

(2) The balance of ordinary deposits remaining after the
repayment thereout of sums withdrawn by depositors shall,
at such intervals as the Treasury may direct, be ascertained
and paid to the Commissioners who shall, after deducting
therefrom—

(*a*) such sums as are mentioned in subsection (1)(*b*)
above; and

(*b*) such sums as are necessary to defray the expenses
incurred by them in the execution of this Act;

invest it.

(3) Sums deducted by the Commissioners in pursuance
of subsection (2)(*a*) above shall be paid into the Consolidated Fund of the United Kingdom.".

(2) This section shall come into operation on the appointed
day.

96. As from the appointed day, section 3 of the Post Office   Consequential
Savings Bank Act 1966 (which requires a separate account to   amendment of
be kept for the purposes of that Act) shall have effect with the   section 3 of
substitution, for subsections (1) and (2) thereof, of the following   the Post Office
subsections:—   Savings Bank
    Act 1966.

" (1) The Director of Savings shall keep a separate   1966 c. 12.
account of all sums received or paid with respect to investment deposits.

(2) The said account shall be known as the National
Savings Bank Investment Account Fund and is in this Act
referred to as ' the Fund ' ",

and with the substitution, for the reference, in subsection (3)(*b*),
to the Postmaster General, of a reference to the Treasury.

97.—(1) There shall be included amongst the sums to be   Debit to the
debited from time to time to the National Savings Bank Invest-   National
ment Account Fund—   Savings Bank
    Investment
(*a*) such sums as the Treasury may determine to be equal   Account Fund
to those expended by the Director of Savings in con-   of expenses of
nection with investment deposits; and   the Director
    of Savings and
(*b*) such sums as may be necessary to secure that, year   contributions
by year, there is contributed to the Exchequers of   in lieu of tax.
the United Kingdom and Northern Ireland as nearly

PART V

1954 c. 63.
1952 c. 10.

as may be what would be contributed thereto in respect of the National Savings Bank by way of corporation tax if that bank were a savings bank certified under the Trustee Savings Banks Act 1954, section 439(1) of the Income Tax Act 1952 (exemption of trustee savings banks' income from tax in respect of interest and dividends arising from investments with the National Debt Commissioners) had not been enacted and the business of that bank were confined to activities concerned with investment deposits.

(2) Sums debited by virtue of paragraph (*a*) or (*b*) of the foregoing subsection shall be paid into the Consolidated Fund, and those debited by virtue of paragraph (*b*) shall be treated, for the purposes of subsection (2) of section 22 of the Government of Ireland Act 1920 (annual determination by Joint Exchequer Board of what part of the proceeds of the reserved taxes is properly attributable to Northern Ireland), as being proceeds of the duties and taxes referred to in subsection (1) of that section.

1920 c. 67.

(3) This section shall come into operation on the appointed day.

Annual statement with respect to ordinary deposits and expenses.

98.—(1) The Director of Savings and the National Debt Commissioners shall, as respects the year in which the appointed day falls and each subsequent year, prepare a statement showing—

(*a*) the aggregate of the sums received and repaid during the year in respect of ordinary deposits ;

(*b*) the aggregate of the sums paid or credited during the year by way of interest on ordinary deposits ;

(*c*) the aggregate liabilities, as at the end of the year, so far as regards ordinary deposits ;

(*d*) the nominal value and the description, as at the end of the year, of the investments held by the Commissioners which have been made under section 16 of the Post Office Savings Bank Act 1954 ;

1954 c. 62.

(*e*) the aggregate of the sums that accrued during the year by way of interest on investments made under that section by the Commissioners ; and

(*f*) the amount of the expenses incurred during that year in the execution of that Act ;

and shall, before the end of May next following, transmit it to the Comptroller and Auditor General who shall examine, certify and report on it and lay copies of it, together with copies of his report on it, before Parliament.

Part V
1954 c. 62.

(2) No accounts or statements shall be made out or prepared under the Post Office Savings Bank Act 1954 as respects the year in which the appointed day falls or any subsequent year ; and anything which, in the first-mentioned year, falls, by virtue of section 15 or 20 of that Act (annual account of ordinary deposits to be laid before Parliament, and annual account of liabilities with respect to such deposits to be so laid), to be done by the Postmaster General shall, if not done before that day, be done instead by the Treasury.

(3) In this section " year " means a period of twelve months ending 31st December.

Adjustment of balances relating to ordinary deposits.

99.—(1) If, in the year in which the appointed day falls or any subsequent year, the aggregate of the sums that accrued by way of interest on investments made under section 16 of the Post Office Savings Bank Act 1954 by the National Debt Commissioners, after deduction of any sum required by the Treasury to be set aside to provide for depreciation in the value of investments so made, exceeds the aggregate of—

(*a*) the aggregate of the sums paid or credited during the year by way of interest on ordinary deposits ; and

(*b*) the amount of the expenses incurred during that year in the execution of that Act ;

the excess shall be paid into the Consolidated Fund ; and if in any such year as aforesaid the aggregate of the sums that accrued as aforesaid, after deduction of any sum required by the Treasury to be set aside as aforesaid, falls short of the second-mentioned aggregate, the deficiency shall be made good out of that fund.

(2) In this section, " year " means a period of twelve months ending 31st December.

Annual accounts with respect to investment deposits.
1966 c. 12.

100.—(1) Anything which, in the year in which the appointed day falls, falls, by virtue of section 5 (preparation and audit of accounts) of the Post Office Savings Bank Act 1966, to be done by or to the Postmaster General shall, if not done before that day, be done instead by or to the Treasury.

(2) The following requirements shall, as respects the year in which the appointed day falls and each subsequent year, have effect in place of those of the said section 5, namely,—

(*a*) the Director of Savings and the National Debt Commissioners shall prepare, for the year, a statement of accounts of the National Savings Bank Investment Account Fund ;

(*b*) the statement of accounts for each year shall, before the end of May next following the expiration of the year, be transmitted to the Comptroller and Auditor

PART V

General who shall examine, certify and report on it and lay copies of it, together with copies of his report on it, before Parliament.

(3) In this section " year " means a period of twelve months ending 31st December.

Ultimate liability of the Consolidated Fund for repayment of deposits.

101. If at any time claims in respect of ordinary or investment deposits cannot be met, the Treasury shall provide the Postmaster General or the Director of Savings with such sum out of the Consolidated Fund as is necessary to meet them.

Certain sums to be treated as expenses incurred by the Director of Savings.

1954 c. 62.
1961 c. 15.

102.—(1) As from the appointed day, section 22(1) of the Post Office Savings Bank Act 1954 (which provides that certain sums are to be deemed to be included amongst the expenses incurred in the execution of that Act by the National Debt Commissioners and, before the passing of the Post Office Act 1961, also provided that certain sums were to be deemed to be included amongst the expenses so incurred by the Postmaster General), shall have effect with the substitution, for the words " the Commissioners " (except where occurring in paragraph (c)), of the words " the Director of Savings and the Commissioners respectively " and with the addition, at the end thereof, of the following paragraph : —

> " (e) any capital expenditure incurred in providing premises or equipment wholly used for the purposes of this Act by the Director of Savings, and such part of any such expenditure incurred in providing premises or equipment partly used as aforesaid as was, in the opinion of the Treasury, incurred for those purposes ".

(2) As from the appointed day, section 22(2) of the Post Office Savings Bank Act 1954 shall have effect with the omission of the words " by the Commissioners ", with the insertion, after the word " premises " (where first occurring) of the words " or equipment " and with the substitution, for the words " the premises or of that part of the premises which was used for the said purposes ", of the words " the premises or equipment or, in the case of premises or equipment partly used for the said purposes, such proportion of that sum as the Treasury determine to be appropriate having regard to the extent to which the premises or equipment were so used ".

Amendment of section 10(1) of the Post Office Savings Bank Act 1954.

103. Section 10(1) of the Post Office Savings Bank Act 1954 (secrecy) shall not prevent the disclosure by a person authorised for the purpose by the Director of Savings of information to any person in connection with an offence committed with reference to the account of a depositor or for the purpose of ascertaining whether or not an offence has been so committed.

104. In subsection (3) of section 12 of the Post Office Savings   PART V
Bank Act 1954 (which requires the necessary financial adjust-   Amendment
ment to be made in the books of the National Debt Commis-   of section 12(3)
sioners in consequence of a depositor in a trustee savings bank   of the Post
having transferred the amount due to him from that bank to a   Office Savings
post office savings bank), for the words from " from the account   Bank Act 1954.
of the first-mentioned savings bank " onwards, there shall be   1954 c. 62.
substituted the words " from the account of the trustee savings
bank in question to that kept for the purposes of this Act ".

105. A statutory instrument containing regulations under the   Parliamentary control of
Post Office Savings Bank Act 1954 or the Post Office Savings   regulation-making powers under the
Bank Act 1966 (not being an instrument whereof a draft has   Post Office Savings
been laid before Parliament before the passing of this Act)   Bank Acts 1954 and 1966.
shall be subject to annulment in pursuance of a resolution of   1966 c. 12.
either House of Parliament.

106. A payment which, if this Act had not passed, would have   Selective
fallen to be made under section 25 of the Finance Act 1967   employment
or section 52(3) of the Finance Act 1968 (refunds of selective   refunds referable to
employment tax) to the Postmaster General on or after the   employment
appointed day shall be made instead to the Post Office ; and no   in the National
payment shall be made under either of those sections on or   Savings Bank.
after that day in respect of a person in respect of a week in which   1967 c. 54.
he was employed in the National Savings Bank and for which a   1968 c. 44.
payment of selective employment tax was paid in respect of him
by someone other than the Postmaster General.

107.—(1) On the appointed day, the land delineated (and   Vesting in the
coloured pink) on the plans deposited in connection with the   Minister of
Bill for this Act with the Minister of Public Building and Works   Public Building and Works
and authenticated by the signature of the Postmaster General   of the
(being land in the London borough of Hammersmith held by   Postmaster
the Postmaster General and appropriated to the exercise and   General's
performance of his functions under the Post Office Savings   interest in
Bank Acts 1954 and 1966) shall, by virtue of this subsection,   certain lands
vest in the Minister of Public Building and Works and shall be   Hammersmith.
taken by him as land necessary for the public service and held
by him for all the estate and interest for which it was previously
held by the Postmaster General.

(2) The Postmaster General may by order provide that the
foregoing subsection shall operate—

   (*a*) to annex to the said land such easements or other rights
      over contiguous land which, immediately before the
      appointed day, may be vested in him for an estate in
      fee simple, as may be specified in the order ; or

PART V

    (*b*) to annex to the last-mentioned land such easements or other rights over the first-mentioned land as may be so specified ;

or to do both of those things.

Replacement of the Postmaster General by the Director of Savings for the Purposes of the National Debt Act 1958 and the National Loans Act 1968, and Provisions consequential thereon

The stock register kept under Part I of the National Debt Act 1958.

1958 c. 6

(7 & 8 Eliz. 2).

    108.—(1) The register of government stock which exists by virtue of section 1(1) of the National Debt Act 1958 shall, instead of being known as the Post Office register, be known as the National Savings Stock Register and (except for such parts thereof as are kept by trustees of trustee savings banks) shall be kept by the Director of Savings ; and, accordingly,—

1915 c. 89.

    (*a*) in section 48 of the Finance (No. 2) Act 1915 (procedure on death of a person entitled to government stock), for the words " the Postmaster General " there shall be substituted the words " the Director of Savings " ;

1916 c. 24.

    (*b*) in sections 66 (transfer of government stock on authority of order of a court) and 67 (indemnity on transfer of government stock) of the Finance Act 1916, for the words " the Postmaster General " there shall be substituted the words " the Director of Savings " ;

1921 c. 32i

    (*c*) in Schedule 3 to the Finance Act 1921 (provisions for carrying out redemption of government stock), for the words " the Post Office Register " (wherever occurring) there shall be substituted the words " the National Savings Stock Register ", for the words " the Postmaster General " (wherever occurring) there shall be substituted the words " the Director of Savings " and for the words " at the General Post Office " there shall be substituted the words " by the Director of Savings " ;

1942 c. 21.

1915 c. 93.

    (*d*) in section 47(4)(*c*) of the Finance Act 1942 (transfer and registration of government stock), for the words " the Post Office register established under the War Loan (Supplemental Provisions) Act 1915 ", there shall be substituted the words " the National Savings Stock Register " ;

    (*e*) in sections 17(4) and 19 of the National Debt Act 1958 (preservation of effect of certain certificates of investment in government stock, and extension to the Isle of Man and the Channel Islands of the provisions of that Act relating to the Post Office register), for

the words " the Post Office register ", there shall be
substituted the words " the National Savings Stock
Register " ;

(f) in section 1(4)(c) of the Stock Transfer Act 1963 1963 c. 18.
(simplified transfer of securities), for the words " the
Post Office register" there shall be substituted the
words " the National Savings Stock Register "; and

(g) any reference to the Postmaster General in a nomination executed under regulations made, or having effect
as if made, under section 2 of the National Debt Act 1958 c. 6
1958 shall be construed as referring to the Director of (7 & 8 Eliz. 2).
Savings.

(2) For the purposes of section 2 of the said Act of 1958
(power to make regulations with respect to the register referred
to in the foregoing subsection), the appropriate authority shall,
instead of being (as prescribed by subsection (3) of that section)
the Treasury in conjunction with the Postmaster General and,
in the case of regulations relating to the National Debt Commissioners, those Commissioners, be, except in the case of
regulations relating to those Commissioners, the Treasury, and,
in the said excepted case, the Treasury in conjunction with those
Commissioners ; and in subsection (2)(b) of that section, for the
reference to issue through the Post Office of bearer bonds, there
shall be substituted a reference to issue by the Director of
Savings of such bonds.

(3) Sections 4 (disputes between the Postmaster General or
the trustees of a savings bank and stockholders) and 5 (transfer
to the register referred to in subsection (1) above of holdings in
names of deceased persons) of the said Act of 1958 shall have
effect with the substitution, for references to the Postmaster
General, of references to the Director of Savings.

(4) For the purposes of section 6 of the said Act of 1958
(acceptance of probate issued in Isle of Man or Channel Islands),
the appropriate authority, in relation to stock registered otherwise than in a part of the register referred to in subsection (1)
above kept by the trustees of a trustee savings bank shall, instead
of being (as prescribed by subsection (3) of that section) the
Postmaster General, be the Director of Savings.

(5) This section shall come into operation on the appointed
day ; but, without prejudice to section 37 of the Interpretation 1889 c. 63.
Act 1889, the power conferred by section 2 of the National
Debt Act 1958, as amended by subsection (2) above, may be
exercised at any time after the passing of this Act as if that
subsection had come into operation on the passing of this Act,
but so that regulations made in exercise of it shall not come into
operation before that day.

PART V
Power of the
Treasury to
raise money
under the
auspices of
the Director
of Savings.
1968 c. 13.
1952 c. 10.

109. The power conferred by section 12 of the National Loans Act 1968 on the Treasury to raise money shall extend to raising money under the auspices of the Director of Savings and, in particular, by the issue, under his auspices, of national savings certificates; and, accordingly, as from the appointed day, references in sections 191(1) (interest on United Kingdom savings certificates to be exempt from tax) and 193(4) (interest on certain Ulster, colonial and other savings certificates issued to local residents to be exempt from tax) of the Income Tax Act 1952 to savings certificates issued by the Treasury through the Post Office shall be construed as including references to savings certificates issued by the Treasury under the auspices of the Director of Savings.

Amendment
of section 12
of the National
Debt Act 1958.
1958 c. 6
(7 & 8 Eliz. 2).
1939 c. 117.

110.—(1) The power conferred by subsection (1) of section 12 of the National Debt Act 1958 on the Treasury to make regulations with respect to the manner in which and the conditions under which, amongst other things, money authorised to be raised under the National Loans Act 1939 or the National Loans Act 1968 may be raised through the Post Office shall include power to make regulations with respect to the manner in which and the conditions under which money authorised to be raised under the last-mentioned Act may be raised under the auspices of the Director of Savings.

(2) In subsection (2)(*a*) of the said section 12, for the words "apply any provision of any Act (including this Act) relating to the Post Office, to savings banks, to the Post Office register or to any other matter under the administration of the Postmaster General", there shall be substituted the words "apply any provision of any Act (including this Act) relating to savings banks or the National Savings Stock Register".

1889 c. 63.

(3) This section shall come into operation on the appointed day; but, without prejudice to section 37 of the Interpretation Act 1889, the power conferred by section 12 of the National Debt Act 1958, as amended by this section, may be exercised at any time after the passing of this Act as if this section had come into operation on the passing of this Act, but so that regulations made in exercise of it shall not come into operation before that day.

Power to
replace lost or
destroyed
bonds issued
by the
Postmaster
General or the
Director of
Savings.

111.—(1) Where the Director of Savings is satisfied that a bond to bearer issued on behalf of the Treasury by him or by the Postmaster General, or a coupon of any such bond, has been lost or destroyed, he may, if he thinks fit, and on such conditions as he thinks fit, but subject to any general directions of the Treasury, issue a new bond or coupon on receiving indemnity to his satisfaction against the claims of all persons deriving title under the bond or coupon lost or destroyed.

(2) This section shall come into operation on the appointed day and have effect in place of section 13 of the National Debt Act 1958.

112. As from the appointed day, section 35 of the Finance Act 1961 (national savings stamps and gift tokens) shall have effect as if, in subsection (1), after the words " the Postmaster General ", there were inserted the words " or the Director of Savings " and as if, in subsection (5), for the words " payable out of the Post Office Fund in respect of those stamps or tokens ", there were substituted the words " payable in respect of the exchange or encashment of those stamps or tokens ".

Credits to the Post Office in respect of certain capital Expenditure incurred by the Postmaster General in Connection with annuity, savings bank and national debt Functions

113.—(1) The Post Office shall, for the purposes of section 33 of this Act, be entitled to credit of—

(*a*) the sum certified by the Minister to be the net book value of buildings erected at the expense of the Postmaster General on the land mentioned in section 107(1) of this Act, being buildings in the case of which expenditure incurred by him after 9th July 1952 with reference to the erection thereof was treated by him as capital expenditure ;

(*b*) the sum so certified to be the net book value of works executed at the expense of the Postmaster General on that land, being works in the case of which expenditure so incurred with reference to the execution thereof was so treated ; and

(*c*) the sum so certified to be the net book value of apparatus installed by the Postmaster General on that land, being apparatus in the case of which expenditure so incurred in the provision and installation thereof was so treated, but not being telegraphic apparatus.

(2) The Post Office shall, for the purposes of section 33 of this Act, be entitled to credit of—

(*a*) the sum certified by the Minister to be the net book value of every such parcel of land as follows, namely,—

(i) every parcel in the case of which an estate or interest subsisting therein of the Postmaster General is, after the passing of this Act, conveyed, assigned or transferred by him to the Minister of Public Building and Works (being a parcel the whole or part of which is occupied, or is intended to be

2 N

occupied, by the Postmaster General in connection with the exercise and performance of his functions under the Government Annuities Act 1929, the Post Office Savings Bank Acts 1954 and 1966, the National Debt Act 1958 or the National Loans Act 1968) ; and

(ii) every parcel in the case of which an estate or interest subsisting therein of the Postmaster General vests in the Post Office by virtue of this Act (being a parcel which, immediately before the appointed day, is the subject of an agreement, to which the parties are the Postmaster General, the Minister of Public Building and Works and the Post Office for the conveyance, assignment or transfer by the Post Office to that Minister of the estate or interest that so vests) ;

(b) the sum so certified to be the net book value of buildings erected, on any such parcel as aforesaid, at the expense of the Postmaster General, being buildings in the case of which the expenditure of the Postmaster General with reference to the erection thereof was treated by him as capital expenditure ; and

(c) the sum so certified to be the net book value of works executed, at his expense, on any such parcel as aforesaid, being works in the case of which the expenditure of the Postmaster General with reference to the execution thereof was so treated.

(3) The Post Office shall, for the purposes of section 33 of this Act, be entitled to credit of—

(a) the sum certified by the Minister to be the net book value of every building erected at the expense of the Postmaster General on land in England in which—

(i) the Minister of Public Building and Works has an estate or interest immediately before the appointed day ; but

(ii) the Postmaster General does not then have, and never previously had, an estate or interest ;

being a building in the case of which the expenditure of the Postmaster General with reference to the erection thereof was treated by him as capital expenditure ; and

(b) the sum so certified to be the net book value of works executed at the expense of the Postmaster General on every parcel of such land as aforesaid, being works in the case of which the expenditure of the Postmaster General with reference to the execution thereof was so treated.

(4) In this section " building " includes part of a building and " net book value " means, in relation to land, buildings, works or apparatus, the value thereof (after deducting depreciation) as shown in the books by reference to which the final statement of accounts under section 12 of the Post Office Act 1961 is 1961 c. 15. prepared.

Extent of Part V and Schedule 6

114. This Part of this Act and Schedule 6 thereto shall extend to the Isle of Man and the Channel Islands. Extent of Part V and Schedule 6.

PART VI

STAMPS AND STAMP DUTIES

Stamps

115.—(1) Any stamp duty which is required or permitted by law to be denoted by adhesive stamps not appropriated by any word or words on the face of them to any particular description of instrument may be denoted by adhesive postage stamps. Use of postage stamps for revenue purposes.

(2) The Post Office shall pay to the Commissioners of Inland Revenue such sums at such times as, in default of agreement between it and them, may be determined by the Treasury to be requisite to secure that, year by year, the Commissioners receive as nearly as may be the difference between the sums received by the Post Office that are attributable to the operation of the foregoing subsection as regards stamp duties chargeable in Great Britain and the sums requisite to remunerate it for having prepared and issued adhesive postage stamps by which duties so chargeable have been denoted.

(3) This section shall come into operation on the appointed day, and subsection (1) thereof shall have effect in place of section 7 of the Stamp Act 1891. 1891 c. 39.

116.—(1) Sections 9 and 10 of the Stamp Duties Management Act 1891 (allowance to be made by the Commissioners of Inland Revenue for spoiled stamps, and allowances to be so made for misused stamps) shall apply to adhesive postage stamps as they apply to other stamps, but subject, in the case of section 9, to the qualification that allowance is not to be made by virtue of this section for stamps not appearing to the Commissioners to have been intended to be used for denoting a duty or fee ; and the second and third references to stamps in section 11 of that Allowance by Commissioners of Inland Revenue for spoiled postage stamps. 1891 c. 38.

2 N 2

PART VI   Act (how allowance is to be made) shall, for the purpose of its operation in relation to allowance made by virtue of this section, be construed as referring to adhesive postage stamps.

(2) This section shall come into operation on the appointed day.

Application of section 9 of the Stamp Act 1891, and provisions as to proceedings thereunder relating to postage stamps.

1891 c. 39.
1890 c. 21.
1898 c. 46.

117.—(1) As from the appointed day, section 9 of the Stamp Act 1891 (penalty for frauds in relation to adhesive stamps) shall have effect as if references therein to such stamps included references to adhesive postage stamps.

(2) The following enactments making provision with respect to the institution of, and otherwise in relation to, proceedings for the recovery of fines under the Acts relating to inland revenue, namely, sections 21, 22 and 35 of the Inland Revenue Regulation Act 1890, section 121 of the Stamp Act 1891 and section 7(5) of the Revenue Act 1898, shall not apply to proceedings in respect of an offence under section 9 of the Stamp Act 1891 committed on or after the appointed day in relation to a postage stamp, but any such proceedings shall be summary ones.

Application of section 13 of the Stamp Duties Management Act 1891 to frauds touching postage stamps, and consequential amendment of section 16 of that Act.

1891 c. 38.

118.—(1) The definitions of " die " and " stamp " in section 27 of the Stamp Duties Management Act 1891 shall, for the purposes of the application thereof, on and after the appointed day, to section 13 of that Act (offences in relation to dies and stamps), have effect as if the reference to the Commissioners of Inland Revenue included a reference to the Post Office and as if references to any duty included references to postage.

(2) Matters or things seized under the authority of a warrant issued under section 16 of the said Act of 1891 on or after the appointed day shall, if they relate to postage, be delivered to the Post Office instead of to the Commissioners of Inland Revenue.

Power of the Commissioners of Inland Revenue to stamp paper for the Post Office.

119. The Commissioners of Inland Revenue may make arrangements with the Post Office whereunder they, in consideration of the making to them by it of such payments as may be agreed between them and it with the approval of the Treasury, stamp paper sent to them for the purpose of its being stamped for use as postcards or reply-postcards or covers or envelopes of postal packets with stamps denoting the appropriate postage.

Validity of existing stamps.

120. Stamps current immediately before the appointed day for denoting duties of postage (whether or not they denote also other duties) shall be deemed for all purposes to be postage stamps.

121.—(1) Section 14 of the National Insurance Act 1965 shall have effect with the substitution, for subsection (2) thereof Amendment (which, amongst other things, makes provision for the prepara- of the tion, issue and sale, under the auspices of the Postmaster Insurance General, of adhesive stamps by means of which contributions Acts as to under that Act are payable), of the following subsection:— payment of

" (2) Where, under regulations made by virtue of sub- contributions. section (1) of this section, contributions under this Act, with 1965 c. 51. or without contributions under the Industrial Injuries Act, are payable by means of adhesive stamps, the Secretary of State may, with the consent of the Treasury, arrange for the preparation and sale of those stamps (hereafter in this Act referred to as 'insurance stamps') and may by regulations provide for applying, with the necessary modifications as respects those stamps, all or any of the provisions of the Stamp Duties Management Act 1891, section 9 of the Stamp 1891 c. 38. Act 1891 and section 63 of the Post Office Act 1953 " ; 1891 c. 39. and the reference in section 67(2) of the National Insurance 1953 c. 36. (Industrial Injuries) Act 1965 (which applies section 14(2) of 1965 c. 52. the first-mentioned Act to insurance stamps within the meaning of the last-mentioned Act) to subsection (2) of the said section 14 shall be construed as referring to the subsection substituted therefor by this subsection.

(2) The foregoing subsection shall come into operation on the appointed day ; but, without prejudice to section 37 of the Interpretation Act 1889, the powers conferred by virtue of 1889 c. 63. that subsection may be exercised at any time after the passing of this Act as if that subsection had come into operation on the passing of this Act, but so that any stamps prepared or regulations made in exercise of the powers shall not be sold or come into operation, as the case may be, before that day.

122.—(1) The Treasury may, by statutory instrument (which Power to apply shall be laid before Parliament), make regulations for applying to to national national savings stamps, with the necessary modifications, all or savings stamps any of the provisions of the Stamp Duties Management Act 1891, respect to section 9 of the Stamp Act 1891 and section 63 of the Post Office revenue and Act 1953. postage stamps.

(2) In this section " national savings stamp " has the meaning assigned to it by section 35(1) of the Finance Act 1961. 1961 c. 36.

123. In the foregoing provisions of this Part of this Act, Meaning of " postage " (except in the expression " duties of postage "), "postage" and means postage chargeable by the Post Office, and " postage "postage stamp " shall be construed accordingly. stamp".

2 N 3

Part VI

Stamp Duties

Composition for stamp duty on the Post Office's money orders.

1891 c. 39.

124.—(1) The Commissioners of Inland Revenue may enter into an agreement with the Post Office for the composition, in accordance with the following provisions of this section, of the stamp duty chargeable in Great Britain under the heading beginning " Bill of Exchange or promissory note of any kind whatsoever " in Schedule 1 to the Stamp Act 1891 on money orders issued by it.

(2) Such an agreement shall require the Post Office to deliver to the Commissioners of Inland Revenue periodical accounts of the orders issued by it and may contain such other terms and conditions as the Commissioners think proper.

(3) Where such an agreement has been made, a money order issued by the Post Office bearing such indication of the payment of stamp duty as the Commissioners of Inland Revenue may require shall not be chargeable with stamp duty, but the Post Office shall pay to the Commissioners, on the delivery of any account under the agreement, such sums as would, but for the provisions of this section, have been chargeable by way of stamp duty in Great Britain on money orders issued by it during the period to which the account relates.

(4) Where the Post Office makes default in delivering an account required by such an agreement or in paying the duty payable on the delivery of any such account, it shall be liable to a fine not exceeding £50 for each day during which the default continues and shall also be liable to pay to Her Majesty, in addition to the duty, interest thereon at the rate of five per cent. per annum from the date when the default begins.

1953 c. 36.

(5) References in this section to money orders issued by the Post Office shall be construed as including references to orders issued by it in pursuance of such an arrangement as is mentioned in section 24 of the Post Office Act 1953, being orders corresponding to money orders issued by the Post Office.

Composition for stamp duty on foreign money orders presented to the Post Office for payment.
1967 c. 54.

125. So far as regards the provision by it of services by means of which money may be remitted by means of money orders, the Post Office shall be deemed to be a banker for the purposes of section 31 of the Finance Act 1967 (composition by bankers of stamp duty chargeable on foreign bills of exchange presented to them for payment).

Postal orders to be exempt from stamp duty.

126. Stamp duty shall not be chargeable on a postal order (whether issued by the Post Office or another postal administration) or on a note, memorandum or writing whereby a postal order (whether issued by the Post Office or another postal administration) is acknowledged to have been paid.

127. For the purposes of section 52 of the Finance Act 1946 (which exempts from stamp duty certain documents connected with nationalisation schemes) any vesting of property in the Post Office after the appointed day effected by virtue of an order under section 17 of this Act shall be deemed to be part of the initial putting into force of such a scheme.

PART VI
Extension of section 52 of the Finance Act 1946.
1946 c. 64.

Special Provisions with respect to Northern Ireland

128. In the application of the foregoing provisions of this Part of this Act to Northern Ireland:—

Application of foregoing provisions of Part VI to Northern Ireland.

(a) for any reference to the Commissioners of Inland Revenue (except in section 119), or to Her Majesty, there shall be substituted a reference to the Ministry of Finance for Northern Ireland;

(b) for any reference to Great Britain there shall be substituted a reference to Northern Ireland;

(c) any reference (except in sections 117 and 122) to the Stamp Duties Management Act 1891 or to the Stamp Act 1891 shall be construed as a reference to that Act as it applies to stamp duties chargeable in Northern Ireland or to stamps which may denote any such duties, as the case may require;

1891 c. 38.
1891 c. 39.

(d) for the reference to the Treasury in section 115 there shall be substituted a reference to the Joint Exchequer Board established under section 32 of the Government of Ireland Act 1920; and

1920 c. 67.

(e) for the reference in section 125 to section 31 of the Finance Act 1967 there shall be substituted a reference to section 8 of the Finance Act (Northern Ireland) 1967.

1967 c. 54.
1967 c. 20 (N.I.).

129.—(1) Section 12 of the Finance Act 1895 (which, in its application to Northern Ireland, requires a person in whom property is, by virtue of an Act, vested by way of sale to produce to the Ministry of Finance for Northern Ireland a copy of the Act stamped with the duty payable on a conveyance on sale) shall not operate to require the delivery to that Ministry of a copy of this Act or any order made under section 17 of this Act or the payment of stamp duty under that section on any copy of this Act or any copy of such an order.

Exemption of Act from stamp duty in Northern Ireland.
1895 c. 16.

(2) Section 9 of the Finance Act (Northern Ireland) 1936 (presentation to the Ministry of Finance for Northern Ireland of particulars relating to transfers of land) shall not apply in relation to any vesting of an estate or interest in land in the Post Office effected by this Act.

1936 c. 33 (N.I.).

(3) This section extends to Northern Ireland only.

PART VII

MISCELLANEOUS AND GENERAL

Power of the
Treasury to
dispose of their
interest in the
shares of Cable
and Wireless
Limited.
1938 c. 57.
1946 c. 82.

130.—(1) The Treasury may dispose, before the appointed day to the Postmaster General or on or after that day to the Post Office, of their interest in the shares of Cable and Wireless Limited in consideration of such sum as they may fix (to be paid, if the disposition is to the Postmaster General, out of the Post Office Fund) ; and sections 1(1) of the Imperial Telegraphs Act 1938 and 3(5) of the Cable and Wireless Act 1946 (which require the payment into the Exchequer of dividends paid on the said shares) shall not apply to dividends so paid after the disposition.

(2) The sum received by the Treasury in consideration of the disposition of their interest in the said shares shall be paid into the Consolidated Fund.

Settlement
of certain
financial
matters
outstanding on
the appointed
day.
1965 c. 54.
1965 c. 62.

1968 c. 13.

131.—(1) The provisions of Schedule 7 to this Act shall have effect for the purpose of securing the settlement on, or as soon as practicable after, the appointed day of outstanding financial matters with which the Postmaster General is concerned and of making provision consequential on the settlement of such of those matters as are connected with the exercise and performance by him of functions under the National Health Service Contributions Act 1965 and the Redundancy Payments Act 1965.

(2) Section 22(2) of the National Loans Act 1968 (construction of references in that Act to the charge of payments on the National Loans Fund with recourse to the Consolidated Fund) shall have effect as if the first reference to that Act included a reference to Schedule 7 to this Act.

Extension of
regulation-
making power
under section
52(2) of the
Government
Annuities
Act 1929.
1929 c. 29.

1889 c. 63.

132.—(1) In section 52(2) of the Government Annuities Act 1929 (which empowers the National Debt Commissioners, with the concurrence of the Treasury, to make regulations for carrying out the provisions of Part II of that Act so far as regards any annuities or insurances granted by the Commissioners, either directly or through any parochial or other society, and so far as the trustees of savings banks are concerned), the words from " so far as regards " to " concerned " shall cease to have effect on the appointed day.

(2) Without prejudice to section 37 of the Interpretation Act 1889, the power to make regulations under the said section 52(2), in so far as it is conferred by virtue of the foregoing subsection, may be exercised at any time after the passing of this Act as if that subsection had come into operation on the passing of this Act, but so that regulations made by virtue of that subsection shall not come into operation before the appointed day.

(3) This section shall extend to the Isle of Man and the Channel Islands.

133.—(1) A fund to which this section applies is one (whether Power of described by the addition thereto of the attribute " welfare ", managers of " benevolent " or " mutual aid " or by the addition thereto of any certain welfare other attribute) the objects of which consist in, or include, the preserve their provision for persons who are, or have been, employed in the scope. department of the Postmaster General, or for such persons of any class or description, or for the relatives or dependants of persons who are, or have been, so employed or of such persons of any class or description, of benefits in case of need, sickness or distress, and a society or organisation to which this section applies is one (however described) the objects of which are similar ; and, in this section, " managers " in relation to a fund, society or organisation, means the trustees, committee or other persons entrusted with its management.

(2) The provisions of the trust deed, rules, regulations or other instrument constituting or regulating a fund, society or organisation to which this section applies may, by resolution of the managers of the fund, society or organisation, be altered—

(*a*) so as to permit persons of any of the following descriptions, namely,—

(i) officers or servants of the Post Office (past or present) ;

(ii) persons who, having been employed in the department of the Postmaster General, are or have been, in consequence of this Act, employed in the department of the Minister ; and

(iii) persons who, having been employed in the department of the Postmaster General, are or have been, in consequence of this Act, employed in the Department for National Savings ;

or persons who are members of a class of persons of any of those descriptions, to become members of, or subscribers to, the fund, society or organisation ;

(*b*) so as, in the case of persons of the said descriptions or persons who are members of a class of persons of any of those descriptions, to entitle them and persons claiming in right of them (subject to such, if any, terms and conditions as may be specified in the resolution) to receive benefits from the fund, society or organisation if, and to the extent that, they would be entitled to receive benefits therefrom if employment by the Post Office, employment in the department of the Minister or, as the case may be, employment in the Department

2 N*

for National Savings were employment in the department of the Postmaster General ;

but so that no alteration be made that alters the character of the fund, society or organisation.

(3) If a resolution of the managers of a fund, society or organisation to which this section applies so provides, any reference in the trust deed, rules, regulations or other instrument constituting or regulating the fund, society or organisation to the Postmaster General or his department (not being a reference in a context referring, in whatever terms, to persons employed in that department or persons so employed of a specified description) shall be construed as referring (or, if the context so requires, as including a reference) to the Post Office, and any reference in that instrument, in whatever terms, to persons so employed or persons so employed of a specified description shall be construed as referring (or, if the context so requires, as including a reference) to officers and servants of the Post Office or, as the case may be, to officers and servants thereof of a corresponding description.

(4) For the purposes of a resolution deriving validity from this section, the definition of a class of persons may be framed by reference to any circumstances whatsoever.

Issue by local authorities in Great Britain of dog and game licences.

134.—(1) As from the appointed day, licences for dogs shall be issued in Great Britain by the councils having power to levy the duties thereon and so, in England and Wales, shall licences for dealing in, or for killing, game.

(2) A council in Great Britain having power to levy the duties on any such licences as aforesaid may employ persons to act as its agents for the purpose of the issue of the licences and may pay to persons employed so to act such reasonable remuneration as it thinks fit.

Remuneration of the Post Office for issuing dog and game licences in England and Wales.

135.—(1) Any sums falling to be paid by the Minister of Housing and Local Government to the Post Office in pursuance of any agreement to which he, it and a council in England or Wales are parties, being—

(a) an agreement providing for the issue by the Post Office, on behalf of the council, of licences of all or any of the following kinds, namely, licences for dogs, licences for dealing in game and licences for killing game, and the payment by that Minister to the Post Office of sums in consideration of its issuing the licences ; or

(b) an agreement providing for the payment by that Minister to the Post Office of sums in consideration of its issuing, on behalf of the council, licences of all or any of those kinds in compliance with a direction under section 12 of this Act ;

shall be paid out of moneys provided by Parliament.

(2) Where licences of any such kinds as aforesaid are, in compliance with a direction under section 12 of this Act, issued by the Post Office on behalf of a council in England or Wales during a period during which an agreement is in force between the council and the Minister of Housing and Local Government providing for the payment to the Post Office by that Minister of sums in consideration of its issuing the licences (not being an agreement to which the Post Office is a party), the Post Office shall be entitled, in consideration of its issuing the licences, to receive payment from that Minister (of an amount to be determined, in the event of a dispute's arising as to the amount thereof, by the Minister) ; and any sums falling to be paid by that Minister in pursuance of this subsection shall be paid out of moneys provided by Parliament.

(3) Where licences of any such kinds as aforesaid are, in compliance with a direction under section 12 of this Act, issued by the Post Office on behalf of a council in England or Wales during a period during which no agreement is in force between the council and the Minister of Housing and Local Government providing for the payment to the Post Office by that Minister of sums in consideration of its issuing the licences, the Post Office shall be entitled, in consideration of its issuing the licences, to receive payment from the council (of an amount to be determined, in the event of a dispute's arising as to the amount thereof, by the Minister).

136. Any increase attributable to the provisions of this Act Expenses. in sums which, under any other enactment (other than the Ministers of the Crown Act 1964), are defrayed out of moneys 1964 c. 98. provided by Parliament shall be defrayed out of moneys so provided, and any increase so attributable in sums which under any other enactment are defrayed out of the Consolidated Fund or the National Loans Fund shall be defrayed out of the first- or last-mentioned fund, as the case may be.

137.—(1) The enactments specified in columns 1 and 2 of Cesser of Part I of Schedule 8 to this Act (which, to the extent specified obsolete, &c. in column 3 of that Part, are obsolete, spent or unnecessary) enactments. shall cease to have effect to that extent on the passing of this Act ; and the enactments specified in columns 1 and 2 of Part II of that Schedule (which, to the extent specified in column 3 of that Part, will, in consequence of this Act, become unnecessary or inappropriate) shall cease to have effect to that extent on the appointed day.

(2) The repeal by this section of section 4 of the Common- 1949 c. 39 wealth Telegraphs Act 1949 shall not affect the title of the Postmaster General to any property vested in him by virtue of that section.

PART VII
1953 c. 36.

(3) The repeal by this section of section 43 of the Post Office Act 1953 and of provisions of sections 44 and 45 thereof shall not operate to annul any provision of a local Act or order requiring the performance of services in regard to the conveyance of mails ; and, accordingly, any such provision shall be construed as if that repeal had not been effected.

(4) This section, and the said Schedule 8, shall extend to the Isle of Man, so far as regards any enactment specified in that Schedule that so extends, and shall extend to the Channel Islands, so far as regards any enactment so specified that so extends.

Transitional
provisions.

138.—(1) The general transitional provisions contained in Schedule 9 to this Act, and the special transitional provisions with respect to patents for inventions and registered designs contained in Schedule 10 to this Act, shall have effect.

(2) This section and the said Schedules 9 and 10 shall extend to the Isle of Man, and this section and the said Schedule 9 shall extend to the Channel Islands.

Application to
Northern
Ireland.

1948 c. 28
(N.I.).

139.—(1) In the application of this Act to Northern Ireland—

(a) any reference to an enactment of the Parliament of Northern Ireland (except a reference to Schedule 5 or 6 to the Roads Act (Northern Ireland) 1948) or to an enactment which that Parliament has power to amend—

(i) shall, except in Schedule 4 to this Act, be construed as including a reference to any enactment of the Parliament of Northern Ireland passed after this Act and re-enacting the said enactment with or without modification ;

(ii) shall, except so far as the context otherwise requires, be construed as a reference to that enactment as amended by any enactment, whether passed before or after this Act, and including a reference thereto as extended or applied by or under any other enactment, including this Act;

(b) " Act " and " enactment " (except in subsection (1) of the next following section) respectively include an Act and an enactment of the Parliament of Northern Ireland.

1920 c. 67.

(2) For the purposes of section 6 of the Government of Ireland Act 1920, this Act shall, so far as it relates to matters within the powers of the Parliament of Northern Ireland, be deemed to be an Act passed before the appointed day within the meaning of that section.

(3) Notwithstanding anything in the Government of Ireland Part VII Act 1920, regulations made by the Minister of Home Affairs 1920 c. 67. for Northern Ireland under the Civil Defence Act (Northern 1950 c. 11 Ireland) 1950 may apply to the Post Office such of the pro- (N.I.). visions of the Civil Defence Act (Northern Ireland) 1939 (except 1939 c. 15 section 7(4) thereof) relating to public utility undertakers as may (N.I.). be specified in the regulations and may specify the Minister or any department of the Government of Northern Ireland as the appropriate department in relation to the Post Office for the purpose of the application of any provisions so specified to the Post Office.

(4) Nothing in this Act (apart from paragraph 25 of Schedule 4 thereto) shall be taken to extend the definition of the expression " postal service " in section 74 of the Government of Ireland Act 1920 (reserved matters).

140.—(1) Any reference in this Act to any other enactment Construction shall, except so far as the context otherwise requires, be con- of references strued as a reference to that enactment as amended, and in- to enactments. cluding a reference thereto as extended or applied, by or under any other enactment, including this Act.

(2) Any reference in an Act passed before the passing of this Act to an enactment which is amended by this Act shall, unless the contrary intention appears, be construed, as from the day on which the amendment takes effect, as referring to that enactment as so amended.

141.—(1) The enactments specified in columns 1 and 2 of Repeals. Part I of Schedule 11 to this Act shall, on the passing of this Act, be repealed to the extent specified in column 3 of that Part (but subject to the provision made at the end of that Part), the enactments specified in columns 1 and 2 of Part II of that Schedule shall, on the appointed day, be repealed to the extent specified in column 3 of that Part and the Orders in Council specified in columns 1 and 2 of Part III of that Schedule shall, on that day, be revoked to the extent specified in column 3 of that Part.

(2) A reference in column 3 of Part II of Schedule 11 to this Act to an enactment shall be taken to refer as well to it as incorporated in any Act or other instrument as to it as originally enacted.

(3) This section, and Parts I and II of the said Schedule 11, shall extend to the Isle of Man, so far as regards any enactment specified in those Parts that so extends, and shall extend to the Channel Islands, so far as regards any enactment so specified that so extends.

142. This Act may be cited as the Post Office Act 1969. Short title.

SCHEDULES

SCHEDULE 1

INCIDENTAL PROVISIONS WITH RESPECT TO THE POST OFFICE AND THE MEMBERS THEREOF

Status

1. The Post Office shall be a body corporate having perpetual succession and a common seal.

Members

2.—(1) A member of the Post Office shall hold and vacate his office in accordance with the terms of his appointment and shall, on ceasing to be a member, be eligible for re-appointment.

(2) As soon as possible after appointing a person to be a member of the Post Office, the Minister shall lay before each House of Parliament a statement of the term for which he has been appointed.

(3) A member may at any time by notice in writing to the Minister resign his office.

3.—(1) Before appointing a person to be a member of the Post Office the Minister shall satisfy himself that that person will have no such financial or other interest as is likely to affect prejudicially the exercise and performance by him of his functions as a member of the Post Office, and the Minister shall also satisfy himself from time to time with respect to every member of the Post Office that he has no such interest ; and a person who is, or whom the Minister proposes to appoint to be, a member of the Post Office shall, whenever requested by the Minister so to do, furnish to him such information as the Minister considers necessary for the performance by the Minister of his duties under this paragraph.

(2) A member of the Post Office who is in any way directly or indirectly interested in a contract made or proposed to be made by the Post Office, or in a contract made or proposed to be made by a subsidiary of the Post Office which is brought up for consideration by the Post Office, shall disclose the nature of his interest at a meeting of the Post Office ; and the disclosure shall be recorded in the minutes of the Post Office, and the member shall not take any part in any deliberation or decision of the Post Office with respect to that contract.

(3) For the purposes of the last foregoing sub-paragraph, a general notice given at a meeting of the Post Office by a member thereof to the effect that he is a member of a specified company or firm and is to be regarded as interested in any contract which may, after the date of the notice, be made with the company or firm, shall be regarded as a sufficient disclosure of his interest in relation to any contract so made or proposed to be so made.

(4) A member of the Post Office need not attend in person at a meeting of the Post Office in order to make a disclosure which he is required to make under this paragraph if he takes reasonable

steps to secure that the disclosure is made by a notice which is SCH. 1 brought up and read at the meeting.

4.—(1) The Post Office—
(a) shall pay to the members thereof such salaries or fees, and such allowances, as the Minister may determine ; and
(b) as regards any member in whose case the Minister may so determine, shall pay such pension, allowance or gratuity to or in respect of him or make such payments towards the provision of such a pension, allowance or gratuity as may be so determined ;

and, if a person ceases to be a member of the Post Office and it appears to the Minister that there are special circumstances which make it right that that person should receive compensation, the Minister may require the Post Office to pay to that person a sum of such amount as the Minister may determine.

(2) The Minister shall, as soon as possible after the first appointment of a person as a member of the Post Office, lay before each House of Parliament a statement of the salary or fees and of the allowances that are or will be payable under this paragraph to him ; and if a subsequent determination by him under this paragraph involves a departure from the terms of that statement, or if a determination by him under this paragraph relates to the payment of, or to payment towards the provision of, a pension, allowance or gratuity to, or in respect of, a member of the Post Office, the Minister shall, as soon as possible after the determination, lay a statement thereof before each House of Parliament.

(3) The approval of the Minister for the Civil Service shall be requisite to a determination under this paragraph by the Minister and to the imposition thereunder by him of a requirement.

5.—(1) If the Minister is satisfied that a member of the Post Office—
(a) has been absent from meetings of the Post Office for a period longer than three consecutive months without the permission of the Post Office ; or
(b) has become bankrupt or made an arrangement with his creditors ; or
(c) is incapacitated by physical or mental illness ; or
(d) is otherwise unable or unfit to discharge the functions of a member ;

the Minister may declare his office as a member of the Post Office to be vacant, and shall notify the fact in such manner as the Minister thinks fit ; and thereupon the office shall become vacant.

(2) In the application of this paragraph to Scotland, for the references in head (b) of sub-paragraph (1) to a member's having become bankrupt and to a member's having made an arrangement with his creditors there shall be substituted respectively references to sequestration of a member's estate having been awarded and to a member's having made a trust deed for behoof of his creditors or a composition contract.

6. Part II of Schedule 1 to the House of Commons Disqualification Act 1957 (which specifies certain commissions, tribunals and other bodies all members of which are disqualified under that Act) shall, in its application to the House of Commons of the United Kingdom, be amended by inserting, at the appropriate point in alphabetical order, the words " The Post Office ".

Proceedings

7. The validity of any proceedings of the Post Office shall not be affected by a vacancy amongst the members thereof or by a defect in the appointment of a member.

8. The quorum of the Post Office shall be three ; and, while a member is disqualified from taking part in a decision or deliberation of the Post Office with respect to a matter, he shall be disregarded for the purpose of constituting a quorum of the Post Office for deciding, or deliberating on, that matter.

9. Subject to the foregoing provisions of this Schedule, the Post Office shall have power to regulate its own procedure.

Staff

10. The Post Office shall appoint a secretary of the Post Office and may appoint such other officers and such servants as it may determine.

11.—(1) Except so far as the Post Office is satisfied that adequate machinery exists for achieving the purposes of this paragraph, being machinery for operation at national level or local level or a level falling between those levels and appearing to the Post Office to be appropriate, it shall be the duty of the Post Office to seek consultation with any organisation appearing to it to be appropriate with a view to the conclusion between it and that organisation of such agreements as appear to the parties to be desirable with respect to the establishment and maintenance, for operation at any such level as aforesaid, of machinery for—

(a) the settlement by negotiation of terms and conditions of employment of persons employed by the Post Office, with provision for reference to arbitration in default of such settlement in such cases as may be determined by or under the agreements ;

(b) the promotion and encouragement of measures affecting efficiency, in any respect, in the carrying on by the Post Office of its activities, including in particular, the promotion and encouragement of the training of persons employed by the Post Office ; and

(c) the promotion and encouragement of measures affecting the safety, health and welfare of persons so employed.

(2) The Post Office shall send to the Minister and the Secretary of State copies of any such agreement as aforesaid and of any instrument varying the terms of any such agreement.

(3) Where it falls to the Post Office to participate in the operation of machinery established under this paragraph and the operation involves discussion of a subject by other persons participating therein, the Post Office shall make available to those persons, at a reasonable time before the discussion is to take place, such information in its possession relating to the subject (other than information whose disclosure to those persons would, in the opinion of the Post Office, be undesirable in the national interest) as, after consultation with those persons, appears to the Post Office to be necessary to enable those persons to participate effectively in the discussion.

(4) Nothing in this paragraph shall be construed as prohibiting the Post Office from taking part together with other employers or organisations of employers in the establishment and maintenance of machinery for the settlement of terms and conditions of employment and the promotion and encouragement of measures affecting efficiency in the carrying on of their activities and the promotion and encouragement of measures affecting the safety, health and welfare of persons employed by them.

(5) In the application of sub-paragraph (2) above to Northern Ireland, for the reference to the Secretary of State there shall be substituted a reference to the Ministry of Health and Social Services for Northern Ireland.

12.—(1) Except with the Minister's consent, the Post Office shall not terminate on security grounds the employment of a person employed by it.

(2) In this paragraph, "security grounds" means grounds which are grounds for dismissal from the civil service of Her Majesty in accordance with any arrangements for the time being in force relating to dismissals from that service for reasons of national security.

Fixing of Seal and Proof of Instruments

13. The fixing of the seal of the Post Office shall be authenticated by the signature of the secretary of the Post Office or of some other person authorised, either generally or specially, by the Post Office to act for that purpose.

14. A certificate signed by the secretary of the Post Office that an instrument purporting to be made or issued by or on behalf of the Post Office was so made or issued shall be conclusive evidence of that fact.

15. Every document purporting to be an instrument made or issued by or on behalf of the Post Office and to be duly executed under the seal of the Post Office, or to be signed or executed by the secretary of the Post Office or a person authorised by the Post Office to act in that behalf shall be received in evidence and deemed, without further proof, to be so made or issued unless the contrary is shown.

SCHEDULE 2

CLASSES OF ASSETS TO BE HELD BY THE POST OFFICE TO MATCH ITS DEBTS TO ITS BANKING CUSTOMERS

PART I

CLASSES OF ASSETS TO BE HELD TO MATCH A PROPORTION, DETERMINED UNDER SECTION 41 OF THIS ACT, OF DEBTS

1. Cash.

2. Money held on current account by other bankers on behalf of the Post Office in its capacity as the provider, in exercise of the power conferred on it by virtue of section 7(1)(b) of this Act, of a banking service.

3. Loans repayable either on demand or not later than the expiration of the period of fourteen days beginning with the day next following that on which notice is given to the borrower requiring repayment, being loans in the case of each of which the following condition is satisfied on each day on which it is outstanding, that is to say, that it is secured on one or more of the following, namely,—

    (a) Treasury bills and bills of Her Majesty's Government in Northern Ireland ;

    (b) accepted and transferable bills of exchange payable at a fixed period after date or sight expiring before the end of the fifth anniversary of that day ;

    (c) marketable fixed interest securities issued by Her Majesty's Government in the United Kingdom, Her Majesty's Government in Northern Ireland or the Government of the Isle of Man, being securities redeemable (otherwise than at the option of the issuer thereof) before the end of that anniversary ;

    (d) marketable fixed interest securities in the case of which the payment of interest thereon is guaranteed by Her Majesty's Government in the United Kingdom, Her Majesty's Government in Northern Ireland or the Government of the Isle of Man, being securities redeemable (otherwise than at the option of the issuer thereof) before the end of that anniversary.

4. Loans of either of the kinds mentioned in paragraph 9 of Part II of Schedule 1 to the Trustee Investments Act 1961, being loans repayable as mentioned in the last foregoing paragraph.

5. Treasury bills payable not more than ninety-one days from date and bills of Her Majesty's Government in Northern Ireland so payable.

6. Assets of such other class as may from time to time be   SCH. 2
designated for the purposes of this Part of this Schedule by the
Post Office with the approval of the Treasury.

PART II

CLASSES OF ASSETS TO BE HELD TO MATCH THE RESIDUE OF DEBTS

7. Cash.

8. Money held as mentioned in paragraph 2 above.

9. Loans of the class specified in paragraph 3 above.

10. Loans of the class specified in paragraph 4 above.

11. Treasury bills and bills of Her Majesty's Government in
Northern Ireland.

12. Assets of a class for the time being designated under paragraph 6 above.

13. Marketable fixed interest securities issued by Her Majesty's
Government in the United Kingdom, Her Majesty's Government in
Northern Ireland or the Government of the Isle of Man, being
securities redeemable (otherwise than at the option of the issuer
thereof) before the end of the fifth anniversary of the day on which
the Post Office acquires them.

14. Marketable fixed interest securities in the case of which the
payment of interest thereon is guaranteed by Her Majesty's Government in the United Kingdom, Her Majesty's Government in Northern
Ireland or the Government of the Isle of Man, being securities
redeemable (otherwise than at the option of the issuer thereof)
before the end of the fifth anniversary of the day on which the Post
Office acquires them.

15. Loans of either of the kinds mentioned in paragraph 9 of
Part II of Schedule 1 to the Trustee Investments Act 1961, being 1961 c. 62.
loans made on terms that they will, without any demands' being
made, or notices' being given, by the persons entitled to repayment,
be repaid before the end of the fifth anniversary of the day on which
they are made.

16. Securities of the kind mentioned in the said paragraph 9,
being securities redeemable (otherwise than at the option of the
issuer thereof) before the end of the fifth anniversary of the day
on which the Post Office acquires them.

17. Assets of such other class as may from time to time be designated for the purposes of this Part of this Schedule by the Post Office
with the approval of the Treasury.

Section 56.

1948 c. 28
(N.I.).

SCHEDULE 3

MODIFICATIONS OF SCHEDULES 5 AND 6 TO THE ROADS ACT
(NORTHERN IRELAND) 1948 FOR THE PURPOSES OF ORDERS MADE
UNDER SECTION 56 OF THIS ACT

1. For any reference in Schedule 5 to the Roads Act (Northern
Ireland) 1948 to an authority or a local authority or to the functions
of a local authority as a road authority there shall be substituted
a reference to the Post Office or to the functions of the Post Office
as the case may require.

2. For any reference in Schedules 5 and 6 to the said Act of 1948
to the Ministry within the meaning of that Act there shall be substituted a reference to the Minister.

3.—(1) Paragraph 2(2) of the said Schedule 5 shall be omitted.

(2) In paragraph 2(3)(*c*) of the said Schedule 5, after the word
" served ", there shall be inserted the words " by post by means of
the recorded delivery service ".

4. For any reference in the said Schedules to the said Act of 1948
there shall be substituted a reference to this Act.

5.—(1) For the purposes of a vesting order in respect of an estate
in land, being an estate less than a fee simple, the said Schedule 5
shall have effect with such modifications as may be necessary to
enable such an estate to be acquired by means of the vesting order
and to enable compensation in respect thereof to be duly paid or
discharged and (without prejudice to the generality of the foregoing
provisions) shall have effect as if for the words in paragraph 5 of
the said Schedule 5 from " A vesting order " to " under this
Schedule " there were substituted the following words—

> " A vesting order shall operate, without further assurance,
> to vest in the Post Office, as from the date on which the
> vesting order becomes operative (in this Schedule referred to
> as ' the date of vesting '), all such estates in, to or over the land
> to which the order relates as are specified in the order, freed
> and discharged from all the estates of any other person
> whosoever therein except in so far as is otherwise expressly
> provided in the order, and the rights and claims of any such
> other person in respect of an estate so vested shall, as from
> the date of vesting be transferred and attached, to the extent
> to which compensation may be payable in accordance with
> this Schedule, to the funds of the Post Office (in this Schedule
> referred to as ' the compensation fund ') and shall be discharged
> by payments made by the Post Office ".

(2) In the said paragraph 5, for the words from " be the date "
onwards there shall be substituted the words " be the date on which
the vesting order becomes operative or the date of the lodgment of
the vesting order with the registering authority under that Act,
whichever is the later ".

6. In paragraph 10 of the said Schedule 5, for the words from Sch. 3
" signed " to the end of head (*b*), there shall be substituted the
words " signed by such person as may be designated for the purposes
of this Schedule by the Post Office ".

SCHEDULE 4

Sections 76,
88, 139.

ADAPTATIONS OF ENACTMENTS AND ORDERS IN COUNCIL CON-
SEQUENTIAL ON THE ASSUMPTION BY THE NEW AUTHORITY FOR THE
CONDUCT OF POSTAL AND TELEGRAPHIC BUSINESS OF FUNCTIONS
EXERCISED AND PERFORMED BEFORE THE APPOINTED DAY BY THE
POSTMASTER GENERAL

PART I

INTERPRETATION

1. In this Schedule " the authority " means the authority established by section 6 of this Act.

PART II

ADAPTATIONS OF PUBLIC GENERAL ENACTMENTS

Adaptations of Enactments relating to the Post

2.—(1) With reference to any point of time after the beginning
of the appointed day, any reference in the provisions of the Post 1953 c. 36.
Office Act 1953 (hereafter in this paragraph referred to as the
" principal Act ") specified in the following table to the Post Office
(except in the expression " an officer of the Post Office ") shall be
construed as referring to the authority, and any reference in those
provisions to an officer of the Post Office shall be construed as
referring to a person engaged in the business of the authority.

TABLE

Provision	*Subject-matter*
Section 3	Exclusive privilege of the Postmaster General.
Section 16	Application of customs Acts to postal packets.
Section 22	Issuing money orders with fraudulent intent.
Section 24	Arrangements with other countries as to money orders.
Section 25	Outward bound ships.
Section 26	Inward bound ships and aircraft.
Section 27	Owners' letters.
Section 28	Retention of postal packets after delivery of part thereof to Post Office.
Section 32	Penalty for opening of mail-bag by master or commander of ship or aircraft.
Section 33	Power to require provision of regular mail-trains.

Provision	*Subject-matter*
Section 34 ...	... Additional provisions as to regular mail-trains.
Section 38 ...	... Conveyance of mail-bags by railway otherwise than as part of regular mail-train services.
Section 41 ...	... Offences relating to conveyance of mails by railway.
Section 42 ...	... Conveyance of mail-bags on ships used by railway undertakers.
Section 45 ...	... Additional provisions as to conveyance of mail-bags by public service vehicles.
Section 53 ...	... Unlawfully taking away or opening mail-bags.
Section 55 ...	... Fraudulent retention of mail-bag or postal packet.
Section 57 ...	... Stealing, embezzlement, destruction, &c., by officer of the Post Office of postal packet.
Section 58 ...	... Opening or delaying of postal packets by officers of the Post Office.
Section 65 ...	... Obstruction and molestation of officers of the Post Office.
Section 76 ...	... Recovery of sums from officers of the Post Office.
Section 79 ...	... Surrender of clothing by officer of the Post Office on ceasing to be officer.
Section 90 ...	... Prosecution of offences in the Isle of Man.

(2) Section 8(3) of the principal Act (mode of dealing with packets posted in contravention of the Act or of regulations thereunder) shall, as from the appointed day, have effect as if, for the references to regulations made under the Act, there were substituted references to the provisions of a scheme made under section 28 of this Act and as if, for the reference to the Postmaster General, there were substituted a reference to the authority.

(3) As from the appointed day, section 11 of the principal Act (prohibition on sending by post certain articles) shall have effect as if,—

    (*a*) in subsection (1)(*a*), for the reference to the Postmaster General, there were substituted a reference to the authority, and, for the reference to an officer of the Post Office, there were substituted a reference to a person engaged in the business of the authority ; and

    (*b*) in subsection (4), for the reference to detention in the Post Office, there were substituted a reference to detention by the authority and, for the reference to any regulations having effect by virtue of that section, there were substituted a reference to any provisions of a scheme made under section 28 of this Act.

(4) As from the appointed day, subsection (2) of section 16 of the principal Act (application of customs Acts to postal packets) shall

have effect with the substitution, for the reference to the Postmaster General, of a reference to the Minister ; but the Minister shall not make a recommendation under that subsection to the Treasury except after consultation with the authority.

(5) Duties of customs or other charges payable in respect of packets to which the said section 16 applies (whether payable to the authority or to any other postal administration) may be recovered by the authority in any court of competent jurisdiction as if they were simple contract debts, and, in any proceedings for the recovery of any charges so payable, a certificate of the authority of the amount thereof shall be evidence (and, in Scotland, sufficient evidence) of that fact.

In the application of this sub-paragraph to Scotland the words " as if they were simple contract debts " shall be omitted.

(6) As from the appointed day, section 17 of the principal Act (power to detain postal packets containing contraband) shall have effect with the substitution, for the reference to the Postmaster General, of a reference to the authority.

(7) As from the appointed day, section 19(1) and (2) of the principal Act (Post Office mark evidence of amount of postage, &c.) shall have effect as if references to the Post Office and the Postmaster General included references to the authority, and section 19(3) of that Act shall have effect as if, for the reference to a certificate signed by or on behalf of the Postmaster General, there were substituted a reference to a certificate of the authority.

(8) Section 21(3) of the principal Act (protection of bankers collecting postal orders) shall, as from the appointed day, have effect as if, after the words " Postmaster General ", there were inserted the words " or the authority established by section 6 of the Post Office Act 1969 ".

(9) References in sections 22 and 23 of the principal Act (issuing money orders with fraudulent intent and forgery and stealing of money orders) to a money order shall, as from the appointed day, be construed as including references to a postal order.

(10) As from the appointed day, section 24 of the principal Act shall have effect as if, for the reference to the Postmaster General, there were substituted a reference to the authority, as if, for the words " money orders ", there were substituted the words " orders for the payment of money " and as if the words " and subject to any prescribed modifications ", the words " within the meaning of those sections " and the proviso were omitted.

(11) References in sections 50 and 51 of the principal Act (extension of postal facilities and accommodation) to the Postmaster General shall, as from the appointed day, be construed as referring to the authority.

(12) With reference to any point of time after the beginning of the appointed day, the reference in section 56 of the principal Act

SCH. 4

(criminal diversion of letters from the addressee) to a person not in the employment of the Postmaster General shall be construed as referring to a person not engaged in the business of the authority.

(13) With reference to any point of time after the beginning of the appointed day, the reference in section 61 of the principal Act (prohibition of affixing placards, notices, &c., on post office letter boxes, &c.) to the Postmaster General shall be construed as referring to the authority.

(14) References in section 62 of the principal Act (prohibition of imitation of post office stamps, envelopes, forms and marks) and section 64 of that Act (prohibition of false notices as to reception of letters, &c.) to the Postmaster General shall, as from the appointed day, be construed as referring to the authority.

(15) As from the appointed day, section 63 of the principal Act (prohibition of fictitious postage stamps) shall have effect as if, in subsection (1), for the words from the beginning to " prescribed ", there were substituted the words " Except for such purposes as may be approved by the Post Office in writing and in accordance with such (if any) conditions as may be attached to the approval, a person shall not ".

(16) With reference to any point of time after the appointed day, the reference in section 65A of the principal Act (fraudulent use of public telephone or telex system) to the Postmaster General shall be construed as referring to the authority.

(17) As from the appointed day, section 72(1) of the principal Act (evidence of thing being a postal packet) shall have effect as if, for the reference to an article's having been accepted on behalf of the Postmaster General for transmission by post, there were substituted a reference to its having been accepted on behalf of him or the authority for transmission by post.

1968 c. 60.

(18) As from the appointed day, section 72(3) of the principal Act (application in certain proceedings of section 27(4) of the Theft Act 1968, and evidence of employment of a vessel, vehicle or aircraft by or under the Post Office for the transmission of postal packets under contract) shall have effect as if, for the reference to a vessel, vehicle or aircraft having been at any time employed by or under the Post Office, there were substituted a reference to its having been at any time employed by or under the Post Office or the authority.

(19) As from the appointed day section 78(1) of the principal Act (provisions as to post office letter boxes) shall have effect as if, for the reference to the Postmaster General, there were substituted a reference to the authority ; and section 78(2) of that Act shall have effect as if the reference to a certificate signed by or on behalf of the Postmaster General included a reference to a certificate of the authority and, for the reference to the permission or authority of the Postmaster General, there were substituted a reference to the permission or authority of the Postmaster General or the authority.

(20) The reference in section 79(1) of the principal Act to the Postmaster General shall, as from the appointed day, be construed as referring to the authority.

(21) As from the appointed day, the definition of "parcel" in section 87(1) of the principal Act (interpretation) shall have effect as if, for the reference to regulations, there were substituted a reference to the provisions of a scheme made under section 28 of this Act.

(22) As from the appointed day, the definition of "post office letter box " in section 87(1) of the principal Act shall have effect as if, after the words "the Postmaster General ", in both places where they occur, there were inserted the words "or the authority established by section 6 of the Post Office Act 1969 ".

(23) As from the appointed day, the reference, in the definition of "the purposes of the Post Office " in section 87(1) of the principal Act, to the execution of any duties for the time being undertaken by the Postmaster General or any of his officers shall be construed as including a reference to the exercise or performance of any powers or duties conferred or imposed by, or by virtue of, this Act on the authority ; and any provision to which that definition is relevant (whether contained in the principal Act or any other Act) shall be construed accordingly.

(24) As from the appointed day, the reference in section 87(2)(*b*) of the principal Act (delivery of postal packet to an officer of the Post Office to be delivery to a post office) to delivery to an officer of the Post Office shall be construed as a reference to delivery to an officer of the Post Office or to a person engaged in the business of the authority.

(25) As from the appointed day, "postage ", in the principal Act, shall, unless the context otherwise requires, mean postage chargeable by the authority.

3. As from the appointed day, section 1 of the Recorded Delivery Service Act 1962 shall have effect as if the reference in subsection (6) thereof (which provides that that section is not to be construed as authorising the sending by that service of anything which, under the Post Office Act 1953 or any instrument thereunder, is not allowed to be so sent) to any instrument under the Post Office Act 1953 included a reference to a scheme under section 28 of this Act, and section 1 of the Recorded Delivery Service Act (Northern Ireland) 1963 shall have effect as if the reference in subsection (5) thereof to such an instrument included a reference to such a scheme.

1962 c. 27.

1953 c. 36.

1963 c. 5 (N.I.).

Adaptations of Enactments relating to Telegraphs

4. References to the company, the Postmaster General or the Post Office in—

   (*a*) section 45 of the Telegraph Act 1863 (omission to transmit or deliver message ; improper divulging of message, &c.) ;

   (*b*) section 20 of the Telegraph Act 1868 (improper disclosure or interception of message) ; and

1863 c. 112.

1868 c. 110.

Sch. 4
1878 c. 76.
(*c*) sections 8, 9 and 10 of the Telegraph Act 1878 (destruction of, or injury to, telegraphic lines ; obstruction of execution of works in connection with such lines ; mode of prosecution of offences under Telegraph Acts) ;

shall, as from the appointed day, be construed as referring to the authority.

1892 c. 59.
5. As from the appointed day, section 5(1) of the Telegraph Act 1892 (application of Acts to licensee of Postmaster General) shall have effect as if, for the words from the beginning to " specified in the licence " (where secondly occurring), there were substituted the words " The Post Office may authorise the holder of a licence granted, or having effect as if it had been granted, under section 27(1) of the Post Office Act 1969 (in this section referred to as ' a licensee ') during the time and within the area specified in the authority to exercise all or any of the powers which are conferred on the Post Office by the Telegraph Acts 1863 and 1878 ".

1899 c. 38.
6. The reference to the Postmaster General in section 2(1) of the Telegraph Act 1899 (payment of expenses of exercise of powers under telephone licence) to the Postmaster General shall, as from the appointed day, be construed as referring to the authority.

7.—(1) Any such notice or counter-notice as follows, namely,—

1863 c. 112.
(*a*) a notice authorised to be given to the authority by any of the following provisions of the Telegraph Act 1863, namely, sections 14 (removal of abandoned works), 15 (removal of works in connection with alterations to streets), 21(3) (alteration of positions of telegraphs in connection with alterations to buildings), 22(3) (removal of telegraphs near dwelling-houses) and 30(1) (removal of work in order to enable building, &c., to take place) ;

(*b*) a notice authorised by section 24 of that Act to be given to the authority objecting to intended works ;

(*c*) a notice required by section 7(1) of the Telegraph Act 1878 to be given to the authority of the time and place at which work will be begun by undertakers or others ;

(*d*) a notice given for the purposes of section 8 of the last-mentioned Act of the intended exercise of a right (not being a notice given in pursuance of some other Act or of an agreement) ;

1908 c. 33.
(*e*) a counter-notice authorised by section 5(2) of the Telegraph (Construction) Act 1908 to be given to the authority objecting to the lopping of a tree ; and

1911 c. 39.
(*f*) a notice given for the purposes of section 1(2)(*d*) of the Telegraph (Construction) Act 1911 to the authority requiring it to remove or alter a telegraphic line constructed or maintained under the authority of that Act ;

may be given by addressing it to the authority (by its name) and by sending it by post to, or leaving it at, the appropriate area office.

(2) In this paragraph " appropriate area office " means—

 (*a*) in the case of such a notice as is mentioned in head (*a*) of the foregoing sub-paragraph, the principal local telecommunications office of the authority for the area in which the works or work to which the notice relates are or is situate ;

 (*b*) in the case of such a notice as is mentioned in head (*b*) of that sub-paragraph, the principal local telecommunications office of the authority for the area in which the works to which the notice relates are intended to be executed ;

 (*c*) in the case of such a notice as is mentioned in head (*c*) of that sub-paragraph, the principal local telecommunications office of the authority for the area in which the work to which the notice relates is to be done ;

 (*d*) in the case of such a notice as is mentioned in head (*d*) of that sub-paragraph, the principal local telecommunications office of the authority for the area in which the right to which the notice relates is intended to be exercised ;

 (*e*) in the case of such a counter-notice as is mentioned in head (*e*) of that sub-paragraph, the principal local telecommunications office of the authority for the area in which the tree to which the notice relates is growing ; and

 (*f*) in the case of such a notice as is mentioned in head (*f*) of that sub-paragraph, the principal local telecommunications office of the authority for the area in which the line to which the notice relates (or any length thereof) is situate.

Adaptations of Enactments relating to the Supply of Electricity

8. As from the appointed day, references to the Postmaster General in the following enactments and regulations (which confer protection for his telegraphic lines and works), namely :—

 (*a*) section 26 of the Electric Lighting Act 1882 ; 1882 c. 56.

 (*b*) section 4 of the Electric Lighting Act 1888 and regulations 1888 c. 12. made under that section ;

 (*c*) sections 10, 14, 60, 69 and 79 of the Schedule to the Electric 1899 c. 19. Lighting (Clauses) Act 1899 and the definition of " telegraphic line " in section 1 of that Schedule ;

 (*d*) section 22(4) and (5) of the Electricity (Supply) Act 1919 ; 1919 c. 100.

 (*e*) section 25(3) of the Electricity (Supply) Act 1922 ; 1922 c. 46.

 (*f*) section 9(3) of the Electricity Act 1947 ; 1947 c. 54.

 (*g*) regulations made, or having effect as if they had been made, under section 60 of the last-mentioned Act ; and

 (*h*) section 28(8) of the Electricity Act 1957 ; 1957 c. 48.

shall be construed as referring to the authority.

9. As from the appointed day, section 26 of the Electric Lighting Act 1882 and the enactments incorporated by that section shall, in

SCH. 4   their application to an Electricity Board, have effect as if references therein which are to be construed as referring to the authority included references to a government department.

1899 c. 19.

10. As from the appointed day, the reference to the Postmaster General in section 62(1)(*b*) of the Schedule to the Electric Lighting (Clauses) Act 1899 (service of notices) shall be construed as referring to the authority.

1919 c. 100.

11. As from the appointed day, references to a private generating station in section 11 of the Electricity (Supply) Act 1919 (restrictions on the establishment of new generating stations) shall be construed as including references to a generating station (within the meaning of that Act) for the generation of electricity for use wholly or mainly for the purposes of the authority's undertaking.

1931 c. 9 (N.I.).

12.—(1) As from the appointed day, references to the Postmaster General in section 37(9) of the Electricity (Supply) Act (Northern Ireland) 1931 (savings) shall be construed as referring to the authority.

(2) As from the appointed day, references to the Postmaster General in section 41 of the said Act of 1931 (electricity supply for certain undertakings not to cause interference with telegraphic lines belonging to, or used by, the Postmaster General) shall be construed as referring to the authority.

1948 c. 18 (N.I.).

13. As from the appointed day, references to the Postmaster General in section 40(2) to (4) of the Electricity (Supply) Act (Northern Ireland) 1948 (saving for power of certain Ministers) shall be construed as referring to the authority.

Adaptations of other Enactments

1862 c. 107.
1871 c. 65.

14. As from the appointed day, section 11 of the Juries Act 1862 and section 22 of the Juries Act (Ireland) 1871 (summoning of jurors by post) shall each have effect as if, for the words from " under such regulations " to the words " the postmaster shall ", there were substituted the words " the postmaster, upon receipt of the fee (if any) exigible for so doing, shall ".

1887 c. 65.

15. As from the appointed day, the reference to the Postmaster General in section 6 of the Military Tramways Act 1887 (which requires the insertion, in certain cases, in a provisional order made under that Act of provisions for the protection of his telegraphs), and any reference to him in a provisional order so made which is in force at the beginning of that day, shall be construed as referring to the authority.

1888 c. 29.

16. As from the appointed day, the reference to the Postmaster General in section 2(2) of Lloyd's Signal Stations Act 1888 (power of the society incorporated under the name of " Lloyd's " to enter into arrangements with the Postmaster General for the purpose of securing telegraphic communication between Lloyd's signal stations themselves

or between those stations and the Postmaster General's telegraph   SCH. 4
stations) and the second reference to him in section 6 of that Act
(saving for his property) shall be construed as referring to the
authority.

17. As from the appointed day, the reference to the Postmaster
General in section 15 (savings) of the Public Health Acts Amend- 1890 c. 59.
ment Act 1890 shall be construed as referring to the authority.

18. As from the appointed day, the reference to Her Majesty's
Postmaster General in section 132 of the Burgh Police (Scotland) 1892 c. 55.
Act 1892 (erection of telegraph poles, &c., in streets) shall be con-
strued as referring to the authority.

19. As from the appointed day, the reference to the Postmaster
General in section 4(1)(*f*) of the Congested Districts (Scotland) Act 1897 c. 53.
1897 (guarantees for telegraph extensions, &c.), shall be construed
as referring to the authority.

20. As from the appointed day, the reference to the Postmaster
General in section 26 of the Local Government (Scotland) Act 1908 c. 62.
1908 (use of machinery in quarries) shall be construed as referring
to the authority.

21.—(1) For the purposes of section 2 of the Official Secrets Act 1911 c. 28.
1911 membership of, or any office or employment under, the authority shall be deemed to be an office under Her Majesty, and a
contract with the authority shall be deemed to be a contract with
Her Majesty ; and, as from the appointed day, any telegraph, telephone, wireless or signal station or office belonging to, or occupied
by, the authority shall be a prohibited place for the purposes of that
Act.

(2) Section 5 of the Official Secrets Act 1920 shall not apply to 1920 c. 75.
the authority ; and, as from the appointed day, the reference in subsection (6) of that section to the Postmaster General shall be construed as referring to the authority.

22. As from the appointed day, section 187 of the Bankruptcy 1913 c. 20.
(Scotland) Act 1913 (letters to bankrupt to be delivered to trustee)
shall have effect as if, for the words " Postmaster General, or the
officers acting under him ", there were substituted the words " Post
Office ".

23. As from the appointed day, references in section 24 of the
Bankruptcy Act 1914 (re-direction of debtor's letters) to the Post- 1914 c. 59.
master General shall be construed as referring to the authority.

24. With reference to any point of time after the beginning of the
appointed day, references in sections 12 and 18 of the Larceny Act 1916 c. 50.
1916 (larceny of postal packets, &c. ; embezzlement by officers of the
Post Office) to an officer of the Post Office shall be construed as referring to a person engaged in the business of the authority.

25. As from the appointed day, the reference in the definition of " postal service " in section 74 of the Government of Ireland Act 1920 to Post Office money orders and postal orders shall be construed as referring to money and postal orders issued by the authority.

26. As from the appointed day, the reference to the Postmaster General in section 194(4) of the Law of Property Act 1925 (which contains a saving for his telegraphic lines) shall be construed as referring to the authority.

27. The reference to the Postmaster General in section 79(3) of the Land Registration Act 1925 (return to the Chief Land Registrar of letters marked outside " Her Majesty's Land Registry " and addressed to persons who cannot be found) shall, as from the appointed day, be construed as referring to the authority.

28. As from the appointed day, section 5 of the Roads Improvement Act 1925 (prescription of building lines) shall have effect as if at the end thereof there were added the following subsection:—

" (9) Nothing in this section shall affect any powers of the Post Office under the enactments relating to telegraphs, or apply to any telegraphic lines placed or maintained by virtue of any of those enactments ".

29. As from the appointed day, the reference in section 10 of the Public Health Act 1925 (Crown rights) to works or apparatus belonging to the Postmaster General shall be construed as referring to works or apparatus belonging to the authority.

30. As from the appointed day, section 2(2)(e) of the Execution of Diligence (Scotland) Act 1926 (execution of arrestment or charge by registered letter) shall have effect as if, for the words from " Postmaster " to " 1908 ", there were substituted the words " Post Office in pursuance of any provision contained in a scheme made under section 28 of the Post Office Act 1969 ".

31. As from the appointed day, section 14 of the Moneylenders Act 1927 and section 14 of the Moneylenders Act (Northern Ireland) 1933 (special provisions as to pawnbrokers' loans) shall each have effect as if, in proviso (i) to subsection (1) thereof, for the words " it would not under the Post Office regulations for the time being in force be received for transmission by parcel post ", there were substituted the words " it would not, under the provisions of a scheme made under section 28 of the Post Office Act 1969 relating to parcel post, be received for transmission by parcel post ".

32. Section 61(1) of the Land Drainage Act 1930 (which protects certain undertakings from works executed under that Act) shall, as from the appointed day, have effect as if, after paragraph (f) thereof, there were added the following paragraph, namely,—

" (g) the undertaking of the Post Office ".

33.—(1) As from the appointed day, references to the Postmaster SCH. 4
General in subsections (1) and (2) of section 2 of the Motor Vehicles 1930 c. 24 (N.I.).
and Road Traffic Act (Northern Ireland) 1930 (conveyance of mails
by public service vehicles) shall be construed as referring to the
authority.

(2) As from the appointed day, references to an officer of the
Post Office in the said subsection (1) shall be construed as referring
to a person engaged in the business of the authority.

34. As from the appointed day, the reference to the Postmaster
General in section 23(2) of the Restriction of Ribbon Development 1935 c. 47.
Act 1935 (saving for Postmaster General) shall be construed as
referring to the authority.

35. As from the appointed day, the reference to the Post Office
in section 20(3) of the Solicitors Act (Northern Ireland) 1938 1938 c. 14 (N.I.).
(service of disciplinary committee's orders) shall be construed as
referring to the authority.

36.—(1) As from the appointed day, the authority shall be
deemed to be public utility undertakers and its undertaking a public
utility undertaking for the purposes of the provisions of the Civil 1939 c. 31.
Defence Act 1939, other than paragraphs (*a*) to (*c*) of section 7(6)
and section 9(4).

(2) As from the appointed day, in the said Act of 1939 the
expression " the appropriate department " shall, in relation to the
authority, mean the Minister.

37.—(1) As from the appointed day, section 22(4) of the Town 1945 c. 33.
and Country Planning (Scotland) Act 1945 shall have effect as if
the first reference to a telegraphic line belonging to or used by the
Postmaster General included a reference to such a line of the authority's, as if for the words " the Postmaster General " in all places
(except the first and third) where they occur, there were substituted
the words " the Post Office " and as if,—

(*a*) in relation to any such period mentioned in paragraph (*a*)
as begins to run before, and is current on, the appointed
day, after the words " the Postmaster General " (where
secondly occurring in that paragraph) there were inserted
the words " or the Post Office ", for the word " he " in
paragraph (*b*), there were substituted the words " the
Postmaster General or the Post Office ", and after the word
" his " in both paragraphs, there were inserted the words
" or its " ;

(*b*) in relation to any such period so mentioned as begins to run
on or after the appointed day, for the words " the
Postmaster General " (where secondly occurring in paragraph (*a*)) and for the word " he " in paragraph (*b*), there
were substituted the words " the Post Office ", and for the
word " his " in both paragraphs, there were substituted
the word " its ".

Sch. 4

(2) As soon as practicable after the making, on or after the appointed day, of an order under the said section 22 extinguishing a public right of way in circumstances in which subsection (4) of that section applies, the Secretary of State shall give notice to the authority of the making of the order.

1945 c. 33.

(3) As from the appointed day, sections 27 and 28 of the Town and Country Planning (Scotland) Act 1945 shall apply to the acquisition of land by the authority under this Act as they apply to the acquisition of land by a purchasing authority under any other enactment.

1945 c. 42.

38.—(1) As from the appointed day, the references to the Postmaster General in sections 4, 5(3) and 70 of Schedule 3 to the Water Act 1945 (which contain savings for his telegraphic lines) shall be construed as referring to the authority.

(2) The reference in the foregoing sub-paragraph to Schedule 3 to the Water Act 1945 shall be construed as including a reference to that Schedule as incorporated or applied by or under any enactment in force at the beginning of the appointed day.

1945 c. 43.

39. As from the appointed day, references to the Postmaster General in section 24 of the Requisitioned Land and War Works Act 1945 (power of owners, &c., to require removal of telegraphic lines) and in subsections (2) and (3) of section 25 of that Act (deep lines) shall be construed as referring to the authority.

1946 c. 42.

40.—(1) As from the appointed day, references to the Postmaster General in paragraphs 4, 5(3) and 36 of Schedule 4 to the Water (Scotland) Act 1946 (which paragraphs contain a protection for telegraphic lines from interference) shall be construed as referring to the authority.

(2) The reference in the foregoing sub-paragraph to Schedule 4 to the Water (Scotland) Act 1946 shall be construed as including a reference to that Schedule as incorporated or applied by or under any enactment in force at the beginning of the appointed day.

1946 c. 7 (N.I.).

41. As from the appointed day, references to Post Office business in proviso (ii) to section 19 (Sunday employment) and in section 33 (application to Post Office business) of the Shops Act (Northern Ireland) 1946 shall be construed as referring to business of any of the kinds that the authority carry on.

1947 c. 53.

42.—(1) The Town and Country Planning (Scotland) Act 1947 shall, as from the appointed day, be amended in accordance with the following sub-paragraphs.

(2) The reference to the Postmaster General in section 111(1) (saving for his powers) shall be construed as referring to the authority.

(3) Section 111(2) (provisions as to telegraphic lines) shall, in relation to an order coming into force on or before the appointed day, have effect as if, for the second reference to the Postmaster

General, there were substituted a reference to the authority, and, in relation to an order coming into force after that day, have effect as if, for each reference to the Postmaster General, there were substituted a reference to the authority.

SCH. 4

(4) Section 111(3) shall, in relation to an order coming into force after the appointed day, have effect as if, for the reference to the Postmaster General, there were substituted a reference to the authority.

43. As from the appointed day, the second reference to the Postmaster General in paragraph 6(1) of the Schedule to the Requisitioned Land and War Works Act 1948 (which paragraph contains a saving for his telegraphic lines) shall be construed as referring to the authority.

1948 c. 17.

44. As from the appointed day, references to the Postmaster General in section 41(1) and (2) of the Roads Act (Northern Ireland) 1948 (Crown rights) shall be construed as referring to the authority.

1948 c. 28 (N.I.).

45.—(1) The Special Roads Act 1949 shall, as from the appointed day, be amended in accordance with the following sub-paragraphs.

1949 c. 32.

(2) The reference to the Postmaster General in section 20(1) (saving for his powers) shall be construed as referring to the authority.

(3) Section 20(2) shall, in relation to an order coming into force on or before the appointed day, have effect as if, for the second reference to the Postmaster General, there were substituted a reference to the authority and, in relation to an order coming into force after that day, have effect as if, for each reference to the Postmaster General, there were substituted a reference to the authority.

(4) Section 20(3) shall, in relation to an order coming into force after the appointed day, have effect as if, for the reference to the Postmaster General, there were substituted a reference to the authority.

46. As from the appointed day, section 28(4)(c) of the Civil Aviation Act 1949 (which modifies the application of Schedule 1 to the Statutory Orders (Special Procedure) Act 1945 in its application to orders stopping up or diverting highways in the interests of civil aviation) shall have effect as if the authority were electricity undertakers.

1949 c. 67.

1945 c. 18.

47.—(1) As from the appointed day, references to the Postmaster General in section 79 of the Representation of the People Act 1949 (candidate's right to send election address post free) shall be construed as referring to the authority.

1949 c. 68.

(2) Section 162 of the Representation of the People Act 1949 (service of notices, &c.) shall, as regards a summons, notice or document sent by post on or after the appointed day, have effect as if, in subsection (2), for the reference to the post office, there were substituted a reference to the authority.

2 O

Sch. 4
1949 c. 74.
48. As from the appointed day, the reference in section 47(*b*) (savings) of the Coast Protection Act 1949 to the Postmaster General shall be construed as referring to the authority.

1949 c. 84.
49. As from the appointed day, section 1(2) of the War Damaged Sites Act 1949 (which precludes a local authority from taking possession compulsorily of any such land as is specified in section 1(2) 1946 c. 49. of the Acquisition of Land (Authorisation Procedure) Act 1946) shall have effect as if the reference to such land included a reference to land acquired by the authority for the purposes of its undertaking.

1949 c. 90.
50. As from the appointed day, the reference in section 17(2) (service of notices) of the Election Commissioners Act 1949 to the Post Office shall be construed as including a reference to the authority.

1950 c. 28.
51. As from the appointed day, references to post office business in the following provisions of the Shops Act 1950, namely, section 22 (Sunday employment), section 44 (exemptions for post office business), Schedule 2 (transactions not affected by general closing hours or by closing orders) and Schedule 5 (transactions for the purposes of which a shop may be open in England and Wales for the serving of customers on Sunday) shall be construed as referring to business of any of the kinds that the authority carry on.

1950 c. 15 (N.I.).
52. As from the appointed day, references to the Postmaster General in section 20 of the Erne Drainage and Development Act (Northern Ireland) 1950 (savings) shall be construed as referring to the authority.

1952 c. 66.
53. As from the appointed day, section 16 of the Defamation Act 1952 (interpretation) shall have effect as if, in subsection (4) thereof, the words " in accordance with a licence granted by the Postmaster 1955 c. 11 (N.I.). General " were omitted and section 14(3) of the Defamation Act (Northern Ireland) 1955 shall have similar effect.

1953 c. 26.
54. As from the appointed day, references in section 6 of the Local Government (Miscellaneous Provisions) Act 1953 (supplementary provisions as to omnibus shelters, &c.) to the Postmaster General shall be construed as referring to the authority.

1953 c. 14 (N.I.).
55. As from the appointed day, the reference to the Post Office in section 12(3)(*b*) of the Criminal Justice Act (Northern Ireland) 1953 (evidence by certificate) shall be construed as including a reference to the authority.

1953 c. 19 (N.I.).
56. As from the appointed day, the reference to the Post Office in section 7(5) of the Juries Act (Northern Ireland) 1953 (service of jurors' summonses) shall be construed as referring to the authority.

57. As from the appointed day, references in paragraph 8 of Sch. 4
Schedule 1 to the Solicitors Act 1957 (re-direction of solicitor's letters 1957 c. 27.
in pursuance of court order) to the Postmaster General shall be
construed as referring to the authority.

58.—(1) Where the alteration of a telegraphic line of the authority
is reasonably necessary for the purpose of enabling a local authority
to exercise any of the powers conferred on them by Part III of the
Housing Act 1957, paragraphs (1) to (8) of section 7 of the Telegraph 1957 c. 56.
Act 1878 (alteration of telegraphic lines in the execution of under- 1878 c. 76.
takings authorised by Act of Parliament) shall apply to the alteration
and accordingly shall have effect, subject to any necessary modifications, as if references therein to undertakers included references to
the local authority.

(2) Where, in pursuance of an order under section 64 of the
Housing Act 1957, that comes into operation on or after the
appointed day, a public right of way over land is extinguished and,
immediately before the day on which the order comes into operation,
there is under, in, on, over, along or across the land a telegraphic
line of the authority's, the authority shall have the same powers in
respect of the line as if the order had not come into operation ; but,
if a person entitled to land over which the right of way subsisted
requires that the line should be altered, paragraphs (1) to (8) of the
said section 7 shall apply to the alteration and accordingly shall
have effect, subject to any necessary modifications, as if references
therein to undertakers included references to the person by whom
the alteration is required.

(3) In the proviso to section 64(3) of the Housing Act 1957, the
expression "apparatus" shall, in relation to the authority, be
construed generally and shall not be limited by the definition thereof
in section 189(1) of that Act.

(4) In this paragraph, "telegraphic line" and "alteration" have
the same meanings as in the Telegraph Act 1878.

59.—(1) Where any work proposed to be done on or after the
appointed day by a relevant authority in pursuance of a clearance
or demolition order or a re-development scheme made by them under
the Housing Acts (Northern Ireland) 1890 to 1967 involves, or is
likely to involve, an alteration in a telegraphic line belonging to, or
used by, the authority, paragraphs (1) to (8) of section 7 of the Telegraph Act 1878 shall apply to the alteration and accordingly shall
have effect, subject to any necessary modifications, as if references
therein to undertakers included references to the relevant authority.

(2) Where, in pursuance of an order under section 22 of the
Housing of the Working Classes Act 1890, section 14 of the Housing 1890 c. 70.
Act (Northern Ireland) 1961, or section 25 of the New Towns Act 1961 c. 12 (N.I.).
(Northern Ireland) 1965, that comes into operation on or after the 1965 c. 13 (N.I.).
appointed day, a public right of way over land is extinguished and,
immediately before the day on which the order comes into operation,

2 O 2

SCH. 4

there is under, in, on, over, along or across the land a telegraphic line of the authority's, the authority shall have the same powers in respect of the line as if the order had not come into operation ; but, if a person entitled to land over which the right of way subsisted requires that the line should be altered, paragraphs (1) to (8) of the said section 7 shall apply to the alteration and accordingly shall have effect, subject to any necessary modifications, as if references therein to undertakers included references to the person by whom the alteration is required.

1878 c. 76.

(3) In this paragraph "relevant authority" means a local authority or the Northern Ireland Housing Trust and "telegraphic line" and "alteration" have the same meanings as in the Telegraph Act 1878.

1957 c. 30 (N.I.).

60. As from the appointed day, the reference in section 8(5) of the Urban Drainage Act (Northern Ireland) 1957 (powers of Postmaster General in relation to streets closed under that section) to a telegraphic line belonging to, or used by, the Postmaster General shall be construed as referring to such a line belonging to, or used by, the authority.

1958 c. 23.

61. As from the appointed day, references in subsections (1) and (4) of section 5 of the Milford Haven Conservancy Act 1958 (powers with respect to dredging, &c.) to a submarine cable placed or maintained by the Postmaster General shall be construed as including references to such a cable placed or maintained by the authority, and the second reference in the said subsection (4) to the Postmaster General shall be construed as referring to the authority.

1958 c. 24.

62. As from the appointed day, the reference to the Postmaster General in paragraph 3 of Schedule 2 to the Land Drainage (Scotland) Act 1958 (saving for telegraphic lines) shall be construed as referring to the authority.

1958 c. 50.

63. As from the appointed day, section 3 of the Local Government (Omnibus Shelters and Queue Barriers) (Scotland) Act 1958 (access to telegraphic lines, &c.) shall have effect as if for the words "Postmaster General" there were substituted the words "Post Office" and as if, in subsection (1), for the words "he" and "him" there were substituted the word "it".

1958 c. 69.

64.—(1) As from the appointed day, references in section 45(1) and (2) of the Opencast Coal Act 1958 (provisions as to telegraphic lines) to the Postmaster General shall be construed as referring to the authority.

(2) Section 45(3) of the said Act of 1958 shall, in relation to an order coming into force on or before the appointed day, have effect as if, for the second reference to the Postmaster General,

there were substituted a reference to the authority and, in relation   SCH. 4
to an order coming into force after that day, have effect as if, for
each reference to the Postmaster General, there were substituted a
reference to the authority.

65.—(1) The Highways Act 1959 shall, as from the appointed day, 1959 c. 25
be amended in accordance with the following sub-paragraphs.

(2) The authority shall be deemed to be undertakers for the purposes of sections 137 to 139 (which contain provision for mitigating
obstruction caused by the execution of works in highways).

(3) The reference to the Postmaster General in section 300(1)
(saving for Postmaster General) shall be construed as referring to
the authority.

(4) Section 300(2) shall, in relation to an order coming into force
on or before the appointed day, have effect as if, for the second
reference to the Postmaster General, there were substituted a reference
to the authority and, in relation to an order coming into force after
that day, have effect as if, for each reference to the Postmaster
General, there were substituted a reference to the authority.

(5) Section 300(3) shall have effect as if, for the words " the Postmaster General ", in all places (except the third) where they occur,
and for the word " he " in paragraph (c), there were substituted the
words " the Post Office " and as if,—

> (a) in relation to any such period mentioned in paragraph (a)
> as begins to run before and is current on the appointed
> day, for the words " the Postmaster General " (where
> secondly occurring in that paragraph) and for the word
> " he ", in paragraph (b), there were substituted the words
> " the Postmaster General or the Post Office " and after the
> word " his ", in both paragraphs, there were inserted the
> words " or its " ; and

> (b) in relation to any such period so mentioned as begins to run
> on or after that day, for the words " the Postmaster
> General " (where secondly occurring in paragraph (a)) and
> for the word " he ", in paragraph (b), there were substituted
> the word " it " and for the word " his ", in both paragraphs,
> there were substituted the word " its ".

(6) The reference in section 300(4) to the Postmaster General
shall be construed as referring to the authority.

(7) Section 300(5) shall, in relation to an order coming into force
after the appointed day, have effect as if, for the reference to the
Postmaster General, there were substituted a reference to the authority.

66. As from the appointed day, references to the Post Office in
subsections (2) and (4) of section 36 of the Mental Health Act 1959 1959 c. 72.
(correspondence of patients) shall be construed as referring to the
authority.

SCH. 4
1960 c. 37.
67. As from the appointed day, section 7(1) of the Payment of Wages Act 1960 (interpretation) shall have effect as if, for the definitions of " money order " and " postal order ", there were substituted the following definitions: —

> " ' money order ' means a money order issued by the Postmaster General or the Post Office and ' postal order ' means a postal order so issued ".

1961 c. 41.
68. As from the appointed day, references to the Postmaster General in paragraph 2 of Schedule 1 and paragraph 3(1)(e) of Schedule 2 to the Flood Prevention (Scotland) Act 1961 (saving for telegraphic lines) shall be construed as referring to the authority.

1961 c. 63.
69. As from the appointed day, the reference to the Postmaster General in section 14(6) of the Highways (Miscellaneous Provisions) Act 1961 (which contains a saving for his telegraphic lines) shall be construed as referring to the authority.

1961 c. 64.
70. As from the appointed day, Schedule 4 to the Public Health Act 1961 (which specifies, in relation to buildings of certain descriptions, the persons who are to be appropriate authorities for the purposes of the provisions of that Act relating to the attachment of street lights to buildings) shall have effect as if the following were added at the end thereof: —

> " A building owned by   The Minister of Posts and
>   the Post Office   Telecommunications ".

1962 c. 38.
71.—(1) The Town and Country Planning Act 1962 shall, as from the appointed day, be amended in accordance with the following sub-paragraphs.

(2) Section 158(1) (which section contains provisions as to telegraphic lines) shall, in relation to an order coming into force on or before the appointed day, have effect as if, for the second reference to the Postmaster General, there were substituted a reference to the authority, and, in relation to an order coming into force after that day, have effect as if, for each reference to the Postmaster General, there were substituted a reference to the authority.

(3) Section 158(2) shall, in relation to an order coming into force after the appointed day, have effect as if, for the reference to the Postmaster General, there were substituted a reference to the authority.

(4) Section 158(3) shall have effect as if the first reference to a telegraphic line belonging to, or used by, the Postmaster General included a reference to such a line of the authority's, as if for the words " the Postmaster General " in all places (except the first and third) where they occur, there were substituted the words " the Post Office " and as if—

> (a) in relation to any such period mentioned in paragraph (a) as begins to run before, and is current on, the appointed day, after the word " the Postmaster General " (where

secondly occurring in that paragraph) there were inserted the
words " or the Post Office ", for the word " he " in paragraph (c), there were substituted the words " the Postmaster
General or the Post Office ", and after the words " his ", in
both paragraphs, there were inserted the words " or its " ;

(b) in relation to any such period so mentioned as begins to
run on or after the appointed day, for the words " the
Postmaster General " (where secondly occurring in paragraph (a)), and for the word " he ", in paragraph (c), there
were substituted the word " it ", and for the word " his ",
in both paragraphs, there were substituted the word " its ".

(5) As soon as practicable after the making, on or after the
appointed day, of an order under section 155 extinguishing a public
right of way in circumstances in which section 158(3) applies, the
Minister of Housing and Local Government shall give notice to the
authority of the making of the order.

(6) The reference to the Postmaster General in paragraph 50 of
Schedule 14 (saving for his powers) shall be construed as referring
to the authority.

72. As from the appointed day, the reference to the Postmaster
General in section 40(1) of the Pipe-lines Act 1962 (avoidance of 1962 c. 58.
interference with telegraphic, &c., lines) shall be construed as
referring to the authority.

73. As from the appointed day, the references to the Postmaster General in section 53 of the Electoral Law Act (Northern 1962 c. 14 (N.I.).
Ireland) 1962 (transmission of election addresses) shall be construed
as referring to the authority.

74.—(1) No order made on or after the appointed day under
section 67 of the Water Resources Act 1963 (compulsory powers for 1963 c. 38.
carrying out engineering or building operations) shall authorise the
doing of anything to, or in relation to, a telegraphic line (within the
meaning of the Telegraph Act 1878) of the authority's. 1878 c. 76.

(2) As from the appointed day, the reference to the Postmaster
General in section 130 of the Water Resources Act 1963 (which
makes provision with respect to alterations of telegraphic lines of his
required by a river authority to be made for the purpose of carrying
out engineering or building operations) shall be construed as referring
to the authority and subsection (2) of that section shall be omitted.

75. As from the appointed day, references to the Postmaster
General in section 28(1) and (2) of the Special Roads Act (Northern 1963 c. 12 (N.I.)
Ireland) 1963 (savings) shall be construed as referring to the authority.

76. As from the appointed day, the reference in subsection (1)
of section 20 of the Airports Authority Act 1965 (which contains 1965 c. 16.

Sch. 4

provisions with respect to telegraphic lines of the Postmaster General's) to a telegraphic line belonging to or used by the Postmaster General shall be construed as including a reference to such a line of the authority's, and the reference in subsection (3) of that section to the Postmaster General shall be construed as referring to the authority.

1965 c. 20.

77. As from the appointed day, the reference in section 1(4) of the Criminal Evidence Act 1965 to the Post Office shall be construed as including a reference to the authority.

1965 c. 59.

78.—(1) Where, on or after the appointed day, the Minister of Housing and Local Government makes an order under section 23 of the New Towns Act 1965 (extinguishment of public rights of way over land acquired) on the application of a development corporation or local highway authority, he shall send a copy thereof to the authority.

(2) As from the appointed day, paragraph 71(4) of this Schedule shall apply to section 24 of the New Towns Act 1965 (which makes provision with respect to telegraphic lines of the Postmaster General's) as it applies to section 158(3) of the Town and Country Planning Act 1962.

(3) As from the appointed day, section 26 of the New Towns Act 1965 (extinguishment of rights of way and rights as to apparatus of statutory undertakers) shall, so far as regards a right of the authority with respect to a telegraphic line and so far as regards a telegraphic line of its, not have effect in a case in which section 24 of that Act has effect.

1878 c. 76.

(4) In this paragraph, " telegraphic line " has the same meaning as in the Telegraph Act 1878.

1965 c. 13 (N.I.).

79. Where, on or after the appointed day, the Ministry of Development for Northern Ireland approves an order made under section 25 of the New Towns Act (Northern Ireland) 1965 (extinguishment of public rights of way over land acquired), that Ministry shall send a copy thereof to the authority.

1966 c. 27.

80. As from the appointed day, the Schedule to the Building Control Act 1966 (which specifies bodies in the case of which work carried out by them is exempt from control under that Act) shall have effect as if, at the end thereof, there were added a reference to the authority.

1966 c. 32.

81.—(1) As from the appointed day, Schedule 1 to the Selective Employment Payments Act 1966 shall have effect as if, in Part I thereof (which sets out the bodies to which section 3 of that Act applies), after paragraph 14, there were inserted the following paragraph: —

" 14A. The Post Office ".

(2) As from the appointed day, Schedule 1 to the Selective Employ- Sch. 4
ment Payments Act (Northern Ireland) 1966 (bodies to which section 1966 c. 32 (N.I.).
4 of that Act applies) shall have effect as if, before the entry relating
to the Ulster Folk Museum, there were inserted the words " The
Post Office ".

82. As from the appointed day, Schedule 2 to the Industrial 1966 c. 34.
Development Act 1966 (which specifies bodies not eligible for certain
grants under Part I of that Act) shall have effect as if the authority
were included amongst the bodies therein specified and Schedule 1
to the Industrial Investment (General Assistance) Act (Northern 1966 c. 41 (N.I.).
Ireland) 1966 shall have similar effect.

83.—(1) Where the alteration of a telegraphic line of the authority's is reasonably necessary for the purpose of enabling a local
authority to exercise any of the powers conferred on them by Part III
of the Housing (Scotland) Act 1966, paragraphs (1) to (8) of section 1966 c. 49.
7 of the Telegraph Act 1878 shall apply to the alteration and 1878 c. 76.
accordingly shall have effect, subject to any necessary modifications,
as if references therein to undertakers included references to the local
authority.

(2) Where, in pursuance of an order under section 51 of the
Housing (Scotland) Act 1966 that comes into operation on or after
the appointed day, a public right of way over land is extinguished
or a street is closed or diverted and, immediately before the day on
which the order comes into operation, there is, under, in, on, over,
along or across the land or street a telegraphic line of the authority's,
the authority shall have the same powers in respect of the line as if
the order had not come into operation ; but, if a person entitled to
land over which the right of way subsisted or on which the street was
situated requires that the line should be altered, paragraphs
(1) to (8) of the said section 7 shall apply to the alteration and
accordingly shall have effect, subject to any necessary modifications,
as if references therein to undertakers included references to the
person by whom the alteration is required.

(3) In the proviso to section 51(4) of the Housing (Scotland) Act
1966, the expression " apparatus " shall, in relation to the authority,
be construed generally and shall not be limited by the definition
thereof in section 208(1) of that Act.

(4) In this paragraph " telegraphic line " and " alteration " have
the same meanings as in the Telegraph Act 1878.

84. As from the appointed day, paragraph 45(*e*) of Schedule 4
to the Land Commission Act 1967 shall have effect as if the reference 1967 c. 1.
to expenditure which has been or is to be met directly or indirectly
by a government department did not include expenditure incurred by
the Postmaster General in relation to land in the case of which an

2 O*

interest therein vests in the Post Office by virtue of section 16 of this Act.

85. As from the appointed day, section 38(7) of the Countryside (Scotland) Act 1967 (provisions as to telegraphic lines) shall, in relation to an order coming into force on or before that day, have effect as if, for the second reference to the Postmaster General, there were substituted a reference to the authority, and, in relation to an order coming into force after that day, have effect as if, for each reference to the Postmaster General, there were substituted a reference to the authority.

86.—(1) Where, on or after the appointed day, the Secretary of State makes an order under section 23 of the New Towns (Scotland) Act 1968 (extinguishment of public rights of way over land acquired) on the application of a development corporation or local highway authority, he shall send a copy thereof to the authority.

(2) As from the appointed day, section 24(1) of the New Towns (Scotland) Act 1968 shall have effect as if the first reference to a telegraphic line belonging to, or used by, the Postmaster General included a reference to such a line of the authority's, as if for the words " the Postmaster General " in all places (except the first and third) where they occur, there were substituted the words " the Post Office " and as if—

> (a) in relation to any such period mentioned in paragraph (a) as begins to run before, and is current on, the appointed day, after the words " the Postmaster General " (where secondly occurring in that paragraph) there were inserted the words " or the Post Office ", for the word " he " in paragraph (c), there were substituted the words " the Postmaster General or the Post Office ", and after the word " his ", in both paragraphs, there were inserted the words " or its " ;

> (b) in relation to any such period so mentioned as begins to run on or after the appointed day, for the words " the Postmaster General " (where secondly occurring in paragraph (a)), and for the word " he ", in paragraph (c), there were substituted the word " it ", and for the word " his ", in both paragraphs, there were substituted the word " its ".

(3) As from the appointed day, section 26 of the New Towns (Scotland) Act 1968 (extinguishment of rights of way, and rights as to apparatus, of statutory undertakers) shall, so far as regards a right of the authority with respect to a telegraphic line and so far as regards a telegraphic line of its, not have effect in a case in which section 24 of that Act has effect.

(4) In this paragraph " telegraphic line " has the same meaning as in the Telegraph Act 1878.

87. As from the appointed day, Schedule 1 to the Industrial Expansion Act 1968 (which specifies bodies to which financial

support is not to be provided under a scheme made under section 2   SCH. 4
of that Act) shall have effect as if the authority were included
amongst the bodies therein specified.

88. As from the appointed day, section 6 of the Transport Act 1968 c. 73.
1968 (the Freight Integration Council) shall have effect as if—

(*a*) in subsection (1), for the reference to the Postmaster General,
there were substituted a reference to the authority ; and

(*b*) in subsection (2), the words " except where that authority is
the Postmaster General " and the words " or, where that
authority is the Postmaster General, may invite him to
appoint a representative so to act " were omitted.

89.—(1) As from the appointed day, section 69(1) of the Town and 1968 c. 72.
Country Planning Act 1968 (new provision as to what is " operational
land " of statutory undertakers) shall, in relation to the authority, have
effect with the substitution, for the reference to section 221(1) of the
Town and Country Planning Act 1962, of a reference to sub-paragraph 1962 c. 38.
(4) of paragraph 93 of this Schedule.

(2) The said section 69 shall not apply to land in the case of which
an interest therein of the Postmaster General vests in the authority
by virtue of section 16 of this Act.

(3) In paragraph 6 of Schedule 9 to the Town and Country Planning Act 1968 (construction of certain statutory references to the
acquisition of land and to land acquired) any reference to an enactment other than the principal Act and that Act and the reference
to a statutory provision shall include a reference to section 55 of
this Act.

90. As from the appointed day, the authority shall be deemed to be
a public utility undertaking for the purposes of section 1 of the Local 1968 c. 30 (N.I.).
Government and Roads Act (Northern Ireland) 1968.

91. As from the appointed day, the reference to the Postmaster
General in section 2(5) of the Vehicle and Driving Licences Act 1969 c. 27.
1969 (which, amongst other things, empowers local authorities to
make arrangements with him for him to issue licences and collect
duty under the Vehicles (Excise) Act 1962 on their behalf) shall be
construed as referring to the authority.

92.—(1) As from the appointed day, section 70(1) of the Town and 1969 c. 30.
Country Planning (Scotland) Act 1969 (new provisions as to what is
" operational land " of statutory undertakers) shall, in relation to the
authority, have effect with the substitution, for the reference to
section 113(1) of the Act of 1947, of a reference to paragraph 93(4)
below.

(2) The said section 70 shall not apply to land in the case of which
an interest therein of the Postmaster General vests in the authority
by virtue of section 16 of this Act.

SCH. 4
1969 c. 30.

(3) In paragraph 5 of Schedule 9 to the Town and Country Planning (Scotland) Act 1969 (construction of certain statutory references to the acquisition of land and to land acquired) any reference to an enactment other than the Act of 1947 and that Act and the reference to a statutory provision shall include a reference to section 55 of this Act.

93.—(1) The authority shall be deemed to be statutory undertakers and its undertaking a statutory undertaking for the purposes of the following enactments, namely,—

1935 c. 47.

(i) section 14 of the Restriction of Ribbon Development Act 1935 ;

1936 c. 5 (1 Edw. & 1 Geo. 6).
1945 c. 33.

(ii) section 3(4) of the Trunk Roads Act 1936 ;

(iii) sections 23 to 26 of, and Schedule 4 to, the Town and Country Planning (Scotland) Act 1945 ;

1946 c. 49.

(iv) the Acquisition of Land (Authorisation Procedure) Act 1946 ;

1947 c. 42.

(v) the Acquisition of Land (Authorisation Procedure) (Scotland) Act 1947 ;

1947 c. 53.

(vi) sections 10, 17, 32(1), (2) and (4), 42(4) and (5), 94 and 99(9) of, and Schedule 5 to, the Town and Country Planning (Scotland) Act 1947 ;

1948 c. 17.

(vii) section 4 of the Requisitioned Land and War Works Act 1948 ;

1948 c. 28 (N.I.).

(viii) the Roads Act (Northern Ireland) 1948 ;

1949 c. 67.

(ix) the Civil Aviation Act 1949 ;

1949 c. 97.

(x) the National Parks and Access to the Countryside Act 1949 ;

1951 c. 65.

(xi) the Reserve and Auxiliary Forces (Protection of Civil Interests) Act 1951 ;

1954 c. 56.

(xii) the Landlord and Tenant Act 1954 ;

1954 c. 73.

(xiii) section 19 of the Town and Country Planning (Scotland) Act 1954 ;

1958 c. 69.

(xiv) section 39(6)(b) of the Opencast Coal Act 1958 ;

1959 c. 25.

(xv) sections 152, 223 and 254(6) of, and Schedule 7 to, the Highways Act 1959 ;

1959 c. 70.

(xvi) sections 31 and 38 of, and paragraph 2(6) of Schedule 5 to, the Town and Country Planning (Scotland) Act 1959 ;

1961 c. 33.

(xvii) section 11 of the Land Compensation Act 1961 ;

1961 c. 41.

(xviii) section 3(4) of the Flood Prevention (Scotland) Act 1961 ;

1962 c. 38.

(xix) sections 12, 41, 70(2), 81, 82, 83, 103, 130 to 133 (both inclusive), 138 and 148(6), Part X and sections 179(7)(b), 189 and 212(6)(b) of the Town and Country Planning Act 1962 ;

1962 c. 58.

(xx) the Pipe-lines Act 1962 ;

1963 c. 51.

(xxi) section 18 of the Land Compensation (Scotland) Act 1963 ;

1964 c. 40.

(xxii) Schedules 3 and 5 to the Harbours Act 1964 ;

(xxiii) Schedule 6 to the Gas Act 1965 ;   Sch. **4**

(xxiv) section 10(4) of the Highlands and Islands Development 1965 c. 36.
(Scotland) Act 1965 ;   1965 c. 46.

(xxv) the New Towns Act 1965 ;   1965 c. 59.

(xxvi) sections 14(2), 15(2), 35(3), 58 and 89(6) of the Land 1967 c. 1.
Commission Act 1967 ;

(xxvii) sections 11(5)(*f*), 54(6) and 75(4) of, and Schedule 3 to, the
Countryside (Scotland) Act 1967 ;   1967 c. 86.

(xxviii) the New Towns (Scotland) Act 1968 ;   1968 c. 16.

(xxix) paragraph 6 of Schedule 2 to the Countryside Act 1968 ;   1968 c. 41.

(xxx) section 22 of the Sewerage (Scotland) Act 1968 ;   1968 c. 47.

(xxxi) sections 33(1), 62, 63, 69 to 73 (both inclusive), 90, 93(3)
and 94(3) of, and paragraphs 13, 14 and 15 of Schedule 5,
Schedules 6 and 7 and paragraph 6 of Schedule 9 to, the
Town and Country Planning Act 1968 ; and   1968 c. 72.

(xxxii) sections 34(1), 62, 63, 70 to 74 (both inclusive), 89, 92(3) and
93(2) of, and paragraphs 12, 13 and 14 of Schedule 4,
Schedules 5 to 7 and paragraph 5 of Schedule 9 to, the Town 1969 c. 30.
and Country Planning (Scotland) Act 1969 ;

subject to this exception, namely, that it shall not be so deemed
for the purposes of section 164 of the Town and Country Planning 1962 c. 38.
Act 1962 as applied by section 13 of the Opencast Coal Act 1958.   1958 c. 69.

(2) In the following enactments, namely,—

(*a*) sections 24 to 26 of the Town and Country Planning (Scot- 1945 c. 33.
land) Act 1945 ;

(*b*) the Acquisition of Land (Authorisation Procedure) Act 1946 ; 1946 c. 49.

(*c*) the Acquisition of Land (Authorisation Procedure) (Scot- 1947 c. 42.
land) Act 1947 ;

(*d*) sections 42 and 99 of, and Schedule 5 to, the Town and 1947 c. 53.
Country Planning (Scotland) Act 1947 ;

(*e*) the Civil Aviation Act 1949 ;   1949 c. 67.

(*f*) section 39(6)(*b*) of the Opencast Coal Act 1958 ;

(*g*) section 254(6) of the Highways Act 1959 ;   1959 c. 25.

(*h*) paragraph 2(6) of Schedule 5 to the Town and Country 1959 c. 70.
Planning (Scotland) Act 1959 ;

(*i*) section 148(6), Part X and section 212(6)(*b*) of the Town and
Country Planning Act 1962 ;

(*j*) the Pipe-lines Act 1962 ;   1962 c. 58.

(*k*) Schedules 3 and 5 to the Harbours Act 1964 ;   1964 c. 40.

(*l*) Schedule 6 to the Gas Act 1965 ;

(*m*) section 10(4) of the Highlands and Islands Development
(Scotland) Act 1965 ;

(*n*) the New Towns Act 1965 ;

(*o*) section 75(4) of the Countryside (Scotland) Act 1967 ;

(*p*) the New Towns (Scotland) Act 1968 ;

(*q*) section 73(5) of, and Schedule 6 and paragraph 4 of Schedule 7 to, the Town and Country Planning Act 1968 ; and

(*r*) section 74(5) of, and Schedule 5 and paragraph 4 of Schedule 7 to, the Town and Country Planning (Scotland) Act 1969 ;

" the appropriate Minister " shall, in relation to the authority, mean the Minister.

(3) The Land Commission Act 1967 shall have effect as if, in sub-section (3) of section 58 thereof in its application to the authority, for the words from " the Minister who " to the end of the subsection, and in subsection (6) of section 89 thereof, in its application to the authority, for the words from " the appropriate Minister " to the end of the subsection, there were substituted the words " the Minister of Posts and Telecommunications ".

(4) In the following enactments, namely,—

(*a*) section 32 of, and Schedule 5 to, the Town and Country Planning (Scotland) Act 1947 ;

(*b*) section 19 of the Town and Country Planning (Scotland) Act 1954 ;

(*c*) section 103(3) and Part X of the Town and Country Planning Act 1962 ;

(*d*) section 13 of the Pipe-lines Act 1962 ;

(*e*) the New Towns Act 1965 ;

(*f*) section 58 of the Land Commission Act 1967 ;

(*g*) the New Towns (Scotland) Act 1968 ;

(*h*) section 71(3) of, and Schedule 6 to, the Town and Country Planning Act 1968 ; and

(*i*) section 72(3) of, and Schedule 5 to, the Town and Country Planning (Scotland) Act 1969 ;

" operational land " shall, in relation to the authority, mean land of its of any such class as may be specified in regulations made jointly by the Minister and the Minister of Housing and Local Government by statutory instrument (which shall be subject to annulment in pursuance of a resolution of either House of Parliament) ; and—

(i) the definition of a class of land for the purposes of regulations made under this sub-paragraph may be framed by reference to any circumstances whatsoever ; and

(ii) if any question arises whether land of the authority's falls within a class specified in regulations so made, it shall be determined by the Minister.

In the application of this sub-paragraph to Scotland, for the reference to the Minister of Housing and Local Government there shall be substituted a reference to the Secretary of State.

(5) This paragraph shall come into operation on the appointed day.

94. Nothing in the Roads Improvement Act (Northern Ireland) 1928 or in the Planning Acts (Northern Ireland) 1931 and 1944 or in any scheme or order made thereunder shall affect any powers of the authority under the enactments relating to telegraphs or apply to any telegraphic lines placed or maintained by virtue of those enactments.   1928 c. 10 (N.I.).

Part III

Adaptations of local Enactments

95.—(1) Whereas the enactments specified in the two Lists below penalize the use of public telephone call boxes for the purpose of making false calls for police assistance, giving false alarms of fire, and the like, but are so framed that, unless amended, they will become of no effect on the appointed day:

Now, therefore, as respects any point of time after the beginning of the appointed day,—

    (*a*) each of the enactments specified in List 1 shall have effect as if, for the reference therein to a call box of the Post Office telephone service, there were substituted a reference to a call box of the authority's telephone service ; and

    (*b*) each of the enactments specified in List 2 shall have effect as if, for the reference therein to the Postmaster General, there were substituted a reference to the authority.

List 1

Section 127(2) of the Tynemouth Corporation Act 1934.	1934 c. lxxvi.
Section 221(2) of the Sunderland Corporation Act 1935.	1935 c. cxxv.
Section 106(2) of the Wolverhampton Corporation Act 1936.	1936 c. cxi.
Section 83(2) of the Rotherham Corporation Act 1937.	1937 c. lxxx.
Section 122(2) of the Wakefield Corporation Act 1938.	1938 c. xl.
Section 176(2) of the Redcar Corporation Act 1938.	1938 c. liv.
Section 167(2) of the Swinton and Pendlebury Corporation Act 1938.	1938 c. lvi.
Section 211(2) of the Clacton Urban District Council Act 1938.	1938 c. lxiii.
Section 89(2) of the Tiverton Corporation Act 1939.	1939 c. lxv.
Section 137(2) of the Walsall Corporation Act 1939.	1939 c. lxxxii.
Section 110(2) of the Macclesfield Corporation Act 1939.	1939 c. lxxxvii.
Section 84(2) of the Coventry Corporation Act 1939.	1939 c. lxxxviii.
Section 101(2) of the Christchurch Corporation Act 1940.	1940 c. xxx.
Section 154(2) of the Preston Corporation Act 1947.	1947 c. xlv.
Section 71(2) of the Brighton Corporation Act 1948.	1948 c. xxxviii.
Section 173(2) of the Ipswich Corporation Act 1948.	1948 c. xli.

SCH. 4
1949 c. xxxvii.
1949 c. xliv.
1949 c. li.

Section 114(2) of the Huddersfield Corporation Act 1949.

Section 86(2) of the Bradford Corporation Act 1949.

Section 89(2) of the Barnsley Corporation Act 1949.

List 2

1951 c. xliv.	Section 178(2) of the Worcester Corporation Act 1951.
1951 c. xlv.	Section 89(2) of the Nottinghamshire County Council Act 1951.
1953 c. xli.	Section 85(2) of the Berkshire County Council Act 1953.
1954 c. xlvii.	Section 117(2) of the Birkenhead Corporation Act 1954.
1956 c. xxxi.	Section 133(2) of the Monmouthshire County Council Act 1956.
1956 c. xl.	Section 97(2) of the Gloucestershire County Council Act 1956.
1956 c. xlix.	Section 96(2) of the Leicester Corporation Act 1956.
1956 c. lxxiii.	Section 26(2) of the Huddersfield Corporation Act 1956.
1958 c. l.	Section 116(2) of the Wallasey Corporation Act 1958.
1958 c. vi.	Section 60(2) of the Kent County Council Act 1958.
1959 c. xli.	Section 73(2) of the Bootle Corporation Act 1959.
1960 c. xliii.	Section 70(2) of the Southampton Corporation Act 1960.
1960 c. xlix.	Section 41(2) of the Hertfordshire County Council Act 1960.
1960 c. lii.	Section 60(2) of the Oldham Corporation Act 1960.
1961 c. xlv.	Section 30(3) of the Devon County Council Act 1961.
1962 c. xxvi.	Section 10(2) of the Grimsby Corporation Act 1962.
1963 c. xxxvii.	Section 44(2) of the Durham County Council Act 1963.
1964 c. xxxv.	Section 28(2) of the Newcastle upon Tyne Corporation Act 1964.
1966 c. xv.	Section 29(2) of the Exeter Corporation Act 1966.

(2) Any enactment contained in a local Act which is not specified in List 1 above but is similar to the enactments so specified shall, as respects any point of time after the beginning of the appointed day, have effect subject to the like amendment as is made by subparagraph (1)(*a*) above ; and any enactment contained in a local Act which is not specified in List 2 above but is similar to the enactments so specified shall, as respects any such point of time as aforesaid, have effect subject to the like amendment as is made by subparagraph (1)(*b*) above.

96.—(1) Nothing in—

(*a*) the London Building Acts 1930 to 1939 or byelaws thereunder ; or

(*b*) a special enactment passed or made before the appointed day (including such an enactment relating to Scotland or Northern Ireland) for purposes similar to those of an enactment contained in Part V or VII of the Highways Act 1959 (except sections 136 to 138) ;

1959 c. 25.

shall affect any powers of the authority under the enactments relating to telegraphs or apply to any telegraphic lines placed or maintained

by the Postmaster General or the authority by virtue of those   Sch. 4
enactments.

(2) In this paragraph, " special enactment " has the same meaning
as in the Highways Act 1959.   1959 c. 25.

97.—(1) As from the appointed day, subsections (2) and (3) of
section 59 of the Metropolitan Water Board (Various Powers) Act 1907 c. clxxiv.
1907 (which empower the Postmaster General to place telegraphic
lines along, over or across the lands, works and undertaking of the
Metropolitan Water Board) shall be construed so as to confer and
impose on the authority the like rights and liabilities as are, immediately before that day, conferred and imposed on the Postmaster
General and so as to render it subject to the like restrictions as those
to which he is subject by virtue thereof immediately before that day ;
and anything done by or to the Postmaster General under those subsections before that day shall, as from that day, be treated as having
been done by or to the authority.

(2) As from the appointed day, the first reference to the Postmaster
General in subsection (4) of the said section 59 (saving for his rights
in relation to the Lee Navigation) and the reference to him in the
proviso to section 11 of the Metropolitan Water Board Act 1915 1915 c. lxxiii.
(which saves his rights under, amongst other enactments, the said Act
of 1907) shall be construed as referring to the authority.

98. As from the appointed day, the references in section 120(1)
and (2) of the Dover Harbour Consolidation Act 1954 (further pro- 1954 c. iv.
tection of Postmaster General) to the Postmaster General shall be
construed as referring to the authority.

99.—(1) Subsection (3) of section 77 of the Kingston upon Hull 1967 c. xxxiii.
Corporation Act 1967 (which provides that byelaws made under
that section with reference to the telephone system maintained by
the Corporation of Kingston upon Hull shall continue in force
only so long as there is in force a licence granted by the Postmaster
General to the Corporation permitting the Corporation to provide
telephonic services) shall, as from the appointed day, have effect
as if, for the reference to a licence so granted and permitting, there
were substituted a reference to a licence so permitting granted, or
having effect as if granted, under section 27 of this Act by the
authority ; and the references in subsection (4) of the said section
77 to any such licence as is mentioned in subsection (3) shall, as
from that day, be construed accordingly.

(2) The power conferred by section 93 of the said Act of 1967
on the Postmaster General to confirm byelaws under the said
section 77 shall, on the appointed day, be transferred to the Minister.

100. A benefit conferred on the Postmaster General by a provision
of a local Act passed in the same session as this Act or a previous
session or of an order confirmed by an Act so passed consisting in

securing that a power conferred by the Act or order to acquire land compulsorily, to secure compulsorily the creation of an easement or other right over land or to execute works on, under or over land shall not, except with his consent or agreement, be exercisable in relation to land specified or described in that provision shall, as from the appointed day, enure for the benefit of the authority.

101.—(1) As from the appointed day, a provision to which this paragraph applies which refers to the rights or powers of the Postmaster General under a provision of an enactment relating to telegraphs or to the exclusive privilege conferred on him by section 3 of the Post Office Act 1953 shall have effect with the substitution, for any reference to the Postmaster General, of a reference to the authority.

(2) A provision to which this paragraph applies that operates to afford protection to, or confer a benefit on, the Postmaster General with reference to, or to accommodation for, telegraphic lines of his or used by him or to communication by means of telegraphic lines of his or used by him, shall, as from the appointed day, be construed so as, in all respects, to afford the like protection to, or confer the like benefit on, the authority with reference to, or to accommodation for, telegraphic lines of its or used by it or, as the case may be, to communication by means of telegraphic lines of its or used by it and subject to the like incidents (if any) as those to which the protection afforded to, or the benefit conferred on, the Postmaster General is subject (references to the authority being, accordingly, substituted where necessary for references to the Postmaster General) ; and, so far as may be necessary to preserve continuity in the giving of effect to that provision, anything done before the appointed day by or to the Postmaster General shall be treated, for the purposes of that provision, as having been done by or to the authority.

(3) The last foregoing sub-paragraph shall apply to a provision to which this paragraph applies that operates to afford protection to the Postmaster General with reference to either of the Post Office underground railways as it applies to any such provision as is therein mentioned ; and any reference in a provision to which this paragraph applies to the rights or interests of the Postmaster General in, or in relation to, either of those railways shall be construed as referring to the rights or interests of the authority in, or, as the case may be, in relation to, it.

(4) A provision to which this paragraph applies that operates to permit vehicles in the service of, or employed by, the Postmaster General to wait on a highway in circumstances in which their waiting there would, apart from that provision, be unlawful, shall, as from the appointed day have effect with the substitution, for any reference to the Postmaster General, of a reference to the authority.

(5) The provisions to which this paragraph applies are those of a local Act passed in the same session as this Act or in a previous session, those of an order confirmed by an Act so passed and those of a scheme or order made before the passing of this Act under any Act (whether public general or local).

(6) In this paragraph, "telegraphic line" means anything falling within the definition of that expression in the Telegraph Act 1878. Scu. 4
1878 c. 76.

102. Nothing in a local Act passed in the same Session as this Act shall authorise the doing of anything constituting an infringement of the privilege conferred by section 24(1) of this Act.

Part IV

Adaptation of Orders in Council

103. As from the appointed day, references in the Parliamentary Writs Order 1944 (which lays down rules for the conveyance through the post of writs for parliamentary elections for constituencies in Great Britain) to the Postmaster General shall be construed as referring to the authority. S.R.&.O.
1944/344.

104. As from the appointed day, Article 7 of the Visiting Forces and International Headquarters (Application of Law) Order 1965 (which empowers the making, by agreement, of exceptions from, inter alia, the exclusive privileges of the Postmaster General with respect to posts and telegraphs) shall have effect as if, in paragraph (*a*), for the reference to the Postmaster General, there were substituted a reference to the authority and as if, for paragraph (*b*), there were substituted the following paragraph:— S.I. 1965/1536.

" (*b*) the transmission of matter within the United Kingdom by the service authorities of that force or by that headquarters shall not constitute an infringement of the privilege conferred by section 24(1) of the Post Office Act 1969, and the prohibition imposed by section 89 of that Act shall not extend to any such transmission ".

SCHEDULE 5 Sections 77, 88.

Repair of minor Deficiencies in certain Acts

1.—(1) In any proceedings against a person in respect of an offence under section 45 of the Telegraph Act 1863 or section 11 of the Post Office (Protection) Act 1884 consisting in the improper divulging of the purport of a message or communication or an offence under section 20 of the Telegraph Act 1868 it shall be a defence for him to prove that the act constituting the offence was done in obedience to a warrant under the hand of a Secretary of State. 1863 c. 112.
1884 c. 76.
1868 c. 110.

(2) Subsection (2) of section 58 of the Post Office Act 1953 (warrants in Northern Ireland and the Isle of Man) shall apply for the purposes of the foregoing sub-paragraph as it applies for the purposes of subsection (1) of that section. 1953 c. 36.

2.—(1) Section 16(1) of the Post Office Act 1953 shall have effect,—

(*a*) in its application to the Channel Islands, in relation to goods contained in postal packets to which that section applies brought into or sent out of the Channel Islands by post from or to the United Kingdom or the Isle of Man or any place outside the British postal area ; and

Sch. 5

    (*b*) in its application to the Isle of Man, in relation to goods contained in postal packets to which that section applies brought into or sent out of the Isle of Man by post from or to the United Kingdom or the Channel Islands or any place outside the British postal area,

as it has effect in relation to goods contained in postal packets brought into or sent out of the United Kingdom by post from or to the Channel Islands, the Isle of Man or any place outside the British postal area.

    (2) In the application of the said section 16 as extended by the foregoing sub-paragraph to the Channel Islands, any reference to the enactments for the time being in force relating to customs shall be construed as a reference to the enactments for the time being in force in the Channel Islands relating to customs.

1953 c. 36.

    (3) This paragraph shall be construed as one with the Post Office Act 1953.

    3. Section 63 of the Post Office Act 1953 shall have effect as if, in subsection (6) thereof, for the words " any stamp for denoting a current rate of postage of any country outside the British postal area ", there were substituted the words " any current stamp for denoting a rate of postage of any country outside the British postal area ".

Sections 94, 114.

SCHEDULE 6

AMENDMENTS OF ACTS CONSEQUENTIAL ON SECTION 94
OF THIS ACT

PART I

1954 c. 62.

AMENDMENTS OF THE POST OFFICE
SAVINGS BANK ACT 1954

Provision amended and Subject-matter thereof	Amendment
Section 2 (general power to make regulations).	In subsection (1), for the words " The Postmaster General, with the consent of the Treasury, may make regulations ", there shall be substituted the words " The Treasury may make regulations ", and the words " in his department " shall be omitted; and, in subsection (2), for the words " post office savings banks " and the words " the Postmaster General ", there shall be substituted, respectively, the words " the National Savings Bank " and the words " the Director of Savings ".
Section 4 (limit on amount of deposits).	In subsection (1), the words " by the Postmaster General " shall be repealed.

Provision amended and Subject-matter thereof	*Amendment*
Section 6 (withdrawal).	For the words "the authority of the Postmaster General" there shall be substituted the word "authority"; and for the words "any Post Office where deposits are received or paid", there shall be substituted the words "any place at which deposits can be withdrawn".
Section 7 (regulations as to deposits).	In subsection (1), for the words "The power of the Postmaster General with the consent of the Treasury to make regulations", there shall be substituted the words "The power of the Treasury to make regulations"; in paragraphs (*a*), (*b*) and (*e*), for the words "a post office savings bank" and the words "any post office savings bank", there shall be substituted the words "the National Savings Bank"; in paragraphs (*d*) and (*g*), for the words "the Postmaster General", there shall be substituted the words "the Director of Savings"; for paragraph (*f*), there shall be substituted the following paragraph:—
	"(*f*) for the purpose of the payment or transfer of any sum, for authorising a person to be treated as having been domiciled in the place in which he was resident at the date of his death";
	and, in paragraph (*l*), the words "the Postmaster General to treat as a depositor in a post office savings bank" shall be omitted, and, at the end of that paragraph, there shall be added the words "to be treated as a depositor"; and, in subsection (2), for the words "a post office savings bank", there shall be substituted the words "the National Savings Bank".
Section 8 (settlement of disputes).	In subsection (1), for the words "the Postmaster General", there shall be substituted the words "the Director of Savings"; in subsection (2), for the words "the Postmaster General" there shall be substituted the words "the Director of Savings"; in subsection (4), for the words "books belonging to the Postmaster General", there shall be substituted the words "books of the

Provision amended and Subject-matter thereof	*Amendment*
Section 8 (settlement of disputes)—*cont.*	National Savings Bank "; and, in subsection (5), for the words " the Postmaster General ", there shall be substituted the words " the Director of Savings ".
Section 10 (secrecy). ...	In subsection (1), for the words " the Postmaster General ", there shall be substituted the words " the Director of Savings ".
Section 11 (transfer of deposits to other savings banks).	In subsection (1), the words " under this Act " shall be repealed, and for the words " the Postmaster General " there shall be substituted the words " the Director of Savings "; in subsections (4) and (5), for the words " the Postmaster General ", there shall be substituted the words " the Director of Savings "; and, in subsection (6), for the words " the post office savings bank ", there shall be substituted the words " the National Savings Bank ".
Section 12 (transfer of deposits from other savings banks).	In subsection (1), for the words " a post office savings bank ", there shall be substituted the words " the National Savings Bank "; in subsection (2), for the words " to any person authorised to receive deposits under this Act ", there shall be substituted the words " at any place where the business of the National Savings Bank is transacted ", and the words " made under this Act " shall be repealed; in subsection (5), for the words " the post office savings bank ", there shall be substituted the words " the National Savings Bank "; and, in subsection (6), for the words " the Postmaster General " there shall be substituted the words " the Director of Savings ".
Section 13 (transfer of deposits from and to **overseas savings** banks).	In subsection (1), for the words " the Postmaster General " there shall be substituted the words " the Director of Savings ", and for the words " the post office savings bank " (in both places where they occur) there shall be substituted the words " the National Savings Bank "; in subsection (2), the reference to an arrangement's having been made under subsection (1) shall be construed as including a reference to an arrangement's

Provision amended and Subject-matter thereof	*Amendment*
Section 13 (transfer of deposits from and to overseas savings banks)—*cont.*	having been made under that subsection by the Postmaster General before the appointed day, and for the words " the Postmaster General may place any amount transferred in pursuance of those arrangements to the post office savings bank ", there shall be substituted the words " the Director of Savings may cause any amount transferred in pursuance of the arrangement to the National Savings Bank to be placed "; and, in subsection (3), for the words " Regulations made under this Act by the Postmaster General with the consent of the Treasury ", there shall be substituted the words " Regulations made under this Act by the Treasury ".
Section 14 (deposits by charitable societies, &c.).	In subsections (1) and (2), for the words " a post office savings bank ", there shall be substituted the words " the National Savings Bank "; in subsection (3), for the words " The Postmaster General " there shall be substituted the words " The Director of Savings ", and, for the words " a post office savings bank " there shall be substituted the words " the National Savings Bank "; and, in subsection (4), for the words " any obligation on the Postmaster General as respects his receiving any funds " there shall be substituted the words " any obligation on the National Savings Bank to receive funds ".

PART II

AMENDMENTS OF THE POST OFFICE SAVINGS BANK ACT 1966

1966 c. 12.

Provision amended and Subject-matter thereof	*Amendment*
Section 1 (investment deposits).	In subsection (1), for the words " received under the Post Office Savings Bank Act 1954 (in this Act referred to as ' the principal Act ') may be so " there shall be substituted the words " may be "; in subsection (2), the words " made in a post office savings bank " shall be repealed; and, in subsection (3), after the words " The following provisions of " there shall be inserted the words " the Post Office Savings Bank Act 1954, in this Act referred to as ".

1954 c. 62.

SCH. 6

Provision amended and Subject-matter thereof	*Amendment*
Section 2 (terms of investment deposits).	In subsection (1), for the words " as the Postmaster General may from time to time by regulations made with the consent of the Treasury prescribe " there shall be substituted the words " as the Treasury may from time to time by regulations prescribe ", and for the words " the Postmaster General " (where secondly occurring) there shall be substituted the words " the Director of Savings "; in subsection (2), the words " the Postmaster General's " shall be omitted; and, in subsection (4), for the words " The Postmaster General " there shall be substituted the words " The Director of Savings ".
Section 4 (investment by National Debt Commissioners).	In subsection (1), for the words " the Postmaster General with the consent of the Treasury " there shall be substituted the words " the Treasury "; in subsection (2), for the words " the Postmaster General with the consent of the Treasury " there shall be substituted the words " the Treasury " and for the words " to the Postmaster General " there shall be substituted the words " to the Director of Savings "; and, in subsection (3), for the words " the Postmaster General " there shall be substituted the words " the Director of Savings ".
Section 6 (making of deposits).	For the words " the Postmaster General " there shall be substituted the words " the Treasury ".

PART III

AMENDMENTS OF OTHER ENACTMENTS

Enactments of the Parliament of the United Kingdom

Enactment amended and Subject-matter thereof	*Amendment*
1879 c. 11. Section 9 of the Bankers' Books Evidence Act 1879 (interpretation of " bank ", " banker " and " bankers' books ").	For the words " any post office savings bank " there shall be substituted the words " the National Savings Bank ".

Enactment amended and Subject-matter thereof	*Amendment*	
Section 2 of the Consolidated Fund (Permanent Charges Redemption) Act 1883 (power of Treasury to borrow from the National Debt Commissioners, out of funds in their hands on account of trustee or post office savings banks, capital sums necessary for carrying into effect contracts made in pursuance of the Consolidated Fund (Permanent Charges Redemption) Act 1873).	In subsection (1), for the words " Trustee or Post Office Savings Banks " there shall be substituted the words " trustee savings banks and the National Savings Bank ".	1883 c. 1. 1873 c. 57.
Section 10 of the Savings Banks Act 1887 (issue, for specially low fee, of certificate of birth, marriage or death for purposes of Acts relating to savings banks and government annuities).	For the words "Post Office Savings Banks " there shall be substituted the words " the National Savings Bank ".	1887 c. 40.
Section 141 of the Merchant Shipping Act 1894 (definition of " savings bank " for the purposes of the provisions of the Act relating to allotment notes).	In subsection (4)(*b*), for the words " a post office savings bank " there shall be substituted the words " the National Savings Bank ".	1894 c. 60.
Section 44 of the Friendly Societies Act 1896 (investment of funds).	In subsection (1)(*a*), for the words " the Post Office Savings Bank " there shall be substituted the words " the National Savings Bank ".	1896 c. 25.
Rule 172 in Schedule 1 to the Sheriff Courts (Scotland) Act 1907 (disposal of money payable to persons under legal disability).	In paragraph (*f*), in sub-paragraph (1), for the words " the Post Office Savings Bank " there shall be substituted the words " the National Savings Bank ", and, in sub-paragraph (4), for the words " the Post Office Savings Bank " there shall be substituted the words " the Director of Savings ".	1907 c. 51.
Section 9 of the Government of Ireland Act 1920 (reserved matters).	In subsection (2)(*b*), for the words " the Post Office Savings Bank ", there shall be substituted the words " the National Savings Bank ".	1920 c. 67.

SCH. 6

Enactment amended and Subject-matter thereof	Amendment
925 c. 23. 1929 c. 29.	Section 47A of the Administration of Estates Act 1925 (right of surviving spouse to have own life interest redeemed).	In subsection (2), in rule 2, for the words " the purchase of an immediate life annuity from the National Debt Commissioners through the Post Office Savings Bank ", there shall be substituted the words " the purchase, under the Government Annuities Act 1929, of an immediate savings bank annuity ".
1947 c. 44.	Section 27 of the Crown Proceedings Act 1947 (attachment of moneys payable by the Crown).	In subsection (1), in the proviso, in paragraph (c), for the words " the Post Office Savings Bank " there shall be substituted the words " the National Savings Bank ".
	Section 46 of the Crown Proceedings Act 1947 (provisions as to arrestment).	In the proviso, in paragraph (c), for the words " the Post Office Savings Bank " there shall be substituted the words " the National Savings Bank ".
1952 c. 10.	Section 29 of the Income Tax Act 1952 (power of surveyor of taxes to obtain information as to interest paid or credited without deduction of tax).	In subsection (3), for the words " the Post Office Savings Bank ", there shall be substituted the words " the National Savings Bank " and for the words " the Postmaster General " there shall be substituted the words " the Director of Savings ".
1954 c. 63.	Section 21 of the Trustee Savings Banks Act 1954 (regulations as to deposits).	In subsection (2), for the words " the post office savings bank " there shall be substituted the words " the National Savings Bank "; and, in subsection (4), for the words " the post office savings bank " there shall be substituted the words " the National Savings Bank ", for paragraph (b), there shall be substituted the following paragraph:— " (b) for the purpose of the payment or transfer of any sum, for authorising a person to be treated as having been domiciled in the place in which he was resident at the date of his death ",

Enactment amended and Subject-matter thereof	*Amendment*
Section 21 of the Trustee Savings Banks Act 1954 (regulations as to deposits)—*cont.*	and, in paragraph (*c*), for the words "the Postmaster General" there shall be substituted the words "the Director of Savings".
Section 54 of the Trustee Savings Banks Act 1954 (trustees of a trustee savings bank who propose to close the bank to give to depositors notice of the facilities afforded by law for transfer of deposits to a post office savings bank).	In subsection (3), for the words " a post office savings bank" there shall be substituted the words "the National Savings Bank".
Section 56 of the Trustee Savings Banks Act 1954 (procedure available on closing a bank).	In subsection (3), for the words " a post office savings bank" there shall be substituted the words "the National Savings Bank"; and, in subsection (4), for the words "any post office savings bank" there shall be substituted the words "the National Savings Bank".
Section 38 of the Administration of Justice Act 1956 (attachment of debts).	In subsection (2), for the words " the Post Office Savings Bank" there shall be substituted the words "the National Savings Bank".
Section 9 of the Finance Act 1956 (relief from income tax on certain savings bank interest).	In subsection (1), for the words " the Post Office savings bank" there shall be substituted the words "the National Savings Bank".
Schedule 3 to the Insurance Companies Act 1958 (rules for valuing policies and liabilities).	In paragraph 5, for the words " the purchase of a life annuity from the National Debt Commissioners through the Post Office Savings Bank" there shall be substituted the words " the purchase under the Government Annuities Act 1929 of a savings bank annuity".
Section 143 of the County Courts Act 1959 (attachment of debts).	In subsection (2), for the words " the Post Office Savings Bank" there shall be substituted the words "the National Savings Bank".

1954 c. 63.

1956 c. 46.

1956 c. 54.

1958 c. 72

1929 c. 29.

1959 c. 22.

SCH. 6

	Enactment amended and Subject-matter thereof	Amendment
1961 c. 62.	Section 17 of the Trustee Investments Act 1961 (extension to the Isle of Man and the Channel Islands of so much of section 16 as relates to the Post Office Savings Bank and to trustee savings banks).	In subsection (3), for the words " the Post Office Savings Bank " there shall be substituted the words " the National Savings Bank ".
	Part I of Schedule 1 to the Trustee Investments Act 1961 (narrower-range investments not requiring advice).	In paragraph 2, for the words " the Post Office Savings Bank " there shall be substituted the words " the National Savings Bank ".
1966 c. 18.	Section 20 of the Finance Act 1966 (exclusion from relief from income tax of interest on Post Office investment deposits).	For the words " the Post Office savings bank " there shall be substituted the words " the National Savings Bank ".

Enactments of the Parliament of Northern Ireland

1957 c. 19 (N.I.).	Section 25 of the Betting and Lotteries Act (Northern Ireland) 1957 (offences in connection with lotteries).	In subsection (4)(c), for the words " the Post Office Savings Bank " there shall be substituted the words " the National Savings Bank ".
1959 c. 25 (N.I.).	Section 98 of the County Courts Act (Northern Ireland) 1959 (investment of funds in court).	In subsection (2)(c), for the words " a Post Office Savings Bank " there shall be substituted the words " the National Savings Bank ".
1968 c. 6 (N.I.).	Schedule 3 to the Insurance Companies Act (Northern Ireland) 1968 (rules for valuing policies and liabilities).	In paragraph 5, for the words " the purchase of a life annuity from the National Debt Commissioners through the Post Office Savings Bank " there shall be substituted the words " the purchase under the Government Annuities Act 1929 of a savings bank annuity ".
1929 c. 29.		

Section 131.

SCHEDULE 7

SETTLEMENT OF FINANCIAL MATTERS OUTSTANDING ON THE APPOINTED DAY

1929 c. 29.

1961 c. 15.

1.—(1) As soon as practicable after the appointed day, the Post Office shall pay sums equal in the aggregate to the difference between the aggregate of the sums paid by the Postmaster General in pursuance of section 2 of the Post Office Act 1961 (contributions by the Postmaster General in lieu of taxes, &c.) and what is agreed between the Treasury and the Post Office to be the aggregate of the sums which, had this Act not passed, would have been paid in pursuance of that section by the Postmaster General in respect of the period beginning with the day on which that Act came into operation and ending with the day immediately preceding the appointed day.

(2) As from the appointed day,—

(*a*) subsection (3) of the said section 2 (destination of payments under that section) shall have effect as if, for the reference to that section, there were substituted a reference to the foregoing sub-paragraph and, for the reference to the Postmaster General, there were substituted a reference to the Post Office; and

(*b*) subsection (4) of that section (apportionment of sums paid under that section between Great Britain and Northern Ireland) shall have effect as if the reference to that section included a reference to the foregoing sub-paragraph.

2.—(1) If, immediately before the appointed day, any sums of money that, by virtue of section 3(1) of the Post Office Act 1961, are subject 1961 c. 15. to be paid by the Postmaster General into the Exchequer of the United Kingdom (that is to say, sums received by him by way of broadcast receiving licence revenue) are in his hands, the Post Office shall, on that day or as soon as practicable thereafter, pay equivalent sums to the Minister, who shall pay them into the Consolidated Fund.

(2) As soon as practicable after the appointed day, the Minister shall pay to the Post Office a sum equal to the difference between the aggregate of the sums paid, under section 3(2) of the Post Office Act 1961, into the Post Office Fund out of moneys provided by Parliament for paying the Postmaster General for discharging his functions under the Wireless Telegraphy Acts 1949 to 1967 and the Television Act 1964 c. 21. 1964, in so far as broadcasting is concerned or otherwise in relation to broadcasting and the amount determined by the Minister, with the approval of the Treasury, to be the aggregate of the sums that, had this Act not passed, would have been paid, under that section, into that fund, out of moneys so provided for that purpose in respect of the period beginning with the day on which the first-mentioned Act came into operation and ending with the day immediately preceding the appointed day.

3.—(1) If, immediately before the appointed day, there are in the hands of the Postmaster General any sums of money received by him from the Secretary of State for the payment on his behalf of benefit (as defined by section 114(1) of the National Insurance Act 1965 or 1965 c. 51. section 86(1) of the National Insurance (Industrial Injuries) Act 1965), 1965 c. 52. allowances under the Family Allowances Act 1965 or allowances or 1965 c. 53. benefit under the Industrial Injuries and Diseases (Old Cases) Act 1967 c. 34. 1967 or received by him in respect of sales of insurance stamps (within the meaning of the first- or second-mentioned Act of 1965), the Post Office shall, on that day, assume a liability to pay equivalent sums to the Secretary of State; and if, immediately before that day, any sums of money are owed by the Secretary of State to the Postmaster General for the purpose of reimbursing him sums paid by him on behalf of the Secretary of State by way of such benefit or allowances as aforesaid, the Secretary of State shall, on that day, assume a liability to pay to the Post Office sums equivalent to those owed.

(2) As soon as practicable after the appointed day, the Secretary of State shall pay to the Post Office a sum equal to the difference between the aggregate of the sums paid by him, the Minister of Social Security and the Minister of Pensions and National Insurance together in pursuance of subsection (2) of section 85 of the National Insurance Act 1965 (payment of the Postmaster General for work done by him in the execution of that Act and the other enactments mentioned in that subsection) to the Postmaster General and the amount agreed between him and the Post Office to be the aggregate of the sums that, had this Act not passed, would have been paid by him and those Ministers together in pursuance of that subsection to the Postmaster General in respect of the period beginning with the day on which that Act came into operation and ending with the day immediately preceding the appointed day.

(3) The payment falling to be made in pursuance of the last foregoing sub-paragraph shall be defrayed as follows, that is to say,—

(*a*) so much as is attributable to work done by the Postmaster General in the execution of the National Health Service Contributions Act 1965, so much as is determined by the Treasury to be attributable to work done by him in the execution of section 28 of the Redundancy Payments Act 1965 and so much as is so determined to be attributable to work done by him in the execution of section 44 of the Finance Act 1966 (selective employment tax) shall be defrayed out of moneys provided by Parliament;

(*b*) the residue shall be defrayed as part of the expenses of the Secretary of State in carrying into effect the enactments mentioned in section 85(2) of the National Insurance Act 1965;

and, for the purpose of determining what part of the residue should be attributed to each respectively of the enactments so mentioned, it shall be apportioned between them in such manner as may be determined by the Secretary of State in accordance with any directions given by the Treasury.

4.—(1) If, immediately before the appointed day, there are in the hands of the Postmaster General any sums of money received by him from the Secretary of State for the payment on his behalf of benefit

(as defined by section 36(1) of the Ministry of Social Security Act 1966), the Post Office shall, on that day, assume a liability to pay equivalent sums to the Secretary of State; and if, immediately before that day, any sums of money are owed to the Postmaster General by the Secretary of State for the purpose of reimbursing him sums paid by him on behalf of the Secretary of State by way of benefit (as so defined), the Secretary of State shall, on that day, assume a liability to pay to the Post Office sums equivalent to those owed.

(2) As soon as practicable after the appointed day, the Secretary of State shall, out of moneys provided by Parliament, pay to the Post Office a sum equal to the difference between the aggregate of the sums paid by him and the Minister of Social Security together in pursuance

of subsection (3) of section 19 of the Post Office Act 1961 (payment of the Postmaster General for work done by him in the execution of

SCH. 7
1966 c. 20.

the Ministry of Social Security Act 1966) to the Postmaster General and the amount agreed between him and the Post Office to be the aggregate of the sums that, had this Act not passed, would have been paid by him and the Minister of Social Security together in pursuance of that subsection to the Postmaster General in respect of the period beginning with the day appointed under section 40(2)(*c*) of the last-mentioned Act by the Minister of Social Security and ending with the day immediately preceding the appointed day.

1962 c. 13.

5.—(1) If, immediately before the appointed day, there are in the hands of the Postmaster General any sums of money received by him on behalf of a county council in respect of licences issued under the Vehicles (Excise) Act 1962, the Post Office shall, on that day, assume a liability to pay equivalent sums to the council.

1961 c. 15.

(2) As soon as practicable after the appointed day, the Minister of Transport shall, out of moneys provided by Parliament, pay to the Post Office a sum equal to the difference between the aggregate of the sums paid by him in pursuance of subsection (4) of section 19 of the Post Office Act 1961 (payment of the Postmaster General for work done by him in the execution of the Vehicles (Excise) Act 1962) to the Postmaster General and the amount agreed between him and the Post Office to be the aggregate of the sums that, had this Act not passed, would have been paid by him in pursuance of that subsection to the Postmaster General in respect of the period beginning with the day on which the first-mentioned Act came into operation and ending with the day immediately preceding the appointed day.

(3) In this paragraph, the expression " county council " shall be construed in like manner as if it were contained in the Vehicles (Excise) Act 1962.

6.—(1) If, immediately before the appointed day, there are in the hands of the Postmaster General any sums of money received by him on behalf of a local authority in England or Wales in respect of licences for dogs or licences to deal in, or for killing, game, the Post Office shall,—

1966 c. 42.

- (*a*) if subsection (3) of section 35 of the Local Government Act 1966 (deduction by Postmaster General, from amount of duties in respect of such licences as aforesaid received by him, of expenses incurred by him on work done in connection with issue thereof) is not in force on that day, assume a liability to pay equivalent sums to the authority;

- (*b*) if that subsection is in force on that day, assume a liability to pay to the authority equivalent sums less such sum as the Minister considers to be equal to that which, had this Act not passed and the first-mentioned sums been paid by the Postmaster General to the authority on that day, would, by virtue of that subsection, have been deducted by him there-from.

(2) If, immediately before the appointed day, there are in the hands of the Postmaster General any sums of money received by him on behalf of a local authority in Scotland in respect of licences for dogs

Sch. 7

or licences for killing game, the Post Office shall pay to the authority equivalent sums, less such sum as the Minister considers to be equal to that which, had this Act not passed and the first-mentioned sums been paid by the Postmaster General to the authority on that day,

1966 c. 57.
S.I. 1967/714
(S. 50).

would, by virtue of section 43(2) of the Local Government (Scotland) Act 1966 or of Article 4(6) of the Game Licences and Gamedealers' Licences (Scotland) Order 1967, have been deducted by him therefrom.

(3) If subsection (3) of section 35 of the Local Government Act

1966 c. 42.

1966 is not in force on the appointed day, the Minister of Housing and Local Government shall, as soon as practicable thereafter, pay to the Post Office, out of moneys provided by Parliament, a sum equal to the difference between the aggregate of the sums paid by him in

1961 c. 15.

pursuance of subsection (5) of section 19 of the Post Office Act 1961 to the Postmaster General and the amount agreed between him and the Post Office to be the aggregate of the sums that, had this Act not passed, would have been paid by him in pursuance of that subsection to the Postmaster General in respect of the period beginning with the day on which that Act came into operation and ending with the day immediately preceding the appointed day.

7.—(1) If, immediately before the appointed day, there are in the hands of the Postmaster General any sums of money received by him by way of ordinary or investment deposits or for the purpose of the repayment of such deposits or the payment of interest thereon, the Post Office shall, on that day, assume a liability to pay equivalent sums to the Director of Savings.

(2) If, immediately before the appointed day, any sums of money are owed to the Postmaster General for the purpose of reimbursing him sums paid by him by way of the repayment of, or the payment of interest on, ordinary deposits, the Director of Savings shall, on that day, assume a liability to pay to the Post Office sums equivalent to the sums owed; and a payment made in or towards discharge of this liability shall be made out of ordinary deposits.

(3) If, immediately before the appointed day, any sums of money are owed to the Postmaster General for the purpose of reimbursing him sums paid by him by way of the repayment of, or the payment of interest on, investment deposits, the Director of Savings shall, on that day, assume a liability to pay to the Post Office sums equivalent to the sums owed; and a payment made in or towards discharge of this liability shall be debited to the National Savings Bank Investment Account Fund.

(4) As soon as practicable after the appointed day, the National Debt Commissioners shall pay to the Post Office a sum equal to the difference between the aggregate of the sums paid by them in pursuance of subsection (6) of section 19 of the Post Office Act 1961 (payment of the Postmaster General for work done by him in the execution of the

1954 c. 62.

Post Office Savings Bank Act 1954) and the amount agreed between the Treasury and the Post Office to be the aggregate of the sums that, had this Act not passed, would have been paid by the Commissioners in pursuance of that subsection to the Postmaster General in respect of the period beginning with the day on which the first-mentioned Act came into operation and ending with the day immediately preceding the appointed day; and the payment of the sum falling to be paid by virtue of the foregoing provisions of this sub-paragraph shall be treated for the purposes of section 16 of the Post Office Savings Bank Act 1954 as part of the expenses incurred by the National Debt Commissioners in the execution of that Act.

Sch. 7

1954 c. 62.

(5) As soon as practicable after the appointed day, there shall be debited to the National Savings Bank Investment Account Fund and paid to the Post Office—

(*a*) a sum equal to the difference between the aggregate of the sums debited in pursuance of paragraph (*a*) of subsection (3) of section 3 of the Post Office Savings Bank Act 1966 (which paragraph operates to secure that the Postmaster General is paid for work done by him in connection with investment deposits) and the amount agreed between the Treasury and the Post Office to be the aggregate of the sums that, had this Act not passed, would have been debited in pursuance of that paragraph in respect of the period beginning with the day on which that Act came into operation and ending with the day immediately preceding the appointed day; and

1966 c. 12.

(*b*) a sum equal to the difference between the aggregate of the sums debited in pursuance of paragraph (*c*) of that subsection (which paragraph operates to secure that the Postmaster General is reimbursed amounts paid by him under section 2 of the Post Office Act 1961 that are attributable to the investment of deposits under the said Act of 1966) and the amount agreed between the Treasury and the Post Office to be the aggregate of the sums that, had this Act not passed, would have been debited in pursuance of that paragraph in respect of the period aforesaid.

1961 c. 15.

8.—(1) If, immediately before the appointed day, there are in the hands of the Postmaster General any sums of money received by him—

(*a*) in respect of purchases or sales of government stock, national savings certificates or relevant securities;

(*b*) for the purpose of the payment of interest on, or the redemption of, government stock or relevant securities;

(*c*) for the purpose of the redemption or repayment of, or the payment of interest on, national savings certificates or war savings certificates; or

(*d*) for the purpose of making, in respect of relevant securities, payments other than payments of principal or interest;

the Post Office shall, on that day, assume a liability to pay equivalent sums to the Director of Savings.

(2) If, immediately before the appointed day, any sums of money are owed to the Postmaster General by the Treasury for the purpose of reimbursing him sums paid by him for any such purpose as is mentioned in sub-paragraph (1)(*b*), (*c*) or (*d*) above, the Director of Savings shall, on that day, assume a liability to pay to the Post Office sums equivalent to the sums owed; and a payment made in or towards

SCH. 7

the discharge of this liability shall be made out of the National Loans Fund with recourse to the Consolidated Fund.

(3) If, immediately before the appointed day, there are in the hands of the Postmaster General any sums of money remitted under section 5 of the National Debt Act 1958 by the Bank of England or Ireland, the Post Office shall, on that day or as soon as practicable thereafter, pay equivalent sums to the Director of Savings.

1958 c. 6.
(7 & 8 Eliz. 2).

(4) In this paragraph—

(*a*) " government stock " means stock registered in the register referred to in section 108(1) of this Act;

(*b*) " national savings certificates " means the certificates issued by that name under section 59 of the Finance Act 1920, Part II of the National Debt Act 1958 or section 12 of the National Loans Act 1968;

1920 c. 18.

1968 c. 13.

(*c*) " relevant securities " means securities (other than national savings certificates) created and issued under the National Loans Act 1939 or section 12 of the National Loans Act 1968 for the purpose of raising money through the department of the Postmaster General; and

1939 c. 117.

(*d*) " war savings certificates " means the certificates issued by that name under the War Loan Act 1915 or section 58 of the Finance Act 1916.

1915 c. 55.
1916 c. 24.

1961 c. 36.

9. If, immediately before the appointed day, any sums of money that, by virtue of section 35(2) of the Finance Act 1961, are subject to be paid into the National Loans Fund are in the hands of the Postmaster General (that is to say, sums received by him from the sale of national savings stamps or gift tokens), the Post Office shall, on that day or as soon as practicable thereafter, pay equivalent sums to the Treasury who shall pay them into that fund; and, if, immediately before that day, any sums are due under the said section 35(2) to the Postmaster General by way of reimbursing him money paid by him in respect of the exchange or encashment of national savings stamps or national savings gift tokens, the Treasury shall, on that day or as soon as practicable thereafter, pay out of that fund equivalent sums to the Post Office.

10.—(1) If, immediately before the appointed day, any sum is due to the Postmaster General for reimbursing him expenses incurred by him of the kind mentioned in section 12(4)(*c*) or 13(4) of the National Loans Act 1968, an equivalent sum shall, on that day or as soon as practicable thereafter, be paid to the Post Office out of the National Loans Fund with recourse to the Consolidated Fund.

(2) If, in any period ending with the day immediately preceding the appointed day, the Postmaster General has done without payment work for whose doing he would, but for this Act, have received payment under subsection (7) of section 16 of the National Loans Act 1968 after the beginning of that day, there shall, on that day or as soon as practicable thereafter, be paid to the Post Office out of the National Loans Fund with recourse to the Consolidated Fund such sum as may

be agreed between the Treasury and the Post Office to be equal to that which, but for this Act, would have been paid under that subsection to the Postmaster General for doing that work.

11.—(1) If, immediately before the appointed day, there are in the hands of the Postmaster General any sums of money paid to him on contracts entered into under Part II of the Government Annuities Act 1929 c. 29. 1929 or received by him from the National Debt Commissioners for the payment of moneys becoming due under contracts so entered into, the Post Office shall, on that day, assume a liability to pay equivalent sums to the National Debt Commissioners.

(2) If, immediately before the appointed day, any sums of money are owed by the National Debt Commissioners to the Postmaster General for the purpose of reimbursing him sums paid by him in satisfaction of payments due under contracts entered into under the said Part II, those Commissioners shall, on that day, assume a liability to pay to the Post Office sums equivalent to those owed; and the Treasury shall, for the purpose of enabling those Commissioners to make payments in or towards discharge of this liability, in so far as it is referable to contracts for the grant of immediate savings bank annuities, provide them with the necessary sums out of the National Loans Fund with recourse to the Consolidated Fund, and shall, for the purpose of enabling them to make payments in discharge of this liability, in so far as it is not so referable, provide them with the necessary sums out of the Consolidated Fund.

(3) As soon as practicable after the appointed day, the National Debt Commissioners shall pay to the Post Office, out of moneys provided by Parliament, a sum equal to the difference between the aggregate of the sums paid by them in pursuance of subsection (7) of section 19 of the Post Office Act 1961 (payment of the Postmaster 1961 c. 15. General for work done by him in the execution of Part II of the Government Annuities Act 1929) and the amount agreed between the Treasury and the Post Office to be the aggregate of the sums that, had this Act not passed, would have been paid by the Commissioners in pursuance of that subsection to the Postmaster General in respect of the period beginning with the day on which the first-mentioned Act came into operation and ending with the day immediately preceding the appointed day.

12. Where, in respect of use before the appointed day of an invention by virtue of section 46 of the Patents Act 1949, a payment has fallen 1949 c. 87. to be, but has not been, made by the Postmaster General, or would, if this Act had not passed, have fallen to be made by him, that payment shall be made instead by the Post Office; and if the amount of the payment has not been agreed or determined as mentioned in subsection (3) of the said section 46 before that day, it shall, in default of agreement between the Post Office and the person to whom the payment is due, be determined in like manner as it would have been determined had this Act not passed.

13. Where, in respect of use before the appointed day of a registered design by virtue of paragraph 1 of Schedule 1 to the Registered Designs 1949 c. 88. Act 1949, a payment has fallen to be, but has not been, made by the

SCH. 7

Postmaster General or would, if this Act had not passed, have fallen to be made by him, that payment shall be made instead by the Post Office; and, if the amount of the payment has not been agreed or determined as mentioned in sub-paragraph (3) of the said paragraph 1 before that day, it shall, in default of agreement between the Post Office and the person to whom the payment is due, be determined in like manner as it would have been determined had this Act not passed.

1953 c. 36.

14. If, immediately before the appointed day, any sums of money are, by virtue of section 77(4) of the Post Office Act 1953 (payment of tolls in Scotland and Northern Ireland), due to be paid by the Postmaster General, the Post Office shall, as soon as practicable after that day, pay such sums to the persons to whom they are due.

1965 c. 62.

15.—(1) Where, under any such arrangements as are mentioned in section 41(3) of the Redundancy Payments Act 1965 (arrangements for securing payments by way of compensation for loss of employment in certain circumstances where no redundancy payment is payable) a payment—

(a) has fallen to be, but has not been, made by the Postmaster General in respect of the termination before the appointed day of the employment of a person in the civil service in the department of the Postmaster General (whether or not in an established capacity) or in any other capacity remunerated out of the Post Office Fund; or

(b) would, if this Act had not passed, have fallen to be made by the Postmaster General in respect of the termination, before the appointed day, of such employment as aforesaid of a person;

that payment shall be made instead by the Post Office.

(2) If, immediately before the appointed day, any sums of money are owed by the Secretary of State to the Post Office Fund under section 41(2) of the Redundancy Payments Act 1965 (which provides for the making of a payment by the Secretary of State out of the Redundancy Fund to certain authorities or funds in a case where he

1965 c. 74.

is satisfied that, in accordance with any provision of the Superannuation Act 1965 or with such arrangements as are referred to in the foregoing sub-paragraph, a payment has been or will be made in respect of the termination of employment of a person) in respect of sums paid by the Postmaster General in respect of the termination of the employment of persons remunerated out of the Post Office Fund, the Secretary of State shall, on that day or as soon as practicable thereafter, pay to the Post Office sums equivalent to those owed.

(3) In the case of a payment falling to be made by the Post Office—

(a) by virtue of sub-paragraph (1) above; or

(b) by virtue of section 44 of this Act, in respect of the termination before the appointed day of such employment of a person as is mentioned in sub-paragraph (1)(a) above,

the said section 41(2) shall have effect in relation thereto with the substitution, for the reference to the appropriate fund or authority, of a reference to the Post Office.

16.—(1) If, immediately before the appointed day, any sums of money are owed by the Ministry of Health and Social Services for Northern Ireland to the Post Office Fund under section 48(2) of the Contracts of Employment and Redundancy Payments Act (Northern Ireland) 1965 (which provides for the making of a payment by that Ministry out of the Northern Ireland Redundancy Fund to certain authorities or funds in a case where it is satisfied that, in accordance with such arrangements as are referred to in sub-paragraph (1) of the last foregoing paragraph, a payment has been or will be made in respect of the termination of employment of a person) in respect of sums paid by the Postmaster General in respect of the termination of the employment of persons remunerated out of the Post Office Fund, that Ministry shall, on that day or as soon as practicable thereafter, pay to the Post Office sums equivalent to those owed.

SCH. 7

1965 c. 19 (N.I.).

(2) In the case of a payment by the Post Office—

> (*a*) by virtue of sub-paragraph (1) of the last foregoing paragraph; or

> (*b*) by virtue of section 44 of this Act, in respect of the termination before the appointed day of such employment of a person as is mentioned in that sub-paragraph;

the said section 48(2) shall have effect in relation thereto with the substitution, for the reference to the appropriate fund or authority, of a reference to the Post Office.

17.—(1) Any payment which, if this Act had not passed, would have fallen to be made under section 3(2) of the Selective Employment Payments Act 1966 or section 4(2) of the Selective Employment Payments Act (Northern Ireland) 1966 to the Postmaster General on or after the appointed day in respect of a contribution week for which he paid selective employment tax before that day shall be made instead to the Post Office.

1966 c. 32.

1966 c. 32 (N.I.).

(2) The difference (if any) on the appointed day between the aggregate of any expenses incurred by the Postmaster General as a designated minister within the meaning of section 3 of the Selective Employment Payments Act 1966 and the aggregate of the amounts paid, by virtue of section 11(2) of that Act, into the Post Office Fund out of moneys provided by Parliament shall, as soon as practicable after that day, be paid to the Post Office out of moneys so provided.

18.—(1) The Secretary of State shall, out of the moneys received by him on account of national health service contributions, set aside sums equal in the aggregate to so much of the payment falling to be made under paragraph 3(2) of this Schedule as is determined by the Treasury to be attributable to work done by the Postmaster General in the execution of section 2 of the National Health Service Contributions Act 1965, and, accordingly, section 3(3) of that Act shall have effect as if the reference therein to subsection (1) of that section included a reference to this sub-paragraph.

1965 c. 54.

(2) The Secretary of State shall, out of the moneys received by him on account of redundancy fund contributions, retain sums equal in the aggregate to so much of the payment falling to be made

under paragraph 3(2) of this Schedule as is determined by the Treasury to be attributable to work done by the Postmaster General in the execution of section 28 of the Redundancy Payments Act 1965, and, accordingly, section 29(5) of that Act shall have effect as if the reference therein to subsection (1) of that section included a reference to this sub-paragraph.

(3) Sums retained in pursuance of either of the foregoing sub-paragraphs by the Secretary of State shall be paid into the Consolidated Fund.

Section 137.

SCHEDULE 8

OBSOLETE, &C., ENACTMENTS CEASING TO HAVE EFFECT

PART I

ENACTMENTS CEASING TO HAVE EFFECT ON THE PASSING OF THIS ACT

Enactment of the Parliament of England

Chapter	Short Title	Extent to which Enactment is to cease to have Effect
1 Anne c. 1.	The Crown Lands Act 1702.	In section 7, the words " in the said general letter office or post office and " and the words " the said general letter office or post office and " (where last occurring).

Enactments of the Parliament of the United Kingdom

Chapter	Title or Short Title	Extent to which Enactment is to cease to have Effect
52 Geo. 3. c. 146.	The Parochial Registers Act 1812.	In section 11, the words from " and all such letters " onwards.
1 Will. 4. c. 27.	An Act for enabling His Majesty's Postmaster General to sell the Premises lately used as the Post Office in Lombard Street, Abchurch Lane, and Sherborne Lane, in the City of London.	The whole Act.
5 & 6 Will. 4. c. 62.	The Statutory Declarations Act 1835.	In section 2, the words " the post office ". In section 5, the words " or post office ".

Chapter	Title or Short Title	Extent to which Enactment is to cease to have Effect
7 Will. 4. & 1 Vict. c. 83.	The Parliamentary Documents Deposit Act 1837.	In the preamble, the words from " and the postmaster " to " Ireland " and the word " postmasters ". In section 1, the word " postmasters ". In section 2, the words " and postmasters " and the words " or postmaster ". In section 3, the word " postmaster " (in both places where it occurs).
2 & 3 Vict. c. 47.	The Metropolitan Police Act 1839.	In section 54, in paragraph 14, the words from " except " to " duty ".
2 & 3 Vict. c. lxxi.	An Act for incorporating certain Persons for the making and maintaining a Railway from the Township of Crook and Billy Row to the Byers Green Branch of the Clarence Railway in the Parish of Saint Andrew Auckland, all in the County of Durham, to be called " The West Durham Railway ".	Section 157.
5 & 6 Vict. c. xci.	An Act for constructing a Low Water Pier and necessary Works at Burntisland in the County of Fife, and establishing a Ferry between the same and Granton in the County of Edinburgh; and for improving the Communication between the said Pier and Kinghorn.	Sections 28 to 37. In section 38, the words " but without prejudice to the authority hereinbefore vested in the Postmaster General ".
7 & 8 Vict. c. 33.	The County Rates Act 1844.	In section 6, the words from " according " to " behalf ".
7 & 8 Vict. c. 85.	The Railway Regulation Act 1844.	Section 14.
11 & 12 Vict. c. lx.	The Chester and Holyhead Railway Act 1848.	Sections 19 and 20.

Chapter	Title or Short Title	Extent to which Enactment is to cease to have Effect
26 & 27 Vict. c. 112.	The Telegraph Act 1863.	Section 2. In section 3, the definition of " the company ". Section 11. In section 14, the words " In the following cases ", the figures (1) and (2), the words " If the company is dissolved, or ceases for six months to carry on business ", the words " (in the former case) ", the words " or (in the latter case) by any of the company's works ", the words " or leave a notice at the last known office or place of business of the company ", the words " in every such case " and the words from " The present section " onwards. Section 31. Section 44. Section 46. Sections 52 and 53.
29 & 30 Vict. c. 3.	The Telegraph Amendment Act 1866.	The whole Act.
31 & 32 Vict. c. 110.	The Telegraph Act 1868.	In section 3, the definition of " any company ". In section 9, paragraphs (1) and (2); in paragraph (6), the words " pay the railway company the following sums by way of compensation ", sub-paragraphs (*a*) to (*f*), in sub-paragraph (*g*) the words " the Postmaster General shall " and in sub-paragraph (*h*) the words from the beginning to " provided " and paragraphs (9), (10) and (11). Section 19. In section 20, the words from " and the Postmaster General " onwards. Section 21. Section 23.
32 & 33 Vict. c. 73.	The Telegraph Act 1869.	In section 3, the definition of " telegraph company ". Section 7. Sections 9 to 11. Sections 23 and 24.
41 & 42 Vict. c. 76.	The Telegraph Act 1878.	In section 13, the words from " except that " to " this Act ".

Chapter	Title or Short Title	Extent to which Enactment is to cease to have Effect
42 & 43 Vict. c. 11.	The Bankers' Books Evidence Act 1879.	In section 9, the words from " the fact ", where last occurring, to " the Post Office ".
43 & 44 Vict. c. xciv.	The South-western (of London) District Post Office Act 1880.	The whole Act.
52 & 53 Vict. c. 34.	The Telegraph (Isle of Man) Act 1889.	In section 1, paragraphs (3), (5) and (10).
55 & 56 Vict. c. 59.	The Telegraph Act 1892.	Section 4(2). In section 12, the words from " The Governor " onwards.
56 & 57 Vict. c. 69.	The Savings Bank Act 1893.	The whole Act.
58 & 59 Vict. c. xxvii.	The Edinburgh and District Waterworks (Additional Supply) Act 1895.	Section 41.
58 & 59 Vict. c. xxxvii.	The Whitby Water Act 1895.	Section 11.
58 & 59 Vict. c. clvi.	The Merthyr Tydfil District Council Waterworks Act 1895.	Section 9.
59 & 60 Vict. c. xxxii.	The Birmingham Corporation Water Act 1896.	Section 24.
59 & 60 Vict. c. ccxlv.	The Barry Urban District Council Act 1896.	In section 21, the words from " The District Council may undertake " onwards.
61 & 62 Vict. c. cxxiii.	The Crawley and District Water Act 1898.	Section 25.
61 & 62 Vict. c. clxxxv.	The Clacton Gas and Water Act 1898.	Section 91.
61 & 62 Vict. c. ccxxv.	The Carlisle Corporation (Water) Act 1898.	Section 48, from " The Corporation may " onwards.
62 & 63 Vict. c. clxxi.	The Woking Water and Gas Act 1899.	Section 20.
1 Edw. 7. c. lvii.	The Aspatria Silloth and District Water Act 1901.	Section 42.
1 Edw. 7. c. ccvii.	The South Essex Waterworks Act 1901.	Section 7

Chapter	Title or Short Title	Extent to which Enactment is to cease to have Effect
1 Edw. 7. c. ccxlii.	The Cromer Water Act 1901.	Section 65.
2 Edw. 7. c. cxxx.	The Bristol Waterworks Act 1902.	Section 21.
2 Edw. 7. c. clxxiv.	The Weardale Water Act 1902.	Section 7.
3 Edw. 7. c. xviii.	The Sutton District Waterworks Act 1903.	Section 6.
4 Edw. 7. c. cciii.	The Thames River Steamboat Service Act 1904.	Section 36.
5 Edw. 7. c. clxii.	The Skegness Water Act 1905.	Section 39.
6 Edw. 7. c. cxlviii.	The Borough of Portsmouth Water-works Act 1906.	Section 10.
7 Edw. 7. c. lxxvii.	The Rawtenstall Cor-poration Act 1907.	Section 34.
7 Edw. 7. c. lxxxiv.	The Great Yarmouth Waterworks and Lowestoft Water and Gas Act 1907.	Section 56.
7 Edw. 7. c. lxxxvi.	The King's Norton and Northfield Urban District Council Act 1907.	Section 23.
7 Edw. 7. c. cii.	The Manchester Cor-poration Tramways Act 1907.	Section 27.
7 Edw. 7. c. cxvii.	The Tramways Orders Confirmation Act 1907.	In the Audenshaw Urban District Council Tramway Order 1907 contained in the Schedule, section 5; in the Huddersfield Corporation Tramway Order 1907 so contained, section 7; in the Leeds Corporation Tram-ways Order 1907 so contained, section 7; in the Taunton Tramways (Extension) Order 1907 so contained, section 11; and in the West Ham Corpora-tion Tramways Order so con-tained, section 10.

Chapter	Title or Short Title	Extent to which Enactment is to cease to have Effect
7 Edw. 7. c. cxxxi.	The Birkenhead Corporation Water Act 1907.	Section 23.
7 Edw. 7. c. cxliv.	The London County Council (Tramways and Improvements) Act 1907.	Section 17.
7 Edw. 7. c. cxlix.	The Dumbarton Borough and County Tramways Order Confirmation Act 1907.	In the Order contained in the Schedule, section 11.
7 Edw. 7. c. clxxiv.	The Metropolitan Water Board (Various Powers) Act 1907.	Section 60.
8 Edw. 7. c. 33.	The Telegraph (Construction) Act 1908.	Section 7.
8 Edw. 7. c. xxii.	The Skegness Urban District Council Act 1908.	In the Schedule, the words " 38. Agreements with the Postmaster General ".
8 Edw. 7. c. lviii.	The Doncaster Corporation Act 1908.	Section 17.
8 Edw. 7. c. lxxv.	The Wolverhampton Corporation Act 1908.	Section 5.
8 Edw. 7. c. xci.	The Metropolitan Electric Tramways Act 1908.	Section 29.
8 Edw. 7. c. xcix.	The Holderness Water Act 1908.	Section 84(2).
8 Edw. 7. c. c.	The London United Tramways Act 1908.	Section 8.
8 Edw. 7. c. cxx.	The Paisley District Tramways Order Confirmation Act 1908.	In the order contained in the Schedule, section 39.
8 Edw. 7. c. cxxxii.	The Tramways Order Confirmation (No. 2) Act 1908.	In the Liverpool Corporation Tramways Extensions Order 1908 contained in the Schedule, section 7; and in the Potteries and North Staffordshire Tramways (Amendment) Order so contained, section 9.

Chapter	Title or Short Title	Extent to which Enactment is to cease to have Effect
9 Edw. 7. c. 20.	The Telegraph (Arbitration) Act 1909.	In section 1, the words " have before the passing of this Act agreed, or hereafter ".
9 Edw. 7. c. xxxiv.	The Preston Chorley and Horwich Tramways Act 1909.	Section 8.
9 Edw. 7. c. xli.	The Wallasey Tramways and Improvements Act 1909.	Section 10.
9 Edw. 7. c. lxx.	The Gateshead and District Tramways Act 1909.	Section 36.
9 Edw. 7. c. lxxxix.	The Oldham Corporation Act 1909.	Section 40.
9 Edw. 7. c. cxliii.	The Tramways Order Confirmation Act 1909.	In the Bolton Corporation Tramways Order 1909 set out in the Schedule, section 8; in the Keighley Corporation Tramways Order 1909 so set out, section 9; in the Portsmouth Corporation Tramways Order so set out, section 8; and in the Whitworth Urban District Council Tramways Order 1909 so set out, section 26.
9 Edw. 7. c. clix.	The Bury Corporation Act 1909.	Section 47.
10 Edw. 7 & 1 Geo. 5. c. lix.	The Dunfermline and District Tramways (Extensions) Order Confirmation Act 1910.	In the order contained in the Schedule, section 23.
10 Edw. 7 & 1 Geo. 5. c. ci.	The Tramways Order Confirmation Act 1910.	In the Milnrow Urban District Council Tramways Order 1910 set out in the Schedule, section 27.
10 Edw. 7 & 1 Geo. 5. c. cv.	The Wemyss and District Water Order Confirmation Act 1910.	In the order contained in the Schedule, sections 44 and 45.
10 Edw. 7 & 1 Geo. 5. c. cxiii.	The Southampton Corporation Act 1910.	Section 13.

Chapter	Title or Short Title	Extent to which Enactment is to cease to have Effect
10 Edw. 7 & 1 Geo. 5. c. cxvii.	The Bradford Corporation Act 1910.	Section 23.
1 & 2 Geo. 5. c. 39.	The Telegraph (Construction) Act 1911.	Section 5.
1 & 2 Geo. 5. c. lv.	The South Lancashire Tramways Act 1911.	Section 16.
1 & 2 Geo. 5. c. lxiv.	The Northampton Corporation Act 1911.	Section 30, and in section 58, the words " Use of tramway posts by Postmaster General ".
1 & 2 Geo. 5. c. lxxxvi.	The Kingston upon Hull Corporation Act 1911.	Section 9.
1 & 2 Geo. 5. c. cix.	The Aberdare Urban District Council Act 1911.	Section 54.
1 & 2 Geo. 5. c. cx.	The Brighton Hove and District Railless Traction Act 1911.	Section 17.
1 & 2 Geo. 5. c. cxiii.	The Halifax Corporation Act 1911.	Section 24.
1 & 2 Geo. 5. c. cxvi.	The Rotherham Corporation Act 1911.	Section 16, and, in section 34, the words " Use of tramway posts by Postmaster General ".
1 & 2 Geo. 5. c. cxviii.	The Metropolitan Water Board (New Works) Act 1911.	Section 26.
1 & 2 Geo. 5. c. clxxi.	The Tramways Order Confirmation Act 1911.	In the Dartford and District Tramways Order 1911 set out in the Schedule, section 31; and in the Dewsbury Corporation Tramways Order 1911 so set out, section 8.
2 & 3 Geo. 5. c. xvii.	The Ramsbottom Urban District Railless Traction Act 1912.	Section 26.
2 & 3 Geo. 5. c. xxxii.	The Stockport Corporation Act 1912.	Section 19.
2 & 3 Geo. 5. c. lv.	The North Ormesby South Bank Normanby and Grangetown Railless Traction Act 1912.	Section 38.

Chapter	Title or Short Title	Extent to which Enactment is to cease to have Effect
2 & 3 Geo. 5. c. lvii.	The Brighton Corporation Act 1912.	Section 19.
2 & 3 Geo. 5. c. lx.	The Hove Corporation Act 1912.	Section 24.
2 & 3 Geo. 5. c. lxxxii.	The Birmingham Corporation Act 1912.	Section 11.
2 & 3 Geo. 5. c. cvii.	The Keighley Corporation Act 1912.	Section 66(1).
2 & 3 Geo. 5. c. cxliv.	The Tramways Order Confirmation Act 1912.	In the Bingley Urban District Council Tramways Order 1912 set out in the Schedule, section 29; in the West Hartlepool Corporation Tramways Order so set out, section 25.
2 & 3 Geo. 5. c. clxvii.	The Sheffield Corporation Act 1912.	In section 38, the words " Section 11 (As to use of posts standards &c. by Postmaster General)".
3 & 4 Geo. 5. c. xxxv.	The Chesterfield Corporation Railless Traction Act 1913.	Section 31.
3 & 4 Geo. 5. c. lxi.	The Rhondda Tramways (Railless Traction) Act 1913.	Section 25.
3 & 4 Geo. 5. c. lxvii.	The Mexborough and Swinton Tramways (Railless Traction) Act 1913.	Section 22.
3 & 4 Geo. 5. c. lxix.	The West Bromwich Corporation Act 1913.	Section 15.
3 & 4 Geo. 5. c. xcii.	The Derby Corporation Act 1913.	Section 10.
3 & 4 Geo. 5. c. xciii.	The Southport Corporation Act 1913.	Section 33.
3 & 4 Geo. 5. c. xcv.	The Huddersfield Corporation Act 1913.	In section 33, the words from " Of the Order " to " Postmaster General ".
3 & 4 Geo. 5. c. ciii.	The Metropolitan Electric Tramways (Railless Traction) Act 1913.	In section 7, the words " Section 29. (Use of tramway posts by Postmaster General) ".

Chapter	Title or Short Title	Extent to which Enactment is to cease to have Effect
3 & 4 Geo. 5. c. cxii.	The Morley Corporation Act 1913.	Section 65.
3 & 4 Geo. 5. c. cxv.	The Western Valleys (Monmouthshire) Railless Electric Traction Act 1913.	Section 35.
3 & 4 Geo. 5. c. cxxiii.	The Tramways Order Confirmation Act 1913.	In the Baildon Urban District Council Tramway Order 1913 set out in the Schedule, section 28; and in the Newcastle-upon-Tyne Corporation Tramways Order 1913 so set out, in section 7, the words " Section 22. Use of tramway posts by Postmaster General ".
4 & 5 Geo. 5. c. lxv.	The Tramways Order Confirmation Act 1914.	In the order set out in the Schedule, in section 6, the words " Section 16. (Use of tramway posts by Postmaster General) ".
4 & 5 Geo. 5. c. lxvii.	The Western Valleys (Monmouthshire) Railless Electric Traction (Extension) Order Confirmation Act 1914.	In the order set out in the Schedule, in section 6, the words " Section 35. Use of trolley vehicle posts by Postmaster General ".
4 & 5 Geo. 5. c. lxxii.	The Preston Corporation Act 1914.	Section 22.
4 & 5 Geo. 5. c. lxxxviii.	The Newport Corporation Act 1914.	Section 34.
4 & 5 Geo. 5. c. ci.	The Reading Corporation Act 1914.	Section 19.
4 & 5 Geo. 5. c. cxlvii.	The West Gloucestershire Water Act 1914.	Section 53.
4 & 5 Geo. 5. c. clx.	The Walsall Corporation Act 1914.	Section 39.
4 & 5 Geo. 5. c. clxxxviii.	The York Corporation Act 1914.	Section 33.
5 & 6 Geo. 5. c. lvii.	The Aberdare Urban District Council Act 1915.	In section 30, the words " Section 54 (Use of tramway posts by Postmaster General) ".

Chapter	Title or Short Title	Extent to which Enactment is to cease to have Effect
5 & 6 Geo. 5. c. lxi.	The Stalybridge Hyde Mossley and Dukinfield Tramways and Electricity Board Act 1915.	Section 18.
5 & 6 Geo. 5. c. lxiii.	The South Shields Corporation Act 1915.	Section 10.
5 & 6 Geo. 5. c. lxxiii.	The Metropolitan Water Board Act 1915.	Section 23.
5 & 6 Geo. 5. c. lxxvii.	The Lincoln Corporation Act 1915.	Section 42.
7 & 8 Geo. 5. c. xx.	The Bristol Waterworks Act 1917.	Section 40(3).
7 & 8 Geo. 5. c. lii.	The Blackpool Improvement Act 1917.	Section 60.
8 & 9 Geo. 5. c. xxi.	The Londonderry Corporation Act 1918.	Section 104.
8 & 9 Geo. 5. c. lxi.	The Sheffield Corporation (Consolidation) Act 1919.	Sections 137 and 157. In section 174, the words " Use of tramway posts by Postmaster General ".
9 & 10 Geo. 5. c. xl.	The Stockton-on-Tees Corporation Act 1919.	Section 18.
9 & 10 Geo. 5. c. 1.	The Birmingham Corporation Tramways Act 1919.	In section 13(3), the words from " and under " to " 1912 ".
9 & 10 Geo. 5. c. lvi.	The Tynemouth Corporation Act 1919.	Section 27.
9 & 10 Geo. 5. c. lviii.	The Middlesborough Corporation Act 1919.	Section 22.
9 & 10 Geo. 5. c. xc.	The Tramways Order Confirmation Act 1919.	In the Thornaby on Tees Corporation Tramways Order 1919 set out in the Schedule, section 25.
10 & 11 Geo. 5. c. liv.	The St. Annes-on-the-Sea Urban District Council Act 1920.	Section 16.
10 & 11 Geo. 5. c. lxvii.	The Pontypridd Urban District Council Act 1920.	Section 11.
10 & 11 Geo. 5. c. lxviii.	The Portsmouth Corporation Act 1920.	In section 54, the words " Section 8 (Use of tramway posts by Postmaster General) ".

Chapter	Title or Short Title	Extent to which Enactment is to cease to have Effect
10 & 11 Geo. 5. c. lxxvi.	The Halifax Corporation Act 1920.	In section 7, the words from " Section 24 " (where last occurring) to " Postmaster General ".
10 & 11 Geo. 5. c. lxxxiii.	The Blackpool Improvement Act 1920.	Section 38(3). Section 41(8)(*i*).
10 & 11 Geo. 5. c. lxxxviii.	The Coventry Corporation Act 1920.	Section 26.
10 & 11 Geo. 5. c. xcii.	The Sheffield Corporation Act 1920.	In section 14(3), the words from " and under " to " 1918 ".
10 & 11 Geo. 5. c. xcvii.	The Manchester Corporation Act 1920.	In section 41, the last entry relating to the Manchester Corporation Tramways Act 1907.
10 & 11 Geo. 5. c. cxix.	The Tramways Orders Confirmation Act 1920.	In the Warrington Corporation Tramways (Extension) Order 1920 set out in the Schedule, section 8.
10 & 11 Geo. 5. c. cxlii.	The Cardiff Corporation Act 1920.	Section 57.
10 & 11 Geo. 5. c. cxlv.	The Huddersfield Corporation (General Powers) Act 1920.	In section 9(1), the entry relating to the Huddersfield Corporation Tramway Order 1907.
10 & 11 Geo. 5. c. cxlviii.	The Salford Corporation Act 1920.	Section 13.
10 & 11 Geo. 5. c. clii.	The Bristol Corporation Act 1920.	Section 47.
11 & 12 Geo. 5. c. xxiv.	The Sutton District Waterworks Act 1921.	Section 18.
11 & 12 Geo. 5. c. lxxiv.	The Liverpool Corporation Act 1921.	Section 141.
11 & 12 Geo. 5. c. lxxvi.	The Grimsby Corporation Act 1921.	Section 45.
11 & 12 Geo. 5. c. lxxxiv.	The South Essex Waterworks Act 1921.	Section 48.
11 & 12 Geo. 5. c. lxxxv.	The Hastings Tramways Act 1921.	Section 10.
11 & 12 Geo. 5. c. xciii.	The Wigan Corporation Act 1921.	Section 42.

SCH. 8

Chapter	Title or Short Title	Extent to which Enactment is to cease to have Effect
11 & 12 Geo. 5. c. cxv.	The Metropolitan Water Board (Various Powers) Act 1921.	Section 38.
12 & 13 Geo. 5. c. xxxiii.	The Colne Valley Water Act 1922.	Section 18.
12 & 13 Geo. 5. c. lii.	The Tramways Order Confirmation Act 1922.	In the order set out in the Schedule, section 12.
12 & 13 Geo. 5. c. lxxvi.	The Birmingham Corporation Act 1922.	In section 24, the words " Section 11 (Use of tramway posts by Postmaster General) ".
12 & 13 Geo. 5. c. lxxxii.	The South Staffordshire Waterworks Act 1922.	Section 12.
12 & 13 Geo. 5. c. xciii.	The Bolton Corporation Act 1922.	Section 42.
13 Geo. 5. Sess. 2. c. 2.	The Irish Free State (Consequential Provisions) Act 1922.	Section 7(3).
13 & 14 Geo. 5. c. ixii.	The Tramways Provisional Orders Act 1923.	In the Leicester Corporation Tramways Order set out in the Schedule, in section 10, the words " Section 15 " (where last occurring) and the words " Use of tramway posts by Postmaster General ".
13 & 14 Geo. 5. c. lxxi.	The Birkenhead Corporation Act 1923.	Sections 44 and 46.
13 & 14 Geo. 5. c. lxxxvi.	The Lytham St. Anne's Corporation Act 1923.	Section 23(a). Section 24.
13 & 14 Geo. 5. c. xcix.	The Chesterfield Corporation Act 1923.	Sections 100 and 102. In section 123, the words "Alteration of telegraph lines of Postmaster General " and the words " Use of tramway posts by Postmaster General ". Section 137(1).
14 & 15 Geo. 5. c. lvi.	The Kingston upon Hull Corporation Act 1924.	Section 13(3).

Chapter	Title or Short Title	Extent to which Enactment is to cease to have Effect
14 & 15 Geo. 5. c. lxv.	The Birmingham Corporation Act 1924.	In section 16(4), the words " and under section 11 (Use of tramway posts by Postmaster General) of the Act of 1912 " and the words " and section respectively ".
14 & 15 Geo. 5. c. lxxxiv.	The St. Helens Corporation (Trolley Vehicles) Order Confirmation Act 1924.	In the Order set out in the Schedule, section 13.
14 & 15 Geo. 5. c. xcv.	The Manchester Corporation Act 1924.	In section 55(1), the words " Section 27 " (where last occurring) and the words " Use of tramway posts by Postmaster General ".
14 & 15 Geo. 5. c. xcviii.	The Croydon Corporation Act 1924.	Section 30.
15 & 16 Geo. 5. c. xlvii.	The Bolton Corporation Act 1925.	In section 39, the words " Section 42 (Use of tramway posts, &c., by Postmaster General) ".
15 & 16 Geo. 5. c. xcvii.	The Oldham Corporation Act 1925.	Sections 52 and 54.
15 & 16 Geo. 5. c. cii.	The Blackpool Improvement Act 1925.	In section 18(2), the words " Section 60 (Use of tramway posts by Postmaster General)".
15 & 16 Geo. 5. c. ciii.	The Ipswich Corporation Act 1925.	Section 7(1). Section 8.
15 & 16 Geo. 5. c. cvii.	The Barrow-in-Furness Corporation Act 1925.	Section 14.
15 & 16 Geo. 5. c. cxvi.	The Darlington Corporation (Transport, &c.) Act 1925.	Section 5.
15 & 16 Geo. 5. c. cxxi.	The Bradford Corporation Act 1925.	In section 33(4), the words " and under section 23 (Use of tramway posts by Postmaster General) of the Act of 1910 " and the words " and section respectively ".
15 & 16 Geo. 5. c. cxxii.	The Walsall Corporation Act 1925.	In section 9, the words " Section 39 (Use of tramway or trolley vehicle posts by Postmaster General) ".
15 & 16 Geo. 5. c. cxxiii.	The Wolverhampton Corporation Act 1925.	In section 18(1), the words from " The Act of 1908 " to " Postmaster General ".

Chapter	Title or Short Title	Extent to which Enactment is to cease to have Effect
16 & 17 Geo. 5. c. ii.	The Dunfermline and District Tramways (Extensions) Order Confirmation Act 1926.	In the order contained in the Schedule, in section 12, the last entry relating to the Order of 1910.
16 & 17 Geo. 5. c. xi.	The Darwen Corporation Act 1926.	Section 14(*a*). Section 15. In section 20, the words " and Use of tramway posts by Postmaster General ".
16 & 17 Geo. 5. c. xxvii.	The Doncaster Corporation Act 1926.	In section 26, the first entry relating to the Doncaster Corporation Act 1908.
16 & 17 Geo. 5. c. xxx.	The Hartlepool Corporation (Trolley Vehicles) Act 1926.	Section 8(*a*). Section 9.
16 & 17 Geo. 5. c. lxiii.	The Tramways Provisional Order Act 1926.	In the order set out in the Schedule, in section 10, the last entry relating to the Act of 1913.
16 & 17 Geo. 5. c. lxxiii.	The Kidderminster and Stourport Electric Tramway Act 1926.	Section 13(*a*). Section 14.
16 & 17 Geo. 5. c. lxxvi.	The Mexborough and Swinton Tramways Act 1926.	In section 9, the words " Section 22 (Use of posts and standards by Postmaster General) ".
16 & 17 Geo. 5. c. xcvii.	The Worcester Corporation Act 1926.	Section 10(1). Section 11.
17 & 18 Geo. 5. c. xvii.	The Matlocks Urban District Council Act 1927.	Section 27(*a*). Section 28. Section 52.
17 & 18 Geo. 5. c. xliii.	The Sheffield Corporation Tramways Order Confirmation Act 1927.	In the order set out in the Schedule, in section 6(3), the words from " and under " to " 1918 " and the words " and section respectively ".
17 & 18 Geo. 5. c. xliv.	The Cardiff Corporation Tramways Order Confirmation Act 1927.	In the order set out in the Schedule, in section 9, the words from " and under " to " 1920 " and the words " and section respectively " and in section 11, the first entry relating to the Act of 1920.
17 & 18 Geo. 5. c. lvii.	The St. Helens Corporation (Trolley Vehicles) Order Confirmation Act 1927.	In the order set out in the Schedule, in section 8(1), the words " Section 13 (Use of posts &c. by Postmaster General) ".

Chapter	Title or Short Title	Extent to which Enactment is to cease to have Effect
17 & 18 Geo. 5. c. lxix.	The Hastings Tramways Company (Trolley Vehicles) Act 1927.	In section 20, the second entry relating to the Act of 1921.
17 & 18 Geo. 5. c. lxxvii.	The Grimsby Corporation Act 1927.	In section 88, the words " Section 45 (Use of tramway posts by Postmaster General) ".
17 & 18 Geo. 5. c. lxxxiv.	The Colchester Corporation Act 1927.	Section 6.
17 & 18 Geo. 5. c. lxxxvi.	The West Bromwich Corporation Act 1927.	In section 82, the words " Section 15 (Use of tramway or trolley vehicle posts by Postmaster General) ".
17 & 18 Geo. 5. c. xc.	The Coventry Corporation Act 1927.	In section 19, the third entry relating to the Act of 1920.
17 & 18 Geo. 5. c. cxxii.	The Wallasey Corporation Act 1927.	In section 18, in subsection (1), the words " the Act of 1909 " (in both places where they occur) and the words " Use of tramway posts by Postmaster General " and, in subsection (2), the words " the Act of 1909 ".
18 & 19 Geo. 5. c. xlviii.	The Exeter Corporation Act 1928.	In section 25(2), the words " Section 21 (Alteration of telegraphic lines of Postmaster General) ". Section 27.
18 & 19 Geo. 5. c. lxxix.	The South Essex Waterworks Act 1928.	Section 48.
18 & 19 Geo. 5. c. cxi.	The Rotherham Corporation Act 1928.	Section 38(*a*). Section 39. In section 65(1), the words " Use of tramway posts by Postmaster General ".
19 & 20 Geo. 5. c. xxvii.	The Southend-on-Sea Corporation (Trolley Vehicles) Order Confirmation Act 1929.	In the order set out in the Schedule, in section 6(1), the words " the Order of 1909 " (in both places where they occur) and the words " Section 10 (As to use of posts by Postmaster General) ".
19 & 20 Geo. 5. c. xlvii.	The Royal Victoria and other Docks Approaches (Improvement) Act 1929.	In section 25, the last entry relating to the London County Council (Tramways and Improvements) Act 1907. In section 26, the second entry relating to the West Ham Corporation Tramways Order 1907.

Chapter	Title or Short Title	Extent to which Enactment is to cease to have Effect
19 & 20 Geo. 5. c. lxxvi.	The Mansfield District Traction Act 1929.	In section 24(1), the first entry relating to the Order of 1920.
19 & 20 Geo. 5. c. lxxxi.	The Manchester Corporation Act 1929.	In section 12(1), the last entry relating to the Manchester Corporation Tramways Act 1907.
19 & 20 Geo. 5. c. lxxxiii.	The South Lancashire Transport Act 1929.	In section 26, the words " The Act of 1911—Section 16 (Use of tramway posts by Postmaster General) ".
19 & 20 Geo. 5. c. xciv.	The Pontypridd Urban District Council Act 1929.	In section 13(1), the first entry relating to the Act of 1920.
20 & 21 Geo. 5. c. xxxviii.	The Birmingham Corporation (General Powers) Act 1929.	Section 16(3).
20 & 21 Geo. 5. c. lii.	The Portsmouth Corporation Act 1930.	In section 28, the second entry relating to the Portsmouth Corporation Tramways Order 1909.
20 & 21 Geo. 5. c. lvii.	The Chester Waterworks Act 1930.	Section 8.
20 & 21 Geo. 5. c. lxvi.	The Derby Corporation Act 1930.	In section 32(1), the second entry relating to the Derby Corporation Act 1913.
20 & 21 Geo. 5. c. lxxviii.	The Newport Corporation (No. 1) Act 1930.	In section 54, the second entry relating to the Newport Corporation Act 1914.
20 & 21 Geo. 5. c. lxxxii.	The Birkenhead Corporation Act 1930.	In section 28, the third entry relating to the Birkenhead Corporation Act 1923.
20 & 21 Geo. 5. c. cxii.	The Liverpool Corporation (General Powers) Act 1930.	In section 12, the eighth entry relating to the Liverpool Corporation Act 1921.
20 & 21 Geo. 5. c. cxix.	The Leeds Corporation Act 1930.	In section 21, the words " and in section 7 (Use of tramway posts by Postmaster General) of the Leeds Corporation Tramways Order 1907 ". In section 23(5), the words " and under section 7 (Use of tramway posts by Postmaster General) of the Leeds Corporation Tramways Order 1907 " and the words " and section respectively ".

Chapter	Title or Short Title	Extent to which Enactment is to cease to have Effect
20 & 21 Geo. 5. c. cxxx.	The Llanelly District Traction Act 1930.	In section 24, the words " The Order of 1910—Section 8 (As to use of posts by Postmaster General) ".
20 & 21 Geo. 5. c. clxxxi.	The Bournemouth Corporation Act 1930.	Section 101.
20 & 21 Geo. 5. c. clxxxiii.	The Southend-on-Sea Corporation Act 1930.	In section 18(1), the words " The Order of 1909—Section 10 (As to use of posts by Postmaster General) ".
20 & 21 Geo. 5. c. clxxxvii.	The London United Tramways Act 1930.	In section 9, the words " The London United Tramways Act 1908—Section 8 (Use of tramway posts by Postmaster General) ".
21 & 22 Geo. 5. c. xiii.	The Preston Corporation Act 1931.	In section 40, the first entry relating to the Preston Corporation Act 1914.
21 & 22 Geo. 5. c. lxxxvii.	The York Corporation (Trolley Vehicles) Order Confirmation Act 1931.	In the order set out in the Schedule, in section 7(1), the words " Section 33 (As to use of posts by Postmaster General) ".
21 & 22 Geo. 5. c. cix.	The Brighton Corporation Act 1931.	Section 102.
22 & 23 Geo. 5. c. vii.	The Edinburgh Corporation Order Confirmation Act 1932.	In the order contained in the Schedule, section 33.
22 & 23 Geo. 5. c. lxix.	The Bury Corporation Act 1932.	In section 76(1), the eighth entry relating to the Bury Corporation Act 1909.
22 & 23 Geo. 5. c. xc.	The Wolverhampton Corporation Act 1932.	In section 78(1), the words " The Act of 1908—Section 5 (Use of tramway posts by Postmaster General) ".
23 & 24 Geo. 5. c. i.	The Public Works Facilities Scheme (Huddersfield Corporation) Confirmation Act 1932.	In the scheme set out in the Schedule, in section 6, the words " Huddersfield Corporation Tramway Order 1907 — Section 7 (Use of tramway posts by Postmaster General) ".
23 & 24 Geo. 5. c. lxxxiii.	The Middlesborough Corporation Act 1933.	Section 89.

Chapter	Title or Short Title	Extent to which Enactment is to cease to have Effect
23 & 24 Geo. 5. c. lxxxix.	The Salford Corporation Act 1933.	In section 43(1), the first entry relating to the Salford Corporation Act 1920.
24 & 25 Geo. 5. c. vii.	The Public Works Facilities Scheme (Huddersfield Corporation) Confirmation Act 1934.	In the scheme set out in the Schedule, in section 5, the words " Huddersfield Corporation Tramway Order 1907—Section 7 (Use of tramway posts by Postmaster General) ".
24 & 25 Geo. 5. c. xlix.	The St. Helens Corporation (Trolley Vehicles) Order Confirmation Act 1934.	In the order set out in the Schedule, in section 6(1), the seventh entry relating to the St. Helens Corporation (Trolley Vehicles) Order 1924.
24 & 25 Geo. 5. c. l.	The Southend-on-Sea Corporation (Trolley Vehicles) Order Confirmation Act 1934.	In the order set out in the Schedule, in section 6(1), the words " The Order of 1909—Section 10 (As to use of posts by Postmaster General) ".
24 & 25 Geo. 5. c. xcv.	The Cardiff Corporation Act 1934.	In section 28(1), the first entry relating to the Cardiff Corporation Act 1920.
24 & 25 Geo. 5. c. xcvi.	The London Passenger Transport Act 1934.	Section 21. In section 22, the words " and ' Conveyance of Mails ' ". Sections 78 to 80.
25 & 26 Geo. 5. c. xc.	The Reading Corporation Act 1935.	In section 11(2), the words " Section 19 (Use of tramway or trolley vehicle posts by Postmaster General) ".
25 & 26 Geo. 5. c. xcvi.	The South Shields Corporation Act 1935.	In section 15(1), the second entry relating to the South Shields Corporation Act 1915.
25 & 26 Geo. 5. c. cviii.	The Blackpool Improvement Act 1935.	In section 20(1), the words " The Blackpool Improvement Act 1917—Section 60 (Use of tramway posts by Postmaster General) ".
25 & 26 Geo. 5. c. cx.	The London Passenger Transport Act 1935.	Section 67(4). In section 76, the words " Section 80 (Use of posts &c. by Postmaster General) ".
25 & 26 Geo. 5. c. cxxiv.	The Newcastle-upon-Tyne Corporation (General Powers) Act 1935.	Section 85.

Chapter	Title or Short Title	Extent to which Enactment is to cease to have Effect
26 Geo. 5 & 1 Edw. 8. c. liii.	The Huddersfield Corporation (Trolley Vehicles) Act 1936.	In section 15, the words " Huddersfield Corporation Tramway Order 1907—Section 7 (Use of tramway posts by Postmaster General) ".
26 Geo. 5 & 1 Edw. 8. c. lv.	The Kingston upon Hull Corporation Act 1936.	In section 11(1), the words " The Kingston upon Hull Corporation Act 1911—Section 9 (Use of tramway posts by Postmaster General) ".
26 Geo. 5 & 1 Edw. 8. c. lxvi.	The Stalybridge Hyde Mossley and Dukinfield Transport and Electricity Board Act 1936.	In section 13(1), the fourth entry relating to the Stalybridge Hyde Mossley and Dukinfield Tramways and Electricity Board Act 1915.
26 Geo. 5 & 1 Edw. 8. c. cxi.	The Wolverhampton Corporation Act 1936.	In section 40(1), the words " The Act of 1908—Section 5 (Use of tramway posts by Postmaster General) ".
26 Geo. 5 & 1 Edw. 8. c. cxviii.	The Manchester Corporation Act 1936.	In section 8(1), the last entry relating to the Manchester Corporation Tramways Act 1907.
1 Edw. 8 & 1 Geo. 6. c. cii.	The Aberdeen Corporation (Water Gas Electricity and Transport) Order Confirmation Act 1937.	In the order contained in the Schedule, section 267.
1 Edw. 8 & 1 Geo. 6. c. cxxii.	The Southampton Corporation Act 1937.	In section 16(1), the last entry relating to the Southampton Corporation Act 1910.
1 & 2 Geo. 6. c. lxxxiii.	The Gateshead and District Tramways and Trolley Vehicles Act 1938.	In section 16, the last entry relating to the Gateshead and District Tramways Act 1909.
1 & 2 Geo. 6. c. lxxxix.	The Brighton Corporation (Transport) Act 1938.	In section 13(1), the words " Section 102—Use of tramway posts by Postmaster General ".
9 & 10 Geo. 6. c. xxvii.	The Newcastle-upon-Tyne Corporation Act 1946.	In section 6, the words " Section 85 (Use of posts by Postmaster General) ".
12, 13 & 14 Geo. 6. c. 11.	The Railway and Canal Commission (Abolition) Act 1949.	Section 6(2).
12, 13 & 14 Geo. 6. c. 39.	The Commonwealth Telegraphs Act 1949.	Section 4. Section 7. Schedule 2.

Chapter	Title or Short Title	Extent to which Enactment is to cease to have Effect
12, 13 & 14 Geo. 6. c. 54.	The Wireless Telegraphy Act 1949	Section 8. Section 14(5). Section 16(2), so far as relating to the power conferred by section 8. Section 18.
12, 13 & 14 Geo. 6. c. lvii.	The Fife County Council Order Confirmation Act 1949.	In the order contained in the Schedule, section 46.
14 Geo. 6. c. 28.	The Shops Act 1950.	Section 44(1)(*b*).
14 Geo. 6. c. 39.	The Public Utilities Street Works Act 1950.	In Schedule 5, the entry relating to section 31 of the Telegraph Act 1863.
15 & 16 Geo. 6 & 1 Eliz. 2. c. xl.	The Newcastle-upon-Tyne Corporation Act 1952.	In section 33, the words " Section 85 (Use of posts by Postmaster General) ".
15 & 16 Geo. 6 & 1 Eliz. 2. c. xliv.	The Llanelly District Traction Act 1952.	Section 4(3).
1 & 2 Eliz. 2. c. 36.	The Post Office Act 1953.	Section 34(3). Section 43. In section 44, in subsection (1), paragraph (*a*), and subsections (3) to (5). In section 45, in subsection (1), the words " any tramway vehicle or ", subsection (2), in subsection (3) the words " any tramway vehicle or ", and, in subsection (4), the words " in a tramway vehicle conveying passengers or ". Section 71. Section 73. Section 75. Section 85. In section 87(1), in the definition of " regular mail train services ", the words " or subsection (3) of section forty-four ".
2 & 3 Eliz. 2. c. 62.	The Post Office Savings Bank Act 1954.	In section 4(2), paragraph (*f*) and the word " and " immediately preceding that paragraph. Section 23. Section 24(2).
5 & 6 Eliz. 2. c. 49.	The Finance Act 1957.	Section 2.

Chapter	Title or Short Title	Extent to which Enactment is to cease to have Effect
5 & 6 Eliz. 2. c. xxxvi.	The Hastings Tramways Act 1957.	Section 12.
6 & 7 Eliz. 2. c. iv.	The Dundee Corporation (Consolidated Powers) Order Confirmation Act 1957.	In the order contained in the Schedule, section 84.
6 & 7 Eliz. 2. c. 63.	The Park Lane Improvement Act 1958.	Section 22.
6 & 7 Eliz. 2. c. 66.	The Tribunals and Inquiries Act 1958.	In Schedule 1, in Part I, in the Annex, the entry relating to the Commonwealth Telegraphs Act 1949.
6 & 7 Eliz. 2. c. 72.	The Insurance Companies Act 1958.	Section 35.
7 & 8 Eliz. 2. c. 6.	The National Debt Act 1958.	Section 16.
9 & 10 Eliz. 2. c. 15.	The Post Office Act 1961.	Section 4. In section 14, in subsection (1), the words from "instead of" onwards, and subsection (2). Section 18. Section 20. Section 24(1). In the Schedule, the entry relating to the Juries Act 1862 and the words in column 2 against it; the entries relating to the Telegraph Act 1869 and the words in column 2 against them; the entries relating to the Post Office (Pneumatic Tubes Acquisition) Act 1922, the Finance Act 1933, the Finance Act 1936, the Finance Act 1937, the Imperial Telegraphs Act 1938, the Finance Act 1940 and the Commonwealth Telegraphs Act 1949 and the words in column 2 against them; the entry relating to section 17 of the Wireless Telegraphy Act 1949 and the words in column 2 against it; the entry relating to section 3 of the Post Office Act 1953 and the words in column 2 against it; the entry relating to section 63 of that Act and the words in column 2 against it;

Chapter	Title or Short Title	Extent to which Enactment is to cease to have Effect
9 & 10 Eliz. 2. c. 15.—*cont.*	The Post Office Act 1961.—*cont.*	the entry relating to section 80 of that Act and the words in column 2 against it; and the entries relating to sections 82 and 83 of that Act and the words in column 2 against them; the entry relating to the Television Act 1954 and the words in column 2 against it; the entry relating to section 23 of the Post Office Savings Bank Act 1954 and the words in column 2 against it; and the entry relating to the Post Office Works Act 1959 and the words in column 2 against it.
1964, c. xliii.	The Glasgow Corporation Consolidation (Water, Transport and Markets) Order Confirmation Act 1964.	In the order contained in the Schedule, section 78.
1965, c. 2.	The Administration of Justice Act 1965.	In Schedule 1, the entry relating to the Telegraph Act 1869.
1965, c. 62.	The Redundancy Payments Act 1965.	In Schedule 7, in paragraph 12, the words " or section 7 of that Act ".
1966, c. 12.	The Post Office Savings Bank Act 1966.	In section 7(3), the words " and 23 ".

Enactments of the Parliament of Northern Ireland

Chapter	Short Title	Extent to which Enactment is to cease to have Effect
14 & 15 Geo. 5. c. 9.	The Private Bill Procedure Act (Northern Ireland) 1924.	Section 1(2)(*b*).
1968, c. 6.	The Insurance Companies Act (Northern Ireland) 1968.	Section 71.

PART II

ENACTMENTS CEASING TO HAVE EFFECT ON THE
APPOINTED DAY

Enactments of the Parliament of the United Kingdom

Chapter	Short Title	Extent to which Enactment is to cease to have Effect
26 & 27 Vict. c. 112.	The Telegraph Act 1863.	Sections 41 to 43. Sections 48 to 51.
33 & 34 Vict. c. 77.	The Juries Act 1870.	In the Schedule, the words " Officers of the Post Office ".
22 & 23 Geo. 5. c. 9.	The Merchant Shipping (Safety and Load Line Conventions) Act 1932.	In section 8, the proviso.
12, 13 & 14 Geo. 6. c. 54.	The Wireless Telegraphy Act 1949.	Section 14(4). In section 15(4), the words from " and criminal proceedings " onwards.
1 & 2 Eliz. 2. c. 36.	The Post Office Act 1953.	In section 4, in subsection (1), the words " without prejudice to subsection (3) of this section ", and subsection (3). Section 56(3). In section 63(3), the proviso. Section 72(2). Section 86.
6 & 7 Eliz. 2. c. 30.	The Land Powers (Defence) Act 1958.	Section 19. In Schedule 2, in paragraph 1, the words " or nineteen "; in paragraph 12, the words " or nineteen " and the words " or, as the case may be, by the Postmaster General "; in paragraph 13, the words " or, as the case may be, the Postmaster General "; and, in paragraph 15, the words " or, as the case may be, the Postmaster General ".
9 & 10 Eliz. 2. c. 15.	The Post Office Act 1961.	In the Schedule, the entry relating to section 72 of the Post Office Act 1953 and the words in column 2 against it.

SCH. 8

Enactment of the Parliament of Northern Ireland

Chapter	Short Title	Extent to which Enactment is to cease to have Effect
16 & 17 Geo. 5. c. 15.	The Jury Laws Amendment Act (Northern Ireland) 1926.	In Schedule 3, the words " Officer of the Post Office ".

Section 138.

SCHEDULE 9

GENERAL TRANSITIONAL PROVISIONS

1949 c. 54.
1964 c. 21.
1967 c. 72.

1.—(1) Section 3(1) of this Act shall not affect the validity of anything done by or in relation to the Postmaster General before the appointed day, being a thing done under or by virtue of the Wireless Telegraphy Act 1949, the Television Act 1964 or the Wireless Telegraphy Act 1967; and anything which, immediately before that day, is, under or by virtue of any of those Acts, in process of being done by or in relation to him (including, in particular, any legal proceeding to which he is a party) may be continued by or in relation to the Minister.

(2) Any notice served, approval or authority given or other thing whatsoever done under or by virtue of the Wireless Telegraphy Act 1949, the Television Act 1964 or the Wireless Telegraphy Act 1967 by the Postmaster General shall, if effective at the appointed day, continue in force and have effect as if similarly served, given or done by the Minister.

2.—(1) Any agreement, and any provision in a document not being an agreement, shall, so far as may be necessary in consequence of the enactment of Part III of this Act, have effect as from the appointed day—

    (*a*) as if references to the Crown, the Postmaster General, the Post Office or the Minister of Public Building and Works (except in cases where they fall to be adapted by head (*b*) or (*c*) below) were (or, if the context so requires, included) references to the authority established by section 6 of this Act;

    (*b*) as if—

1953 c. 36.

        (i) references in general terms (however worded) to officers of the Postmaster General, to officers of the Post Office (otherwise than as defined by section 87(1) of the Post Office Act 1953), to officers of the Crown or to servants of the Postmaster General, the Post Office or the Crown were (or, if the context so requires, included) references to persons employed by the authority established by section 6 of this Act;

        (ii) references in general terms (however worded) to officers of the Post Office as so defined were (or, if the context so requires, included) references to persons engaged in the business of the said authority;

(iii) references in general terms (however worded) to agents of the Postmaster General, the Post Office or the Crown were (or, if the context so requires, included) references to agents of the said authority;

(iv) references (however worded) to an officer of the Postmaster General or the Post Office holding a specified office were (or, if the context so requires, included) references to the person employed by the said authority who corresponds, as nearly as may be, to the first-mentioned officer; and

(v) references (however worded) to a servant of the Postmaster General, the Post Office or the Crown serving in a specified capacity were (or, if the context so requires, included) references to the person employed by the said authority who corresponds, as nearly as may be, to the first-mentioned servant;

(c) as if references (whether express or implied and, if express, however worded) to property of the Crown or the Postmaster General or his department were (or, if the context so requires, included) references to property of the said authority and references (whether express or implied and, if express, however worded) to land or premises occupied by the Crown, the Postmaster General, his department or an officer or servant of the Crown or Postmaster General were (or, if the context so requires, included) references to land or premises occupied by the said authority;

(d) as if any reference to the making, under a government provision, of a payment to or in respect of a person in consequence of his becoming ill, being injured or dying, were a reference to the making, to or in respect of him in consequence of his becoming ill, being injured or dying, of a payment falling to be made by virtue of a condition of his service (whether binding in law or not) providing for the making, in consequence of his becoming ill, being injured or dying, of a payment to or in respect of him.

(2) Without prejudice to the foregoing sub-paragraph, any agreement to which the Crown is a party, whether in writing or not, and whether or not of such a nature that rights and liabilities thereunder could be assigned by it, shall, as from the appointed day, have effect, so far as may be necessary for, or in consequence of, the vesting by virtue of Part III of this Act of property, rights or liabilities in the Post Office, as if the Post Office had been a party thereto.

(3) Without prejudice to sub-paragraph (1) above, where, by the operation of the said Part III, a right or liability becomes a right or liability of the Post Office, it and all other persons shall have the same rights, powers and remedies (and, in particular, the same rights, powers and remedies as to taking or resisting legal proceedings or the making or resisting of applications to any authority) for ascertaining, perfecting or enforcing it as they would have had if it had at all times been the right or liability of the Post Office; and legal proceedings or applications by or against the Crown, in so far as they relate to any property,

SCH. 9   rights or liabilities vested in the Post Office by virtue of sections 16 to 20 of this Act, or to any agreement or document which has effect in accordance with the foregoing provisions of this paragraph, shall not abate by reason of the Crown's ceasing to be interested in the subject-matter thereof but may be continued by or against the Post Office to the exclusion of the Crown.

3.—(1) Any such regulations as follows that are in force immediately before the appointed day, that is to say,—

1862 c. 107.

(*a*) regulations under section 11 of the Juries Act 1862;

1871 c. 65.

(*b*) regulations under section 22 of the Juries Act (Ireland) 1871;

1953 c. 36.

1947 c. 44.

(*c*) any such regulations made, or having effect as if made, under section 81 of the Post Office Act 1953 as have effect by virtue of section 5(2), 6(1) or (2), 8(1), 10, 11(3), 15, 20, 21 or proviso (*b*) to section 24 of that Act or of section 9(5) of the Crown Proceedings Act 1947;

1951 c. 52.

(*d*) regulations under the Telephone Act 1951;

1962 c. 14.

(*e*) regulations made, or having effect as if made, under the Telegraph Act 1962;

and are not revoked by virtue of sub-paragraph (4) below shall, with the substitution, for references to the Postmaster General, of references to the Post Office, with the omission of provisions as to evidence, deductions of money payable to bankers for or on account or in respect of money orders and limitation or exclusion of liability (except liability in respect of money orders that have become void by effluxion of time) and with any requisite modifications, have effect on and after that day as if they were provisions of schemes made under section 28 of this Act and coming into operation on that day and may be revoked or amended accordingly, and any charges fixed under any such regulations as aforesaid that are not revoked by virtue of that sub-paragraph shall have effect as if fixed under schemes so made and coming into operation.

(2) Subsection (3) of section 10 of the Post Office Act 1953 (consequence of failure to pay sums payable in respect of a cash on delivery packet) shall (unless repealed by virtue of sub-paragraph (4) below), with the omission of the reference to a British postal agency, with the substitution, for the references to the Postmaster General, of references to the Post Office and with the omission of the words " as a debt due to him ", have effect on and after the appointed day as if it were a provision of a scheme made under section 28 of this Act and coming into operation on that day, and may be repealed or amended accordingly; and, as from that day, the expression " cash on delivery packet " in that subsection shall mean a packet on whose delivery a sum falls to be collected by the Post Office for remission to the sender of the packet.

(3) Conclusive evidence of charges fixed under regulations made under the Telephone Act 1951 or regulations made, or having effect as if made, under section 81 of the Post Office Act 1953 or under the Telegraph Act 1962 may be given in all courts of justice and in all legal proceedings by the production of a copy of the London, Edinburgh or Belfast Gazette in which they were published.

(4) A scheme made under section 28 of this Act which is to come into effect on the appointed day may revoke or amend any such regulations as are referred to in sub-paragraph (1) above, and may repeal section 10(3) of the Post Office Act 1953.

(5) Any reference in an agreement or licence in force on the appointed day to a provision of any such regulations as are mentioned in sub-paragraph (1)(*d*) or (*e*) above (other than a provision relating to evidence or to limitation or exclusion of liability) shall, if during the currency of the agreement or licence that provision is revoked, be construed (unless the context otherwise requires) as referring to the corresponding provision for the time being in force of a scheme made under section 28 of this Act; and any reference in any such agreement or licence to a provision of any such regulations relating to limitation or exclusion of liability shall, as from that day, be construed in like manner as if that provision had not ceased to be in force.

(6) For the purposes of section 69 of this Act, proceedings instituted by or against the Postmaster General which are continued by or against the Post Office shall be treated as having been instituted by or against the Post Office; and the reference in subsection (1) of that section to a sum due to the Post Office under such provisions as are therein mentioned shall be taken to include a reference to a sum that, having been due to the Postmaster General under any such regulations as are mentioned in sub-paragraph (1)(*d*) or (*e*) above, has, by virtue of section 16 of this Act, become due to the Post Office.

4. Any postage or other sum payable under the Post Office Act 1953 in respect of a postal packet which has not been paid before the appointed day shall, on that day, become payable to the Post Office and be treated for the purposes of this Act as if it were exigible under a scheme made under section 28 thereof; and any proceedings instituted by the Crown for the recovery of any such sum as aforesaid that are pending on that day may be continued by the Post Office in like manner as if they had been instituted by it.

5.—(1) References in sections 70 and 71 of this Act to a money order issued by the Post Office shall include references to—

(*a*) a money order issued by the Postmaster General but not paid before the appointed day; and

(*b*) an order issued by him in pursuance of such an arrangement as is mentioned in section 24 of the Post Office Act 1953 (as in force immediately before the appointed day) but not so paid, being an order which is for the payment of money in the British Islands and corresponds to a money order issued by him;

and the reference in the said section 71 to payment by the Post Office shall include a reference to payment by the Postmaster General.

(2) References in section 70 of this Act to a postal order issued by the Post Office shall include references to a postal order issued by the Postmaster General but not paid before the appointed day.

(3) In this paragraph " the British Islands " means the United Kingdom, the Isle of Man and the Channel Islands.

6. An authorisation given under section 3(1), 61, 62 or 64 of the Post Office Act 1953 by the Postmaster General which is effective at the appointed day shall have effect as from that day as if given by the Post Office, and a declaration under section 78(1) of that Act by the Postmaster General which is so effective shall so have effect as if made by the Post Office.

7. An undertaking given under section 51(2) or (3) of the Post Office Act 1953 to the Postmaster General shall, if effective at the appointed day, have effect, as from that day, as if given to the Post Office.

8. Where, on the appointed day there are in progress any proceedings for the settlement or determination, under the Telegraph Act 1863 or the Telegraph Act 1878, of a difference, dispute, matter or question or the amount or application of compensation, being proceedings to which the Postmaster General is a party, the Post Office shall be substituted for the Postmaster General as a party to the proceedings; and where, on that day, there are in progress any proceedings under section 8 of the last-mentioned Act for the recovery by the Postmaster General of either or both of the following, namely, expenses incurred by him in making good destruction of, or injury to, a telegraphic line and a daily fine in respect of the interruption of telegraphic communication, the Post Office shall be similarly substituted.

9.—(1) This paragraph applies to the following instruments, namely,—

(*a*) the agreement dated 2nd April 1962 whereto the parties are the Postmaster General and the Commercial Cable Company, Incorporated (a company incorporated under the law of the State of New York of the United States of America);

(*b*) the agreement dated 1st April 1963 whereto the parties are the Postmaster General and the Compagnie Française des Câbles Télégraphiques S.A. (a company incorporated under the law of France);

(*c*) the agreement dated 27th December 1965 whereto the parties are the Postmaster General and Western Union International, Incorporated (a company incorporated under the law of the State of Delaware of the United States of America); and

(*d*) the licence dated 1st March 1966 whereto the parties are Her Majesty, the Crown Estate Commissioners, the Postmaster General and Det Store Nordiske Telegraf-Selskab Aktieselskab (a company incorporated under the law of the Kingdom of Denmark and commonly known in the United Kingdom, and in that licence referred to, as the Great Northern Telegraph Company Limited).

(2) Nothing done, on or after the appointed day, under, and in accordance with the terms of, an instrument to which this paragraph applies, shall constitute an infringement of the privilege conferred by section 24(1) of this Act.

Sch. 9

10.—(1) Any licence operating by way of exception from the exclusive privilege conferred by section 4 of the Telegraph Act 1869 on the 1869 c. 73. Postmaster General which is effective at the appointed day (not being a licence under the Wireless Telegraphy Act 1949) shall, as from that 1949 c. 54. day, have effect as if it had been granted under section 27(1) of this Act and—

(*a*) as if references to the Crown (except in contexts referring to a Minister of the Crown) or to the Postmaster General or the Post Office (except in cases where they fall to be adapted by head (*b*) below) were references to the authority established by section 6 of this Act; and

(*b*) as if—

(i) references in general terms (however worded) to officers of the Postmaster General, to officers of the Post Office (otherwise than as defined by section 87(1) of the Post 1953 c. 36. Office Act 1953), or to servants of the Postmaster General or the Post Office were (or, if the context so requires, included) references to persons employed by the authority established by section 6 of this Act;

(ii) references in general terms (however worded) to officers of the Post Office as so defined were (or, if the context so requires, included) references to persons engaged in the business of the said authority;

(iii) references in general terms (however worded) to agents of the Postmaster General or the Post Office were (or, if the context so requires, included) references to agents of the said authority;

(iv) references (however worded) to an officer of the Postmaster General or the Post Office holding a specified office were references to the person employed by the said authority who corresponds, as nearly as may be, to the first-mentioned officer; and

(v) references (however worded) to a servant of the Postmaster General or the Post Office serving in a specified capacity were references to the person employed by the said authority who corresponds, as nearly as may be, to the first-mentioned servant.

(2) Any instrument issued in pursuance of a licence falling within the foregoing sub-paragraph, being an instrument effective at the appointed day, shall, as from that day, have effect subject to the like modifications as those provided for by heads (*a*) and (*b*) of that sub-paragraph in the case of the licence.

11. A notice or certificate given, request made or requirement imposed under any provision of the enactments relating to telegraphs by, to or on the Postmaster General which is effective at the appointed day shall, as from that day, have effect as if given, made or imposed by, to or on the Post Office.

12. An authority granted under section 5(1) of the Telegraph Act 1892 c. 59. 1892 which is effective at the appointed day shall, as from that day, have effect as if it had been granted under that section as amended by paragraph 5 of Schedule 4 to this Act.

Sch. 9
1899 c. 38.

13. Any such council as is mentioned in the Telegraph Act 1899 which, at the beginning of the appointed day, is licensed by the Postmaster General to provide a system of public telephonic communication, shall, so long as the licence continues in force, be deemed, for the purposes of that Act, to be licensed by the Post Office so to provide.

1882 c. 56.

14.—(1) A notice given under section 26 of the Electric Lighting Act 1882 by undertakers to the Postmaster General which is effective at the appointed day shall, as from that day, have effect as if given to the Post Office; any requirements made under that section by the Postmaster General which are so effective shall, as from that day, have effect as if made by the Post Office; and any arbitration on a difference under that section which is in progress immediately before that day may be continued with the substitution of the Post Office for the Postmaster General as a party thereto.

1888 c. 12.

(2) A requirement imposed under section 4(2) of the Electric Lighting Act 1888 by the Postmaster General which is effective at the appointed day shall, as from that day, have effect as if imposed by the Post Office.

1899 c. 19.

(3) An approval given under section 10(c) of the Schedule to the Electric Lighting (Clauses) Act 1899 with the concurrence of the Postmaster General which is effective at the appointed day shall, as from that day, have effect as if given with the concurrence of the Post Office; a notice served under section 14 of that Schedule by undertakers on the Postmaster General which is so effective shall, as from that day, have effect as if served on the Post Office; a requirement imposed or approval or disapproval notified under that section by the Postmaster General which is effective at the appointed day shall, as from that day, have effect as if imposed or notified by the Post Office; and a requirement imposed under section 60 of that Schedule which is effective at the appointed day shall, as from that day, have effect as if imposed by the Post Office.

(4) Any notice given under section 20 of the Schedule to the Electric Lighting (Clauses) Act 1899 to the Postmaster General which is effective at the appointed day shall, as from that day, have effect as if given to the Post Office, any requisition served under that section by the Postmaster General which is effective at that day shall, as from that day, have effect as if served by the Post Office and any arbitration under that section which is in progress immediately before that day, being an arbitration to which the Postmaster General is a party, may be continued with the substitution of the Post Office for the Postmaster General.

1913 c. 20.
1914 c. 59.

15. An order under section 187 of the Bankruptcy (Scotland) Act 1913 or section 24 of the Bankruptcy Act 1914 which is effective at the appointed day shall, as from that day, have effect as if, for any reference therein to the Postmaster General, there were substituted a reference to the Post Office.

1945 c. 43.

16. A notice given under section 24 of the Requisitioned Land and War Works Act 1945 by or to the Postmaster General which is effective at the appointed day shall, as from that day, have effect as if given by or to the Post Office.

17.—(1) No steps shall be taken for the enforcement of a building SCH. 9 law with respect to works on land that vests in the Post Office by virtue of section 16 of this Act, being works begun before the appointed day, or with respect to works on land begun by the Post Office before the expiration of six months beginning with that day; nor shall any proceedings for the recovery of a fine or other penalty be brought against the Post Office for having carried out or retained any such works as aforesaid which do not comply with a building law.

(2) In the foregoing sub-paragraph, "building law" means any obligation or restriction as to the construction, nature or situation of works on land or as to any other circumstances of such works (including the use of the land) having effect by virtue of—

(*a*) section 17 of the Restriction of Ribbon Development Act 1935; 1935 c. 47.

(*b*) an enactment contained in Part II or IV of the Public Health 1936 c. 49. Act 1936 or Part II of the Public Health Act 1961 or byelaws 1961 c. 64. or regulations made under an enactment so contained;

(*c*) the London Building Acts 1930 to 1939 or byelaws made thereunder;

(*d*) the Thermal Insulation (Industrial Buildings) Act 1957 or 1957 c. 40. regulations made thereunder;

(*e*) section 72, 73, 74, 75, 81 or 159 of the Highways Act 1959; 1959 c. 25.

(*f*) paragraph 13, 15 or 18 of Part III of Schedule 9 to the London 1963 c. 33. Government Act 1963 or byelaws made under paragraph 6 of that Part of that Schedule; or

(*g*) any enactment contained in a local Act made for purposes similar to the purposes of any of the aforesaid enactments or any byelaws made under any enactment contained in a local Act so made;

and "works" includes any building, structure, excavation or other work on land.

(3) Any reference in this paragraph to non-compliance with a building law means, in relation to any works on land, that the construction, nature or situation of the works or any other circumstances thereof (including the use of the land) are such either that the works do not comply with the building law in question or that, by virtue of that law, the rejection of plans for the works is expressly required or authorised.

(4) Any reference in this paragraph to the enforcement of a building law shall be construed as a reference to securing (whether by the doing of work on land or the requiring, by injunction or otherwise, that some other person shall do work on land) that works on land not complying with the building law in question shall either be demolished or removed or be altered so as to comply therewith.

(5) In the application of this paragraph to Scotland, the following shall be substituted for heads (*a*) to (*g*) of sub-paragraph (2):—

" (*a*) an enactment contained in the Burgh Police (Scotland) Acts 1892 to 1903 or under the Public Health (Scotland) Act 1897 1897 c. 38. or byelaws made under any such enactment;

(b) the Roads Improvement Act 1925;

(c) section 17 of the Restriction of Ribbon Development Act 1935;

(d) section 53 of the Water (Scotland) Act 1946;

(e) the Thermal Insulation (Industrial Buildings) Act 1957 or regulations made thereunder;

(f) the Building (Scotland) Act 1959 or regulations made thereunder;

(g) the Sewerage (Scotland) Act 1968;

(h) any enactment contained in a local Act made for purposes similar to the purposes of any of the aforesaid enactments or any byelaws made under any enactment contained in a local Act so made; or

(i) any enactment or rule of the common law conferring powers on a dean of guild court ".

(6) In the application of this paragraph to Northern Ireland, the following shall be substituted for heads (a) to (g) of sub-paragraph (2):—

" (a) section 9 of the Summary Jurisdiction (Ireland) Act 1851;

(b) an enactment contained in the Public Health Acts (Northern Ireland) 1878 to 1967 or byelaws made under an enactment so contained;

(c) an enactment contained in the Housing Acts (Northern Ireland) 1890 to 1967;

(d) the Roads Improvement Act (Northern Ireland) 1928; or

(e) any enactment contained in a local Act made for purposes similar to the purposes of any of the aforesaid enactments or any byelaws or orders made under any enactment contained in a local Act so made ".

18.—(1) Any regulations under section 79 of the Representation of the People Act 1949 which are effective at the appointed day shall, as from that day, have effect as if, for references therein to the Post Office or the Postmaster General, there were substituted references to the authority established by section 6 of this Act.

(2) Any security given under any such regulations as aforesaid which is effective at the appointed day shall, as from that day, have effect as if given to the said authority.

19.—(1) Any regulations under section 53 of the Electoral Law Act (Northern Ireland) 1962 which are effective at the appointed day shall, as from that day, have effect as if, for references therein to the Post Office or the Postmaster General, there were substituted references to the authority established by section 6 of this Act.

(2) Any security given under any such regulations as aforesaid which is effective at the appointed day shall, as from that day, have effect as if given to the said authority.

20.—(1) Nothing in Part III of this Act shall affect the validity of anything done by, or in relation to, the Postmaster General before the appointed day under or by virtue of the Public Utilities Street Works Act 1950; and anything which, immediately before that day, is in process of being done under, or by virtue of, that Act by or in relation to him (including, in particular, any legal proceedings to which he is a party) may be continued by, or in relation to, the Post Office.

(2) Any notice or direction given or other thing whatsoever done under the said Act of 1950 by the Postmaster General shall, if effective at the appointed day, continue in force and have effect as if similarly given or done by the Post Office.

21. A notice served under section 29 of the Income Tax Act 1952 (power to obtain information as to interest paid or credited without deduction of tax) on the Postmaster General before the appointed day shall, if it has not been complied with before that day, be deemed to have been served on the Director of Savings; and subsection (1) of that section shall, in its application on and after that day to the National Savings Bank, have effect as if the reference to interest paid or credited by the Director of Savings included, as regards any period before that day, a reference to interest paid or credited by the Postmaster General to depositors.

22. A notice given under section 6 of the Local Government (Miscellaneous Provisions) Act 1953 (supplementary provisions as to omnibus shelters, &c.) by the Postmaster General which is effective at the appointed day shall, as from that day, have effect as if given by the Post Office; and any proceedings for the settlement of a dispute under that section in progress at the appointed day, being proceedings to which the Postmaster General is a party, may be continued with the substitution of the Post Office for the Postmaster General.

23. In relation to an agreement which, on the appointed day, becomes subject to registration under Part I of the Restrictive Trade Practices Act 1956 by reason of its having effect as from that day as if the Post Office had been a party thereto, section 10 of that Act (particulars to be furnished for registration) and section 7 of the Restrictive Trade Practices Act 1968 (consequences of failure to register) shall have effect with the substitution, for references to the time within which particulars are required to be furnished under section 6 of the last-mentioned Act (time for registration of agreements), of references to the period of three months beginning with that day and the said section 6 shall not apply.

24. An order under paragraph 8 of Schedule 1 to the Solicitors Act 1957 which is effective at the appointed day shall, as from that day, have effect as if, for any reference therein to the Postmaster General, there were substituted a reference to the Post Office.

25. A notice given under section 5(4) of the Milford Haven Conservancy Act 1958 by the Milford Haven Conservancy Board to the Postmaster General which is effective at the appointed day shall, as from that day, have effect as if given to the Post Office.

26. A notice given under section 3 of the Local Government (Omnibus Shelters and Queue Barriers) (Scotland) Act 1958 by the Postmaster General which is effective at the appointed day shall, as from that day, have effect as if given by the Post Office; and any proceedings for the settlement of a dispute under that section in progress immediately before the appointed day, being proceedings to which the Postmaster General is a party, may be continued with the substitution of the Post Office for the Postmaster General.

27.—(1) Where, between the passing of this Act and the appointed day, the Postmaster General notifies a local planning authority in writing of a proposal to carry out development of land, and, before that day and the expiration of the relevant period, that authority notifies the Postmaster General in writing that it has no objection to the proposal, planning permission for the development shall be deemed to be granted by that authority on that day subject to the relevant condition as to time.

(2) Where, between the passing of this Act and the appointed day, the Postmaster General notifies a local planning authority in writing of a proposal to carry out development of land, and, before that day and the expiration of the relevant period, that authority notifies the Postmaster General in writing that it has no objection to the proposal provided that conditions specified by it in the notification are complied with (not being conditions containing a stipulation as to the time at which the development must be begun or completed), planning permission for the development shall—

(*a*) except in a case in which those conditions are subsequently either modified as mentioned in the following provisions of this sub-paragraph or withdrawn as so mentioned, be deemed to be granted by that authority on the appointed day subject to those conditions and to the relevant condition as to time;

(*b*) in a case in which those conditions are subsequently modified by that authority in writing with the written concurrence of the Postmaster General, be deemed to be granted by that authority on the appointed day subject to those conditions as so modified and to the relevant condition as to time;

(*c*) in a case in which those conditions are withdrawn by that authority in writing addressed to the Postmaster General, be deemed to be granted by that authority on the appointed day subject to the relevant condition as to time.

(3) Where, between the passing of this Act and the appointed day, the Postmaster General notifies a local planning authority in writing of a proposal to carry out development of land, and before that day and the expiration of the relevant period, that authority notifies the Postmaster General in writing that it has no objection to the proposal provided that conditions specified by it in the notification are complied

with (being conditions containing a stipulation as to the time at which
the development must be begun or completed), planning permission
for the development shall—

  (*a*) except in a case in which those conditions are subsequently
    either modified as mentioned in the following provisions of
    this sub-paragraph or withdrawn as so mentioned, be deemed
    to be granted by that authority on the appointed day subject
    to those conditions;

  (*b*) in a case in which those conditions are subsequently modified
    by that authority in writing with the written concurrence
    of the Postmaster General (otherwise than by withdrawing
    the stipulation as to time), be deemed to be granted by that
    authority on the appointed day subject to those conditions
    as so modified;

  (*c*) in a case in which those conditions (except so far as containing
    the stipulation as to time) are withdrawn by that authority
    in writing addressed to the Postmaster General, be deemed to
    be granted by that authority on the appointed day subject
    to the condition containing that stipulation.

(4) Where, between the passing of this Act and the appointed day,
the Postmaster General notifies a local planning authority in writing
of a proposal to carry out development of land, and—

  (*a*) the relevant period expires with the day immediately preceding
    the appointed day or with an earlier day; and

  (*b*) that authority does not, before the expiration of that period,
    notify the Postmaster General in writing as mentioned in
    sub-paragraph (1), (2) or (3) above or that it objects to the
    proposal;

planning permission for the development shall be deemed to be granted
by the authority on the appointed day subject to the relevant condition
as to time.

(5) The foregoing sub-paragraphs shall, with requisite modifications,
apply in a case where, before the passing of this Act, the Postmaster
General has notified a local planning authority in writing of a proposal
to carry out development of land (but that development has not been
carried out before the appointed day) as they apply in a case where
he does so between the passing of this Act and that day.

(6) Where, by virtue of sub-paragraph (2) or (3) above, planning
permission for the carrying out of development of land consisting in
the erection, extension or alteration of a building is deemed to be
granted by a local planning authority subject to a condition that the
Postmaster General should consult that authority with respect to any
matters relating to the siting, design or external appearance of the
building or means of access thereto, then, so far as regards any of those
matters as to which, before the appointed day, the Postmaster General
has not been notified by that authority in writing that it is satisfied with
the way in which that matter is to be dealt with, it shall be deemed, as

2 Q*

from that day, to be a matter in the case of which the approval of that authority to the manner in which it is to be dealt with is required under a development order and the planning permission shall be deemed to be granted subject to a condition that application for approval must be made not later than the expiration of three years beginning with that day.

1962 c. 38.

(7) Parts VI and XI of the Town and Country Planning Act 1962 shall not have effect in a case in which planning permission is deemed, by virtue of this paragraph, to be granted.

In the application of this sub-paragraph to Scotland, for the reference to Parts VI and XI of the Town and Country Planning Act 1962 there shall be substituted a reference to the following provisions—

1954 c. 73.

(*a*) sections 1 and 2, Part II, sections 50, 65 and 66 of the Town and Country Planning (Scotland) Act 1954; and

1959 c. 70.

(*b*) section 31 of the Town and Country Planning (Scotland) Act 1959.

1965 c. 33.

(8) Section 7 of the Control of Office and Industrial Development Act 1965 shall not have effect in relation to planning permission deemed, by virtue of this paragraph, to be granted.

(9) Every local planning authority shall, with respect to each case in which planning permission is deemed, by virtue of this paragraph, to be granted by it, include, in that part of the register kept by it under section 19(4) of the Town and Country Planning Act 1962 that contains entries relating to applications for planning permission that have been finally disposed of, the following particulars, namely,—

(*a*) the date on which the permission is deemed to be granted;

(*b*) a general description of the development to which the permission relates and of the land to be developed in accordance with the permission;

(*c*) in a case in which the authority approves, in relation to the development to which the permission relates, anything which, by virtue of sub-paragraph (6) above, falls to be approved by it, the date on which it does so;

(*d*) in a case in which, in consequence of the operation of that sub-paragraph, an appeal as to any matter relating to the development to which the permission relates is entertained by the Minister of Housing and Local Government or an application is referred to him, the date on which the appeal or reference is disposed of, and the decision on the appeal or reference.

In the application of this sub-paragraph to Scotland, for the references to section 19(4) of the Town and Country Planning Act 1962 and to the Minister of Housing and Local Government there shall be

1947 c. 53.

substituted respectively references to section 12(5) of the Town and Country Planning (Scotland) Act 1947 and to the Secretary of State.

(10) For the purposes of section 99(3) of the Land Commission Act 1967, planning permission which, by virtue of sub-paragraph (2) or (3) above, is deemed to be granted subject to approval on any matter, shall be deemed to be granted on an outline application.

Sch. 9
1967 c. 1.

(11) Section 69 of the Town and Country Planning Act 1968 and section 70 of the Town and Country Planning (Scotland) Act 1969 shall have effect in relation to the Post Office as if, at the end of paragraph (*d*) of subsection (3) thereof, there were added the following—

1968 c. 72.
1969 c. 30.

" or
> (*e*) deemed to be granted by virtue of paragraph 27 of Schedule 9 to the Post Office Act 1969 ".

(12) In this paragraph,—

(*a*) " development ", " development order ", " local planning authority " and " planning permission " have, in the application of this paragraph to England and Wales, the same meanings as they have for the purposes of the Town and Country Planning Act 1962 and, in the application of this paragraph to Scotland, the same meanings as in the Town and Country Planning (Scotland) Act 1947;

1962 c. 38.

1947 c. 53

(*b*) " the relevant condition as to time "—

> (i) except in a case in which planning permission is, by virtue of sub-paragraph (6) above, deemed to be granted subject to a condition that application for the approval of matters must be made not later than the expiration of three years beginning with the appointed day, means a condition that the development to which the permission relates must be begun not later than the expiration of five years beginning with that day;

> (ii) in the said excepted case, means a condition that the development must be begun not later than whichever is the later of the following dates, namely, the expiration of five years from the appointed day and the expiration of two years from the final approval of matters which are the subject of the condition subject to which planning permission is, by virtue of that sub-paragraph, deemed to be granted (or, in the case of approval on different dates, the final approval of the last such matter to be approved);

(*c*) " relevant period ", in relation to a notification to a local planning authority of a proposal to carry out development, means the period of two months from the day on which the notification is received by the authority or such longer period as may, before the expiration of the first-mentioned period, be agreed in writing between the authority and the Postmaster General.

(13) For the purposes of this paragraph, development shall be taken to be begun on the earliest date on which any specified operation (as defined in section 64(3) of the Land Commission Act 1967) comprised in the development begins to be carried out.

(14) Sections 65 and 66 of the Town and Country Planning Act 1968 and sections 66 and 67 of the Town and Country Planning (Scotland) Act 1969 (which relate to the duration of planning permission) shall not apply to planning permission deemed, by virtue of this paragraph, to be granted.

(15) Subsections (3) and (5) of section 67 of the Town and Country Planning Act 1968 (which respectively define final approval of reserved matters and invalidate development carried out, and applications for approval made, out of time) shall have effect for the purposes of this paragraph with the substitution for any reference to a reserved matter of a reference to such a matter as is referred to in sub-paragraph (12)(*b*)(ii) above, and, for the reference to planning permission having conditions attached to it by or under provisions of section 65 or 66 of that Act, of a reference to planning permission deemed, by virtue of this paragraph, to be granted.

In the application of this sub-paragraph to Scotland, for the references to subsections (3) and (5) of section 67 of the Town and Country Planning Act 1968 and to sections 65 and 66 of that Act there shall be substituted respectively references to subsections (3) and (5) of section 68 of the Town and Country Planning (Scotland) Act 1969 and to sections 66 and 67 of that Act.

(16) For the purposes of the general application of this paragraph to Scotland, in sub-paragraphs (1), (2) and (3) the words " and the expiration of the relevant period " and sub-paragraphs (4) and (12)(*c*) shall be omitted.

(17) This paragraph does not extend to Northern Ireland.

28.—(1) Notwithstanding section 83 of the Town and Country Planning (Scotland) Act 1947 or section 199 of the Town and Country Planning Act 1962 (exercise of powers in relation to Crown land), planning permission for the development by the Post Office of land which is Crown land within the meaning of that section by reason only of the subsistence therein of an interest of the Postmaster General may be granted under either Act in pursuance of an application therefor made by the Post Office before the appointed day, and section 36 of

the Town and Country Planning (Scotland) Act 1959 and section 16 of the said Act of 1962 (certificates required to accompany application) shall not apply to an application that may be granted by virtue of this sub-paragraph or to an appeal from a decision to refuse to grant planning permission in pursuance of such an application or to grant it subject to conditions.

(2) Any approval required under a development order (within the meaning of the said Act of 1947 or of the said Act of 1962) in relation to development of such land as is mentioned in the foregoing sub-paragraph, being development proposed to be carried out by the Post Office, may be granted in pursuance of an application therefor made by the Post Office before the appointed day.

SCH. 9

29. No enforcement notice shall be served by virtue of section 72(1) of the Town and Country Planning (Scotland) Act 1947 or under paragraph 12 of Schedule 13 to the Town and Country Planning Act 1962 in respect of works carried out on land that vests in the Post Office by virtue of section 16 of this Act or in respect of use of land that so vests; and no enforcement notice shall be served under section 15 of the Town and Country Planning Act 1968 or section 15 of the Town and Country Planning (Scotland) Act 1969 in respect of development carried out before the appointed day on land that so vests.

1947 c. 53.

1962 c. 38.

1968 c. 72.

1969 c. 30.

30. Neither an interim development authority, nor, where the Ministry of Development for Northern Ireland is exercising any of the functions of such an authority, that Ministry, shall take any action under section 4 of the Planning (Interim Development) Act (Northern Ireland) 1944 (enforcement of interim development control) in respect of any development carried out before the appointed day in or on land that vests in the Post Office by virtue of section 16 of this Act.

1944 c. 3 (N.I.).

31.—(1) Subsection (2) of section 57 of the Landlord and Tenant Act 1954 (modification on grounds of public interest of rights under Part II of that Act) shall not preclude the giving, in relation to a tenancy, of a certificate under subsection (1) or (5) of that section by the Minister if, in relation to the tenancy, a notice has been given under the first-mentioned subsection by the Postmaster General; but in a case in which this paragraph applies, the Minister shall, before determining whether to give the certificate, consider any representations made in writing by the tenant to the Postmaster General within twenty-one days of the giving of the notice.

1954 c. 56.

(2) A certificate given by the Postmaster General under subsection (1) or (5) of the said section 57 with respect to property in which, immediately before the appointed day, the landlord's interest belongs to him, shall not be rendered ineffective by reason of the vesting, on that day, by virtue of section 16 of this Act, of that interest in the Post Office.

32.—(1) A licensing authority to whom an application is made before the appointed day by the Post Office for an A licence or for a B licence shall not refuse the application if it is accompanied by a certificate of the Postmaster General certifying that the vehicles proposed to be used under the licence are in use by him.

(2) Section 168(2) of the Road Traffic Act 1960 (which authorises a licensing authority to attach conditions to a B licence) shall not apply to a B licence granted in pursuance of an application which, by virtue of the foregoing sub-paragraph, the authority is bound to grant, but it shall be a condition of the licence that no vehicle which is for the time being an authorised vehicle shall be used for the carriage for hire or reward of goods other than—

1960 c. 16.

(*a*) goods consigned for carriage by post; or

SCH. 9

(*b*) goods that are the subject of an agreement between the Post Office and another person who carries on business as a carrier of goods whereunder the Post Office undertakes to carry on his behalf goods consigned to him for carriage;

and accordingly, in relation to a B licence so granted, section 166(3) of that Act (which specifies the purposes for which a B licence entitles the holder thereof to use the authorised vehicles) shall have effect with the substitution, for paragraph (*b*), of the following paragraph, namely,—

" (*b*) for the carriage of goods for hire or reward ".

1960 c. 16.

(3) This paragraph shall be construed as one with Part IV of the Road Traffic Act 1960.

1963 c. 49.

33.—(1) Where a person enters the employment of the Post Office on the appointed day and, immediately before that day, was occupied in the department of the Postmaster General in employment to which this paragraph applies, then, for the purpose of ascertaining the length of the period of his employment for the purposes of sections 1 and 2 of the Contracts of Employment Act 1963, Schedule 1 to that Act shall have effect—

(*a*) as if, in a case where he was so occupied otherwise than under a contract of service, employment of his to which this paragraph applies in which he was occupied otherwise than as aforesaid before the appointed day, whether or not in the department of the Postmaster General, had been employment within the meaning of the said Act of 1963, and, while he was occupied therein, he had been an employee within the meaning of that Act, but as if for paragraph 4 of that Schedule there were substituted the following paragraph:—

" 4. Any week during the whole or part of which the terms of his employment normally involve employment for twenty-one hours or more weekly shall count in computing a period of employment ";

and

(*b*) as if, in any case, subject to the next following sub-paragraph, the period, ending immediately before the appointed day, of employment of his to which this paragraph applies, whether or not in the department of the Postmaster General, counted as a period of employment with the Post Office (if, apart from this provision, it would not so count) and his transfer to employment with the Post Office did not break the continuity of the period of employment (if, apart from this provision, the transfer would do so).

1965 c. 74.

1965 c. 62.

(2) Where, before the appointed day, a person's employment to which this paragraph applies was terminated and a payment made to him in respect of the termination in accordance with the Superannuation Act 1965 or any enactment repealed by that Act, or under such arrangements as are mentioned in section 41(3) of the Redundancy Payments Act 1965, then, whether or not he was re-employed in employment to

which this paragraph applies immediately following that termination, Schedule 1 to the said Act of 1963 shall have effect as if the period of his employment before that termination in employment to which this paragraph applies did not count as a period of employment with the Post Office.

(3) In the application of paragraph 7 of Schedule 2 to the said Act of 1963 (calculation of rates of remuneration) to a person in whose case sub-paragraph (1) above applies, references in that paragraph to a former employer and a period of employment with a former employer shall be construed in accordance with the foregoing sub-paragraphs, and the reference in that paragraph to paragraph 10 of Schedule 1 to that Act shall include a reference to head (*b*) of that sub-paragraph.

(4) Section 7 of the said Act of 1963 (power to vary number of weekly hours of employment necessary to qualify for rights) shall have effect as if the references therein to paragraph 4 of Schedule 1 to that Act included references to the paragraph substituted therefor by sub-paragraph (1) above and to the next following sub-paragraph.

(5) This paragraph applies to employment of a person in the civil service of the State in an established or unestablished capacity within the meaning of the Superannuation Act 1965, and to employment of a 1965 c. 74. person therein in part-time service, where he gives personal service of at least twenty-one hours a week and the remuneration in respect thereof is defrayed entirely out of the Post Office Fund or moneys provided by Parliament.

34.—(1) For the purpose of computing, for the purposes of the Redundancy Payments Act 1965, a period of employment of a person 1965 c. 62. in whose case sub-paragraph (1) of the last foregoing paragraph applies, any reference in that Act to Schedule 1 or 2 to the Contracts of Employ- 1963 c. 49. ment Act 1963 shall, in relation to employment of his to which the last foregoing paragraph applies, being employment before the appointed day, be construed as a reference to the said Schedule 1 or 2, as the case may be, as it has effect by virtue of the last foregoing paragraph.

(2) Where a person enters the employment of the Post Office on the appointed day and, immediately before that day, was occupied in the department of the Postmaster General in employment to which the last foregoing paragraph applies, then, for the purposes of computing a period of employment for the purposes of Schedule 1 to the said Act of 1963 as applied by the said Act of 1965, a period in which he was occupied in employment to which the last foregoing paragraph applies shall, notwithstanding the provisions of section 16(4) of the said Act of 1965 (which excludes the application of section 1 of that Act to a person in respect of certain employment) be treated as if it had been a period in respect of which section 1 of that Act had applied.

SCH. 9

1965 c. 19
(N.I.).

35.—(1) Where a person enters the employment of the Post Office on the appointed day and immediately before that day was occupied in the department of the Postmaster General in employment to which this paragraph applies, then, for the purpose of ascertaining the length of the period of his employment for the purposes of sections 1 and 2 of the Contracts of Employment and Redundancy Payments Act (Northern Ireland) 1965, Schedule 1 to that Act shall have effect—

(a) as if, in a case where he was so occupied otherwise than under a contract of service, employment of his to which this paragraph applies in which he was occupied otherwise than as aforesaid before the appointed day, whether or not in the department of the Postmaster General, had been employment within the meaning of the said Act of 1965, and, while he was occupied therein, he had been an employee within the meaning of that Act, but as if, for paragraph 4 of that Schedule, there were substituted the following paragraph:—

" 4. Any week during the whole or a part of which the terms of his employment normally involve employment for twenty-one hours or more weekly shall count in computing a period of employment ";

and

(b) as if, in any case, subject to the next following sub-paragraph, the period, ending immediately before the appointed day, of employment of his to which this paragraph applies, whether or not in the department of the Postmaster General, counted as a period of employment with the Post Office (if, apart from this provision, it would not so count) and his transfer to employment with the Post Office did not break the continuity of the period of employment (if, apart from this provision, the transfer would do so).

1965 c. 74.

1965 c. 62.

(2) Where, before the appointed day a person's employment to which this paragraph applies was terminated and a payment made to him in respect of the termination in accordance with the Superannuation Act 1965 or any enactment repealed by that Act, or under such arrangements as are mentioned in section 41(3) of the Redundancy Payments Act 1965, then, whether or not he was re-employed in employment to which this paragraph applies immediately following that termination, Schedule 1 to the Contracts of Employment and Redundancy Payments Act (Northern Ireland) 1965 shall have effect as if the period of his employment before that termination in employment to which this paragraph applies did not count as a period of employment with the Post Office.

(3) In the application of paragraph 7 of Schedule 2 to the Contracts of Employment and Redundancy Payments Act (Northern Ireland) 1965 (calculation of rates of remuneration) to a person in whose case sub-paragraph (1) above applies, references in that paragraph to a former employer and a period of employment with a former employer shall be construed in accordance with the foregoing sub-paragraphs, and the reference in that paragraph to paragraph 10 of Schedule 1 to that Act shall include a reference to head (b) of that sub-paragraph.

(4) Section 7 of the Contracts of Employment and Redundancy Payments Act (Northern Ireland) 1965 (power to vary number of weekly hours of employment necessary to qualify for rights) shall have effect as if the reference therein to paragraph 4 of Schedule 1 to that Act included a reference to the paragraph substituted therefor by sub-paragraph (1) above and to sub-paragraph (7) below.

(5) For the purpose of computing, for the purposes of the Contracts of Employment and Redundancy Payments Act (Northern Ireland) 1965, a period of employment of a person in whose case sub-paragraph (1) of this paragraph applies, any reference in that Act to Schedule 1 or 2 to that Act shall, in relation to employment to which this paragraph applies of his before the appointed day, be construed as a reference to the said Schedule 1 or 2, as the case may be, as it has effect by virtue of sub-paragraphs (1) to (4) above.

(6) Where a person enters the employment of the Post Office on the appointed day and, immediately before that day, was occupied in the department of the Postmaster General in employment to which this paragraph applies, then, for the purpose of computing a period of employment for the purposes of the said Schedule 1 as applied by Schedule 3 to the said Act of 1965, a period in which he was occupied in employment to which this paragraph applies shall, notwithstanding the provisions of section 26(3) of the said Act of 1965 (which excludes the application of section 11 of that Act to a person in respect of certain employment), be treated as if it had been a period in respect of which section 11 of that Act had applied.

(7) This paragraph applies to employment of a person in the civil service of the State in an established or unestablished capacity within the meaning of the Superannuation Act 1965, and to employment of a person therein in part-time service where he gives personal service of at least twenty-one hours a week and the remuneration in respect thereof is defrayed entirely out of the Post Office Fund or moneys provided by Parliament.

36.—(1) Notwithstanding paragraph 82 of Schedule 4 to this Act, the Board of Trade may, out of moneys provided by Parliament, make to the Post Office in respect of an asset provided by the Postmaster General for the purposes of his business a grant of the like amount as they might have made to him under section 1 or 2 of the Industrial Development Act 1966 if this Act had not passed.

(2) For the purposes of the foregoing sub-paragraph, an asset shall not be deemed not to have been provided as therein mentioned by reason of the fact that it is delivered to the Post Office on or after the appointed day and is so delivered in fulfilment of a contract entered into before that day by the Postmaster General.

(3) Section 8 of the Industrial Development Act 1966 (conditions) shall have effect as if references therein to Part I of that Act included references to sub-paragraph (1) above.

37.—(1) Notwithstanding paragraph 82 of Schedule 4 to this Act, the Ministry of Commerce for Northern Ireland may, if the Parliament of Northern Ireland makes provision for the defrayal

SCH. 9

1966 c. 41
(N.I.).

out of moneys provided by that Parliament of any expenses which may be incurred by that Ministry under this paragraph, make to the Post Office in respect of an asset provided by the Postmaster General for the purposes of his business a grant of the like amount as it might have made to him under section 1, 2 or 5 of the Industrial Investment (General Assistance) Act (Northern Ireland) 1966 if this Act had not passed.

(2) For the purposes of the foregoing sub-paragraph, an asset shall not be deemed not to have been provided as therein mentioned by reason of the fact that it is delivered to the Post Office on or after the appointed day and is so delivered in fulfilment of a contract entered into before that day by the Postmaster General.

(3) Sections 10 and 11 of the Industrial Investment (General Assistance) Act (Northern Ireland) 1966 (conditions and fraudulent applications) shall have effect as if references therein to that Act included references to sub-paragraph (1) above.

1967 c. 1.

38. Where an interest of the Postmaster General in land vests in the Post Office by virtue of section 16 of this Act and, at a time when the interest was vested in the Postmaster General, the land fell within any of such descriptions of land as, for the purposes of section 84 of the Land Commission Act 1967, were agreed between him and the Treasury as being at that time descriptions of land which, in relation to functions of his, corresponded as nearly as may be to the descriptions of land which were operational land in relation to statutory undertakers, then, for the purposes of section 58 of that Act, the land shall be treated as if, at that time, it had been operational land of the Post Office.

1961 c. 15.

39.—(1) Where—

    (*a*) in relation to relevant land, an act or event falling within Case C occurs between the passing of this Act and the appointed day or has occurred before the passing of this Act and occurs or occurred in circumstances in which, but for the exemptions enjoyed by the Postmaster General as mentioned in section 2(1) of the Post Office Act 1961, a credit would be, or have been, taken to have arisen from the act or event by reason of the case falling within paragraph 2 of Schedule 11 to the Land Commission Act 1967 (carry forward of credit from previous chargeable act or event); or

    (*b*) in relation to land in the case in which an interest therein vests in the Post Office by virtue of section 16 of this Act, an act or event falling within Case E occurs between the passing of this Act and the appointed day or has occurred before the passing of this Act, and occurs or occurred in circumstances in which, but for the exemptions aforesaid, a credit would be, or have been, taken to have arisen from the act or event by reason of the case falling within paragraph 3 of the said Schedule 11;

and a sum is certified by the Treasury to be the sum agreed between them and the Postmaster General or between them and the Post Office as the amount which is to be treated as subsisting or having subsisted on the appointed day in respect of the act or event by way of credit

under the said Schedule 11, then paragraph 6 and Parts II and III   Sch. 9
of the said Schedule 11 shall have effect as if a credit of that amount
were taken to have arisen from a previous chargeable act or event
falling within such of the cases distinguished as Cases A to F in the
Table in section 27(2) of the Land Commission Act 1967 as is certified 1967 c. 1.
by the Treasury as being the Case within which the act or event falls.

(2) For the purposes of the said Schedule 11 as it has effect in any
case by virtue of the foregoing sub-paragraph the original chargeable
interest and the original chargeable unit shall respectively be the
interest in land, and the land, designated in that behalf by the Treasury,
and the original chargeable owner shall be taken to be the Post Office.

(3) Sub-paragraph (1) above shall have effect in relation to an act
or event falling within Case F as it does in relation to one falling
within Case E, with the modifications that for the reference to paragraph 3 of Schedule 11 there shall be substituted a reference to
any provision of regulations made under paragraph 15 of that Schedule
providing for a credit's being taken to have arisen from an act or
event falling within Case F, and for the reference to paragraph 6
and Parts II and III of the said Schedule 11, there shall be substituted
a reference to that paragraph and those Parts as they have effect
by virtue of the said paragraph 15.

(4) In sub-paragraph (1) above, " relevant land " means land in
the case of which an interest therein vests in the Post Office by virtue
of section 16 of this Act or land (other than as aforesaid) in which
the Post Office acquires, after the appointed day, an interest, being an
interest in the case of which the Postmaster General was immediately
before the appointed day under an enforceable contract to purchase
it or had before that day served (and had not before that day withdrawn) a notice to treat for the compulsory purchase thereof, or a
tenancy which on that day the Postmaster General was under an
enforceable contract to take and " Case C," " Case E " and
" Case F " have the same meanings respectively as in Part III of the
Land Commission Act 1967.

40.—(1) Where work begun before the passing of this Act, or
between the passing of this Act and the appointed day, constitutes
development for which planning permission is, by virtue of paragraph
27 of this Schedule, deemed to be granted on that day, then, notwithstanding that the work was so begun it shall, for the purposes of
paragraph 21(7) of Schedule 4 to the Land Commission Act 1967 and
of paragraph 7(2) of Schedule 6 to that Act be treated as if planning
permission for its carrying out had been granted before it was begun.

(2) Where work falling within the foregoing sub-paragraph constitutes the carrying out of a project of material development of
relevant land, other than one which is relevant for the purposes of
paragraph 21 of Schedule 4 to the Land Commission Act 1967, and is
uncompleted at the date which, for the purposes of that paragraph, is
the relevant date in relation to the carrying out of a project of
material development of that land which is relevant for those purposes,
then, notwithstanding anything in sub-paragraph (6) of that paragraph,

SCH. 9

in calculating the rent referred to in paragraph 16 of that Schedule, account shall be taken of the planning permission deemed to have been granted in respect of the development constituted by the work in so far as it authorises the carrying out of the first-mentioned project.

1967 c. 1.

(3) Where work falling within sub-paragraph (1) above constitutes a project of material development of relevant land, then, notwithstanding anything in sub-paragraph (1) of paragraph 7 of Schedule 6 to the Land Commission Act 1967 (but subject to paragraph 8 of that Schedule where that paragraph applies), in calculating any such value as is referred to in paragraph 6 of that Schedule account shall, if the project was begun before, but remained uncompleted at, the relevant date, be taken of the planning permission deemed to have been granted in respect of the development constituted by the work in so far as it relates to the land comprised in that project; and for that purpose sub-paragraph (3) of paragraph 7 shall apply as it applies where account of planning permission is taken by virtue of sub-paragraph (2) thereof.

(4) In this paragraph, " project of material development " has the same meaning as it has for the purposes of Part III of the Land Commission Act 1967.

1967 c. 9.

41.—(1) If, in the case of a hereditament vested in the Post Office by virtue of section 16 of this Act, there is, in compliance with section 37(1) of the General Rate Act 1967, entered in the valuation list immediately before the appointed day, as representing the rateable value of the hereditament, the value upon which is computed any contribution made by the Crown in lieu of rates, then there shall be ascribed in that list to the hereditament under section 19 of that Act a net annual value equal to the value so entered.

(2) Where alterations fall to be made in a valuation list in consequence of the foregoing sub-paragraph, the valuation officer shall cause those alterations to be made therein without any proposal under section 69 of the General Rate Act 1967, and section 87 of that Act (duty of rating authority to give effect to directions as to alteration of a valuation list) shall have effect in relation to this paragraph as it does in relation to any provision of that Act.

(3) No proposal shall be made under section 69 of the General Rate Act 1967 for an alteration of the rateable value ascribed by virtue of this paragraph in a list to—

(a) a hereditament occupied by the Post Office by any such property as follows, namely, posts, wires, underground cables and ducts, telephone kiosks and other equipment not within a building, being property used for the purposes of telecommunications services; or

(b) a hereditament occupied by the Post Office by the underground railway.

(4) Expressions used in this paragraph and in the General Rate Act 1967 have the same meaning in this paragraph as in that Act; and the expression " the underground railway " means the railway constructed, and the works executed, by the Postmaster General in exercise of

the powers conferred by the Post Office (London) Railway Act 1913, SCH. 9
and the railway constructed, and the works associated therewith 1913 c. cxvi.
executed, by him in exercise of the powers conferred by the Post Office 1954 c. xxix.
(Site and Railway) Act 1954.

(5) This paragraph extends to England and Wales only.

42.—(1) If, in the case of lands and heritages vested in the Post Office
by virtue of section 16 of this Act, there is entered in the valuation
roll immediately before the appointed day, as representing the rateable
value of the lands and heritages, the value upon which is computed any
contribution made by the Crown in lieu of rates, then the rateable
value of the lands and heritages on the appointed day shall be taken
to be the value so entered in the valuation roll.

(2) The rateable values of lands and heritages described in section
53(1) of this Act shall remain unaltered until an apportionment as
mentioned in section 53(2) of this Act is made, and the rate to be
levied by a county council on the rateable value entered in the valuation roll in respect of such lands and heritages shall be the mean of
the county rate and the highest aggregate rate levied in the separately
rated areas of the landward area of the county.

(3) In this paragraph " county rate " has the same meaning as in
section 224(1) of the Local Government (Scotland) Act 1947 and other 1947 c. 43.
expressions have the same meanings as in the Local Government 1966 c. 51.
(Scotland) Act 1966.

(4) This paragraph extends to Scotland only.

43.—(1) If, in the case of a hereditament vested in the Post Office
by virtue of section 16 of this Act, there is entered in the valuation
lists immediately before the appointed day, as representing the net
annual value of the hereditament, the amount upon which is computed
any contribution made by the Crown in lieu of rates, then the net
annual value of the hereditament on the appointed day shall be taken
to be the amount so entered in the valuation lists.

(2) A hereditament vested in the Post Office by virtue of section 16
of this Act which, immediately before the appointed day, was, under
section 2 of the Valuation (Ireland) Act 1854, distinguished as exempt 1854 c. 8.
from rates shall, as from that day, be deemed not to be so distinguished.

(3) The Commissioner of Valuation for Northern Ireland shall not,
during the period beginning with the appointed day and ending with
the 31st March next following, make any interim revision of the net
annual value of any hereditament (other than any such hereditament
as is mentioned in section 54(1) of this Act) vested in the Post Office
by virtue of section 16 of this Act unless during that period the Post
Office ceases to occupy the hereditament or there is a change in the
use of the hereditament by the Post Office.

(4) In this paragraph " interim revision " means a revision under
section 13 of the Local Government (Finance) Act (Northern Ireland) 1936 c. 10 (N.I).
1936 or section 4 of the Valuation Acts Amendment Act (Northern 1953 c. 10 (N.I).
Ireland) 1953.

(5) This paragraph extends to Northern Ireland only.

44.—(1) If an order made by virtue of section 67 of the Town and Country Planning Act 1962 or section 29 of the Town and Country Planning Act 1968 for the acquisition by the Postmaster General of any land or rights is effective at the appointed day, proceedings for the acquisition may be continued by the Post Office as if section 55 of this Act had been in force when the order became operative, the order were one made by virtue of that section and confirmed by the Minister, and anything done by or to the Postmaster General after the order became operative had been done by or to the Post Office.

1946 c. 49.

(2) If, at the appointed day, the provisions compliance with which is, by virtue of Schedule 1 to the Acquisition of Land (Authorisation Procedure) Act 1946, requisite in order for an order prepared in draft by a Minister to be made by him, are in course of being complied with with reference to an order prepared in draft by virtue of the said section 67 or the said section 29 for the acquisition by the Postmaster General of any land or rights, then, upon compliance with those provisions being completed, the order may (with any adaptations rendered requisite in consequence of the provisions of this paragraph) be made by the Minister and shall take effect as if it were an order made by the Post Office by virtue of section 55 of this Act and confirmed by him, being an order that authorised the acquisition by the Post Office of that land or, as the case may be, those rights.

1947 c. 42.

1947 c. 53.
1969 c. 30.

(3) In the application of this paragraph to Scotland, for references to the Acquisition of Land (Authorisation Procedure) Act 1946 there shall be substituted references to the Acquisition of Land (Authorisation Procedure) (Scotland) Act 1947 and for references to section 67 of the Town and Country Planning Act 1962 and to section 29 of the Town and Country Planning Act 1968 there shall be substituted respectively references to section 34 of the Town and Country Planning (Scotland) Act 1947 and to section 30 of the Town and Country Planning (Scotland) Act 1969.

1968 c. 73.

45. An application by the Post Office made before the appointed day for an operator's licence under Part V of the Transport Act 1968 shall, if accompanied by a certificate of the Postmaster General certifying that the vehicles proposed to be used under the licence are in use by him, be treated for the purposes of section 94(1) of that Act as an application made by the holder of a carrier's licence in respect of the vehicles.

46.—(1) The Postmaster General shall be under obligation to provide the Post Office with such money as it requires during the period beginning with the day on which this Act is passed and ending with the day immediately preceding the appointed day; and payments in discharge of this obligation shall be made out of the Post Office Fund.

1961 c. 15.

(2) The power conferred by section 9 of the Post Office Act 1961 on the Treasury to make, out of the National Loans Fund, advances to the Postmaster General shall include power to make, out of that

fund, advances to him for the purpose of enabling him to discharge the obligation imposed on him by the foregoing sub-paragraph.

47. All expenses incurred by the Post Office before the appointed day shall, for the purposes of its accounts, be treated as expenses incurred in the first accounting year; and all sums received by the Post Office before that day shall be treated for those purposes as receipts attributable to that year.

48. The following enactments, namely,—

(*a*) section 107(1) of the National Insurance Act 1965 and section 4(8)(*a*) of the Industrial Injuries and Diseases (Old Cases) Act 1967 (which provide that certain orders, regulations and schemes shall not be made unless a draft thereof has been laid before Parliament and approved by resolution of each House);   1965 c. 51. 1967 c. 34.

(*b*) section 108 of the said Act of 1965 (which requires a preliminary draft of any regulations under that Act to be submitted to the National Insurance Advisory Committee); and

(*c*) section 62(2) of the National Insurance (Industrial Injuries) Act 1965 (which requires any proposal to make regulations under that Act to be referred to the Industrial Injuries Advisory Council for consideration and advice);   1965 c. 52.

shall not apply to any regulations or scheme contained in a statutory instrument made before the appointed day if that instrument states that it is made in consequence of this Act; but any such regulations or scheme to which the said section 107(1) or 4(8)(*a*) would otherwise apply shall instead be subject to annulment in pursuance of a resolution of either House of Parliament.

49. Where works on land vested in the Post Office by virtue of this Act are executed by it so as injuriously to affect another person who would, had the works been executed by the Postmaster General, have had a right to receive from him compensation in respect of the injurious affection, that person shall have the right to receive from the Post Office compensation in respect of the injurious affection.

50.—(1) Where, on the appointed day, a matter in dispute between the Postmaster General and another stands referred, under section 8 of the Post Office Savings Bank Act 1954 to the Registrar (as defined by that Act) or to a person to whom the powers and duties under that section of the Registrar have been transferred by virtue of subsection (5) thereof, the Director of Savings shall be substituted for the Postmaster General as a party to the reference; and an award, order or determination made under that section before that day shall, as from that day, bind the Director of Savings.   1954 c. 62.

(2) Where, on the appointed day, a matter in dispute between the Postmaster General and the holder of stock stands referred, under section 4 of the National Debt Act 1958, to the Chief Registrar of friendly societies, the Assistant Registrar of friendly societies in Scotland or a deputy appointed by the Chief Registrar of friendly societies, the Director of Savings shall be substituted for the Postmaster General   1958 c. 6 (7 & 8 Eliz. 2).

SCH. 9

as a party to the reference; and an award made under that section before that day that binds the Postmaster General shall, as from that day, bind the Director of Savings.

1958 c. 6
(7 & 8 Eliz. 2).

51. An indemnity given under section 13 of the National Debt Act 1958 to the Postmaster General shall, if effective at the appointed day, have effect, as from that day, as if given to the Director of Savings.

1939 c. 117.
1968 c. 13.

52. Any reference to the Postmaster General in a prospectus issued with respect to securities issued under the National Loans Act 1939 or the National Loans Act 1968 shall, as from the appointed day, be construed as referring to the Director of Savings.

1925 c. 20.

1881 c. 41.

53. Where the Crown retains possession of any documents of title to any land any part of which is vested by virtue of section 16 of this Act in the Post Office, the Minister shall be assumed to have given to the Post Office an acknowledgment in writing of the right of the Post Office to production of those documents and to delivery of copies thereof, and, so far as relates to land in England or Wales, section 64 of the Law of Property Act 1925 shall have effect accordingly, and on the basis that the acknowledgment did not contain any such expression of contrary intention as is mentioned in that section and, so far as relates to land in Northern Ireland, section 9 of the Conveyancing Act 1881 shall have similar effect.

1947 c. 44.

54. Any legal proceedings or applications pending on the appointed day by or against the Crown, being proceedings or applications instituted or made by or against the Postmaster General or his department (but not being proceedings in the case of which express provision is made by some other provision of this Act with respect to the continuance thereof) may be continued by or against the appropriate government department authorised for the purposes of the Crown Proceedings Act 1947.

Section 138.

SCHEDULE 10

SPECIAL TRANSITIONAL PROVISIONS WITH RESPECT TO PATENTS FOR INVENTIONS AND REGISTERED DESIGNS

PART I

PATENTS FOR INVENTIONS

1949 c. 87.

1. For the purposes of so much of section 32(1) of the Patents Act 1949 as provides that a patent may be revoked on the grounds that the invention, so far as claimed in any claim of the complete specification, was secretly used in the United Kingdom before the priority date of that claim, no account shall be taken of any use, on or after the appointed day, of the invention by the Post Office or a person authorised by it, in consequence of the applicant for the patent or any person from whom he derives title having communicated or disclosed the invention directly or indirectly,—

(*a*) before the appointed day, to a government department or person authorised by a government department ; or (*b*) on or after the appointed day, in pursuance of an agreement in the case of which rights and liabilities thereunder vest in the Post Office by virtue of sections 16 to 18 of this Act, to the Post Office or a person authorised by it.

2.—(1) Where an agreement in the case of which rights and liabilities thereunder vest in the Post Office by virtue of sections 16 to 18 of this Act contains provision—

(*a*) conferring authority under section 46(1) of the Patents Act 1949 c. 87. 1949 for the making, use or exercise of an invention for a purpose referable to the functions of the Postmaster General ; or

(*b*) providing for the conferring by the Postmaster General on a person of such an authority under that section,

then, on and after the appointed day,—

(i) the authority conferred by the agreement, and any authority conferred before that day in pursuance of such a provision as is mentioned in head (*b*) above, shall continue in force and shall have effect so as to authorise the making, use and exercise of the invention for a purpose referable to the functions of the Post Office, being a purpose corresponding to that mentioned in head (*a*) above ; and

(ii) the provision described in head (*b*) above shall have effect as if it provided for the conferring by the Post Office of an authority having such effect as is mentioned in the last foregoing head.

(2) For the purpose of fulfilling obligations imposed on it by virtue of this paragraph, the Post Office shall, on and after the appointed day, have power to confer such an authority as is mentioned in head (ii) of the foregoing sub-paragraph.

(3) Nothing in the Patents Act 1949 shall be taken to prevent the use by the Post Office, for a purpose referable to its functions, of any articles made and supplied to it in the exercise of an authority continued in force by, or conferred by virtue of, this paragraph.

3. Where, by an agreement in force immediately before the appointed day and made in pursuance of subsection (3) of section 46 of the Patents Act 1949, terms are agreed upon which use of an invention may be made by virtue of that section for the manufacture of articles by the department of the Postmaster General, or the manufacture and supply to that department of articles by a person authorised by it,—

(*a*) the agreement shall (so far as it relates to the use of the invention by, or with the authority of, that department) have effect as from the appointed day as if, for any reference to use by virtue of that section, whether or not it is expressed to be for any purpose referable to functions of the Postmaster General, there were substituted a reference to use by virtue of this paragraph for any purpose referable to functions of the Post Office corresponding to a purpose

SCH. 10

referable to functions of the Postmaster General, being a purpose in the case of which use of the invention therefor fell within the agreement, and the rights and liabilities of the Postmaster General subsisting immediately before the appointed day under the agreement shall, on that day, vest in the Post Office by virtue of this paragraph, and paragraph 2 of Schedule 9 to this Act shall apply as it does where rights and liabilities so vest by virtue of sections 16 to 18 of this Act ;

(b) the Post Office shall have power to use the invention for the manufacture of articles on the terms of the agreement as it has effect by virtue of this paragraph, and any person authorised by the Post Office in writing shall have power to use the invention for manufacture and supply to the Post Office on such terms, and the Post Office shall, accordingly, have power to use, for purposes referable to its functions, articles so manufactured by, or supplied to, it.

1949 c. 87.

4.—(1) If an obligation of the department of the Postmaster General incurred under section 46(5) of the Patents Act 1949 to give a notification or furnish information to a person has not been fulfilled before the appointed day, the Post Office shall, on that day, become under obligation to give the notification or furnish the information to that person ; and the Post Office shall, on and after that day, be under obligation to furnish to any person who requires it such other information as to the extent of use before that day of an invention as that department could have been required under the said section 46(5) to furnish to that person if this Act had not passed.

(2) Subject to sub-paragraph (4) below, where, on or after the appointed day, use of an invention is begun under an authority continued in force by, or conferred by virtue of, paragraph 2 of this Schedule, the Post Office shall notify the patentee as soon as practicable after the use is begun.

(3) Subject as aforesaid, the Post Office shall furnish the patentee with such information as he may from time to time require as to the extent of use, if any, of the invention after the beginning of the appointed day under such an authority as is mentioned in the last foregoing sub-paragraph or by virtue of paragraph 3 of this Schedule.

(4) Nothing in the foregoing provisions of this paragraph shall impose on the Post Office an obligation to give notification or furnish information if the Minister notifies it that it is contrary to the public interest to do so.

5. Where, in the case of an invention, an authority for its use is continued in force by, or is conferred by virtue of, paragraph 2 of this Schedule, then—

(a) if and so far as the invention has, before the priority date of the relevant claim of the complete specification, been duly recorded by or tried by or on behalf of a government department otherwise than in consequence of the communication thereof, directly or indirectly, by the patentee or a person from whom he derives title, any use of the invention by virtue of the said paragraph 2 may be made free of any royalty or other payment to the patentee ;

(*b*) if and so far as the invention has not been so recorded or tried as aforesaid, any use of the invention by virtue of the said paragraph 2 at any time after the acceptance of the complete specification in respect of the patent or in consequence of any such communication as aforesaid, shall—

(i) except where an agreement as to terms for the use of the invention was made before the appointed day under section 46(3) of the Patents Act 1949 or a deter- mination as to those terms was made by the court under section 48 of that Act, be made upon such terms as may be agreed upon, either before or after the use, between the Post Office and the patentee, or as may, in default of such an agreement, be determined by the court on a reference under paragraph 9 of this Schedule ;

(ii) in the said excepted case, be made upon the terms of the said agreement or determination.

6. The authority of the Post Office in respect of an invention may be given under paragraph 2 or 3 of this Schedule either before or after the patent is granted and either before or after the acts in respect of which the authority is given are done, but not so as to authorise the doing before the appointed day of any act ; and such authority may be given to any person whether or not he is authorised, directly or indirectly, by the patentee to make, use, exercise or vend the invention.

7.—(1) The Post Office shall have power to use, for a purpose referable to its functions, any article vested in it and made before the appointed day, in the exercise of the powers conferred by section 46 of the Patents Act 1949, by a government department, or a person authorised by a government department.

(2) In the case of articles described in the foregoing sub-paragraph, and articles vested in the Post Office and made on or after the appointed day under an authority continued in force by, or conferred by virtue of, paragraph 2 of this Schedule, the Post Office, if the circumstances are such that their supply to the government of a country outside the United Kingdom is, by virtue of section 46(6) of the Patents Act 1949 included among the services of the Crown, shall have power to sell them to that government, and if the circumstances are such that their supply to the United Nations is, by virtue of that section, so included, shall have power to sell them to that organisation.

(3) In the case of articles mentioned in the last foregoing sub-paragraph and articles vested in the Post Office and made on or after the appointed day by virtue of paragraph 3 of this Schedule, the Post Office shall have power to sell to any person such, if any, of them as are not required for a purpose referable to functions of the Post Office.

(4) The purchaser of any articles sold in the exercise of powers conferred by this paragraph, and any person claiming through him, shall have power to deal with them in the same manner as if the patent were held by or on behalf of the Post Office.

8 —(1) In relation to any use of a patented invention or an invention in respect of which an application for a patent is pending, being a use made on or after the appointed day for purposes referable to functions of the Post Office—

> (*a*) by the Post Office under any power conferred by, or by virtue of, the foregoing provisions of this Act, or by its using articles supplied to it by the patentee or applicant for the patent under an agreement in the case of which rights and liabilities thereunder vest in the Post Office by virtue of sections 16 to 18 of this Act ;

> (*b*) by a person authorised by an authority continued in force by paragraph 2 above or conferred by virtue of that paragraph or paragraph 3 above ;

> (*c*) by the patentee or applicant for the patent, for the purpose of satisfying a liability under an agreement in the case of which rights and liabilities thereunder vest in the Post Office by virtue of sections 16 to 18 of this Act ;

the provisions of any licence, assignment or agreement made—

> (i) before the appointed day, between the patentee or applicant for the patent or any person who derives title from him or from whom he derives title, and any person other than a government department ; or

> (ii) on or after the appointed day, between the patentee or applicant for the patent or any person who derives title from him or from whom he derives title, and any person other than the Post Office ;

shall be of no effect so far as those provisions restrict or regulate the use of the invention, or any model, document or information relating thereto, or provide for the making of payments in respect of any such use, or calculated by reference thereto ; and the reproduction or publication of any model or document in connection with the said use shall not be deemed to be an infringement of any copyright subsisting in the model or document.

(2) Where an exclusive licence granted otherwise than for royalties or other benefits determined by reference to the use of the invention is in force under the patent, then,—

> (*a*) in relation to any use of the invention which, but for the provisions of this paragraph and paragraph 2 of this Schedule would constitute an infringement of the rights of the licensee, paragraph 5 of this Schedule shall have effect as if, for the reference in sub-paragraph (*b*) thereof to the patentee, there were substituted a reference to the licensee ; and

(*b*) in relation to any use of the invention by the licensee by virtue of an authority continued in force by, or conferred by virtue of, paragraph 2 of this Schedule, paragraph 5 thereof shall have effect as if sub-paragraph (*b*) were omitted.

(3) Subject to the provisions of the last foregoing sub-paragraph, where the patent, or the right to apply for or obtain the patent, has been assigned to the patentee in consideration of royalties or other benefits determined by reference to the use of the invention, then—

(*a*) in relation to any use of the invention by virtue of paragraph 2 of this Schedule, paragraph 5 thereof shall have effect as if, in sub-paragraph (*b*), the reference to the patentee included a reference to the assignor, and any sum payable by virtue of that paragraph or an agreement referred to in paragraph 3 of this Schedule shall—

(i) except where an agreement was made before the appointed day between the patentee and the assignor as to the proportions in which any sum payable in relation to the use of the invention by or under the authority of the department of the Postmaster General by virtue of section 46 of the Patents Act 1949 should be divided 1949 c. 87. or a determination as to those proportions was made by the court under section 48 of that Act before the appointed day, be divided between the patentee and the assignor in such proportions as may be agreed between them or as may in default of agreement be determined by the court on a reference under paragraph 9 of this Schedule ;

(ii) in the said excepted case, be divided in such proportions as may be provided for by the said agreement or determination ; and

(*b*) in relation to any use of the invention made after the beginning of the appointed day, being use referable to the functions of the Post Office and made by the patentee for the purpose mentioned in sub-paragraph (1)(*c*) above, paragraph 5(*b*) of this Schedule shall have effect as if that use were made by virtue of an authority continued in force by paragraph 2 of this Schedule.

(4) Where, under paragraph 5 of this Schedule or such an agreement as is referred to in paragraph 3 thereof, payments are required to be made by the Post Office to a patentee in respect of any use of an invention, any person, being the holder of an exclusive licence under the patent (not being such a licence as is mentioned in sub-paragraph (2) of this paragraph) authorising him to make that use of the invention, shall—

(*a*) except where an agreement as to the recovery from the patentee of a part of the payments made under section 46(3) of the Patents Act 1949 by the department of the Postmaster General in respect of the use of the invention was made before the appointed day under section 47(4) of that Act or a determination was made before that day under section 48 of that Act by the court as to such recovery, be entitled to recover from the patentee such part (if any) of those payments as may be agreed upon between that person and the patentee or as may, in default of agreement, be determined by the court on a reference under paragraph 9 of this Schedule to be just having regard to any expenditure incurred by that person—

(i) in developing the said invention, or

(ii) in making payments to the patentee, other than royalties or other payments determined by reference to the use of the invention, in consideration of the licence ;

(b) in the said excepted case, be entitled to recover such part, if any, of the payments as may be provided for by the said agreement or determination ;

and if that person, at any time before the amount of any such payment has been settled, gives to the Post Office notice in writing of his interest, any agreement as to the amount of that payment shall be of no effect unless it is made with his consent ; and, for the purposes of this sub-paragraph, a notice given before the appointed day to the department of the Postmaster General in pursuance of section 47(4) of the Patents Act 1949 shall have effect as if it had been given to the Post Office.

(5) Where any models, documents or information relating to an invention are used in connection with any such use of the invention as is described in sub-paragraph (1) above, paragraph 5 of this Schedule shall, whether or not it applies to the use of the invention, apply to the use of the models, documents or information as if, for the reference therein to the patentee, there were substituted a reference to the person entitled to the benefit of any provision of a licence, assignment or agreement which is rendered inoperative by the said sub-paragraph (1) in relation to that use.

(6) Nothing in this paragraph shall be construed as authorising the disclosure to the Post Office or any other person of any model, document or information to the use of which this paragraph applies in contravention of any such licence, assignment or agreement as aforesaid.

9.—(1) Any dispute as to the exercise by the Post Office or a person authorised by it of powers subsisting by virtue of the foregoing provisions of this Schedule, or as to terms for use thereunder of an invention or any models, documents or information relating to an invention, or as to the right of any person to receive any part of a payment made in pursuance of paragraph 5 of this Schedule or any such agreement as is referred to in paragraph 3 thereof may be referred to the court by either party to the dispute in such manner as is prescribed by the rules for the time being in force for the purposes of section 48(1) of the Patents Act 1949.

(2) Subsections (2) to (5) of section 48 of the Patents Act 1949 shall have effect in relation to proceedings under the foregoing sub-paragraph and disputes that may be determined thereunder as

they do in relation to proceedings and disputes that may be determined under subsection (1) of the said section 48, but subject to the modifications that—

    (*a*) in subsection (2), for references to a government department there shall be substituted references to the Post Office ;

    (*b*) in subsection (3), for the references to section 46 of that Act and to the opinion of the government department there shall be substituted respectively references to paragraph 5(*a*) of this Schedule and to the opinion of the Minister stated in a certificate signed by him ; and

    (*c*) in subsection (4), for the first reference to a government department there shall be substituted a reference to the Post Office, for the second such reference there shall be substituted a reference to the department of the Postmaster General or the Post Office, and the reference to the services of the Crown shall include a reference to the purposes of the Post Office.

(3) Any proceedings under the said section 48 which are in progress immediately before the appointed day, being proceedings to which the department of the Postmaster General is a party, may be continued with the substitution of the Post Office for that department ; but in relation to such proceedings, subsection (3) of the said section 48 shall have effect with the substitution, for the reference to the opinion of a government department, of a reference to the opinion of the Minister stated in a certificate signed by him.

10.—(1) Where, in pursuance of an agreement made before the appointed day in relation to an invention claimed under a complete specification, between the department of the Postmaster General and the applicant for the patent, or any person from whom he derives title, being an agreement to which the Post Office has become a party by virtue of this Act, communication of the invention is made to the Post Office or a person authorised by it to investigate the invention or its merits, the invention shall not be deemed to have been anticipated by reason only of that communication or of anything done in consequence thereof for the purposes of the investigation.

(2) An authorisation to investigate an invention given under subsection (1) of section 51 of the Patents Act 1949 by the department of the Postmaster General and in force immediately before the appointed day shall remain in force on and after that day as if given by the Post Office and, in relation to that invention, the said subsection (1) shall have effect as if references to a government department included references to the Post Office.

11. Expressions to which meanings are assigned by the Patents Act 1949 for the purposes of that Act have those meanings also for the purposes of this Part of this Schedule.

Part II

Registered Designs

12.—(1) Where an agreement in the case of which rights and liabilities thereunder vest in the Post Office by virtue of sections 16 to 18 of this Act contains provision—

(*a*) conferring authority under paragraph 1(1) of Schedule 1 to the Registered Designs Act 1949 for the use of a registered design for a purpose referable to the functions of the Postmaster General ; or

(*b*) providing for the conferring by the Postmaster General on a person of such an authority under that paragraph,

then, on and after the appointed day,—

(i) the authority conferred by the agreement, and any authority conferred before that day in pursuance of such a provision as is mentioned in head (*b*) above, shall continue in force and shall have effect so as to authorise the use of the design for a purpose referable to the functions of the Post Office, being a purpose corresponding to that mentioned in head (*a*) above ; and

(ii) the provision described in head (*b*) above shall have effect as if it provided for the conferring by the Post Office of an authority having such effect as is mentioned in the last foregoing head.

(2) For the purpose of fulfilling obligations imposed on it by virtue of this paragraph, the Post Office shall, on and after the appointed day, have power to confer such an authority as is mentioned in head (ii) of the foregoing sub-paragraph.

13. Where, by an agreement in force immediately before the appointed day and made in pursuance of sub-paragraph (3) of paragraph 1 of Schedule 1 to the Registered Designs Act 1949, terms are agreed upon which use of a design may be made by virtue of that paragraph for the manufacture of articles by the department of the Postmaster General, or the manufacture and supply to that department of articles by a person authorised by it,—

(*a*) the agreement shall (so far as it relates to the use of the design by, or with the authority of, that department) have effect as from the appointed day as if, for any reference to use by virtue of that paragraph, whether or not it is expressed to be for any purpose referable to functions of the Postmaster General, there were substituted a reference to use by virtue of this paragraph for any purpose referable to functions of the Post Office corresponding to a purpose referable to functions of the Postmaster General, being a purpose in the case of which use of the design therefor fell within the agreement, and the rights and liabilities of the Postmaster General subsisting immediately before the appointed day under the agreement shall on that day vest in the Post Office by virtue of this paragraph, and paragraph 2 of Schedule 9 to this Act shall apply as it does where rights and liabilities so vest by virtue of sections 16 to 18 of this Act ;

SCH. 10

(*b*) the Post Office shall have power to use the design for the manufacture of articles on the terms of the agreement as it has effect by virtue of this paragraph, and any person authorised by the Post Office in writing shall have power to use the design for manufacture and supply to the Post Office on such terms.

14.—(1) If an obligation of the department ot the Postmaster General incurred under paragraph 1(5) of Schedule 1 to the Registered Designs Act 1949 to give a notification or furnish information to a person has not been fulfilled before the appointed day, the Post Office shall, on that day, become under obligation to give the notification or furnish the information to that person ; and the Post Office shall, on and after that day, be under obligation to furnish to any person who requires it such other information as to the extent of use before that day of a registered design as that department could have been required under the said paragraph 1(5) to furnish to that person if this Act had not passed.

1949 c. 88.

(2) Subject to sub-paragraph (4) below, where, on or after the appointed day, use of a registered design is begun under an authority continued in force by, or conferred by virtue of, paragraph 12 of this Schedule the Post Office shall notify the registered proprietor as soon as practicable after the use is begun.

(3) Subject as aforesaid, the Post Office shall furnish the registered proprietor with such information as he may from time to time require as to the extent of use, if any, of the registered design after the beginning of the appointed day under such an authority as is mentioned in the last foregoing sub-paragraph or by virtue of paragraph 13 of this Schedule.

(4) Nothing in the foregoing provisions of this paragraph shall impose on the Post Office an obligation to give notification or furnish information if the Minister notifies it that it is contrary to the public interest to do so.

15. Where, in the case of a design, an authority for its use is continued in force by, or is conferred by virtue of, paragraph 12 of this Schedule, then—

(*a*) if and so far as the design has, before the date of registration thereof, been duly recorded by or applied by or on behalf of a government department otherwise than in consequence of the communication of the design, directly or indirectly, by the registered proprietor or a person from whom he derives title, any use of the design by virtue of the said paragraph 12 may be made free of any royalty or other payment to the registered proprietor ;

2 R

(*b*) if and so far as the design has not been so recorded or applied as aforesaid, any use of the design by virtue of the said paragraph 12 at any time after the date of registration thereof or in consequence of any such communication as aforesaid, shall—

(i) except in a case where an agreement as to terms for the use of the design was made before the appointed day under paragraph 1(3) of Schedule 1 to the Registered Designs Act 1949 or a determination as to those terms was made by the court under paragraph 3 of that Schedule, be made upon such terms as may be agreed upon, either before or after the use, between the Post Office and the registered proprietor or as may, in default of such an agreement, be determined by the court on a reference under paragraph 19 of this Schedule ;

(ii) in the said excepted case, be made upon the terms of the said agreement or determination.

16. The authority of the Post Office in respect of a design may be given under paragraph 12 or 13 of this Schedule either before or after the design is registered and either before or after the acts in respect of which the authority is given are done, but not so as to authorise the doing before the appointed day of any act ; and such authority may be given to any person whether or not he is authorised, directly or indirectly, by the registered proprietor to use the design.

17.—(1) In the case of articles vested in the Post Office and made before the appointed day, in the exercise of the powers conferred by paragraph 1 of Schedule 1 to the Registered Designs Act 1949, and articles so vested and made on or after the appointed day under an authority continued in force by, or conferred by virtue of, paragraph 12 of this Schedule, the Post Office, if the circumstances are such that their supply to the government of a country outside the United Kingdom is, by virtue of paragraph 1(6) of the said Schedule 1 included among the services of the Crown, shall have power to sell them to that government, and if the circumstances are such that their supply to the United Nations is, by virtue of that paragraph, so included, shall have power to sell them to that organisation.

(2) In the case of articles mentioned in the last foregoing sub-paragraph and articles vested in the Post Office and made on or after the appointed day by virtue of paragraph 13 of this Schedule, the Post Office shall have power to sell to any person such, if any, of them as are not required for a purpose referable to functions of the Post Office.

(3) The purchaser of any articles sold in the exercise of powers conferred by this paragraph, and any person claiming through him, shall have power to deal with them in the same manner as if the rights in the registered design were held by or on behalf of the Post Office.

18.—(1) In relation to any use of a registered design or a design in respect of which an application for registration is pending, being a use made on or after the appointed day for purposes referable to functions of the Post Office—

(*a*) by the Post Office under any power conferred by or by virtue of the foregoing provisions of this Act ;

(*b*) by a person authorised by an authority continued in force by paragraph 12 above or conferred by virtue of that paragraph or paragraph 13 above ;

(*c*) by the registered proprietor or applicant for registration for the purpose of satisfying a liability under an agreement in the case of which rights and liabilities thereunder vest in the Post Office by virtue of sections 16 to 18 of this Act ;

the provisions of any licence, assignment or agreement made,—

(i) before the appointed day, between the registered proprietor or applicant for registration or any person who derives title from him or from whom he derives title and any person other than a government department ; or

(ii) on or after the appointed day, between the registered proprietor or applicant for registration or any person who derives title from him or from whom he derives title and any person other than the Post Office ;

shall be of no effect so far as those provisions restrict or regulate the use of the design, or any model, document or information relating thereto, or provide for the making of payments in respect of any such use, or calculated by reference thereto ; and the reproduction or publication of any model or document in connection with the said use shall not be deemed to be an infringement of any copyright subsisting in the model or document.

(2) Where an exclusive licence granted otherwise than for royalties or other benefits determined by reference to the use of the design is in force under the registered design, then—

(*a*) in relation to any use of the design which, but for the provisions of this paragraph and paragraph 12 of this Schedule would constitute an infringement of the rights of the licensee, paragraph 15 of this Schedule shall have effect as if, for the reference in sub-paragraph (*b*) thereof to the registered proprietor, there were substituted a reference to the licensee ; and

(*b*) in relation to any use of the design by the licensee by virtue of an authority continued in force by, or conferred by virtue of, paragraph 12 of this Schedule, paragraph 15 thereof shall have effect as if sub-paragraph (*b*) were omitted.

(3) Subject to the provisions of the last foregoing sub-paragraph, where the registered design or the right to apply for or obtain

Sch. 10

registration of the design has been assigned to the registered proprietor in consideration of royalties or other benefits determined by reference to the use of the design, then—

(*a*) in relation to any use of the design by virtue of paragraph 12 of this Schedule, paragraph 15 thereof shall have effect as if, in sub-paragraph (*b*), the reference to the registered proprietor included a reference to the assignor, and any sum payable by virtue of that paragraph or an agreement referred to in paragraph 13 of this Schedule shall—

(i) except in a case where an agreement was made before the appointed day between the registered proprietor and the assignor as to the proportions in which any sum payable in relation to the use of the design by or under the authority of the department of the Postmaster General by virtue of paragraph 1 of Schedule 1 to the Registered Designs Act 1949 should be divided or a determination as to those proportions was made by the court under paragraph 3 of that Schedule before the appointed day, be divided between them in such proportions as may be agreed between them or as may in default of agreement be determined by the court on a reference under paragraph 19 of this Schedule ;

1949 c. 88.

(ii) in the said excepted case, be divided in such proportions as may be provided for by the said agreement or determination ; and

(*b*) in relation to any use of the design made after the beginning of the appointed day, being use referable to the functions of the Post Office and made by the registered proprietor for the purpose mentioned in sub-paragraph (1)(*c*) above, paragraph 15(*b*) of this Schedule shall have effect as if that use were made by virtue of an authority continued in force by paragraph 12 of this Schedule.

(4) Where, under paragraph 15 of this Schedule or such an agreement as is referred to in paragraph 13 thereof, payments are required to be made by the Post Office to a registered proprietor in respect of any use of a design, any person, being the holder of an exclusive licence under the registered design (not being such a licence as is mentioned in sub-paragraph (2) of this paragraph) authorising him to make that use of the design, shall—

(*a*) except where an agreement as to the recovery from the registered proprietor of a part of the payments made under paragraph 1(3) of the said Schedule 1 by the department of the Postmaster General in respect of the use of the design was made before the appointed day under paragraph 2(4) of that Schedule or a determination was made before that day under paragraph 3 of that Schedule by the court as to such recovery, be entitled to recover from the registered proprietor such part (if any) of those payments as may be agreed upon between that person and the registered proprietor or as may, in default of agreement be determined by the court on a reference under paragraph 19 of this Schedule, to be just having regard to any expenditure incurred by that person—

(i) in developing the said design ; or

(ii) in making payments to the registered proprietor, other than royalties or other payments determined by reference to the use of the design, in consideration of the licence ;

(*b*) in the said excepted case, be entitled to recover such part, if any, of the payments as may be provided for by the said agreement or determination ;

and if, at any time before the amount of any such payment has been settled, that person gives to the Post Office notice in writing of his interest, any agreement as to the amount of that payment shall be of no effect unless it is made with his consent ; and for the purposes of this sub-paragraph, a notice given before the appointed day to the department of the Postmaster General in pursuance of paragraph 2(4) of the said Schedule 1 shall have effect as if it had been given to the Post Office.

(5) Where any models, documents or information relating to a registered design are used in connection with any such use of the design as is described in sub-paragraph (1) above, paragraph 15 of this Schedule shall, whether or not it applies to the use of the design, apply to the use of the models, documents or information as if, for the reference therein to the registered proprietor, there were substituted a reference to the person entitled to the benefit of any provision of a licence, assignment or agreement which is rendered inoperative by the said sub-paragraph (1) in relation to that use.

(6) Nothing in this paragraph shall be construed as authorising the disclosure to the Post Office or any other person of any model, document or information to the use of which this paragraph applies in contravention of any such licence, assignment or agreement as aforesaid.

19.—(1) Any dispute as to the exercise by the Post Office or a person authorised by it of powers subsisting by virtue of this Part of this Schedule, or as to terms for use thereunder of a design, or any models, documents or information relating to a design, or as to the right of any person to receive any part of a payment made in pursuance of paragraph 15 of this Schedule or any such agreement as is referred to in paragraph 13 thereof may be referred to the court by either party to the dispute in such manner as is prescribed by the rules for the time being in force for the purposes of paragraph 3(1) of Schedule 1 to the Registered Designs Act 1949.

(2) Sub-paragraphs (2) to (5) of paragraph 3 of the said Schedule 1 shall have effect in relation to proceedings under the foregoing sub-paragraph and disputes that may be determined thereunder as they

SCH. 10

do in relation to proceedings and disputes that may be determined under sub-paragraph (1) of the said paragraph 3, but subject to the modifications that—

(*a*) in sub-paragraph (2), for references to a government department there shall be substituted references to the Post Office ;

(*b*) in sub-paragraph (3), for the references to paragraph 1 of that Schedule and to the opinion of the government department there shall be substituted respectively references to paragraph 15(*a*) of this Schedule and to the opinion of the Minister stated in a certificate signed by him ; and

(*c*) in sub-paragraph (4), for the first reference to a government department there shall be substituted a reference to the Post Office, for the second such reference there shall be substituted a reference to the department of the Postmaster General or the Post Office, and the reference to the services of the Crown shall include a reference to the purposes of the Post Office.

(3) Any proceedings under the said paragraph 3 which are in progress immediately before the appointed day, being proceedings to which the department of the Postmaster General is a party, may be continued with the substitution of the Post Office for that department ; but in relation to such proceedings, sub-paragraph (3) of the said paragraph 3 shall have effect with the substitution, for the reference to the opinion of a government department, of a reference to the opinion of the Minister stated in a certificate signed by him.

20.—(1) Where, in pursuance of an agreement made before the appointed day in relation to a design between the department of the Postmaster General and the proprietor of the design or any person from whom he derives title, being an agreement to which the Post Office has become a party by virtue of this Act, communication of the design is made to the Post Office or a person authorised by it to consider the merits of the design, an application for the registration of the design shall not be refused and the registration of the design shall not be invalidated by reason only of that communication or of anything done in consequence thereof.

1949 c. 88.

(2) An authorisation to consider the merits of a design given under subsection (3) of section 6 of the Registered Designs Act 1949 by the department of the Postmaster General and in force immediately before the appointed day shall remain in force on and after that day as if given by the Post Office and, in relation to that design, the said subsection (3) shall have effect as if references to a government department included references to the Post Office.

21. Expressions to which meanings are assigned by the Registered Designs Act 1949 for the purposes of that Act have those meanings also for the purposes of this Part of this Schedule.

SCHEDULE 11

Section 141.

REPEALS AND REVOCATIONS

PART I

ENACTMENTS REPEALED ON THE PASSING OF THIS ACT

Chapter	Short Title	Extent of Repeal
1 & 2 Eliz. 2. c. 36.	The Post Office Act 1953.	Section 66.
2 & 3 Eliz. 2. c. 62.	The Post Office Savings Bank Act 1954.	Section 19(3). In section 24(1), the words from " and a draft " onwards.
1966, c. 12.	The Post Office Savings Bank Act 1966.	Section 3(4).

The above repeal of section 24(1) of the Post Office Savings Bank Act 1954 shall not render section 6(1) of the Statutory Instruments 1964 c. 36. Act 1946 inoperative as respects an instrument whereof a draft has been laid before Parliament before the passing of this Act.

PART II

ENACTMENTS REPEALED ON THE APPOINTED DAY

Enactment of the Parliament of Great Britain

Chapter	Title	Extent of Repeal
39 Geo. 3. c. lxxiii.	An Act for making and maintaining a Tunnel or Road under the River Thames, from or near to the Town of Gravesend, in the County of Kent, to or near to Tilbury Fort, in the County of Essex.	In section 43, the words from " or for or in respect of " (where last occurring) to " Deputies ".

Enactments of the Parliament of the United Kingdom

Chapter	Title or Short Title	Extent of Repeal
43 Geo. 3. c. cxxviii.	An Act for the Improvement of the Town of Bedford, in the County of Bedford, and for rebuilding the Bridge over the River Ouze, in the said Town.	In section 69, the words from " or any Horses or Carriages " (where secondly occurring) to " conveying the same ".

Chapter	Title or Short Title	Extent of Repeal
46 Geo. 3. c. xlv.	An Act for taking down and rebuilding the Bridge across the River Severn at Gloucester, called the Westgate Bridge, and for opening convenient Avenues thereto.	In section 24, the words from " for any Horse " (where first occurring) to " conveying the same; or ".
47 Geo. 3. Sess. 2. c. xxxv.	An Act to enable the Reverend Alban Thomas Jones Gwynne, his Heirs and Assigns, to repair and enlarge or rebuild the Quay or Pier within the Harbour or Port of Aberayron, in the County of Cardigan; and to improve the said Harbour, and to regulate the Moorings of Ships and Vessels therein.	In section 14, the words from " nor any Ship " (where first occurring) to " Postmaster General ".
49 Geo. 3. c. cxliii.	An Act for taking down and rebuilding the Whole or Part of a certain Bridge called Wallingford Bridge, in the Borough of Wallingford, in the County of Berks; and for opening, widening and improving the Avenues or Approaches to the said Bridge.	In section 23, the words from " nor for any Horse " (where secondly occurring) to " conveying the same ".
49 Geo. 3. c. cxliv.	An Act for taking down and rebuilding certain Parts of North Bridge and Tickford Bridge, in the Parishes of Newport Pagnell and Lathbury in the County of Buckingham; and for widening and making more commodious the said Bridge, and the Approaches thereto.	In section 21, the words from " or any Horses " (where secondly occurring) to " conveying the same ".

Chapter	Title or Short Title	Extent of Repeal
53 Geo. 3. c. cxxv.	An Act for further improving the Communication between the County of Edinburgh and the County of Fife, by the Ferries cross the Frith of Forth, between Leith and Newhaven, in the County of Edinburgh, and Kinghorn and Bruntisland in the County of Fife.	In section 41, the words from " for Horses " (where first occurring) to " conveying the same, nor ".
57 Geo. 3. c. lxx.	An Act for improving the Harbour of Blakeney, within the Port of Blakeney and Clay, in the County of Norfolk.	In section 35, the words " Post Office ".
60 Geo. 3 & 1 Geo. 4. c. iii.	An Act to continue and amend several Acts for building a Bridge over the River Lea, at Jeremy's Ferry, and for repairing Roads from there into the great Roads at Snaresbrooke, in the County of Essex, and at Clapton, in the County of Middlesex.	In section 13, the words from " or for any Horse " (where first occurring) to " guarding the same ".
1 Geo. 4. c. v.	An Act for repealing an Act of His late Majesty's Reign, for making a Harbour in the Cove of Beer, in the County of Devon, and for granting more effectual powers for effecting the Purpose aforesaid.	In section 14, the words " or Post Office ".
1 Geo. 4. c. xl.	An Act for repairing or taking down and rebuilding the Bridge within the Borough and Town of Weymouth and Melcombe Regis, in the County of Dorset.	In section 26, the words from " or for any Horses " (where secondly occurring) to " guarding the same ".

2 R*

Chapter	Title or Short Title	Extent of Repeal
1 Geo. 4. c. li.	An Act for building a Bridge over the River Wensum, in the City of Norwich, at or near the Duke's Palace in the said City.	In section 55, the words from "for any Horse" (where first occurring) to "guarding the same; or ".
1 & 2 Geo. 4. c. xcviii.	An Act for more effectually enlarging, deepening, improving, and maintaining the Harbour of Saltcoats, in the County of Ayr.	In section 21, the words " of His Majesty's Postmaster or Postmasters General ".
1 & 2 Geo. 4. c. xcix.	An Act for improving and maintaining the Harbour, Pier or Cobb, at the Port and Borough of Lyme Regis, in the County of Dorset.	In section 21, the words " or Post-Office ".
1 & 2 Geo. 4. c. cxv.	An Act to alter and amend an Act of His late Majesty's Reign, intituled An Act to enable His Majesty to vest the Sands of Traeth Mawr, dividing the Counties of Carnarvon and Merioneth, in William Alexander Madocks Esquire, and for building Quays and other Works, and for the Purpose of facilitating the landing, loading, and unloading of Ships and Vessels frequenting the Harbour of Port Madoc, in the said County of Carnarvon.	In section 20, the words " or Post Office ".
3 Geo. 4. c. cii.	An Act for erecting and maintaining a Chain Pier and other Works connected therewith, at the Town of Brighthelmston, in the County of Sussex.	In section 36, the words " or the Postmaster General for the Time being ", the words " or Postmaster respectively" and the words "nor the Master only of the Vessel employed in carrying the Mail to and from Brighthelmston aforesaid ".

Chapter	Title or Short Title	Extent of Repeal
4 Geo. 4. c. i.	An Act for building a Bridge over the River Severn, at or near the Haw Passage, in the County of Gloucester, and for making convenient Roads thereto.	In section 62, the words from " for any Horse " (where first occurring) to " guarding the same, or ".
4 Geo. 4. c. ix.	An Act for building a Bridge and making a Causeway from Langstone in the Parish of Havant in the County of Southampton, to Hayling Island in the Parish of Hayling North in the said County, at or near a certain House there, called the Ferry House; and for forming and making proper Roads, Approaches, or Avenues thereto.	In section 74, the words from " nor for any Horse " to " guarding the same ".
4 Geo. 4. c. xix.	An Act for the Improvement, more effectual Security, and Maintenance of the Harbour of Bridport, in the County of Dorset.	In section 37, the words " or Post Office ".
4 Geo. 4. c.xxxii.	An Act for altering and enlarging the Powers of Two Acts of the Ninth and Nineteenth Years of His late Majesty King George the Third, for building and completing a Bridge at Worcester over the River Severn, and for opening convenient Avenues thereto.	In section 12, the words from " for any Horse " (where first occurring) to " guarding the same; or ".
5 Geo. 4. c. xciii.	An Act for maintaining the Harbour of the Burgh of Dingwall, and regulating the Police of the said Burgh.	In section 26, the words " or Post Office ".

2 R* 2

Chapter	Title or Short Title	Extent of Repeal
5 Geo. 4. c. xciv.	An Act for establishing a Ferry over the River Arun at Littlehampton in the County of Sussex, and making Roads to communicate therewith.	In section 62, the words from " for any Horse " (where first occurring) to " guarding the same; or ".
5 Geo. 4. c. cxiv.	An Act for building a Bridge over the River Teign at Teignmouth in the County of Devon; and for making Approaches to the same.	In section 79, the words from " or for any Horse " (where first occurring) to " guarding the same ".
6 Geo. 4. c. lix.	An Act for building a Bridge over the River Don, near the village of Balgownie or Polgownie, in the Parish of Old Machar and County of Aberdeen.	In section 25, the words from " nor for any horses " to " such tolls ".
6 Geo. 4. c. cxxiv.	An Act for erecting an additional Bridge over the River Dee, in the City of Chester; for opening and making convenient Roads and Approaches thereto; and for taking down and rebuilding the Parish Church of Saint Bridget within the said City; and for repairing the present Bridge over the River Dee.	In section 48, the words from " or for any horse " (where first occurring) to " guarding the same ".
7 Geo. 4. c. xliii.	An Act for erecting and maintaining a Harbour, and Works connected therewith, in the Frith of Cromarty, at or near the Village of Invergordon in the County of Ross.	In section 22, the words " or Post Office ".
7 Geo. 4. c. lix.	An Act for building a Bridge over the River Severn, at or near Holt Fleet, in the Parishes of Holt and Ombersley in the County of Worcester; and for making approaches to such Bridge.	In section 86, the words from " or for any Horse " (where first occurring) to " guarding the same ".

Chapter	Title or Short Title	Extent of Repeal
7 & 8 Geo. 4. c. xix.	An Act for more effectually repairing and improving the Road from Shillingford in the County of Oxford, through Wallingford and Pangborne, to Reading in the County of Berks; and for repairing and maintaining a Bridge over the River Thames at or near Shillingford Ferry.	In section 25, the words from " or for any Horses " to " guarding the same ".
9 Geo. 4. c. xxxix.	An Act for regulating and fixing the Rates to be paid for Goods imported at and exported from the Quay of Bideford in the County of Devon, and for Keyage and Keelage of Ships and Vessels in the Harbour of Bideford, and for more easily levying and collecting the same; and also for regulating Ships and Vessels in the said Harbour.	In section 10, the words " or of the Post Office ".
9 Geo. 4. c. lviii.	An Act for maintaining, enlarging, improving, and regulating the Harbour of the Burgh of Kirkwall in Orkney.	In section 11, the words " or any of His Majesty's Postmaster General ".
9 Geo. 4. c. lxxxv.	An Act for more effectually repairing the Road from the Town and Port of Sandwich in the County of Kent, to the Towns of Margate and Ramsgate in the Isle of Thanet in the said County; and for reducing for a limited Time the Tolls and Duties payable at Sandwich Bridge.	In section 25, the words " or for any Horses " to " guarding the same ".

Chapter	Title or Short Title	Extent of Repeal
10 Geo. 4. c. xxxiv.	An Act for the Improvement of the Harbour of Aberdeen.	In section 35, the words from " o any Ship " to " Postmaster General ".
10 Geo. 4. c. xliii.	An Act for erecting a Bridge over the River Dee, at the Craiglug, in the Parish of Old Machar in the County of Aberdeen, and of Nigg in the County of Kincardine; and for making a Road from Cairnrobin, by the said Bridge, toward the City of Aberdeen.	In section 31, the words from " or for any Horses " (where secondly occurring) to " such Tolls ".
10 Geo. 4. c. xlix.	An Act for making and maintaining a Pier at or near Southend in the Parish of Prittlewell in the County of Essex, and for making convenient Approaches to and from the same.	In section 93, the words from " nor of any Ship " to " Postmaster General ".
10 Geo. 4. c. l.	An Act to regulate, repair and maintain the Ferry of Kincardine across the Frith of Forth, and the Accesses connected therewith.	In section 29, the words " or wholly in the Service of the Post Offiee " and the words " or for any Carriage carrying the Mails ".
10 Geo. 4. c. xcviii.	An Act for establishing a Ferry across the River Tyne, between North Shields in the County of Northumberland and South Shields in the County of Durham, and for opening and making proper Roads, Avenues, Ways, and Passages to communicate therewith.	In section 79, the words from " for any Horse " (where first occurring) to " guarding the same; or ".
10 Geo. 4. c. xcix.	An Act for the Improvement, Maintenance and Regulation of the Harbour of Kirkcaldy in the County of Fife.	In section 33, the words "or Post Office ".

Chapter	Title or Short Title	Extent of Repeal
10 Geo. 4. c. c.	An Act for building a Bridge over the River Wansbeck at the Town of Morpeth in the County of Northumberland.	In section 61, the words from " or for any Horse " (where first occurring) to " guarding the same ".
11 Geo. 4 & 1 Will. 4. c. xlix.	An Act for the Improvement and Preservation of the River Wear, and Port and Haven of Sunderland, in the County Palatine of Durham.	In section 85, the words " or of His Majesty's Postmaster General ".
11 Geo. 4 & 1 Will. 4. c. lxi.	An Act for making a Railway from the Cowley Hill Colliery in the Parish of Prescot to Runcorn Gap in the same Parish (with several Branches therefrom), all in the County Palatine of Lancaster; and for constructing a Wet Dock at the Termination of the said Railway at Runcorn Gap aforesaid.	In section 122, the words " or of His Majesty's Postmaster General ".
11 Geo. 4 & 1 Will. 4. c. lxiii.	An Act for more effectually repairing and improving the Road from Brighton to Shoreham, for building a Bridge over the River Adur at New Shoreham, and for making a Road to Lancing and a Branch Road therefrom, all in the County of Sussex.	In section 51, the words from " or for any Beast " (where first occurring) to " guarding the same".
11 Geo. 4 & 1 Will. 4. c. lxvi.	An Act for building a Bridge over the River Trent, from Dunham in the County of Nottingham to the opposite Shore in the County of Lincoln.	In section 81, the words from " for any Horse " (where first occurring) to " guarding the same; or ".

2 R* 4

Chapter	Title or Short Title	Extent of Repeal
11 Geo. 4 & 1 Will. 4. c. lxvii	An Act for building a Bridge over the River Wensum, in the Hamlet of Heigham and the Parish of Saint Clement, in the County of the City of Norwich.	In section 63, the words from " or for any Horse " (where first occurring) to " guarding the same ".
11 Geo. 4 & 1 Will. 4. c. lxviii.	An Act for erecting and maintaining a Bridge over Stonehouse Mill Pool, at or near Stonehouse Mills in the County of Devon.	In section 13, the words from " or for any Horse " (where first occurring) to " guarding the same ".
11 Geo. 4 & 1 Will. 4. c. lxix.	An Act for building a Bridge over the River Avon, from Clifton in the County of Gloucester to the opposite Side of the River in the County of Somerset, and for making convenient Roads and Approaches to communicate therewith.	In section 67, the words from " or for any Horse " (where first occurring) to " guarding the same ".
2 & 3 Will. 4. c. xliv.	An Act for constructing and maintaining a pier or Harbour at Largs in the County of Ayr.	In section 65, the words " or Post Office ".
3 & 4 Will. 4. c. lxvii.	An Act to alter and amend the Powers of several Acts passed relating to the Harbour of Rye in the County of Sussex, and for granting further Powers for improving and completing the said Harbour and the Navigation thereof.	In section 75, the words from " or any Ship " to " Postmaster General ".
4 & 5 Will. 4. c. xliii.	An Act for improving the Port and Harbour of Aberavon in the County of Glamorgan.	In section 59, the words " or of His Majesty's Postmaster General ".

Chapter	Title or Short Title	Extent of Repeal
4 & 5 Will. 4. c. lxxxv.	An Act for establishing a Floating Bridge over the River Itchen from or near a place called Cross House, within the Liberties of the Town of Southampton, to the Opposite Shore in the County of Southampton, with proper Approaches thereto, and for making Roads to communicate therewith.	In section 89, the words from " for any Horse " (where first occurring) to " guarding the same; or ".
5 & 6 Will. 4. c. xii.	An Act for constructing and maintaining a Harbour at New Quay in the County of Cardigan.	In section 73, the words " or of His Majesty's Postmaster General ".
5 & 6 Will. 4. c. xiii.	An Act for making and maintaining a Pier and other Works at Deptford in the County of Kent.	In section 89, the words " or of His Majesty's Postmaster General ".
5 & 6 Will. 4. c. lxxviii.	An Act for erecting and maintaining a Pier or Harbour at Gourock in the County of Renfrew.	In section 71, the words " or Post Office ".
6 & 7 Will. 4. c. 28.	The Government Offices Security Act 1836.	In the preamble, the words " Revenues of the Post Office ". In section 1, the words " of the postmaster general or ". In section 2, the words " for the said postmaster general upon the certificate of the accountant general of the post office and ". In section 3, the words " his Majesty's postmaster general or " and the words " as the case may be ". In section 5, the words " by the postmaster general or " and the words " with the said postmaster general or ". In section 7, the words " nor the said postmaster general ". In section 8, the words " the said postmaster general or of ", the word " respectively " and the words " in the postmaster general and ".

Chapter	Title or Short Title	Extent of Repeal
6 & 7 Will. 4. c. 28.—*cont.*	The Government Offices Security Act 1836.—*cont.*	In section 10, the words " for the said postmaster general and ", the word " respectively " and the words " of the accountant general of the post office or ". In the Schedule, in the Form of Certificate, the words " His Majesty's Postmaster General or ", and the words " as the case may be ".
6 & 7 Will. 4. c. xxxix.	An Act for building a Bridge over the River Aire at Leeds, and for making convenient Roads, Avenues, and Approaches thereto.	In section 82, the words from "or for any Horse" (where first occurring) to " guarding the same ".
6 & 7 Will. 4. c. lxvi.	An Act for regulating, preserving and improving the Port or Harbour at Newport in the County of Monmouth.	In section 73, the words " or Post Office ".
6 & 7 Will. 4. c. cxiii.	An Act for making and maintaining a Harbour and other Works at Sidmouth in the County of Devon.	In section 77, the words " or of His Majesty's Postmaster General ".
6 & 7 Will. 4. c. cxxviii.	An Act for making and maintaining a Pier Wharf and other Works at Greenwich in the County of Kent.	In section 57, the words " or of His Majesty's Postmaster General ".
7 Will. 4. & 1 Vict. c. lx.	An Act for building a Bridge over the River Tweed, at or near to Mertoun Mill in the County of Berwick, and for making Avenues and Approaches thereto.	In section 34, the words from " or for any Horse " to " such Tolls ".
7 Will. 4. & 1 Vict. c. xcix.	An Act for improving the Harbour of the Burgh of Montrose in the County of Forfar.	In section 87, the words from " nor in respect " to " Postmaster General ".

Chapter	Title or Short Title	Extent of Repeal
1 & 2 Vict. c. 61.	The Government Offices Security Act 1838.	In the preamble, the words " of the Postmaster General, or ", the words " Postmaster General or " (where secondly occurring), the words " His said Majesty's Postmaster General " and the words " the Postmaster General, or " (where secondly occurring). In section 1, the words " of the said Postmaster General, or " and the words " of such Post-Master general, or ". In section 2, the words " for the said postmaster general, upon the certificate of the accountant general of the Post Office and ", the words " postmaster general or " (in the first place in which they occur), the words " as the case may be ", and the words " postmaster general, or " (in the second place in which they occur).
1 & 2 Vict. c. i.	An Act for making and maintaining a Harbour and other Works at Paington in the County of Devon.	In section 80, the words " or of Her Majesty's Postmaster General ".
1 & 2 Vict. c. x.	An Act for building a Bridge over the River Thames from Cookham in the County of Berks to the opposite Shore in the County of Bucks.	In section 75, the words from " or for any Horse " (where first occurring) to " guarding the same ".
1 & 2 Vict. c. xxxi.	An Act for building a Bridge over the River Wye at a Place called Boughrood Ferry in the Counties of Brecon and Radnor, and for making convenient Approaches thereto.	In section 78, the words from " or for any Horse " (where first occurring) to " guarding the same ".
2 & 3 Vict. c. xvi.	An Act for extending, improving, regulating, and managing the Harbour of the Royal Burgh of Aberbrothwick in the County of Forfar.	In section 78, the words " or Post Office ".

Chapter	Title or Short Title	Extent of Repeal
2 & 3 Vict. c. lxv.	An Act for further improving and maintaining the Harbour of the Burgh of the Regality of Fraserburgh in the County of Aberdeen.	In section 56, the words from " or employed " to " Postmaster General ".
2 & 3 Vict. c. lxxii.	An Act for enlarging the Town Quay of the Borough of Portsmouth, and for improving that Portion of the Harbour of Portsmouth called The Camber.	In section 68, the words " in Her Majesty's Service in carrying the Mails of Letters or Express under the Authority of Her Majesty's Postmaster General or ".
3 & 4 Vict. c. xxvi.	An Act for making and maintaining a new Bridge over the River Aire at Leeds, at or near the place called Crown Point, with suitable Approaches thereto; and for making certain Drains or Watercourses under the Road leading to such Bridge, and through the adjoining Lands, to communicate with the River Aire below the Leeds Locks.	In section 69, the words from " or for any Horse " (where first occurring) to " guarding the same ".
3 & 4 Vict. c. xliv.	An Act for regulating and preserving the Harbour of Workington in the County of Cumberland, and for other purposes relating thereto.	In section 28, the words " or of Her Majesty's Postmaster General ".
3 & 4 Vict. c. lxxiii.	An Act for improving, enlarging and maintaining the Harbour of Fisherrow in the County of Edinburgh.	In section 31, the words from " or employed " to " Postmaster General ".
3 & 4 Vict. c. cxi.	An Act for erecting and maintaining a Pier and other Works in Mill Bay in the Port of Plymouth in the County of Devon.	In section 22, the words " or of Her Majesty's Postmaster General ".

Chapter	Title or Short Title	Extent of Repeal
4 & 5 Vict. c. xlix.	An Act for maintaining Gourdon Harbour in the County of Kincardine.	In section 55, the words " or of Her Majesty's Postmaster General ".
4 & 5 Vict. c. l.	An Act for making and maintaining a Harbour at Scrabster Roads, in the Bay of Thurso and County of Caithness, and Road thereto.	In section 79, the words from " nor in respect " to " Postmaster General ".
6 & 7 Vict. c. xlii.	The Pile Pier Act 1843.	In section 194, the words " or of Her Majesty's Postmaster General ".
6 & 7 Vict. c. lxxi.	An Act for improving and maintaining the Port or Harbour of Neath in the County of Glamorgan.	In section 234, the words " or of Her Majesty's Postmaster General ".
7 & 8 Vict. c. lxxvii.	An Act for making a Landing Place at or near Hythe in the Parish of Fawley, and extra-parochial Places adjoining thereto in the County of Southampton.	In section 207, the words " or Post Office ".
7 & 8 Vict. c. xciii.	An Act for improving the Harbour and Quay at Wells in the County of Norfolk; and for extending and altering some of the Provisions of the Act relating to the said Harbour and Quay.	In section 127, the words " or of Her Majesty's Postmaster General ".
8 & 9 Vict. c. xxv.	An Act for improving and maintaining the Harbour or Port of Boddam in the County of Aberdeen.	In section 84, the words " or of Her Majesty's Postmaster General ".
9 & 10 Vict. c. xvi.	An Act for improving and maintaining the Port and Harbour of Helensburgh in the County of Dumbarton.	In section 110, the words " or of Her Majesty's Postmaster General ".

Chapter	Title or Short Title	Extent of Repeal
9 & 10 Vict. c. xciv.	An Act for improving and maintaining the Harbour of Port Ellen in the County of Argyll.	In section 82, the words " or Post Office ".
9 & 10 Vict. c. cviii.	The Portsmouth Harbour Pier Act 1846.	In section 38, the words " and for all Persons in charge of Her Majesty's Mail Bags ".
9 & 10 Vict. c. cxlvi.	The Herculaneum Dock Act 1846.	In section 83, the words " or Post Office ".
9 & 10 Vict. c. cccxliv.	The Portbury Pier and Railway Act 1846.	Section 35.
9 & 10 Vict. c. ccclxiv.	The Campbeltown Harbour and Burgh Act 1846.	In section 50, the words " Post Office ".
10 & 11 Vict. c. 27.	The Harbours, Docks and Piers Clauses Act 1847.	In section 28, the words from " or any packet " to " whatsoever " and the words " or Post Office ".
10 & 11 Vict. c. vi.	The Pile Pier Act 1847.	In section 12, the words " or Post Office ".
10 & 11 Vict. c. ix.	The Newhaven Harbour and Ouse Lower Navigation Act 1847.	Section 75.
10 & 11 Vict. c. ccix.	The Inverness Harbour Act 1847.	In section 59, the words " or Post Office ".
12 & 13 Vict. c. 45.	The Quarter Sessions Act 1849.	In sections 2, 12 and 13, the words " or Post Office ".
14 & 15 Vict. c. xlix.	The Briton Ferry Dock and Railway Act 1851	In section 46, the words " or belonging to or in the Service of Her Majesty's Postmaster General ".
16 & 17 Vict. c. cxlvi.	The Llynvi Valley Railway Act 1853.	In section 21, the words from " or any Packet Boat " to " whatsoever " and the words " or Post Office ".
17 & 18 Vict. c. cxxvi.	The Swansea Harbour Act 1854.	In section 144, the words from " or any Beast " to " Employment; or " (where first occurring).

Chapter	Title or Short Title	Extent of Repeal
18 & 19 Vict. c. v.	The Hoarwithy Bridge Act 1855.	In section 34, the words from " or for any Horse " (where first occurring) to " guarding the same ".
20 & 21 Vict. c. 44.	The Crown Suits (Scotland) Act 1857.	In section 4, the words " the Post Office ".
20 & 21 Vict. c. xlviii.	The Fownhope and Holme Lacy Bridge Act 1857.	In section 48, the words from " Secondly " to " guarding the same ".
21 & 22 Vict. c. 40.	The New General Post Office, Edinburgh, Act 1858.	The whole Act.
22 Vict. c. vii.	The Londonderry Bridge Act 1859.	In section 64, the words from " or for any Mail Carriage " to " guarding the same ".
24 & 25 Vict. c. cxii.	The Clifton Suspension Bridge Act 1861.	In section 31, the words from " or for any Horse or Carriage " to " guarding the same; or ".
25 & 26 Vict. c. lxi.	The Shard Bridge Act 1862.	In section 56, the words from " Secondly " to " guarding the same ".
26 & 27 Vict. c. 112.	The Telegraph Act 1863.	Section 5(2), so far as relating to service of notices on the company.
26 & 27 Vict. c. lxiii.	The Rixton and Warburton Bridge Act 1863.	In section 56, the words from " Secondly " to " guarding the same ".
27 & 28 Vict. c. lxviii.	The Scarborough Valley Bridge Company's Act 1864.	In section 42, the words from " or for any Horse " (where first occurring) to " guarding the same ".
31 & 32 Vict. c. 72.	The Promissory Oaths Act 1868.	In the Schedule, in Part I, the words " Postmaster General ".
31 & 32 Vict. c. 110.	The Telegraph Act 1868.	Section 22.
31 & 32 Vict. c. cxxviii.	The Portsmouth Camber Quays Act 1868.	In section 23, the words from " nor of any ship " to " Postmaster General ".
32 & 33 Vict. c. 73.	The Telegraph Act 1869.	The whole Act.
32 & 33 Vict. c. lxv.	The Cricksea Bridge Act 1869.	In section 32, the words from " or for any horse or carriage " to " guarding the same ".

Chapter	Title or Short Title	Extent of Repeal
33 & 34 Vict. c. lxv.	The Cawood Bridge Act 1870.	In section 53, the words from " or for any horse or carriage " to " guarding the same ".
34 & 35 Vict. c. 65.	The Juries Act (Ireland) 1871.	In section 22, the word " registration " (where last occurring).
34 & 35 Vict. c. xxxii.	The Clayhithe Bridge Act 1871.	In section 42, the words from " or for any horse or carriage " to " guarding the same ".
36 & 37 Vict. c. xii.	The Shrewsbury (Kingsland) Bridge Act 1873.	In section 31, the words from " or for any horse, beast " to " guarding the same ".
41 & 42 Vict. c. 76.	The Telegraph Act 1878.	In section 12, the words from " A notice required to be given under this Act to the Postmaster General " to " usual place of abode ".
44 & 45 Vict. c. clxxiv.	The Medway Conservancy Act 1881.	In section 122, in the second proviso, paragraph (*b*).
45 & 46 Vict. c. 56.	The Electric Lighting Act 1882.	In section 32, the definition of " telegram ". Section 35.
47 & 48 Vict. c. 76.	The Post Office (Protection) Act 1884.	In section 11, the words " the post office, or ".
48 & 49 Vict. c. clxxxviii.	The Manchester Ship Canal Act 1885.	Section 210.
51 & 52 Vict. c. 29.	Lloyd's Signal Stations Act 1888.	In section 6, the words from " to acquire " to " land, or ". Section 7.
54 & 55 Vict. c. 39.	The Stamp Act 1891.	Section 7.
55 & 56 Vict. c. 55.	The Burgh Police (Scotland) Act 1892.	In section 288, the words " post office or other " (in both places where they occur).
55 & 56 Vict. c. cxxxii.	The Bradford Corporation Waterworks Act 1892.	Section 10.
56 & 57 Vict. c. xlvii.	The Ilkley Local Board Act 1893.	In section 16, the proviso.
56 & 57 Vict. c. clxxviii.	The Belfast Water Act 1893.	In section 6, the proviso.
56 & 57 Vict. c. ccxvii.	The Fleetwood Improvement Act 1893.	Section 44.

SCH. 11

Chapter	Title or Short Title	Extent of Repeal
57 & 58 Vict. c. lviii.	The Fulwood Local Board (Water) Act 1894.	In section 5, the proviso.
57 & 58 Vict. c. lxi.	The Southend Waterworks Act 1894.	In section 6, the proviso.
57 & 58 Vict. c. lxxviii.	The Kendal Corporation Gas and Water Act 1894.	In section 37, the proviso.
57 & 58 Vict. c. xci.	The Gloucester Corporation Act 1894.	In section 8, the proviso.
58 & 59 Vict. c. xxvii.	The Edinburgh and District Waterworks (Additional Supply) Act 1895.	In section 40, the words " or in contravention of any exclusive privilege by law vested for the time being in the Postmaster General ".
58 & 59 Vict. c. xxxvii.	The Whitby Water Act 1895.	In section 10, the proviso.
58 & 59 Vict. c. clvi.	The Merthyr Tydfil District Council Waterworks Act 1895.	In section 8, the proviso.
59 & 60 Vict. c. lxxii.	The Malvern Link (Extension and Water) Act 1896.	In section 40, the proviso.
59 & 60 Vict. c. clxxxvii.	The Eastbourne Waterworks Act 1896.	In section 6, the proviso.
59 & 60 Vict. c. cxc.	The Sheffield Corporation Water Act 1896.	In section 15, the proviso.
59 & 60 Vict. c. ccxlv.	The Barry Urban District Council Act 1896.	In section 21, the words from " Provided that " to " 1869 ".
60 & 61 Vict. c. 53.	The Congested Districts (Scotland) Act 1897.	In section 4(1)(f), the words " and savings bank ".
60 & 61 Vict. c. xxviii.	The Loughborough Corporation Act 1897.	In section 6, the proviso.
60 & 61 Vict. c. cix.	The Carnarvon Corporation Act 1897.	Section 33(1)(b).
60 & 61 Vict. c. cxvii.	The Crowborough District Water Act 1897.	In section 25, the proviso.
60 & 61 Vict. c. cxxiv.	The Eastbourne Waterworks Act 1897.	In section 4, the proviso.
60 & 61 Vict. c. clxviii.	The Newport Corporation Act 1897.	In section 8, the proviso.

Chapter	Title or Short Title	Extent of Repeal
60 & 61 Vict. c. clxxxix.	The Belfast Water Act 1897.	In section 23, the proviso.
60 & 61 Vict. c. cc.	The Nottingham Corporation Water Act 1897.	In section 6, the first proviso.
60 & 61 Vict. c. ccv.	The Pwllheli Corporation Act 1897.	In section 37, the proviso.
61 & 62 Vict. c. 46.	The Revenue Act 1898.	Section 10(3).
61 & 62 Vict. c. lxx.	The Ilkeston Corporation Act 1898.	In section 5, the proviso.
61 & 62 Vict. c. cviii.	The Carmarthen Improvement Act 1898.	In section 20, the proviso.
61 & 62 Vict. c. cxxiii.	The Crawley and District Water Act 1898.	In section 24, the second proviso.
61 & 62 Vict. c. cxlvii.	The Folkestone Water Act 1898.	In section 6, the proviso.
61 & 62 Vict. c. clvi.	The Bacup Corporation Water Act 1898.	In section 15, the proviso.
61 & 62 Vict. c. ccxxv.	The Carlisle Corporation (Water) Act 1898.	Section 48, from the beginning to " 1869 ".
61 & 62 Vict. c. cclx.	The Wey Valley, Frimley, and Farnham Water Act 1898.	In section 40, the proviso.
62 & 63 Vict. c. xxi.	The Nuneaton and Chilvers Coton Urban District Council Waterworks Act 1899.	In section 5, the proviso.
62 & 63 Vict. c. xxiv.	The Glastonbury Water Act 1899.	In section 11, the proviso.
62 & 63 Vict. c. lxx.	The Lanarkshire (Middle Ward District) Water Act 1899.	In section 24, the words " or in contravention of any exclusive privilege by law vested for the time being in the Postmaster General ".
62 & 63 Vict. c. clxiv.	The Ayr Burgh Act 1899.	In section 5, the proviso.
62 & 63 Vict. c. clxxi.	The Woking Water and Gas Act 1899.	In section 19, the proviso.
62 & 63 Vict. c. ccxxv.	The Warrington Corporation Act 1899.	In section 7, the proviso.

Chapter	Title or Short Title	Extent of Repeal
62 & 63 Vict. c. cclxix.	The Derwent Valley Water Act 1899.	In section 47, in the proviso, the words from " shall not be used " to " 1869 and ".
63 & 64 Vict. c. xcvi.	The Mountain Ash Water and Gas Act 1900.	In section 7, the proviso.
1 Edw. 7. c. lxxxiv.	The Burgess Hill Water Act 1901.	In section 4, the proviso.
1 Edw. 7. c. lxxxv.	The Kettering Urban District Water Act 1901.	In section 5, the second proviso.
1 Edw. 7. c. xciii.	The Faversham Water Act 1901.	In section 46, the proviso.
1 Edw. 7. c. xcvi.	The Llandrindod Wells Water Act 1901.	In section 21, the proviso.
1 Edw. 7. c. cxxv.	The Swanage Gas and Water Act 1901.	In section 59, the proviso.
1 Edw. 7. c. cxcviii.	The Stockport Corporation Water Act 1901.	In section 14, the proviso.
1 Edw. 7. c. ccvii.	The South Essex Waterworks Act 1901.	In section 6, in the proviso, the words from " be used " to " 1869 or ".
1 Edw. 7. c. ccxviii.	The Barrow-in-Furness Corporation Act 1901.	In section 6, the proviso.
1 Edw. 7. c. ccxlii.	The Cromer Water Act 1901.	In section 64, the proviso.
1 Edw. 7. c. ccl.	The Ilkeston and Heanor Water Act 1901.	In section 30, the proviso.
1 Edw. 7. c. cclvi.	The Leeds Corporation Water Act 1901.	In section 5, the proviso.
1 Edw. 7. c. cclxvii.	The Derby Corporation Act 1901.	In section 97, the proviso.
1 Edw. 7. c. cclxx.	The Loch Leven Water Power Act 1901.	In section 10, the proviso.
2 Edw. 7. c. v.	The Finedon Urban District Water Act 1902.	In section 7, the proviso.
2 Edw. 7. c. ix.	The Wrexham Waterworks Act 1902.	In section 23, the proviso.
2 Edw. 7. c. xi.	The Darley Dale Water Act 1902.	In section 6, the words from " any telegraphs " to " 1869 and ".

Chapter	Title or Short Title	Extent of Repeal
2 Edw. 7. c. xxxii.	The Street Urban District Water Act 1902.	In section 9, the proviso.
2 Edw. 7. c. xlviii.	The Abertillery Urban District Council Act 1902.	In section 4, the proviso.
2 Edw. 7. c. cxxv.	The Buxton Urban District Council Water Act 1902.	In section 7, the proviso.
2 Edw. 7. c. cxxx.	The Bristol Waterworks Act 1902.	In section 5, the proviso.
2 Edw. 7. c. cxxxvii.	The Huddersfield Corporation Act 1902.	In section 8, the first proviso.
2 Edw. 7. c. clxi.	The Consett Waterworks Act 1902.	In section 7, the proviso.
2 Edw. 7. c. clxii.	The Rhondda Urban District Council (Tramways &c.) Act 1902.	In section 60, the proviso.
2 Edw. 7. c. clxxiv.	The Weardale Water Act 1902.	In section 6, the proviso.
3 Edw. 7. c. xviii.	The Sutton District Waterworks Act 1903.	In section 5, the proviso.
3 Edw. 7. c. xciii.	The Scunthorpe Urban District Water Act 1903.	In section 6, the second proviso.
3 Edw. 7. c. xcvi.	The New Hunstanton Improvement Act 1903.	In section 9, the proviso.
3 Edw. 7. c. cxiv.	The Merthyr Tydfil Urban District Council Act 1903.	In section 6, the proviso.
3 Edw. 7. c. ccvii.	The Bath Corporation Water Act 1903.	Section 22(2).
4 Edw. 7. c. xxiv.	The Gosport Water Act 1904.	In section 5, the proviso.
4 Edw. 7. c. xlv.	The Chesterfield Gas and Water Board Act 1904.	In section 13, the proviso.
4 Edw. 7. c. cl.	The Thurles Urban District Council Water Act 1904.	In section 6, the proviso.

Chapter	Title or Short Title	Extent of Repeal
4 Edw. 7. c. cli.	The Ebbw Vale Water Act 1904.	In section 6, in the proviso, the words from " no telegraph " to " and that ".
4 Edw. 7. c. cxcvi.	The Derwent Valley Water Act 1904.	In section 11, the first proviso.
4 Edw. 7. c. ccxxxiv.	The Swindon Corporation Act 1904.	In section 5, the proviso.
4 Edw. 7. c. ccxxxv.	The Manchester Corporation (General Powers) Act 1904.	In section 11, the first proviso.
4 Edw. 7. c. ccxli.	The Loch Leven Water Power (Amendment) Act 1904.	In section 9, the proviso.
5 Edw. 7. c. xiii.	The Truro Water Act 1905.	In section 5, the proviso.
5 Edw. 7. c. xl.	The Accrington District Gas and Water Board Act 1905.	In section 7, the proviso.
5 Edw. 7. c. lxiii.	The Morley Corporation Act 1905.	Section 14(2).
5 Edw. 7. c. xcvi.	The Hythe Corporation Act 1905.	In section 20, the proviso.
5 Edw. 7. c. ci.	The Mansfield Corporation Act 1905.	In section 6, the proviso.
5 Edw. 7. c. clxii.	The Skegness Water Act 1905.	Section 29.
5 Edw. 7. c. clxxxiv.	The Malvern Water Act 1905.	In section 11, the first proviso.
5 Edw. 7. c. cxcvi.	The Bangor (County Down) Water and Improvement Act 1905.	In section 6, the proviso.
6 Edw. 7. c. xxxvi.	The North East Lincolnshire Water Act 1906.	Section 53.
6 Edw. 7. c. xci.	The Manchester Corporation Act 1906.	In section 13, the proviso.
7 Edw. 7. c. lxxxi.	The Leeds Corporation Act 1907.	Section 20.

Chapter	Title or Short Title	Extent of Repeal
7 Edw. 7. c. lxxxiv.	The Great Yarmouth Waterworks and Lowestoft Water and Gas Act 1907.	Section 8.
7 Edw. 7. c. lxxxviii.	The Penrith Urban District Council Act 1907.	In section 6, the proviso.
7 Edw. 7. c. clxxiv.	The Metropolitan Water Board (Various Powers) Act 1907.	In section 5, the words from "Any telegraphic" onwards. In section 58, the words " or in contravention of any exclusive privilege by law vested for the time being in the Postmaster General ".
8 Edw. 7. c. 62.	The Local Government (Scotland) Act 1908.	In section 11(7), the words "or of any postal " to the end.
8 Edw. 7. c. xxxiii.	The Lincoln Corporation (Water &c.) Act 1908.	In section 9, the proviso.
8 Edw. 7. c. lxix.	The Pontypridd Waterworks and Tramroad Act 1908.	In section 4, the proviso.
8 Edw. 7. c. lxxxix.	The Burnley Corporation Act 1908.	In section 5, in the proviso, the words from " and that " onwards.
8 Edw. 7. c. xcix.	The Holderness Water Act 1908.	Section 84(1).
8 Edw. 7. c. ciii.	The Criccieth Water and Improvement Act 1908.	In section 15, the proviso.
9 Edw. 7. c. xxv.	The Clevedon Water Act 1909.	Section 46.
9 Edw. 7. c. xlix.	The South Staffordshire Waterworks Act 1909.	Section 13.
9 Edw. 7. c. lxv.	The Pontypridd Waterworks (Amendment) Act 1909.	In section 4, in the proviso, the words from " and shall " onwards.
9 Edw. 7. c. lxxxii.	The Llanelly Waterworks Act 1909.	In section 6, the words from " Provided always " onwards.
9 Edw. 7. c. lxxxiii.	The Northallerton Waterworks Act 1909.	In section 4, the proviso.

Chapter	Title or Short Title	Extent of Repeal
9 Edw. 7. c. xci.	The Stourbridge and District Water Board Act 1909.	Section 39.
9 Edw. 7. c. clxi.	The Cardiff Corporation Act 1909.	In section 5, in the proviso, the words from " and shall " onwards.
9 Edw. 7. c. cxlii.	The Gas and Water Orders Confirmation Act 1909.	In the Gravesend and Milton Water Order 1909 set out in the Schedule, in section 8, in the proviso, the words from " shall not " to " 1908 and ".
10 Edw. 7 & 1 Geo. 5. c. xxxix.	The Exmouth Urban District Water Act 1910.	In section 6, the proviso.
10 Edw. 7 & 1 Geo. 5. c. cvii.	The Mountain Ash Water Act 1910.	Section 40.
10 Edw. 7 & 1 Geo. 5. c. cxx.	The Pontypridd and Rhondda Water Act 1910.	Section 43.
10 Edw. 7 & 1 Geo. 5. c. cxxii.	The Fylde Water Board Act 1910.	Section 23.
10 Edw. 7 & 1 Geo. 5. c. cxxv.	The Abertillery and District Water Board Act 1910.	Section 32.
10 Edw. 7 & 1 Geo. 5. c. cxxvi.	The Slough Waterworks Act 1910.	In section 10, the proviso.
1 & 2 Geo. 5. c. 48.	The Finance Act 1911.	Section 20.
1 & 2 Geo. 5. c. ix.	The Felixstowe and Walton Waterworks Act 1911.	In section 5, the proviso.
1 & 2 Geo. 5. c. xxxix.	The Hastings Corporation (Water and Finance) Act 1911.	In section 7, the proviso.
1 & 2 Geo. 5. c. xlv.	The Chesterfield Gas and Water Board Act 1911.	In section 5, the proviso.
1 & 2 Geo. 5. c. lxxxvi.	The Kingston upon Hull Corporation Act 1911.	In section 23, the words from " shall not " to " 1909 and "

Chapter	Title or Short Title	Extent of Repeal
1 & 2 Geo. 5. c. xcii.	The Gloucester Corporation Act 1911.	In section 20, the words from " shall not be used " to " 1869 and ".
1 & 2 Geo. 5. c. xcvii.	The Merthyr Tydfil Corporation Water Act 1911.	Section 9.
1 & 2 Geo. 5. c. cv.	The Ipswich Corporation Act 1911.	Section 20.
1 & 2 Geo. 5. c. cxviii.	The Metropolitan Water Board (New Works) Act 1911.	Section 7, from " Any telegraphic " onwards.
2 & 3 Geo. 5. c. xvi.	The Egremont Urban District Water Act 1912.	Section 11.
2 & 3 Geo. 5. c. xxxiv.	The Windermere District Gas and Water Act 1912.	In section 30, the proviso.
2 & 3 Geo. 5. c. lvi.	The Shipley Urban District Council Act 1912.	In section 59, the proviso.
2 & 3 Geo. 5. c. lx.	The Hove Corporation Act 1912.	Section 26.
2 & 3 Geo. 5. c. lxx.	The Swanage Gas and Water Act 1912.	In section 5, the proviso.
2 & 3 Geo. 5. c. xcvii.	The Fylde Water Board Act 1912.	Section 34.
2 & 3 Geo. 5. c. cvii.	The Keighley Corporation Act 1912.	Section 25.
2 & 3 Geo. 5. c. cix.	The Blyth Harbour Act 1912.	In section 73, the words from " or of any mail bag as defined by the Post Office Act 1908 ".
3 & 4 Geo. 5. c. 27.	The Forgery Act 1913.	In section 18(1), in the definition of " revenue paper ", the words " Post Office money orders, or postal orders ".
3 & 4 Geo. 5. c. xv.	The Northampton Corporation Water Act 1913.	Section 18.
3 & 4 Geo. 5. c. xvii.	The South Staffordshire Waterworks Act 1913.	In section 4, in the proviso, the words from " shall not be used " to " 1869 and ".

Chapter	Title or Short Title	Extent of Repeal
3 & 4 Geo. 5. c. xxxv.	The Chesterfield Corporation Railless Traction Act 1913.	Section 32(1).
3 & 4 Geo. 5. c. xliii.	The Leeds Corporation Act 1913.	Section 12.
3 & 4 Geo. 5. c. xlvi.	The Brighton Corporation Act 1913.	Section 11(3).
3 & 4 Geo. 5. c. lxxxv.	The Ebbw Vale Water Act 1913.	In section 4, in the proviso, the words from " that no " to " 1869 and ".
3 & 4 Geo. 5. c. xcviii.	The Metropolitan Water Board Act 1913.	In section 8, the words from "Any telegraphic or " to " 1869 and ".
3 & 4 Geo. 5. c. xcix.	The Barry Urban District Council Act 1913.	Section 16.
3 & 4 Geo. 5. c. cxxvi.	The Gas and Water Orders Confirmation (No. 2) Act 1913.	In the Wey Valley Water Order 1913 set out in the Schedule, in section 6, the words from " Provided that " to " 1869 ".
4 & 5 Geo. 5. c. cl.	The Northwich Urban District Council Act 1914.	Section 26.
5 & 6 Geo. 5. c. 24.	The Injuries in War (Compensation) Act 1915.	The whole Act.
5 & 6 Geo. 5. c. xiv.	The Blyth Harbour Act 1915.	In section 44, the words " or for any mail bag as defined by the Post Office Act 1908 ".
5 & 6 Geo. 5. c. lxii.	The Ashington Urban District Council Act 1915.	Section 12.
5 & 6 Geo. 5. c. lxiv.	The Wolverhampton Corporation Water Act 1915.	Section 23.
5 & 6 Geo. 5. c. lxv.	The Barnoldswick Urban District Council Water Act 1915.	Section 12.
5 & 6 Geo. 5. c. lxxii.	The Weardale and Consett Water Act 1915.	In section 7, the proviso.
5 & 6 Geo. 5. c. lxxiii.	The Metropolitan Water Board Act 1915.	In section 6, the words from " Any telegraphic " to " 1869 and ".

Chapter	Title or Short Title	Extent of Repeal
6 & 7 Geo. 5. c. xx.	The Wakefield Corporation Act 1916.	Section 24.
6 & 7 Geo. 5. c. xli.	The Tynemouth Corporation Act 1916.	Section 34.
7 & 8 Geo. 5. c. xx.	The Bristol Waterworks Act 1917.	In section 40(1), the words from " shall not " to " 1869 and ".
7 & 8 Geo. 5. c. xlv.	The Chepstow Water Act 1917.	Section 42.
8 & 9 Geo. 5. c. 15.	The Finance Act 1918.	Section 43.
8 & 9 Geo. 5. c. x.	The Pontypool Gas and Water Act 1918.	Section 50.
8 & 9 Geo. 5. c. xxi.	The Londonderry Corporation Act 1918.	Section 14.
8 & 9 Geo. 5. c. xxiv.	The Nelson Corporation Water Act 1918.	Section 45.
8 & 9 Geo. 5. c. lx.	The Lancaster Corporation Act 1918.	Section 23.
9 & 10 Geo. 5. c. 75.	The Ferries (Acquisition by Local Authorities) Act 1919.	In section 4, the words " or for any mail bag as defined by the Post Office Act 1908 ".
9 & 10 Geo. 5. c. xlix.	The Sheffield Corporation Act 1919.	Section 13.
9 & 10 Geo. 5. c. cxiii.	The Glasgow Water Order Confirmation Act 1919.	In the order contained in the Schedule, section 13.
9 & 10 Geo. 5. c. cxix.	The Manchester Corporation Act 1919.	Section 47.
9 & 10 Geo. 5. c. cxxii.	The Gosport and Alverstoke Urban District Council Act 1919.	In section 52, the words " or for any mail bag as defined by the Post Office Act 1908 ".
10 & 11 Geo. 5. c. 67.	The Government of Ireland Act 1920.	In section 74, in the definition of " postal service ", the words from " but " onwards.
10 & 11 Geo. 5. c. 75.	The Official Secrets Act 1920.	In section 5(6), the words " or the Telegraph Acts 1863 to 1920 ".
10 & 11 Geo. 5. c. lvii.	The Newport Corporation Act 1920.	In section 44(1), the words from " shall be used " to " 1869 or ".

Chapter	Title or Short Title	Extent of Repeal
10 & 11 Geo. 5. c. lviii.	The Liverpool Corporation Waterworks Act 1920.	In section 9, the words " the exclusive privilege conferred upon the Postmaster General by the Telegraph Act 1869 or of ".
10 & 11 Geo. 5. c. xcv.	The Norwich Corporation Act 1920.	Section 27.
11 & 12 Geo. 5. c. xxii.	The Cambridge University and Town Waterworks Act 1921.	In section 12, the proviso.
11 & 12 Geo. 5. c. lxxiv.	The Liverpool Corporation Act 1921.	In section 60, the words from " shall not be used " to " 1869 and ".
11 & 12 Geo. 5. c. lxxix.	The Southampton Corporation Water Act 1921.	In section 26, the words from " shall not be used " to " 1869 and ".
11 & 12 Geo. 5. c. lxxxii.	The Rhymney Valley Water Act 1921.	Section 69(1).
11 & 12 Geo. 5. c. cxiii.	The Batley Corporation Act 1921.	In section 8, the words from " and shall " onwards.
12 & 13 Geo. 5. c. 43.	The Post Office (Pneumatic Tubes Acquisition) Act 1922.	The whole Act.
12 & 13 Geo. 5. c. xix.	The Newhaven and Seaford Water Act 1922.	In section 15, the proviso.
12 & 13 Geo. 5. c. xxxiii.	The Colne Valley Water Act 1922.	In section 17, the words from " shall not " to " 1869 and ".
12 & 13 Geo. 5. c. liv.	The Worthing Corporation Act 1922.	In section 30, the words from " shall not be used " to " 1869 and ".
12 & 13 Geo. 5. c. lxviii.	The Staffordshire Potteries Waterworks Act 1922.	In section 46, the first proviso.
12 & 13 Geo. 5. c. lxxxii.	The South Staffordshire Waterworks Act 1922.	In section 11, the words from " shall not " to " 1869 and ".
12 & 13 Geo. 5. c. xciii.	The Bolton Corporation Act 1922.	In section 10, the words from " and shall not " onwards.
13 & 14 Geo. 5. c. lxxx.	The Felixstowe Dock and Railway Act 1923.	In section 18, the words " or for any mail bag as defined by the Post Office Act 1908 ".

2 S 2

Chapter	Title or Short Title	Extent of Repeal
13 & 14 Geo. 5. c. lxxxviii.	The Bournemouth-Swanage Motor Road and Ferry Act 1923.	In section 88(1), the words " or for any mail bag as defined by the Post Office Act 1908 ".
13 & 14 Geo. 5. c. lxxxix.	The Barnsley Corporation Act 1923.	In section 9, the words from " and shall " onwards.
13 & 14 Geo. 5. c. xci.	The Chelmsford Corporation Water Act 1923.	In section 29, the words from " shall not be used " to " 1869 and ".
13 & 14 Geo. 5. c. xcix.	The Chesterfield Corporation Act 1923.	In section 46, the words from " shall not be used " to " 1869 and ".
13 & 14 Geo. 5. c. cvi.	The Macclesfield Corporation Act 1923.	Section 30.
14 & 15 Geo. 5. c. lxxxviii.	The Hastings Corporation Act 1924.	In section 16, the words from " shall not be used " to " 1869 and ".
14 & 15 Geo. 5. c. xcix.	The Tynemouth Corporation Act 1924.	In section 12, the words " Section 34 (For protection of Postmaster General) ".
15 & 16 Geo. 5. c. 71.	The Public Health Act 1925.	In section 10, the words " any privilege of the Postmaster General under the Telegraph Act 1869 or ".
15 & 16 Geo. 5. c. civ.	The Leek Urban District Council Water Act 1925.	In section 16(2), the words from " shall not " to " 1869 and ".
15 & 16 Geo. 5. c. cx.	The Mersey Tunnel Act 1925.	In section 72, the words " or for any mail bag as defined by the Post Office Act 1908 ".
15 & 16 Geo. 5. c. cxxi.	The Bradford Corporation Act 1925.	In section 14, the words from " and shall " onwards.
16 & 17 Geo. 5. c. 51.	The Electricity (Supply) Act 1926.	Section 24(2).
16 & 17 Geo. 5. c. lxxi.	The Teignmouth and Shaldon Bridge Act 1926.	In section 62(1), the words " or for any mail bag as defined by the Post Office Act 1908 ".
17 & 18 Geo. 5. c. lxiv.	The Bristol Waterworks Act 1927.	Section 5.
17 & 18 Geo. 5. c. lxxvii.	The Grimsby Corporation Act 1927.	In section 103, the first proviso.

SCH. 11

Chapter	Title or Short Title	Extent of Repeal
17 & 18 Geo. 5. c. lxxxiii.	The Chepping Wycombe Corporation Act 1927.	In section 85, the proviso.
18 & 19 Geo. 5. c. xlvi.	The Lewes Water Act 1928.	In section 23, the words from " shall not " to " 1869 and ".
18 & 19 Geo. 5. c. lxx.	The Windermere District Gas and Water Act 1928.	In section 13, the words from " shall not " to " 1869 and ".
19 & 20 Geo. 5. c. 29.	The Government Annuities Act 1929.	Section 51(1). In section 52, in subsection (2), the words " or by the Postmaster General with the consent of the Commissioners ", and subsection (3). In section 54(4), the words " other than a post office savings bank ".
19 & 20 Geo. 5. c. xiii.	The Llanelly Corporation Act 1929.	In section 82, the proviso.
19 & 20 Geo. 5. c. xxxvii.	The Blackburn Corporation Act 1929.	In section 71(1), the proviso.
19 & 20 Geo. 5. c. xlv.	The Llanfrechfa Upper and Llantarnam Water Board Act 1929.	In section 24, the words from " be used " to " 1869 or ".
19 & 20 Geo. 5. c. lxiii.	The Lewes Corporation Act 1929.	In section 23, in the proviso, the words from " shall not " to " 1869 and ".
19 & 20 Geo. 5. c. lxxix.	The Warrington Corporation Water Act 1929.	In section 28, the words from " shall not be used " to " 1869 and ".
19 & 20 Geo. 5. c. lxxx.	The Galloway Water Power Act 1929.	Section 77(3).
19 & 20 Geo. 5. c. xcvi.	The Chester Corporation Act 1929.	In section 131, the proviso.
20 & 21 Geo. 5. c. lvii.	The Chester Waterworks Act 1930.	In section 9, in the first proviso, the words from " shall not " to " 1869 and ".
20 & 21 Geo. 5. c. lviii.	The Milford Haven Urban District Council Act 1930.	In section 5(2), in the proviso, the words from " shall not " to " 1869 and ".
20 & 21 Geo. 5. c. lxvii.	The Portsmouth Water Act 1930.	In section 12, in the second proviso, the words from " shall not " to " 1869 and ".

Chapter	Title or Short Title	Extent of Repeal
20 & 21 Geo. 5. c. lxix.	The Tees Valley Water Act 1930.	In section 13, in the first proviso, the words from " shall not " to " 1869 and ".
20 & 21 Geo. 5. c. cxix.	The Leeds Corporation Act 1930.	In section 36(1), the proviso.
20 & 21 Geo. 5. c. clxxi.	The Falmouth Corporation Water Act 1930.	In section 20, in the proviso, the words from " shall not " to " 1869 and "
20 & 21 Geo. 5. c. clxxvi.	The Rotherham Corporation Act 1930.	In section 64, the first proviso.
20 & 21 Geo. 5. c. clxxviii.	The Manchester Corporation (General Powers) Act 1930.	In section 51(1), the words from " but nothing " to " 1869 ".
20 & 21 Geo. 5. c. clxxx.	The Bristol Corporation (No. 2) Act 1930.	In section 55, the first proviso.
20 & 21 Geo. 5. c. clxxxi.	The Bournemouth Corporation Act 1930.	In section 146, the proviso.
20 & 21 Geo. 5. c. clxxxviii.	The Southport Corporation Act 1930.	In section 49, the proviso.
21 & 22 Geo. 5. c. xvii.	The Gillingham Corporation Act 1931.	In section 32, the first proviso.
21 & 22 Geo. 5. c. xxvii.	The Lowestoft Water and Gas Act 1931.	In section 13, in the first proviso, the words from " shall not " to " 1869 and ".
21 & 22 Geo. 5. c. xliii.	The Portsmouth Corporation Act 1931.	In section 38(1), the proviso.
21 & 22 Geo. 5. c. lvii.	The Doncaster Corporation Act 1931.	In section 84, the first proviso.
21 & 22 Geo. 5. c. lxxiii.	The Public Works Facilities Scheme (Swindon Corporation) Confirmation Act 1931.	In the scheme set out in the Schedule, in section 9, the words from " shall not " to " 1869 and ".
21 & 22 Geo. 5. c. xci.	The Bacup Corporation Act 1931.	In section 19, in the proviso, the words from " shall not " to " 1869 and ".
21 & 22 Geo. 5. c. xcvi.	The Seaton Urban District Council Act 1931.	In section 14, the words from " shall not " to " 1869 and ".

Chapter	Title or Short Title	Extent of Repeal
21 & 22 Geo. 5. c. xcix.	The Southampton Corporation Act 1931.	In section 26, in the second proviso, the words from " be used " to " 1869 or ". In section 101(1), the proviso.
21 & 22 Geo. 5. c. civ.	The Corby (Northants) and District Water Act 1931.	In section 32, the words from " be used " to " 1869 or ".
21 & 22 Geo. 5. c. cv.	The Felixstowe and District Water Act 1931.	In section 32, in the first proviso, the words from " shall not " to " 1869 and ".
21 & 22 Geo. 5. c. cvi.	The Scarborough Corporation Act 1931.	In section 16, in the proviso, the words from " shall not " to " 1869 and ".
22 & 23 Geo. 5. c. xxxi.	The Rhyl Urban District Council Act 1932.	In section 18, the words from " shall not " to " 1869 and ".
22 & 23 Geo. 5. c. xl.	The Public Works Facilities Scheme (Shrewsbury Corporation) Confirmation Act 1932.	In the scheme set out in the Schedule, in section 20, the words from " shall not be used " to " 1869 and ".
22 & 23 Geo. 5. c. lxviii.	The Sidmouth Water Act 1932.	In section 21, the words from " be used " to " 1869 or ".
22 & 23 Geo. 5. c. lxxxvii.	The Chesterfield and Bolsover Water Act 1932.	In section 46, the words from " be used " to " 1869 or ".
23 & 24 Geo. 5. c. xxiv.	The Lyme Regis District Water Act 1933.	In section 38, the words from " shall not be used " to " 1869 and ".
23 & 24 Geo. 5. c. xl.	The Sidmouth Urban District Council Act 1933.	In section 24(2), in the proviso, the words from " shall not be used " to " 1869 and ".
23 & 24 Geo. 5. c. xlii.	The Worksop Corporation Act 1933.	In section 25, in the second proviso, the words from " shall not be used " to " 1869 and ".
23 & 24 Geo. 5. c. lxxxiii.	The Middlesbrough Corporation Act 1933.	In section 424, the words " or for any mail bag as defined by the Post Office Act 1908 ".
24 & 25 Geo. 5. c. i.	The Public Works Facilities Scheme (Witney Urban District Council) Confirmation Act 1933.	In the scheme set out in the Schedule, in section 14, in the first proviso, the words from " shall not " to " 1869 and ".

Chapter	Title or Short Title	Extent of Repeal
24 & 25 Geo. 5. c. viii.	The Public Works Facilities Scheme (Boston Corporation) Confirmation Act 1934.	In section 21 of the scheme set out in the Schedule, in the proviso, the words from " shall not " to " 1869 and ".
24 & 25 Geo. 5. c. xviii.	The East Worcestershire Water Act 1934.	In section 10, in the first proviso, the words from " shall not be used " to " 1869 and ".
24 & 25 Geo. 5. c. xxvi.	The Workington Corporation Act 1934.	In section 11, in the second proviso, the words from " shall not be used " to " 1869 and ".
24 & 25 Geo. 5. c. xxxvi.	The South West Suburban Water Act 1934.	In section 20, in the first proviso, the words from " shall not " to " 1869 and ".
24 & 25 Geo. 5. c. lxxiii.	The Chailey Rural District Council Act 1934.	In section 27, in the proviso, the words from " shall not " to " 1869 and ".
24 & 25 Geo. 5. c. lxxvi.	The Tynemouth Corporation Act 1934.	In section 208(1), the words " Section 34 (For protection of Postmaster General) ".
24 & 25 Geo. 5. c. xci.	The North Lindsey Water Act 1934.	In section 109, the words from " be used " to " 1869 or ".
24 & 25 Geo. 5. c. xciv.	The Weston-super-Mare Urban District Council Act 1934.	In section 15, the words from " shall not be used " to " 1869 and ".
24 & 25 Geo. 5. c. xcvii.	The Manchester Corporation Act 1934.	In section 18, the words " and section 47 (For protection of Postmaster General) ".
25 & 26 Geo. 5. c. xl.	The Baildon Urban District Council Act 1935.	In section 17, the words from " shall not be used " to " 1869 and ".
25 & 26 Geo. 5. c. li.	The West Hampshire Water Act 1935.	In section 14, in the first proviso, the words from " shall not " to " 1869 and ".
25 & 26 Geo. 5. c. lxxxix.	The Maidstone Corporation Act 1935.	In section 26(1), the first proviso.
25 & 26 Geo. 5. c. xci.	The Fylde Water Board Act 1935.	In section 8, the words " Section 34 (For protection of Postmaster General) ".
25 & 26 Geo. 5. c. xciii.	The Chichester Corporation Act 1935.	In section 29, the words from " shall not " to " 1869 and ".
25 & 26 Geo. 5. c. cvii.	The Harrogate Corporation Act 1935.	In section 30, the first proviso.

Chapter	Title or Short Title	Extent of Repeal
25 & 26 Geo. 5. c. cx.	The London Passenger Transport Act 1935.	Section 67(1).
25 & 26 Geo. 5. c. cxxv.	The Sunderland Corporation Act 1935.	In section 220, the first proviso.
26 Geo. 5 & 1 Edw. 8. c. v.	The Dundee Corporation Order Confirmation Act 1935.	In the order contained in the Schedule, in section 8, the proviso.
26 Geo. 5 & 1 Edw. 8. c. xxx.	The South East Cornwall Water Board Act 1936.	In section 45, the words from " shall not " to " 1869 and ".
26 Geo. 5 & 1 Edw. 8. c. xxxviii.	The Winchester Corporation Act 1936.	In section 21, in the first proviso, the words from " shall not " to " 1869 and ".
26 Geo. 5 & 1 Edw. 8. c. lvi.	The Rickmansworth and Uxbridge Valley Water Act 1936.	In section 17(1), the words from " shall not " to " 1869 and ".
26 Geo. 5 & 1 Edw. 8. c. lviii.	The Fishguard and Goodwick Urban District Council Act 1936.	In section 45(2), the words from " shall not " to " 1869 and ".
26 Geo. 5 & 1 Edw. 8. c. cvii.	The Wrexham and East Denbighshire Water Act 1936.	In section 11, the words from " shall not be used " to " 1869 or ".
26 Geo. 5 & 1 Edw. 8. c. cxiii.	The Hereford Corporation Act 1936.	In section 8, in the first proviso, the words from " shall not " to " 1869 and ".
1 Edw. 8 & 1 Geo. 6. c. liv.	The Newquay and District Water Act 1937.	In section 11, the words from " shall not " to " 1869 and ".
1 Edw. 8 & 1 Geo. 6. c. lxvi.	The Pontypool Gas and Water Act 1937.	In section 31, in the proviso, the words from " shall not " to " 1869 and ".
i Edw. 8 & 1 Geo. 6. c. lxix.	The Huddersfield Corporation Act 1937.	In section 33, the words from " shall not " to " 1869 and ".
1 Edw. 8 & 1 Geo. 6. c. lxxxvii.	The Ministry of Health Provisional Order Confirmation (Tonbridge Water) Act 1937.	In the order set out in the Schedule, in section 10, the words from " shall not be used " to " 1869 and ".
1 Edw. 8 & 1 Geo. 6. c. lxxxviii.	The Banbury Waterworks Act 1937.	In section 26, the words from " shall not be used " to " 1869 and ".

2 S*

Chapter	Title or Short Title	Extent of Repeal
1 Edw. 8 & 1 Geo. 6. c. xcv.	The Bucks Water Act 1937.	In section 63, the words from " shall not be used " to " 1869 and ".
1 Edw. 8 & 1 Geo. 6. c. cii.	The Aberdeen Corporation (Water Gas Electricity and Transport) Order Confirmation Act 1937.	In the order contained in the Schedule, in section 17, the words from " shall not " to " 1869 and ".
1 Edw. 8 & 1 Geo. 6. c. civ.	The Paisley Corporation Order Confirmation Act 1937.	In the order contained in the Schedule, in section 30(1), the words from " shall not be used " to " 1869 and ".
1 Edw. 8 & 1 Geo. 6. c. cxx.	The North Cotswold Rural District Council Act 1937.	In section 14, in the first proviso, the words from " shall not " to " 1869 and ".
1 Edw. 8 & 1 Geo. 6. c. cxxiii.	The Staffordshire Potteries Water Board Act 1937.	In section 10, in the first proviso, the words from " shall not " to " 1869 and ".
1 & 2 Geo. 6. c. xxxiv.	The Irwell Valley Water Board Act 1938.	In section 19, the proviso. In section 24, the words from " shall not " to " 1869 and ".
1 & 2 Geo. 6. c. xxxvii.	The Rickmansworth and Uxbridge Valley Water Act 1938.	In section 19, the words from " shall not " to " 1869 and ".
1 & 2 Geo. 6. c. xl.	The Wakefield Corporation Act 1938.	In section 121, the first proviso.
1 & 2 Geo. 6. c. liv.	The Redcar Corporation Act 1938.	In section 175, the words from " Provided that nothing " to " 1869 ".
1 & 2 Geo. 6. c. lxxxii.	The Newcastle and Gateshead Waterworks Act 1938.	In section 6, the words from " shall not be used " to " 1869 and ".
1 & 2 Geo. 6. c. xcviii.	The Warrington Corporation Water Act 1938.	In section 13, the words from " shall not be used " to " 1869 and ".
2 & 3 Geo. 6. c. xlvi.	The Ministry of Health Provisional Order Confirmation (Heywood and Middleton Water Board) Act 1939.	In the order set out in the Schedule, in section 6(1), in the proviso, the words from " shall not be used " to " 1869 and ".
2 & 3 Geo. 6. c. lxii.	The South Staffordshire Waterworks Act 1939.	In section 40, the words from " shall not be used " to " 1869 and ".

Chapter	Title or Short Title	Extent of Repeal
2 & 3 Geo. 6. c. lxv.	The Tiverton Corporation Act 1939.	In section 15, the words from "shall not be used" to "1869 and ". In section 88(1), the first proviso.
2 & 3 Geo. 6. c. lxvii.	The Stroud District Water Board &c. Act 1939.	In section 70, in the first proviso, the words from "shall not" to "1869 and ".
2 & 3 Geo. 6. c. lxxviii.	The Colne Valley Water Act 1939.	In section 94, the words from "shall not be used" to "1869 and ".
2 & 3 Geo. 6. c. lxxxii.	The Walsall Corporation Act 1939.	In section 136, the first proviso.
2 & 3 Geo. 6. c. lxxxvii.	The Macclesfield Corporation Act 1939.	In section 19, the words from "shall not" to "1869 and ". In section 109, the first proviso.
2 & 3 Geo. 6. c. xcii.	The Lanarkshire County Council Order Confirmation Act 1939.	In the order contained in the Schedule, in section 97(1), the words "or in contravention of any exclusive privilege by law vested for the time being in the Postmaster General ".
2 & 3 Geo. 6. c. cii.	The Folkestone Water Act 1939.	In section 18, in the second proviso, the words from "shall not" to "1869 and ".
2 & 3 Geo. 6. c. ciii.	The Sheffield Corporation Act 1939.	In section 73(3), the words from "shall not be used" to "1869 and ".
3 & 4 Geo. 6. c. ii.	The Glasgow Water and Tramways Order Confirmation Act 1940.	In the order set forth in the Schedule, in section 49, the words from "shall not" to "1869 and ".
3 & 4 Geo. 6. c. xxviii.	The Bournemouth Gas and Water Act 1940.	In section 16, the words from "be used" to "1869 or ".
3 & 4 Geo. 6. c. xxxi.	The Gosport Water Act 1940.	In section 12, the words from "be used" to "1869 or ".
4 & 5 Geo. 6. c. xiii.	The Ebbw Vale Urban District Council Act 1941.	In section 21, the words from "shall not be used" to "1869 and ".
5 & 6 Geo. 6. c. x.	The Pembrokeshire County Council Act 1942.	In section 43(1), the words "or for any mail bag as defined by the Post Office Act 1908 ".
5 & 6 Geo. 6. c. xv.	The Bilston Corporation Act 1942.	In section 12, the words from "shall not be used" to "1869 and ".

Chapter	Title or Short Title	Extent of Repeal
6 & 7 Geo. 6. c. xv.	The Northampton Corporation Act 1943.	In section 125, the words from " shall not " (where first occurring) to " 1869 and ".
7 & 8 Geo. 6. c. xx.	The Anglesey County Council (Water &c.) Act 1944.	In section 50, the words from " be used " to " 1869 or ".
8 & 9 Geo. 6. c. 42.	The Water Act 1945.	In Schedule 3, in section 5(3), the words from " be used " to " 1869, or ".
8 & 9 Geo. 6. c. 43.	The Requisitioned Land and War Works Act 1945.	In section 4, the words " the Postmaster General ". In section 32, the words " the Postmaster General ".
9 & 10 Geo. 6. c. vi.	The North Devon Water Board Act 1945.	In section 83, the words from " be used " to " 1869 or ".
9 & 10 Geo. 6. c. viii.	The Colne Valley Water Act 1945.	In section 64, the words from " shall not be used " to " 1869 and ".
9 & 10 Geo. 6. c. xii.	The East Grinstead Gas and Water Act 1945.	In section 61, the words from " shall not be used " to " 1869 and ".
9 & 10 Geo. 6. c. xiv.	The Plympton St. Mary Rural District Council Act 1945.	In section 30, the words from " be used " to " 1869 or ".
9 & 10 Geo. 6. c. 42.	The Water (Scotland) Act 1946.	In Schedule 4, in paragraph 5(3), the words from " be used " to " 1869, or ".
9 & 10 Geo. 6. c. xvii.	The Metropolitan Water Board Act 1946.	Section 83(2).
9 & 10 Geo. 6. c. xxxviii.	The Manchester Corporation Act 1946.	Section 6(5), from the beginning to " 1869 and ".
9 & 10 Geo. 6. c. liii.	The Tees Conservancy Act 1946.	In section 46(1), the words from " shall not " to " 1869 and ".
10 & 11 Geo. 6. c. 41.	The Fire Services Act 1947.	Section 3(2)(*c*).

SCH. 11

Chapter	Title or Short Title	Extent of Repeal
10 & 11 Geo. 6. c. 44.	The Crown Proceedings Act 1947.	Section 9.
10 & 11 Geo. 6. c. 54.	The Electricity Act 1947.	In Schedule 4, in Part I, in the entry relating to section 24 of the Electricity (Supply) Act 1926, the words " in both places where they occur ".
10 & 11 Geo. 6. c. xxxiii.	The Southend-on-Sea Corporation Act 1947.	In section 219, the words from " shall not " to " 1869 and ".
10 & 11 Geo. 6. c. xlv.	The Preston Corporation Act 1947.	In section 153, the first proviso.
11 & 12 Geo. 6. c. xli.	The Ipswich Corporation Act 1948.	In section 172(1), the proviso.
12, 13 & 14 Geo. 6. c. 39.	The Commonwealth Telegraphs Act 1949.	Section 9.
12, 13 & 14 Geo. 6. c. li.	The Barnsley Corporation Act 1949.	In section 88(1), the proviso.
14 Geo. 6. c. 39.	The Public Utilities Street Works Act 1950.	In section 33(2)(*b*), the words from " other than " onwards.
14 & 15 Geo. 6. c. 52.	The Telephone Act 1951.	The whole Act.
14 & 15 Geo. 6. c. xxxix.	The British Transport Commission Act 1951.	Section 16.
15 & 16 Geo. 6 & 1 Eliz. 2. c. 47.	The Rating and Valuation (Scotland) Act 1952.	Section 2.
15 & 16 Geo. 6 & 1 Eliz. 2. c. xx.	The Dundee Harbour and Tay Ferries Order Confirmation Act 1952.	In the order contained in the Schedule, in section 91, the words from " be used " to " 1869 or " and in section 213(1), the words " or for any mail bag as defined by the Post Office Act 1908 ".
15 & 16 Geo. 6 & 1 Eliz. 2. c. xli.	The Clifton Suspension Bridge Act 1952.	Section 44(1)(*e*).
15 & 16 Geo. 6 & 1 Eliz. 2. c. xlvi.	The North Wales Hydro-Electric Power Act 1952.	Section 35(2).

Chapter	Title or Short Title	Extent of Repeal
1 & 2 Eliz. 2. c. 36.	The Post Office Act 1953.	Sections 1 and 2. Sections 5 to 7. Section 8(1), (2) and (4). Section 9. Section 10 (except subsection (3)). Section 11(3). Sections 12 to 15. Section 16(3). Section 18. In section 19(1), the words from " and the sum " onwards. Section 20. Section 21 (except subsection (3)). Section 31. Sections 46 to 49. In section 76, the words from " and any such " onwards. Section 81. Section 84. In section 87(1), the definitions of " British postal agency ", " mandated territory ", " postage ", " prescribed ", " regulations " and " trust territory " and, in the definition of " mail bag ", the words " a parcel, an envelope and ". Schedule 1.
2 & 3 Eliz. 2. c. 36.	The Law Reform (Limitation of Actions, &c.) Act 1954.	In section 5, subsection (3), and, in subsection (4), the words " and subsection (2) of section nine ".
2 & 3 Eliz. 2. c. 62.	The Post Office Savings Bank Act 1954.	In section 25, the definitions of " post office savings bank " and " Post Office Savings Banks Fund ".
4 & 5 Eliz. 2. c. xi.	The Kent Water Act 1955.	In section 165(1)(*d*), the words from " be used " to " 1869 or ".
4 & 5 Eliz. 2. c. xxv.	The North Wales Hydro-Electric Power Act 1955.	Section 40(2).
4 & 5 Eliz. 2. c. xlix.	The Leicester Corporation Act 1956.	Section 95(2).
4 & 5 Eliz. 2. c. lxix.	The Millport Piers (Amendment) Order Confirmation Act 1956.	In the order contained in the Schedule, section 5.
4 & 5 Eliz. 2. c. lxxiii.	The Huddersfield Corporation Act 1956.	Section 25(2).

SCH. 11

Chapter	Title or Short Title	Extent of Repeal
5 & 6 Eliz. 2. c. 20.	The House of Commons Disqualification Act 1957.	In Schedule 2, the words " Postmaster General " and the words "Assistant Postmaster General ".
5 & 6 Eliz. 2. c. xxix.	The B P Trading Act 1957.	Section 5(8).
5 & 6 Eliz. 2. c. xxxviii.	The Esso Petroleum Company Act 1957.	Section 6(7).
6 & 7 Eliz. 2. c. xix	The Seaham Harbour Dock Act 1958.	Section 27.
6 & 7 Eliz. 2. c. xlviii.	The Shell (Stanlow to Partington Pipeline) Act 1958.	Section 4(7).
6 & 7 Eliz. 2. c. l.	The Wallasey Corporation Act 1958.	Section 115(2).
7 & 8 Eliz. 2. c. 6.	The National Debt Act 1958.	In section 1(1), the words " by the name of the Post Office register ". Section 13.
7 & 8 Eliz. 2. c. vi.	The Kent County Council Act 1958.	Section 59(2).
7 & 8 Eliz. 2. c. 25.	The Highways Act 1959.	In section 152(4), the words " or the Postmaster General ". In section 236(1)(c), the words from " other than " onwards.
7 & 8 Eliz. 2. c. 50.	The Pensions (Increase) Act 1959.	In the Schedule, in Part I, paragraph 22.
7 & 8 Eliz. 2. c. 55.	The Dog Licences Act 1959.	Section 7(3) to (8).
7 & 8 Eliz. 2. c. viii.	The Angle Ore and Transport Company Act 1959.	Section 5(7).
7 & 8 Eliz. 2. c. xxxii.	The Bucks Water Board Act 1959.	In section 38(2), the words from " be used " to " 1869 or ".
7 & 8 Eliz. 2. c. xxxiii.	The Reading and Berkshire Water &c. Act 1959.	In section 52(ii), the words from " be used " to " 1869 or ".
7 & 8 Eliz. 2. c. xliv.	The British Transport Commission Act 1959.	Section 13(4)(b).

2 S* 4

Chapter	Title or Short Title	Extent of Repeal
7 & 8 Eliz. 2. c. xlvi.	The Humber Bridge Act 1959.	Section 68(2)(*e*).
7 & 8 Eliz. 2. c. xlvii.	The Shell-Mex and B.P. (London Airport Pipeline) Act 1959.	Section 4(7).
7 & 8 Eliz. 2. c. li.	The Lee Valley Water Act 1959.	In section 83(1)(*d*), the words from " be used " to " 1869 or ".
8 & 9 Eliz. 2. c. xxxix.	The Tyne Tunnel Act 1960.	Section 41(2)(*e*).
8 & 9 Eliz. 2. c. lii.	The Oldham Corporation Act 1960.	Section 59(2).
9 & 10 Eliz. 2. c. i.	The Aberdeen Harbour Order Confirmation Act 1960.	In the order contained in the Schedule, in section 141, the words from " and for " onwards.
9 & 10 Eliz. 2. c. 15.	The Post Office Act 1961.	Section 1. Section 2(1) and (2). Sections 3 to 7. Section 8(1) and (3). Sections 9, 10 and 11. Section 13. Section 15(2) and (3). Sections 16 and 17. Section 19. Sections 21 and 22. Section 23(3). Section 25. Section 26(1). Section 27(3) and (4). Section 28(2). Section 29. In the Schedule, the entries relating to section 4 of the Exchequer and Audit Departments Act 1921, the Government Annuities Act 1929, the Bank of England Act 1946, the Crown Proceedings Act 1947, Schedule 1 to the Wireless Telegraphy Act 1949, the Telephone Act 1951, and sections 5 to 10 of the Post Office Act 1953 and the words in column 2 against them; in the entry relating to section 11 of the last-mentioned Act, the words from " in subsection (3) " to " by

Chapter	Title or Short Title	Extent of Repeal
9 & 10 Eliz. 2. c. 15—*cont.*	The Post Office Act 1961—*cont.*	regulations and "; and the entries relating to sections 12, 14, 15, 16, 20, 21, 24, 47, 48, 49, 77, 81 and 87 of the last-mentioned Act and sections 16 and 22 of the Post Office Savings Bank Act 1954 and the words in column 2 against them.
9 & 10 Eliz. 2. c. 36.	The Finance Act 1961.	Section 35(2).
9 & 10 Eliz. 2. c. vi.	The Esso Petroleum Company Act 1961.	Section 16(8).
9 & 10 Eliz. 2. c. xlv.	The Devon County Council Act 1961.	Section 29(2).
10 & 11 Eliz. 2. c. 13.	The Vehicles (Excise) Act 1962.	In section 22(1)(*b*), the words " other than the Postmaster General ".
10 & 11 Eliz. 2. c. 14.	The Telegraph Act 1962.	The whole Act.
10 & 11 Eliz. 2. c. 38.	The Town and Country Planning Act 1962.	In section 193(3), the proviso.
10 & 11 Eliz. 2. c. 58.	The Pipe-lines Act 1962.	In section 68(2), the words " other than the Postmaster General ".
10 & 11 Eliz. 2. c. xxxiii.	The Tay Road Bridge Order Confirmation Act 1962.	In the order contained in the Schedule, section 98(2)(*f*).
10 & 11 Eliz. 2. c. xliv.	The Regent Refining Company Act 1962.	Section 5(7).
1963, c. 11.	The Agriculture (Miscellaneous Provisions) Act 1963.	In section 27(*a*), the words form " other than " onwards.
1963, c. 31.	The Weights and Measures Act 1963.	In section 64(1)(*a*), the words " other than expenses incurred by the Postmaster General ".
1964, c. 21.	The Television Act 1964.	In section 2(6), the words " or section 5 of the Telegraph Act 1869 " and the word " respectively ". Section 29(2).
1964, c. 98.	The Ministers of the Crown Act 1964.	In Schedule 2, in Part II, the words " Postmaster General " and the words " Assistant Postmaster General ".

Chapter	Title or Short Title	Extent of Repeal
1964, c. xliii.	The Glasgow Corporation Consolidation (Water, Transport and Markets) Order Confirmation Act 1964.	In the order contained in the Schedule, in section 45, the words from " shall not " to " 1869 and ".
1965, c. 51.	The National Insurance Act 1965.	In section 52(1), the words from " and regulations " onwards. In section 85(1), the words "except the Postmaster General ", and paragraph (*a*).
1965, c. 52.	The National Insurance (Industrial Injuries) Act 1965.	In section 27(1), the words from " and regulations " onwards. In section 61(1), the words "except the Postmaster General ".
1965, c. 53.	The Family Allowances Act 1965.	In section 7(1), the words " whether through the Post Office or otherwise ". In section 13(1), the words " and in conjunction with the Postmaster General so far as relates to the Post Office ". In section 16, in subsection (1)(*b*), the words "other than expenses incurred by the Postmaster General", and subsection (2)(*b*).
1965, c. 54.	The National Health Service Contributions Act 1965.	In section 3(1), the words " except the Postmaster General ". In section 4, the words " except the Postmaster General ".
1965, c. 58.	The Ministerial Salaries Consolidation Act 1965.	In section 8(1), in the definition of " Parliamentary Secretary ", the words " and the Assistant Postmaster General ". In Schedule 1, the entries relating to the Postmaster General and the Assistant Postmaster General.
1965, c. 62.	The Redundancy Payments Act 1965.	In section 29, in subsection (1), the words " except the Postmaster General ", and, in subsection (3), the words " of section 19(2)(*b*) of the Post Office Act 1961 ". Section 41(6)(*b*). In section 55, in subsection (1), the words " other than the Postmaster General ", in subsection (2)(*a*), the words " other than the Postmaster General ", subsection (4), and, in subsection (6), the words " and the Postmaster General ".

Chapter	Title or Short Title	Extent of Repeal
1965, c. 78.	The Pensions (Increase) Act 1965	In Schedule 1, in Part I, paragraph 22.
1965, c. xxiv.	The Gulf Oil Refining Act 1965.	Section 16(7).
1965, c. xxviii.	The Crude Oil Terminals (Humber) Act 1965.	Section 15(7).
1965, c. xxxvi.	The Pembrokeshire County Council Act 1965.	Section 46(2)(*b*).
1965, c. xlv.	The Clyde Port Authority Order Confirmation Act 1965.	In the order set out in the Schedule, in section 80, in subsection (1), in paragraph (*a*)(iii), the words " the Postmaster General or " and paragraph (*c*).
1966, c. 12.	The Post Office Savings Bank Act 1966.	Section 1(3)(*c*). Section 3(3)(*a*) and (*c*). Section 7(4) and (5). Section 8(1) and (3).
1966, c. 18.	The Finance Act 1966.	In section 44, in subsection (4), the words " except the Postmaster General ", and subsection (5). Section 48.
1966, c. 20.	The Ministry of Social Security Act 1966.	Section 17(2). In Schedule 6, paragraph 17.
1966, c. 32.	The Selective Employment Payments Act 1966.	Section 3(1)(*b*). In Schedule 1, in Part II, the words " The Post Office Savings Bank ".
1966, c. 34.	The Industrial Development Act 1966.	Section 13(2). Section 30(2).
1966, c. 42.	The Local Government Act 1966.	Section 35(3) and (4).
1966, c. 51.	The Local Government (Scotland) Act 1966.	In section 43, in subsection (1)(*b*), the words " and to the Minister of Housing and Local Government " and the words " and to the Secretary of State ", and subsection (2). Section 44(2)(*b*) and (*c*).
1966, c. xv.	The Exeter Corporation Act 1966.	Section 28(2).

SCH. 11

Chapter	Title or Short Title	Extent of Repeal
1966, c. xxv.	The Tees and Hartlepools Port Authority Act 1966.	In section 81(1), in paragraph (*a*)(iii), the words " the Postmaster General or " and paragraph (*c*).
1967, c. 1.	The Land Commission Act 1967.	In section 2(3), the words " except the Postmaster General ". In section 4(4), the words " except the Postmaster General ". Section 84.
1967, c. 13.	The Parliamentary Commissioner Act 1967.	In Schedule 2, the words " Post Office " (where first occurring), and Note 3.
1967, c. 15.	The Post Office (Borrowing Powers) Act 1967.	The whole Act.
1967, c. 32.	The Development of Inventions Act 1967.	In section 11(1), the words " other than the Post Office ".
1967, c. 62.	The Post Office (Data Processing Service) Act 1967.	Sections 1 and 3(2).
1967, c. 72.	The Wireless Telegraphy Act 1967.	Section 14(1).
1967, c. 80.	The Criminal Justice Act 1967.	In Schedule 3, the entry relating to section 66 of the Post Office Act 1953.
1967, c. xxxiii.	The Kingston upon Hull Corporation Act 1967.	In section 77(1), the words " under licence from the Postmaster General ".
1968, c. 13.	The National Loans Act 1968.	In section 16(7), the words " and into the Post Office Fund ", and the words " and the Postmaster General ". In Schedule 1, the entries relating to the Post Office Act 1961. In Schedule 5, the entry relating to section 35(2) of the Finance Act 1961.
1968, c. 18.	The Consular Relations Act 1968.	Section 9.
1968, c. 34.	The Agriculture (Miscellaneous Provisions) Act 1968.	In section 53(*a*), the words " (except the Postmaster General) ".
1968, c. 47.	The Sewerage (Scotland) Act 1968.	In section 55(3), the words " or the Postmaster General ".

Chapter	Title or Short Title	Extent of Repeal
1968, c. 59.	The Hovercraft Act 1968.	In section 6(1), the words " (except the Postmaster General) ".
1968, c. 61.	The Civil Aviation Act 1968.	Section 27(3).
1968, c. 72.	The Town and Country Planning Act 1968.	In section 29, subsection (2), and, in subsection (4), the words " or the Postmaster General ".
1968, c. xxiv.	The Crosby Corporation Act 1968.	Section 14(7).
1968, c. xxxi.	The Mid-Glamorgan Water Act 1968.	In section 18(1), the words from " be used " to " 1869 or ".
1968, c. xxxii.	The Port of London Act 1968.	In section 28, in paragraph (*a*) (iii), the words " the Postmaster General or ", and paragraph (*c*).
1968, c. xxxiii.	The Medway Water (Bewl Bridge Reservoir) Act 1968.	In section 41(4), the words from " be used " to " 1869 and ".
1969, c. 30.	The Town and Country Planning (Scotland) Act 1969.	In section 30, subsection (2), and, in subsection (4), the words " or the Postmaster General ".

Enactments of the Parliament of Northern Ireland

Chapter	Short Title	Extent of Repeal
18 & 19 Geo. 5. c. 10.	The Roads Improvement Act (Northern Ireland) 1928.	In section 18, the words from " and in particular " onwards.
1946, c. 7.	The Shops Act (Northern Ireland) 1946.	Section 33(1)(*b*).
1948, c. 28.	The Roads Act (Northern Ireland) 1948.	In section 41(3), the words from " Except " to " section ".
1956, c. 19.	The Criminal Injuries Act (Northern Ireland) 1956.	In section 10, in the definition of " property ", the words " includes the property of the Postmaster General but ", and the word " other " (in both places where it occurs).
1956, c. v.	The River Bann Navigation Act (Northern Ireland) 1956.	Section 13.

Chapter	Short Title	Extent of Repeal
1966, c. 32.	The Selective Employ-ment Payments Act (Northern Ireland) 1966.	Section 4(1)(*b*).
1966, c. 41.	The Industrial Invest-ment (General Assistance) Act (Northern Ireland) 1966.	Section 14(4).

PART III

ORDERS IN COUNCIL REVOKED ON THE APPOINTED DAY

Number	Title or Short Title	Extent of Revocation
S.R. & O. 1908/844.	Order in Council fixing date of transfer of certain local taxation licence duties to county councils and county boroughs under section 6 of the Finance Act 1908 (8 Edw. 7. c. 16), and making provisions therefor.	Articles IV and V.
S.R. & O. 1921/221.	The Road Vehicles (Registration and Licensing) Order 1921.	In Article 2(*f*), the words from " Provided that " onwards.
S.R. & O. 1922/213.	The Local Taxation (Licence Officers) Order 1922.	The whole Order.

Education (Scotland) Act 1969

1969 CHAPTER 49

An Act to amend the law relating to education in Scotland, and for connected purposes.   [25th July 1969]

Be it enacted by the Queen's most Excellent Majesty, by and with the advice and consent of the Lords Spiritual and Temporal, and Commons, in this present Parliament assembled, and by the authority of the same, as follows:—

Part I

Provision of Education by Education Authorities

1.—(1) In the Education (Scotland) Act 1962 (hereafter in this Act called " the principal Act "), for sections 1 to 3 (provision of educational facilities by education authorities) there shall be substituted the following sections:—

Functions of education authorities.
1962 c. 47

" Duty of education authorities to secure provision of education.

1.—(1) It shall be the duty of every education authority to secure that there is made for their area adequate and efficient provision of school education and further education.

(2) In this Act—

(*a*) ' school education ' means progressive education appropriate to the requirements of pupils in attendance at schools, regard being had to the age, ability and aptitude of such pupils, and includes—

(i) activities in schools and classes (hereafter in this Act called ' nursery schools ' and ' nursery classes '), being activities of a kind suitable in the ordinary case for pupils who, for the purpose of school attendance, are under school age ;

(ii) special education ;

(iii) the teaching of Gaelic in Gaelic speaking areas ; and

(b) ' further education ' has the meaning assigned to it by section 4 of this Act.

(3) Every education authority—

(a) shall have power to secure for their area, and

(b) without prejudice to the duty imposed on them by subsection (1) above, shall be under a duty to secure for pupils in attendance at schools in their area,

the provision of adequate facilities for social, cultural and recreative activities and for physical education and training.

Secretary of State may prescribe standards, etc., for education authorities.

2. The Secretary of State may make regulations prescribing the standards and general requirements to which every education authority shall conform in discharging their functions under section 1 of this Act.

Fees not to be charged in public schools, etc.: exceptions.

3. School education and compulsory further education provided by an education authority shall be so provided without payment of fees, but an education authority shall have (and shall be deemed always to have had) power to charge fees in respect of the use of some or all of—

(a) any facilities for voluntary further education provided by them ;

(b) any facilities provided by them under section 1(3) of this Act.

Duty of education authorities to provide child guidance service.

3A. It shall be the duty of every education authority to provide for their area a child guidance service in child guidance clinics or elsewhere, and the functions of that service shall include—

(a) the study of handicapped, backward and difficult children ;

(b) the giving of advice to parents and teachers as to appropriate methods of education and training for such children ;

(c) in suitable cases, the provision of special education for such children in child guidance clinics ;

1968 c. 49.

(*d*) the giving of advice to a local authority within the meaning of the Social Work (Scotland) Act 1968 regarding the assessment of the needs of any child for the purposes of any of the provisions of that or any other enactment."

(2) Any reference in any enactment or other instrument (including this Act and, unless the contrary intention appears, any enactment or other instrument passed or made after the commencement of this Act) to—

(*a*) primary education shall be construed as a reference to school education of a kind which is appropriate in the ordinary case to the requirements of pupils who have not attained the age of twelve years ;

(*b*) secondary education shall be construed as a reference to school education of a kind which is appropriate in the ordinary case to the requirements of pupils who have attained that age ;

and any reference in any such enactment or other instrument as aforesaid to primary or secondary schools or departments or classes shall be construed accordingly.

(3) Notwithstanding the provisions of section 3 of the principal Act (as set out in subsection (1) above)—

(*a*) the power to charge fees in public schools conferred on education authorities by the proviso to section 1(3) of that Act (as originally enacted) shall continue to be available to, and may be exercised by, education authorities after the commencement of this Act, so, however, that this paragraph shall cease to have effect on 1st August 1970 ;

(*b*) where—

(i) an education authority have, at any time in the year ending with 1st August 1970, provided school education in any school under their management for an outwith-area pupil and have charged fees in respect of that education, and

(ii) the said pupil is on 1st October 1970 in attendance at a class in a secondary school, or in the secondary department of a school, under the management of that education authority,

the said education authority may charge fees in respect of any school education provided by them for that pupil in any school under their management at any time after 1st August 1970 when he is an outwith-area pupil :

> Provided that the education authority shall not have power under this paragraph to charge fees in respect of education provided by them for any pupil if a contribution in respect of such provision is payable to them by another education authority.

In this subsection " outwith-area pupil " means, in relation to any education authority, a pupil who is not deemed to belong for the purposes of section 24 of the principal Act to the area of that authority.

Provision of museums by education authorities.

2.—(1) An education authority (other than the town council of a burgh being a county of a city) may provide and maintain museums within their area, and shall have power—

(*a*) to acquire any objects which, in their opinion, it is desirable to include in a collection contained in a museum maintained by them under this section ;

(*b*) to lend any object vested in them and comprised in any such collection, on such terms and conditions as they think fit, to any person for any purpose ;

(*c*) subject to subsection (3) below, to transfer any object vested in them and comprised in any such collection to the governing body of a museum maintained by a person other than the education authority, for the purpose of being included in a collection contained in that museum ;

(*d*) subject to subsection (3) below, to sell, exchange, give away or otherwise dispose of any object vested in them and comprised in a collection contained in a museum maintained by them under this section, if for any reason that object is not, in their opinion, required for retention in any such collection ;

(*e*) to co-operate with any other education authority or the town council of any burgh in the provision or maintenance of a museum ;

(*f*) generally to do all such things as they may consider necessary or expedient for or in connection with the provision and maintenance of museums under this section.

(2) An education authority may, if they think fit, make such charge as they consider reasonable for admission to a museum maintained by them under this section, and in determining whether, and in what manner, to exercise their powers under this subsection in relation to any museum, an authority shall take into account the need to secure that the museum plays its full part in the promotion of education in their area, and shall have particular regard to the interests of children and students.

(3) Where an object has become vested in an education authority subject to any trust or condition—

(*a*) that object shall, on being transferred under subsection (1)(*c*) above, be subject to the like trust or condition in the hands of the transferee ;

(*b*) the powers conferred by subsection (1)(*d*) above shall not be exercisable in relation to that object in a manner inconsistent with that trust or condition.

3. For subsection (1) of section 19 of the principal Act (requirements as to premises of educational establishments) there shall be substituted the following subsection : —

　" (1) The Secretary of State may make regulations prescribing standards and general requirements which are to apply to the premises and equipment of educational establishments under the management of education authorities, and regulations under this subsection may prescribe different standards or requirements in respect of such different classes (however defined) of educational establishment as may be specified in the regulations."

4. In section 20 of the principal Act (acquisition of land and execution of works), after subsection (1) there shall be inserted the following subsection :—

　"(1A) An education authority shall not—

(*a*) acquire any land for use as the site of an educational establishment, or of playing fields to be used in connection with such an establishment, or of an extension to any such establishment or playing fields (whether contiguous to the establishment or playing fields or detached therefrom), or

(*b*) except in such cases as may be prescribed by regulations made by the Secretary of State, cause or permit works to be commenced for the erection of any building on land acquired by them for any such use as aforesaid, or for the extension or alteration of any building on land so acquired by them,

without the approval of the Secretary of State given in writing before such acquisition or commencement, as the case may be, and—

(i) an application by an education authority to the Secretary of State for an approval under this subsection shall be in such form, and shall contain such particulars, as may be prescribed, and

PART I

(ii) the Secretary of State may give his approval unconditionally, or subject to such conditions as he may think fit."

Discontinuance of educational establishments.

5.—(1) In section 22 of the principal Act (discontinuance of educational establishments), after subsection (1) there shall be inserted the following subsections:—

" (1A) Where an education authority propose to discontinue any educational establishment under their management, or to discontinue the use, in connection with such an educational establishment, of any part of that establishment, or of any building or part of a building ancillary to the establishment, and land forming the site, or part of the site, of that establishment or of that part of the establishment or of that building or part of a building, as the case may be, is subject to—

1841 c. 38.

(*a*) the third proviso to section 2 of the School Sites Act 1841 (which provides that, if any land granted in accordance with the provisions of that section ceases to be used for the purposes mentioned in that Act, that land shall revert to the grantor), or

(*b*) any condition of a similar nature in any Act, deed or other instrument,

the Secretary of State, on the application in that behalf of the education authority, may by order direct that the said proviso or condition shall not have effect in relation to that land:

Provided that such a direction shall not be given in relation to any land unless the Secretary of State is satisfied either—

(i) that the person to whom the land would revert in accordance with the said proviso or condition cannot after due inquiry be found, or

(ii) that, if that person can be found, he has consented to relinquish his rights in relation to the land under the said proviso or condition, and that, if he has consented to do so in consideration of the payment of a sum of money to him, adequate provision can be made for the payment to him of that sum.

(1B) A direction given by the Secretary of State under subsection (1A) above in relation to any land may make provision for the payment out of the proceeds of any sale of that land of any sum which is payable to any person in consideration of the relinquishment of his rights in relation to the land under the said proviso or condition."

(2) Section 119(3) of the principal Act (certain school land to be deemed to be an educational endowment) shall cease to have effect in so far as it relates to land forming the site or part of the site of an educational establishment under the management of an education authority or of any building ancillary to such an educational establishment.

6. For sections 25 and 26 of the principal Act (contributions by education authorities to schools, universities, etc.) there shall be substituted the following section:—

Power of education authorities to make payments to persons providing education, etc.

" Power of education authorities to make payments to persons providing education, etc.

25.—(1) An education authority may, for the purpose of promoting education generally, or of improving the facilities for education available, or the education provided, for their area in particular, make payments—

    (*a*) to another education authority,

    (*b*) to a university, or to the managers of a hostel or other residence used by students attending a university,

    (*c*) with the approval of the Secretary of State, to the managers of any school (other than a public school),

    (*d*) to the managers of any educational establishment (other than a school),

    (*e*) to any other person providing education or educational services,

    (*f*) to any person to assist the carrying out of educational research,

and any such payment may be made either unconditionally or subject to such conditions as may be agreed between the parties.

(2) Notwithstanding paragraph (*c*) of subsection (1) above, the approval of the Secretary of State shall not be required for the making by an education authority, by virtue of the power conferred on them by that paragraph, of payments to the managers of schools (other than public schools) in order to secure the admission thereto and education therein free of charge of pupils nominated by the education authority.

(3) Where—

    (*a*) it is agreed between an education authority and the managers of any educational establishment, as a condition of the making of payments under subsection (1) above, that the authority shall have representation or additional representation on the governing body of that establishment, but

(*b*) the provisions of any trust deed or other instrument relating to the establishment will not, unless they are modified, permit provision to be made for such representation or additional representation as aforesaid,

the Secretary of State may, on being requested to do so by the managers of the establishment, by order make such modifications in the provisions of that trust deed or other instrument as may be necessary to enable provision to be made for such representation or additional representation, as the case may be, as aforesaid, and any such trust deed or other instrument shall, so long as the said payments continue to be made, have effect subject to any modifications so made."

Part II

Rights and Duties of Parents and Functions of Education Authorities in Relation to Individual Pupils

Transfer schemes.

7. For section 30 of the principal Act (transfer schemes) there shall be substituted the following section:—

" Transfer schemes.

30. An education authority may at any time, and shall if and when so required by the Secretary of State, prepare and submit for his approval under section 70 of this Act a scheme or a revised scheme (hereafter in this Act called a ' transfer scheme ') relating to the schools under their management, and a transfer scheme shall—

(*a*) set out the arrangements which the education authority propose to adopt in relation to the transfer of pupils from one stage of school education and their admission to a subsequent stage of school education, and

(*b*) fix a single date (to be known as a ' transfer date ') on which such transfer shall take place in every year:

Provided that the Secretary of State may, if in the circumstances of any particular case he thinks it expedient to do so, approve a scheme which fixes more than one transfer date."

8. In section 33(1) of the principal Act (under which the Secretary of State may require an education authority to fix for their area two or more fixed dates for commencing school attendance and two school leaving dates), for the words from " Provided that " to the end there shall be substituted the following words: —

" Provided that—

>   (i) if in relation to the area of any education authority the Secretary of State is satisfied, either of his own accord or on the application of that authority, that, having regard to all the circumstances, it is desirable that a single date for commencing school attendance, or a single school leaving date, should be fixed for that area, he may require the authority to fix for the area a single date for commencing school attendance or, as the case may be, a single school leaving date ;

>   (ii) an education authority may, in pursuance of any requirement under paragraph (*a*) or paragraph (*b*) of this subsection or paragraph (i) of this proviso, fix different dates for different schools in their area."

9. After section 58 of the principal Act there shall be inserted the following section: —

" Dental inspection and supervision of pupils and young persons.

58A.—(1) It shall be the duty of an education authority to provide for the dental inspection, at appropriate intervals, and for the dental supervision of all pupils in attendance at any school under their management and of all young persons in attendance at any junior college or other educational establishment under their management, and an education authority shall have power to provide also for the dental inspection and supervision of other pupils in attendance at any educational establishment under their management who desire such inspection and supervision.

(2) For the purpose of securing the proper dental inspection of the pupils and young persons for whom it is their duty under this section to provide such inspection, an education authority may require the parent of any pupil in attendance at any school under their management to submit the pupil for dental inspection in accordance with arrangements made by the authority, and may require any young person in attendance at any junior college or other educational establishment under their management to submit himself for dental inspection.

PART II

(3) If any person fails without reasonable excuse to comply with a requirement made by an education authority under subsection (2) above, he shall be guilty of an offence and shall be liable on conviction by a court of summary jurisdiction to a fine not exceeding ten pounds."

Handicapped children.

10. For sections 62 to 66 of the principal Act (handicapped children) there shall be substituted the following sections:—

" Classification and educational arrangements.

62. The Secretary of State may make regulations defining the several categories of pupils requiring special education and making provision as to the special educational arrangements appropriate for pupils of each category.

Functions of education authority in relation to ascertainment of handicapped children.

63.—(1) An education authority—

(a) shall have power, as regards children in their area who have not attained the age of five years, and

(b) shall be under a duty, as regards children in their area who have attained that age,

to ascertain—

(i) which of those children require special education, and

(ii) which of those children are suffering from a disability of such a nature or to such an extent as to make them unsuitable for education or training either by ordinary methods of education or by special education.

(2) It shall be the duty of an education authority to disseminate in their area information as to the importance to any child who requires special education of the early ascertainment of his need, and of the opportunity for medical examination and psychological examination available under the following provisions of this Act.

Examination of children.

64.—(1) It shall not be lawful for an education authority to decide that a child requires special education, or that a child is suffering from a disability of such a nature or to such an extent as is mentioned in paragraph (ii) of section 63(1) of this Act, unless that child has undergone a medical examination and a psychological examination for the purpose of affording to the authority advice as to whether or not they ought so to decide ; and accordingly, before so deciding in the case of any child, an education authority shall—

    (*a*) invite the parent of that child to submit the child for a medical examination and a psychological examination for the said purpose, and

    (*b*) (in the case of a child who has attained the age of five years) if the parent fails to submit the child as aforesaid, by notice in writing served upon the parent require him to submit the child for a medical examination and a psychological examination for the said purpose.

(2) A parent who submits his child for a medical examination under subsection (1) above shall be entitled to be present at that examination if he so desires.

(3) If any parent on whom a notice has been served under paragraph (*b*) of subsection (1) above fails without reasonable excuse to comply with the requirements of the notice, he shall be guilty of an offence and liable on conviction by a court of summary jurisdiction to a fine not exceeding ten pounds.

(4) A notice served under paragraph (*b*) of subsection (1) above in respect of any child shall—

    (*a*) state that the purpose of the examinations is to afford to the education authority advice as to whether or not they ought to decide that that child requires special education or is suffering from a disability of such a nature or to such an extent as is mentioned in paragraph (ii) of section 63(1) of this Act ;

    (*b*) specify the times and places at which the examinations will be held ;

    (*c*) inform the parent of his right to be present at the medical examination if he so desires ;

    (*d*) inform the parent of the penalty to which he will be liable if he fails without reasonable excuse to comply with the requirements of the notice.

(5) If the parent of any child requests the education authority for the area to cause that child to be

medically and psychologically examined for the purpose of affording to the authority advice as to whether or not they ought to decide that the child requires special education or is suffering from a disability of such a nature or to such an extent as is mentioned in paragraph (ii) of section 63(1) of this Act, the authority shall comply with the request unless in their opinion the request is unreasonable.

65.—(1) An education authority shall take into consideration—

> (*a*) the advice given to them with respect to any child in consequence of the medical and psychological examinations undergone by that child under section 64 of this Act;

> (*b*) the views of the parent of the child, so far as these can be obtained;

> (*c*) if the child has been at any time in attendance at any school, any reports or other information with respect to the child which they are able to obtain from the records of the school or from teachers at the school;

> (*d*) any other reports or information which they are able to obtain with respect to the ability or aptitude of the child;

and the education authority may thereafter decide that the child requires special education, and if they so decide shall—

> (i) forthwith give to the parent of the child notice in writing of their decision, and

> (ii) thereafter ensure that any education provided by them for the child is special education.

(2) A notice given by an education authority to a parent in pursuance of paragraph (i) of subsection (1) above shall inform the parent of his right under subsection (1) of section 66A of this Act to require the authority to issue to him a statement of the reasons for their decision, and of his right under that subsection to refer the case to the Secretary of State.

Review by education authority of cases of children requiring special education.

66.—(1) It shall be the duty of an education authority to keep generally under consideration the cases of all children in their area who the authority have decided require special education, and—

(a) when in the discharge of that duty in relation to such a child the education authority think it expedient, or

(b) if the education authority are at any time requested to do so by notice in writing given to them by the parent of such a child,

the education authority shall review their decision that the said child requires special education:

Provided that the parent of a child who the education authority have decided requires special education shall not, by virtue of paragraph (b) above, be entitled to request the authority to review their decision earlier than the expiry of the period of 12 months from the date of that decision or more often than once in any period of 12 months subsequent to the expiry of the first-mentioned period.

(2) For the purpose of obtaining advice in connection with a review, under subsection (1) above, of their decision that a child requires special education, an education authority may—

(a) invite the parent of that child to submit the child for a medical examination and a psychological examination, and

(b) (in the case of a child who has attained the age of five years) if the parent fails to submit the child as aforesaid, by notice in writing served upon the parent require him to submit the child for a medical examination and a psychological examination.

(3) Subsections (2) to (4) of section 64 of this Act (examination of child) shall apply for the purposes of this section as they apply for the purposes of that section, with the substitution, for the references to subsection (1) of that section, of references to subsection (2) of this section, and subject to any other necessary modifications.

(4) In reviewing, under subsection (1) above, their decision that a child requires special education an education authority shall take into consideration—

(a) the advice given to them with respect to that child in consequence of medical and psychological examinations undergone by the child ;

(b) if either the review is being carried out in pursuance of a request made to them by the parent of the child by virtue of paragraph (b) of subsection (1) above or the parent was invited, under paragraph (a) of subsection (2) above, to submit the child for medical and psychological examination in connection with the review, the views of the parent of the child, so far as these can be obtained ;

(c) if the child has been at any time in attendance at any school, any reports or other information with respect to the child which they are able to obtain from the records of the school or from teachers at the school ;

(d) any other reports or information which they are able to obtain with respect to the ability or aptitude of the child ;

and the education authority shall thereafter either—

(i) revoke the said decision, in which case they shall forthwith give to the parent of the child notice in writing of its revocation, and their duty to ensure that any education provided by them for the child is special education shall thereupon cease ; or

(ii) determine not to revoke the decision, in which case, if either the review was carried out in pursuance of a request made to them by the parent of the child by virtue of paragraph (b) of subsection (1) above or the parent was invited, under paragraph (a) of subsection (2) above, to submit the child for medical and psychological examination in connection with the review, they shall forthwith give to the parent such notice of their determination as is mentioned in subsection (5) below; or

(iii) subject to subsection (6) below, revoke the decision but decide that the child is suffering from a disability of such a nature or to such an extent as is mentioned in paragraph (ii) of section 63(1) of this Act and that a report to the local authority should be issued by them under section 66B of this Act with respect to the child.

(5) A notice given by an education authority to a parent in pursuance of paragraph (ii) of subsection (4) above shall be in writing and shall inform the parent of his right under subsection (1) of section 66A of this Act to require the authority to issue to him a statement of the reasons for their determination, and of his right under that subsection to refer the case to the Secretary of State.

(6) An education authority shall not make, in relation to any child, a determination under paragraph (iii) of subsection (4) above unless—

(*a*) the child has attained the age of two years at the date of the determination, and

(*b*) the review was carried out in pursuance of paragraph (*a*) of subsection (1) above, and

(*c*) the child has undergone a medical examination and a psychological examination in connection with the review.

(7) In this section and in sections 66B, 66C, 66D and 66E of this Act the expression " local authority " 1968 c. 49. shall have the same meaning as in the Social Work (Scotland) Act 1968:

Provided that until section 1(4) of the said Act of 1968 comes into operation the expression " local authority " shall mean a local health authority with- 1947 c. 27. in the meaning of the National Health Service (Scotland) Act 1947 (including a joint committee or board constituted under section 20 of that Act).

Reference to Secretary of State of cases under ss. 65 and 66.
66A.—(1) Where an education authority—

(*a*) decide under section 65 of this Act that a child requires special education, or

(*b*) determine under section 66 of this Act not to revoke a decision made by them that a child requires special education and give to the parent of that child, in pursuance of paragraph (ii) of section 66(4) of this Act, notice in writing of their determination,

the education authority shall, if so required by the parent of the child, issue to the parent a statement of the reasons for their decision or determination, as the case may be, and where such a statement is so issued the parent may, if he is aggrieved by the decision or determination—

   (i) in the case of a decision, within the period of twenty-eight days from the date on which the statement was issued or such longer period therefrom as the Secretary of State may, either during or after the expiry of the twenty-eight days, allow,

   (ii) in the case of a determination, within the said period of twenty-eight days,

refer the case to the Secretary of State.

(2) On any reference under subsection (1) above the Secretary of State shall either confirm or refuse to confirm the decision or determination of the education authority.

(3) Where under subsection (2) above the Secretary of State refuses to confirm the decision or determination of an education authority with respect to any child, the authority shall be deemed to have revoked their decision that that child requires special education, and—

   (*a*) they shall forthwith give to the parent of the child notice in writing of the revocation of the decision, and

   (*b*) their duty to ensure that any education provided by them for the child is special education shall thereupon cease.

Ascertainment by education authority of children unsuitable for education: reference to Secretary of State.

66B.—(1) An education authority may, after considering, in accordance with section 65(1) of this Act, the advice and any reports or other information received by them with respect to any child who has attained the age of two years, and the views of the parent of that child (so far as these can be obtained), decide that the child is suffering from a disability of such a nature or to such an extent as is mentioned in paragraph (ii) of section 63(1) of this Act.

(2) Where an education authority decide as aforesaid in relation to any child, either under subsection (1) above or under paragraph (iii) of section 66(4) of this Act, they shall, subject to the following provisions of this section, issue to the local authority a report of their decision, together with a copy of any

document which they took into consideration in making their decision.

(3) Before issuing a report under this section with respect to any child, an education authority shall give to the parent of that child notice in writing—

(a) stating their intention to issue such a report with respect to the child ;

(b) setting out the functions of the local authority with respect to the making of arrangements for the treatment, care and training of the child in the event of the report's being issued ;

(c) specifying (if they are known to the education authority) the arrangements proposed to be made by the local authority for the discharge of those functions ;

(d) informing the parent of his right under the following provisions of this section to require the authority to issue to him a statement of the reasons for their decision in relation to the child, and of his right under those provisions to refer the case to the Secretary of State ;

and the education authority shall not issue such a report with respect to the child—

(i) earlier than the expiry of the period of twenty-eight days from the date on which the notice was served,

(ii) if within the said period the parent requires them, under subsection (4) below, to issue to him a statement of the reasons for their decision in relation to the child, earlier than the expiry of the period of twenty-eight days from the date on which that statement was issued,

(iii) if within either of the said periods the parent refers the case to the Secretary of State, except by the direction of the Secretary of State.

(4) Where an education authority have given notice to the parent of any child in pursuance of subsection (3) above, they shall, if so required by the parent within the period of twenty-eight days from the date on which the notice was served, issue

to the parent a statement of the reasons for their decision in relation to the child, and the parent may, if he is aggrieved by the decision—

    (*a*) where such a statement has been so required, within the period of twenty-eight days from the date on which that statement was issued,

    (*b*) where such a statement has not been so required, within the period of twenty-eight days from the date on which the said notice was served,

refer the case to the Secretary of State.

(5) On any reference under subsection (4) above the Secretary of State shall either—

    (*a*) direct the education authority to issue to the local authority a report under this section with respect to the child in question ; or

    (*b*) refuse to direct the education authority to issue such a report ; or

    (*c*) in the case of a child who the education authority have decided under subsection (1) above is suffering from a disability of such a nature or to such an extent as is mentioned in paragraph (ii) of section 63(1) of this Act, refuse to direct the authority to issue such a report but substitute for that decision a decision that the child requires special education ; or

    (*d*) in the case of a child in relation to whom the education authority have decided as aforesaid under paragraph (iii) of section 66(4) of this Act, refuse to direct the authority to issue such a report but confirm their determination under that paragraph so far as relating to the revocation of the decision that the child requires special education.

(6) Where under paragraph (*a*) of subsection (5) above the Secretary of State directs an education authority to issue to the local authority a report under this section with respect to any child, the education authority shall forthwith comply with that direction.

(7) Where under paragraph (*b*) of subsection (5) above the Secretary of State refuses to direct an education authority to issue such a report with respect to any child, being a child who the authority have decided, under paragraph (iii) of section 66(4) of this Act, is suffering from a disability of such a nature or to such an extent as is mentioned in paragraph (ii) of section 63(1) of this Act, the authority shall be deemed not to have revoked their decision that the child requires special education and shall continue to ensure that any education provided by them for the child is special education.

(8) Where under paragraph (*c*) of subsection (5) above the Secretary of State substitutes for any decision of an education authority in relation to any child a decision that the child requires special education, the authority shall be deemed to have decided under section 65(1) of this Act that the child requires special education and shall thereafter ensure that any education provided by them for the child is special education.

(9) An education authority shall as soon as practicable give to the parent of any child notice in writing of any decision made by the Secretary of State in relation to that child on a reference under subsection (4) above and of the effect of that decision.

Review by education authority of cases of children unsuitable for education.

66C.—(1) An education authority shall, if they are at any time requested to do so by notice in writing given to them—

(*a*) by the parent of a child with respect to whom the education authority have issued a report under section 66B of this Act, or

(*b*) by the local authority, as regards such a child, or

(*c*) by any authority or body responsible for the management of an institution in which such a child is under care,

review their decision that the said child is suffering from a disability of such a nature or to such an extent as is mentioned in paragraph (ii) of section 63(1) of this Act:

Provided that the parent of a child with respect to whom the education authority have issued a report under section 66B of this Act shall not, by

2 T*

virtue of paragraph (*a*) above, be entitled to request the education authority to review their decision earlier than the expiry of the period of 12 months from the date of that report or more often than once in any period of 12 months subsequent to the expiry of the first-mentioned period.

(2) Where an education authority review, under subsection (1) above, their decision in relation to any child, they shall, for the purpose of obtaining advice in connection with that review—

> (*a*) invite the parent of that child to submit the child for a medical examination and a psychological examination, and

> (*b*) if the parent fails to submit the child as aforesaid, by notice in writing served upon the parent require him to submit the child for a medical examination and a psychological examination.

(3) Subsections (2) to (4) of section 64 of this Act (examination of child) shall apply for the purposes of this section as they apply for the purposes of that section, with the substitution, for the references to subsection (1) of that section, of references to subsection (2) of this section, and subject to any other necessary modifications.

(4) In reviewing, under subsection (1) above, their decision in relation to any child an education authority shall take into consideration—

> (*a*) the advice given to them with respect to that child in consequence of medical and psychological examinations undergone by the child ;

> (*b*) any reports or other information with respect to the child which they are able to obtain from the parent of the child, or from the local authority, or from any authority or body responsible for the management of an institution in which the child is under care, or from any other person ;

and the education authority shall thereafter either—

> (i) cancel the report issued by them under section 66B of this Act with respect to the child, in which case they shall forthwith give notice in writing of its cancellation to the parent of the child, to the local

authority and to any authority or body responsible for the management of an institution in which the child is under care ; or

(ii) cancel the said report but decide that the child requires special education, in which case they shall forthwith give notice in writing of their determination to the persons mentioned in paragraph (i) above and shall thereafter ensure that any education provided by them for the child is special education ; or

(iii) determine not to cancel the report, in which case they shall forthwith give notice in writing of their determination to the persons mentioned in paragraph (i) above.

(5) A notice given by an education authority to a parent in pursuance of paragraph (ii) or paragraph (iii) of subsection (4) above shall inform the parent of his right under subsection (1) of section 66D of this Act to require the education authority to issue to him a statement of the reasons for their determination, and of his right under that subsection to refer the case to the Secretary of State.

Reference to Secretary of State of cases under s. 66C.

66D.—(1) Where an education authority, acting under section 66C of this Act—

(a) cancel a report issued by them under section 66B of this Act with respect to any child, but decide that the child requires special education, or

(b) determine not to cancel a report issued by them under the said section 66B with respect to any child,

the education authority shall, if so required by the parent of the child, issue to the parent a statement of the reasons for their determination, and where such a statement is so issued the parent may, if he is aggrieved by the determination, within the period of twenty-eight days from the date on which the statement was issued refer the case to the Secretary of State.

(2) On any reference under subsection (1) above the Secretary of State shall either—

(a) confirm the determination of the education authority, or (*b*) refuse to confirm their determination, or

(*c*) (where the education authority have determined not to cancel the report in question) refuse to confirm the determination of the education authority and substitute therefor a determination that the report should be cancelled but that the child to whom the report relates requires special education.

(3) Where under paragraph (*b*) of subsection (2) above the Secretary of State refuses to confirm the determination of an education authority with respect to any child, the education authority shall be deemed to have cancelled the report issued by them under section 66B of this Act with respect to that child, and they shall forthwith give notice in writing of its cancellation to the persons mentioned in paragraph (i) of section 66C(4) of this Act.

(4) Where under paragraph (*c*) of subsection (2) above the Secretary of State refuses to confirm the determination of an education authority with respect to any child and substitutes therefor a determination that the report in question should be cancelled but that the child to whom the report relates requires special education, the education authority shall be deemed to have cancelled the said report but to have decided that the child requires special education, and they shall forthwith give notice in writing to this effect to the persons mentioned in paragraph (i) of section 66C(4) of this Act and shall thereafter ensure that any education provided by them for the child is special education.

Children who may benefit by local authority services after leaving school.

66E.—(1) Where an education authority decide that a child to whom this section applies is suffering from mental deficiency to such an extent that he may, on leaving school, benefit from services which it is the function of a local authority to provide or secure the provision of, it shall be the duty of the education authority to issue, not earlier than six months, or later than one month, before the child ceases to be of school age—

(*a*) to the parent of the child, a report of their decision, and

(*b*) to the local authority, a report of their decision together with a copy of any document which was taken into account in making the decision.

(2) For the purpose of obtaining advice as to the carrying out of the duty imposed on them by subsection (1) above in relation to any child, an education authority may—

> (*a*) invite the parent of the child to submit the child for a medical examination and (if the education authority think it expedient) a psychological examination, and

> (*b*) if the parent fails to submit the child for any examination on being invited to do so under paragraph (*a*) above, by notice in writing served upon the parent require him to submit the child for such an examination.

(3) Subsections (2) to (4) of section 64 of this Act (examination of child) shall apply for the purposes of this section as they apply for the purposes of that section, with the substitution, for the references to subsection (1) of that section, of references to subsection (2) of this section, and subject to any other necessary modifications.

(4) This section applies to—

> (*a*) any child in attendance at a school under the management of the education authority concerned ;

> (*b*) any child in attendance at a school (other than such a school as is mentioned in paragraph (*a*) above) in the area of the education authority concerned ;

> (*c*) any child who is receiving education at a school by virtue of arrangements made by the education authority concerned with the managers of that school."

Part III

Administration and Finance

11. In section 67 of the principal Act (which imposes a duty on the Secretary of State to cause inspection to be made of educational establishments), in subsection (1), for the words " It shall be the duty of the Secretary of State " there shall be substituted the words " The Secretary of State shall have power ".

Amendment of s. 67 of Education (Scotland) Act 1962.

Part III

Power of Secretary of State to make grants to education authorities and others.

12.—(1) For section 75 of the principal Act (application of moneys provided by Parliament for education in Scotland) there shall be substituted the following section:—

" Power of Secretary of State to make grants to education authorities and others.

75. The Secretary of State may out of moneys provided by Parliament apply, in accordance with regulations made by him, such sums as he thinks necessary or expedient for any or all of the following purposes:—

(a) the payment of grants to education authorities ;

(b) the payment of grants to universities ;

(c) the payment of grants to the managers of educational establishments ;

(d) the payment of grants to any other persons providing education or educational services ;

(e) the payment of grants to persons to assist the carrying out of educational research ;

(f) the payment of allowances to or in respect of persons attending courses of education ;

(g) providing for any other educational expenditure approved by him."

(2) Notwithstanding the provisions of subsection (1) above, the power conferred on the Secretary of State by section 75(2) of the principal Act (as originally enacted) to make payments to universities out of moneys provided by Parliament shall continue to be available to, and may be exercised by, him until 1st August 1972.

1929 c. 25.

(3) Section 52(3) of, and Schedule 6 to, the Local Government (Scotland) Act 1929, so far as they relate to the payment of moneys to the universities of Scotland, shall cease to have effect.

Abolition of highland schools grant, and compensation therefor.

13.—(1) No payment shall be made under section 77 of the principal Act (highland schools grant) by the Treasury to any education authority after 11th November 1969, and the said section 77 and Schedule 2 to the principal Act shall cease to have effect immediately after that date.

(2) The sums mentioned in Schedule 1 to this Act shall be charged on the Consolidated Fund of the United Kingdom, and the Treasury shall, as soon as practicable after 11th November 1969, pay out of that Fund to the education authority of each education area mentioned in the first column of the said Schedule, by way of compensation for the loss occasioned to that authority by the cessation of payment of grants under the said section 77, the sum shown in the second column of that Schedule opposite to the name of that area.

14. Section 78 of the principal Act (appointment of account-ant) and section 80 of that Act (accountant's annual report) shall cease to have effect.

15. For section 81 of the principal Act (training of teachers) there shall be substituted the following section:—

" Power of Secretary of State to make regulations with respect to certain institutions providing further education.

81.—(1) The Secretary of State may make regula-tions with respect to grant-aided colleges, and such regulations may—

(*a*) make provision with regard to the constitu-tion of the governing bodies of such colleges, and in particular provide that the governing bodies shall be bodies corporate having a common seal;

(*b*) prescribe the general functions to be dis-charged by the governing bodies, and confer on the governing bodies such powers as the Secretary of State may consider neces-sary or expedient for the efficient discharge of those functions;

and without prejudice to the generality of the fore-going provisions of this subsection, such regulations may—

(i) prescribe the administrative and other arrangements to be adopted by the govern-ing bodies for the purpose of discharging their functions and, in particular, provide for the delegation by the governing bodies of such of their functions as may be pre-scribed in the regulations to persons or bodies of persons to be appointed in such manner as may be so prescribed;

(ii) provide for the appointment, remuneration, discipline and dismissal by the governing bodies of administrative, teaching and other staff, and for the payment by the governing bodies of pensions, allowances or gratuities to or in respect of members of such staff on their death or retirement;

(iii) make provision with regard to fees and other payments to be made by students in attendance at such colleges;

(iv) provide for the constitution of bodies repre-sentative of students in attendance at such colleges and confer on any such bodies such functions as may be prescribed in the regulations ;

(v) prescribe the procedure to be followed in cases of alleged breaches of discipline by students in attendance at such colleges.

(2) The Secretary of State may by regulations establish institutions for the provision of any form of further education, and such regulations may make provision with regard to any of the matters mentioned in paragraphs (*a*) and (*b*), and paragraphs (i) to (v), of subsection (1) above ; and where any institution established by regulations under this subsection becomes a grant-aided college, those regulations shall continue to apply to that institution until varied or revoked by regulations made under subsection (1) above or subsection (3) below.

(3) The Secretary of State may by regulations dissolve any grant-aided college.

(4) Regulations made under subsection (1) above may—

(*a*) apply to all grant-aided colleges, or to certain grant-aided colleges only, or to a single grant-aided college only ;

(*b*) make different provision in respect of different classes of grant-aided college or in respect of different grant-aided colleges ;

(*c*) vary or revoke the provisions of any enactment (including any regulations made under subsection (2) above), scheme, articles of association, trust deed or other instrument relating to any grant-aided college to which the regulations apply, in so far as those provisions are, in the opinion of the Secretary of State, inconsistent with the regulations ;

and regulations under any of the foregoing provisions of this section may contain such incidental, supplementary and consequential provisions as appear to the Secretary of State to be necessary or expedient.

(5) In this section the expression ' grant-aided college ' means a central institution, a college of education or an institution established under subsection (2) above, the managers of which are for the time being receiving grant in respect of that institution or college under section 75(*c*) of this Act."

16.—(1) Except where his employer otherwise determines, every teacher to whom this section applies and who holds a post of special responsibility shall retire from that post—

    (*a*) on the date on which he attains the age of sixty-five years, or

    (*b*) in the case of a teacher holding such a post at the commencement of this section of this Act who has attained the age of sixty-five years before such commencement, on the date of such commencement,

so, however, that nothing in this subsection shall prevent the employer of a teacher who has, by virtue of this subsection, retired from a post of special responsibility from offering to that teacher, or the teacher from accepting, appointment to another post, not being a post of special responsibility.

(2) Except where his employer otherwise determines, every teacher to whom this section applies shall retire from the post in which he is employed—

    (*a*) on the date on which he attains the age of seventy years, or

    (*b*) in the case of a teacher employed in any post at the commencement of this section of this Act who has attained the age of seventy years before such commencement, on the date of such commencement.

(3) This section applies to every teacher employed by an education authority or by the managers of a grant-aided school, and the references in this section to a post of special responsibility shall be construed as references to a post which attracts a responsibility allowance in terms of the memorandum referred to in an order made by the Secretary of State under section 2(4) of the Remuneration of Teachers (Scotland) Act 1967 and for the time being in force.

(4) This section shall come into force on such date as the Secretary of State may appoint by an order made by statutory instrument.

17. Sections 84 and 87 of the principal Act (retiring allowances, etc.) shall cease to have effect.

18.—(1) In section 85 of the principal Act (dismissal of teachers), for the word "certificated", wherever it occurs, there shall be substituted the word "registered".

(2) Notwithstanding the provisions of subsection (1) above, subsections (1) and (2) of the said section 85 shall after the commencement of this Act continue to apply in relation to

PART III certificated teachers employed in an institution providing any form of further education, but this subsection shall cease to have effect on such date as the Secretary of State may appoint by an order made by statutory instrument.

PART IV

REORGANISATION OF ENDOWMENTS

Schemes for reorganisation of educational endowments: procedure, appeal, making and effect.

19. For sections 125 to 127 of the principal Act (procedure, etc., relating to schemes for reorganisation of educational endowments) there shall be substituted the following sections:—

" Procedure in preparation of reorganisation schemes.

125.—(1) Before making a scheme for the reorganisation of any educational endowment the Secretary of State shall prepare a draft scheme and shall—

(*a*) send copies of the draft scheme to the governing body of the endowment to which it relates ; and

(*b*) cause the draft scheme to be published in such manner as he thinks sufficient for giving information to all persons interested in the scheme ;

and the governing body of that endowment or any other person interested in the scheme may, not later than the expiry of the period of one month from the first publication of the draft scheme, send in writing to the Secretary of State objections to the draft scheme, or proposed amendments thereto, or both.

(2) If within the period referred to in subsection (1) above no objection and no proposed amendment to the draft scheme is received by him, the Secretary of State may by statutory instrument make the scheme in the terms of the draft scheme published under subsection (1) above.

(3) If within the said period objections or proposed amendments to the draft scheme are received by him, the Secretary of State shall consider those objections and proposed amendments and may thereafter, if he thinks fit, frame a scheme in such form as he thinks expedient.

(4) If the Secretary of State frames a scheme under subsection (3) above, he shall as soon as practicable thereafter—

(*a*) give to the persons who made the objections or, as the case may be, proposed the amendments to the draft scheme notice in writing of his decision with respect to those objections or amendments, together with a statement in writing of the reasons for his decision ;

(b) send copies of the scheme to the governing body of the endowment to which it relates ;

(c) cause the scheme to be published in such manner as he thinks sufficient for giving information to all persons interested in the scheme ;

(d) cause to be published, along with the scheme, a notice—

(i) stating that, unless not later than the expiry of the period of one month from the first publication of the scheme a petition or appeal is presented to the Court of Session in accordance with the following provisions of this section, the Secretary of State proposes by statutory instrument to make the scheme in the terms in which it has been published, and

(ii) drawing attention to the provisions of subsection (6) below in such a way as to inform all persons concerned of their right under that subsection to present a petition to the Secretary of State and of the effect of their so doing.

(5) If within the period referred to in paragraph (d)(i) of subsection (4) above no petition or appeal is presented as aforesaid to the Court of Session, or if any petition or appeal so presented is refused by the Court, the Secretary of State may by statutory instrument make the scheme in the terms in which it was published under subsection (4) above.

(6) If within the said period a petition praying that the scheme be laid before Parliament is presented to the Secretary of State by any of the persons mentioned below, the Secretary of State shall lay the statutory instrument containing the scheme before Parliament, and that statutory instrument shall be subject to annulment in pursuance of a resolution of either House thereof.

The persons referred to above are—

(a) the governing body of the endowment to which the scheme relates,

(b) the town council of any burgh directly affected by the scheme,

(c) any education authority directly affected by the scheme,

(d) any ratepayers (not being less than twenty) of any burgh or parish or place directly affected by the scheme,

(e) any person having a vested interest in the said endowment or any part of it.

(7) If within the said period there is presented to the Court of Session by the governing body of the endowment a petition for amendment of the scheme or for the substitution of a new scheme, the Court may amend the scheme and make it as so amended, or may make a new scheme, and for those purposes the Court of Session shall have the like powers as are conferred by this Part of this Act on the Secretary of State regarding schemes for the future government and management of educational endowments.

(8) If within the said period an appeal is presented to the Court of Session by—

(a) the governing body of the endowment to which the scheme relates, or any other person directly affected by the scheme, on the ground that the scheme is not within the scope of, or is not made in conformity with, this Part of this Act, or

(b) any person holding any office, place or employment, or receiving any pension, compensation allowance, bursary or emolument, under or arising out of the endowment to which the scheme relates, on the ground that the scheme does not comply with the provisions of this Part of this Act as to saving or making due compensation for his vested interests,

and the Court of Session decides that the scheme is contrary to law on any of the grounds mentioned in paragraphs (a) and (b) above, the Secretary of State shall not make the scheme but may, if he thinks fit, frame an amended scheme in such form as he thinks expedient, and the provisions of subsections (4) to (7) above, and of this subsection, shall apply in relation to an amended scheme framed under this subsection as they apply to a scheme framed under subsection (3) above.

(9) Where the Secretary of State causes a draft scheme or a scheme to be published under this section, he shall cause to be prefixed to that draft scheme or scheme a memorandum setting out—

> (*a*) the reasons why, in his view, the reorganisation of the endowment to which the draft scheme or scheme relates is necessary ;

> (*b*) the respects in which the draft scheme or scheme involves any substantial alteration of the purposes to which the said endowment is applied or applicable ; and

> (*c*) the reasons for any such alteration ;

and for the purposes of the provisions of this section relating to publication, that memorandum shall be deemed to be part of the draft scheme or scheme, as the case may be.

Procedure in preparation of reorganisation schemes by Scottish Universities Committee of Privy Council by virtue of s.118(5).

126.—(1) Before making, by virtue of section 118(5) of this Act, a scheme for the reorganisation of any endowment the Scottish Universities Committee of the Privy Council (hereafter in this section called " the Committee ") shall prepare a draft scheme and shall—

> (*a*) send copies of the draft scheme to the governing body of the endowment to which the draft scheme relates ; and

> (*b*) cause the draft scheme to be published in such manner as it thinks sufficient for giving information to all persons interested in the scheme ;

and the governing body of that endowment or any other person interested in the scheme may, not later than the expiry of the period of one month from the first publication of the draft scheme, send in writing to the Committee objections to the draft scheme, or proposed amendments thereto, or both.

(2) If within the period referred to in subsection (1) above no objection and no proposed amendment to the draft scheme is received by it, the Committee may make the scheme in the terms of the draft scheme published under that subsection, and it shall be lawful for Her Majesty by Order in Council to approve the scheme so made.

(3) If within the said period objections or proposed amendments to the draft scheme are received by it, the Committee shall consider those objections and proposed amendments and may thereafter, if it thinks fit, frame a scheme in such form as it thinks expedient.

(4) If the Committee frames a scheme under subsection (3) above, it shall as soon as practicable thereafter—

(*a*) give to the persons who made the objections or, as the case may be, proposed the amendments to the draft scheme notice in writing of its decision with respect to those objections or amendments;

(*b*) send copies of the scheme to the governing body of the endowment to which the scheme relates;

(*c*) cause the scheme to be published in such manner as it thinks sufficient for giving information to all persons interested in the scheme;

(*d*) cause to be published, along with the scheme, a notice—

(i) stating that, unless not later than the expiry of the period of one month from the first publication of the scheme an appeal is presented to the Court of Session in accordance with the following provisions of this section, the Committee proposes to make the scheme in the terms in which it has been published, and that the scheme when so made may be approved by Her Majesty by Order in Council; and

(ii) drawing attention to the provisions of subsection (6) below in such a way as to inform all persons concerned of their right under that subsection to present a petition to the Committee and of the effect of their so doing.

(5) If within the period referred to in paragraph (*d*)(i) of subsection (4) above no appeal is presented as aforesaid to the Court of Session, or if any appeal so presented is refused by the Court, the

Committee may make the scheme in the terms in which it was published under that subsection, and, subject to subsection (6) below, it shall be lawful for Her Majesty by Order in Council to approve the scheme so made.

(6) If within the said period a petition praying that the scheme be laid before Parliament is presented to the Committee by any of the persons mentioned below, the Committee shall cause the scheme to be laid before both Houses of Parliament, and it shall be lawful for Her Majesty, after the scheme has so lain for forty days (in reckoning which period no account is to be taken of any time during which Parliament is dissolved or prorogued or during which both Houses are adjourned for more than four days), by Order in Council to approve the scheme unless within that period either House has resolved that the scheme shall not be proceeded with, in which case no further proceedings shall be taken thereon, without prejudice, however, to the making of a new scheme.

The persons referred to above in relation to a scheme under this section are those mentioned in paragraphs (*a*) to (*e*) of section 125(6) of this Act in relation to a scheme under that section.

(7) Subsection (8) of section 125 of this Act shall apply for the purposes of this section as it applies for the purposes of that section, with the substitution, for the references to the Secretary of State and to subsections (4) to (7) and (3) of that section, of references to the Committee and to subsections (4) to (6) and (3) of this section respectively.

(8) Subsection (9) of section 125 of this Act shall apply for the purposes of this section as it applies for the purposes of that section, with the substitution, for the references to the Secretary of State and to that section, of references to the Committee and to this section respectively.

(9) For the purposes of this section, references to an endowment shall be construed as references to a university endowment or the Carnegie Trust and references to the governing body of an endowment shall be construed as references to the founder or the governing body of the university court of any university, with respect to a university endowment, and to the Carnegie Trustees, with respect to the Carnegie Trust.

PART IV

Effect of schemes.

127.—(1) Any scheme made or approved under the foregoing provisions of this Part of this Act shall come into operation—

(a) except as provided in paragraph (b) below, on the date of the making of the statutory or other instrument containing, or (as the case may be) the Order in Council approving, the scheme ;

(b) in the case of a scheme contained in a statutory instrument laid before Parliament in pursuance of section 125(6) of this Act, on such date as may be specified in that statutory instrument ;

and shall have effect in the same manner as if it had been enacted in this Act, and accordingly, from the said date, any enactment, letters patent, deed, instrument, trust or direction relating to the subject-matter of the scheme, so far as inconsistent with the provisions thereof, shall cease to have effect.

(2) A statutory or other instrument containing a scheme made (otherwise than by the Scottish Universities Committee of the Privy Council), or an Order in Council or other instrument approving a scheme, under this Part of this Act shall be conclusive evidence that that scheme is within the scope of, and was made in conformity with, this Act, and the validity of the scheme shall not be questioned in any legal proceedings whatever."

Schemes for small endowments.

20. In section 128 of the principal Act (which provides a shortened procedure for the making of schemes for the reorganisation of educational endowments of an annual value of less than fifty pounds), for the word " fifty " there shall be substituted the words " five hundred ".

PART V

MISCELLANEOUS PROVISIONS

Power of Secretary of State to relax certain regulations.

21.—(1) If it appears to the Secretary of State, on an application in that behalf made to him—

(a) in relation to regulations made under section 2 or section 19(1) of the principal Act, by an education authority ;

(*b*) in relation to regulations made under section 76(1) of the principal Act, by any education authority or other person to whom any grant is payable under that Act

that it is unreasonable that any provision of those regulations should apply in relation to that authority or person or to such educational establishment under the management of that authority or person as may be specified in the application, or should so apply without modification, he may, subject to subsection (2) below, direct that the said provision shall not apply in relation to that authority or person or that educational establishment or, as the case may be, shall so apply subject to such modification as may be specified in the direction.

(2) A direction under subsection (1) above—

(*a*) may be given either unconditionally or subject to such conditions as may be specified in the direction ;

(*b*) shall not be given in respect of any provision of any regulations which is described in those regulations as not being subject to the giving of a direction under this section ;

(*c*) may be varied or revoked by a subsequent direction given by the Secretary of State either of his own accord or on the application of the education authority or other person on whose application the original direction was given.

22. In section 137 of the principal Act (power of education authorities to prohibit or restrict employment of children), in subsection (3) (penalties), for the words " five pounds " there shall be substituted the words " twenty pounds " and for the words " twenty pounds " there shall be substituted the words " fifty pounds ".

23. In section 144 of the principal Act (regulations) subsections (2) and (3) shall cease to have effect.

Part VI

Supplementary Provisions

24.—(1) Subject to the provisions of this section, any notice required or authorised by the principal Act or this Act to be served or given to any person may be served or given by delivering it to him, or by leaving it at his proper address, or by sending it to him by post.

(2) For the purposes of this section and of section 26 of the Interpretation Act 1889 (service by post) in its application to this section, the proper address of a person on or to whom any such notice as aforesaid is to be served or given shall, in the case

PART VI

of an education authority, be the address of any office of that authority and, in any other case, be the last known address of the person on or to whom the notice is to be served or given.

(3) Any notice which, in accordance with the provisions of subsection (1) of this section, is left for a person at his proper address shall, unless the contrary is proved, be presumed to have been received by him on the day on which it was left there.

Financial provisions.

25. There shall be paid out of moneys provided by Parliament—

(a) all sums payable and all expenses incurred by the Secretary of State under this Act, and

(b) all sums which, in consequence of the provisions of this Act, fall to be paid out of moneys so provided under any other enactment.

Interpretation. 1962 c. 47.

26.—(1) In this Act the expression " the principal Act " means the Education (Scotland) Act 1962.

(2) Except in so far as the context otherwise requires, expressions used in this Act and in the principal Act have the same meaning in this Act as in that Act.

(3) Any reference in this Act to any enactment shall be construed as a reference to that enactment as amended or extended, and as including a reference thereto as applied, by or under any other enactment including, unless the context otherwise requires, this Act.

Amendments and repeals.

27.—(1) The enactments mentioned in Schedule 2 to this Act shall have effect subject to the amendments specified in that Schedule, being minor amendments and amendments consequential on the provisions of this Act:

Provided that—

(a) paragraph 7(1) of Part I of that Schedule shall cease to have effect on, and paragraph 7(2) of the said Part I shall not have effect until, 1st August 1970 ; and

(b) paragraph 26 of Part I, and paragraph 4 of Part II, of that Schedule shall not have effect until 1st August 1972.

(2) The enactments specified in Schedule 3 to this Act are hereby repealed to the extent specified in relation thereto in the third column of that Schedule:

Provided that—

(a) the repeal of section 11(2) of the principal Act shall not take effect until 1st August 1970 ;

(*b*) the repeal of section 76(3) of the principal Act and of PART VI
paragraph 4 of Part I of Schedule 1 to the Local 1966 c. 51.
Government (Scotland) Act 1966 shall not take effect
until 1st August 1972 ;

(*c*) the repeal of section 77 of, and Schedule 2 to, the
principal Act shall not take effect until 12th November
1969.

28. The transitional and savings provisions set out in Schedule Transitional
4 to this Act shall have effect. and savings
provisions.

29.—(1) This Act may be cited as the Education (Scotland) Short title
Act 1969, and the Education (Scotland) Acts 1939 to 1967 and citation,
this Act may be cited together as the Education (Scotland) Acts commence-
1939 to 1969. ment and
extent.

(2) Except as provided in sections 16 and 27 of this Act, this
Act shall come into force on the expiry of the period of one
month beginning with the date on which it is passed.

Any reference in this Act or in any other enactment to the
commencement of this Act shall be construed as a reference to
the date on which this Act (except section 16 thereof and except
as provided in section 27 thereof) comes into force.

(3) This Act shall extend to Scotland only.

SCHEDULES

Section 13.

SCHEDULE 1

Sᴜᴍs ᴛᴏ ʙᴇ ᴘᴀɪᴅ ʙʏ ᴡᴀʏ ᴏғ Cᴏᴍᴘᴇɴsᴀᴛɪᴏɴ ғᴏʀ Aʙᴏʟɪᴛɪᴏɴ
ᴏғ Hɪɢʜʟᴀɴᴅ Sᴄʜᴏᴏʟs Gʀᴀɴᴛ

Serial Number	Education Area	Sum £
1	Argyll	4,942
2	Banff	420
3	Caithness	812
4	Inverness	1,792
5	Orkney	420
6	Perth	868
7	Ross and Cromarty	2,086
8	Sutherland	1,246
		12,586

Section 27.

SCHEDULE 2

Mɪɴᴏʀ ᴀɴᴅ Cᴏɴsᴇǫᴜᴇɴᴛɪᴀʟ Aᴍᴇɴᴅᴍᴇɴᴛs

Pᴀʀᴛ I

1962 c. 47.

Aᴍᴇɴᴅᴍᴇɴᴛ ᴏғ ᴛʜᴇ Eᴅᴜᴄᴀᴛɪᴏɴ (Sᴄᴏᴛʟᴀɴᴅ) Aᴄᴛ 1962

1. In section 4 (further education)—

    (a) in paragraph (a), for the words " subsection (2) of section one " there shall be substituted the words " section 2 ";

    (b) for paragraph (c) there shall be substituted the following paragraph:—

        " (c) social, cultural and recreative activities and physical education and training, either as part of a course of instruction or as organised voluntary leisure-time occupation ; and ".

2. For section 5 (special education) there shall be substituted the following section:—

" Special education.   5.—(1) In this Act the expression " special education " means education by special methods appropriate to the requirements of pupils whose physical, intellectual, emotional or social development cannot, in the opinion of the education authority, be adequately promoted by ordinary methods of education, and shall be given in special schools or by other appropriate means.

    (2) Regulations under section 2 of this Act may prescribe the requirements to be complied with by an education authority in providing special education for their area.".

3. For section 6 of the principal Act (recreation, etc.) there shall be substituted the following section: —

" Social activities, physical education, etc.

6.—(1) For the purpose of securing the provision of facilities for social, cultural and recreative activities and physical education and training, an education authority may—

    (*a*) establish, maintain and manage camps, play-grounds, playing fields, gymnasiums, swimming baths, play centres, social and cultural centres and other places at which any such facilities as aforesaid are available ;

    (*b*) organise holiday classes, games, expeditions and other activities.

(2) In the exercise of their powers under subsection (1) above an education authority—

    (*a*) may assist any body whose objects include the provision of any such facilities as aforesaid ;

    (*b*) shall, so far as practicable, co-operate with local authorities and with any voluntary societies or bodies whose objects include the provision of any such facilities as aforesaid.

(3) In this section the expression ' local authority ' means a county, town or district council.".

4. In section 7 (provision of educational facilities to be in accordance with schemes)—

    (*a*) in subsection (1), in paragraph (*c*), for the words " special educational treatment " there shall be substituted the words " special education " ;

    (*b*) in subsections (4), (6) and (8), for the words " primary and secondary ", wherever they occur, and for the words " primary or secondary ", wherever they occur, there shall be substituted the word " school ".

5. In section 9 (conscience clause), subsection (2) shall cease to have effect.

6. In section 10 (safeguards for religious beliefs), in subsection (2), for the words " subsection (2) of section one " there shall be substituted the words " section 2 ".

7.—(1) In section 11 (provision of books, etc., free of charge), in subsection (1), for the words " in accordance with subsection (3) of section one of this Act " there shall be substituted the words " by virtue of arrangements made by the authority with the managers of those schools ".

(2) In section 11—

    (*a*) in subsection (1), for the words from " are given " to " books " there shall be substituted the following words: —

        " (*a*) are in attendance at schools or junior colleges under their management, or

        (*b*) are receiving free education at other schools by virtue of arrangements made by the education authority with the managers of those schools,

       books " ;

    (*b*) subsection (2) shall cease to have effect ;

    (*c*) in subsection (3), for the words from " training " to the end there shall be substituted the words " education or training provided by the authority under section 1(3) of this Act, articles of clothing suitable for such physical education or training.".

8. In section 12 (county library service)—

    (*a*) in subsection (1), after the word " books " there shall be inserted the words " and other printed matter, pictures, gramophone records, tape recordings, films and other materials " ;

    (*b*) in subsection (2), after the word " may " there shall be inserted the following words : —

        " (*a*) make such arrangements as they consider necessary for the management of a library service provided by them, including the accommodation and distribution of books and other materials, and

          (*b*) ".

9. In section 14 (provision of education elsewhere than at an educational establishment), the words " with the approval of the Secretary of State " shall cease to have effect.

10. In section 15 (transfer of endowed schools to education authorities)—

    (*a*) in subsection (1), the words " extending over at least three years ", wherever they occur, shall cease to have effect ;

    (*b*) subsection (2) shall cease to have effect.

11. In section 18 (improvements as to premises of educational establishments for the safety of pupils)—

    (*a*) in subsection (1), the words " and with the approval of the Secretary of State " shall cease to have effect ;

    (*b*) in subsection (3), in the proviso, for the words " or shall satisfy the Secretary of State that " there shall be substituted the word " unless ".

12. In section 19 (requirements as to premises of educational establishments)—

    (*a*) subsection (2) shall cease to have effect ;

    (*b*) for subsection (3) there shall be substituted the following subsection : —

        " (3) It shall be the duty of an education authority to secure that the premises and equipment of any educational establishment under their management conform to the standards and requirements applicable to that establishment and, in particular, that the premises and equipment of all educational establishments under their management are maintained in such a condition as to conduce to the good health and safety of all persons occupying or frequenting the premises or using the equipment." ;

(c) for subsection (4) there shall be substituted the following subsection—

"(4) Where the premises or equipment of any educational establishment under the management of an education authority do not conform to the standards or requirements applicable to that establishment or are not maintained as mentioned in subsection (3) above, the Secretary of State may, after consultation with the authority, direct that the premises or equipment be brought into conformity with the said standards or requirements or into the state of maintenance mentioned in that subsection (as the case may be) within a period to be specified in the direction ; and it shall thereupon be the duty of the authority to comply with the direction." ;

(d) subsection (5) shall cease to have effect.

13. In section 20 (acquisition of land and execution of works), in subsection (1), after the word "may" there shall be inserted the words "subject to the provisions of subsection (1A) below,".

14. In section 24 (provision by education authority for education of pupils belonging to other areas)—

(a) in subsection (1), for the words "primary, secondary" there shall be substituted the words "school education" ;

(b) in subsections (2) and (3), for the words "primary or secondary", wherever they occur, there shall be substituted the word "school" ;

(c) in subsection (4), for the words "for the primary or secondary education of" there shall be substituted the words "school education for" ;

(d) subsection (5) shall cease to have effect.

15. In section 28 (educational conferences), the words "Subject to any regulations made by the Secretary of State" shall cease to have effect.

16. In section 32 (school age), in subsection (4), for the words from "section fifty-five" to "treatment" there shall be substituted the words "the Act of 1946 or this Act that a child requires special education", and for the word "rescinded" there shall be substituted the word "revoked".

17. In section 35 (failure by parent to secure regular attendance by his child at a public school), subsection (2) shall cease to have effect.

18. In section 38 (attendance orders)—

(a) in subsection (1), for the words "being a school" there shall be substituted the words "being either a public school or a school (other than a public school)" ;

(b) in subsection (2), in paragraph (b), for the words from "a certificate" to the end there shall be substituted the words "the education authority have decided under the Act of 1946 or this Act that the child requires special education.".

19. In section 40 (period of operation of attendance orders), in the proviso, for the words from " certificate " to " withdrawn " there shall be substituted the words " decision of an education authority under the Act of 1946 or this Act that a child requires special education is revoked ".

20. In section 49 (power of education authorities to assist persons to take advantage of educational facilities)—

    (*a*) for the words " primary or secondary ", wherever they occur, there shall be substituted the word " school " ;

    (*b*) in subsection (1), for the words " Great Britain ", wherever they occur, there shall be substituted the word " Scotland ".

21. In section 50 (education of pupils in exceptional circumstances), in subsection (1), for the words " primary or secondary ", wherever they occur, there shall be substituted the word " school ".

22. In section 54 (provision of clothing for pupils at public schools), in subsection (4), in paragraph (*b*), for the words " special educational treatment " there shall be substituted the words " special education ".

23. For section 57 (regulations as to medical examination and inspection) there shall be substituted the following section : —

"Regulations as to medical and dental examination and inspection.
    57. The Secretary of State may make regulations as to the conduct of medical and dental examinations and medical and dental inspections for the purposes of this Act, and such regulations may, in particular, prescribe the special qualifications or experience to be possessed by—

    (*a*) the medical or (as the case may be) dental practitioners by whom any class of examination may be conducted,

    (*b*) the persons who may assist in the conduct of any such examinations,

    (*c*) the medical practitioners by whom or under whose directions any class of medical inspection may be conducted,

    (*d*) the dental practitioners by whom any class of dental inspection may be conducted.".

24. In section 58 (medical inspection, etc., of pupils)—

    (*a*) in subsection (1), the words " or junior college " shall cease to have effect, and after the words " persons in attendance at any " there shall be inserted the words " junior college or " ;

    (*b*) in subsection (2), after the word " pupils " there shall be inserted the words " and young persons ", and after the word " duty " there shall be inserted the words " under this section ".

25. In section 60 (provisions supplementary to school health provisions)—

    (*a*) in subsection (2), the words " primary or secondary " shall cease to have effect, and after the word " dental " there shall be inserted the words " inspection, supervision and " ;

SCH. 2

(b) in subsection (3), after the word "medical", in the first place where it occurs, there shall be inserted the words "and dental";

(c) in subsection (4), after the word "dental" there shall be inserted the words "examination, inspection, supervision and".

26. In section 76 (payment of grants to be subject to conditions), subsection (3) shall cease to have effect.

27. In section 79 (examination of accounts), for the words "and report to the accountant" there shall be substituted the words "to the Secretary of State".

28. In section 85 (dismissal of teachers)—

(a) in subsection (1), for the words "first class service or of first class service and second class service" there shall be substituted the words "reckonable service or of reckonable service and external service";

(b) subsection (5)(b) shall cease to have effect.

29. In section 91 (incidental expenses of education authorities)—

(a) in subsection (1), for the word "duties" there shall be substituted the word "functions";

(b) in subsection (2), at the end there shall be inserted the following paragraph:—

"(d) expenses incurred by the parent of any child in connection with any medical or dental inspection, or any medical or psychological examination, of that child, or by any young person in connection with any medical or dental inspection of that young person, under any provision of this Act.".

30. Section 94 (education authorities to administer revenues of endowments applicable to bursaries) shall cease to have effect.

31. In section 97 (returns by registrars)—

(a) in subsection (1), after the words "education authority" there shall be inserted the words "on a form to be provided by the authority";

(b) subsection (2) shall cease to have effect.

32. Section 98 (service of notices) shall cease to have effect.

33. In section 118 (schemes for reorganisation of educational endowments), in subsection (5), for the words "so, however" to the end there shall be substituted the words "and—

(a) except as mentioned in paragraph (b) below, the provisions of this Part of this Act shall, with any necessary modifications, apply for that purpose;

(b) section 126 of this Act shall apply in place of section 125 thereof in relation to the procedure to be followed by the Scottish Universities Committee in preparing a scheme under this Part of this Act.".

34. In section 123 (provisions as to beneficiaries and teachers), in subsection (2), for the word "certificated", in both places where it occurs, there shall be substituted the word "registered".

2 U

35. In section 124 (accounts and audit of educational endowments)—

    (*a*) in subsection (3), the words " of the Secretary of State, or " shall cease to have effect, and at the end there shall be inserted the words " and no person shall be qualified to be appointed auditor as aforesaid unless he is a member of one or more of the following bodies:—

        (*a*) the Institute of Chartered Accountants of Scotland ;

        (*b*) the Institute of Chartered Accountants in England and Wales ;

        (*c*) the Association of Certified and Corporate Accountants ;

        (*d*) the Institute of Chartered Accountants in Ireland ;

1948 c. 38.   (*e*) any other body of accountants established in the United Kingdom and for the time being recognised for the purposes of section 161(1)(*a*) of the Companies Act 1948 by the Board of Trade ;

    but a Scottish firm may be so appointed if each of the partners therein is qualified to be so appointed." ;

    (*b*) in subsections (4) and (5), for the word " accountant ", wherever it occurs, there shall be substituted the words " Secretary of State " ;

    (*c*) subsection (6) shall cease to have effect ;

    (*d*) in subsection (7), for the words from the beginning to " such accounts " there shall be substituted the words " The Registrar of Educational Endowments shall make the audited accounts of every endowment to which this section applies ".

36. In section 128 (schemes for small endowments), for the words " approved by Order in Council under this Part of this Act " there shall be substituted the words " made under section 125 of this Act ".

37. In section 129 (amending schemes), for the words " framed and " there shall be substituted the words " made or ", and after the words " any scheme " there shall be inserted the words " made or ".

38. In section 133 (default of governing body)—

    (*a*) after the words " any scheme " there shall be inserted the words " made or " ;

    (*b*) for the words " without undue delay " there shall be substituted the words " within such time as may be specified in the requisition ".

39. In section 135 (interpretation of Part VI)—

    (*a*) in subsection (1), after paragraph (*a*) there shall be inserted the following paragraph :—

        " (*aa*) the expression ' charitable purposes ' shall be construed in the same way as if it were contained in the Income Tax Acts ; " ;

(*b*) in subsection (1), for paragraph (*c*) there shall be substituted the following paragraph:—

" (*c*) ' Educational purposes ' includes—

(i) payments towards the cost of professional training and apprenticeship fees,

(ii) the provision of maintenance, clothing and other benefits, and

(iii) the payment of grants for travel ; " ;

(*c*) after subsection (2) there shall be inserted the following subsection:—

" (3) Any reference in this Act to the endowment to which a scheme under this Part of this Act relates shall, in the case of a scheme relating to more than one endowment, be construed as a reference to every endowment, or (as the context may require) to any endowment, to which the scheme relates.".

40. In section 141 (saving as to persons suffering from mental disorder), in subsection (2), for paragraph (*b*) there shall be substituted the following paragraph:—

" (*b*) any child who is for the time being the subject of a report issued by an education authority under the Act of 1946 or this Act to the effect that they have decided that the child is suffering from a disability of such a nature or to such an extent as to make him unsuitable for education or training either by ordinary methods of education or by special education ; and ".

41. In section 145 (general definitions)—

(*a*) paragraph (1) shall cease to have effect ;

(*b*) in paragraph (11), for the words " subsection (2) of section seventy-seven of the Act of 1946 or section eighty-one of " there shall be substituted the words " the Act of 1946 or " ;

(*c*) for paragraph (14) there shall be substituted the following paragraph:—

" (14) ' College of education ' means an educational establishment in which further education is provided and the primary purpose of which is the education and training of teachers ; " ;

(*d*) after paragraph (15) there shall be inserted the following paragraphs:—

" (15A) ' Dental examination ' means examination by a registered dentist, so however that in conducting an examination of any such class as may be prescribed, such dentist may be assisted by other persons having such special qualifications or experience as may be prescribed ;

(15B) ' Dental inspection ' and ' dental supervision ' mean, respectively, inspection and supervision by a registered dentist ;

(15C) 'Dental treatment' includes prevention and treatment of dental diseases by or (so far as permitted by law) under the direction of any registered dentist, and the supply of appliances on the recommendation of such dentist, but does not, in relation to any pupil other than a pupil receiving school education elsewhere than at school under arrangements made by an education authority under section 14 of this Act, include treatment in that pupil's home ; " ;

(e) in paragraph (17), for the words from " or organising " to " Act " there shall be substituted the words " for social, cultural or recreative activities or for physical education or training, " ;

(f) after paragraph (19) there shall be inserted the following paragraph : —

"(19A) 'Enactment' includes an order, regulation, rule or other instrument having effect by virtue of an Act ; " ;

(g) in paragraph (21), the words " facilities described in subsection (4) of section one and the " and the word " both " shall cease to have effect ;

(h) in paragraph (22), for the words " managers' contributions under Part IV of this Act " there shall be substituted the words " employers' contributions under the Teachers Superannuation (Scotland) Act 1968 " ;

1968 c. 12.

(i) in paragraph (28), the words " or in appropriate cases by a person registered under the Dentists Act 1957 " shall cease to have effect ;

1957 c. 28.

(j) in paragraph (30), for the words " primary or secondary " there shall be substituted the word " school " ;

(k) in paragraph (31), for the words " paragraph (a) of subsection (2) of section two " there shall be substituted the words " section 1(2)(a)(i) " ;

(l) in paragraph (35), the words " except in Part IV of this Act " shall cease to have effect ;

(m) in paragraph (36), for the words " subsection (2) of section two of this Act " there shall be substituted the words " section 1(2)(a) of the Education (Scotland) Act 1969 " ;

(n) after paragraph (38) there shall be inserted the following paragraph : —

"(38A) 'Psychological examination' means an examination by an educational or clinical psychologist appointed by an education authority for the purpose ; " ;

(o) after paragraph (41) there shall be inserted the following paragraph : —

"(41A) 'Registered teacher' means a teacher registered under the Teaching Council (Scotland) Act 1965 ; " ;

1965 c. 19.

(p) after paragraph (43) there shall be inserted the following paragraph : —

"(43A) 'School education' has the meaning assigned to it by section 1(2) of this Act ; " ;

(*q*) in paragraph (44), for the words "subsection (2) of section three of this Act" there shall be substituted the words "section 1(2)(*b*) of the Education (Scotland) Act 1969";

(*r*) in paragraph (45), for the words "Special educational treatment" there shall be substituted the words "Special education";

(*s*) for paragraph (48) there shall be substituted the following paragraph:—

"(48) 'Teachers (Superannuation) Regulations' means regulations made under the Teachers Superannuation (Scotland) Act 1968;".

1968 c. 12.

PART II
AMENDMENT OF OTHER ENACTMENTS
The Physical Training and Recreation Act 1937

1937 c. 46.

1. In section 10 (application to Scotland), after subsection (5) there shall be inserted the following subsection:—

"(5A) Section 4 of this Act shall have effect as if in subsection (4) after the words 'another local authority' there were inserted the words 'or by an education authority within the meaning of the Education (Scotland) Act 1962'.".

1962 c. 47.

The Teaching Council (Scotland) Act 1965

1965 c. 19.

2. In section 7—

(*a*) in subsection (5), for the words "section 144(2) of the Act of 1962" there shall be substituted the words "subsection (8A) of this section";

(*b*) in subsection (7), for the words "section 144(2) of the Act of 1962" there shall be substituted the words "subsection (8A) of this section";

(*c*) in subsection (8), for the words from the beginning to "thereof)" there shall be substituted the words "Subsections (1), (4) and (5) of section 144 of the Act of 1962", and for the words "it applies" there shall be substituted the words "they apply";

(*d*) after subsection (8) there shall be inserted the following subsection:—

"(8A) The Secretary of State shall, not less than forty days before making regulations under this section, cause a draft of the regulations to be published and send a copy thereof to every education authority, and shall have regard to any representations made by an education authority or by any person interested before he makes the regulations; and the regulations may be made in the same form as in the published draft or in an amended form.".

3. Section 16 (amendment of Education (Scotland) Act 1962) shall cease to have effect.

The Local Government (Scotland) Act 1966

1966 c. 51.

4. In Schedule 1 (rate support grants), in Part I, paragraph 4 shall cease to have effect.

The Social Work (Scotland) Act 1968

5. In section 30 (definition of child for Part III), in subsection (1), at the end there shall be inserted the following words:—

" and for the purposes of the application of this Part of this Act to a person who has failed to attend school regularly without reasonable excuse includes a person who is over the age of sixteen years but who is not over school age.".

6. In Schedule 8, for paragraph 61 there shall be substituted the following paragraph:—

" 61. In section 36(3), for the words from ' if satisfied ' to the end of the subsection there shall be substituted the words—

' refer the child to the reporter of the appropriate local authority.

In this subsection the expression " local authority " has the same meaning as in the Social Work (Scotland) Act 1968.'.".

7. In Schedule 8, for sub-paragraph (1) of paragraph 62 there shall be substituted the following sub-paragraph:—

" (1) In section 44(1), for the words from ' that the child be brought ' to the end of the subsection there shall be substituted the words—

' that the case be referred to the reporter of the appropriate local authority and, if so referred, shall certify the said failure as a ground established for the purposes of Part III of the Social Work (Scotland) Act 1968.

In this subsection the expression " local authority " has the same meaning as in the said Act of 1968.'.".

8. In Schedule 8, paragraphs 63 and 64 shall cease to have effect.

9. In Schedule 8, for paragraph 65 there shall be substituted the following paragraph:—

" 65. In section 85, in subsection (5), for paragraph (c) there shall be substituted the following paragraph:—

' (c) the persons responsible for the management of an establishment or residential establishment within the meaning of the Social Work (Scotland) Act 1968 and the registered teachers employed therein in the provision of school education.'.".

10. In Schedule 8, in paragraph 67, for the words from the beginning to the end of head (b) there shall be substituted the following words:—

" In section 145—

(a) after definition (41A) there shall be inserted—

' (41B) " residential establishment " has the same meaning as in the Social Work (Scotland) Act 1968 ;';

(b) in definition (42), for the words ' an approved school within the meaning of the Act of 1937 ' there shall be substituted the words ' an establishment or residential establishment within the meaning of the Social Work (Scotland) Act 1968.' ; ".

SCHEDULE 3

ENACTMENTS REPEALED

Chapter	Short Title	Extent of Repeal
19 & 20 Geo. 5. c. 25.	The Local Government (Scotland) Act 1929.	Section 52(3) and Schedule 6, so far as those provisions relate to the payment of moneys to the universities of Scotland.
10 & 11 Eliz. 2. c. 47.	The Education (Scotland) Act 1962.	In section 9, subsection (2). In section 11, subsection (2). In section 14, the words " with the approval of the Secretary of State ". In section 15, in subsection (1), the words " extending over at least three years ", wherever they occur, and subsection (2). In section 18, in subsection (1), the words " and with the approval of the Secretary of State ". In section 19, subsections (2) and (5). In section 24, subsection (5). In section 28, the words " Subject to any regulations made by the Secretary of State ". In section 35, subsection (2). In section 58, in subsection (1), the words " or junior college". In section 60, in subsection (2), the words " primary or secondary ". In section 76, subsection (3). Section 77. Section 78. Section 80. Section 84. In section 85, in subsection (5), paragraph (*b*). Section 87. Section 94. In section 97, subsection (2). Section 98. In section 119, subsection (3), in so far as it relates to land forming the site of an educational establishment under the management of an education authority. In section 124, in subsection (3), the words " of the Secretary of State, or ", and subsection (6). In section 144, subsections (2) and (3).

Chapter	Short Title	Extent of Repeal
10 & 11 Eliz. 2. c. 47.—*cont.*	The Education (Scotland) Act 1962—*cont.*	In section 145— paragraph (1), in paragraph (21), the words " facilities described in sub-section (4) of section one and the " and the word " both ", in paragraph (28), the words " or in appropriate cases by a person registered under the Dentists Act 1957 ", in paragraph (35), the words " except in Part IV of this Act ". Schedule 2.
1965 c. 19.	The Teaching Council (Scotland) Act 1965.	Section 16.
1966 c. 51.	The Local Government (Scotland) Act 1966.	In Schedule 1, in Part I, paragraph 4.
1968 c. 49.	The Social Work (Scotland) Act 1968.	In Schedule 8, paragraphs 63 and 64.

SCHEDULE 4

TRANSITIONAL AND SAVINGS PROVISIONS

General

1. In this Schedule " an original provision " means any provision of the principal Act as in force immediately before the commencement of this Act, and " a new provision " means any provision of the principal Act as amended by or set out in this Act.

2. Any regulations, scheme or other instrument or any decision made, direction or notice given, report issued or other thing done, or deemed to have been made, given, issued or done, under or for the purposes of an original provision and in force at the commencement of this Act shall, in so far as it could have been made, given, issued or done under or for the purposes of a new provision, continue in force and be deemed to have been made, given, issued or done under or for the purposes of that new provision.

3. So much of any enactment or other document as refers expressly or by implication to an original provision shall, in so far as the context permits and as may be necessary to preserve the effect of the said enactment or other document, be construed as referring, or (as the case may require) as including a reference, to any new provision which corresponds to that original provision.

4. Any reference in any provision of this Act (including any new provision) to, or to things done or falling to be done under, a new provision shall, in so far as the context permits, be construed as including, in relation to times, circumstances and purposes in relation to which an original provision had effect, a reference to, or to things done or falling to be done under, that original provision.

School leaving dates

5.—(1) Any date fixed before the commencement of this Act under proviso (i) to section 33(1) of the principal Act and in force at the commencement of this Act shall be deemed to have been fixed under proviso (ii) to the said section 33(1) as set out in this Act.

(2) Any date fixed before the commencement of this Act under proviso (ii) to the said section 33(1) and in force at the commencement of this Act shall have effect until a new date or dates is or are fixed under the said section 33(1) as amended by this Act.

Handicapped children

6. Any reference in any enactment or other instrument passed or made before the commencement of this Act to special educational treatment shall be construed as a reference to special education, and any reference in any such enactment or other instrument to a child who is suffering from a disability of mind of such a nature or to such an extent as to make him unsuitable for education or training in a special school shall be construed as a reference to a child who is suffering from a disability of such a nature or to such an extent as to make him unsuitable for education or training either by ordinary methods of education or by special education.

7.—(1) Any decision made before the commencement of this Act by an education authority—

(a) to the effect that a child requires special educational treat-ment, or

(b) to the effect that a child is suffering from a disability of mind of such a nature or to such an extent as to make him incapable of receiving education or training in a special school or as to make it inexpedient that he should be educated or trained in association with other children either in his own interests or in those of the other children, or that a child is suffering from a disability of mind of such a nature or to such an extent as to make him unsuitable for education or training in a special school,

and any report of any such decision as is mentioned in head (b) above issued by an education authority to a local health authority before such commencement, being a decision made or a report issued under the Education (Scotland) Act 1946 or under the principal 1946 c. 72. Act as in force immediately before such commencement, and in force at such commencement, shall, subject to paragraph 8 below, continue in force and be deemed to be—

(i) in the case of such a decision as is mentioned in head (a) above, a decision under section 65 of the principal Act as set out in this Act to the effect that the child requires special education, being a decision duly notified to the parent of the child under paragraph (i) of subsection (1) of that section ;

(ii) in the case of any such decision as is mentioned in head (b) above, a decision under section 66B of the principal Act

SCH. 4

as set out in this Act to the effect that the child is suffering from a disability of such a nature or to such an extent as to make him unsuitable for education or training either by ordinary methods of education or by special education ;

(iii) in the case of any such report as aforesaid, a report of a decision under the said section 66B as so set out issued by the education authority to the local authority ;

but so however that section 66A of the principal Act as set out in this Act shall not (except in so far as it relates to a determination under section 66 of the principal Act as so set out) apply in relation to a decision deemed by virtue of paragraph (i) above to be a decision under section 65 of the principal Act as so set out.

1968 c. 49.

(2) In this paragraph the expression " local authority " shall have the same meaning as in the Social Work (Scotland) Act 1968:

1947 c. 27.

Provided that until section 1(4) of the said Act of 1968 comes into operation the expression " local authority " shall mean a local health authority within the meaning of the National Health Service (Scotland) Act 1947 (including a joint committee or board constituted under section 20 of that Act).

8. Where immediately before the commencement of this Act there is pending—

(a) a reference to the Secretary of State under section 64(2) of the principal Act, or

(b) an appeal to the sheriff under section 64(4) of that Act, or

(c) a review of a decision of an education authority under section 65(4) of that Act, or

(d) an appeal to the Secretary of State under section 65(6) of that Act,

any such reference, appeal or review may be proceeded with in accordance with the provisions of the principal Act as if this Act had not been passed.

Educational endowments

9. Any scheme for the reorganisation of an educational endowment approved by Order in Council, or amended or framed by the Court of Session, under section 125 or section 127 of the principal Act before the commencement of this Act and in force at such commencement shall continue in force and have effect as if made or approved under the corresponding provision of Part VI of the principal Act as set out in this Act.

10. Where before the commencement of this Act the Secretary of State or the Scottish Universities Committee of the Privy Council has prepared the draft of a scheme for the reorganisation of any educational endowment in pursuance of section 125(2) of the principal Act, such scheme may be proceeded with in accordance with the provisions of the principal Act as if this Act had not been passed.

Savings

11. The repeal by this Act of sections 84 and 87 of the principal Act shall not affect the payment after the commencement of this Act of any pension, gratuity or retiring allowance which was payable immediately before such commencement under either of the said sections.

12. The repeal by this Act of section 94 of the principal Act shall not affect the application of that section to any part of the annual revenue of any scheme, being a part to which that section applied immediately before the commencement of this Act.

Trustee Savings Banks Act 1969

1969 CHAPTER 50

An Act to consolidate the Trustee Savings Banks Acts 1954 to 1968, with amendments to give effect to recommendations of the Law Commission and the Scottish Law Commission.   [25th July 1969]

BE IT ENACTED by the Queen's most Excellent Majesty, by and with the advice and consent of the Lords Spiritual and Temporal, and Commons, in this present Parliament assembled, and by the authority of the same, as follows:—

Establishment of trustee savings banks

1.—(1) A savings bank shall have the benefit of this Act (including the privilege of paying money into the Bank of England or the Bank of Ireland in return for interest-bearing receipts) if the conditions set out in this section and section 2 of this Act are fulfilled.

Conditions under which a savings bank may obtain the benefit of this Act.

(2) A savings bank shall not have the benefit of this Act unless its formation was sanctioned and approved by the National Debt Commissioners (hereafter in this Act referred to as "the Commissioners") or on their behalf by the Comptroller General or Assistant Comptroller of the National Debt Office; but this subsection shall not apply to any savings bank formed before 28th July 1863 (that is to say the date on which the Trustee Savings Banks Act 1863 was passed).

1863 c. 87.

(3) In this section and in sections 2 and 3 of this Act "savings bank" means a society formed in the United Kingdom, the Isle of Man or any of the Channel Islands for the purpose of establishing and maintaining an institution in the nature of a bank—

(*a*) to accept deposits of money for the benefit of the persons making the deposits and deposits of money by a trustee, and

(b) to accumulate the produce of the deposits (so far as not withdrawn) at compound interest, and

(c) to return the deposits and produce to the depositors after deducting any necessary expenses of management but without deriving any benefit from the deposits or produce.

Requirements as to bank rules.

2.—(1) A savings bank shall not have the benefit of this Act unless the rules of the bank expressly provide for the matters set out in Schedule 1 to this Act nor unless those rules—

(a) have been certified and deposited with the Commissioners in pursuance of this section, and

(b) have been entered in a book to be kept by an officer of the bank appointed for that purpose which is to be open at all proper times for inspection by depositors.

(2) For the purpose of ascertaining whether the rules are in conformity with law and with the provisions of this Act, two copies of all the rules of the bank signed by two trustees of the bank shall be submitted by the trustees and managers of the bank to the Registrar.

(3) The Registrar shall certify on each copy that the rules are in conformity with law and with the provisions of this Act or point out in what respect they are repugnant thereto.

(4) One of the copies when so certified shall be returned to the savings bank and the other copy shall be deposited by the Registrar with the Commissioners.

(5) Rules made under section 76, 80 or 81 of this Act shall not be taken as forming part of the rules of a bank for the purposes of this section.

Certification of a trustee savings bank.

1954 c. 63.
1863 c. 87.

3. A savings bank established under this Act shall be certified under this Act by the title of " savings bank certified under the Trustee Savings Banks Act 1969 ", and a bank certified under this Act, the Trustee Savings Banks Act 1954 or the Trustee Savings Banks Act 1863 is hereafter in this Act referred to as a " trustee savings bank ".

The Inspection Committee

Constitution of the Inspection Committee.

4.—(1) There shall continue to be an Inspection Committee of trustee savings banks with the several powers and duties conferred by the following provisions of this Act.

(2) The Inspection Committee shall, with the approval of the Commissioners, make a scheme which, subject to the provisions of this Act, makes provision—

(a) with respect to the composition of the Committee, and to the appointment, tenure of office and vacation of

office of members of the Committee, and to the
procedure of the Committee ;

(*b*) for revoking the scheme made under section 2 of the
Savings Banks Act 1891 (which established an Inspec- 1891 c. 21.
tion Committee of trustee savings banks and required
certain persons to frame a scheme for the appointment
of the Committee).

(3) The Committee may, with the approval of the Commissioners, modify the scheme made under this section.

(4) A paid officer of a trustee savings bank shall not be
eligible to be a member of the Committee.

(5) The Committee may act by a majority of the members
present and voting at any meeting of the Committee, and may
signify their acts by an instrument in writing signed by any
two of the members of the Committee, and an act of the
Committee shall not be invalid by reason only of any vacancy
in their number.

(6) The Committee may, with the approval of the Minister
for the Civil Service, appoint such officers as may appear to be
required for the execution of the duties of the Committee under
this Act.

(7) The members of the Committee shall be entitled to such
remuneration by way of fees or otherwise, and to such reasonable
travelling expenses in respect of attendance at meetings of the
Committee, as may be approved by the said Minister.

(8) The power to make a scheme under this section, and the
power to modify it, shall be exercisable by statutory instrument
which shall be laid before Parliament, and the Statutory 1946 c. 36.
Instruments Act 1946 shall apply to a statutory instrument
containing such a scheme or modification in like manner as if
the scheme or modification had been made by a Minister of
the Crown.

General provisions as to conduct of trustee savings banks

5. A trustee savings bank may not be designated or described Title of a
in any manner which imports that the Government is respon- trustee savings
sible or liable to depositors for money placed in the safe keeping bank.
of the bank, and may not bear any title other than that of
" savings bank certified under the Act of 1863 " or, as the
case may be, " savings bank certified under the Trustee Savings 1954 c. 63.
Banks Act 1954 " or " savings bank certified under the Trustee

Savings Banks Act 1969 " with such additional local description, if any, as may be required for the sake of distinctiveness.

Alteration of
bank rules.

6.—(1) No alteration of the rules of a trustee savings bank shall take effect until it has been entered in the book mentioned in section 2 of this Act.

(2) Subject to subsection (3) below, two copies of any alterations of the rules signed by two trustees shall as soon as possible be submitted by the trustees of the bank to the Registrar and the Registrar shall certify on each copy that they are in conformity with law and with the provisions of this Act or point out in what respect they are repugnant thereto.

(3) An alteration as respects the days or hours of attendance need not be submitted to the Registrar.

(4) One of the copies when so certified shall be returned to the trustee savings bank and the other copy shall be deposited by the Registrar with the Commissioners.

(5) The foregoing provisions of this section shall not apply in relation to any alteration of rules made under section 76, 80 or 81 of this Act.

(6) In this section " alteration " includes repeal.

General
provisions as
to bank
rules.

7.—(1) Subject to section 6(1) of this Act, the rules of a trustee savings bank, and any alterations of those rules, shall, from the time when they are certified by the Registrar, be binding on the trustees, managers and officers of the bank and on the depositors.

(2) The copy of any rules of a trustee savings bank, transmitted under this Act to the Commissioners, or a true copy examined with the original copy so transmitted, and proved to be a true copy, shall be admissible as evidence of the rules in all cases.

Objects on
which a
trustee
savings bank
may expend
money.

8.—(1) Any expenditure incurred by a trustee savings bank which, in the opinion of the Commissioners, is calculated to further the objects of the bank shall be deemed to be necessary expenses within the meaning of section 1 of this Act.

(2) The trustees of a trustee savings bank may, with the consent of the Commissioners given after consultation with the Inspection Committee and the Association, and subject to such conditions as the Commissioners after such consultation as aforesaid may impose either generally or in the case of any

particular bank, undertake any business which is, in the opinion of the Commissioners, calculated to encourage thrift and within the financial capacity of the bank.

(3) The trustees of a trustee savings bank may defray all or any of the expenses of a penny savings bank which has a deposit account with the trustee savings bank.

(4) Any expenses properly incurred by a bank in carrying on such a business as is mentioned in subsection (2) above and any expenses defrayed under subsection (3) above shall be deemed to be necessary expenses within the meaning of section 1 of this Act.

(5) In this Act " the Association " means the association registered under the Companies Acts 1908 to 1917, by the name of the Trustee Savings Banks Association.

9.—(1) All property of whatsoever description belonging to a trustee savings bank, including things in action or interests arising out of or incident to any property, shall be vested in the custodian trustees of the bank to be appointed under this section. *Bank property to be held by custodian trustees.*

(2) It shall be the duty of the trustees of every trustee savings bank (in this section referred to as " the general trustees ") as soon as may be to appoint out of their own number four persons to be the custodian trustees of the bank, and from time to time, when a vacancy occurs in the number of the custodian trustees, to appoint out of their own number a person to fill the vacancy.

(3) If the general trustees of a trustee savings bank fail, within three months after the occurrence of a vacancy in the number of the custodian trustees, to fill the vacancy the power of the general trustees to fill the vacancy shall be transferred to the Inspection Committee, and the Committee shall fill the vacancy accordingly.

(4) The Inspection Committee may, on the application of the general trustees of a trustee savings bank, remove any custodian trustee of the bank if, in the opinion of the Committee, he is unfit to continue in office or incapable of performing his duties, and a custodian trustee may, with the approval of the Inspection Committee, resign his office as such.

(5) A custodian trustee may continue to hold office as a general trustee, and may continue to hold office as custodian trustee notwithstanding that he has ceased to be a general trustee.

(6) All property of whatsoever description vested in any person in trust for a trustee savings bank at the date of the first appointment of the custodian trustees of the bank shall, by virtue of this Act, vest in the custodian trustees so appointed, and thereafter all property of whatsoever description vested in the custodian trustees of a trustee savings bank shall, on the occurrence of any vacancy in the number of custodian trustees or any change in the persons who are custodian trustees, by virtue of this Act, vest in the custodian trustees of the bank for the time being ; but on there ceasing to be any custodian trustees of a bank the property shall thereupon, by virtue of this Act, vest in the general trustees of the bank until the appointment of new custodian trustees.

(7) The management of the property and the exercise of any power or discretion exercisable by the general trustees shall remain vested in the general trustees, and the custodian trustees shall concur in and perform all acts necessary to enable the general trustees to exercise their powers of management or other power or discretion vested in them.

(8) Documents executed and things done by the custodian trustees of a trustee savings bank in relation to property vested in those trustees for the bank, or on or in connection with the acquisition of property to be so vested, shall be conclusively presumed to have been executed or done by them by the direction and on behalf of the trustees of the bank.

(9) Any document to be executed by the custodian trustees of a trustee savings bank may be executed by any three in the name of all of them.

(10) The custodian trustees of a trustee savings bank may sue and be sued by the name of " the Custodian Trustees for the Trustee Savings Bank " without further description, and in all legal proceedings concerning any property of the bank the property may be stated to be the property of the custodian trustees of the bank ; but nothing in this section shall affect any proceedings by or against or relating to the property of a trustee savings bank, which are pending at the time of the first appointment of custodian trustees for that bank.

Register of
custodian
trustees and
certificates
as to
custodian
trustees and
property.

10.—(1) The Commissioners shall in respect of each trustee savings bank keep a register of the custodian trustees of the bank, and shall enter in the register the date of the appointment of each custodian trustee and, on his vacating office, the date on which he vacates office.

(2) A certificate purporting to be signed by the Comptroller General or Assistant Comptroller of the National Debt Office to the effect that the persons named in the certificate were on any specified date custodian trustees of a trustee savings bank

or that any property mentioned in the certificate was, at the date of the first appointment of custodian trustees for a trustee savings bank, held by a person named in the certificate in trust for that bank shall be conclusive evidence for all purposes of the facts stated in the certificate.

(3) The general trustees of every trustee savings bank shall forthwith, after the appointment of custodian trustees, send to the Commissioners such particulars as the Commissioners may require for the purposes of subsections (1) and (2) above, and thereafter shall from time to time send to the Commissioners such particulars as the Commissioners may require for the purposes of the said register.

(4) Any person acting in pursuance of any such certificate shall not by reason only of anything contained therein be affected with notice of any trust or of the fiduciary character of the persons named therein or of any fiduciary obligation attached to the holding of any property.

11.—(1) The trustees of a trustee savings bank shall have power, with the consent of the Commissioners, to purchase land or erect buildings for the purposes of the bank, and with the like consent to sell, exchange or lease any land or buildings acquired for the purposes of the bank, or any part of such land or buildings. *Power to purchase and dispose of property, erect buildings, etc.*

(2) The power of the trustees of a trustee savings bank to purchase land or erect buildings for the purposes of the bank shall include power to incur expenditure of a capital nature on the doing of work to land or buildings provided for the purposes of the bank.

(3) No purchaser, assignee or tenant shall be entitled to inquire as to the authority for, or consent of the Commissioners to, any sale, exchange or lease under this section and the receipt of the custodian trustees for the time being shall be a discharge for all moneys accruing from or in connection with such a sale, exchange or lease.

(4) A certificate signed by the Comptroller General or Assistant Comptroller of the National Debt Office stating that a purchase of land has been made with the consent of the Commissioners and with the money belonging to a trustee savings bank shall be conclusive evidence thereof for all purposes.

Distinction between ordinary deposits and sums received for special investment and between different kinds of ordinary deposits

12.—(1) Save as otherwise provided by this Act, all sums of money deposited with the trustees of a trustee savings bank shall be invested with the Commissioners in accordance with the provisions of this Act in that behalf. *Ordinary deposits and special investments.*

(2) Notwithstanding the provisions of subsection (1) above, the trustees of a trustee savings bank may under the conditions laid down by the following provisions of this Act, and if the rules of the bank so provide, receive any sum of money from a depositor and apply it in any other manner for the benefit of the depositor.

(3) Deposits for investment under subsection (1) above are in this Act referred to as " ordinary deposits " and the investment of money received under subsection (2) above is in this Act referred to as " special investment ".

Current
account
deposits and
meaning of
" savings
account
deposit ".

13.—(1) The provisions of this Act shall not be construed as preventing a trustee savings bank from having the benefit of this Act by reason only of the acceptance by the bank of ordinary deposits of money to be placed in the books of the bank to the credit of an account (in this Act referred to as a " current account ") opened on the terms that—

(a) the money is to be available for payment of any cheque drawn on, or against any other written order given to, the bank by the person in whose name the account stands ; and

(b) no interest shall be paid by the bank on money standing to the credit of the account.

(2) Section 1(3)(c) of this Act shall not be construed as requiring a trustee savings bank to return to depositors the produce of ordinary deposits accepted by the bank as mentioned in subsection (1) above.

(3) The matters for which, under section 2 of this Act, the rules of a trustee savings bank must expressly provide shall, in the case of a bank by which a service consisting of the operation of current accounts for depositors of money with the bank is provided, include the matters set out in Schedule 2 to this Act.

(4) Hereafter in this Act—

" current account deposit " means an ordinary deposit accepted by a trustee savings bank as mentioned in subsection (1) above ;

" savings account deposit " means an ordinary deposit, not being a current account deposit ;

" current account service " means such a service as is mentioned in subsection (3) above.

Ordinary deposits

Limits on
amount of
ordinary
deposits.

14.—(1) The Treasury may by order limit the amount which may be received by a trustee savings bank from any person whatsoever by way of savings account deposit either in any one year or in the aggregate.

(2) The Treasury may by order limit the amount which may be received by a trustee savings bank from any person by way of current account deposit in any one year, or the amount which at any time may stand in its books to the credit of the current account of a person.

(3) For the purposes of this section a person who is a trustee shall be treated separately in his personal capacity and in his capacity as trustee, and in the latter capacity separately in respect of each separate trust fund.

(4) An order under this section—

(a) may fix different limits as respects different classes of persons ;

(b) may provide that any limit fixed by the order shall have effect subject to any exceptions or exclusions specified in the order ;

(c) may contain special provisions with respect to depositors whose deposits, at the date on which the order takes effect, exceed the limit fixed by the order as respects deposits ;

(d) may contain such consequential and supplemental provisions as appear to the Treasury to be necessary for giving full effect to the order ; and

(e) may be revoked or varied by a subsequent order.

(5) The power to make orders conferred by this section shall be exercisable by statutory instrument and a draft of every statutory instrument made under that power shall be laid before Parliament.

15.—(1) The interest payable to depositors by the trustees of a trustee savings bank in respect of ordinary deposits shall not exceed the rate of £2 10s. 0d. per cent. per annum. *Payment of interest on ordinary deposits.*

(2) The said interest shall be computed half yearly to 20th May and 20th November, or yearly to 20th November in each year, as the case may be, and to no other period.

(3) The trustees and managers of a trustee savings bank may direct that all interest payable to the depositors in the bank shall yearly, or twice in each year, be carried to the credit of the respective depositors and become principal and carry interest like other principal moneys.

16.—(1) A depositor in a trustee savings bank who desires to transfer an ordinary deposit belonging to him to another trustee savings bank shall, on application to the first bank, be furnished with a certificate stating the whole amount due to him, with interest, and thereupon his account at that bank shall be closed. *Transfer of deposits to other trustee savings banks.*

(2) When the certificate has been delivered to the trustees or managers of the other bank and the depositor has signed the declaration required in the case of a new depositor, they shall forthwith open an account for the amount stated in the certificate, and the amount so stated shall, upon the certificate being forwarded to the Commissioners, be transferred in the books of the Commissioners from the first bank to the other bank.

(3) In subsection (1) above, the second reference to a trustee savings bank shall include a reference to a trustee savings bank in the Republic of Ireland.

Sums received for special investment

Restriction on power to receive money for special investment and limits on amount which may be received.

17.—(1) The trustees of a trustee savings bank shall not have power under section 12(2) of this Act to receive money for special investment except by way of deposit repayable in cash and not otherwise.

(2) The Treasury may by order under this section limit the amount which may be received by a trustee savings bank from any person for special investment either in any one year or in the aggregate.

(3) For the purposes of this section a person who is a trustee shall be treated separately in his personal capacity and in his capacity as trustee, and in the latter capacity separately in respect of each separate trust fund.

(4) An order under this section—

    (a) may fix different limits as respects different classes of persons ;

    (b) may provide that any limit fixed by the order shall have effect subject to any exceptions or exclusions specified in the order ;

    (c) may contain special provisions with respect to persons to whose credit there stand, at the date on which the order takes effect, amounts exceeding the limit fixed by the order ;

    (d) may contain such consequential and supplemental provisions as appear to the Treasury to be necessary for giving full effect to the order ; and

    (e) may be revoked or varied by a subsequent order.

(5) The power to make orders conferred by this section shall be exercisable by statutory instrument, and a draft of every statutory instrument made under that power shall be laid before Parliament.

18.—(1) A special investment shall not be made on behalf of any person unless he is at the time of the making of the investment a depositor in the bank to the extent of not less than £50, but nothing in this subsection shall prevent the continuance of special investments on behalf of a person who was before 3rd July 1891 (being the date of the passing of the Savings Banks Act 1891) a depositor under section 16 of the Trustee Savings Banks Act 1863 (being the section which then authorised the making of special investments).

(2) The rules of a trustee savings bank making special investments shall, as respects those investments, provide that the trustees shall have power to demand at least one month's notice in advance of any repayment, of whatever amount, required by a depositor.

(3) The trustees of a trustee savings bank making special investments shall cause to be printed, in the pass-books in use for the purpose of special investments, a notice stating that the security of any special investment is not in any way guaranteed by the Government.

Current account service

19.—(1) A current account shall not be opened in the books of a trustee savings bank in the name of a person except upon a written application by him, and no such application shall be granted unless—

    (*a*) it appears to the bank, after undertaking such inquiries as appear to the bank to be necessary, that the applicant is a suitable person to operate a current account; and

    (*b*) the applicant has, immediately before the application is granted, a savings account deposit with the bank of not less than such amount as the rules of the bank may provide, or has had, throughout a period ending with the granting of the application and of not less than such length as the said rules may provide, a savings account deposit with the bank.

(2) A current account shall not be opened in the books of a trustee savings bank in the names of two or more persons if any of those persons, but not the other or others, is described in the account as a trustee.

(3) An application for the opening of a current account in the books of a trustee savings bank must contain a declaration by the applicant that he will not operate the account either wholly or partly as a trade or business account.

(4) A trustee savings bank shall have the right at any time, after giving reasonable notice of its intention so to do, to close

any current account standing in the books of the bank ; and, if at any time the person in whose name a current account stands in the books of a trustee savings bank operates that account either wholly or partly as a trade or business account, or ceases to have a savings account deposit at the bank, no sums shall after that time be debited by the bank to the current account except in pursuance of instructions to the bank the giving of which appears to the bank to have been initiated before that time, and the bank shall, after giving reasonable notice of its intention so to do, close the current account.

(5) The rules of a bank made for the purposes of paragraph (*b*) of subsection (1) above may provide for different amounts and periods of different lengths for different classes of person.

Operation of current accounts.

20.—(1) No sum shall, in pursuance of instructions in that behalf, be debited to the current account of a person at a trustee savings bank, if, on the date on which the instructions are given, the amount of the sum is not ascertained.

(2) No sum shall, in pursuance of instructions in that behalf, be debited to the account of the savings account deposits of a person or the special investments of a person and credited to the current account of that or any other person at the bank, if, on the date on which the instructions are given, the amount of the sum is not ascertained.

(3) No sum, other than a sum due to the bank in respect of a charge duly imposed by virtue of a charges scheme made by the bank under section 21 of this Act, shall be debited to the current account of a person at a trustee savings bank at any time unless there then stands to the credit of that account an amount not less than that sum.

1882 c. 61.

(4) Section 53(2) of the Bills of Exchange Act 1882 (which provides that in Scotland presentment of a bill of exchange operates as an assignment in favour of the holder of the bill of funds held by the drawee) shall not have effect in relation to funds being savings account deposits or special investments of a person at a trustee savings bank.

Charges schemes for contributing to defrayal of expenses of current account service.

21.—(1) A trustee savings bank shall not provide a current account service unless there is for the time being in force a scheme (hereafter in this Act referred to as a " charges scheme ") made by the bank and approved by the Commissioners for the purpose of securing contributions towards the expenses incurred by the bank in providing that service which are defrayable under this Act.

(2) A trustee savings bank may, by virtue of a charges scheme, impose on persons in whose names current accounts stand in

its books charges of such amounts and in respect of such matters as may be specified in the scheme, including, without prejudice to the generality of the provisions of this subsection,—

(*a*) the issue of cheque forms ;

(*b*) the use of any instrument requiring the bank to pay sums from moneys standing to the credit of a current account ;

(*c*) the carrying out of any transaction made in compliance with an instrument requiring the bank to debit to a current account sums of specified amounts at different times ;

(*d*) the maintenance of a current account.

(3) A charges scheme may be varied or revoked by a subsequent scheme made by the bank and approved by the Commissioners.

(4) Before approving a charges scheme made by a bank, the Commissioners must be satisfied that it is reasonable to expect that the aggregate of the following amounts, that is to say—

(*a*) the amounts received by the bank in respect of charges imposed by virtue of the scheme ;

(*b*) the amount of the interest credited to the account of the bank in the books of the Commissioners under section 35 of this Act in respect of moneys paid into the Fund for the Banks for Savings and representing current account deposits ; and

(*c*) the amount of any other sums paid or credited to the bank so far as, in the opinion of the Commissioners, they represent produce of such deposits ;

will be not less than sufficient to meet the expenses mentioned in subsection (1) above, taking one year with another.

(5) Approval under this section of a charges scheme may be given subject to such limitations or conditions as the Commissioners think fit.

(6) If a trustee savings bank by which a current account service is provided ceases to provide that service, any sums which, after payment in accordance with the provisions of this Act of the expenses incurred by the bank in providing that service, stand in the books of the bank and represent amounts received by the bank in respect of charges imposed by virtue of a charges scheme made by the bank shall be deemed to be moneys forming part of the assets of the bank in respect of ordinary deposits.

Power of
Commissioners
to require
variation
of charges
scheme or
cesser of
current
account
service.

22. If, at any time, in the case of a trustee savings bank which provides a current account service, the aggregate of the amounts mentioned in section 21(4) of this Act is not sufficient to meet the expenses mentioned in section 21(1) of this Act, and it appears to the Commissioners that the aggregate of those amounts will not be sufficient to defray those expenses, taking one year with another, the Commissioners—

(*a*) unless it appears to them that the charges scheme for the time being in force cannot be so varied as to satisfy them that it will be reasonable to expect that the aggregate of those amounts will be so sufficient taking one year with another, may direct the bank to vary, within such period as may be specified in the direction, that charges scheme so as so to satisfy them ; or

(*b*) if it so appears to them, may direct the bank to cease, within such period as may be specified in the direction, to provide a current account service.

Defrayal of
expenses of,
or ancillary
to, current
account
service.

23.—(1) The expenses incurred by a trustee savings bank during each year ending with the 20th November in providing a current account service, being expenses which in the opinion of the Commissioners are properly so incurred, shall be defrayed,—

(*a*) if those expenses are less than the amounts obtained by way of charges imposed by virtue of a charges scheme made by the bank and not expended by them under this section, out of those amounts ; and

(*b*) in any other case, to the extent of those amounts, by means thereof, and, to the extent, if any, by which those amounts are insufficient to defray those expenses, as part of the necessary expenses of the bank within the meaning of section 1 of this Act.

(2) For the purposes of this Act, there shall be included among the expenses incurred by a bank in providing a current account service—

(*a*) so much of any expenses incurred by the bank which are attributable both to the provision of that service and to other matters as is, in the opinion of the Commissioners, attributable to that service ; and

(*b*) any expenses incurred by the bank which, in the opinion of the Commissioners, are calculated to further the effectiveness of that service.

General provisions as to deposits

Prohibition
on making a
deposit in
more than
one bank.

24.—(1) Subject to the provisions of this section, it shall not be lawful for a person—

(*a*) who has a deposit in a trustee savings bank, or

(*b*) who is entitled to any benefit from the funds of a trustee savings bank, not being a benefit derived solely as personal representative of a deceased depositor,

to make a deposit in another trustee savings bank.

(2) For the purposes of this section a person who is a trustee shall be treated separately in his personal capacity and in his capacity as trustee, and in the latter capacity separately in respect of each separate trust fund.

(3) If a person at any time has a deposit in more than one trustee savings bank, he shall be liable to forfeit any amount illegally deposited, either as to the whole thereof, or to such extent as the Commissioners may think just in the circumstances of the case, and any money so forfeited shall be paid to the Commissioners and applied to the reduction of the National Debt.

(4) Where a bank has suspended payment, nothing in this section shall prevent a depositor in that bank from subsequently opening or having an account in another bank.

(5) Nothing in this section shall prevent a friendly society from having deposits in more than one bank.

(6) Nothing in this section shall prevent a depositor from belonging to or being interested in the funds of any friendly society or charitable institution or penny savings bank which has invested its funds in a trustee savings bank.

(7) Nothing in this section shall prevent a depositor, having closed his account in a bank, from making a deposit in another bank.

25. No sum shall be paid into a trustee savings bank by a person by ticket or number or otherwise, without disclosing his name together with his profession, business, occupation or calling, and residence, all of which shall be entered in the books of the bank.

Particulars to be disclosed by a depositor.

26.—(1) The Commissioners may, in the case of any trustee savings bank, authorise the receipt and repayment of deposits in accordance with arrangements approved by the Inspection Committee.

Power to relax requirements of rules as to receipt and repayment of deposits.

(2) Where any such authority is given, deposits may be received and repaid accordingly, notwithstanding anything in the rules of the bank and in particular notwithstanding anything included therein by virtue of paragraph 2 of Schedule 1 to this Act or by virtue of the provision in paragraph 9 of that Schedule for the presence of a second party in every transaction when money is paid or received.

27.—(1) If a dispute arises between the trustees and managers of a trustee savings bank and—

(a) a depositor, or

(b) a person who is or claims to be the personal representative or next of kin or creditor of a depositor or the successor in the trusts of any depositor, being a trustee, or

(c) the trustee in bankruptcy or assignee of a depositor who is bankrupt or insolvent, or

(d) a person who claims to be entitled to money deposited in the bank,

the matter in dispute shall be referred in writing to the Registrar.

(2) Upon the reference of the dispute the Registrar shall have power to proceed ex parte on giving notice in writing to the trustees of the bank left at, or sent by post to, the office of the bank.

(3) Any award, order or determination made by the Registrar shall be binding and conclusive on all parties and shall be final to all intents and purposes, without any appeal.

(4) On a reference under this section the Registrar may inspect any books belonging to the trustee savings bank relating to the matter in dispute, and may administer an oath to any witness appearing before him.

28.—(1) Regulations may be made by the Treasury with the concurrence of the Commissioners prescribing what declarations shall be required from a depositor on opening an account in a trustee savings bank, and may require different declarations from a depositor on opening an account in respect of savings account deposits and on opening a current account.

(2) The Treasury shall make regulations for the purpose of extending to trustee savings banks any regulations made with respect to the National Savings Bank so far as those regulations provide—

(a) for the payment or transfer of sums which belong to persons appearing to be under the age of majority or incapable through disorder or disability of mind of managing their property and affairs, or form part of the personal estate of any persons appearing to be deceased ; or

(b) for the transfer of deposits from one account to another account, whether an existing or a new account ; or

(c) for determining the receipts which are to be a good discharge in the case of the payment or transfer of any sum.

(3) Regulations under this section may also provide—

(*a*) for the addition of one or more names to an account already in a trustee savings bank ;

(*b*) for the nomination by a depositor not being under sixteen years of age of any person or persons to whom any sum or sums payable to the depositor at his decease (including any portion of any savings bank annuity or accrued interest payable to the representatives of the depositor) is or are to be paid at his decease ;

(*c*) for the manner in which any such nomination may be revoked by the depositor, and for the circumstances in which it is to be treated as having ceased to be operative and for the payment of the specified amount to any nominee so nominated ;

(*d*) for directing that any person acting as witness to a nomination shall be disqualified from taking thereunder ;

(*e*) for authorising the trustee savings bank to treat as a depositor in the bank any person named as a nominee in any nomination who dies after the death of the nominator, but before receiving payment of the sum to be paid to him under the nomination ;

(*f*) for providing that where any person to whom any sum, being the whole or any part of the deposit of a deceased depositor, is payable is unable by reason of any incapacity whatsoever to give a legal discharge therefor, the sum may be paid to any person undertaking to maintain the incapacitated person.

(4) The Treasury may make regulations applying to trustee savings banks, with or without modifications, the provisions of any regulations made with respect to the National Savings Bank so far as those regulations provide—

(*a*) for prescribing the means by which particular facts may be proved and the mode in which evidence thereof may be given, and for authorising proof of any particular facts given in the manner prescribed by the regulations to be treated as conclusive evidence of those facts for the purpose of the payment or transfer of any sum ;

(*b*) for the purpose of the payment or transfer of any sum, for authorising a person to be treated as having been domiciled in the place in which he was resident at the date of his death ;

(c) for directing that, except as provided by the regulations, no entry with respect to any trust, express, implied or constructive, shall be made in the account of any depositor, and that except as aforesaid no notice of any such trust shall be receivable by the Director of Savings;

(d) for determining the date on which a deposit is to be deemed to be withdrawn, and for prescribing the method by which payment of sums withdrawn is to be made;

but paragraph (d) above shall not have effect in relation to transactions concerning current accounts.

(5) Where the sum in a trustee savings bank which forms part of the personal estate of a person appearing to be deceased does not exceed £500, then, if the regulations under this section so provide, and subject to such regulations, probate, or other proof of the title of the personal representative of the deceased person may be dispensed with, and that sum may be paid or distributed to or among the persons appearing in manner provided by the regulations to be beneficially entitled to the personal estate of the deceased person, whether under such nomination of the deceased person as is allowed by the regulations, or by law, or as next of kin, or as creditors or otherwise, or to or among any one or more of such persons, exclusively of the others; and the person making such a payment shall be discharged from all liability in respect of the sum paid in accordance with the said regulations.

(6) The power to make regulations conferred by this section shall be exercisable by statutory instrument a draft of which shall be laid before Parliament.

Power to increase amount disposable on death without representation.

29.—(1) The Treasury may from time to time by order direct that section 28(5) of this Act shall have effect as if for the reference to £500 there were substituted a reference to such higher amount as may be specified in the order.

(2) Any order under this section shall apply in relation to deaths occurring after the expiration of a period of one month beginning with the date on which the order comes into force.

(3) Any order under this section may be revoked by a subsequent order and shall be made by statutory instrument; and no such order shall be made unless a draft of the order has been laid before Parliament and approved by a resolution of each House of Parliament.

30.—(1) Where the trustees and managers of a trustee savings bank accept a deposit from a person acting as trustee for some other person, they shall open an account in the names of both of those persons, but the person making a deposit under this section shall, on behalf of the beneficiary, make the declaration required in the case of a person making a deposit on his own account. Joint account in names of trustee and beneficiary.

(2) Subject to subsection (4) below, repayment of any sum deposited in an account opened under subsection (1) above, or any part thereof, shall not be made—

> (a) during the joint lives of the persons in whose names the account stands, without the receipt of both of those persons, or
>
> (b) after the death of either or both of those persons, without the receipt of the survivor or the personal representative of the survivor ;

and the receipt may be given either in person or, subject to subsection (6) below, by an agent appointed in writing in a form approved by the trustees of the bank.

(3) Subject to subsection (4) below, a receipt given in accordance with subsection (2) above shall alone be a good discharge to the trustees and managers of a bank in respect of the repayment of any sum deposited in an account opened under subsection (1) above.

(4) Where either of the persons in whose names an account opened under subsection (1) above stands becomes incapable through disorder or disability of mind of managing his property and affairs, repayment of the deposit or any part thereof shall be made in accordance with regulations made under section 28(2) of this Act determining the receipts which are to be a good discharge in the case of the payment of any sum belonging to a person who has become incapable as aforesaid.

(5) A person under the age of seven shall not be capable of giving a receipt under this section.

(6) A person under the age of fourteen shall not be capable of appointing an agent for the purpose of giving a receipt under this section, but the appointment of an agent for that purpose by a person who is not of full age but is aged fourteen or over shall be as effective as it would be if he were of full age.

(7) An abstract of the provisions of this section shall be included as one of the rules of every trustee savings bank.

31.—(1) Without prejudice to the provisions of section 31 of the Industrial and Provident Societies Act 1965 (Investment of funds of registered society), and subject to those provisions, the treasurer of any charitable or provident institution or society, or charitable donation or bequest for the maintenance, Deposits by, and payments to, certain institutions, etc. 1965 c. 12.

education or benefit of the poor, or of any penny savings bank, may invest the funds of the institution or society in the funds of a trustee savings bank.

(2) Where a payment is made by a trustee savings bank to a trustee, treasurer or other officer of a provident institution or society or of a charity, friendly society or penny savings bank, who is apparently authorised to require that payment, his receipt shall be a sufficient discharge, and neither the trustee savings bank nor any of its trustees, managers or officers shall be responsible for any misapplication or for any want of authority of the person requiring or receiving the payment.

Investment by trustee savings banks of ordinary deposit moneys

Investment of moneys forming part of assets in respect of ordinary deposits.

32.—(1) Subject to subsection (2) below and to any other provision of this Act, the sums of money which the trustees of a trustee savings bank are authorised to invest under this Act or under any rules of the bank and which form part of the assets of the bank in respect of ordinary deposits shall be invested under section 33 of this Act and shall not be invested in any other manner.

(2) Subsection (1) above shall not apply to such sums of money as are needed to answer the exigencies of the bank.

The Fund for the Banks for Savings

Investment in Fund for the Banks for Savings.

33.—(1) There shall continue to be an account raised in the name of the Commissioners in the books of the Banks of England and Ireland respectively, called the Fund for the Banks for Savings (hereafter in this Act referred to as " the Fund ").

(2) The sums of money which the trustees of a trustee savings bank are by section 32 of this Act to invest under this section shall be paid into the Fund.

(3) Sums of money representing current account deposits shall be paid into the Fund separately from any other sums so paid for the bank, and the Commissioners shall keep a separate account of those sums.

Issue of interest-bearing receipts.

34.—(1) The officer of the Commissioners shall have power to issue a receipt signed by a cashier of the Bank of England or Bank of Ireland, as the case may be, in respect of a payment under section 33 of this Act.

(2) Subject to subsections (3) and (5) below, the receipt shall carry interest at such rate not being less than £2 15s. 0d. per cent. per annum and not exceeding £3 13s. 0d. per cent. per annum as the Treasury may fix by order.

(3) The power to make an order under subsection (2) above shall include power to fix a rate for a receipt in respect of a payment of a sum of money representing current account deposits different from, but not greater than, that for the time being fixed by such an order for a receipt in respect of a payment of money representing savings account deposits.

(4) The power of making orders under subsection (2) above shall include power to vary or revoke an order and shall be exercisable by statutory instrument, subject to annulment in pursuance of a resolution of either House of Parliament.

(5) So long as there is in operation a scheme prepared by the Association and approved by the Commissioners for mutual assistance between trustee savings banks in the United Kingdom, the Isle of Man and the Channel Islands no rate fixed under subsection (2) above, or fixed under that subsection by virtue of subsection (3) above, shall apply to banks qualified to participate but not participating in that scheme, and in the case of any such bank—

(*a*) the rate of interest to be carried by a receipt in respect of a payment of money representing savings account deposits shall be such rate (not exceeding the rate fixed for such a receipt by an order under subsection (2) above) as the Treasury may from time to time direct, having regard in particular to the expenses of management of that bank ; and

(*b*) the rate of interest to be carried by a receipt in respect of a payment of money representing current account deposits shall be such rate (not exceeding the rate having effect in relation to such a receipt by virtue of subsection (2) or (3) above) as the Treasury may from time to time direct, having regard in particular to the expenses of the provision by that bank of a current account service.

(6) The principal and interest of all sums mentioned in any receipt shall be charged on all money in the Fund and on any moneys produced by the sale of any securities standing to the credit of the Fund.

(7) The receipt shall be in such form as the Commissioners may direct.

Management of the Fund

35.—(1) All sums credited to an account of a trustee savings bank in the books of the Commissioners shall carry interest (at the rate for the time being fixed for such of the sums credited to that account as represent payments under section 33 of this

Interest on sums in the Fund.

Act) from the day at which they are credited to the account to the day preceding that at which they are debited to it; but no interest shall be allowed on any fraction of a pound of the balance for the time being standing to the credit of the account.

(2) The officer of the Commissioners shall, within six weeks from 20th November and 20th May in each year, calculate the interest due on the said sums for the six months ending with that day, and that interest shall be credited to the account as at the following day (any fraction of a penny being disregarded); and within sixty days from 20th November and 20th May in each year he shall issue, in a form approved by the Commissioners, a receipt signed by him for the amount of the interest so credited as if that amount had been a payment made by the trustees of the bank under section 33 of this Act on the 21st day of that month.

Investment of money in the Fund.

36.—(1) The Commissioners, subject to reserving such sums as they think fit, shall invest money paid into the Fund—

(a) in Parliamentary securities created or issued under the authority of an Act of Parliament where those securities are securities for the interest on which provision is made by Parliament or are securities directly chargeable on the National Loans Fund, with recourse to the Consolidated Fund of the United Kingdom, or

(b) in stock or debentures or other securities expressly guaranteed by authority of Parliament or the due payment of the interest on which is expressly guaranteed by authority of Parliament, or

(c) in securities which are issued in respect of a loan raised by the Government of Northern Ireland or securities the interest on which is for the time being guaranteed by the Parliament of Northern Ireland.

(2) The interest on such investments shall also be invested under this section.

Power to hold cash balance in Bank of Ireland.

37. Notwithstanding the provisions of section 36 of this Act, the Commissioners may, in accordance with arrangements made by them with the Bank of Ireland, pay any sums of money into the Bank of England to be placed to the credit of the Fund in the Bank of Ireland, and those sums shall be applied as if they had originally been paid into the Fund in the Bank of Ireland under section 33 of this Act.

Withdrawal of sums from the Fund.

38. The Commissioners with the concurrence of the Treasury may by statutory instrument make regulations as to the manner in which sums standing to the credit of a trustee savings bank in the books of the Commissioners may be withdrawn, the manner in which payments may be made on any such withdrawal and the manner in which a valid discharge is to be given to the Commissioners for any such payment.

39.—(1) The Commissioners shall annually make out an account in such form as the Treasury may direct with respect to the year ending on 20th November— Annual account as between Commissioners and trustee savings banks.

(a) showing on the one side the interest accrued from the securities standing to the credit of the Fund, and

(b) showing on the other side the interest paid and credited to trustee savings banks.

(2) The account shall, not later than 31st May in each year, be transmitted to the Comptroller and Auditor General.

40.—(1) The Commissioners shall in every year, out of the amount by which the gross amount of the interest accrued during the preceding year on the securities standing to the credit of the Fund appears by the account under section 39 of this Act to have exceeded the gross amount of interest paid and credited in that year to trustee savings banks, apply, in accordance with the directions of the Treasury, such sum as the Treasury may from time to time authorise towards defraying— Certain expenses to be defrayed out of surplus income of the Fund.

(a) in the first place, the expenses incurred by the Inspection Committee in the exercise of any powers conferred by this Act,

(b) in the second place, the expenses incurred by the Commissioners in the execution of this Act.

(2) For the purposes of this section the expenses incurred by the Commissioners in the execution of this Act shall be deemed to include—

(a) such sum as, in the opinion of the Treasury, approximately represents the amount in each year of the accruing liability in respect of the benefits for which any officers or persons employed by the Commissioners in the execution of this Act will on their retirement become eligible under the Superannuation Act 1965 ; 1965 c. 74.

(b) such proportion of the salary, or of the said accruing liability in respect of superannuation benefits, of any officer or person who is so employed in part only in the execution of this Act as, in the opinion of the Treasury, is attributable to the execution of this Act :

(c) any capital expenditure incurred in providing premises wholly used by the Commissioners for the purposes of this Act and such part of any such expenditure incurred in providing premises partly used as aforesaid as was, in the opinion of the Treasury, incurred for those purposes ;

(*d*) in the case of any premises occupied by the Commissioners wholly or partly for the purposes of this Act and in respect of which no rent is payable, such an amount as is estimated by the Treasury to represent the rental value of the premises or of that part of the premises used for the said purposes, after allowing for any capital expenditure incurred as aforesaid which has been charged to the Fund.

(3) If, in any case where any capital expenditure incurred as aforesaid has been charged to the Fund, the premises in respect of which the expenditure was incurred are sold or cease to be used for the said purposes, there shall be deducted from the amount thereafter chargeable to the Fund such sum as may be determined by the Treasury to represent the then value of the premises or of that part of the premises which was used for the said purposes.

Adjustment of balances.

41.—(1) Where the annual account mentioned in section 39 of this Act shows that in the year for which the account is made up the gross amount of interest accrued from the securities standing to the credit of the Fund exceeded—

(*a*) the gross amount of interest paid and credited during the year to trustee savings banks in pursuance of this Act, together with

(*b*) a sum, to be determined by the Treasury, to provide against the depreciation in the value of the securities, and

(*c*) any amount applied under section 40(1) of this Act,

the Commissioners shall cause the amount of the surplus to be paid out of the Fund into the Consolidated Fund of the United Kingdom in such manner as may from time to time be agreed on between the Treasury and the Commissioners.

(2) Where the said account shows that, with respect to the year for which the account is made up, the gross amount of interest accrued from the securities standing to the credit of the Fund was less than—

(*a*) the gross amount of interest paid or credited to trustee savings banks in pursuance of this Act, together with

(*b*) a sum, to be determined by the Treasury, to provide against the depreciation in the value of the securities, and

(*c*) such of the expenses (including the remuneration of members and officers) incidental to the exercise by the Inspection Committee of the powers conferred on them by this Act as may be sanctioned by the Treasury on the recommendation of the Commissioners, and

(d) the expenses incurred by the Commissioners in the execution of this Act,

an amount equal to the deficiency shall, at such times as the Treasury may direct, be paid out of the Consolidated Fund of the United Kingdom and shall be applied in defraying the said expenses of the Inspection Committee and the Commissioners and, so far as not so applied, shall be paid into the said Fund.

The reference in this subsection to the Commissioners' expenses shall be construed in accordance with section 40(2) and (3) of this Act.

(3) If the Fund is insufficient to meet its liabilities the Treasury may, on being informed thereof by the Commissioners, issue the amount of the deficiency out of the Consolidated Fund of the United Kingdom and the Treasury shall certify the deficiency to Parliament.

42.—(1) The Commissioners shall at the close of each year ending on 20th November prepare a statement in such form as the Treasury may direct showing the aggregate of the liabilities of the Government to trustee savings banks and the nature and amount of the securities held by the Commissioners to meet those liabilities.

Annual statement of liabilities of Government to banks.

(2) The statement shall, not later than 31st May in each year, be transmitted to the Comptroller and Auditor General.

Special investments

43.—(1) A trustee savings bank may not exercise the power to make special investments unless—

(a) it exercised that power before 1st June 1891, or

(b) the Commissioners on the recommendation of the Inspection Committee authorise the bank to do so.

Conditions subject to which a bank may make special investments.

(2) Before the Commissioners give their authority under subsection (1) above, they must be satisfied—

(a) that the bank is open daily ; and

(b) that it has an aggregate cash liability to its depositors, irrespective of the amount of any special investments, of not less than £200,000.

The Commissioners may withdraw their authority if at any time in their opinion either of these conditions is not for the time being complied with.

(3) Paragraph (b) of subsection (2) above shall not apply if—

(a) the Association concur in the recommendation of the Inspection Committee required under subsection (1) above ; and

2 X 3

   (*b*) the Commissioners, having regard to the financial position of the bank and to the size and importance of the area served by it, think it expedient in the interests of the depositors of the bank that their authority should be given under that subsection.

(4) The accounts of a trustee savings bank making special investments shall be kept so as to distinguish between the receipts and expenditure on account of special investments and the receipts and expenditure on account of the general business of the bank.

(5) The rules of a trustee savings bank making special investments shall provide to the satisfaction of the Inspection Committee for the audit, examination and publication of the accounts relating to special investments and for the safe custody of the securities held by the bank on account of special investments.

(6) Assets of a trustee savings bank in respect of ordinary deposits shall not be chargeable with any part of the expenditure on account of special investments and, subject to the following provisions of this Act, shall not be liable for any loss or deficiency in respect of special investments.

Commissioners' power of control.

44.—(1) Every trustee savings bank which carries on the business of making special investments shall so far as respects that business be subject to the control of the Commissioners and shall comply with any directions which may from time to time be given by the Commissioners with respect to that business, including directions as to the manner in which the total expenses of management are to be apportioned in the bank's accounts as between the business of making special investments and the handling of ordinary deposits.

If a bank to which any such directions are given neglects or refuses to comply therewith the Commissioners may themselves take the necessary steps for giving effect thereto, and for that purpose may do all such things and exercise all such powers as may be done and exercised by the trustees, managers and other officers of the bank.

(2) Without prejudice to the general power of control given to the Commissioners by subsection (1) above, the following provisions shall have effect with respect to the special investment business of a trustee savings bank—

   (*a*) no money received for investment or forming part of the assets held by a bank on account of special investments shall be invested, and no securities held on account of special investments shall be sold, except with the approval of the Commissioners;

(*b*) no change shall be made in the rate of interest allowed to depositors in respect of special investments except with the approval of the Commissioners ;

(*c*) the amount to be expended by the bank for expenses of management on account of the special investment business shall not exceed such an amount as may be allowed by the Commissioners ;

(*d*) there shall be transmitted to the Commissioners, together with the statement required to be transmitted to them under section 56 of this Act, a valuation of the securities held by the bank on account of special investments, and for the purpose of the valuation the value of those securities shall be calculated according to the current market price at the date of the valuation, or, in the case of securities for which there is at that date no current market price, shall be taken to be such an amount as the Commissioners fix, having regard to the date of repayment of, and to the rate of interest payable in respect of, the securities.

45.—(1) Moneys received for special investment shall not be invested except in accordance with sections 46 and 47 of this Act.

(2) The provisions of subsection (1) above and of the said sections 46 and 47 shall be taken to apply to the investment of any moneys forming part of the assets held by a bank on account of special investments.

Investment of moneys received for special investment and certain other moneys.

46.—(1) The trustees of a trustee savings bank may, subject to regulations made by the Treasury and to the powers of control conferred on the Commissioners by section 44 of this Act, invest moneys received for special investment in any such manner for the time being specified in Part II of Schedule 1 to the Trustee Investments Act 1961 as may be specified in the regulations.

Securities in which moneys received for special investment may be invested.
1961 c. 62.

(2) Without prejudice to subsection (1) above—

(*a*) the trustees of a trustee savings bank may, subject to regulations so made and to the Commissioners' said powers of control, invest moneys so received in any securities of which principal and interest are charged on the National Loans Fund, with recourse to the Consolidated Fund of the United Kingdom, or on the Consolidated Fund of Northern Ireland, whether directly or by virtue of any guarantee, notwithstanding that the securities are excluded from Part II of Schedule 1 to the Trustee Investments Act 1961 by the operation of paragraph 2 of Part IV of that Schedule ; and (*b*) the trustees of a trustee savings bank in the island of Jersey or Guernsey may, subject as aforesaid, invest moneys so received in any security issued by the States of that island of which principal and interest are charged on the general revenues of the States.

(3) The power of the Treasury to make regulations for the purposes of this section shall be exercisable by statutory instrument and a draft of any statutory instrument made in the exercise of the power shall be laid before Parliament.

Powers to transfer moneys received for special investment to another trustee savings bank for investment and to deposit such moneys with a bank other than a trustee savings bank.

47.—(1) Notwithstanding anything in section 12(2) of this Act, the Commissioners may, on the application of the trustees of a trustee savings bank, authorise all or any of the moneys received by the trustees for special investment to be paid to and received by the trustees of another trustee savings bank for special investment, but subject to the following conditions:—

(*a*) a bank shall not be permitted to make a payment under this subsection if its total liabilities to depositors in respect of special investments apart from this subsection are more than £1 million or if the amounts standing to its credit with other banks under this subsection would with that payment be more than £200,000 ;

(*b*) a bank shall not be permitted to receive a payment under this subsection if its total liabilities to depositors in respect of special investments apart from this subsection are less than £4 million or less than ten times the amount which its total liabilities to other banks in respect of special investments under this subsection would attain with that payment ;

(*c*) the terms of any investment by one bank with another under this subsection shall be stated in the application to the Commissioners and shall be such as may be agreed between the banks concerned, except that—

(i) the money shall be repayable by the bank receiving it on six months or some shorter notice, and on one month or some shorter notice if the trustees of the other bank certify that it is necessary for them to call in investments in order to meet an unusual demand on the bank ; and

(ii) the rate of interest shall be not less than that from time to time allowed by the bank receiving the money on moneys which are received on the same date for special investment apart from this subsection and are repayable on one month's notice ;

(*d*) a bank shall at any time withdraw any money invested by it or repay any money invested with it under this subsection if so directed by the Commissioners.

For the purpose of paragraphs (*a*) and (*b*) above, the amount of a bank's liability to any person in respect of special investments shall be taken to be the amount for the time being standing to his credit in respect thereof in the books of the bank.

(2) The trustees of a trustee savings bank shall have power to deposit moneys received by them for special investment in a bank other than a savings bank, either on deposit account or on current account.

48.—(1) For the purpose of providing for any deficiency which may arise in respect of special investments made by trustee savings banks, there shall continue to be a guarantee fund under the control of the Commissioners.

(2) The guarantee fund shall consist of—

(*a*) the reserves both in respect of general business and of special investments of all trustee savings banks which make special investments, and

(*b*) the closed banks fund,

and for the purpose aforesaid the reserves of every such trustee savings bank shall be at the disposal of the Commissioners, and the bank shall comply with any directions given by the Commissioners with respect to those reserves for the purpose of giving effect to the provisions of this section.

(3) If, on any valuation of the assets belonging to any bank on account of special investments, it appears that there is a deficiency, that deficiency shall, in the event of the bank being closed or wound up, or discontinuing, with the consent of the Commissioners, the business of making special investments, be a charge on and be made good out of the guarantee fund, as follows—

(*a*) recourse shall be had in the first instance to the amount standing to the credit of the guarantee fund in respect of the reserves of the bank in question and, so far as that amount is insufficient for the purpose, to the amount standing to the credit of the guarantee fund in respect of the reserves of other banks and to the closed banks fund pari passu, and

(*b*) as between the reserves of a bank in connection with special investments and the reserves of a bank in connection with its general business, recourse shall be had in the first instance to the reserves in connection with special investments, and as between the banks other than the bank in connection with whose account the deficiency has arisen the amount falling to be

2 X*

charged on the reserves of those banks shall be allocated pro rata to those reserves according to their several amounts.

49.—(1) Where a trustee savings bank discontinues the business of making special investments—

    (*a*) the like results shall follow as would have followed if, immediately before the discontinuance, every depositor had, in pursuance of a previous notice duly given in that behalf, withdrawn the whole amount which he is entitled to withdraw in respect of special investments and had immediately redeposited the amount withdrawn as a savings account deposit with the bank, and

    (*b*) all assets and liabilities of the bank in respect of the business of making special investments, other than its liabilities to depositors, shall be deemed to be assets and liabilities in respect of savings account deposits, notwithstanding anything in this Act restricting the investment of the funds of any such bank, and

    (*c*) the bank shall comply with any directions of the Commissioners as to any of the assets referred to in paragraph (*b*) above ;

and, save so far as the contrary is expressly provided by an order under section 14 of this Act, the amounts deemed to be deposited under paragraph (*a*) above shall be left out of account for the purposes of every order made under that section.

(2) Where a trustee savings bank discontinues the business of making special investments, the assets and liabilities thereof shall be valued as at the date of the discontinuance but without regard to the operation of subsection (1) above.

For the purpose of the valuation, the value of any securities shall be calculated according to the current market price at the date of the discontinuance or, in the case of securities for which there is at that date no current market price, shall be taken to be such amount as the Commissioners shall fix, having regard to the date of repayment of, and to the rate of interest payable in respect of, the securities, and the value of any land or buildings shall be taken at such amount as the Commissioners shall fix.

(3) If, on any such valuation, it appears that there is a deficiency, the deficiency shall be made good out of the guarantee fund under section 48(3) of this Act and, without prejudice to the generality of the provisions of that subsection, the deficiency, if and so far as it exceeds the reserve of the bank in respect of ordinary deposits, shall be made good to the bank out of that fund.

(4) If, on any such valuation as aforesaid, it appears that there is a surplus, an amount equal to the surplus shall be carried to the closed banks fund and the bank shall have no claim to the principal thereof or any interest thereon.

(5) Where a trustee savings bank carrying on the business of making special investments is wholly closed or is ordered to be wound up, the bank shall for the purpose of this section be deemed to have discontinued the business of making special investments immediately before the closing or the commencement of the winding up, as the case may be.

50. The trustees of a trustee savings bank may, with the approval of the Commissioners, borrow, whether by way of temporary loan or of overdraft from bankers or otherwise, on the security of the funds, or any part of the funds, held on account of special investments.

Power to borrow on security of special investment funds.

Financing of capital expenditure for bank purposes

51.—(1) Without prejudice to sections 53 and 54 of this Act, the cost to a trustee savings bank of purchasing any land or erecting any building for the purposes of the bank under section 11 of this Act may be defrayed out of—

Ways of defraying cost of purchasing land, etc.

(a) surplus moneys forming part of the assets of the bank in respect of ordinary deposits, including moneys received by way of advance or grant from another trustee savings bank, from the mutual assistance account or from the closed banks fund, or

(b) moneys applied for those purposes under section 52 of this Act,

or partly in one way and partly in the other.

(2) Any expenditure incurred by a trustee savings bank in the doing of work to land or buildings provided for the purposes of the bank or in the acquisition of equipment or machinery required for the conduct of the business of the bank, being expenditure of a capital nature, may be defrayed in the same manner as the cost of purchasing land may be defrayed under this section.

(3) Where the whole or part of the cost to a trustee savings bank of—

(a) purchasing any land or erecting any building, or

(b) doing any work to land or buildings provided for the purposes of the bank,

is defrayed out of an advance from another trustee savings bank, the repayment of the sum advanced and the payment of any sums payable under the terms of the advance by way of interest or otherwise to the bank making the advance may be secured by mortgage of or charge on the land or building; and in relation to moneys which by virtue of any such mortgage or charge ought to be paid to the trustees of the bank making the advance the reference to the custodian trustees in section 11(3) of this Act shall be construed as referring to the custodian trustees of that bank.

Purchase of property out of special investment surplus.

52.—(1) The trustees of a trustee savings bank may, with the consent of the Commissioners, apply a part of the surplus capital held by the bank on account of special investments towards the purchase of land or the provision of buildings for the purposes of the bank under section 11 of this Act.

(2) The Commissioners shall not give their consent in any case if the amount proposed to be applied would, when added to any sums already applied under this section (excluding sums applied towards the purchase of any land or the provision of any buildings which have been sold) exceed twenty per cent. of the surplus capital as shown on the last annual valuation.

(3) All moneys accruing from or in connection with the sale, exchange or lease of any land purchased or buildings provided under this section, or of any part of such land or buildings, shall be invested by the trustees as if they were moneys received for special investment.

(4) The value of any land purchased or buildings provided under the provisions of this section shall be taken at such an amount as the Commissioners may from time to time fix and shall be included in the annual valuation.

(5) If the cost of purchasing any land or erecting any building is or has been defrayed partly but not wholly out of moneys applied under this section, subsection (3) above shall apply to such part of the moneys first referred to in that subsection as appears to the trustees, with the approval of the Commissioners, to be referable on a just apportionment to the sums applied under this section, and such part of the value of that land or building as appears to the trustees, with the said approval, to be so referable shall be included in the annual valuation.

(6) The whole or part of the cost of any land purchased or buildings erected for the purposes of a bank making special investments may, with the consent of the Commissioners, be transferred to or from moneys applied under this section by applying a sum representing the whole or a proportionate part of the value of the land or buildings out of moneys available for the purchase of land under this section or out of moneys otherwise available for the purchase of land, as the case may be; and in the case of a transfer from moneys applied under this section that sum shall be invested as if it were money received for special investment.

(7) Expenditure of a capital nature incurred by a trustee savings bank on the doing of work to land or buildings provided for the purposes of the bank shall be treated for the purposes of this section as incurred on the purchase of the land or erection of the building.

(8) In this section " annual valuation " means a valuation required to be made under section 44(2)(*d*) of this Act, and " surplus capital " means the amount by which the value of the assets held by a bank on account of special investments at the date of the annual valuation is found on that valuation to exceed the aggregate liability of the bank on account of or in connection with special investments.

53.—(1) The Commissioners may make to a trustee savings bank advances out of the Fund in order to meet expenditure incurred by the bank in purchasing land or erecting buildings for the purposes of the bank or any expenditure of a capital nature incurred by the bank—

Advances by Commissioners out of the Fund for the Banks for Savings.

> (*a*) on the doing of work to land or buildings provided for the said purposes ; or
>
> (*b*) in the acquisition of equipment or machinery required for the conduct of the business of the bank.

(2) Advances made by virtue of this section shall be on such terms and for such period as the Commissioners may with the approval of the Treasury direct, but the total of the advances so made shall not exceed £10 million.

54.—(1) Where the Commissioners, in pursuance of section 1 of this Act, approve the formation of a new trustee savings bank, they may, after consultation with the Association and the Inspection Committee, advance to the trustees of that bank out of the closed banks fund such sums as they think fit for the purpose of providing for expenses incurred in connection with the formation and initial working of the bank ; and for the purposes of this subsection expenses incurred in the purchase of land or erection of buildings for the purposes of a new bank shall be deemed to be incurred in connection with the formation and initial working of the bank.

Advances by Commissioners out of closed banks fund.

(2) The Commissioners may also, after consultation with the Association, advance to the trustees of a trustee savings bank out of the closed banks fund such sums as the Commissioners think fit for the purpose of enabling the operations of that bank to be extended.

(3) Any advance under this section may be made on such terms and conditions and for such period as the Commissioners with the consent of the Treasury may determine.

(4) The Commissioners may, with the consent of the Treasury, release the whole or any part of the principal of and interest on any advance made by the Commissioners under this section.

(5) The amount for the time being outstanding in respect of advances from the closed banks fund under this section shall not be treated as forming part of that fund for the purposes of section 48 of this Act.

Returns and accounts to be prepared by trustee savings banks

Weekly
returns.

55. The trustees and managers of every trustee savings bank shall transmit weekly returns to the Commissioners, in such form and giving such particulars as the Commissioners may direct, showing the amounts of the week's transactions of the bank and the amount of the cash balances in the hands of the treasurer or any other person on account of the bank.

Annual
statements.

56.—(1) The trustees and managers of every trustee savings bank shall annually prepare a general statement of the sums standing to the credit of the bank in the books of the Commissioners up to 20th November in each year, and of expenses incurred.

(2) The said annual statement shall show the balance or principal sum due to depositors in the bank collectively and identify the persons holding the said balance.

(3) The said annual statement shall contain, or be accompanied by, such particulars with respect to the special investments of the bank as the Commissioners direct.

(4) The said annual statement shall be signed by two managers or two trustees, or by one manager and one trustee, of the bank and shall be countersigned by the secretary or actuary of the bank.

(5) The said annual statement shall be in such form and contain, or be accompanied by, such particulars as the Commissioners direct and shall be transmitted to the office of the Commissioners within nine weeks after 20th November in each year.

(6) A similar statement shall be transmitted to the Inspection Committee within the said period of nine weeks.

(7) If the said annual statement is not prepared and transmitted to the Commissioners within the said period of nine weeks, the Commissioners, or the Comptroller General or Assistant Comptroller of the National Debt Office, shall for the information of the depositors forthwith publish, in the London

Gazette and in any newspapers published in the county in which the bank is established, the name of the bank in default, in such form and words, and under such conditions as the Commissioners or the said Comptroller General or Assistant Comptroller may think fit.

(8) If it appears in the said annual statement that any money belonging to a trustee savings bank is in the hands of a treasurer or other person, the statement shall be accompanied by a certificate, signed by the treasurer or other person, stating that the money therein mentioned is in his possession.

(9) The trustees and managers of every trustee savings bank shall cause a duplicate of any annual statement under this section, accompanied by a list of the trustees and managers of the bank, signed and countersigned in the same manner as the statement, to be publicly affixed and exhibited in some conspicuous part of the office or place where the deposits of the bank are usually received, for the information of all persons making deposits therein, and the duplicate shall remain so affixed and exhibited until the ensuing annual statement is in like manner affixed and exhibited under this subsection.

(10) Every depositor shall be entitled to receive from the bank a printed copy of the annual statement.

57. The Commissioners or the Comptroller General or Assistant Comptroller of the National Debt Office may require from the trustees and managers of a trustee savings bank a detailed statement of all the expenses whatever incurred by the trustees and managers in the management of the bank or otherwise.

Statements of expenses.

Supervision of trustee savings banks

58.—(1) The Inspection Committee may appoint persons to inspect the books and accounts of trustee savings banks, and to examine and ascertain and report to the Committee from time to time, with respect to each bank, whether the bank has complied with the requirements of this Act and of the rules of the bank as to the security to be taken from officers, the accounts of the bank and the conduct of its business, and whether any part of the expenditure is excessive or unnecessary ; and every trustee savings bank shall give all due facilities for enabling any such inspection or examination to be made.

Powers and duties of Inspection Committee.

(2) If on the report of any such person it appears to the Committee that a trustee savings bank has made default in giving such facilities or complying with any of the requirements aforesaid, or that any part of the expenditure of the bank is excessive or unnecessary, the Committee shall call upon the

bank to remedy the default or, as the case may be, to reduce the expenditure within a specified time, and if the default is not remedied or the expenditure is not reduced within that time the Committee shall report the matter to the Commissioners.

(3) Thereupon the Commissioners may, subject to subsection (4) below, at their discretion—

(a) close the account of the bank and proceed under section 60 of this Act, or

(b) report the matter to the Treasury with a view to action being taken under section 59 of this Act,

or adopt both of these courses.

(4) The power conferred by subsection (3) above to close the account of a bank shall—

(a) in the case of default in complying with a current account service requirement, be limited to the closing of the separate account of the bank of moneys representing current account deposits mentioned in section 33(3) of this Act, and

(b) in the case of default in complying with any other requirement of this Act mentioned in subsection (1) above, be construed as extending to the closing of that separate account.

In this subsection " current account service requirement " means a requirement of any of the following sections of this Act, that is to say, sections 13, 19, 20, 21, 22 and 23.

(5) If, on any report of the Committee, any question arises as to what constitutes the necessary expenses of a trustee savings bank within the meaning of section 1 of this Act, the decision of the Commissioners on that question shall be conclusive.

(6) The Committee may, with the approval of the Commissioners, make rules for regulating the duties of persons appointed by the Committee under this section.

(7) The trustees of every trustee savings bank shall, at the request of the Committee, supply the Committee with a copy of the pass book in use by the bank for the purpose of savings account deposits or special investments, as the case may require, and of the rules of the bank and of any alterations thereof.

(8) If, in the opinion of the Committee, the rules of a trustee savings bank are insufficient for the purpose of maintaining an efficient audit, the bank shall, with all convenient speed, make such additional rules as may, in the opinion of the Committee, be required for the purpose.

(9) If the bank do not, within a time specified by the Committeee, from the date of being required to make any such rules, comply with the requirement, the Committee may make the rules, and shall submit the rules so made to the Registrar, to be certified by him; and, when so certified, they shall be binding on the trustees.

(10) The Committee shall, not later than 31st May in each year, send to the Commissioners a report of the proceedings of the Committee under this Act during the year ending on the previous 20th November, and the report shall be laid before Parliament.

59.—(1) The Treasury may, if satisfied on the representation either of such number of the depositors in any trustee savings bank as appears to them sufficient, or of the Commissioners, that there is good reason for causing an examination to be made into the affairs of any trustee savings bank, apply ex parte to any judge of the High Court, or to any judge of the Court of Session in Scotland, who, if satisfied that such examination is desirable, may thereupon appoint a master of the Supreme Court or a barrister of not less than seven years standing in England or Northern Ireland, or an advocate of not less than five years standing or writer to the signet of not less than five years standing in Scotland, as a commissioner to hold a local inquiry into the affairs of that bank, and to report thereon; but such notice of any representation by depositors under this section shall be given to the trustees of the bank as the Treasury may direct.

Appointment of commissioner to examine affairs of trustee savings bank.

(2) Every such commissioner shall, for the purposes of the examination which he is authorised to conduct, have power—

(*a*) to require by summons under his hand a person to send a written return to any inquiry, or to attend as a witness before him, and to examine any witness on oath, and to require any witness to take an oath and to answer any question; and

(*b*) to require production of all books, papers and documents which appear to him to relate to the affairs of the bank, and the production of which appears to him necessary.

(3) If any person, after having had a tender made to him of the expenses (if any) to which he is entitled, fails, without lawful excuse, to comply with any requirement of the commissioner under this section, he shall, on summary conviction, for each offence be liable to a fine not exceeding £10.

(4) Every witness shall be allowed such expenses as would be allowed to him when attending to give evidence before any superior court, and in case of dispute the amount shall be

referred by the commissioner to a master or taxing officer of the Supreme Court, or to the Queen's and Lord Treasurer's Remembrancer in Scotland, who, on request under the hand of the commissioner, shall ascertain and certify the proper amount of the expenses.

(5) The Treasury may, if they think fit, where a representation is made by depositors, require such security for costs to be given as they think proper, but except so far as costs may be recovered under any such security, all costs incurred in or incidental to any proceedings under this section shall be paid out of moneys provided by Parliament.

Default powers of Commissioners.

60.—(1) Subject to subsection (2) below, if—

(a) the trustees of a trustee savings bank neglect or refuse to obey any orders or directions given by the Commissioners, whether or not through their officers, in pursuance of this Act, or

(b) default is made in complying with the requirements of section 5 of this Act as respects any trustee savings bank, or

(c) the trustees of a trustee savings bank neglect or refuse to make out and transmit to the Commissioners the annual statement mentioned in section 56 of this Act within the period of nine weeks mentioned in that section, or

(d) the Inspection Committee have under section 58(2) of this Act reported to the Commissioners that a trustee savings bank has failed to remedy such a default, or reduce such expenditure, as is mentioned in that section,

the Commissioners may close the account of the trustee savings bank and may direct that no further sum shall be accepted at the Bank of England or at the Bank of Ireland from the trustees of that trustee savings bank to the Commissioners' account until such time as the Commissioners think fit.

(2) If—

(a) a trustee savings bank fails to comply with a direction given under section 22 of this Act, or

(b) the Inspection Committee report to the Commissioners under section 58(2) of this Act that a trustee savings bank has failed to remedy a default in complying with a current account service requirement,

subsection (1) above shall not apply, but the Commissioners may close the separate account of the bank of moneys representing current account deposits mentioned in section 33(3) of this Act and may direct that no further sums of money representing current account deposits shall be accepted at the Bank of England or at the Bank of Ireland from the trustees of that bank to the Commissioners' account until such time as the Commissioners think fit.

In this subsection " current account service requirement " has the same meaning as in section 58(4) of this Act.

(3) Without prejudice to subsection (2) above, the power of closing the account of a trustee savings bank conferred by subsection (1) above shall be construed as extending to the closing of the separate account of that bank referred to in subsection (2) above.

(4) After the Commissioners have closed an account under subsection (1) or (2) above they may, if the trustees of the trustee savings bank comply with the directions of the Commissioners or their officers, re-open the said account and again authorise the acceptance of money at the Bank of England or at the Bank of Ireland ; and they may allow the payment of compound interest on the account during the period when it was closed.

Amalgamation and mutual assistance

61.—(1) Any two or more trustee savings banks may, with the assent of the Commissioners, on the recommendation of the Inspection Committee, by special resolution of both or all such banks, become amalgamated together as one bank with or without dissolution or division of the funds and property of the banks, or either or any of them, and all the funds and property of the banks, so far as not already vested in the custodian trustees of the amalgamated bank, shall become vested in them without the necessity of any form of conveyance or assignment other than the special resolution for amalgamation.

Power to amalgamate.

(2) For the purposes of the amalgamation a special resolution shall mean a resolution passed by not less than three-fourths of the trustees of the bank present at a general meeting of which notice specifying the intention to propose the resolution has been duly given according to the rules, and confirmed by a majority of the trustees present at a subsequent meeting, of which notice has been duly given, held not less than fourteen days nor more than a month from the date of the first-mentioned meeting.

(3) Notwithstanding anything in section 9 of this Act, on any amalgamation of two or more trustee savings banks which is to be effected not by merging with one of the existing banks the other or others of them, but by establishing a new bank, the special resolutions for the amalgamation shall appoint four of the trustees of the amalgamated bank to be the custodian trustees of that bank.

Advances by trustee savings banks for development.

62.—(1) The trustees of a trustee savings bank may, with the approval of the Commissioners, make advances of such amounts, on such terms and conditions and for such period as may be approved by the Commissioners,—

    (*a*) to the trustees of another trustee savings bank for the purpose of enabling the operations of that other bank to be extended ;

    (*b*) to any persons proposing to form a new trustee savings bank for the purpose of providing for expenses incurred or to be incurred in connection with the formation and initial working of the new bank.

(2) For the purposes of this section expenses incurred in the purchase of land or erection of buildings for the purpose of a new bank shall be deemed to be incurred in connection with the formation and initial working of the bank.

(3) The trustees of a trustee savings bank who have made an advance under this section may release the whole or any part of the principal of and interest on that advance.

Grants by trustee savings banks for benefit of other trustee savings banks.

63.—(1) A trustee savings bank may, with the approval of the Commissioners, make a grant to the Commissioners of such amount as may be approved by the Commissioners, to be applied for the benefit of other trustee savings banks.

(2) The Commissioners shall, as part of the Fund, maintain a separate account known as the mutual assistance account, and shall credit to that account any sums granted to the Commissioners under subsection (1) above.

(3) Notwithstanding anything in section 34(3) or (5) of this Act, the mutual assistance account shall carry interest at the rate fixed by order of the Treasury under subsection (2) of the said section 34 for a receipt in respect of a payment of money representing savings account deposits ; and in addition to that interest there shall be credited to that account on 21st November and 21st May in each year a sum equal to that by which the interest credited to trustee savings banks for the preceding six months is reduced in consequence of the said section 34(5), and the sum so credited shall be treated as if it were interest credited to the mutual assistance account.

(4) Any interest credited to the mutual assistance account shall, for the purposes of the annual account to be prepared by the Commissioners under section 39 of this Act, be treated as interest credited to trustee savings banks.

(5) The Commissioners, upon the application of the Association, may if they think fit, debit the mutual assistance account with any amount not exceeding that specified in the application,

and credit that amount to the account in the books of the Commissioners of any trustee savings banks so specified.

(6) In addition to the power conferred by subsection (1) above, a trustee savings bank shall have power, with the approval of the Commissioners, to make direct to another trustee savings bank a grant of such amount and on such conditions as may be approved by the Commissioners.

(7) The Commissioners may, at the request of a bank which makes a grant under this section, debit that bank's account in the books of the Commissioners with the amount of the grant and credit that amount in those books to the account of the bank to which the grant is to be made, or to the mutual assistance account, as the case may be.

Closing of trustee savings banks

64.—(1) It shall not be lawful for the trustees of a trustee savings bank to close or dissolve the bank or cease to carry on the business of the bank or to carry on business only for the purpose of winding up its affairs unless— Consent of Commissioners required for closing a bank.

(a) the Commissioners consent, or

(b) the bank is ordered to be wound up in pursuance of section 399 of the Companies Act 1948 (winding up of unregistered companies) or a corresponding enactment forming part of the law of Northern Ireland. 1948 c. 38.

(2) The consent of the Commissioners under this section shall not be given unless and until they have satisfied themselves, after consultation with the Inspection Committee and the Association, that there are no proper persons able and willing to act as trustees and managers of the bank.

(3) Where the trustees of a trustee savings bank propose to close the bank, they shall give to depositors such notice as the Commissioners may require of the facilities afforded by law to depositors for transferring their deposits to the National Savings Bank.

65.—(1) When a trustee savings bank is finally closed, the trustees, or any two or more of them, shall forthwith notify the Commissioners in writing, and shall, with the consent of the Commissioners, convert into money any property held by the said trustees or by any person as trustee for the bank. Sale of property on closing a bank.

(2) The trustees of the bank, after paying the expenses of the conversion and any claims thereon, shall account for and pay over the residue to the Commissioners.

(3) The Commissioners shall continue to keep a distinct account of money standing to the credit of closed banks (in this Act referred to as " the closed banks fund ").

(4) The Commissioners shall carry the residue paid over to them under subsection (2) above to the closed banks fund.

(5) The moneys carried on account of each bank to the closed banks fund under this section shall be subject to any claim that may thereafter be substantiated on account of any depositor in the bank.

(6) The trustees of a bank desiring to close the bank may with the consent of the Commissioners compensate their officers out of money which would otherwise be carried to the closed banks fund under this section.

Procedure available on closing a bank.

66.—(1) If the trustees of a trustee savings bank—

(*a*) give public notice of their intention to close the bank by posting a letter to each depositor at his residence when known, and by advertisement in a newspaper circulating in the district where the bank is situated and by affixing notice of their intention to close the bank on the outer door of the building in which the business of the bank is carried on, and

(*b*) transmit to the Commissioners a certified list (signed by two trustees and three managers of the bank) of the depositors who have not applied to them to receive their deposits or for transfer certificates, and of the amount due to them respectively,

the Commissioners may accept from the said trustees all money remaining in the hands of the said trustees or their treasurer.

(2) If the said money with the money belonging to the bank in the hands of the Commissioners, together with the proceeds of sale of other property as referred to in section 65 of this Act, is sufficient to discharge the whole of the liabilities of the trustees to the depositors, as set out in the said list, the certificate of the Commissioners shall be a sufficient discharge to the trustees in respect of all money so paid over or in the hands of the Commissioners.

(3) All the said moneys shall be held by the Commissioners subject to the rights and claims of the depositors named in the list, and those depositors shall thereafter be considered to be depositors in the National Savings Bank.

(4) The said depositors, on presenting their deposit books at the National Savings Bank, shall be entitled to claim payment of the sums due to them respectively, with the interest due to

them thereon, and on establishing their claim shall be paid out of the moneys so paid over by the trustees under section 65 of this Act and this section and the moneys in the hands of the Commissioners as above referred to.

The reference in this subsection to deposit books shall be construed as a reference to deposit books in use by the bank for the purpose of savings account deposits or special investments, as the case may require.

(5) The surplus of the said moneys, if any, after providing for the sums due to the said depositors, shall be carried to the closed banks fund in the books of the Commissioners and shall be subject to any claim that may thereafter be substantiated on account of any depositor in the bank.

(6) The trustees shall not close the bank before the expiration of one month from the giving of the notice required by this section.

Officers, employees, etc., of trustee savings banks

67.—(1) Subject to subsection (2) below, the following persons, that is to say—

(*a*) every treasurer of a trustee savings bank, and

(*b*) every officer or other person receiving any salary or allowance for his services from the funds of a trustee savings bank,

shall give good and sufficient security to be approved of by not less than two trustees of the bank for the just and faithful execution of his office or trust.

Security to be given by officers and others.

(2) Subsection (1) above shall not apply to such persons or classes of persons as the Commissioners may direct, and paragraph (*b*) of that subsection shall not apply to supernumerary assistants employed at the periods of balancing the accounts.

(3) The security required by this section shall comprise security in respect of the amount received on account of special investments and the rules of the bank shall provide to the satisfaction of the Inspection Committee for the security in respect of that amount.

(4) The security to be given under this section by an officer or other person receiving any salary or allowance for his services shall be either—

(*a*) by bond, with one or more sureties, to the Comptroller General of the National Debt Office ; or (*b*) with the permission of the Commissioners, by the deposit of money or of Government securities or by the bond of a guarantee society; or

(*c*) if the Commissioners and the Inspection Committee approve, by a single bond of a guarantee society guaranteeing all the persons employed by the bank or at any branch thereof who are required to give security;

and where security is given under paragraph (*c*) above, the annual premium on the bond shall be paid by the trustees of the bank, and the trustees of the bank shall be entitled to recover from each person covered by the bond such proportion of the premium as that person's annual salary bears to the total amount of the annual salaries of the persons covered by the bond.

(5) In case of forfeiture the trustees or managers of the trustee savings bank may sue on the bond in the name of the said Comptroller General, and carry on the proceedings at the costs and charges and on behalf of the bank, fully indemnifying the Comptroller General from all costs and charges in respect of the proceedings.

(6) A bond given under this section shall, when executed, be deposited with the Commissioners and the Commissioners may, on application signed by not less than two trustees in such form as the Commissioners shall direct, deliver up to the bank any such bond deposited with them for the purpose of being cancelled.

Persons
failing to
account for
money
received from
depositors.
    68.—(1) If an actuary, cashier, secretary, officer or other person holding a situation or appointment in a trustee savings bank receives any sum of money from or on account of a depositor, or person desirous of becoming a depositor, or on account of the bank, and does not forthwith, or, in the case of local receivers acting on behalf of a trustee savings bank, within the time specified in the rules of that bank, duly account for and pay over the money to the trustees and managers or to such person as may be directed by the rules of the bank, he shall be guilty of an offence.

(2) A person convicted on indictment of an offence under this section by a court in England, Wales or Northern Ireland shall be liable to a fine or to imprisonment for a term not exceeding two years or both.

Liability of
trustees and
managers.
    69.—(1) No trustee or manager of a trustee savings bank shall be personally liable, except—

(*a*) for money actually received by him on account of or for the use of the bank which is not paid over and disposed of as directed by the rules of the bank, or (*b*) for neglect or omission in complying with the rules required by Schedule 1 to this Act to be adopted in the maintenance of checks, the audit and examination of accounts, the holding of meetings and the keeping of the minutes of proceedings thereat, or

(*c*) for neglect or omission in taking security under section 67 of this Act from officers.

(2) The reference to any neglect or omission in paragraphs (*b*) and (*c*) of subsection (1) above shall not include a reference to any act or omission in pursuance of an authority or direction given by the Commissioners under section 26 or 67(2) of this Act.

70. Where any payment or act is, or has before the commencement of this Act been, made or done by the trustees of a trustee savings bank in accordance with the enactments and regulations relating to trustee savings banks for the time being in force, and in accordance with the rules of the bank, the trustees of the bank are hereby indemnified against all claims on the part of any person in respect of the payment or act, but any person may nevertheless recover any sum lawfully due to him from the person to whom the trustees of the bank have paid it.

Indemnity for trustees against claims in respect of certain acts.

71. A person who—

(*a*) holds or receives any part of the money, effects or funds belonging to a trustee savings bank, or

(*b*) is in any manner entrusted with the disposition, management or custody of such money, effects or funds or of any securities, books or papers, or property relating thereto,

Recovery of property of a bank from certain persons.

and his personal representative and assigns shall on demand made in pursuance of an order of not less than two trustees and three managers of the bank or at any general meeting of the trustees or managers thereof—

(i) give in his or their account to the said trustees or managers or general meeting, or to such other person as may be nominated to receive the account, to be examined and allowed or disallowed by the said trustees or managers, and

(ii) pay over all the money remaining in his or their hands and assign and transfer or deliver all securities and effects, books, papers and property in his or their hands or custody to such person as the said trustees or managers may appoint.

Priority of debts owed by bank officers to the bank.

72.—(1) If an officer of a trustee savings bank who is entrusted with the keeping of the accounts or who has in his hands or possession by virtue of his office or employment any money or effects belonging to the bank, or any deeds or securities relating thereto—

(a) dies, or

(b) becomes bankrupt, or makes any assignment of his property for the benefit of his creditors, or

(c) has any execution or attachment or other process issued against his property,

his personal representative or, as the case may be, his trustee in bankruptcy or assignee, or the sheriff or other officer executing such process as aforesaid shall, within forty days after demand made by two of the trustees of the bank,—

(i) deliver and pay over all moneys and other things belonging to the bank to such person as the said trustees appoint, and

(ii) pay out of the estate, assets or effects of the said person all sums of money remaining due which he received by virtue of his office or employment, before any other of his debts are paid or satisfied, or, as the case may be, before the money directed to be levied by the said process is paid over to the party issuing the process.

(2) Subsection (1) above, so far as it relates to bankruptcy or the administration of insolvent estates, shall not apply in Scotland.

Office of trustee to be vacated for non-attendance at meetings.

73.—(1) If a trustee of a trustee savings bank is absent from all the meetings of the trustees and of the committee of management (if any) held during any period of twelve months ending with 20th November, and has not during that period performed any of the duties imposed on trustees and managers by paragraph 2 of Schedule 1 to this Act, his office as trustee shall at the end of that period become vacant.

(2) The person whose office as trustee so becomes vacant shall not, unless he has before the end of the said period explained to the satisfaction of the Inspection Committee his absence or the non-performance of his duties, be eligible for re-appointment until the expiration of one year from the end of that period, and until he is re-appointed his name shall not be allowed to continue in the list of trustees, but the vacation of his office shall not affect any liability which he may have incurred as trustee before the date at which he vacates office.

(3) Where a vacancy occurs in pursuance of this section, the trustees of the bank shall forthwith send notice of the vacancy to the Commissioners and to the Inspection Committee.

74. An auditor of a trustee savings bank shall be appointed for a term not exceeding one year, but a retiring auditor shall be eligible for re-appointment. Appointment of auditors.

Superannuation of officers and employees

75.—(1) The trustees of a trustee savings bank may with the consent of the Inspection Committee— Superannuation allowances to, and gratuities in case of death of, officers of trustee savings banks.

    (*a*) grant to an officer of the bank who has served for not less than ten years as an officer of trustee savings banks, and who retires from his office after attaining the age of sixty years or on becoming incapable of discharging the duties thereof by reason of permanent infirmity of mind or body:—

        (i) an annual allowance not exceeding one-eightieth of the average annual amount of the salary and emoluments of his office during the last three years of his service for each year of service as such an officer, subject to a maximum of forty-eightieths thereof ; and

        (ii) an allowance by way of lump sum not exceeding three-eightieths of the average annual amount of the salary and emoluments of his office during the last three years of his service for each year of such service, subject to a maximum of one hundred and twenty eightieths thereof ; and

    (*b*) grant to the personal representative of any such officer who, after five years' service as such, dies while still employed in the service of the bank, a gratuity not exceeding whichever may be the greater of :—

        (i) the average annual amount of the salary and emoluments of his office during the last three years of his service ; or

        (ii) the amount of the allowance by way of lump sum which might have been granted to him if he had retired from his office on the ground of ill health at the date of his death ; and

    (*c*) grant to the personal representative of any such officer who after becoming entitled to an annual allowance, dies after he has retired from the service, and in whose case the sums actually received by him at the time of his death on account of the annual allowance together with the sum received by him by way of lump sum allowance are less than the average annual amount of the salary and emoluments of his office during the last three years of his service, a gratuity not exceeding the deficiency.

(2) An annual allowance under this section shall only be continued so long as, in the opinion of the Inspection Committee, the funds of the bank admit of its payment.

Allocation of part of superannuation benefits to dependants.

76.—(1) An officer of a trustee savings bank who retires from the service of the bank, otherwise than on the ground of ill health, at any time after the coming into operation for that bank of rules under this section shall be allowed to surrender, as from the date of his retirement, such part (not exceeding one-third) of any annual allowance which the trustees of the bank may grant to him under section 75 of this Act as may be provided by the rules in return for the trustees granting to the wife or husband, as the case may be, of the officer or to a dependant of the officer a pension, payable from the like source as the said allowance, of such value as according to tables for the time being in force for the purposes of section 43 of the Superannuation Act 1965 (which provides for the allocation of superannuation benefits) is actuarially equivalent, on the date of the officer's retirement, to the value of that part of the said annual allowance which is surrendered.

1965 c. 74.

(2) Rules under this section may with the approval of the Commissioners be made for any trustee savings bank by the trustees of the bank, and may provide—

(*a*) for the application thereof to officers of the bank generally or to any class of such officers;

(*b*) for the circumstances in which, and the conditions as to proof of good health and other matters subject to which, an officer to whom the rules apply may surrender an allowance in accordance with subsection (1) above;

(*c*) for the application, in relation to any pension granted in return for such a surrender, of the provisions of section 75(2) of this Act subject to such modifications as appear to the trustees requisite for excluding from the application of that subsection so much of the pension as represents deductions in respect thereof made from instalments of the annual allowance of the retiring officer already paid to him.

(3) Any such pension as aforesaid for the benefit of a dependant, not being the spouse of the retiring officer, shall be

payable in respect of the period, if any, for which the dependant survives the retiring officer, and any such pension as aforesaid for the benefit of the spouse of the retiring officer shall, according as the retiring officer may in conformity with the rules of the bank under this section elect, be payable either—

(a) in respect of the period, if any, for which the spouse survives the retiring officer, or

(b) in respect both of the period of their joint lives subsequent to the retirement and of the period, if any, for which the spouse survives the retiring officer,

and the rules may provide that a pension payable thereunder in respect of the periods mentioned in paragraph (b) above shall be paid at one rate in respect of the first of those periods and at a higher rate in respect of the second.

(4) If any person has, in accordance with rules under this section, surrendered part of an allowance, then for the purpose of calculating the amount of any gratuity which may be granted to his personal representative under paragraph (c) of section 75(1) of this Act the sums paid or payable to him at the time of his death on account of the said allowance shall be deemed to be the sums which would have been so paid or payable but for the surrender.

77.—(1) Subject to the consent of the Minister for the Civil Service given on the recommendation of the Commissioners, the Inspection Committee shall have the same power of granting superannuation allowances and gratuities to officers of the Committee and to the personal representatives of such officers as is by section 75(1) of this Act conferred on the trustees of a trustee savings bank with respect to officers of the bank and their personal representatives. *Officers of Inspection Committee.*

(2) Section 76 of this Act shall apply to the Inspection Committee and officers thereof as it applies to a trustee savings bank and officers thereof, with the substitution for references to the trustees of a trustee savings bank or to such a bank of references to the Committee, and for references to the said section 75, and any provision thereof, of references to that section or provision as applied by subsection (1) above.

(3) The amounts payable under this section shall, for the purpose of section 40 of this Act, be deemed to be expenses incurred by the Committee in the exercise of their powers.

78.—(1) Where an officer of the Inspection Committee, the Association or the Savings Banks Institute (hereafter in this section referred to as " the Institute ") has been transferred to service with a trustee savings bank, or an officer of a trustee *Superannuation payments for transferred officers.*

savings bank, the Association or the Institute has been transferred to service with the Inspection Committee, then, for the purposes of sections 75, 76 and 77 of this Act the period of continuous trustee savings bank service of the officer ending with the transfer shall, subject to the provisions of this section, be reckoned as if it were a period of service with the bank or Committee to service with which the officer is transferred.

(2) In this section "trustee savings bank service" means service with any trustee savings bank institution, that is to say, any trustee savings bank, the Inspection Committee, the Association or the Institute, and trustee savings bank service shall be treated as continuous if interrupted only on transfer from one trustee savings bank institution to another.

(3) In respect of the transfer of an officer of a trustee savings bank to service with another such bank or the Inspection Committee, the Association or the Institute, or of an officer of the Committee to service with a trustee savings bank, the Association or the Institute, the trustees of the bank from service with which he is transferred or the Committee, as the case may be, may, with the approval of the Commissioners, pay to the bank, Committee, Association or Institute to service with which the officer is transferred such amount as may with the like approval be determined by the trustees or Committee making the payment to represent the superannuation value, at the date of the transfer, of the continuous trustee savings bank service of the officer ending with that date.

Any payment under this subsection by trustees or the Inspection Committee may be defrayed in the like manner as sums payable by the trustees or Committee under sections 75, 76 and 77 of this Act.

(4) No payment shall be made—

(a) by the trustees of a trustee savings bank under the said sections by reference to previous service of an officer of the bank with the Inspection Committee, the Association or the Institute, or

(b) by the Inspection Committee under the said sections by reference to previous service of an officer of the Committee with a trustee savings bank, the Association or the Institute,

unless on the transfer of the officer in question to service with the bank or the Committee, as the case may be, payment was made to them in respect of the officer by the bank, Committee, Association or Institute from service with which the officer was transferred of an amount equal to the superannuation value, at the date of the transfer, of the said previous service.

(5) For the purposes of this section, the superannuation value, at the date of any transfer, of any service of a transferred officer

shall be an amount, calculated in accordance with rules for the purposes of this section made by the Commissioners by statutory instrument, equivalent to the actuarial value at that date of the superannuation benefits, so far as attributable to the service in question, which would be payable in respect of him if he continued to serve with the bank, Committee, Association or Institute from service with which he is transferred at the remuneration payable to him immediately before the transfer until his trustee savings bank service was terminated by death or retirement.

(6) In this section " the Savings Banks Institute " means the body constituted by that name in January 1948.

79.—(1) Where an institution established as a savings bank Reckoning (as defined in section 1(3) of this Act) is certified under this for super-Act, or was certified under the Trustee Savings Banks Act 1954, annuation as a trustee savings bank, and a person is or was serving as of certain an officer of the bank both immediately before and immediately savings bank after the time when it is or was certified, his service as an not certified officer of the bank before that time may, to such extent as the as trustee Commissioners with the approval of the Minister for the Civil savings bank. Service may determine, be reckoned for the purpose of sections 1954 c. 63. 75, 76, 77 and 78 of this Act as if it were a period of service as an officer of the trustee savings bank.

(2) In subsection (1) above the reference to sections 75, 76, 77 and 78 of this Act shall include any order modifying those sections under section 82 of this Act, except in so far as the contrary is provided by any order made under that section.

80.—(1) The trustees of a trustee savings bank, or of two Establishment or more such banks acting jointly, may, with the approval of of super-the Inspection Committee and in accordance with rules made by annuation the trustees with the consent of the Commissioners, establish a reserves. reserve fund to be known as the superannuation reserve.

(2) Where such a reserve has been established any superannuation payment falling to be made by the trustees of the bank, or of any of the banks, for which the reserve was established shall, in such cases and to such extent as may be provided by rules under this subsection, be defrayed out of the superannuation reserve.

(3) Rules made as aforesaid shall provide for the source from which and the manner in which the trustees shall make payments to the superannuation reserve and for the application of the assets thereof otherwise than in defraying superannuation payments either where it is determined in accordance with the rules that the assets of the superannuation reserve exceed the

amount likely to be required for defraying such payments or in the event of the winding up of the bank, or of any of the banks, for which the reserve was established, or in such other circumstances as may be provided by the rules.

(4) Save as may be provided by rules made as aforesaid the assets of the superannuation reserve shall not be applicable except for the purpose of defraying superannuation payments and any expenses of managing the reserve.

(5) Section 75(2) of this Act shall, notwithstanding anything in that subsection or in rules made under section 76 of this Act, not apply to so much of any superannuation payment as is payable out of the superannuation reserve.

(6) The assets of any superannuation reserve established under this section shall be invested with the Commissioners on the same terms and in the like manner as assets of the bank in question which are invested with the Commissioners in pursuance of section 33 of this Act, and the fixing of a rate of interest by virtue of section 34(3) or (5) of this Act shall not be taken to affect those terms.

(7) The Commissioners, after consultation with the Inspection Committee, may require any trustees to amend rules made by them for the purposes of this section in such manner as the Commissioners may specify, and if it appears to the Commissioners that the trustees have failed within a reasonable time to comply with any such requirement the Commissioners may direct that the rules shall have effect as if amended in accordance with the requirement.

(8) Rules under this section may contain such incidental and supplementary provisions as appear requisite for the purposes of this section.

(9) Where superannuation reserves have been established, whether jointly or separately, for two or more trustee savings banks, the reserves may, with the approval of the Commissioners, be amalgamated on such terms as to the making of payments out of the amalgamated reserves as may be agreed between the trustees of the banks in question, and where superannuation reserves have been amalgamated in pursuance of this subsection, they shall be treated as if they were a single superannuation reserve established by the said banks acting jointly, and the foregoing provisions of this section shall apply accordingly.

(10) In this section " superannuation payment " means a payment under sections 75, 76, 77 and 78 of this Act.

81.—(1) The trustees of a trustee savings bank, or of two or more such banks acting jointly, may in accordance with rules made by them with the consent of the Commissioners establish a contributory superannuation fund, to be vested in trustees appointed in accordance with the rules, to which contributions shall be made, of such amounts and payable at such times and in such manner as may be provided by the rules,— Establishment of contributory superannuation funds.

(a) by the persons for whom provision can be made out of the fund and who are employed in the service of the bank or banks by whom the fund is established ;

(b) by the trustees of the said bank or banks, from such source as may be provided by the rules.

(2) The assets of any fund established under this section shall be applied—

(a) in providing, in respect of persons employed in the service of the bank or banks in question or any class of such persons, as may be provided by the rules, benefits of all or any of the descriptions provided for by section 75 of this Act of amounts not exceeding those which could be paid under that section or under that section as extended by section 79 of this Act ;

(b) in repaying, in such cases and to such extent as may be provided by the rules, the amount of contributions made to the fund by persons in the service of the bank, or any of the banks, in question, together with compound interest thereon calculated at such rate and in such manner as may be provided by the rules but subject to the deduction (in so far as the rules so provide) of sums due from such persons to the bank by whom they have been employed ;

(c) in defraying, in so far as the rules so provide, the cost of payments under section 78(3) of this Act ;

(d) in defraying the expenses of management of the fund :

Provided that where it is determined in accordance with the rules that the assets of the fund exceed the amount likely to be required under paragraphs (a), (b), (c) and (d) above, or in the event of the winding up of the bank, or of any of the banks, for which the fund was established, or in such other circumstances as may be provided by the rules, the assets shall become applicable in such other manner as may be so specified.

(3) Subsections (6), (7), (8) and (9) of section 80 of this Act shall apply for the purposes of this section with the substitution for references to a superannuation reserve of references to a contributory superannuation fund and for references to that section of references to this section.

Power to make orders as to super-annuation benefits.

82.—(1) The Minister for the Civil Service may, after consulting the Commissioners, by order extend or modify the superannuation benefits payable under sections 75, 76, 77, 78, 80 and 81 of this Act.

1965 c. 74.
1967 c. 28.

(2) The said Minister may, in particular, by an order under this section authorise the payment of superannuation benefits corresponding to those payable under the Superannuation Acts 1965 and 1967, or under any other enactment whether past or future, which relates to the superannuation benefits payable in respect of the service of civil servants, but shall not make an order which in his opinion would authorise the payment of superannuation benefits superior to those payable in respect of the service of civil servants.

(3) Subject to the restrictions imposed by subsection (2) above, an order under this section may in particular—

(a) authorise the granting of pensions for widows, children and other dependants of deceased employees, and of lump sums payable on retirement, or on death before retirement, and

1944 c. 21.

(b) authorise the increase of pensions in cases corresponding to those where civil service pensions have been increased by the Pensions (Increase) Act 1944 or any subsequent Act relating to the increase of current pensions, and

(c) make provision as to the kinds of service which may be treated as pensionable service, and as to payments in respect of employees transferred from one service to another, and

(d) amend any of the provisions of the sections specified in subsection (1) above, and

(e) make provision for transitional, supplemental or incidental matters ;

1952 c. 10.

and an order making provision corresponding to Part III or IV of the Superannuation Act 1965 (which provide for the payment of contributions in return for the benefits thereby conferred), may apply section 384 of the Income Tax Act 1952 (which provides that relief from income tax shall not be allowed in respect of such contributions).

(4) An order under this section may be varied or revoked by a subsequent order and the power of making such orders shall be exercisable by statutory instrument which shall be subject to annulment in pursuance of a resolution by either House of Parliament.

(5) In this section " civil servant " has the meaning assigned to it by section 98(2) of the Superannuation Act 1965.

Miscellaneous

83.—(1) The Commissioners shall at the close of each year ending on 20th November prepare an account with respect to trustee savings banks containing such particulars and in such form as the Treasury may direct.

Account to be prepared by Commissioners.

(2) The account shall, not later than 31st May in each year, be transmitted to the Comptroller and Auditor General.

84. The Comptroller and Auditor General shall each year examine, certify and report on the account transmitted to him under section 39 or 83 of this Act, and on the statement transmitted to him under section 42 thereof, and shall lay copies of them, together with copies of his report, before each House of Parliament.

Comptroller and Auditor General to report on certain accounts, etc.

85.—(1) Any ledger, book of account, register or minute book required by any provisions of this Act or by the rules of a trustee savings bank, to be kept by a trustee savings bank may be kept by making entries in a bound book or by recording the matters in question in any other manner.

Keeping by banks of ledgers, accounts and registers and minute books.

(2) Where any such ledger, book of account, register or minute book is not kept by making entries in a bound book but by some other means, precautions shall be taken to the satisfaction of the Inspection Committee for guarding against falsification and facilitating its discovery.

86.—(1) The Treasury shall have power, with the concurrence of the Commissioners, to make regulations prescribing the manner in which and the persons by whom any document required by this Act to be used in connection with a trustee savings bank is to be signed or executed, and the provisions of this Act with respect to the manner in which or person by whom any particular document is to be signed or executed shall, in so far as they conflict with any regulations under this subsection, cease to have effect as from the date when the regulations come into force.

Forms of documents.

(2) Except in so far as regulations under subsection (1) above otherwise provide, all receipts, orders, certificates, indorsements, accounts, returns or instruments, or other matters or things required for carrying into execution this Act shall contain such particulars and shall be made in such form and manner and under such conditions as shall be directed or required or approved by the Commissioners or their officers.

(3) The power to make regulations under this section shall be exercisable by statutory instrument a draft of which shall be laid before Parliament.

Rules of
bank for
authentication
of documents.

87. Except in so far as regulations under section 86(1) of this Act otherwise provide, the rules of a trustee savings bank may provide for the execution and signing of instruments and documents on behalf of the trustees by not less than four trustees authorised for the purpose by the trustees, and any such rules, if duly certified shall be binding on all persons, and be operative for all purposes, but shall not affect anything contained in any regulations made by the Commissioners under section 38 of this Act.

Fees taken
by Registrar.

88.—(1) The Treasury may by warrant direct that there shall be charged upon any certificate or authority given, and any award, order or determination made by the Registrar under this Act, such reasonable fee as may be fixed by the warrant of the Treasury.

(2) Every such fee shall be paid into the Consolidated Fund, and shall be paid by such persons and in such manner as may be directed by the warrant.

(3) No fee which is not allowed by the warrant shall be charged or taken in respect of any matter for which a fee can be charged under this section.

1946 c. 36.

(4) The power of making warrants under this section shall be exercisable by statutory instrument and a draft statutory instrument under this section shall be laid before both Houses of Parliament for at least forty days before the statutory instrument is made, but section 6 of the Statutory Instruments Act 1946 shall not apply to a statutory instrument under this section.

Exemption
from stamp
duty.

89. No stamp duty shall be charged on—

(a) a power, warrant or letter of attorney given by a person as trustee of a trustee savings bank or by a depositor in a trustee savings bank authorising a person to make a deposit on behalf of the depositor or to sign a document or instrument required by the rules of the bank on making a deposit, or to withdraw a deposit, or the interest on a deposit,

(b) a receipt, or entry in a receipt book, for a deposit in a trustee savings bank, or for any money received by a depositor, or his personal representatives, assigns or attornies, from the funds of a trustee savings bank, or

(c) a draft or order, an appointment of an agent, an instrument for the revocation of any such appointment, a surety-bond, or any other instrument or document whatever required or authorised to be given, issued signed, made or produced in pursuance of this Act.

90. Neither the Bank of England nor the Bank of Ireland nor the Commissioners shall be under any liability in respect of anything required or permitted to be done in pursuance of this Act. Indemnity for Bank of England, etc.

91. The Commissioners may employ such clerks and other officers as may be necessary for the purposes of this Act, and the Minister for the Civil Service may determine the remuneration of those clerks or other officers. Commissioners' staff.

92.—(1) If any person, not being a trustee savings bank, takes or uses, in connection with any business carried on by him, the title of " savings bank certified under the Act of 1863 ", " savings bank certified under the Trustee Savings Banks Act 1954 " or " savings bank certified under the Trustee Savings Banks Act 1969 ", he shall be guilty of an offence. Use of title of certified savings bank by unauthorised persons.
1954 c. 63.

(2) A person convicted on indictment of an offence under this section by a court in England, Wales or Northern Ireland shall be liable to a fine or to imprisonment for a term not exceeding two years or both.

(3) Where an offence under this section which has been committed by a body corporate is proved to have been committed with the consent or connivance of or is attributable to any neglect on the part of any director, manager, secretary or other similar officer of the body corporate, or any person who was purporting to act in any such capacity, he as well as the body corporate shall be deemed to be guilty of the offence and shall be liable to be proceeded against and punished accordingly.

93.—(1) In section 9(3) of the Finance Act 1956 (which provides for the extension to deposits with a savings bank maintained under a local Act of the relief given to an individual by that section from income tax on ordinary deposits with a trustee savings bank where the Treasury are satisfied that the deposits with the savings bank so maintained correspond with ordinary deposits in a trustee savings bank and in connection with that relief applies certain provisions of the Trustee Savings Banks Act 1954 to a savings bank so maintained)— Modification of s. 9(3) of Finance Act 1956 and of certain other enactments which refer to ordinary deposits in trustee savings banks.
1956 c. 54.

(*a*) any reference to an ordinary deposit in a trustee savings bank shall be construed as a reference to a savings account deposit in such a bank, and

(*b*) the reference to sections 25 to 38 of the said Act of 1954 shall be construed as referring to sections 32, 33(1) and (2), 34 (except subsections (3) and (5)), 35 to 37 and 39 to 42 of this Act and the reference to section 27(2) of that Act shall be construed as referring to section 34(2) of this Act.

(2) The Treasury may by order under the said section 9(3) make for any bank or department of a bank for the time being certified under that subsection the like provision as may be made for trustee savings banks by regulations under section 38 of this Act.

(3) In any enactment whereby a power is conferred on any person to invest in ordinary deposits in a trustee savings bank any reference to an ordinary deposit in a trustee savings bank shall be construed as a reference to a savings account deposit in such a bank.

Rate of interest on deposits in seamen's savings banks. 1894 c. 60.

94. Notwithstanding anything in section 34(3) or (5) of this Act, the interest to be paid by the Commissioners to the account of the Board of Trade on money representing deposits in seamen's savings banks under section 149(2) of the Merchant Shipping Act 1894 (which requires interest to be paid at the same rate as on the money received from trustee savings banks) shall continue to be paid at the rate fixed by order of the Treasury under section 34(2) of this Act for a receipt in respect of a payment of money representing savings account deposits.

Supplemental and general

Interpretation.

95.—(1) In this Act, unless the context otherwise requires—
" the Association " has the meaning assigned to it by section 8(5) of this Act ;
" charges scheme " has the meaning assigned to it by section 21(1) of this Act ;
" closed banks fund " has the meaning assigned to it by section 65(3) of this Act ;
" the Commissioners " means the National Debt Commissioners ;
" current account " has the meaning assigned to it by section 13(1) of this Act ;
" current account deposit " has the meaning assigned to it by section 13(4) of this Act ;
" current account service " has the meaning assigned to it by the said section 13(4) ;
" enactment " includes an enactment of the Parliament of Northern Ireland ;
" friendly society " means a friendly society registered in the manner required by the Acts for the time being in force relating to friendly societies and includes a registered branch of a friendly society ;
" the Fund " has the meaning assigned to it by section 33(1) of this Act ;

" Inspection Committee " means the Committee established under section 4 of this Act ;

" land " includes hereditaments and chattels real and in Scotland heritable subjects of any description ;

" ordinary deposit " has the meaning assigned to it by section 12(3) of this Act ;

" penny savings bank " means a bank the rules of which fix a sum not exceeding £5 as the maximum amount which may stand to the credit of any one depositor therein at any one time, and which provide, upon the attainment of that maximum amount, for its transfer to an account opened in the depositor's own name in the savings bank where the deposit account of the penny savings bank is kept ;

" Registrar " has the meaning assigned to it by section 106 of the Friendly Societies Act 1896 ;   1896 c. 25.

" reserves " means as respects any bank the whole of the assets of the bank, less the amount necessary to discharge in full all liability to depositors in the bank and outstanding management expenses ;

" savings account deposit " has the meaning assigned to it by section 13(4) of this Act ;

" special investment " has the meaning assigned to it by section 12(3) of this Act ;

" trustee " in relation to a trustee savings bank does not include a custodian trustee ;

" trustee savings bank " means a bank certified under this Act, the Trustee Savings Banks Act 1954 or the Trustee 1954 c. 63. Savings Banks Act 1863.   1863 c. 87.

(2) Any reference in this Act to any enactment is a reference to it as amended by or under any other enactment.

96.—(1) The enactments specified in Part I of Schedule 3 Repeals, to this Act are hereby repealed to the extent specified in the revocation, third column of that Part of that Schedule, and the order savings and specified in Part II of that Schedule is hereby revoked to the consequential extent specified in the third column of that Part of that Schedule. amendment.

(2) In so far as any instrument made or other thing whatsoever done under any enactment repealed by this Act could have been made or done under a corresponding enactment in this Act, it shall not be invalidated by the repeal of that enactment but shall have effect as if made or done under that corresponding enactment ; and for the purposes of this provision anything which under section 82(2) of the Trustee Savings Banks Act 1954 had effect as if done under any enactment in that Act

shall, so far as may be necessary for the continuity of the law, be treated as done under the corresponding enactment in this Act.

(3) Subject to the provisions of this Act, the term of office of members of the Inspection Committee and the making of appointments, and the powers, procedure and duties of that Committee, shall continue to be governed by the scheme made under section 2 of the Savings Banks Act 1891 in the same manner as immediately before the commencement of this Act, but on the date on which a scheme made under section 4 of this Act comes into force this subsection shall cease to have effect.

1891 c. 21.

(4) Nothing in the repeals made by section 82 of the Trustee Savings Banks Act 1954 shall affect—

1954 c. 63.

(a) the application of an Act passed in the fifty-ninth year of the reign of King George the Third intituled an Act for the Protection of Banks for Savings in Scotland to any savings bank established under that Act before 28th July 1863 unless and until that bank becomes a trustee savings bank ; or

1819 c. 62.

(b) the savings on the repeal of sections 12 and 51 to 54 of the Trustee Savings Banks Act 1863 contained in section 12 of the Savings Banks Act 1949 ; or

1863 c. 87.
1949 c. 13.

(c) the savings on the repeal of provisions in section 41 of the said Act of 1863 contained in Schedule 11 to the Finance Act 1949.

1949 c. 47.

(5) Nothing in sections 45 and 46 of this Act shall apply to or affect any investment made before 5th July 1968 or any investment previously made in the exercise of powers conferred by section 2 of the Trustee Savings Banks Act 1958 or section 41 of the Trustee Savings Banks Act 1954.

1958 c. 8.

(6) Any reference in section 51(1) or 52(5) or (6) of this Act to the said section 52 includes, in relation to moneys applied before 25th January 1955, a reference to section 8 of the Savings Banks Act 1929.

1929 c. 27.

(7) Any enactment or other document referring to an enactment repealed by this Act or by the Trustee Savings Banks Act 1954 shall, so far as may be necessary for preserving its effect, be construed as referring, or as including a reference, to the corresponding enactment in this Act.

(8) In section 33(9) of the Bankruptcy Act 1914 for the words " section fourteen of the Trustee Savings Banks Act 1863 " there shall be substituted the words " section 72 of the Trustee Savings Banks Act 1969".

1914 c. 59.

(9) In section 398 of the Companies Act 1948 after the words " 1863 " there shall be inserted the words " the Trustee Savings Banks Act 1954 or the Trustee Savings Banks Act 1969 ", and in section 399(8) of the said Act of 1948 for the words

1948 c. 38.

" Trustee Savings Banks Act 1887 " there shall be substituted the words " Trustee Savings Banks Act 1969 ".

(10) In section 5(1) of the Administration of Estates (Small 1965 c. 32. Payments) Act 1965, after the words " section 2 of this Act " there shall be inserted the words " or to section 28(5) of the Trustee Savings Banks Act 1969 ", and in section 6(3) of the said Act of 1965 after the words " this section " there shall be inserted the words " or section 29 of the Trustee Savings Banks Act 1969 ".

(11) Nothing in the foregoing provisions of this section shall be taken as prejudicing the operation of section 38 of the Interpretation Act 1889 (which relates to the effect of repeals). 1889 c. 63.

97.—(1) It is hereby declared that this Act extends to Northern Ireland. | Application to Northern Ireland.

(2) In the application of this Act to Northern Ireland, the provisions of this Act relating to stamp duties (being matters with respect to which the Parliament of Northern Ireland may make laws) shall be treated for the purposes of section 6 of the Government of Ireland Act 1920 (which provides that that 1920 c. 67. Parliament may amend laws of the Parliament of the United Kingdom passed before the day appointed for the purposes of that section) as passed before that day.

98.—(1) In relation to sums of money which at the com- Application mencement of this Act stand in the books of the Commissioners of Act to to the credit of a trustee savings bank in the Republic of banks in Ireland or which may thereafter be credited in those books to Ireland. such a trustee savings bank in pursuance of section 16 of this Act or any other enactment, references in this Act to trustee savings banks shall include references to trustee savings banks in the Republic of Ireland.

(2) Save as otherwise expressly provided by subsection (1) above or any other provision of this Act, references in this Act to trustee savings banks shall not include references to trustee savings banks in the Republic of Ireland.

99.—(1) This Act shall extend to the Isle of Man and the Application to Channel Islands and shall have effect in those Islands subject Isle of Man to such adaptations and modifications as Her Majesty may by and Channel Order in Council specify. | Islands.

(2) Any Order in Council made under subsection (1) above may be varied or revoked by a subsequent Order in Council so made.

100.—(1) This Act may be cited as the Trustee Savings Banks Short title Act 1969. | and com-mencement.

(2) This Act shall come into force on such day as the Treasury may by order made by statutory instrument appoint, being a day not earlier than the day appointed for the purposes of the Post Office Act 1969. | 1969 c. 48.

SCHEDULES

SCHEDULE 1

MATTERS TO BE COVERED BY THE RULES OF A BANK WHICH IS TO
HAVE THE BENEFIT OF THIS ACT

The rules of a trustee savings bank must expressly provide for the
following matters.

1.—(1) That a person who is a treasurer, trustee or manager of
the bank, or who has any control in the management of the bank,
shall not derive any benefit from any deposit made in the bank.

(2) That the persons depositing money in the bank shall have the
whole benefit of those deposits and the produce thereof, except for
such salaries and allowances or other necessary expenses as may,
according to the rules of the bank, be provided for the charges of
managing the bank and for remuneration to officers employed in the
management of the bank, so, however, that the treasurer, trustees,
managers or other persons having direction of the management of
the bank shall not directly or indirectly have any salary, allowance,
profit or benefit whatsoever therefrom, beyond their actual expenses
for the purposes of the bank.

In this sub-paragraph the reference to the benefit of deposits and
the produce thereof shall be construed as not including a reference
to the benefit of current account deposits or the produce thereof.

2.—(1) That not less than two persons who are trustees, managers
or paid officers appointed for that specific purpose shall be present
on all occasions of public business, and be parties to every transaction of deposit and repayment, so as to form at least a double check
on every such transaction with depositors.

(2) That where the bank is open for not more than six hours
in every week, and there are only two such persons, one of them
shall be a trustee or manager.

*Note.—Notwithstanding that this provision is contained in
the rules, receipts and repayments of deposits may be carried
out in accordance with section 26 of this Act.*

3. That the depositor's pass book shall be compared with the
ledger on every transaction of repayment, and in each year on its
first production at the bank after 20th November.

In this paragraph the reference to a transaction of repayment shall
not include a reference to a transaction of repayment of moneys
standing to the credit of a current account, and the reference to a
pass book shall be construed as a reference to the pass book in
use by the bank for the purpose of savings account deposits or
special investments, as the case may require.

4. That every depositor in the bank shall once at least in every
year cause his deposit book to be produced at the office of the bank
for the purpose of being examined.

In this paragraph the reference to a deposit book shall be construed as a reference to a deposit book in use by the bank for the purpose of savings account deposits or special investments, as the case may require.

5. That no money be received from or paid to depositors except at the office or branch offices where the business of the bank is carried on under the authority of the board of managers, and during the usual hours for public business :

Provided that the rules of the bank may, if the Commissioners approve, provide for payments to and by depositors being made at the office of another bank, whether that other bank is a trustee savings bank or not.

6. That a public accountant or one or more auditors be appointed by the trustees and managers, but not out of their own body,—

    (*a*) to examine the books of the bank, and

    (*b*) to report in writing to the board or committee of management the result of the audit not less than once in every half-year, and

    (*c*) to examine an extracted list of the depositors' balances made up every year to 20th November and to certify as to the correct amount of the liabilities and assets of the bank.

In this paragraph the reference to an extracted list of the depositors' balances shall be construed as a reference to an extracted list of the balances of the depositors standing to the credit of the accounts of their savings account deposits and special investments, and paragraph 7 below shall be construed accordingly.

7. That a book containing such an extracted list as aforesaid of every depositor's balance, omitting the name, but giving the distinctive number and amount of each, and showing the aggregate number and amount of the whole, checked and certified by the said public accountant or auditors, be open at any time during the hours of public business for the inspection of every depositor as respects his own account, to examine his own deposit book therewith, and the general results of the same.

In this paragraph the reference to a deposit book shall be construed as a reference to a deposit book in use by the bank for the purpose of savings account deposits or special investments, as the case may require.

8. That the trustees and managers or committee of management shall hold meetings once at least in every half year, and shall keep minutes of their proceedings in a separate book provided for that purpose.

9. That where a bank is established with agents or local receivers elsewhere than at the head office, those agents and local receivers shall duly receive and account for all moneys on account of the bank, that a second party shall be present in every transaction

SCH. 1   where money is paid or received, and that the depositors' books shall be periodically examined with the ledger, at least once in every year.

> *Note.—Notwithstanding that this provision is contained in the rules, receipts and repayments of deposits may be carried out in accordance with section 26 of this Act.*

> *General note.—Additional requirements as to the contents of the rules are imposed by sections 18, 30, 43 and 67 of this Act.*

Section 13.

SCHEDULE 2

MATTERS TO BE COVERED BY THE RULES OF A BANK PROVIDING A CURRENT ACCOUNT SERVICE

The rules of a trustee savings bank which provides a current account service must expressly provide for the following matters.

1. That, except for such salaries and allowances or other expenses or such part thereof as may, according to the rules of the bank and the provisions of this Act, be defrayed therefrom, neither the treasurer, trustees, managers or other persons having direction of the management of the bank shall, directly or indirectly, have any salary, allowance, profit or benefit whatsoever from any current account deposits or their produce or any amounts obtained under any charges scheme.

2. That a current account of a person shall be kept in the books of the bank separately from the account of the savings account deposits, or the special investments, of that person.

3. That, as soon as possible after the end of each accounting period in relation to a current account, that is to say the period beginning with the opening of the account and ending with such day falling not later than six months later as the bank may determine, and any subsequent period of not more than six months from the end of the previous accounting period, which the bank may determine, the bank shall cause to be delivered to the person in whose name the account stands a statement of each sum credited and debited to that account during that period and of the balance on the account at the end of that period.

SCHEDULE 3

Section 96.

REPEALS AND REVOCATION

PART I

ENACTMENTS REPEALED

Chapter	Short Title	Extent of Repeal
2 & 3 Eliz. 2. c. 63.	The Trustee Savings Banks Act 1954.	The whole Act.
3 & 4 Eliz. 2. c. 12.	The Trustee Savings Banks (Pensions) Act 1955.	The whole Act.
6 & 7 Eliz. 2. c. 8.	The Trustee Savings Banks Act 1958.	The whole Act.
9 & 10 Eliz. 2. c. 62.	The Trustee Investments Act 1961.	In Schedule 4, in paragraph 4(1), the words from the beginning to "trustee and" and the words "and subsection (1) of section twenty of the Trustee Savings Banks Act 1954", paragraph 4(2), in paragraph 4(3), the words "and subsection (1) of section twenty-four of the Trustee Savings Banks Act 1954" and, in paragraph 5, the words "and the Trustee Savings Banks Act 1954" and the words from "or ordinary" to "bank".
1964 c. 4.	The Trustee Savings Banks Act 1964.	The whole Act.
1965 c. 32.	The Administration of Estates (Small Payments) Act 1965.	In Schedule 1, in Part II, the entry relating to the Trustee Savings Banks Act 1954.
1968 c. 6.	The Trustee Savings Banks Act 1968.	The whole Act.

PART II

ORDER REVOKED

Reference	Title	Extent of Revocation
S.I. 1955/842	The Trustee Savings Banks (Pensions) Order 1955.	Article 2.

2 Y* 3

Development of Tourism Act 1969

1969 CHAPTER 51

An Act to provide for the establishment of a British Tourist Authority and Tourist Boards for England, Scotland and Wales with responsibility for promoting the development of tourism to and within Great Britain; to provide for the giving of financial assistance out of public funds for the provision of new hotels and the extension, alteration and improvement of existing hotels; to enable provision to be made for the registration of hotels and other establishments at which sleeping accommodation is provided by way of trade or business and for securing that the prices charged there for such accommodation are brought to the notice of persons seeking to avail themselves of it; and for connected purposes.   [25th July 1969]

BE IT ENACTED by the Queen's most Excellent Majesty, by and with the advice and consent of the Lords Spiritual and Temporal, and Commons, in this present Parliament assembled, and by the authority of the same, as follows:—

PART I

THE TOURIST AUTHORITY AND THE TOURIST BOARDS

1.—(1) For the purposes of this Act there shall be established four bodies to be known respectively as the British Tourist Authority, the English Tourist Board, the Scottish Tourist Board and the Wales Tourist Board.

(2) The British Tourist Authority shall consist of—

    (a) a chairman and not more than five other members appointed by the Board of Trade ; and

    (b) the chairman of the English Tourist Board, the chairman of the Scottish Tourist Board and the chairman of the Wales Tourist Board.

Establishment of British Tourist Authority, English Tourist Board, Scottish Tourist Board and Wales Tourist Board.

PART I

(3) The English Tourist Board shall consist of a chairman and not more than six other members appointed by the Board of Trade, the Scottish Tourist Board shall consist of a chairman and not more than six other members appointed by the Secretary of State for Scotland, and the Wales Tourist Board shall consist of a chairman and not more than six other members appointed by the Secretary of State for Wales.

1957 c. 20.

(4) In Part III of Schedule 1 to the House of Commons Disqualification Act 1957 (offices the holders of which are disqualified under that Act), in its application to the House of Commons of the Parliament of the United Kingdom, there shall be inserted at the appropriate point in alphabetical order the words " Any member in receipt of remuneration of the British Tourist Authority, the English Tourist Board, the Scottish Tourist Board or the Wales Tourist Board ".

(5) Schedule 1 to this Act shall have effect in relation to each of the bodies established by this section.

(6) In this Act " Tourist Board " means any of the bodies established by this section, and " the relevant Minister " means, in relation to the British Tourist Authority and the English Tourist Board, the Board of Trade, in relation to the Scottish Tourist Board, the Secretary of State for Scotland and, in relation to the Wales Tourist Board, the Secretary of State for Wales.

General functions and powers.

2.—(1) It shall be the function of the British Tourist Authority—

    (*a*) to encourage people to visit Great Britain and people living in Great Britain to take their holidays there; and

    (*b*) to encourage the provision and improvement of tourist amenities and facilities in Great Britain;

and the English Tourist Board, the Scottish Tourist Board and the Wales Tourist Board shall have the like functions as respects England, Scotland and Wales respectively.

(2) In addition to the specific powers conferred on it by or under the subsequent provisions of this Act but subject to subsections (3) and (4) of this section, each Tourist Board shall have power to do anything for the purpose of discharging the functions conferred on it by this section or which is incidental or conducive to the discharge of those functions and in particular (but without prejudice to the generality of the foregoing provisions) for that purpose—

    (*a*) to promote or undertake publicity in any form;

    (*b*) to provide advisory and information services;

(c) to promote or undertake research ;

(d) to establish committees to advise them in the performance of their functions ;

(e) to contribute to or reimburse expenditure incurred by
any other person or organisation in carrying on any
activity which the Board has power to carry on under
paragraph (a), (b) or (c) oɪ this subsection.

(3) Only the British Tourist Authority shall have power by
virtue of subsection (2) of this section to carry on any activities
outside the United Kingdom for the purpose of encouraging
people to visit Great Britain or any part of it but this subsection shall not prevent the other Tourist Boards engaging in
such activities on behalf of the Authority.

(4) None of the Tourist Boards shall have power, except as
provided by sections 3 and 4 of this Act, to give financial
assistance for the carrying out of, or itself to carry out, any
project for providing or improving tourist amenities and facilities
in Great Britain.

(5) In discharging their functions under this section the English
Tourist Board, the Scottish Tourist Board and the Wales Tourist
Board shall have regard to the desirability of fostering and, in
appropriate cases, co-operating with organisations discharging
functions corresponding to those of the Boards in relation to
particular areas within the countries for which the Boards are
respectively responsible ; and, without prejudice to the
foregoing provisions of this section, each of those Boards shall
have power to provide such organisations with financial or other
assistance.

(6) In discharging its functions under this section each
Tourist Board shall have regard to the desirability of undertaking appropriate consultation with the other Tourist Boards and
with persons and organisations, including those mentioned in
the last foregoing subsection, who have knowledge of, or are
interested in, any matters affecting the discharge of those
functions.

(7) A Tourist Board may charge for its services and receive
contributions towards its expenses in carrying out any of its
functions.

(8) A Tourist Board shall not borrow money except with the
consent of the relevant Minister and the Treasury.

(9) In this Part of this Act " tourist amenities and facilities "
means, in relation to any country, amenities and facilities for
visitors to that country and for other people travelling within
it on business or pleasure.

Part I
General
schemes of
assistance
for tourist
projects.

3.—(1) The British Tourist Authority may, after consultation with the English Tourist Board, the Scottish Tourist Board and the Wales Tourist Board, prepare schemes providing for the giving of financial assistance by those Boards for the carrying out of projects of such classes as may be specified in the schemes, being projects which in the opinion of the Authority will provide or improve tourist amenities and facilities in Great Britain.

(2) Any scheme prepared under subsection (1) of this section shall be submitted to the Board of Trade who may, subject to subsection (6) of this section, by order confirm it with or without modification ; and if a scheme is so confirmed it shall thereupon have effect.

(3) A scheme under this section may provide for financial assistance to be given by way of grant or loan or by any combination of those methods.

(4) In making a grant or loan under any scheme made by virtue of this section a Tourist Board may, subject to the provisions of the scheme and to any directions under section 19 of this Act, impose such terms and conditions as it thinks fit, including conditions for the repayment of a grant in specified circumstances ; and Schedule 2 to this Act shall have effect for securing compliance with conditions subject to which any such grant is made.

(5) A scheme which has effect under this section may be varied or revoked by a subsequent scheme prepared, submitted and confirmed in like manner or, subject to subsection (6) of this section, by an order made by the Board of Trade after consultation with the British Tourist Authority, the English Tourist Board, the Scottish Tourist Board and the Wales Tourist Board.

(6) Any power of the Board of Trade to make orders under this section shall be exercisable by statutory instrument and any order under subsection (2) of this section shall set out the scheme which the order confirms ; and no order shall be made under this section except with the consent of the Treasury and unless a draft of it has been laid before Parliament and approved by a resolution of each House.

Execution
of particular
tourist
projects.

4.—(1) A Tourist Board shall have power—

    (*a*) in accordance with arrangements approved by the relevant Minister and the Treasury, to give financial assistance for the carrying out of any project which in the opinion of the Board will provide or improve tourist amenities and facilities in the country for which the Board is responsible ;

    (*b*) with the approval of the relevant Minister and the Treasury, to carry out any such project as aforesaid.

(2) Financial assistance under subsection (1)(*a*) of this section may be given by way of grant or loan or, if the project is being or is to be carried out by a company incorporated in Great Britain, by subscribing for or otherwise acquiring shares or stock in the company, or by any combination of those methods.

(3) In making a grant or loan in accordance with arrangements approved under subsection (1)(*a*) of this section a Tourist Board may, subject to the arrangements, impose such terms and conditions as it thinks fit, including conditions for the repayment of a grant in specified circumstances ; and Schedule 2 to this Act shall have effect for securing compliance with conditions subject to which any such grant is made.

(4) A Tourist Board shall not dispose of any shares or stock acquired by it by virtue of this section except—

> (*a*) after consultation with the company in which the shares or stock are held ; and

> (*b*) with the approval of the relevant Minister and the Treasury.

5.—(1) It shall be the duty of the British Tourist Authority to advise any Minister or public body on such matters relating to tourism in Great Britain as a whole as the Minister or body may refer to it or as the Authority may think fit ; and the English Tourist Board, the Scottish Tourist Board and the Wales Tourist Board shall have the like duty as respects matters relating to tourism in England, Scotland and Wales respectively.

Miscellaneous duties and powers.

(2) In the last foregoing subsection " public body " includes any local authority or statutory undertaker, and any trustees, commissioners, board or other persons, who, as a public body and not for their own profit, act under any enactment for the improvement of any place or the production or supply of any commodity or service.

(3) The British Tourist Authority shall have power to carry on, at the request of any corresponding body established under the law of Northern Ireland, any of the Channel Islands or the Isle of Man and on such terms as may be agreed upon between the Authority and that body, activities outside the United Kingdom and those Islands for encouraging people to visit Northern Ireland or those Islands.

(4) Each Tourist Board shall have power, with the consent of the relevant Minister, to enter into and carry out agreements with the Minister of Overseas Development whereunder the Board acts, at the expense of that Minister, as the instrument by means of which technical assistance is furnished by him in exercise of the power conferred on him by section 1(1) of the Overseas Aid Act 1966.

1966 c. 21.

6.—(1) Each Tourist Board shall keep proper accounts and other records in relation to the accounts and shall prepare in respect of each of its financial years a statement of account in such form as the relevant Minister may, with the approval of the Treasury, determine.

(2) The statement of account prepared by each Tourist Board for each financial year shall be submitted to the relevant Minister at such time as he may, with the approval of the Treasury, direct.

(3) The relevant Minister shall, on or before 30th November in any year, transmit to the Comptroller and Auditor General the statement of account prepared by each Tourist Board under this section for the financial year last ended.

(4) The Comptroller and Auditor General shall examine and certify each statement of account transmitted to him under this section and lay before Parliament copies of the statement of account together with his report thereon.

(5) Each Tourist Board shall provide the relevant Minister with such information relating to the activities or proposed activities of the Board as the Minister may from time to time require, and for that purpose shall permit any person authorised in that behalf by the Minister to inspect and make copies of its accounts, books, documents or papers and shall afford to that person such explanation thereof as he may reasonably require.

(6) Each Tourist Board shall as soon as possible after the end of each financial year make to the relevant Minister a report dealing with the activities of the Board during that year, and the Minister shall lay a copy of the report before each House of Parliament.

(7) In this section " financial year " means the period beginning with the commencement of this Act and ending with 31st March 1970, and each subsequent period of twelve months ending with 31st March.

Part II

Financial Assistance for Hotel Development

Hotel development grants

7.—(1) Subject to the provisions of this Act, a person who has incurred eligible expenditure in providing a new hotel in Great Britain shall be entitled to receive from the appropriate Tourist Board, after the completion of the hotel, a grant in respect of the eligible expenditure which he has so incurred.

(2) No grant shall be payable under this section unless the appropriate Tourist Board is satisfied that the hotel in question

complies, or as from its opening will comply, with the following requirements, that is to say—

(a) that it has not less than ten (or, if it is in Greater London, twenty-five) letting bedrooms and that the sleeping accommodation offered at the hotel consists wholly or mainly of letting bedrooms ;

(b) that breakfast and an evening meal are provided at reasonable times on the premises for persons staying at the hotel ;

(c) that there is on the premises a lounge (whether a room or part of a room) for the common use at all reasonable times of persons staying at the hotel ;

(d) that hotel services appropriate to the establishment (but including in every case the cleaning of rooms and making of beds) are provided for persons staying at the hotel ;

(e) that the accommodation is in a building or buildings of a permanent nature.

(3) For the purposes of this Part of this Act, a hotel shall be treated as complying with the requirements specified in subsection (2) of this section if it complies with them throughout the period in each year between 1st April and 31st October (or throughout every part of that period for which the premises are open) even though it does not comply with them at other times.

(4) The expenditure eligible for grant under this section is approved capital expenditure on constructional work and on the purchase and installation of fixed equipment.

8.—(1) Subject to the provisions of this Act, a person who has incurred eligible expenditure in extending or altering an existing hotel in Great Britain shall, if the extension or alteration consists of or includes the provision of not less than five additional letting bedrooms, be entitled to receive from the appropriate Tourist Board, after the completion of the extension or alteration, a grant in respect of the eligible expenditure which he has so incurred.

Grants for extension or alteration of existing hotels.

(2) No grant shall be payable under this section unless the appropriate Tourist Board is satisfied that on the completion of the extension or alteration the hotel in question complies, or as from its opening thereafter will comply, with the requirements specified in section 7(2) of this Act.

(3) Where the extension or alteration of a hotel includes, but is not confined to, the provision of letting bedrooms and

PART II

any such bedroom is provided by the alteration (as distinct from the extension) of existing accommodation in the hotel, no grant shall be payable under this section, unless the appropriate Tourist Board in any case otherwise determines, in respect of expenditure which is not attributable to the provision of the bedrooms and any bathroom or bathrooms appearing to the Board to be provided in association with the bedrooms.

(4) The expenditure eligible for grant under this section is approved capital expenditure on constructional work and on the purchase and installation of fixed equipment.

Grants for provision of certain fixed equipment.

9.—(1) Subject to the provisions of this Act, a person who has incurred approved capital expenditure in purchasing and installing in an existing hotel in Great Britain fixed equipment of a description specified in Schedule 3 to this Act, not being expenditure in respect of which he is entitled to a grant under the foregoing provisions of this Part of this Act, shall be entitled to receive from the appropriate Tourist Board, after the completion of the installation, a grant in respect of the approved capital expenditure which he has so incurred.

(2) No grant shall be payable under this section unless the appropriate Tourist Board is satisfied that on the completion of the installation of the equipment the hotel in question complies, or as from its opening thereafter will comply, with the requirements specified in section 7(2) of this Act.

(3) Any grant under this section shall be in respect of the total expenditure eligible for grant under this section which the applicant has incurred in a complete financial year, and no such grant shall be payable to any applicant in respect of any hotel unless the total expenditure eligible for grant under this section which the applicant has incurred in that year in respect of that hotel is £1,000 or more.

(4) In subsection (3) of this section " financial year " means the period of twelve months ending with 31st March but, in relation to an applicant who so elects, the period beginning with 1st April 1969 and ending with the date of the commencement of this Act shall be treated as if it formed part of the preceding financial year and not of the financial year ending with 31st March 1970.

Recipient of grant to be occupier or lessor of hotel

10.—(1) No grant shall be payable under the foregoing provisions of this Part of this Act to any person who, at the relevant time, is not either—

(*a*) the occupier of the hotel in question, that is to say the person in possession of it ; or (*b*) a lessor of the hotel, that is to say a person who is entitled to an interest in reversion (whether freehold or leasehold) expectant, whether immediately or not, on the termination of a leasehold interest by virtue of which the occupier is in possession.

(2) Schedule 4 to this Act shall have effect in relation to cases where some or all of the expenditure eligible for a grant under the foregoing provisions of this Part of this Act has been incurred by a predecessor in title of a person who is the occupier or a lessor of the hotel at the relevant time or by a lessor of the hotel who grants a lease for a capital consideration.

(3) In this section " the relevant time " means—

(*a*) in relation to a grant under section 7 of this Act, the time when the hotel in respect of which the grant is to be made is first opened after completion ;

(*b*) in relation to a grant under section 8 or 9 of this Act, the time when the extension, alteration or installation of equipment, as the case may be, in respect of which the grant is to be made is completed or, if the hotel in question is then closed, when it is first opened thereafter,

except that the relevant time shall be the date of the commencement of this Act in any case in which the time mentioned in paragraph (*a*) or (*b*) of this subsection falls before that date.

(4) In the application of this section to Scotland, for paragraph (*b*) of subsection (1) there shall be substituted the following paragraph : —

(*b*) a lessor of the hotel, that is to say, in a case where the occupier is in possession of the hotel by virtue of a lease, a person holding the interest of landlord under any lease under which the hotel is let.

11.—(1) Subject to subsection (2) of this section, the grant Rates of payable under section 7 or 8 of this Act in respect of any grant. expenditure shall be of an amount equal to—

(*a*) twenty per cent. of that expenditure ; or

(*b*) £1,000 for each letting bedroom in the new hotel or, as the case may be, each additional letting bedroom provided by the alteration or extension of the existing hotel,

whichever is the less ; and the grant payable under section 9 of this Act in respect of any expenditure shall be of an amount equal to twenty per cent. of that expenditure.

(2) In relation to a grant in respect of a new or existing hotel in an area which is a development area—

    (*a*) at the time of the making of the contract or contracts under which the expenditure (or the main part of the expenditure) eligible for grant was incurred ; or

    (*b*) at the time when the relevant work was begun,

subsection (1) of this section shall have effect with the substitution for the references to twenty per cent. and £1,000 of references to twenty-five per cent. and £1,250 respectively.

(3) In subsection (2) of this section " development area " means an area specified as such under subsection (2) of section 15 of the Industrial Development Act 1966 and includes any such locality outside that area as is specified in subsection (6) of that section.

1966 c. 34.

(4) In paragraph (*b*) of subsection (2) of this section " the relevant work " means work on the site in question for the purpose of providing the new hotel, extending or altering the existing hotel or installing fixed equipment in the existing hotel, as the case may be ; and for the purposes of that paragraph no account shall be taken of work for the purpose of clearing the site or erecting temporary fencing for it.

(5) Where a grant has been paid under section 7 or 8 of this Act in respect of the provision of a new hotel or the extension or alteration of an existing hotel, no grant shall be payable under section 9 of this Act in respect of the purchase and installation of any equipment if the appropriate Tourist Board considers that the purchase and installation of that equipment ought properly to be regarded as part of the provision of the hotel or of that extension or alteration, as the case may be.

(6) Where two or more persons are entitled to grants under section 7 or 8 of this Act in respect of expenditure incurred by them in providing a particular new hotel or in carrying out a particular alteration or extension of an existing hotel, the total amount of the grants shall be calculated as for a single grant in respect of the total of the expenditure incurred by those persons and that total shall be apportioned between the grants by reference to the amount of the expenditure which each recipient has incurred.

Conditions of grant.

12.—(1) In making a grant under this Part of this Act a Tourist Board may, subject to any directions under section 19 of this Act, impose such conditions as it thinks fit.

(2) Conditions imposed under this section may provide for the repayment of a grant in specified circumstances and, in particular, if the number of letting bedrooms in the hotel in

question is reduced or the hotel ceases to comply with the requirements mentioned in section 7(2) of this Act before the expiration of such period as may be specified in the conditions ; and different periods may be so specified in different classes of case.

(3) Schedule 2 to this Act shall have effect for securing compliance with conditions imposed under this section.

Loans for hotel development

13.—(1) Subject to the provisions of this Act and to any directions under section 19 thereof, the appropriate Tourist Board may, if it thinks fit, make a loan or loans to any person for assisting him—

(*a*) to provide a new hotel in Great Britain ; or

(*b*) to extend or alter an existing hotel in Great Britain or to provide and install fixed equipment in any such hotel,

where it appears to the Board that the total eligible expenditure incurred or to be incurred by him in carrying out the project in question exceeds, in a case within paragraph (*a*) of this subsection, £20,000 or, in a case within paragraph (*b*) of this subsection, £10,000.

(2) No loan shall be made under this section unless the appropriate Tourist Board is satisfied that the hotel in question complies or will comply, on the completion of the project or as from its opening thereafter, with the requirements specified in section 7(2) of this Act.

(3) Subject to subsection (4) of this section, the total amount lent under this section in respect of any project shall not exceed—

(*a*) the following percentage of the eligible expenditure incurred or to be incurred on the project, that is to say—

(i) in the case of a project within subsection (1)(*a*) of this section, thirty per cent. ;

(ii) in any other case, fifty per cent. ; or

(*b*) £500,000,

whichever is the less.

(4) If the relevant Minister is satisfied by the appropriate Tourist Board that a particular project within subsection (1)(*a*) of this section will not be carried out unless the total amount lent exceeds the amount permitted by subsection (3) of this section, he may, with the consent of the Treasury, authorise the Board

Part II

to make loans in respect of that project to such total amount in excess of the amount so permitted as may be specified by him, but the total amount so specified shall not exceed what would be permitted by the said subsection (3) if the percentage mentioned in paragraph (*a*)(i) thereof were forty per cent.

(5) Subject to any directions under section 19 of this Act, a loan under this section shall be made on such terms and conditions as the Tourist Board concerned may determine, but the period within which any such loan is to be repaid shall not exceed twenty years in a case within subsection (1)(*a*) of this section or fifteen years in any other case.

(6) In this section " eligible expenditure " means approved capital expenditure on constructional work and on the purchase and installation of fixed equipment.

Supplementary provisions

General restrictions on the making of grants and loans.

14.—(1) No grant or loan shall be made under this Part of this Act to a local authority, and no loan shall be so made to, or to a subsidiary of, any body established by or under any enactment for the purpose of carrying on under national ownership any industry or undertaking or part of an industry or undertaking.

(2) In the foregoing subsection " local authority " means—

1875 c. 83.

(*a*) in relation to England and Wales, any authority being, within the meaning of the Local Loans Act 1875, an authority having power to levy a rate, and includes a joint board or joint committee of such authorities ;

1947 c. 43.

(*b*) in relation to Scotland, any county council, town council or district council, and any statutory authority, commissioners or trustees having power to levy a rate as defined in section 379 of the Local Government (Scotland) Act 1947 or to issue a requisition for payment of money to be raised out of such a rate and includes any joint board or joint committee of such authorities appointed under any enactment, order or scheme ;

1948 c. 38.

and " subsidiary " means a subsidiary as defined by section 154 of the Companies Act 1948.

(3) A Tourist Board shall not without the consent of the relevant Minister and the Treasury make a grant or loan under this Part of this Act in respect of any project if it appears to the Board that financial assistance from public funds (whether by way of grant or loan) otherwise than under this Part of this Act has already been accepted in respect of capital expenditure incurred or to be incurred in the execution of that project or of any larger project of which it forms part.

(4) Where it appears to the appropriate Tourist Board that any expenditure has been incurred—

(*a*) partly for the purpose of providing a new hotel or for any other purpose in relation to which a grant or loan can be made under this Part of this Act ; and

(*b*) partly for other purposes,

so much of the expenditure as, in the opinion of the Board, is attributable to those other purposes shall be disregarded for the purposes of any such grant or loan and the Board shall make all such apportionments as may be required for giving effect to this subsection.

15.—(1) Subject to the provisions of this section, a Tourist Board shall not make a grant or loan under this Part of this Act except on an application received by it before 1st April 1973 and unless satisfied that the relevant work—

(*a*) was begun not earlier than 1st April 1968 and not later than 31st March 1971 ; and

(*b*) has been, or in the case of a loan has been or will be, completed not later than 31st March 1973.

(2) Paragraph (*b*) of subsection (1) of this section shall not prevent the making of a grant or loan in any case in which the Tourist Board is satisfied that the relevant work would have been completed as required by that paragraph but for circumstances outside the applicant's control and that the work has been, or in the case of a loan has been or will be, completed with reasonable despatch thereafter.

(3) In this section " the relevant work " means work on the site in question for the purpose of providing the new hotel, extending or altering the existing hotel or installing fixed equipment in the existing hotel, as the case may be ; and for the purposes of subsection (1)(*a*) of this section no account shall be taken of work for the purpose of clearing the site or erecting temporary fencing for it.

(4) If in any case it appears to the Tourist Board concerned that although the relevant work was not begun before 1st April 1968 other work had then already been carried out on the site in question in the execution of a project to which the relevant work is also referable, this section shall have effect in relation to that case as if the relevant work had been begun before that date.

16.—(1) In this Part of this Act—

" the appropriate Tourist Board " means, in relation to England, the English Tourist Board, in relation to Scotland, the Scottish Tourist Board and, in relation to Wales, the Wales Tourist Board ;

" approved capital expenditure ", in relation to any grant or loan, means expenditure appearing to the Tourist Board concerned to be of a capital nature and approved by it for the purposes of the grant or loan ;

" building " includes part of a building ;

" expenditure on constructional work " includes expenditure in respect of professional fees (other than legal fees) and other matters incidental to the carrying out of the work ;

" fixed equipment " means equipment, including furniture, which in the opinion of the Tourist Board concerned is fixed to, or incorporated in, a building in such a manner as not to be easily detachable therefrom ;

" letting bedroom " means a private bedroom which—

> (*a*) if booked in advance, does not have to be so booked for more than seven consecutive nights ; and

> (*b*) if not so booked, can be taken, if desired, for a single night ;

> and which is not normally in the same occupation for more than twenty-one consecutive nights ;

" purchase ", in relation to any equipment, includes purchase under a hire-purchase agreement within the meaning of the Hire-Purchase Act 1965 or, as the case may be, the Hire-Purchase (Scotland) Act 1965.

1965 c. 66.
1965 c. 67.

(2) For the purposes of this Part of this Act an establishment shall not be treated as a hotel unless its services and facilities are offered to the public generally, that is to say, to any person who wishes to avail himself of, and appears able and willing to pay a reasonable sum for, those services and facilities and is in a fit state to be received.

(3) In this Part of this Act references to providing a new hotel include references to providing it by converting into a hotel a building or buildings previously used for a different purpose.

(4) For the purposes of this Part of this Act a person who instead of purchasing any fixed equipment for installation in a hotel manufactures it himself shall be treated as having purchased it for such sum as appears to the Tourist Board concerned to be properly attributable to its manufacture by him.

(5) For the purposes of this Part of this Act expenditure shall be treated as incurred at the time when the sum of which it consists becomes payable or, in the case of expenditure not consisting of a sum payable to another person, at such time as

the Tourist Board concerned considers appropriate having regard to the time when the matters giving rise to the expenditure occurred.

PART III

MISCELLANEOUS AND GENERAL

17.—(1) Her Majesty may by Order in Council make pro-vision for the registration by the Tourist Boards of, or of any class of, hotels and other establishments in Great Britain at which sleeping accommodation is provided by way of trade or business.

(2) An Order under this section may in particular make provision—

(a) as to the form and contents of the register or registers to be maintained under the Order and as to the estab-lishments to be registered therein ;

(b) for requiring the person carrying on an establishment which is required to be registered to furnish, at such time or times as may be specified in the Order, to the body responsible for registering it such information as may be so specified ;

(c) for the charging of annual or other periodical fees for registration ;

(d) for the issue and display of certificates of registration and the display of signs indicating that an establish-ment is registered ;

(e) for the inspection of establishments and for powers of entry for that purpose ;

(f) for exemptions from any of the requirements of the Order ;

(g) for securing compliance with any requirement of the Order by the imposition of a penalty not exceeding a fine of £200.

(3) If provision is made by an Order under this section for the classification or grading of the establishments entered in a register, the Order shall also make provision—

(a) for requiring the criteria in accordance with which the classification or grading is carried out, so far as not prescribed by the Order, to be determined from time to time by the British Tourist Authority after consulta-tion with the English Tourist Board, the Scottish Tourist Board, the Wales Tourist Board and such other

PART III

organisations as appear to the Authority to be representative of trade and consumer interests likely to be affected ;

(b) for the publication of any criteria so determined ;

(c) for enabling the person carrying on an establishment registered with any Tourist Board to make representations to the Board before any classification or grade is accorded to the establishment and before its classification or grade is altered or cancelled.

(4) An Order under this section may contain such supplementary and incidental provisions as appear to Her Majesty to be necessary or expedient, and may authorise the Board of Trade, the Secretary of State for Scotland and the Secretary of State for Wales to make regulations as respects England, Scotland and Wales respectively for such purposes of the Order as may be specified therein ; and the Statutory Instruments Act 1946 shall apply in relation to any such regulations as if they were made under powers conferred by an Act of Parliament.

1946 c. 36.

(5) An Order under this section and any regulations made thereunder may make different provision for different cases and, in particular, provision may be made for an Order to come into force at different times in relation to, or to different parts of, England, Scotland and Wales respectively.

(6) Any Order under this section shall be subject to annulment in pursuance of a resolution of either House of Parliament and may be revoked or varied by a subsequent Order under this section.

(7) A Tourist Board maintaining a register by virtue of an Order under this section shall have power to publish, or make available for publication, any information furnished to it by virtue of the Order and any information as to any classification or grade accorded under the Order to any establishment ; and such information may be published or made available for publication either gratuitously or for consideration.

Notification of prices of accommodation.

18.—(1) Her Majesty may, by an Order in Council applying to, or to any class of, hotels and other establishments in Great Britain at which sleeping accommodation is provided by way of trade or business, make provision for requiring the display at the establishments of information with respect to the prices charged there for such accommodation as aforesaid or otherwise for securing that such information is brought to the notice of persons seeking to avail themselves of the accommodation.

(2) Subsection (2)(e), (f) and (g) and subsections (4), (5) and (6) of section 17 of this Act shall apply to an Order under this section as they apply to an Order under that section.

19.—(1) The relevant Minister may, after consultation with a Tourist Board, give to it directions of a general character as to the exercise of its functions.

(2) Subject to the provisions of any scheme under section 3 and to the provisions of Part II of this Act, the relevant Minister may, with the approval of the Treasury, give to a Tourist Board directions as to—

(a) the matters with respect to which that Board must be satisfied before making a loan under the scheme or that Part ;

(b) the terms on which and the conditions subject to which any such loan is to be made ;

(c) the conditions to be imposed in making any grant under the scheme or that Part ;

and such directions may distinguish between different classes of case.

(3) Without prejudice to the generality of paragraph (a) of subsection (2) of this section, directions given by virtue of that paragraph may require a Tourist Board to be satisfied that the applicant cannot obtain a loan for the purpose in question from any other source, whether on terms which are more or less favourable than those of any loan which might be made by the Board.

(4) A Tourist Board shall give effect to any directions given to it under this section.

20.—(1) The relevant Minister may pay to a Tourist Board such sums in respect of its expenditure as he may with the consent of the Treasury determine.

(2) Any sums required by a relevant Minister for making payments under subsection (1) of this section and any other expenses of a relevant Minister under this Act shall be defrayed out of moneys provided by Parliament.

(3) Any sums received by a Tourist Board—

(a) in repayment of, or as interest on, any loan made by it under this Act ;

(b) in repayment of any grant made by it under this Act ; or

(c) as dividend on, or otherwise in respect of, any shares or stock acquired by it under this Act,

shall be paid to the relevant Minister.

(4) Any sums received by a relevant Minister under subsection (3) of this section shall be paid into the Consolidated Fund.

PART III
Short title,
interpretation,
commencement and
extent.

21.—(1) This Act may be cited as the Development of Tourism Act 1969.

(2) In this Act "Wales" includes Monmouthshire and references to England shall be construed accordingly.

(3) This Act shall come into force at the expiration of the period of one month beginning with the day on which it is passed.

(4) This Act, except section 1(4), does not extend to Northern Ireland.

SCHEDULES

SCHEDULE 1

THE TOURIST BOARDS

Incorporation and status

1. Each of the Tourist Boards (in this Schedule referred to as " the Board ") shall be a body corporate having perpetual succession and a common seal.

2. The Board shall not be regarded as the servant or agent of the Crown or as enjoying any status, immunity or privilege of the Crown or as exempt from any tax, duty, levy or other charge whatsoever, and its property shall not be regarded as the property of, or property held on behalf of, the Crown.

Membership

3. A member of the Board shall hold and vacate his office in accordance with the terms of his appointment.

4. Any member of the Board may at any time by notice in writing to the relevant Minister resign his office.

5.—(1) If the relevant Minister is satisfied that a member of the Board—

    (*a*) has been absent from meetings of the Board for a period longer than three consecutive months without the permission of the Board ; or

    (*b*) has become bankrupt or made an arrangement with his creditors ; or

    (*c*) is incapacitated by physical or mental illness ; or

    (*d*) is otherwise unable or unfit to discharge the functions of a member,

the relevant Minister may declare his office as a member of the Board to be vacant and shall notify the fact in such manner as he thinks fit ; and thereupon the office shall become vacant.

(2) In the application of this paragraph to Scotland, for the references in the last foregoing sub-paragraph to a member's having become bankrupt and to a member's having made an arrangement with his creditors there shall be substituted respectively references to sequestration of a member's estate having been awarded and to a member's having made a trust deed for behoof of his creditors or a composition contract.

Remuneration

6. The Board shall pay to its members such salaries, fees or allowances as the relevant Minister may determine.

7. The Board shall, as regards any members in whose case the relevant Minister may so determine, make provision for, or pay to or in respect of them, such pensions or gratuities as may be so determined.

8. If a person ceases to be a member of the Board and it appears to the relevant Minister that there are special circumstances which make it right that that person should receive compensation, the Minister may require the Board to pay to that person a sum of such amount as the Minister may determine.

9. The relevant Minister shall, as soon as possible after the first appointment of any person as a member of the Board, lay before each House of Parliament a statement of the sums that are or will be payable to or in respect of that member under paragraph 6 of this Schedule ; and if any subsequent determination by the relevant Minister under that paragraph involves a departure from the terms of that statement, or if the relevant Minister makes a determination under paragraph 7 or 8 of this Schedule, he shall, as soon as possible after the determination, lay a statement before each House of Parliament of the sums that are or will be payable in consequence of that determination.

Staff

10. The Board may appoint such officers and servants as it may, with the consent of the relevant Minister as to numbers and remuneration, determine.

11. The Board shall, in the case of such of its officers and servants as the relevant Minister may determine, pay such pensions or gratuities to or in respect of them as may be so determined, make such payments towards the provision of such pensions or gratuities as may be so determined or provide and maintain such schemes (whether contributory or not) for the payment of such pensions or gratuities as may be so determined.

Proceedings

12. The validity of any proceedings of the Board shall not be affected by any vacancy among the members or by any defect in the appointment of any member.

13. The quorum of the Board and the arrangements relating to meetings of the Board shall be such as the Board may determine.

14. A member of the Board who is in any way directly or indirectly interested in a transaction or project of the Board shall disclose the nature of his interest at a meeting of the Board ; and the disclosure shall be recorded in the minutes of the Board, and the member shall not take any part in any deliberation or decision of the Board with respect to that transaction or project.

15. The fixing of the seal of the Board shall be authenticated by the signature of the secretary of the Board or of some other person authorised either generally or specially by the Board to act for that purpose.

16. Any document purporting to be a document duly executed under the seal of the Board shall be received in evidence and shall, unless the contrary is proved, be deemed to be a document so executed.

Requirement of approval of Minister for the Civil Service

17. The approval of the Minister for the Civil Service shall be required for the making by the relevant Minister of any determination under paragraph 6, 7, 8 or 11 of this Schedule, for the imposition by him of any requirement under the said paragraph 8 and for the giving by him of any consent under paragraph 10 of this Schedule.

Interpretation

18. In paragraphs 3 to 9 of this Schedule, references to a member of the Board do not include, in the case of the British Tourist Authority, references to persons who are members thereof by virtue of section 1(2)(*b*) of this Act.

SCHEDULE 2

ENFORCEMENT OF CONDITIONS OF GRANT

Power to call for information

1.—(1) A Tourist Board may by notice require any person who has received a grant from the Board under this Act, and any person acting on his behalf, to furnish to the Board such information, or to produce for examination on behalf of the Board such books, records or other documents, as may be specified in the notice for the purpose of enabling the Board to determine whether any condition subject to which the grant was made is satisfied or is being complied with or whether the grant has become repayable in whole or in part in accordance with any such condition.

(2) A notice under this paragraph may require the information to which it relates to be furnished within such time as may be specified in the notice, and may require the documents to which it relates to be produced at such time and place as may be so specified:

Provided that the time specified in such a notice for furnishing any information or producing any document shall not be earlier than the end of the period of twenty-eight days beginning with the service of the notice.

(3) A notice under this paragraph may be served—

    (*a*) by delivering it to the person on whom it is to be served ;

    (*b*) by leaving it at the usual or last known place of abode of that person ;

    (*c*) by sending it in a prepaid registered letter, or by the recorded delivery service, addressed to that person at his usual or last known place of abode ; or

    (*d*) in the case of an incorporated company or body, by delivering it to the secretary or clerk of the company or body at their registered or principal office, or sending it in a prepaid registered letter, or by the recorded delivery service, addressed to the secretary or clerk of the company or body at that office.

SCH. 2   (4) Any person who without reasonable excuse fails to comply with a notice under this paragraph shall be guilty of an offence and liable on summary conviction to a fine not exceeding £100 or, on a second or subsequent conviction, £400.

Power to enter and inspect premises

2.—(1) Any person duly authorised in that behalf by a Tourist Board may, on production (if so required) of written evidence of his authority, at all reasonable times enter and inspect any premises in relation to which a grant has been made by the Board under this Act for the purpose of determining whether any condition subject to which the grant was made is satisfied or is being complied with or whether the grant has become repayable in whole or in part in accordance with any such condition.

(2) Any person who wilfully obstructs any person in the exercise of a right of entry conferred by this paragraph shall be guilty of an offence and liable on summary conviction to a fine not exceeding £50.

Failure to comply with condition requiring notification of event on which grant becomes repayable

3.—(1) Any person who without reasonable excuse fails to comply with any condition subject to which a grant was made to him under this Act requiring him to inform a Tourist Board of any event whereby the grant becomes repayable in whole or in part shall be guilty of an offence and liable to a fine which, if imposed on summary conviction, shall not exceed £400.

1952 c. 55.   (2) Notwithstanding anything in section 104 of the Magistrates' Courts Act 1952 (time limit for proceedings), summary proceedings in England and Wales for an offence under this paragraph may be taken by the Director of Public Prosecutions at any time within three years after the commission of the offence and within twelve months after the date on which evidence sufficient in the opinion of the Director to justify the proceedings comes to his knowledge.

1954 c. 48.   (3) Summary proceedings in Scotland for an offence under this paragraph shall not be commenced after the expiration of three years from the commission of the offence, but subject to the foregoing limitation and notwithstanding anything in section 23 of the Summary Jurisdiction (Scotland) Act 1954, such proceedings may be commenced at any time within twelve months after the date on which evidence sufficient in the opinion of the Lord Advocate to justify the proceedings comes to his knowledge ; and subsection (2) of the said section 23 shall apply for the purposes of this sub-paragraph as it applies for the purposes of that section.

(4) For the purposes of sub-paragraphs (2) and (3) of this paragraph, a certificate of the Director of Public Prosecutions or the Lord Advocate, as the case may be, as to the date on which such evidence as aforesaid came to his knowledge shall be conclusive evidence of that fact.

Offences by bodies corporate

4.—(1) Where an offence under this Schedule committed by a body corporate is proved to have been committed with the consent or connivance of, or to be attributable to any neglect on the part of, any director, manager, secretary or other similar officer of the body corporate, or any person who was purporting to act in any such capacity, he as well as the body corporate shall be guilty of that offence and shall be liable to be proceeded against and punished accordingly.

(2) In this paragraph " director ", in relation to a body corporate established by or under any enactment for the purpose of carrying on under national ownership any industry or undertaking or part of an industry or undertaking, being a body corporate whose affairs are managed by its members, means a member of that body.

SCHEDULE 3

Section 9.

FIXED EQUIPMENT ELIGIBLE FOR GRANT UNDER SECTION 9 OF THIS ACT

Centrally-installed plant for water heating, space heating, ventilation or air-conditioning.

Centrally-installed plant for water softening or filtering.

Plant for the preparation, storage or serving on the premises of food and other refreshment.

Mechanically-operated lifts, hoists, escalators and luggage-handling equipment.

Baths, showers, wash-hand basins, bidets and lavatory equipment.

SCHEDULE 4

Section 10.

EXPENDITURE INCURRED BY PREDECESSOR IN TITLE OR LESSOR

Interpretation

1.—(1) In this Schedule—

" lease " includes a sublease and an agreement for a lease or sublease and references to the grant of a lease shall be construed accordingly ;

" transferred " includes transferred by operation of law ;

and references to the occupier or a lessor of a hotel and to the relevant time shall be construed in the same manner as in section 10 of this Act.

(2) Where by virtue of this Schedule expenditure is treated as if it had been incurred by any person it shall be treated as incurred by him to the exclusion of anyone else.

Expenditure incurred by predecessor in title of occupier or lessor

2. Subject to paragraph 3 of this Schedule, where—

   (*a*) a person has incurred expenditure eligible for a grant under Part II of this Act in respect of a hotel ; and

   (*b*) after the execution of the work which gave rise to the expenditure but before the relevant time his interest in the hotel has been directly or indirectly transferred to a person who at that time is the occupier or a lessor of the hotel,

the expenditure shall be treated, for the purposes of the grant, as if it had been incurred by the person (whether the occupier or a lessor) in whom the interest is vested at the relevant time.

Expenditure incurred by lessor

3.—(1) This paragraph applies where expenditure eligible for a grant under Part II of this Act has been incurred, or would (but for this paragraph) be treated under paragraph 2 of this Schedule as if it had been incurred, by a person who at the relevant time is a lessor (in this paragraph referred to as " the relevant lessor ") of the hotel in respect of which the expenditure was incurred.

(2) The expenditure shall be treated, for the purposes of the grant, as if it had been incurred by any person (whether the occupier of the hotel at the relevant time or, if he holds indirectly under the relevant lessor, an intermediate lessor) in whose case the following requirements are satisfied, that is to say—

   (*a*) that he (and each intermediate lessor, if any, between himself and the relevant lessor) holds under a lease which—

      (i) began after the execution of the work which gave rise to the expenditure ; and

      (ii) was granted for a consideration which consisted of or included a capital sum of an amount not less than the amount of that expenditure ; and

   (*b*) in the case of an intermediate lessor, that the expenditure cannot by virtue of the foregoing provisions of this paragraph be treated as if it had been incurred by a person holding under him.

(3) In the application of the foregoing provisions of this paragraph to a relevant lessor who himself holds under a lease the expenditure mentioned in sub-paragraph (2)(*a*)(ii) shall include any expenditure which would be treated under those provisions as if it had been incurred by the relevant lessor if he were himself the occupier of the hotel at the relevant time.

Statute Law (Repeals) Act 1969

1969 CHAPTER 52

An Act to promote the reform of the statute law by the repeal, in accordance with recommendations of the Law Commission, of certain enactments which (except in so far as their effect is preserved) are no longer of practical utility, and by making other provision in connection with the repeal of those enactments.

[22nd October 1969]

BE IT ENACTED by the Queen's most Excellent Majesty, by and with the advice and consent of the Lords Spiritual and Temporal, and Commons, in this present Parliament assembled, and by the authority of the same, as follows:—

1. The enactments mentioned in the Schedule to this Act are hereby repealed to the extent specified in column 3 of the Schedule. *Repeal of enactments.*

2.—(1) In proceedings by way of quare impedit commenced within six months of induction, judgment shall be given for the removal of an incumbent instituted to fill the vacancy, if he was instituted on a presentation made without title and is made a defendant to the proceedings. *Advowsons.*

(2) Where the Crown presents to a benefice which is full of an incumbent, effect shall not be given to the presentation without judgment having been given for the removal of the incumbent in proceedings by way of quare impedit brought by or on behalf of the Crown.

Subsection (1) above shall apply in relation to proceedings so brought whether or not they are commenced within the period of six months therein referred to.

(3) The provisions of this section shall have effect in place of chapter 5 of the Statute of Westminster, the Second, chapter 10 of the statute of uncertain date concerning the King's prerogative and chapter 1 of 13 Ric. 2. Statute 1.

Rentcharges, etc. under Copyhold Act 1894.

1894 c. 46.

3. Notwithstanding the repeal by this Act of the Copyhold Act 1894—

> (*a*) the owner for the time being of a rentcharge created under the provisions of that Act or of a certificate of charge under that Act shall have for the recovery of the rentcharge or, as the case may be, any sum in the nature of interest or periodical payment becoming due under the certificate the like remedies as are provided by section 121 of the Law of Property Act 1925;

1925 c. 20.

> (*b*) the owner for the time being of such a certificate of charge shall also have, in respect of every sum whether in the nature of interest or periodical payment or principal sum secured by the certificate, the like remedies as a chargee by deed expressed to be by way of legal mortgage of an estate in fee simple has in respect of the principal sum and interest secured by his charge; and
>
> (*c*) a certificate of charge under that Act and the charge made thereby shall be transferable by endorsement on the certificate.

Savings.

1448 c. 5.

4.—(1) The repeal by this Act of the Sunday Fairs Act 1448 shall not have the effect of requiring any market or fair to be held on a Sunday, Good Friday, Ascension Day, Corpus Christi Day, the Feast of the Assumption of Our Blessed Lady or All Saints' Day; and a market or fair may continue to be held on any day on which it might lawfully have been held if that Act had not been repealed.

1558 c. 1.

1533 c. 19.
1533 c. 20.
1533 c. 21.
1534 c. 14.
1558 c. 1.
1547 c. 1.

(2) The repeal by this Act of section 2 of the Act of Supremacy shall not affect the continued operation so far as unrepealed of the Submission of the Clergy Act 1533, the Appointment of Bishops Act 1533, the Ecclesiastical Licences Act 1533 and the Suffragan Bishops Act 1534; and the repeal by this Act of section 5 of the Act of Supremacy shall not affect the continued operation so far as unrepealed of the Sacrament Act 1547.

1662 c. 4.

1548 c. 1.

(3) The repeal by this Act of section 20 of the Act of Uniformity 1662 shall not affect the continued operation of section 7 of the Act of Uniformity 1548 in relation to the Book of Common Prayer annexed to the said Act of 1662.

1542 c. 20.

(4) The repeal by this Act of section 1 of the Feigned Recoveries Act 1542 shall not make barrable any entail existing at the passing of this Act which was unbarrable by reason of that section.

Provisions relating to Northern Ireland.

1920 c. 67.

5.—(1) The following provisions of this Act, that is to say, sections 2 to 4, and so much of this Act as repeals the enactments mentioned in Parts III and IV of the Schedule shall not extend to Northern Ireland; but notwithstanding anything in the Government of Ireland Act 1920, the Parliament of Northern Ireland shall have power to make laws for purposes similar to the purposes of those provisions.

(2) Save as expressly provided by subsection (1) above, this Act extends to Northern Ireland and shall, as respects matters within the powers of the Parliament of Northern Ireland, be subject to alteration by that Parliament as if it had been an Act passed before the day appointed for the purposes of section 6 of the Government of Ireland Act 1920. 1920 c. 67.

(3) The repeal by this Act of any enactment mentioned in Part II of the Schedule to this Act shall not affect the continued operation of section 20 of the Irish Church Act 1869. 1869 c. 42.

6. This Act, in so far as it repeals any of the provisions of the Societies (Miscellaneous Provisions) Act 1940, shall extend to the Channel Islands and the Isle of Man.

Application to Channel Islands and Isle of Man 1940 c. 19.

7.—(1) This Act may be cited as the Statute Law (Repeals) Act 1969.

(2) This Act shall come into force on 1st January 1970.

Short title and commencement.

SCHEDULE

ENACTMENTS REPEALED

PART I

Constitutional Enactments

Statute, etc.	Title, short title or subject	Extent of repeal
25 Edw. 1. (1297).	(Confirmation of Magna Carta).	The whole statute, so far as unrepealed, except articles 1, 9, 29 and 37.
25 Edw. 1. (1297).	(Confirmation of the Charters).	The whole statute except chapters 1 and 6.
25 Edw. 1. (1297).	A Statute concerning Tallage.	The whole statute except chapter 1.
28 Edw. 1. (1300).	Articles upon the Charters.	The whole statute, so far as unrepealed.
1 Edw. 3. Stat. 2. (1327).	(Borough liberties).	Chapter 9.
2 Edw. 3. (1328).	Statute of Northampton.	Chapter 8.
5 Edw. 3. (1331).	(Unlawful attachment).	Chapter 9.
14 Edw. 3. Stat. 1. (1340).	(Confirmation of liberties).	Chapter 1.
1 Mary Sess. 3. c. 1.	The Queen Regent's Prerogative Act 1554.	The whole Act.
5 Eliz. 1. c. 18.	The Lord Keeper Act 1562.	The whole Act.
16 Chas. 1. c. 14.	The Ship Money Act 1640.	The whole Act, so far as unrepealed.
12 Chas. 2. c. 1.	The Parliament Act 1660.	The whole Act.
12 Chas. 2. c. 30. (1660).	An Act for the attainder of several persons guilty of the horrid murder of His late sacred Majesty King Charles the First.	The whole Act, so far as unrepealed.
13 Chas. 2. Stat. 1. c. 6. (1661).	An Act declaring the sole right of the Militia to be in the King and for the present ordering and disposing of the same.	The preamble, so far as unrepealed.

Part II

Ecclesiastical Enactments

Statute, etc.	Title, short title or subject	Extent of repeal
13 Edw. 1. (1285).	(Statute of Westminster, the Second).	Chapter 5.
13 Edw. 1. (1285).	(Statute of Winchester).	Chapter 6.
9 Edw. 2. Stat. 1. (1315).	Articles for the Clergy.	The whole statute, so far as unrepealed.
[Of uncertain date].	Of the King's Prerogative.	Chapter 10.
25 Edw. 3. Stat. 6. (1351).	An Ordinance for the Clergy.	The whole statute, so far as unrepealed.
13 Ric. 2. Stat. 1. (1389).	(Royal presentations to benefices).	Chapter 1, so far as unrepealed.
15 Ric. 2. (1391).	(Appropriation of benefices).	Chapter 6, so far as unrepealed.
4 Hen. 4. (1402).	(Appropriation of benefices).	Chapter 12, so far as unrepealed.
8 Hen. 6. c. 1. (1429).	(Convocation to have privilege of Parliament).	The whole chapter, so far as unrepealed.
23 Hen. 8. c. 20. (1531).	An Act concerning restraint of payment of annates to the See of Rome.	The whole Act, so far as unrepealed.
24 Hen. 8 c. 12.	The Ecclesiastical Appeals Act 1532.	The whole Act, so far as unrepealed.
25 Hen. 8. c. 19.	The Submission of the Clergy Act 1533.	The whole Act, so far as unrepealed, except sections 1 and 3.
25 Hen. 8. c. 20.	The Appointment of Bishops Act 1533.	The preamble and sections 1 and 2.
25 Hen. 8. c. 21.	The Ecclesiastical Licences Act 1533.	The preamble and sections 1, 2, 15, 21 and 23.
27 Hen. 8. c. 28.	The Suppression of Religious Houses Act 1535.	The whole Act, so far as unrepealed.
28 Hen. 8. c. 16.	The Ecclesiastical Licences Act 1536.	The whole Act, so far as unrepealed.
31 Hen. 8. c. 13.	The Suppression of Religious Houses Act 1539.	The whole Act, except section 19.

Statute, etc.	Title, short title or subject	Extent of repeal
32 Hen. 8. c. 7.	The Tithe Act 1540.	Section 5, so far as unrepealed.
32 Hen. 8. c. 20. (1540).	The Liberties to be used.	The whole Act.
37 Hen. 8. c. 4.	The Dissolution of Colleges Act 1545.	The whole Act, so far as unrepealed.
1 Edw. 6. c. 1.	The Sacrament Act 1547.	The whole Act, so far as unrepealed, except section 8.
2 & 3 Edw. 6. c. 1.	The Act of Uniformity 1548.	The whole Act, so far as unrepealed, except section 7.
2 & 3 Edw. 6. c. 21.	The Clergy Marriage Act 1548.	The whole Act, so far as unrepealed.
5 & 6 Edw. 6. c. 1.	The Act of Uniformity 1551.	The whole Act, so far as unrepealed.
5 & 6 Edw. 6. c. 3.	The Holy Days and Fasting Days Act 1551.	The whole Act, so far as unrepealed.
5 & 6 Edw. 6. c. 12.	The Clergy Marriage Act 1551.	The whole Act, so far as unrepealed.
1 Eliz. 1. c. 1. (1558).	The Act of Supremacy.	The whole Act, so far as unrepealed, except section 8.
1 Eliz. 1. c. 2.	The Act of Uniformity 1558.	The whole Act, so far as unrepealed, except section 13.
13 Eliz. 1. c. 2. (1571).	An Act against the bringing in and putting in execution of bulls and other instruments from the See of Rome.	The whole Act, so far as unrepealed.
13 Eliz. 1. c. 12.	The Ordination of Ministers Act 1571.	The whole Act, so far as unrepealed.
35 Eliz. 1. c. 3. (1592).	An Act explaining the Statute of 34 Hen. 8. touching grants.	The whole Act.
13 Chas. 2. Stat. 1. c. 12.	The Ecclesiastical Jurisdiction Act 1661.	The whole Act, so far as unrepealed.

Statute, etc.	Title, short title or subject	Extent of repeal
14 Chas. 2. c. 4.	The Act of Uniformity 1662.	The following provisions, so far as unrepealed:— Sections 2 and 3. In section 10 the words from " upon pain " onwards. Section 17. In section 20 the words " and statutes of this realm " and the words " have beene formerly made and ".
15 Chas. 2. c. 6.	The Act of Uniformity (Explanation) Act 1663.	The whole Act, so far as unrepealed.
1 Will. & Mar. c. 18.	The Toleration Act 1688.	The whole Act, so far as unrepealed.
7 & 8 Will. 3. c. 34. (1695).	An Act that the solemn affirmation and declaration of the people called Quakers shall be accepted instead of an oath in the usual form.	The whole Act, so far as unrepealed.
7 Ann. c. 18.	The Advowsons Act 1708.	The whole Act.
1 Geo. 1. Stat. 2. c. 6.	The Tithes and Church Rates Recovery Act 1714.	The whole Act, so far as unrepealed.
19 Geo. 3. c. 44.	The Nonconformist Relief Act 1779.	The whole Act, so far as unrepealed.
9 & 10 Vict. c. 59.	The Religious Disabilities Act 1846.	Section 1, so far as unrepealed.
23 & 24 Vict. c. 32.	The Ecclesiastical Courts Jurisdiction Act 1860.	Section 6.
26 & 27 Vict. c. 120. (1863).	The Lord Chancellor's Augmentation Act.	The whole Act.

PART III

Law of Property Enactments

Statute, etc.	Title, short title or subject	Extent of repeal
32 Hen. 8. c. 37.	The Cestui que vie Act 1540.	The whole Act, so far as unrepealed.
32 Hen. 8. c. 51.	The Queen Consort Act 1540.	The whole Act, so far as unrepealed.

Statute, etc.	Title, short title or subject	Extent of repeal
34 & 35 Hen. 8. c. 20.	The Feigned Recoveries Act 1542.	The whole Act, so far as unrepealed.
12 Chas. 2. c. 24.	The Tenures Abolition Act 1660.	The whole Act, so far as unrepealed, except sections 4 and 9.
3 & 4 Will. 4. c. 74.	The Fines and Recoveries Act 1833.	In section 27 the words from " (except " to " thirty-three) ". In section 40 the words from " and if " onwards. In section 58 the words " except so far as the same may be varied by the clause next hereinafter contained." Section 71 from " and all the previous clauses in this Act " onwards. In section 72 the words from " but every deed to be executed " to " Ireland ", where next occurring. Sections 77 and 78. Section 91.
7 Will. 4 and 1 Vict. c. 26.	The Wills Act 1837.	In section 1, in the definition of " will " the words from " by virtue of an Act ", where first occurring to " knights service " where last occurring; and in the definition of " real estate " the words from " whether freehold " to " tenure, and ". In section 3 the words from " upon the heir " to " ancestor or "; and the words from " to all real estate " to " hereditament; and also ". Sections 4 to 6. Section 8. In section 26 the words " customary, copyhold or " and the words " customary, copyhold and " in both places.
5 & 6 Vict. c. 94.	The Defence Act 1842.	Section 8. In section 10, the words " feoffees or ", the words from " tenants for life " to

Statute, etc.	Title, short title or subject	Extent of repeal
5 & 6 Vict. c. 94—*cont.*	The Defence Act 1842—*cont.*	" curators or ", the words from " femes covert " to " idiots or ", the word " surrender ", the words " enfranchisements, surrenders " and the words from " and shall be a complete bar " onwards. In sections 12, 13 and 14 the word " surrender " wherever occurring, and in section 14 the word " surrendered ". In section 15 the words from " or being femes covert " to " for that purpose ", and the word " discovert ". In section 18 the words " feoffees or ", the words from " tenants for life " to " curators or ", the words from " femes covert " to " idiots or ", the word " surrender " and the word " surrenders ". In section 25 the words " enfranchisement of any copyhold or ".
9 & 10 Vict. c. 70.	The Inclosure Act 1846.	Section 6, except the words " such Assistant Commissioner shall frame a draft award ", and the words from " with a map or plan annexed thereto " to " under their seal ". Section 7. In section 8 the words from " and any such authority " to " may require " where next occurring, the words " shall insert a declaration in his draft award or ", and the words " as the case may require ". Section 9. In section 10 the words " authorised to take surrenders or grant admittance of or to copyhold or customary lands in such manor ".
12 & 13 Vict. c. 49.	The School Sites Act 1849.	Section 6.

Statute, etc.	Title, short title or subject	Extent of repeal
17 & 18 Vict. c. 112.	The Literary and Scientific Institutions Act 1854.	Section 15.
20 & 21 Vict. c. 57.	The Married Women's Reversionary Interests Act 1857.	The whole Act, so far as unrepealed.
22 & 23 Vict. c. 35.	The Law of Property Amendment Act 1859.	Section 25.
45 & 46 Vict. c. 75.	The Married Women's Property Act 1882.	Sections 6 to 9. In section 11 the words from " If at the time of the death of the insured " to " the same ". Section 13. In section 17 the words from " or any such bank " to " are standing ", and the final proviso. Sections 18 and 19. In section 24 the words from the beginning to " administration ". Section 25.
57 & 58 Vict. c. 46.	The Copyhold Act 1894.	The whole Act.
59 & 60 Vict. c. 25.	The Friendly Societies Act 1896.	Section 48.
7 Edw. 7. c. 18.	The Married Women's Property Act 1907.	Section 2.
4 & 5 Geo. 5. c. 59.	The Bankruptcy Act 1914.	Section 55(5), so far as it relates to any provision repealed by this Act in the Fines and Recoveries Act 1833.
12 & 13 Geo. 5. c. 16.	The Law of Property Act 1922.	Section 43(4) to (7). Sections 128 to 136. Sections 138 to 143. In section 188, paragraphs (2) to (5), (7), (8), (10) to (18), (20) to (22) and (24) to (29); paragraph (30) from " trustees for sale " onwards; and paragraph (32). Section 189. Schedules 12 to 14.

Statute, etc.	Title, short title or subject	Extent of repeal
15 & 16 Geo. 5. c. 5.	The Law of Property (Amendment) Act 1924.	In Schedule 2, paragraphs 3 and 4. In Schedule 9, paragraph 6 in column 1 and 2.
15 & 6 Geo. 5. c. 18.	The Settled Land Act 1925.	Section 38(ii). In section 58(1) the words "manorial incidents". Section 62(1) to (3). In section 64(2) the words "extinguishment of manorial incidents". In section 71(1) paragraphs (iv) and (v). In section 73(1) paragraphs (vi) and (vii).
15 & 16 Geo. 5. c. 20.	The Law of Property Act 1925.	Section 133. Sections 167 to 170. Section 178.
15 & 16 Geo. 5. c. 24.	The Universities and College Estates Act 1925.	In section 2(1), paragraph (ii). In section 26(1), paragraphs (v) and (vi).
15 & 16 Geo. 5. c. 76.	The Expiring Laws Act 1925.	In Schedule 1, the entry relating to 34 & 35 Hen. 8. c. 20.
16 & 17 Geo. 5. c. 11.	The Law of Property (Amendment) Act 1926.	In the Schedule, so much of the entry relating to the Law of Property Act 1922 as amends Schedule 13.
25 & 26 Geo. 5. c. 30.	The Law Reform (Married Women and Tortfeasors) Act 1935.	Schedule 1 except so far as it amends section 11 of the Married Women's Property Act 1882.
3 & 4 Geo. 6. c. 2.	The Postponement of Enactments (Miscellaneous Provisions) Act 1939.	The whole Act, so far as unrepealed.
11 & 12 Geo. 6. c. 38.	The Companies Act 1948.	Section 217. In section 401(2) the words "or marriage of any female contributory" and the words "and to the liabilities of husbands and wives".
11 & 12 Geo. 6. c. 63.	The Agricultural Holdings Act 1948.	Section 85.

Statute, etc.	Title, short title or subject	Extent of repeal
12, 13 & 14 Geo. 6. c. 78.	The Married Women (Restraint upon Anticipation) Act 1949.	Section 1(3). Schedule 1.
5 & 6 Eliz. 2. c. 27.	The Solicitors Act 1957.	Section 74(*b*).
7 & 8 Eliz. 2. c. 22.	The County Courts Act 1959.	In Schedule 1, the entry relating to the Law of Property Act 1922, and in the entry relating to the Law of Property Act 1925, the words " one hundred and sixty-nine " in column 1.
7 & 8 Eliz. 2. c. 72.	The Mental Health Act 1959.	In Schedule 5 the entries relating to the Defence Act 1842 and the Copyhold Act 1894. In Schedule 7, in the entry relating to the Fines and Recoveries Act 1833, the words from " In section ninety-one " onwards.
8 & 9 Eliz. 2. c. 58.	The Charities Act 1960.	In Schedule 6, the entry relating to the Copyhold Act 1894.

Part IV

Enactments relating to Sunday Observance

Statute, etc.	Title, short title or subject	Extent of repeal
27 Hen. 6. c. 5.	The Sunday Fairs Act 1448.	The whole chapter.
1 Chas. 1. c. 1.	The Sunday Observance Act 1625.	The whole Act, so far as unrepealed.
3 Chas. 1. c. 2. (1627).	An Act for the further reformation of sundry abuses committed on the Lord's Day commonly called Sunday.	The whole Act, so far as unrepealed.

Statute, etc.	Title, short title or subject	Extent of repeal
29 Chas. 2. c. 7.	The Sunday Observance Act 1677.	The whole Act, so far as unrepealed.
34 & 35 Vict. c. 87.	The Sunday Observation Prosecution Act 1871.	The whole Act, so far as unrepealed.
12 & 13 Geo. 5. c. 50.	The Expiring Laws Act 1922.	In Schedule 1, the entry relating to the Sunday Observation Prosecution Act 1871.
14 Geo. 6. c. 28.	The Shops Act 1950.	Section 59(2).
2 & 3 Eliz. 2. c. 57.	The Baking Industry (Hours of Work) Act 1954.	Section 12(1).
6 & 7 Eliz. 2. c. 65.	The Children Act 1958.	In section 7(2), the words " notwithstanding anything in section six of the Sunday Observance Act 1677 ".
7 & 8 Eliz. 2. c. 5.	The Adoption Act 1958.	In section 43(2), the words " notwithstanding anything in section six of the Sunday Observance Act 1677 ".

PART V

Hallmarking Enactments

Statute, etc.	Title, short title or subject	Extent of repeal
18 Eliz. 1. c. 15. (1575).	An Act for Reformation of Abuses in Goldsmiths.	The whole Act, so far as unrepealed.
8 & 9 Will. 3. c. 8. (1696).	An Act for encouraging the bringing in wrought plate to be coined.	In section 8, the words from " and if any silversmith, goldsmith or other person " onwards.
1 Ann. c. 3. (1702).	(Assay of plate).	Sections 3 and 5.

Statute, etc.	Title, short title or subject	Extent of repeal
12 Geo. 2. c. 26.	The Plate (Offences) Act 1738.	In section 11 the words from " or to and for any warden " to " Newcastle-upon-Tyne "; the words " such warden, deputy warden or assayer ", and the words " or assayers ". Section 18. In section 20 the words from " or any assayer at York " to " Newcastle - upon - Tyne,"; and the words " or any warden of the company at any of the cities or places aforesaid ". In section 21 the words from " or in the assay office at York " to " Newcastle-upon-Tyne,".
38 Geo. 3. c. 69.	The Gold Plate (Standard) Act 1798.	In section 3 the words from " and the wardens and assayer " to " Newcastle upon Tyne ".
7 & 8 Vict. c. 22.	The Gold and Silver Wares Act 1844.	In section 7 the words from " or any of the several companies" to "Newcastle-upon-Tyne,". In section 15 the words from " and by the several companies " to " Newcastle-upon-Tyne,".

PART VI

Enactments relating to the Commonwealth

Statute, etc.	Title, short title or subject	Extent of repeal
24 & 25 Geo. 5. c. 2.	The Newfoundland Act 1933.	Section 3.
11 & 12 Geo. 6. c. 7.	The Ceylon Independence Act 1947.	In section 4, in subsection (1) the words from " and His Majesty " to " section one of this Act "; and subsections (3) and (4).

Statute, etc.	Title, short title or subject	Extent of repeal
11 & 12 Geo. 6. c. 8.	The Mandated and Trust Territories Act 1947.	In section 1, in subsection (1) the words " Subject to subsection (2) of this section "; subsection (2); in subsection (5) the words " and an Order in Council thereunder may modify "; and subsection (6).
12, 13 & 14 Geo. 6. c. 22.	The British North America Act 1949.	Section 2.
14 Geo. 6. c. 5.	The Newfoundland (Consequential Provisions) Act 1950.	Sections 1 and 3. The Schedule.
4 & 5 Eliz. 2. c. 31.	The Pakistan (Consequential Provision) Act 1956.	In section 1, in subsection (1) the words " and subject to the provisions of subsection (3) of this section "; and subsection (3).
5 & 6 Eliz. 2. c. 6.	The Ghana Independence Act 1957.	In section 4(4), the words from " and Her Majesty " to " that day ".
6 & 7 Eliz. 2. c. 45.	The Prevention of Fraud (Investments) Act 1958.	In section 28(7), the words " subsection (3) of section one of the Pakistan (Consequential Provision) Act 1956 ".
8 & 9 Eliz. 2. c. 55.	The Nigeria Independence Act 1960.	In section 3(4), the words from " and Her Majesty " to " that day ".
9 & 10 Eliz. 2. c. 16.	The Sierra Leone Independence Act 1961.	In section 3(3), the words from " and Her Majesty " to " that day ".
10 & 11 Eliz. 2. c. 1.	The Tanganyika Independence Act 1961.	In section 3(4), the words from " and Her Majesty " to " that day ".
10 & 11 Eliz. 2. c. 40.	The Jamaica Independence Act 1962.	In section 3(5), the words from " and Her Majesty " onwards.
10 & 11 Eliz. 2. c. 54.	The Trinidad and Tobago Independence Act 1962.	In section 3(4), the words from " and Her Majesty " onwards.
10 & 11 Eliz. 2. c. 57.	The Uganda Independence Act 1962.	In section 3(4), the words from " and Her Majesty " onwards.

Statute, etc.	Title, short title or subject	Extent of repeal
11 & 12 Eliz. 2. c. 1	The Tanganyika Republic Act 1962.	In section 1, in subsection (1) the words " and subject to the following provisions of this section "; and subsections (2) and (3).
1963 c. 54.	The Kenya Independence Act 1963.	In section 4, in subsection (4) the words from " and Her Majesty " onwards; and in subsection (5) the words " and any Order in Council made under the said subsection (4) ".
1963 c. 55.	The Zanzibar Act 1963.	Section 4. In section 5(1) and (2) the words " or section 4 ".
1963 c. 57.	The Nigeria Republic Act 1963.	In section 2, subsection (1); in subsection (2) the words "Any Order in Council made under subsection (1) of this section, and "; and subsection (3).
1964 c. 20.	The Uganda Act 1964.	In section 2, subsection (1); in subsection (2) the words "Any Order in Council made under subsection (1) of this section, and "; and subsection (3).
1964 c. 46.	The Malawi Independence Act 1964.	In section 4, in subsection (4) the words from " and Her Majesty " onwards; subsection (5); and in subsection (6) the words " and any Order in Council made under the said subsection (4) ".
1964 c. 65.	The Zambia Independence Act 1964.	Section 9. In section 10(1) and (2), the words " or section 9 ".
1964 c. 86.	The Malta Independence Act 1964.	In section 4, in subsection (4) the words from " and Her Majesty " onwards; subsection (5); and subsection (7) except the words " Schedule 2 to this Act and subsection (4) of this section shall not extend to Malta as part of its law ".

Statute, etc.	Title, short title or subject	Extent of repeal
1964 c. 93.	The Gambia Independence Act 1964.	In section 4, in subsection (4) the words from " and Her Majesty " onwards; subsection (5); and subsection (6) except the words " Schedule 2 to this Act and subsection (4) of this section shall not extend to The Gambia as part of its law ".
1965 c. 5.	The Kenya Republic Act 1965.	In section 2, subsection (1); in subsection (2) the words "Any Order in Council made under subsection (1) of this section, and "; and subsection (3).
1966 c. 29.	The Singapore Act 1966.	In section 4, subsection (1); in subsection (2) the words "An Order in Council under this section and "; and subsection (3).

PART VII

Miscellaneous Enactments

Statute, etc.	Title, short title or subject	Extent of repeal
3 Edw. 1. (1275).	(Statute of Westminster, the First).	Chapter 16.
13 Edw. 1. (1285).	(Statute of Westminster, the Second).	Chapters 37 and 42.
2 Edw. 3. (1328).	Statute of Northampton.	Chapter 15.
7 Hen. 4. (1405).	(Sales by wholesale in City of London).	Chapter 9.
18 Hen. 6. c. 1. (1439).	(Date of letters patent).	The whole chapter.

Statute, etc.	Title, short title or subject	Extent of repeal
28 Hen. 8. c. 5.	The Apprentices Act 1536.	The whole Act, so far as unrepealed.
1 & 2 Phil. & Mar. c. 12.	The Distress Act 1554.	The whole Act, so far as unrepealed.
7 Jas. 1. c. 12.	The Shop-books Evidence Act 1609.	The whole Act, so far as unrepealed.
7 Jas. 1. c. 15.	The Crown Debts Act 1609.	The whole Act, so far as unrepealed.
21 Jas. 1. c. 3. (1623).	The Statute of Monopolies.	In the preamble, the words from " and of the benefitt " to " the forfeiture ". In section 1, the words from " or to give licence " to " the same or any of them,". Sections 2 to 4.
29 Chas. 2. c. 3. (1677).	The Statute of Frauds.	Section 22.
5 Will. & Mar. c. 6.	The Royal Mines Act 1693.	Section 2.
55 Geo. 3. c. 134.	The Crown Pre-emption of Lead Ore Act 1815.	The whole Act, so far as unrepealed.
6 Geo. 4. c. 97.	The Universities Act 1825.	In section 3, the words " and night walker ".
5 & 6 Will. 4. c. 24.	The Naval Enlistment Act 1835.	The whole Act, so far as unrepealed.
1 & 2 Vict. c. 43.	The Dean Forest (Mines) Act 1838.	The preamble. Sections 1 to 13. Section 16 from " and a list " onwards. In section 17 the words " to the said Commissioners hereby appointed ". Section 18. Section 19 from the beginning to the words " London Gazette, then ". In section 20 the words " by the ꞁ said Commissioners or ". In section 22 the words from " or from " to " Buildings ". Sections 24 to 26.

Statute, etc.	Title, short title or subject	Extent of repeal
1 & 2 Vict. c. 43—*cont.*	The Dean Forest (Mines) Act 1838—*cont.*	Section 27 from the beginning to the words "the passing of this Act and" in the proviso; the words from "for the term", where first occurring in the proviso to "paid to Her Majesty, Her Heirs and Successors" except the words "and the yearly rent"; the words "respectively as aforesaid"; and the words "to Her Majesty" wherever afterwards occurring. Section 28. Sections 30 to 44. Sections 50 and 51. In section 53 the words from the beginning to "successors, and" except the words "it shall be lawful for the said gaveller"; and the words from "the said commissioners", in the second place where they occur to "their agents" except the words "the gaveller". Section 55. In section 56 the words from "with the previous approbation and allowance" to "under their hands and seals"; and the first proviso. Section 57 from "and the gaveller" onwards. In section 60 the words from "and when" to "direct". Section 63. In section 65, in the first proviso the words "and enrolled in the office of land revenue records and enrolments". Section 66. In section 68 the words from "by the said Commissioners hereby appointed" to "determined" where next occurring; the words from "after the time limited" to "ten days", where next occurring; and the proviso

Statute, etc.	Title, short title or subject	Extent of repeal
1 & 2 Vict. c. 43—*cont.*	The Dean Forest (Mines) Act 1838—*cont.*	from " and that for the purposes of this Act " onwards. Sections 70 to 82. Section 83 from the beginning to " provided nevertheless, that ". Sections 84 to 89. Section 91.
3 & 4 Vict. c. 65.	The Admiralty Court Act 1840.	The whole Act, so far as unrepealed.
5 & 6 Vict. c. 83. (1842).	An Act to abolish the court of Saint Briavel's, and for the more easy and speedy recovery of small debts within the hundred of Saint Briavel's in the county of Gloucester.	The whole Act, so far as unrepealed.
16 & 17 Vict. c. 69.	The Naval Enlistment Act 1853.	The whole Act, so far as unrepealed.
16 & 17 Vict. c. 107.	The Customs Consolidation Act 1853.	Sections 332 and 333, 335 to 341 and 343 to 345.
24 & 25 Vict. c. 40. (1861).	An Act to make further provision for the management of Her Majesty's Forest of Dean, and of the mines and quarries therein and in the hundred of Saint Briavel's in the county of Gloucester.	The preamble. Section 2. Sections 5 and 6. Section 17. Section 22. Section 27.
34 & 35 Vict. c. 85.	The Dean Forest (Mines) Act 1871.	The preamble. Section 2 except in so far as it defines " principal Acts ". Sections 5 to 32 (but without prejudice to the award thereunder).
37 & 38 Vict. c. 42.	The Building Societies Act 1874.	Section 7.
39 & 40 Vict. c. 36.	The Customs Consolidation Act 1876.	Section 275, so far as unrepealed.
40 & 41 Vict. c. 40.	The Writs Execution (Scotland) Act 1877.	Section 4.
42 & 43 Vict. c. 36.	The Customs Buildings Act 1879.	Section 4 and, so far as unrepealed, section 6.

Statute, etc.	Title, short title or subject	Extent of repeal
42 & 43 Vict. c. 44.	The Lord Clerk Register (Scotland) Act 1879.	Section 4.
45 & 46 Vict. c. 17.	The Customs and Inland Revenue Buildings (Ireland) Act 1882.	Sections 3 and 5.
58 & 59 Vict. c. 19.	The Court of Session Consignations (Scotland) Act 1895.	In section 2, the words " or by any of the clerks of court, as the case may be ". In section 3, from the beginning to the words " provided that " and the words from " and the Clerk " to " such clerk ". In section 16, the words " or any of the Clerks of Court". Section 17.
59 & 60 Vict. c. 19.	The Public Health Act 1896.	The whole Act, so far as unrepealed.
60 & 61 Vict. c. 24.	The Finance Act 1897.	The whole Act, so far as unrepealed.
4 Edw. 7. c. 7.	The Finance Act 1904.	The whole Act, so far as unrepealed.
4 Edw. 7. c. 16.	The Public Health Act 1904.	The whole Act, so far as unrepealed.
4 Edw. 7. c. clvi.	The Dean Forest (Mines) Act 1904.	Section 5. Section 7(3). Section 8.
9 & 10 Geo. 5. c. 82.	The Irish Land (Provision for Sailors and Soldiers) Act 1919.	Section 2.
10 & 11 Geo. 5. c. 18.	The Finance Act 1920.	Section 57, so far as unrepealed.
15 & 16 Geo. 5. c. 36.	The Finance Act 1925.	Section 5(4).
15 & 16 Geo. 5. c. 88.	The Coastguard Act 1925.	Section 1(3).
17 & 18 Geo. 5. c. 18.	The Royal Naval Reserve Act 1927.	Section 1(2).
19 & 20 Geo. 5. c. 21.	The Finance Act 1929.	The whole Act, so far as unrepealed.

Statute, etc.	Title, short title or subject	Extent of repeal
22 & 23 Geo. 5. c. 46.	The Children and Young Persons Act 1932.	Sections 70, 77 and 87, so far as unrepealed. In section 90, the words in subsection (1) from " and the Children Acts " onwards and, in subsection (2), the words from the beginning to " except that ". Schedule 2.
2 & 3 Geo. 6. c. 21.	The Limitation Act 1939.	In section 31(2), the words from " or a convict " onwards.
3 & 4 Geo. 6. c. 19.	The Societies (Miscellaneous Provisions) Act 1940.	The following provisions, so far as unrepealed:— Sections 1 to 7. In section 8(1), the words from " or any " to " 1928 ". In section 10(1), the definitions of " building society ", " emergency ", " period of emergency ", "society" and " trade union ". Section 12(3). The Schedule.
12, 13 & 14 Geo. 6. c. 47.	The Finance Act 1949.	Section 17.
14 & 15 Geo. 6. c. 39.	The Common Informers Act 1951.	In the Schedule, the entries relating to 2 Hen. 6. c. 17, the Apprentices Act 1536, and the Leases by Corporations Act 1541.
14 & 15 Geo. 6. c. 59.	The Price Control and other Orders (Indemnity) Act 1951.	The whole Act.
4 & 5 Eliz. 2. c. 35.	The Validation of Elections (Northern Ireland) Act 1956.	The whole Act.
6 & 7 Eliz. 2. c. 65.	The Children Act 1958.	Sections 38 and 40(2). Schedule 3.
8 & 9 Eliz. 2. c. 64.	The Building Societies Act 1960.	Section 63. In Schedule 5, the entry relating to the Friendly Societies Act 1829.

Statute, etc.	Title, short title or subject	Extent of repeal
10 & 11 Eliz. 2. c. 37.	The Building Societies Act 1962.	Section 125(2) and (4). Section 133(2) and (5).
1964 c. 24.	The Trade Union (Amalgamations, etc.) Act 1964.	Section 11(2) and (3). Schedule 3.
1967 c. 86.	The Countryside (Scotland) Act 1967.	In section 11(1) the words from " In this subsection " onwards.

PART VIII

Acts of the Parliament of Ireland

Statute, etc.	Title, short title or subject	Extent of repeal
37 Hen. 6. c. 1.	The Warrants and Patents Act (Ireland) 1459.	The whole Act.
2 Eliz. 1. c. 1.	The Act of Supremacy (Ireland) 1560.	Section 14.
4 Ann. c. 12.	The Royal Mines Act (Ireland) 1705.	Section 4.
10 Geo. 1. c. 5.	The Mines Act (Ireland) 1723.	Section 12.

PART IX

Church Assembly Measures

Statute, etc.	Title, short title or subject	Extent of repeal
2 & 3 Geo. 6. No. 1.	The Queen Anne's Bounty (Powers) Measure 1939.	In section 1, paragraph (vi).

Late Night Refreshment Houses Act 1969

1969 CHAPTER 53

An Act to consolidate certain enactments relating to refreshment houses within the meaning of the Refreshment Houses Act 1860, with corrections and improvements made under the Consolidation of Enactments (Procedure) Act 1949.   [22nd October 1969]

BE IT ENACTED by the Queen's most Excellent Majesty, by and with the advice and consent of the Lords Spiritual and Temporal, and Commons, in this present Parliament assembled, and by the authority of the same, as follows:—

1. For the purposes of this Act, a " late night refreshment house " is a house, room, shop or building kept open for public refreshment, resort and entertainment at any time between the hours of 10 o'clock at night and 5 o'clock of the following morning, other than a house, room, shop or building which is licensed for the sale of beer, cider, wine or spirits.

Meaning of
" late night
refreshment
house ".

2.—(1) A person who keeps a late night refreshment house shall take out annually a licence to do so, granted by the licensing authority under this Act.

Requirement
of licence
to keep late
night
refreshment
house.

(2) The licensing authorities under this Act are county and county borough councils and, in the case of Greater London, the councils of London boroughs and the Common Council of City of London ; and in the following provisions of this Act—

  (*a*) " licence " means a licence under this Act to keep a late night refreshment house ; and

  (*b*) " licensed " and " licensee " shall be construed accordingly.

(3) It is an offence for a person to keep a late night refreshment house without having a licence in force under this Act.

Annual duty
on licence,
and power
to vary.

3.—(1) Subject to the provisions of this Act, on every licence under this Act there shall be charged a duty of one guinea payable to the licensing authority; and a licence shall be granted by the licensing authority on payment of the duty (except where there is for the time being in force in relation to the person or premises concerned a disqualification order under section 100

1964 c. 26.

of the Licensing Act 1964 or section 11(4) of this Act).

(2) Subsection (1) of this section may be amended by an order made by the Secretary of State so as to vary the sum specified thereby or so as to provide that the sum payable thereunder shall cease to be so payable; and an order under this section may be revoked or varied by a subsequent order thereunder.

(3) The power of the Secretary of State to make orders under this section shall be exercisable by statutory instrument, and any statutory instrument containing such an order shall be subject to annulment in pursuance of a resolution of either House of Parliament.

Reduced
duty on
beginner's
part-year
licence.

4. Where a licence is granted on or after 1st July in any year—

> (a) to a person who has not within two years immediately preceding held a licence; or
>
> (b) in respect of premises in respect of which the person to whom the licence is granted has not within the said period held a licence,

the licensing authority may grant the licence on payment of a proportion of the full duty, the proportion being as follows—

> (i) if the licence is taken out in July, August or September, three-quarters;
>
> (ii) if it is taken out in October, November or December, one-half; and
>
> (iii) if it is taken out in January, February or March, one-quarter.

Date of
licence and
period of
validity.

5.—(1) A licence granted between 31st March and 1st May in any year shall have effect from 1st April in that year; and a licence granted at any other time shall have effect from the date of the grant.

(2) Every licence, whenever granted, shall have effect until the end of 31st March next following the date of the grant and shall be renewable annually on payment of the duty chargeable, if any.

(3) On the death of a person licensed under this Act to keep a late night refreshment house the licensing authority may, by endorsement or otherwise, authorise his personal representative or his widow or child, if possessed of and occupying the premises

to which the licence relates, to continue to keep the refreshment house until the end of the following 31st March, without taking out a fresh licence or paying any additional duty ; and a person so authorised shall then be deemed to be the holder of the licence.

6.—(1) There shall be kept by every licensing authority a list or register of licences granted by them for late night refreshment houses in their area, showing in respect of each licence the name and place of abode of the licensee and the name and description of the premises which are the subject of the licence.

Local register of licences.

(2) The authority shall, whenever required, give to the clerk to the justices for their area or any part of it a copy of or extract from the list or register.

(3) The licensee of a late night refreshment house shall, on any change of address which affects the list or register kept by a licensing authority under this section, notify the authority in writing of the new address to be entered in the list or register as his place of abode ; and he shall be guilty of an offence if he fails to do so within two weeks after the change of address.

7.—(1) A licensing authority, if satisfied that it is desirable to do so in order to avoid unreasonable disturbance to residents of the neighbourhood, may on the grant or renewal of a licence for a late night refreshment house impose a condition prohibiting the opening or keeping open of the refreshment house for public refreshment, resort or entertainment at any time between such time (not earlier than 11 o'clock at night) as may be specified in the condition and 5 o'clock in the morning.

Power of licensing authority to impose conditions as to opening after 11 p.m.

(2) In the event of a contravention of a condition imposed by the licensing authority under this section, the licensee of the refreshment house shall be guilty of an offence.

(3) A person aggrieved by a condition imposed under this section on the grant or renewal of a licence may appeal to a magistrates' court ; and—

(a) the court may on the appeal give such directions as it thinks proper with respect to the condition subject to which the licence is to be granted or renewed (including a direction that no condition is to be imposed) ; and

(b) a party to an appeal under this subsection may appeal from the decision of the magistrates' court to a court of quarter sessions.

8.—(1) Where this subsection applies to a late night refreshment house, it shall not be lawful to make any charge for or in connection with the entertainment of persons in the refreshment house during the hours of late opening, whether for the supply

Conditions of licence as to charges and touting.

3 A

of food or drink, for admission, for service of any description or for any other matter, except any reasonable charge for the use of cloakroom or toilet facilities, unless—

(a) a tariff of charges made in the refreshment house is during those hours kept displayed in such position and in such manner that it can be conveniently read by persons frequenting the refreshment house and, if so required by subsection (4) of this section, can be so read by any such person before entering ; and

(b) the charge is specified for the matter in question in the tariff or is less than a charge so specified.

(2) Where this subsection applies to a late night refreshment house it shall not be lawful to seek to obtain custom for the refreshment house by means of personal solicitation outside or in the vicinity of the refreshment house.

(3) Subsection (1) or (2) above, or both, shall apply to a late night refreshment house if, but only if, the licensing authority have made that a condition of the grant or renewal of a licence for the refreshment house, and have not revoked the condition ; and a licensing authority may impose such a condition in any case where it appears to them desirable in order to ensure that persons frequenting the refreshment house are not misled as to the nature or cost of the entertainment provided.

(4) Where subsection (1) applies, the tariff of charges must be able to be read before entering by any person frequenting the refreshment house, if it is so stated by the condition applying the subsection, and on any renewal of the licence the condition may be varied so as to include or omit any such statement.

(5) In the event of a contravention of subsection (1) or (2) of this section the keeper of the refreshment house and any person responsible for the contravention (other than a person who did not know of the condition applying the subsection) shall be guilty of an offence ; and where a person is charged with such an offence, it shall be for him to show that he did not know of the condition.

(6) In this section " the hours of late opening " means any period between the hours of 10 o'clock at night and 5 o'clock on the following morning during which the refreshment house is open.

Illegal and disorderly conduct.

9.—(1) If the licensee of a late night refreshment house knowingly permits unlawful gaming therein or knowingly permits prostitutes, thieves, or drunken and disorderly persons to assemble at, or continue in or upon, his premises, he shall be guilty of an offence.

(2) In subsection (1) of this section the reference to unlawful gaming is to the playing of any game in such circumstances that

an offence is committed under Part II of the Betting, Gaming 1963 c. 2. and Lotteries Act 1963.

(3) As from the date on which there comes into force so much of section 53 of, and Part I of Schedule 11 to, the Gaming Act 1968 c. 65. 1968 as amends section 40 of the Betting, Gaming and Lotteries Act 1963, subsection (2) of this section shall have effect as if for the reference to Part II of the said Act of 1963 there were substituted a reference to the said Act of 1968.

(4) If a person who is drunk, riotous, quarrelsome or disorderly in a late night refreshment house licensed under this Act refuses or neglects to leave it on being requested to do so by the manager or occupier, or his agent or servant, or by any constable, he shall be guilty of an offence.

10.—(1) A constable may, at any time when he thinks fit, Power of enter a late night refreshment house licensed under this Act and constable to go upon any premises belonging thereto ; and the licensee or any enter and keep order. other person being his employee or acting by his direction shall be guilty of an offence if he fails or refuses to admit a constable demanding admittance under this subsection.

(2) Every constable is hereby authorised and required, on the demand of the manager or occupier of a late night refreshment house licensed under this Act, or of any servant or agent of the manager or occupier, to assist in expelling from the refreshment house drunken, riotous, quarrelsome and disorderly persons.

11.—(1) A person guilty of an offence under section 2(3), Punishment 7(2), 8(5), 9(1) or 10(1) of this Act shall be liable on summary of offences. conviction to a fine of not more than £200 or to imprisonment for a term of not more than three months, or both.

(2) A person guilty of an offence under section 6(3) of this Act shall be liable on summary conviction to a fine of not more than £20.

(3) A person guilty of an offence under section 9(4) of this Act shall be liable on summary conviction to a fine of not more than £5.

(4) On a person's conviction in relation to any premises of any of the following offences, that is to say—

(a) an offence under section 2(3), 7(2), 8(5), 9(1) or 10(1) of this Act ;

(b) an offence under section 160 of the Licensing Act 1964 1964 c. 26. (sale of intoxicating liquor without licence) committed by the keeper of a late night refreshment house ; or

(c) an offence under section 84(2) of that Act (supply or consumption of intoxicating liquor at parties organised for gain) committed by the keeper of a late night refreshment house in connection with parties at the refreshment house,

1964 c. 26. the court by or before which he is convicted may make a disqualification order, and sections 100(2) and 101 of the Licensing Act 1964 shall apply to a disqualification order under this subsection as they apply to a disqualification order under section 100 of that Act.

Power to apply provisions of Customs and Excise Act 1952.

1952 c. 44.
1949 c. 47.

12. Section 313(3) of the Customs and Excise Act 1952 (under which the Treasury may by order apply provisions of that Act to the duties transferred to county and county borough councils by section 15 of the Finance Act 1949), and any order made before the commencement of this Act under that subsection, shall continue to have effect in relation to the duties chargeable on licences under this Act and to councils levying those duties and to the officers of such councils, subject in the case of any order so made to its being varied or revoked under section 313(4) of the said Act of 1952.

Transitional provisions and saving.

13.—(1) Any licence granted or renewed, or condition imposed, or other thing done, under an enactment repealed by this Act shall have effect as if granted, renewed, imposed or done under the corresponding enactment in this Act.

(2) Any enactment or other document referring—

    (a) to an enactment repealed by this Act ; or

1860 c. 27.   (b) to a refreshment house within the meaning of the Refreshment Houses Act 1860 or a licence for such a refreshment house, or to a person keeping or being licensed to keep such a refreshment house,

shall, so far as such a construction is necessary for preserving the effect of the document, be construed as referring to the corresponding enactment in this Act or to a late night refreshment house within the meaning of this Act, or to a licence under this Act for such a refreshment house, or to a person keeping or being licensed to keep such a refreshment house, as the case may be.

(3) Without prejudice to subsection (2) of this section, in subsection (2)(a) of section 100 of the Licensing Act 1964 (disqualification orders) for the words " the Refreshment Houses Act 1860 " there shall be substituted the words " the Late Night Refreshment Houses Act 1969 ".

1889 c. 63. (4) The mention of particular matters in this section shall not be taken to affect the general application of section 38 of the Interpretation Act 1889 with regard to the effect of repeals.

(5) A power under any enactment to amend or repeal an enactment repealed by this Act shall include power to amend or repeal the corresponding provision of this Act.

14. The enactments specified in the Schedule to this Act are Repeals. hereby repealed to the extent specified in the third column of that Schedule.

15.—(1) This Act may be cited as the Late Night Refreshment Citation, Houses Act 1969. commencement and extent.

(2) This Act shall come into force on 1st January 1970.

(3) Nothing in this Act extends to Scotland or Northern Ireland.

Section 14.

SCHEDULE

ENACTMENTS REPEALED

Chapter	Short Title	Extent of Repeal
23 & 24 Vict. c. 27.	The Refreshment Houses Act 1860.	Sections 1, 2, 6, 9 to 12, 16, 18, 32 and 41.
24 Vict. c. 91.	The Revenue (No. 2) Act 1861.	Sections 8 and 9.
27 & 28 Vict. c. 18.	The Revenue (No. 1) Act 1864.	Section 5.
12, 13 & 14 Geo. 6. c. 47.	The Finance Act 1949.	In section 15, paragraph (*d*) of subsection (1), subsection (4), and, in subsection (9) the words " and references to licences to keep refreshment houses shall not apply ".
15 & 16 Geo. 6 and 1 Eliz. 2. c. 44.	The Customs and Excise Act 1952.	In section 237(2), the words " the Refreshment Houses Act 1860 or ".
10 & 11 Eliz. 2. c. 52.	The Penalties for Drunkenness Act 1962.	In section 1(2)(*a*), the words " section forty-one of the Refreshment Houses Act 1860 ".
1963 c. 2.	The Betting, Gaming and Lotteries Act 1963.	In section 40, the words " section 32 of the Refreshment Houses Act 1860 ".
1964 c. 88.	The Refreshment Houses Act 1964.	The whole Act, except so much of the Schedule as provides a new subsection (1) for section 100 of the Licensing Act 1964.
1966 c. 42.	The Local Government Act 1966.	In Part II of Schedule 3, the entry (numbered 2) relating to the Revenue (No. 2) Act 1861.
1967 c. 38.	The Refreshment Houses Act 1967.	The whole Act.

Children and Young Persons Act 1969

1969 CHAPTER 54

An Act to amend the law relating to children and young persons; and for purposes connected therewith.

[22nd October 1969]

BE IT ENACTED by the Queen's most Excellent Majesty, by and with the advice and consent of the Lords Spiritual and Temporal, and Commons, in this present Parliament assembled, and by the authority of the same, as follows:—

PART I

CARE AND OTHER TREATMENT OF JUVENILES THROUGH COURT PROCEEDINGS

Care of children and young persons through juvenile courts

1.—(1) Any local authority, constable or authorised person who reasonably believes that there are grounds for making an order under this section in respect of a child or young person may, subject to section 2(3) and (8) of this Act, bring him before a juvenile court.

Care proceedings in juvenile courts.

(2) If the court before which a child or young person is brought under this section is of opinion that any of the following conditions is satisfied with respect to him, that is to say—

(*a*) his proper development is being avoidably prevented or neglected or his health is being avoidably impaired or neglected or he is being ill-treated ; or

(*b*) it is probable that the condition set out in the preceding paragraph will be satisfied in his case, having regard to the fact that the court or another court has found that that condition is or was satisfied in the case of another child or young person who is or was a member of the household to which he belongs ; or

(*c*) he is exposed to moral danger ; or

3 A 4

(*d*) he is beyond the control of his parent or guardian ; or

(*e*) he is of compulsory school age within the meaning of the Education Act 1944 and is not receiving efficient full-time education suitable to his age, ability and aptitude ; or

(*f*) he is guilty of an offence, excluding homicide,

and also that he is in need of care or control which he is unlikely to receive unless the court makes an order under this section in respect of him, then, subject to the following provisions of this section and sections 2 and 3 of this Act, the court may if it thinks fit make such an order.

(3) The order which a court may make under this section in respect of a child or young person is—

(*a*) an order requiring his parent or guardian to enter into a recognisance to take proper care of him and exercise proper control over him ; or

(*b*) a supervision order ; or

(*c*) a care order (other than an interim order) ; or

(*d*) a hospital order within the meaning of Part V of the Mental Health Act 1959 ; or

(*e*) a guardianship order within the meaning of that Act.

(4) In any proceedings under this section the court may make orders in pursuance of paragraphs (*c*) and (*d*) of the preceding subsection but subject to that shall not make more than one of the orders mentioned in the preceding subsection, without prejudice to any power to make a further order in subsequent proceedings of any description ; and if in proceedings under this section the court makes one of those orders and an order so mentioned is already in force in respect of the child or young person in question, the court may discharge the earlier order unless it is a hospital or guardianship order.

(5) An order under this section shall not be made in respect of a child or young person—

(*a*) in pursuance of paragraph (*a*) of subsection (3) of this section unless the parent or guardian in question consents ;

(*b*) in pursuance of paragraph (*d*) or (*e*) of that subsection unless the conditions which, under section 60 of the said Act of 1959, are required to be satisfied for the making of a hospital or guardianship order in respect of a person convicted as mentioned in that section are satisfied in his case so far as they are applicable ;

(*c*) if he has attained the age of sixteen and is or has been married.

(6) In this section "authorised person" means a person authorised by order of the Secretary of State to bring proceedings in pursuance of this section and any officer of a society which is so authorised, and in sections 2 and 3 of this Act "care proceedings" means proceedings in pursuance of this section and "relevant infant" means the child or young person in respect of whom such proceedings are brought or proposed to be brought.

2.—(1) If a local authority receive information suggesting that there are grounds for bringing care proceedings in respect of a child or young person who resides or is found in their area, it shall be the duty of the authority to cause enquiries to be made into the case unless they are satisfied that such enquiries are unnecessary.

(2) If it appears to a local authority that there are grounds for bringing care proceedings in respect of a child or young person who resides or is found in their area, it shall be the duty of the authority to exercise their power under the preceding section to bring care proceedings in respect of him unless they are satisfied that it is neither in his interest nor the public interest to do so or that some other person is about to do so or to charge him with an offence.

(3) No care proceedings shall be begun by any person unless that person has given notice of the proceedings to the local authority for the area in which it appears to him that the relevant infant resides or, if it appears to him that the relevant infant does not reside in the area of a local authority, to the local authority for any area in which it appears to him that any circumstances giving rise to the proceedings arose ; but the preceding provisions of this subsection shall not apply where the person by whom the notice would fall to be given is the local authority in question.

(4) Without prejudice to any power to issue a summons or warrant apart from this subsection, a justice may issue a summons or warrant for the purpose of securing the attendance of the relevant infant before the court in which care proceedings are brought or proposed to be brought in respect of him ; but subsections (3) and (4) of section 47 of the Magistrates' Courts Act 1952 (which among other things restrict the circumstances in which a warrant may be issued) shall apply with the necessary modifications to a warrant under this subsection as they apply to a warrant under that section and as if in subsection (3) after the word "summons" there were inserted the words "cannot be served or".

(5) Where the relevant infant is arrested in pursuance of a warrant issued by virtue of the preceding subsection and cannot be brought immediately before the court aforesaid, the person in whose custody he is—

(a) may make arrangements for his detention in a place of safety for a period of not more than seventy-two hours from the time of the arrest (and it shall be lawful for him to be detained in pursuance of the arrangements) ; and

(b) shall within that period, unless within it the relevant infant is brought before the court aforesaid, bring him before a justice ;

and the justice shall either make an interim order in respect of him or direct that he be released forthwith.

1952 c. 55.

(6) Section 77 of the Magistrates' Courts Act 1952 (under which a summons or warrant may be issued to secure the attendance of a witness) shall apply to care proceedings as it applies to the hearing of a complaint.

(7) In determining whether the condition set out in subsection (2)(b) of the preceding section is satisfied in respect of the relevant infant, it shall be assumed that no order under that section is to be made in respect of him.

(8) In relation to the condition set out in subsection (2)(e) of the preceding section the references to a local authority in that section and subsections (1), (2) and (11) (b) of this section shall be construed as references to a local education authority ; and in any care proceedings—

(a) the court shall not entertain an allegation that that condition is satisfied unless the proceedings are brought by a local education authority ; and

(b) the said condition shall be deemed to be satisfied if the relevant infant is of the age mentioned in that condition and it is proved that he—

1944 c. 31.

(i) is the subject of a school attendance order which is in force under section 37 of the Education Act 1944 and has not been complied with, or

(ii) is a registered pupil at a school which he is not attending regularly within the meaning of section 39 of that Act , or

(iii) is a person whom another person habitually wandering from place to place takes with him,

unless it is also proved that he is receiving the education mentioned in that condition ;

but nothing in paragraph (*a*) of this subsection shall prevent any evidence from being considered in care proceedings for any purpose other than that of determining whether that condition is satisfied in respect of the relevant infant.

(9) If on application under this subsection to the court in which it is proposed to bring care proceedings in respect of a relevant infant who is not present before the court it appears to the court that he is under the age of five and either—

   (*a*) it is proved to the satisfaction of the court, on oath or in such other manner as may be prescribed by rules under section 15 of the Justices of the Peace Act 1949, that notice of the proposal to bring the proceedings at the time and place at which the application is made was served on the parent or guardian of the relevant infant at what appears to the court to be a reasonable time before the making of the application ; or

1949 c. 101.

   (*b*) it appears to the court that his parent or guardian is present before the court

the court may if it thinks fit, after giving the parent or guardian if he is present an opportunity to be heard, give a direction under this subsection in respect of the relevant infant ; and a relevant infant in respect of whom such a direction is given by a court shall be deemed to have been brought before the court under section 1 of this Act at the time of the direction, and care proceedings in respect of him may be continued accordingly.

(10) If the court before which the relevant infant is brought in care proceedings is not in a position to decide what order, if any, ought to be made under the preceding section in respect of him, the court may make an interim order in respect of him.

(11) If it appears to the court before which the relevant infant is brought in care proceedings that he resides in a petty sessions area other than that for which the court acts, the court shall, unless it dismisses the case and subject to subsection (5) of the following section, direct that he be brought under the preceding section before a juvenile court acting for the petty sessions area in which he resides ; and where the court so directs—

   (*a*) it may make an interim order in respect of him and, if it does so, shall cause the clerk of the court to which the direction relates to be informed of the case ;

   (*b*) if the court does not make such an order it shall cause the local authority in whose area it appears to the court that the relevant infant resides to be informed of the case, and it shall be the duty of that authority to give effect to the direction within twenty-one days.

Part I

(12) The relevant infant may appeal to quarter sessions against any order made in respect of him under the preceding section except such an order as is mentioned in subsection (3)(*a*) of that section.

(13) Such an order as is mentioned in subsection (3)(*a*) of the preceding section shall not require the parent or guardian in question to enter into a recognisance for an amount exceeding fifty pounds or for a period exceeding three years or, where the relevant infant will attain the age of eighteen in a period shorter than three years, for a period exceeding that shorter period ; and section 96 of the Magistrates' Courts Act 1952 (which relates to the forfeiture of recognisances) shall apply to a recognisance entered into in pursuance of such an order as it applies to a recognisance to keep the peace.

1952 c. 55.

(14) For the purposes of this Act, care proceedings in respect of a relevant infant are begun when he is first brought before a juvenile court in pursuance of the preceding section in connection with the matter to which the proceedings relate.

Further supplementary provisions relating to s. 1(2)(*f*).

3.—(1) In any care proceedings, no account shall be taken for the purposes of the condition set out in paragraph (*f*) of subsection (2) of section 1 of this Act (hereafter in this section referred to as " the offence condition ") of an offence alleged to have been committed by the relevant infant if—

(*a*) in any previous care proceedings in respect of him it was alleged that the offence condition was satisfied in consequence of the offence ; or

(*b*) the offence is a summary offence within the meaning of the Magistrates' Courts Act 1952 and, disregarding section 4 of this Act, the period for beginning summary proceedings in respect of it expired before the care proceedings were begun ; or

(*c*) disregarding section 4 of this Act, he would if charged with the offence be entitled to be discharged under any rule of law relating to previous acquittal or conviction.

(2) In any care proceedings the court shall not entertain an allegation that the offence condition is satisfied in respect of the relevant infant unless the proceedings are brought by a local authority or a constable ; but nothing in this or the preceding subsection shall prevent any evidence from being considered in care proceedings for any purpose other than that of determining whether the offence condition is satisfied in respect of the relevant infant.

(3) If in any care proceedings the relevant infant is alleged to have committed an offence in consequence of which the offence

condition is satisfied with respect to him, the court shall not find the offence condition satisfied in consequence of the offence unless, disregarding section 4 of this Act, it would have found him guilty of the offence if the proceedings had been in pursuance of an information duly charging him with the offence and the court had had jurisdiction to try the information; and without prejudice to the preceding provisions of this subsection the same proof shall be required to substantiate or refute an allegation that the offence condition is satisfied in consequence of an offence as is required to warrant a finding of guilty, or as the case may be, of not guilty of the offence.

(4) A person shall not be charged with an offence if in care proceedings previously brought in respect of him it was alleged that the offence condition was satisfied in consequence of that offence.

(5) If in any care proceedings in which it is alleged that the offence condition is satisfied in respect of the relevant infant it appears to the court that the case falls to be remitted to another court in pursuance of subsection (11) of the preceding section but that it is appropriate to determine whether the condition is satisfied before remitting the case, the court may determine accordingly; and any determination under this subsection shall be binding on the court to which the case is remitted.

(6) Where in any care proceedings the court finds the offence condition satisfied with respect to the relevant infant in consequence of an indictable offence within the meaning of the Magistrates' Courts Act 1952 then, whether or not the court 1952 c. 55. makes an order under section 1 of this Act—

(a) section 34 of that Act (which relates to compensation for loss of property or damage to it) shall apply as if the finding were a finding of guilty of the offence and as if the maximum amount of an award under that section were one hundred pounds; and

(b) the court shall if the relevant infant is a child, and may if he is not, order any sum awarded by virtue of this subsection to be paid by his parent or guardian instead of by him unless it is satisfied that the parent or guardian cannot be found or has not conduced to the commission of the offence by neglecting to exercise due care or control of him, so however that an order shall not be made in pursuance of this paragraph unless the parent or guardian has been given an opportunity of being heard or has been required to attend the proceedings and failed to do so; and

(c) any sum payable by a parent or guardian by virtue of the preceding paragraph may be recovered from him in like manner as if he had been convicted of the offence in question ;

but where the finding in question is made in pursuance of the preceding subsection, the powers conferred by this subsection shall be exercisable by the court to which the case is remitted instead of by the court which made the finding.

For the purposes of this subsection an offence under section 14(1) of the Criminal Justice Administration Act 1914 (which provides for damage committed wilfully or maliciously to be punishable on summary conviction) shall be treated as an indictable offence within the meaning of the said Act of 1952.

(7) Where in any care proceedings the court finds the offence condition satisfied with respect to the relevant infant and he is a young person, the court may if it thinks fit and he consents, instead of making such an order as is mentioned in section 1(3) of this Act, order him to enter into a recognisance for an amount not exceeding twenty-five pounds and for a period not exceeding one year to keep the peace or to be of good behaviour ; and such an order shall be deemed to be an order under section 1 of this Act but no appeal to quarter sessions may be brought against an order under this subsection.

(8) Where in any care proceedings the court finds the offence condition satisfied with respect to the relevant infant in consequence of an offence which was not admitted by him before the court, then—

(a) if the finding is made in pursuance of subsection (5) of this section and the court to which the case is remitted decides not to make any order under section 1 of this Act in respect of the relevant infant ; or

(b) if the finding is not made in pursuance of that subsection and the court decides as aforesaid,

the relevant infant may appeal to quarter sessions against the finding, and in a case falling within paragraph (a) of this subsection any notice of appeal shall be given within fourteen days after the date of the decision mentioned in that paragraph ; and a person ordered to pay compensation by virtue of subsection (6) of this section may appeal to quarter sessions against the order.

(9) An appeal in pursuance of the preceding subsection or subsection (12) of the preceding section against an order made by a court in consequence of a finding made by another court by virtue of subsection (5) of this section shall lie to the same

quarter sessions as would have had jurisdiction to entertain PART I
an appeal under subsection (8) of this section against the finding
if the court had decided not to make any order.

Consequential changes in criminal proceedings etc.

4. A person shall not be charged with an offence, except Prohibition of
homicide, by reason of anything done or omitted while he was a criminal proceedings for offences
child. by children.

5.—(1) A person other than a qualified informant shall not Restrictions
lay an information in respect of an offence if the alleged offender on criminal
is a young person. proceedings for offences

(2) A qualified informant shall not lay an information in by young
respect of an offence if the alleged offender is a young person persons.
unless the informant is of opinion that the case is of a description prescribed in pursuance of subsection (4) of this section
and that it would not be adequate for the case to be dealt with
by a parent, teacher or other person or by means of a caution
from a constable or through an exercise of the powers of a
local authority or other body not involving court proceedings
or by means of proceedings under section 1 of this Act.

(3) A qualified informant shall not come to a decision in
pursuance of the preceding subsection to lay an information
unless—

(*a*) he has told the appropriate local authority that the
laying of the information is being considered and has
asked for any observations which the authority may
wish to make on the case to the informant ; and

(*b*) the authority either have notified the informant that they
do not wish to make such observations or have not
made any during the period or extended period indi-
cated by the informant as that which in the circumstances he considers reasonable for the purpose or the
informant has considered the observations made by the
authority during that period ;

but the informant shall be entitled to disregard the foregoing
provisions of this subsection in any case in which it appears to
him that the requirements of the preceding subsection are satisfied and will continue to be satisfied notwithstanding any observations which might be made in pursuance of this subsection.

(4) The Secretary of State may make regulations specifying,
by reference to such considerations as he thinks fit, the descriptions of cases in which a qualified informant may lay an information in respect of an offence if the alleged offender is a young
person ; but no regulations shall be made under this subsection
unless a draft of the regulations has been approved by a resolution of each House of Parliament.

(5) An information laid by a qualified informant in a case where the informant has reason to believe that the alleged offender is a young person shall be in writing and shall—

   (a) state the alleged offender's age to the best of the informant's knowledge ; and

   (b) contain a certificate signed by the informant stating that the requirements of subsections (2) and (3) of this section are satisfied with respect to the case or that the case is one in which the requirements of the said subsection (2) are satisfied and the informant is entitled to disregard the requirements of the said subsection (3).

(6) If at the time when justices begin to inquire into a case, either as examining justices or on the trial of an information, they have reason to believe that the alleged offender is a young person and either—

   (a) it appears to them that the person who laid the information in question was not a qualified informant when he laid it ; or

   (b) the information is not in writing or does not contain such a certificate as is mentioned in subsection (5)(b) of this section,

it shall be their duty to quash the information, without prejudice to the laying of a further information in respect of the matter in question ; but no proceedings shall be invalidated by reason of a contravention of any provision of this section and no action shall lie, by reason only of such a contravention, in respect of proceedings in respect of which such a contravention has occurred.

(7) Nothing in the preceding provisions of this section applies to an information laid with the consent of the Attorney General or laid by or on behalf or with the consent of the Director of Public Prosecutions.

(8) It shall be the duty of a person who decides to lay an information in respect of an offence in a case where he has reason to believe that the alleged offender is a young person to give notice of the decision to the appropriate local authority unless he is himself that authority.

(9) In this section—

   " the appropriate local authority ", in relation to a young person, means the local authority for the area in which it appears to the informant in question that the young person resides or, if the young person appears to the informant not to reside in the area of a local authority, the local authority in whose area it is alleged that the relevant offence or one of the relevant offences was committed ; and

" qualified informant " means a servant of the Crown, a police officer and a member of a designated police force acting in his capacity as such a servant, officer or member, a local authority, the Greater London Council, the council of a county district and any body designated as a public body for the purposes of this section ;

and in this subsection " designated " means designated by an order made by the Secretary of State ; but nothing in this section shall be construed as preventing any council or other body from acting by an agent for the purposes of this section.

6.—(1) Where a person under the age of seventeen appears Summary or is brought before a magistrates' court on an information trial of young charging him with an offence, other than homicide, which is an persons. indictable offence within the meaning of the Magistrates' Courts 1952 c. 55. Act 1952, he shall be tried summarily unless—

(*a*) he is a young person and the offence is such as is mentioned in subsection (2) of section 53 of the Act of 1933 (under which young persons convicted on indictment of certain grave crimes may be sentenced to be detained for long periods) and the court considers that if he is found guilty of the offence it ought to be possible to sentence him in pursuance of that subsection ; or

(*b*) he is charged jointly with a person who has attained the age of seventeen and the court considers it necessary in the interests of justice to commit them both for trial ;

and accordingly in a case falling within paragraph (*a*) or paragraph (*b*) of this subsection the court shall, if it is of opinion that there is sufficient evidence to put the accused on trial, commit him for trial.

(2) In sections 18(1) and 25(1) of the said Act of 1952 (which provide for the trial on indictment of persons aged fourteen or over who are charged with certain summary offences within the meaning of that Act) for the word " fourteen " there shall be substituted the word " seventeen ".

(3) If on trying a person summarily in pursuance of subsection (1) of this section the court finds him guilty, it may impose a fine of an amount not exceeding fifty pounds or may exercise the same powers as it could have exercised if he had been found guilty of an offence for which, but for section 107(2) of the said Act of 1952, it could have sentenced him to imprisonment for a term not exceeding three months.

PART I
Alterations in
treatment
of young
offenders etc.
1948 c. 58.
1952 c. 55.

7.—(1) The minimum age at conviction which qualifies for a sentence of borstal training under section 20 of the Criminal Justice Act 1948 shall be seventeen instead of fifteen years ; and accordingly in subsection (1) of that section and section 28(1) of the Magistrates' Courts Act 1952 for the word " fifteen " there shall be substituted the word " seventeen ".

(2) In section 3(1) of the said Act of 1948 (which authorises the court by or before which a person is convicted of an offence to make a probation order in respect of him) after the word " person " there shall be inserted the words " who has attained the age of seventeen ".

(3) If a court having power to order children or young persons of any class or description to be detained in a detention centre in pursuance of section 4 of the Criminal Justice Act 1961 or to attend at an attendance centre in pursuance of section 19 of the said Act of 1948 is notified in pursuance of this subsection by the Secretary of State that a detention centre or, as the case may be, an attendance centre will not be available for the reception from that court of children or young persons of that class or description after a date specified in the notification, the power in question shall not be exercisable by that court after that date ; and the Secretary of State shall cause a copy of any notification under this subsection to be published in the London Gazette before the date specified in the notification.

(4) Section 5 of the said Act of 1961 (which provides for detention for defaults) shall cease to apply to young persons.

(5) An order sending a person to an approved school shall not be made after such day as the Secretary of State may by order specify for the purposes of this subsection.

(6) Sections 54 and 57 of the Act of 1933 (which among other things enable a child or young person found guilty of an offence to be sent to a remand home or committed to the care of a fit person) shall cease to have effect.

(7) Subject to the enactments requiring cases to be remitted to juvenile courts and to section 53(1) of the Act of 1933 (which provides for detention for certain grave crimes), where a child is found guilty of homicide or a young person is found guilty of any offence by or before any court, that court or the court to which his case is remitted shall have power—

    (*a*) if the offence is punishable in the case of an adult with imprisonment, to make a care order (other than an interim order) in respect of him ; or

    (*b*) to make a supervision order in respect of him ; or

(c) with the consent of his parent or guardian, to order the parent or guardian to enter into a recognisance to take proper care of him and exercise proper control over him,

and, if it makes such an order as is mentioned in this subsection while another such order made by any court is in force in respect of the child or young person, shall also have power to discharge the earlier order; and subsection (13) of section 2 of this Act shall apply to an order under paragraph (c) of this subsection as it applies to such an order as is mentioned in that subsection.

(8) Without prejudice to the power to remit any case to a juvenile court which is conferred on a magistrates' court other than a juvenile court by section 56(1) of the Act of 1933, in a case where such a magistrates' court finds a person guilty of an offence and either he is a young person or was a young person when the proceedings in question were begun it shall be the duty of the court to exercise that power unless the court decides to deal with the case by exercising a power to make one or more of the following orders, that is to say, an order discharging him absolutely or conditionally, an order for the payment of a fine, damages or costs, an order requiring his parent or guardian to enter into a recognisance to take proper care of him and exercise proper control over him or an order under section 5 or 7 of the Road Traffic Act 1962 (which relate respectively to the dis- 1962 c. 59. qualification of drivers and the endorsement of licences).

8.—(1) If a police officer not below the rank of inspector Finger- makes an application on oath to a justice stating— printing of

(a) that there is evidence sufficient to justify the laying of an suspected information that a young person has or is suspected of young having committed an offence punishable with imprison- persons. ment in the case of an adult; and

(b) that with a view to deciding, in accordance with section 5 of this Act, whether the information should be laid it is appropriate in the opinion of the officer for an order under subsection (2) of this section to be made in respect of the young person,

the justice may if he thinks fit issue a summons or warrant for the purpose of securing the attendance of the young person before a magistrates' court with a view to the making of such an order in respect of him.

(2) The court before which a young person appears in pursuance of a summons or warrant under the preceding subsection may if it thinks fit order his finger and palm prints to be taken by a constable.

(3) Subsections (2) and (4) of section 40 of the Magistrates' Courts Act 1952 (which respectively relate to the taking and destruction of finger and palm prints) shall have effect as if references to an order under that section included references to an order under the preceding subsection and, in relation to an order under the preceding subsection, as if for the words from " remanded " to " committed " in subsection (2) there were substituted the words " lawfully detained at any place, at that place " and as if the reference to acquittal in subsection (4) included a reference to a finding of a court that the condition set out in section 1(2)(*f*) of this Act is not satisfied in consequence of the offence specified in the application mentioned in subsection (1) of this section.

Investigations by local authorities.

9.—(1) Where a local authority or a local education authority bring proceedings under section 1 of this Act or proceedings for an offence alleged to have been committed by a young person or are notified that any such proceedings are being brought, it shall be the duty of the authority, unless they are of opinion that it is unnecessary to do so, to make such investigations and provide the court before which the proceedings are heard with such information relating to the home surroundings, school record, health and character of the person in respect of whom the proceedings are brought as appear to the authority likely to assist the court.

(2) If the court mentioned in subsection (1) of this section requests the authority aforesaid to make investigations and provide information or to make further investigations and provide further information relating to the matters aforesaid, it shall be the duty of the authority to comply with the request.

Further limitations on publication of particulars of children and young persons etc.

10.—(1) In subsection (1) of section 49 of the Act of 1933 (which among other things imposes restrictions on reports of certain court proceedings concerning children or young persons but authorises the court or the Secretary of State, if satisfied that it is in the interests of justice to do so, to dispense with the requirements of that section)—

(*a*) the references to a young person concerned in the proceedings as the person in respect of whom they are taken shall be construed as including references to any person who has attained the age of seventeen but not eighteen and against or in respect of whom the proceedings are taken and, in the case of proceedings under Part I of this Act, any other person in respect of whom those proceedings are taken ; and

(*b*) the references to a juvenile court shall, in relation to proceedings in pursuance of the provisions of sections 15 and 16 of this Act or on appeal from such proceedings, be construed as including a reference to any other magistrates' court or, as the case may be, the court in which the appeal is brought; and

(c) for the words " in the interests of justice so to do " there shall be substituted the words " appropriate to do so for the purpose of avoiding injustice to a child or young person " and after the word " section " there shall be inserted the words " in relation to him ".

(2) Where by virtue of paragraph (b) of the preceding subsection the said section 49 applies to any proceedings, it shall be the duty of the court in which the proceedings are taken to announce in the course of the proceedings that that section applies to them; and if the court fails to do so that section shall not apply to the proceedings in question.

(3) A notice displayed in pursuance of section 4 of the Criminal Justice Act 1967 (which requires the publication of 1967 c. 80. a notice stating the result of proceedings before examining justices and containing particulars of the person to whom the proceedings related) shall not contain the name or address of any child or young person unless the justices in question have stated that in their opinion he would be mentioned in the notice apart from the foregoing provisions of this subsection and should be mentioned in it for the purpose of avoiding injustice to him.

Supervision

11. Any provision of this Act authorising a court to make a Supervision supervision order in respect of any person shall be construed as orders. authorising the court to make an order placing him under the supervision of a local authority designated by the order or of a probation officer; and in this Act " supervision order " shall be construed accordingly and " supervised person " and " supervisor ", in relation to a supervision order, mean respectively the person placed or to be placed under supervision by the order and the person under whose supervision he is placed or to be placed by the order.

12.—(1) A supervision order may require the supervised Power to person to reside with an individual named in the order who include agrees to the requirement, but a requirement imposed by a requirements in supervision order in pursuance of this subsection shall be subject supervision to any such requirement of the order as is authorised by the orders. following provisions of this section.

(2) Subject to section 19(6) of this Act, a supervision order may require the supervised person to comply with such directions of the supervisor as are mentioned in paragraph (a) or (b) or paragraphs (a) and (b) of this subsection, that is to say—

(a) directions requiring the supervised person to live for a single period specified in the directions at a place so specified;

(*b*) directions given from time to time requiring him to do all or any of the following things—

(i) to live at a place or places specified in the directions for a period or periods so specified,

(ii) to present himself to a person or persons specified in the directions at a place or places and on a day or days so specified,

(iii) to participate in activities specified in the directions on a day or days so specified ;

but it shall be for the supervisor to decide whether and to what extent he exercises any power to give directions conferred on him by virtue of the preceding provisions of this subsection and to decide the form of any directions ; and a requirement imposed by a supervision order in pursuance of this subsection shall be subject to any such requirement of the order as is authorised by subsection (4) of this section.

(3) The periods specified in directions given by virtue of subsection (2) of this section in pursuance of a supervision order shall be in accordance with the following provisions, that is to say—

(*a*) the aggregate of the periods specified in directions given by virtue of paragraph (*a*) and paragraph (*b*) of that subsection shall not exceed ninety days ;

(*b*) the period specified in directions given by virtue of the said paragraph (*a*) shall not exceed ninety days and subject to paragraph (*e*) below shall not begin after the expiration of one year beginning with the date of the order or, if the directions are authorised solely by a variation of the order, with the date of the variation ;

(*c*) the aggregate of the periods specified in directions given by virtue of the said paragraph (*b*) shall not exceed thirty days in the year beginning with the date aforesaid and thirty days in any year beginning with an anniversary of that date ;

(*d*) if the order provides that any of the preceding paragraphs of this subsection is to have effect in relation to the order as if for a reference to ninety days or thirty days there were substituted a reference to a shorter period specified in the order, the paragraph in question shall have effect accordingly ;

(*e*) for the purpose of calculating the period or periods in respect of which directions may be given in pursuance of the order—

(i) the supervisor shall be entitled to disregard any day in respect of which directions were previously given in pursuance of the order and on which the directions were not complied with ;

(ii) a direction given in respect of one or more parts of a day shall be treated as given in respect of the whole of the day,

and if during the year mentioned in paragraph (*b*) of this subsection the supervised person is given such directions as are there mentioned specifying a period beginning in that year but does not begin to comply with the directions during that year, the supervisor shall be entitled to disregard so much of that paragraph as prevents that period from beginning after the expiration of that year.

(4) Where a court which proposes to make a supervision order is satisfied, on the evidence of a medical practitioner approved for the purposes of section 28 of the Mental Health Act 1959, 1959 c. 72. that the mental condition of a supervised person is such as requires and may be susceptible to treatment but is not such as to warrant his detention in pursuance of a hospital order under Part V of that Act, the court may include in the supervision order a requirement that the supervised person shall, for a period specified in the order, submit to treatment of one of the following descriptions so specified, that is to say—

(*a*) treatment by or under the direction of a fully registered medical practitioner specified in the order ;

(*b*) treatment as a non-resident patient at a place specified in the order ; or

(*c*) treatment as a resident patient in a hospital or mental nursing home within the meaning of the said Act of 1959, but not a special hospital within the meaning of that Act.

(5) A requirement shall not be included in a supervision order in pursuance of the preceding subsection—

(*a*) in any case, unless the court is satisfied that arrangements have been or can be made for the treatment in question and, in the case of treatment as a resident patient, for the reception of the patient ;

(*b*) in the case of an order made or to be made in respect of a person who has attained the age of fourteen, unless he consents to its inclusion ;

and a requirement so included shall not in any case continue in force after the supervised person becomes eighteen.

13.—(1) A court shall not designate a local authority as the supervisor by a provision of a supervision order unless the authority agree or it appears to the court that the supervised person resides or will reside in the area of the authority.

Selection of supervisor.

(2) A court shall not insert in a supervision order a provision placing a child under the supervision of a probation officer unless the local authority of which the area is named or to be named in the order in pursuance of section 18(2)(*a*) of this Act so request and a probation officer is already exercising or has exercised, in relation to another member of the household to which the child belongs, duties imposed by paragraph 3(5) of Schedule 5 to the Criminal Justice Act 1948 or by rules under paragraph 6(*b*) of that Schedule.

1948 c. 58.

(3) Where a provision of a supervision order places a person under the supervision of a probation officer, the supervisor shall be a probation officer appointed for or assigned to the petty sessions area named in the order in pursuance of section 18(2)(*a*) of this Act and selected under arrangements made by the probation and after-care committee ; but if the probation officer selected as aforesaid dies or is unable to carry out his duties or if the case committee dealing with the case think it desirable that another officer should take his place, another probation officer shall be selected as aforesaid for the purposes of the order.

Duty of supervisor.

14. While a supervision order is in force it shall be the duty of the supervisor to advise, assist and befriend the supervised person.

Variation and discharge of supervision orders.

15.—(1) If while a supervision order is in force in respect of a supervised person who has not attained the age of eighteen it appears to a juvenile court, on the application of the supervisor or the supervised person, that it is appropriate to make an order under this subsection, the court may make an order discharging the supervision order or varying it by—

(*a*) cancelling any requirement included in it in pursuance of section 12 or section 18(2)(*b*) of this Act ; or

(*b*) inserting in it (either in addition to or in substitution for any of its provisions) any provision which could have been included in the order if the court had then had power to make it and were exercising the power,

and may on discharging the supervision order make a care order (other than an interim order) in respect of the supervised person ; but the powers of variation conferred by this subsection do not include power to insert in the supervision order, after the expiration of twelve months beginning with the date when the order was originally made, a requirement in pursuance of section 12(2)(*a*) of this Act or, after the expiration of three months beginning with that date, a requirement in pursuance of section 12(4) of this Act, unless in either case it is in substitution for such a requirement already included in the order.

(2) If on an application in pursuance of the preceding sub-section, in a case where the supervised person has attained the age of seventeen and the supervision order was not made by virtue of section 1 of this Act or on the occasion of the discharge of a care order, it appears to the court appropriate to do so it may proceed as if the application were in pursuance of sub-section (3) or, if it is made by the supervisor, in pursuance of subsections (3) and (4) of this section and as if in that subsection or those subsections, as the case may be, the word " seventeen " were substituted for the word " eighteen " and the words " a magistrates' court other than " were omitted.

(3) If while a supervision order is in force in respect of a supervised person who has attained the age of eighteen it appears to a magistrates' court other than a juvenile court, on the application of the supervisor or the supervised person, that it is appropriate to make an order under this subsection, the court may make an order discharging the supervision order or varying it by—

(a) inserting in it a provision specifying the duration of the order or altering or cancelling such a provision already included in it ; or

(b) substituting for the provisions of the order by which the supervisor is designated or by virtue of which he is selected such other provisions in that behalf as could have been included in the order if the court had then had power to make it and were exercising the power ; or

(c) substituting for the name of an area included in the order in pursuance of section 18(2)(a) of this Act the name of any other area of a local authority or petty sessions area, as the case may be, in which it appears to the court that the supervised person resides or will reside ; or

(d) cancelling any provision included in the order by virtue of section 18(2)(b) of this Act or inserting in it any provision prescribed for the purposes of that paragraph ; or

(e) cancelling any requirement included in the order in pursuance of section 12(1) or (2) of this Act.

(4) If while a supervision order is in force in respect of a supervised person who has attained the age of eighteen it is proved to the satisfaction of a magistrates' court other than a juvenile court, on the application of the supervisor, that the supervised person has failed to comply with any requirement

Part I included in the supervision order in pursuance of section 12 or section 18(2)(*b*) of this Act, the court may—

(*a*) whether or not it also makes an order under subsection (3) of this section, order him to pay a fine of an amount not exceeding twenty pounds or, subject to subsection (10) of the following section, make an attendance centre order in respect of him;

(*b*) if it also discharges the supervision order, make an order imposing on him any punishment which it could have imposed on him if it had then had power to try him for the offence in consequence of which the supervision order was made and had convicted him in the exercise of that power;

and in a case where the offence in question is of a kind which the court has no power to try or has no power to try without appropriate consents, the punishment imposed by virtue of paragraph (*b*) of this subsection shall not exceed that which any court having power to try such an offence could have imposed in respect of it and shall not in any event exceed imprisonment for a term of six months and a fine of four hundred pounds.

(5) If a medical practitioner by whom or under whose direction a supervised person is being treated for his mental condition in pursuance of a requirement included in a supervision order by virtue of section 12(4) of this Act is unwilling to continue to treat or direct the treatment of the supervised person or is of opinion—

(*a*) that the treatment should be continued beyond the period specified in that behalf in the order; or

(*b*) that the supervised person needs different treatment; or

(*c*) that he is not susceptible to treatment; or

(*d*) that he does not require further treatment,

the practitioner shall make a report in writing to that effect to the supervisor; and on receiving a report under this subsection the supervisor shall refer it to a juvenile court, and on such a reference the court may make an order cancelling or varying the requirement.

(6) The preceding provisions of this section shall have effect subject to the provisions of the following section.

Provisions supplementary to s. 15.

16.—(1) Where the supervisor makes an application or reference under the preceding section to a court he may bring the supervised person before the court, and subject to subsection (5) of this section a court shall not make an order under that section unless the supervised person is present before the court.

(2) Without prejudice to any power to issue a summons or warrant apart from this subsection, a justice may issue a summons or warrant for the purpose of securing the attendance of a supervised person before the court to which any application or reference in respect of him is made under the preceding section ; but subsections (3) and (4) of section 47 of the Magis- trates' Courts Act 1952 (which among other things restrict the circumstances in which a warrant may be issued) shall apply with the necessary modifications to a warrant under this sub-section as they apply to a warrant under that section and as if in subsection (3) after the word " summons " there were inserted the words " cannot be served or " .

(3) Where the supervised person is arrested in pursuance of a warrant issued by virtue of the preceding subsection and cannot be brought immediately before the court referred to in that subsection, the person in whose custody he is—

> (a) may make arrangements for his detention in a place of safety for a period of not more than seventy-two hours from the time of the arrest (and it shall be lawful for him to be detained in pursuance of the arrangements) ; and

> (b) shall within that period, unless within it the relevant infant is brought before the court aforesaid, bring him before a justice ;

and the justice shall either direct that he be released forthwith or—

> (i) if he has not attained the age of eighteen, make an interim order in respect of him ;

> (ii) if he has attained that age, remand him.

(4) If on an application to a court under subsection (1) of the preceding section—

> (a) the supervised person is brought before the court under a warrant issued or an interim order made by virtue of the preceding provisions of this section ; or

> (b) the court considers that it is likely to exercise its powers under that subsection to make an order in respect of the supervised person but, before deciding whether to do so, seeks information with respect to him which it considers is unlikely to be obtained unless the court makes an interim order in respect of him,

the court may make an interim order in respect of the supervised person.

(5) A court may make an order under the preceding section in the absence of the supervised person if the effect of the order is confined to one or more of the following, that is to say—

> (a) discharging the supervision order ;

(*b*) cancelling a provision included in the supervision order in pursuance of section 12 or section 18(2)(*b*) of this Act ;

(*c*) reducing the duration of the supervision order or any provision included in it in pursuance of the said section 12 ;

(*d*) altering in the supervision order the name of any area ;

(*e*) changing the supervisor.

(6) A juvenile court shall not—

(*a*) exercise its powers under subsection (1) of the preceding section to make a care order or an order discharging a supervision order or inserting in it a requirement authorised by section 12 of this Act or varying or cancelling such a requirement except in a case where the court is satisfied that the supervised person either is unlikely to receive the care or control he needs unless the court makes the order or is likely to receive it notwithstanding the order ;

(*b*) exercise its powers to make an order under subsection (5) of the preceding section except in such a case as is mentioned in paragraph (*a*) of this subsection ;

(*c*) exercise its powers under the said subsection (1) to make an order inserting a requirement authorised by section 12(4) of this Act in a supervision order which does not already contain such a requirement unless the court is satisfied as mentioned in the said section 12(4) on such evidence as is there mentioned.

(7) Where the supervised person has attained the age of fourteen, then except with his consent a court shall not make an order under the preceding section containing provisions which insert in the supervision order a requirement authorised by section 12(4) of this Act or which alter such a requirement already included in the supervision order otherwise than by removing it or reducing its duration.

(8) The supervised person may appeal to quarter sessions against—

(*a*) any order made under the preceding section, except an order made or which could have been made in the absence of the supervised person and an order containing only provisions to which he consented in pursuance of the preceding subsection ;

(*b*) the dismissal of an application under that section to discharge a supervision order.

(9) Where an application under the preceding section for the discharge of a supervision order is dismissed, no further application for its discharge shall be made under that section by any

person during the period of three months beginning with the date of the dismissal except with the consent of a court having jurisdiction to entertain such an application.

(10) In paragraph (*a*) of subsection (4) of the preceding section " attendance centre order " means such an order to attend an attendance centre as is mentioned in subsection (1) of section 19 of the Criminal Justice Act 1948 ; and the provisions of that 1948 c. 58. section shall accordingly apply for the purposes of that paragraph as if for the words from " has power " to " probation order " in subsection (1) there were substituted the words " considers it appropriate to make an attendance centre order in respect of any person in pursuance of section 15(4) of the Children and Young Persons Act 1969 " and for references to an offender there were substituted references to the supervised person and as if subsection (5) were omitted.

(11) In this and the preceding section references to a juvenile court or any other magistrates' court, in relation to a supervision order, are references to such a court acting for the petty sessions area for the time being named in the order in pursuance of section 18(2)(*a*) of this Act ; and if while an application to a juvenile court in pursuance of the preceding section is pending the supervised person to whom it relates attains the age of seventeen or eighteen, the court shall deal with the application as if he had not attained the age in question.

17. A supervision order shall, unless it has previously been Termination of discharged, cease to have effect— supervision.

    (*a*) in any case, on the expiration of the period of three years, or such shorter period as may be specified in the order, beginning with the date on which the order was originally made ;

    (*b*) if the order was made by virtue of section 1 of this Act or on the occasion of the discharge of a care order and the supervised person attains the age of eighteen on a day earlier than that on which the order would expire under paragraph (*a*) above, on that earlier day.

18.—(1) A court shall not make a supervision order unless Supplementary it is satisfied that the supervised person resides or will reside provisions in the area of a local authority ; and a court shall be entitled relating to to be satisfied that the supervised person will so reside if he supervision is to be required so to reside by a provision to be included in orders. the order in pursuance of section 12(1) of this Act.

(2) A supervision order—

    (*a*) shall name the area of the local authority and the petty sessions area in which it appears to the court making the order, or to the court varying any provision included in the order in pursuance of this paragraph, that the supervised person resides or will reside ; and

(b) may contain such prescribed provisions as the court aforesaid considers appropriate for facilitating the performance by the supervisor of his functions under section 14 of this Act, including any prescribed provisions for requiring visits to be made by the supervised person to the supervisor,

and in paragraph (b) of this subsection " prescribed " means prescribed by rules under section 15 of the Justices of the Peace Act 1949.

(3) A court which makes a supervision order or an order varying or discharging a supervision order shall forthwith send a copy of its order—

(a) to the supervised person and, if the supervised person is a child, to his parent or guardian ; and

(b) to the supervisor and any person who has ceased to be the supervisor by virtue of the order ; and

(c) to any local authority who is not entitled by virtue of the preceding paragraph to such a copy and whose area is named in the supervision order in pursuance of the preceding subsection or has ceased to be so named by virtue of the court's order ; and

(d) where the supervised person is required by the order, or was required by the supervision order before it was varied or discharged, to reside with an individual or to undergo treatment by or under the direction of an individual or at any place, to the individual or the person in charge of that place ; and

(e) where a petty sessions area named in the order or discharged order in pursuance of subsection (2) of this section is not that for which the court acts, to the clerk to the justices for the petty sessions area so named ;

and, in a case falling within paragraph (e) of this subsection, shall also send to the clerk to the justices in question such documents and information relating to the case as the court considers likely to be of assistance to them.

(4) Where a supervision order requires compliance with such directions as are mentioned in section 12(2) of this Act, any expenditure incurred by the supervisor for the purposes of the directions shall be defrayed by the local authority of which the area is named in the order in pursuance of subsection (2) of this section.

19.—(1) It shall be the duty of the children's regional planning committee for each planning area (hereafter in this section
referred to as " the committee ") to make arrangements, with
such persons as the committee thinks fit, for the provision by
those persons of facilities for enabling directions given by
virtue of section 12(2) of this Act to persons resident in the area
to be carried out effectively.

(2) The committee shall specify the arrangements made in
pursuance of the preceding subsection in a scheme and shall
submit the scheme to the Secretary of State for him to determine
the date on which it is to come into force ; and the Secretary
of State shall, after consultation with the committee and the
relevant authorities, determine that date and notify his determination to the committee.

(3) On receiving a notification in pursuance of subsection (2)
of this section in respect of a scheme, the committee shall send
copies of the scheme and notification to each of the relevant
authorities and to the clerk to the justices for each petty sessions
area of which any part is included in the planning area in
question ; and each of the relevant authorities shall, as soon
as practicable after receiving those documents, keep a copy
of them available at their principal offices for inspection by
members of the public at all reasonable hours and on demand
by any person furnish him with a copy of them free of charge.

(4) If, after the scheme prepared by the committee under
this section has come into force, any arrangements specified in
it are cancelled or the committee makes arrangements for the
purposes of this section other than arrangements so specified,
the committee shall send notice of the cancellations or other
arrangements, stating the date on which they are to come into
force and the alterations in the scheme which they entail,
to the Secretary of State and the authorities and clerks mentioned in subsection (3) of this section ; and on and after that
date the scheme shall have effect subject to those alterations
and the relevant authorities shall have, in relation to the notice,
the same duty as is imposed on them by that subsection in
relation to the scheme.

(5) Arrangements in pursuance of this section shall not be
made for any facilities unless the facilities are approved or
are of a kind approved by the Secretary of State for the purposes of this section ; but where arrangements in pursuance
of this section are made by the committee with any of the
relevant authorities for the provision of facilities by the authority
it shall be the duty of the authority to provide those facilities
while the scheme is in force and those arrangements are specified
in it.

(6) A court shall not include in a supervision order any such requirements as are mentioned in section 12(2) of this Act unless the court is satisfied that a scheme under this section is in force for the planning area in which the supervised person resides or will reside or that the date on which such a scheme is to come into force has been determined ; and a supervisor authorised to give directions by virtue of any such requirements shall not, in pursuance of those requirements, give directions involving the use of facilities which are not for the time being specified in a scheme in force under this section for the planning area aforesaid.

Committal to care of local authorities

Orders for committal to care of local authorities.

20.—(1) Any provision of this Act authorising the making of a care order in respect of any person shall be construed as authorising the making of an order committing him to the care of a local authority ; and in this Act " care order " shall be construed accordingly and " interim order " means a care order containing provision for the order to expire with the expiration of twenty-eight days, or of a shorter period specified in the order, beginning—

(a) if the order is made by a court, with the date of the making of the order ; and

(b) if it is made by a justice, with the date when the person to whom it relates was first in legal custody in connection with the matter in consequence of which the order is made.

(2) The local authority to whose care a person is committed by a care order shall be—

(a) except in the case of an interim order, the local authority in whose area it appears to the court making the order that that person resides or, if it does not appear to the court that he resides in the area of a local authority, any local authority in whose area it appears to the court that any offence was committed or any circumstances arose in consequence of which the order is made ; and

(b) in the case of an interim order, such one of the local authorities mentioned in paragraph (a) of this subsection as the court or justice making the order thinks fit (whether or not the person in question appears to reside in their area).

(3) Subject to the provisions of the following section, a care order other than an interim order shall cease to have effect—

(a) if the person to whom it relates had attained the age of sixteen when the order was originally made, when he attains the age of nineteen ; and (*b*) in any other case, when that person attains the age of eighteen.

(4) A care order shall be sufficient authority for the detention by any local authority or constable of the person to whom the order relates until he is received into the care of the authority to whose care he is committed by the order.

21.—(1) If it appears to a juvenile court, on the application of a local authority to whose care a person is committed by a care order which would cease to have effect by virtue of subsection (3)(*b*) of the preceding section, that he is accommodated in a community home or a home provided by the Secretary of State and that by reason of his mental condition or behaviour it is in his interest or the public interest for him to continue to be so accommodated after he attains the age of eighteen, the court may order that the care order shall continue in force until he attains the age of nineteen; but the court shall not make an order under this subsection unless the person in question is present before the court.

(2) If it appears to a juvenile court, on the application of a local authority to whose care a person is committed by a care order or on the application of that person, that it is appropriate to discharge the order, the court may discharge it and on discharging it may, unless it was an interim order and unless the person to whom the discharged order related has attained the age of eighteen, make a supervision order in respect of him.

(3) Where an application under the preceding subsection for the discharge of a care order is dismissed, then—

(*a*) in the case of an interim order, no further application for its discharge shall be made under that subsection except with the consent of a juvenile court (without prejudice to the power to make an application under subsection (4) of the following section); and

(*b*) in any other case, no further application for its discharge shall be made under this subsection by any person during the period of three months beginning with the date of the dismissal except with the consent of a juvenile court.

(4) The person to whom the relevant care order relates or related may appeal to quarter sessions against an order under subsection (1) of this section or a supervision order made in pursuance of subsection (2) of this section or the dismissal of an application under the said subsection (2) for the discharge of the care order.

(5) The local authority to whose care a person is committed by a care order (other than an interim order) may, within the period of three months beginning with the date of the order,

PART I

appeal to quarter sessions against the provision of the order naming their area on the ground that at the time the order was made the person aforesaid resided in the area of another local authority named in the notice of appeal; but no appeal shall be brought by a local authority under this subsection unless they give notice in writing of the proposal to bring it to the other local authority in question before giving notice of appeal.

(6) References in this section to a juvenile court, in relation to a care order, are references to a juvenile court acting for any part of the area of the local authority to whose care a person is committed by the order or for the place where that person resides.

Special provisions relating to interim orders.

22.—(1) A juvenile court or a justice shall not make an interim order in respect of any person unless either—

(a) that person is present before the court or justice; or

(b) the court or justice is satisfied that he is under the age of five or cannot be present as aforesaid by reason of illness or accident.

(2) An interim order shall contain provision requiring the local authority to whose care a person is committed by the order to bring that person before a court specified in the order on the expiration of the order or at such earlier time as the specified court may require, so however that the said provision shall, if the court making the order considers it appropriate so to direct by reason of the fact that that person is under the age of five or by reason of illness or accident, require the local authority to bring him before the specified court on the expiration of the order only if the specified court so requires.

(3) A juvenile court acting for the same area as a juvenile court by which or a justice by whom an interim order has been made in respect of any person may, at any time before the expiration of the order, make a further interim order in respect of him; and the power to make an interim order conferred by this subsection is without prejudice to any other power to make such an order.

(4) The High Court may, on the application of a person to whom an interim order relates, discharge the order on such terms as the court thinks fit; but if on such an application the discharge of the order is refused, the local authority to whose care he is committed by the order shall not exercise in his case their powers under section 13(2) of the Children Act 1948 (which enables them to allow a parent or other person to be in charge of him) except with the consent and in accordance with any directions of the High Court.

1948 c. 43.

(5) If a court which has made or, apart from this subsection, would make an interim order in respect of a person who has attained the age of fourteen certifies that he is of so unruly a character that he cannot safely be committed to the care of a local authority and has been notified by the Secretary of State that a remand centre is available for the reception from the court of persons of his class or description, then, subject to the following provisions of this section, the court shall commit him to a remand centre for twenty-eight days or such shorter period as may be specified in the warrant; but in a case where an interim order is in force in respect of the person in question, a warrant under this subsection shall not be issued in respect of him except on the application of the local authority to whose care he is committed by the order and shall not be issued for a period extending beyond the date fixed for the expiration of the order, and on the issue of a warrant under this subsection in such a case the interim order shall cease to have effect.

In this subsection " court " includes a justice.

(6) Subsections (1), (3) and (4) of this section, so much of section 2(11)(*a*) as requires the clerk to be informed and section 21(2) to (4) of this Act shall apply to a warrant under subsection (5) of this section as they apply to an interim order but as if the words " is under the age of five or " in subsection (1) of this section were omitted.

23.—(1) Where a court—

    (*a*) remands or commits for trial a child charged with homicide or remands a child convicted of homicide ; or

    (*b*) remands a young person charged with or convicted of one or more offences or commits him for trial or sentence,

and he is not released on bail, then, subject to the following provisions of this section, the court shall commit him to the care of a local authority in whose area it appears to the court that he resides or that the offence or one of the offences was committed.

(2) If the court aforesaid certifies that a young person is of so unruly a character that he cannot safely be committed to the care of a local authority under the preceding subsection, then if the court has been notified by the Secretary of State that a remand centre is available for the reception from the court of persons of his class or description, it shall commit him to a remand centre and, if it has not been so notified, it shall commit him to a prison.

(3) If, on the application of the local authority to whose care a young person is committed by a warrant under subsection (1)

PART I   of this section, the court by which he was so committed or any magistrates' court having jurisdiction in the place where he is for the time being certifies as mentioned in subsection (2) of this section, the provisions of the said subsection (2) relating to committal shall apply in relation to him and he shall cease to be committed in pursuance of the said subsection (1).

1952 c. 55.   (4) The preceding provisions of this section shall have effect subject to the provisions of section 28 of the Magistrates' Courts Act 1952 (which relates to committal to quarter sessions with a view to a borstal sentence).

(5) In this section " court " and " magistrates' court " include a justice ; and notwithstanding anything in the preceding provisions of this section, section 105(5) of the said Act of 1952 (which provides for remands to the custody of a constable for periods not exceeding three clear days) shall have effect in relation to a child or young person as if for the reference to three clear days there were substituted a reference to twenty-four hours.

Powers and duties of local authorities etc. with respect to persons committed to their care.   **24.**—(1) It shall be the duty of a local authority to whose care a person is committed by a care order or by a warrant under subsection (1) of the preceding section to receive him into their care and, notwithstanding any claim by his parent or guardian, to keep him in their care while the order or warrant is in force.

(2) A local authority shall, subject to the following provisions of this section, have the same powers and duties with respect to a person in their care by virtue of a care order or such a warrant as his parent or guardian would have apart from the order or warrant and may (without prejudice to the preceding provisions of this subsection but subject to regulations made in pursuance of section 43 of this Act) restrict his liberty to such extent as the authority consider appropriate.

(3) A local authority shall not cause a person in their care by virtue of a care order to be brought up in any religious creed other than that in which he would have been brought up apart from the order.

(4) It shall be the duty of a local authority to comply with any provision included in an interim order in pursuance of section 22(2) of this Act and, in the case of a person in their care by virtue of the preceding section, to permit him to be removed from their care in due course of law.

(5) If a person who is subject to a care order and has attained the age of five is accommodated in a community home or other establishment which he has not been allowed to leave during the preceding three months for the purpose of ordinary

attendance at an educational institution or at work and it appears
to the local authority to whose care he is committed by the
order that—

(a) communication between him and his parent or guardian
has been so infrequent that it is appropriate to appoint
a visitor for him ; or

(b) he has not lived with or visited or been visited by either
of his parents or his guardian during the preceding
twelve months,

it shall be the duty of the authority to appoint an independent
person to be his visitor for the purposes of this subsection ; and
a person so appointed shall—

(i) have the duty of visiting, advising and befriending the
person to whom the care order relates ; and

(ii) be entitled to exercise on behalf of that person his powers
under section 21(2) of this Act ; and

(iii) be entitled to recover from the authority who appointed
him any expenses reasonably incurred by him for the
purposes of his functions under this subsection.

In this section " independent person " means a person satisfying such conditions as may be prescribed by regulations made by
the Secretary of State with a view to securing that he is independent of the local authority in question and unconnected with any
community home.

(6) A person's appointment as a visitor in pursuance of the
preceding subsection shall be determined if the care order in
question ceases to be in force or he gives notice in writing to the
authority who appointed him that he resigns the appointment or
the authority give him notice in writing that they terminate it ;
but the determination of such an appointment shall not prejudice
any duty under the preceding subsection to make a further
appointment.

(7) The functions conferred on a local authority by the preceding provisions of this section in respect of any person are in
addition to the functions which, by virtue of section 27 of this
Act, are conferred on the authority in respect of him by Part II
of the Children Act 1948.   1948 c. 43.

(8) While a care order other than an interim order is in
force in respect of a person who has not attained the age of
eighteen, it shall be the duty of his parent to keep the local
authority to whose care he is committed by the order informed
of the parent's address ; and if the parent knows of the order
and fails to perform his duty under this subsection, the parent
shall be liable on summary conviction to a fine not exceeding
ten pounds unless he shows that at the material time he was

Part I

residing at the address of the other parent and had reasonable cause to believe that the other parent had kept the authority informed of their address.

Transfer

Transfers between England or Wales and Northern Ireland.

25.—(1) If it appears to the Secretary of State, on the application of the welfare authority or the managers of the training school to whose care a person is committed by a fit person order or by virtue of a training school order, that his parent or guardian resides or will reside in the area of a local authority in England or Wales, the Secretary of State may make an order committing him to the care of that local authority ; and while an order under this subsection is in force it shall have effect as if it were a care order and as if sections 20(2) and (3) and 21(1) and (5) of this Act were omitted and in section 31(3)(*a*) of this Act for the reference to section 20(3) there were substituted a reference to subsection (3) of this section.

(2) If it appears to the Minister of Home Affairs for Northern Ireland, on the application of the local authority to whose care a person is committed by a care order other than an interim order, that his parent or guardian resides or will reside in Northern Ireland, the said Minister may make an order committing him to the care of the managers of a training school or to the care of the welfare authority in whose area his parent or guardian resides or will reside ; and the provisions of the Children and Young Persons Act (Northern Ireland) 1968 (except sections 83(3)(*a*), 88(3), 90 and 91(3)) shall apply to an order under this subsection as if it were a training school order made on the date of the care order or, as the case may be, a fit person order.

1968 c. 34. (N.I.).

If an order under this subsection commits a person to the care of the managers of a training school, the contributions to be made in respect of him under section 161 of the said Act of 1968 shall be made by such council as may be named in that order, being the council within whose district his parent proposes to reside or is residing at the time of the order.

(3) When a person is received into the care of a local authority or welfare authority or the managers of a training school in pursuance of an order under this section, the training school order, fit person order or care order in consequence of which the order under this section was made shall cease to have effect ; and the order under this section shall, unless it is discharged earlier, cease to have effect—

   (*a*) in the case of an order under subsection (1), on the earlier of the following dates, that is to say, the date when the person to whom the order relates attains the age of nineteen or the date when, by the effluxion of time, the

fit person order aforesaid would have ceased to have PART I
effect or, as the case may be, the period of his detention
under the training school order aforesaid would have
expired ;

(*b*) in the case of an order under subsection (2), on the date
when the care order aforesaid would have ceased to
have effect by the effluxion of time or—

(i) if the person to whom the order relates is
committed by it to the care of a welfare authority
and will attain the age of eighteen before that date,
when he attains that age ;

(ii) if the order has effect by virtue of subsection (2)
as a training school order and the period of supervision following the detention of the person in
question in pursuance of the order expires before that
date, when that period expires.

(4) An order under this section shall be sufficient authority for
the detention in Northern Ireland, by any constable or by a
person duly authorised by a local authority or welfare authority
or the managers of a training school, of the person to whom the
order relates until he is received into the care of the authority or
managers to whose care he is committed by the order.

(5) In this section "training school", "training school
order" and "welfare authority" have the same meaning as in
the said Act of 1968, and "fit person order" means an order
under that Act committing a person to the care of a fit person.

26.—(1) The Secretary of State may by order designate for Transfers
the purposes of this section an order of any description which— between
England or
(*a*) a court in the Isle of Man or any of the Channel Islands Wales and
is authorised to make by the law for the time being in the Channel
force in that country ; and Islands or
Isle of Man.
(*b*) provides for the committal to the care of a public
authority of a person who has not attained the age of
eighteen ; and

(*c*) appears to the Secretary of State to be of the same nature
as a care order other than an interim order ;

and in this section "relevant order" means an order of a
description for the time being so designated and "the relevant
authority ", in relation to a relevant order, means the authority
in the Isle of Man or any of the Channel Islands to whose care
the person to whom the order relates is, under the law of that
country, committed by the order.

(2) The Secretary of State may authorise a local authority to
receive into their care any person named in the authorisation who
is the subject of a relevant order ; and while such an authorisa-

PART I

tion is in force in respect of any person he shall, subject to the following subsection, be deemed to be the subject of a care order committing him to the care of the local authority.

(3) This Act shall have effect, in relation to a person in respect of whom an authorisation under this section is in force, as if sections 20(2) and (3), 21 and 31 and in section 27(4) the words from " and if " onwards were omitted ; and it shall be the duty of a local authority who propose, in exercise of their powers under

1948 c. 43.

section 13(2) of the Children Act 1948, to allow such a person to be under the charge and control of a person residing outside England and Wales to consult the relevant authority before exercising those powers.

(4) An authorisation given to a local authority under this section shall cease to have effect when—

(a) the local authority is informed by the Secretary of State that he has revoked it ; or

(b) the relevant order to which the authorisation relates ceases to have effect by the effluxion of time under the law of the place where the order was made or the local authority is informed by the relevant authority that the order has been discharged under that law ; or

(c) the person to whom the relevant order relates is again received into the care of the relevant authority ;

and if a local authority having by virtue of this section the care of a person to whom a relevant order relates is requested by the relevant authority to make arrangements for him to be received again into the care of the relevant authority, it shall be the duty of the local authority to comply with the request.

Consequential modifications of ss. 11 and 12 of Children Act 1948

Consequential modifications of 1948 c. 43 ss. 11 and 12.

27.—(1) For section 11 of the Children Act 1948 (which specifies the children in respect of whom functions are conferred on local authorities by Part II of that Act) there shall be substituted the following section : —

Children to whom Part II applies.

11. Except where the contrary intention appears, any reference in this Part of this Act to a child who is or was in the care of a local authority is a reference to a child who is or was in the care of the authority under section 1 of this Act or by virtue of a care order within the meaning of the Children and Young Persons Act 1969 or a warrant under section 23(1) of that Act (which relates to remands in the care of local authorities). ;

but nothing in the said section 11 as replaced by this subsection prejudices the application of any provision of the said Part II to any person by virtue of an enactment passed after that Act and before this Act.

(2) If it appears to a local authority that it is necessary, for the purpose of protecting members of the public, to exercise their powers in relation to a particular child in their care in a manner which may not be consistent with their general duty under section 12(1) of the said Act of 1948 to further his best interests and afford him opportunity for proper development, the authority may, notwithstanding that duty, act in that manner.

(3) If the Secretary of State considers it necessary, for the purpose of protecting members of the public, to give directions to a local authority with respect to the exercise of their powers in relation to a particular child in their care, he may give such directions to the authority; and it shall be the duty of the authority, notwithstanding their general duty aforesaid, to comply with any such directions.

(4) Without prejudice to their general duty aforesaid, it shall be the duty of a local authority who have at any time had a child in their care throughout the preceding six months and have not during that period held a review of his case in pursuance of this subsection to review his case as soon as is practicable after the expiration of that period and, if a care order is in force with respect to him, to consider in the course of the review whether to make an application for the discharge of the order.

Detention

28.—(1) If, upon an application to a justice by any person Detention of for authority to detain a child or young person and take him child or young to a place of safety, the justice is satisfied that the applicant has person in reasonable cause to believe that— place of safety.

(a) any of the conditions set out in section 1(2)(a) to (e) of this Act is satisfied in respect of the child or young person ; or

(b) an appropriate court would find the condition set out in section 1(2)(b) of this Act satisfied in respect of him ; or

(c) the child or young person is about to leave the United Kingdom in contravention of section 25 of the Act of 1933 (which regulates the sending abroad of juvenile entertainers),

the justice may grant the application ; and the child or young person in respect of whom an authorisation is issued under this subsection may be detained in a place of safety by virtue of the

3 B*

authorisation for twenty-eight days beginning with the date of authorisation, or for such shorter period beginning with that date as may be specified in the authorisation.

(2) Any constable may detain a child or young person as respects whom the constable has reasonable cause to believe that any of the conditions set out in section 1(2)(*a*) to (*d*) of this Act is satisfied or that an appropriate court would find the condition set out in section 1(2)(*b*) of this Act satisfied or that an offence is being committed under section 10(1) of the Act of 1933 (which penalises a vagrant who takes a juvenile from place to place).

(3) A person who detains any person in pursuance of the preceding provisions of this section shall, as soon as practicable after doing so, inform him of the reason for his detention and take such steps as are practicable for informing his parent or guardian of his detention and of the reason for it.

(4) A constable who detains any person in pursuance of subsection (2) of this section or who arrests a child without a warrant otherwise than for homicide shall as soon as practicable after doing so secure that the case is enquired into by a police officer not below the rank of inspector or by the police officer in charge of a police station, and that officer shall on completing the enquiry either—

(*a*) release the person in question ; or

(*b*) if the officer considers that he ought to be further detained in his own interests or, in the case of an arrested child, because of the nature of the alleged offence, make arrangements for his detention in a place of safety and inform him, and take such steps as are practicable for informing his parent or guardian, of his right to apply to a justice under subsection (5) of this section for his release ;

and subject to the said subsection (5) it shall be lawful to detain the person in question in accordance with any such arrangements.

(5) It shall not be lawful for a child arrested without a warrant otherwise than for homicide to be detained in consequence of the arrest or such arrangements as aforesaid, or for any person to be detained by virtue of subsection (2) of this section or any such arrangements, after the expiration of the period of eight days beginning with the day on which he was arrested or, as the case may be, on which his detention in pursuance of the said subsection (2) began ; and if during that period the person in question applies to a justice for his release, the justice shall direct that he be released forthwith unless the justice considers

that he ought to be further detained in his own interests or, in the case of an arrested child, because of the nature of the alleged offence.

(6) If while a person is detained in pursuance of this section an application for an interim order in respect of him is made to a magistrates' court or a justice, the court or justice shall either make or refuse to make the order and, in the case of a refusal, may direct that he be released forthwith.

29.—(1) Where a person is arrested with or without a warrant and cannot be brought immediately before a magistrates' court, then if either— Release or further detention of arrested child or young person.

   (*a*) he appears to be a child and his arrest is for homicide ; or

   (*b*) he appears to be a young person and his arrest is for any offence,

the police officer in charge of the police station to which he is brought or another police officer not below the rank of inspector shall forthwith enquire into the case and, subject to subsection (2) of this section, shall release him unless—

   (i) the officer considers that he ought in his own interests to be further detained ; or

   (ii) the officer has reason to believe that he has committed homicide or another grave crime or that his release would defeat the ends of justice or that if he were released (in a case where he was arrested without a warrant) he would fail to appear to answer to any charge which might be made.

(2) A person arrested in pursuance of a warrant shall not be released in pursuance of subsection (1) of this section unless he or his parent or guardian (with or without sureties) enters into a recognisance for such amount as the officer aforesaid considers will secure his attendance at the hearing of the charge ; and a recognisance entered into in pursuance of this subsection may, if the said officer thinks fit, be conditioned for the attendance of the parent or guardian at the hearing in addition to the person arrested.

(3) An officer who enquires into a case in pursuance of subsection (1) of this section and does not release the person to whom the enquiry relates shall, unless the officer certifies that it is impracticable to do so or that he is of so unruly a character as to make it inappropriate to do so, make arrangements for him to be taken into the care of a local authority and detained by the authority, and it shall be lawful to detain him in pursuance of the arrangements ; and a certificate made under this subsection in respect of any person shall be produced to the court before which that person is first brought thereafter.

(4) Where an officer decides in pursuance of subsection (1) of this section not to release a person arrested without a warrant and it appears to the officer that a decision falls to be taken in pursuance of section 5 of this Act whether to lay an information in respect of an offence alleged to have been committed by that person, it shall be the duty of the officer to inform him that such a decision falls to be taken and to specify the offence.

(5) A person detained by virtue of subsection (3) of this section shall be brought before a magistrates' court within seventy-two hours from the time of his arrest unless within that period a police officer not below the rank of inspector certifies to a magistrates' court that by reason of illness or accident he cannot be brought before a magistrates' court within that period.

(6) Where in pursuance of the preceding subsection a person is brought before a court or a certificate in respect of any person is produced to a court and the court does not proceed forthwith to inquire into the case, then—

(*a*) except in a case falling within paragraph (*b*) of this subsection, the court shall order his release ; and

(*b*) in a case where he was arrested in pursuance of a warrant or the court considers that he ought in his own interests to be further detained or the court has reason to believe as mentioned in subsection (1)(ii) of this section, the court shall remand him ;

and where a court remands a person in pursuance of this subsection otherwise than on bail it shall, if he is not represented by counsel or a solicitor, inform him that he may apply to a judge of the High Court to be admitted to bail and shall, if he is not so represented or his counsel or solicitor so requests, give him a written notice stating the reason for so remanding him.

Detention of young offenders **in** community homes.

30.—(1) The power to give directions under section 53 of the Act of 1933 (under which young offenders convicted on indictment of certain grave crimes may be detained in accordance with directions given by the Secretary of State) shall include power to direct detention by a local authority specified in the directions in a home so specified which is a community home provided by the authority or a controlled community home for the management, equipment and maintenance of which the authority are responsible ; but a person shall not be liable to be detained in the manner provided by this section after he attains the age of nineteen.

(2) It shall be the duty of a local authority specified in directions given in pursuance of this section to detain the person to whom the directions relate in the home specified in the

directions subject to and in accordance with such instructions relating to him as the Secretary of State may give to the authority from time to time ; and the authority shall be entitled to recover from the Secretary of State any expenses reasonably incurred by them in discharging that duty.

31.—(1) Where a person who has attained the age of fifteen is for the time being committed to the care of a local authority by a care order (other than an interim order) and accommodated in a community home and the authority consider that he ought to be removed to a borstal institution under this section, they may with the consent of the Secretary of State bring him before a juvenile court.

Removal to borstal institutions of persons committed to care of local authorities.

(2) If the court before which a person is brought in pursuance of this section is satisfied that his behaviour is such that it will be detrimental to the persons accommodated in any community home for him to be accommodated there, the court may order him to be removed to a borstal institution.

(3) Where an order is made under subsection (2) of this section with respect to any person, the care order aforesaid shall cease to have effect and he shall be treated as if he had been sentenced to borstal training on the date of the other order, except that—

(*a*) where the day on which the care order would have ceased to have effect by virtue of section 20(3) of this Act (disregarding section 21(1)) is earlier than the end of the period of two years beginning with the date aforesaid he shall, subject to paragraph (*b*) of this subsection, not be liable to be detained by virtue of this subsection after that day ; and

(*b*) section 45(4) of the Prison Act 1952 shall apply to him as if for the reference to two years from the date of his sentence there were substituted a reference to that day.

1952 c. 52.

(4) If the court before which a person is brought in pursuance of this section is not in a position to decide whether to make an order under subsection (2) of this section in respect of him, it may make an order for his detention in a remand centre for a period not exceeding twenty-one days.

(5) An order under the preceding subsection may from time to time be varied or extended by the court which made the order or by any other magistrates' court acting for the same area as that court, but a court shall not exercise its powers under this subsection—

(*a*) if the person to whom the order relates is not before the court, unless the court is satisfied that by reason of illness or accident he cannot be present ;

(*b*) so as to authorise the detention of that person after the expiration of the period of eight weeks beginning with the date when the order was originally made.

1952 c. 55.

(6) The provisions of the Magistrates' Courts Act 1952 and of any other enactment relating to summary proceedings (other than provisions relating to remand or legal aid) shall apply to proceedings for the removal of a person under this section as they apply to proceedings against a person charged with a summary offence.

(7) Where immediately before an order under paragraph (*f*) of section 34(1) of this Act comes into force an order under this section is in force with respect to any person, the order under that paragraph shall not affect the other order or the application of this section to that person while the other order remains in force.

Detention
of absentees.

32.—(1) If any of the following persons, that is to say—

(*a*) a person committed to the care of a local authority by a care order or by a warrant under section 23 of this Act ; or

(*b*) a person who, in pursuance of section 2(5), 16(3) or 28 of this Act, has been taken to a place of safety which is a community home provided by a local authority or a controlled community home ; or

(*c*) a person in the care of a local authority in pursuance of arrangements under section 29(3) of this Act ; or

(*d*) a person sent to a remand home, special reception centre or training school or committed to the care of a fit person under the Children and Young Persons Act (Northern Ireland) 1968,

1968 c. 34.
(N.I.).

is absent from premises at which he is required by the local authority or the relevant Northern Ireland authority to live, or as the case may be is absent from the home, remand home, special reception centre or training school, at a time when he is not permitted by the local authority or the managers of the home or the relevant Northern Ireland authority to be absent from it, he may be arrested by a constable anywhere in the United Kingdom or the Channel Islands without a warrant and shall if so arrested be conducted, at the expense of the authority or managers, to the premises or other place aforesaid or such other premises as the authority or managers may direct.

(2) If a magistrates' court is satisfied by information on oath that there are reasonable grounds for believing that a person specified in the information can produce a person who is absent as mentioned in subsection (1) of this section, the court may issue a summons directed to the person so specified and requiring him to attend and produce the absent person before the court ; and a person who without reasonable excuse fails

to comply with any such requirement shall, without prejudice to PART I any liability apart from this subsection, be guilty of an offence and liable on summary conviction to a fine of an amount not exceeding twenty pounds.

In the application of this subsection to Northern Ireland, " magistrates' court " means a magistrates' court within the 1964 c. 21 meaning of the Magistrates' Courts Act (Northern Ireland) 1964. (N.I.).

(3) A person who knowingly compels, persuades, incites or assists another person to become or continue to be absent as mentioned in subsection (1) of this section shall be guilty of an offence and liable on summary conviction to imprisonment for a term not exceeding six months or a fine of an amount not exceeding one hundred pounds or both.

(4) The reference to a constable in subsection (1) of this section includes a reference to a person who is a constable under the law of any part of the United Kingdom, to a member of the police in Jersey and to an officer of police within the meaning of section 43 of the Larceny (Guernsey) Law 1958 or any corresponding law for the time being in force, and in that subsection " the relevant Northern Ireland authority " means in the case of a person committed to the care of a fit person, the fit person, and in the case of a person sent to a remand home, special reception centre or training school, the person in charge of that home or centre or the managers of that school.

(5) Nothing in this section authorises the arrest in Northern Ireland of, or the taking there of any proceedings in respect of, such a person as is mentioned in paragraph (*d*) of subsection (1) of this section.

Legal aid

33.—(1) Part IV of the Criminal Justice Act 1967 (which Legal aid. relates to legal aid in criminal proceedings) shall have effect 1967 c. 80. subject to the provisions of Schedule 1 to this Act (being provisions for applying the said Part IV to certain proceedings under this Part of this Act and for modifying the said Part IV in certain minor respects in relation to juveniles).

(2) Legal aid in pursuance of the Legal Aid and Advice 1949 c. 51. Act 1949 shall not be given in respect of any proceedings in respect of which legal aid may be given by virtue of the preceding subsection.

Transitional modifications of Part I for persons of specified ages

34.—(1) The Secretary of State may by order provide—

(*a*) that any reference to a child in section 4, 13(2) or 28(4) or (5) of this Act shall be construed as excluding a child who has attained such age as may be specified in the order ;

(*b*) that any reference to a young person in section 5 of this Act (except subsection (8)) shall be construed as including a child, or excluding a young person, who has attained such age as may be so specified ;

(*c*) that any reference to a young person in section 5(8), 7(7), 7(8), 9(1), 23(1) or 29(1) of this Act shall be construed as including a child who has attained such age as may be so specified ;

(*d*) that section 7(1) of this Act shall have effect as if for references to seventeen years there were substituted references to sixteen years ;

(*e*) that section 23(2) or (3) of this Act shall have effect as if the references to a young person excluded a young person who has not attained such age as may be so specified ;

(*f*) that section 22(5) of this Act shall have effect as if for the reference to the age of fourteen, or section 31(1) of this Act shall have effect as if for the reference to the age of fifteen, there were substituted a reference to such greater age as may be so specified.

(2) In the case of a person who has not attained the age of seventeen but has attained such lower age as the Secretary of State may by order specify, no proceedings under section 1 of this Act or for an offence shall be begun in any court unless the person proposing to begin the proceedings has, in addition to any notice falling to be given by him to a local authority in pursuance of section 2(3) or 5(8) of this Act, given notice of the proceedings to a probation officer for the area for which the court acts ; and accordingly in the case of such a person the reference in section 1(1) of this Act to the said section 2(3) shall be construed as including a reference to this subsection.

(3) In the case of a person who has attained such age as the Secretary of State may by order specify, an authority shall, without prejudice to subsection (2) of section 9 of this Act, not be required by virtue of subsection (1) of that section to make investigations or provide information which it does not already possess with respect to his home surroundings if, by direction of the justices or probation and after-care committee

acting for any relevant area, arrangements are in force for PART I information with respect to his home surroundings to be furnished to the court in question by a probation officer.

(4) Except in relation to section 13(2) of this Act, references to a child in subsection (1) of this section do not include references to a person under the age of ten.

(5) In relation to a child tried summarily in pursuance of section 6 of this Act, for the words " fifty pounds " in subsection (3) of that section there shall be substituted the words " ten pounds ".

(6) Without prejudice to the generality of section 69(4) of this Act, an order under this section may specify different ages for the purposes of different provisions of this Act specified in the order.

(7) A draft of any order proposed to be made under this section shall be laid before Parliament and, in the case of an order of which the effect is that the reference to a child in section 4 of this Act includes a child who has attained an age of more than twelve, shall not be made unless the draft has been approved by a resolution of each House of Parliament.

PART II

ACCOMMODATION ETC. FOR CHILDREN IN CARE, AND FOSTER
CHILDREN

Community homes

35.—(1) With a view to the preparation, in pursuance of Regional the provisions of this Part of this Act, of regional plans for planning of the provision of accommodation for children in the care of accommodation for local authorities and for the equipment and maintenance of the children in care. accommodation, the Secretary of State may by order provide that any area specified in the order shall be a separate area (in this Act referred to as a " planning area ") for the purposes of those provisions.

(2) Before making an order under subsection (1) of this section, the Secretary of State shall consult each local authority whose area or any part of whose area is included in the planning area which he proposes should be specified in the order and such other local authorities, if any, as he thinks fit.

(3) It shall be the duty of the local authorities whose areas are wholly or partly included in a planning area (in this Act referred to, in relation to such an area, as " the relevant authorities ") to establish for the area, within such period as may be provided by the order specifying the planning area or such longer period as the Secretary of State may allow, a body to be called the children's regional planning committee.

(4) The provisions of Schedule 2 to this Act shall have effect in relation to children's regional planning committees.

(5) In the case of an order under subsection (1) of this section which (by virtue of section 69(3) of this Act) varies or revokes a previous order under that subsection—

(a) the reference in subsection (2) of this section to the planning area which the Secretary of State proposes should be specified in the order shall be construed as a reference to the planning area as it would be if the variation were made or, as the case may be, to the planning area as it is before the revocation ; and

(b) the order may contain such transitional provisions (including provisions as to the expenses and membership of any existing or former children's regional planning committee for a planning area) as the Secretary of State thinks fit.

Regional plans for community homes.

36.—(1) The children's regional planning committee for a planning area (in this and the following section referred to as " the committee ") shall prepare and submit to the Secretary of State, in accordance with the following provisions of this section, a plan (in this Act referred to as a " regional plan ") for the provision and maintenance of homes, to be known as community homes, for the accommodation and maintenance of children in the care of the relevant authorities.

(2) The community homes for which provision may be made by a regional plan shall be—

(a) community homes provided by the relevant authorities ; and

(b) voluntary homes provided by voluntary organisations but in the management of each of which the plan proposes that a relevant authority should participate in accordance with an instrument of management.

(3) Where a regional plan makes provision for any such voluntary home as is referred to in paragraph (b) of subsection (2) of this section, the plan shall designate the home as either a controlled community home or an assisted community home, according as it is proposed in the plan that the management, equipment and maintenance of the home should be the responsibility of one of the relevant authorities or of the voluntary organisation by which the home is provided.

(4) Every regional plan shall contain proposals—

(a) with regard to the nature and purpose of each of the community homes for which the plan makes provision ; and

(b) for the provision of facilities for the observation of the physical and mental condition of children in the care of the relevant authorities and for the assessment of the most suitable accommodation and treatment for those children.

(5) Before including provision in a regional plan that a community home should be provided by any of the relevant authorities or that a voluntary home provided by a voluntary organisation should be designated as a controlled or assisted community home, the committee shall obtain the consent of the authority or voluntary organisation by which the home is or is to be provided and, in the case of a home which is to be designated as a controlled or assisted community home, the consent of the local authority which it is proposed should be specified in the instrument of management for the home.

(6) A regional plan shall be prepared in such form and shall contain such information as the Secretary of State may direct, either generally or in relation to a particular planning area or particular kinds of plans ; and the Secretary of State may direct that the regional plan for a particular planning area shall be submitted to him within such period as may be specified in the direction or such longer period as he may allow.

37.—(1) After considering any regional plan submitted to him under section 36 of this Act and after making in the plan such modifications (if any) as he may agree with the committee by which the plan was submitted and as he may consider appropriate for securing that the plan makes proper provision for the accommodation and maintenance of children in the care of the relevant authorities, the Secretary of State may approve the plan.

Approval and variation of regional plans.

(2) Where the Secretary of State considers that, either with or without such modifications as are referred to in subsection (1) of this section, part but not the whole of a plan submitted to him under section 36 of this Act makes proper provision for the accommodation and maintenance of the children to whom that part of the plan relates, the Secretary of State may approve that part of the plan.

(3) Where the Secretary of State has approved part only of a regional plan, the committee for the planning area concerned shall prepare and submit to him under section 36 of this Act a further regional plan containing proposals to supplement that part of the previous plan which was approved by the Secretary of State.

(4) If, at any time after the approval of the whole or part of a regional plan by the Secretary of State, the committee for the planning area concerned consider that the plan, or such part of it as was approved, should be varied or replaced, they shall prepare and submit to the Secretary of State under section

36 of this Act a further regional plan for that purpose ; and any such further regional plan may—

> (a) take the form of a replacement for the regional plan or part thereof which was previously approved by the Secretary of State ; or
>
> (b) contain proposals for the amendment of that regional plan or part thereof.

(5) In relation to a further regional plan which contains proposals for supplementing or amending a regional plan or part of a regional plan which has been previously approved by the Secretary of State (in this subsection referred to as " the approved plan ")—

> (a) section 36(4) of this Act shall have effect as if references to a regional plan were references to the approved plan as it would have effect if supplemented or amended in accordance with the proposals contained in the further regional plan ; and
>
> (b) subsection (1) of this section shall have effect as if the reference therein to children in the care of the relevant authorities were a reference to the children to whom the proposals in the plan relate ; and
>
> (c) in so far as the further regional plan contains proposals under which a home would cease to be a community home, or would become a community home of a different description, or would be used for a purpose different from that provided for in the approved plan, the committee preparing the further plan shall, before submitting it to the Secretary of State, obtain the consent of the local authority or voluntary organisation by which the home is provided and, if the proposal is for a home to become or to cease to be a controlled or assisted community home, the consent of the local authority which it is proposed should be, or which is, specified in the instrument of management for the home.

(6) Where the Secretary of State approves a regional plan, in whole or in part, he shall give notice in writing of his approval to the committee for the planning area concerned specifying the date on which the plan is to come into operation, and the committee shall send a copy of the notice to each of the relevant authorities and to any voluntary organisation whose consent was required to any provision of the plan.

Provision of community homes by local authorities.

38. Where a regional plan for a planning area includes provision for a community home to be provided by one of the relevant authorities, it shall be the duty of the local authority concerned to provide, manage, equip and maintain that home.

39.—(1) The Secretary of State may by order make an instrument of management providing for the constitution of a body of managers for any voluntary home which, in accordance with a regional plan approved by him, is designated as a controlled or assisted community home.

(2) Where in accordance with a regional plan approved by the Secretary of State, two or more voluntary homes are designated as controlled community homes or as assisted community homes, then if—

(a) those homes are, or are to be, provided by the same voluntary organisation ; and

(b) the same local authority is to be represented on the body of managers for those homes,

a single instrument of management may be made by the Secretary of State under this section constituting one body of managers for those homes or for any two or more of them.

(3) The number of persons who, in accordance with an instrument of management under this section, constitute the body of managers for a voluntary home shall be such number, being a multiple of three, as may be specified in the instrument of management, but the instrument shall provide that a proportion of the managers shall be appointed by such local authority as may be so specified and—

(a) in the case of a voluntary home which is designated in a regional plan as a controlled community home, the proportion shall be two-thirds ; and

(b) in the case of a voluntary home which is so designated as an assisted community home, the proportion shall be one-third.

(4) An instrument of management shall provide that the " foundation managers ", that is to say, those of the managers of the voluntary home to which the instrument relates who are not appointed by a local authority in accordance with subsection (3) of this section, shall be appointed, in such manner and by such persons as may be specified in the instrument,—

(a) so as to represent the interests of the voluntary organisation by which the home is, or is to be, provided ; and

(b) for the purpose of securing that, as far as practicable, the character of the home as a voluntary home will be preserved and that, subject to section 40(3) of this Act, the terms of any trust deed relating to the home are observed.

(5) An instrument of management under this section shall come into force on such date as may be specified in the instrument, and if such an instrument is in force in relation to a

Part II

voluntary home the home shall be and be known as a controlled community home or an assisted community home, according to its designation in the regional plan.

Supplementary provioiono ao to instruments of management and trust deeds.

40.—(1) An instrument of management for a controlled or assisted community home shall contain such provisions as the Secretary of State considers appropriate for giving effect to the provisions of the regional plan by which the home is designated as a controlled or assisted community home, but nothing in the instrument of management for such a home shall affect the purposes for which the premises comprising the home are held.

(2) Without prejudice to the generality of subsection (1) of this section, an instrument of management may contain—

(*a*) provisions specifying the nature and purpose of the home or each of the homes to which it relates ;

(*b*) provisions requiring a specified number or proportion of the places in that home or those homes to be made available to local authorities and to any other body specified in the instrument ; and

(*c*) provisions relating to the management of that home or those homes and the charging of fees in respect of children placed therein or places made available to any local authority or other body.

(3) Subject to subsection (1) of this section, in the event of any inconsistency between the provisions of any trust deed and the instrument of management relating to a controlled or assisted community home, the instrument of management shall prevail over the provisions of the trust deed in so far as they relate to that home.

(4) After consultation with the voluntary organisation by which a controlled or assisted community home is provided and with the local authority specified in the instrument of management for the time being in force for that home, the Secretary of State may vary or revoke any provisions of that instrument of management by a further instrument of management.

(5) In this Act the expression " trust deed ", in relation to a voluntary home, means any instrument (other than an instrument of management) regulating the maintenance, management or conduct of the home or the constitution of a body of managers or trustees of the home.

Management of controlled community homes.

41.—(1) The management, equipment and maintenance of a controlled community home shall be the responsibility of the local authority specified in the instrument of management for that home, and in the following provisions of this section " the responsible authority ", in relation to such a home, means the local authority responsible for its management, equipment and maintenance.

(2) Subject to the following provisions of this section, the PART II
responsible authority shall exercise their functions in relation to a
controlled community home through the body of managers constituted by the instrument of management for the home, and any
thing done, liability incurred or property acquired by the managers shall be done, incurred or acquired by the managers as
agents of the responsible authority.

(3) In so far as any matter is reserved for the decision of the
responsible authority, either by subsection (4) of this section
or by the instrument of management for the controlled community home in question or by the service by the responsible
authority on the managers or any of them of a notice reserving
any matter, that matter shall be dealt with by the responsible
authority themselves and not by the managers, but in dealing with
any matter so reserved, the responsible authority shall have
regard to any representations made to them by the managers.

(4) The employment of persons at a controlled community
home shall be a matter reserved for the decision of the responsible authority, but where the instrument of management so
provides the responsible authority may enter into arrangements
with the voluntary organisation by which the home is provided
whereby, in accordance with such terms as may be agreed
between the responsible authority and the voluntary organisation,
persons who are not in the employment of the responsible
authority shall undertake duties at the home.

(5) The accounting year of the managers of a controlled community home shall be such as may be specified by the responsible
authority and, before such date in each accounting year as may
be so specified, the managers of a controlled community home
shall submit to the responsible authority estimates, in such form
as the authority may require, of expenditure and receipts in
respect of the next accounting year ; and any expenses incurred
by the managers of a controlled community home with the
approval of the responsible authority shall be defrayed by that
authority.

(6) The managers of a controlled community home shall
keep proper accounts in respect of that home and proper records
in relation to the accounts, but where an instrument of
management relates to more than one controlled community
home, one set of accounts and records may be kept in respect
of all the homes to which the instrument relates.

42.—(1) The management, equipment and maintenance of Management
an assisted community home shall be the responsibility of the of assisted
voluntary organisation by which the home is provided, and community
in the following provisions of this section " the responsible homes.

organisation ", in relation to such a home, means the voluntary organisation responsible for its management, equipment and maintenance.

(2) Subject to the following provisions of this section, the responsible organisation shall exercise its functions in relation to the home through the body of managers constituted by the instrument of management for the home, and any thing done, liability incurred or property acquired by the managers shall be done, incurred or acquired by the managers as agents of the responsible organisation.

(3) In so far as any matter is reserved for the decision of the responsible organisation, either by subsection (4) of this section or by the instrument of management for the assisted community home in question or by the service by the responsible organisation on the managers or any of them of a notice reserving any matter, that matter shall be dealt with by the responsible organisation itself and not by the managers, but in dealing with any matter so reserved the responsible organisation shall have regard to any representations made to the organisation by the managers.

(4) The employment of persons at an assisted community home shall be a matter reserved for the decision of the responsible organisation but, subject to subsection (5) of this section,—

    (*a*) where the responsible organisation proposes to engage any person to work at the home or to terminate without notice the employment of any person at the home, the responsible organisation shall consult the local authority specified in the instrument of management and, if the local authority so directs, the responsible organisation shall not carry out its proposal without the consent of the local authority ; and

    (*b*) the local authority may, after consultation with the responsible organisation, require the organisation to terminate the employment of any person at the home.

(5) Paragraphs (*a*) and (*b*) of subsection (4) of this section shall not apply—

    (*a*) in such cases or circumstances as may be specified by notice in writing given by the local authority to the responsible organisation ; and

    (*b*) in relation to the employment of any persons or class of persons specified in the instrument of management.

(6) The accounting year of the managers of an assisted community home shall be such as may be specified by the responsible organisation and, before such date in each accounting year as may be so specified, the managers of an assisted community home

shall submit to the responsible organisation estimates, in such
form as the organisation may require, of expenditure and receipts
in respect of the next financial year ; and all expenses incurred
by the managers of an assisted community home with the
approval of the responsible organisation shall be defrayed by the
organisation.

(7) The managers of an assisted community home shall keep
proper accounts in respect of that home and proper records in
relation to those accounts, but where an instrument of management relates to more than one assisted community home, one
set of accounts and records may be kept in respect of all the
homes to which the instrument relates.

43.—(1) The Secretary of State may make regulations with Control of
respect to the conduct of community homes and for securing premises
the welfare of the children in community homes.   used for, and
conduct of,
community
(2) Without prejudice to the generality of subsection (1) of this homes.
section, regulations under this section may—

(*a*) impose requirements as to the accommodation and
equipment to be provided in community homes and
as to the medical arrangements to be made for protecting the health of the children in the homes ;

(*b*) impose requirements as to the facilities which are to
be provided for giving religious instruction to children
in community homes ;

(*c*) require the approval of the Secretary of State for the
provision and use of accommodation for the purpose
of restricting the liberty of children in community
homes and impose other requirements as to the placing
of a child in accommodation provided for that purpose, including a requirement to obtain the permission
of the local authority or voluntary organisation in
whose care the child is ;

(*d*) authorise the Secretary of State to give and revoke
directions requiring the local authority by whom a
community home is provided or who are specified in
the instrument of management for a controlled community home or the voluntary organisation by which
an assisted community home is provided to accommodate in the home a child in the care of a local
authority for whom no places are made available in
that home or to take such action in relation to a child
accommodated in the home as may be specified in the
directions ;

(e) require reviews of any permission given in pursuance of paragraph (c) above and provide for such a review to be conducted in a manner approved by the Secretary of State by a committee of persons representing the local authority or voluntary organisation in question but including at least one person satisfying such conditions as may be prescribed by the regulations with a view to securing that he is independent of the authority or organisation and unconnected with any community home containing such accommodation as is mentioned in the said paragraph (c) ;

(f) prescribe standards to which premises used for community homes are to conform ;

(g) require the approval of the Secretary of State to the use of buildings for the purpose of community homes and to the doing of anything (whether by way of addition, diminution or alteration) which materially affects the buildings or grounds or other facilities or amenities available for children in community homes ;

(h) provide that, to such extent as may be provided for in the regulations, the Secretary of State may direct that any provision of regulations under this section which is specified in the direction and makes any such provision as is referred to in paragraph (a), (f) or (g) above shall not apply in relation to a particular community home or the premises used for it, and may provide for the variation or revocation of any such direction by the Secretary of State.

(3) Without prejudice to the power to make regulations under this section conferring functions on the local authority or voluntary organisation by which a community home is provided or on the managers of a controlled or assisted community home, regulations under this section may confer functions in relation to a controlled or assisted community home on the local authority named in the instrument of management for the home.

(4) Where it appears to the Secretary of State that any premises used for the purposes of a community home are unsuitable for those purposes, or that the conduct of a community home is not in accordance with regulations made by him under this section or is otherwise unsatisfactory, he may by notice in writing served on the responsible body, direct that as from such date as may be specified in the notice the premises shall not be used for the purposes of a community home.

(5) Where the Secretary of State has given a direction in relation to a controlled or assisted community home under subsection (4) of this section and the direction has not been revoked,

the Secretary of State may at any time by order revoke the   PART II
instrument of management for that home.

(6) For the purposes of subsection (4) of this section the
responsible body—

(a) in relation to a community home provided by a local
authority, is that local authority ;

(b) in relation to a controlled community home, is the
local authority specified in the instrument of management for that home ; and

(c) in relation to an assisted community home, is the
voluntary organisation by which the home is provided.

44. While a voluntary home is a controlled or assisted com-   Controlled
munity home, the following enactments shall not apply in relation   and assisted
to it, that is to say,—   community
                                                                     homes

(a) sections 29 and 30 of the Children Act 1948 (compul-   exempted from
sory registration of voluntary homes) ;   certain
                                                            provisions as
(b) section 31 of that Act (regulations as to conduct of   to voluntary
voluntary homes) ; and   homes.

(c) section 93 of the Act of 1933 and section 32 of the   1948 c. 43.
Children Act 1948 (notification to Secretary of State
of certain particulars relating to voluntary homes).

45.—(1) Subject to subsection (5) of this section, where any   Determination
dispute relating to a controlled community home arises between   of disputes
the local authority specified in the instrument of management   relating to
and either the voluntary organisation by which the home is   controlled
provided or any other local authority who have placed, or desire   and assisted
                                                                 community
or are required to place, a child in their care in the home, the   homes.
dispute may be referred by either party to the Secretary of State
for his determination.

(2) Subject to subsection (5) of this section, where any dispute
relating to an assisted community home arises between the
voluntary organisation by which the home is provided and any
local authority who have placed, or desire to place, a child in
their care in the home, the dispute may be referred by either
party to the Secretary of State for his determination.

(3) Where a dispute is referred to the Secretary of State
under this section he may, in order to give effect to his determination of the dispute, give such directions as he thinks fit
to the local authority or voluntary organisation concerned.

(4) The provisions of this section shall apply notwithstanding
that the matter in dispute may be one which, under or by
virtue of the preceding provisions of this Part of this Act, is

Part II　reserved for the decision, or is the responsibility, of the local authority specified in the instrument of management or, as the case may be, the voluntary organisation by which the home is provided.

(5) Where any trust deed relating to a controlled or assisted community home contains provision whereby a bishop or any other ecclesiastical or denominational authority has power to decide questions relating to religious instruction given in the home, no dispute which is capable of being dealt with in accordance with that provision shall be referred to the Secretary of State under this section.

Discontinuance of approved schools etc. on establishment of community homes.

1948 c. 58.

46.—(1) If in the case of any approved school, remand home, approved probation hostel or approved probation home within the meaning of the Criminal Justice Act 1948 (hereafter in this section referred to as an " approved institution ") it appears to the Secretary of State that in consequence of the establishment of community homes for a planning area the institution as such is no longer required, he may by order provide that it shall cease to be an approved institution on a date specified in the order.

(2) The provisions of Schedule 3 to this Act shall have effect in relation to institutions which are, or by virtue of this section have ceased to be, approved institutions.

Discontinuance by voluntary organisation of controlled or assisted community home.

47.—(1) The voluntary organisation by which a controlled or assisted community home is provided shall not cease to provide the home except after giving to the Secretary of State and the local authority specified in the instrument of management not less than two years' notice in writing of their intention to do so.

(2) A notice under subsection (1) of this section shall specify the date from which the voluntary organisation intends to cease to provide the home as a community home ; and where such a notice is given and is not withdrawn before the date specified in it, then, subject to subsection (4) of this section the instrument of management for the home shall cease to have effect on that date and accordingly the home shall then cease to be a controlled or assisted community home.

(3) Where a notice is given under subsection (1) of this section, the local authority to whom the notice is given shall inform the children's regional planning committee responsible for the regional plan under which the voluntary home in question was designated as a controlled or assisted community home of the receipt and content of the notice.

(4) Where a notice is given under subsection (1) of this section and the body of managers for the home to which the notice relates give notice in writing to the Secretary of State that they are unable or unwilling to continue as managers of the home until the date specified in the first-mentioned notice, the Secretary of State may by order—

(a) revoke the instrument of management ; and

(b) require the local authority who were specified in that instrument to conduct the home, until the date specified in the notice under subsection (1) of this section or such earlier date (if any) as may be specified for the purposes of this paragraph in the order, as if it were a community home provided by the local authority.

(5) Where the Secretary of State makes such a requirement as is specified in subsection (4)(b) of this section,—

(a) nothing in the trust deed for the home in question shall affect the conduct of the home by the local authority ; and

(b) the Secretary of State may by order direct that for the purposes of any provision specified in the direction and made by or under any enactment relating to community homes (other than this section) the home shall, until the date or earlier date specified as mentioned in subsection (4)(b) of this section, be treated as an assisted community home or as a controlled community home, but except in so far as the Secretary of State so directs, the home shall until that date be treated for the purposes of any such enactment as a community home provided by the local authority ; and

(c) on the date or earlier date specified as mentioned in subsection (4)(b) of this section the home shall cease to be a community home.

48.—(1) Where the instrument of management for a con- Financial trolled or assisted community home ceases to have effect by provisions virtue either of an order under section 43(5) of this Act or of applicable on subsection (2) or subsection (4)(a) of section 47 of this Act, the cessation voluntary organisation by which the home was provided or, if of controlled the premises used for the purposes of the home are not vested or assisted in that organisation, the persons in whom those premises are community vested (in this section referred to as " the trustees of the home "), home. shall become liable, in accordance with the following provisions of this section, to make repayment in respect of any increase in the value of the premises and other property belonging to the voluntary organisation or the trustees of the home which is attributable to the expenditure of public money thereon.

(2) Where an instrument of management has ceased to have effect as mentioned in subsection (1) of this section and the instrument related—

(a) to a controlled community home ; or

(b) to an assisted community home which, at any time before that instrument of management came into force, was a controlled community home,

then, on the home ceasing to be a community home, the voluntary organisation by which the home was provided or, as the case may be, the trustees of the home, shall pay to the local authority specified in that instrument of management a sum equal to that part of the value of any relevant premises which is attributable to expenditure by the local authority who at the time the expenditure was incurred had responsibility for the management, equipment and maintenance of the home by virtue of section 41(1) of this Act.

(3) For the purposes of subsection (2) of this section, " relevant premises ", in relation to a controlled or assisted community home, means premises used for the purposes of the home and belonging to the voluntary organisation or the trustees of the home but erected, extended or improved, at any time while the home was a controlled community home, by the local authority having, at that time, such responsibility in relation to the home as is mentioned in subsection (2) of this section.

(4) Where an instrument of management has ceased to have effect as mentioned in subsection (1) of this section and the instrument related—

(a) to an assisted community home ; or

(b) to a controlled community home which, at any time before that instrument of management came into force, was an assisted community home,

then, on the home ceasing to be a community home, the voluntary organisation by which the home was provided or, as the case may be, the trustees of the home, shall pay to the Secretary of State a sum equal to that part of the value of the premises and any other property used for the purposes of the home which is attributable to the expenditure of money provided by way of grant under section 65 of this Act.

(5) Where an instrument of management has ceased to have effect as mentioned in subsection (1) of this section and the controlled or assisted community home to which it related was conducted in premises which formerly were used as an approved school or were an approved probation hostel or home but which were designated as a community home in a regional plan approved by the Secretary of State, then, on the home ceasing to be a community home, the voluntary organisation by which

the home was provided or, as the case may be, the trustees of PART II
the home, shall pay to the Secretary of State a sum equal to
that part of the value of the premises concerned and of any
other property used for the purposes of the home and belonging
to the voluntary organisation or the trustees of the home which
is attributable to the expenditure—

> (*a*) of sums paid towards the expenses of the managers of
> an approved school under section 104 of the Act of
> 1933 ; or
>
> (*b*) of sums paid under section 77(3)(*b*) of the Criminal 1948 c. 58.
> Justice Act 1948 in relation to expenditure on approved
> probation hostels or homes.

(6) The amount of any sum payable under this section by
the voluntary organisation by which a controlled or assisted
community home was provided or by the trustees of the home
shall be determined in accordance with such arrangements—

> (*a*) as may be agreed between the voluntary organisation
> by which the home was provided and the local authority
> concerned or, as the case may be, the Secretary of
> State ; or
>
> (*b*) in default of agreement, as may be determined by the
> Secretary of State ;

and with the agreement of the local authority concerned or the
Secretary of State, as the case may be, the liability to pay any
sum under this section may be discharged, in whole or in part,
by the transfer of any premises or other property used for the
purposes of the home in question.

(7) The provisions of this section shall have effect notwithstanding anything in any trust deed for a controlled or assisted
community home and notwithstanding the provisions of any
enactment or instrument governing the disposition of the property
of a voluntary organisation.

(8) Any sums received by the Secretary of State under this
section shall be paid into the Consolidated Fund.

Consequential modifications of ss. 13 and 19 of
Children Act 1948

49. For section 13 of the Children Act 1948 there shall be Provision of
substituted the following section : — accommoda-
tion and
Provision of **13.**—(1) A local authority shall discharge their maintenance
accommo- duty to provide accommodation and maintenance for children
dation and for a child in their care in such one of the following in care.
maintenance
for children ways as they think fit, namely,— 1948 c. 43.
in care.
> (*a*) by boarding him out on such terms as to
> payment by the authority and otherwise as

the authority may, subject to the provisions of this Act and regulations thereunder, determine ; or

(*b*) by maintaining him in a community home or in any such home as is referred to in section 64 of the Children and Young Persons Act 1969 ; or

(*c*) by maintaining him in a voluntary home (other than a community home) the managers of which are willing to receive him ;

or by making such other arrangements as seem appropriate to the local authority.

(2) Without prejudice to the generality of subsection (1) of this section, a local authority may allow a child in their care, either for a fixed period or until the local authority otherwise determine, to be under the charge and control of a parent, guardian, relative or friend.

(3) The terms, as to payment and other matters, on which a child may be accommodated and maintained in any such home as is referred to in section 64 of that Act shall be such as the Secretary of State may from time to time determine.

Accommodation of persons over school age in convenient community home.

1948 c. 43.

50. For section 19 of the Children Act 1948 there shall be substituted the following section:—

Accommodation of persons over school age in convenient community home.

19. A local authority may provide accommodation in a community home for any person who is over compulsory school age but has not attained the age of twenty-one if the community home is provided for children who are over compulsory school age and is near the place where that person is employed or seeking employment or receiving education or training.

Foster children

Modification of general duty of local authorities with respect to foster children.

1958 c. 65.

51. For section 1 of the Children Act 1958 (which imposes a duty on every local authority to secure that foster children are visited by officers of the authority) there shall be substituted the following section:—

Duty of local authorities to ensure well-being of foster children.

1. It shall be the duty of every local authority to satisfy themselves as to the well-being of children within their area who are foster children within the meaning of this Part of this Act and, for that purpose, to secure that, so far as appears to the authority to be appropriate, the children are visited from time to

time by officers of the authority and that such advice PART II
is given as to the care and maintenance of the
children as appears to be needed.

52.—(1) In subsection (1) of section 2 of the Children Act Amendments
1958 (which, subject to the following provisions of that section, of definitions
defines a foster child for the purposes of Part I of that Act as a of " foster
child below the upper limit of the compulsory school age whose " protected
care and maintenance are undertaken for reward for a period child ".
exceeding one month by a person who is not a relative or 1958 c. 65.
guardian of his) the words from " for reward " to " one month "
shall be omitted.

(2) At the end of paragraph (*c*) of subsection (3) of the said
section 2 (which provides that a child is not a foster child while
he is in the care of any person in a school) there shall be added
the words " in which he is receiving full time education ".

(3) After subsection (3) of the said section 2 there shall be
inserted the following subsection:—

(3A) A child is not a foster child within the meaning of
this Part of this Act at any time while his care and
maintenance are undertaken by a person, other than a
relative or guardian of his, if at that time—

(*a*) that person does not intend to, and does not in
fact, undertake his care and maintenance for a
continuous period of more than six days ; or

(*b*) that person is not a regular foster parent and does
not intend to, and does not in fact, undertake his
care and maintenance for a continuous period of
more than twenty-seven days ;

and for the purposes of this subsection a person is a regular
foster parent if, during the period of twelve months immediately preceding the date on which he begins to undertake the care and maintenance of the child in question, he
had, otherwise than as a relative or guardian, the care and
maintenance of one or more children either for a period of,
or periods amounting in the aggregate to, not less than
three months or for at least three continuous periods each
of which was of more than six days.

(4) Section 37 of the Adoption Act 1958 (which defines 1958 c. 5. (7 &
" protected child " for the purposes of Part IV of that Act) shall 8 Eliz. 2.)
have effect subject to the following modifications:—

(*a*) in paragraph (*a*) of subsection (1) (which refers to
arrangements for placing a child in the care of a

person who is not a parent, guardian or relative of his) after the words " relative of his " there shall be inserted the words " but who proposes to adopt him " ;

(b) in subsection (1) (which among other matters excludes a foster child from the definition of " a protected child ") the words " but is not a foster child within the meaning of Part I of the Children Act 1958 " shall be omitted ; and

(c) in subsection (2) (which excludes certain children from the definition of protected child, including children only temporarily in the care and possession of a person under such arrangements as are referred to in sub-section (1)(a) of that section) the words from " by reason " to " that subsection, nor " shall be omitted.

(5) In consequence of the modifications of the definition of " protected child " specified in subsection (4) of this section,

after subsection (4) of section 2 of the Children Act 1958 there shall be inserted the following subsection : —

" (4A) A child is not a foster child for the purposes of this Part of this Act while he is placed in the care and possession of a person who proposes to adopt him under arrangements made by such a local authority or registered adoption society as is referred to in Part II of the Adoption

Act 1958 or while he is a protected child within the meaning of Part IV of that Act."

Modification
of duty of
persons
maintaining
foster
children to
notify local
authority.
53.—(1) Section 3 of the Children Act 1958 (which requires any person maintaining foster children to notify the local authority on each occasion on which he receives a foster child) shall have effect subject to the following provisions of this section.

(2) In subsection (1) of the section (which requires at least two weeks advance notice of, or, in an emergency, notice within one week after, the reception of a foster child) at the beginning there shall be inserted the words " Subject to the following pro-visions of this section ", after the words " two weeks " there shall be inserted the words " and not more than four weeks " and for the words " one week " there shall be substituted the words " forty-eight hours ".

(3) In subsection (2) of the section (which relates to the content of the notice) after the word " specify " there shall be inserted the words " the date on which it is intended that the child should be received or, as the case may be, on which the child was in fact received or became a foster child and ".

(4) After subsection (2) of the section there shall be inserted the following subsection :—

(2A) A person shall not be required to give notice under subsection (1) of this section in relation to a child if—

(a) he has on a previous occasion given notice under that subsection in. respect of that or any other child, specifying the premises at which he proposes to keep the child in question ; and

(b) he has not, at any time since that notice was given, ceased to maintain at least one foster child at those premises and been required by virtue of the following provisions of this section to give notice under subsection (5A) of this section in respect of those premises.

(5) In subsection (3) of the section (which relates to notification of changes of address of foster parents and requires similar periods of notice as under subsection (1))—

(a) for the words " a foster child " there shall be substituted the words " one or more foster children " ;

(b) for the words " the child is kept " there shall be substituted the words " the child is, or the children are, kept " ;

(c) after the words " two weeks " there shall be inserted the words " and not more than four weeks " ; and

(d) for the words " one week " there shall be substituted the words " forty-eight hours ".

(6) So much of subsection (4) of the section as requires notification that a foster child has been removed or has removed himself from the care of the person maintaining him shall cease to have effect and, accordingly, in that subsection for the words " that person " there shall be substituted the words " the person who was maintaining him " and in subsection (5) of the section (which dispenses with the need for such a notice where a child ceases to be a foster child on his removal from a foster parent but empowers the local authority concerned to require certain particulars in such a case)—

(a) for the words " ceases to be a foster child on his removal " there shall be substituted the words " is removed or removes himself " ;

(b) the words " need not give notice under subsection (4) of this section but " shall be omitted ; and

(c) for the words from " the same " onwards there shall be substituted the words " the name and address, if known, of the person (if any) into whose care the child has been removed ".

3 C 2

(7) After subsection (5) of the section there shall be inserted the following subsections: —

(5A) Subject to the provisions of the following subsection, where a person who has been maintaining one or more foster children at any premises ceases to maintain foster children at those premises and the circumstances are such that no notice is required to be given under subsection (3) or subsection (4) of this section, that person shall, within forty-eight hours after he ceases to maintain any foster child at those premises, give notice in writing thereof to the local authority.

(5B) A person need not give the notice required by the preceding subsection in consequence of his ceasing to maintain foster children at any premises if, at the time he so ceases, he intends within twenty-seven days again to maintain any of them as a foster child at those premises ; but if he subsequently abandons that intention or the said period expires without his having given effect to it he shall give the said notice within forty-eight hours of that event.

Inspection of premises in which foster children are kept.

1958 c. 65.

54.—(1) In section 4(1) of the Children Act 1958 (which empowers an officer of a local authority to inspect premises in the local authority's area in which foster children are being kept) after the word " in " in the second place where it occurs there shall be inserted the words " the whole or any part of ".

(2) After the said section 4(1) there shall be inserted the following subsection: —

(1A) If it is shown to the satisfaction of a justice of the peace on sworn information in writing—

(a) that there is reasonable cause to believe that a foster child is being kept in any premises, or in any part thereof, and

(b) that admission to those premises or that part thereof has been refused to a duly authorised officer of the local authority or that such a refusal is apprehended or that the occupier is temporarily absent,

the justice may by warrant under his hand authorise an officer of the local authority to enter the premises, if need be by force, at any reasonable time within forty-eight hours of the issue of the warrant, for the purpose of inspecting the premises.

(3) At the end of paragraph (b) of section 14(1) of the Children Act 1958 (which makes it an offence under that section to refuse to allow an inspection of any premises under section 4(1) of that Act) there shall be added the words " or wilfully

obstructs a person entitled to enter any premises by virtue of a PART II
warrant under subsection (1A) of that section ".

55.—(1) In section 4(2) of the Children Act 1958 (which Imposition of
empowers a local authority to impose certain requirements on a requirements
person who keeps or proposes to keep foster children in premises and
used wholly or mainly for that purpose) for the word " mainly " prohibitions
there shall be substituted the word " partly ". relating to
the keeping
of foster
(2) After paragraph (*f*) of the said section 4(2) there shall be children.
inserted the following paragraphs:— 1958 c. 65.

   (*g*) the fire precautions to be taken in the premises ;

   (*h*) the giving of particulars of any foster child received in
      the premises and of any change in the number or
      identity of the foster children kept therein.

(3) In the words following the several paragraphs of the said
section 4(2), after the word " but " there shall be inserted the
words " any such requirement may be limited to a particular
class of foster children kept in the premises and " and for the
words " (*b*) to (*f*) " there shall be substituted the words " (*b*) to
(*h*) ".

(4) For subsection (3) of section 4 of the Children Act 1958
(which empowers a local authority to prohibit a person from
keeping a particular foster child or any foster children at
particular premises) there shall be substituted the following subsections:—

   (3) Where a person proposes to keep a foster child in
any premises and the local authority are of the opinion
that—

   (*a*) the premises are not suitable premises in which
      to keep foster children ; or

   (*b*) that person is not a suitable person to have the
      care and maintenance of foster children ; or

   (*c*) it would be detrimental to that child to be kept
      by that person in those premises ;

the local authority may impose a prohibition on that
person under subsection (3A) of this section.

   (3A) A prohibition imposed on any person under this
subsection may—

   (*a*) prohibit him from keeping any foster child in
      premises specified in the prohibition ; or

   (*b*) prohibit him from keeping any foster child in any
      premises in the area of the local authority ; or

   (*c*) prohibit him from keeping a particular child
      specified in the prohibition in premises so
      specified.

PART II

(3B) Where a local authority have imposed a prohibition on any person under subsection (3A) of this section, the local authority may, if they think fit, cancel the prohibition, either of their own motion or on an application made by that person on the ground of a change in the circumstances in which a foster child would be kept by him.

1958 c. 65.

(5) In section 5(1) of the Children Act 1958 (which confers a right of appeal to a juvenile court within fourteen days of the imposition of a requirement or prohibition under section 4 of that Act) after the word " prohibition ", in the second place where it occurs, there shall be inserted the words " or, in the case of a prohibition imposed under subsection (3A) of that section, within fourteen days from the refusal by the local authority to accede to an application by him for the cancellation of the prohibition ".

Extension of disqualification for keeping foster children.

56.—(1) In section 6 of the Children Act 1958 (which provides that a person shall not, without the consent of the local authority, maintain a foster child if one or more of a variety of orders has been made against him) there shall be made the following amendments, that is to say—

(a) in paragraph (b), after the word " 1933 ", there shall be inserted the words " the Children and Young Persons Act 1969 " and for the words from " in respect of " to " of which the " there shall be substituted the words " and by virtue of the order or requirement a " ;

(b) at the end of paragraph (c) there shall be inserted the words " or has been placed on probation or discharged absolutely or conditionally for any such offence " ;

(c) in paragraph (e), after the word " subsection " there shall be inserted the words " (3) or " and for the words from " refusing " onwards there shall be substituted the words " refusing, or an order under section five of that Act cancelling, the registration of any premises occupied by him or his registration " ; and

(d) after paragraph (e) there shall be inserted the following paragraph : —

1958 c. 5. (7 & 8 Eliz. 2.)

(f) an order has been made under section 43 of the Adoption Act 1958 for the removal of a protected child who was being kept or was about to be received by him.

(2) At the end of the said section 6 there shall be added the following subsection : —

(2) Where this section applies to any person, otherwise than by virtue of this subsection, it shall apply also to any

other person who lives in the same premises as he does or
who lives in premises at which he is employed ;
and accordingly the said section 6 as amended by the preceding
subsection shall be subsection (1) of that section.

57.—(1) After subsection (1) of section 14 of the Children   Modifications
Act 1958 (which, among other matters, makes it an offence to   of provisions
maintain a foster child in contravention of section 6 of that   as to offences.
Act) there shall be inserted the following subsection :—   1958 c. 65.

(1A) Where section 6 of this Act applies to any
person by virtue only of subsection (2) of that section,
he shall not be guilty of an offence under paragraph (*d*)
of subsection (1) of this section if he proves that he did
not know, and had no reasonable ground for believing, that
a person living or employed in the premises in which he
lives was a person to whom that section applies.

(2) After subsection (2) of the said section 14 (which provides that offences under that section are punishable summarily)
there shall be added the following subsection :—

(2A) If any person who is required, under any provision of
this Part of this Act, to give a notice fails to give the notice
within the time specified in that provision, then, notwithstanding anything in section 104 of the Magistrates' Courts   1952 c. 55.
Act 1952 (time limit for proceedings) proceedings for the
offence may be brought at any time within six months
from the date when evidence of the offence came to the
knowledge of the local authority.

Inspection

58.—(1) Subject to subsection (2) of this section, the Secretary   Inspection of
of State may cause to be inspected from time to time—   children's
homes etc.
(*a*) any community home provided by a local authority   by persons
under section 38 of this Act ;   authorised
(*b*) any voluntary home (whether a community home or   Secretary
not) ;   State.
(*c*) any other premises at which one or more children in
the care of a local authority are being accommodated
and maintained ;
(*d*) any other premises at which one or more children are
being boarded out by a voluntary organisation ; and
(*e*) any other premises where a foster child within the
meaning of Part I of the Children Act 1958 or a
child to whom any of the provisions of that Part are
extended by section 12 or section 13 of that Act, or a

protected child within the meaning of Part IV of the Adoption Act 1958 is being accommodated or maintained.

(2) Subsection (1) of this section does not apply to any home or other premises which is, as a whole, subject to inspection by or under the authority of a government department.

(3) An inspection under this section shall be conducted by a person authorised in that behalf by the Secretary of State, but an officer of a local authority shall not be so authorised except with the consent of that authority.

(4) Any person inspecting a home or other premises under this section may inspect the children therein and make such examination into the state and management of the home or other premises and the treatment of children therein as he thinks fit.

Powers of entry supplemental to s. 58.
59.—(1) A person authorised to inspect any home or other premises under section 58 of this Act shall have a right to enter the home or other premises for that purpose and for any other purpose specified in subsection (4) of that section, but shall if so required produce some duly authenticated document showing his authority to exercise the power of entry conferred by this subsection.

(2) A person who obstructs the exercise by a person authorised as mentioned in subsection (1) of this section of a power of entry conferred thereby shall be liable on summary conviction to a fine not exceeding five pounds or, in the case of a second or subsequent conviction, to a fine not exceeding twenty pounds.

(3) A refusal to allow any such person as is mentioned in subsection (1) of this section to enter any such home or other premises as are mentioned in section 58(1) of this Act shall be deemed, for the purposes of section 40 of the Act of 1933 (which relates to search warrants), to be a reasonable cause to suspect that a child or young person in the home or other premises is being neglected in a manner likely to cause him unnecessary suffering or injury to health.

Part III

Miscellaneous and general

Miscellaneous

Extradition offences.

1870 c. 52.
60.—(1) There shall be included—

    (*a*) in the list of extradition crimes contained in Schedule 1 to the Extradition Act 1870 ; and

(*b*) among the descriptions of offences set out in Schedule 1 PART III
to the Fugitive Offenders Act 1967, 1967 c. 68.
any offence of the kind described in section 1 of the Act of 1933
(which relates to cruelty to persons under sixteen) and any
offence of the kind described in section 1 of the Indecency with 1960 c. 33.
Children Act 1960.

(2) Nothing in this Act shall be construed as derogating from
the provisions of section 17 of the said Act of 1870 or section
16(2) or 17 of the said Act of 1967 in their application to any
provisions of those Acts respectively as amended by the preceding
subsection.

61.—(1) Without prejudice to the generality of the power to Rules relating
make rules under section 15 of the Justices of the Peace Act 1949 to juvenile
relating to the procedure and practice to be followed by magis- court panels
trates' courts, provision may be made by such rules with respect composition
to any of the following matters, namely,— of juvenile

    (*a*) the formation and revision of juvenile court panels, courts.
        that is to say, panels of justices specially qualified to 1949 c. 101.
        deal with juvenile cases and the eligibility of justices to
        be members of such panels ;

    (*b*) the appointment of persons as chairmen of juvenile
        courts ; and

    (*c*) the composition of juvenile courts.

(2) Rules making any such provisions as are referred to in
subsection (1) of this section may confer powers on the Lord
Chancellor with respect to any of the matters specified in the
rules and may, in particular, provide for the appointment of
juvenile court panels by him and for the removal from a juvenile
court panel of any justice who, in his opinion, is unsuitable to
serve on a juvenile court.

(3) Rules made by virtue of this section may make different
provision in relation to different areas for which juvenile court
panels are formed ; and in the application of this section to the
county palatine of Lancaster, for any reference in the preceding
subsection to the Lord Chancellor there shall be substituted a
reference to the Chancellor of the Duchy.

(4) Nothing in this section or in any rules made under section
15 of the said Act of 1949 shall affect—

    (*a*) the areas for which juvenile court panels are formed
        and juvenile courts are constituted ;

    (*b*) the provisions of Part I of Schedule 2 to the Act of
        1963 (and, as it has effect by virtue of section 17(1)
        of that Act, Part I of Schedule 2 to the Act of 1933)

3 C*

with respect to the making of recommendations and orders relating to the formation of combined juvenile court panels ; or

(c) the provisions of paragraph 14 of that Schedule relating to the divisions of the metropolitan area for which juvenile courts sit ;

but rules under the said section 15 may repeal, either generally or with respect to any part of the metropolitan area, any provision contained in paragraphs 15 to 18 of that Schedule (which contain provisions applicable in the metropolitan area with respect to certain of the matters referred to in subsection (1) of this section)

and in subsections (2) and (3) of section 12 of the Administration of Justice Act 1964 (which amend those paragraphs).

(5) In this section " the metropolitan area " means the inner London area and the City of London.

Contributions in respect of children and young persons in care.

62.—(1) The provisions of sections 86 to 88 of the Act of 1933 (which, as originally enacted, provided for contributions in respect of children and young persons committed to the care of a fit person or sent to an approved school) shall apply in relation to children and young persons committed to the care of a local authority by a care order which is not an interim order.

(2) Whether or not a contribution order has been made in respect of any child or young person in the care of a local authority, no contribution shall be payable in respect of him for any period during which he is allowed by the local authority to be under the charge and control of a parent, guardian, relative or friend, although remaining in the care of the local authority.

(3) Where a person (in this section referred to as a " contributory ") is liable under section 86 of the Act of 1933 to make a contribution in respect of a child or young person in the care of a local authority, then, subject to the following provisions of this section, the amount of his contribution shall be such as may be proposed by the local authority and agreed by the contributory or, in default of agreement, as may be determined by a court in proceedings for, or for the variation of, a contribution order.

(4) The maximum contribution which may be proposed by a local authority in respect of a child or young person in their care shall be a weekly amount equal to the weekly amount which, in the opinion of the local authority, they would normally be prepared to pay if a child or young person of the same age were boarded out by them (whether or not the child or young person in respect of whom the contribution is proposed is in fact so boarded out and, if he is, whether or not the local authority are in fact paying that amount).

(5) No contribution order shall be made on a contributory in
respect of a child or young person unless—

(a) the local authority in whose care he is have, by notice in writing given to the contributory, proposed an amount as the amount of his contribution ; and

(b) either the contributory and the local authority have not, within the period of one month beginning with the day on which the notice was given to the contributory, agreed on the amount of his contribution or the contributory has defaulted in making one or more contributions of an amount which has been agreed.

(6) In proceedings for a contribution order, the court shall not order a contributory to pay a contribution greater than that proposed in the notice given to him under subsection (5)(a) of this section.

(7) In proceedings for the variation of a contribution order, the local authority concerned shall specify the weekly amount which, having regard to subsection (4) of this section, they propose should be the amount of the contribution and the court shall not vary the contribution order so as to require the contributory to pay a contribution greater than that proposed by the local authority.

(8) In this section—

" contribution " means a contribution under section 86 of the Act of 1933 ; and

" contribution order " means an order under section 87 of that Act.

63.—(1) Every local authority shall, at such times and in such form as the Secretary of State may direct, transmit to the Secretary of State such particulars as he may require—

(a) with respect to the performance by the local authority of all or any of the functions specified in section 39(1) of the Children Act 1948 (which relates to the establishment of children's committees) ; and

(b) with respect to the children in relation to whom the authority have exercised those functions.

(2) Every voluntary organisation shall, at such times and in such form as the Secretary of State may direct, transmit to him such particulars as he may require with respect to the children who are accommodated and maintained in voluntary homes provided by the organisation or who have been boarded out by the organisation.

(3) The clerk of each juvenile court shall, at such times and in such form as the Secretary of State may direct, transmit to

Returns of information and presentation of reports etc. to Parliament. 1948 c. 43.

PART III   him such particulars as he may require with respect to the proceedings of the court.

(4) The Secretary of State shall in each year lay before Parliament a consolidated and classified abstract of the information transmitted to him under the preceding provisions of this section.

(5) The Secretary of State shall lay before Parliament in 1973 and in every third subsequent year a report with respect to the exercise by local authorities of the functions specified in 1948 c. 43.   section 39(1) of the Children Act 1948, the provision by voluntary organisations of facilities for children and such other matters relating to children as he thinks fit.

Financial provisions

Expenses of Secretary of State in providing homes offering specialised facilities.   **64.** There shall be defrayed out of moneys provided by Parliament any expenses incurred by the Secretary of State in providing, equipping and maintaining homes for the accommodation of children who are in the care of local authorities and are in need of particular facilities and services which are provided in those homes and are, in the opinion of the Secretary of State, unlikely to be readily available in community homes.

Grants to voluntary organisations etc.   **65.**—(1) The Secretary of State may make out of moneys provided by Parliament grants to voluntary organisations of such amounts and subject to such conditions as he may with the consent of the Treasury determine towards expenditure incurred by them in connection with the establishment, maintenance or improvement of voluntary homes which at the time the expenditure was incurred were assisted community homes or were designated as such in a regional plan which was then in operation, including expenses incurred by them in respect of the borrowing of money to defray any such expenditure.

(2) The power of the Secretary of State to make grants to voluntary organisations under section 46 of the Children Act 1948 (which relates to grants in respect of certain expenses incurred in connection with voluntary homes) shall not apply to expenditure incurred in connection with a voluntary home which, at the time the expenditure was incurred, was a controlled or assisted community home or was designated as such in a regional plan which was then in operation.

(3) Where an order has been made under section 46 of this Act in relation to an approved institution within the meaning of that section and no such provision as is referred to in paragraph 9(1) of Schedule 3 to this Act is made by a regional plan in relation to any part of the premises of the institution, the Secretary of State may with the consent of the Treasury

make out of moneys provided by Parliament grants towards the discharge by any person of any liability, other than an obligation to which paragraph 11 of that Schedule applies, which was incurred by that person in connection with the establishment, maintenance or improvement of the institution.

(4) No grant shall be made under subsection (3) of this section in respect of a liability relating to an institution unless it appears to the Secretary of State that, on or within a reasonable time after the date specified in the order referred to in that subsection, the premises of the institution are to be used for a purpose which is of benefit to children ; and any grant made under that subsection shall be subject to such conditions as the Secretary of State may with the approval of the Treasury determine, including conditions with respect to the repayment in whole or in part of the grant, either by the person to whom the grant was made or by some other person who, before the grant was made, consented to accept the liability.

(5) Any sums received by the Secretary of State by virtue of any such condition as is referred to in subsection (4) of this section shall be paid into the Consolidated Fund.

66.—(1) The power to make an order under section 3(1) of Increase of the Local Government Act 1966 increasing the amounts fixed rate support by a rate support grant order for a particular year shall be grants. exercisable, in accordance with subsection (2) of this section, in 1966 c. 42. relation to any rate support grant order made before the date of the coming into operation of any provision of this Act (in this section referred to as " the relevant provision ") for a grant period ending after that date.

(2) Without prejudice to subsection (4) of the said section 3 (which empowers an order under subsection (1) of that section to vary the matters prescribed by a rate support grant order), an order under subsection (1) of that section made by virtue of this section may be made for such year or years comprised in the grant period concerned as may be specified in the order and in respect of the year or each of the years so specified shall increase the amounts fixed by the relevant rate support grant order as the aggregate amounts of the rate support grants and any elements of the grants for that year to such extent and in such a manner as may appear to the Minister of Housing and Local Government to be appropriate, having regard to any additional expenditure incurred or likely to be incurred by local authorities in consequence of the coming into operation of the relevant provision.

(3) In this section " grant period " means the period for which a rate support grant order is made.

Part III   (4) There shall be defrayed out of moneys provided by Parliament any increase in rate support grants attributable to this Act.

Administrative expenses.   **67.** Any administrative expenses of the Secretary of State under this Act shall be defrayed out of moneys provided by Parliament.

Supplemental

Compulsory acquisition of land.   **68.**—(1) A local authority other than a county council may be authorised by the Secretary of State to purchase compulsorily any land, whether situated inside or outside their area, for the purposes of their functions under this Act or section 1 of the Act of 1963.

1946 c. 49.   (2) The Acquisition of Land (Authorisation Procedure) Act 1946 shall apply in relation to the compulsory purchase of land in pursuance of subsection (1) of this section as if that subsection were contained in an Act in force immediately before the commencement of that Act.

1933 c. 51.   (3) In the application to the functions of a county council under this Act or section 1 of the Act of 1963 of section 159(1) of the Local Government Act 1933 (under which a county council may be authorised to purchase land compulsorily) the power to authorise a compulsory purchase shall be vested in the Secretary of State.

Orders and regulations etc.   **69.**—(1) Any power conferred on the Secretary of State by this Act to make an order or regulations, except an order under section 25, 39 or 43(5) or paragraph 23 or 24 of Schedule 4, shall be exercisable by statutory instrument; and any statutory instrument made in pursuance of this subsection, except an instrument containing only regulations under paragraph 8(2) of Schedule 3 or an order under section 1(6), 26, 46, 47, 72(2) or 73(2), or paragraph 11(2) of Schedule 3, shall be subject to annulment in pursuance of a resolution of either House of Parliament.

(2) A statutory instrument containing regulations under subsection (4) of section 5 or an order under section 34 of this Act shall not be subject to annulment as aforesaid, but no such regulations or order shall be included in a statutory instrument containing provisions which do not require approval in pursuance of the said subsection (4) or, as the case may be, to which subsection (7) of the said section 34 does not apply.

(3) An order made or directions given by the Secretary of State under any provision of this Act, except an order under section 7(5), may be revoked or varied by a subsequent order or subsequent directions under that provision.

(4) Any order or regulations made by the Secretary of State Part III under this Act may—

(a) make different provision for different circumstances;

(b) provide for exemptions from any provisions of the order or regulations; and

(c) contain such incidental and supplemental provisions as the Secretary of State considers expedient for the purposes of the order or regulations.

70.—(1) In this Act, unless the contrary intention appears, the Interpretation following expressions have the following meanings:— and ancillary provisions.

"the Act of 1933" means the Children and Young Persons 1933 c. 12. Act 1933;

"the Act of 1963" means the Children and Young Persons 1963 c. 37. Act 1963;

"approved school order", "guardian" and "place of safety" have the same meanings as in the Act of 1933;

"care order" has the meaning assigned to it by section 20 of this Act;

"child", except in Part II (including Schedule 3) and sections 27, 63, 64 and 65 of this Act, means a person under the age of fourteen, and in that Part (including that Schedule) and those sections means a person under the age of eighteen and a person who has attained the age of eighteen and is the subject of a care order;

"instrument of management" means an instrument of management made under section 39 of this Act;

"interim order" has the meaning assigned to it by section 20 of this Act;

"local authority" means the council of a county, county borough or London borough or the Common Council of the City of London;

"petty sessions area" has the same meaning as in the Magistrates' Courts Act 1952 except that, in relation 1952 c. 55. to a juvenile court constituted for the metropolitan area within the meaning of Part II of Schedule 2 to the Act of 1963, it means such a division of that area as is mentioned in paragraph 14 of that Schedule;

"planning area" has the meaning assigned to it by section 35(1) of this Act;

"police officer" means a member of a police force;

"regional plan" has the meaning assigned to it by section 36(1) of this Act;

3 C* 4

" the relevant authorities ", in relation to a planning area, has the meaning assigned to it by section 35(3) of this Act ;

" reside " means habitually reside, and cognate expressions shall be construed accordingly except in section 12(4) and (5) of this Act ;

" supervision order ", " supervised person " and " supervisor " have the meanings assigned to them by section 11 of this Act ;

"trust deed ", in relation to a voluntary home, has the meaning assigned to it by section 40(5) of this Act ;

" voluntary home " has the same meaning as in Part V of the Act of 1933 ;

" voluntary organisation " has the same meaning as in the Children Act 1948 ; and

" young person " means a person who has attained the age of fourteen and is under the age of seventeen ;

and it is hereby declared that, in the expression " care or control ", " care " includes protection and guidance and " control " includes discipline.

(2) Without prejudice to any power apart from this subsection to bring proceedings on behalf of another person, any power to make an application which is exercisable by a child or young person by virtue of section 15(1), 21(2), 22(4) or (6) or 28(5) of this Act shall also be exercisable on his behalf by his parent or guardian ; and in this subsection " guardian " includes any person who was a guardian of the child or young person in question at the time when any supervision order, care order or warrant to which the application relates was originally made.

(3) In section 99(1) of the Act of 1933 (under which the age which a court presumes or declares to be the age of a person brought before it is deemed to be his true age for the purposes of that Act) the references to that Act shall be construed as including references to this Act.

(4) Subject to the following subsection, any reference in this Act to any enactment is a reference to it as amended, and includes a reference to it as applied, by or under any other enactment including this Act.

(5) Any reference in this Act to an enactment of the Parliament of Northern Ireland shall be construed as a reference to that enactment as amended by any Act of that Parliament, whether passed before or after this Act, and to any enactment of that Parliament for the time being in force which re-enacts the said enactment with or without modifications.

71. This Act shall have effect, in its application to the Isles
of Scilly, with such modifications as the Secretary of State may Application
by order specify.   to Isles of
Scilly.

72.—(1) The transitional provisions and savings set out in Transitional
Part I of Schedule 4 to this Act shall have effect.   provisions,
minor
(2) The transitional provisions set out in Part II of Schedule amendments
4 to this Act shall have effect until such day as the Secretary of and repeals
State may by order specify for the purposes of this subsection etc.
(being the day on and after which those provisions will in his
opinion be unnecessary in consequence of the coming into
force of provisions of the Social Work (Scotland) Act 1968) and 1968 c. 49.
shall be deemed to have been repealed on that day by an Act of
Parliament passed after this Act.

(3) The enactments mentioned in Schedule 5 to this Act shall
have effect subject to the amendments specified in that Schedule
(which are minor amendments and amendments consequential
on the provisions of this Act).

(4) Subject to subsection (1) of this section, the enactments
mentioned in the first and second columns of Schedule 6 to
this Act are hereby repealed to the extent specified in the
third column of that Schedule.

(5) In accordance with Part II of this Act and the said
Schedules 5 and 6, sections 1 to 6 and 14 of the Children Act 1958 c. 65.
1958 are to have effect, after the coming into force of so much
of that Part and those Schedules as relates to those sections,
as set out in Schedule 7 to this Act, but without prejudice to
any other enactment affecting the operation of those sections.

73.—(1) This Act may be cited as the Children and Young Citation,
Persons Act 1969, and this Act and the Children and Young commence-
Persons Acts 1933 to 1963 may be cited together as the Children ment and
and Young Persons Acts 1933 to 1969.   extent.

(2) This Act shall come into force on such day as the
Secretary of State may by order appoint, and different days
may be appointed under this subsection for different provisions
of this Act or for different provisions of this Act so far as
they apply to such cases only as may be specified in the order.

(3) Without prejudice to the generality of section 69(4) of
this Act, an order under the preceding subsection may make such
transitional provision as the Secretary of State considers appropriate in connection with the provisions brought into force by the
order, including such adaptations of those provisions and of any
other provisions of this Act then in force as appear to him appropriate for the purposes or in consequence of the operation of any

provision of this Act before the coming into force of any other
provision of this Act or of a provision of the Social Work (Scotland) Act 1968.

(4) This section and the following provisions only of this
Act extend to Scotland, that is to say—

(a) sections 10(1) and (2), 32(1), (3) and (4), 56 and 57(1);

(b) section 72(2) and Part II of Schedule 4;

(c) paragraphs 25, 26, 33, 35, 38, 42, 43, 53, 54 and 57 to
83 of Schedule 5 and section 72(3) so far as it relates
to those paragraphs;

(d) section 72(4) and Schedule 6 so far as they relate to the
Merchant Shipping Act 1894, the Superannuation
(Miscellaneous Provisions) Act 1948, sections 10, 53, 55
and 59 of the Act of 1963, the Family Allowances Act
1965 and the Social Work (Scotland) Act 1968.

(5) This section and the following provisions only of this
Act extend to Northern Ireland, that is to say—

(a) sections 25 and 32;

(b) section 72(3) and Schedule 5 so far as they relate to
section 29 of the Criminal Justice Act 1961 and provisions of the Social Work (Scotland) Act 1968 which
extend to Northern Ireland; and

(c) section 72(4) and Schedule 6 so far as they relate to
section 83 of the Act of 1933, paragraph 13 of Schedule
2 to the Children and Young Persons (Scotland) Act
1937, section 29 of the Criminal Justice Act 1961,
sections 10(1) and (2), 53(1) and 65(5) of, and paragraphs 27, 34 and 50 of Schedule 3 to, the Act of 1963
and sections 73(2), 76(1) and (2) and 77(1)(b) of the
Social Work (Scotland) Act 1968;

and section 32(2) and (3) of this Act shall be treated for the
purposes of section 6 of the Government of Ireland Act 1920 as
if it had been passed before the day appointed for the said
section 6 to come into operation.

(6) Section 26 of this Act and this section, and section
72(4) of this Act and Schedule 6 to this Act so far as they
relate to paragraph 13 of Schedule 2 to the Children and Young
Persons (Scotland) Act 1937 and section 53(1) of, and paragraph
34 of Schedule 3 to, the Act of 1963, extend to the Channel
Islands and the Isle of Man, and section 32(1) and (4) of this
Act and this section extend to the Channel Islands.

(7) It is hereby declared that the provisions of sections 69
and 70 of this Act extend to each of the countries aforesaid so
far as is appropriate for the purposes of any other provisions of
this Act extending to the country in question.

SCHEDULES

SCHEDULE 1

Section 33(1).

MODIFICATIONS OF PART IV OF CRIMINAL JUSTICE ACT 1967   1967 c. 80.

1.—(1) In section 73(1), after the word " proceedings " there shall be inserted the words " and the proceedings mentioned in subsections (3A) and (3B) of this section ".

(2) At the end of section 73(2) there shall be inserted the words " and any other magistrates' court to which the case is remitted in pursuance of section 56(1) of the Children and Young Persons Act 1933 ". 1933 c. 12.

(3) In section 73, after subsection (3) there shall be inserted the following subsections:—

(3A) Where a person—

(a) is or is to be brought before a juvenile court under section 1 of the Children and Young Persons Act 1969 ; or

(b) is the subject of an application to a magistrates' court under section 15 or section 21 of that Act ; or

(c) is or is to be brought before a juvenile court under section 31 of that Act,

the court may order that he shall be given legal aid for the purpose of proceedings before the court and, in a case falling within paragraph (a) of this subsection, before any juvenile court to which the case is remitted.

(3B) Where a person desires to appeal to a court of quarter sessions in pursuance of section 2(12), 3(8), 16(8), 21(4) or 31(6) of the said Act of 1969, that court or the court from whose decision the appeal lies may order that he be given legal aid for the purpose of the appeal.

2.—(1) At the end of section 74(2) there shall be inserted the words " and except in the case of proceedings under section 1 of the Children and Young Persons Act 1969 where it is alleged that the condition set out in subsection (2)(f) of that section is satisfied in consequence of an indictable offence and where the court is of the opinion aforesaid ".

(2) In section 74(3), after " (3) " there shall be inserted the word " (3B) " and for the word " either " there shall be substituted the word " any ".

(3) In section 74(5), after the word " (2) " there shall be inserted the words " or (3A) ".

(4) In section 74(6), after the word " section ", there shall be inserted the words " or to any person by a legal aid order under subsection (3B) of that section " and after the word " sentence " there shall be inserted the words " or, as the case may be, dismissing the appeal mentioned in the said subsection (3B) or otherwise altering the order to which the appeal relates ".

3. In section 75, after subsection (4) there shall be inserted the following subsection: —

(4A) Subsections (3) and (4) of this section shall have effect, in their application to a person who has not attained the age of sixteen, as if the words " he ", " him " and " his " referred to that person and a person who is an appropriate contributor in relation to him or such of them as the court selects, and as if for the word " shall " in subsection (4) there were substituted the word " may " ; and the court may require that a statement furnished by an appropriate contributor in pursuance of subsection (4) shall specify both his means and those of the other person aforesaid.

4.—(1) In section 76, after subsection (1) there shall be inserted the following subsection: —

(1A) In a case where a legally assisted person has not attained the age of sixteen, the power conferred by the last foregoing subsection to order him to pay contributions in respect of the relevant costs shall include power to order any person who is an appropriate contributor in relation to him to pay such contributions ; and for the purposes of any order proposed to be made by virtue of this subsection in connection with a legal aid order, an appropriate contributor who has failed to furnish a statement which he was required to furnish in pursuance of section 75(4) of this Act in connection with the legal aid order shall be deemed to have resources and commitments which are such that he may reasonably be ordered to pay the whole amount of the costs in question.

(2) In section 76(4)(a), after the words " that magistrates' court " there shall be inserted the words ", or any other magistrates' court to which the case is remitted in pursuance of section 56(1) of the Children and Young Persons Act 1933."

(3) At the end of section 76 there shall be inserted the following subsection: —

(5) Nothing in subsection (4) of this subsection applies in a case where the legal aid order in question was made by virtue of section 73(3A) or (3B) of this Act, and in such a case an order under this section may be made—

(a) where the legal aid was ordered to be given for the purpose of proceedings before a magistrates' court, by that court, or any other magistrates' court to which the case is remitted in pursuance of section 2(11) of the Children and Young Persons Act 1969, after disposing of the case ; and

(b) where the legal aid was ordered to be given for the purposes of an appeal to a court of quarter sessions, by that court after disposing of the appeal.

5. In section 77(1), after the words " assisted person ", there shall be inserted the words ", or a person who is an appropriate contributor in relation to him,", for the words " into his means " there

shall be substituted the words "into the means of that person and any such contributor or of either or any of them" and the words "on his means" shall be omitted.

6. In section 78(1), after the words "that he" there shall be inserted the words "or any other person".

7.—(1) In section 79(2), after the word "by" there shall be inserted the words "or in respect of", and for the words "to him" there shall be substituted the words—

"(*a*) where the contribution was made by one person only, to him ; and

(*b*) where the contribution was made by two or more persons, to them in proportion to the amounts contributed by them".

(2) In section 79(3) and section 79(6) after the words "assisted person" there shall be inserted the words "or an appropriate contributor".

8.—(1) In section 84, in the definition of "appropriate authority", after paragraph (*a*) there shall be inserted the following paragraph:—

(*aa*) in relation to legal aid ordered by virtue of section 73(3A) or (3B) of this Act, the clerk of the magistrates' court before which the proceedings were heard or from which the appeal was brought or the clerk of the magistrates' court nominated for the purposes of this paragraph by the first-mentioned court.

(2) In section 84, after the definition aforesaid there shall be inserted the following:—

"appropriate contributor", in relation to a person who has not attained the age of sixteen, means his father, any person who has been adjudged to be his putative father and (whether or not he is legitimate) his mother.

(3) At the end of section 84 there shall be inserted the following subsections:—

(2) Any power to make an application in pursuance of this Part of this Act which is exercisable by a person who has not attained the age of seventeen shall also be exercisable by his parent or guardian on his behalf, without prejudice to any powers of the parent or guardian apart from this subsection ; and in this subsection "guardian" has the same meaning as in section 70(2) of the Children and Young Persons Act 1969.

(3) A person who attains the age of sixteen after a legal aid order is made in respect of him or, in a case where such an order is made in pursuance of an application, after the application is made, shall be treated for the purposes of this Part of this Act, in relation to the order, as not having attained that age.

and accordingly the said section 84 as amended by sub-paragraphs (1) and (2) of this paragraph shall be subsection (1) of that section.

SCHEDULE 2

CHILDREN'S REGIONAL PLANNING COMMITTEES

1.—(1) Subject to the following provisions of this Schedule, the children's regional planning committee for a planning area (in this Schedule referred to as " the committee ") shall consist of such number of persons selected and appointed in such manner and holding office on such terms as the relevant authorities may from time to time approve.

(2) No person who is disqualified by virtue of section 59 of the Local Government Act 1933 from being a member of any local authority which is one of the relevant authorities for a planning area may be a member of the committee for that area.

2.—(1) Subject to sub-paragraph (2) of this paragraph, the relevant authorities for a planning area shall so exercise their powers under paragraph 1(1) of this Schedule as to secure that each authority nominates as a member of the committee for the area at least one person who is not so nominated by any other of the relevant authorities.

(2) If the Secretary of State considers that owing to special circumstances the requirement.imposed by sub-paragraph (1) of this paragraph should be dispensed with in the case of a particular authority he may direct accordingly.

(3) The members of the committee for a planning area who are nominated by the relevant authorities are in the following provisions of this Schedule referred to as " the nominated members ".

3.—(1) Without prejudice to any power of co-option conferred on the committee for a planning area under paragraph 1(1) of this Schedule, but subject to paragraph 4 of this Schedule, the nominated members of the committee may co-opt other persons to serve as members of the committee, either generally or in relation only to such matters as may be specified by the nominated members.

(2) Where any persons are co-opted to serve as members of the committee for a planning area in relation only to such matters as are specified by the nominated members then, subject to any directions given by the relevant authorities, the extent to which those persons shall be entitled to attend, speak and vote at meetings of the committee shall be such as may be determined by the nominated members.

4. The relevant authorities for a planning area shall so exercise their powers under paragraph 1(1) of this Schedule, and the nominated members of the committee for a planning area shall so limit any exercise of their power under paragraph 3 of this Schedule, as to secure that at all times a majority of the members of the committee for the planning area are members of the relevant authorities.

5. Subject to any directions given by the relevant authorities, the procedure and quorum of the committee for a planning area shall be such as may be determined by the nominated members.

6. Section 93(1) of the Local Government Act 1933 (which relates   SCH. 2
to the expenses of joint committees of local authorities) shall apply 1933 c. 51.
to the committee for a planning area as it applies to such a joint
committee as is mentioned in that section, but as if—

(*a*) for references to the local authorities by whom the committee is appointed there were substituted references to the
relevant authorities ; and

(*b*) for paragraphs (*a*) and (*b*) of subsection (1) of that section
there were substituted the words " by the Secretary of
State " ;

and Part X of that Act (which relates to accounts and audit) shall
apply to the accounts of the committee for a planning area as it
applies to the accounts of such a joint committee as is mentioned
in section 219(*c*) of that Act.

SCHEDULE 3   Section 46(2).

APPROVED SCHOOLS AND OTHER INSTITUTIONS

Provisions as to staff

1.—(1) This paragraph applies where it appears to the Secretary
of State that on the date specified in an order under section 46 of
this Act (in the following provisions of this Schedule referred to as
a " section 46 order ") all or any of the premises used for the purposes of the institution to which the order relates are to be used for
the purposes—

(*a*) of a community home, or

(*b*) of a school of any of the following descriptions, namely,
a county school, a voluntary school which is a controlled
or aided school, or a special school ;

and in this Schedule " the specified date ", in relation to an institution
to which a section 46 order relates, means the date specified in that
order.

(2) Where this paragraph applies the Secretary of State may, by
the section 46 order, make such provision as he considers appropriate
with respect to—

(*a*) the transfer of existing staff to the employment of the
authority, voluntary organisation or other body of persons
responsible for the employment of persons at the community home or school, as the case may be ; and

(*b*) the transfer to a local authority or voluntary organisation
specified in the order of any liabilities (including contingent
and future liabilities) with respect to the payment of superannuation and other benefits to or in respect of existing
staff and retired staff.

(3) If any such superannuation or other benefits as are referred to
in sub-paragraph (2)(*b*) of this paragraph are not benefits to which the
Pensions (Increase) Acts 1920 to 1969 or any of those Acts apply, the

1558   CH. **54**   *Children and Young Persons Act 1969*

SCH. 3   section 46 order may contain such provisions as the Secretary of State considers appropriate—

> (a) for securing the continued payment of additional amounts (calculated by reference to increases under those Acts) which were paid before the specified date in respect of any such benefits ; and
>
> (b) for securing the payment of additional amounts (calculated by reference to increases under those Acts) in respect of any such benefits to which any person became entitled before the specified date but in respect of which no similar additional amounts were paid before that date.

(4) Where this paragraph applies the section 46 order—

> (a) shall contain provisions for the protection of the interests of any existing staff whose employment is transferred as mentioned in sub-paragraph (2)(a) of this paragraph ;
>
> (b) may contain provisions for the protection of the interests of existing staff whose employment is not so transferred ; and
>
> (c) may contain provisions applying, amending or repealing any provision made by or under any enactment and relating to the conditions of service of existing staff or the payment of superannuation and other benefits to or in respect of existing or retired staff ;

and in a case falling within sub-paragraph (1)(b) of this paragraph any provisions made under paragraph (a) of this sub-paragraph shall have effect notwithstanding any provision made by or under any enactment and relating to the remuneration of teachers.

(5) In this paragraph " existing staff " in relation to a section 46 order means persons who, immediately before the specified date, were employed for the purposes of the institution to which the order relates, and " retired staff " in relation to such an order means persons who, at some time before the specified date, were employed for those purposes but ceased to be so employed before the specified date.

1958 c. 55.   2.—(1) Regulations under section 60 of the Local Government Act 1958 may make provision in relation to persons who suffer loss of employment or loss or diminution of emoluments as a result of a section 46 order and, if in such a case the Minister by whom the regulations are made thinks fit, the regulations may provide for the payment of compensation by the Secretary of State instead of by an authority prescribed by or determined under the regulations.

(2) In accordance with sub-paragraph (1) of this paragraph, sub-section (2) of the said section 60 shall be amended as follows :

> (a) after the words " under the regulations " there shall be inserted the words " or, in a case to which paragraph 2 of Schedule 3 to the Children and Young Persons Act 1969 applies, by the Secretary of State " ; and
>
> (b) after the words " order under Part I of the Police Act 1964 " there shall be inserted the words " or of an order under section 46 of the Children and Young Persons Act 1969 ".

(3) Where a section 46 order is made in relation to an approved institution but paragraph 1 of this Schedule does not apply in relation to that institution, the section 46 order may make such provision as the Secretary of State considers appropriate with respect to the transfer to him of any such liabilities as are referred to in sub-paragraph (2)(*b*) of that paragraph and the payment by him of any such additional amount as is referred to in sub-paragraph (3) of that paragraph.

Use of premises as homes for children in care

3.—(1) If on the day specified for the purposes of section 7(5) of this Act premises are used for the purposes of an approved school, then during the period (in this Schedule referred to, in relation to an approved school, as " the interim period ") beginning immediately after that day and ending on the day on which the school ceases to be an approved school (whether by virtue of a section 46 order or otherwise) those premises may be used for the accommodation and maintenance of children in the care of local authorities.

(2) If during the interim period the premises of an approved school are used for the accommodation and maintenance of children in the care of a local authority then, during that period,

(*a*) any reference in section 21(1) or section 31 of this Act to a community home includes a reference to those premises ; and

(*b*) for the reference in section 18(1)(*c*) of the Criminal Justice Act 1961 (directions of Secretary of State as to management of approved schools) to persons under the care of the managers there shall be substituted a reference to the children in the care of local authorities who are accommodated and maintained in those premises.

(3) At the request of the managers of an approved school the Secretary of State may, at any time during the interim period, give a direction—

(*a*) that so much as may be specified in the direction of any rules made under paragraph 1(1) of Schedule 4 to the Act of 1933 (approved school rules) and of any rules made by the managers and approved by him under paragraph 1(2) of that Schedule shall no longer apply in relation to that school ; and

(*b*) that, in place of those rules, so much as may be specified in the direction of any regulations made under section 43 of this Act shall apply, subject to such adaptations and modifications as may be so specified, in relation to the approved school as if it were a community home.

(4) If the effect of the application, by a direction under sub-paragraph (3) above, of any provision of regulations made under section 43 of this Act in relation to an approved school would be to impose any duty or confer any power on a local authority in relation to that school, the Secretary of State shall not give a direction applying that provision except with the consent of the local authority concerned.

4.—(1) If on the day specified for the purposes of section 7(5) of this Act a remand home was designated under section 11 of the Act of 1963 as a classifying centre then, during the period beginning immediately after that day and ending on the date specified in a section 46 order relating to that home, the home may be used for the accommodation and maintenance of children in the care of local authorities.

(2) In this Schedule " classifying centre " means a remand home designated as mentioned in sub-paragraph (1) of this paragraph and, in relation to a classifying centre, the period specified in that sub-paragraph is referred to as " the interim period ".

(3) During the interim period—

    (*a*) the expenses of a local authority in providing and maintaining a classifying centre in relation to the whole or part of the expenses of which a direction has been given by the Secretary of State under section 11(3) of the Act of 1963 shall be treated for the purposes of section 104 of the Act of 1933 as if they were expenses incurred by the authority as managers of an approved school ;

    (*b*) subsections (4) and (5) of section 106 of the Act of 1933 shall apply in relation to a classifying centre as they apply in relation to an approved school the managers of which are a local authority ; and

    (*c*) any reference in section 21(1) or section 31 of this Act to a community home includes a reference to a classifying centre.

5.—(1) Where a section 46 order is made in relation to an approved school or approved probation hostel or home and, in a regional plan approved by the Secretary of State, the whole or any part of the premises of the institution is designated as a controlled or assisted community home, the premises so designated may, after the specified date, be used for the purpose specified in the regional plan.

(2) Without prejudice to any power to vary the provisions of a trust deed relating to a community home consisting of premises designated as mentioned in sub-paragraph (1) of this paragraph, the purpose referred to in that sub-paragraph shall be deemed to be included among the purposes for which the premises are held in accordance with a trust deed relating to that home.

6.—(1) Where a section 46 order is made in relation to an approved institution (other than an institution provided by a local authority) and, in a regional plan approved by the Secretary of State, the whole or any part of the premises of the institution is designated as a community home to be provided by a local authority, then if the Secretary of State is satisfied that the premises so designated were to a substantial extent provided with the assistance of grants under section 104 of the Act of 1933 or section 77 of the Criminal Justice Act 1948, he may, by an authorisation in writing under this paragraph, authorise the transfer of the premises so designated to that local authority.

(2) The transfer of any premises in pursuance of an authorisation under this paragraph—

(a) shall be on such terms, as to payment and other matters, as may be agreed between the local authority concerned and the trustees or other persons in whom the premises are vested and, if the authorisation so provides, as may be approved by the Secretary of State ;

(b) shall not take effect before the specified date ; and

(c) shall operate to vest the premises transferred in the local authority free from any charitable trust and from any other obligation requiring the use of the premises for the purposes of an approved institution.

(3) Before giving an authorisation under this paragraph authorising the transfer of any premises belonging to a charity or otherwise held on charitable trusts, the Secretary of State shall consult the Charity Commissioners.

7. The provisions of paragraphs 3 to 6 of this Schedule shall have effect notwithstanding anything in the law relating to charities or in any deed or other instrument regulating the purposes for which any premises may be used.

Financial provisions

8.—(1) During the period which is the interim period in relation to an approved school or to a classifying centre falling within paragraph 4(3)(a) of this Schedule contributions shall be payable by local authorities to the managers of that school or, as the case may be, the local authority providing the classifying centre in respect of children in the care of the authorities who are accommodated and maintained in the school premises or the classifying centre in accordance with paragraph 3(1) or paragraph 4(1) of this Schedule.

(2) The contributions payable by a local authority under sub-paragraph (1) above in respect of a child in their care shall be payable throughout the time during which the child is accommodated and maintained in the approved school or classifying centre concerned and shall be such as may be prescribed by regulations made by the Secretary of State.

9.—(1) Where a section 46 order is made in relation to an approved institution, other than an institution provided by a local authority, and in a regional plan approved by the Secretary of State the whole or any part of the premises of the approved institution is designated as a community home, then,—

(a) on the coming into force of an instrument of management for a voluntary home which consists of or includes the premises so designated ; or

(b) on the transfer of the premises so designated to a local authority in pursuance of an authorisation under paragraph 6 of this Schedule,

any such obligation relating to that institution as is referred to in sub-paragraph (2) of this paragraph shall cease.

(2) Sub-paragraph (1) of this paragraph applies to any obligation arising by virtue of a condition imposed under either of the following enactments, namely,—

    (*a*) section 104 of the Act of 1933 (expenses of managers of an approved school) ; or

(*b*) section 77 of the Criminal Justice Act 1948 (expenditure in connection with approved probation hostels or homes).

(3) In a case falling within sub-paragraph (1) of this paragraph, the section 46 order may contain provisions requiring the responsible authority or organisation or, as the case may be, the local authority to whom the premises are transferred, to pay to the Secretary of State such sum as he may determine in accordance with sub-paragraph (4) of this paragraph by way of repayment of a proportion of any grants made in relation to the former approved institution under either of the enactments referred to in sub-paragraph (2) of this paragraph, but where the community home concerned is an assisted community home, the section 46 order may provide that, with the consent of the Treasury, the Secretary of State may reduce the sum to be paid to him in accordance with the preceding provisions of this sub-paragraph to such sum as he thinks fit.

(4) For the purpose of determining any such sum as is mentioned in sub-paragraph (3) of this paragraph, the Secretary of State shall assess—

    (*a*) the amount which in his opinion represents the proportion of the total amount of the grants paid in respect of expenditure in connection with the former approved institution which was attributable to expenditure of a capital nature ; and

    (*b*) the amount which in his opinion represents the proportion of the contributions paid by local authorities under section 90 of the Act of 1933 or, as the case may be, the proportion of the sums paid by probation committees under rules made under Schedule 5 to the Criminal Justice Act 1948 which (in either case) should be treated as having been paid on account of expenditure of a capital nature in connection with the former approved institution ;

and the sum determined by the Secretary of State for the purpose of sub-paragraph (3) of this paragraph shall be equal to the amount by which the amount assessed under paragraph (*a*) above exceeds twice the amount assessed under paragraph (*b*) above.

(5) If the instrument of management for an assisted community home ceases to have effect as mentioned in subsection (1) of section 48 of this Act there shall be deducted from any sum which is payable to the Secretary of State under subsection (5) of that section any sums paid to him by the responsible organisation in respect of the assisted community home in pursuance of any such provisions of a section 46 order relating to the former approved institution as are referred to in sub-paragraph (3) of this paragraph.

(6) In this paragraph " the former approved institution ", in relation to a community home, means the approved institution the whole
or part of the premises of which are comprised in that home.

10.—(1) The provisions of this paragraph apply where in a regional
plan approved by the Secretary of State, the whole or any part of
the premises of an approved institution to which a section 46 order
relates is designated as a controlled or assisted community home and
an instrument of management for a community home which consists
of or includes the premises so designated has come into force ; and
in this paragraph " the former approved institution ", in relation to
such a community home, means the approved institution the whole
or part of the premises of which are comprised in that home.

(2) Where this paragraph applies and the community home con‹
cerned is a controlled community home, then—

> (*a*) the Secretary of State may, by the section 46 order, make
> such provision as he considers appropriate for the transfer to
> the responsible authority of any rights, liabilities and obliga-
> tions which, immediately before the specified date, were
> rights, liabilities and obligations of the managers of, or the
> society or person carrying on, the former approved institu-
> tion ; and

> (*b*) except in so far as the section 46 order otherwise provides,
> any legal proceedings pending immediately before the speci-
> fied date by or against those managers or that society or
> person shall be continued on and after that date, with the
> substitution of the responsible authority for those managers
> or that society or person as a party to the proceedings.

(3) Where this paragraph applies and the community home concerned is an assisted community home but the responsible organisation does not consist of the persons who were the managers of or, as
the case may be, is not the society or person who carried on, the
former approved institution, paragraphs (*a*) and (*b*) of sub-paragraph
(2) of this paragraph shall apply with the substitution for any reference to the responsible authority of a reference to the responsible
organisation.

(4) If any liabilities of a voluntary organisation which is the
responsible organisation in relation to an assisted community home
falling within sub-paragraph (1) of this paragraph were incurred by
the organisation before the specified date or were transferred to the
organisation by the section 46 order (by virtue of sub-paragraph (3)
of this paragraph) and, in either case, had the former approved institution continued to be an approved institution, any expenditure
incurred in meeting those liabilities would have been eligible for a
grant out of moneys provided by Parliament—

> (*a*) under section 104(1)(*a*) of the Act of 1933 as the expenses
> of the managers of an approved school, or

> (*b*) under section 77(3)(*b*) of the Criminal Justice Act 1948, as
> expenditure falling within that section and relating to an
> approved probation hostel or home,

SCH. 3   then any expenditure incurred after the specified date by the responsible organisation in meeting those liabilities shall be deemed for the purposes of section 65(1) of this Act to be expenditure incurred by the responsible organisation in connection with the assisted community home in question.

11.—(1) Where a section 46 order is made in relation to an approved institution and no such provision as is referred to in sub-paragraph (1) of paragraph 9 of this Schedule is made by a regional plan in relation to any part of the premises of the institution, the person or persons on whom falls any such obligation (in this paragraph referred to as a " repayment obligation ") relating to the institution as is referred to in sub-paragraph (2) of that paragraph may apply to the Secretary of State for an order under this paragraph.

(2) If, on an application under sub-paragraph (1) of this paragraph, it appears to the Secretary of State that on or within a reasonable time after the specified date the premises of the institution concerned or the proceeds of sale of the whole or any part of those premises are to be used for a purpose which is of benefit to children, he may with the consent of the Treasury make an order—

(a) substituting for the conditions under which the repayment obligation arose such different conditions as he considers appropriate with respect to the repayment of any sum to which the repayment obligation relates ; and

(b) if the person or persons on whom the repayment obligation falls so request, imposing any liability to repay a sum in pursuance of the substituted conditions referred to in paragraph (a) above on such other person or persons as consent to accept the liability and as, in the opinion of the Secretary of State, will be able to discharge that liability.

Interpretation

12. In this Schedule—

" approved institution " has the same meaning as in section 46 of this Act ;

" the responsible authority ", in relation to a controlled community home, has the same meaning as in section 41 of this Act ;

" the responsible organisation ", in relation to an assisted community home, has the same meaning as in section 42 of this Act ; and

" section 46 order " and, in relation to an institution to which such an order relates, " specified date " have the meanings assigned to them by paragraph 1(1) of this Schedule.

SCHEDULE 4

TRANSITIONAL PROVISIONS AND SAVINGS

PART I

GENERAL

1. For the purposes of subsection (4) of section 1 and subsection (7) of section 7 of this Act, any order under the Act of 1933 committing a child or young person to the care of a fit person other than a local authority, any supervision order under that Act and any order to enter into recognisances in pursuance of section 62(1)(*c*) of that Act shall be deemed to be such an earlier order as is mentioned in those subsections.

2.—(1) Nothing in section 4 of this Act affects any proceedings against a person for an offence with which by virtue of that section he has ceased to be chargeable since the' proceedings were begun ; but where a person is found guilty of an offence and by reason of that section could not have been charged with it on the date of finding, then, subject to sections 1(5) and 2(13) of this Act, the court may make an order under section 1 of this Act in respect of the offender or an order discharging him absolutely but shall not have power to make any other order in consequence of the finding.

(2) Nothing in section 4 of this Act shall be construed as preventing any act or omission which occurred outside the United Kingdom from being a civil offence for the purposes of the Army Act 1955, 1955 c. 18. the Air Force Act 1955, or the Naval Discipline Act 1957, or from 1955 c. 19. being dealt with under any of those Acts.   1957 c. 53.

3. Nothing in section 5 of this Act affects any information laid in respect of a person before the date on which apart from this paragraph the information would have been required by virtue of that section to contain a statement of his age.

4. Where a person is committed for trial by a jury before subsection (1) of section 6 of this Act comes into force, or claims to be tried by a jury before subsection (2) of that section comes into force, proceedings in respect of the offence in question shall not be affected by the coming into force of that subsection.

5.—(1) The coming into force of section 7(1) or of an order under section 34(1)(*d*) of this Act shall not affect any sentence of borstal training passed before the date when the said section 7(1) or the order came into force or any committal for sentence before that date under section 28(1) of the Magistrates' Courts Act 1952 ; 1952 c. 55. but a sentence of borstal training shall not be passed on any person (including a person to whom such a committal relates) if on the date of the relevant conviction he had not attained the minimum age which is for the time being specified in section 20(1) of the Criminal Justice Act 1948.   1948 c. 58.

(2) Nothing in section 7(2) of this Act affects a probation order made before the coming into force of the said section 7(2).

6. No order shall be made under section 19(1) of the Criminal Justice Act 1948, at any time after the coming into force of this paragraph and before the coming into force of paragraph 23 of Schedule 5 to this Act, in respect of a person under the age of seventeen in consequence of a default within the meaning of the Criminal Justice Act 1961.

7.—(1) Every approved school order in force on the specified day shall cease to have effect at the end of that day ; and after that day—

(*a*) no person shall be detained by virtue of section 73 or section 82 of the Act of 1933 or an order under paragraph 2 of Schedule 2 to the said Act of 1961 or be subject to supervision in pursuance of that Schedule ; and

(*b*) no person who has attained the age of nineteen shall be detained by virtue of a warrant under section 15 of the said Act of 1961.

(2) A person who has not attained the age of nineteen on the specified day and who, but for sub-paragraph (1) of this paragraph, would after that day have been the subject of an approved school order or liable to be detained or subject to supervision as mentioned in that sub-paragraph shall be deemed from the end of that day—

(*a*) to be the subject of a care order made by the court which made the approved school order in question on the same day as that order and committing him to the care of the local authority named in the approved school order in pursuance of section 70(2) of the Act of 1933 or, if no authority is so named, of a local authority nominated in relation to him by the Secretary of State ; and

(*b*) in the case where he would have been subject to supervision as aforesaid, to have been allowed by the said local authority to be under the charge and control of the person last nominated in relation to him in pursuance of paragraph 1(1) of Schedule 2 to the said Act of 1961 ;

but nothing in this paragraph shall be construed as affecting the validity of a warrant under the said section 15 in relation to a person who has not attained the age of nineteen.

In relation to a person in respect of whom two or more approved school orders would have been in force after the specified day but for sub-paragraph (1) of this paragraph, references to such an order in paragraph (*a*) of this sub-paragraph are to the later or latest of the orders.

(3) The Secretary of State may from time to time nominate another local authority in the place of a local authority nominated by him in pursuance of the preceding sub-paragraph or this sub-paragraph.

(4) A person who is the subject of a care order by virtue of sub-paragraph (2) of this paragraph and who was unlawfully absent on the specified day from an approved school in which he was then required to be shall, until the local authority to whose care he is committed by the order direct otherwise, be deemed for the purposes

of section 32 of this Act to be duly required by the authority to   SCH. 4
live after that day in the premises which on that day constituted the
school.

(5) A person who on the specified day is the subject of an
approved school order or subject to supervision in pursuance of the
said Schedule 2 or eligible for assistance under paragraph 7 of that
Schedule and is not the subject of a care order from the end of that
day by virtue of sub-paragraph (2) of this paragraph shall be deemed
for the purposes of section 20 of the Children Act 1948 and section 1948 c. 43.
58 of the Act of 1963 (which authorise local authorities to provide
assistance for persons formerly in care) to have been in the care of a
local authority under the Children Act 1948 on that day, notwithstanding that he may then have attained the age of eighteen ; and in
relation to such a person the reference in the said section 58 to the
local authority shall be construed as a reference to any local
authority.

(6) If an order under section 88 of the Act of 1933 is in force
at the end of the specified day in respect of payments under an
affiliation order made for the maintenance of a person who is deemed
by virtue of this paragraph to be subject to a care order after that
day, the order under that section shall after that day be deemed to
have been made, by virtue of the care order, under that section as
modified by this Act.

(7) A direction restricting discharge which was given under section
74 of the Mental Health Act 1959 in respect of a person detained by 1959 c. 72.
virtue of an approved school order and which is in force at the end
of the specified day shall cease to have effect at the end of that day.

(8) References to an approved school order in this paragraph,
except in sub-paragraph (2)(*a*), include references to an order of
the competent authority under subsection (1) of section 83 of the Act
of 1933 and such an order as is mentioned in subsection (3) of that
section ; and in relation to those orders this paragraph shall have
effect as if for sub-paragraph (2)(*a*) there were substituted the
following—

" (*a*) to be the subject of a care order made by a court in England
on the date when the order for his detention in a school
was made under the relevant law mentioned in section 83
of the Act of 1933 and committing him to the care of a
local authority nominated in relation to him by the Secretary
of State ; and "

(9) In this paragraph " the specified day " means the day specified
for the purposes of section 7(5) of this Act.

8.—(1) An order under the Act of 1933 committing a child or young
person to the care of a local authority as a fit person and in force
on the date when section 7(6) of this Act comes into force shall
be deemed on and after that date to be a care order committing him
to the care of that authority.

3 D

(2) Sub-paragraph (6) of the preceding paragraph shall have effect for the purposes of this paragraph as if for references to that paragraph and the specified day there were substituted respectively references to this paragraph and the day preceding the date mentioned in the preceding sub-paragraph.

9. Except as provided by paragraph 1 of this Schedule and this paragraph, nothing in this Act affects—

> (*a*) an order under the Act of 1933 committing a child or young person to the care of a fit person other than a local authority and in force on the date when section 7(6) of this Act comes into force ; or
>
> (*b*) the operation of any enactment in relation to such an order ;

but where an application for the variation or revocation of the order is considered on or after that date by a juvenile court in pursuance of section 84(6) of the Act of 1933, the court shall have power (to the exclusion of its powers under the said section 84(6)) to refuse the application or to revoke the order and, where it revokes the order, to make a care order in respect of the child or young person in question.

10. Without prejudice to the preceding paragraph, a person who is subject to such an order as is mentioned in sub-paragraph (*a*) of that paragraph is not a foster-child within the meaning of Part I

of the Children Act 1958.

11. Notwithstanding anything in section 20(3) or 21(1) of this Act, an order which is a care order by virtue of paragraph 8 of this Schedule and a care order made by virtue of paragraph 9 of this Schedule shall, unless previously revoked, cease to have effect when the child or young person in question attains the age of eighteen.

12.—(1) Where a supervision order under the Children and Young Persons Acts 1933 to 1963 is in force on the date when this paragraph comes into force or where an order under section 52 of the Act of 1963 (whether made before, on or after that date) falls to be treated by virtue of subsection (3) of that section as a supervision order under the Act of 1933, the order and, in relation to the order, any enactment amended or repealed by this Act shall, subject to the following provisions of this paragraph, have effect as if this Act had not been passed ; and the order may be altered or revoked accordingly.

(2) A juvenile court before which the person to whom such a supervision order relates is brought after the date aforesaid in pursuance of subsection (1) of section 66 of the Act of 1933 shall not have power to make such an order as is mentioned in that subsection in respect of him but shall instead have power to revoke the supervision order and make a care order in respect of him on being satisfied that he is unlikely to receive the care or control he needs unless the court makes a care order ; and section 6(1) of the Act of 1963 shall not apply in a case where the court exercises its power under this sub-paragraph.

(3) Where such a supervision order contains a provision requiring residence in an institution which has become a community home, the

provision shall be construed as requiring residence in the home ; and   SCH. 4
in such a case any reference to an institution of the kind in question
in rules under the Criminal Justice Act 1948 providing for the making 1948 c. 58.
of payments to the body or person by whom the institution is managed shall be construed as a reference to the home.

(4) References to a supervision order in sub-paragraphs (2) and (3)
of this paragraph include references to an order under the said
section 52.

13.—(1) During the period beginning with the coming into force
of section 35 of this Act and ending with the coming into operation
of a regional plan for a particular planning area—

(*a*) sections 15 and 16 of the Children Act 1948 shall continue 1948 c. 43.
to apply in relation to each of the relevant authorities ; and

(*b*) each of the relevant authorities may continue to exercise the
power conferred by subsection (2) of section 19 of that Act,
as it had effect immediately before the passing of this
Act, to accommodate persons in hostels provided under
that section ; and

(*c*) section 77(1) of the Act of 1933 shall continue to apply in
relation to each of the relevant authorities as if for the words
" the duty of " there were substituted the words " lawful
for ".

(2) Where different parts of the area of a local authority are comprised in different planning areas then, in relation to that local
authority, the period specified in sub-paragraph (1) of this paragraph
shall not expire until a regional plan has come into operation for
each of those planning areas.

(3) If on the submission of a regional plan for a planning area to
the Secretary of State part only of the plan is approved by him, any
reference in the preceding provisions of this paragraph to the coming
into operation of a regional plan for that area shall be construed as
a reference to the coming into operation of a further regional plan
containing all necessary supplementary proposals for that area.

14. If immediately before the coming into force of section 49 of
this Act any person has, under section 3(3) of the Children Act 1948,
the care and control of a child (within the meaning of that Act) with
respect to whom a resolution under section 2 of that Act is in
force, then after the coming into force of that section the child shall
again be in the care of the local authority by whom the resolution
was passed but shall be deemed to have been allowed by that
authority, under section 13(2) of that Act (as substituted by the said
section 49), to be under the charge and control of that person, on the
same terms as were applicable under the said section 3(3).

15. It shall be lawful for a person detained in any place in pursuance of section 27 of the Criminal Justice Act 1948 at the time
when paragraph 24 of Schedule 5 to this Act comes into force to be
detained there thereafter, until he is next delivered thence in due
course of law, as if that paragraph had not come into force.

SCH. 4
1958 c. 65.
1937 c. 37.

16. Nothing in paragraph 29 of Schedule 5 to this Act affects the operation of section 2(4) of the Children Act 1958 in relation to a supervision order made under the Children and Young Persons (Scotland) Act 1937.

1958 c. 5
(7 & 8 Eliz. 2).

17. Nothing in Schedule 6 to this Act affects the operation of section 15(3) of the Adoption Act 1958 in relation to a fit person order made under the Children and Young Persons (Scotland) Act 1937.

18. Nothing in any provision of Schedule 6 to this Act affects any order which, immediately before the coming into force of that provision, is in force by virtue of any enactment repealed by that provision.

PART II

INTERIM PROVISIONS PENDING COMMENCEMENT OF PROVISIONS OF
SOCIAL WORK (SCOTLAND) ACT 1968

1968 c. 49.

19. Where a court in England or Wales by which a child or young person is found guilty of an offence is satisfied that he resides or will reside in Scotland, the court shall have power, without prejudice to its other powers and notwithstanding anything in section 7(2) of this Act, to make a probation order in respect of him in accordance with sections 3 and 9 of the Criminal Justice Act 1948.

1948 c. 58.

20. In section 51(1) of the Act of 1963, for the words " principal Act " there shall be substituted the words " Children and Young Persons Act 1969 in proceedings under section 1 of that Act."

21. In section 51(2) of the Act of 1963, for the words from " proposes " to " this Act " there shall be substituted ", or a supervision order under the Children and Young Persons Act 1969 has been made in proceedings under section 1 of that Act, proposes to reside or is residing in Scotland " and for the words " specified in the supervision order " there shall be substituted the words " for which the supervision order would have continued in force if it had been allowed to continue in force until it ceased to have effect by the effluxion of time."

22. Where a juvenile court in England or Wales is satisfied that a person who has not attained the age of eighteen and in respect of whom a supervision order made by virtue of section 7(7)(*b*) of this Act or section 7A(4) of the Criminal Justice (Scotland) Act 1949 is in force resides or will reside in Scotland, the court may discharge the order and exercise the like powers to make a probation order in accordance with sections 3 and 9 of the Criminal Justice Act 1948 in respect of him as if in the proceedings it had duly found him guilty of the offence in consequence of which the supervision order was made and section 7(2) of this Act had not been passed ; but a probation order made by virtue of this paragraph shall not continue in force after the date on which the discharged supervision order would have ceased to have effect by the effluxion of time.

1949 c. 94.

23.—(1) Where it appears to the local authority to whose care a   SCH. 4
person is committed by a care order that his parent or guardian
resides or will reside in Scotland and that it is appropriate to transfer
him to the care of the managers of an approved school in Scotland,
the authority shall make a report on the case to the Secretary of
State ; and thereupon the Secretary of State may, if he thinks fit,
make an order transferring the person in question to the care of
the managers of such a school.

(2) The provisions of the Children and Young Persons (Scotland)
Acts 1937 to 1963 shall apply to an order made under this paragraph as if it were an approved school order made by a juvenile court
in Scotland on the date on which the care order in question was
originally made ; but notwithstanding anything in section 75 of the
said Act of 1937 such an order shall cease to have effect on the date
when the care order in question would have ceased to have effect by
the effluxion of time and the contributions to be made under section
94 of the said Act of 1937 in respect of the person to whom the
order under this paragraph relates shall be made by the authority
nominated for the purpose in the order under this paragraph, being
the education authority within whose area it appears to the Secretary
of State at the time that order is made that his parent or guardian
resides or will reside.

(3) When a person is received into the care of the managers of an
approved school in pursuance of an order under this paragraph, the
care order in question shall cease to have effect.

24. If it appears to the Secretary of State that the parent or
guardian of a person who has not attained the age of nineteen and
is the subject of an approved school order in force under the Children
and Young Persons (Scotland) Act 1937, or such other order as is 1937 c. 37.
mentioned in subsection (1) or subsection (3) of section 87 of that
Act, resides or will reside in the area of a local authority in England
or Wales, the Secretary of State may make an order committing
that person to the care of that authority ; and an order under this
paragraph shall have effect as if it were a care order made on the
date on which the approved school or other order was made, but as
if sections 20(2) and 21(5) of this Act were omitted.

SCHEDULE 5   Section 72(3).

MINOR AND CONSEQUENTIAL AMENDMENTS OF ENACTMENTS

The Police (Property) Act 1897   1897 c. 30.

1. The Police (Property) Act 1897 (which makes provision for the
disposal of property in the possession of the police) shall apply to
property which has come into the possession of the police in connection with an allegation, in proceedings under section 1 of this
Act, that the condition set out in subsection (2)(*f*) of that section
is satisfied as it applies to property which has come into the possession
of the police in the circumstances mentioned in that Act.

3 D 3

The Act of 1933

2. In section 10 of the Act of 1933, after subsection (1) there shall be inserted the following subsection:—

(1A) Proceedings for an offence under this section shall not be instituted except by a local education authority; and before instituting such proceedings the authority shall consider whether it would be appropriate, instead of or as well as instituting the proceedings, to bring the child or young person in question before a juvenile court under section 1 of the Children and Young Persons Act 1969.

3. In section 34(2) of the Act of 1933, after the words " be taken " there shall be inserted the words " by the person who arrested him ".

4. In section 46 of the Act of 1933, after subsection (1) there shall be inserted the following subsection:—

1957 c. 29.

(1A) If a notification that the accused desires to plead guilty without appearing before the court is received by the clerk of a court in pursuance of section 1 of the Magistrates' Courts Act 1957 and the court has no reason to believe that the accused is a child or young person, then, if he is a child or young person he shall be deemed to have attained the age of seventeen for the purposes of subsection (1) of this section in its application to the proceedings in question.

5. In section 55(1) of the Act of 1933, for the words " charged with " there shall be substituted the words " found guilty of " and after the word " care " there shall be inserted the words " or control ".

6. In section 56(1) of the Act of 1933, for the word " resides " there shall be substituted the words " habitually resides ".

7. Section 63 of the Act of 1933 shall cease to have effect.

8. In section 86(1) of the Act of 1933 for the words from " an order " to " approved school " there shall be substituted the words " a care order which is not an interim order has been made in respect of a child or young person ".

9.—(1) In subsection (1) of section 87 of the Act of 1933, for the words from " an order has " to " same time, and " there shall be substituted the words " a care order which is not an interim order has been made in respect of a child or young person then, subject to section 62 of the Children and Young Persons Act 1969 ".

(2) For subsection (2) of that section, there shall be substituted the following subsection:—

(2) A contribution order in respect of a child or young person may be made on the application of the local authority entitled to receive contributions in respect of him.

(3) In subsection (3) of that section for the words from "in the case ", in the first place where they occur, onwards there shall be substituted the words " as long as the child or young person to whom it relates is in the care of the local authority concerned ".

10.—(1) In subsection (1) of section 88 of the Act of 1933 for the words from " ordered " to " approved school " there shall be substituted the words " the subject of a care order (other than an interim order) " ; for the words " that court " there shall be substituted the words " the court which makes the order " ; for the words " the person who is " there shall be substituted the words " the local authority who are ", and for the words " the persons by whom, and in the circumstances in which " there shall be substituted the words " the local authorities by whom ".

(2) In subsection (2)(c) of that section, for the words " person who was " there shall be substituted the words " local authority who were ".

(3) In subsection (4) of that section, for paragraphs (a) and (b) there shall be substituted the words " after the child or young person to whom that order relates has ceased to be the subject of the care order by virtue of which the order under this section was made or, where this section applies by virtue of section 23 of the Children 1948 c. 43. Act 1948, after he has ceased to be in the care of a local authority under section 1 of that Act or, in either case, if he is allowed by the local authority to be under the charge and control of a parent, guardian, relative or friend, although remaining in the care of the local authority ".

11. In section 106(2)(a) of the Act of 1933, for the words from " fifty-seven " to " Schedule to " there shall be substituted the words " eighty-seven and eighty-eight of ".

12.—(1) In section 107(1) of the Act of 1933, after the words " that is to say " there shall be inserted the following words : —

" care order " and " interim order " have the same meanings as in the Children and Young Persons Act 1969.

(2) In the said section 107(1), in the definition of " place of safety ", for the words " any home provided by a local authority under Part II of the Children Act 1948 any remand home or " there shall be substituted the words " a community home provided by a local authority or a controlled community home, any ".

(3) Section 107(2) of the Act of 1933 shall cease to have effect.

The Education Act 1944

13. For subsections (2) to (5) of section 40 of the Education Act 1944 there shall be substituted the following subsections : —

(2) Proceedings for such offences as aforesaid shall not be instituted except by a local education authority ; and before instituting such proceedings the authority shall

SCH. 5

consider whether it would be appropriate, instead of or as well as instituting the proceedings, to bring the child in question before a juvenile court under section 1 of the Children and Young Persons Act 1969.

(3) The court by which a person is convicted of an offence against section 37 of this Act or before which a person is charged with an offence against section 39 of this Act may if it thinks fit direct the authority who instituted the proceedings to bring the child to whom the proceedings relate before a juvenile court under the said section 1 ; and it shall be the duty of the authority to comply with the direction.

(4) Where a child in respect of whom a school attendance order is in force is brought before a juvenile court by a local education authority under the said section 1 and the court finds that the condition set out in subsection (2)(*e*) of that section is not satisfied with respect to him, the court may direct that the order shall cease to be in force.

1948 c. 43.

The Children Act 1948

14. In section 4(3) of the Children Act 1948, the proviso shall cease to have effect.

15. In section 20(1) of the said Act of 1948, for the words " any such person as is mentioned in subsection (1) of the last foregoing section " there shall be substituted the words " any person over compulsory school age but under the age of twenty one who is, or has at any time after ceasing to be of compulsory school age been, in the care of a local authority ".

16. In section 23(1) of the said Act of 1948 for the words from " committed " in the second place where it occurs to the end of the subsection there shall be substituted the words " in the care of a local authority by virtue of such an order as is mentioned in subsection (1) of the said section 86 ".

17.—(1) In section 26(1) of the said Act of 1948 for paragraph (*b*) there shall be substituted the following paragraph : —

1933 c. 12.

(*b*) an illegitimate child is in the care of a local authority by virtue of such an order as is mentioned in section 86(1) of the Children and Young Persons Act 1933, or.

(2) In subsections (3) and (4)(*b*) of the said section 26, for the words " person who is " there shall be substituted the words " local authority who are ", and in subsection (4) of that section for the words " (*b*) or (*c*) " there shall be substituted the words " or (*b*) ".

18. In section 39(1) of the said Act of 1948 after paragraph (*h*) there shall be inserted the following paragraph : —

(*i*) the Children and Young Persons Act 1969.

19. In section 43(1) of the said Act of 1948 for the words from   SCH. **5**
" Parts IV and V " onwards there shall be substituted the words 1958 c. 5
" the Children and Young Persons Acts 1933 to 1969, the Adoption (7 & 8 Eliz. 2).
Act 1958 and the Adoption Act 1968 ".   1968 c.53.

20.—(1) In subsection (1) of section 51 of the said Act of 1948,
for the words from " homes " to " this Act " there shall be substituted the words " community homes provided by them or in controlled community homes " and at the end of that subsection there
shall be added the words " or sections 2(5), 16(3) or 28 of the
Children and Young Persons Act 1969 and of children detained by
them in pursuance of arrangements under section 29(3) of that Act ".

(2) In subsection (3) of the said section 51, for the words from
" home " to " this Act " there shall be substituted the words " community home provided by a local authority or a controlled community home ".

21.—(1) In subsection (3) of section 54 of the said Act of 1948,
after the word " area " in the first place where it occurs there shall
be inserted the words " other than community homes " and after
the word " any " in the last place where it occurs, there shall be
inserted the word " such ".

(2) In subsection (4) of that section, for the words from " as a fit
person " to the end of the subsection there shall be substituted the
words " by a care order within the meaning of the Children and
Young Persons Act 1969 or by a warrant under section 23(1) of
that Act."

(3) In subsection (5) of that section, for the words from " ninety-
four " to " 1933 " there shall be substituted the words " section 58
of the Children and Young Persons Act 1969 ".

22. In section 59(1) of the said Act of 1948, at the end of the
definition of " child " there shall be added the words " and any
person who has attained that age and is the subject of a care order
within the meaning of the Children and Young Persons Act 1969 ".

The Criminal Justice Act 1948   1948 c. 58.

23. In section 19(1) of the Criminal Justice Act 1948, after the
words " who is " there shall be inserted the words " not less than
seventeen but ".

24. For section 27 of the said Act of 1948 there shall be substituted
the following section : —

Remand of   27.—(1) Where a court remands a person charged with
persons   or convicted of an offence or commits him for trial or
aged 17 to   sentence and he is not less than seventeen but under
20.   twenty-one years old and is not released on bail, then,
if the court has been notified by the Secretary of State
that a remand centre is available for the reception from

3 D*

SCH. 5

the court of persons of his class or description, it shall commit him to a remand centre and, if it has not been so notified, it shall commit him to a prison.

(2) Where a person is committed to a remand centre in pursuance of this section, the centre shall be specified in the warrant and he shall be detained there for the period for which he is remanded or until he is delivered thence in due course of law.

1952 c. 55.

(3) In this section "court" includes a justice; and nothing in this section affects the provisions of section 105(5) of the Magistrates' Courts Act 1952 (which provides for remands to the custody of a constable).

1949 c. 94.

The Criminal Justice (Scotland) Act 1949

25. In section 7 of the Criminal Justice (Scotland) Act 1949, after the words "that the offender" in subsection (1) and "that the probationer" in subsection (2) there shall be inserted the words "has attained the age of seventeen and".

26. After section 7 of the said Act of 1949 there shall be inserted the following section:—

Further provisions as to probation orders relating to persons residing or formerly residing in England.

7A.—(1) Where the court by which a probation order is made under section 2 of this Act or subsection (6) of this section is satisfied that the person to whom the order relates is under the age of seventeen and resides or will reside in England, subsection (2) of the said section 2 shall not apply to the order but the order shall name the petty sessions area in which that person resides or will reside and the court shall send notification of the order to the clerk to the justices for that area.

(2) Where a probation order has been made under section 2 of this Act or subsection (6) of this section and the court which made the order or the appropriate court is satisfied that the person to whom the order relates is under the age of seventeen and proposes to reside or is residing in England, the power of that court to amend the order under Schedule 2 to this Act shall include power, without summoning him and without his consent, to insert in the order the name of the petty sessions area aforesaid; and where the court exercises the power conferred on it by virtue of this subsection it shall send notification of the order to the clerk aforesaid.

(3) A court which sends a notification to a clerk in pursuance of the foregoing provisions of this section shall send to him with it three copies of the probation order in question and such other documents and information relating to the case as it considers likely to be of assistance to the juvenile court mentioned in the following subsection.

(4) It shall be the duty of the clerk to whom a noti- Sch. 5
fication is sent in pursuance of the foregoing provisions
of this section to refer the notification to a juvenile court
acting for the petty sessions area named in the order,
and on such a reference the court—

> (a) may make a supervision order under the Child-
> ren and Young Persons Act 1969 in respect of
> a person to whom the notification relates ; and

> (b) if it does not make such an order, shall dismiss
> the case.

(5) A supervision order made by virtue of the foregoing subsection shall not include a requirement authorised by section 12 of the said Act of 1969 unless the
supervised person is before the court when the supervision
order is made, and in relation to a supervision order made
by virtue of that subsection—

> (a) section 15 of that Act shall have effect as if in
> subsection (4) paragraph (b) and the words
> following it were omitted ; and

> (b) section 17(a) of that Act shall have effect as if
> the second reference to the supervision order
> were a reference to the probation order in con-
> sequence of which the supervision order is
> made ;

and when a juvenile court disposes of a case referred
to it in pursuance of the foreging subsection, the probation order in consequence of which the reference was
made shall cease to have effect.

(6) The court which, in pursuance of subsection (1) of
section 73 of the Social Work (Scotland) Act 1968, con- 1968 c. 49.
siders a case referred to it in consequence of a notification under paragraph (i) of that subsection (which relates
to a case in which a person subject to a supervision order
made by virtue of this section moves to Scotland)—

> (a) may, if it is of opinion that the person to whom
> the notification relates should continue to be
> under supervision, make a probation order in
> respect of him for a period specified in the
> order ; and

> (b) if it does not make such an order, shall dismiss
> the case ;

and when the court disposes of a case in pursuance of
this subsection the supervision order aforesaid shall cease
to have effect.

(7) Notwithstanding any provision to the contrary in
section 2 of this Act, a probation order made by virtue
of the foregoing subsection which includes only requirements having the like effect as any requirement or provision of the supervision order to which the notification

relates may be made without summoning the person to whom the notification relates and without his consent, and shall specify a period of supervision which shall expire not later than the date on which that supervision order would have ceased to have effect by the effluxion of time ; and, except as aforesaid, Part I of this Act shall apply to that probation order.

(8) In this section " petty sessions area " has the same meaning as in the said Act of 1969.

The Sexual Offences Act 1956

27. In section 37(7) of the Sexual Offences Act 1956, for the words " section twenty or twenty-one of the Magistrates' Courts Act 1952 (which relate " in paragraph (*a*) there shall be substituted the words " section 6 of the Children and Young Persons Act 1969 (which relates " and for the words " that Act " in paragraph (*b*) there shall be substituted the words " the Magistrates' Courts Act 1952 ".

The Affiliation Proceedings Act 1957

28.—(1) In section 5(2)(*a*) of the Affiliation Proceedings Act 1957, for the words from " fit person " to " school " there shall be substituted the words " local authority ".

(2) In section 7(4) of that Act, for paragraph (*a*) there shall be substituted the following paragraph : —
> (*a*) subject to the next following subsection, so as to require payments thereunder to be made in respect of any period when the child is in the care of a local authority under section 1 of the Children Act 1948 or by virtue of a care order (other than an interim order) within the meaning of the Children and Young Persons Act 1969 ;

(3) In section 7(6) of that Act, for the words from " a person " onwards there shall be subsituted the words " by virtue of such a care order as aforesaid ".

The Children Act 1958

29. In section 2(4) of the Children Act 1958, for the words " supervision order or " there shall be substituted the words " supervision order within the meaning of the Children and Young Persons Act 1969 or a ".

30. In section 9 of the said Act of 1958, after the words " foster child " there shall be inserted the words " for reward ".

31. In section 12(1) of the said Act of 1958, for the words " one month " there shall be substituted the words " two weeks ".

32. In section 17 of the said Act of 1958, after the words " that is to say " there shall be inserted the words " " approved school " has the same meaning as in the Children and Young Persons (Scotland)

Act 1937 ; " and, in the definition of " place of safety ", for the word   Sch. 5
" home " in the first place where it occurs there shall be substituted
the words " community home " and for the words " under Part II
of the Children Act 1948, remand " there shall be substituted the
words " a controlled community ".

The Adoption Act 1958

1958 c. 5 (7 & 8 Eliz. 2).

33.—(1) In section 4(3) of the Adoption Act 1958, for paragraph
(*a*) there shall be substituted the following paragraph :—

   (*a*) section 24 of the Children and Young Persons Act 1969
   (which relates to the powers and duties of local authorities
   with respect to persons committed to their care in pursuance
   of that Act).

34. In section 15(3) of the said Act of 1958, for the words " the
last mentioned order " there shall be substituted the words " or to
the care of a local authority by a care order (other than an interim
order) in force under the Children and Young Persons Act 1969,
the fit person order or care order as the case may be ".

35. In section 37(2) of the said Act of 1958, for the words " (4) or
(5) " there shall be substituted the words " or (4) ".

36. In section 57(1) of the said Act of 1958, in the definition of
" place of safety ", for the word " home " in the first place where
it occurs there shall be substituted the words " community home "
and for the words " under Part II of the Children Act 1948, remand "
there shall be substituted the words " a controlled community ".

The Mental Health Act 1959

1959 c. 72.

37.—(1) In subsection (1) of section 9 of the Mental Health Act
1959 for the words from " or other accommodation " to " section
fifteen of that Act " there shall be substituted the words " provided
under section 38 of the Children and Young Persons Act 1969 " and
for the words " that Act " there shall be substituted the words " the
Children Act 1948 ".

(2) In subsection (2) of the said section 9, for the words " or other
accommodation provided under the said section fifteen " there shall
be substituted the words " provided under the said section 38 ".

38. In section 10(1)(*a*) of the said Act of 1959 for sub-paragraph
(i) there shall be substituted the following sub-paragraph :—

   (i) section 24 of the Children and Young Persons Act 1969
   (which relates to the powers and duties of local authorities
   with respect to persons committed to their care in pursuance
   of that Act).

39. In section 50 of the said Act of 1959, for paragraph (*a*) there
shall be substituted the following paragraph :—

   (*a*) section 24 of the Children and Young Persons Act 1969
   (which relates to the powers and duties of local authorities

Sch. 5

with respect to persons committed to their care in pursuance of that Act).

40. In section 60(6) of the said Act of 1959, after the word " offence " there shall be inserted the words " or make any such order as is mentioned in paragraphs (*b*) or (*c*) of section 7(7) of the Children and Young Persons Act 1969 in respect of the offender ".

41. In section 62(4) of the said Act of 1959 for the words " section 62 of the Children and Young Persons Act 1933 " there shall be substituted the words " section 1 of the Children and Young Persons Act 1969 ".

1960 c. 61.

The Mental Health (Scotland) Act 1960

42. In section 10(1)(*a*) of the Mental Health (Scotland) Act 1960, for sub-paragraph (ii) there shall be substituted the following sub-paragraph : —

  (ii) section 24 of the Children and Young Persons Act 1969 (which relates to the powers and duties of local authorities in England and Wales with respect to persons committed to their care).

43. In section 46 of the said Act of 1960, for paragraph (*b*) there shall be substituted the following paragraph : —

  (*b*) section 24 of the Children and Young Persons Act 1969 (which relates to the powers and duties of local authorities in England and Wales with respect to persons committed to their care).

1961 c. 39.

The Criminal Justice Act 1961

44. For section 5(1) of the Criminal Justice Act 1961 there shall be substituted the following : —

Defaulters already detained in detention centre.

5.—(1) Where a court has power to commit a person to prison for any term for a default and that person has attained the age of seventeen and is detained in a detention centre under a previous sentence or warrant, the court may, subject to the provisions of this section, commit him to a detention centre for a term not exceeding the term aforesaid or six months, whichever is the shorter.

and subsection (3) of section 6 of that Act shall be subsection (6) of section 5 of that Act.

45. In section 9 of the said Act of 1961, for the words from the beginning to " that Act ", where they first occur, there shall be substituted the words " Where an order for conditional discharge under section seven of the Criminal Justice Act 1948 ".

1948 c. 58.

46. In section 29(3)(*a*) of the said Act of 1961, for the words " that Act " there shall be substituted the words " the Children and Young Persons Act 1933 ".

47. In section 3(1) of the Act of 1963, for the words " section 62 of the principal Act " there shall be substituted the words " section 1 of the Children and Young Persons Act 1969 ".

48. In section 23 of the Act of 1963, in subsection (1)(*b*), for the words " that Act " there shall be substituted the words " the principal Act " and, in subsection (5), for the words from " for his detention " onwards there shall be substituted the words " within the meaning of the Children and Young Persons Act 1969 ".

49. In section 29(1) of the Act of 1963, for the words " before a juvenile court under section 62 or section 65 of the principal Act " there shall be substituted the words " under section 1 of the Children and Young Persons Act 1969 or for an offence " ; and section 29(2) of the Act of 1963 shall cease to have effect.

50.—(1) In subsection (1) of section 30 of the Act of 1963, for the words " the person who " there shall be substituted the words " the local authority who ".

(2) In subsection (3) of that section, for the words " subsections (3) and (4) " there shall be substituted " subsection (3) " and at the end of that subsection there shall be added the words " section 62 of the Children and Young Persons Act 1969 ".

(3) In subsection (4) of that section for the words from " a magistrates' court ", in the first place where they occur, to the end of the subsection there shall be substituted the words " a magistrates' court acting for the area or part of the area of the local authority which is the applicant."

(4) In subsection (5) of that section for the words " 14(1) of this Act keep the person " there shall be substituted the words " 24(8) of the Children and Young Persons Act 1969 keep the local authority ".

51. In section 45(1) of the Act of 1963, after the words " the Children Act 1958 " there shall be inserted the words " the Children and Young Persons Act 1969 ".

52. In section 49(1) of the Act of 1963, for the words " section 3(3) ", there shall be substituted the words " section 13(2) " and for the words " over the care " in both places there shall be substituted the word " charge ".

53. For subsection (3) of section 57 of the Act of 1963 there shall be substituted the following subsection : —

(3) The said sections 39 and 49 shall extend to Scotland and the said sections 46 and 54 shall extend to England and Wales, but—

(*a*) references to a court in the said sections 39 and 49 shall not include a court in Scotland ; and

3 D* 4

(b) references to a court in the said sections 46 and 54 shall not include a court in England or Wales.

1965 c. 53.   *The Family Allowances Act* 1965

54.—(1) In subsection (1)(b) of section 11 of the Family Allowances Act 1965, for the words " said Act of " there shall be substituted the words " Children and Young Persons Act ".

(2) In subsection (2) of that section for the words " said Act of 1933 " there shall be substituted the words " Children and Young Persons Act 1969 (other than an interim order) " and for the words from " 5(1) " to " 1956 " there shall be substituted the words " 13(2)
1948 c. 43.   of the Children Act 1948 ".

(3) In subsection (3) of that section, for the words " 3 or 4 " there shall be substituted the words " 4 or 13(2) ".

1967 c. 80.   *The Criminal Justice Act* 1967

55. In sections 2 and 9 of the Criminal Justice Act 1967, after subsection (3) of each section there shall be inserted the following subsection : —

(3A) In the case of a statement which indicates in pursuance of subsection (3)(a) of this section that the person making it has not attained the age of fourteen, subsection (2)(b) of this section shall have effect as if for the words from " made " onwards there were substituted the words " understands the importance of telling the truth in it."

56. In section 3(3) of the Criminal Justice Act 1967, for the words " 19 or 20 of the Magistrates' Courts Act 1952 " there shall be sub-
1952 c. 55.   stituted the words " or 19 of the Magistrates' Courts Act 1952 or section 6 of the Children and Young Persons Act 1969 ".

1968 c. 49.   *The Social Work (Scotland) Act* 1968

57. After section 44(1) of the Social Work (Scotland) Act 1968, there shall be inserted the following subsection : —

(1A) A supervision requirement imposing a condition as to the place where a child is to reside in England or Wales shall be a like authority as in Scotland for the person in charge of the place to restrict the child's liberty to such an extent as that person may consider appropriate having regard to the terms of the supervision requirement.

58.—(1) In section 72 of the said Act of 1968, after subsection (1) there shall be inserted the following subsection : —

(1A) The juvenile court in England or Wales to which notification of a supervision requirement is sent under this section may make a supervision order in respect of the person to whom the notification relates but, notwithstanding anything in section 76(1) of this Act, shall not include in the order a requirement authorised by section 12 of the Children and Young Persons

Act 1969 unless that person is before the court when the supervision order is made ; and in relation to a supervision order
made by virtue of this subsection—

(*a*) section 15 of that Act shall have effect as if subsection
(2) were omitted ; and

(*b*) section 17 of that Act shall have effect as if in paragraph
(*a*) the references to three years and the date on which
the order was originally made were respectively references to one year and the date on which the said
notification was sent and as if in paragraph (*b*) the
words from " the order was " to " and " were omitted.

(2) In subsection (2) of that section, after the word " court " there
shall be inserted the words " in Northern Ireland ".

(3) In subsection (4) of that section for the words from " includes "
to " 1963 " there shall be substituted the words ", in relation to
England and Wales, has the same meaning as in the said Act of
1969 ".

59.—(1) In section 73 of the said Act of 1968, in subsection (1),
after the word " reporter ", in the second place where it occurs, there
shall be inserted the following words : —

(i) in the case of a supervision order made by virtue of
section 7A(4) of the Criminal Justice (Scotland) Act 1949, to
notify the appropriate court and to transmit to that court all
documents and certified copies of documents relating to the
case which the reporter has received by virtue of section 76 of
this Act ;

(ii) in any other case.
and at the end of that subsection there shall be inserted the following
paragraph : —

In this subsection " the appropriate court " means the sheriff
having jurisdiction in the area in which the child proposes to
reside or is residing or, where the original probation order was
imposed by the High Court of Justiciary, that Court.

(2) After subsection (1) of that section there shall be inserted the
following subsection : —

(1A) Where a court in England or Wales is satisfied that a
child in respect of whom the court proposes to make a supervision order is residing or proposes to reside in Scotland, the
court may make the order notwithstanding anything in subsection
(1) of section 18 of the Children and Young Persons Act 1969
(which relates to residence of the supervised person in England
or Wales) ; and where the court makes a supervision order by
virtue of this subsection—

(*a*) the areas to be named in the order in pursuance of subsection (2)(*a*) of the said section 18 shall be those in
which the court is sitting ;

(*b*) the order may require the supervised person to
comply with directions of the supervisor with respect to

his departure to Scotland, and any such requirement
shall, for the purposes of sections 15 and 16 of that
Act (which relate to the variation and discharge of
supervision orders), be deemed to be included in the
order in pursuance of section 12(2) of that Act ; and

(*c*) the court shall send notification of the order as mentioned
in paragraph (*b*) of the foregoing subsection and the
provisions of that subsection relating to the duty of the
reporter shall apply accordingly.

(3) In subsection (2) of that section for the word " subsection " there
shall be substituted the words " provisions of this section."

60. In section 74 of the said Act of 1968, after subsection (5)
there shall be inserted the following subsection : —

(6) An order under this section committing a child to the care
of a local authority shall have effect as if it were a care order
under the Children and Young Persons Act 1969, but as if
sections 20(2) and 21(5) of that Act and in section 20(3) of that
Act paragraph (*a*) and the words ' in any other case ' in paragraph (*b*) were omitted.

61.—(1) In section 75 of the said Act of 1968, in subsection (1)
after the word " order " there shall be inserted the words " or an
order under section 74(3) of this Act relating to a training school ".

(2) In subsection (2) of that section, for the words from " under ",
where it first occurs, to " 1944 " there shall be substituted the words
" by a care order (other than an interim order) within the meaning
of the Children and Young Persons Act 1969 or an order under
section 74(3) of this Act " and after the word " 1947 " there shall be
inserted the words " or the said section 74(3) ".

(3) In subsection (3) of that section, after the words " training
school order " there shall be inserted the words " or order under
the said section 74(3) relating to a training school ".

(4) In subsection (4) of that section after the word " order " there
shall be inserted the words " under the said section 74(3) or ".

62. In section 76(4) of the said Act of 1968, after the word " order "
there shall be inserted the words " or order under section 74(3) of
this Act relating to a training school ".

63. In section 90(1) of the said Act of 1968, the words " or to
prescribe any matter," shall be omitted.

64. In section 94(1) of the said Act of 1968—

(1) after the definition of " place of safety " there shall be
inserted the words—

" prescribed " means—

(*a*) in section 3, prescribed by regulations,

(*b*) in section 44, prescribed by rules, and

(*c*) in sections 62(2), 66(1) and (2), 94, paragraphs 2(2)
and (3), 4(3) and (4) of Schedule 7, prescribed by
order,

(2) in the definition of "supervision order" after the word "1963" there shall be inserted the words "and includes a supervision order within the meaning of the Children and Young Persons Act 1969".

65. In section 97(1) of the said Act of 1968—

(1) after the words "that is to say—" there shall be inserted the words "section 44(1) (except head (*b*)) and (1A)",

(2) after the words "Part V" there shall be inserted the words "section 98(3)" and "Schedule 2, paragraphs 7 and 13".

66. In section 98 of the said Act of 1968, after subsection (2) there shall be inserted the following subsection:—

(3) An order under this section may make such transitional provisions as appear to the Secretary of State to be necessary or expedient in connection with the provisions thereby brought into force, including such adaptations of those provisions or of any provision of this Act then in force as appear to the Secretary of State necessary or expedient for the purposes or in consequence of the operation of any provision of this Act before the coming into force of any other provision of this Act or of the Children and Young Persons Act 1969.

67. In Schedule 2 to the said Act of 1968, in paragraph 10, to section 50 of the Children and Young Persons (Scotland) Act 1937 1937 c. 37. as substituted by that paragraph, there shall be added the following subsection:—

(2) The provisions of the foregoing subsection so far as they relate to section 54 of this Act shall extend to England and Wales.

68. In Schedule 2 to the said Act of 1968, in paragraph 19, after the word "'children'" there shall be inserted the words ", for the word 'offenders' there shall be substituted the word 'children', and for the word 'offender' in the three places where that word occurs there shall be substituted the word 'child'".

69. In Schedule 7 to the said Act of 1968, in paragraph 1(1)(*a*), for the words "section 63" there shall be substituted the words "section 62".

70. In Schedule 8 to the said Act of 1968, in paragraph 7—

(*a*) for sub-paragraph (1) of that paragraph there shall be substituted the following sub-paragraph:—

(1) In section 87, for subsection (1), there shall be substituted the following subsection—

(1) Any person detained in a training school under the law in force in Northern Ireland may, with the consent of the Secretary of State, be transferred by order of the competent authority in Northern Ireland to such place in Scotland as the Secretary of State may direct for the purposes of undergoing residential training, and shall be

subject to the provisions of this Act and of the Criminal Justice (Scotland) Act 1963 as if the order sending him to the school in Northern Ireland were an order for committal for residential training made under section 58A of this Act made upon the same date, and as if the order were an authority for his detention for a period not exceeding the period for which he might be detained under the training school order made in respect of him.;

(b) in sub-paragraph (2) of that paragraph at the end there shall be inserted the words " ; and in section 87(2) and (4) the words " England or ", wherever they occur, shall be omitted " ;

(c) in sub-paragraph (3) of that paragraph the words " to such " shall be omitted ;

(d) after sub-paragraph (3) of that paragraph there shall be inserted the following sub-paragraphs—

(4) In section 87(5) the words " in relation to England, the Secretary of State, and," shall be omitted.

(5) In section 87 subsection (6) shall be omitted.

71. In Schedule 8 to the said Act of 1968, in paragraph 9(2), for the word " for " there shall be substituted the word " of ".

72. In Schedule 8 to the said Act of 1968, in paragraph 10, at the end there shall be inserted the following words—

" after the definition of " Street " there shall be inserted the following definition—

' Training school order ' has the same meaning as in the Social Work (Scotland) Act 1968 ' ".

73. In Schedule 8 to the said Act of 1968, in paragraph 17(1), for the words " in Scotland " there shall be substituted the words ", within the meaning of the Social Work (Scotland) Act 1968 ".

74. In Schedule 8 to the said Act of 1968, in paragraph 38, for the words " In section 15(4) " there shall be substituted the words—

" (1) In section 15(3), for the words " the last mentioned order " there shall be substituted the words " or to the care of a local authority by a care order (other than an interim order) in force under the Children and Young Persons Act 1969, the fit person order or care order as the case may be ".

(2) In subsection (4) ".

75. In Schedule 8 to the said Act of 1968, in sub-paragraph (1) of paragraph 51, for the words from " include " where it secondly occurs to the end of the sub-paragraph there shall be substituted the words " include ' ; and paragraph (e) shall be omitted."

76. In Schedule 8 to the said Act of 1968, in paragraph 54, for the word " and " where that word first occurs there shall be substituted the word " or " and after the words " " by virtue of " " there shall be inserted the words " where those words secondly occur ".

77. In Schedule 8 to the said Act of 1968, after paragraph 59,   SCH. 5
there shall be inserted the following paragraph:—

> *Criminal Justice Act* 1961   1961 c. 39.
> 59A. In section 32(2), after paragraph (*g*), there shall be
> inserted the following paragraph—
> > (*h*) section 58A of the Children and Young Persons 1937 c. 37.
> > (Scotland) Act 1937.

78. In Schedule 8 to the said Act of 1968, for paragraph 74(1),
there shall be substituted the following sub-paragraph—

> 74.—(1) For section 11(1)(*a*) there shall be substituted the
> following paragraph—
> > (*a*) during which his or her residence in a residential
> > establishment is required by a supervision require-
> > ment made under section 44 of the Social Work
> > (Scotland) Act 1968, and the child is not absent from 1968 c. 49.
> > the residential establishment under supervision ;
> in paragraph (*b*), for the words " the said Act of 1937 ", there
> shall be substituted the words " the Children and Young Persons
> (Scotland) Act 1937 ", after paragraph (*b*) there shall be inserted
> the following paragraph:—
> > (*bb*) during which the child is liable to undergo residential
> > training under committal by virtue of section 58A of
> > the said Act of 1937, and is not released under that
> > section ;
> and for paragraph (*c*) there shall be substituted the following
> paragraph:—
> > (*c*) during which the child is accommodated by virtue
> > of rules made by the Secretary of State under section
> > 45 of the Social Work (Scotland) Act 1968 ".

79. In Part I of Schedule 9 to the said Act of 1968, in the entry
relating to the Children and Young Persons (Scotland) Act 1937,
in the third column, after the words " Sections 68 to 86 " there shall
be inserted the following words:—

> " In section 87(2) and (4) the words " England or " wherever
> they occur, in subsection (5) the words " in relation to England,
> the Secretary of State, and " and subsection (6)."

80. In Part I of Schedule 9 to the said Act of 1968, in the entry
relating to the Children Act 1958, in the third column, for the
words " Section 2(6) and (7) " there shall be substituted the words—

> In section 2, in subsection (4) the words from " or by virtue
> of " to " of an approved school ", and subsections (6) and (7).

81. In Part I of Schedule 9 to the said Act of 1968, in the entry
relating to section 15(3) of the Adoption Act 1958, in the third 1958 c. 5
column, for the words " ' or the Children ' to ' 1937 ' " there shall (7 & 8 Eliz. 2).
be substituted the following words " ' fit person by ' to ' care of a '
and the words ' fit person order or ' and ' as the case may be ' ".

SCH. 5   82. In Part II of Schedule 9 to the said Act of 1968, in the entry relating to the Children Act 1958, in the third column, the entry relating to section 17 shall be omitted.

83. In Part II of Schedule 9 to the said Act of 1968, in the entry relating to the Family Allowances Act 1965, in the third column, for the words from " 11," to " (2)," there shall be substituted the word " 11(2),".

Section 72(4).   **SCHEDULE 6**

REPEALS

Chapter	Short title	Extent of repeal
1894 c. 60.	The Merchant Shipping Act 1894.	In section 183(3), the proviso.
1918 c. 57.	The War Pensions (Administrative Provisions) Act 1918.	Section 9(4).
1920 c. 23.	The War Pensions Act 1920.	Section 9.
1933 c. 12.	The Children and Young Persons Act 1933.	In section 10(2) the words from " and may " onwards. Sections 26(6), 29(3) and 32. In section 34(2) the words " or taken to a place of safety ". Section 35. In section 44, in subsection (1) the words from " being " to " as ", and subsection (2). In section 48(2) the words " a probationer or " and " any failure to comply with the requirements of the probation order or " and the words from " or to amend " onwards. Section 54. In section 55 the words " child or " wherever they occur, in subsection (1) the words " in any case and shall if the offender is a child," subsection (2), and in subsection (4) the words " or on forfeiture of any such security as aforesaid ". In section 56(1) the words " child or ". Sections 57 and 58. In section 59(1) the words " children and " and " child or ". Sections 62 to 85.

Chapter	Short title	Extent of repeal
1933 c. 12— *cont.*	The Children and Young Persons Act 1933—*cont.*	In section 86, subsection (2), in subsection (3) the words " or ordered to be sent to an approved school" and the words from " and ", in the first place where it occurs, to the end of the subsection, and subsection (4). Sections 89(1), 90, 91 and 94. In section 102, paragraphs (*a*) and (*b*) of subsection (1), and in subsection (2) the words from " the rights " to " Act or ". Sections 103 and 104. In section 106, subsections (3) to (5). In section 107(1) the definitions of " approved school ", " approved school order ", " managers " and " special reception centre ". Section 107(2). Section 108(2) and (3). Schedule 4.
1937 c. 37.	The Children and Young Persons (Scotland) Act 1937.	Sections 82, 86, 87 and 89. In Schedule 2, paragraph 13.
1938 c. 40.	The Children and Young Persons Act 1938.	The whole Act.
1944 c. 31.	The Education Act 1944.	Section 40A.
1948 c. 33.	The Superannuation (Miscellaneous Provisions) Act 1948.	Section 14.
1948 c. 40.	The Education (Miscellaneous Provisions) Act 1948.	In Schedule 1, the entries relating to section 40 of the Education Act 1944.
1948 c. 43.	The Children Act 1948.	Section 3(3) to (5). In section 4(3), the proviso. Sections 5, 6(3) and (4), 7, 15 and 16. In section 23, in subsection (1), the words from " (which " to " aliment) " and subsection (3). Section 25. In section 26(1), paragraph (*c*), and in paragraph (ii) the words " or (*c*) " and the words from " or ", in the second place where it occurs, onwards. Section 39(1)(*e*). In section 49(1), the words from " other than " onwards. Section 51(2). Section 54(1) and (2).

Chapter	Short title	Extent of repeal
1948 c. 43— *cont.*	The Children Act 1948— *cont.*	In section 59, in subsection (1) the definition of " approved school order ", and subsection (2). In Schedule 3, the entries relating to sections 70, 82, 84, 90 and 107 of the Act of 1933.
1948 c. 58.	The Criminal Justice Act 1948.	In section 3(5), the words from " if the " to " age ". In section 11(1) the words from the beginning to " behaviour " in the first place where it occurs. In sections 46(1) and 47(1) the words " or a supervision order". Sections 48(4), 49, 71, 72 and 75. In section 77, in subsection (1) the words " or in remand homes or approved schools ", in subsection (4)(*c*) the words " in remand homes or " and " or in approved schools ", and subsection (6). In section 80(1), the definitions of " approved school " " remand home " and " supervision order " and in the definition of " sentence " the words from " an ", in the second place where it occurs, to " school ". In Schedule 9, the entries relating to sections 54, 58, 70, 77, 78, 82 and 90 of the Act of 1933, in the entry relating to section 48(2) of the Act of 1933 the words " a probationer or " and " any failure to comply with the requirements of the probation order or " and the words from " or to amend " to the end of the entry, and the entry relating to the Children and Young Persons Act 1938.
1949 c. 101.	The Justices of the Peace Act 1949.	Section 14.
1950 c. 37.	The Maintenance Orders Act 1950.	In Schedule 1, in the entry relating to section 86 of the Act of 1933, the words from " or as " onwards.
1952 c. 50.	The Children and Young Persons (Amendment) Act 1952.	Sections 2 to 5. In the Schedule, paragraphs 2, 3, 5, 8, 9 and 11 to 16.

Chapter	Short title	Extent of repeal
1952 c. 52.	The Prison Act 1952.	In section 49(2) the words " remand home or", where they first occur, and the words " remand home " wherever else they occur. In section 50, the words from " and subsection " onwards. In section 53(1) the definition of " remand home ".
1952 c. 55.	The Magistrates' Courts Act 1952.	Sections 20, 21 and 26(2). Section 32. In section 38(1), the words from " The provisions of this " onwards.
1953 c. 33.	The Education (Miscellaneous Provisions) Act 1953.	Section 11.
1956 c. 24.	The Children and Young Persons Act 1956.	The whole Act.
1956 c. 50.	The Family Allowances and National Insurance Act 1956.	Section 5.
1957 c. 55.	The Affiliation Proceedings Act 1957.	In section 5(2)(*d*) the words from " or " onwards. In section 7(5), the words " Sub-paragraph (ii) of ".
1958 c. 55.	The Local Government Act 1958.	In Schedule 8, in paragraph 2, sub-paragraph (3), in sub-paragraph (4) the words " paragraph (*b*) of ", and sub-paragraph (5).
1958 c. 65.	The Children Act 1958.	In section 2, in subsection (1) the words from " for reward " to " one month ", in subsection (2) the words from " by " in the first place where it occurs to " or " where that word first subsequently occurs, in subsection (4) the words " the Children and Young Persons Act 1933 or of ", and subsections (6) and (7). In section 3, in subsection (4), the words from " or is removed " to " maintaining him " and the words from " or removal " onwards, in subsection (5) the words " need not give a notice under subsection (4) of this section but ", and subsection (6). In section 17, in the definition of " fit person order " the words " the Children and Young Persons Act 1933 or ". In Schedule 2 the entry relating to section 54 of the Children Act 1948.

Chapter	Short title	Extent of repeal
1958 c. 5 (7 & 8 Eliz. 2).	The Adoption Act 1958	In section 15(3) the words from " fit person by " to " care of a " and the words " fit person order or " and " as the case may be ". In section 37, in subsection (1) the words " but is not a foster child within the meaning of Part I of the Children Act 1958 ", in subsection (2) the words from " by reason " to "subsection nor ", and in subsection (3) the words " in an approved school or ".
1959 c. 72.	The Mental Health Act 1959.	In section 60(6) the words from " including " onwards. Section 61. Section 70(2). In section 72(6)(a) the words from " or made " to " Act 1933 " and from " or an order " onwards. In section 75(1), the words "(other than a person detained in a remand home) " and in paragraph (b) the words from " or as " to " have been remitted ", and in section 75(2) the words from " including " to " 1963 ". Section 79. In section 80(1), the definitions of " approved school " and " remand home ".
1961 c. 39.	The Criminal Justice Act 1961.	In section 1, subsection (1) and the proviso to subsection (2). In section 4, in subsection (1) the words " but not less than fourteen ", and in subsection (2)(a) the words from " the offender " to " and ". In section 5(2), paragraph (a) and the words following paragraph (b), and section 5(3). In section 6, subsections (1) and (2), and in subsection (3) the words from " or ordering " to " home " in paragraph (a), the words from " or " to " home " in paragraph (b), and the words " or remand home " and " a prison is so named and ". In section 7, subsection (2), and in subsection (3) the words from " and where " onwards.

Chapter	Short title	Extent of repeal
1961 c. 39— *cont.*	The Criminal Justice Act 1961—*cont.*	Section 8(1) and (2). In section 9, paragraph (*a*). In section 10(2)(*a*), the words from " except " to " excessive ". Sections 14 to 19, 22(4) and 25. In section 29(1), the words " remand home " and " special reception centre or other " and in section 29(3) the words from " special " to " 1933 and ". Schedule 2. In Schedule 4 the entries relating to sections 54, 72, 78, 82, 83 and 88 of the Act of 1933 and to Schedule 4 to that Act and the entries relating to the Children and Young Persons Act 1938, section 72 and the change in the definition of " sentence " in section 80(1) of the Criminal Justice Act 1948, sections 20 and 32 of the Magistrates' Courts Act 1952, and section 79 of the Mental Health Act 1959.
1963 c. 33.	The London Government Act 1963.	In section 47, in subsection (1) the words " and in the definition of ' remand home ' in any enactment ", and in subsection (3) the reference in paragraph (*c*) to section 49 of the Criminal Justice Act 1948. In Schedule 17, paragraph 18(*c*).
1963 c. 37.	The Children and Young Persons Act 1963.	Sections 1(4), 2 and 4 to 15. Section 22. In section 23, in subsection (1), paragraph (*a*) and the word " authority ", subsection (2), in subsection (3) the words " or subsection (2) " in both places and the words " takes refuge there or ", and subsections (6) to (8). Section 24. In section 25(1) the words " or taken to a place of safety ", and section 25(2). In section 29, in subsection (1) the words " continue to " and subsection (2). Section 33. Section 53(1) and (2).

SCH. 6

Chapter	Short title	Extent of repeal
1963 c. 37— cont.	The Children and Young Persons Act 1963—cont.	In section 55 the words from "section 84(5)" to "principal Act", the word "or" immediately preceding the words "section 17" and the words from "(which relate" onwards. Sections 59 and 61. In section 65(5), the words "subsections (1) and (2) of section 10 and", "and 53(1)" and "27" and "34". Schedule 1. In Schedule 3, paragraphs 10, 15 to 23, 25 to 27, 33, 34, 35, 36, 44, 46, 48 and 49, and in paragraph 50 the words "special reception centre or other", and "'special reception centre' has the same meaning as in the Children and Young Persons Act 1933 and".
1963 c. 39.	The Criminal Justice (Scotland) Act 1963.	In Schedule 5, the entry relating to the Children Act 1948.
1965 c. 53.	The Family Allowances Act 1965.	In section 11(1), sub-paragraph (i) of paragraph (a) and in paragraph (c) the words from "made" to "order".
1967 c. 80.	The Criminal Justice Act 1967.	In section 55, the words "or any provision of the Children and Young Persons Act 1933" and the words from "and accordingly" onwards. In section 77(1), the words "on his means". In Part I of Schedule 3, the entries relating to sections 72(5) and 82(5) of the Act of 1933 and section 14 of the Act of 1963.
1968 c. 49.	The Social Work (Scotland) Act 1968.	In section 72(2), the words "of the Children and Young Persons Acts 1933 to 1963 or, as the case may be", the word "respectively" and the words "to a supervision order within the meaning of section 5 of the Children and Young Persons Act 1963 or". In section 73(2), the word "juvenile". In section 74, in subsection (3) the words "in England or Wales or" and "if he thinks fit" and the words from "an approved" to "be" where it

SCH. 6

Chapter	Short title	Extent of repeal
1968 c. 49—*cont.*	The Social Work (Scotland) Act 1968—*cont.*	first occurs, in subsection (4) the words from " the Children " to " be of ", the words " an approved school or " in the first, second and third places where they occur, the word " of " and " in " following those words in the first and third of those places respectively and the words " section 71 of the said Act of 1933 or " and " section 90 of the said Act of 1933 or under ", and in subsection (5) the words " of the Acts of 1933 to 1963 or, as the case may be ", the words " of a local authority or, as the case may be " and the words " those Acts or ". In section 75, in subsection (1) the words " the Secretary of State or " and " approved school or ", and in subsection (3) the words " approved school or ". In section 76, in subsections (1) and (2) the word " juvenile " wherever it occurs, and in subsection (4) the words " approved school or " and " of the approved school or ". Section 77(1)(*b*). In section 90(1) the words " or to prescribe any matter ". In Schedule 2, in paragraph 10 the words from " and " to " 1933 ". In Schedule 8, paragraphs 2 to 5, 18, 21 and 35.

SCHEDULE 7

Section 72(5).

SECTIONS 1 TO 6 AND 14 OF THE CHILDREN ACT 1958
AS AMENDED

1958 c. 65.

1. It shall be the duty of every local authority to satisfy themselves as to the well-being of children within their area who are foster children within the meaning of this Part of this Act and, for that purpose, to secure that, so far as appears to the authority to be appropriate, the children are visited from time to time by officers of the authority and that such advice is given as to the care and maintenance of the children as appears to be needed.

Duty of local authorities to ensure well-being of foster children.

2.—(1) In this Part of this Act " foster child " means, subject to the following provisions of this section, a child below the upper limit of the compulsory school age whose care and maintenance are undertaken by a person who is not a relative or guardian of his.

(2) A child is not a foster child within the meaning of this Part of this Act while he is in the care of a local authority or a voluntary organisation or is boarded out by a local health authority or a local education authority (or, in Scotland, an education authority).

(3) A child is not a foster child within the meaning of this Part of this Act while he is in the care of any person—

(a) in premises in which any parent, adult relative or guardian of his is for the time being residing ;

(b) in any voluntary home within the meaning of Part V of the Children and Young Persons Act, 1933, or in any residential establishment within the meaning of the Social Work (Scotland) Act 1968 ;

(c) in any school within the meaning of the Education Acts, 1944 to 1953, or the Education (Scotland) Acts 1939 to 1956 in which he is receiving full-time education ;

(d) in any hospital or in any nursing home registered or exempted from registration under Part VI of the Public Health Act, 1936, Part XI of the Public Health (London) Act, 1936, or the Nursing Homes Registration (Scotland) Act, 1938 ; or

(e) in any home or institution not specified in this section but maintained by a public or local authority.

(3A) A child is not a foster child within the meaning of this Part of this Act at any time while his care and maintenance are undertaken by a person, other than a relative or guardian of his, if at that time—

(a) that person does not intend to, and does not in fact, undertake his care and maintenance for a continuous period of more than six days ; or

(b) that person is not a regular foster parent and does not intend to, and does not in fact, undertake his care and maintenance for a continuous period of more than twenty-seven days ;

and for the purposes of this subsection a person is a regular foster parent if, during the period of twelve months immediately preceding the date on which he begins to undertake the care and maintenance of the child in question, he had, otherwise than as a relative or guardian, the care and maintenance of one or more children either for a period of, or periods amounting in the aggregate to, not less than three months or for at least three continuous periods each of which was of more than six days.

(4) A child is not a foster child within the meaning of this Part of this Act while he is in the care of any person in compliance with a supervision order within the meaning of the Children and

Young Persons Act 1969 or a probation order or supervision requirement or by virtue of a fit person order or while he is in an approved
school or is deemed for the purposes of the Children and Young
Persons (Scotland) Act, 1937, to be under the care of the managers
of an approved school or while he is liable to be detained or subject
to guardianship under the Mental Health Act, 1959, or the Mental
Health (Scotland) Act, 1960, or is resident in a residential home for
mentally disordered persons within the meaning of Part III of the
Mental Health Act, 1959, or in a residential home for persons suffering from mental disorder within the meaning of Part III of the
Mental Health (Scotland) Act, 1960.

(4A) A child is not a foster child for the purposes of this Part
of this Act while he is placed in the care and possession of a
person who proposes to adopt him under arrangements made by
such a local authority or registered adoption society as is referred
to in Part II of the Adoption Act 1958 or while he is a protected
child within the meaning of Part IV of that Act.

3.—(1) Subject to the following provisions of this section, a Duty of persons
person who proposes to maintain as a foster child a child not maintaining
already in his care shall give written notice thereof to the local foster children
authority not less than two weeks and not more than four weeks to notify local
before he receives the child, unless he receives him in an emergency ; authority.
and a person who maintains a foster child whom he received in
an emergency or who became a foster child while in his care shall
give written notice thereof to the local authority not later than forty-
eight hours after he receives the child or, as the case may be, after
the child becomes a foster child.

(2) Every such notice shall specify the date on which it is intended
that the child should be received or, as the case may be, on which
the child was in fact received or became a foster child and the
premises in which the child is to be or is being kept and shall be
given to the local authority for the area in which those premises
are situated.

(2A) A person shall not be required to give notice under subsection (1) of this section in relation to a child if—

(*a*) he has on a previous occasion given notice under that subsection in respect of that or any other child, specifying the
premises at which he proposes to keep the child in question ; and

(*b*) he has not, at any time since that notice was given, ceased
to maintain at least one foster child at those premises and
been required by virtue of the following provisions of this
section to give notice under subsection (5A) of this section
in respect of those premises.

(3) Where a person who is maintaining one or more foster
children changes his permanent address or the premises in which the
child is, or the children are, kept he shall, not less than two weeks
and not more than four weeks before the change or, if the change
is made in an emergency, not later than forty-eight hours after the
change, give written notice to the said local authority, specifying
the new address or premises, and if the new premises are in the

Sch. 7

area of another local authority, the authority to whom the notice is given shall inform that other local authority and give them such of the particulars mentioned in subsection (7) of this section as are known to them.

(4) If a foster child dies the person who was maintaining him shall, within forty-eight hours thereof, give to the local authority and to the person from whom the child was received notice in writing of the death.

(5) Where a foster child is removed or removes himself from the care of the person maintaining him, that person shall at the request of the local authority give them the name and address, if known, of the person (if any) into whose care the child has been removed.

(5A) Subject to the provisions of the following subsection, where a person who has been maintaining one or more foster children at any premises ceases to maintain foster children at those premises and the circumstances are such that no notice is required to be given under subsection (3) or subsection (4) of this section, that person shall, within forty-eight hours after he ceases to maintain any foster child at those premises, give notice in writing thereof to the local authority.

(5B) A person need not give the notice required by the preceding subsection in consequence of his ceasing to maintain foster children at any premises if, at the time he so ceases, he intends within twenty-seven days again to maintain any of them as a foster child at those premises ; but if he subsequently abandons that intention or the said period expires without his having given effect to it he shall give the said notice within forty-eight hours of that event.

(7) A person maintaining or proposing to maintain a foster child shall at the request of the local authority give them the following particulars, so far as known to him, that is to say, the name, sex, and date and place of birth of the child, and the name and address of every person who is a parent or guardian or acts as a guardian of the child or from whom the child has been or is to be received.

Power to inspect premises, impose conditions, or prohibit the keeping of foster children.

4.—(1) Any officer of a local authority authorised to visit foster children may, after producing, if asked to do so, some duly authenticated document showing that he is so authorised, inspect any premises in the area of the authority in the whole or any part of which foster children are to be or are being kept.

(1A) If it is shown to the satisfaction of a justice of the peace on sworn information in writing—

> (a) that there is reasonable cause to believe that a foster child is being kept in any premises, or in any part thereof ; and

> (b) that admission to those premises or that part thereof has been refused to a duly authorised officer of the local authority or that such a refusal is apprehended or that the occupier is temporarily absent,

the justice may by warrant under his hand authorise an officer of the local authority to enter the premises if need be by force, at any reasonable time within forty-eight hours of the issue of the warrant, for the purpose of inspecting the premises.

(2) Where a person is keeping or proposes to keep foster children in premises used (while foster children are kept therein) wholly or partly for that purpose, the local authority may impose on him requirements, to be complied with, after such time as the authority may specify, whenever a foster child is kept in the premises, as to—

(a) the number, age and sex of the foster children who may be kept at any one time in the premises or any part thereof ;

(b) the accommodation and equipment to be provided for the children ;

(c) the medical arrangements to be made for protecting the health of the children ;

(d) the giving of particulars of the person for the time being in charge of the children ;

(e) the number, qualifications or experience of the persons employed in looking after the children ;

(f) the keeping of records ;

(g) the fire precautions to be taken in the premises ;

(h) the giving of particulars of any foster child received in the premises and of any change in the number or identity of the foster children kept therein ;

but any such requirement may be limited to a particular class of foster children kept in the premises and any requirement imposed under paragraphs (b) to (h) of this subsection may be limited by the authority so as to apply only when the number of foster children kept in the premises exceeds a specified number.

(3) Where a person proposes to keep a foster child in any premises and the local authority are of the opinion that—

(a) the premises are not suitable premises in which to keep foster children ; or

(b) that person is not a suitable person to have the care and maintenance of foster children ; or

(c) it would be detrimental to that child to be kept by that person in those premises ;

the local authority may impose a prohibition on that person under subsection (3A) of this section.

(3A) A prohibition imposed on any person under this subsection may—

(a) prohibit him from keeping any foster child in premises specified in the prohibition ; or

(b) prohibit him from keeping any foster child in any premises in the area of the local authority ; or

(c) prohibit him from keeping a particular child specified in the prohibition in premises so specified.

SCH. 7

(3B) Where a local authority have imposed a prohibition on any person under subsection (3A) of this section, the local authority may, if they think fit, cancel the prohibition, either of their own motion or on an application made by that person on the ground of a change in the circumstances in which a foster child would be kept by him.

(4) Where a local authority impose a requirement on any person under subsection (2) of this section as respects any premises, they may prohibit him from keeping foster children in the premises after the time specified for compliance with the requirement unless the requirement is complied with.

(5) Any requirement or prohibition imposed under this section shall be imposed by notice in writing addressed to the person on whom it is imposed.

Appeal to juvenile court against requirement or prohibition imposed under section four.

5.—(1) Any person aggrieved by any requirement or prohibition imposed under section four of this Act may, within fourteen days from the date on which he is notified of the requirement or prohibition, or, in the case of a prohibition imposed under subsection (3A) of that section, within fourteen days from the refusal by the local authority to accede to an application by him for the cancellation of the prohibition, appeal to a juvenile court, and where the appeal is against such a requirement the requirement shall not have effect while the appeal is pending.

(2) Where the court allows such an appeal it may, instead of cancelling the requirement or prohibition, vary the requirement or allow more time for compliance with it or, where an absolute prohibition has been imposed, substitute for it a prohibition to use the premises after such time as the court may specify unless such specified requirements as the local authority had power to impose under section four of this Act are complied with.

(3) Any notice by which a requirement or prohibition is imposed on any person under section four of this Act shall contain a statement informing him of his right to appeal against the requirement or prohibition and of the time within which he may do so.

(4) Any requirement or prohibition specified or substituted under this section by the court shall be deemed for the purposes of this Part of this Act other than this section to have been imposed by the local authority under section four of this Act.

(5) In the application of this section to Scotland, for references to a juvenile court there shall be substituted references to the sheriff.

Disqualification for keeping foster children.

6.—(1) A person shall not maintain a foster child if—

(a) an order has been made against him under this Part of this Act removing a child from his care ;

(b) an order has been made under the Children and Young Persons Act, 1933, the Children and Young Persons Act 1969, or the Children and Young Persons (Scotland) Act, 1937, or a supervision requirement has been made under the Social Work (Scotland) Act 1968 and by virtue of the order or requirement a child was removed from his care ;

(c) he has been convicted of any offence specified in the First Sch 7
Schedule to the said Act of 1933 or the First Schedule to the
said Act of 1937 or has been placed on probation or discharged absolutely or conditionally for any such offence ;

(d) his rights and powers with respect to a child have been
vested in a local authority under section two of the
Children Act, 1948 or under section 16 of the Social Work
(Scotland) Act 1968 ;

(e) a local health authority or in Scotland a local authority
have made an order under subsection (3) or (4) of section
one of the Nurseries and Child-Minders Regulation Act
1948 refusing, or an order under section five of that Act
cancelling, the registration of any premises occupied by him
or his registration ;

(f) an order has been made under section 43 of the Adoption
Act 1958 for the removal of a protected child who was
being kept or was about to be received by him,

unless he has disclosed that fact to the local authority and obtained
their consent.

(2) Where this section applies to any person, otherwise than
by virtue of this subsection, it shall apply also to any other person
who lives in the same premises as he does or who lives in premises
at which he is employed.

14.—(1) A person shall be guilty of an offence if— Offences.

(a) being required, under any provision of this Part of this
Act, to give any notice or information, he fails to give
the notice within the time specified in that provision or
fails to give the information within a reasonable time, or
knowingly makes or causes or procures another person
to make any false or misleading statement in the notice or
information ;

(b) he refuses to allow the visiting of any foster child by a
duly authorised officer of a local authority or the inspection, under the power conferred by subsection (1) of section four of this Act, of any premises or wilfully obstructs
a person entitled to enter any premises by virtue of a
warrant under subsection (1A) of that section ;

(c) he fails to comply with any requirement imposed by a local
authority under this Part of this Act or keeps any foster
child in any premises in contravention of a prohibition
so imposed ;

(d) he maintains a foster child in contravention of section six
of this Act ; or

(e) he refuses to comply with an order under this Part of this
Act for the removal of any child or obstructs any person
in the execution of such an order.

(1A) Where section 6 of this Act applies to any person by virtue
only of subsection (2) of that section, he shall not be guilty of
an offence under paragraph (d) of subsection (1) of this section

if he proves that he did not know, and had no reasonable ground for believing, that a person living or employed in the premises in which he lives was a person to whom that section applies.

(2) A person guilty of an offence under this section shall be liable on summary conviction to imprisonment for a term not exceeding six months or a fine not exceeding one hundred pounds or both.

(2A) If any person who is required, under any provision of this Part of this Act, to give a notice fails to give the notice within the time specified in that provision, then, notwithstanding anything in section 104 of the Magistrates' Courts Act 1952 (time limit for proceedings) proceedings for the offence may be brought at any time within six months from the date when evidence of the offence came to the knowledge of the local authority.

(3) In England and Wales, a local authority may institute proceedings for an offence under this section.

Divorce Reform Act 1969

1969 CHAPTER 55

An Act to amend the grounds for divorce and judicial separation; to facilitate reconciliation in matrimonial causes; and for purposes connected with the matters aforesaid.   [22nd October 1969]

BE IT ENACTED by the Queen's most Excellent Majesty, by and with the advice and consent of the Lords Spiritual and Temporal, and Commons, in this present Parliament assembled, and by the authority of the same, as follows:—

1. After the commencement of this Act the sole ground on which a petition for divorce may be presented to the court by either party to a marriage shall be that the marriage has broken down irretrievably. *Breakdown of marriage to be sole ground for divorce.*

2.—(1) The court hearing a petition for divorce shall not hold the marriage to have broken down irretrievably unless the petitioner satisfies the court of one or more of the following facts, that is to say— *Proof of breakdown.*

(*a*) that the respondent has committed adultery and the petitioner finds it intolerable to live with the respondent;

(*b*) that the respondent has behaved in such a way that the petitioner cannot reasonably be expected to live with the respondent;

(*c*) that the respondent has deserted the petitioner for a continuous period of at least two years immediately preceding the presentation of the petition;

(*d*) that the parties to the marriage have lived apart for a continuous period of at least two years immediately preceding the presentation of the petition and the respondent consents to a decree being granted;

3 E 3

(e) that the parties to the marriage have lived apart for a continuous period of at least five years immediately preceding the presentation of the petition.

(2) On a petition for divorce it shall be the duty of the court to inquire, so far as it reasonably can, into the facts alleged by the petitioner and into any facts alleged by the respondent.

(3) If the court is satisfied on the evidence of any such fact as is mentioned in subsection (1) of this section, then, unless it is satisfied on all the evidence that the marriage has not broken down irretrievably, it shall, subject to section 4 of this Act and section 5(5) of the Matrimonial Causes Act 1965, grant a decree nisi of divorce.

1965 c. 72.

(4) For the purpose of subsection (1)(c) of this section the court may treat a period of desertion as having continued at a time when the deserting party was incapable of continuing the necessary intention if the evidence before the court is such that, had that party not been so incapable, the court would have inferred that his desertion continued at that time.

(5) For the purposes of this Act a husband and wife shall be treated as living apart unless they are living with each other in the same household.

(6) Provision shall be made by rules of court for the purpose of ensuring that where in pursuance of subsection (1)(d) of this section the petitioner alleges that the respondent consents to a decree being granted the respondent has been given such information as will enable him to understand the consequences to him of his consenting to a decree being granted and the steps which he must take to indicate that he consents to the grant of a decree.

Provisions designed to encourage reconciliation.

3.—(1) Provision shall be made by rules of court for requiring the solicitor acting for a petitioner for divorce to certify whether he has discussed with the petitioner the possibility of a reconciliation and given him the names and addresses of persons qualified to help effect a reconciliation between parties to a marriage who have become estranged.

(2) If at any stage of proceedings for divorce it appears to the court that there is a reasonable possibility of a reconciliation between the parties to the marriage, the court may adjourn the proceedings for such period as it thinks fit to enable attempts to be made to effect such a reconciliation.

The power conferred by the foregoing provision is additional to any other power of the court to adjourn proceedings.

(3) Where the parties to the marriage have lived with each other for any period or periods after it became known to the

petitioner that the respondent had, since the celebration of the marriage, committed adultery, then,—

(a) if the length of that period or of those periods together was six months or less, their living with each other during that period or those periods shall be disregarded in determining for the purposes of section 2(1)(a) of this Act whether the petitioner finds it intolerable to live with the respondent; but

(b) if the length of that period or of those periods together exceeded six months, the petitioner shall not be entitled to rely on that adultery for the purposes of the said section 2(1)(a).

(4) Where the petitioner alleges that the respondent has behaved in such a way that the petitioner cannot reasonably be expected to live with him, but the parties to the marriage have lived with each other for a period or periods after the date of the occurrence of the final incident relied on by the petitioner and held by the court to support his allegation, that fact shall be disregarded in determining for the purposes of section 2(1)(b) of this Act whether the petitioner cannot reasonably be expected to live with the respondent if the length of that period or of those periods together was six months or less.

(5) In considering for the purposes of section 2(1) of this Act whether the period for which the respondent has deserted the petitioner or the period for which the parties to a marriage have lived apart has been continuous, no account shall be taken of any one period (not exceeding six months) or of any two or more periods (not exceeding six months in all) during which the parties resumed living with each other, but no period during which the parties lived with each other shall count as part of the period of desertion or of the period for which the parties to the marriage lived apart, as the case may be.

(6) References in this section to the parties to a marriage living with each other shall be construed as references to their living with each other in the same household.

4.—(1) The respondent to a petition for divorce in which the petitioner alleges any such fact as is mentioned in paragraph (e) of section 2(1) of this Act may oppose the grant of a decree nisi on the ground that the dissolution of the marriage will result in grave financial or other hardship to him and that it would in all the circumstances be wrong to dissolve the marriage.

Decree to be refused in certain circumstances.

(2) Where the grant of a decree nisi is opposed by virtue of this section, then,—

(a) if the court is satisfied that the only fact mentioned in the said section 2(1) on which the petitioner is entitled

3 E 4

to rely in support of his petition is that mentioned in the said paragraph (*e*), and

(*b*) if apart from this section it would grant a decree nisi,

the court shall consider all the circumstances, including the conduct of the parties to the marriage and the interests of those parties and of any children or other persons concerned, and if the court is of opinion that the dissolution of the marriage will result in grave financial or other hardship to the respondent and that it would in all the circumstances be wrong to dissolve the marriage it shall dismiss the petition.

(3) For the purposes of this section hardship shall include the loss of the chance of acquiring any benefit which the respondent might acquire if the marriage were not dissolved.

Power to rescind decree nisi in certain cases.

5. Where the court on granting a decree of divorce held that the only fact mentioned in section 2(1) of this Act on which the petitioner was entitled to rely in support of his petition was that mentioned in paragraph (*d*), it may, on an application made by the respondent at any time before the decree is made absolute, rescind the decree if it is satisfied that the petitioner misled the respondent (whether intentionally or unintentionally) about any matter which the respondent took into account in deciding to consent to the grant of a decree.

Financial protection for respondent in certain cases.

6.—(1) The following provisions of this section shall have effect where—

(*a*) the respondent to a petition for divorce in which the petitioner alleged any such fact as is mentioned in paragraph (*d*) or (*e*) of section 2(1) of this Act has applied to the court under this section for it to consider for the purposes of subsection (2) hereof the financial position of the respondent after the divorce ; and

(*b*) a decree nisi of divorce has been granted on the petition and the court has held that the only fact mentioned in the said section 2(1) on which the petitioner was entitled to rely in support of his petition was that mentioned in the said paragraph (*d*) or (*e*).

(2) The court hearing an application by the respondent under this section shall consider all the circumstances, including the age, health, conduct, earning capacity, financial resources and financial obligations of each of the parties, and the financial position of the respondent as, having regard to the divorce, it is likely to be after the death of the petitioner should the petitioner die first ; and notwithstanding anything in the foregoing provisions of this Act but subject to subsection (3) of this section, the

court shall not make absolute the decree of divorce unless it is satisfied—

   (a) that the petitioner should not be required to make any financial provision for the respondent, or

   (b) that the financial provision made by the petitioner for the respondent is reasonable and fair or the best that can be made in the circumstances.

(3) The court may if it thinks fit proceed without observing the requirements of subsection (2) of this section if—

   (a) it appears that there are circumstances making it desirable that the decree should be made absolute without delay, and

   (b) the court has obtained a satisfactory undertaking from the petitioner that he will make such financial provision for the respondent as the court may approve.

7.—(1) Provision may be made by rules of court for enabling Rules may the parties to a marriage, or either of them, on application made enable certain either before or after the presentation of a petition for divorce, agreements or to refer to the court any agreement or arrangement made or pro- to be referred posed to be made between them, being an agreement or arrange- to the court. ment which relates to, arises out of, or is connected with, the proceedings for divorce which are contemplated or, as the case may be, have begun, and for enabling the court to express an opinion, should it think it desirable to do so, as to the reasonableness of the agreement or arrangement and to give such directions, if any, in the matter as it thinks fit.

(2) In section 3 of the Matrimonial Causes Act 1967 (con- 1967 c. 56. sideration of agreements or arrangements by divorce county courts) after the word " 1965 " there shall be inserted the words " or of section 7 of the Divorce Reform Act 1969 ".

8.—(1) After the commencement of this Act the existence of Judicial any such fact as is mentioned in section 2(1) of this Act shall separation. be a ground on which either party to a marriage may present a petition for judicial separation ; and the ground of failure to comply with a decree for restitution of conjugal rights and any ground on which a decree of divorce a mensa et thoro might have been pronounced immediately before the commencement of the Matrimonial Causes Act 1857 shall cease to be a ground on 1857 c. 85. which such a petition may be presented.

(2) Accordingly for subsection (1) of section 12 of the Matri- 1965 c. 72. monial Causes Act 1965 there shall be substituted the following subsection : —

   " (1) A petition for judicial separation may be presented to the court by either party to a marriage on the ground that any such fact as is mentioned in section 2(1) of the

Divorce Reform Act 1969 exists, and sections 2(2), (4), (5) and (6), 3 and 7 of that Act and paragraph 2 of Schedule 1 to this Act shall, with the necessary modifications, apply in relation to such a petition as they apply in relation to a petition for divorce."

(3) The court hearing a petition for judicial separation shall not be concerned to consider whether the marriage has broken down irretrievably, and if it is satisfied on the evidence of any such fact as is mentioned in section 2(1) of this Act, it shall, subject to section 33 of the Matrimonial Causes Act 1965 (restrictions on decrees for dissolution or separation affecting children), grant a decree of judicial separation.

1965 c. 72.

Consequential amendments, repeals and saving.
9.—(1) The provisions of the Matrimonial Causes Act 1965 specified in Schedule 1 to this Act shall have effect subject to the amendments set out in that Schedule, being amendments consequential on the foregoing provisions of this Act.

(2) Each of the provisions of the Matrimonial Causes Act 1965 specified in column 1 of Schedule 2 to this Act is, to the extent specified in relation to it in column 2 of that Schedule, hereby repealed.

(3) Without prejudice to any provision of this Act or of the Matrimonial Causes Act 1965, as amended by this Act, which empowers or requires the court to dismiss a petition for divorce or judicial separation or to dismiss an application for a decree nisi of divorce to be made absolute, nothing in section 32 of the Supreme Court of Judicature (Consolidation) Act 1925 (rules as to exercise of jurisdiction) or in any rule of law shall be taken as empowering or requiring the court to dismiss such a petition or application on the ground of collusion between the parties in connection with the presentation or prosecution of the petition or the obtaining of the decree nisi or on the ground of any conduct on the part of the petitioner.

1925 c. 49.

Saving for petitions presented before commencement of Act.
10. This Act (including the repeals and amendments made by it) shall not have effect in relation to any petition for divorce or judicial separation presented before the commencement of this Act.

Short title, construction, commencement and extent.
11.—(1) This Act may be cited as the Divorce Reform Act 1969.

(2) This Act shall be construed as one with the Matrimonial Causes Act 1965.

(3) This Act shall come into operation on 1st January 1971.

(4) This Act does not extend to Scotland or Northern Ireland.

SCHEDULES

SCHEDULE 1

CONSEQUENTIAL AMENDMENTS OF THE MATRIMONIAL
CAUSES ACT 1965

1. In section 3(1) after the word "petitioner" there shall be inserted the words "or respondent".

2. In section 4(1) and (2) for the words "on the ground of adultery" there shall be substituted the words "in which adultery is alleged" and in section 4(1) for the words "on that ground" there shall be substituted the words "and alleging adultery".

3. In section 5(6) for the words from "opposes" to "desertion" there shall be substituted the words "alleges against the petitioner and proves any such fact as is mentioned in section 2(1) of the Divorce Reform Act 1969".

4. In section 15(*b*) for the words "on the ground of her husband's insanity" there shall be substituted the words "and alleging any such fact as is mentioned in section 2(1)(*e*) of the Divorce Reform Act 1969 where the court is satisfied on proof of such facts as may be prescribed by rules of court that her husband is insane".

5. In section 16(3) for the words from the beginning to "insanity" there shall be substituted the words "Where on a petition for divorce presented by a wife the court granted her a decree and held that the only fact mentioned in section 2(1) of the Divorce Reform Act 1969 on which she was entitled to rely was that mentioned in paragraph (*e*), then if the court is satisfied on proof of such facts as may be prescribed by rules of court that the husband is insane".

6. In section 17(2) for the words from the beginning to "she" there shall be substituted the words "Where on a petition for divorce presented by the husband he satisfies the court of any such fact as is mentioned in section 2(1)(*a*), (*b*) or (*c*) of the Divorce Reform Act 1969 and the court grants him a decree of divorce, then if it appears to the court that the wife" and for the words "innocent party" there shall be substituted the word "husband".

7. In section 20(1)(*b*) for the words "on the ground of her husband's insanity" there shall be substituted the words "and the court held that the only fact mentioned in section 2(1) of the Divorce Reform Act 1969 on which she was entitled to rely was that mentioned in paragraph (*e*) and the court is satisfied on proof of such facts as may be prescribed by rules of court that the husband is insane".

8. In section 26(6), as amended by the Family Provision Act 1966, in the definition of "court", after the word "court", where first occurring, there shall be inserted the words "means the High Court and".

9. In section 30(2)—

    (*a*) in paragraph (*a*) for the words "on the ground of her husband's insanity" there shall be substituted the words

SCH. 1

" and the court is satisfied on proof of such facts as may be prescribed by rules of court that her husband is insane ";

(b) in paragraph (b) the word " divorce " and the words " or judicial separation " shall be omitted ; and

(c) after paragraph (a) there shall be inserted the following paragraph : —

" (aa) a petition for divorce or judicial separation is presented by a husband and the court is satisfied on proof of such facts as may be prescribed by rules of court that his wife is insane ; or ".

10. In section 34(3) for the words " on the ground of the husband's insanity " there shall be substituted the words " in favour of a wife where the court held that the only fact mentioned in section 2(1) of the Divorce Reform Act 1969 on which she was entitled to rely was that mentioned in paragraph (e) and the court is satisfied on proof of such facts as may be prescribed by rules of court that the husband is insane."

11. In section 46(2) after the definition of " adopted " there shall be inserted the following definition :—

1967 c. 56.

" ' the court ' (except in sections 26, 27, 28 and 28A) means the High Court or, where a county court has jurisdiction by virtue of the Matrimonial Causes Act 1967, a county court ; and ".

12. In Schedule 1, in paragraph 2 after the word " Act " there shall be inserted the words " or of section 2(1)(c) of the Divorce Reform Act 1969."

Section 9(2).

1965 c. 72.

SCHEDULE 2

REPEALS IN THE MATRIMONIAL CAUSES ACT 1965

Provision		Extent of Repeal
Section 1	...	The whole section.
Section 5	...	Subsections (1), (2), (3) and (4).
Section 6	...	In subsection (1), except as applied by section 10 or 14 of the said Act of 1965, paragraph (c).
Section 7	...	In subsection (1), except as applied by the said section 10 or 14, the words from " either " to " collusion or ".
Section 30	...	In subsection (2)(b), the word " divorce " and the words " or judicial separation ".
Section 42	...	Subsections (1) and (3) so far as they apply in relation to proceedings for divorce or judicial separation.
		In subsection (2), the words " this Act and ".

Auctions (Bidding Agreements) Act 1969

1969 CHAPTER 56

An Act to amend the law with respect to proceedings for offences under the Auctions (Bidding Agreements) Act 1927; to make fresh provision as to the rights of a seller of goods by auction where an agreement subsists that a person or persons shall abstain from bidding for the goods; and for connected purposes.

[22nd October 1969]

BE IT ENACTED by the Queen's most Excellent Majesty, by and with the advice and consent of the Lords Spiritual and Temporal, and Commons, in this present Parliament assembled, and by the authority of the same, as follows:—

1.—(1) Offences under section 1 of the Auctions (Bidding Agreements) Act 1927 (which, as amended by the Criminal Justice Act 1967, renders a dealer who agrees to give, or gives, or offers a gift or consideration to another as an inducement or reward for abstaining, or for having abstained, from bidding at a sale by auction punishable on summary conviction with a fine not exceeding £400 or imprisonment for a term not exceeding six months, or both, and renders similarly punishable a person who agrees to accept, or accepts, or attempts to obtain from a dealer any such gift or consideration as aforesaid) shall be triable on indictment as well as summarily; and the penalty that may be imposed on a person on conviction on indictment of an offence under that section shall be imprisonment for a term not exceeding two years or a fine or both. *Offences under Auctions (Bidding Agreements) Act 1927 to be indictable as well as triable summarily, and extension of time for bringing summary proceedings. 1927 c. 12. 1967 c. 80.*

(2) Notwithstanding anything in section 104 of the Magistrates' Courts Act 1952, an information relating to an offence under the said section 1 may be tried by a magistrates' court in England or Wales if it is laid at any time within five years after the commission of the offence and within three months after the date on which evidence sufficient in the opinion of the Attorney General to justify the proceedings comes to his knowledge. *1952 c. 55.*

(3) Summary proceedings in Scotland for an offence under the said section 1 shall not be commenced after the expiration of five years from the commission of the offence, but, subject to the foregoing limitation and notwithstanding anything in section 23 of the Summary Jurisdiction (Scotland) Act 1954, such proceedings may be commenced at any time within three months after the date on which evidence sufficient in the opinion of the Lord Advocate to justify the proceedings comes to his knowledge, and subsection (2) of the said section 23 shall apply for the purposes of this subsection as it applies for the purposes of that section.

1954 c. 48.

(4) For the purposes of subsection (2) above, a certificate of the Attorney General as to the date on which evidence sufficient in his opinion to justify proceedings came to his knowledge shall be conclusive evidence and so, for the purposes of the last foregoing subsection, shall be a corresponding certificate of the Lord Advocate.

(5) This section applies only to offences committed after the commencement of this Act.

Persons convicted not to attend or participate in auctions.

2.—(1) On any such summary conviction or conviction on indictment as is mentioned in section 1 above, the court may order that the person so convicted or that person and any representative of him shall not (without leave of the court) for a period from the date of such conviction—

(*a*) in the case of a summary conviction, of not more than one year, or

(*b*) in the case of a conviction on indictment, of not more than three years,

enter upon any premises where goods intended for sale by auction are on display or to attend or participate in any way in any sale by auction.

(2) In the event of a contravention of an order under this section, the person who contravenes it (and, if he is the representative of another, that other also) shall be guilty of an offence and liable—

(*a*) on summary conviction, to a fine not exceeding £400;

(*b*) on conviction on indictment, to imprisonment for a term not exceeding two years or to a fine or to both.

(3) In any proceedings against a person in respect of a contravention of an order under this section consisting in the entry upon premises where goods intended for sale by auction were on display, it shall be a defence for him to prove that he did not know, and had no reason to suspect, that goods so intended were on display on the premises, and in any proceedings against a person in respect of a contravention of such an order consisting

in his having done something as the representative of another, it shall be a defence for him to prove that he did not know, and had no reason to suspect, that that other was the subject of such an order.

(4) A person shall not be guilty of an offence under this section by reason only of his selling property by auction or causing it to be so sold.

3.—(1) Where goods are purchased at an auction by a person who has entered into an agreement with another or others that the other or the others (or some of them) shall abstain from bidding for the goods (not being an agreement to purchase the goods bona fide on a joint account) and he or the other party, or one of the other parties, to the agreement is a dealer, the seller may avoid the contract under which the goods are purchased.

(2) Where a contract is avoided by virtue of the foregoing subsection, then, if the purchaser has obtained possession of the goods and restitution thereof is not made, the persons who were parties to the agreement that one or some of them should abstain from bidding for the goods the subject of the contract shall be jointly and severally liable to make good to the seller the loss (if any) he sustained by reason of the operation of the agreement.

(3) Subsection (1) above applies to a contract made after the commencement of this Act whether the agreement as to the abstention of a person or persons from bidding for the goods the subject of the contract was made before or after that commencement.

(4) Section 2 of the Auctions (Bidding Agreements) Act 1927 (right of vendors to treat certain sales as fraudulent) shall not apply to a sale the contract for which is made after the commencement of this Act.

(5) In this section, " dealer " has the meaning assigned to it by section 1(2) of the Auctions (Bidding Agreements) Act 1927.

4. Section 3 of the Auctions (Bidding Agreements) Act 1927 (copy of Act to be exhibited at sale) shall have effect as if the reference to that Act included a reference to this Act.

5.—(1) This Act may be cited as the Auctions (Bidding Agreements) Act 1969.

(2) This Act shall come into force at the expiration of one month beginning with the day on which it is passed.

(3) This Act shall not extend to Northern Ireland.

Employers' Liability (Compulsory Insurance) Act 1969

1969 CHAPTER 57

An Act to require employers to insure against their liability for personal injury to their employees; and for purposes connected with the matter aforesaid.

[22nd October 1969]

Be it enacted by the Queen's most Excellent Majesty, by and with the advice and consent of the Lords Spiritual and Temporal, and Commons, in this present Parliament assembled, and by the authority of the same, as follows:—

1.—(1) Except as otherwise provided by this Act, every employer carrying on any business in Great Britain shall insure, and maintain insurance, under one or more approved policies with an authorised insurer or insurers against liability for bodily injury or disease sustained by his employees, and arising out of and in the course of their employment in Great Britain in that business, but except in so far as regulations otherwise provide not including injury or disease suffered or contracted outside Great Britain. *Insurance against liability for employees.*

(2) Regulations may provide that the amount for which an employer is required by this Act to insure and maintain insurance shall, either generally or in such cases or classes of case as may be prescribed by the regulations, be limited in such manner as may be so prescribed.

(3) For the purposes of this Act—

(a) "approved policy" means a policy of insurance not subject to any conditions or exceptions prohibited for those purposes by regulations;

(b) "authorised insurer" means a person or body of persons lawfully carrying on in Great Britain insurance business of any class relevant for the purposes of Part II of the Companies Act 1967 and issuing the policy or policies in the course thereof; *1967 c. 81.*

(c) " business " includes a trade or profession, and includes any activity carried on by a body of persons, whether corporate or unincorporate;

(d) except as otherwise provided by regulations, an employer not having a place of business in Great Britain shall be deemed not to carry on business there.

Employees to be covered.

2.—(1) For the purposes of this Act the term " employee " means an individual who has entered into or works under a contract of service or apprenticeship with an employer whether by way of manual labour, clerical work or otherwise, whether such contract is expressed or implied, oral or in writing.

(2) This Act shall not require an employer to insure—

(a) in respect of an employee of whom the employer is the husband, wife, father, mother, grandfather, grandmother, step-father, step-mother, son, daughter, grandson, grand-daughter, stepson, stepdaughter, brother, sister, half-brother or half-sister; or

(b) except as otherwise provided by regulations, in respect of employees not ordinarily resident in Great Britain.

Employers exempted from insurance.

3.—(1) This Act shall not require any insurance to be effected by—

(a) any such authority as is mentioned in subsection (2) below; or

(b) any body corporate established by or under any enactment for the carrying on of any industry or part of an industry, or of any undertaking, under national ownership or control; or

(c) in relation to any such cases as may be specified in the regulations, any employer exempted by regulations.

(2) The authorities referred to in subsection (1)(a) above are the Common Council of the City of London, the Greater London Council, the council of a London borough, the council of a county, county borough or county district in England or Wales, a county, town or district council in Scotland, any joint board or joint committee in England and Wales or joint committee in Scotland which is so constituted as to include among its members representatives of any such council, and any police authority.

Certificates of insurance.

4.—(1) Provision may be made by regulations for securing that certificates of insurance in such form and containing such particulars as may be prescribed by the regulations, are issued by insurers to employers entering into contracts of insurance in accordance with the requirements of this Act and for the surrender in such circumstances as may be so prescribed of certificates so issued.

(2) Where a certificate of insurance is required to be issued to an employer in accordance with regulations under subsection (1) above, the employer (subject to any provision made by the regulations as to the surrender of the certificate) shall during the currency of the insurance and such further period (if any) as may be provided by regulations—

(a) comply with any regulations requiring him to display copies of the certificate of insurance for the information of his employees;

(b) produce the certificate of insurance or a copy thereof on demand to any inspector duly authorised by the Secretary of State for the purposes of this Act and produce or send the certificate or a copy thereof to such other persons, at such place and in such circumstances as may be prescribed by regulations;

(c) permit the policy of insurance or a copy thereof to be inspected by such persons and in such circumstances as may be so prescribed.

(3) A person who fails to comply with a requirement imposed by or under this section shall be liable on summary conviction to a fine not exceeding £50.

5. An employer who on any day is not insured in accordance with this Act when required to be so shall be guilty of an offence and shall be liable on summary conviction to a fine not exceeding two hundred pounds; and where an offence under this section committed by a corporation has been committed with the consent or connivance of, or facilitated by any neglect on the part of, any director, manager, secretary or other officer of the corporation, he, as well as the corporation shall be deemed to be guilty of that offence and shall be liable to be proceeded against and punished accordingly. *Penalty for failure to insure.*

6.—(1) The Secretary of State may by statutory instrument make regulations for any purpose for which regulations are authorised to be made by this Act, but any such statutory instrument shall be subject to annulment in pursuance of a resolution of either House of Parliament. *Regulations.*

(2) Any regulations under this Act may make different provision for different cases or classes of case, and may contain such incidental and supplementary provisions as appear to the Secretary of State to be necessary or expedient for the purposes of the regulations.

7.—(1) This Act may be cited as the Employers' Liability (Compulsory Insurance) Act 1969.

(2) This Act shall not extend to Northern Ireland.

(3) This Act shall come into force for any purpose on such date as the Secretary of State may by order contained in a statutory instrument appoint, and the purposes for which this Act is to come into force at any time may be defined by reference to the nature of an employer's business, or to that of an employee's work, or in any other way.

Administration of Justice Act 1969

1969 CHAPTER 58

An Act to increase the jurisdiction of county courts and to amend the County Courts Act 1959; to make further provision for appeals from the High Court (whether in England and Wales or in Northern Ireland) to the House of Lords; to enable wills and codicils to be made for mentally disordered persons; to make provision for interim payments to be made where proceedings are pending, and for conferring powers to be exercisable by the court before the commencement of an action, and to make further provision with respect to interest on damages; to enable any jurisdiction of the High Court to be assigned to two or more Divisions concurrently; to enable the Appeal Tribunals under the Patents Act 1949 and the Registered Designs Act 1949 to consist of two or more judges; to change the title and qualification of clerks to registrars of the Chancery Division; to make further provision with respect to miscellaneous matters, that is to say, certain employments in the offices of the Supreme Court, records of grants of probate and grants of administration and the making of second and subsequent grants, admission as a public notary, pension rights and related matters in connection with certain judicial offices, and the stipend and fees of the Chancellor of the County Palatine of Durham; to extend the legislative power of the Parliament of Northern Ireland with respect to grand juries and indictments; and for purposes connected with the matters aforesaid.

[22nd October 1969]

B E IT ENACTED by the Queen's most Excellent Majesty, by and with the advice and consent of the Lords Spiritual and Temporal, and Commons, in this present Parliament assembled, and by the authority of the same, as follows:—

PART I

AMENDMENTS OF COUNTY COURTS ACT 1959

Increase of general jurisdiction in contract and tort and in respect of money recoverable by statute.
1959 c. 22.

1. In sections 39 and 40 of the County Courts Act 1959 (in this Part of this Act referred to as " the principal Act ") for each reference to five hundred pounds there shall be substituted the words " £750 ".

Corresponding increases under other provisions.

2. In the following provisions of the principal Act, that is to say, section 41 (abandonment of part of claim to give court jurisdiction), section 45(2) (transfer of actions of contract or tort from High Court to county court), section 68 (transfer of interpleader proceedings from High Court to county court), section 80 (actions by persons under 21 for payment of remuneration) and section 146 (transfer from High Court of applications to attach debts or levy executions against members of firms), and, in Schedule 1 to that Act, in the entry relating to section 136 of the Law of Property Act 1925, for each reference to five hundred pounds there shall be substituted the words " £750 ".

1925 c. 20.

Transfer of certain actions of contract or tort from county court to High Court at defendant's instance.

3. In section 44 of the principal Act, in subsection (1), for the words " forty pounds " there shall be substituted the words " £100 ", and in subsection (2), for the words from " the amount claimed and the costs of trial " to the end of paragraph (*a*) there shall be substituted the words " such amount as the registrar may determine, and ".

Costs of proceedings commenced in High Court which could have been commenced in county court.

4.—(1) In section 47 of the principal Act (costs of actions of contract or tort commenced in High Court which could have been commenced in county court), in subsection (1),—

(*a*) the words " and the action is not referred for trial to an official referee " shall cease to have effect ;

(*b*) in paragraph (*a*), for the reference to four hundred pounds there shall be substituted the words " £500 " ; and

(*c*) in paragraph (*b*), for the words " seventy-five pounds " there shall be substituted the words " £100 ",

and after that subsection there shall be inserted the following subsection :—

" (1A) In relation to an action brought to enforce a right to recover possession of goods, or to enforce such a right and to claim payment of a debt or other demand

or damages, subsection (1) of this section shall have effect
as if—

(a) in paragraph (a) of that subsection, for the words
' he recovers a sum less than £500 ' there were
substituted the words ' the aggregate amount
recovered by him in the action, including the value
of any goods ordered in the action to be delivered
to him, is less than £500 ', and

(b) in paragraph (b) of that subsection, for the words
' he recovers a sum less than £100 ' there were
substituted the words ' the aggregate amount
recovered by him in the action, including the
value of any goods ordered in the action to be
delivered to him, is less than £100 ',

and as if, in the words so substituted, any reference to an
order for the delivery of goods to the plaintiff included a
reference to an order to deliver goods to the plaintiff or to
pay their value to him."

(2) Subsection (4) of the said section 47 shall cease to have
effect.

(3) In section 60 of the principal Act (costs of certain Ad-
miralty proceedings commenced in High Court which could
have been commenced in county court), in subsection (3), for
the words " seventy-five pounds " there shall be substituted the
words " £100 ".

5. In section 52(1) of the principal Act (equity jurisdic-   Increase of
tion) and in Schedule 1 to that Act (excluding the entry in that jurisdiction
Schedule relating to section 136 of the Law of Property Act in equity and
1925) for the words " five hundred pounds ", in each place certain related
where they occur, there shall be substituted the words " £5,000 ", proceedings.
and for the words " thirty pounds ", in each place where they 1925 c. 20.
occur, there shall be substituted the words " £300 ".

6. In section 74 of the principal Act the words " in any General
proceedings before it " shall cease to have effect, and at the end ancillary
of that section there shall be added the following subsection: — jurisdiction.

" (2) For the purposes of this section it shall be assumed
(notwithstanding any enactment to the contrary) that any
proceedings which can be commenced in a county court
could be commenced in the High Court."

7.—(1) In section 89 of the principal Act, in paragraph (c), Right of
for the words " but not a solicitor retained as an advocate by a audience.
solicitor so acting " there shall be substituted the words " (in this
paragraph referred to as a ' solicitor on the record '), any solicitor
employed by a solicitor on the record, any solicitor engaged as
an agent by a solicitor on the record and any solicitor employed

PART I

by a solicitor so engaged ", and paragraph (i) of the proviso shall be omitted.

(2) At the end of the said section 89 there shall be added the following subsections: —

" (2) Where an action is brought in a county court by a local authority for either or both of the following, that is to say—

    (a) the recovery of possession of a house belonging to the authority ;

    (b) the recovery of any rent, mesne profits, damages or other sum claimed by the authority in respect of the occupation by any person of such a house,

then, in so far as the proceedings in the action are heard by the registrar, any officer of the authority authorised by the authority in that behalf, not being a person entitled to address the court by virtue of subsection (1) of this section, may address the registrar as if he were a person so entitled.

(3) In this section ' local authority ' means the council of a county, county borough, London borough or county district, the Greater London Council or the Common Council of the City of London, ' house ' includes a part of a house, a flat or any other dwelling and also includes any yard, garden, outhouse or appurtenance occupied with a house or part of a house or with a flat or other dwelling, and any reference to the occupation of a house by a person includes a reference to anything done by that person, or caused or permitted by him to be done, in relation to the house as occupier of the house, whether under a tenancy or licence or otherwise."

Assessors.

8. In section 91 of the principal Act, at the beginning of subsection (2) there shall be inserted the words " Subject to the next following subsection ", and after that subsection there shall be inserted the following subsection: —

" (2A) For the purpose of assisting the judge in reviewing the taxation by the registrar of the costs of any proceedings, the power conferred by subsection (1) of this section shall be exercisable by the judge without any application being made by any party to the proceedings; and, where one or more assessors are summoned for that purpose otherwise than on the application of a party to the proceedings, the remuneration of any such assessor—

    (a) shall be at such rate as may be determined by the Lord Chancellor with the approval of the Treasury, and

    (b) shall be payable out of moneys provided by Parliament."

9.—(1) In section 102 of the principal Act (county court PART I rules), in subsection (3)(*c*)(iii) (under which county court rules County may authorise the registrar, by leave of the judge and in the court rules. absence of objection by the parties, to hear and determine actions in which the sum claimed or the amount involved does not exceed £30), for the words " thirty pounds " there shall be substituted the words " £75 ".

(2) For paragraph (*d*) of subsection (3) of the said section 102 (under which rules may authorise a judge of county courts in certain circumstances to direct that the hearing in proceedings pending in one of his courts shall take place in the court for another district of which he is the judge) there shall be substituted the following paragraph : —

" (*d*) authorising directions to be given as follows, where the same judge is the judge for two or more districts, that is to say—

(i) authorising the judge to direct that the hearing in proceedings pending in the court for one of those districts, being proceedings which are to be heard and determined by the judge, shall take place in the court for another of those districts, or

(ii) authorising the registrar for one of those districts to direct that the hearing in proceedings pending in the court for the district for which he is the registrar, being proceedings which are to be heard and determined by the judge, shall take place in the court for another of those districts."

(3) After paragraph (*e*) of subsection (3) of the said section 102 there shall be inserted the following paragraph : —

" (*f*) making, with respect to proceedings in county courts, any provision regarding solicitors of the Supreme Court which could be made by rules of court with respect to proceedings in the High Court ".

10.—(1) For subsection (1) of section 192 of the principal Power to Act (which enables the limits specified in certain provisions of raise limits of that Act and in section 73(2) of the Solicitors Act 1957 to be jurisdiction. raised by Order in Council to an extent specified in that sub- 1957 c. 27. section), there shall be substituted the following subsection : —

" (1) If it appears to Her Majesty in Council that a sum specified in any of the enactments mentioned in the next following subsection (as that enactment has effect for the time being, whether by virtue of the Administration of Justice Act 1969 or this subsection or otherwise) should be increased, Her Majesty may by Order in Council, specifying the enactment and the sum in question, direct that the enactment shall be amended so as to substitute for that sum such larger sum as may be specified in the Order."

(2) For subsection (2) of the said section 192 (which specifies the enactments in relation to which the power conferred by subsection (1) is exercisable) there shall be substituted the following subsection.—

" (2) The said enactments are—

(a) sections 39, 40, 41, 44(1), 45, 47, 52, 60(3), 68, 80, 102(3)(c)(iii) and 146 of this Act, and Schedule 1 to this Act except so much of it as relates to sections 146 and 147 of the Law of Property Act 1925;

1925 c. 20.

1925 c. 18.   (b) section 113(3) of the Settled Land Act 1925; and

1957 c. 27.   (c) section 73(2) of the Solicitors Act 1957 ".

Miscellaneous amendments of principal Act.

11.—(1) In section 36(1) of the principal Act (which provides for the holding of additional courts at places where an office is kept open by the registrar) the words " at which an office is kept open by the registrar " shall cease to have effect.

(2) Section 46 of the principal Act (transfer from High Court to county court of actions of tort where plaintiff impecunious) shall cease to have effect.

(3) In sections 31(3) and 84(1) of the principal Act (each of which provides for a fine not exceeding £10) for the words " ten pounds " there shall be substituted the words " £50 ".

(4) In section 95(4) of the principal Act (under which a person summoned as a juror and failing to attend may forfeit a sum not exceeding £5) for the words " five pounds " there shall be substituted the words " £20 ".

Part II

Appeal from High Court to House of Lords

Grant of certificate by trial judge.

12.—(1) Where on the application of any of the parties to any proceedings to which this section applies the judge is satisfied—

(a) that the relevant conditions are fulfilled in relation to his decision in those proceedings, and

(b) that a sufficient case for an appeal to the House of Lords under this Part of this Act has been made out to justify an application for leave to bring such an appeal, and

(c) that all the parties to the proceedings consent to the grant of a certificate under this section,

the judge, subject to the following provisions of this Part of this Act, may grant a certificate to that effect.

(2) This section applies to any civil proceedings in the High
Court which are either—

(*a*) proceedings before a single judge of the High Court
(including a person acting as such a judge under section 3 of the Judicature Act 1925), or

(*b*) proceedings before a commissioner acting under a
commission issued under section 70 of the Judicature
Act 1925, or

(*c*) proceedings before a Divisional Court.

(3) Subject to any Order in Council made under the following
provisions of this section, for the purposes of this section the
relevant conditions, in relation to a decision of the judge
in any proceedings, are that a point of law of general public
importance is involved in that decision and that that point of
law either—

(*a*) relates wholly or mainly to the construction of an enactment or of a statutory instrument, and has been fully
argued in the proceedings and fully considered in the
judgment of the judge in the proceedings, or

(*b*) is one in respect of which the judge is bound by
a decision of the Court of Appeal or of the House of
Lords in previous proceedings, and was fully considered in the judgments given by the Court of Appeal
or the House of Lords (as the case may be) in those
previous proceedings.

(4) Any application for a certificate under this section shall
be made to the judge immediately after he gives judgment in
the proceedings:

Provided that the judge may in any particular case entertain any such application made at any later time before the end
of the period of fourteen days beginning with the date on which
that judgment is given or such other period as may be prescribed
by rules of court.

(5) No appeal shall lie against the grant or refusal of a certificate under this section.

(6) Her Majesty may by Order in Council amend subsection
(3) of this section by altering, deleting, or substituting one or
more new paragraphs for, either or both of paragraphs (*a*) and
(*b*) of that subsection, or by adding one or more further paragraphs.

(7) Any Order in Council made under this section shall be
subject to annulment in pursuance of a resolution of either House
of Parliament.

PART II

(8) In this Part of this Act " civil proceedings " means any proceedings other than proceedings in a criminal cause or matter, and " the judge ", in relation to any proceedings to which this section applies, means the judge or commissioner referred to in paragraph (*a*) or paragraph (*b*) of subsection (2) of this section, or the Divisional Court referred to in paragraph (*c*) of that subsection, as the case may be.

Leave to appeal to House of Lords.

13.—(1) Where in any proceedings the judge grants a certificate under section 12 of this Act, then, at any time within one month from the date on which that certificate is granted or such extended time as in any particular case the House of Lords may allow, any of the parties to the proceedings may make an application to the House of Lords under this section.

(2) Subject to the following provisions of this section, if on such an application it appears to the House of Lords to be expedient to do so, the House may grant leave for an appeal to be brought directly to the House ; and where leave is granted under this section—

    (*a*) no appeal from the decision of the judge to which the certificate relates shall lie to the Court of Appeal, but

    (*b*) an appeal shall lie from that decision to the House of Lords.

(3) Applications under this section shall be determined without a hearing.

(4) Any order of the House of Lords which provides for applications under this section to be determined by a committee of the House—

    (*a*) shall direct that the committee shall consist of or include not less than three of the persons designated as Lords of Appeal in accordance with section 5 of the Appellate Jurisdiction Act 1876, and

    (*b*) may direct that the decision of the committee on any such application shall be taken on behalf of the House.

1876 c. 59.

(5) Without prejudice to subsection (2) of this section, no appeal shall lie to the Court of Appeal from a decision of the judge in respect of which a certificate is granted under section 12 of this Act until—

    (*a*) the time within which an application can be made under this section has expired, and

    (*b*) where such an application is made, that application has been determined in accordance with the preceding provisions of this section.

14. In relation to any appeal which lies to the House of
Lords by virtue of subsection (2) of section 13 of this Act—

(*a*) section 4 of the Appellate Jurisdiction Act 1876 (which
provides for the bringing of appeals to the House of
Lords by way of petition),

(*b*) section 5 of that Act (which regulates the composition
of the House for the hearing and determination of
appeals), and

(*c*) except in so far as those orders otherwise provide, any
orders of the House of Lords made with respect to the
matters specified in section 11 of that Act (which
relates to the procedure on appeals),

shall have effect as they have effect in relation to appeals under
that Act.

15.—(1) No certificate shall be granted under section 12 of
this Act in respect of a decision of the judge in any proceedings
where by virtue of any enactment, apart from the provisions of
this Part of this Act, no appeal would lie from that decision
to the Court of Appeal, with or without the leave of the judge
or of the Court of Appeal.

(2) No certificate shall be granted under section 12 of this
Act in respect of a decision of the judge where—

(*a*) the decision is in proceedings other than proceedings
under the Matrimonial Causes Act 1965, and

(*b*) by virtue of any enactment, apart from the provisions
of this Part of this Act, no appeal would (with or
without the leave of the Court of Appeal or of the
House of Lords) lie from any decision of the Court
of Appeal on an appeal from the decision of the judge.

(3) Where by virtue of any enactment, apart from the provisions of this Part of this Act, no appeal would lie to the
Court of Appeal from the decision of the judge except with
the leave of the judge or of the Court of Appeal, no certificate
shall be granted under section 12 of this Act in respect of that
decision unless it appears to the judge that apart from the
provisions of this Part of this Act it would be a proper case for
granting such leave.

(4) No certificate shall be granted under section 12 of this
Act where the decision of the judge, or any order made by
him in pursuance of that decision, is made in the exercise of
jurisdiction to punish for contempt of court.

PART II
Application
of Part II to
Northern
Ireland.

16.—(1) In the application of this Part of this Act to Northern Ireland—

" the Court of Appeal " means Her Majesty's Court of Appeal in Northern Ireland ;

" the High Court " means the High Court of Justice in Northern Ireland ;

" statutory instrument " includes an instrument made under an enactment of the Parliament of Northern Ireland ;

1962 c. 30.
1877 c. 57.

for the references in section 12(2) to sections 3 and 70 of the Judicature Act 1925 there shall be substituted respectively references to section 5(1) of the Northern Ireland Act 1962 and to sections 29 and 41 of the Supreme Court of Judicature Act (Ireland) 1877 ; and

1965 c. 72.

1939 c. 13
(N.I.).

for the reference in section 15(2)(*a*) to the Matrimonial Causes Act 1965 there shall be substituted a reference to the Matrimonial Causes Act (Northern Ireland) 1939 or any enactment re-enacting that Act (whether with or without modifications).

(2) Nothing in this Part of this Act shall affect the operation of—

(*a*) any enactment of the Parliament of Northern Ireland having effect after the commencement of this Act by virtue of section 1(8) or section 2(3) of the Northern Ireland Act 1962, or

1922 c. 2.

(*b*) paragraph 6(2) of Schedule 1 to the Irish Free State (Consequential Provisions) Act 1922 (Session 2) (appeals to the Court of Appeal in Northern Ireland where validity of Acts of the Northern Ireland Parliament is involved and an appeal would not otherwise lie).

PART III

POWER TO MAKE WILLS AND CODICILS FOR MENTALLY DISORDERED PERSONS

Provision
for executing
will for
patient.
1959 c. 72.

17.—(1) In the Mental Health Act 1959 (in this Part of this Act referred to as " the principal Act "), in section 103(1) (powers of the judge as to patient's property and affairs) the following paragraph shall be inserted after paragraph (*d*) : —

" (*dd*) the execution for the patient of a will making any provision (whether by way of disposing of property or exercising a power or otherwise) which could be made by a will executed by the patient if he were not mentally disordered, so however that in such cases as a nominated judge may direct the powers conferred by this paragraph shall not be exercisable except by the Lord Chancellor or a nominated judge ; ".

(2) At the end of section 103(3) of the principal Act there shall be inserted the words " and the power of the judge to make or give an order, direction or authority for the execution of a will for a patient—

    (*a*) shall not be exercisable at any time when the patient is an infant, and

    (*b*) shall not be exercised unless the judge has reason to believe that the patient is incapable of making a valid will for himself ".

18. The following section shall be inserted in the principal Act after section 103 :—

" 103A.—(1) Where under section 103(1) of this Act the judge makes or gives an order, direction or authority requiring or authorising a person (in this section referred to as ' the authorised person ') to execute a will for a patient, any will executed in pursuance of that order, direction or authority shall be expressed to be signed by the patient acting by the authorised person, and shall be—

    (*a*) signed by the authorised person with the name of the patient, and with his own name, in the presence of two or more witnesses present at the same time, and

    (*b*) attested and subscribed by those witnesses in the presence of the authorised person, and

    (*c*) sealed with the official seal of the Court of Protection.

(2) The Wills Act 1837 shall have effect in relation to any such will as if it were signed by the patient by his own hand, except that in relation to any such will—

    (*a*) section 9 of that Act (which makes provision as to the manner of execution and attestation of wills) shall not apply, and

    (*b*) in the subsequent provisions of that Act any reference to execution in the manner thereinbefore required shall be construed as a reference to execution in the manner required by subsection (1) of this section.

(3) Subject to the following provisions of this section, any such will executed in accordance with subsection (1) of this section shall have the like effect for all purposes as if the patient were capable of making a valid will and the will had been executed by him in the manner required by the Wills Act 1837.

(4) So much of subsection (3) of this section as provides for such a will to have effect as if the patient were capable of making a valid will—

(*a*) shall not have effect in relation to such a will in so far as it disposes of any immovable property, other than immovable property in England or Wales, and

(*b*) where at the time when such a will is executed the patient is domiciled in Scotland or Northern Ireland or in a country or territory outside the United Kingdom, shall not have effect in relation to that will in so far as it relates to any other property or matter, except any property or matter in respect of which, under the law of his domicile, any question of his testamentary capacity would fall to be determined in accordance with the law of England and Wales.

(5) For the purposes of the application of the Inheritance (Family Provision) Act 1938 in relation to a will executed in accordance with subsection (1) of this section, in section 1(7) of that Act (which relates to the deceased's reasons for disposing of his estate in a particular way)—

(*a*) any reference to the deceased's reasons for which anything is done or not done by his will shall be construed as a reference to the reasons for which it is done or (as the case may be) not done by that will, and

(*b*) any reference to a statement in writing signed by the deceased shall be construed as a reference to a statement in writing signed by the authorised person in accordance with a direction given in that behalf by the judge."

19.—(1) In section 107 of the principal Act (preservation of interests in patient's property), in subsection (3), after the words " or other dealing " there shall be inserted the words " (otherwise than by will) ".

(2) In section 117 of the principal Act (reciprocal arrangements in relation to Scotland and Northern Ireland as to exercise of powers), after subsection (2) there shall be inserted the following subsection: —

" (2A) Nothing in this section shall affect any power to execute a will under section 103(1)(*dd*) of this Act or the effect of any will executed in the exercise of such a power ".

(3) In section 119 of the principal Act (interpretation of Part VIII), at the end of subsection (1) there shall be inserted the words " ' will ' includes a codicil ".

Part IV

Miscellaneous and Supplementary Provisions

20.—(1) The power to make rules of court under section 99 Orders for of the Judicature Act 1925, and the power to make county interim court rules under section 102 of the County Courts Act 1959, payment. shall each include power by any such rules to make provision 1959 c. 22. for enabling the court in which any proceedings are pending, in such circumstances as may be specified in the rules, to make an order requiring a party to the proceedings to make an interim payment of such amount as may be specified in the order, either by payment into court or (if the order so provides) by paying it to another party to the proceedings.

(2) Where any such rules make provision in accordance with subsection (1) of this section, the rules may include provision for enabling a party to any proceedings who, in pursuance of such an order, has made an interim payment to recover the whole or part of the amount of the payment in such circumstances, and from such other party to the proceedings, as may be determined in accordance with the rules.

(3) Any rules made by virtue of this section may include such incidental, supplementary and consequential provisions as the authority making the rules may consider necessary or expedient.

(4) Nothing in this section shall be construed as affecting the exercise of any power relating to costs, including any power to make rules of court or county court rules relating to costs.

(5) In its application to Northern Ireland, this section shall have effect as if for the reference to section 99 of the Judicature Act 1925 there were substituted a reference to section 7 of the Northern Ireland Act 1962, and as if any reference to county 1962 c. 30. court rules were omitted.

(6) In this section "interim payment", in relation to a party to any proceedings, means a payment on account of any damages, debt or other sum (excluding any costs) which that party may be held liable to pay to or for the benefit of another party to the proceedings if a final judgment or order of the court in the proceedings is given or made in favour of that other party; and any reference to a party to any proceedings includes a reference to any person who for the purposes of the proceedings acts as next friend or guardian of a party to the proceedings.

21.—(1) On the application of any person in accordance with Powers of rules of court, the High Court shall, in such circumstances as court may be specified in the rules, have power to make an order exercisable providing for any one or more of the following matters, that is commence-to say— ment of
 action.

    (*a*) the inspection, photographing, preservation, custody and detention of property which appears to the court

3 F

PART IV

to be property which may become the subject-matter of subsequent proceedings in the court, or as to which any question may arise in any such proceedings, and

(b) the taking of samples of any such property as is mentioned in the preceding paragraph and the carrying out of any experiment on or with any such property.

(2) The power to make rules of court under section 99 of the Judicature Act 1925 shall include power to make rules of court as to the manner in which an application for such an order can be made, and as to the circumstances in which such an order can be made ; and any such rules may include such incidental, supplementary and consequential provisions as the authority making the rules may consider necessary or expedient.

(3) The preceding provisions of this section shall have effect in relation to county courts in England and Wales as they have effect in relation to the High Court, as if in those provisions references to rules of court and to section 99 of the Judicature
1959 c. 22.   Act 1925 included references to county court rules and to section 102 of the County Courts Act 1959.

(4) In the application of this section to Northern Ireland, " the High Court " means the High Court of Justice in Northern Ireland, the reference in subsection (2) to section 99 of the Judicature Act 1925 shall be construed as a reference to section 7
1962 c. 30.   of the Northern Ireland Act 1962, and subsection (3) shall be omitted.

(5) In this section " property " includes any land, chattel or other corporeal property of any description.

Interest on
damages.
1934 c. 41.

22. In section 3 of the Law Reform (Miscellaneous Provisions) Act 1934 (power of courts of record to award interest on debts and damages), after subsection (1) there shall be inserted the following subsections : —

" (1A) Where in any such proceedings as are mentioned in subsection (1) of this section judgment is given for a sum which (apart from interest on damages) exceeds £200 and represents or includes damages in respect of personal injuries to the plaintiff or any other person, or in respect of a person's death, then (without prejudice to the exercise of the power conferred by that subsection in relation to any part of that sum which does not represent such damages) the court shall exercise that power so as to include in that sum interest on those damages or on such part of them as the court considers appropriate, unless the court is satisfied that there are special reasons why no interest should be given in respect of those damages.

(1B) Any order under this section may provide for interest to be calculated at different rates in respect of different parts of the period for which interest is given, whether that Part IV period is the whole or part of the period mentioned in subsection (1) of this section.

(1C) For the avoidance of doubt it is hereby declared that in determining, for the purposes of any enactment contained in the County Courts Act 1959, whether an 1959 c. 22. amount exceeds, or is less than, a sum specified in that enactment, no account shall be taken of any power exercisable by virtue of this section or of any order made in the exercise of such a power.

(1D) In this section ' personal injuries ' includes any disease and any impairment of a person's physical or mental condition, and any reference to the County Courts Act 1959 is a reference to that Act as (whether by virtue of the Administration of Justice Act 1969 or otherwise) that Act has effect for the time being ".

23.—(1) Section 57 of the Judicature Act 1925 (which enables Power of Lord the Lord Chancellor by order to direct that any jurisdiction of Chancellor to the High Court which by any enactment, rule or order is assigned assign any to any Division shall be assigned to another Division) shall be particular jurisdiction of amended as follows. the High Court

(2) In subsection (1) for the words " shall, notwithstanding that to two or more Divisions enactment, rule or order, be assigned to such other Division as concurrently. may be specified in the order and shall be exercised either by any special judge or judges or by all the judges of that other Division " there shall be substituted the words—

" (*a*) shall, notwithstanding that enactment, rule or order, be assigned to such other Division or Divisions as may be specified in the order (whether in addition to the Division or Divisions to which the jurisdiction is at the time assigned or by way of transfer therefrom) ; and

(*b*) shall be exercised either by any special judge or judges or by all the judges of any Division to which the jurisdiction in question is assigned by the order or by which it continues to be exercisable ".

(3) In the proviso to subsection (1) (which precludes the making of an order under that subsection except with the concurrence of the president of the Division to which the jurisdiction is at the time assigned and of the president of the Division to which the jurisdiction is to be transferred)—

(*a*) for the words " the Division ", in both places where they occur, there shall be substituted the words " any Division " ;

(*b*) after the words " to which the jurisdiction is to be transferred " there shall be inserted the words " or with which it is to be shared ".

(4) In subsection (2) (which enables the Lord Chancellor, in cases where there is under any enactment a right of appeal from the county court to the High Court or to any Division, by order to direct to which Division the appeal shall lie) for the words " to which Division " there shall be substituted the words " to which Division or Divisions ".

Appeal
Tribunals
under Patents
Act 1949 and
Registered
Designs Act
1949.
1949 c. 87.
1949 c. 88.

24.—(1) Section 85 of the Patents Act 1949 and section 28 of the Registered Designs Act 1949 (each of which provides for an Appeal Tribunal) shall be amended in accordance with the following provisions of this section.

(2) For subsection (2) of each of those sections (which provides that the Appeal Tribunal shall be a judge of the High Court nominated by the Lord Chancellor) there shall be substituted the following subsections : —

" (2) The Appeal Tribunal shall consist of one or more judges of the High Court nominated for the purpose by the Lord Chancellor.

(2A) At any time when it consists of two or more judges, the jurisdiction of the Appeal Tribunal—

(*a*) where in the case of any particular appeal the senior of those judges so directs, shall be exercised in relation to that appeal by both of the judges, or (if there are more than two) by two of them, sitting together, and

(*b*) in relation to any appeal in respect of which no such direction is given, may be exercised by any one of the judges ;

and, in the exercise of that jurisdiction, different appeals may be heard at the same time by different judges ".

(3) After subsection (8) of each of those sections (which empowers the Appeal Tribunal to make rules) there shall be inserted the following subsection : —

" (8A) At any time when the Appeal Tribunal consists of two or more judges, the power to make rules under sub-section (8) of this section shall be exercisable by the senior of those judges :

Provided that another of those judges may exercise that power if it appears to him that it is necessary for rules to be made and that the judge (or, if more than one, each of the judges) senior to him is for the time being prevented by illness, absence or otherwise from making them ".

(4) At the end of each of those sections there shall be inserted (as subsection (11) in the case of the said section 85 and as

subsection (10) in the case of the said section 28) the following PART IV
provision: —
    " For the purposes of this section the seniority of judges
    shall be reckoned by reference to the dates on which they
    were appointed judges of the High Court respectively ".

25.—(1) The clerks to the registrars of the Chancery Division Clerks to
of the High Court shall cease to be called by that name and registrars of
shall instead be called assistant registrars; and accordingly— Chancery
    (a) in section 123 of the Judicature Act 1925, for the words Division.
    " clerks to the registrars " and " clerks ", wherever
    they occur, there shall be substituted the words " assis-
    tant registrars ", and
    (b) in section 126(2) of that Act, for the words " clerks to
    the registrars " and " clerk to the registrars " there
    shall be substituted respectively the words " assistant
    registrars " and " assistant registrar ".

(2) A solicitor shall be qualified to be appointed as an
assistant registrar of the Chancery Division of the High Court
notwithstanding that he is of less than two years' standing;
and accordingly in section 126(2) of the Judicature Act 1925
the words " of not less than two years' standing " shall cease
to have effect.

26.—(1) In section 106 of the Judicature Act 1925 (appoint- Provisions
ment and removal of officers), in subsection (1) (under which as to other
the right to fill certain vacancies may be exercised by the Lord employments
Chancellor, the Lord Chief Justice and the Master of the Rolls in Supreme
in rotation) the words " or in any clerkship in the central office " Court.
shall cease to have effect, and after subsection (2) there shall be
inserted the following subsection: —
    " (2A) The right of filling any vacancy in any clerkship
    in the central office shall be vested in the Lord Chancellor ".

(2) Section 117 of the Judicature Act 1925 (notice of vacancies
in offices) shall cease to have effect.

(3) In section 128(1)(b) of the Judicature Act 1925 (which
relates to the Superannuation Act 1909) the words " section 1909 c. 10.
three of that Act (which provides for the application of the Act
to existing male civil servants) " shall cease to have effect.

27.—(1) The following section shall be substituted for section Records of
156 of the Judicature Act 1925: — grants of
    " **156.**—(1) Records shall be kept of all grants of probate probate and
    and grants of administration which are made in the grants of
    principal probate registry or in any of the district probate administration.
    registries.

3 F 3

PART IV

(2) Any such records shall be in such form, and shall contain such particulars, as the President of the Probate Division may direct."

1958 c. 51.

(2) Section 8(3) of the Public Records Act 1958 (which relates to inspection by the public of calendars of grants) shall cease to have effect.

(3) The following section shall be substituted for section 72 of the Probates and Letters of Administration Act (Ireland) 1857 :—

1857 c. 79.

" **72.**—(1) Records shall be kept of all grants of probate and grants of administration which are made in the principal registry or in any district registry of the Court.

(2) Any such records shall be in such form, and shall contain such particulars, as the Lord Chief Justice of Northern Ireland may direct."

(4) Section 73 of the said Act of 1857 (registrar to transmit printed copies to certain offices etc.) shall cease to have effect.

1876 c. 70.

(5) Where a calendar has been prepared under section 45 of the Sheriff Courts (Scotland) Act 1876 or under section 156 of the Judicature Act 1925 (as for the time being in force apart from this section), and a copy of that calendar is kept in the principal probate registry of the High Court of Justice in Northern Ireland, the Lord Chief Justice of Northern Ireland—

(*a*) may direct that the copy shall be removed to the Public Record Office of Northern Ireland, or

(*b*) in the case of a copy of a calendar prepared under the said section 45, may, with the agreement of the authority responsible for the management of the place in question, direct that it shall be removed to such place in Scotland as may be specified in the direction.

(6) Any direction under subsection (5) of this section may be given either in respect of a particular copy to which that subsection is applicable or in respect of a class of such copies.

(7) In relation to copies of calendars prepared as mentioned in subsection (5) of this section which—

(*a*) are removed to the Public Record Office of Northern Ireland in pursuance of a direction given under that subsection, or

(*b*) have been removed to that Office before the commencement of this Act,

1923 c. 20 (N.I.).

the Public Records Act (Northern Ireland) 1923 shall have effect as it has effect in relation to documents which are Northern Ireland records within the meaning of that Act and which have been removed to that Office in accordance with that Act.

28. Section 153 of the Judicature Act 1925 (which limits the   PART IV
district probate registries in which second and subsequent grants   Second and
of probate and administration may be made) shall cease to   subsequent
have effect.   grants of
probate and
administration.

29. In relation to clerks and apprentices to persons who are   Reduction
members of the Incorporated Company of Scriveners and have   of period of
been admitted to practise as public notaries within the juris-   apprenticeship
diction of that Company, section 3 of the Public Notaries   for public
Act 1843 (which provides for admission as a public notary after   notaries in
five years' service as clerk or apprentice to a notary, instead of   London.
seven years' service as previously provided) shall, notwithstanding   1843 c. 90.
anything in section 6 of that Act (which limits the operation
of that Act in relation to practice within the jurisdiction of the
Company), have effect in respect of admission to practise as a
public notary within the jurisdiction of that Company as it
has effect in respect of admission to practise elsewhere.

30. In the Superannuation Act 1965 the following section   Superannua-
shall be inserted after section 39 :—   tion benefits
in respect
" **39A.**—(1) The Lord Chancellor may with the consent   of certain
of the Minister for the Civil Service make rules with respect   judicial
to the superannuation benefits payable to or in respect of   offices.
persons who have been employed—   1965 c. 74.

(*a*) in two or more offices falling within paragraphs (*a*)
to (*i*) of subsection (3) of this section, or

(*b*) in one or more such offices and in one or more
judicial offices remunerated out of central funds.

(2) The Secretary of State may with the consent of the
Minister for the Civil Service make rules with respect to the
superannuation benefits payable to or in respect of persons
who have been employed—

(*a*) in two or more offices falling within paragraphs (*j*)
and (*k*) of subsection (3) of this section, or

(*b*) in one or more such offices and in one or more
judicial offices remunerated out of central funds.

(3) The offices referred to in subsections (1)(*a*) and (2)(*a*)
of this section are the following, that is to say—

(*a*) Recorder of London ;

(*b*) Common Serjeant ;

(*c*) additional judge of the Central Criminal Court ;

(*d*) recorder of Liverpool ;

(*e*) recorder of Manchester ;

(f) assistant judge of the Mayor's and City of London Court;

(g) presiding judge of the Court of Passage of the City of Liverpool;

(h) chairman or deputy chairman of a court of quarter sessions where under any enactment (whether passed before or after this Act) a person may qualify for a pension by virtue of service in that office;

(i) stipendiary magistrate in England or Wales, other than metropolitan stipendiary magistrate;

(j) stipendiary magistrate appointed under section 455 of the Burgh Police (Scotland) Act 1892;

1892 c. 55.

(k) stipendiary magistrate appointed under section 24 of the Glasgow Corporation and Police Act 1895.

1895 c. cxliii.

(4) Subsections (2) to (5) of section 38 of this Act shall have effect in relation to rules made under this section as they have effect in relation to rules under that section, as if—

(a) in subsection (2) of that section any reference to a public office were a reference to an office which is either an office specified in subsection (3) of this section or a judicial office remunerated out of central funds, and the reference to such supplemental and incidental provisions as are mentioned in that subsection were a reference to such supplemental and incidental provisions as appear to the Lord Chancellor or to the Secretary of State (as the case may be) to be expedient, and

(b) in subsections (3) and (4) of that section any reference to different public offices, or to ceasing to be employed in one public office and becoming employed in another, were a reference to different offices or (as the case may be) to ceasing to be employed in one office and becoming employed in another ('office' for this purpose being taken to mean any office which is either an office specified in subsection (3) of this section or a judicial office remunerated out of central funds).

(5) Where any rules under this section make provision for any pension to be defrayed partly by one authority and partly by one or more other authorities, whether by way of contribution or otherwise, nothing in section 10(2) of the Criminal Justice Administration Act 1956 (which requires contributions to be paid by the city councils of Liverpool and Manchester in respect of the Crown Courts and recorders of those cities) shall be construed as preventing the rules from applying that provision to, or making any

1956 c. 34.

such provision specially in respect of, persons whose employment includes employment as recorder of Liverpool or recorder of Manchester.

(6) In this section ' judicial office remunerated out of central funds ' means any of the following, that is to say—

> (a) any office listed in Schedule 1 to the Administration of Justice (Pensions) Act 1950, with the exception of the offices of stipendiary magistrate referred to in the last two entries in that Schedule, and

1950 c. 11. (14 & 15 Geo. 6.)

> (b) any office in relation to which sections 2 to 8 of that Act have effect as if it were listed in that Schedule, with the exception of the offices of recorder of Liverpool and recorder of Manchester,

and ' pension ' has the meaning assigned to it by section 38(6) of this Act."

31.—(1) In Schedule 1 to the Administration of Justice (Pensions) Act 1950, before the entry " Clerk of Assize " there shall be inserted the entries " Registrar of Criminal Appeals " and " Assistant Registrar of Criminal Appeals ".

Further provisions as to pension rights and related matters.

(2) In section 3 of the Superannuation (Miscellaneous Provisions) Act 1967 (effect of pension in respect of public office on remuneration in judicial or related office), in subsection (4) (which specifies the offices to which that section applies), after paragraph (a) there shall be inserted the following paragraph : —

1967 c. 28.

> " (aa) chairman or deputy chairman of a court of quarter sessions where under any enactment (whether passed before or after this Act) a person may qualify for a pension by virtue of service in that office ".

(3) For paragraphs 1 to 3 of Part II of Schedule 1 to the County Courts Act 1934 (which prescribe the maximum superannuation allowances of registrars of county courts and, by virtue of section 25(2) of the Administration of Justice Act 1956, apply also to the superannuation allowances of assistant registrars of county courts) there shall be substituted the following paragraph : —

1934 c. 53.

1956 c. 34.

> " 1. After the completion of a period of service of not less than five years, an annual allowance may be granted as follows, that is to say—

>> (a) where the period of service is five years, fifteen-eightieths of the last annual salary ;

Part IV

(b) where that period exceeds five years but is less than ten, fifteen-eightieths of that salary plus one-eightieth for each completed year of service exceeding five ;

(c) where that period is or exceeds ten years but is less than twenty, one-fourth of that salary plus one fortieth for each completed year of service exceeding ten ;

(d) where that period is twenty years or more, one-half of the last annual salary ".

Transfer of liability for stipend and fees of Chancellor of County Palatine of Durham.

32. If an agreement is made between the Lord Chancellor and the Church Commissioners whereby, in consideration of a capital sum to be paid by the Commissioners, any future liability of the Commissioners to pay any stipend or fees to the Chancellor of the County Palatine of Durham is transferred to the Lord Chancellor, the Lord Chancellor may with the concurrence of the Treasury pay out of moneys provided by Parliament any sums required to be paid by him for giving effect to that agreement.

Extension of legislative power of Parliament of Northern Ireland with respect to grand juries and indictments.

1920 c. 67.

33. The reservation by section 47 of the Government of Ireland Act 1920 of matters relating to the Supreme Court of Judicature of Northern Ireland shall not preclude the Parliament of Northern Ireland from making any law for the purpose of—

(a) abolishing grand juries, or

(b) amending the law relating to the presentment of indictments,

or of making any provision related to or consequential upon either or both of those matters.

Interpretation, application to Crown, and provisions as to orders.

1925 c. 49.

34.—(1) In this Act " enactment ", unless the context otherwise requires, includes an enactment of the Parliament of Northern Ireland, and " the Judicature Act 1925 " means the Supreme Court of Judicature (Consolidation) Act 1925.

(2) Except in so far as the context otherwise requires, any reference in this Act to an enactment shall be construed as a reference to that enactment as amended or extended by or under any other enactment, including this Act.

(3) Section 20 of this Act shall bind the Crown so far as (but no further than) any proceedings to which that section is applicable can be brought by or against the Crown in accordance with the Crown Proceedings Act 1947, and section 22 of this Act shall bind the Crown so far as (but no further than) by virtue of section 24(3) of that Act section 3 of the Law Reform (Miscellaneous Provisions) Act 1934 applies to proceedings by or against the Crown.

1947 c. 44.

1934 c. 41.

(4) Any power conferred on the Lord Chancellor by this Act to make an order shall include power to revoke or vary the order by a subsequent order.

(5) Any power of the Lord Chancellor to make an order under this Act shall be exercisable by statutory instrument.

(6) In the application to Northern Ireland of so much of subsection (3) of this section as relates to section 20 of this Act, the reference to the Crown Proceedings Act 1947 is a 1947 c. 44. reference to that Act as it applies in Northern Ireland in relation to the Crown in right of Her Majesty's Government in the United Kingdom and in right of Her Majesty's Government in Northern Ireland.

35.—(1) The enactments specified in Schedule 1 to this Act Minor and shall have effect subject to the amendments set out in that consequential Schedule, being minor amendments and amendments conse- amendments and repeals. quential upon the preceding provisions of this Act.

(2) The enactments and instrument specified in Schedule 2 to this Act are hereby repealed to the extent specified in the third column of that Schedule.

36.—(1) This Act may be cited as the Administration of Short title, Justice Act 1969. extent and commence-

(2) This Act (except section 24, subsections (1) and (2) of ment. section 27, sections 30, 31, 34, 35 and this section and Schedules 1 and 2) shall not extend to Scotland.

(3) This Act (except Part II and sections 20, 21, 24, 27, 30, 31, 33 to 35 and this section and Schedules 1 and 2) shall not extend to Northern Ireland.

(4) Section 24 of this Act shall extend to the Isle of Man.

(5) The provisions of this Act shall come into operation on such day as the Lord Chancellor may by order appoint, and different days may be so appointed for different provisions of this Act or for different purposes (including, in the case of any provision of section 35 of this Act, the amendment or repeal of different enactments to which that provision is applicable) ; and any reference in any provision of this Act to the commencement of this Act shall be construed as a reference to the day so appointed for the coming into operation of that provision.

(6) Any order made under this section may make such transitional provision as appears to the Lord Chancellor to be necessary or expedient in connection with the provisions of this Act which are thereby brought (wholly or in part) into force, including such adaptations of those provisions or of any provision of this Act then in force as appears to him to be necessary or expedient in consequence of the partial operation of this Act (whether before, on or after the day appointed by the order).

SCHEDULES

SCHEDULE 1

Enactments Amended

Enactment	Amendment
The Settled Land Act 1925 (1925 c. 18)	In section 113(3), for the words " five hundred pounds ", in each place where they occur, there shall be substituted the words " £5,000 ", and for the words " thirty pounds " there shall be substituted the words " £300 ".
The Patents Act 1949 (12, 13 and 14 Geo. 6. c. 87)	In section 101(1), for the definition of " Appeal Tribunal " there shall be substituted the words, " ' Appeal Tribunal ' means the Appeal Tribunal constituted and acting in accordance with section 85 of this Act as amended by the Administration of Justice Act 1969 ".
The Registered Designs Act 1949 (12, 13 and 14 Geo. 6. c. 88)	In section 44(1), for the definition of " Appeal Tribunal " there shall be substituted the words " ' Appeal Tribunal ' means the Appeal Tribunal constituted and acting in accordance with section 28 of this Act as amended by the Administration of Justice Act 1969 ".
The Solicitors Act 1957 (1957 c. 27)	In section 73(2), for the reference to five hundred pounds there shall be substituted the words " £750 ".
The County Courts Act 1959 (1959 c. 22)	In section 47(1), for the words " subsections (3) and (4) " there shall be substituted the words " subsection (3) ".
The Northern Ireland Act 1962 (1962 c. 30)	In section 2(1), after paragraph (*i*) there shall be inserted the following paragraph:— " (*j*) from a decision granting or refusing a certificate under section 12 of the Administration of Justice Act 1969 ".
The Superannuation Act 1965 (1965 c. 74)	In section 97(1)(*a*) after the word " offices " there shall be inserted the words " (including section 39A of this Act) ".

SCHEDULE 2 Section 35(2).

REPEALS

Acts

Chapter	Short Title	Extent of Repeal
20 & 21 Vict. c. 79.	The Probates and Letters of Administration Act (Ireland) 1857.	Section 73.
15 & 16 Geo. 5. c. 49.	The Supreme Court of Judicature (Consolidation) Act 1925.	In section 106(1) the words " or in any clerkship in the central office ". Section 117. In section 126(2) the words " of not less than two years' standing ". In section 128(1)(*b*) the words " section three of that Act (which provides for the application of the Act to existing male civil servants) ". Section 153.
14 & 15 Geo. 6. c. 11.	The Administration of Justice (Pensions) Act 1950.	In Schedule 2, in the entry relating to the County Courts Act 1934, the words from " and in Part II " to the end of the entry.
6 & 7 Eliz. 2. c. 51.	The Public Records Act 1958.	Section 8(3).
7 & 8 Eliz. 2. c. 22.	The County Courts Act 1959.	In section 36(1) the words " at which an office is kept open by the registrar ". Section 46. In section 47(1), the words " and the action is not referred for trial to an official referee ". Section 47(4). In section 74, the words " in any proceedings before it ". In section 89, paragraph (i) of the proviso.
7 & 8 Eliz. 2. c. 72.	The Mental Health Act 1959.	In section 107(1), the words " or any codicil thereto ".
10 & 11 Eliz. 2. c. 30.	The Northern Ireland Act 1962.	In Schedule 1, the entry relating to section 73 of the Probates and Letters of Administration Act (Ireland) 1857.
1967 c. 28.	The Superannuation (Miscellaneous Provisions) Act 1967.	In section 3(4), sub-paragraphs (v), (ix), (xi) and (xii) of paragraph (*a*), and paragraph (*b*).

                         Instrument

No.	Title	Extent of Repeal
S.I. 1965 No. 2141.	The County Courts Jurisdiction Order 1965.	The whole Order.

Law of Property Act 1969

1969 CHAPTER 59

An Act to amend Part II of the Landlord and Tenant Act 1954; to provide for the closing of the Yorkshire deeds registries; to amend the law relating to dispositions of estates and interests in land and to land charges; to make further provision as to the powers of the Lands Tribunal and court in relation to restrictive covenants affecting land; and for purposes connected with those matters. [22nd October 1969]

BE IT ENACTED by the Queen's most Excellent Majesty, by and with the advice and consent of the Lords Spiritual and Temporal, and Commons, in this present Parliament assembled, and by the authority of the same, as follows:—

PART I

AMENDMENT OF PART II OF LANDLORD AND TENANT ACT 1954   1954 c. 56.

Provisions as to rent

1.—(1) In section 34 of the Act of 1954 (rent under new tenancy) the following paragraph shall be substituted for paragraph (c) (improvements to be disregarded):— Improvements to be disregarded in fixing rent.

" (c) any effect on rent of an improvement to which this paragraph applies "

and the following subsection shall be added (the present section, as amended by the foregoing provisions, becoming subsection (1)):—

" (2) Paragraph (c) of the foregoing subsection applies to any improvement carried out by a person who at the time it was carried out was the tenant, but only if it was carried out otherwise than in pursuance of an obligation

3 F* 4

to his immediate landlord, and either it was carried out during the current tenancy or the following conditions are satisfied, that is to say,—

(a) that it was completed not more than twenty-one years before the application for the new tenancy was made ; and

(b) that the holding or any part of it affected by the improvement has at all times since the completion of the improvement been comprised in tenancies of the description specified in section 23(1) of this Act ; and

(c) that at the termination of each of those tenancies the tenant did not quit."

(2) In section 41(1)(b) and section 42(2)(b) of the Act of 1954 the words " subsection (1) of " shall be inserted before the words " section 34 ".

Determination of variable rent.

2. At the end of section 34 of the Act of 1954 (rent under new tenancy) there shall be added the following subsection :—

"(3) Where the rent is determined by the court the court may, if it thinks fit, further determine that the terms of the tenancy shall include such provision for varying the rent as may be specified in the determination."

Rent while tenancy continues by virtue of s. 24 of Act of 1954.

3.—(1) After section 24 of the Act of 1954 there shall be inserted the following section :—

" **24A.**—(1) The landlord of a tenancy to which this Part of this Act applies may,—

(a) if he has given notice under section 25 of this Act to terminate the tenancy ; or

(b) if the tenant has made a request for a new tenancy in accordance with section 26 of this Act ;

apply to the court to determine a rent which it would be reasonable for the tenant to pay while the tenancy continues by virtue of section 24 of this Act, and the court may determine a rent accordingly.

(2) A rent determined in proceedings under this section shall be deemed to be the rent payable under the tenancy from the date on which the proceedings were commenced or the date specified in the landlord's notice or the tenant's request, whichever is the later.

(3) In determining a rent under this section the court shall have regard to the rent payable under the terms of the tenancy, but otherwise subsections (1) and (2) of section

34 of this Act shall apply to the determination as they would apply to the determination of a rent under that section if a new tenancy from year to year of the whole of the property comprised in the tenancy were granted to the tenant by order of the court."

(2) In section 24(1)(*a*) of the Act of 1954 for the words " the next following section " there shall be substituted the words " section 25 of this Act ".

Termination of tenancy and right to new tenancy

4.—(1) At the end of section 24(2) of the Act of 1954 (which Restriction on includes notice to quit by the tenant and surrender among the termination of means by which a tenancy to which Part II of that Act applies tenancy by agreement. can be brought to an end) there shall be added the words " unless—

(*a*) in the case of a notice to quit, the notice was given before the tenant had been in occupation in right of the tenancy for one month ; or

(*b*) in the case of an instrument of surrender, the instrument was executed before, or was executed in pursuance of an agreement made before, the tenant had been in occupation in right of the tenancy for one month."

(2) Section 27 of the Act of 1954 (termination by tenant of tenancy for fixed term) shall be amended as follows: —

(*a*) at the end of subsection (1) (notice by tenant that he does not desire tenancy to be continued) there shall be added the words " unless the notice is given before the tenant has been in occupation in right of the tenancy for one month " ; and

(*b*) in subsection (2) (termination on quarter day by tenant's notice) the words " before or " shall be omitted and at the end of the subsection there shall be added the words " or before that date, but not before the tenant has been in occupation in right of the tenancy for one month ".

5. In subsection (1) of section 38 of the Act of 1954 (restric-Exclusion of tion on agreements excluding provisions of Part II) after the provisions of Part II of Act words " shall be void " there shall be inserted the words " (except of 1954 by as provided by subsection (4) of this section) " and at the end authorised of the section there shall be added the following subsection: — agreement.

" (4) The court may—

(*a*) on the joint application of the persons who will be the landlord and the tenant in relation to a tenancy to be granted for a term of years certain which will be a tenancy to which this Part of this Act applies, authorise an agreement excluding in relation to that tenancy the provisions of sections 24 to 28 of this Act ; and

(b) on the joint application of the persons who are the landlord and the tenant in relation to a tenancy to which this Part of this Act applies, authorise an agreement for the surrender of the tenancy on such date or in such circumstances as may be specified in the agreement and on such terms (if any) as may be so specified ;

if the agreement is contained in or endorsed on the instrument creating the tenancy or such other instrument as the court may specify ; and an agreement contained in or endorsed on an instrument in pursuance of an authorisation given under this subsection shall be valid notwithstanding anything in the preceding provisions of this section."

Business carried on by company controlled by landlord.

6. At the end of section 30 of the Act of 1954 there shall be added the following subsection : —

" (3) Where the landlord has a controlling interest in a company any business to be carried on by the company shall be treated for the purposes of subsection (1)(g) of this section as a business to be carried on by him.

For the purposes of this subsection, a person has a controlling interest in a company if and only if either—

(a) he is a member of it and able, without the consent of any other person, to appoint or remove the holders of at least a majority of the directorships ; or

(b) he holds more than one-half of its equity share capital, there being disregarded any shares held by him in a fiduciary capacity or as nominee for another person ;

and in this subsection ' company ' and ' share ' have the meanings assigned to them by section 455(1) of the Companies Act 1948 and ' equity share capital ' the meaning assigned to it by section 154(5) of that Act."

1948 c. 38.

Grant of new tenancy in some cases where section 30(1)(f) applies.

7.—(1) After section 31 of the Act of 1954 there shall be inserted the following section : —

" **31A.**—(1) Where the landlord opposes an application under section 24(1) of this Act on the ground specified in paragraph (f) of section 30(1) of this Act the court shall not hold that the landlord could not reasonably carry out the

demolition, reconstruction or work of construction intended Part I
without obtaining possession of the holding if—

> (a) the tenant agrees to the inclusion in the terms of the new tenancy of terms giving the landlord access and other facilities for carrying out the work intended and, given that access and those facilities, the landlord could reasonably carry out the work without obtaining possession of the holding and without interfering to a substantial extent or for a substantial time with the use of the holding for the purposes of the business carried on by the tenant ; or
>
> (b) the tenant is willing to accept a tenancy of an economically separable part of the holding and either paragraph (a) of this section is satisfied with respect to that part or possession of the remainder of the holding would be reasonably sufficient to enable the landlord to carry out the intended work.

> (2) For the purposes of subsection (1)(b) of this section a part of a holding shall be deemed to be an economically separable part if, and only if, the aggregate of the rents which, after the completion of the intended work, would be reasonably obtainable on separate lettings of that part and the remainder of the premises affected by or resulting from the work would not be substantially less than the rent which would then be reasonably obtainable on a letting of those premises as a whole."

(2) In section 32 of the Act of 1954 (property to be comprised in new tenancy) for the words " Subject to the next following subsection " there shall be substituted the words " Subject to the following provisions of this section " ; and after subsection (1) there shall be inserted the following subsection : —

> " (1A) Where the court, by virtue of paragraph (b) of section 31A(1) of this Act, makes an order under section 29 of this Act for the grant of a new tenancy in a case where the tenant is willing to accept a tenancy of part of the holding, the order shall be an order for the grant of a new tenancy of that part only."

8. At the end of section 32(3) of the Act of 1954 (rights to Power to be included in new tenancy) there shall be added the words exclude rights " except as otherwise agreed between the landlord and the enjoyed with tenant or, in default of such agreement, determined by the court." holding.

9. After section 41 of the Act of 1954 there shall be inserted the following section:—

"**41A.**—(1) The following provisions of this section shall apply where—

    (*a*) a tenancy is held jointly by two or more persons (in this section referred to as the joint tenants); and

    (*b*) the property comprised in the tenancy is or includes premises occupied for the purposes of a business; and

    (*c*) the business (or some other business) was at some time during the existence of the tenancy carried on in partnership by all the persons who were then the joint tenants or by those and other persons and the joint tenants' interest in the premises was then partnership property; and

    (*d*) the business is carried on (whether alone or in partnership with other persons) by one or some only of the joint tenants and no part of the property comprised in the tenancy is occupied, in right of the tenancy, for the purposes of a business carried on (whether alone or in partnership with other persons) by the other or others.

(2) In the following provisions of this section those of the joint tenants who for the time being carry on the business are referred to as the business tenants and the others as the other joint tenants.

(3) Any notice given by the business tenants which, had it been given by all the joint tenants, would have been—

    (*a*) a tenant's request for a new tenancy made in accordance with section 26 of this Act; or

    (*b*) a notice under subsection (1) or subsection (2) of section 27 of this Act;

shall be treated as such if it states that it is given by virtue of this section and sets out the facts by virtue of which the persons giving it are the business tenants; and references in those sections and in section 24A of this Act to the tenant shall be construed accordingly.

(4) A notice given by the landlord to the business tenants which, had it been given to all the joint tenants, would have been a notice under section 25 of this Act shall be treated as such a notice, and references in that section to the tenant shall be construed accordingly.

(5) An application under section 24(1) of this Act for a new tenancy may, instead of being made by all the joint

tenants, be made by the business tenants alone; and
where it is so made—

(*a*) this Part of this Act shall have effect, in relation
to it, as if the references therein to the tenant
included references to the business tenants alone;
and

(*b*) the business tenants shall be liable, to the exclusion
of the other joint tenants, for the payment of rent
and the discharge of any other obligation under
the current tenancy for any rental period beginning
after the date specified in the landlord's notice
under section 25 of this Act or, as the case may
be, beginning on or after the date specified in their
request for a new tenancy.

(6) Where the court makes an order under section 29(1)
of this Act for the grant of a new tenancy on an application
made by the business tenants it may order the grant to be
made to them or to them jointly with the persons carrying
on the business in partnership with them, and may order
the grant to be made subject to the satisfaction, within a
time specified by the order, of such conditions as to
guarantors, sureties or otherwise as appear to the court
equitable, having regard to the omission of the other joint
tenants from the persons who will be the tenant under the
new tenancy.

(7) The business tenants shall be entitled to recover any
amount payable by way of compensation under section 37
or section 59 of this Act."

10. For subsection (3) of section 42 of the Act of 1954 Group of
(Group of companies) there shall be substituted the following companies.
subsection:—

" (3) Where the landlord's interest is held by a member
of a group—

(*a*) the reference in paragraph (*g*) of subsection (1) of
section 30 of this Act to intended occupation by
the landlord for the purposes of a business to be
carried on by him shall be construed as including
intended occupation by any member of the group
for the purposes of a business to be carried on by
that member; and

(*b*) the reference in subsection (2) of that section to
the purchase or creation of any interest shall be
construed as a reference to a purchase from or
creation by a person other than a member of the
group."

PART I
Compensation
where no
application
to court is
made.

11. In section 37(1) of the Act of 1954 (compensation where court precluded from making an order for new tenancy on any of the grounds specified in paragraphs (*e*), (*f*) and (*g*) of section 30(1)) after the words " of that subsection " there shall be inserted the words "or where no other ground is specified in the landlord's notice under section 25 of this Act or, as the case may be, under section 26(6) thereof, than those specified in the said paragraphs (*e*), (*f*) and (*g*) and either no application under the said section 24 is made or such an application is withdrawn ".

Duration
of short
tenancies
excluded from
Part II of
Act of 1954.

12.—(1) In section 43(3) of the Act of 1954 (exclusion of certain tenancies granted for not more than three months) for the words " three months ", in both places where they occur, there shall be substituted the words " six months " and for the words " six months " (in paragraph (*b*)) the words " twelve months ".

(2) Subsection (1) of this section does not apply to tenancies granted before the commencement of this Act.

Jurisdiction
of county
court to make
declaration.

13. After section 43 of the Act of 1954 there shall be inserted the following section :—

" 43A. Where the rateable value of the holding is such that the jurisdiction conferred on the court by any other provision of this Part of this Act is, by virtue of section 63 of this Act, exercisable by the county court, the county court shall have jurisdiction (but without prejudice to the jurisdiction of the High Court) to make any declaration as to any matter arising under this Part of this Act, whether or not any other relief is sought in the proceedings."

Definition
of landlord
and further
provisions
where
immediate
landlord is
not the
freeholder.

14.—(1) In section 44(1) of the Act of 1954 the following paragraph shall be substituted for paragraph (*b*):—

" (*b*) that it is either the fee simple or a tenancy which will not come to an end within fourteen months by effluxion of time and, if it is such a tenancy, that no notice has been given by virtue of which it will come to an end within fourteen months or any further time by which it may be continued under section 36(2) or section 64 of this Act ".

(2) The following shall be added at the end of Schedule 6 to the Act of 1954 :—

" *Withdrawal by competent landlord of notice given by mesne landlord*

6. Where the competent landlord has given a notice under section 25 of this Act to terminate the relevant

tenancy and, within two months after the giving of the PART I
notice, a superior landlord—

(a) becomes the competent landlord ; and

(b) gives to the tenant notice in the prescribed form
that he withdraws the notice previously given ;

the notice under section 25 of this Act shall cease to have
effect, but without prejudice to the giving of a further notice
under that section by the competent landlord.

Duty to inform superior landlords

7. If the competent landlord's interest in the property
comprised in the relevant tenancy is a tenancy which will
come or can be brought to an end within sixteen months
(or any further time by which it may be continued under
section 36(2) or section 64 of this Act) and he gives to
the tenant under the relevant tenancy a notice under
section 25 of this Act to terminate the tenancy or is given
by him a notice under section 26(3) of this Act :—

(a) the competent landlord shall forthwith send a copy
of the notice to his immediate landlord ; and

(b) any superior landlord whose interest in the property
is a tenancy shall forthwith send to his immediate
landlord any copy which has been sent to him
in pursuance of the preceding sub-paragraph or
this sub-paragraph ".

15. Sections 24, 27, 30, 32, 34, 37, 38, 42 and 44 of the Act of Certain
1954 and Schedule 6 to that Act, and section 43(3) of that Act as provisions
it applies to tenancies granted after the commencement of this of Part II of
Act, are set out as amended by this Part of this Act in Schedule Act of 1954
1 to this Act. set out as
amended.

PART II

CLOSING OF YORKSHIRE DEEDS REGISTRIES

16.—(1) The deeds register maintained at a Yorkshire deeds Closing of
registry shall be closed as respects the registration of instruments Yorkshire
made on or after the date which under this section is the relevant deeds
date in relation to that registry ; and accordingly the Act of 1884 registries.
and section 11 of the Law of Property Act 1925 (instruments 1925 c. 20.
capable of registration in a local deeds registry) shall not apply
to any instrument made on or after that date so far as it affects
land within the jurisdiction of that registry.

(2) At the expiration of the period of two years beginning
with the date which under this section is the relevant date in

relation to a Yorkshire deeds registry the deeds register maintained there shall be closed for all purposes; and thereupon the enactments specified in Part I of Schedule 2 to this Act shall, to the extent specified in the third column of that Schedule, be repealed as respects that register, that registry and the area which was within its jurisdiction.

(3) For the purposes of this section the relevant date in relation to a Yorkshire deeds registry is the date of the coming into force, as respects any part of the area within its jurisdiction, of any Order in Council made after the commencement of this Act under section 120 of the Land Registration Act 1925 (power to extend area of compulsory registration of title to land) except that the Lord Chancellor may, at the request of the county council, by an order made by statutory instrument direct that it shall be such earlier date as may be specified in the order.

17.—(1) As from the date which under section 16(3) of this Act is the relevant date in relation to a Yorkshire deeds registry—

    (a) section 10(6) of the Land Charges Act 1925 (certain land charges affecting land in any of the three ridings to be registered in the appropriate local deeds registry) shall not apply to the registration of any charge so far as it affects land which is then within the jurisdiction of the registry; and

    (b) section 97 of the Law of Property Act 1925 (priorities as between certain mortgages of unregistered land not within the jurisdiction of a local deeds registry to be determined according to dates of registration under the Land Charges Act 1925) shall apply in relation to land which is then within the jurisdiction of the registry as it applies to land which was never within the jurisdiction of any local deeds registry;

and accordingly as from that date the enactments specified in Part II of Schedule 2 to this Act shall, to the extent specified in the third column of that Schedule, be repealed as respects that registry and the area which is then within its jurisdiction.

(2) As soon as may be after subsection (1) of this section has come into force in relation to a Yorkshire deeds registry, the register of land charges maintained there pursuant to section 10(6) of the Land Charges Act 1925 shall be transferred to the Land Charges Department of Her Majesty's Land Registry in accordance with directions given for the purpose by the Chief Land Registrar.

(3) The Chief Land Registrar may direct that, during such period (not exceeding seven days) as he considers requisite for effecting the transfer of a register under subsection (2) of this

section, no search shall be permitted in that register under
section 16 of the Land Charges Act 1925 and that any certificate
issued during that period under section 17 of that Act shall not
be conclusive as to the existence or otherwise of any entry of
a matter or document whereof entries were required or allowed
to be made in that register.

(4) The Chief Land Registrar shall give notice of any direction
under the last foregoing subsection in such manner as appears
to him to be appropriate.

(5) A puisne mortgage registered in the deeds register maintained at a Yorkshire deeds registry shall be registrable under
the Land Charges Act 1925 to the same extent as a puisne
mortgage not registered in any local deeds register, and accordingly in section 10(1) of that Act, in Class C(i), the words " and
(where the whole of the land affected is within the jurisdiction
of a local deeds registry) not being registered in the local deeds
register " are hereby repealed.

(6) No fee shall be payable on the registration as a land
charge under the Land Charges Act 1925 of a mortgage which
becomes capable of registration under that Act by virtue of
subsection (5) of this section.

(7) Where before the commencement of this Act a person has
purported to register under the Land Charges Act 1925 a
mortgage which was incapable of such registration because
already registered in the deeds register maintained at a Yorkshire
deeds registry, the purported registration shall be treated as
valid notwithstanding the prior registration in the deeds register.

18.—(1) A deeds register which under section 16(2) of this Disposal of
Act has been closed for all purposes shall be treated, in relation registers
to the county council concerned, as included among the records of closed
and documents to which section 279(1) of the Local Government registries.
Act 1933 (custody of county records) applies. 1933 c. 51.

(2) A county council shall preserve any document forming
part of a register to which subsection (1) of this section applies
which they consider deserves preservation on historical or other
grounds and shall, before destroying or otherwise disposing of
any other document forming part of such a register, make and
preserve a copy (which may be a microfilm) of that document
if they consider that on historical or other grounds a copy of
it should be preserved.

(3) In this section " a deeds register " includes any books,
indexes or other documents connected with the business of deeds
registration at the registry in question.

19.—(1) As respects anything falling to be done by or to a registrar under section 49 of the Act of 1884 (actions for neglect, etc.) after the date on which his appointment terminates by virtue of section 16(2) of this Act, the said section 49 shall have effect as if for references to the registrar there were substituted references to the clerk of the county council; and any action pending on that date in which by virtue of that section the registrar is sued as nominal defendant may be continued against the said clerk as nominal defendant.

(2) The Lord Chancellor may make regulations requiring the county council to pay compensation (subject to such exceptions or conditions as may be prescribed in the regulations) to or in respect of persons who are or were employed for the purposes of a Yorkshire deeds registry and who suffer loss of employment, or loss or diminution of emoluments, in consequence of this Part of this Act.

(3) Regulations under subsection (2) of this section may include provision as to the manner in which and the person to whom any claim for compensation under the regulations is to be made, and for the determination of all questions arising under the regulations.

(4) The power to make regulations under subsection (2) of this section shall be exercisable by statutory instrument, and any statutory instrument containing regulations so made shall be subject to annulment in pursuance of a resolution of either House of Parliament.

20.—(1) If the expenses incurred by the county council in respect of a Yorkshire deeds registry during the period of two years beginning with the date which under section 16(3) of this Act is the relevant date in relation to that registry (including expenses in consequence of any regulations made under section 19(2) of this Act) exceed the receipts of the council in respect of the registry during that period, the Treasury shall pay to the council a sum equal to the excess.

(2) Any dispute under this section shall be determined by arbitration.

Indemnity
for members
of the public
who suffer
loss.
1925 c. 20.

21.—(1) Subject to the provisions of this section, any person suffering loss by reason of—

(a) section 16(2) of this Act so far as it repeals sections 19 and 20 of the Act of 1884 (searches) or section 197 of the Law of Property Act 1925 (registration in local deeds registry to constitute actual notice); or

(b) section 17(1)(b), (5) or (7) of this Act,

shall be entitled to be indemnified in respect of that loss.

(2) No indemnity shall be payable under this section in respect of any loss where the applicant has himself caused or substantially contributed to the loss by his act, neglect or default.

(3) Subsection (2) of this section shall not apply to any failure on the part of the applicant to register under the Land Charges Act 1925 a puisne mortgage which became capable of such registration by virtue of section 17(5) of this Act, but if—

(a) the mortgage is not registered under that Act before the expiration of two years beginning with the date which under section 16(3) of this Act is the relevant date in relation to the Yorkshire deeds registry in question; and

(b) the loss could have been prevented by the registration or earlier registration thereof,

no indemnity shall be payable unless there is reasonable excuse for the failure to register the mortgage in time to prevent the loss.

(4) Any indemnity under this section shall include a reasonable sum in respect of any costs or expenses properly incurred by the applicant in relation to the matter.

(5) If any question arises as to whether a person is entitled to an indemnity under this section, or as to the amount of any such indemnity, he may apply to the High Court to have that question determined.

(6) Any indemnity under this section shall be paid by the Chief Land Registrar; and where an indemnity is paid the Chief Land Registrar shall be entitled, on behalf of the Crown—

(a) to recover the amount paid from any person who has caused or substantially contributed to the loss by his fraud; and

(b) to enforce any express or implied covenant or other right which the person who is indemnified would have been entitled to enforce in relation to the matter in respect of which the indemnity was paid.

22.—(1) A certificate of the registration of an instrument in Proof of a deeds register maintained at a Yorkshire deeds registry en- registration. dorsed on the instrument by an officer of the registry shall, after the register has been closed for all purposes under section 16(2) of this Act, be conclusive evidence for all purposes of the facts certified.

(2) A writing endorsed on an instrument and purporting to be such a certificate as aforesaid shall be received in evidence and be deemed to be such a certificate without further proof unless the contrary is shown.

Part III

Amendment of Law Relating to Dispositions of Estates and Interests in Land and to Land Charges

Reduction of
statutory
period of
title.
1925 c. 20.

23. Section 44(1) of the Law of Property Act 1925 (under which the period of commencement of title which may be required under a contract expressing no contrary intention is thirty years except in certain cases) shall have effect, in its application to contracts made after the commencement of this Act, as if it specified fifteen years instead of thirty years as the period of commencement of title which may be so required.

Contracts for
purchase of
land affected
by land
charge, etc.
1925 c. 21.

1925 c. 22.

24.—(1) Where under a contract for the sale or other disposition of any estate or interest in land the title to which is not registered under the Land Registration Act 1925 or any enactment replaced by it any question arises whether the purchaser had knowledge, at the time of entering into the contract, of a registered land charge, that question shall be determined by reference to his actual knowledge and without regard to the provisions of section 198 of the Law of Property Act 1925 (under which registration under the Land Charges Act 1925 or any enactment replaced by it is deemed to constitute actual notice).

(2) Where any estate or interest with which such a contract is concerned is affected by a registered land charge and the purchaser, at the time of entering into the contract, had not received notice and did not otherwise actually know that the estate or interest was affected by the charge, any provision of the contract shall be void so far as it purports to exclude the operation of subsection (1) above or to exclude or restrict any right or remedy that might otherwise be exercisable by the purchaser on the ground that the estate or interest is affected by the charge.

(3) In this section—

" purchaser " includes a lessee, mortgagee or other person acquiring or intending to acquire an estate or interest in land ; and

" registered land charge " means any instrument or matter registered, otherwise than in a register of local land charges, under the Land Charges Act 1925 or any Act replaced by it.

(4) For the purposes of this section any knowledge acquired in the course of a transaction by a person who is acting therein as counsel, or as solicitor or other agent, for another shall be treated as the knowledge of that other.

(5) This section does not apply to contracts made before the commencement of this Act.

25.—(1) Where a purchaser of any estate or interest in land
under a disposition to which this section applies has suffered
loss by reason that the estate or interest is affected by a registered land charge, then if—

Part III

Compensation
in certain
cases for loss
due to
undisclosed
land charges.

(*a*) the date of completion was after the commencement of
this Act ; and

(*b*) on that date the purchaser had no actual knowledge of
the charge ; and

(*c*) the charge was registered against the name of an owner
of an estate in the land who was not as owner of any
such estate a party to any transaction, or concerned
in any event, comprised in the relevant title ;

the purchaser shall be entitled to compensation for the loss.

(2) For the purposes of subsection (1)(*b*) above, the question
whether any person had actual knowledge of a charge shall
be determined without regard to the provisions of section 198
of the Law of Property Act 1925 (under which registration under
the Land Charges Act 1925 or any enactment replaced by it is
deemed to constitute actual notice).

(3) Where a transaction comprised in the relevant title was
effected or evidenced by a document which expressly provided
that it should take effect subject to an interest or obligation
capable of registration in any of the relevant registers, the transaction which created that interest or obligation shall be treated
for the purposes of subsection (1)(*c*) above as comprised in the
relevant title.

(4) Any compensation for loss under this section shall be
paid by the Chief Land Registrar, and where the purchaser of the
estate or interest in question has incurred expenditure for the
purpose—

(*a*) of securing that the estate or interest is no longer
affected by the registered land charge or is so affected
to a less extent ; or

(*b*) of obtaining compensation under this section ;
the amount of the compensation shall include the amount of the
expenditure (so far as it would not otherwise fall to be treated
as compensation for loss) reasonably incurred by the purchaser
for that purpose.

(5) In the case of an action to recover compensation under
this section, the cause of action shall be deemed for the purposes of the Limitation Act 1939 to accrue at the time when
the registered land charge affecting the estate or interest in
question comes to the notice of the purchaser.

PART III　　(6) Any proceedings for the recovery of compensation under this section shall be commenced in the High Court; and if in such proceedings the High Court dismisses a claim to compensation it shall not order the purchaser to pay the Chief Land Registrar's costs unless it considers that it was unreasonable for the purchaser to commence the proceedings.

1925 c. 22.　　(7) Rules under the Land Charges Act 1925 may include provision—

(a) requiring the Chief Land Registrar to take steps in relation to any registered land charge in respect of which compensation has been claimed under this section which would be likely to bring the charge to the notice of any person who subsequently makes a search, or requires a search to be made, of the relevant registers in relation to the estate or interest affected by the charge; and

(b) authorising the use of the alphabetical index kept under that Act in any manner which will serve that purpose, notwithstanding that its use in that manner is not otherwise authorised by or by virtue of that Act.

(8) Where compensation under this section has been paid in a case where the purchaser would have had knowledge of the registered land charge but for the fraud of any person, the Chief Land Registrar, on behalf of the Crown, may recover the amount paid from that person.

(9) This section applies to the following dispositions, that is to say—

(a) any sale or exchange and, subject to the following provisions of this subsection, any mortgage of an estate or interest in land;

(b) any grant of a lease for a term of years derived out of a leasehold interest;

(c) any compulsory purchase, by whatever procedure, of land; and

1967 c. 88.　　(d) any conveyance of a fee simple in land under Part I of the Leasehold Reform Act 1967;

but does not apply to the grant of a term of years derived out of the freehold or the mortgage of such a term by the lessee; and references in this section to a purchaser shall be construed accordingly.

(10) In this section—

" date of completion ", in relation to land which vests in the Land Commission or another acquiring authority

by virtue of a general vesting declaration under the Part III
Land Commission Act 1967 or the Town and Country 1967 c. 1.
Planning Act 1968, means the date on which it so 1968 c. 72.
vests ;

" mortgage " includes any charge ;

" registered land charge " means any instrument or matter
registered, otherwise than in a register of local
land charges, under the Land Charges Act 1925 or 1925 c. 22.
any Act replaced by it, except that—

> (a) in relation to an assignment of a lease or
> underlease or a mortgage by an assignee under such
> an assignment, it does not include any instrument
> or matter affecting the title to the freehold or to any
> relevant leasehold reversion ; and

> (b) in relation to the grant of an underlease or the
> mortgage by the underlessee of the term of years
> created by an underlease, it does not include any
> instrument or matter affecting the title to the free-
> hold or to any leasehold reversion superior to the
> leasehold interest out of which the term of years
> is derived ;

" relevant registers " means the registers kept under section
1 of the Land Charges Act 1925 ;

" relevant title " means—

> (a) in relation to a disposition made under a con-
> tract, the title which the purchaser was, apart from
> any acceptance by him (by agreement or otherwise)
> of a shorter or an imperfect title, entitled to require ;
> or

> (b) in relation to any other disposition, the title
> which he would have been entitled to require if
> the disposition had been made under a contract to
> which section 44(1) of the Law of Property Act 1925 1925 c. 20.
> applied and that contract had been made on the date
> of completion.

(11) For the purposes of this section any knowledge acquired
in the course of a transaction by a person who is acting therein
as counsel, or as solicitor or other agent, for another shall be
treated as the knowledge of that other.

26. Section 10(5) of the Land Charges Act 1925 (by virtue Registration
of which registration under section 95 of the Companies Act of land charges
1948 takes effect, in the case of a land charge for securing money created by
created by a company, as if it were registration under the Land companies.
Charges Act 1925) shall not apply to any charge created 1948 c. 38.
after the commencement of this Act other than one created

Part III

as a floating charge, and accordingly in that subsection, after the words " created by a company ", there shall be inserted the words " before 1st January 1970 or so created at any time as a floating charge ".

Land
improvement
charges.
1925 c. 22.

27. After section 11 of the Land Charges Act 1925 (under which certain land charges take effect as charges by way of legal mortgage) there shall be inserted the following section:—

" 11A.—(1) The following provisions shall have effect with respect to land improvement charges registered as land charges of Class A:—

(*a*) if the charge is registered after 31st December 1969, section 11 of this Act shall not apply to it;

(*b*) if the charge was registered before 1st January 1970, any body corporate which, but for the charge, would have power to advance money on the security of the estate or interest affected by it shall have that power notwithstanding the charge

1864 c. 114.

1899 c. 46.

(2) In this section " land improvement charge " means any charge under the Improvement of Land Act 1864 or under any special improvement Act within the meaning of the Improvement of Land Act 1899 ".

Part IV

Restrictive Covenants

Powers of
Lands Tribunal
and court in
relation to
restrictive
covenants
affecting land.
1925 c. 20.

28.—(1) In section 84 of the Law of Property Act 1925—

(*a*) for the words " The Authority hereinafter defined " in subsection (1), and for the words " the Authority " wherever else they occur, (which now refer to the Lands Tribunal) there shall be substituted the words " the Lands Tribunal "; and

(*b*) there shall be made the further amendments provided for by subsections (2) to (9) below;

and accordingly section 84 shall have effect as it is set out in Schedule 3 to this Act with the amendments made by section

1954 c. 56.

52(1) of the Landlord and Tenant Act 1954 and by this section (and the omission of repealed provisions), subject however to any other enactments affecting the operation of section 84 and to subsection (11) below.

(2) So much of section 84(1)(*a*) as follows the words " obsolete or " shall be a separate paragraph (*aa*) and shall be amended as follows:—

(*a*) after the word " that " there shall be inserted the words " in a case falling within subsection (1A) below ";

(*b*) for the words " the reasonable user " there shall be
substituted the words " some reasonable user " ; and

(*c*) the words " without securing practical benefits to other persons " shall be omitted ;

and after section 84(1) there shall be inserted as new subsections (1A), (1B) and (1C) :—

" (1A) Subsection (1)(*aa*) above authorises the discharge or modification of a restriction by reference to its impeding some reasonable user of land in any case in which the Lands Tribunal is satisfied that the restriction, in impeding that user, either—

(*a*) does not secure to persons entitled to the benefit of it any practical benefits of substantial value or advantage to them ; or

(*b*) is contrary to the public interest ;

and that money will be an adequate compensation for the loss or disadvantage (if any) which any such person will suffer from the discharge or modification.

(1B) In determining whether a case is one falling within subsection (1A) above, and in determining whether (in any such case or otherwise) a restriction ought to be discharged or modified, the Lands Tribunal shall take into account the development plan and any declared or ascertainable pattern for the grant or refusal of planning permissions in the relevant areas, as well as the period at which and context in which the restriction was created or imposed and any other material circumstances.

(1C) It is hereby declared that the power conferred by this section to modify a restriction includes power to add such further provisions restricting the user of or the building on the land affected as appear to the Lands Tribunal to be reasonable in view of the relaxation of the existing provisions, and as may be accepted by the applicant ; and the Lands Tribunal may accordingly refuse to modify a restriction without some such addition."

(3) In section 84(1) there shall be omitted the words " (subject or not to the payment by the applicant of compensation to any person suffering loss in consequence of the order) " and the proviso, and after paragraph (*c*) there shall be inserted the words " and an order discharging or modifying a restriction under this subsection may direct the applicant to pay to any person entitled to the benefit of the restriction such sum by way of consideration as the Tribunal may think it just to award under one, but not both, of the following heads, that is to say, either—

(i) a sum to make up for any loss or disadvantage suffered by that person in consequence of the discharge or modification ; or

3 G

(ii) a sum to make up for any effect which the restriction had, at the time when it was imposed, in reducing the consideration then received for the land affected by it."

(4) In section 84(2), in the phrase " is affected " in paragraph (a), and in the phrase " is enforceable " in paragraph (b), there shall in each case be inserted after the word " is " the words " or would in any given event be " ; and at the end of section 84(2) there shall be added the words : —

"Neither subsections (7) and (11) of this section nor, unless the contrary is expressed, any later enactment providing for this section not to apply to any restrictions shall affect the operation of this subsection or the operation for purposes of this subsection of any other provisions of this section."

(5) In section 84(3) in the phrase " any local authority " there shall be inserted after the word " any " the words " government department or ".

(6) After section 84(3) there shall be inserted as a new subsection (3A) :—

" (3A) On an application to the Lands Tribunal under this section the Lands Tribunal shall give any necessary directions as to the persons who are or are not to be admitted (as appearing to be entitled to the benefit of the restriction) to oppose the application, and no appeal shall

1949 c. 42.   lie against any such direction ; but rules under the Lands Tribunal Act 1949 shall make provision whereby, in cases in which there arises on such an application (whether or not in connection with the admission of persons to oppose) any such question as is referred to in subsection (2)(a) or (b) of this section, the proceedings on the application can and, if the rules so provide, shall be suspended to enable the decision of the court to be obtained on that question by an application under that subsection, or by means of a case stated by the Lands Tribunal, or otherwise, as may be provided by those rules or by rules of court."

(7) In section 84(8) for the words " when made " there shall

1925 c. 21.   be substituted the words " in accordance with the Land Registration Act 1925 " ; and in section 50(3) of the Land Registration Act 1925 (which provides for the alteration of the register where a covenant or agreement is discharged or modified by an order

1925 c. 20.   under the Law of Property Act 1925 and in other cases) for the words " or modified " there shall be substituted the words " modified or dealt with ".

(8) In section 84(11) at the end of paragraph (b) there shall

1949 c. 67.   be added the words " or of section 19 or 23 of the Civil Aviation Act 1949 ".

(9) In section 84(11) after the word "nor" there shall be inserted the words "subject to subsection (11A) below"; and after section 84(11) there shall be inserted as a new subsection (11A):—

> "(11A) Subsection (11) of this section—
>
> (a) shall exclude the application of this section to a restriction falling within subsection (11)(a), and not created or imposed in connection with the use of any land as an aerodrome, only so long as the restriction is enforceable by or on behalf of the Crown; and
>
> (b) shall exclude the application of this section to a restriction falling within subsection (11)(b), or created or imposed in connection with the use of any land as an aerodrome, only so long as the restriction is enforceable by or on behalf of the Crown or any public or international authority."

(10) In section 38(3) of the Requisitioned Land and War Works Act 1945 (under which section 84 of the Law of Property 1945 c. 43. Act 1925 does not apply to a covenant obtained under the 1925 c. 20. Defence Acts, so long as the covenant is enforceable on behalf of the Crown) for the words "any covenant obtained under the Defence Acts" there shall be substituted the words "any restriction created or imposed under the Defence Acts or under section 13 (acquisition of land for oil installations) of the Land Powers 1958 c. 30. (Defence) Act 1958", and for the words "the covenant" there shall be substituted the words "the restriction".

(11) This section applies to restrictions whether subsisting at the time it comes into force or created or imposed thereafter, but—

(a) the coming into force of any provision of this section other than subsection (6) shall not affect proceedings then pending; and

(b) subsection (6) shall not come into force until such date as the Lord Chancellor may appoint by order made by statutory instrument, which shall be laid before Parliament after being made.

PART V

SUPPLEMENTARY PROVISIONS

29. There shall be paid out of moneys provided by Parliament Expenses. any expenses of the Treasury or the Chief Land Registrar under this Act and any increase in the sums so payable under any other Act.

PART V
Interpretation.
1884 c. 54
1954 c. 56.

30.—(1) In this Act—

"the Act of 1884" means the Yorkshire Registries Act 1884;

"the Act of 1954" means the Landlord and Tenant Act 1954;

"county council", in relation to a Yorkshire deeds registry, means the county council of the riding for which the registry is or was maintained;

"instrument" includes any document which is, or but for Part II of this Act would be, capable of registration under the Act of 1884, and references to the registration of an instrument include references to the registration of a memorial of an instrument;

"puisne mortgage" means a legal mortgage not protected by a deposit of documents relating to the legal estate affected;

"Yorkshire deeds registry" means a registry maintained under the Act of 1884.

(2) Any reference in this Act to any enactment shall be construed as a reference thereto as amended by any other enactment, including, except where the context otherwise requires, this Act.

Short title, commencement and extent.

31.—(1) This Act may be cited as the Law of Property Act 1969.

(2) This Act, except section 28(6), shall come into force on 1st January 1970.

(3) This Act does not extend to Scotland or Northern Ireland.

SCHEDULES

SCHEDULE 1   Section 15.

CERTAIN PROVISIONS OF PART 2 OF ACT OF 1954 SET OUT AS AMENDED

24.—(1) A tenancy to which this Part of this Act applies shall
not come to an end unless terminated in accordance with the provisions of this Part of this Act; and, subject to the provisions of
section 29 of this Act, the tenant under such a tenancy may apply
to the court for a new tenancy— *Continuation of tenancies to which Part II applies and grant of new tenancies.*

   (a) if the landlord has given notice under section 25 of this Act
       to terminate the tenancy, or

   (b) if the tenant has made a request for a new tenancy in
       accordance with section 26 of this Act.

(2) The last foregoing subsection shall not prevent the coming
to an end of a tenancy by notice to quit given by the tenant, by
surrender or forfeiture, or by the forfeiture of a superior tenancy,
unless—

   (a) in the case of a notice to quit, the notice was given before
       the tenant had been in occupation in right of the tenancy for
       one month ; or

   (b) in the case of an instrument of surrender, the instrument was
       executed before, or was executed in pursuance of an agree-
       ment made before, the tenant had been in occupation in
       right of the tenancy for one month.

(3) Notwithstanding anything in subsection (1) of this section,—

   (a) where a tenancy to which this Part of this Act applies ceases
       to be such a tenancy, it shall not come to an end by reason
       only of the cesser, but if it was granted for a term of years
       certain and has been continued by subsection (1) of this
       section then (without prejudice to the termination thereof
       in accordance with any terms of the tenancy) it may be
       terminated by not less than three nor more than six months'
       notice in writing given by the landlord to the tenant ;

   (b) where, at a time when a tenancy is not one to which this
       Part of this Act applies, the landlord gives notice to quit,
       the operation of the notice shall not be affected by reason
       that the tenancy becomes one to which this Part of this Act
       applies after the giving of the notice.

27.—(1) Where the tenant under a tenancy to which this Part of
this Act applies, being a tenancy granted for a term of years certain,
gives to the immediate landlord, not later than three months before
the date on which apart from this Act the tenancy would come to
an end by effluxion of time, a notice in writing that the tenant does
not desire the tenancy to be continued, section 24 of this Act shall
not have effect in relation to the tenancy, unless the notice is given
before the tenant has been in occupation in right of the tenancy
for one month. *Termination by tenant of tenancy for fixed term.*

3 G 3

SCH. 1

(2) A tenancy granted for a term of years certain which is continuing by virtue of section 24 of this Act may be brought to an end on any quarter day by not less than three months' notice in writing given by the tenant to the immediate landlord, whether the notice is given after the date on which apart from this Act the tenancy would have come to an end or before that date, but not before the tenant has been in occupation in right of the tenancy for one month.

Opposition by landlord to application for new tenancy.

30.—(1) The grounds on which a landlord may oppose an application under subsection (1) of section 24 of this Act are such of the following grounds as may be stated in the landlord's notice under section 25 of this Act or, as the case may be, under subsection (6) of section 26 thereof, that is to say :—

(a) where under the current tenancy the tenant has any obligations as respects the repair and maintenance of the holding, that the tenant ought not to be granted a new tenancy in view of the state of repair of the holding, being a state resulting from the tenant's failure to comply with the said obligations ;

(b) that the tenant ought not to be granted a new tenancy in view of his persistent delay in paying rent which has become due ;

(c) that the tenant ought not to be granted a new tenancy in view of other substantial breaches by him of his obligations under the current tenancy, or for any other reason connected with the tenant's use or management of the holding ;

(d) that the landlord has offered and is willing to provide or secure the provision of alternative accommodation for the tenant, that the terms on which the alternative accommodation is available are reasonable having regard to the terms of the current tenancy and to all other relevant circumstances, and that the accommodation and the time at which it will be available are suitable for the tenant's requirements (including the requirement to preserve goodwill) having regard to the nature and class of his business and to the situation and extent of, and facilities afforded by, the holding ;

(e) where the current tenancy was created by the sub-letting of part only of the property comprised in a superior tenancy and the landlord is the owner of an interest in reversion expectant on the termination of that superior tenancy, that the aggregate of the rents reasonably obtainable on separate lettings of the holding and the remainder of that property would be substantially less than the rent reasonably obtainable on a letting of that property as a whole, that on the termination of the current tenancy the landlord requires possession of the holding for the purpose of letting or otherwise disposing of the said property as a whole, and that in view thereof the tenant ought not to be granted a new tenancy ;

(*f*) that on the termination of the current tenancy the landlord intends to demolish or reconstruct the premises comprised in the holding or a substantial part of those premises or to carry out substantial work of construction on the holding or part thereof and that he could not reasonably do so without obtaining possession of the holding ;

(*g*) subject as hereinafter provided, that on the termination of the current tenancy the landlord intends to occupy the holding for the purposes, or partly for the purposes, of a business to be carried on by him therein, or as his residence.

(2) The landlord shall not be entitled to oppose an application on the ground specified in paragraph (*g*) of the last foregoing subsection if the interest of the landlord, or an interest which has merged in that interest and but for the merger would be the interest of the landlord, was purchased or created after the beginning of the period of five years which ends with the termination of the current tenancy, and at all times since the purchase or creation thereof the holding has been comprised in a tenancy or successive tenancies of the description specified in subsection (1) of section 23 of this Act.

(3) Where the landlord has a controlling interest in a company any business to be carried on by the company shall be treated for the purposes of subsection (1)(*g*) of this section as a business to be carried on by him.

For the purposes of this subsection, a person has a controlling interest in a company if and only if either—

(*a*) he is a member of it and able, without the consent of any other person, to appoint or remove the holders of at least a majority of the directorships ; or

(*b*) he holds more than one-half of its equity share capital, there being disregarded any shares held by him in a fiduciary capacity or as nominee for another person ;

and in this subsection " company " and " share " have the meanings assigned to them by section 455(1) of the Companies Act 1948 and " equity share capital " the meaning assigned to it by section 154(5) of that Act.

1948 c. 38.

32.—(1) Subject to the following provisions of this section, an order under section 29 of this Act for the grant of a new tenancy shall be an order for the grant of a new tenancy of the holding ; and in the absence of agreement between the landlord and the tenant as to the property which constitutes the holding the court shall in the order designate that property by reference to the circumstances existing at the date of the order.

Property to be comprised in new tenancy.

(1A) Where the court, by virtue of paragraph (*b*) of section 31A(1) of this Act, makes an order under section 29 of this Act for the grant of a new tenancy in a case where the tenant is willing to accept a tenancy of part of the holding, the order shall be an order for the grant of a new tenancy of that part only.

(2) The foregoing provisions of this section shall not apply in a case where the property comprised in the current tenancy includes other property besides the holding and the landlord requires any new tenancy ordered to be granted under section 29 of this Act to be a tenancy of the whole of the property comprised in the current tenancy ; but in any such case—

(a) any order under the said section 29 for the grant of a new tenancy shall be an order for the grant of a new tenancy of the whole of the property comprised in the current tenancy, and

(b) references in the following provisions of this Part of this Act to the holding shall be construed as references to the whole of that property.

(3) Where the current tenancy includes rights enjoyed by the tenant in connection with the holding, those rights shall be included in a tenancy ordered to be granted under section 29 of this Act, except as otherwise agreed between the landlord and the tenant or, in default of such agreement, determined by the court.

Rent under
new tenancy.
34.—(1) The rent payable under a tenancy granted by order of the court under this Part of this Act shall be such as may be agreed between the landlord and the tenant or as, in default of such agreement, may be determined by the court to be that at which, having regard to the terms of the tenancy (other than those relating to rent), the holding might reasonably be expected to be let in the open market by a willing lessor, there being disregarded—

(a) any effect on rent of the fact that the tenant has or his predecessors in title have been in occupation of the holding,

(b) any goodwill attached to the holding by reason of the carrying on thereat of the business of the tenant (whether by him or by a predecessor of his in that business),

(c) any effect on rent of an improvement to which this paragraph applies,

(d) in the case of a holding comprising licensed premises, any addition to its value attributable to the licence, if it appears to the court that having regard to the terms of the current tenancy and any other relevant circumstances the benefit of the licence belongs to the tenant.

(2) Paragraph (c) of the foregoing subsection applies to any improvement carried out by a person who at the time it was carried out was the tenant, but only if it was carried out otherwise than in pursuance of an obligation to his immediate landlord and either it was carried out during the current tenancy or the following conditions are satisfied, that is to say,—

(a) that it was completed not more than twenty-one years before the application for the new tenancy was made ; and (*b*) that the holding or any part of it affected by the improvement has at all times since the completion of the improvement been comprised in tenancies of the description specified in section 23(1) of this Act ; and

(*c*) that at the termination of each of those tenancies the tenant did not quit.

(3) Where the rent is determined by the court the court may, if it thinks fit, further determine that the terms of the tenancy shall include such provision for varying the rent as may be specified in the determination.

37.—(1) Where on the making of an application under section 24 of this Act the court is precluded (whether by subsection (1) or subsection (2) of section 31 of this Act) from making an order for the grant of a new tenancy by reason of any of the grounds specified in paragraphs (*e*), (*f*) and (*g*) of subsection (1) of section 30 of this Act and not of any grounds specified in any other paragraph of that subsection, or where no other ground is specified in the landlord's notice under section 25 of this Act or, as the case may be, under section 26(6) thereof, than those specified in the said paragraphs (*e*), (*f*) and (*g*) and either no application under the said section 24 is made or such an application is withdrawn, then, subject to the provisions of this Act, the tenant shall be entitled on quitting the holding to recover from the landlord by way of compensation an amount determined in accordance with the following provisions of this section.

(2) The said amount shall be as follows, that is to say,—

(*a*) where the conditions specified in the next following subsection are satisfied it shall be twice the rateable value of the holding,

(*b*) in any other case it shall be the rateable value of the holding.

(3) The said conditions are—

(*a*) that, during the whole of the fourteen years immediately preceding the termination of the current tenancy, premises being or comprised in the holding have been occupied for the purposes of a business carried on by the occupier or for those and other purposes ;

(*b*) that, if during those fourteen years there was a change in the occupier of the premises, the person who was the occupier immediately after the change was the successor to the business carried on by the person who was the occupier immediately before the change.

(4) Where the court is precluded from making an order for the grant of a new tenancy under this Part of this Act in the circumstances mentioned in subsection (1) of this section, the court shall on the application of the tenant certify that fact.

3 G*

SCH. 1

(5) For the purposes of subsection (2) of this section the rateable value of the holding shall be determined as follows:—

(*a*) where in the valuation list in force at the date on which the landlord's notice under section 25 or, as the case may be, subsection (6) of section 26 of this Act is given a value is then shown as the annual value (as hereinafter defined) of the holding, the rateable value of the holding shall be taken to be that value;

(*b*) where no such value is so shown with respect to the holding but such a value or such values is or are so shown with respect to premises comprised in or comprising the holding or part of it, the rateable value of the holding shall be taken to be such value as is found by a proper apportionment or aggregation of the value or values so shown;

(*c*) where the rateable value of the holding cannot be ascertained in accordance with the foregoing paragraphs of this subsection, it shall be taken to be the value which, apart from any exemption from assessment to rates, would on a proper assessment be the value to be entered in the said valuation list as the annual value of the holding;

and any dispute arising, whether in proceedings before the court or otherwise, as to the determination for those purposes of the rateable value of the holding shall be referred to the Commissioners of Inland Revenue for decision by a valuation officer.

An appeal shall lie to the Lands Tribunal from any decision of a valuation officer under this subsection, but subject thereto any such decision shall be final.

(6) The Commissioners of Inland Revenue may by statutory instrument make rules prescribing the procedure in connection with references under this section.

(7) In this section—

the reference to the termination of the current tenancy is a reference to the date of termination specified in the landlord's notice under section 25 of this Act or, as the case may be, the date specified in the tenant's request for a new tenancy as the date from which the new tenancy is to begin;

the expression " annual value " means rateable value except that where the rateable value differs from the net annual value the said expression means net annual value;

the expression " valuation officer " means any officer of the Commissioners of Inland Revenue for the time being authorised by a certificate of the Commissioners to act in relation to a valuation list.

Restriction on agreements excluding provisions of Part II.

38.—(1) Any agreement relating to a tenancy to which this Part of this Act applies (whether contained in the instrument creating the tenancy or not) shall be void (except as provided by subsection (4) of this section) in so far as it purports to preclude the tenant from making an application or request under this Part of this Act

or provides for the termination or the surrender of the tenancy   Sch. 1
in the event of his making such an application or request or for the
imposition of any penalty or disability on the tenant in that event.

(2) Where—

(a) during the whole of the five years immediately preceding
the date on which the tenant under a tenancy to which
this Part of this Act applies is to quit the holding, premises
being or comprised in the holding have been occupied for
the purposes of a business carried on by the occupier or
for those and other purposes, and

(b) if during those five years there was a change in the occupier
of the premises, the person who was the occupier immediately after the change was the successor to the business
carried on by the person who was the occupier immediately
before the change,

any agreement (whether contained in the instrument creating the
tenancy or not and whether made before or after the termination
of that tenancy) which purports to exclude or reduce compensation
under the last foregoing section shall to that extent be void, so however that this subsection shall not affect any agreement as to the
amount of any such compensation which is made after the right
to compensation has accrued.

(3) In a case not falling within the last foregoing subsection the
right to compensation conferred by the last foregoing section may
be excluded or modified by agreement.

(4) The court may—

(a) on the joint application of the persons who will be the landlord and the tenant in relation to a tenancy to be granted
for a term of years certain which will be a tenancy to which
this Part of this Act applies, authorise an agreement excluding in relation to that tenancy the provisions of sections
24 to 28 of this Act ; and

(b) on the joint application of the persons who are the landlord and the tenant in relation to a tenancy to which this
Part of this Act applies, authorise an agreement for the
surrender of the tenancy on such date or in such circumstances as may be specified in the agreement and on such
terms (if any) as may be so specified ;

if the agreement is contained in or endorsed on the instrument
creating the tenancy or such other instrument as the court may
specify ; and an agreement contained in or endorsed on an instrument in pursuance of an authorisation given under this subsection
shall be valid notwithstanding anything in the preceding provisions
of this section.

42.—(1) For the purposes of this section two bodies corporate shall   Groups of
be taken to be members of a group if and only if one is a sub-   companies.
sidiary of the other or both are subsidiaries of a third body corporate.

3G* 2

In this subsection " subsidiary " has the same meaning as is assigned to it for the purposes of the Companies Act 1948 by section 154 of that Act.

(2) Where a tenancy is held by a member of a group, occupation by another member of the group, and the carrying on of a business by another member of the group, shall be treated for the purposes of section 23 of this Act as equivalent to occupation or the carrying on of a business by the member of the group holding the tenancy : and in relation to a tenancy to which this Part of this Act applies by virtue of the foregoing provisions of this subsection—

(a) references (however expressed) in this Part of this Act and in the Ninth Schedule to this Act to the business of or to use occupation or enjoyment by the tenant shall be construed as including references to the business of or to use occupation or enjoyment by the said other member ;

(b) the reference in paragraph (d) of subsection (1) of section 34 of this Act to the tenant shall be construed as including the said other member ; and

(c) an assignment of the tenancy from one member of the group to another shall not be treated as a change in the person of the tenant.

(3) Where the landlord's interest is held by a member of a group—

(a) the reference in paragraph (g) of subsection (1) of section 30 of this Act to intended occupation by the landlord for the purposes of a business to be carried on by him shall be construed as including intended occupation by any member of the group for the purposes of a business to be carried on by that member ; and

(b) the reference in subsection (2) of that section to the purchase or creation of any interest shall be construed as a reference to a purchase from or creation by a person other than a member of the group.

Tenancies excluded from Part II.

43.—

(3) This Part of this Act does not apply to a tenancy granted for a term certain not exceeding six months unless—

(a) the tenancy contains provision for renewing the term or for extending it beyond six months from its beginning ; or

(b) the tenant has been in occupation for a period which, together with any period during which any predecessor in the carrying on of the business carried on by the tenant was in occupation, exceeds twelve months.

Meaning of " the landlord " in Part II, and provisions as to mesne landlords, etc.

44.—(1) Subject to the next following subsection, in this Part of this Act the expression " the landlord ", in relation to a tenancy (in this section referred to as " the relevant tenancy "), means the person (whether or not he is the immediate landlord) who is the owner of that interest in the property comprised in the relevant

tenancy which for the time being fulfils the following conditions, SCH. 1
that is to say—

    (*a*) that it is an interest in reversion expectant (whether immediately or not) on the termination of the relevant tenancy, and

    (*b*) that it is either the fee simple or a tenancy which will not come to an end within fourteen months by effluxion of time and, if it is such a tenancy, that no notice has been given by virtue of which it will come to an end within fourteen months or any further time by which it may be continued under section 36(2) or section 64 of this Act,

and is not itself in reversion expectant (whether immediately or not) on an interest which fulfils those conditions.

(2) References in this Part of this Act to a notice to quit given by the landlord are references to a notice to quit given by the immediate landlord.

(3) The provisions of the Sixth Schedule to this Act shall have effect for the application of this Part of this Act to cases where the immediate landlord of the tenant is not the owner of the fee simple in respect of the holding.

SIXTH SCHEDULE

PROVISIONS FOR PURPOSES OF PART II WHERE IMMEDIATE LANDLORD IS NOT THE FREEHOLDER

Definitions

1. In this Schedule the following expressions have the meanings hereby assigned to them in relation to a tenancy (in this Schedule referred to as " the relevant tenancy "), that is to say : —

" the competent landlord " means the person who in relation to the tenancy is for the time being the landlord (as defined by section 44 of this Act) for the purposes of Part II of this Act ;

" mesne landlord " means a tenant whose interest is intermediate between the relevant tenancy and the interest of the competent landlord ; and

" superior landlord " means a person (whether the owner of the fee simple or a tenant) whose interest is superior to the interest of the competent landlord.

Power of court to order reversionary tenancies

2. Where the period for which in accordance with the provisions of Part II of this Act it is agreed or determined by the court that a new tenancy should be granted thereunder will extend beyond the date on which the interest of the immediate landlord will come to an end, the power of the court under Part II of this Act to order

3 G* 3

such a grant shall include power to order the grant of a new tenancy until the expiration of that interest and also to order the grant of such a reversionary tenancy or reversionary tenancies as may be required to secure that the combined effects of those grants will be equivalent to the grant of a tenancy for that period ; and the provisions of Part II of this Act shall, subject to the necessary modifications, apply in relation to the grant of a tenancy together with one or more reversionary tenancies as they apply in relation to the grant of one new tenancy.

Acts of competent landlord binding on other landlords

3.—(1) Any notice given by the competent landlord under Part II of this Act to terminate the relevant tenancy, and any agreement made between that landlord and the tenant as to the granting, duration, or terms of a future tenancy, being an agreement made for the purposes of the said Part II, shall bind the interest of any mesne landlord notwithstanding that he has not consented to the giving of the notice or was not a party to the agreement.

(2) The competent landlord shall have power for the purposes of Part II of this Act to give effect to any agreement with the tenant for the grant of a new tenancy beginning with the coming to an end of the relevant tenancy, notwithstanding that the competent landlord will not be the immediate landlord at the commencement of the new tenancy, and any instrument made in the exercise of the power conferred by this sub-paragraph shall have effect as if the mesne landlord had been a party thereto.

(3) Nothing in the foregoing provisions of this paragraph shall prejudice the provisions of the next following paragraph.

Provisions as to consent of mesne landlord to acts of competent landlord

4.—(1) If the competent landlord, not being the immediate landlord, gives any such notice or makes any such agreement as is mentioned in sub-paragraph (1) of the last foregoing paragraph without the consent of every mesne landlord, any mesne landlord whose consent has not been given thereto shall be entitled to compensation from the competent landlord for any loss arising in consequence of the giving of the notice or the making of the agreement.

(2) If the competent landlord applies to any mesne landlord for his consent to such a notice or agreement, that consent shall not be unreasonably withheld, but may be given subject to any conditions which may be reasonable (including conditions as to the modification of the proposed notice or agreement or as to the payment of compensation by the competent landlord).

(3) Any question arising under this paragraph whether consent has been unreasonably withheld or whether any conditions imposed on the giving of consent are unreasonable shall be determined by the court.

*Consent of superior landlord required for agreements affecting
his interest*

5. An agreement between the competent landlord and the tenant
made for the purposes of Part II of this Act in a case where—

   (*a*) the competent landlord is himself a tenant, and

   (*b*) the agreement would apart from this paragraph operate as
   respects any period after the coming to an end of the interest
   of the competent landlord,

shall not have effect unless every superior landlord who will be the
immediate landlord of the tenant during any part of that period
is a party to the agreement.

*Withdrawal by competent landlord of notice given by
mesne landlord*

6. Where the competent landlord has given a notice under
section 25 of this Act to terminate the relevant tenancy and, within
two months after the giving of the notice, a superior landlord—

   (*a*) becomes the competent landlord ; and

   (*b*) gives to the tenant notice in the prescribed form that he
   withdraws the notice previously given ;

the notice under section 25 of this Act shall cease to have effect, but
without prejudice to the giving of a further notice under that section
by the competent landlord.

Duty to inform superior landlords

7. If the competent landlord's interest in the property comprised in
the relevant tenancy is a tenancy which will come or can be brought
to an end within sixteenth months (or any further time by which it
may be continued under section 36(2) or section 64 of this Act)
and he gives to the tenant under the relevant tenancy a notice under
section 25 of this Act to terminate the tenancy or is given by him a
notice under section 26(3) of this Act : —

   (*a*) the competent landlord shall forthwith send a copy of the
   notice to his immediate landlord ; and

   (*b*) any superior landlord whose interest in the property is a
   tenancy shall forthwith send to his immediate landlord any
   copy which has been sent to him in pursuance of the
   preceding sub-paragraph or this sub-paragraph.

SCHEDULE 2

Yorkshire Registries : Repeals

Part I

Enactments Relating to Registration of Deeds

Chapter	Short Title	Extent of Repeal
47 & 48 Vict. c. 54.	The Yorkshire Registries Act 1884.	The whole Act, except section 49.
48 & 49 Vict. c. 4.	The Yorkshire Registries Amendment Act 1884.	The whole Act.
48 & 49 Vict. c. 26.	The Yorkshire Registries Amendment Act 1885.	The whole Act.
51 & 52 Vict. c. 41.	The Local Government Act 1888.	Section 46(4).
10 Edw. 7. & 1 Geo. 5. c. cxviii.	The East Riding County Council Act 1910.	Section 3.
7 & 8 Geo. 5. c. v.	The Yorkshire Registries (North Riding) Amendment Act 1917.	The whole Act.
15 & 16 Geo. 5. c. 20.	The Law of Property Act 1925.	Section 11. In section 94(2) the words " or in a local deeds registry ". In section 96(2) the words " or in a local deeds register ". Section 197.
15 & 16 Geo. 5. c. 21.	The Land Registration Act 1925.	Sections 125, 135 and 136.
16 & 17 Geo. 5. c. 11.	The Law of Property (Amendment) Act 1926.	In the Schedule, in the entry relating to section 96 of the Law of Property Act 1925, the words " or in a local deeds register ".
7 & 8 Geo. 6. c. i.	The Yorkshire Registries (West Riding) Amendment Act 1944.	The whole Act.
5 & 6 Eliz. 2. c. 56.	The Housing Act 1957.	In section 15(6) the words from " or of the Yorkshire Registries Act 1884 " onwards.
1965 c. 64.	The Commons Registration Act 1965.	In section 13, the words from " and may exclude " onwards.
1966 c. xxvi.	The Yorkshire Registries Amendment Act 1966.	The whole Act.
1969 c. xxxviii.	The York Corporation Act 1969.	Section 24.

Part II

Enactments Relating to Land Charges

Chapter	Short Title	Extent of Repeal
15 & 16 Geo. 5. c. 20.	The Law of Property Act 1925.	In section 97 the words " or of land within the jurisdiction of a local deeds registry ".

Chapter	Short Title	Extent of Repeal
15 & 16 Geo. 6. c. 22.	The Land Charges Act 1925.	Section 10(6). Section 20(12).
16 & 17 Geo. 5. c. 11.	The Law of Property (Amendment) Act 1926.	In the Schedule, the second entry relating to section 10 of the Land Charges Act 1925.
1967 c. 75.	The Matrimonial Homes Act 1967.	In the Schedule, paragraph 1.

SCHEDULE 3

Section 28.

LAW OF PROPERTY ACT 1925 SECTION 84 REPRINTED WITH AMENDMENTS

1925 c. 20.

84.—(1) The Lands Tribunal shall (without prejudice to any concurrent jurisdiction of the court) have power from time to time, on the application of any person interested in any freehold land affected by any restriction arising under covenant or otherwise as to the user thereof or the building thereon, by order wholly or partially to discharge or modify any such restriction on being satisfied—

(a) that by reason of changes in the character of the property or the neighbourhood or other circumstances of the case which the Lands Tribunal may deem material, the restriction ought to be deemed obsolete ; or

(aa) that (in a case falling within subsection (1A) below) the continued existence thereof would impede some reasonable user of the land for public or private purposes or, as the case may be, would unless modified so impede such user ; or

(b) that the persons of full age and capacity for the time being or from time to time entitled to the benefit of the restriction, whether in respect of estates in fee simple or any lesser estates or interests in the property to which the benefit of the restriction is annexed, have agreed, either expressly or by implication, by their acts or omissions, to the same being discharged or modified ; or

(c) that the proposed discharge or modification will not injure the persons entitled to the benefit of the restriction ;

and an order discharging or modifying a restriction under this subsection may direct the applicant to pay to any person entitled to the benefit of the restriction such sum by way of consideration as the Tribunal may think it just to award under one, but not both, of the following heads, that is to say, either—

(i) a sum to make up for any loss or disadvantage suffered by that person in consequence of the discharge or modification ; or

(ii) a sum to make up for any effect which the restriction had, at the time when it was imposed, in reducing the consideration then received for the land affected by it.

(1A) Subsection (1)(*aa*) above authorises the discharge or modification of a restriction by reference to its impeding some reasonable user of land in any case in which the Lands Tribunal is satisfied that the restriction, in impeding that user, either—

(*a*) does not secure to persons entitled to the benefit of it any practical benefits of substantial value or advantage to them ; or

(*b*) is contrary to the public interest ;

and that money will be an adequate compensation for the loss or disadvantage (if any) which any such person will suffer from the discharge or modification.

(1B) In determining whether a case is one falling within subsection (1A) above, and in determining whether (in any such case or otherwise) a restriction ought to be discharged or modified, the Lands Tribunal shall take into account the development plan and any declared or ascertainable pattern for the grant or refusal of planning permissions in the relevant areas, as well as the period at which and context in which the restriction was created or imposed and any other material circumstances.

(1C) It is hereby declared that the power conferred by this section to modify a restriction includes power to add such further provisions restricting the user of or the building on the land affected as appear to the Lands Tribunal to be reasonable in view of the relaxation of the existing provisions, and as may be accepted by the applicant ; and the Lands Tribunal may accordingly refuse to modify a restriction without some such addition.

(2) The court shall have power on the application of any person interested—

(*a*) to declare whether or not in any particular case any freehold land is, or would in any given event be, affected by a restriction imposed by any instrument ; or

(*b*) to declare what, upon the true construction of any instrument purporting to impose a restriction, is the nature and extent of the restriction thereby imposed and whether the same is, or would in any given event be, enforceable and if so by whom.

Neither subsections (7) and (11) of this section nor, unless the contrary is expressed, any later enactment providing for this section not to apply to any restrictions shall affect the operation of this subsection or the operation for purposes of this subsection of any other provisions of this section.

(3) The Lands Tribunal shall, before making any order under this section, direct such enquiries, if any, to be made of any government department or local authority, and such notices, if any, whether by way of advertisement or otherwise, to be given to such

of the persons who appear to be entitled to the benefit of the restriction intended to be discharged, modified, or dealt with as, having regard to any enquiries, notices or other proceedings previously made, given or taken, the Lands Tribunal may think fit.

(3A) On an application to the Lands Tribunal under this section the Lands Tribunal shall give any necessary directions as to the persons who are or are not to be admitted (as appearing to be entitled to the benefit of the restriction) to oppose the application, and no appeal shall lie against any such direction ; but rules under the Lands Tribunal Act 1949 shall make provision whereby, in cases in which there arises on such an application (whether or not in connection with the admission of persons to oppose) any such question as is referred to in subsection (2)(*a*) or (*b*) of this section, the proceedings on the application can and, if the rules so provide, shall be suspended to enable the decision of the court to be obtained on that question by an application under that subsection, or by means of a case stated by the Lands Tribunal, or otherwise, as may be provided by those rules or by rules of court.

(5) Any order made under this section shall be binding on all persons, whether ascertained or of full age or capacity or not, then entitled or thereafter capable of becoming entitled to the benefit of any restriction, which is thereby discharged, modified or dealt with, and whether such persons are parties to the proceedings or have been served with notice or not.

(6) An order may be made under this section notwithstanding that any instrument which is alleged to impose the restriction intended to be discharged, modified, or dealt with, may not have been produced to the court or the Lands Tribunal, and the court or the Lands Tribunal may act on such evidence of that instrument as it may think sufficient.

(7) This section applies to restrictions whether subsisting at the commencement of this Act or imposed thereafter, but this section does not apply where the restriction was imposed on the occasion of a disposition made gratuitously or for a nominal consideration for public purposes.

(8) This section applies whether the land affected by the restrictions is registered or not, but, in the case of registered land, the Land Registrar shall give effect on the register to any order under this section in accordance with the Land Registration Act 1925.

(9) Where any proceedings by action or otherwise are taken to enforce a restrictive covenant, any person against whom the proceedings are taken, may in such proceedings apply to the court for an order giving leave to apply to the Lands Tribunal under this section, and staying the proceedings in the meantime.

(11) This section does not apply to restrictions imposed by the Commissioners of Works under any statutory power for the protection of any Royal Park or Garden or to restrictions of a like character imposed upon the occasion of any enfranchisement effected before the commencement of this Act in any manor vested

in His Majesty in right of the Crown or the Duchy of Lancaster, nor (subject to subsection (11A) below) to restrictions created or imposed—

    (*a*) for naval, military or air force purposes,

    (*b*) for civil aviation purposes under the powers of the Air

1920 c. 80.
1949 c. 67.
          Navigation Act, 1920 or of section 19 or 23 of the Civil Aviation Act 1949.

(11A) Subsection (11) of this section—

    (*a*) shall exclude the application of this section to a restriction falling within subsection (11)(*a*), and not created or imposed in connection with the use of any land as an aerodrome, only so long as the restriction is enforceable by or on behalf of the Crown ; and

    (*b*) shall exclude the application of this section to a restriction falling within subsection (11)(*b*), or created or imposed in connection with the use of any land as an aerodrome, only so long as the restriction is enforceable by or on behalf of the Crown or any public or international authority.

(12) Where a term of more than forty years is created in land (whether before or after the commencement of this Act) this section shall, after the expiration of twenty-five years of the term, apply to restrictions affecting such leasehold land in like manner as it would have applied had the land been freehold:

    Provided that this subsection shall not apply to mining leases.

Transport (London) Amendment Act 1969

1969 CHAPTER 60

An Act to repeal certain provisions of section 19 of the Transport (London) Act 1969.   [11th December 1969]

BE IT ENACTED by the Queen's most Excellent Majesty, by and with the advice and consent of the Lords Spiritual and Temporal, and Commons, in this present Parliament assembled, and by the authority of the same, as follows:—

1. So much of section 19 of the Transport (London) Act 1969 as provides—

> (*a*) for the Greater London Council to assume a debt due to the Minister of Transport which, when aggregated with the increase under that section in the commencing capital debt of the National Bus Company, is equal to one tenth of the debt of the London Transport Board which is extinguished under subsection (1)(*a*) of that section, and

> (*b*) for the creation of a corresponding capital debt due from the London Transport Executive to the Greater London Council and for the said increase in the commencing capital debt of the National Bus Company,

shall cease to have effect; and accordingly paragraphs (*b*) to (*d*) of subsection (1) and subsections (2) to (7) of that section are hereby repealed.

Extinguishment of transferred capital debt under section 19 of Transport (London) Act 1969.

2.—(1) This Act may be cited as the Transport (London) Amendment Act 1969.

(2) This Act extends to England and Wales only.

Short title and extent.

Expiring Laws Act 1969

1969 CHAPTER 61

An Act to make permanent certain expiring laws and continue others. [11th December 1969]

BE IT ENACTED by the Queen's most Excellent Majesty, by and with the advice and consent of the Lords Spiritual and Temporal, and Commons, in this present Parliament assembled, and by the authority of the same, as follows:—

1. The Accommodation Agencies Act 1953 and the Children and Young Persons (Harmful Publications) Act 1955 (which are limited to expire at the end of December 1969) shall become permanent and, accordingly,— *(Enactments made permanent. 1953 c. 23. 1955 c. 28.)*

   (a) in the former Act, in section 1(1), the words " during the continuance in force of this Act ", and section 2(4); and

   (b) in the latter Act, section 5(5);

shall cease to have effect.

2.—(1) Section 1 of the Aliens Restriction (Amendment) Act 1919 and Part I of, and Schedule 1 to, the Commonwealth Immigrants Act 1962 (which are limited to expire at the end of December 1969) shall continue in force till the end of December 1970. *(Enactments continued in force. 1919 c. 92. 1962 c. 21.)*

   (2) Part VII of the Licensing Act 1964 (which is limited to expire at the end of March 1970) shall continue in force till the end of March 1971. *(1964 c. 26.)*

3.—(1) This Act may be cited as the Expiring Laws Act 1969. *(Short title and application to Northern Ireland.)*

   (2) Except in so far as it makes permanent section 4 of the Children and Young Persons (Harmful Publications) Act 1955 and continues in force the enactments mentioned in section 2(1) above, this Act shall not extend to Northern Ireland.

Rent (Control of Increases) Act 1969

1969 CHAPTER 62

An Act to limit increases in rents for local authority houses or payable under regulated tenancies.

[11th December 1969]

BE IT ENACTED by the Queen's most Excellent Majesty, by and with the advice and consent of the Lords Spiritual and Temporal, and Commons, in this present Parliament assembled, and by the authority of the same, as follows:—

PART I

LOCAL AUTHORITY RENTS

1.—(1) A local authority shall not, for any period beginning before 1st July 1971 or such earlier date as the Minister may by order specify, charge in respect of houses to which this Part of this Act applies rents exceeding the former rents except where— *Restrictions on increases in local authority rents.*

(a) neither the limit specified in paragraph (a) of section 2(1) of this Act nor, where it applies, that specified in paragraph (b) thereof is exceeded ; or

(b) the increases accord with proposals submitted to and passed by the Minister under section 3 of this Act ; or

(c) the increases are excepted from the provisions of this section by subsection (4) thereof.

(2) The houses to which this Part of this Act applies (in this Part of this Act referred to as " local authority houses ") are those of which the rents fall to be carried to the local authority's Housing Revenue Account kept under the Housing (Financial *1958 c. 42.* Provisions) Act 1958 or the Housing (Financial Provisions) *1968 c. 31.* (Scotland) Act 1968, other than houses occupied, under the terms of their tenancies, for other as well as residential purposes.

(3) Any reference in this Part of this Act to the former rent of a local authority house is, in relation to any date, a reference

Part I

to the rent payable for the house as a local authority house fifty-two weeks before that date or, if there was then no rent so payable, the rent first so payable for it thereafter.

(4) An increase in the rent for a house is excepted from the provisions of this section if it is attributable to improvements or extensions to the house ; and if part of an increase is so attributable that part is excepted from the provisions of this section.

(5) Where, after the coming to an end of a tenancy of a local authority house, the house is let under a new tenancy and the tenant under the new tenancy is neither the person who was the tenant under the first-mentioned tenancy nor a member of that person's family who resided with him, this Part of this Act shall have effect as if no rent payable for the house before the beginning of the new tenancy had been payable for it as a local authority house.

(6) The power to make an order under this section shall be exercisable by statutory instrument, but no such order shall be made unless a draft thereof has been laid before and approved by resolution of each House of Parliament.

Limits of
unrestricted
increases.

2.—(1) The limits referred to in section 1(1)(*a*) of this Act are—

    (*a*) a limit on the rent for each local authority house ; and

    (*b*) a limit on the average of the increased rents for the local authority houses of each local authority.

(2) The limit, at any date, on the rent for each local authority house is a rent the weekly rate of which is ten shillings more than the weekly rate of the former rent.

(3) The limit, at any date, on the average of the increased rents for the local authority houses of any local authority is an average the weekly rate of which is seven shillings and sixpence more than that of the average of the former rents ; and any such average shall be calculated by taking the aggregate of the rents for those of the local authority houses of the local authority the rents for which exceed their former rents and dividing that aggregate by the number of those houses.

(4) The limit on the average of the increased rents for the local authority houses of a local authority does not apply where the houses to be taken into account in calculating that average would be ten per cent. or less of the total of the local authority houses of that authority.

Proposals for
other rent
increases.

3.—(1) Any proposals submitted by a local authority to the Minister under this section—

    (*a*) shall be accompanied by such information and be in such form as may be required by any general or special directions of the Minister ; and (*b*) may include provision for making rent increases by stages over a period or for limiting the proposed increases (or those proposed for any stage) in any way, whether by reference to a fixed amount or to a proportion of any rent to be increased, or by reference to a total or average amount or proportion for all the rents or some part of them, or otherwise.

(2) If, on submission of proposals under this section to the Minister, he notifies the local authority of his agreement to the proposals (or two months elapse without his notifying them that he is unable to agree), then subject to any condition attached to the agreement effect may be given to the proposals as proposals passed by the Minister ; but where it appears to the Minister that he ought not to agree to the proposals, or not without further information from the authority or further consideration of the proposals by the authority, he may within the two months notify the authority that he is unable to agree, and the submission shall then lapse.

(3) Where the Minister notifies a local authority that he is unable to agree to proposals submitted to him under this section, the local authority may, if they see fit having regard to any observations of the Minister, resubmit all or any of the proposals with or without modification ; and the provisions of this section shall apply on the resubmission of any proposals as if they had not previously been submitted.

(4) A local authority shall comply with any general or special directions given by the Minister as to the information to be published, or to be given to persons concerned, about proposals submitted by the authority under this section and any steps taken thereon.

4.—(1) In this Part of this Act—

Supplementary provisions.
1958 c. 42.
1968 c. 31.

" house " has the same meaning as in the Housing (Financial Provisions) Act 1958 or, in the application of this Act to Scotland, the Housing (Financial Provisions) (Scotland) Act 1968 ;

" local authority " means any authority keeping a Housing Revenue Account under either of those Acts ; and

" the Minister " means, in relation to authorities in Scotland or in Wales and Monmouthshire, the Secretary of State and, in relation to other authorities, the Minister of Housing and Local Government.

(2) In calculating, for the purposes of this Part of this Act, the rent payable at any date there shall be excluded—

(*a*) any amount expressed under the terms of the tenancy to be payable for the use of furniture ;

PART I

(b) any amount so expressed to be payable for, or attributable on a proper apportionment to, rates, or water rates or charges ; and

(c) any amount which, at that date, is expressed under the terms of the tenancy to be payable for services, but only if an amount is so expressed also at the other date concerned ;

and where the rent which would otherwise be payable is increased or reduced according to the circumstances of the tenant (including the earnings of other persons in the house or of members of his family, or the presence of a lodger in the house) rent shall be calculated as if the increase or reduction had not been made.

(3) If a local authority contravenes or fails to comply with any provisions of this Part of this Act or any requirement imposed thereunder, proceedings for the enforcement of those provisions or that requirement by mandamus, injunction, interdict or otherwise (including, in Scotland, proceedings under 1868 c. 100. section 91 of the Court of Session Act 1868) may be instituted by or on behalf of the Minister.

(4) In a case where, by virtue of paragraph 6 of Schedule 3 1968 c. 42. to the Prices and Incomes Act 1968, the expiration of section 10 of that Act does not affect the operation of that section in relation to any rent accruing in the interval mentioned in that paragraph, the submission and passing under that section of any proposals with regard to that rent shall be deemed for the purposes of this Act to be the submission and passing of proposals under section 3 thereof.

(5) Any administrative expenses incurred by the Minister in consequence of the provisions of this Part of this Act shall be defrayed out of moneys provided by Parliament.

PART II

RENTS UNDER REGULATED TENANCIES

Restrictions on increases in rents under regulated tenancies.
1968 c. 23.
1965 c. 75.

5.—(1) Where a rent for a dwelling which is subject to a regulated tenancy is registered under Part IV of the Rent Act 1968 or Part II of the Rent Act 1965 in the year 1970 or 1971 and the provisions of this subsection apply, there shall be a period of delay determined in accordance with the Schedule to this Act and the rent payable for a statutory period of the tenancy beginning during the period of delay shall not be increased by a notice of increase except to the extent (if any) permitted under that Schedule ; and any such notice which purports to increase it further shall have effect to increase it to the extent so permitted but no further.

(2) Where a tenant under a regulated tenancy of a dwelling, or a person who might succeed him as a statutory tenant, becomes the tenant under a new regulated tenancy of the dwelling and, whether before or after he becomes the tenant under the new regulated tenancy, a rent for the dwelling is registered, then, if the provisions of subsection (1) of this section apply—

(a) the rent limit for any contractual period of the new tenancy beginning during the period of delay shall be the amount to which, if the first-mentioned tenancy had continued, the rent payable thereunder could have been increased in accordance with this Act for a statutory period beginning at the same time, and in relation to such a contractual period the reference in section 47(3) of the Rent Act 1968 to section 20(2) of that Act, and the reference in section 28(2) of the Rent Act 1965 to section 3(2) of that Act, shall be construed as a reference to this subsection ; and

(b) in relation to any statutory period of the new tenancy subsection (1) of this section and the Schedule to this Act shall have effect as if it were a statutory period of the first-mentioned tenancy.

(3) The provisions of subsection (1) of this section apply in every case, except—

(a) where the rent is registered as mentioned in paragraph 1, 6 or 8 of Schedule 3 to the Housing Act 1969 or paragraph 1, 6 or 8 of Schedule 4 to the Housing (Scotland) Act 1969 ; or

(b) where the rent is registered on an application made under section 45(4) of the Rent Act 1968 or paragraph 16 of Schedule 3 to the Rent Act 1965 (certificates of fair rent) and is so registered otherwise than in substitution for a rent with respect to which the provisions of subsection (1) of this section apply ; or

(c) where the rent is registered (by virtue of paragraph 5 of Schedule 9 to the Housing Act 1969) under section 49 of the Rent Act 1968 (dwellings improved under repealed enactments) ; or

(d) where the regulated tenancy is one which has arisen by virtue of Part I of the Landlord and Tenant Act 1954 on the termination of a long tenancy and the rent is registered while the rent for the dwelling continues to be that last payable under the long tenancy.

6.—(1) In the application of this Part of this Act to England and Wales, " notice of increase " means a notice of increase under section 22(2) of the Rent Act 1968 and other expressions shall be construed as in that Act.

PART II

1965 c. 75.

(2) In the application of this Part of this Act to Scotland, " notice of increase " means a notice of increase under section 7 of the Rent Act 1965 and other expressions shall be construed as in that Act.

1968 c. 23.

(3) The power to make regulations under section 50 of the Rent Act 1968 for the purposes of Part IV of that Act shall extend to this Part of this Act in its application to England and Wales.

(4) The power to make regulations under section 46 of the Rent Act 1965 for the purposes of that Act shall extend to this Part of this Act in its application to Scotland.

PART III

GENERAL

Short title, commencement and extent.

7.—(1) This Act may be cited as the Rent (Control of Increases) Act 1969.

(2) This Act shall come into force on 1st January 1970.

(3) This Act does not extend to Northern Ireland.

SCHEDULE

PHASING OF RENT INCREASES

Period of delay

1. The period of delay with respect to any rent shall be—

   (*a*) if the rent is registered in the year 1970, a period of two years ;

   (*b*) if the rent is registered in the year 1971, a period of one year ;

ginning with the date on which the rent is registered.

Permitted increases

2.—(1) The rent for any rental period may be increased to the gregate of the following : —

   (*a*) the amount of the previous limit, calculated in accordance with paragraph 3 of this Schedule ; and

   (*b*) the amount (if any) apportioned to services in accordance with paragraph 4 of this Schedule ; and

   (*c*) the appropriate proportion of the difference between the registered rent and the aggregate of the amounts specified in paragraphs (*a*) and (*b*) above.

(2) The appropriate proportion mentioned in sub-paragraph (1)(*c*) this paragraph is—

   (*a*) one-third if the rental period begins in the first year of the period of delay ; and

   (*b*) (in a case where the period of delay is two years) two-thirds if the rental period begins in the second year of the period of delay.

(3) Notwithstanding anything in the preceding provisions of this iragraph, the amount to which the rent for any rental period may ɛ increased shall not in any case be less than seven shillings and xpence a week above the following, that is to say,—

   (*a*) if the rental period begins in the first year of the period of delay, the aggregate of the amounts specified in sub-paragraphs (1)(*a*) and (1)(*b*) of this paragraph ;

   (*b*) if, in a case where the period of delay is two years, the rental period begins in the second year, the amount to which the rent for a rental period beginning in the first year could be increased ;

ıt nothing in this paragraph shall be taken to enable the rent to be creased above the amount registered.

Previous limit

3.—(1) For the purposes of this Schedule the previous limit of a nt shall be taken to be, subject to sub-paragraph (2) of this para-ʻaph, the amount which at the date of registration was recoverable y way of rent or would have been so recoverable if all notices of increase authorised by the Rent Act 1965, the Rent Act 1968 or regulations under section 9 of the Prices and Incomes Act 1968 had been served.

(2) Where the rent includes an amount payable in respect of rates, the amount so payable, ascertained in accordance with Schedule 4 to the Rent Act 1968, or in accordance with Schedule 2 to the Rent Act 1957 as applied by section 47(2) of the Rent Act 1965, shall be deducted from the amount specified in sub-paragraph (1) of this paragraph in calculating the previous limit of the rent.

Amount to be apportioned to services

4.—(1) Where the registered rent includes a payment in respect of services provided by the landlord or a superior landlord, then if—

    (*a*) the rent is not registered as a variable rent in accordance with section 47(4) of the Rent Act 1968 or section 28(3) of the Rent Act 1965; but

    (*b*) not less than 10 per cent. of the amount of the registered rent is in the opinion of the rent officer or rent assessment committee fairly attributable to the provision of the services;

the amount so attributable shall be noted in the register.

(2) Where it appears to the rent officer or rent assessment committee that some amount was in the previous limit attributable to the provision of services by the landlord or a superior landlord and was less than the amount noted in pursuance of sub-paragraph (1) of this paragraph, then—

    (*a*) if the amount so attributable can be ascertained the difference between it and the amount so noted shall be the amount apportioned to the services ;

    (*b*) if the amount so attributable cannot be ascertained it shall be taken to be an amount bearing to the previous limit the same proportion as the amount noted in pursuance of sub-paragraph (1) of this paragraph bears to the amount of the registered rent, and the difference between the amount so taken and the amount so noted shall be the amount apportioned to the services ;

and the amount apportioned to the services in accordance with this sub-paragraph shall also be noted in the register.

(3) Where it appears to the rent officer or rent assessment committee that no amount was in the previous limit attributable to the provision of services by the landlord or a superior landlord, the amount noted in pursuance of sub-paragraph (1) of this paragraph shall be the amount apportioned to the services and shall be noted as such in the register.

Successive rents

5. Where the provisions of section 5(1) of this Act apply with respect to the rent for a dwelling (in this paragraph referred to as the first rent) and, during the period of delay, a higher rent for the

dwelling is registered with respect to which those provisions also
apply, then if—

    (*a*) the higher rent is registered on an application made under
section 45(4) of the Rent Act 1968 or paragraph 16 of
Schedule 3 to the Rent Act 1965 (certificates of fair rent) ;
or

    (*b*) the whole of the difference between the first rent and the
higher rent is apportioned to services ;

the rent for any statutory period beginning after the registration of
the higher rent may be increased to an amount arrived at by adding
the difference between that rent and the first rent to the amount to
which the rent for that period could have been increased had the
first rent remained registered.

Adjustment for rental periods of different lengths

6. In ascertaining for the purposes of this Schedule whether there
is any difference between amounts or what that difference is such
adjustments shall be made as may be necessary to take account of
periods of different lengths ; and for that purpose a month shall be
treated as one twelfth and a week as one fifty-second of a year.

Substitution of rent determined by rent assessment committee

7. Where a rent determined by a rent assessment committee is
registered in substitution for a rent determined by the rent officer,
the preceding provisions of this Schedule shall have effect as if only
the rent determined by the rent assessment committee had been
registered ; but the date of registration shall be deemed for the
purposes of section 5 of this Act and of this Schedule (but not for
the purposes of section 22(3) of the Rent Act 1968 or section 7(*b*)
of the Rent Act 1965) to be the date on which the rent determined
by the rent officer was registered.

Procedural provisions

8. Any amount to be noted in the register in pursuance of paragraph 4 of this Schedule as an amount fairly attributable to the
provision of services shall be included among the matters to be
specified in an application for the registration, and any such amount
and any amount to be so noted as an amount apportioned to the
services shall be included among the matters with respect to which
representations may be made or consultations are to be held or
notices to be given under Schedule 6 to the Rent Act 1968 or under
paragraphs 4 to 12 of Schedule 3 to the Rent Act 1965.

Police Act 1969

1969 CHAPTER 63

An Act to enable assistance to be given to the Royal Ulster Constabulary by home police forces and empower the Parliament of Northern Ireland to enable assistance to be given to home police forces by the Royal Ulster Constabulary; to make provision in connection with the giving of assistance to home police forces by the Royal Ulster Constabulary; to establish a Police Council for the United Kingdom in place of the Police Council for Great Britain; and to enable certain police pensions regulations to be made with retrospective effect and alter the mode of exercising parliamentary control of the power to make them.

[11th December 1969]

BE IT ENACTED by the Queen's most Excellent Majesty, by and with the advice and consent of the Lords Spiritual and Temporal, and Commons, in this present Parliament assembled, and by the authority of the same, as follows:—

Aid by home police forces of the Royal Ulster Constabulary and vice versa

1829 c. 44.
1839 c. xciv.
1964 c. 48.
1967 c. 77.

1.—(1) The chief officer of police of a police force maintained under the Metropolitan Police Act 1829, the Act of the second and third years of Queen Victoria intituled " An Act for regulating the Police in the City of London " (commonly known as the City of London Police Act 1839), the Police Act 1964 or the Police (Scotland) Act 1967 (hereafter in this Act referred to as a " home police force ") may, on the application of the Inspector General of the Royal Ulster Constabulary or of such other person as may be designated for the purposes of this subsection by order of the Secretary of State, provide constables or other assistance for the purpose of enabling the last-mentioned force to meet a special demand on its resources.

(2) The Secretary of State, if satisfied by the Minister of Home Affairs for Northern Ireland that it is expedient in the interests of public safety or order that the Royal Ulster Constabulary should be reinforced or should receive other assistance for the purpose of enabling it to meet a special demand on its resources and that satisfactory arrangements under the foregoing sub-section cannot be made or cannot be made in time, may, at his request, direct the chief officer of a home police force to provide such constables or other assistance for that purpose as may be specified in the direction.

(3) A constable shall, during any period during which he is provided under this section for the assistance of the Royal Ulster Constabulary be under the like direction and control as a member of that force notwithstanding section 5(1) of the Police Act 1964 or section 17(2) of the Police (Scotland) Act 1967 (controlling powers of chief constables).

1964 c. 48.
1967 c. 77.

(4) An enactment of the Parliament of Northern Ireland which makes provision for the Royal Ulster Constabulary to assist a home police force shall be deemed to be within the powers of that Parliament notwithstanding anything in the Government of Ireland Act 1920.

1920 c. 67.

2.—(1) The following provisions shall have effect with respect to a member (other than the chief officer) of a home police force who, with the consent of the appropriate authority and the Secretary of State, engages for a period of service in the Royal Ulster Constabulary, namely:—

Provisions for facilitating the engagement of members of home police forces for periods of service in the Royal Ulster Constabulary.

(*a*) during that period (or if, during the course thereof, he is dismissed from the Royal Ulster Constabulary or is required to resign as an alternative to dismissal, during such part of that period as ends when he is dismissed or required to resign) he shall, except for the purpose of his being promoted in his home force, be treated as if he were not a member thereof; and

(*b*) he shall, when, by virtue of the foregoing paragraph, he ceases (except for the purpose aforesaid) to be treated as if he were not a member of his home force, be entitled to revert to that force—

(i) if he has not been promoted in that force during his period of service in the Royal Ulster Constabulary, in the rank in which he was serving immediately before he engaged for a period of service in the last-mentioned force;

(ii) if he has been so promoted, in the rank to which he has been promoted.

3 H

(2) Where, in the case of a person to whom the foregoing subsection applies, the period of service in the Royal Ulster Constabulary for which he engages is, with the consent of the appropriate authority and the Secretary of State, extended or curtailed, paragraph (*a*) of that subsection shall have effect in relation to him as if, for the references to that period, there were substituted references, as the case requires, to the extended period or the curtailed period.

(3) A person to whom subsection (1) above applies who is dismissed or required to resign as mentioned in paragraph (*a*) of that subsection shall, for the purposes of the Police (Discipline) Regulations, be deemed to have committed, as a member of his home force, an offence against discipline, and may be dealt with under those Regulations accordingly; and for the purposes of this subsection a certificate that such a person has been so dismissed or required to resign, being a certificate given by or on behalf of the Inspector General of the Royal Ulster Constabulary or such other person, or such authority, as may be designated for the purposes of this subsection by order of the Secretary of State, shall be evidence (and, in Scotland, sufficient evidence) of that fact.

1964 c. 48.   (4) Paragraph 2 of Schedule 4 to the Police Act 1964 (which, in a case where, at a time when a member of a police force in England or Wales is on central service or is serving overseas, that force is amalgamated with another, converts his right of reversion to his force into a right of reversion to the amalgamated force) shall have effect as if, after sub-paragraph (*b*) thereof, there were inserted the following words—

" or

(*c*) section 2 of the Police Act 1969 ",

1967 c. 77.   and section 24(1) of the Police (Scotland) Act 1967 (which makes similar provision in the case of a member of a police force in Scotland) shall have effect as if, after paragraph (*b*) thereof, there were inserted the same words.

(5) In this section—

    (*a*) " appropriate authority ", in relation to a member of a home police force, other than an assistant chief constable or a deputy chief constable, means the chief officer of that force acting with the consent of the police authority therefor and, in the case of an assistant chief constable or deputy chief constable of such a force, means that authority;

    (*b*) " Police (Discipline) Regulations " means, in relation to a police force within the meaning of the Police Act 1964, the regulations relating to discipline for the time being in force under section 33 of that Act and, in

relation to a police force within the meaning of the
Police (Scotland) Act 1967, the regulations relating to 1967 c. 77.
discipline for the time being in force under section 26
of that Act.

3.—(1) Where, under arrangements authorised by, or in Provisions
compliance with directions given under, an enactment of the with respect
Parliament of Northern Ireland, a member of the Royal Ulster to aid given
Constabulary is provided for the purpose of enabling a home to a home
police force to meet a special demand on its resources, he shall, by the Royal
while serving with that force— Ulster
Constabulary.
    (*a*) be under the direction and control of the chief officer
        thereof; and

    (*b*) have in any place the like (if any) powers and privileges
        as a member of that force has therein as a constable.

(2) The police authority maintaining a police force for which
assistance is provided under such arrangements, or in compliance
with such directions, as are mentioned in the foregoing subsection,
shall pay, to such authority in Northern Ireland as may be
designated for the purposes of this subsection by order of the
Secretary of State, such contribution as may be agreed between
the police authority and the authority so designated or as may,
in default of agreement, be determined jointly by the Secretary
of State and the Minister of Home Affairs for Northern Ireland.

4.—(1) For the consideration, by persons representing the The Police
interests of the authorities who between them maintain the home Council
police forces and the Royal Ulster Constabulary and those of for the
the persons who are members of home police forces or of that Kingdom.
Constabulary or are police cadets, of questions relating to hours
of duty, leave, pay and allowances, pensions or the issue, use and
return of police clothing, personal equipment and accoutrements,
there shall be a council, to be known as the Police Council for
the United Kingdom, which shall be established in accordance
with such arrangements made after consultations between the
Secretary of State and organisations representing those interests
as appear to him to be satisfactory.

(2) The arrangements shall regulate the procedure for reaching
agreement on a recommendation to be made by the Council for
the purposes of subsection (4) of this section and shall include
provision for arriving at such a recommendation by arbitration
in such circumstances as may be determined by or under the
arrangements.

(3) The Secretary of State may, out of moneys provided by
Parliament, defray any expenses incurred by the Council.

(4) Before making, with respect to any of the matters mentioned in subsection (1) above (other than pensions),—

1964 c. 48.
    (*a*) regulations under section 33 or 35 of the Police Act 1964;

1967 c. 77.
    (*b*) regulations under section 26 or 27 of the Police (Scotland) Act 1967 (other than regulations relating to special constables); or

1836 c. 13.
1919 c. 68.
    (*c*) rules, orders or regulations under section 6 of the Constabulary (Ireland) Act 1836 or orders under subsection (1) of section 4 of the Constabulary and Police (Ireland) Act 1919;

the Secretary of State or, as the case may be, the Minister of Home Affairs for Northern Ireland, shall take into consideration any recommendation made by the Police Council for the United Kingdom and furnish the Council with a draft of the regulations, rules or orders.

1948 c. 24.
(5) The Police Council for the United Kingdom shall be taken to be the Police Council referred to in section 1(1) of the Police Pensions Act 1948; and—

    (*a*) no regulations relating to pensions shall be made under section 35 of the Police Act 1964 or section 27 of the Police (Scotland) Act 1967 by the Secretary of State except after consultation with that Council; and

    (*b*) no order so relating shall be made under subsection (1) of section 4 of the Constabulary and Police (Ireland) Act 1919 by the Minister of Home Affairs for Northern Ireland except after the like consultation.

(6) Section 46(3) of the Police Act 1964 (which requires that, before making regulations under section 33 or 35 of that Act, other than regulations to which subsection (4) of section 45 of that Act applies, the Secretary of State shall furnish a draft of the regulations to the Police Advisory Board for England and Wales and take into consideration any representations made by that Board) shall have effect with the substitution, for the words " other than regulations to which subsection (4) of section 45 of this Act applies ", of the words " other than regulations with respect to any of the matters mentioned in section 4(1) of the Police Act 1969 "; and section 26(9) of the Police (Scotland) Act 1967 (which requires that, before making regulations under that section, other than regulations in relation to the making of which subsection (8) of that section applies, the Secretary of State shall submit a draft either to the Police Advisory Board for Scotland or to the three central committees of the Police Federation for Scotland sitting together as a joint committee and to such bodies or associations as appear to him to be representative of police authorities, chief constables and superintendents, including chief superintendents, respectively,

and shall consider any representations made as to the draft by that Board or, as the case may be, by the joint committee or any of those bodies or associations) shall have effect with the substitution, for the words " other than regulations in relation to the making of which subsection (8) of this section applies " of the words " other than regulations with respect to any of the matters mentioned in section 4(1) of the Police Act 1969 ".

(7) The references in subsections (4) and (5) above to sub-section (1) of section 4 of the Constabulary and Police (Ireland) 1919 c. 68 Act 1919 shall be construed as including references to that sub-section as amended or re-enacted (with or without modification) by any enactment of the Parliament of Northern Ireland and the reference in subsection (4) above to section 6 of the Con- 1836 c. 13. stabulary (Ireland) Act 1836 shall be similarly construed.

(8) Upon the establishment of the Police Council for the United Kingdom, the Police Council for Great Britain established under section 45 of the Police Act 1964 shall cease to exist and 1964 c. 48. the following provisions shall cease to have effect, namely:—

 (*a*) that section; and

 (*b*) in the Police (Scotland) Act 1967, in section 26, sub- 1967 c. 77. section (8), in section 27(3) the words " (8) and " and, in Schedule 4, the third paragraph under the heading " The Police Act 1964 ".

5.—(1) Regulations made under section 1 of the Police Power to give Pensions Act 1948 may, if the instrument containing them retrospective satisfies the condition that it is made before the expiration of effect to the period of twelve months beginning with the day on which certain police this Act is passed and either states that it is made in consequence pensions of the enactment of section 2 of this Act or states that it is made regulations, in consequence of the enactment by the Parliament of Northern and Ireland of provisions relating to the Royal Ulster Constabulary, parliamentary be made so as to take effect from such day, whether before or after control of the the making of the regulations, as may be specified therein, not power to being earlier than the day on which this Act is passed. make them.
1948 c. 24.

(2) Subsection (7) of section 1 of the Police Pensions Act 1948 (which provides that regulations made under that section shall not be made unless a draft thereof has been laid before Parliament and approved by resolution of each House) shall not apply to regulations so made contained in an instrument that satisfies the condition mentioned in the foregoing subsection, but the instrument shall be subject to annulment in pursuance of a resolution of either House of Parliament.

6. A power conferred by this Act to make an order shall be Orders. exercisable by statutory instrument, and a power conferred by any of the foregoing provisions of this Act to make an order shall be construed as including a power, exercisable in the like manner, to vary or revoke the order.

Short title and commencement.

7.—(1) This Act may be cited as the Police Act 1969.

(2) This Act shall come into operation on such day as the Secretary of State may by order appoint; and different days may be appointed for different provisions.

Customs (Import Deposits) Act 1969

1969 CHAPTER 64

An Act to extend for one year the period for which the duty imposed by the Customs (Import Deposits) Act 1968 may remain in force subject to the like exemptions and reliefs as were provided for by that Act, but to reduce the amount of that duty from fifty per cent. to forty per cent. of the value of the goods on which it is charged.   [11th December 1969]

Most Gracious Sovereign,

WE, Your Majesty's most dutiful and loyal subjects, the Commons of the United Kingdom in Parliament assembled, towards raising the necessary supplies to defray Your Majesty's public expenses, and making an addition to the public revenue, have freely and voluntarily resolved to give and grant unto Your Majesty the duties hereinafter mentioned; and do therefore most humbly beseech Your Majesty that it may be enacted by the Queen's most Excellent Majesty, by and with the advice and consent of the Lords Spiritual and Temporal, and Commons, in this present Parliament assembled, and by the authority of the same, as follows:—

1.—(1) In section 3(4) of the Customs (Import Deposits) Act 1968 (which provides that duty under section 1 of that Act shall cease to be in force at the expiration of a period of one year beginning with the date on which that Act was passed) for the words " one year " there shall be substituted the words " two years "; but, as from 5th December 1969, in subsection (1) of the said section 1 (which provides that the duty shall be fifty per cent. of the value of the goods on which it is charged) for the words " fifty per cent." there shall be substituted the words " forty per cent.". *Amendments of Customs (Import Deposits) Act 1968.*

1968 c. 74.

S.I. 1958/1976. (2) The reference in paragraph 7(1) of Schedule 2 to the said Act of 1968 to the Import Duty Reliefs (No. 4) Order 1958 shall be construed as including, and as having always included, a reference to so much of any subsequent order as re-enacts the provisions of the said Order of 1958 with or without modification.

Short title
and extent.

2.—(1) This Act may be cited as the Customs (Import Deposits) Act 1969.

(2) It is hereby declared that this Act extends to Northern Ireland.

Ulster Defence Regiment Act 1969

1969 CHAPTER 65

An Act to establish the Ulster Defence Regiment and for purposes connected therewith.   [18th December 1969]

B E IT ENACTED by the Queen's most Excellent Majesty, by and with the advice and consent of the Lords Spiritual and Temporal, and Commons, in this present Parliament assembled, and by the authority of the same, as follows:—

1.—(1) It shall be lawful for Her Majesty to establish and maintain a force to be called the Ulster Defence Regiment (hereafter in this Act referred to as " the force ") consisting of such number as may from time to time be determined by Parliament of such men as may voluntarily undertake to serve therein and as may be accepted for such service.

Establishment and status of Ulster Defence Regiment.

(2) Members of the force shall be members of the armed forces of the Crown; and—

(a) any holder of a land forces commission who is for the time being assigned for duty with the force, and any other member of the force when serving on the permanent staff of the force, shall be subject to military law;

(b) any member of the force to whom paragraph (a) of this subsection does not apply shall be subject to military law—

(i) at all times when called out for service under section 2 of this Act or when undergoing training whether in pursuance of an obligation under that section or not; and

(ii) at any other time when he is in possession, or when, in pursuance of any order given or permission granted by a superior officer of his, he is required or authorised to be in possession, of any arms or ammunition or of any prescribed description of equipment, being arms, ammunition or equipment belonging to Her Majesty.

1955 c. 18.

(3) References in Parts II to V of the Army Act 1955 to the regular forces shall include references to members of the force while subject to military law but save as aforesaid references in that Act to the regular forces shall not include references to the force.

(4) The following provisions shall have effect as to the enrolment, re-engagement and resignation of members of the force otherwise than as officers thereof, namely—

    (*a*) a person volunteering and accepted for service in the force shall be enrolled for a prescribed period not exceeding three years;

    (*b*) a member of the force may, if he so desires and is accepted for re-engagement, re-engage from time to time for a further such period;

    (*c*) a member of the force may if he so desires cease to be a member thereof upon the expiration of one month's notice of his desire so to cease given in writing to his commanding officer;

but a person shall not cease to be a member of the force by virtue of paragraph (*a*), (*b*) or (*c*) of this subsection if immediately before the expiration of the period for which he was enrolled, or the period for which he re-engaged, or the period of his notice, as the case may be, he is on permanent service in pursuance of section 2(3) or (4) of this Act.

(5) Subject to the provisions of subsection (4) of this section, the conditions for the acceptance of persons as members of the force and the conditions of service of members thereof (including conditions as to pay, allowances and pensions or other grants in respect of death or disablement) shall be such as may be prescribed; and orders or regulations shall make provision for the organisation, administration, government and duties of the force, but shall not require members of the force to give whole-time service except during any period during which the force or the part of it to which they belong is called out under subsection (2), (3) or (4), or they are undergoing training under paragraph (*a*) of subsection (5), of section 2 of this Act and shall not require members of the force to serve or train outside Northern Ireland.

1948 c. 21.

(6) Section 3(1) of the Army and Air Force (Women's Service) Act 1948 (which provides for the application to women of certain enactments relating to men) shall not apply to this Act.

Liabilities for service and training.

2.—(1) The Secretary of State may grant authority in writing to any designated officer of the regular forces within the meaning of the Army Act 1955 of a rank not lower than major to exercise the powers conferred by subsection (2) of this section with or without authority for that officer in turn to authorise any other officer designated by him, being such an officer of the regular forces as aforesaid, to exercise those powers; and any authorisation in pursuance of this subsection may be given either in general terms or subject to specified limitations.

(2) Any officer authorised in accordance with subsection (1) of this section to exercise the powers conferred by this subsection may, subject to the terms of his authority, call out the force or any part of it for emergency service in Northern Ireland if, and for so long as, it appears to that officer to be necessary or expedient for the defence of life or property in Northern Ireland against armed attack or sabotage, whether actual or apprehended.

(3) The force shall be liable to be called out for permanent service in Northern Ireland in defence of the United Kingdom against actual or apprehended attack; and this subsection shall be a relevant enactment within the meaning of section 9 of the Reserve Forces Act 1966 (which relates to call-out notices).   1966 c. 30.

(4) An order under section 5(1) of the said Act of 1966 (which relates to the calling out of reserves where it appears to Her Majesty that national danger is imminent or that a great emergency has arisen) may authorise the calling out of the force for permanent service in Northern Ireland; and, for the purposes of this subsection, the said section 9 shall apply as if the force were a reserve force within the meaning of the said section 5.

(5) Subject to subsection (6) of this section any member of the force may, in accordance with regulations, be required to undergo training in Northern Ireland in any year—

(*a*) for one or more periods which shall not exceed twelve days in the aggregate and of which—

(i) none shall exceed eight consecutive days; and

(ii) except with his consent, not more than two shall exceed thirty-six consecutive hours; and

(*b*) for such other periods as may be prescribed, none of which shall except with his consent exceed two hours,

and may while so undergoing training be attached to and trained with any body of Her Majesty's forces which is for the time being in Northern Ireland.

(6) Regulations may make provision—

(*a*) for securing that subsection (5) of this section shall not apply to persons of such descriptions as may be prescribed to whom but for the regulations that subsection would apply;

(*b*) for relaxing, in such cases as may be prescribed, the liability imposed by the said subsection (5) on members of the force.

(7) Where any person is, or is liable to be, called out under subsection (2), (3) or (4) of this section, the provisions of the Reinstatement in Civil Employment Act 1950 shall apply to that person as they apply to a person who has entered, or, as the case may be, may be required to enter, upon a period of whole-time service in the armed forces of the Crown in the circumstances mentioned in section 1(*a*) of that Act; and any service rendered by virtue of the said subsection (2), (3) or (4), and any continuous period of training of seven days or longer performed as a member of the force, whether in pursuance of an obligation under subsection (5) of this section or under voluntary arrangements, shall be relevant service within the meaning of the Reserve and Auxiliary Forces (Protection of Civil Interests) Act 1951; and, in the application of this subsection to Northern Ireland, references to the said Act of 1950 or 1951 shall be construed as references to that Act as it applies in Northern Ireland.

1950 c. 10.

1951 c. 65.

Punishment for certain offences.

3.—(1) Any member of the force who—

(*a*) when required by or in pursuance of regulations under section 2(5) of this Act to attend at any place fails without reasonable excuse to attend in accordance with the requirement, or

(*b*) fails without reasonable excuse to comply with orders or regulations made under this Act,

shall, whether otherwise subject to military law or not, be guilty of an offence and liable on conviction by court-martial to a fine not exceeding £5; and the offence shall, for all purposes of and incidental to the trial of the offender, including the summary disposal of the case otherwise than by court-martial, be deemed to be an offence under the Army Act 1955.

1955 c. 18.

(2) Any person who, in Northern Ireland or elsewhere—

(*a*) procures or persuades any member of the force to desert within the meaning of section 37 of the Army Act 1955 or to absent himself without leave; or

(*b*) knowing that any member of the force is about to desert as aforesaid or to absent himself without leave, assists him in so doing; or

(*c*) knowing any person to be a deserter within the meaning of the said section 37 or an absentee without leave from the force, procures or persuades or assists him to remain such a deserter or absentee, or assists in his rescue from custody,

shall be liable on summary conviction to a fine not exceeding £50 or to imprisonment for a term not exceeding three months or to both, or on conviction on indictment to a fine not exceeding £500 or to imprisonment for a term not exceeding two years or to both.

4.—(1) In this Act—

   (*a*) the expression " prescribed " means prescribed by orders or regulations;

   (*b*) except in section 6(2), references to orders are references to orders of Her Majesty signified under the hand of the Secretary of State; and

   (*c*) references to regulations are references to regulations made by the Secretary of State.

Orders and regulations.

(2) Any power conferred by this Act to make an order shall include power to vary or revoke an order.

(3) Any order or regulations made under this Act shall be laid before Parliament after being made.

5. Any expenditure incurred by any government department which is attributable to the provisions of this Act shall be defrayed out of moneys provided by Parliament.

Expenses.

6.—(1) This Act may be cited as the Ulster Defence Regiment Act 1969.

(2) This Act shall come into force on such date as the Secretary of State may by order made by statutory instrument appoint.

Short title and commence-ment.

1969 No. 1

A MEASURE passed by the National Assembly of the Church of England to amend the Clergy Pensions Measure 1961 in respect of the entitlement to pension and rate of pension of clerks in Holy Orders who retire before the retiring age.   [25th July 1969]

1. Section 1(1)(*c*) of the Clergy Pensions Measure 1961 and Part III of Schedule 1 to that Measure (which relate to entitlement to pension and rate of pension of clerks in Holy Orders retiring before the retiring age) shall each be amended by substituting for the words " but not more than five years before he would have attained that age " the words " but not before attaining pensionable age within the meaning of the enactments relating to national insurance as for the time in force ". *Amendment of Clergy Pensions Measure 1961 in respect of clerks retiring before the retiring age. 1961 No. 3.*

2.—(1) This Measure may be cited as the Clergy Pensions (Amendment) Measure 1969. *Short title and citation.*

(2) The Clergy Pensions Measure 1961, the Clergy Pensions (Amendment) Measure 1967 and this Measure may be cited together as the Clergy Pensions Measures 1961 to 1969. *1967 No. 1*

1969 No. 2

A MEASURE passed by The National Assembly of the Church of England to provide for the vesting by Canon of the functions, authority, rights and privileges of the Convocations of Canterbury and York in the General Synod of the Church of England, and for the modification by Canon of the functions of the said Convocations when sitting separately for their provinces; to rename and reconstitute the Church Assembly as the General Synod, and to make further provision for the synodical government of the Church of England, and for purposes connected with the matters aforesaid.
[25th July 1969]

WHEREAS the Convocations of Canterbury and York, on the 8th day of October 1968, resolved that the functions, authority, rights and privileges of the said Convocations should, by Canons made by them with Her Majesty's Licence and Assent, vest in the Church Assembly to be renamed and reconstituted as the General Synod of the Church of England.

AND WHEREAS it is expedient to give effect to the said resolution and to bring to an end the present dual exercise of functions by the Church Assembly and the Convocations, and to provide a system of synodical government for the Church of England.

1.—(1) It shall be lawful for the Convocations of Canterbury and York to submit for Her Majesty's Licence and Assent Canons in the form set out in Schedule 1 to this Measure providing—

Vesting of functions and authority of Convocations in a General Synod.

(a) for vesting in the General Synod of the Church of England, being the Church Assembly renamed and reconstituted in accordance with this Measure, the functions, authority, rights and privileges of the said Convocations:

(b) for modifying the functions of the said Convocations when sitting separately for their provinces;

and, if Her Majesty is pleased to grant Her Licence and Assent, it shall be lawful for the said Convocations to make, promulge and execute the said Canons, which shall have full force and effect.

(2) The functions so vested shall be exercisable in accordance with the Constitution of the General Synod set out in Schedule 2 to this Measure and shall be exercisable for the Church of

England as a whole, instead of being exercisable provincially, but without prejudice to the making of different provision, where appropriate, for the two provinces.

(3) The provisions of sections 1 and 3 of the Submission of the Clergy Act 1533—

1533 c. 19.

(a) requiring the Queen's Assent and Licence to the making, promulging and executing of Canons by the said Convocations, and

(b) providing that no Canons shall be made or put in execution by the said Convocations which are contrary or repugnant to the Royal prerogative or the customs, laws or statutes of this realm,

shall apply in like manner to the making, promulging and executing of Canons by the General Synod.

(4) The dissolution and calling together of the said Convocations in pursuance of the Royal Writ (or otherwise under the Church of England Convocations Act 1966) shall have the effect, in accordance with the said Constitution, of dissolving and bringing into being the General Synod.

1966 c. 2.

(5) The functions vested in the General Synod by the said Canons—

(a) shall include the power of the said Convocations as declared by the Convocations of the Clergy Measure 1920, to make, promulge and execute Canons for the amendment of the Constitution of the Lower Houses thereof ;

1920 No. 1.

(b) shall not include the functions of the said Convocations under the Measures mentioned in section 3 of this Measure, which shall be exercisable in accordance with that section.

Renaming and reconstitution of the Church Assembly as the General Synod.

2.—(1) As from the appointed day, the Church Assembly shall be renamed the General Synod of the Church of England (and may be referred to as " the General Synod ") and shall be reconstituted in accordance with the Constitution of the General Synod set out in Schedule 2 to this Measure.

1919 c. 76.

(2) References in sections 3 and 4 of the Church of England Assembly (Powers) Act 1919 and in other Measures, enactments and instruments to the Church Assembly and to its Constitution and Legislative Committee shall, as from the appointed day, be construed as references or, where the contexts so require, as including references to the General Synod and its Constitution and the Legislative Committee appointed thereunder, respectively, and any definitions of the said expressions and of " the National Assembly of the Church of England " in section 1

of the said Act and in the Interpretation Measure 1925 shall 1925 No. 1.
cease to apply or be limited to the said contexts.

3.—(1) The powers of the Convocations of Canterbury and Functions
York to approve forms of Service with the agreement of the under the
House of Laity under section 1 of the Prayer Book (Alternative Prayer Book
and Other Services) Measure 1965, and the powers of the Measures and
Convocations and the House of Laity to extend or renew the tical Jurisdic-
period of use of any such form of Service, shall be exercisable by tion Measure.
the General Synod with a majority in each House thereof of not 1965 No. 1.
less than two-thirds of those present and voting, and the said
section shall take effect accordingly with the necessary
modifications.

(2) The powers of the said Convocations to approve forms of
Service under section 2 of the said Measure shall be exercisable
by the General Synod, but the powers to approve forms of
Service under section 4(1) thereof and to make regulations
under section 4(2) and section 6 thereof shall continue to be
exercisable by the said Convocations for their respective
provinces.

(3) The powers of the said Convocations to give directions
under section 1(2) of the Prayer Book (Miscellaneous Provisions) 1965 No. 3.
Measure 1965, shall continue to be exercisable by them for their
respective provinces.

(4) The powers exercisable by the said Convocations with
the concurrence of the House of Laity under the Prayer Book 1965 No. 4.
(Versions of the Bible) Measure 1965 shall be exercisable by the
General Synod.

(5) The powers exercisable by the said Convocations with the
concurrence of the Church Assembly under section 2(1) of
the Prayer Book (Further Provisions) Measure 1968, and the 1968 No. 2.
powers exercisable by the said Convocations with the concurrence of the House of Laity under section 4 of the said
Measure, shall be exercisable by the General Synod.

(6) The powers exercisable by the said Convocations or the
Houses thereof under the Ecclesiastical Jurisdiction Measure 1963 No. 1.
1963 shall continue to be exercisable by them for their respective
provinces.

(7) Section 1(2) of this Measure shall apply to the functions
exercisable by the General Synod under this section, and accordingly the exercise of those functions shall be subject, in particular,
to Article 7 of the Constitution of the General Synod.

(8) This section shall have effect as from the appointed day,

Constitution
and functions
of Diocesan
Synods.

4.—(1) Diocesan synods shall be constituted for all dioceses in accordance with Part IV of the Church Representation Rules contained in Schedule 3 to this Measure and the transitional provisions contained in Schedule 4.

(2) The functions of the diocesan synod shall be—

(*a*) to consider matters concerning the Church of England and to make provision for such matters in relation to their diocese, and to consider and express their opinion on any other matters of religious or public interest ;

(*b*) to advise the bishop on any matters on which he may consult the synod ;

(*c*) to consider and express their opinion on any matters referred to them by the General Synod, and in particular to approve or disapprove provisions referred to them by the General Synod under Article 8 of the Constitution :

Provided that the functions referred to in paragraph (*a*) hereof shall not include the issue of any statement purporting to declare the doctrine of the Church on any question.

(3) It shall be the duty of the bishop to consult with the diocesan synod on matters of general concern and importance to the diocese.

(4) Except as may be provided by standing orders or directions of the diocesan synod, the advisory and consultative functions of the synod under subsections (2)(*b*) and (3) of this section may be discharged on behalf of the synod by the bishops council and standing committee appointed in accordance with rule 28 of the Church Representation Rules contained in Schedule 3 to this Measure, but either the bishop or the body so appointed may require any matter to be referred to the synod.

(5) The diocesan synod shall keep the deanery synods of the diocese informed of the policies and problems of the diocese and of the business which is to come before meetings of the diocesan synod, and may delegate executive functions to deanery synods ; and shall keep themselves informed, through the deanery synods, of events and opinion in the parishes, and shall give opportunities for discussing at meetings of the diocesan synod matters raised by deanery synods and parochial church councils.

(6) The General Synod may by Canon or Regulation extend, amend or further define the functions of diocesan synods, and if any question arises as to whether any matter falls within the functions of a diocesan synod as laid down by subsection (2) of this section or any such Canon or Regulation relating to that subsection, it shall be decided by the bishop.

(7) As soon as a diocesan synod has been constituted, the diocesan conference shall be dissolved and all functions exercisable by the diocesan conference shall be transferred to the diocesan synod, and any reference in any Measure or instrument to diocesan conferences shall be construed as references to diocesan synods:

Provided that nothing herein shall prevent the bishop from summoning a conference of persons appearing to him to be representative of the clergy and laity of the diocese, on such occasions and for such purposes as he thinks fit.

5.—(1) Deanery synods shall be constituted for all deaneries Constitution in accordance with Part III of the Church Representation Rules and functions contained in Schedule 3 to this Measure and the transitional of Deanery provisions contained in Schedule 4. Synods.

(2) Deanery synods shall, as soon as they are constituted, take the place of ruri-decanal conferences where they exist, and those conferences shall thereupon be dissolved, and any references in any Measure to ruri-decanal conferences shall be construed as references to deanery synods.

(3) The functions of a deanery synod shall be—
   (*a*) to consider matters concerning the Church of England and to make provision for such matters in relation to their deanery, and to consider and express their opinion on any other matters of religious or public interest;
   (*b*) to bring together the views of the parishes of the deanery on common problems, to discuss and formulate common policies on those problems, to foster a sense of community and interdependence among those parishes, and generally to promote in the deanery the whole mission of the Church, pastoral, evangelistic, social and ecumenical;
   (*c*) to make known and so far as appropriate put into effect any provision made by the diocesan synod;
   (*d*) to consider the business of the diocesan synod, and particularly any matters referred to that synod by the General Synod, and to sound parochial opinion whenever they are required or consider it appropriate to do so;
   (*e*) to raise such matters as the deanery synod consider appropriate with the diocesan synod:

Provided that the functions referred to in paragraph (*a*) hereof shall not include the issue of any statement purporting to declare the doctrine of the Church on any question.

(4) If the diocesan synod delegate to deanery synods functions in relation to the parishes of their deaneries, and in particular

3 I 4

the determination of parochial shares in quotas allocated to the deaneries, the deanery synod shall exercise those functions.

In this subsection " quota " means an amount to be subscribed to the expenditure authorised by diocesan synods.

(5) The General Synod may by Canon or Regulation extend, amend or further define the functions of deanery synods.

Functions of
Parochial
Church
Councils.
1956 No. 3.

6. For section 2 of the Parochial Church Councils (Powers) Measure 1956 (which relates to the general functions of a parochial church council), there shall be substituted the following section: —

"General
functions of
council.

2.—(1) It shall be the duty of the incumbent and the parochial church council to consult together on matters of general concern and importance to the parish.

(2) The functions of parochial church councils shall include—

(*a*) co-operation with the incumbent in promoting in the parish the whole mission of the Church, pastoral, evangelistic, social and ecumenical ;

(*b*) the consideration and discussions of matters concerning the Church of England or any other matters of religious or public interest, but not the declaration of the doctrine of the Church on any question ;

(*c*) making known and putting into effect any provision made by the diocesan synod or the deanery synod, but without prejudice to the powers of the council on any particular matter ;

(*d*) giving advice to the diocesan synod and the deanery synod on any matter referred to the council ;

(*e*) raising such matters as the council consider appropriate with the diocesan synod or deanery synod.

(3) In the exercise of its functions the parochial church council shall take into consideration any expression of opinion by any parochial church meeting.".

Church
Representation
Rules.

7.—(1) The rules contained in Schedule 3 to this Measure, which may be cited as the Church Representation Rules, shall have effect for the purpose of providing for the constitution and proceedings of diocesan and deanery synods and making further provision for the synodical government of the Church, including the matters hitherto provided for by the Rules for the Representation of the Laity:

Provided that the said rules may at any time be amended by a resolution of the General Synod passed by a majority in each House of not less than two-thirds of those present and voting.

(2) The Statutory Instruments Act 1946 shall apply to any such resolution as if it were a statutory instrument and as if this Measure were an Act providing that it should be subject to annulment in pursuance of a resolution of either House of Parliament. 1946 c. 36.

(3) The Representation of the Laity Measure 1956 and the Diocesan Conferences Regulation 1958 shall cease to have effect except as may be temporarily provided by Schedule 4 to this Measure. 1956 No. 2.

8. The transitional provisions contained in Schedule 4 to this Measure shall have effect with respect to matters arising on the transfer of functions from the Convocations, the reconstitution of the Church Assembly as the General Synod, the changes affecting diocesan and ruri-decanal conferences, and the coming into operation of the Church Representation Rules, but nothing in the said Schedule shall be taken as prejudicing section 38 of the Interpretation Act 1889 as applied by the Interpretation Measure 1925. Transitional Provisions.

1889 c. 63.
1925 No. 1.

9.—(1) This Measure may be cited as the Synodical Government Measure 1969. Short title, interpretation and extent.

(2) In this Measure 'the appointed day' means such day as may be appointed by the Archbishops of Canterbury and York, following the completion of the first elections after the passing of this Measure of the Lower Houses of the Convocations and of the House of Laity, and " deanery " means rural deanery.

(3) This Measure shall extend to the Provinces of Canterbury and York, except that it shall only extend to the Isle of Man and the Channel Islands in accordance with the following provisions of this section.

(4) Sections 1, 2 and 3, Schedules 1 and 2, and so much of Schedule 4 as relates to those provisions, shall extend to the Isle of Man and the remainder of the Measure may by Act of Tynwald be extended to the Isle of Man, with such exceptions, adaptations and modifications, if any, as may be specified in such Act.

(5) This Measure may be applied to the Channel Islands or either of them, as defined in the Channel Islands (Church Legislation) Measures 1931 and 1957, in accordance with the pro-visions of those Measures, and any scheme made for the purpose of such application may provide for such modifications of the

1931 No. 5.
1931 No. 4.

Channel Islands (Representation) Measure 1931 and of the said Channel Islands (Church Legislation) Measure 1931 as may be necessary or expedient in consequence of the provisions of this Measure.

SCHEDULES

SCHEDULE 1

FORM OF PROPOSED CANON

Of the General Synod and the Convocations

1. On such day as may be appointed by the Archbishops of Canterbury and York under the Synodical Government Measure 1969, the powers to legislate by Canon and other functions of the Convocation of Canterbury [York], and the authority, rights and privileges of the said Convocation, shall vest in the General Synod of the Church of England, being the Church Assembly renamed and reconstituted by the said Measure.

2. Notwithstanding such vesting as aforesaid, the said Convocation may continue to meet separately, within the province or elsewhere at such places and times as they may determine, for the purpose of considering matters concerning the Church of England and making provision by appropriate instruments for such matters in relation to their province or referring such matters to the General Synod, and shall meet for the purpose of discharging their functions under section 3 of this Measure and their functions under Article 7 of the Constitution of the General Synod in respect of provisions touching doctrinal formulae or the services or ceremonies of the Church of England or the administration of the Sacraments or sacred rites thereof, or to consider any other matter referred to them by the General Synod:

Provided that the power to make provision as aforesaid shall not be exercisable by Canon, and shall (without prejudice to the said Article 7) be exercisable consistently with the exercise of functions by the General Synod and, in the event of any inconsistency, the provision made by the General Synod shall prevail.

3. The said Convocation may, by their Standing Orders or otherwise, make provision for joining to their two Houses, at such sittings and for the purposes of such of their functions as they may determine, a House of Laity composed of—

(*a*) such of the members of the House of Laity of the General Synod as are elected for areas in the province ;

(*b*) such of the ex-officio and co-opted members of the said House as may be allocated to the province for the purposes of this paragraph by the President and the Prolocutor of the Houses of the said Convocation and the Prolocutor and Pro-Prolocutor of the House of Laity of the General Synod ; and

(*c*) the member of the said House chosen by the lay members of religious communities in the said province :

Provided that the House of Laity joined as aforesaid to the two Houses of the said Convocation shall not be given any power to vote on any matter referred to the Convocation under Article 7 of the said Constitution, or any matter in respect of which powers are exercisable by the Convocation in accordance with section 3 of the said Measure.

4. The vesting of rights and privileges of the said Convocation in the General Synod by this Canon shall not affect the right of the said Convocation (which shall be exercisable also by the General Synod) to present addresses to Her Majesty, or the right of the Lower House of the said Convocation to present gravamina to the Upper House thereof.

Section 2.

SCHEDULE 2

Constitution of the General Synod

1. The General Synod shall consist of the Convocations of Canterbury and York joined together in a House of Bishops and a House of Clergy and having added to them a House of Laity.

2. The House of Bishops and the House of Clergy shall accordingly comprise the Upper and the Lower Houses respectively of the said Convocations, and the House of Laity shall be elected and otherwise constituted in accordance with the Church Representation Rules.

3.—(1) The General Synod shall meet in session at least twice a year, and at such times and places as it may provide, or, in the absence of such provision, as the Joint Presidents of the Synod may direct.

(2) The General Synod shall, on the dissolution of the Convocations, itself be automatically dissolved, and shall come into being on the calling together of the new Convocations.

(3) Business pending at the dissolution of the General Synod shall not abate, but may be resumed by the new Synod at the stage reached before the dissolution, and any Boards, Commissions, Committees or other bodies of the Synod may, so far as may be appropriate and subject to any Standing Orders or any directions of the Synod or of the Archbishops of Canterbury and York, continue their proceedings during the period of the dissolution, and all things may be done by the Archbishops or any such bodies or any officers of the General Synod as may be necessary or expedient for conducting the affairs of the Synod during the period of dissolution and for making arrangements for the resumption of business by the new Synod.

(4) A member of the General Synod may continue to act during the period of the dissolution as a member of any such Board, Commission, Committee or body :

Provided that, if a member of the Synod who is an elected proctor of the clergy or an elected member of the House of Laity does not stand for re-election or is not re-elected, this paragraph shall cease to apply to him with effect from the date on which the election of his successor is announced by the presiding officer.

4.—(1) The Archbishops of Canterbury and York shall be joint Presidents of the General Synod, and they shall determine the occasions on which it is desirable that one of the Presidents shall

be the chairman of a meeting of the General Synod, and shall
arrange between them which of them is to take the chair on any
such occasion :

Provided that one of the Presidents shall be the Chairman when
any motion is taken for the final approval of a provision to which
Article 7 of this Constitution applies and in such other cases as may
be provided in Standing Orders.

(2) The Presidents shall, after consultation with the Standing
Committee of the General Synod, appoint from among the members
of the Synod a panel of not less than 3 or more than 8 chairmen,
who shall be chosen for their experience and ability as chairmen of
meetings and may be members of any House ; and it shall be the
duty of one of the chairmen on the panel, in accordance with
arrangements approved by the Presidents and subject to any special
directions of the Presidents, to take the chair at meetings of the
General Synod at which neither of the Presidents take the chair.

(3) The Provincial Registrars shall be Joint Registrars of the
General Synod.

5.—(1) A motion for the final approval of any Measure or Canon
shall not be deemed to be carried unless, on a division by Houses, it
receives the assent of the majority of the members of each House
present and voting:

Provided that by permission of the chairman and with the leave
of the General Synod given in accordance with Standing Orders this
requirement may be dispensed with.

(2) All other motions of the General Synod shall, subject as
hereinafter provided, be determined by a majority of the members of
the Synod present and voting, and the vote may be taken by a show
of hands or a division :

Provided that, except in the case of a motion relating solely to
the course of business or procedure, any 25 members present may
demand a division by Houses and in that case the motion shall not
be deemed to be carried unless, on such a division, it receives the
assent of the majority of the members of each House present and
voting.

(3) This Article shall be subject to any provision of this Con-
stitution or any Measure requiring a two-thirds majority of each
House, and in that case the vote shall be taken on a division by
Houses.

6. The functions of the General Synod shall be as follows : —

    (*a*) to consider matters concerning the Church of England and
    to make provision in respect thereof—

        (i) by Measure intended to be given, in the manner
prescribed by the Church of England Assembly (Powers) 1919 c. 76.
Act 1919, the force and effect of an Act of Parliament,
or

        (ii) by Canon made, promulged and executed in
accordance with the like provisions and subject to the
like restrictions and having the like legislative force as

Canons heretofore made, promulged and executed by the Convocations of Canterbury and York, or

(iii) by such order, regulation or other subordinate instrument as may be authorised by Measure or Canon ; or

(iv) by such Act of Synod, regulation or other instrument or proceeding as may be appropriate in cases where provision by or under a Measure or Canon is not required ;

(b) to consider and express their opinion on any other matters of religious or public interest.

7.—(1) A provision touching doctrinal formulae or the services or ceremonies of the Church of England or the administration of the Sacraments or sacred rites thereof shall, before it is finally approved by the General Synod, be referred to the House of Bishops, and shall be submitted for such final approval in terms proposed by the House of Bishops and not otherwise.

(2) A provision touching any of the matters aforesaid shall, if the Convocations or either of them or the House of Laity so require, be referred, in the terms proposed by the House of Bishops for final approval by the General Synod, to the two Convocations sitting separately for their provinces and to the House of Laity ; and no provision so referred shall be submitted for final approval by the General Synod unless it has been approved, in the terms so proposed, by each House of the two Convocations sitting as aforesaid and by the House of Laity.

(3) The question whether such a reference is required by a Convocation shall be decided by the President and Prolocutor of the Houses of that Convocation, and the Prolocutor shall consult the Standing Committee of the Lower House of Canterbury or, as the case may be, the Assessors of the Lower House of York, and the decision of the President and Prolocutor shall be conclusive:

Provided that if, before such a decision is taken, either House of a Convocation resolves that the provision concerned shall be so referred or both Houses resolve that it shall not be so referred, the resolution or resolutions shall be a conclusive decision that the reference is or is not required by that Convocation.

(4) The question whether such a reference is required by the House of Laity shall be decided by the Prolocutor and Pro-Prolocutor of that House who shall consult the Standing Committee of that House, and the decision of the Prolocutor and the Pro-Prolocutor shall be conclusive:

Provided that if, before such a decision is taken, the House of Laity resolves that the reference is or is not required, the resolution shall be a conclusive decision of that question.

(5) Standing Orders of the General Synod shall provide for ensuring that a provision which fails to secure approval on a reference under this Article by each of the four Houses of the Convocations or by the House of Laity of the General Synod is not proposed again in the same or a similar form until a new General Synod comes into being,

except that, in the case of objection by one House of one Convocation only, provision may be made for a second reference to the Convocations and, in the case of a second objection by one House only, for reference to the Houses of Bishops and Clergy of the General Synod for approval by a two-thirds majority of the members of each House present and voting, in lieu of such approval by the four Houses aforesaid.

(6) If any question arises whether the requirements of this Article or Standing Orders made thereunder apply to any provision, or whether those requirements have been complied with, it shall be conclusively determined by the Presidents and Prolocutors of the Houses of the Convocations and the Prolocutor and Pro-Prolocutor of the House of Laity of the General Synod.

8.—(1) A Measure providing for permanent changes in the Services of Baptism or Holy Communion or in the Ordinal, or a scheme for a constitutional union or a permanent and substantial change of relationship between the Church of England and another Christian body, shall not be finally approved by the General Synod unless, at a stage determined by the Archbishops, the Measure or scheme, or the substance of the proposals embodied therein, has been approved by a majority of the dioceses at meetings of their Diocesan Synods.

(2) Any question whether this Article applies to any Measure or scheme, or whether its requirements have been complied with, shall be conclusively determined by the Archbishops, the Prolocutors of the Lower Houses of the Convocations and the Prolocutor and Pro-Prolocutor of the House of Laity of the General Synod.

9.—(1) Standing Orders of the General Synod may provide for separate sittings of any of the three Houses or joint sittings of any two Houses, and as to who is to take the chair at any such separate or joint sitting.

(2) The House of Laity shall elect a Chairman and Vice-Chairman of that House who shall also discharge the functions assigned by this Constitution and the Standing Orders and by or under any Measure or Canon to the Prolocutor and Pro-Prolocutor of that House.

10.—(1) The General Synod shall appoint a Legislative Committee from members of all three Houses, to whom shall be referred all Measures passed by the General Synod which it is desired should be given, in accordance with the procedure prescribed by the Church of England Assembly (Powers) Act 1919, the force of an Act of Parliament ; and it shall be the duty of the Legislative Committee to take such steps with respect to any such Measure as may be so prescribed.

1919 c. 76.

(2) The General Synod may appoint or provide by their Standing Orders for the appointment of a Standing Committee and such other Committees, Commissions and bodies, which may include persons who are not members of the Synod, and such officers as they think fit.

(3) Each House may appoint or provide by their Standing Orders for the appointment of such Committees of their members as they think fit.

11.—(1) The General Synod may make, amend and revoke Standing Orders providing for any of the matters for which such provision is required or authorised by this Constitution to be made, and consistently with this Constitution, for the meetings, business and procedure of the General Synod.

(2) Each House may make, amend and revoke Standing Orders for the matter referred to in Article 10(3) hereof and consistently with this Constitution and with any Standing Orders of the General Synod, for the separate sittings, business and procedure of that House.

(3) Subject to this Constitution and to any Standing Orders, the business and procedure at any meeting of the General Synod or any House or Houses thereof shall be regulated by the chairman of the meeting.

12.—(1) References to final approval shall, in relation to a Canon or Act of Synod be construed as referring to the final approval by the General Synod of the contents of the Canon or Act, and not to the formal promulgation thereof:

Provided that the proviso to Article 4(1) shall apply both to the final approval and to the formal promulgation of a Canon or Act of Synod.

(2) Any question concerning the interpretation of this Constitution, other than questions for the determination of which express provision is otherwise made, shall be referred to and determined by the Archbishops of Canterbury and York.

(3) No proceedings of the General Synod or any House or Houses thereof, or any Board, Commission, Committee or body thereof shall be invalidated by any vacancy in the membership of the body concerned or by any defect in the qualification, election or appointment of any member thereof.

13. Any functions exercisable under this Constitution by the Archbishops of Canterbury and York, whether described as such or as Presidents of the General Synod, may, during the absence abroad or incapacity through illness of one Archbishop or a vacancy in one of the Sees, be exercised by the other Archbishop alone.

Section 4.

SCHEDULE 3

Church Representation Rules

Part I

Church Electoral Roll

Formation of Roll

1.—(1) There shall be a church electoral roll (in these rules referred to as " the roll ") in every parish, on which the names of lay persons shall be entered as hereinafter provided. The roll shall be available for inspection by bona-fide inquirers.

(2) A lay person shall be entitled to have his name entered on the electoral roll of a parish, if he—

(*a*) is baptised ;

(*b*) is a member of the Church of England or another Church of the Anglican Communion or an overseas Church in communion with the Church of England, and is not a member of any other religious body which is not in communion with the Church of England ;

(*c*) is of seventeen years or upwards ;

(*d*) is resident in the parish, or, if not so resident, has habitually attended public worship in the parish during a period of six months prior to enrolment ; and

(*e*) has signed the form of application for enrolment set out in section 1 of Appendix I to these rules.

(3) No person shall be entitled to have his name on the roll of more than one parish at the same time :

Provided that where : —

(*a*) a person has the qualifications required under these rules for having his name on the roll of two parishes ;

(*b*) his name is on the roll of one of those parishes ;

(*c*) he applies in accordance with these rules to have his name entered on the roll of the other parish ;

(*d*) the parochial church councils of both parishes consent to his name being on the roll of both parishes ;

then, for so long as he rtains the necessary qualifications, he shall be entitled to have his name on the roll of both the parishes concerned. The granting of such consent shall be in the discretion of the councils hereinbefore mentioned, and there shall be no right of appeal if it is withheld.

No person shall in any circumstances be entitled to have his name on the roll of more than two parishes at the same time.

(4) The roll shall, until a parochial church council has been constituted in a parish, be formed and revised by the minister and churchwardens (if any), and shall, after such council has been constituted, be kept and revised by or under the direction of the council. Reference in this rule to a parochial church council shall, so far as may be necessary for giving effect to these rules, be construed as including references to the minister and churchwardens (if any).

(5) The parochial church council shall appoint an electoral roll officer to act under its directions for the purpose of carrying out its functions with regard to the electoral roll.

(6) The names of persons who are entitled to have their names entered upon the roll of the parish shall, subject to the provisions of these rules, be from time to time added to the roll. No name shall be added to or removed from the roll except by the authority of the parochial church council and it shall be the duty of that council to keep the roll constantly up to date and to cause names to be added and removed as from time to time required by these rules.

(7) Subject to the provisions of this rule, a person's name shall, as the occasion arises, be removed from the roll, if he: —

(*a*) has died ; or

(*b*) becomes a clerk in Holy Orders ; or

(*c*) signifies in writing his desire that his name should be removed ; or

(*d*) becomes a member of any religious body which is not in communion with the Church of England ; or

(*e*) ceases to reside in the parish, unless after so ceasing he continues habitually to attend public worship in the parish ; or

(*f*) is not resident in the parish and has not attended public worship in the parish during the preceding six months, not having been prevented from doing so by illness or other sufficient cause ; or

(*g*) at any time after the entry of his name on the roll has his name entered on the roll of another parish except in accordance with the proviso to paragraph (3) of this rule ; or

(*h*) was not entitled to have his name entered on the roll at the time when it was entered.

(8) The removal of a person's name from the roll under any of the provisions of these rules shall be without prejudice to his right to have his name entered again, if he is entitled to do so.

(9) The roll shall where practicable contain a record of the address of every person whose name is entered on the roll, but a failure to comply with this requirement shall not prejudice the validity of any entry on the roll.

Revision of Roll and Preparation of New Roll

2.—(1) Except in a year in which a new roll is prepared, the roll of a parish shall be revised annually by or under the direction of the council. Notice of the intended revision in the form set out in section 2 of Appendix I to these rules shall be affixed by the minister or under his direction on or near the principal door of every church in the parish and every building in the parish licensed for public worship and remain so affixed for a period of not less than fourteen days before the commencement of the revision. The revision shall be completed not less than fifteen days or more than twenty-eight days before the annual parochial church meeting.

(2) Upon every revision all enrolments or removals from the roll which have been effected since the date of the last revision (or since the formation of the roll, if there has been no previous revision) shall be reviewed, and such further enrolments or removals from the rolls as may be required shall be effected.

(3) After the completion of the revision, a copy of the roll as revised shall, together with a list of the names removed from the roll since the last revision (or since the formation of the roll, if there has been no previous revision), be published by being exhibited

continuously for not less than fourteen days before the annual parochial church meeting on or near the principal door of the parish church in such manner as the council shall appoint. No name shall be entered upon or removed from the roll during the period in any year between the completion of the revision and the close of the annual parochial church meeting.

(4) Not less than two months before the annual parochial church meeting in the year 1972 and every succeeding sixth year notice in the form set out in section 3 of Appendix 1 to these rules shall be affixed by the minister or under his direction on or near the principal door of every church in the parish and every building in the parish licensed for public worship and remain so affixed for a period of not less than fourteen days. On the affixing of the notice a new roll shall be prepared.

(5) The parochial church council shall be responsible for ensuring that all persons whose names are entered on the previous electoral roll are informed of the preparation of the new roll either by the notice affixed under the preceding paragraph, or by public announcement, or by communication in writing or verbally to the person concerned.

(6) The new roll shall be prepared by entering upon it the names of persons entitled to entry under rule 1(2), and a fresh application shall be required from persons whose names were entered on the previous roll. A person whose name was so entered shall not be disqualified for entry on the new roll by reason only of his failure to comply with the conditions specified in rule 1(2)(*d*), if he was prevented from doing so by illness or other sufficient cause, and the circumstances shall be stated on the application form. The preparation of the new roll shall be completed not less than fifteen days or more than twenty-eight days before the annual parochial church meeting.

(7) After the completion of the new roll, a copy shall be published by being exhibited continuously for not less than fourteen days before the annual parochial church meeting on or near the principal door of the parish church in such manner as the council shall appoint. No name shall be entered upon or removed from the roll during the period in any year between the completion of the new roll and the close of the annual parochial church meeting. On the publication of the new roll the previous roll shall cease to have effect.

(8) Upon the alteration of the boundaries of any parishes the parochial church council of the parish from which any area is transferred shall enquire from the persons resident in that area whose names are entered on the roll of the parish, whether they wish to have their names transferred to the roll of the other parish. The parochial church council shall remove the names of persons answering in the affirmative from its own roll and shall inform the parochial church council of the parish in which such persons now reside, which shall enter the names on its roll without any application for enrolment being required.

Procedural provisions relating to entry and removal of names

3.—(1) When a person applying for enrolment on the roll of any parish signifies his desire that his name should be removed from the roll of any other parish, notice of that fact shall be sent by the parochial church council receiving the application to the parochial church council of that other parish.

(2) When the name of any person is removed from the roll of the parish owing to his having become resident in another parish, notice of that fact shall, whenever possible, be sent by the parochial church council of the first mentioned parish to the parochial church council of the last mentioned parish.

(3) When a person wishes to have his name on the rolls of two parishes in accordance with rule 1(3), his name must first be on the roll of one of those two parishes.

He must then :—

(*a*) apply to the parochial church council of that parish for its consent to his name being entered on the roll of the other parish concerned ; and

(*b*) if such consent is given, apply for entry on the roll of the other parish concerned.

The parochial church council of that other parish shall then decide whether or not to give its consent to his name being on the roll of both parishes and, if it does not give consent, the application for entry on the roll of that parish shall be refused.

(4) For so long as the name of any person is on the roll of two parishes pursuant to rule 1(3), a note to that effect shall be entered upon the roll of each of the parishes concerned. Where consent is given by the parochial church council of the parish to an application under sub-paragraph (*a*) of the preceding paragraph such note may be added immediately on the roll of that parish, but if so added, must be cancelled immediately on notification being given that the parochial church council of the other parish concerned has refused its consent to the name of the person in question being on the rolls of both parishes.

(5) An omission to comply with the requirements of this rule shall not disqualify any person whose name has been entered upon any roll.

Certification of Numbers on Rolls

4.—(1) Not later than the first day of July—

(*a*) in any year immediately preceding a year in which elections of members of deanery synods or diocesan synods will fall due,

(*b*) in any year being the fourth year after the last preceding election of members of the House of Laity of the General Synod,

the number of names on the roll of each parish shall be certified to the secretary of the diocesan synod and the secretary of the deanery synod, and the certificate shall be signed by the chairman, vice-chairman, secretary or electoral roll officer of the parochial church council:

Provided that, if the General Synod is at any time dissolved before the fourth year after the last preceding election of the House of Laity or before this rule has taken effect during that year, the General Synod or the Presidents thereof may give directions requiring the number of names on the roll of each parish to be certified as aforesaid within such time as may be specified, and the directions may, if the dissolution is known to be impending, be given before it occurs.

(2) A copy of such certificate shall be affixed at or near to the principal door of every church in the parish and every building licensed for public worship in the parish when the certificate is sent to the secretary of the diocesan synod, and shall remain so affixed for a period of not less than fourteen days.

(3) Every certificate under this rule shall include a special statement certifying how many of the total number of names included in the certificate relate to persons whose names are entered on the rolls of two parishes.

(4) In calculating for the purposes of these rules the number of names on the roll of the parish or on the rolls of the parishes in the deanery or diocese the person who receives the certificate shall adjust the total number of names certified by deducting therefrom one half of the number of names included in the special statement.

(5) Any question as to the accuracy of any certificate given under this rule shall be decided in such manner as the diocesan synod or the bishop's council and standing committee shall determine.

Part II

Parochial Church Meetings and Councils

Annual Meetings

5.—(1) In every parish there shall be held not later than the 30th April in each year the annual parochial church meeting (hereafter in these rules referred to as " the annual meeting ").

(2) All lay persons whose names are entered on the roll of the parish shall be entitled to attend the annual meeting and to take part in its proceedings, and no other lay person shall be so entitled.

(3) A clerk in Holy Orders shall be entitled to attend the annual meeting of a parish and take part in its proceedings—

   (a) if he is either beneficed in or licensed to the parish or any other parish in the area of the benefice to which the parish belongs ; or

   (b) if the parish is in the area of a group ministry and he is an incumbent of any benefice in the group ; or

   (c) if he is resident in the parish and is not beneficed in or licensed to any other parish.

Convening of Meeting

6.—(1) The annual meeting shall be convened by the minister of the parish by a notice in the form set out in section 4 of Appendix 1 to these rules affixed on or near to the principal door of every church in the parish and every building licensed for public worship in the parish, for a period including the last two Sundays before the day of the meeting.

(2) The annual meeting shall be held at such place on such date and at such hour as shall be directed by the previous annual meeting, or by the parochial church council (which may vary any direction given by a previous annual meeting) or in the absence of any such direction as shall be appointed by the minister.

(3) During the vacancy of the benefice or curacy or when the minister is absent or incapacitated by illness or any other cause, the vice-chairman of the parochial church council, or if there is no vice-chairman, or if he is unable or unwilling to act, the secretary of or some other person appointed by that council shall have all the powers vested in the minister under this rule.

(4) The annual meeting shall be held at a place within the parish unless the parochial church council decide otherwise.

Chairman

7. The minister, if present, or if he is not present, the vice-chairman of the parochial church council, or, if he also is not present, a chairman chosen by the annual meeting shall preside thereat. In case of an equal division of votes, the chairman of the meeting shall have a second or casting vote ; but no clerical chairman shall have a vote in the election of the parochial representatives of the laity.

Business

8.—(1) The annual meeting shall receive from the parochial church council and shall be free to discuss : —

(*a*) a copy or copies of the roll ;

(*b*) an annual report on the proceedings of the parochial church council ;

(*c*) an annual report on the financial affairs of the parish ;

(*d*) the audited accounts of the parochial church council for the year ending on the 31st December immediately preceding the meeting ;

(*e*) an audited statement of the funds and property, if any, remaining in the hands of the parochial church council at the said date ;

(*f*) a report upon the fabric, goods and ornaments of the church or churches of the parish ; and

(*g*) a report on the proceedings of the deanery synod.

(2) The council shall cause a copy of the said audited accounts
and the said audited statement to be affixed on or near the principal
door of every church in the parish and every building licensed for
public worship in the parish at least seven days before the annual
meeting.

(3) Such accounts and statement shall be submitted to the annual
meeting for approval. If approved, they shall be signed by the
chairman of the meeting, who shall then deliver them to the parochial
church council for publication, and the parochial church council shall
forthwith cause them to be published and affixed on or near the
principal door of every church in the parish and every building
licensed for public worship in the parish and at such other conspicuous place or places in the parish as the parochial church council
think appropriate.

(4) The annual meeting shall in the manner provided by rule 10 of
these rules : —

> (*a*) elect in every third year parochial representatives of the
> laity to the deanery synod ;
> (*b*) elect parochial representatives of the laity to the parochial
> church council ;
> (*c*) elect sidesmen ;

and the elections shall be carried out in the above order.

(5) The annual meeting shall appoint the auditors to the council.

(6) Any person entitled to attend the annual meeting may ask
any question about parochial church matters, or bring about a discussion of any matter of parochial or general church interest, by
moving a general resolution or by moving to give any particular
recommendation to the council in relation to its duties.

(7) The annual meeting shall have power to adjourn and to
determine its own rules of procedure.

(8) The secretary of the parochial church council (or another
person appointed by the meeting in his place) shall act as a clerk
of the annual meeting, and shall record the minutes thereof.

Qualifications of persons to be chosen or elected by annual meetings

9.—(1) The qualifications of a person to be elected a parochial
representative of the laity to either of the bodies referred to in the
last preceding rule are that—

> (*a*) his name is entered on the roll of the parish ; and
> (*b*) he is an actual communicant member of the Church of
> England or, in the case of election to the parochial church
> council, of any other Church of the Anglican Communion
> or of an overseas Church in communion with the Church
> of England ; and
> (*c*) in the case of election to the deanery synod, he is of age to
> vote at a Parliamentary election:

Provided that—

> (i) if his name is entered on the rolls of two parishes, he must
> choose one of those parishes for the purpose of qualification

SCH. 3

for election to a deanery synod, but may serve on the parochial church councils of both parishes ;

(ii) the registrar of the diocese shall not be qualified for election to any of the said bodies in that diocese.

(2) The qualification of a person to be elected a sidesman is that his name is entered on the roll of the parish.

(3) No person shall be elected under the last preceding rule unless he has signified his consent to serve or there is in the opinion of the meeting sufficient evidence of his willingness to serve.

Conduct of Elections at Annual Meetings

10.—(1) This rule shall apply to all elections at annual meetings.

(2) All candidates for election at an annual meeting must be nominated and seconded by persons entitled to attend the annual meeting, and in the case of parochial representatives of the laity, by persons whose names are entered on the roll of the parish. A candidate shall be nominated or seconded either before the meeting in writing or at the meeting.

(3) If the number of candidates nominated is not greater than the number of seats to be filled, the candidates nominated shall forthwith be declared elected.

(4) If more candidates are nominated than there are seats to be filled, the election shall take place at the annual meeting.

(5) No clerk in Holy Orders shall be entitled to vote in the election of any parochial representatives of the laity.

(6) Each person entitled to vote shall have as many votes as there are seats to be filled but may not give more than one vote to any one candidate.

(7) Votes may be given:—

(a) on voting papers, which must be signed by the voter ; or

(b) if no person present objects thereto, by show of hands.

(8) Where owing to an equality of votes an election is not decided, the decision between the persons for whom the equal numbers of votes have been cast shall be taken by lot.

(9) The result of any election by an annual meeting shall be announced as soon as practicable by the person presiding over the election, and a notice of the result shall in every case be affixed on or near the principal door of every church in the parish and every building licensed for public worship in the parish, and shall bear the date on which the result is declared. The notice shall remain affixed for not less than fourteen days.

(10) Returns of parochial representatives of the laity elected to the deanery synod shall be sent to the secretary of that synod.

CONDUCT OF ELECTIONS OF CHURCHWARDENS   SCH. 3

11.—(1) If elections of churchwardens take place at meetings of parishioners under section 3 of the Churchwardens (Appointment 1964 No. 3. and Resignation) Measure 1964 either because there has been no joint consent under section 2 of that Measure or because there is no minister, the elections shall be conducted, announced and notified in the same manner as elections under the preceding rule except that all persons entitled to attend the meeting of parishioners other than the minister shall be entitled to nominate and vote at such elections of churchwardens.

(2) The Churchwardens (Appointment and Resignation) Measure 1964 shall be amended as follows:—

(a) in section 2(1) for the words "not later in the year than during the week following Easter week" there shall be substituted the words "not later than the 30th April in each year";

(b) sections 4, 5, 6 and 11(3) shall be repealed; and

(c) section 3(6) shall not apply to elections of churchwardens.

PAROCHIAL CHURCH COUNCIL

Members

12.—(1) The parochial church council shall consist of:—

(a) all clerks in Holy Orders beneficed in or licensed to the parish, including in the case of a team ministry all vicars in the team;

(b) any deaconess or woman worker licensed to the parish or any male lay worker licensed to the parish and receiving a stipend in respect of work for the cure of souls in the parish;

(c) the churchwardens, being actual communicant members of the Church of England whose names are on the roll of the parish;

(d) any reader whose name is on the roll of the parish, if the annual meeting so determines;

(e) all persons whose names are on the roll of the parish and who are lay members of any deanery synod, diocesan synod or the General Synod;

(f) such number of representatives of the laity as the annual meeting may decide, and so that the number determined may be altered from time to time by a resolution passed at any annual meeting, but such resolution shall not take effect before the next ensuing annual meeting; and

(g) co-opted members, if the parochial church council so decides, not exceeding in number one-fifth of the representatives of the laity elected under the last preceding sub-paragraph of this paragraph, and being either clerks in Holy Orders or actual lay communicant members of the Church of England of seventeen years of age or upwards. The term of office of a co-opted member shall be until the conclusion of the next annual meeting ; but without prejudice to his being co-opted on subsequent occasions for a similar term, subject to and in accordance with the provisions of these rules.

(2) Any elected representative of the laity whose name is removed from the roll under rule 1 shall forthwith cease to be a member of the parochial church council, without prejudice to any right that the council may have to make him a co-opted member : provided that, where a person's name is removed from the roll under sub-paragraph (c) of rule 1(7) he shall not cease to be a member of the council by virtue of that fact unless the council so resolves.

(3) Where a group ministry is established the incumbents of all benefices in the group shall be entitled to attend meetings of the parochial church councils of all the parishes in the area for which the group ministry is established. They shall be entitled to receive documents circulated to members of councils of which they are not themselves members and to speak but not to vote at meetings of such councils.

General Provisions relating to Parochial Church Councils

13. The provisions in Appendix II to these rules shall have effect with respect to parochial church councils, and with respect to the officers, the meetings and the proceedings thereof:

Provided that a parochial church council may, with the consent of the diocesan synod, vary the said provisions, in their application to the council.

Term of office

14. Representatives of the laity on the parochial church council of a parish shall hold office from the conclusion of the annual meeting until the conclusion of the next annual meeting of the parish:

Provided that the annual meeting may decide that one-third only (or the number nearest to one-third) of the representatives of the laity elected to the council shall retire from office in every year. In any case where it is so decided, the representatives of the laity to retire from office at each annual meeting shall be those who have been longest in office since last elected, and as between representatives of the laity elected on the same day, those to retire shall (unless they otherwise agree among themselves) be selected by lot. A representative of the laity shall in any event retire at the conclusion of the third annual meeting after that at which he was elected.

Limitation on years of service

15. The annual meeting may decide that no representative of the laity on the parochial church council may hold office for more than a specified number of years continuously and may also decide that after a specified interval a person who has ceased to be eligible by reason of such decision may again stand for election as a representative of the laity on the council.

Parishes with more than one Place of Worship

16.—(1) In any parish where there are two or more churches or buildings licensed for public worship the annual meeting may make a scheme, either: —

(*a*) for the election of representatives of the laity to the parochial church council in such manner as to ensure due representation of the congregation of each such church or building ; or

(*b*) for the election of district church councils for any district in the parish in which a church (other than the parish church) or building licensed as aforesaid is situated.

(2) A scheme for the election of any district church council or councils under the preceding paragraph shall provide for the election of representatives of the laity on to such council, for ex-officio members and for the chairmanship of such council and shall contain such other provisions as to membership and procedure as shall be considered appropriate by the annual meeting.

(3) Such a scheme may also provide for the delegation by the parochial church council to a district church council of such functions as it may specify and subject to the scheme the parochial church council may delegate to a district church council such of its functions as it shall think fit.

(4) Such a scheme may also provide for the election or choice of one or two deputy churchwardens in respect of any such church or building, and for the delegation to him or them of such functions of the churchwardens relating to that church or building as the scheme may specify, and the churchwardens may, subject to the scheme, delegate such of their said functions as they think fit to the deputy churchwarden or churchwardens.

(5) No scheme under this rule shall be valid unless approved by at least two-thirds of the persons present and voting at the annual meeting, nor shall it be operative until the next ensuing annual meeting. Every such scheme shall, on its approval, be communicated to the secretary of the diocesan synod, who may if he considers it appropriate lay the scheme before the bishop's council and standing committee of that synod, which may determine that the scheme shall not come into operation.

(6) This rule shall be without prejudice to the establishment of a district church council and deputy churchwardens in the area of a team ministry by a scheme or by an instrument made by the bishop under paragraph 3(2) of Schedule 3 to the Pastoral Measure 1968, 1968 No. 1. or to the appointment, in parishes with more than one parish church, of two churchwardens for each parish church under section 27(3) of the said Measure.

Joint Parochial Church Councils and Group Councils

17. These rules shall, in relation to a joint parochial church council established by a scheme or order under paragraph 13 of Schedule 3 to the Pastoral Measure 1968, have effect subject to the scheme or

SCH. 3 order, and, in relation to a group council established by a scheme or an instrument of the bishop under paragraph 3(4) of the said Schedule, have effect subject to the scheme or instrument.

SPECIAL AND EXTRAORDINARY MEETINGS

18.—(1) In addition to the annual meeting, the minister of a parish may convene a special parochial church meeting, and he shall do so on a written representation by not less than one-third of the lay members of the parochial church council ; and the provisions of these rules relating to the convening and conduct of the annual meeting shall, with the necessary modifications, apply to a special parochial church meeting.

(2) On a written representation made to the archdeacon by not less than one-third of the lay members of the parochial church council, or by one-tenth of the persons whose names are on the roll of the parish, and deemed by the archdeacon to have been made with sufficient cause, the archdeacon shall convene an extraordinary meeting of the parochial church council or an extraordinary parochial church meeting, and shall either take the chair himself or shall appoint a chairman to preside. The chairman, not being otherwise entitled to attend such meeting, shall not be entitled to vote upon any resolution before the meeting.

(3) In any case where the archdeacon is himself the minister, any representation under paragraph (2) of this rule shall be made to the bishop, and in any such case the references to the archdeacon in paragraph (2) of this rule shall be construed as references to the bishop, or to a person appointed by him to act on his behalf.

(4) The persons entitled to attend any special or extraordinary parochial church meeting shall be those entitled to attend the annual meeting.

PART III

DEANERY SYNODS

Membership

19.—(1) A deanery synod shall consist of a house of clergy and a house of laity.

(2) The members of the house of clergy of a deanery synod shall consist of—

    (*a*) the clerks in Holy Orders beneficed in or licensed to any parish in the deanery ;

    (*b*) any clerks in Holy Orders licensed to institutions in the deanery under the Extra-Parochial Ministry Measure 1967 ;

1967 No. 2.

    (*c*) any clerical members of the General Synod or diocesan synod resident in the deanery ;

    (*d*) such other clerks in Holy Orders holding the bishop's licence and resident or working in any part of the deanery as may be determined by or in accordance with a resolution of the diocesan synod.

(3) The members of the house of laity of a deanery synod shall consist of—

(*a*) the parochial representatives elected to the synod by the annual meetings of the parishes of the deanery ;

(*b*) any lay members of the General Synod or diocesan synod whose names are entered on the roll of any parish in the deanery ;

(*c*) such other lay persons, being deaconesses or whole-time lay workers licensed by the bishop to work in any part of the deanery, as may be determined by or in accordance with a resolution of the diocesan synod.

(4) The house of clergy and house of laity of a deanery synod may co-opt additional members of their respective houses, being clerks in Holy Orders or, as the case may be, lay persons who shall be actual communicant members of the Church of England of age to vote at a Parliamentary election:

Provided that the number of members co-opted by either house shall not exceed five per cent. of the total members of that house.

Election and choice of members

20.—(1) The parochial representatives of the laity elected by annual meetings shall be so elected every three years, and shall hold office for a term of three years beginning with the 1st June next following their election.

(2) The numbers to be so elected from the several parishes shall be determined by resolution of the diocesan synod not later than the 1st December in the year preceding any such elections, and those numbers shall be related to the numbers of names on the rolls of the parishes as certified and adjusted under rule 4 and provision may be made by the resolution for the separate representation of a district for which there is a district church council.

(3) Not later than the 31st December in the year preceding any such elections, the secretary of the diocesan synod shall certify to the secretary of each parochial church council the number of such representatives to be elected at the annual meeting of the parish and inform him of any provision for the separate representation of such a district as aforesaid and shall send to the secretary of each deanery synod copies of the certificates and information relating to the parishes of the deanery.

(4) A resolution of the diocesan synod making provision under paragraph (2)(*d*) or (3)(*c*) of the last preceding rule for the membership of the clerks in Holy Orders or the deaconesses or lay workers therein mentioned may provide for the choice by a class of such

persons of some of their number to be members, and for the term of office of persons so chosen.

(5) The diocesan synod shall exercise their powers under this and the last preceding rule so as to secure that the total number of members of any deanery synod in the diocese shall not be more than 150 and, so far as practicable, shall not be less than 50:

Provided that the maximum number of 150 may be exceeded for the purpose of securing that the house of laity is not less in number than the house of clergy.

Variation of Membership of Deanery Synods by Scheme

21.—(1) If it appears to the diocesan synod that the preceding rules in this Part relating to the membership of deanery synods ought to be varied to meet the special circumstances of the diocese or the deaneries and to secure better representation of clergy or laity or both on the deanery synods, they may make a scheme for such variation, and, if the scheme comes into operation under this rule, the said rules shall have effect subject to the scheme:

Provided that no scheme shall be made under this rule so as to come into operation before the end of the first term of office of the members of the synods who are parochial representatives except for the purposes of the elections at the end of that term.

(2) Copies of every such scheme must be sent to members of the diocesan synod at least fourteen days before the session at which they are considered, and every such scheme shall require the assent of the bishop and of a two-thirds majority of the members of each house of the synod present and voting.

(3) A scheme approved by the diocesan synod as aforesaid shall be laid before a session of the General Synod and shall be subject to annulment by resolution of the General Synod, and if not so annulled shall come into operation on the day after the session or such later date as may be specified in the scheme.

Representation of Cathedral Clergy and Laity

22.—(1) Any diocesan synod may provide by scheme for the representation on such deanery synod as may be determined by or under the scheme—

(a) of the dean or provost, the residentiary canons and other ministers of the cathedral church of the diocese, or any of them; and

(b) of lay persons who

(i) in a parish church cathedral are on the electoral roll prepared under rule 1(1); or

(ii) in any other cathedral are declared by the dean to be habitual worshippers at the cathedral church of the diocese and whose names are not entered on the roll of any parish.

(2) Paragraph (2) of the last preceding rule shall apply to schemes made under this rule.

Procedure

23.—(1) The diocesan synod shall make rules for deanery synods which shall provide—

(*a*) that the rural dean and a member of the house of laity elected by that house shall be joint chairmen of the deanery synod ;

(*b*) that there shall be a secretary of the deanery synod ;

(*c*) that a specified minimum number of meetings shall be held by the deanery synod in each year ;

(*d*) that on such matters and in such circumstances as may be specified in the rules, voting shall be by houses, but that otherwise decisions shall be taken by a majority of the members of the synod present and voting ;

(*e*) that there shall be a standing committee of the synod with such membership and functions as the rules may provide ;

(*f*) that the synod shall prepare and circulate to all parochial church councils in the deanery a report of its proceedings ;

and may provide for such other matters consistent with these rules as the diocesan synod think fit.

(2) Subject to any such rules, the deanery synod shall have power to determine its own procedure.

Pᴀʀᴛ IV

Dɪᴏᴄᴇsᴀɴ Sʏɴᴏᴅs

Membership of Diocesan Synods

24.—(1) A diocesan synod shall consist of three authorities, the bishop, who shall be president, a house of clergy and a house of laity.

(2) The members of the house of clergy shall consist of—

(*a*) the following ex-officio members, that is to say : —

(i) the suffragan bishop or bishops and any full-time assistant bishop or bishops ;

(ii) the dean or provost of the cathedral (including in appropriate dioceses, the Dean of Westminster, the Dean of Windsor and the Deans of Jersey and Guernsey) ;

(iii) the archdeacons ;

(iv) the proctors elected from the diocese or from any university in the diocese (the University of London being for this purpose wholly in the diocese of London) to the Lower House of the Convocation of the Province, excluding the registrar of the diocese (if so elected) ;

(v) the chancellor of the diocese (if in Holy Orders) ; and

(vi) the chairman of the diocesan board of finance (if in Holy Orders) ;

SCH. 3

(b) members elected by the houses of clergy of the deanery synods in the diocese in accordance with the next following rules ; and

(c) not more than five members (being clerks in Holy Orders) co-opted by the house of clergy of the diocesan synod.

(3) The members of the house of laity shall consist of : —

(a) the following ex-officio members, that is to say : —

(i) the chancellor of the diocese (if not in Holy Orders) ;

(ii) the chairman of the diocesan board of finance (if not in Holy Orders) ;

(iii) the members elected from the diocese to the House of Laity of the General Synod, excluding the registrar of the diocese (if so elected) ;

(b) members elected by the houses of laity of the deanery synods in the diocese in accordance with the next following rules ; and

(c) not more than five members co-opted by the house of laity of the diocesan synod, who shall be actual communicant members of the Church of England of age to vote at a Parliamentary election.

(4) The bishop of the diocese may nominate ten additional members of the diocesan synod, who may be of the clergy or the laity and shall be members of the appropriate house.

Elections of Members of Diocesan Synods by Deanery Synods

25.—(1) The elections of members of the diocesan synod by the houses of clergy and laity of the deanery synods in the diocese shall taken place every three years, and the members so elected shall hold office for a term ending with the election of their successors.

(2) Any clerk in Holy Orders who is a member of the deanery synod or is working or residing in the deanery shall be qualified to be so elected by the house of clergy of a deanery synod, and the electors shall be the members of that house other than the co-opted members:

Provided that no clerk shall stand for election by more than one deanery synod.

(3) Any lay person who is an actual communicant member of the Church of England of age to vote at a Parliamentary election and whose name is entered on the roll of any parish in the deanery or who is a lay person declared by the dean to be a habitual worshipper at the cathedral church of the diocese and to be associated with the deanery, shall be qualified to be so elected by the house of laity of a deanery synod, and the electors shall be the members of that house other than the co-opted members:

Provided that a person whose name is entered on the roll of two parishes in different deaneries must choose one of those parishes for the purpose of such qualification.

(4) The diocesan synod shall, not later than the 1st December in the year preceding any such election determine the numbers of members to be so elected by the houses of the several deanery synods in the diocese, and the numbers shall—

(*a*) in the case of elections by the houses of clergy, be related to the numbers of members of those houses in the respective deanery synods ;

(*b*) in the case of elections by the houses of laity, be related to the total numbers of names on the rolls of the parishes in the respective deaneries as certified and adjusted under rule 4 :

Provided that at least two members shall be elected by each house of every deanery synod.

(5) For the purposes of such determination by the diocesan synod, the secretary of every deanery synod shall, not later than the 1st July in the year preceding any such election, certify the number of members of the house of clergy of the synod to the secretary of the diocesan synod.

(6) The diocesan synod shall so exercise their powers under this rule as to secure that the number of members of the synod is not less than 150 and not more than 270 and that the numbers of the two houses are approximately equal :

Provided that for the purposes of the first two elections after the passing of this Measure of the diocesan synod for the diocese of London, and the filling of casual vacancies among the persons then elected, this paragraph shall have effect with the substitution of the number 500 for the number 270.

(7) Not later than the 31st December in each year preceding any such elections, the secretary of the diocesan synod shall certify to the secretary of every deanery synod the numbers determined under this rule for that deanery synod.

26.—(1) Elections of members of the diocesan synod by the houses of the deanery synods shall be carried out in each diocese during such period between the 1st day of June and the last day of July (both inclusive) as shall be fixed by the bishop of the diocese.

(2) The presiding officers for the deaneries in each diocese shall be appointed by the bishop, and the expenses of elections shall be paid out of diocesan funds.

(3) Every candidate must be nominated and seconded by a quali- fied elector. A notice in the form set out in section 5 of Appendix I indicating the number of seats to be filled and inviting nominations shall be dispatched to every elector by the presiding officer not earlier than 1st June in each election year. Nominations in the form set out in section 6 of Appendix I shall be sent to the presiding officer in writing within such period not being less than 14 days as he shall specify and be accompanied by a statement signed by the candidate of his willingness to serve.

(4) If more candidates are nominated than there are seats to be filled the names of the candidates nominated shall be circulated on a voting paper in the form set out in section 7 of Appendix I to every qualified elector.

(5) The voting paper marked and signed by the elector shall be returnable to the presiding officer within such period not being less than 14 days as he shall specify. Only one vote may be given to any one candidate and no elector may give more votes than there are seats to be filled. No vote shall be counted if given on a voting paper not in accordance with this paragraph.

(6) Where owing to an equality of votes an election is not decided, the decision between the persons for whom the equal numbers of votes have been cast shall be taken by lot by the presiding officer.

(7) A return of the result of the election shall be sent by the presiding officer to the secretary of the diocesan synod and a statement of the result shall be sent by him to every candidate not later than the 1st September in each election year.

Variation of Membership of Diocesan Synods by Scheme

27.—(1) If it appears to the diocesan synod that the preceding rules in this Part relating to the membership of diocesan synods ought to be varied to meet the special circumstances of the diocese and to secure better representation of clergy or laity or both on the diocesan synod, they may make a scheme for such variation, and if the scheme comes into operation in accordance with the provisions hereinafter applied, the said rules shall have effect subject to the scheme :

Provided that no scheme shall be made under this rule so as to come into operation before the end of the first term of office of elected members of the synod except for the purposes of the elections at the end of that term.

(2) Paragraphs (2) and (3) of rule 21 shall apply to schemes under this rule as it applies to schemes under that rule.

Procedure of Diocesan Synods

28.—(1) The diocesan synod shall make standing orders which shall provide—

(a) that the bishop need not be chairman of its meetings if and to the extent that standing orders otherwise provide ;

(b) that there shall be a secretary of the diocesan synod ;

(c) that a specified minimum number of meetings being not less than two shall be held in each year ;

(d) that a meeting of the diocesan synod shall be held if not less than a specified number of members of the synod so request ;

(e) that subject to the two next following sub-paragraphs, nothing shall be deemed to have the assent of the diocesan synod unless the three authorities which constitute the synod have assented thereto ;

(f) that questions relating only to the conduct of business shall be decided by the votes of all the members of the diocesan synod present and voting, and every other question shall be decided in like manner, the assent of the three authorities being presumed, unless any ten members present demand that a separate vote of each of the houses of clergy and laity be taken, or unless the bishop requires his distinct opinion to be recorded ;

(*g*) that if the votes of the houses of clergy and laity are in favour of any matter referred to the diocesan synod by the General Synod under the provisions of Article 8 of Schedule 2 of this Measure, that matter shall be deemed to have been approved for the purposes of the said Article ;

(*h*) that there shall be a bishop's council and standing committee of the diocesan synod with such membership as may be provided by standing orders and with the functions exercisable by it under section 4(4) of the Measure and such other functions as may be provided by the standing orders or by these rules or by any Measure or Canon ;

and may contain such further provisions consistent with these rules as the diocesan synod shall consider appropriate.

(2) The registrar of the diocese shall be the registrar of the diocesan synod, and may appoint a deputy.

PART V

HOUSE OF LAITY OF GENERAL SYNOD

29.—(1) The House of Laity of the General Synod shall consist of—

(*a*) the members elected by the diocesan electors of each diocese as hereinafter provided ;

(*b*) two members, one from each province, chosen by the lay members of religious communities from among their number in such manner as may be provided by a resolution of the General Synod ;

(*c*) such ex-officio and co-opted members as are hereinafter provided.

(2) For the purposes of this Part of these rules, the diocesan electors of a diocese shall be the members of the houses of laity of all the deanery synods in the diocese other than the co-opted members :

Provided that if any person is a member (other than a co-opted member) of more than one deanery synod, whether or not in the same diocese, he shall choose one deanery synod only for the purpose of voting at elections to the General Synod.

ELECTIONS OF MEMBERS

Number of Elected Members

30.—(1) The total number of members to be elected by the diocesan electors of all the dioceses, which shall not exceed 250, shall be fixed by resolution of the General Synod not later than the last day of November in the fourth year after the last preceding election of the House of Laity (but subject as hereinafter provided), and the resolution shall then—

SCH. 3

(*a*) apportion the number so fixed to the provinces of Canterbury and York in a proportion of sixty-eight to thirty-two or as nearly as possible thereto ;

(*b*) divide the number so apportioned to each province among the dioceses of that province so that the number of members to be elected by the several dioceses are as nearly as possible proportionate to the total numbers of names certified for them under the next following paragraph, but so that no diocese (other than the diocese of Sodor and Man) shall elect less than three members.

(2) The secretary of each diocesan synod shall, not later than the first day of August in the fourth year after the last preceding election of the House of Laity, certify to the secretary of the General Synod the total number of names on the rolls of the parishes of the diocese as adjusted under rule 4.

(3) The number of members of the House of Laity to be elected by each diocese, when fixed by the General Synod as aforesaid, shall forthwith be certified to the secretaries of the diocesan synods.

(4) If the General Synod is at any time dissolved before the fourth year after the last preceding election of the House of Laity or before the fixing of numbers under this rule by the General Synod during that year, the General Synod or the Presidents thereof may give directions with respect to the fixing and certifying of the numbers of members to be elected to the House of Laity by each diocese, and the directions may provide that the numbers so fixed and certified on the last previous occasion shall be deemed to have been fixed and certified for the purpose of the election following the dissolution, and the directions may, if the dissolution is known to be impending, be given before it occurs.

Qualification of Elected Members

31. Any lay person who is an actual communicant member of the Church of England of age to vote at a Parliamentary election and whose name is entered on the roll of any parish or who is declared by the dean of any cathedral church to be a habitual worshipper at that cathedral church shall be qualified for election for any diocese by the diocesan electors of the diocese in which the parish or cathedral church is situated :

Provided that a person whose name is entered on the roll of two parishes in different dioceses must choose one of those parishes for the purposes of such qualification.

Electoral Areas

32.—(1) Subject to any division of a diocese under this rule every diocese shall be an electoral area for the purposes of elections to the House of Laity.

(2) So far as is consistent with any rule made under the Standing Orders of the General Synod under paragraph (4) of the next following rule a diocesan synod may, for the purposes of any election,

divide a diocese into two or more areas, and apportion the number of members of the House of Laity to be elected for the diocese among such areas, and the election shall be conducted in each area as if such area were a separate diocese. Where a diocese is so divided, a diocesan elector who is a representative of the laity shall vote in the area to which the body by which he was elected belongs, and a diocesan elector who is not a representative of the laity shall vote in such area as the diocesan synod may decide. Any such division shall remain in force until it is revoked by the diocesan synod.

Conduct of Elections

33.—(1) Subject to any directions by the General Synod or the Presidents thereof, elections to the House of Laity shall be carried out during the three months immediately following any dissolution of the General Synod and shall be so carried out in each diocese during such period within the said three months as shall be fixed by the archbishops of Canterbury and York.

(2) The presiding officer in each diocese or each area of a diocese shall be the registrar of the diocese or a person appointed by him, except that, if the said registrar is a candidate in the election, the presiding officer shall be a person appointed by the registrar of the province. The expenses of the elections shall be paid out of diocesan funds.

(3) Every candidate must be nominated and seconded by diocesan electors qualified to vote in the area in which the candidate is seeking to be elected. All nominations shall be in writing and shall be sent to the presiding officer of the area, together with evidence of the candidate's consent to serve, on or before a date to be specified by the presiding officer. If any of the candidates so request the presiding officer shall despatch to every elector election addresses from those candidates, sufficient copies of the addresses to be provided by the candidates at their own expense.

(4) If more candidates are nominated for any area than there are seats to be filled, the election shall be conducted by voting papers upon the principle of proportional representation (unless the number of candidates to be elected be less than three) under rules to be made from time to time as provided by the Standing Orders of the General Synod.

(5) A candidate or a person nominated by him has the right to be present at the counting of the votes, and the presiding officer of the area shall give notice to each candidate of the time and place at which the votes are to be counted.

(6) A full statement of the result of each election shall be furnished to every candidate within the area, and published in such manner as the bishop may approve.

Term of Office of Elected and Representative Members

34. The term of office of elected members of the House of Laity and of members chosen by the lay members of religious communities shall be for the lifetime of the General Synod for which they are elected or chosen, but without prejudice to their acting under Article

SCH. 3   3(4) of the Constitution during the period of the dissolution of the General Synod or as ex-officio members of other bodies constituted under these rules during that period.

EX-OFFICIO AND CO-OPTED MEMBERS OF THE HOUSE OF LAITY

35.—(1) The following persons, if they are not in Holy Orders, shall be ex-officio members of the House of Laity:—

(*a*) the Dean of the Arches and Auditor ;

(*b*) the Vicar-General of the Province of York ;

(*c*) the three Church Estate Commissioners ;

(*d*) the Chairman of the Central Board of Finance.

(2) The House of Laity shall have power to co-opt persons who are actual lay communicant members of the Church of England of age to vote at a Parliamentary election to be members of the House of Laity :

Provided that :—

(*a*) the co-opted members shall not at any time exceed five in number ; and,

(*b*) no person shall be qualified to become a co-opted member unless not less than two-thirds of the members of the Standing Committee of the House of Laity shall have first consented to his being co-opted, either at a meeting of the Standing Committee or in writing.

(3) Except in regard to their appointment, the ex-officio and co-opted members shall have the same rights and be subject to the same rules and regulations as elected members:

Provided that no ex-officio or co-opted member shall, by reason only of his membership of the House of Laity, be a member of any other body constituted under these rules.

(4) Co-opted members shall continue to be members of the House of Laity until the next dissolution of the General Synod, but without prejudice to their acting under Article 3(4) of the Constitution during the period of the dissolution:

Provided that the House of Laity may, in the case of any co-opted member, fix a shorter period of membership.

(5) The House of Laity may make standing orders for regulating the procedure of and incidental to the appointment of co-opted members and otherwise for carrying this rule into effect.

PART VI

APPEALS AND DISQUALIFICATIONS

Appeals

36.—(1) Subject to the provisions of rule 1(3) of these rules there shall be a right of appeal by any person aggrieved against:—

(*a*) any enrolment, or refusal of enrolment, on the roll of a parish ;

(*b*) the removal of any name, or the refusal to remove any name, from the roll of a parish (*c*) the allowance or disallowance of any vote given or tendered in an election under these rules or to a body constituted under or in accordance with these rules ;

(*d*) the result of any election or choice held or made or purporting to be held or made under these rules, or any election or choice of members of a body constituted under or in accordance with these rules.

(2) In the case of an appeal arising out of an election to the House of Laity of the General Synod or the diocesan synod notice of the appeal shall be given in writing to the bishop. In any other case, notice of the appeal shall be given in writing to the rural dean, or, if there be no rural dean, to the archdeacon. Notices under this paragraph shall be given : —

(*a*) in the case of an appeal against an enrolment or a refusal of an enrolment, or in the case of an appeal against the removal of any name or the refusal to remove any name from the roll, not later than fourteen days after the date of the enrolment, removal or refusal or, if the appeal arises on the revision of the roll or the preparation of a new roll, not later than fourteen days after the first publication of the revised or new roll under rule 2(3) or (7) ;

(*b*) in the case of an appeal against the allowance or disallowance of a vote, not later than fourteen days after such allowance or disallowance ;

(*c*) in the case of an appeal against the result of an election, not later than fourteen days after the result thereof has been announced by the presiding officer.

(3) An error in the electoral roll shall not be a ground of appeal against the result of any election unless—

(i) either it has been determined under this rule that there has been such an error or the question is awaiting determination under this rule ; and

(ii) the error would or might be material to the result of the election ;

and the allowance or disallowance of a vote shall not be a ground of appeal against the result of an election unless the allowance or disallowance would or might be material to the result of the election.

(4) An appeal arising out of an election or choice of members of the House of Laity of the General Synod shall be referred to the standing committee of the Synod who shall appoint two or more of their members to consider and decide the appeal.

(5) In each diocese there shall be an electoral commission constituted by the diocesan synod. The bishop or the archdeacon or the rural dean, as the case may be, shall, unless the parties agree to a settlement of their dispute, refer any appeal under this rule except an appeal arising out of an election to the House of Laity to the commission. The commission shall appoint two or more of its members to consider and decide any appeal so referred. All or the majority of the members appointed shall be laymen, save when the

question arises in connection with an election or choice of members of the house of clergy of the diocesan synod or a deanery synod when all or the majority so appointed shall be clerks in Holy Orders. The decision of such members shall be final.

(6) For the purpose of the consideration and decision of any appeal under this rule, the members of the standing committee or commission so appointed shall consider all the relevant circumstances, and shall be entitled to inspect all documents and papers relating to the subject matter of the appeal, and be furnished with all information respecting the same which they may require. They shall give to the parties to the appeal an opportunity of appearing before them in person or through a legal or other representative.

(7) The members of the standing committee or the commission appointed in any diocese under this rule shall have power at any time to extend the time within which a notice of appeal is given.

Vacation of Seat by Member ceasing to be Qualified for Election

37. Where—

　(a) any lay member of a deanery synod, being a parochial representative or a representative under rule 22, ceases to be entered on the roll of the parish by which he was elected or, as the case may be, to be declared under the said rule to be a habitual worshipper at the cathedral church ;

　(b) any member of a diocesan synod elected by the house of clergy of a deanery synod ceases to be qualified for election by that house ;

　(c) any lay member of a diocesan synod elected by the house of laity of a deanery synod ceases to have the qualification of entry on the roll of any parish in that deanery or (in appropriate cases) of being declared a habitual worshipper at the cathedral church of the diocese under rule 22 ;

　(d) any elected member of the House of Laity of the General Synod ceases to have the qualification of entry on the roll of any parish in the diocese for which he was elected or of being declared a habitual worshipper as aforesaid ;

his seat shall forthwith be vacated:

Provided that, if the bishop's council and standing committee has determined that a person to whom paragraph (d) applies should remain a member of the House of Laity, his seat shall not be vacated under this rule.

Ex-Officio Membership not to Disqualify for Election

38. No lay person shall be disqualified from being elected or chosen a member of any body under these rules by the fact that he is also a member ex-officio of that body ; and no lay person shall be deemed to vacate his seat as such an elected or chosen member of any body by reason only of the fact that subsequently to his election or choice he has become a member of that body ex-officio.

PART VII

SUPPLEMENTARY AND INTERPRETATION

Casual Vacancies

39.—(1) Elections to fill casual vacancies among persons elected under these rules shall be conducted in the same manner as ordinary elections, a special meeting of the electing body being held, if necessary, for the purpose, provided that in the case of a casual vacancy among the parochial representatives elected to the parochial church council or deanery synod, such vacancy may be filled by the parochial church council. Such elections shall, where possible, be held at such times as will enable all casual vacancies among representatives of the laity who are electors to be filled at the time of every election to the House of Laity of the General Synod, but so that no such election shall be invalid by reason of any casual vacancies not having been so filled up.

(2) Elections to fill casual vacancies shall be held as soon as reasonably practicable after the vacancy has occurred, and elections to fill a casual vacancy in the House of Laity of the General Synod or either house of the diocesan synod shall be completed within six months from the occurrence of the vacancy: Provided that where a casual vacancy occurs in any of these three houses and the period for holding a general election to that house is due to begin within nine months of the vacancy, such vacancy shall not be filled unless the bishop so directs.

(3) The preceding provisions of this rule shall apply, so far as applicable and with the necessary modifications, to the choosing of persons under these rules as it applies to the election of persons thereunder, and shall also apply to the election or choosing of members of any body constituted under or in accordance with these rules.

(4) Any person elected or chosen to fill a casual vacancy shall hold office only for the unexpired portion of the term of office of the person in whose place he is elected or chosen.

Resignations

40. Persons holding office under these rules or members of bodies constituted by or in accordance with these rules may resign at will.

Notices

41. Any notice or other document required or authorised to be sent or given under these rules shall be deemed to have been duly sent or given if sent through the post addressed to the person to whom it is required or authorised to be sent or given at that person's last known address.

Revocation and Variation of Rules, etc.

42. Subject to the provisions of these rules any power conferred by these rules to make, approve, frame, pass or adopt any rule, order, resolution, determination, decision, appointment or scheme,

SCH. 3   or to give any consent or settle any constitution, or to prescribe the manner of doing anything, shall be construed as including a power, exercisable in a like manner and subject to the like conditions, to revoke or vary any such rule, order, resolution determination, decision, appointment, scheme, consent or constitution, or anything so prescribed.

Special Provisions

43.—(1) In the carrying out of these rules in any diocese the bishop of such diocese shall have power :—

(a) to make provision for any matter not herein provided for ;

(b) to appoint a person to do any act in respect of which there has been any neglect or default on the part of any person or body charged with any duty under these rules ;

(c) so far as may be necessary for the purpose of giving effect to the intention of these rules, to extend or alter the time for holding any meeting or election or to modify the procedure laid down by these rules in connection therewith ;

(d) in any case in which there has been no valid election, to direct a fresh election to be held and to give such directions in connection therewith as he may think necessary ; and

(e) in any case in which any difficulties arise, to give any directions which he may consider expedient for the purpose of removing the difficulties.

(2) The powers of the bishop under this rule shall not enable him :—

(a) to validate anything that was invalid at the time when it was done ;

(b) to give any direction that is contrary to any resolution of the General Synod.

(3) No proceedings of any body constituted under these rules shall be invalidated by any vacancy in the membership of that body or by any defect in the qualification, election or appointment of any members thereof.

(4) No proceedings shall be invalidated by the use of a form which differs from that prescribed by these rules if the form which has in fact been used is to a substantially similar effect. Any question as to whether the form which has been used is to a substantially similar effect shall be determined by the bishop.

(5) In the case of an omission in any parish to prepare or maintain a roll or form or maintain a council or to hold the annual meeting, the rural dean upon such omission being brought to his notice shall ascertain and report to the bishop the cause thereof.

(6) During a vacancy in an archbishopric or diocesan bishopric the functions of an archbishop or a diocesan bishop under these rules shall be exercisable by the guardian of the spiritualities.

(7) An archbishop or diocesan bishop or, during a vacancy, the guardian of the spiritualities may for any period of absence abroad

or incapacity through illness appoint a commissary and delegate   Sch. 3
to him all or any of the functions of the archbishop or bishop under
these rules, and, where during a vacancy, the guardian of the
spiritualities is a corporation aggregate, it shall appoint a commissary and delegate to him such functions as cannot appropriately
be exercised by the corporation.

Meaning of Minister, Parish and other words and phrases

44.—(1) In these rules :—

" actual communicant member " means a member who has
received Communion according to the use of the Church
of England or of another Church of the Anglican Communion or any overseas Church in communion with the
Church of England at least three times during the twelve
months preceding the date of his election or appointment ;

" the Measure " means the Synodical Government Measure
1969 ;

" minister " means :—

    (*a*) the incumbent of a parish ;

    (*b*) a curate licensed to the charge of a parish or a
minister acting as priest-in-charge of a parish in respect
of which rights of presentation are suspended ; and

    (*c*) a vicar in a team ministry to the extent that the
duties of a minister are assigned to him by a scheme
under the Pastoral Measure 1968 or his license from the   1968 No. 1.
bishop ;

" parish " means :—

    (*a*) an ecclesiastical parish ; and

    (*b*) a district which is constituted a " conventional
district " for the cure of souls and has a separate curate
licensed thereto.

" public worship " means public worship according to the rites
and ceremonies of the Church of England.

(2) Any reference in these rules to the laity shall be construed
as a reference to persons other than Clerks in Holy Orders, and
the expression " lay " in these rules shall be construed accordingly.

(3) References in these rules to the cathedral church of the
diocese shall include, in the case of the dioceses of London and
Oxford, references to Westminster Abbey and St. George's Chapel,
Windsor, respectively.

(4) If any question arises as to whether a Church is a Church
of the Anglican Communion or an overseas Church in communion
with the Church of England, it shall be conclusively determined
for the purposes of these rules by the Archbishops of Canterbury
and York.

(5) In these rules words importing residence include residence of
a regular nature but do not include residence of a casual nature.

(6) Any reference herein to " these rules " shall be construed as
including a reference to the Appendices hereto.

APPENDIX I

Section 1

APPLICATION FOR ENROLMENT ON CHURCH ELECTORAL ROLL

(Full Christian name and surname)

I ....

(Full postal address)

of ....

declare:—

    (i) I am baptised.

    (ii) I am a member of the Church of England.

or

I am a member of
    , being a Church of the Anglican Communion or an overseas Church in communion with the Church of England.*

    (iii) I am not a member of any other religious body which is not in communion with the Church of England.

    (iv) I have attained the age of seventeen years.

    (v) I am resident in the parish to which this application relates.

or

I am not resident in the parish and have habitually attended public worship in the parish in the last six months.*

    (vi) My name is not on the church electoral roll of any other parish.

or

my name is not on the church electoral roll of any other parish except that of the parish of .... from which roll I desire my name to be removed.

or

my name is not on the church electoral roll of any other parish except that of the parish of .... The parochial church council of that parish has given its consent to my name being on the rolls of both parishes for so long as I retain the necessary qualifications.*

I hereby apply to have my name entered on the Church Electoral Roll of the parish of ....

in the diocese of ....

Signed ....

Date ....

---

* Strike out whichever of the two or three possibilities is not applicable.

Section 2

Rule 2(1)

FORM OF NOTICE OF REVISION OF CHURCH ELECTORAL ROLL

Diocese of ....

Parish of ....

* NOTE— Notice is hereby given that the Church Electoral Roll
The Revision of the above parish will be revised by the Parochial
must be
completed Church Council,* beginning on .... the ....
not less than day of .... 19...... and ending on
15 days or
more than ...., the .... day of ....
28 days
before the 19......
Annual After such Revision, a copy of the Roll will forth-
Parochial
Church with be exhibited on, or near to, the principal door of
Meeting. the Parish Church for inspection.

Under the Church Representation Rules any persons are entitled
to have their names entered on the roll, if they : —

(i) are baptised,

(ii) are members of the Church of England or another Church
of the Anglican Communion or an overseas Church in
communion with the Church of England, and are not
members of any other religious body which is not in
communion with the Church of England,

(iii) are seventeen or over,

(iv) are resident in the parish, or, not being resident in the
parish, have habitually attended public worship in the
parish during the six months before the date of application
for enrolment, and

(v) have signed a form of application for enrolment.

Entry on the Rolls of two parishes at the same time is subject
to special conditions. No person's name may be on the Rolls of
more than two parishes at once.

Forms of application for enrolment can be obtained from the
undersigned, and should be returned, if possible, in time for the
Revision.

Any error discovered in the Roll should at once be reported to the
undersigned.

* Not less Dated this* .... day of ....
than 14 days
notice must 19......
be given.

Electoral Roll Officer

Address ....

Sch. 3   Section 3

Rule 2(4)

FORM OF NOTICE OF PREPARATION OF NEW ROLL

Diocese of ....

Parish of ....

* NOTE—   Notice is hereby given that under the Church Repre-
The new roll sentation Rules a new Church Electoral Roll is being
must be   prepared. All persons who wish to have their names
completed   entered on the new Roll, whether their names are entered
not less than
15 days or   on the present Roll or not, are requested to apply for
more than   enrolment if possible not later than...........................
28 days
before the   ....
Annual
Parochial   The new roll will come into operation on ....
Church
Meeting.   ....
              Forms of application for enrolment can be obtained
              from the undersigned.

Under the Church Representation Rules any persons are entitled
to have their names entered on the Roll, if they :—

   (i) are baptised,

   (ii) are members of the Church of England or another Church
        of the Anglican Communion or an overseas Church in
        communion therewith, and are not members of any other
        religious body which is not in communion with the Church
        of England,

   (iii) are seventeen or over,

   (iv) are resident in the parish, or, not being resident in the
        parish, have habitually attended public worship in the
        parish during the six months before the date of application
        for enrolment, and

   (v) have signed a form of application for enrolment.

Entry on the Rolls of two parishes at the same time is subject
to special conditions. No person's name may be on the Rolls of
more than two parishes at once.

Any error discovered on the Roll should at once be reported to
the undersigned.

              Dated this .... day of ....
              19......

                              Electoral Roll Officer
                       Address ....

Section 4   Rule 6(1)   Sᴄʜ. 3

NOTICE OF ANNUAL PAROCHIAL CHURCH MEETING

Parish of ....

The Annual Parochial Church Meeting will be held in ....

....

on .... day of ....

.... at ....

For the election of Parochial representatives of the laity as follows : —

To the Parochial Church Council .... representatives.

*To the Deanery Synod .... representatives.

For the election of Sidesmen.

For the consideration of : —

    (*a*) A copy or copies of the Roll ;

    (*b*) An Annual Report of the proceedings of the Council ;

    (*c*) An Annual Report on the financial affairs of the parish ;

    (*d*) The audited Accounts of the Council for the year ending on the 31st December immediately preceding the meeting ;

    (*e*) An audited Statement of the funds and property of the Council ;

    (*f*) A Report upon the fabric, goods and ornaments of the church or churches of the parish ;

    (*g*) A Report on the proceedings of the Deanery Synod ;

and other matters of parochial or general Church interest.

All persons whose names are entered upon the Church Electoral Roll of the parish (and such persons only) are entitled to vote at the election of parochial representatives of the laity.

Such persons may object to the inclusion on or omission from the roll of any name but must do so before the commencement of elections.

Parochial representatives of the laity must be lay persons who have communicated at least three times in the year before the annual meeting in the Church of England or another Church of the Anglican Communion or an overseas Church in communion with the Church of England. For the parochial church council they must be at least seventeen and have their names on the electoral roll of the parish. For the deanery synod they must be of age to vote at a Parliamentary election and have their names on the roll of one of the parishes in the area in question.

Any person whose name is on the roll may be a sidesman.

                Signed ....

              **Minister of the parish.

---

 * Include where applicable.

 ** Or " Vice-Chairman of the Parochial Church Council " as the case may be (see rule 6(3) of the Church Representation Rules).

Section 5

Rule 26(3)

NOTICE OF ELECTION TO HOUSE OF CLERGY OR HOUSE OF LAITY OF DIOCESAN SYNOD

Diocese of ....

Deanery of ....

1. An election of...... members of the House of Clergy/Laity of the Diocesan Synod will be held in the above Deanery on...............

2. Candidates must be nominated and seconded by qualified electors on forms to be obtained from.....................................

3. Nominations must be received by no later than 12 o'clock (noon) on ....

Date.....................................

....
Presiding Officer.

Section 6

Rule 26(3)

FORM OF NOMINATION TO THE HOUSE OF CLERGY OR HOUSE OF LAITY OF THE DIOCESAN SYNOD

Diocese of ....

Deanery of ....

Election of members of the House of Clergy/Laity of the Diocesan Synod

We the undersigned, being qualified electors, hereby nominate the following person as a candiate at the election in the above Deanery.

Surname	Other Names	Address and Description

Proposer's signature ....

Proposer's full name ....

Address ....

Seconder's signature ....

Seconder's full name ....

Address ....

I, the above named .... hereby signify my willingness to serve as a member of the House of Clergy/Laity of the Diocesan Synod if elected.

Candidate's signature ....

Note: This nomination must be sent to ....
so as to be received no later than 12 noon on ....

Section 7

Rule 26(4)

FORM OF VOTING PAPER FOR ELECTIONS TO THE HOUSE
OF CLERGY OR THE HOUSE OF LAITY OF THE
DIOCESAN SYNOD

.... Diocesan Synod

Election of members of the House of Clergy/Laity

Deanery of ....

.... members to be elected.

Voting Paper

Candidates' names, addresses and descriptions	Mark your vote in this column

Instructions to Voters

1. This voting paper must be signed.

2. You have as many votes as there are members to be elected.

3. You may not give more than one vote to any one candidate.

4. You vote by placing an " X " opposite the name(s) of the candidate(s) of your choice.

5. If you inadvertently spoil your voting paper you may return it to the Presiding Officer who will give you another paper.

6. This voting paper duly voted upon and signed must be delivered (by post or otherwise) to ....
so as to arrive by no later than ....

Signature of Voter ....
Full name ....
Address ....
....

APPENDIX II

General Provisions Relating to Parochial Church Councils

Officers of the council.

1.—(*a*) The minister of the parish shall be chairman of the parochial church council (hereinafter referred to as " the council ").

(*b*) A lay member of the council shall be elected as vice-chairman of the council.

(*c*) During the vacancy of the benefice and when the chairman is incapacitated by absence or illness or any other cause the vice-chairman of the council shall act as chairman and have all the powers vested in the chairman.

(*d*) The council may appoint one of their number to act as secretary of the council. If no member is appointed so to act the council shall appoint some other fit person with such remuneration (if any) as they shall think fit. The secretary shall have charge of all documents relating to the current business of the council except that, unless he is the electoral roll officer, he shall not have charge of the roll. He shall be responsible for keeping the minutes, shall record all resolutions passed by the council and shall keep the secretary of the diocesan synod and deanery synod informed as to his name and address.

(*e*) The council may appoint one or more of their number to act as treasurer solely or jointly. Failing such appointment, the office of treasurer shall be discharged jointly by such of the churchwardens as are members of the council, or, if there is only one such churchwarden, by the churchwarden solely. No remuneration shall be paid to any person in respect of his appointment as treasurer

(*f*) The council shall appoint an electoral roll officer, who may but need not be a member of the council and may be the secretary, and if he is not a member may pay to him such remuneration as it shall think fit. He shall have charge of the roll.

(*g*) If auditors to the council are not appointed by the annual meeting, or if auditors appointed by the annual meeting are unable or unwilling to act, auditors shall be appointed by the council. The remuneration (if any) of the auditors shall be paid by the council.

Meetings of Council.

2. The council shall hold not less than four meetings in each year. Meetings shall be convened by the chairman and if not more than four meetings are held they shall be at quarterly intervals so far as possible.

Power to call meetings.

3. The chairman may at any time convene a meeting of the council. If he refuse or neglect to do so within seven days after a requisition for that purpose signed by not less than one-third of the members of the council has been presented to him those members may forthwith convene a meeting.

Notices relating to meetings.

4.—(*a*) Except as provided in paragraph 8 of this Appendix, at least ten clear days before any meeting of the council notice thereof specifying the time and place of the intended meeting and signed by or on behalf of the chairman of the council or the persons convening the meeting shall be posted at or near the principal door of every church, or building licensed for public worship in the parish.

(b) Not less than seven days before the meeting a notice thereof specifying the time and place of the meeting signed by or on behalf of the secretary shall be sent to every member of the council. Such notice shall contain the agenda of the meeting including any motion or other business proposed by any member of the council of which notice has been received by the secretary.

5. Subject to the provisions of rule 18 the chair at a meeting of the council shall be taken:—

(a) by the chairman of the council if he is present ;

(b) if the chairman of the council is not present, or his office is vacant, by the vice-chairman of the council if he is present :

Provided that at any such meeting the chairman or the vice-chairman of the council shall, if he thinks it expedient to do so or the meeting so resolves, vacate the chair either generally or for the purposes of any business in which he has a personal interest or for any other particular business.

Should neither the chairman or vice-chairman be available to take the chair for any meeting or for any particular item on the agenda during a meeting then a chairman shall be chosen by those members present from among their number and the person so chosen shall preside for that meeting or for that particular item.

6. No business shall be transacted at any meeting of the council unless at least one-third of the members are present thereat and no business which is not specified in the agenda shall be transacted at any meeting except by the consent of three-quarters of the members present at the meeting.

7. The business of a meeting of the council shall be transacted in the order set forth in the agenda unless the council by resolution otherwise determine.

8. In case of sudden emergency or other special circumstances requiring immediate action by the council a meeting may be convened by the chairman of the council at not less than three days' notice in writing to the members of the council but the quorum for the transaction of any business at such meetings shall be a majority of the then existing members of the council and no business shall be transacted at such meeting except as is specified in the notice convening the meeting.

9. The meeting of the council shall be held at such place as the council may direct or in the absence of such direction as the chairman may direct.

10. The business of the Council shall be decided by a majority of the members present and voting thereon.

11. In the case of an equal division of votes the chairman of the meeting shall have a second or casting vote.

12.—(a) The names of the members present at any meeting of the council shall be recorded in the minutes.

SCH. 3

(*b*) If one-fifth of the members present and voting on any resolution so require, the minutes shall record the names of the members voting for and against that resolution.

(*c*) Any member of the council shall be entitled to require that the minutes shall contain a record of the manner in which his vote was cast on any resolution.

(*d*) Members of the council shall have access to the minutes of all meetings, but no other person other than the bishop or a person authorised by him in writing, or the archdeacon, shall have access to the minutes without the authority of the council.

Adjournments.

13. Any meeting of the council may adjourn its proceedings to such time and place as may be determined at such meeting.

Standing committee.

14.—(*a*) The council shall have a standing committee consisting of not less than five persons. The minister and such of the churchwardens as are members of the council shall be ex-officio members of the standing committee, and the council shall by resolution appoint at least two other members of the standing committee from among its own members and may remove any person so appointed.

(*b*) The standing committee shall have power to transact the business of the council between the meetings thereof subject to any directions given by the council.

Other committees.

15. The council may appoint other committees for the purpose of the various branches of church work in the parish and may include therein persons who are not members of the council. The minister shall be a member of all committees ex-officio.

Validity of proceedings.

16. No proceedings of the council shall be invalidated by any vacancy in the membership of the council or by any defect in the qualification or election of any member thereof.

Interpretation.

17. Any question arising on the interpretation of this Appendix shall be referred to the bishop of the diocese and any decision given by him or by any person appointed by him on his behalf shall be final.

Section 4.

SCHEDULE 4

TRANSITIONAL PROVISIONS

Transfer of Functions from Convocations

1.—(1) The transfer of functions from the Convocations of Canterbury and York to the General Synod on the appointed day shall not affect the validity of anything done by the Convocations before the appointed day in the exercise of those functions ; and any Canons, Acts of Convocation, regulations, directions, instruments or other things made, given or done by the said Convocations in the exercise of those functions shall, if in force immediately before that day, continue in force and have effect as if they had been made, given or done by the General Synod.

(2) Any business of the said Convocations in the exercise of the functions aforesaid, being business which was pending immediately before the dissolution of the said Convocations preceding the appointed day, shall not abate by reason of the dissolution but may be resumed by the General Synod at the stage which the business had reached immediately before the dissolution.

Reconstitution of Church Assembly

2.—(1) The reconstitution of the Church Assembly as the General Synod shall not affect the validity of anything done by the Assembly before the appointed day ; and any orders, regulations, rules, directions, instruments or other things made, given or done by the Church Assembly and in force immediately before the appointed day shall continue in force and have effect as if they had been made, given or done by the Church Assembly reconstituted as the General Synod.

(2) The reconstitution of the Church Assembly as the General Synod shall not affect any Boards, Commissions, Committees or other bodies of the Church Assembly which would otherwise continue in being, or any officers of the Church Assembly (which expression includes all persons in receipt of salaries paid from the Church Assembly Fund) ; and they shall continue as the Boards, Commissions, Committees, bodies and officers of the General Synod, but without prejudice to the making of such changes as the General Synod may determine in accordance with its constitution and standing orders.

(3) Any business pending before the Church Assembly immediately before the appointed day may be continued by the Assembly reconstituted as the General Synod.

(4) The Archbishops of Canterbury and York may, before the appointed day, make or authorise the making of all such temporary appointments and arrangements and the doing of all such things as they may think necessary to enable the functions of the General Synod to be discharged effectively as from the appointed day.

Changes affecting Diocesan and Ruridecanal Conferences

3.—(1) The dissolution of a diocesan conference and the transfer of functions from the conference to a diocesan synod shall not affect the validity of anything done by the conference before its dissolution or affect the continuance in being of any other diocesan body ; and any scheme, direction, appointment, election, resolution, notice, instrument or other thing given, made or done by the diocesan conference which could have been given, made or done by the diocesan synod shall, if in force immediately before the conference was dissolved, continue in force and have effect as given, made or done by the diocesan synod.

(2) The repeal of the Representation of the Laity Measure 1956 and the Diocesan Conferences Regulation 1958 shall not take effect as respects any diocesan conference or ruridecanal conference until that conference is dissolved under this Measure. 1956 No. 2.

(3) It shall not be necessary to hold any further elections of members of diocesan conferences and ruridecanal conferences and the term of office of the existing elected members thereof shall be extended until the conferences are dissolved under this Measure, and this provision shall be deemed to have had effect as from the 1st January 1969.

Commencement of Church Representation Rules

4.—(1) The repeal of the Rules for the Representation of the Laity by this Measure shall not affect any person's membership of the House of Laity or of any other body, or the tenure of any office, or the contents of any church electoral roll, until such membership is terminated, or such office is vacated, or such roll is revised or replaced, under the Church Representation Rules.

(2) The references in rule 12(1)(e) of the said Rules to lay members of any deanery synod, diocesan synod or the General Synod shall, until the said synods are respectively constituted, be construed as references to lay members of any ruridecanal conference, diocesan conference or the Church Assembly, and references in rule 19(2) and (3) and Rule 24(3) to the General Synod shall, until it is constituted, be construed as references to the Church Assembly.

(3) Any determination, resolution, appointment, ruling, consent or other thing made, given or done for the purposes of any provision of the Rules for the Representation of the Laity shall, if in effect immediately before the commencement of this Measure, continue to have effect, so far as applicable, for the purposes of any corresponding provision of the Church Representation Rules, and may be revoked or varied as if made under the last-mentioned Rules.

5.—(1) The first elections of parochial representatives of the laity to deanery synods under the Church Representation Rules shall take place at the annual meetings of parishes in the year 1970, and the first choosing of members of deanery synods under any such resolution as is mentioned in Part III of the said Rules shall be completed not later than thirtieth April in that year, and the powers of diocesan synods under the said Part III shall, for the purposes of the first elections and choosing as aforesaid, be exercised by diocesan conferences.

(2) The first elections by the members of deanery synods of members of diocesan synods under Part IV of the Church Representation Rules shall take place in the year 1970; and the diocesan synods shall forthwith after those elections be constituted in accordance with the said Part IV, and the powers of diocesan synods under that Part shall, for the purposes of those first elections, be exercised by diocesan conferences.

(3) The election of members of the House of Laity due to take place in the year 1970 under the Rules for the Representation of the Laity shall be held during the periods in that year fixed under rule 25(1) of those Rules, and rule 25(4) thereof shall apply to that

election instead of rule 33(4) of the Church Representation Rules, but in other respects the election and matters connected therewith shall be held and carried out in accordance with the Church Representation Rules, subject to the modification that the powers exercisable by the General Synod shall be exercisable by the Church Assembly (as constituted at the passing of this Measure) ; and the House of Laity then elected and constituted shall, on the appointed day, be the House of Laity of the General Synod.

(4) Any certificate or information required by the Church Representation Rules to be given to or by the secretaries of deanery synods, diocesan synods or the General Synod shall, before the said synods are constituted, be given to or by the secretaries of ruridecanal conferences, diocesan conferences or the Church Assembly, as the case may be, and the certificate required to be given under rule 25(5) shall certify the number of beneficed or licensed clergy of the chapter of clergy of the ruridecanal conference, which shall be treated as if it were the house of clergy of the deanery synod ; and any certificates received by the secretaries of the said conferences shall, where necessary, be given or sent to the secretaries of the said synods when they are constituted.

(5) The powers of diocesan synods under rule 23 and rule 28 of the said rules to make rules of procedure for deanery synods and diocesan synods respectively shall be exercisable by diocesan conferences before the constitution of diocesan synods, without prejudice to any rules so made being amended or replaced by diocesan synods when constituted.

Power to Remove Transitional Difficulties

6. (1) If any difficulty arises on or in connection with any of the transitional matters for which this Schedule provides, it shall be referred to the Archbishops of Canterbury and York who may give any directions which they may consider expedient for the purpose of removing the difficulty, and such directions may extend the time for doing anything required by the Church Representation Rules for or in connection with the first elections or choosing of members of any bodies constituted under or in accordance with those Rules.

(2) Rule 43(6) and (7) of the said Rules shall extend to the functions of the Archbishops under this paragraph.

TABLE V

Tables of the Derivations of the Consolidation Acts of 1969

CONTENTS

THE CUSTOMS DUTIES (DUMPING AND SUBSIDIES) ACT 1969 (c. 16)

Note:—The following abbreviations are used in this Table:—

1957 = The Customs Duties (Dumping and Subsidies) Act 1957
(1957 c. 18)

1958 = The Import Duties Act 1958
(1958 c. 6)

1968 = The Customs Duties (Dumping and Subsidies) Amendment
Act 1968
(1968 c. 33)

Section of 1969 Act	Derivation
1(1), (2)	1957 s. 1(1), (2); 1968 s. 2(1), (6).
(3)	1957 s. 2(1), (2); 1968 s. 2(1), (2), (5).
(4), (5)	1968 s. 2(2), (3).
2(1)–(5)	1957 s. 3(1), (2), (3), (4), (6).
3(1)–(4)	1957 s. 6(1)–(4).
4(1)–(3)	1957 s. 7(1)–(3); 1968 s. 3(1), (2).
(4)	1968 s. 3(2).
(5)	1957 s. 7(2); 1968 s. 3(2).
(6)	1957 s. 7(4).
5(1)	1957 s. 8(1).
(2)	1957 s. 8(1), (3).
(3)	1957 ss. 6, 7, 8(2); 1968 s. 3.
6(1)	1957 s. 9(2).
(2)	1957 ss. 6, 7; 1968 s. 3.
7(1)	1957 s. 1(1), 2(1), (2); 1968 s. 2(1), (2), (6).
(2)	1957 s. 1(3).
(3)	1957 s. 3(5).
8(1)–(3)	1968 s. 1(1)–(3).
(4)	1968 s. 1(2).
(5)	1968 s. 2(1), (3), (4).
9(1)	1968 s. 1(4), Sch. §1.
(2)	1968 Sch. §2.
(3)	1968 Sch. §3(1).
(4)	1968 Sch. §1.
10(1)	1957 s. 2(4).
(2)	1957 s. 2(5).
(3)	1957 s. 2(3); 1968 s. 4(1).
(4)	1957 s. 2(3).
(5)	1957 s. 2(4); 1958 s. 3(1).
11(1), (2)	1957 s. 4(1), (2).
(3)	1968 Sch. §3(2).
12(1), (2), (3)	1958 s. 7(4); Finance Act 1965 (c. 25) s. 2(1), (2), (3); Finance Act 1966 (c. 18) s. 1(1).

CUSTOMS DUTIES (DUMPING AND SUBSIDIES) ACT—*cont.*

Section of 1969 Act	Derivation
13(1)	1957 s. 9(1).
(2), (3)	1957 s. 8(4).
14(1)–(4)	1957 s. 5(1), (2).
15(1)	1957 s. 11(1); 1958 s. 13(6); 1968 ss. 1(5), 4(2).
(2)	1957 s. 11(1); 1958 s. 13(6); 1968 s. 4(2).
(3)	1957 s. 11(1); 1958 s. 13(6).
(4)	1957 s. 11(1).
16(1)	1957 s. 11(2); 1968 s. 1(6).
(2)	1968 s. 1(6).
17	1957 s. 9(1); 1968 s. 2(5).

THE LATE NIGHT REFRESHMENT HOUSES ACT 1969 (c. 53)

Note: The following abbreviations are used in this Table:—

1860	=	The Refreshment Houses Act 1860 (c. 27).
1861	=	The Revenue (No. 2) Act 1861 (c. 91).
1949	=	The Finance Act 1949 (c. 47), section 15.
1952	=	The Customs and Excise Act 1952 (c. 44).
1964	=	The Refreshment Houses Act 1964 (c. 88).
1967	=	The Refreshment Houses Act 1967 (c. 38).
Memo	=	Lord Chancellor's Memorandum under the Consolidation of Enactments (Procedure) Act 1949

Section of 1969 Act	Derivation
1	1860 s. 6; 1861 s. 8; Memo.
2	1860 ss. 6, 9; 1949.
3	1861 s. 9; 1949; Local Government Act 1966 (c. 42) ss. 3(52), 40(2), Sch. 3 Part II; Transfer of Functions (Refreshment House Licences Order 1969 (S.I. 1969 No. 377).
4	1952 s. 237.
5	1860 ss. 11, 12; Memo.
6	1860 s. 16; 1964 s. 2; 1967 s. 4(3).
7	1967 ss. 1, 2.
8	1964 s. 1.
9	1860 ss. 32, 41; Betting, Gaming and Lotteries Act 1963 (c. 2) s. 40; Gaming Act 1968 (c. 65), s. 53, Sch. 11 Part I.
10	1860 ss. 18, 41.
11	1860 s. 41; 1964 ss. 2, 3; 1967 ss. 1(2), 3; Penalties for Drunkenness Act 1962 (c. 52).
12	1952 s. 313.
13	—
14	—
15	—

THE TRUSTEE SAVINGS BANKS ACT 1969 (c. 50)

Note:—The following abbreviations are used in this Table—

1954	= The Trustee Savings Banks Act 1954 (2 & 3 Eliz. 2. c. 63)
1955	= The Trustee Savings Banks (Pensions) Act 1955 (3 & 4 Eliz. 2. c. 12)
1958	= The Trustee Savings Banks Act 1958 (6 & 7 Eliz. 2. c. 8)
1961	= The Trustee Investments Act 1961 (9 & 10 Eliz. 2. c. 62)
1964	= The Trustee Savings Banks Act 1964 (1964 c. 4)
1965	= The Administration of Estates (Small Payments) Act 1965 (1965 c. 32)
1968	= The Trustee Savings Banks Act 1968 (1968 c. 6)
1968 (c. 13)	= The National Loans Act 1968 (1968 c. 13)
S.I. 1955	= The Trustee Savings Banks (Pensions) Order 1955 (S.I. 1955/842 II, p. 2388)
S.I. 1968	= The Minister for the Civil Service Order (S.I. 1968/1656)
R (followed by a number)	= The recommendation set out in the paragraph of that number in the Appendix to the Report of the Law Commissions (Cmnd. 4004)

Section of 1969 Act	Derivation
1	1954, ss. 1, 85; 1961, s. 16, Sch. 4, para. 4(1).
2	1954, s. 2; **R. 1.**
3	1954, s. 3.
4	1954, s. 4; S.I. 1968; **R. 2.**
5	1954, s. 5.
6	1954, s. 6; **R. 1, 3.**
7	1954, s. 7; **R. 3.**
8	1954, s. 8.
9	1954, s. 9(1)–(8); 1958, s. 5(1), (2).
10	1954, s. 9(9)–(12).
11(1) (2) (3) (4)	1954, s. 10(1). 1958, s. 4(2). 1954, s. 10(2); 1958, s. 5(4). 1954, s. 10(5); 1958, s. 5(6).
12	1954, s. 11.
13	1964, ss. 1, 9, Sch. 2, para. 1.

TRUSTEE SAVINGS BANKS ACT—*cont.*

Section of 1969 Act	Derivation
14(1)	1954, s. 12(1); 1964, s. 9, Sch. 2, para. 2.
(2)	1964, s. 9, Sch. 2, para. 2.
(3)	1961, s. 16, Sch. 4, para. 5.
(4)	1954, s. 12(2); 1964, s. 9, Sch. 2, para. 2; **R. 4.**
(5)	1954, s. 12(3); 1964, s. 9, Sch. 2, para. 2.
15	1954, s. 13.
16	1954, s. 14.
17(1)	1958, s. 2(4).
(2)	1954, s. 15(1).
(3)	1961, s. 16, Sch. 4, para. 5.
(4)	1954, s. 15(2).
(5)	1954, s. 15(3).
18	1954, s. 16.
19	1964, ss. 2, 9, Sch. 2, para. 4
20	1964, s. 3.
21	1964, s. 4.
22	1964, s. 5.
23	1964, s. 6.
24	1954, s. 17; 1961, s. 16, Sch. 4, para. 5.
25	1954, s. 18.
26	1954, s. 19.
27	1954, s. 20; 1961, s. 16, Sch. 4, para. 4(1), (2); **R. 5.**
28(1)–(4)	1954, s. 21(1)–(4); 1964, s. 9, Sch. 2, paras. 3, 4; Post Office Act, 1969 c. 48, s. 94, Sch. 6, Pt. III, **R. 6, 7.**
(5), (6)	1954, s. 21(5), (6); 1965, s. 1, Sch. 1 Pt. II; **R. 4, 8.**
29	1965, s. 6(1), (2), (4).
30	1954, s. 22; 1958, s. 5(7); **R. 10.**
31	1954, s. 24; 1961, s. 16, Sch. 4, para. 4(3); **R. 11.**
32	1954, s. 25; **R. 12.**
33	1954, s. 26; 1964, s. 7(1), (2).
34(1)	1954, s. 27(1).
(2)	1954, s. 27(2); 1968, s. 1.
(3)	1964, s. 7(3).
(4)	1954, s. 27(2).
(5)	1954, s. 85; 1958, s. 1(2); 1964, s. 7(4).
(6)	1954, s. 27(3).
(7)	1954, s. 27(4).
35	1958, s. 3(2), (3); 1964, s. 9, Sch. 2, para. 10.
36	1954, s. 32; 1968 (c. 13), s. 13(7).
37	1954, s. 33.

TRUSTEE SAVINGS BANKS ACT—*cont.*

Section of 1969 Act	Derivation
38	1958, s. 3(4).
39	1954, s. 34; 1968, s. 5(1), (2).
40	1954, s. 35.
41	1954, s. 36; 1968 (c. 13), s. 1(8).
42	1954, s. 37; 1968, s. 5(1), (2).
43	1954, s. 39.
44(1)	1954, s. 40(1); 1968, s. 6.
(2)	1954, s. 40(2); 1958, s. 2(5).
45	1958, s. 2(5); 1968, s. 3(4), (5).
46	1968, s. 3(1), (2), (6); 1968 (c. 13), s. 13(7).
47	1958, s. 2(2), (3).
48	1954, s. 42; 1958, s. 3, Sch. 2, para. 2.
49	1954, s. 43; 1958, s. 3, Sch. 2, para. 2; 1964, s. 9, Sch. 2, para. 5.
50	1954, s. 44.
51(1)	1958, s. 4(1).
(2)	1958, s. 4(2); 1968, s. 2(3).
(3)	1958, s. 4(2), (3).
52(1)	1954, s. 45(1).
(2)	1954, s. 45(1).
(3)	1954, s. 45(1).
(4)	1954, s. 45(2).
(5)	1958, s. 4(4).
(6)	1958, s. 4(5).
(7)	1958, s. 4(2).
(8)	1954, s. 45(3).
53	1968, s. 2(1), (2).
54(1)	1954, s. 75(1); 1958, ss. 3(5), 4(6), Sch. 2, para. 2.
(2)	1954, s. 75(1); 1958, s. 4(7).
(3)	1954, s. 75(1).
(4)	1954, s. 75(2).
(5)	1958, s. 4(8).
55	1954, s. 46.
56	1954, s. 47; 1968, s. 8; **R. 13.**
57	1954, s. 48.
58	1954, s. 49; 1964, ss. 8(1), (4), 9, Sch. 2, para. 6; **R. 14.**
59	1954, s. 50.
60	1954, s. 70; 1964, s. 8(2)–(4).
61	1954, s. 51; 1958, s. 5(3).
62	1954, s. 52; 1958, s. 4(6).

Table of Derivations

TRUSTEE SAVINGS BANKS ACT—*cont.*

Section of 1969 Act	Derivation
63	1954, s. 53, 1958, s. 1(3); 1964, s. 7(5)(*a*).
64	1954, s. 54; Post Office Act 1969 c. 48, s. 94, Sch. 6 Pt. III.
65	1954, s. 55; 1958, s. 3(5), Sch. 2, paras. 2, 3; **R. 15.**
66	1954, s. 56; 1958, s. 3(5), Sch. 2, para. 2; 1964, s. 9, Sch. 2, para. 6; Post Office Act 1969 c. 48, s. 94, Sch. 6 Pt. III.
67	1954, s. 57; **R. 16.**
68	1954, s. 58; **R. 17**
69	1954, s. 59.
70	1958, s. 5(9).
71	1954, s. 60; **R. 18.**
72	1954, s. 61; **R. 19.**
73	1954, s. 62.
74	1954, s. 63.
75	1954, s. 64; S.I. 1955.
76	1954, s. 65.
77	1954, s. 66; S.I. 1968.
78	1954, s. 67; 1968, s. 7(1), (2), (4).
79	1958, s. 6; S.I. 1968.
80	1954, s. 68; 1964, s. 7(5)(*b*).
81	1954, s. 69; 1958, s. 6(1).
82	1955, s. 1; 1958, s. 6(2); S.I. 1968.
83	1954, s. 71; 1968, s. 5(2).
84	1968, s. 5(2).
85	1954, s. 72.
86	1954, s. 73; **R. 4.**
87	1954, s. 74; 1958, s. 3(4).
88	1954, s. 6; 1968 (c. 13), s. 1(8).
89	1954, s. 77.
90	1954, s. 78.
91	1954, s. 79; S.I. 1968.
92	1954, s. 80; **R. 20.**
93	1958, s. 3(7); 1964, s. 12.

TRUSTEE SAVINGS BANKS ACT—*cont.*

Section of 1969 Act	Derivation
94	1958, s. 1(5); 1964, s. 7(5)(*c*); Transfer of Functions (Shipping and Construction of Ships) Order: S.I. 1965/145, I p. 438.
95	1954, ss. 10(5), 81; 1958, s. 4(9); 1964, s. 11; 1968, s. 10.
96(1)	[Repeals and revocation.]
(2)	[Savings.]
(3)	1954, s. 4(2); **R. 2.**
(4)	1954, s. 82(3), (4).
(5)	1958, s. 2(7); 1968, s. 3(3).
(6)	1958, s. 4(9).
(7)	[Consequential amendments.]
(8)	[Consequential amendments.]
(9)	[Consequential amendments.]
(10)	[Consequential amendment.]
(11)	[Saving.]
97	1954, s. 83; 1955, s. 2(2); 1958, s. 8(2); 1964, s. 13(2); 1968, s. 12(2).
98	1954, s. 84.
99	1954, s. 85; 1955, s. 2(2); 1958, s. 8(2); 1964, s. 13(2); 1968, s. 12(2); **R. 21.**
100	[Short title and commencement.]
Sch. 1	1954, Sch. 1.
2	1964, Sch. 1.
3	[Repeals and revocation. **R. 4, 5, 7, 9, 12, 13, 18.**]

TABLE VI

Effect of Legislation

Acts and Measures (in chronological order)
repealed, amended or otherwise affected
by those Acts and Statutory Instruments
which received the Royal Assent or were made during 1969.

LIST OF ABBREVIATIONS

am.	amended		ext.	extended
appl.	applied		incorp. ...	incorporated
appl. (mod.) ...	applied with modifications		mod. ...	modified
C.A.M. ...	Church Assembly Measures		restr. ...	restricted
cont.	continued		rep.	repealed
excl.	excluded		S.I.	Statutory Instrument
expld. ...	explained		subst. ...	substituted

Session and Chap. or No. of Measure	Short title or Subject	How affected	Chapter of 1969 Act or number of Measure or Statutory Instrument
3 Edw. 1: c. 16	Statute of Westminster, the First [1275].	Rep.	52, S.L. (Repeals).
13 Edw. 1 c. 5	Statute of Westminster, the Second [1285].	Rep. and superseded ...	52, ss. 1, 2, sch. Pt. II.
c. 6	Statute of Winchester [1285].	Rep.	52, S.L. (Repeals).
c. 37	Distress Act 1285 ...	Rep.	52, S.L. (Repeals).
c. 42	Fees of the King's Marshall [1285].	Rep.	52, S.L. (Repeals).
25 Edw. 1	Confirmation of Magna Carta [1297].	Residue rep. (exc. chapters 1, 9, 29, 37).	52, S.L. (Repeals).
	Confirmation of the Charters [1297].	Rep. (exc. chapters 1, 6)	52, S.L. (Repeals).
	Statute concerning Tallage [1297].	Rep. (exc. chapter 1) ...	52, S.L. (Repeals).
28 Edw. 1	Articles upon the Charters [1300].	Residue rep.	52, S.L. (Repeals).
9 Edw. 2 Stat. 1 ...	Articles for the Clergy [1315].	Residue rep.	52, S.L. (Repeals).
17 Edw. 2 c. 10	King's presentation to vacant churches (Temp. Incert.).	Rep. and superseded ...	52, ss. 1, 2, sch. Pt. II.

Session and Chap. or No. of Measure	Short title or Subject	How affected	Chapter of 1969 Act or number of Measure or Statutory Instrument
1 Edw. 3 **Stat. 2** c. 9	Borough liberties [1327]	Rep.	52, S.L. (Repeals).
2 Edw. 3 c. 8	Statute of Northampton (Commands in delay of Justice) [1328].	Rep.	52, S.L. (Repeals).
c. 15	Statute of Northampton (Keeping of fairs) [1328].	Rep.	52, S.L. (Repeals).
5 Edw. 3 c. 9	Unlawful attachment [1331].	Rep.	52, S.L. (Repeals).
14 Edw. 3 **Stat. 1** c. 1	Confirmation of liberties [1340].	Rep.	52, S.L. (Repeals).
25 Edw. 3 **Stat. 6** ...	Ordinance for the Clergy [1351].	Residue rep.	52, S.L. (Repeals).
13 Ric. 2 **Stat. 1** c. 1	Royal presentations to Benefices [1389].	Residue rep. and superseded.	52, ss. 1, 2, sch. Pt. II.
15 Ric. 2 c. 6	Appropriation of Benefices [1391].	Residue rep.	52, S.L. (Repeals).
4 Hen. 4 c. 12	Appropriation of Benefices [1402].	Residue rep.	52, S.L. (Repeals).
7 Hen. 4 c. 9	Sales by Wholesale in City of London [1405].	Rep.	52, S.L. (Repeals).
8 Hen. 6 c. 1	Convocation to have privilege of Parliament [1429].	Residue rep.	52, S.L. (Repeals).
18 Hen. 6 c. 1	Date of letters patent [1439].	Rep.	52, S.L. (Repeals).
27 Hen. 6 c. 5	Sunday Fairs Act 1448	Rep. (saving)	52, ss. 1, 4(1), sch. Pt. IV.
23 Hen. 8 c. 20	An Act concerning restraint of payment of annates to the See of Rome [1531].	Residue rep.	52, S.L. (Repeals).

Session and Chap. or No. of Measure	Short title or Subject	How affected	Chapter of 1969 Act or number of Measure or Statutory Instrument
24 Hen. 8 c. 12	Ecclesiastical Appeals Act 1532.	Residue rep.	52, S.L. (Repeals).
25 Hen. 8 c. 19	Submission of the Clergy Act 1533.	Residue rep. (exc. ss. 1, 3)	52, S.L. (Repeals).
		Ss. 1, 3 saved	52, s. 4(2).
		Ss. 1, 3 appl.	C.A.M. No. 2, s. 1(3).
c. 20	Appointment of Bishops Act 1533.	Preamble, ss. 1, 2 rep. ...	52, S.L. (Repeals).
		Ss. 3, 4, 7 saved... ...	52, s. 4(2).
c. 21	Ecclesiastical Licences Act 1533.	Preamble, ss. 1, 2, 15, 21, 23 rep.	52, S.L. (Repeals).
		Ss. 3–14, 17, 18 saved ...	52, s. 4(2).
26 Hen. 8 c. 14	Suffragan Bishops Act 1534.	Saved	52, s. 4(2).
27 Hen. 8 c. 28	Suppression of Religious Houses Act 1535.	Residue rep.	52, S.L. (Repeals).
28 Hen. 8 c. 5	Apprentices Act 1536 ...	Residue rep.	52, S.L. (Repeals).
c. 16	Ecclesiastical Licences Act 1536.	Residue rep.	52, S.L. (Repeals).
31 Hen. 8 c. 13	Suppression of Religious Houses Act 1539.	Rep. (exc. s. 19) ...	52, S.L. (Repeals).
32 Hen. 8 c. 7	Tithe Act 1540	S. 5 residue rep. ...	52, S.L. (Repeals).
c. 20	Liberties to be used [1540]	Rep.	52, S.L. (Repeals).
c. 37	Cestui que vie Act 1540...	Residue rep.	52, S.L. (Repeals).
c. 51	Queen Consort Act 1540	Residue rep.	52, S.L. (Repeals).
34 & 35 Hen. 8: c. 20 ...	Feigned Recoveries Act 1542.	Residue rep.	52, S.L. (Repeals).
37 Hen. 8: c. 4	Dissolution of Colleges Act 1545.	Residue rep.	52, S.L. (Repeals).
1 Edw. 6: c.1	Sacrament Act 1547 ...	Residue rep. (exc. s. 8)...	52, S.L. (Repeals).
		S. 8 saved	52, s. 4(2).

Session and Chap. or No. of Measure	Short title or Subject	How affected	Chapter of 1969 Act or number of Measure or Statutory Instrument
2 & 3 Edw. 6:			
c. 1	Act of Uniformity 1548	Residue rep. (exc. s. 7)...	52, S.L. (Repeals).
		S. 7 saved	52, s. 4(3).
c. 21	Clergy Marriage Act 1548	Residue rep.	52, S.L. (Repeals).
5 & 6 Edw. 6:			
c. 1	Act of Uniformity 1551...	Residue rep.	52, S.L. (Repeals).
c. 3	Holy Days and Fasting Days Act 1551.	Residue rep.	52, S.L. (Repeals).
c. 12	Clergy Marriage Act 1551	Residue rep.	52, S.L. (Repeals).
1 Mary: Sess. 3			
c. 1	Queen Regent's Prerogative Act 1554.	Rep.	52, S.L. (Repeals).
1 & 2 Phil. & Mar.:			
c. 12	Distress Act 1554 ...	Residue rep.	52, S.L. (Repeals).
1 Eliz 2:			
c. 1	Act of Supremacy 1558	Residue rep. (exc. s. 8)...	52, S.L. (Repeals).
c. 2	Act of Uniformity 1558...	Residue rep. (exc. s. 13)...	52, S.L. (Repeals).
5 Eliz. 1:			
c. 18	Lord Keeper Act 1562...	Rep.	52, S.L. (Repeals).
13 Eliz. 1:			
c. 2	An Act against the bringing in and putting in execution of bulls and other instruments from the See of Rome [1571].	Residue rep.	52, S.L. (Repeals).
c. 12	Ordination of Ministers Act 1571.	Residue rep.	52, S.L. (Repeals).
18 Eliz. 1:			
c. 15	An Act for Reformation of Abuses in Goldsmiths [1575].	Resdiue rep.	52, S.L. (Repeals).
35 Eliz. 1:			
c. 3	An Act explaining the Statute of 34 Hen. 8 touching grants [1592].	Rep.	52, S.L. (Repeals).
7 Jas. 1:			
c. 12	Shop-books Evidence Act 1609.	Residue rep.	52, S.L. (Repeals).
c. 15	Crown Debts Act 1609...	Residue rep. ...	52, S.L. (Repeals).

Session and Chap. or No. of Measure	Short title or Subject	How affected	Chapter of 1969 Act or number of Measure or Statutory Instrument
21 Jas. 1:			
c. 3	Statute of Monopolies [1623].	Preamble, Ss. 1 rep. in pt., 2–4 rep.	52, S.L. (Repeals).
1 Chas. 1:			
c. 1	Sunday Observance Act 1625.	Residue rep.	52, S.L. (Repeals).
3 Chas. 1:			
c. 2	An Act for the further reformation of sunday abuses committed on the Lord's Day commonly called Sunday [1627].	Residue rep.	52, S.L. (Repeals).
16 Chas. 1:			
c. 14	Ship Money Act 1640 ...	Residue rep.	52, S.L. (Repeals).
12 Chas. 2:			
c. 1	Parliament Act 1660 ...	Rep.	52, S.L. (Repeals).
c. 24 ...	Tenures Abolition Act 1660.	Residue rep. (exc. ss. 4, 9)	52, S.L. (Repeals).
		S. 9 am.	46, s. 1(3), sch. 1 Pt. I.
c. 30 ...	An Act for the attainder of several persons guilty of the horrid murder of His late sacred Majesty King Charles the First [1660].	Residue rep.	52, S.L. (Repeals).
13 Chas. 2, Stat. 1:			
c. 6	King's sole right over the militia [1661].	Preamble residue rep. ...	52, S.L. (Repeals).
c. 12	Ecclesiastical Jurisdiction Act 1661.	Residue rep.	52, S.L. (Repeals).
14 Chas. 2:			
c. 4	Act of Uniformity 1662...	Ss. 2, 3 rep., 10 rep. in pt., 17 rep., 20 rep. in pt.	52, S.L. (Repeals).
15 Chas. 2:			
c. 6	Act of Uniformity (Explanation) Act 1663.	Residue rep.	52, S.L. (Repeals).
29 Chas. 2:			
c. 3	Statute of Frauds [1677]	S. 22 rep.	52, S.L. (Repeals).
c. 7	Sunday Observance Act 1677.	Residue rep.	52, S.L. (Repeals).
1 Will. & Mar.:			
c. 18	Toleration Act 1688 ...	Residue rep.	52, S.L. (Repeals).
5 Will. & Mar.:			
c. 6	Royal Mines Act 1693...	S. 2 rep.	52, S.L. (Repeals).

3 M* 4

Session and Chap. or No. of Measure	Short title or Subject	How affected	Chapter of 1969 Act or number of Measure or Statutory Instrument
7 & 8 Will. 3:			
c. 25	Parliamentary Elections Act 1695.	S. 7 saved	46, s. 1(4), sch. 2 para. 2.
c. 34	An Act that the solemn affirmation and declaration of the people called Quakers shall be accepted instead of an oath in the usual form [1695].	Residue rep.	52, S.L. (Repeals).
8 & 9 Will. 3:			
c. 8	An Act for encouraging the bringing in wrought plate to be coined [1696].	S. 8 rep. in pt.	52, S.L. (Repeals).
1 Anne:			
c. 1	Crown Lands Act 1702	S. 7 rep. in pt.	48, s. 137(1), sch. 8 Pt. I.
c. 3	Assay of Plate [1702] ...	Ss. 3, 5 rep.	52, S.L. (Repeals).
7 Anne:			
c. 18	Advowsons Act 1708 ...	Rep.	52, S.L. (Repeals).
1 Geo. 1, Stat. 2:			
c. 6	Tithes and Church Rates Recovery Act 1714.	Residue rep.	52, S.L. (Repeals).
12 Geo. 2:			
c. 26	Plate (Offences) Act 1738	Ss. 11 rep in pt., 18 rep., 20, 21. rep in pt.	52, S.L. (Repeals.)
19 Geo. 3:			
c. 44	Nonconformist Relief Act 1779.	Residue rep.	52, S.L. (Repeals).
38 Geo. 3:			
c. 69	Gold Plate (Standard) Act 1798.	S. 3 rep. in pt.	52, S.L. (Repeals).
52 Geo. 3:			
c. 146 ...	Parochial Register Act 1812.	S. 11 rep. in pt. ...	48, s. 137(1), sch. 8 Pt. I.
55 Geo. 3:			
c. 134 ...	Crown Pre-emption of Lead Ore Act 1815.	Residue rep.	52, S.L. (Repeals).
57 Geo. 3:			
c. 97	Land Revenues of the Crown Act 1817.	S. 25 am.	10, s. 32(2)(*c*).
1 Geo. 4:			
c. 100 ...	Militia (City of London) Act 1820.	S. 35 am. (15.2.1971) ...	19, s. 10(3), sch. 2 para. 1.

Session and Chap. or No. of Measure	Short title or Subject	How affected	Chapter of 1969 Act or number of Measure or Statutory Instrument
6 Geo. 4:			
c. 97	Universities Act 1825 ...	S. 3 rep. in pt.	52, S.L. (Repeals).
c. 120 ...	Court of Session Act 1825	S. 25 am.	39, s. 1(3), sch. 1 Pt. I.
1 Will. 4:			
c. 27	An Act for enabling His Majesty's Postmaster General to sell the Premises lately used as the Post Office in Lombard Street, Abchurch Lane and Sherbourne Lane, in the City of London [1831].	Rep.	48, s. 137(1), sch. 8 Pt. I.
2 & 3 Will. 4:			
c. 111 ...	Lord Chancellor's Pension Act 1832.	Pensions increase ...	7, s. 1(1), sch. 1 Pt. I para. 3.
3 & 4 Will. 4:			
c. 74	Fines and Recoveries Act 1833.	Ss. 27, 40, 58, 71, 72 rep. in pt., 77, 78, 91 rep.	52, S.L. (Repeals).
5 & 6 Will. 4:			
c. 24	Naval Enlistment Act 1835.	Residue rep.	52, S.L. (Repeals).
c. 62	Statutory Declarations Act 1835.	Ss. 2, 5 rep. in pt. ...	48, s. 137(1), sch. 8 Pt. I.
6 & 7 Will. 4:			
c. 28	Government Offices Security Act 1836.	Preamble, Ss. 1–3, 5 7, 8, 10, sch. rep. in pt.	48, s. 141, sch. 11 Pt. II.
7 Will. 4 & 1 Vict.:			
c. 26	Wills Act 1837	Appl. (mod.) ... ... Ss. 1 definitions of " will ", " real estate ", 3 rep. in pt. (E.), 4–6 rep. (E.). S. 7 am. (E.) ... ... Ss. 8 rep. (E.), 26 rep. in pt. (E.). S. 33 am. (E.)	58, s. 18. 52, S.L. (Repeals). 46, s. 3. 52, S.L. (Repeals). 46, s. 16(1).
c. 83	Parliamentary Documents Deposit Act 1837.	Preamble, Ss. 1–3 rep. in pt.	48, s. 137(1), sch. 8 Pt. I.
1 & 2 Vict.:			
c. 43	Dean Forest (Mines) Act 1838.	Preamble, Ss. 1–3 rep., 16, 17 rep. in pt., 18 rep., 19, 20, 22 rep. in pt., 24–26 rep., 27 rep. in pt., 28, 30–44, 50, 51 rep., 53 rep. in pt., 55 rep., 56, 57, 60 rep. in pt., 63 rep., 65 rep. in pt., 66 rep., 68 rep. in pt., 70–82 rep., 83 rep. in pt., 84–89, 91 rep.	52, S.L. (Repeals).

Session and Chap. or No. of Measure	Short title or Subject	How affected	Chapter of 1969 Act or number of Measure or Statutory Instrument
1 & 2 Vict.: *—cont.*			
c. 61	Government Offices Security Act 1838.	Preamble, Ss. 1, 2 rep. in pt.	48, s. 141, sch. 11 Pt. II.
2 & 3 Vict.:			
c. 47	Metropolitan Police Act 1839.	S. 54 para. 14 rep. in pt.	48, s. 137(1), sch. 8 Pt. I.
3 & 4 Vict.:			
c. 65	Admiralty Court Act 1840.	Residue rep.	52, S.L. (Repeals).
5 & 6 Vict.:			
c. 83	St. Brivals small debts court [1842].	Residue rep.	52, S.L. (Repeals).
c. 94	Defence Act 1842 ...	Ss. 8 rep. (E.) (S.), 10, 12–15, 18, 25 rep. in pt. (E.) (S.).	52, S.L. (Repeals).
6 & 7 Vict.:			
c. 90	Public Notaries Act 1843	S. 3 am.	58, s. 29.
		S. 6 excl.	58, s. 29.
7 & 8 Vict.:			
c. 22	Gold and Silver Wares Act 1844.	Ss. 7, 15 rep. in pt. ...	52, S.L. (Repeals).
c. 32	Bank Charter Act 1844	S. 21 excl.	48, s. 40.
c. 33	County Rates Act 1844	S. 6 rep. in pt.	48, s. 137(1), sch. 8 Pt. I.
c. 85	Railway Regulation Act 1844.	S. 14 rep.	48, s. 137(1), sch. 8 Pt. I.
8 & 9 Vict.:			
c. 18	Lands Clauses Consolidation Act 1845.	Incorp. (N.I.) (exc. ss. 127–133).	48, s. 60(3).
c. 19	Lands Clauses Consolidation (Scotland) Act 1845.	Appl.	30, s. 31, sch. 2 para. 6.
		S. 90 saved	30, s. 36(7).
c. 33	Railways Clauses Consolidation (Scotland) Act 1845.	S. 6 appl.	30, s. 31, sch. 2 para. 6.
c. 38	Bank Notes (Scotland) Act 1845.	S. 13 excl.	48, s. 40.
9 & 10 Vict.:			
c. 59	Religious Disabilities Act 1846.	S. 1 residue rep. ...	52, S.L. (Repeals).
c. 70	Inclosure Act 1846 ...	Ss. 6 rep. in pt., 7 rep., 8 rep. in pt., 9 rep., 10 rep. in pt.	52, S.L. (Repeals).
10 & 11 Vict.:			
c. 27	Harbours, Docks and Piers Clauses Act 1847.	Transfer of functions ...	S.I. No. 388.
		S. 28 rep. in pt.	48, s. 141, sch. 11 Pt. II.
11 & 12 Vict.:			
c. 36	Entail Amendment Act 1848.	Ss. 1–3 am.	39, s. 1(3), sch. 1 Pt. I.

Session and Chap. or No. of Measure	Short title or Subject	How affected	Chapter of 1969 Act or number of Measure or Statutory Instrument
12 & 13 Vict.:			
c. 45	Quarter Sessions Act 1849.	Ss. 2, 12, 13 rep. in pt....	48, s. 141, sch. 11 Pt. II.
c. 49	School Sites Act 1849 ...	S. 6 rep.	52, S.L. (Repeals).
14 & 15 Vict.:			
c. 42	Crown Lands Act 1851	S. 22 Transfer of functions.	S.I. No. 383.
16 & 17 Vict.:			
c. 69	Naval Enlistment Act 1853.	Residue rep.	52, S.L. (Repeals).
c. 107... ...	Customs Consolidation Act 1853.	Ss. 332, 333, 335–341, 343–345 rep.	52, S.L. (Repeals).
17 & 18 Vict.:			
c. 112... ...	Literary and Scientific Institutions Act 1854.	S. 15 rep. (E.)	52, S.L. (Repeals).
18 & 19 Vict.:			
c. 43	Infant Settlements Act 1855.	Rep.	46, s. 11.
c. 81	Places of Worship Registration Act 1855.	Ext.	38, s. 6(1).
20 & 21 Vict.:			
c. 44	Crown Suits (Scotland) Act 1857.	S. 4 rep. in pt.	48, s. 141, sch. 11 Pt. II.
c. 57	Married Women's Reversionary Interests Act 1857.	Residue rep. (E.) ...	52, S.L. (Repeals).
c. 79	Probates and Letters of Administration Act (Ireland) 1857.	S. 72 subst. ... ... S. 73 rep.	58, s. 27(3). 58, ss. 27(4), 35 (2), sch. 2.
21 & 22 Vict.:			
c. 40	New General Post Office, Edinburgh Act 1858.	Rep.	48, s. 141, sch. 11 Pt. II.
22 & 23 Vict.:			
c. 35	Law of Property Amendment Act 1859.	S. 25 rep. (E.)	52, S.L. (Repeals).
23 & 24 Vict.:			
c. 27	Refreshment Houses Act 1860.	Ss. 1, 2, 6, 9–12, 16, 18, 32, 41 rep.	53, s. 14, sch.
c. 32	Ecclesiastical Courts Jurisdiction Act 1860.	S. 6 rep.	52, S.L. (Repeals).
24 & 25 Vict.:			
c. 40	Forest of Dean [1861] ...	Preamble, ss. 2, 5, 6, 17, 22, 27 rep.	52, S.L. (Repeals).
c. 91	Revenue (No. 2) Act 1861	Ss. 8, 9 rep. (E.) ...	53, s. 14, sch.
25 & 26 Vict.:			
c. 107... ...	Juries Act 1862	S. 11 am.	48, s. 76, sch. 4 para. 14.

Session and Chap. or No. of Measure	Short title or Subject	How affected	Chapter of 1969 Act or number of Measure or Statutory Instrument
26 & 27 Vict.:			
c. 49	Duchy of Cornwall Management Act 1863.	S. 8 am.	10, s. 32(2)(*d*).
		S. 38 am.	46, s. 10(3).
c. 112... ...	Telegraph Act 1863 ...	Expld.	48, s. 21(1).
		S. 2 rep.	48, s. 137(1), sch. 8 Pt. I
		S. 3 definition of " the company " rep.	48, s. 137(1), sch. 8 Pt. I.
		S. 5(2) rep. in pt. ...	48, s. 141, sch. 11 Pt. II.
		Ss. 11 rep., 14 rep. in pt.	48, s. 137(1), sch. 8 Pt. I.
		Ss. 14, 15, 21(3), 22(3), 24 am.	48, s. 76, sch. 4 para. 7.
		S. 30(1) am.	48, s. 76, sch. 4 para. 7.
		S. 31 rep.	48, s. 137(1), sch. 8 Pt. I.
		Ss. 41–43 rep.	48, s. 137(1), sch. 8 Pt. II.
		S. 44 rep.	48, s. 137(1), sch. 8 Pt. I.
		S. 45 expld.	48, s. 76, sch. 4 para. 4.
		am.	48, s. 77, sch. 5 para. 1(1).
		S. 46 rep.	48, s. 137(1), sch. 8 Pt. I.
		Ss. 48–51 rep.	48, s. 137(1), sch. 8 Pt. II.
		Ss. 52, 53 rep.	48, s. 137(1), sch. 8 Pt. I.
c. 120... ...	Lord Chancellor's Augmentation Act 1863.	Rep.	52, S.L. (Repeals).
27 & 28 Vict.:			
c. 18	Revenue (No. 1) Act 1864	S. 5 rep. (E.)	53, s. 14, sch.
28 & 29 Vict.:			
c. 87	Post Office Extension Act 1865.	Am.	48, s. 22(1).
29 & 30 Vict.:			
c. 3	Telegraph Act Amendment Act 1866.	Rep.	48, s. 137(1), sch. 8 Pt. I.
30 & 31 Vict.:			
c. 17	Lyon King of Arms Act 1867.	Sch. B. subst.	S.I. No. 1454.
31 & 32 Vict.:			
c. 100 ...	Court of Session Act 1868	S. 91 appl.	62, s. 4(3).
c. 110 ...	Telegraph Act 1868 ...	Expld.	48, s. 21(1).
		S. 2 rep. in pt.	48, s. 21(1)(*a*).
		Ss. 3 definition of " any company ", 9 paras. (1) (2) rep., (6) rep. in pt.	48, s. 137(1), sch. 8 Pt. I.
		S. 9 paras. (6)(*g*), (7), (8) rep.	48, s. 83.
		S. 9 paras. (9)–(11) rep.	48, s. 137(1), sch. 8 Pt. I.

Session and Chap. or No. of Measure	Short title or Subject	How affected	Chapter of 1969 Act or number of Measure or Statutory Instrument
31 & 32 Vict.:			
c. 110—*cont.*	Telegraph Act 1868 —*cont.*	S. 12 rep.	48, s. 83.
		Ss. 19 rep., 20 rep. in pt.	48, s. 137(1), sch. 8 Pt. I.
		S. 20 expld.	48, s. 76, sch. 4 para. 4.
		am.	48, s. 77, sch. 5 para. 1(1).
		S. 21 rep.	48, s. 137(1), sch. 8 Pt. I.
		S. 22 rep.	48, s. 141, sch. 11 Pt. II.
		S. 23 rep.	48, s. 137(1), sch. 8 Pt. I.
32 & 33 Vict.:			
c. 42	Irish Church Act 1869 ...	S. 20 saved.	52, s. 5(3).
c. 43	Diplomatic Salaries &c. Act 1869.	Pensions Increase ...	7, s. 1(1), sch. 1 Pt. I para. 35.
c. 73	Telegraph Act 1869 ...	Rep.	48, ss. 137(1), 141 sch. 8 Pt. I, sch. 11 Pt. II.
33 & 34 Vict.:			
c. 10	Coinage Act 1870 ...	S. 3 am. (15.2.1971) ...	19, s. 15(1).
		S. 4 rep. in pt. (15.2.1971)	19, ss. 15(2), 17 (2), sch. 4.
		am. (15.2.1971) ...	19, s. 15(2).
		S. 6 rep. (15.2.1971) ...	19, s. 17(2), sch. 4.
		S. 11 am. (15.2.1971) ...	19, ss. 1(5), 15(5).
		saved	19, s. 17(2).
		S. 11 para. 4 rep. (15.2.1971).	19, ss. 15(3), 17 (2), sch. 4.
		para. 6 rep. (15.2.1971).	19, s. 17(2), sch. 4.
		para. 9 am. (15.2.1971).	19, s. 15(4).
		Sch. 1 am. (15.2.1971) ...	19, s. 15(1)(*b*), sch. 3.
		rep. in pt. (15.2.1971).	19, ss. 15(6), 17 (2), sch. 4.
c. 52	Extradition Act 1870 ...	S. 3(1) expld. (genocide)	12, s. 2(2).
		S. 17 ext.	12, s. 3(1).
		expld.	54, s. 60(2).
		S. 22 ext.	12, s. 3(1).
		Sch. 1 am. ...	12, s. 2(1). 54, s. 60(1).
c. 77	Juries Act 1870	Sch. rep. in pt.	48, s. 137(1), sch. 8 Pt. II.
c. 88	Telegraph Act 1870 ...	Expld.	48, s. 21(1)
34 & 35 Vict.:			
c. 65	Juries Act (Ireland) 1871	S. 22 rep. in pt.	48, s. 141, sch. 11 Pt. II.
c. 85	Dean Forest (Mines) Act 1871.	Preamble rep., 2 rep. in pt., 5–32 rep. (saving).	52, S.L. (Repeals).
c. 87	Sunday Observation prosecution Act 1871.	Residue rep.	52, S.L. (Repeals).

Session and Chap. or No. of Measure	Short title or Subject	How affected	Chapter of 1969 Act or number of Measure or Statutory Instrument
35 & 36 Vict.:			
c. 15	Parks Regulation Act 1872.	Transfer of functions ...	S.I. No. 383.
c. 93	Pawnbrokers Act 1872...	Schs. 3 Pt. II, 4 Pt. I am. (15.2.1971).	19, s. 10(3), sch. 2 para. 2.
36 & 37 Vict.:			
c. 60	Extradition Act 1873 ...	S. 5 expld. (genocide) ...	12, s. 2(2).
37 & 38 Vict.:			
c. 42	Building Societies Act 1874.	S. 7 rep.	52, S.L. (Repeals).
c. 84	Works and Public Buildings Act 1874.	S. 5. Transfer of functions	S.I. No. 383.
c. 94	Conveyancing (Scotland) Act 1874.	S. 61 ext.	30, s. 31, sch. 2 para. 1(2).
38 & 39 Vict.:			
c. 61	Entail Amendment (Scotland) Act 1875.	S. 4 rep.	39, s. 1(9).
c. 90	Employers and Workmen Act 1875.	S. 6 rep. in pt.	46, ss. 11, 28(4) (*e*).
39 & 40 Vict.:			
c. 22	Trade Union Act Amendment Act 1876.	S. 9 am. (S.)	39, s. 1(3), sch. 1 Pt. I.
		(E.)	46, s. 1(3), sch. 1 Pt. I.
c. 36	Customs Consolidation Act 1876.	S. 275 residue rep. ...	52, S.L. (Repeals).
c. 59	Appellate Jurisdiction Act 1876.	S. 3 excl.	20, s. 3(8).
		Ss. 4, 5, 11 ext.	58, s. 14.
40 & 41 Vict.:			
c. 40	Writs Execution (Scotland) Act 1877.	S. 4 rep.	52, S.L. (Repeals).
41 & 42 Vict.:			
c. 76	Telegraph Act 1878 ...	Expld.	48, s. 21(1).
		S. 7(1)–(8) appl. (mod.)	48, s. 76, sch. 4 paras. 58(1)(2), 59(1)(3), 83 (1)(2).
		Ss. 7(1), 8 am.	48, s. 76, sch. 4 para. 7.
		Ss. 8–10 expld.	48, s. 76, sch. 4 para. 4.
		S. 12 rep. in pt. ...	48, s. 141, sch. 11 Pt. II.
		S. 13 rep. in pt. ...	48, s. 137(1), sch. 8 Pt. I.
42 & 43 Vict.:			
c. 11	Bankers' Books Evidence Act 1879.	S. 9 am.	48, s. 94(2)(*c*), sch. 6 Pt. III.
		rep. in pt.	48, s. 137(1), sch. 8 Pt. I.

Session and Chap. or No. of Measure	Short title or Subject	How affected	Chapter of 1969 Act or number of Measure or Statutory Instrument
42 & 43 Vict.: *—cont.*			
c. 36	Customs Buildings Act 1879.	Ss. 4 rep., 6 residue rep.	52, S.L. (Repeals).
c. 44	Lord Clerk Register (Scotland) Act 1879.	S. 4 rep.	52, S.L. (Repeals).
43 & 44 Vict.:			
c. 26	Married Women's Policies of Assurance (Scotland) Act 1880.	S. 2 am.	46, s. 19(1).
44 & 45 Vict.:			
c. 12	Customs and Inland Revenue Act 1881.	S. 38(2)(c) rep.	32, s. 61(6), sch. 21 Pt. V.
c. 17	Customs and Inland Revenue Buildings (Ireland) Act 1882.	Ss. 3, 5 rep.	52, S.L. (Repeals).
c. 56	Electric Lighting Act 1882	S. 26 expld.	48, s. 76, sch. 4 para. 8.
		am.	48, s. 76, sch. 4 para. 9.
		Ss. 32 definition of "telegram", 35 rep.	48, s. 141, sch. 11 Pt. II.
c. 61	Bills of Exchange Act 1882.	S. 3 am. (15.2. 1971) ...	19, s. 2.
		S. 14 excl. (*temp.*) ...	19, s. 13(2).
		S. 53(2) excl.	50, s. 20(4).
		S. 64 expld. (15.2.1971)	19, s. 3(2).
		S. 92 am. (*temp.*) ...	19, s. 13(1).
c. 72	Revenue, Friendly Societies and National Debt Act 1882.	S. 18 am. (15.2.1971) ...	19, s. 10(3), sch. 2 para. 3.
c. 75	Married Women's Property Act 1882.	Ss. 6–9 rep. (E.), 11 rep. in pt. (E.).	52, S.L. (Repeals).
		S. 11 am. (E.)	46, s. 19(1).
		Ss. 13 rep. (E.), 17 rep. in pt. (E.), 18, 19 rep. (E.), 24 rep. in pt. (E.), 25 rep. (E.).	52, S.L. (Repeals).
c. 77	Citation Amendment (Scotland) Act 1882	Sch. 2B. paras. 1, 2(1) am. (15.2.1971).	19, s. 19(3), sch. 2 para. 4.
46 & 47 Vict.:			
c. 1	Consolidated Fund (Permanent Charges Redemption) Act 1883.	S. 2(1) am.	48, s. 94(2)(c), sch. 6 Pt. III.
47 & 48 Vict.:			
c. 54	Yorkshire Registries Act 1884.	Rep. (exc. s. 49) (*prosp.*)	59, s. 16(2), sch. 2 Pt. I.
		S. 49 am.	59, s. 19(1).
c. 76	Post Office (Protection) Act 1884.	S. 11 am.	48, s. 77, sch. 5 para. 1(1).
		rep. in pt. ...	48, s. 141, sch. 11 Pt. II.

Session and Chap. or No. of Measure	Short title or Subject	How affected	Chapter of 1969 Act or number of Measure or Statutory Instrument
48 & 49 Vict. ...			
c. 4	Yorkshire Registries Amendment Act 1884.	Rep. (prosp.)	59, s. 16(2), sch. 2 Pt. I.
c. 26	Yorkshire Registries Amendment Act 1885.	Rep. (prosp.)	59, s. 16(2), sch. 2 Pt. I.
50 & 51 Vict.:			
c. 40	Savings Banks Act 1887	S. 10 am.	48, s. 94(2)(*c*), sch. 6 Pt. III.
c. 65	Military Tramways Act 1887.	S. 6 expld.	48, s. 76, sch. 4 para. 15.
51 & 52 Vict.:			
c. 12	Electric Lighting Act 1888	S. 4 expld.	48, s. 76, sch. 4 para. 8.
c. 29	Lloyd's Signal Stations Act 1888.	S. 2(2) expld.	48, s. 76, sch. 4 para. 16.
		Ss. 6 rep. in pt., 7 rep....	48, s. 141, sch. 11 Pt. II.
c. 41	Local Government Act 1888.	S. 46(4) rep. (*prosp.*) ...	59, s. 16(2), sch. 2 Pt. I.
52 & 53 Vict.:			
c. 7	Customs and Inland Revenue Act 1889.	S. 11(1) rep. in pt. ...	32, s. 61(6), sch. 21 Pt. V.
c. 34	Telegraph (Isle of Man) Act 1889.	Expld.	48, s. 21(1).
		S. 1 paras. (3)(5)(10) rep.	48, s. 137(1), sch. 8 Pt. I.
c. 55	Universities (Scotland) Act 1889.	Transfer of functions ...	S.I. No. 383.
c. 63	Interpretation Act 1889	S. 26 expld. ...	10, s. 30(3). 40, s. 14(1).
		S. 26 expld. (S.) ...	49, s. 24(2).
		S. 26 expld. (*prosp.*) ...	27, s. 35.
		S. 37 saved	48, ss. 94(4), 108 (5), 110(3), 121 (2), 132(2).
		S. 38 saved ...	16, s. 18(4). 50, s. 96(11).
		S. 38 saved (E.)	C.A.M. No. 2, s. 8.
		S. 38(1) saved	32, s. 60, sch. 20 para. 29.
		S. 38(2) appl.	29, s. 5(3).
53 & 54 Vict.:			
c. 21	Inland Revenue Regulation Act 1890.	S. 4A added	32, s. 60, sch. 20 para. 11.
		Ss. 21, 22 rep. (capital gains tax and corporation tax).	32, s. 61(6), sch. 21 Pt. X.
		Ss. 21, 22 excl.	48, s. 117(2).
		S. 24(4) added	32, s. 60, sch. 20 para. 11.
		S. 35 excl.	48, s. 117(2).
		S. 35(2) rep. (capital gains tax and corporation tax).	32, s. 61(6), sch. 21 Pt. X.
c. 59	Public Health Acts Amendment Act 1890.	S. 15 expld. (N.I.) ...	48, s. 76, sch. 4 para. 17.

Session and Chap. or No. of Measure	Short title or Subject	How affected	Chapter of 1969 Act or number of Measure or Statutory Instrument
54 & 55 Vict.:			
c. 38	Stamp Duties Management Act 1891.	Power to appl. (mod.) ...	48, ss. 121(1), 122(1).
		Ss. 9, 10 appl.	48, s. 116(1)
		S. 11 expld.	48, s. 116(1).
		S. 13 am.	48, s. 118(1).
		S. 16 am.	48, s. 118(2).
c. 39	Stamp Act 1891... ...	S. 7 rep.	48, s. 141, sch. 11 Pt. II.
		superseded	48, s. 115(3).
		S. 9 am.	48, s. 117(1).
		Power to appl. (mod.)	48, ss. 121(1), 122(1).
		S. 12 appl. (London) ...	35, s. 44(3).
		S. 112 excl. (London) ...	35, s. 44(2).
		S. 121 excl.	48, s. 117(2).
		Sch. 1 " Bill of exchange or promissory note of any kind whatsoever " expld.	48, s. 124.
c. 72	Coinage Act 1891 ...	Sch. rep in pt. (15.2.1971)	19, s. 17(2), sch. 4.
55 & 56 Vict.:			
c. 23	Foreign Marriage Act 1892.	S. 7(c) am.	46, ss. 2(1)(a), 28(4)(b).
c. 55	Burgh Police (Scotland) Act 1892.	S. 132 expld.	48, s. 76, sch. 4 para. 18.
		S. 288 rep. in pt. ...	48, s. 141, sch. 11 Pt. II.
c. 59	Telegraph Act 1892 ...	Expld.	48, s. 21(1).
		S. 4(2) rep.	48, s. 137(1), sch. 8 Pt. I.
		S. 5(1) am.	48, s. 76, sch. 4 para. 5.
		S. 12 rep. in pt. ...	48, s. 137(1), sch. 8 Pt. I.
56 & 57 Vict.:			
c. 69	Savings Bank Act 1893	Rep.	48, s. 137(1), sch. 8 Pt. I.
57 & 58 Vict.:			
c. 30	Finance Act 1894 ...	Pt. I (ss. 1–24) expld. ...	32, s. 35(2).
		S. 1 rep. in pt.	32, s. 61(6), sch. 21 Pt. V.
		S. 2(1) am.	32, ss. 36–38, 40, sch. 17 Pt. II para. 9.
		S. 2(1)(d) rep.	32, s. 61(6), sch. 21 Pt. V.
		S. 2(3) subst.	32, s. 40(1), sch. 17 Pt. III para. 1.
		S. 3 saved	32, s. 37(5).
		S. 3(3) added	32, s. 40(1), sch. 17 Pt. III para. 2.

Session and Chap. or No. of Measure	Short title or Subject	How affected	Chapter of 1969 Act or number of Measure or Statutory Instrument
57 & 58 Vict.: c. 30—*cont.*	Finance Act 1894—*cont.*	S. 4 rep. in pt.	32, s. 61(6), sch. 21 Pt. V.
		S. 5(2) expld.	32, s. 40(1), sch. 17 Pt. II para. 6(1).
		S. 5(3) rep.	32, s. 61(6), sch. 21 Pt. V.
		S. 6(2) ext.	32, s. 23(1)(4).
		S. 7(5) ext.	32, s. 38(2).
		S. 7(6) restr.	32, s. 38(2).
		S. 7(6) rep. in pt., (7) rep.	32, s. 61(6), sch. 21 Pt. V.
		S. 7(10) excl.	32, s. 38(2).
		S. 8(4) ext.	32, s. 40(1), sch. 17 Pt. II para. 14.
		Ss. 8(7), 11(2)(3) rep. in pt., 15(1)(3) rep.	32, s. 61(6), sch. 21 Pt. V.
		S. 16(3) am.	32, s. 40(1), sch. 17 Pt. III para. 3(a)(b).
		S. 16(3) rep. in pt. ...	32, ss. 40(1), 61(6), sch. 17 Pt. III para. 3(c)(d), sch. 21 Pt. V.
		S. 22(1)(i) am.	32 s. 36(4), (5)(a).
		S. 22(1)(j) mod. ...	32, s. 36(5)(b).
		S. 22(1)(l) rep.	32, s. 61(6), sch. 21 Pt. V.
		S. 22(2)(a) rep. in pt. ...	32, ss. 40(1), 61(6), sch. 17 Pt. III para. 4, sch. 21 Pt. V.
		S. 23(12)(14)–(16) rep. ...	32, s. 61(6), sch. 21 Pt. V.
c. 46	Copyhold Act 1894 ...	Rep.	52, S.L. (Repeals).
c. 60	Merchant Shipping Act 1894.	S. 141(4)(b) definition of " savings bank " am.	48, s. 94(2)(c), sch. 6 Pt. III.
		S. 149(2) saved	50, s. 94.
		S. 183(3) proviso rep. ...	54, ss. 72(4), 73(4)(d), sch. 6.
58 & 59 Vict.: c. 16	Finance Act 1895 ...	S. 12 excl. (N.I.) ...	48, s. 129(1).
		S. 12 excl. (London) ...	35, s. 44(1).
c. 19	Court of Session Consignations (Scotland) Act 1895.	Ss. 2, 3, 16 rep. in pt., 17 rep.	52, S.L. (Repeals).
59 & 60 Vict.: c. 19	Public Health Act 1896	Residue rep.	52, S.L. (Repeals).
c. 25	Friendly Societies Act 1896.	S. 36(1) am. (S.) ...	39, s. 1(3), sch. 1 Pt. I.
		(E.) ...	46, s. 1(3), sch. 1 Pt. I.

Session and Chap. or No. of Measure	Short title or Subject	How affected	Chapter of 1969 Act or number of Measure or Statutory Instrument
59 & 60 Vict.: c. 25—*cont.*	Friendly Societies Act 1896—*cont.*	S. 44(1)(*a*) am.	48, s. 94(2)(*c*), sch. 6 Pt. III.
		S. 48 rep. (E.), (S.) ...	52, S.L. (Repeals).
		S. 56 expld.	19, s. 7(3).
		S. 57 ext.	19, s. 7(3).
		S. 58 ext.	19, s. 7(4).
c. 28	Finance Act 1896 ...	S. 14 rep.	32, s. 61(6), sch. 21 Pt. V.
		S. 15(1)(3) am.	32, s. 40(1), sch. 17 Pt. III para. 5.
		Ss. 15(4), 16 rep. ...	32, s. 61(6), sch. 21 Pt. V.
60 & 61 Vict.: c. 24	Finance Act 1897 ...	Residue rep.	52, S.L. (Repeals).
c. 30	Police (Property) Act 1897.	Appl. (*prosp.*)	54, s. 72(3), sch. 5 para. 1.
c. 38	Public Health (Scotland) Act 1897.	S. 166 ext.	10, s. 34(3).
c. 53	Congested Districts (Scotland) Act 1897.	S. 4(1)(*f*) expld. ...	48, s. 76, sch. 4 para. 19.
		rep. in pt. ...	48, s. 141, sch. 11 Pt. II.
61 & 62 Vict.: c. 44	Merchant Shipping (Mercantile Marine Fund) Act 1898.	Sch. 2 scale subst., rules 1, 7, exemptions am.	S.I. No. 386.
c. 46	Revenue Act 1898 ...	S. 7(5) excl.	48, s. 117(2).
		S. 10(3) rep.	48, s. 141, sch. 11 Pt. II.
c. 57	Elementary School Teachers (Superannuation) Act 1898.	Pensions increase ...	7, s. 1(1), sch. 1 Pt. 1 para. 13.
62 & 63 Vict.: c. 9	Finance Act 1899 ...	S. 8 excl.	32, s. 56.
		S. 8 excl. (London) ...	35, s. 44(2).
c. 19	Electric Lighting (Clauses) Act 1899.	Sch.– ss. 1 definition of "telegraphic line", 10, 14, 60 expld.	48, s. 76, sch. 4 para. 8.
		S. 62 (1)(*b*) expld.	48, s. 76, sch. 4 para. 10.
		Ss. 69, 79 expld. ...	48, s. 76, sch. 4 para. 8.
c. 38	Telegraph Act 1899 ...	S. 2(1) expld.	48, s. 76, sch. 4 para. 6.
c. 44	Small Dwellings Acquisition Act 1899.	S. 9(4) am. (15.2.1971)...	19, s. 10(3), sch 2. para. 5.
63 & 64 Vict.: c. 7	Finance Act 1900 ...	S. 12 rep.	32. s. 61(6), sch. 21 Pt. V.

Session and Chap. or No. of Measure	Short title or Subject	How affected	Chapter of 1969 Act or number of Measure or Statutory Instrument
4 Edw. 7:			
c. 7	Finance Act 1904 ...	Residue rep.	52, S.L. (Repeals).
c. 16	Public Health Act 1904...	Residue rep.	52, S.L. (Repeals).
6 Edw. 7:			
c. 40	Marriage with Foreigners Act 1906.	Sch. Pt. I. 1 para. 2(*c*) am.	46, ss. 2(1)(*b*), 28 (4)(*b*).
7 Edw. 7:			
c. 18	Married Women's Property Act 1907.	S. 2 rep. (E.)	52, S.L. (Repeals).
c. 51	Sheriff Courts (Scotland) Act 1907.	S. 20 Pensions increase...	7, s. 1(1), sch. 1, Pt. I para. 6.
		Sch. 1 rule 172(*f*)(1)(4) am.	48, s. 94(2)(*c*), sch. 6 Pt. III.
8 Edw. 7:			
c. 33	Telegraph (Construction) Act 1908.	Expld.	48, s. 21(1).
		S. 5(2) am.	48, s. 76, sch. 4 para. 7.
		S. 7 rep.	48, s. 137(1), sch. 8 Pt. 1.
c. 62	Local Government (Scotland) Act 1908.	S. 11(7) rep. in pt. ...	48, s. 141, sch. 11 Pt. II.
		S. 26 expld.	48, s. 76, sch. 4 para. 20.
9 Edw. 7:			
c. 20	Telegraph (Arbitration) Act 1909.	Expld.	48, s. 21(1).
		S. 1 rep. in pt.	48, s. 137(1), sch. 8 Pt. I.
10 Edw. 7 & 1 Geo. 5:			
c. 8	Finance (1909–10) Act 1910.	S. 57 rep.	32, s. 61(6), sch. 21 Pt. V.
		S. 59(2) am., (3) subst....	32, s. 40(1), sch. 17 Pt. III para. 6.
		S. 61(5) am.	32, s. 40(1), sch. 17 Pt. III para. 7.
1 & 2 Geo. 5:			
c. 28	Official Secrets Act 1911	S. 2 expld.	48, s. 76, sch. 4 para. 21(1).
c. 39	Telegraph (Construction) Act 1911.	Expld.	48, s. 21(1).
		S. 1(2)(*d*) am. ...	48, s. 86, sch. 4 para. 7.
		S. 5 rep.	48, s. 137(1), sch. 8 Pt. I.
c. 48	Finance Act 1911 ...	S. 20 rep.	48, s. 141, sch. 11 Pt. II.
2 & 3 Geo. 5:			
c. 12	Elementary School Teachers (Superannuation) Act 1912.	Pensions Increase ...	7, s. 1(1), sch. 1 Pt. I para. 13.

Session and Chap. or No. of Measure	Short title or Subject	How affected	Chapter of 1969 Act or number of Measure or Statutory Instrument
3 & 4 Geo. 5:			
c. 20	Bankruptcy (Scotland) Act 1913.	S. 118 ext.	32, s. 3(9), sch. 9 para. 16.
		S. 187 am.	48, s. 76, sch. 4 para. 22.
c. 27	Forgery Act 1913 ...	S. 18(1) definition of " revenue paper " rep. in pt.	48, s. 141, sch. 11 Pt. II.
c. 32	Ancient Monuments Consolidation and Amendment Act 1913.	Transfer of functions ...	S.I. No. 383, 388.
4 & 5 Geo. 5:			
c. 10	Finance Act 1914 ...	S. 13(1) rep.	32, s. 61(6), sch. 21 Pt. V.
c. 12	Aliens Restriction Act 1914.	S. 1 am. (*prosp.*)... ...	21, ss. 14, 21(5).
c. 58	Criminal Justice Act 1914	S. 14(1) mod. (*prosp.*) ...	54, s. 3(6).
c. 59	Bankruptcy Act 1914 ...	S. 24 expld.	48, s. 76, sch. 4 para. 23.
		S. 33 ext.	32, s. 3(9), sch. 9 para. 16.
		S. 33(9) am.	50, s. 96(8).
		S. 55(5) rep. in pt. ...	52, S.L. (Repeals).
5 & 6 Geo. 5:			
c. 18	Injuries in War (Compensation) Act 1914 (Session 2).	Pensions increase ...	7, ss. 1(1), 2(1), sch. 1 Pt. I para. 42, sch. 3 para. 2.
c. 24	Injuries in War (Compensation) Act 1915.	Rep.	48, s. 141, sch. 11 Pt. II.
		Pensions increase ...	7, s. 1(1), sch. 1 Pt. I para. 43.
c. 74	Police Magistrates (Superannuation) Act 1915.	Pensions increase ...	7, s. 1(1), sch. 1 Pt. I para. 12.
c. 89	Finance (No. 2) Act 1915	S. 48 am.	48, s. 108(1)(*a*).
		S. 51(1) rep.	32, s. 61(6), sch. 21 Pt. X.
6 & 7 Geo. 5:			
c. 12	Local Government (Emergency Provisions) Act 1916.	Ss. 2, 3 Pensions increase	7, s. 1(1)(3), sch. 1 Pt. II para. 1.
c. 24	Finance Act 1916 ...	Ss. 66, 67 am.	48, s. 108(1)(*b*).
c. 40	Telegraph (Construction) Act 1916.	Expld.	48, s. 21(1).
c. 50	Larceny Act 1916 ...	Ss. 12, 18 expld. (N.I.)...	48, s. 76, sch. 4 para. 24.
7 & 8 Geo. 5:			
c. 58	Wills (Soldiers and Sailors) Act 1918.	Ss. 1, 3(1) am. (E.) ...	46, s. 3.
8 & 9 Geo. 5:			
c. 15	Finance Act 1918 ...	S. 43 rep.	48, s. 141, sch. 11 Pt. II.
c. 57	War Pensions (Administrative Provisions) Act 1918.	S. 9(4) rep.	54, s. 72(4), sch. 6.

Session and Chap. or No. of Measure	Short title or Subject	How affected	Chapter of 1969 Act or number of Measure or Statutory Instrument
9 & 10 Geo. 5:			
c. 21	Ministry of Health Act 1919.	S. 2 Transfer of functions, S. 5 rep.	S.I. No. 388.
c. 75	Ferries (Acquisition by Local Authorities) Act 1919.	S. 4 rep. in pt.	48, s. 141, sch. 11 Pt. II.
c. 76	Church of England Assembly (Powers) Act 1919.	Ss. 1, 3, 4 am. (*prosp.*)...	C.A.M. No. 2, s. 2(2).
c. 82	Irish Land (Provision for Sailors and Soldiers) Act 1919.	S. 2 rep.	52, S.L. (Repeals).
c. 92	Aliens Restriction (Amendment) Act 1919.	S. 1 cont. until 31.12.1970	61, s. 2(1).
c. 100 ...	Electricity (Supply) Act 1919.	S. 11 expld.	48, s. 76, sch. 4 para. 11.
		S. 22(4)(5) expld. ...	48, s. 76, sch. 4 para. 8.
10 & 11 Geo. 5:			
c. 3	Coinage Act 1920 ...	S. 1(1) rep. (15.2.1971)...	19, s. 17(2), sch. 4.
c. 17	Increase of Rent and Mortgage Interest (Restrictions) Act 1920.	S. 2(1)(*a*) saved ... ... S. 17(1) ext.	34, s. 52(1). 34, s. 56(2).
c. 18	Finance Act 1920 ...	S. 57 residue rep. ...	52, S.L. (Repeals).
c. 23	War Pensions Act 1920...	S. 9 rep.	54, s. 72(4), sch. 6.
c. 67	Government of Ireland Act 1920.	S. 4 mod.	48, s. 139(3).
		S. 6 mod. ...	32, s. 50(3). 42, s. 4(2). 48, s. 139(2). 50, s. 92(2). 52, s. 5(2). 54, s. 73(5).
		S. 9(2)(*b*) am.	48, s. 94(2)(*c*), sch. 6 Pt. III.
		S. 22(2) ext. ... ... S. 47 am.	48, s. 97(2). 58, s. 33.
		S. 74 definition of "postal service "— expld.	48, s. 76, sch. 4 para. 25.
		rep. in pt.	48, s. 141, sch. 11 Pt. II.
		Sch. 8 Pensions increase	7, ss. 1(1), 5(3)(*a*), sch. 1 Pt. I para. 36.
c. 70	Gold and Silver (Export Control, &c.) Act 1920.	Residue rep. (saving for s. 2) (15.2.1971).	19, s. 17(2)(3), sch. 4.
c. 72	Roads Act 1920... ...	Ss. 3(4), 17 definitions of " county ", " county council ", 18 rep. (prosp.).	27, s. 37, sch. 3.
c. 75	Official Secrets Act 1920	S. 5 excl.	48, s. 76, sch. 4 para. 21(2).
		S. 5(6) expld.	48, s. 76, sch. 4 para. 21(2).
		rep. in pt. ...	48, s. 141, sch. 11 Pt. II.

Session and Chap. or No. of Measure	Short title or Subject	How affected	Chapter of 1969 Act or number of Measure or Statutory Instrument
10 & 11 Geo. 5: *—cont.* C.A.M. No. 1	Convocations of the Clergy Measure 1920.	Am.	C.A.M. No. 2, s. 1(5).
11 & 12 Geo. 5: c. 31	Police Pensions Act 1921	Pensions increase ...	7, s. 1(1)(3)(4), sch. 1 Pt. II para. 13, sch. 2 para. 5.
c. 32	Finance Act 1921 ...	Sch. 3 am.	48, s. 108(1)(*c*).
12 & 13 Geo. 5: c. 16	Law of Property Act 1922	Ss. 43(4)–(7), 128–136, 138–143, 188 paras. (2)–(5), (7)(8)(10)–(18), (20)–(22) (24)–(29) rep., (30) rep. in pt. (32), 189, schs. 12–14 rep.	52, S.L. (Repeals).
c. 43	Post Office (Pneumatic Tubes Acquisition) Act 1922.	Rep.	48, s. 141, sch. 11 Pt. II.
c. 46	Electricity (Supply) Act 1922.	S. 25(3) expld.	48, s. 76, sch. 4 para. 8.
c. 50	Expiring Laws Act 1922	Sch. 1 rep. in pt. ...	52, S.L. (Repeals).
c. 51	Allotments Act 1922 ...	S. 16(1) am. (15.2.1971)	19, s. 10(3), sch. 2 para. 6.
c. 55	Constabulary (Ireland) Act 1922	Pensions increase ...	7, s. 1(1), sch. 1 Pt. I para. 38.
13 Geo. 5: c. 2	Irish Free State (Consequential Provisions) Act 1922 (Sess. 2).	S. 7(3) rep. ... ... Sch. 1 para. 6(2) saved.	48, s. 137(1), sch. 8 Pt. I. 58, s. 16(2).
13 & 14 Geo. 5: c. 16	Salmon and Freshwater Fisheries Act 1923.	Pts. IV (ss. 37–43), VI (ss. 59, 60) Transfer of functions.	S.I. No. 388.
c. 18	War Memorials (Local Authorities' Powers) Act 1923.	S.2 am. (15.2.1971) ...	19, s. 10(3), sch. 2 para. 7.
14 & 15 Geo. 5: c. 27	Conveyancing (Scotland) Act 1924.	S. 2(1)(*b*) appl. (mod.) (" heritable security ")	10, s. 35.
15 & 16 Geo. 5: c. 5	Law of Property (Amendment) Act 1924.	Sch. 2 paras. 3, 4, sch. 9 para. 6 cols. 1, 2 rep.	52, S.L. (Repeals).

Session and Chap. or No. of Measure	Short title or Subject	How affected	Chapter of 1969 Act or number of Measure or Statutory Instrument
15 & 16 Geo. 5: *—cont.*			
c. 18	Settled Land Act 1925 ...	S. 27(3) rep.	46, s. 11.
		Ss. 38(ii) rep., 58(1) rep. in pt., 62(1)–(3) rep., 64(2) rep. in pt.	52, S.L. (Repeals).
		S. 71 am.	10, s. 32(2)(*b*).
		S. 71 paras. (iv) (v) rep....	52, S.L. (Repeals).
		S. 73 am.	10, s. 32(2)(*a*).
		S. 73(1) paras. (vi) (vii) rep.	52, S.L. (Repeals).
		S. 113(3) am. (prosp.) ...	58, s. 35(1), sch. 1.
c. 19	Trustee Act 1925 ...	S. 31(1)(ii), (2)(i)(*a*)(*b*) am.	46, s. 1(3), sch. 1 Pt. I.
		S. 33 am.	46, s. 15(3).
c. 20	Law of Property Act 1925	S. 11 rep. (prosp.) ...	59, s. 16(2), sch. 2 Pt. I.
		S. 44(1) mod.	59, s. 23.
		S. 64 ext. (L.T.E.) ...	35, s. 16(3), sch. 2 para. 14.
		S. 84 reprinted as am. ...	59, s. 28 (1), sch. 3.
		S. 84 am.	59, s. 28(1).
		S. 84(1) rep. in pt. and am.	59, s. 28(3).
		S. 84(1)(*aa*) rep. in pt. and am.	59, s. 28(2).
		S. 84(1A)–(1C) added ...	59, s. 28(2).
		S. 84(2) am.	59, s. 28(4).
		S. 84(3) am.	59, s. 28(5).
		S. 84(3A) added (prosp.)	59, s. 28(6)(11).
		S. 84(8) am.	59, s. 28(7).
		S. 84(11) am.	59, s. 28(9).
		S. 84(11)(*b*) am. ...	59, s. 28(8).
		S. 84(11A) added ...	59, s. 28(9).
		Ss. 94(2), 96(2) rep. in pt. (prosp.).	59, s. 16(2), sch. 2 Pt. I.
		S. 97 rep. in pt. (prosp.)	59, ss. 16(2), 17(1), sch. 2 Pt. II.
		S. 121 ext.	52, s. 3.
		S. 133 rep.	52, S.L. (Repeals).
		S. 134(1) am.	46, s. 1(3), sch. 1 Pt. I.
		Ss. 167–170, 178 rep. ...	52, S.L. (Repeals).
		S. 194(4) expld. ...	48, s. 76, sch. 4 para. 26.
		S. 197 rep. (prosp.) ...	59, s. 16(2), sch. 2 Pt. I.
		S. 198 excl.	59, ss. 24(1), 25(2).
c. 21	Land Registration Act 1925.	S. 50(3) am.	59, s. 28(7).
		S. 79(3) expld.	48, s. 76, sch. 4 para. 27.
		Ss. 125, 135, 136 rep. (prosp.).	59, s. 16(2), sch. 2 Pt. I.

Session and Chap. or No. of Measure	Short title or Subject	How affected	Chapter of 1969 Act or number of Measure or Statutory Instrument
15 & 16 Geo. 5:			
—*cont.*			
c. 22	Land Charges Act 1925	S. 10(1) Class C(i) rep. in pt.	59, s. 17(5).
		S. 10(5) am.	59, s. 26.
		S. 10(6) rep. (prosp.) ...	59, ss. 16(2), 17(1), sch. 2 Pt. II.
		S. 11A added	59, s. 27.
		S. 16 excl. (*temp.*) ...	59, s. 17(3).
		S. 17 expld.	59, s. 17(3).
		S. 19 am.	59, s. 25(7).
		S. 20(12) rep. (prosp.) ...	59, ss. 16(2), 17(1), sch. 2 Pt. II.
c. 23	Administration of Estates Act 1925.	Pt. IV (ss. 45–52) am. ...	46, s. 14(3).
		S. 47(1)(i) am.	46, s. 3(2).
		S. 47A(2) rule 2 am. ...	48, s. 94(2)(*c*), sch. 6 Pt. III.
		S. 50(1) am.	46, s. 14(6).
c. 24	Universities and College Estates Act 1925.	S. 2(1) para. (ii) rep. ...	52, S.L. (Repeals).
		S. 26 am.	10, s. 32(2)(*a*).
		S. 26(1) paras. (v) (vi) rep.	52, S.L. (Repeals).
		S. 30 am.	10, s. 32(2)(*b*).
c. 36	Finance Act 1925 ...	S. 5(4) rep.	52, S.L. (Repeals).
		S. 23(1) am.	32, s. 40(1), sch. 17 Pt. III para. 8.
		S. 23(1)(4) rep. in pt. ...	32, s. 61(6), sch. 21 Pt. V.
c. 45	Guardianship of Infants Act 1925.	Ss. 3(2), 5(4), 6 expld. ...	46, s. 4(1).
c. 49	Supreme Court of Judicature (Consolidation) Act 1925.	S. 32 restr. (1.1.1971) ...	55, s. 9(3).
		S. 57(1) am.	58, s. 23(2)(3).
		S. 57(2) am.	58, s. 23(4).
		S. 99 am.	58, ss. 20, 21(2).
		S. 106(1) rep. in pt. ...	58, ss. 26(1), 35 (2), sch. 2.
		S. 106(2A) added ...	58, s. 26(1).
		S. 117 rep.	58, ss. 26(2), 35 (2), sch. 2.
		Ss. 123, 126(2) am. ...	58, s. 25(1).
		S. 126(2) rep. in pt. ...	58, ss. 25(2), 35 (2), sch. 2.
		S. 128(1)(*b*) rep. in pt. ...	58, ss. 26(3), 35 (2), sch. 2.
		S. 153 rep.	58, ss. 28, 35(2), sch. 2.
		S. 156 subst.	58, s. 27(1).
		S. 165(1) am.	46, s. 1(3), sch. I Pt. I.
c. 59	Teachers (Superannuation) Act 1925.	S. 14(3)(*b*) Pensions increase.	7, s. 1(1)(3), sch. 1 Pt. II para. 7.
c. 68	Roads Improvement Act 1925.	S. 5(9) added	48, s. 76, sch. 4 para. 28.

Session and Chap. or No. of Measure	Short title or Subject	How affected	Chapter of 1969 Act or number of Measure or Statutory Instrument
15 & 16 Geo. 5:			
—cont.			
c. 71	Public Health Act 1925	S. 10 expld.	48, s. 76, sch. 4 para. 29.
		rep. in pt. ...	48, s. 141, sch. 11 Pt. II.
c. 76	Expiring Laws Act 1925	Sch. 1 Pt. II rep. in pt.	52, S.L. (Repeals).
c. 88	Coastguard Act 1925 ...	S. 1(3) rep.	52, S.L. (Repeals).
C.A.M. No. 1	Interpretation Measure 1925.	Am. (*prosp.*)	C.A.M. No. 2, s. 2(2).
16 & 17 Geo. 5:			
c. 11	Law of Property (Amendment) Act 1926.	Sch. rep. in pt.	52, S.L. (Repeals).
		Sch. rep. in pt. (*prosp.*)	59, ss. 16(2), 17(1), sch. 2.
c. 16	Execution of Diligence (Scotland) Act 1926.	S. 2(2)(*e*) am.	48, s. 76, sch. 4 para. 30.
c. 36	Parks Regulation (Amendment) Act 1926.	Transfer of functions ...	S.I. No. 383.
c. 51	Electricity (Supply) Act 1926.	S. 24(2) rep.	48, s. 141, sch. 11 Pt. II.
c. 59	Coroners (Amendment) Act 1926.	S. 6 Pensions increase ...	7, s. 1(1), sch. 1 Pt. II para. 16.
c. 60	Legitimacy Act 1926 ...	S. 3(1)(*b*), (2) excl. ...	46, s. 15(4).
		S. 9 rep.	46, s. 14(7).
17 & 18 Geo. 5:			
c. 12	Auctions (Bidding Agreements) Act 1927.	S. 1 am.	56, s. 1.
		S. 2 excl.	56, s. 3(4).
		S. 3 ext.	56, s. 4.
c. 18	Royal Naval Reserve Act 1927.	S. 1(2) rep.	52, S.L. (Repeals).
c. 21	Moneylenders Act 1927	S. 14(1) proviso (i) am.	48, s. 76, sch. 4 para. 31.
19 & 20 Geo. 5:			
c. 17	Local Government Act 1929.	S. 75 excl. (15.2.1971) ...	19, s. 10(3), sch. 2 paras. 5–7.
c. 21	Finance Act 1929 ...	Residue rep.	52, S.L. (Repeals).
c. 25	Local Government (Scotland) Act 1929.	S. 52(3), sch. 6 rep. in pt.	49, ss. 12(3), 27(2), sch. 3.
c. 29	Government Annuities Act 1929.	S. 51(1) rep.	48, s. 141, sch. 11 Pt. II.
		S. 52(2) rep. in pt. ...	48, ss. 132(1), 141, sch. 11 Pt. II.
		Ss. 52(3) rep., 54(4) rep. in pt.	48, s. 141, sch. 11 Pt. II.
c. 37	Police Magistrates Superannuation (Amendment) Act 1929.	Pensions Increase ...	7, s. 1(1), sch. 1 Pt. I para. 12.
20 & 21 Geo. 5:			
c. 28	Finance Act 1930 ...	S. 40 excl.	32, s. 39(2)(3).
c. 44	Land Drainage Act 1930	S. 61(1)(*g*) added ...	48, s. 76, sch. 4 para. 32.
		Sch. 3 Pt. II para. 2 Transfer of functions.	S.I. No. 388.

Session and Chap. or No. of Measure	Short title or Subject	How affected	Chapter of 1969 Act or number of Measure or Statutory Instrument
20 & 21 Geo. 5: —*cont.*			
c. 51	Reservoirs (Safety Provisions) Act 1930.	Ss. 2(8)(9), 8(2)(3) am., (4) rep., 10(1) definition of " prescribed " subst.	S.I. No. 1067.
21 & 22 Geo. 5:			
c. 17	Local Authorities (Publicity) Act 1931.	S. 1(1) am. (15.2.1971) ...	19, s. 10(3), sch. 2 para. 8.
c. 33	Architects (Registration) Act 1931.	S. 13(3)(4) appl.... ...	42, s. 1(2)(3).
		S. 14 rep.	42, s. 2.
22 & 23 Geo. 5:			
c. 9	Merchant Shipping (Safety and Load Line Conventions) Act 1932.	S. 8 proviso rep. ...	48, s. 137(1), sch. 8 Pt. II.
		S. 24(4) expld.	48, s. 3(1).
		S. 36 am.	48, s. 3(6).
c. 12	Destructive Imported Animals Act 1932.	Ss. 1, 2, 10 Transfer of functions.	S.I. No. 388.
c. 25	Finance Act 1932 ...	S. 29 Pensions increase...	7, s. 1(1), sch. 1 Pt. I para. 23.
c. 46	Children and Young Persons Act 1932.	Ss. 70, 77, 87 residue rep., 90 rep. in pt., sch. 2 rep.	52, S.L. (Repeals).
23 & 24 Geo. 5:			
c. 12	Children and Young Persons Act 1933.	S. 10(1) appl. (*prosp.*) ...	54, s. 28(2).
		S. 10(1A) added (*prosp.*)	54, s. 72(3), sch. 5 para. 2.
		Ss. 10(2) rep. in pt. (*prosp.*), 26(6), 29(3), 32 rep. (*prosp.*), 34(2) rep. in pt. (*prosp.*).	54, s. 72(4), sch. 6.
		S. 34(2) am. (*prosp.*) ...	54, s. 72(3), sch. 5 para. 3.
		S. 35 rep. (*prosp.*) ...	54, s. 72(4), sch. 6.
		S. 40 expld.	54, s. 59(3).
		S. 44(1) rep. in pt. (*prosp.*) (2) rep. (*prosp.*) ...	54, s. 72(4), sch. 6.
		S. 46(1A) added ...	54, s. 72(3), sch. 5 para. 4.
		S. 48(2) rep. in pt. (*prosp.*)	54, s. 72(4), sch. 6.
		S. 49(1) am. and expld. (*prosp.*).	54, ss. 10(1)(2), 73(4)(a).
		S. 53 am. (*prosp.*) ...	54, s. 30(1).
		S. 54 rep. (*prosp.*) ...	54, ss. 7(6), 72(4), sch. 6.
		S. 55 rep. in pt. (*prosp.*)	54, s. 72(4), sch. 6.
		S. 55(1) am. (*prosp.*) ...	54, s. 72(3), sch. 5 para. 5.
		S. 56(1) rep. in pt. (*prosp.*)	54, s. 72(4), sch. 6.
		am. (*prosp.*) ...	54, s. 72(3), sch. 5 para. 6.
		mod. (*prosp.*) ...	54, s. 7(8).
		S. 57 rep. (*prosp.*) ...	54, ss. 7(6), 72(4), sch. 6.

Session and Chap. or No. of Measure	Short title or Subject	How affected	Chapter of 1969 Act or number of Measure or Statutory Instrument
23 & 24 Geo. 5: c. 12—*cont.*	Children and Young Persons Act 1933—*cont.*	Ss. 58 rep. (*prosp.*), 59(1) rep. in pt. (*prosp.*), 62 rep. (*prosp.*).	54, s. 72(4), sch. 6.
		S. 63 rep. (*prosp.*) ...	54, s. 72(3)(4), sch. 5 para. 7, sch. 6.
		Ss. 64–76 (1B) rep. (*prosp.*), 76(2), 77(1) rep., (2)–(4), 78–85 rep. (*prosp.*)	54, s. 72(4), sch. 6.
		S. 86 appl. (mod.) (*prosp.*)	54, s. 62(3).
		Ss. 86–88 ext. (*prosp.*) ...	54, s. 62(1).
		S. 86(1) am. (*prosp.*) ...	54, s. 72(3), sch. 5 para. 8.
		S. 86(2) rep. (*prosp.*) (3) rep. in pt. (*prosp.*), (4) rep. (*prosp.*)	54, s. 72(4), sch. 6.
		S. 87(1) am. (*prosp.*), (2) subst. (*prosp.*) (3) am. (*prosp.*)	54, s. 72(3), sch. 5 para. 9.
		S. 88(1), (2)(*c*) am. (*prosp.*), (4)(*a*)(*b*) replaced (*prosp.*)	54, s. 72(3), sch. 5 para. 10.
		Ss. 89(1), 90, 91 rep. (*prosp.*)	54, s. 72(4), sch. 6.
		S. 93 excl.	54, s. 44.
		S. 94 rep.	54, s. 72(4), sch. 6.
		S. 99(1) ext.	54, s. 70(3).
		Ss. 102(1)(*a*)(*b*) rep. (*prosp.*), (2) rep. in pt. (*prosp.*), 103, 104 rep. (*prosp.*)	54, s. 72(4), sch. 6.
		S. 106(2)(*a*) am. (*prosp.*)	54, s. 72(3), sch. 5 para. 11.
		Ss. 106(3)–(5), 107(1) definitions of–" approved school ", " approved school order ", " managers," " special reception centre " rep. (*prosp.*)	54, s. 72(4), sch. 6.
		S. 107(1) definitions of– " care order " and " interim order " added, " place of safety " am. (*prosp.*)	54, s. 72(3), sch. 5 para. 12(1) (2).
		S. 107(2) rep. (*prosp.*) ...	54, s. 72(3)(4), sch. 5 para. 12 (3), sch. 6.
		S. 108(2)(3), sch. 4 rep. (*prosp.*)	54, s. 72(4), sch. 6.
c. 14	London Passenger Transport Act 1933.	Ss. 16, 17, 25, 26, 107(1) definition of " Special Area ", sch. 7 Pts. II–IV, rep.	35, s. 47(2), sch. 6.
c. 51	Local Government Act 1933.	S. 57 saved	46, s. 1(4), sch. 2 para. 2.
		S. 57(*b*) rep. (16.2.1970)...	15, ss. 15, 24 (4)(5), sch. 3 Pt. II.

Session and Chap. or No. of Measure	Short title or Subject	How affected	Chapter of 1969 Act or number of Measure or Statutory Instrument
23 & 24 Geo. 5: c. 51—*cont.*	Local Government Act 1933—*cont.*	S. 57(*c*)(*d*) am. (16.2.1970)	15, ss. 16, 24(5).
		S. 59 appl.	54, s. 35(4), sch. 2 para. 1(2).
		S. 67(5)(*b*) rep. (16.2.1970)	15, s. 24(4), sch. 3 Pt. II.
		S. 72(1)(*a*) am. (16.2.1970)	15, s. 13(4).
		S. 93(1) appl. (mod.) ...	54, s. 35(4), sch. 2 para. 6.
		S. 159(1) mod.	54, s. 68(3).
		S. 193(3)(5) am. (15.2.1971).	19, s. 10(3), sch. 2 para. 9.
		S. 203 appl.	35, s. 8(8).
		Pt. X (ss. 219–243) appl.	54, s. 35(4), sch. 2 para. 6.
		S. 279(1) ext.	59, s. 18(1).
		S. 287A excl.	10, s. 30(5).
		S. 287B saved	10, s. 30(5).
		S. 290(2)–(5) appl. ...	30, s. 64(7), sch. 6 para. 15(2). 35, s. 36, sch. 5 paras. 4(1), 16 (2).
		S. 295 am. (16.2.1970) ...	15, s. 18(5).
		Sch. 3 Pt. VI para. 5(5) am. and ext.	15, s. 24(3).
24 & 25 Geo. 5: c. 2	Newfoundland Act 1933	S. 3 rep.	52, S.L. (Repeals).
c. 32	Finance Act 1934 ...	S. 28 rep.	32, s. 61(6), sch. 21 Pt. V.
c. 38 ...	Architects (Registration) Act 1934.	Rep.	42, s. 2.
c. 41	Law Reform (Miscellaneous Provisions) Act 1934.	S. 3(1A)–(D) added ...	58, s. 22.
c. 49	Whaling Industry (Regulation) Act 1934.	S. 17(1) definition of " British ship " am. (retrosp.).	29, s. 3(2)(3).
c. 53	County Courts Act 1934	S. 9 Pensions increase ...	7, s. 1(1), sch. 1 Pt. I para. 5.
		Sch. 1 Pt. II paras. 1–3 replaced (prosp.).	58, s. 31(3).
25 & 26 Geo. 5: c. 9	Herring Industry Act 1935.	Sch. 1 para. 6 Transfer of functions.	S.I. No. 388.
c. 24	Finance Act 1935 ...	S. 33 rep.	32, s. 61(6), sch. 21 Pt. V.
c. 30	Law Reform (Married Women and Tortfeasors) Act 1935.	Sch. 1 rep. in pt. ...	52, S.L. (Repeals).
c. 47	Restriction of Ribbon Development Act 1935.	S. 14 ext.	48, s. 76, sch. 4 para. 93(1).
		S. 23(2) expld.	48, s. 76, sch. 4 para. 34.
26 Geo. 5 & 1 Edw. 8: c. 48	Health Resorts and Watering Places Act 1936.	S. 1(1)(*b*) am. (15.2.1971)	19, s. 10(3), sch. 2 para. 10.

Session and Chap. or No. of Measure	Short title or Subject	How affected	Chapter of 1969 Act or number of Measure or Statutory Instrument
26 Geo. 5 & 1 Edw. 8—*cont.*			
c. 49	Public Health Act 1936...	Pt. III (ss. 91–110) (exc. s. 99) appl. (mod.).	25, s. 3.
		Pt. III (ss. 91–110) ext....	25, s. 4(2).
		S. 94 ext.	25, s. 2.
		S. 94(3) excl.	25, s. 3(2).
		S. 268(3) expld.	25, s. 4(5).
		Ss. 272, 274, 275, 277, 304, 305, 341 ext.	10, s. 33.
1 Edw. 8 & 1 Geo. 6:			
c. 5	Trunk Roads Act 1936...	S. 3(4) ext.	48, s. 76, sch. 4 para. 93(1).
c. 16	Regency Act 1937 ...	Saved (S.)	39, s. 1(4), sch. 2 para. 1.
		Saved (E.)	46, s. 1(4), sch. 2 para. 1.
c. 37	Children and Young Persons (Scotland) Act 1937.	Ss. 82, 86, 87, 89, sch. 2 para. 13 rep. (*prosp.*).	54, s. 72(4), sch. 6.
c. 46	Physical Training and Recreation Act 1937.	Functions transfd. to Min. of Housing and Local Government.	S.I. No. 1497.
		S. 10(5A) added ...	49, s. 27(1), sch. 2 Pt. II para. 1.
c. 54	Finance Act 1937 ...	S. 31(3) rep. in pt. ...	32, s. 61(6), sch. 21 Pt. V.
		S. 31(3)(*b*) am. ...	32, s. 40(1), sch. 17 Pt. III para. 9.
c. 68	Local Government Superannuation Act 1937.	S. 6(5) expld.	27, s. 2(4).
		S. 12(3) Pensions increase.	7, s. 1(1)(3), sch. 1 Pt. II para. 1.
c. 69	Local Government Superannuation (Scotland) Act 1937.	S. 6(5) expld.	27, s. 2(4).
		S. 12(3) Pensions increase.	7, s. 1(1)(3), sch. 1 Pt. II para. 1.
c. 70	Agriculture Act 1937 ...	Pt. I (ss. 1–5) Transfer of functions.	S.I. No. 388.
1 & 2 Geo. 6:			
c. 40	Children and Young Persons Act 1938.	Rep. (*prosp.*)	54, s. 72(4), sch. 6.
c. 42	Herring Industry Act 1938.	Ss. 1, 2 Transfer of functions.	S.I. No. 388.
c. 44	Road Haulage Wages Act 1938.	Pt. II (ss. 4, 5) excl. ...	48, s. 81(2).
		S. 4(2) am. (L.T.E.) ...	35, s. 17(1), sch. para. 1(1)(2). 3
c. 45	Inheritance (Family Provision) Act 1938.	S. 1(1)(*c*), (2)(*c*) am. ...	46, s. 5(1).
		S. 1(7) expld.	58, s. 18.
		S. 5(1) definition of " son " and " daughter " am.	46, s. 18(1).
c. 46	Finance Act 1938 ...	S. 47 expld.	32, s. 40(1), sch. 17 Pt. II para. 12.
		S. 47(1)–(6) am. ...	32, s. 40(1), sch. 17 Pt. III para. 10.

Session and Chap. or No. of Measure	Short title or Subject	How affected	Chapter of 1969 Act or number of Measure or Statutory Instrument
1 & 2 Geo. 6:			
c. 46—*cont.*	Finance Act 1938—*cont.*	Ss. 47(7), 48 rep. ...	32, s. 61(6), sch. 21 Pt. V.
		Sch. 4 Pt. 1 ext. ...	32, s. 30(5), sch. 15 para. 6(*d*).
c. 57	Imperial Telegraphs Act 1938.	S. 1(1) excl.	48, s. 130(1).
2 & 3 Geo. 6:			
c. 18	Local Government Superannuation Act 1939.	S. 1(1)(2) Pensions increase.	7, s. 1(1)(3) sch. 1 Pt. II para. 1.
c. 21	Limitation Act 1939 ...	Pt. I (ss. 1–21) ext. ...	10, s. 20(6), sch. 3 para. 6(2).
		S. 7 expld.	59, s. 25(5).
		S. 31(2) rep. in pt. ...	52, S.L. (Repeals).
c. 31	Civil Defence Act 1939	Expld. (exc. ss. 7(6)(*a*)–(*c*), 9(4).	48, s. 76, sch. 4 para. 36.
c. 38	Ministry of Supply Act 1939.	Ss. 2, 4 Transfer of functions.	S.I. No. 1498.
c. 41	Finance Act 1939 ...	S. 30(1) rep. (saving), (2)(4) rep.	32, s. 61(6), sch. 21 Pt. V.
		S. 31 excl.	32, s. 38(7).
		S. 31(2) rep. in pt. ...	32, s. 61(6), sch. 2 Pt. V.
c. 70	Ships and Aircraft (Transfer Restriction) Act 1939.	Restr. (*retrosp.*) ...	29, s. 3(1)(3).
c. 89	Trading with the Enemy Act 1939.	S. 7 am.	20, s. 1.
c. 94	Local Government Staff (War Service) Act 1939.	S. 3 Pensions increase ...	7, s. 1(1)(3), sch. 1 Pt. II para.
c. 96	Education (Scotland) (War Service Superannuation) Act 1939.	Pensions increase ...	7, s. 1(1), sch. 1 Pt. I para. 15.
C.A.M. No. 1	Queen Anne's Bounty (Powers) Measure 1939.	S. 1 para. (vi) rep. ...	52, S.L. (Repeals).
3 & 4 Geo. 6:			
c. 2	Postponement of Enactments (Miscellaneous Provisions) Act 1939.	Residue rep.	52, S.L. (Repeals).
c. 14	Agriculture (Miscellaneous War Provisions) Act 1940.	S. 15 Transfer of functions	S.I. No. 388.
c. 19	Societies (Miscellaneous Provisions) Act 1940.	Ss. 1–7 residue rep., 8(1) rep. in pt., 10(1) definitions of " building society", "emergency", "period of emergency", " society ", " trade union ", 12(3), sch. residue rep.	52, S.L. (Repeals).
c. 29	Finance Act 1940 ...	Ss. 43, 45(3) rep. ...	32, s. 61(6), sch. 21 Pt. V.
		S. 46(1) am.	32, s. 40(1), sch. 17 Pt. III para. 11.
		S. 51(2A) rep. in pt. ...	32, s. 61(6), sch. 21 Pt. V.

Session and Chap. or No. of Measure	Short title or Subject	How affected	Chapter of 1969 Act or number of Measure or Statutory Instrument
3 & 4 Geo. 6: c. 29—*cont.*	Finance Act 1940—*cont.*	S. 51(2c) am.	32, s. 40(1), sch. 17 Pt. III para. 12.
		S. 52 rep.	32, s. 61(6), sch. 21 Pt. V.
		S. 55 ext.	32, s. 23(2).
		S. 56(2) rep. in pt. ...	32, s. 61(6), sch. 21 Pt. V.
c. 48	Finance (No. 2) Act 1940	S. 17(1) am.	32, s. 40(1), sch. 17 Pt. III para. 13.
4 & 5 Geo. 6: c. 50	Agriculture (Miscellaneous Provisions) Act 1941.	S. 11(1)(2) Transfer of functions.	S.I. No. 388.
5 & 6 Geo. 6: c. 21	Finance Act 1942 ...	S. 47(4)(c) am. ...	48, s. 108(1)(d).
6 & 7 Geo. 6 c. 28	Finance Act 1943 ...	S. 26 am.	32, s. 40(1), sch. 17 Pt. III para. 14.
c. 32	Hydro-Electric Development (Scotland) Act 1943.	Sch. 1 para. 11 am. ...	1, s. 2.
C.A.M. No. 1	New Parishes Measures 1943.	Ss. 13, 14 excl.	38, s. 3(3).
7 & 8 Geo. 6 c. 21	Pensions (Increase) Act 1944.	S. 4 Pensions increase ...	7, s. 1(1)(3) sch. 1 Pt. II para. 15.
		Sch. 1 Pt. 1 ext. ...	7, s. 2(1), sch. 2 para. 2.
c. 23	Finance Act 1944 ...	S. 38(2A) rep. in pt., sch. 4 Pt. II para. 4 rep.	32, s. 61(6), sch. 21 Pt. V.
c. 28	Agriculture (Miscellaneous Provisions) Act 1944.	S. 2(3) Transfer of functions.	S.I. No. 388.
c. 31	Education Act 1944 ...	S. 40(2)–(5) replaced (*prosp.*)	54, s. 72(3), sch. 5 para. 13.
		S. 40A rep. (*prosp.*) ...	54, s. 72(4), sch. 6.
8 & 9 Geo. 6 c. 19	Ministry of Fuel and Power Act 1945.	Ss. 1(1) am., 2, 3, 5 rep.	S.I. No. 1498.
c. 33	Town and Country Planning (Scotland) Act 1945.	S. 18(4) am. ...	30, s. 105, sch. 9 para. 8.
		S. 18(5) am.	30, s. 105, sch. 9 para. 9.
		S. 22(3)–(5) appl. (*prosp.*)	30, ss. 90(2), 91(7).
		S. 22(4) am.	48, s. 76, sch. 4 para. 37(1).
		Ss. 23–26 ext.	48, s. 76, sch. 4 para. 93(1).
		S. 24 am.	30, ss. 73, 74.

Session and Chap. or No. of Measure	Short title or Subject	How affected	Chapter of 1969 Act or number of Measure or Statutory Instrument
8 & 9 Geo. 6: c. 33—*cont.*	Town and Country Planning (Scotland) Act 1945—*cont.*	Ss. 24–26 expld.... ...	48, s. 76, sch. 4 para. 93(2).
		Ss. 24–28 expld.... ...	30, s. 105, sch. 9 para. 5(*a*).
		S. 24(7) rep. (saving) ...	30, ss. 71(3), 107, sch. 11.
		Ss. 27, 28 appl.	48, s. 76, sch. 4 para. 37(3).
		S. 50(4)–(6) appl. (*prosp.*)	30, s. 8(1).
		S. 50(4)–(9) appl. (*prosp.*)	30, ss. 25(3), 63 (6), 64(7) sch. 6 para. 15(1).
		Sch. 4 ext.	48, s. 76, sch. 4 para. 93(1).
		Sch. 4 para. 1(*a*)(*b*) excl. in pt.	30, s. 72.
		para. 2 appl. (mod.)	30, s. 74(7)(8).
		Sch. 6 rep.	30, s. 107, sch. 11.
c. 42	Water Act 1945 ...	Sch. 3 (s. 4) expld. ...	48, s. 76, sch. 4 para. 38.
		(s. 5(3)) rep. in pt.	48, s. 141, sch. 11 Pt. II.
		(ss. 5(3), 70) expld.	48, s. 76, sch. 4 para. 38.
c. 43	Requisitioned Land and War Works Act 1945.	S. 4(2) rep. in pt. ...	48, s. 141, sch. 11 Pt. II.
		Ss. 24, 25(2)(3) expld. ...	48, s. 76, sch. 4 para. 39.
		S. 32(1) rep. in pt. ...	48, s. 141, sch. 11 Pt. II.
		S. 38(3) am.	59, s. 28(10).
9 & 10 Geo. 6: c. 3	Coatbridge and Springburn Elections (Validation) Act 1945.	Rep.	15, s. 24(4), sch. 3 Pt. I.
c. 13	Finance (No. 2) Act 1945	S. 60 Pensions increase	7, s. 1(1) sch. 1 Pt. 1 para. 23.
c. 17	Police (Overseas Service) Act 1945.	Pensions increase ...	7, s. 1(1), sch. 1 Pt. I para. 18.
c. 36	Statutory Instruments Act 1946.	Appl.	{ 19, s. 6(10). 50, s. 4(8). 51, s. 17(4).
		Appl. (E.)	C.A.M. No. 2, s. 7(2).
		S. 6 excl.	50, s. 88(4).
c. 42	Water (Scotland) Act 1946	Sch. 4 paras. 4, 5(3) expld.	48, s. 76, sch. 4 para. 40.
		para. 5(3) rep. in pt.	48, s. 141, sch. 11 Pt. II.
		para. 36 expld. ...	48, s. 76, sch. 4 para. 40.

3 N*

Session and Chap. or No. of Measure	Short title or Subject	How affected	Chapter of 1969 Act or number of Measure or Statutory Instrument
9 & 10 Geo. 6:— *cont.*			
c. 43	Camberwell, Bristol and Nottingham Elections (Validation) Act 1946.	Rep.	15, s. 24(4), sch. 3 Pt. I.
c. 49	Acquisition of Land Authorisation Procedure) Act 1946.	Appl.	$\begin{cases} 33, \text{ s. } 32(2). \\ 54, \text{ s. } 68(2). \end{cases}$
		Appl. (mod.)	48, s. 55.
		Ext.	48, s. 76, sch. 4 para. 93(1).
		Expld.	48, s. 76, sch. 4 para. 93(2).
		Sch. 1 para. 12 Transfer of functions.	S.I. No. 388.
c. 58	Borrowing (Control and Guarantees) Act 1946.	S. 1 ext. (L.T.E.) ...	35, s. 8(7).
		S. 1 saved.	48, s. 35(5).
c. 64	Finance Act 1946 ...	S. 52 ext.	48, s. 127.
		S. 62 Pensions increase	7, s. 1(1), sch. 1 Pt. I para. 23.
c. 73	Hill Farming Act 1946...	Transfer of functions ...	S.I. No. 388.
c. 74	Coinage Act 1946 ...	Ss. 1–3 rep. (15.2.1971)...	19, s. 17(2), sch. 4.
		S. 1 am. (temp.) ...	19, s. 15(7).
		S. 4(1) am.	19, s. 15(8).
		Ss. 5(1) rep. in pt. (15.2.1971), 6, sch. rep. (15.2.1971).	19, s. 17(2), sch. 4.
c. 81	National Health Service Act 1946.	Transfer of functions ...	S.I. No. 388.
		S. 6 Pensions increase...	7, s. 1(1), sch. 1 Pt. I para. 24.
		S. 11(9) Pensions increase.	7, s. 1(1), sch. 1 Pt. I para. 29.
		Ss. 67, 68 Pensions increase.	7, s. 1(1), sch. 1 Pt. 1 para. 25.
c. 82	Cable and Wireless Act 1946.	S. 3(5) excl.	48, s. 130(1).
10 & 11 Geo. 6: c. 7	Pensions (Increase) Act 1947.	S. 1 ext.	7, s. 2(1), sch. 3 para. 2.
		S. 2(1) rep.	7, s. 2(6).
c. 14	Exchange Control Act 1947.	Saved	48, s. 35(5).
c. 26	Cotton (Centralised Buying) Act 1947.	S. 5(8) Pensions increase	7, s. 1(1), sch. 1 Pt. III para. 2.
c. 27	National Health Service (Scotland) Act 1947.	S. 6 Pensions increase...	7, s. 1(1), sch. 1 Pt. I para. 26.
		Ss. 66, 67 Pensions increase.	7, s. 1(1), sch. 1 Pt. I para. 27.

Session and Chap. or No. of Measure	Short title or Subject	How affected	Chapter of 1969 Act or number of Measure or Statutory Instrument
10 & 11 Geo. 6: *—cont.*			
c. 35	Finance Act 1947 ...	S. 51 am.	32, s. 40(1), sch. 17 Pt. III para. 15.
		expld.	32, s. 40(1), sch. 17 Pt. II para. 12.
c. 39	Statistics of Trade Act 1947.	S. 17(3) am. and rep. in pt.	S.I. No. 1498.
c. 40	Industrial Organisation and Development Act 1947.	Ss. 1, 9 Transfer of functions.	S.I. No. 1498.
c. 41	Fire Services Act 1947...	S. 3(2)(*c*) rep.	48, s. 141, sch. 11 Pt. II.
		S. 26 Pensions increase...	7, s. 1(1)(4), sch. 1 Pt. I para. 22, Pt. II para. 11, sch. 2 para. 5.
c. 42	Acquisition of Land (Authorsation Procedure) (Scotland) Act 1947.	Appl. (mod.) ...	30, s. 29(4). 34, s. 7(3). 48, s. 55.
		Appl.	30, s. 30(4). 34, ss. 58(2), 69 (2), sch. 6 para. 7(*b*).
		Appl. (retrosp.) (prosp.)	30, s. 53(3).
		Ext.	48, s. 76, sch. 4 para. 93(1).
		Expld.	48, s. 76, sch. 4 para. 93(2).
		S. 1(4)(*d*)(*e*) rep. ...	34, s. 69(3), sch. 7.
		Sch. 1 para. 3(*b*) mod. (prosp.).	30, s. 53(3).
		para. 6 ext. ...	30, s. 31, sch. 2 para. 2(1).
		para. 7 mod. (prosp.).	30, s. 53(3).
		para. 11(1)(*b*) am.	30, s. 32(1).
		para. 12 expld. (prosp.).	30, s. 59.
		para. 12 Transfer of functions.	S.I. No. 383.
		Sch. 2 para. 4 saved ...	30, s. 36(8).
c. 43	Local Government (Scotland) Act 1947.	S. 50 saved	39, s. 1(4), sch. 2 para. 2.
		S. 63 am. (15.2.1970) ...	15, s. 13(4).
		S. 156 ext.	34, s. 7(2).
		S. 158 appl.	34, s. 7(2).
		S. 163 ext.	34, s. 13.
		S. 173 excl.	34, s. 7(2).
		Ss. 191(2), (3)(*c*)(*f*)(*g*), 236 am. (15.2.1971).	19. s. 10(3), sch. 2 para. 11.
		S. 278 appl.	35, s. 8(8).
		S. 339(1)(*a*) am. (15.2. 1971).	19, s. 10(3), sch. 2 para. 11.
		S. 347 saved	10, s. 30(5).
		S. 349 excl.	10, s. 30(5).

Session and Chap. or No. of Measure	Short title or Subject	How affected	Chapter of 1969 Act or number of Measure or Statutory Instrument
10 & 11 Geo. 6: —*cont.*			
c. 44	Crown Proceedings Act 1947.	S. 9 rep.	48, s. 141, sch. 11 Pt. II.
		S. 27(1)(*c*) am.	48, s. 94(2)(*c*)(3), sch. 6 Pt. III.
		S. 43(*b*) appl.	48, s. 29(4).
		S. 46 proviso (*c*) am. ...	48, s. 94(2)(*c*), sch. 6 Pt. III.
c. 48	Agriculture Act 1947 ...	Ss. 2, 71, 97–99, Sch. 9 paras. 7–12, 21 Transfer of functions.	S.I. No. 388.
c. 53	Town and Country Planning (Scotland) Act 1947.	Ext.	30, s. 102(2).
		Pt. II (ss. 3–33)—	
		ext. (*prosp.*)	30, ss. 90–95.
		appl. (*prosp.*)	30, s. 44(4), sch. 4 para. 17(6).
		expld. (*prosp.*) ...	30, s. 105, sch. 9 para. 4.
		Ss. 3–9 rep. (*prosp.*) ...	30, s. 107, sch. 11.
		S. 10 ext.	48, s. 76, sch. 4 para. 93(1).
		S. 10(2)(*a*) excl. ...	30, s. 75.
		S. 10(5) mod.	30, s. 76.
		S. 10(5) proviso (i) rep. (*prosp.*).	30, s. 107, sch. 11.
		S. 12 mod.	30, s. 65(1).
		S. 12(1) appl. (*prosp.*) ...	30, s. 26.
		mod. (*prosp.*) ...	30, s. 41(4).
		am.	30, s. 105, sch. 9 para. 11(*a*).
		S. 12(2) saved	30, s. 66(4).
		appl. (*prosp.*) ...	30, s. 26.
		S. 12(3)(*a*) am.	30, s. 105, sch. 9 para. 11(*b*).
		am. (*retrosp.*)	30, s. 78.
		S. 12(4) appl. (*prosp.*) ...	30, s. 26.
		S. 12(4) Transfer of functions.	S.I. No. 1498.
		S. 12(5) ext.	30, s. 16(7)(*c*).
		Power to am. ...	30, s. 79(2).
		am. (*prosp.*) ...	30, s. 18(6), sch. 1 para. 6.
		appl. (*prosp.*) ...	30, s. 44(4), sch. 4 para. 17(6).
		S. 13 mod.	30, s. 62, 63.
		am.	30, s. s80.
		appl. (mod.) ...	30, s. 64(7), sch. 6 para. 8(2).
		S. 13(2) excl. (*prosp.*) ...	30, ss. 22(6), 62(8), 64(7), sch. 6 para. 11(1).
		S. 14 Power to mod. (*prosp.*).	30, s. 22.
		appl. (mod.) (*prosp.*).	30, s. 23(3).
		restr. (*prosp.*) ...	30, s. 26.
		mod.	30, ss. 62, 63.
		saved	30, s. 68(4).
		appl. (mod.) ...	30, s. 64(7), sch. 6 para. 8(2).

Session and Chap. or No. of Measure	Short title or Subject	How affected	Chapter of 1969 Act or number of Measure or Statutory Instrument
10 & 11 Geo. 6: c. 53—*cont.*	Town and Country Planning (Scotland) Act 1947—*cont.*	S. 14(1) proviso rep. (*prosp.*).	30, s. 107, sch. 11.
		S. 15 mod.	30, s. 65(1).
		S. 16 saved	30, s. 66(4).
		S. 16(5) proviso rep. in pt.	30, ss. 76(3)(*b*), 107, sch. 11.
		S. 16(6) rep. in pt. ...	30, ss. 76(3)(*c*), 107, sch. 11.
		S. 17 am. (*prosp.*) ...	30, s. 51(4).
		mod. (*prosp.*) ...	30, s. 42(1), sch. 4 para. 13(8).
		ext.	48, s. 76, sch. 4 para. 93(1)
		S. 17(1AA) added, (1B) am.	30, s. 105, sch. 9 para. 12(*a*)(*b*).
		S. 17(1B)(2) expld. ...	30, s. 105, sch. 9 para. 5(*b*).
		S. 17(2) mod. (*prosp.*) ...	30, s. 33(3).
		S. 17(3) rep. in pt. ...	30, ss. 105, 107, sch. 9 para. 12(*c*), sch. 11.
		S. 17(5)(7) appl. (mod.) (*prosp.*).	30, s. 42(1), sch. 4 para. 12(3).
		S. 17(7) am.	30, s. 105, sch. 9 para. 12(*d*).
		S. 19 am. (*prosp.*) ...	30, s. 81.
		S. 20(3) excl.	30, s. 72(3).
		S. 21 rep.	30, s. 107, sch. 11.
		S. 22(1)(2) am.	30, s. 105, sch. 9 para. 13.
		S. 22(3) am.	30, s. 100, sch. 8.
		S. 22(4) excl.	30, s. 76(4).
		S. 22(5) ext. (*prosp.*) ...	30, s. 46(3).
		S. 23(1) rep. in pt. ...	30, ss. 105, 107, sch. 9 para. 14, sch. 11.
		S. 24 expld.	30, s. 68(2).
		S. 24(4) am.	30, s. 100, sch. 8.
		S. 26 mod.	30, s. 65(1).
		am. (*prosp.*) ...	30, s. 82.
		S. 26(5) rep. in pt. (*prosp.*)	30, s. 107, sch. 11.
		S. 27 rep. (*prosp.*) ...	30, ss. 40(9), 107, sch. 11.
		S. 28 ext. (*prosp.*) ...	30, ss. 48, 49.
		am. (*prosp.*) ...	30, ss. 54, 60(1).
		S. 28(4) am. (*prosp.*) ...	30, s. 105, sch. 9 para. 15.
		S. 28(5)–(8) rep. (*prosp.*)	30, ss. 40(9), 107, sch. 11.
		S. 29 mod.	30, s. 65(1).
		S. 29(1)(*d*) am.	30, s. 105, sch. 9 para. 16.
		S. 29(4) rep. in pt. ...	30, ss. 105, 107, sch. 9 para. 17, sch. 11.
		S. 30(2) am. (*prosp.*) ...	30, s. 105, sch. 9 para. 18.
		proviso rep. (*prosp.*).	30, s. 107, sch. 11.
		S. 30(3) am.	30, s. 100, sch. 8.

Session and Chap. or No. of Measure	Short title or Subject	How affected	Chapter of 1969 Act or number of Measure or Statutory Instrument
10 & 11 Geo. 6: c. 53—*cont.*	Town and Country Planning (Scotland) Qct 1947—*cont.*	S. 32 mod.	30, ss. 62, 63.
		expld.	30, s. 68(2).
		expld. (" operational land ").	48, s. 76, sch. 4 para. 93(4).
		appl. (mod.) ...	30, s. 64(7), sch. 6 para. 8(3).
		S. 32(1)(2) ext. ...	48, s. 76, sch. 4 para. 93(1).
		S. 32(3) am.	30, s. 105, sch. 9 para. 19.
		S. 32(4) ext.	48, s. 76, sch. 4 para. 93(1).
		S. 33 rep. (*prosp.*) ...	30, s. 107, sch. 11.
		Pt. III (ss. 34–46) expld. (*prosp.*).	30, s. 105, sch. 9 para. 5.
		Ss. 34, 35 rep. and superseded.	30, ss. 28, 107, sch. 11.
		S. 36 rep.	30, s. 107, sch. 11.
		S. 37 appl.	30, s. 94(2).
		am.	30, s. 105, sch. 9 para. 10.
		S. 37(1) rep. in pt. ...	30, s. 107, sch. 11.
		S. 37(2) appl.	48, s. 60(2).
		S. 38(1)–(4) rep. (*prosp.*)	30, s. 107, sch. 11.
		S. 38(5) am. (*prosp.*) ...	30, s. 105, sch. 9 para. 20.
		S. 38(6) rep. (*prosp.*) ...	30, s. 107, sch. 11.
		S. 39(1) rep. in pt. ...	30, ss. 105, 107, sch. 9 para. 21, sch. 11.
		S. 40 am.	30, s. 105, sch. 9 para. 10.
		S. 42 expld.	48, s. 76, sch. 4 para. 93(2).
		S. 42(1) am.	30, s. 105, sch. 9 para. 22.
		S. 42(2) am.	30, s. 105, sch. 9 para. 10.
		S. 42(3) rep., (4) rep. in pt.	30, s. 107, sch. 11.
		S. 42(4) ext.	48, s. 76, sch. 4 para. 93(1).
		S. 42(4)(*b*) rep. (saving)	30, ss. 71(3), 107, sch. 11.
		S. 42(5) ext.	48, s. 76, sch. 4 para. 93(1).
		S. 42(6) rep.	30, s. 107, sch. 11.
		S. 46 am.	30, s. 89.
		S. 46(2)–(5) appl. (*prosp.*)	30, s. 91(7).
		S. 46(2)–(7) appl. ...	30, s. 90(2).
		S. 46(4) am.	30, s. 96(1).
		S. 72(9) rep.	30, ss. 76(3)(*d*), 107, sch. 11.
		S. 73(2) am.	30, s. 105, sch. 9 para. 23.
		S. 78(1) am.	30, s. 105, sch. 9 para. 24.
		S. 83 ext. (*prosp.*) ...	30, s. 60(2).

Session and Chap. or No. of Measure	Short title or Subject	How affected	Chapter of 1969 Act or number of Measure or Statutory Instrument
10 & 11 Geo. 6: c. 53—*cont.*	Town and Counrty Planning (Scotland) Act 1947—*cont.*	S. 83(2)(*a*) rep. in pt. (*prosp.*).	30, s. 107, sch. 11.
		S. 83(3)(*a*) am.	30, s. 105, sch. 9 para. 25(*a*).
		S. 83(3)(*b*) rep. (*prosp.*)	30, s. 107, sch. 11.
		S. 83(4) am. (*prosp.*), (5) replaced (*prosp.*).	30, s. 105, sch. 9 para. 25(*b*)(*c*).
		S. 84 proviso (*a*) rep. in pt.	30, ss. 99, 107, sch. 11.
		S. 86(1) am.	30, s. 105, sch. 9 para. 26.
		S. 93 am. (*prosp.*) ...	30, s. 105, sch. 9 para. 27.
		S. 94 ext.	48, s. 76, sch. 4 para. 93(1).
		S. 94(1)(*b*) am. (*prosp.*)...	30, s. 105, sch. 9 para. 28.
		S. 95(2) am.	30, s. 105, sch. 9 para. 29.
		S. 96 mod.	30, s. 83.
		S. 96(1) am. (*prosp.*) ...	30, s. 105, sch. 9 para. 30(*a*).
		S. 96(2)(*e*) rep. (*prosp.*)...	30, s. 107, sch. 11.
		S. 96(4)(*a*) subst. (*prosp.*)	30, s. 105, sch. 9 para. 30(*b*).
		S. 99 expld.	48, s. 76, sch. 4 para. 93(2).
		S. 99(1)(*c*) am. (*prosp.*), (1A)(1B) added (*prosp.*), (2)(3)(*a*) am. (*prosp.*).	30, s. 105, sch. 9 para. 31.
		S. 99 (4)–(6) appl. (mod.)	48, s. 58(2).
		S. 99(6) am.	30, s. 100, sch. 8.
		S. 99(9) appl. (mod.) ...	48, s. 58(2).
		ext.	48, s. 76, sch. 4 para. 93(1).
		S. 102 am.	30, s. 100, sch. 8.
		S. 105(1) am. (*prosp.*) ...	30, s. 105, sch. 9 para. 32.
		S. 107(4) rep. in pt. ...	30, s. 107, sch. 11.
		S. 111(1) expld.	48, s. 76, sch. 4 para. 93(1).
		S. 111(2)(3) am. ...	48, s. 76, sch. 4 para. 42(3)(4).
		S. 111(2)–(4) appl. (*prosp.*)	30, ss. 90(2), 91 (7).
		S. 113(1) definitions of— " Act of 1969 " added	30, s. 105, sch. 9 para. 33.
		" building preservation order ", " development plan " rep. (*prosp.*).	30, s. 107, sch. 11.
		" operational land " mod.	30, s. 70.
		Sch. 1 Pt. III para. 1 am. (*prosp.*).	30, s. 105, sch. 9 para. 34.
		Sch. 4 para. 1 am. (*prosp.*)	30, s. 105, sch. 9 para. 35.

Session and Chap. or No. of Measure	Short title or Subject	How affected	Chapter of 1969 Act or number of Measure or Statutory Instrument
10 & 11 Geo. 6:			
c. 53 _cont._	Town and Country Planning (Scotland) Act 1947—_cont._	Sch. 3 ext.	48, s. 76, sch. 4 para. 93(1).
		expld.	48, s. 76, sch. 4 para. 93(2).
		expld. (" operational land ").	48, s. 76, sch. 4 para. 93(4).
		para. 1(1) ext. ...	30, s. 71(1).
		para. 1(1) am., (1A) added.	30, s. 105, sch. 9 para. 36.
		paras. 1(2), 2(1)(_a_), 3(2), 4(2) rep. (saving).	30, ss. 71(3), 107, sch. 11.
		Sch. 6 am.	30, s. 89.
		paras. 1(_b_), 4 am.	30, s. 96(2).
		para. 7 rep.	30, s. 107, sch. 11.
		Sch. 10 para. 17 rep.	
c. 54	Electricity Act 1947 ...	S. 9(3) expld.	48, s. 76, sch. 4 para. 8.
		S. 47(7) am.	1, s. 1(1).
		S. 60 expld.	48, s. 76, sch. 4 para. 8.
		Sch. 4 Pt. I rep. in pt. ...	48, s. 141, sch. 11 Pt. II.
11 & 12 Geo. 6:			
c. 7	Ceylon Independence Act 1947.	S. 4(1) rep. in pt., (3)(4) rep.	52, S.L. (Repeals).
c. 8	Mandated and Trust Territories Act 1947.	S. 1(1) rep. in pt., (2) rep., (5) rep. in pt., (6) rep.	52, S.L. (Repeals).
c. 17	Requisition Land and War Works Act 1948.	S. 4 ext.	48, s. 76, sch. 4 para. 93(1).
		Sch. para. 6(1) expld. ...	48, s. 76, sch. 4 para. 43.
c. 21	Army and Air Force (Women's Service) Act 1948.	S. 3(1) excl.	65, s. 1(6).
c. 24	Police Pensions Act 1948	Pensions increase ...	7, s. 1(1)(4), sch. 1 Pt. I paras. 18–20, Pt. II para. 8, sch. 2 para. 6.
		S. 1(1) expld. (_prosp._) ...	63, s. 4(5).
		S. 1(7) excl.	63, s. 5(2).
c. 26	Local Government Act 1948.	S. 47 Pensions increase	7, ss. 1(1)(3), 2(1), sch. 1 Pt. II para. 17, sch. 3 para. 5.
		Pt. VI (ss. 111–119) appl. (L.T.E.).	35, s. 14(5).
		S. 130 ext.	35, s. 9(1).
		S. 132 ext. (S.)	41, s. 1.
		S. 137 rep. (15.2.1971) ...	19, s. 17(2), sch. 4.
c. 33	Superannuation (Miscellaneous Provisions) Act 1948.	S. 3 Pensions increase ...	7, s. 1(1), sch. 1 Pt. I para. 30.
		S. 14 rep. (_prosp._) ...	54, ss. 72(4), 73(4)(_d_), sch. 6.
c. 37	Radioactive Substances Act 1948.	Ss. 3(7)(9), 4(2)(4), 12 am.	S.I. No. 388.

Session and Chap. or No. of Measure	Short title or Subject	How affected	Chapter of 1969 Act or number of Measure or Statutory Instrument
11 & 12 Geo. 6: —*cont.*			
c. 38	Companies Act 1948 ...	S. 94 ext.	32, s. 3(9), sch. 9 para. 16.
		S. 154 ext.	48, s. 86(2).
		S. 217 rep.	52, S.L. (Repeals).
		S. 319 ext.	32, s. 3(9), sch. 9 para. 16.
		Ss. 398, 399(8) am. ...	50, s. 96(9).
		S. 401(2) rep. in pt. ...	52, S.L. (Repeals).
c. 39	Industrial Assurance and Friendly Societies Act 1948.	S. 2(2) expld.	19, s. 7(2).
		S. 8(2) am.	19, s. 7(5).
c. 40	Education (Miscellaneous Provisions) Act 1948.	Sch. 1 rep. in pt. (*prosp.*)	54, s. 72(4), sch. 6.
c. 43	Children Act 1948 ...	S. 3(3)–(5) rep.	54, s. 72(4), sch. 6.
		S. 4(3) proviso rep. ...	54, s. 72(3)(4), sch. 5 para. 14, sch. 6.
		Ss. 5, 6(3)(4) rep. (*prosp.*)	54, s. 72(4), sch. 6.
		S. 7 rep.	54, s. 72(4), sch. 6.
		Pt. II (ss. 11–22) ext. (E.)	46, s. 7(2)(3).
		S. 11 subst. (*prosp.*) ...	54, s. 27(1).
		S. 11 as subst. excl. (*prosp.*).	54, s. 27(1).
		S. 12(1) excl. (*prosp.*) ...	54, s. 27(2).
		S. 13 subst.	54, s. 49.
		S. 13(2) ext. (*prosp.*) ...	54, s. 26(3).
		mod. (*prosp.*) ...	54, s. 22(4).
		Ss. 15, 16 rep.	54, s. 72(4), sch. 6.
		S. 19 subst.	54, s. 50.
		S. 20(1) am.	54, s. 72(3), sch. 5 para. 15.
		S. 23(1) am. (*prosp.*) ...	54, s. 72(3), sch. 5 para. 16.
		Ss. 23(1) rep. in pt. (*prosp.*), (3), 25 rep. (*prosp.*), 26(1) rep. in pt. (*prosp.*).	54, s. 72(4), sch. 6.
		S. 26(1)(*b*) subst. (*prosp.*), (3)(4) am. (*prosp.*).	54, s. 72(3), sch. 5 para. 17.
		Ss. 29–32 excl.	54, s. 44.
		S. 39(1) am.	54, s. 63.
		S. 39(1)(*e*) rep.	54, s. 72(4), sch. 6.
		S. 39(1)(i) added ...	54, s. 72(3), sch. 5 para. 18.
		S. 43(1) am.	54, s. 72(3), sch. 5 para. 19.
		S. 46 restr.	54, s. 65(2).
		S. 49(1) rep. in pt. (*prosp.*)	54, s. 72(4), sch. 6.
		S. 51(1) am. (*prosp.*) ...	54, s. 72(3), sch. 5 para. 20(1).

Session and Chap. or No. of Measure	Short title or Subject	How affected	Chapter of 1969 Act or number of Measure or Statutory Instrument
11 & 12 Geo. 6: c. 43—*cont.*	Children Act 1948—*cont.*	S. 51(2) rep.	54, s. 72(4), sch. 6.
		S. 51(3) am.	54, s. 72(3), sch. 5 para. 20(2).
		S. 54(1)(2) rep.	54, s. 72(4), sch. 6.
		S. 54(3) am., (4) am. (*prosp.*), (5) am.	54, s. 72(3), sch. 5 para. 21.
		S. 59(1) definitions of— " approved school order " rep. (*prosp.*) " child " am. (*prosp.*)	54, s. 72(4), sch. 6. 54, s. 72(3), sch. 5 para. 22.
		S. 59(2) rep. (*prosp.*), sch. 3 rep. in pt. (*prosp.*).	54, s. 72(4), sch. 6.
c. 45	Agriculture (Scotland) Act 1948.	S. 50(4) am. ... ... S. 50(4)(5) rep. (*prosp.*)...	26, s. 2. 26, ss. 1, 3.
c. 56	British Nationality Act 1948.	S. 1(3) am. (*retrosp.*) and rep. in pt. (*retrosp.*).	29, s. 1(1).
		S. 6(1) excl. (*prosp.*) ...	21, s. 18(1)(2).
		S. 32(1) definition of " minor ", (9) am.	46, ss. 1(3), 28 (4)(*a*), sch. 1 Pt. I.
c. 58	Criminal Justice Act 1948	S. 3(1) am. (*prosp.*) ...	54, s. 7(2).
		Ss. 3(5), 11(1) rep. in pt. (*prosp.*).	54, s. 72(4), sch. 6.
		S. 19 am. (*prosp.*)	54, s. 7(3).
		S. 19(1) am. (*prosp.*) ...	54, s. 72(3), sch. 5 para. 23.
		appl. (mod.) (*prosp.*)	54, s. 16(10).
		S. 19(5) excl. (*prosp.*) ...	54, s. 16(10).
		S. 20(1) am. (*prosp.*) ...	54, s. 7(1).
		S. 27 subst. (*prosp.*) ...	54, s. 72(3), sch. 5 para. 24.
		Ss. 46(1), 47(1) rep. in pt. (*prosp.*), 48(4), 49, 71, 72, 75 rep. (*prosp.*).	54, s. 72(4), sch. 6.
		S. 77 ext.	54, s. 46(2), sch. 3 paras. 6(1), 9 (2)(*b*).
		Ss. 77(1), (4)(*c*) rep. in pt. (*prosp.*) (6), 80(1) definitions of " approved school ", " remand home ", " supervision order " rep. (*prosp.*) " sentence " rep. in pt. (*prosp.*).	54, s. 72(4), sch. 6.
		Sch. 9 rep. in pt. (*prosp.*).	54, s. 72(4), sch. 6.
c. 63	Agriculture Holdings Act 1948.	S. 2 Transfer of functions.	S.I. No. 388.
		S. 85 rep.	52, S.L. (Repeals).
c. 65	Representation of the People Act 1948.	S. 57(3) proviso subst. (*prosp.*).	15, s. 18(1).

Session and Chap. or No. of Measure	Short title or Subject	How affected	Chapter of 1969 Act or number of Measure or Statutory Instrument
11 & 12 Geo. 6:			
—cont.			
c. 66	Monopolies and Restrictive Practices (Inquiry and Control) Act 1948.	Transfer of functions ...	S.I. No. 1534.
c. 67	Gas Act 1948	S. 48(1) am.	32, s. 60, sch. 20 para. 26.
12, 13 & 14 Geo. 6:			
c. 4	Judges Pensions (India and Burma) Act 1948.	Pensions increase ...	7, s. 1(1), sch. 1 Pt. I para. 34.
c. 11	Railway and Canal Commission (Abolition) Act 1949.	S. 6(2) rep.	48, s. 137(1), sch. 8 Pt. I.
c. 16	National Theatre Act 1949.	S. 1 am.	11, s. 1.
c. 22	British North America Act 1949.	S. 2 rep.	52, S.L. (Repeals).
c. 32	Special Roads Act 1949...	S. 20(1) expld.	48, s. 76, sch. 4 para. 45(2).
		S. 20(2)(3) am.	48, s. 76, sch. 4 para. 45(3)(4),
c. 39	Commonwealth Telegraphs Act 1949.	S. 4 rep. (saving) ...	48, s. 137(1)(2). sch. 8 Pt. I.
		S. 6 expld.	48, s. 4.
		S. 6(2)–(4) appl. (mod.)...	48, s. 49(2).
		S. 6(2)(*c*)(*d*)(iv)–(vi) am.	48, s. 48.
		S. 6(5)(7)(8) appl. (mod.)	48, s. 49(2).
		S. 7 rep.	48, s. 137(1), sch. 8 Pt. I.
		S. 9 rep....	48, s. 141, sch. 11 Pt. II.
		Sch. 2 rep.	48, s. 137(1), sch. 8 Pt. I.
c. 42	Lands Tribunal Act 1949.	S. 2(6) Pensions increase	7, s. 1(1), sch. 1 Pt. I para. 11.
c. 46	House of Commons (Indemnification of Certain Members) Act 1949.	Rep.	15, s. 24(4), sch. 3 Pt. I.
c. 47	Finance Act 1949 ...	S. 15(1)(*d*) rep. (4) rep. (E.) (9), rep. in pt.	53, s. 14, sch.
		S. 17 rep.	52, S.L. (Repeals).
		S. 28(1) rep. in pt. ...	32, s. 61(6), sch. 21 Pt. V.
		S. 28(2) ext.	32, s. 36(6).
		S. 29 saved	32, s. 35(2).
		S. 29(5) am.	32, s. 40(1), sch. 17 Pt III para. 16.
		S. 33(1) am.	32, s. 40(1), sch. 17 Pt. III para. 17.
c. 51	Legal Aid and Advice Act 1949.	Apptd. day for Pt. I (ss. 1–17) relating to certain matters (1.1.1970).	S.I. No. 1709.
		Excl. (*prosp.*)	54, s. 33(2).

Session and Chap. or No. of Measure	Short title or Subject	How affected	Chapter of 1969 Act or number of Measure or Statutory Instrument
12, 13 & 14 Geo. 6;—*cont.*			
c. 54	Wireless Telegraphy Act 1949.	Expld.	48, s. 3(1).
		S. 2(1) restored as originally enacted.	48, s. 3(2)(a).
		S. 2(1) am.	48, s. 3(3).
		S. 8 rep.	48, s. 137(1), sch. 8 Pt. I.
		S. 14(4) rep.	48, s. 137(1), sch. 8 Pt. II.
		S. 14(5) rep.	48, s. 137(1), sch. 8 Pt. I.
		S. 15(4) rep. in pt. ...	48, s. 137(1), sch. 8 Pt. II.
		Ss. 16(2) rep. in pt., 18 rep.	48, s. 137(1), sch. 8 Pt. I.
		S. 20(3) am.	48, s. 3(6).
		Sch. 1 para. 3 subst. ...	48, s. 3(2)(b).
c. 67	Civil Aviation Act 1949	Am.	48, s. 76, sch. 4 para. 93(2).
		Ext.	48, s. 76, sch. 4 para. 93(1).
		S. 28(4)(c) ext.	48, s. 76, sch. 4 para. 46.
		S. 67(1) ext.	48, s. 88(3).
c. 68	Representation of the People Act 1949.	Saved (S.)	39, s. 1(4), sch. 2 para. 2.
		Saved (E.)	46, s. 1(4), sch. 2 para. 2.
		S. 1 am.	15, s. 1.
		expld.	15, s. 3(1).
		S. 1(1) am.	15, s. 24(1), sch. 2 para. 1.
		S. 1(2) proviso rep. ...	15, s. 24(4), sch. 3 Pt. I.
		S. 2 am.	15, s. 1.
		expld.	15, s. 3(1).
		S. 2(1) am.	15, s. 24(1)(5) sch. 2 para. 1.
		S. 5 rep.	15, ss. 23(4), 24 (4)(5), sch. 3 Pt. II.
		S. 7 ext.	15, s. 7(1).
		S. 8(1) proviso am. ...	15, s. 24(1), sch. 2 para. 2(1).
		S. 8(2) proviso paras. (a)(b) rep.	15, s. 24(1)(4), sch. 2 para. 2(2), sch. 3 Pt. II.
		S. 8(2) proviso para. (c) am.	15, s. 24(1), sch. 2 para. 2(1).
		rep. in pt.	15, s. 24(4), sch. 3 Pt. II.
		S. 9(1)(c) am.	15, s. 24(1), sch. 2 para. 3.
		S. 10 mod. (London) ...	15, s. 23(3).
		S. 10(1)(bb) added, (c) am.	15, s. 24(1), sch. 2 para. 4(1).
		S. 10(3) rep. in pt. ...	15, s. 24(4), sch. 3 Pt. II.

Session and Chap. or No. of Measure	Short title or Subject	How affected	Chapter of 1969 Act or number of Measure or Statutory Instrument
12,13 &14 Geo.6: c. 68—*cont.*	Representation of the People Act 1949.— *cont.*	S. 10(5)(*a*)–(*d*) replaced, (6)(9) am.	15, s. 24(1), sch. 2 para. 4(2)–(4).
		S. 10(10) rep.	15, s. 24(4), sch. 3 Pt. II.
		S. 12(1) am.	15, s. 5(1)(2).
		S. 12(1)(*c*) am. ...	15, s. 24(1), sch. 2 para. 5.
		S. 12(2) rep. in pt. (16.2.1970).	15, s. 24(4), sch. 3 Pt. II.
		S. 12(4) ext.	15, s. 6(2).
		S. 12(5) rep. (16.2.1970)	15, s. 24(4), sch. 3 Pt. II.
		S. 12(7)(*a*) subst. ...	15, s. 6(1).
		S. 13 ext.	15, s. 5(3).
		S. 14(2), (5)(*a*) am. ...	15, s. 24(1), sch. 2 para. 6.
		S. 15 ext.	15, s. 6(4).
		am. and rep. in pt.	15, s. 24(1), sch. 2 para. 7.
		S. 15(3)(*a*) subst. ...	15, s. 6(1).
		S. 23(1) am.	15, s. 5(1)(2).
		S. 23(1)(*c*) am. ...	15, s. 24(1), sch. 2 para. 8(1).
		S. 23(2)(3) rep. in pt. (16.2.1970).	15, s. 24(4), sch. 3 Pt. II.
		S. 23(4) ext. (16.2.1970)	15, s. 6(2).
		am. (16.2.1970)	15, s. 24(1), sch. 2 para. 8(2).
		S. 23(5) rep. (16.2.1970)	15, s. 24(4), sch. 3 Pt. II.
		S. 23(7) rep. in pt. (16.2.1970).	15, s. 6(5).
		S. 24(2) am. (16.2.1970)	15, s. 24(1), sch. 2 para. 9.
		S. 24(3)(*b*) rep. in pt. ...	15, s. 24(4), sch. 3 Pt. II.
		S. 25 ext.	15, s. 6(4).
		S. 25(3) am.	15, s. 24(1), sch. 2 para. 10.
		S. 25(4)(6) rep. in pt. (16.2.1970).	15, s. 24(4), sch. 3 Pt. II.
		S. 26(7) am.	15, s. 19(4).
		S. 29 ext.	15, s. 26(2).
		S. 29(4) rep.	15, s. 24(4), sch. 3 Pt. I.
		S. 30(5) am.	15, s. 19(4).
		S. 36(2) appl.	15, s. 13(1)(*b*).
		S. 36(4) appl.	15, s. 26(3).
		S. 38 rep.	15, s. 24(4), sch. 3 Pt. II.
		S. 39(2)(*a*) subst., (3A) added, (4) am.	15, s. 24(1), sch. 2 para. 11.
		S. 39(4) rep. in pt. ...	15, s. 24(1)(4), sch. 2 para. 11 (3), sch. 3 Pt. II.
		S. 39(2)(*c*) rep. in pt. (*d*) rep.	15, s. 24(4), sch. 3 Pt. II.
		S. 42 am.	15, s. 3(2).
		S. 45(1)(*c*) rep. in pt. ...	15, s. 24(4), sch. 3 Pt. II.

Session and Chap. or No. of Measure	Short title or Subject	How affected	Chapter of 1969 Act or number of Measure or Statutory Instrument
12, 13 & 14 Geo. 6: c. 68—*cont.*	Representation of the People Act 1949— *cont.*	S. 46(4)(*b*) am.	15, s. 24(1), sch. 2 para. 12(1).
		S. 46(4) proviso rep. ...	15, s. 24(1)(4), sch. 2 para. 12(1), sch. 3 Pt. II.
		S. 46(4A) added ...	15, s. 24(1), sch. 2 para. 12(2).
		S. 48(1) am.	15, s. 24(1)(2), sch. 2 para. 13(1).
		S. 48(1) proviso rep. ...	15, s. 24(1)(4), sch. 2 para. 13(1), sch. 3 Pt. II.
		S. 48(2)(*b*) am. (16.2. 1970), (*c*) rep. in pt. (16.2.1970), (3)(*c*) rep. in pt., (*d*) added (16.2. 1970).	15, s. 24(1)(2), sch. 2 para. 13(2).
		Pt. II (ss. 55–106) ext. ...	15, ss. 9(3), 11(6).
		S. 55 am.	15, s. 11(1)(5).
		S. 56(1)(2) am. (16.2. 1970), (2) rep. in pt. (16.2.1970), (5) added (16.2.1970).	15, s. 24(1), sch. 2 para. 14.
		S. 57 am.	15, s. 11(3).
		S. 57(2) rep. (16.2.1970)	15, s. 24(4), sch. 3 Pt. II.
		S. 58(4)(6) am. (16.2. 1970).	15, s. 24(1), sch. 2 para. 15.
		S. 63(1) proviso (i) am.	15, s. 9(4).
		S. 64(2)(3) appl.... ...	15, s. 8(1).
		S. 64(2)(*a*)–(*d*) replaced, (4A) added.	15, s. 24(1), sch. 2 para. 16.
		S. 65(2) rep. in pt. ...	15, s. 24(4), sch. 3 Pt. II.
		S. 66(6) rep. in pt. ...	15, s. 24(4), sch. 3 Pt. I.
		S. 70 am.	15, s. 8(4).
		S. 70(1)(2) rep. in pt. ...	15, s. 24(4), sch. 3 Pt. II.
		Ss. 73(3), 74(9) rep. in pt.	15, s. 24(4), sch. 3 Pt. I.
		S. 76 subst. (16.2.1970)	15, s. 8(5).
		S. 77(1) am. (16.2.1970)	15, s. 8(6).
		S. 79 expld.	48, s. 76, sch. 4 para. 47(1).
		S. 79(4) am.	15, s. 24(1), sch. 2 para. 17.
		S. 80 excl. in pt. (City of London).	15, s. 9(6).
		S. 80(1) am.	15, s. 9(5).
		Ss. 87(2) rep., 91(6) rep. in pt.	15, s. 24(4), sch. 3 Pt. I.
		S. 97 rep.	15, ss. 10, 24(4), sch. 3 Pt. II.
		S. 102 rep.	15, s. 24(4), sch. 3 Pt. I.

Session and Chap. or No. of Measure	Short title or Subject	How affected	Chapter of 1969 Act or number of Measure or Statutory Instrument
12, 13 & 14 Geo. 6: c. 68—*cont.*	Representation of the People Act 1949—*cont.*	S. 106(2) am. (16.2.1970), (3) added (16.2.1970).	15, s. 24(1), sch. 2 para. 18.
		S. 109(3)(*a*), (4) am. (16.2.1970).	15, s. 24(1), sch. 2 para. 19.
		S. 109(8) rep. in pt. ...	15, s. 24(4), sch. 3 Pt. I.
		S. 115(2) rep. in pt. ...	15, ss. 22(1), 24(4), sch. 3 Pt. II.
		S. 116(2) rep. in pt. ...	15, s. 24(4), sch. 3 Pt. I.
		S. 122(3) am.	15, s. 22(2).
		Ss. 128(6), 145(4) rep. in pt., 146(7) rep., 152(1), 152(6), 154(1) rep. in pt.	15, s. 24(4), sch. 3 Pt. I.
		S. 155(1) rep. in pt. ...	15, s. 21(1).
		S. 159(5) rep. in pt. ...	15, ss. 21(2), 24(4), sch. 3 Pt. II.
		S. 162(2) am.	48, s. 76, sch. 4 para. 47(2).
		S. 165(2) appl.	15, s. 26(3).
		S. 165(3) rep. in pt. ...	15, s. 24(4), sch. 3 Pt. II.
		S. 165(4) appl.	15, s. 26(3).
		S. 167 saved	15, s. 23(1).
		S. 167(4) subst.	15, s. 24(1), sch. 2 para. 20.
		S. 171(1) definitions of— " election commissioners " rep.	15, s. 24(4), sch. 3 Pt. I.
		" elector " am., " service voter " subst.	15, s. 24(1), sch. 2 para. 21.
		S. 172(3) proviso rep. in pt.	15, s. 24(4), sch. 3 Pt. I.
		S. 172(4) appl.	15, s. 26(3).
		S. 174(2)(3) appl. ...	15, s. 26(4).
		Schs. 2, 3 am. and rep. in pt.	15, ss. 11(4), 12, 13(3)(5), 14, 17(2), 18(2)(3), 24(1)(4), schs. 1, 2 paras. 22–37, sch. 3.
		Sch. 2 Parliamentary election rules— rule 1 ext.	15, s. 13(1)(*a*)(ii).
		rules 7(1), 12(1)(3) excl.	15, s. 14, sch. 1 Pt. II para. 5(1).
		Sch. 4 para. 2 am. ...	15, s. 24(1), sch. 2 para. 38(1).
		para. 5(2) rep. in pt.	15, ss. 7(3), 24(4), sch. 3 Pt. II.
		para. 5(2)(*b*), (3) am.	15, s. 24(1), sch. 2 para. 38(2)(3).
		Sch. 5 am.	15, s. 24(1), sch. 2 para. 39.
		Sch. 6 para. 8(1) am. ...	15, s. 8(6).

Session and Chap. or No. of Measure	Short title or Subject	How affected	Chapter of 1969 Act or number of Measure or Statutory Instrument
12, 13 & 14 Geo. 6:			
c. 68—*cont.*	Representation of the People Act 1949—*cont.*	Sch. 8 paras. 1(1), 7(2) am.	15, s. 24(1), sch. 2 para. 40.
c. 72	Iron and Steel Act 1949	S. 41(1) am.	45, s. 8(3).
		S. 59(1) definition of " financial year " para. (*a*) rep.	45, s. 16(3) sch.
		Sch. 1 para. 5 subst. ...	45, s. 14.
c. 74	Coast Protection Act 1949	S. 47(*b*) expld.	48, s. 76, sch. 4 para. 48.
c. 76	Marriage Act 1949 ...	Appl. (mod.)	38, s. 6, sch. 1.
		S. 3 ext.	46, s. 2(3).
		S. 3(5) am.	46, s. 2(2).
		Pt. II (ss. 5–25) appl. ...	38, s. 6(2).
		S. 20 appl.	38, s. 6(2)(*b*).
		S. 21 appl.	38, s. 6(4).
		S. 26(2) excl.	38, s. 6(3).
		S. 78(1) am.	46, s. 2(1)(*c*).
c. 78	Married Women (Restraint upon Anticipation) Act 1949.	S. 1(3), sch. 1 rep. ...	52, S.L. (Repeals).
c. 84	War Damaged Sites Act 1949.	S. 1(2) am.	48, s. 76, sch. 4 para. 49.
c. 86	Electoral Registers Act 1949.	S. 1(6) rep. in pt., (7) rep.	15, s. 24(4), sch. 3 Pt. I.
		S. 2, sch. 1 rep.	15, s. 24(4), sch. 3 Pt. II.
c. 87	Patents Act 1949 ...	S. 40(3) am.	S.I. No. 1534.
		S. 85(2) replaced, (8A) (11) added.	58, s. 24.
		S. 101(1) definition of " Appeal Tribunal " subst.	58, s. 35(1), sch. 1.
c. 88	Registered Designs Act 1949.	S. 28(2) replaced, (8A) (10) added.	58, s. 24.
		S. 44(1) definition of " Appeal Tribunal " subst.	58, s. 35(1), sch. 1.
c. 90	Election Commissioners Act 1949.	Rep.	15, s. 24(4), sch. 3 Pt. I.
c. 94	Criminal Justice (Scotland) Act 1949.	S. 7(1)(2) am. (*prosp.*) ...	54, ss. 72(3), 73 (4)(*c*), sch. 5 para. 25.
		S. 7A added (*prosp.*) ...	54, ss. 72(3), 73 (4)(*c*), sch. 5 para. 26.
c. 97	National Parks and Access to the Countryside Act 1949.	Ext.	48, s. 76, sch. 4 para. 93(1).
c. 101 ...	Justices of the Peace Act 1949.	S. 14 rep. (*prosp.*) ...	54, s. 72(4), sch. 6.
		S. 15 am. (*prosp.*) ...	54, ss. 18(2), 61.
		S. 27 expld. (*prosp.*) ...	21, s. 12, sch. 3 para. 8(4).
		S. 33 Pensions increase	7, s. 1(1), sch. 1 Pt. II para. 2.

Session and Chap. or No. of Measure	Short title or Subject	How affected	Chapter of 1969 Act or number of Measure or Statutory Instrument
14 Geo. 6:			
c. 5	Newfoundland (Consequential Provisions) Act 1950.	Ss. 1, 3, sch. rep. ...	52, S.L. (Repeals).
c. 12	Foreign Compensation Act 1950.	S. 2(3) rep.	20, s. 2(4).
		S. 3 am.	20, s. 2(1)–(3).
		Ss. 3(*b*), 4(2) ext. ...	20, s. 3.
		S. 4(4) excl.	20, s. 3(12).
c. 15	Finance Act 1950 ...	S. 43 rep.	32, s. 61(6), sch. 21 Pt. V.
		S. 44 expld.	32, s. 40(1), sch. 17 Pt. II para. 12.
		S. 44(1)–(5)(8) am. ...	32, s. 40(1), sch. 17 Pt. III para. 18.
		S. 45 rep.	32, s. 61(6), sch. 21 Pt. V.
		S. 48 excl.	32, s. 39(2)(3).
		S. 48(4) excl.	32, s. 39(4).
		Sch. 7 rep.	32, s. 61(6), sch. 21 Pt. V.
c. 21	Miscellaneous Financial Provisions Act 1950.	S. 2(1) am.	32, s. 57.
c. 28	Shops Act 1950 ...	Ss. 22, 44 expld. ...	48, s. 76, sch. 4 para. 51.
		S. 44(1)(*b*) rep.	48, s. 137(1), sch. 8 Pt. I.
		S. 59(2) rep.	52, S.L. (Repeals).
		Schs. 2, 5 expld. ...	48, s. 76, sch. 4 para. 51.
c. 31	Allotments Act 1950 ...	S. 11(1) rep. (15.2.1971)	19, s. 17(2), sch. 4.
c. 34	Housing (Scotland) Act 1950.	S. 125 proviso rep. ...	34, s. 69(3), sch. 7.
c. 36	Diseases of Animals Act 1950.	Ext.	28, s. 2(2).
		S. 37(4A) added, (5) am.	28, s. 1.
		S. 40A added	28, s. 3(1).
		S. 41 am.	28, s. 3(2).
		S. 84(4) definition of " pony " added.	28, s. 1.
c. 37	Maintenance Orders Act 1950.	S. 16 ext.	46, ss. 4(5)(*a*), 6(7), 28(4)(*c*).
		Sch. 1 rep. in pt. (*prosp.*)	54, s. 72(4), sch. 6.
c. 39	Public Utilities Street Works Act 1950.	Expld. (L.T.E.)	35, s. 34(9).
		S. 20 expld.	48, s. 21(1)(*b*).
		S. 33(2)(*b*) rep. in pt. ...	48, s. 141, sch. 11 Pt. II.
		Sch. 5 rep. in pt. ...	48, s. 137(1), sch. 8 Pt. I.
14 & 15 Geo. 6:			
c. 10	Re-instatement in Civil Employment Act 1950.	Appl.	65, s. 2(7).
c. 11	Administration of Justice (Pensions) Act 1950.	Pt. I (ss. 1–20) Pensions increase.	7, ss. 1(1), 2(1), sch. 1 Pt. I para. 4, Pt. II para. 3 sch. 3 para. 3.

Session and Chap. or No. of Measrue	Short title or Subject	How affected	Chapter of 1969 Act or number of Measure or Statutory Instrument
14 & 15 Geo 6: c. 11—*cont.*	Administration of Justice (Pensions) Act 1950— *cont.*	S. 22 Pensions increase	7, s. 1(1), sch. 1 Pt. II para. 4.
		Sch. 1 am.	58, s. 31(1).
		Sch. 2 rep. in pt. ...	58, s. 35(2), sch. 2.
c. 30	Sea Fish Industry Act 1951.	Ss. 1(2), 3(2), 17(5) Transfer of functions.	S.I. No. 388.
c. 39	Common Informers Act 1951.	Sch. rep. in pt.	{ 15, s. 24(4), sch. 3 Pt. I. 52, S.L. (Repeals).
c. 46	Courts-Martial (Appeals) Act 1951.	S. 34(1) Pensions increase	7, s. 1(1), sch. 1 Pt. I para. 7.
c. 52	Telephone Act 1951 ...	Rep.	48, s. 141, sch. 11 Pt. I.
c. 55	Nurses (Scotland) Act 1951.	Ss. 2(4), 3(2) am. ...	47, s. 10(1), sch. 1 para. 1.
		S. 4 rep.	47, s. 10(2), sch. 2.
		S. 5(1)(3) subst. (1.12.1970)	47, s. 4(3).
		S. 6(1) am.	47, s. 7(1).
		S. 7(1) am.	47, s. 7(2).
		rep. in pt.	47, ss. 7(2), 10(2), sch. 2.
		S. 8(2) rep.	47, ss. 8, 10(2), sch. 2.
		S. 10 rep. in pt. ...	47, s. 10(2), sch. 2.
		S. 11(3) am.	47, s. 10(1), sch. 1 para. 2.
		S. 12(3)(*b*) subst. ...	47, s. 10(1), sch. 1 para. 3.
		S. 15 am.	47, s. 10(1), sch. 1 para. 4.
		Ss. 15, 33(2) rep. in pt. ...	47, s. 10(2), sch. 2.
		S. 34 appl.	47, s. 9(1).
		S. 34 definition of " registered general nurse " added.	47, s. 10(1), sch. 1 para. 5.
		Sch. 1 para. 1(*a*)(*b*) am. (1.12.1970).	47, s. 3(1).
		para. 2 subst. (1.12.1970).	47, s. 3(2).
		Schs. 2, 3 rep.	47, s. 10(2), sch. 2.
		Sch. 4 para. 2(*c*) rep. ...	47, ss. 6, 10(2), sch. 2.
c. 59	Price Control and other Orders (Indemnity) Act 1951.	Rep.	52, S.L. (Repeals)
c. 60	Mineral Workings Act 1951.	S. 32(1)(2) appl. (mod.) (S.).	30, s. 93(4).
		S. 32(3) am. (S.) ...	30, s. 90(3).
c. 65	Reserve and Auxiliary Forces (Protection of Civil Interests) Act 1951.	Ext.	48, s. 76, sch. 4 para. 93(1).
		S. 2(1)(*d*) ext.	46, ss. 4(5)(*b*), 6(7).
		Sch. 1 am.	65, s. 2(7).

Session and Chap. or No. of Measure	Short title or Subject	How affected	Chapter of 1969 Act or number of Measure or Statutory Instrument
15 & 16 Geo. 6 & Eliz. 2:			
c. 10	Income Tax Act 1952 ...	Excl. (Albert & Edward medallists).	32, s. 12.
		S. 2(2)(*a*) am.	32, s. 18(7), sch. 13 para. 21.
		rep. in pt. ...	32, s. 18(1).
		S. 5(2) rep., 12(1) rep. in pt.	32, s. 61(6), sch. 21 Pt. X.
		S. 12(4) rep. (6.4.1970) ...	32, ss. 60, 61(6), sch. 20 para. 17(1), sch. 21 Pt. VIII.
		S. 17 rep. in pt. ...	32, s. 61(6), sch. 21 Pt. X.
		S. 27(2) am.	32, s. 60, sch. 20 para. 9(1).
		S. 29(3) am.	48, s. 94(2)(*c*), sch. 6 Pt. III.
		S. 31(1) rep. in pt., 32 rep.	32, s. 61(6), sch. 21 Pt. X.
		Ss. 51, 52(2)(*b*) rep. (6.4.1970).	32, s. 61(6), sch. 21 Pt. VIII.
		S. 52(4) am.	32, s. 60, sch. 20 para. 13(5).
		S. 59(1) rep. (6.4.1970) ...	32, s. 61(6), sch. 21 Pt. VIII.
		S. 59(3)(*b*) rep. in pt. (6.4.1970).	32, ss. 60, 61(6), sch. 20 para. 13(4), sch. 21 Pt. VIII.
		S. 59(3) proviso ext. ...	32, s. 60, sch. 20 para. 13(4).
		Ss. 62, 63(1) rep. (6.4.1970)	32, s. 61(6), sch. 21 Pt. VIII.
		S. 65(2) appl. (mod.) ...	32, s. 60, sch. 20 para. 17(2).
		S. 66(1) rep. in pt. (6.4.1970).	32, ss. 60, 61(6), sch. 20 para. 17(3), sch. 21 Pt. VIII.
		S. 72(2)(*c*) rep.	32, ss. 60, 61(6), sch. 20 para. 17(4), sch. 21 Pt. IX.
		S. 74(2)(5) rep. in pt. ...	32, s. 61(6), sch. 21 Pt. X.
		S. 83 sch. B para. 2 rep.	32, s. 61, sch. 21 Pt. IX.
		S. 115(1) rep.	32, s. 61(6), sch. 21 Pt. IX.
		S. 117 sch. C para. 6 rep.	32, ss. 60, 61(6), sch. 20 para. 17(6), sch. 21 Pt. IX.
		para. 7 rep.	32, s. 61(6), sch. 21 Pt. X.
		S. 119(1)(2) am. ...	32, s. 60, sch. 20 para. 17(6).

Session and Chap. or No. of Measure	Short title or Subject	How affected	Chapter of 1969 Act or number of Measure or Statutory Instrument
15 & 16 Geo. 6 & Eliz. 2: c. 10—*cont.*	Income Tax Act 1952—*cont.*	S. 120 subst.	32, s. 60, sch. 20 para. 17(5).
		S. 121 definition of " dividends " rep. in pt.	32, ss. 60, 61, sch. 20 para. 17(6), sch. 21 Pt. IX.
		am. ...	32, s. 60, sch. 20 para. 17(6).
		S. 122 Sch. D— para. 1 rep. in pt. ...	32, s. 61(6), sch. 21 Pt. X.
		para. 1(*b*) am. ...	32, s. 60, sch. 20 para. 1(1)(*b*).
		para. 1 proviso rep. ...	32, s. 61(6), sch. 21 Pt. IX.
		S. 123 Sch. D— Case I ext.	32, ss. 18(7), 32(6)(7), sch. 13 para. 6(1).
		Case II ext.	32, s. 18(7), sch. 13 para. 6(1).
		Case III ext.	32, s. 24(1).
		am.	32, s. 26(1)(2).
		Case V ext.	32, s. 60, sch. 20 para. 5(3).
		Case VI ext.	32, ss. 18(7), 31(2), 32(3), sch. 13 para. 12(3)(4).
		Case VII excl. ...	32, s. 41(7), sch. 18 Pt. III para. 5(2).
		Ss. 124(3), 126 rep. ...	32, s. 61(6), sch. 21 Pt. X.
		S. 127(3) am.	32, s. 60, sch. 20 para. 17(7).
		S. 129(3) am.	32, s. 60, sch. 20 para. 17(8).
		S. 131 expld.	32, s. 18(7), sch. 13 para. 2.
		S. 132(1) rep. in pt. ...	32, s. 61(6), sch. 21 Pt. X.
		S. 132(1)(*b*) rep. ...	32, s. 61(6), sch. 21 Pt. IX.
		S. 132(1)(*c*) am. ...	32, s. 18(7), sch. 13 para. 21.
		rep. in pt. ...	32, s. 18(6).
		S. 137(*c*) am., (*c*)(i) rep. in pt.	32, ss. 60, 61(6), sch. 20 para. 17(10), sch. 21 Pt. IX.
		S. 137(*f*) expld. ...	32, s. 18(7), sch. 13 para. 4(1).
		S. 137(*l*) rep. in pt. ...	32, s. 18(4).
		am.	32, s. 18(7), sch. 13 para. 22.
		S. 137(*ll*) added ...	32, s. 18(7), sch. 13 para. 4(2).
		S. 138 am.	32, s. 18(7), sch. 13 para. 5(3).

Session and Chap. or No. of Measure	Short title or Subject	How affected	Chapter of 1969 Act or number of Measure or Statutory Instrument
15 & 16 Geo. 6 & Eliz. 2: c. 10—*cont.*	Income Tax Act 1952—*cont.*	S. 138(1) ext.	32, s. 18(7), sch. 13 para. 5(1).
		rep. in pt. (6.4. 1970), (2) rep. (6.4.1970).	32, s. 61(6), sch. 21 Pt. II.
		S. 144(4) am.	32, s. 60, sch. 20 para. 17(11).
		S. 155(2) excl.	32, s. 60, sch. 20 para. 17(13).
		S. 156 Sch. E— para. 1A rep. in pt. ...	32, s. 61(6), sch. 21 Pt. X.
		paras. 2, 3, subst. ...	32, s. 60, sch. 20 para. 5(1)(2).
		S. 157 saved	32, s. 10(9).
		S. 157(4) rep.	32, s. 61(6), sch. 21 Pt. X.
		S. 165(1) rep. in pt. (6.4.1970).	32, s. 61(6), sch. 21 Pt. VIII.
		S. 169 restr.	32, s. 25(8).
		excl.	32, s. 26(7).
		S. 169(1) rep. in pt. ...	32, s. 18(1).
		am.	32, ss. 18(7), 60, sch. 13 para. 21, sch. 20 para. 17(14).
		S. 169(2)(4) rep. ...	32, ss. 60, 61(6), sch. 20 para. 17(14), sch. 21 Pt. IX.
		S. 169(5) rep. (15.8.1970)	32, s. 61(6), sch. 21 Pt. II.
		S. 170 restr.	32, s. 25(8).
		appl.	32, s. 32(13), sch. 16 para. 7(3).
		excl.	32, s. 26(7).
		S. 170(1)(a) rep. in pt. ...	32, s. 26(3).
		am. ...	32, ss. 18(7), 60, sch. 13 para. 21, sch. 20 para. 17(14).
		S. 170(2)(4) appl. ...	32, s. 26(4).
		S. 170(5) rep.	32, ss. 60, 61(6), sch. 20 para. 17(14), sch. 21 Pt. IX.
		S. 187(1)(b) rep.	32, s. 61(6), sch. 21 Pt. X.
		S. 190 subst.	32, s. 60, sch. 20 para. 17(15).
		S. 191(1) expld.	48, s. 109.
		S. 193(2) rep. in pt. (3)(b) (c) rep.	32, ss. 60, 61(6), sch. 20 para. 17(16), sch. 21 Pt IX.
		S. 193(4) expld.	48, s. 109.
		S. 193(5) rep. in pt. ...	32, ss. 60, 61(6), sch. 20 para. 17(16), sch. 21 Pt. IX.

Session and Chap. or No. of Measure	Short title or Subject	How affected	Chapter of 1969 Act or number of Measure or Statutory Instrument
15 & 16 Geo. 6 & Eliz. 2: c. 10—*cont.*	Income Tax Act 1952—*cont.*	S. 200 rep.	32, ss. 18(2), 61 (6), sch. 21 Pt. II.
		S. 202(5) rep.	32, s. 61(6), sch. 21 Pt. X.
		S. 203 excl.	32, s. 18(7), sch. 13 para. 12(7).
		S. 203(1)(ii) rep. in pt. ...	32, s. 60, sch. 20 para. 17(17).
		S. 207(1)(*b*) am.	32, s. 60, sch. 20 para. 17(18).
		S. 210 am.	32, s. 10(2).
		S. 211(2)(3) am.	32, s. 10(4).
		S. 212(1) am.	32, s. 11(2).
		S. 212(2) subst.	32, s. 11(3).
		S. 212(5) am.	32, s. 60, sch. 20 para. 17(19).
		S. 212(6) added	32, s. 11(4).
		S. 214(1) rep. in pt.	32, ss. 60, 61(6), sch. 20 para. 17(20), sch. 21 Pt. IX.
		am.	32, s. 60, sch. 20 para. 17(20).
		S. 214(2) rep.	32, s. 61(6), sch. 21 Pt. IX.
		S. 216(1) am.	32, s. 10(5).
		S. 218(4) am.	32, s. 10(8).
		S. 219(2)(*a*)(*i*) am. ...	32, s. 60, sch. 20 para. 17(21).
		S. 220(1) Table subst. ...	32, s. 10(3).
		S. 220(1) rep. in pt. ...	32, s. 61(6), sch. 21 Pt. IV.
		S. 222 rep.	32, s. 61(6), sch. 21 Pt. IX.
		S. 223 proviso (*i*) rep. ...	32, s. 61(6), sch. 21 Pt. X.
		S. 225(2)(*a*)(*i*) am. ...	32, s. 60, sch. 20 para. 17(21).
		S. 226(5) am.	32, s. 60, sch. 20 para. 17(22).
		S. 227(2)(*b*) am.... ...	32, s. 60, sch. 20 para. 17(23).
		S. 228 expld.	32, s. 11(5).
		S. 229(1) am.	32, s. 60, sch. 20 para. 17(24).
		S. 229(4) rep. in pt. (6.4. 1970).	32, s. 61(6), sch. 21 Pt. VIII.
		S. 229(6)(7) rep. (6.4.1970)	32, ss. 60, 61(6), sch. 20 para. 17(25), sch. 21 Pt. VIII.
		S. 232 am.	32, s. 60, sch. 20 para. 17(25).
		S. 233(3) rep. (6.4.1970)	32, s. 61(6), sch. 21 Pt. VIII.
		S. 237(7)(*b*) am. ...	32, s. 60, sch. 20 para. 17(26).
		S. 244(6) rep. in pt. (6.4. 1970).	32, s. 61(6), sch. 21 Pt. VIII.

Session and Chap. or No. of Measure	Short title or Subject	How affected	Chapter of 1969 Act or number of Measure or Statutory Instrument
15 & 16 Geo. 6 & Eliz. 2: c. 10—*cont.*	Income Tax Act 1952—*cont.*	Pt. IX Ch. III (ss. 245–264) am.	32, s. 60, sch. 20 para. 9(1).
		S. 249(2)(*a*) rep. ...	32, ss. 60, 61(6), sch. 20 para 17 (27), sch. 21 Pt. IX.
		S. 249(2)(*b*) am.	32, s. 60, sch. 20 para. 17(27).
		S. 249(3),(4)(*b*) proviso, (5) rep. in pt.	32, s. 61(6), sch. 21 Pt. X.
		S. 258(3) proviso appl. (mod.).	32, s. 60, sch. 20 para. 6(2).
		S. 258(3) proviso (i) (ii) rep. in pt.	32, s. 61(6), sch. 21 Pt. IX.
		Ss. 316(1), (2), 317(1)–(4), 318(1)(2) rep. in pt., 319 rep.	32, s. 61(6), sch. 21, Pt. X.
		S. 342(4) expld.	32, s. 60, sch. 20 para. 17(28).
		Ss. 341, 342 am. (*retrosp.*)	32, s. 34(6).
		S. 342 ext.	32, s. 18(7), sch. 13 para. 6(1).
		S. 347(1)(*b*), (4) expld. ...	32, s. 60, sch. 20 para. 17(29).
		S. 348(5) rep.	32, s. 61(6), sch. 21 Pt. IX.
		S. 352(1)(2) am. ...	32, s. 60, sch. 20 para. 17(30).
		S. 352(3) rep.	32, s. 61(6), sch. 21 Pt. IX.
		S. 354(2) am. ...	32, s. 60, sch. 20 para. 17(31).
		S. 355(1) am.	32, s. 60, sch. 20 para. 17(32).
		S. 359(1)(2) am. ...	32, s. 60, sch. 20 para. 17(31).
		Ss. 359(5) rep. in pt. (6.4. 1970), (6), 360(3) rep. (6.4.1970) 362(2), 367 (1)(2) rep. in pt. (6.4. 1970).	32, s. 61(6), sch. 21 Pt. VIII
		Ss. 368 rep. in pt., 373(1) (*b*) rep.	32, s. 61(6), sch. 21 Pt. X.
		S. 379(1) expld.	32, s. 60, sch. 20 para. 17(33).
		S. 379(4)(*c*) rep. in pt. ...	32, s. 61(6), sch. 21 Pt. IX.
		S. 384 Power to apply ...	50, s. 82(3).
		S. 392 rep. in pt. ...	32, s. 61(6), sch. 21 Pt. X.
		Pt. XVIII Ch. II (ss. 397–403) expld.	32, s. 16(3).
		am.	32, s. 18(7), sch. 13, para. 11.
		S. 397(1) excl.	32, s. 16(5).
		S. 411 appl. (mod.) ...	32, s. 18(7), sch. 13 para. 11(4).
		S. 411(3)(*b*) appl. (mod.)	32, s. 18(7), sch. 13 para. 9(1).

Session and Chap. or No. of Measure	Short title or Subject	How affected	Chapter of 1969 Act or number of Measure or Statutory Instrument
15 & 16 Geo. 6 & Eliz. 2: c. 10—*cont.*	Income Tax Act 1952— *cont.*	S. 412(1) am.	32, s. 33(2).
		S. 412(6) am.	32, s. 33(3).
		S. 413(4) added	32, s. 33(4).
		S. 416(3) rep. in pt. ...	32, s. 60, sch. 20 para. 17(17).
		S. 419 expld.	32, s. 60, sch. 20 para. 17(34).
		S. 425(6)(*b*) am.... ...	32, s. 60, sch. 20 para. 17(35).
		S. 429(2) am.	32, s. 14(3).
		S. 430 ext. (*retrosp.*) ...	32, s. 29, sch. 14 para. 9(2).
		S. 430(1) appl. (*retrosp.*)	32, s. 29, sch. 14 para. 9(4).
		S. 430(2) subst.	32, s. 29, sch. 14 para. 8(2).
		expld.	32, s. 29, sch. 14 para. 8(4).
		S. 430(4)(5) rep. and superseded.	32, ss. 29, 61(6), sch. 14 para. 8 (7), sch. 21 Pt. IV.
		Ss. 434(1), 435(1) am. ...	32, s. 60, sch. 20 para. 17(36).
		Ss. 437 definition of " assurance company " subst. " life assurance business " am.	32, s. 60, sch. 20 para. 17(37).
		S. 439(2) proviso (*b*) rep.	32, s. 61(6), sch. 21 Pt. X.
		Ss. 439(2), 440(1)(2) rep. in pt.	32, ss. 60, 61(6), sch. 20 para. 17(38) sch. 21 Pt. IX.
		S. 440(1)(2) am. ...	32, s. 60, sch. 20 para. 17(38).
		S. 442 ext.	32, s. 18(7), sch. 13 para. 23.
		S. 442(1) am.	32, s. 60, sch. 20 para. 17(39).
		S. 442(2)(3) rep. in pt. ...	32, ss. 60, 61(6), sch. 20 para. 17(39), sch. 21 Pt. IX.
		S. 442(3) am.	32, s. 60, sch. 20 para. 17(39).
		S. 442(4) rep. in pt. ...	32, s. 61(6), sch. 21 Pt. X.
		S. 444 am.	32, s. 60, sch. 20 para. 9(1).
		S. 444(1)(2) rep. in pt. ...	32, s. 61(6), sch. 21 Pt. IX.
		S. 444(3) rep.	32, s. 61(6), sch. 21 Pt. X.
		S. 444(4) rep.	32, s. 61(6), sch. 21 Pt. IX.
		S. 445 ext.	32, s. 18(7), sch. 13 para. 23.

Session and Chap. or No. of Measure	Short title or Subject	How affected	Chapter of 1969 Act or number of Measure or Statutory Instrument
15 & 16 Geo. 6 & Eliz. 2: c. 10—*cont.*	Income Tax Act 1952—*cont.*	S. 445 am.	32, s. 60, sch. 20 para. 17(41).
		S. 445(1) am.	32, s. 60, sch. 20 para. 17(40).
		S. 445(3)(*b*) rep.... ...	32, ss. 18(3), 61 (6), sch. 21 Pt. II.
		S. 445(3) definition of " dividend " rep.	32, s. 61(6), sch. 21 Pt. IX.
		S. 457(1) rep. in pt. (3)(*b*) rep.	32, s. 61(6), sch. 21 Pt. X.
		S. 461 rep.	32, ss. 60, 61(6), sch. 20 para. 8 (4), sch. 21 Pt. IX.
		S. 463 Transfer of functions.	S.I. No. 1498.
		Ss. 463(5) rep., 469(1)(2) rep. in pt.	32, s. 61(6), sch. 21 Pt. X.
		S. 471(1A) added	32, s. 13(1).
		S. 472 ext.	32, s. 60, sch. 20 para. 17(42).
		S. 495(5) rep. in pt. ...	32, s. 61(6), sch. 21 Pt. X.
		S. 496 ext.	32, s. 60, sch. 20 para. 14.
		S. 498(1) proviso(*b*) rep.	32, s. 61(6), sch. 21 Pt. X.
		S. 510 appl. (mod.) ...	32, s. 60, sch. 20 para. 17(43).
		S. 511(1)(*b*) am.... ...	32, s. 18(7), sch. 13 para. 21.
		S. 514(1)–(3) rep. in pt....	32, s. 61(6), sch. 20 Pt. X.
		S. 515(2)–(4)(6)(7) rep. (6.4.1970).	32, s. 61(6), sch. 21 Pt. VIII.
		S. 524(4) ext.	32, s. 18(7), sch. 13 para. 24.
		S. 524(5)(*c*) rep.... ...	32, s. 61(6), sch. 21 Pt. II.
		S. 525(2)(*e*) rep.... ...	32, s. 61(6), sch. 21 Pt. X.
		S. 526(1) definition of— " farmland " am. ...	32, s. 15.
		" relative " restr. ...	32, s. 60, sch. 20 para. 17(44).
		Ss. 528(3)(*b*), 529(3)(4), 530(1)(2) rep.	32, s. 61(6), sch. 21 Pt. X.
		Sch. 8 para. 1(1) rep. in pt. (6.4.1970).	32, ss. 60, 61(6), sch. 20 para. 17(45), sch. 21 Pt. VIII.
		paras. 1(3) added (6.4.1970), 4 am. (6.4.1970).	32, s. 60, sch. 20 para. 17(45).
		Sch. 9 paras. 1, 2 rep. ...	32, s. 61(6), sch. 21 Pt. X.
		Sch. 10 paras. 4–9 replaced.	32, s. 60, sch. 20 para. 17(46).

Session and Chap. or No. of Measure	Short title or Subject	How affected	Chapter of 1969 Act or number of Measure or Statutory Instrument
15 & 16 Geo. 6 & Eliz. 2:			
c. 10—*cont.*	Income Tax Act 1952—*cont.*	Sch. 16 para. 1 rep. in pt.	32, s. 61(6), sch. 21 Pt. X.
		para. 10 am. ...	32, s. 60, sch. 20 para. 9(2).
		para. 13 ext. ...	32, s. 60, sch. 20 para. 17(47).
		Sch. 17 para. 3 am. ...	32, s. 60, sch. 20 para. 9(2).
		Sch. 18 Pt. III para. 2(1) rep. in pt.	32, s. 61(6), sch. 21 Pt. X.
		para. 2(1) (*b*) rep. in pt.	32, s. 18(7), sch. 13 para. 19(2).
		para. 2(1) (*b*) am.	32, s. 18(7), sch. 13 para. 21.
		Sch. 19 para. 1(1) definition of " payment ", " contribution " rep. in pt. Sch. 20 para. 2(3) proviso rep. Sch. 22 (residue) rep. Sch. 23 Pt. II paras. 4, 5 rep.	32, s. 61(6), sch. 21 Pt. X.
		Sch. 24 am.	32, s. 18(7), sch. 13 para. 21.
		rep. in pt. ...	32, s. 61(6), sch. 21 Pt. X.
c. 15	Agriculture (Fertilisers) Act 1952.	Transfer of functions ...	S.I. No. 388.
c. 33	Finance Act 1952 ...	S. 15(2) am.	32, s. 10(7).
		S. 17 rep.	32, s. 61(6), sch. 21 Pt. X.
		S. 18 expld.	32, s. 18(7), sch. 13 para. 2.
		Ss. 18(6)(*c*) rep., (7) rep. in pt., 67(1) proviso rep.	32, s. 61(6), sch. 21 Pt. X.
c. 35	Agriculture (Ploughing Grants) Act 1952.	Transfer of functions ...	S.I. No. 388.
c. 37	Civil List Act 1952 ...	S. 2(2)(*a*) rep. in pt. (*b*) rep.	46, s. 10(1).
		S. 4(1)(*a*) am.	46, s. 10(2).
c. 44	Customs and Excise Act 1952.	S. 34 excl.	16, s. 9(2).
		S. 142 am.	32, s. 1(5), sch. 7 para. 2.
		S. 199 am.	32, s. 1(3)(*b*).
		S. 234 appl. (mod.) ...	32, ss. 2(9), 5(13), sch. 8 para. 4, sch. 11 para. 17.
		S. 237 appl.	32, s. 2(9), sch. 8 para. 4.
		expld.	32, s. 2(9), sch. 8 paras. 4–8.
		S. 237(2) rep. in pt. ...	53, s. 14, sch.
		S. 243(1)(*b*) rep. and replaced.	32, s. 1(5), sch. 7 para. 1.
		S. 244(2)(*a*) am. (S) ...	39, s. 1(3), sch. 1 Pt. I.
		am. (E.) ...	46, s. 1(3), sch. 1 Pt. I.

Session and Chap. or No. of Measure	Short title or Subject	How affected	Chapter of 1969 Act or number of Measure or Statutory Instrument
15 & 16 Geo. 6 & Eliz. 2:			
c. 44—*cont.*	Customs and Excise Act 1952—*cont.*	S. 255 ext.	16, s. 9(2)(*c*).
		S. 259 excl.	16, s. 10(2).
		S. 313 ext. (E.) ...	53, s. 12.
c. 45	Pensions (Increase) Act 1952.	Sch. 1 Pts. I, II ext. ...	7, s. 2(1), sch. 3 paras. 2, 5.
c. 46	Hypnotism Act 1952 ...	S. 3 am. (S.)	39, s. 1(3), sch. 1 Pt. I.
		S. 3 am. (E.)	46, s. 1(3), sch. 1 Pt. I.
c. 47	Rating and Valuation (Scotland) Act 1952.	S. 2 rep.	48, s. 141, sch. 11 Pt. II.
c. 50	Children and Young Persons (Amendment) Act 1952.	Ss. 2–5 rep. (*prosp.*) sch. rep. in pt (*prosp.*)	54, s. 72(4), sch. 6.
c. 52	Prison Act 1952... ...	S. 45(4) appl. (mod.) (*prosp.*).	54, s. 31(3)(*b*).
		Ss. 49(2), 50 rep. in pt., (*prosp.*), 53(1) definition of " remand home " rep. (*prosp.*)	54, s. 72(4), sch. 6.
c. 55	Magistrates' Courts Act 1952.	Appl. (*prosp.*)	54, s. 31(6).
		S. 18(1) am. (*prosp.*) ...	54, s. 6(2).
		Ss. 20, 21 rep. (*prosp.*) ...	54, s. 72(4), sch. 6.
		S. 25(1) am. (*prosp.*) ...	54, s. 6(2).
		S. 26(2) rep. (*prosp.*) ...	54, s. 72(4), sch. 6.
		S. 28 ext. (*prosp.*) ...	54, s. 23(4).
		S. 28(1) am. (*prosp.*) ...	54, s. 7(1).
		S. 32 rep. (*prosp.*) ...	54, s. 72(4), sch. 6.
		S. 34 appl. (mod.) (*prosp.*)	54, s. 3(6).
		S. 38(1) rep. in pt. (*prosp.*)	54, s. 72(4), sch. 6.
		S. 40(2)(4) am. (*prosp.*) ...	54, s. 8(3).
		S. 47(3)(4) appl. (mod.) (*prosp.*).	54, ss. 2(4), 16(2).
		S. 77 ext. (*prosp.*) ...	54, s. 2(6).
		S. 96 ext. (*prosp.*) ...	54, s. 2(13).
		S. 104 excl ...	51, s. 12(3), sch. 2 para. 3(2). 56, s. 1(2).
		S. 104 excl. (*prosp.*) ...	54, s. 57(2).
		S. 105(5) mod. (*prosp.*)...	54, s. 23(5).
		saved (*prosp.*)	54, s. 72(4), sch. 5 para. 24.
		S. 107(2) saved (*prosp.*)...	54, s. 6(3).
c. 62	Agriculture (Calf Subsidies) Act 1952.	Transfer of functions ...	S.I. No. 388.
c. 66	Defamation Act 1952 ...	S. 9(3) expld.	48, s. 3(1).
		S. 16(4) rep. in pt. ...	48, s. 76, sch. 4 para. 53.
1 & 2 Eliz. 2:			
c. 17	White Fish and Herring Industries Act 1953.	Ss. 1, 5, 6 Transfer of functions.	S.I. No. 388.
c. 20	Births and Deaths Registration Act 1953.	S. 9 am.	46, s. 27(3).
		S. 10 am.	46, s. 27(1).
		S. 14(1)(*a*) am.	46, s. 27(5).
c. 23	Accommodation Agencies Act 1953.	Ss. 1(1) rep. in pt., 2(4) rep.	61, s. 1.

Session and Chap. or No. of Measure	Short title or Subject	How affected	Chapter of 1969 Act or number of Measure or Statutory Instrument
1 & 2 Eliz. 2:— *cont.*			
c. 25	Local Government Superannuation Act 1953.	S. 15 ext. (L.T.E.) ...	35, s. 4(5).
c. 26	Local Government (Miscellaneous Provisions) Act 1953.	S. 2(2) am. (15.2.1971) ...	19, s. 10(3), sch. 2 para. 12.
		S. 6 expld.	48, s. 76, sch. 4 para. 54.
c. 33	Education (Miscellaneous Provisions) Act 1953.	S. 11 rep. (*prosp.*) ...	54, s. 72(4), sch. 6.
		S. 12(1)(*a*) proviso am. (London).	35, s. 17(1), sch. 3 para. 11.
		S. 12(3) rep.	35, s. 47(2), sch. 6.
c. 34	Finance Act 1953 ...	S. 22 excl.	32, s. 13(2).
		S. 25(8) rep.	32, s. 61(6), sch. 21 Pt. X.
c. 36	Post Office Act 1953 ...	Ss. 1, 2 rep.	48, s. 141, sch. 11 Pt. II.
		S. 3 am.	48, ss. 23(1), 76, sch. 4 para. 101(1).
		expld.	48, s. 76, sch. 4 para. 2(1).
		S. 4 am.	48, s. 23(1).
		S. 4(1) rep. in pt., (3) rep.	48, s. 137(1), sch. 8 Pt. II.
		Ss. 5–7, 8(1)(2) rep. ...	48, s. 141, sch. 11 Pt. II.
		S. 8(3) am.	48, s. 76, sch. 4 para. 2(2).
		Ss. 8(4), 9, 10(1)(2)(4)(5) rep.	48, s. 141, sch. 11 Pt. II.
		S. 11(1)(*a*) am.	48, s. 76, sch. 4 para. 2(3).
		S. 11(3) rep.	48, s. 141, sch. 11 Pt. II.
		S. 11(4) am.	48, s. 76, sch. 4 para. 2(3).
		Ss. 12–15 rep.	48, s. 141, sch. 11 Pt. II.
		S. 16 expld.	48, s. 76, sch. 4 para. 2(1).
		S. 16(1) ext.	48, s. 77, sch. 5 para. 2(1).
		S. 16(2) am.	48, s. 76, sch. 4 para. 2(4).
		S. 16(3) rep.	48, s. 141, sch. 11 Pt. II.
		S. 17 am.	48, s. 76, sch. 4 para. 2(6).
		Ss. 18 rep., 19(1) rep. in pt.	48, s. 141, sch. 11 Pt. II.
		S. 19(1)–(3) am. ...	48, s. 76, sch. 4 para. 2(7).
		Ss. 20, 21(1)(2) rep. ...	48, s. 141, sch. 11 Pt. II.
		S. 21(3) am.	48, s. 76, sch. 4 para. 2(8).

Session and Chap. or No. of Measure	Short title or Subject	How affected	Chapter of 1969 Act or number of Measure or Statutory Instrument
1 & 2 Eliz. 2: —*cont.*	Post Office Act 1953— *cont.*	S. 21(4)(5) rep.	48, s. 141, sch. 11 Pt. II.
		S. 22 expld.	48, s. 76, sch. 4 para. 2(1).
		Ss. 22, 23 am.	48, s. 76, sch. 4 para. 2(9).
		S. 24 am. and rep. in pt.	48, s. 76, sch. 4 para. 2(10).
		S. 24 ext.	48, s. 124(5).
		Ss. 24–28 expld.... ...	48, s. 76, sch. 4 para. 2(1).
		S. 29 am.	48, s. 20.
		S. 31 rep.	48, s. 141, sch. 11 Pt. II.
		Ss. 32–34 expld.... ...	48, s. 76, sch. 4 para. 2(1).
		Ss. 33–36 am.	48, s. 20.
		S. 34(3) rep.	48, s. 137(1), sch. 8 Pt. I.
		S. 38 expld.	48, s. 76, sch. 4 para. 2(1).
		Ss. 38–41 am.	48, s. 20.
		Ss. 41, 42 expld. ...	48, s. 76, sch. 4 para. 2(1).
		S. 43 rep. (saving) ...	48, s. 137(1)(3), sch. 8 Pt. I.
		S. 44(1)(*a*) (3)–(5) rep. (saving).	48, s. 137(1)(3), sch. 8 Pt. I.
		S. 45 am.	48, s. 20.
		expld.	48, s, 76, sch. 4 para. 2(1).
		S. 45(1) rep. in pt.(saving), (2) rep. (saving), (3)(4) rep. in pt. (saving).	48, s. 137(1)(3), sch. 8 Pt. I.
		Ss. 46–49 rep.	48, s. 141, sch. 11 Pt. II.
		Ss. 50, 51 am.	48, s. 76, sch. 4 para. 2(11).
		Ss. 53, 55 expld. ...	48, s. 76, sch. 4 para. 2(1).
		S. 56 expld.	48, s. 76, sch. 4 para. 2(12).
		S. 56(3) rep.	48, s. 137(1), sch. 8 Pt. II.
		Ss. 57, 58 expld. ...	48, s. 76, sch. 4 para. 2(1).
		S. 58(2) appl. ...	48, s. 77, sch. 5 para. 1(2).
		S. 61 expld.	48, s. 76, sch. 4 para. 2(13).
		S. 62 expld.	48, s. 76, sch. 4 para. 2(14).
		S. 63 Power to appl. (mod.).	48, ss. 121(1), 122(1).
		S. 63(1) am.	48, s. 76, sch. 4 para. 2(15).
		S. 63(3) proviso rep. ...	48, s. 137(1), sch. 8 Pt. II.
		S. 63(6) am.	48, s. 77, sch. 5 para. 3.

Session and Chap. or No. of Measure	Short title or Subject	How affected	Chapter of 1969 Act or number of Measure or Statutory Instrument
1 & 2 Eliz. 2; —*cont.*	Post Office Act 1953— *cont.*	S. 64 expld.	48, s. 76, sch. 4 para. 2(14).
		S. 65 expld.	48, s. 76, sch. 4 para. 2(1).
		S. 65A expld.	48, s. 76, sch. 4 para. 2(16).
		S. 66 rep.	48, s. 141, sch. 11 Pt. I.
		S. 71 rep.	48, s. 137(1), sch. 8 Pt. I.
		S. 72(1) am.	48, s. 76, sch. 4 para. 2(17).
		S. 72(2) rep.	48, s. 137(1), sch. 8 Pt. II.
		S. 72(3) am.	48, s. 76, sch. 4 para. 2(18).
		Ss. 73, 75 rep. ...	48, s. 137(1), sch. 8 Pt. I.
		S. 76 rep. in pt.	48, s. 141, sch. 11 Pt. II.
		expld.	48, s. 76, sch. 4 para. 2(1).
		S. 77 rep.	48, s. 68.
		S. 78(1)(2) am.	48, s. 76, sch. 4 para. 2(19).
		S. 79 expld.	48, s. 76, sch. 4 para. 2(1).
		S. 79(1) expld. ...	48, s. 76, sch. 4 para. 2(20).
		Ss. 81, 84 rep.	48, s. 141, sch. 11 Pt. II.
		S. 85 rep.	48, s. 137(1), sch. 8 Pt. I.
		S. 86 rep.	48, s. 137(1), sch. 8 Pt. II.
		S. 87(1) definitions of— "British postal agency", " mandated territory," " postage ", " pre-scribed ", " regula-tions ", " trust terri-tory " rep., " mail bag" rep. in pt.	48, s. 141, sch. 11 Pt. II.
		" regular mail train services " rep. in pt.	48, s. 137(1), sch. 8 Pt. I.
		" parcel " am. ...	48, s. 76, sch. 4 para. 2(21).
		" post office letter box " am.	48, s. 76, sch. 4 para. 2(22).
		" postage " am. ...	48, s. 76, sch. 4 para. 2(25).
		" the purposes of the Post Office " expld.	48, s. 76, sch. 4 para. 2(23).
		S. 87(2)(*b*) expld. ...	48, s. 76, sch. 4 para. 2(24).
		S. 87(2)(*c*) am.	48, s. 79.
		S. 90 expld.	48, s. 76, sch. 4 para. 2(1).
		Sch. 1 rep.	48, s. 141, sch. 11 Pt. II.

Session and Chap. or No. of Measure	Short title or Subject	How affected	Chapter of 1969 Act or number of Measure or Statutory Instrument
1 & 2 Eliz. 2: —*cont.*			
c. 49	Historic Buildings and Ancient Monuments Act 1953.	S. 5 Power to ext.(E.) ... S. 7 restr. (E.)	22, ss. 4, 5. 22, s.6.
c. 52	Enemy Property Act 1953	S. 3(4)(5) restr. ... ... S. 4(1) excl.	20, s. 1(6). 20, s. 1(3).
2 & 3 Eliz. 2:			
c. 8	Electoral Registers Act 1953.	S. 1(2)(3) rep.	15, s. 24(4), sch. 3 Pt. II.
		S. 1(4) rep.	15, s. 24(4), sch. 3 Pt. I.
		Sch. rep.	15, s. 24(4), sch. 3 Pt. II.
c. 10	Navy, Army and Air Force Reserves Act 1954.	S. 1(1) am. ... ... Ss. 2(1)(5), 3(1)(4) rep., (5) rep. in pt., 6(5)(6) (*a*), (*c*) rep.	23, s. 1(1). 23, s. 1(2).
c. 24	Cotton Act 1954 ...	S. 4(2) Pensions increase	7, s. 1(1), sch. 1 Pt. III para. 2.
c. 29	Niall Macpherson Indemnity Act 1954.	Rep.	15, s. 24(4), sch. 3 Pt. I.
c. 30	Protection of Birds Act 1954.	S.10 Transfer of functions	S.I. No. 388.
c. 32	Atomic Energy Authority Act 1954.	S. 6(2)(*a*)–(*e*) replaced ...	32, s. 60, sch. 20 para. 27.
c. 36	Law Reform (Limitation of Actions, &c.) Act 1954.	S. 5(3) rep., (4) rep. in pt.	48, s. 141, sch. 11 Pt. II.
c. 37	Superannuation (President of the Industrial Court) Act 1954.	Pensions increase ...	7, s. 1(1), sch. 1 Pt. I para 10.
c. 39	Agriculture (Miscellaneous Provisions) Act 1954.	S. 11(1), sch. 2 am. ...	28, s. 4(3).
c. 44	Finance Act 1954 ...	S. 18 ext....	32, s. 18(7), sch. 13 para. 6(1).
		S. 25 rep.	32, s. 61(6), sch. 21 Pt. X.
		S. 28(1),(2)(*b*) am. ...	32, s. 40(1), sch. 17 Pt. III para. 19.
		S. 29(5) am.	32, s. 40(1), sch. 17 Pt. III para. 20.
		expld.	32, s. 40(1), sch. 17 Pt. II para. 12.
		S. 33(1) rep. in pt. ...	32, s. 61(6), sch. 21 Pt. V.
c. 46 ...	Landlord and Tenant Act 1954.	S. 24 ext.	33, s. 43(3).
c. 48 ...	Summary Jurisdiction (Scotland) Act 1954.	S. 23 excl. ...	{ 27, s. 26(4). 51, s. 12(3), sch. 2 para. 3(3). 56, s. 1(3).
		S. 23(2) appl. ...	{ 27, s. 26(4). 51, s. 12(3), sch. 2 para. 3(3). 56, s. 1(3).

Session and Chap. or No. of Measure	Short title or Subject	How affected	Chapter of 1969 Act or number of Measure or Statutory Instrument
2 & 3 Eliz. 2: —*cont.*			
c. 50	Housing Repairs and Rents (Scotland) Act 1954.	S. 39(2) replaced ...	34, s. 69(2), sch. 6 para. 1.
c. 56	Landlord and Tenant Act 1954.	Ext.	48, s. 76, sch. 4 para. 93(1).
		S. 24 reprinted as am. ...	59, s. 15, sch. 1.
		S. 24(1)(*a*) am.	59, s. 3(2).
		S. 24(2) am.	59, s. 4(1).
		S. 24A added	59, s. 3(1).
		S. 27 reprinted as am. ...	59, s. 15, sch. 1.
		S. 27(1)(2) am., (2) rep. in pt.	59, s. 4(2).
		S. 30 reprinted as am. ...	59, s. 15, sch. 1.
		S. 30(3) added	59, s. 6.
		S. 31A added	59, s. 7(1).
		S. 32 reprinted as am. ...	59, s. 15, sch. 1.
		S. 32(1) am. (1A) added	59, s. 7(2).
		S. 32(3) am.	59, s. 8.
		S. 34 reprinted as am. ...	59, s. 15, sch. 1.
		S. 34 para. (*c*) subst., (2) added.	59, s. 1(1).
		S. 34(3) added	59, s. 2.
		S. 37 reprinted as am. ...	59, s. 15, sch. 1.
		S. 37(1) am.	59, s. 11.
		S. 38 reprinted as am. ...	59, s. 15, sch. 1.
		S. 38(1) am., (4) added ...	59, s. 5.
		S. 41A added	59, s. 9.
		S. 41(1)(*b*) am.	59, s. 1(2).
		S. 42 reprinted as am. ...	59, s. 15, sch. 1.
		S. 42(2)(*b*) am.	59, s. 1(2).
		S. 42(3) subst.	59, s. 10.
		S. 43(3) reprinted as am.	59, s. 15, sch. 1.
		S. 43(3) am.	59, s. 12(1).
		S. 43A added	59, s. 13.
		S. 44 reprinted as am. ...	59, s. 15, sch. 1.
		S. 44(1)(*b*) subst. ...	59, s. 14(1).
		S. 60 Transfer of functions	S.I. No. 1498.
		Sch. 6 reprinted as am....	59, s. 15, sch. 1.
		Sch. 6 paras. 6, 7 added...	59, s. 14(2).
c. 57	Baking Industry (Hours of Work) Act 1954.	S. 12(1) rep.	52, S.L. (Repeals).
c. 62	Post Office Savings Bank Act 1954.	Expld.	48, s. 94(2).
		S. 1 rep. (saving) ...	48, s. 94(1).
		Ss. 2(1) rep. in pt., (1)(2) am., 4(1) rep. in pt. ...	48, s. 94(2)(*a*), sch. 6 Pt. I.
		S. 4(2) rep. in pt. ...	48, s. 137(1), sch. 8 Pt. I.
		Ss. 6, 7 am., (1)(*l*) rep. in pt., 8(1)(2)(4)(5), 10(1) am.	48, s. 94(2)(*a*), sch. 6 Pt. I.
		S. 10(1) am.	48, s. 103.
		Ss. 11(1) rep. in pt., (1) (4)–(6), 12(1)(2) am., 12(2) rep. in pt	48, s. 94(2)(*a*), sch. 6 Pt. I.
		S. 12(3) am.	48, s. 104.
		Ss. 12(5)(6), 13(1)–(3) am., 13(2) expld., 14 am.	48, s. 94(2)(*a*), sch. 6 Pt. I.
		S. 16 subst.	48, s. 95(1).

Session and Chap. or No. of Measure	Short title or Subject	How affected	Chapter of 1969 Act or number of Measure or Statutory Instrument
2 & 3 Eliz. 2: c. 62—*cont.*	Post Office Savings Bank Act 1954—*cont.*	S. 19(3) rep.	48, s. 141, sch. 11 Pt. I.
		S. 22(1) am.	48, s. 102(1).
		S. 22(2) rep. in pt. and am.	48, s. 102(2).
		S. 23 rep.	48, s. 137(1), sch. 8 Pt. I.
		S. 24 am.	48, s. 105.
		S. 24(1) rep. in pt. ...	48, s. 141, sch. 11 Pt. I.
		S. 24(2) rep. ...	48, s. 137(1), sch. 8 Pt. I.
		S. 25 definitions of " post office savings bank ", " Post Office Savings Banks Fund " rep.	48, s. 141, sch. 11 Pt. II.
c. 63	Trustee Savings Banks Act 1954.	Rep.	50, s. 96(1), sch. 3 Pt. I.
c. 68	Pests Act 1954	S. 1(1) Transfer of functions.	S.I. No. 388.
c. 70	Mines and Quarries Act 1954.	Am.	10, s. 1(3).
		S. 1(1) am. ...	10, s. 1(3)(b), sch. 1 para. 1.
		Ss. 2(2), 11(2) am. ...	10, s. 1(3)(b), sch. 1 para. 2.
		S. 89 am.	10, s. 1(3)(b), sch. 1 para. 3.
		S. 99 am.	10, s. 1(3)(b), sch. 1 para. 2.
		S. 115(a) mod. (tips) ...	10, s. 1(3)(b), sch. 1 para. 3.
		Pt. VI (ss. 116–122) am.	10, s. 1(3)(b), sch. 1 para. 4(1).
		S. 116 expld. (tips) ...	10, s. 1(3)(b), sch. 1 para. 4(2).
		S. 135 am.	10, s. 1(3)(b), sch. 1 para. 5.
		Ss. 145, 146 am. ...	10, s. 1(3)(b), sch. 1 para. 6(1)(2).
		S. 146 expld. (tips) ...	10, s. 1(3)(b), sch. 1 para. 6(3).
		S. 151(2)(3) expld. (E.) ...	25, s. 4(3).
		Pt. XIV (ss. 152–167) expld.	10, s. 1(3)(b), sch. 1 para. 7.
		S. 152(1)(2) excl. ...	10, s. 3(2).
		S. 155 mod. (tips) ...	10, s. 9.
		S. 170 appl.	10, ss. 3(6), 5(4).
		S. 180(4) excl. ...	10, s. 2(5).
c. 73	Town and Country Planning (Scotland) Act 1954.	Pt. II (ss. 16–30) excl. ...	30, s. 68(6).
		S. 19 ext.	48, s. 76, sch. 4 para. 93(1).
		expld. (" operational land ").	48, s. 76, sch. 4 para. 93(4).
C.A.M. No. 1... ...	New Housing Areas (Church Buildings) Measure 1954.	S. 1 excl.	38, s. 3(3).

3 O*

Session and Chap. or No. of Measure	Short title or Subject	How affected	Chapter of 1969 Act or number of Measure or Statutory Instrument
3 & 4 Eliz. 2:			
c. 7	Fisheries Act 1955 ...	S.2 Transfer of functions	S.I. No. 388.
c. 12	Trustee Savings Banks (Pensions) Act 1955.	Rep.	50, s. 96(1), sch. 3 Pt. I.
c. 18	Army Act 1955	Cont. until 31.12.1970 ...	S.I. No. 1683.
		Pts. II (ss. 24–143) to V (ss. 177–204) am.	65, s. 1(3).
		S. 37 appl.	65, s. 3(2).
		S. 70(3)(*a*)(*b*) added, (4) (5) am.	12, s. 1(6).
c. 19	Air Force Act 1955 ...	Cont. until 31.12.1970 ...	S.I. No. 1682.
		S. 70(3)(*a*)(*b*) added, (4) (5) am.	12, s. 1(6).
c. 22	Pensions (India, Pakistan and Burma) Act 1955.	Sch. 2 Pts. I, II Power to apply.	7, s. 1(4), sch. 2 para. 13.
c. 28	Children and Young Persons (Harmful Publications) Act 1955.	S. 5(5) rep.	61, s. 1.
4 & 5 Eliz. 2:			
c. 6	Miscellaneous Financial Provisions Act 1955.	Sch. 1 rep. in pt. (*prosp.*)	27, s. 37, sch. 3.
c. 10	Validation of Elections Act 1955.	Rep.	15, s. 24(4), sch. 3 Pt. I.
c. 12	Validation of Elections (No. 2) Act 1955.	Rep.	15, s. 24(4), sch. 3 Pt. I.
c. 13	Validation of Elections (No. 3) Act 1955.	Rep.	15, s. 24(4), sch. 3 Pt. I.
c. 17	Finance (No. 2) Act 1955	S. 3 (1) proviso rep. ...	32, s. 61(6), sch. 21 Pt. X.
c. 24	Children and Young Persons Act 1956.	Rep. (*prosp.*)	54, s. 72(4), sch. 6.
c. 27	Charles Beattie Indemnity Act 1956.	Rep.	15, s. 24(4), sch. 3 Pt. I.
c. 31	Pakistan (Consequential Provisions) Act 1956.	S. 1 (1) rep. in pt., (3) rep.	52, S.L. (Repeals).
c. 34	Criminal Justice Administration Act 1956.	S. 4(5) Pensions increase	7, ss. 1(1), 2(1), sch. 1 Pt. I para. 9, sch. 3 para. 1.
		S. 10(2) excl.	58, s. 30.
c. 35	Validation of Elections (Northern Ireland) Act 1956.	Rep.	52, S.L. (Repeals).
c. 39	Pensions (Increase) Act 1956.	Sch. 1 Pts. I, II ext. ...	7, s. 2(1), sch. 3 paras. 2, 5.
c. 43	Local Government Elections Act 1956.	Ss. 1(1)(2), 2(1) rep. in pt. (2) rep., 3 rep. in pt., 4(4), 5(2) rep.	15, s. 24(4), sch. 3 Pt. I.
		S. 6(1) am. and rep. in pt. (1A) added.	15, s. 18(4).
		S. 6(2) rep.	15, s. 24(4), sch. 3 Pt. I.
c. 46	Administration of Justice Act 1956.	S. 38(2) am.	48, s. 94(2)(*c*), sch. 6 Pt. III.
c. 50	Family Allowances and National Insurance Act 1956.	S. 5 rep. (E.)	54, s. 72(4), sch. 6.
c. 53	Teachers (Superannuation) Act 1956.	Pensions increase ...	7, s. 1(1), sch. 1 Pt. I para. 14.

Session and Chap. or No. of Measure	Short title or Subject	How affected	Chapter of 1969 Act or number of Measure or Statutory Instrument
4 & 5 Eliz. 2: —*cont.*			
c. 54	Finance Act 1956 ...	S. 9(1) am.	48, s. 94(2)(*c*), sch. 6 Pt. III.
		S. 9(3) am.	50, s. 93(1).
		S. 19(3) am.	32, s. 40(1), sch. 17 Pt. III para. 21.
		S. 19(4), (7)(*a*) rep. ...	32, ss. 40(1), 61 (6), sch. 17 Pt. III para. 21, sch. 21 Pt. V.
		S. 20(3) restr.	32, s. 60, sch. 20 para. 23(3).
		S. 22(8) am.	32, s. 60, sch. 20 para. 18(1).
		S. 24(2)(*b*) rep. in pt. ...	32, s. 61(6), sch. 21 Pt. X.
		S. 24(4) am.	32, s. 29, sch. 14 para. 8(3).
		expld.	32, s. 29, sch. 14 para. 8(4).
		ext. (*retrosp.*) ...	32, s. 29, sch. 14 para. 9(2).
		S. 28(1) restr.	32, s. 60, sch. 20 para. 18(2).
		S. 28(1) proviso rep. in pt.	32, s. 61(6), sch. 21 Pt. IX.
		S. 28(2)–(4) am. ...	32, s. 60, sch. 20 para. 18(3).
		S. 28(5) am.	32, s. 60, sch. 20 para. 18(4).
		S. 32 rep.	32, s. 61(6), sch. 21 Part V.
		S. 34(2) am.	S.I. Nos. 383, 388.
		S. 35 rep.	32, s. 61(6), sch. 21 Pt. V.
		Sch. 2 para. 7(1) am. ...	32, s. 18(7), sch. 13 para. 25.
c. 60	Valuation and Rating (Scotland) Act 1956.	S. 35 rep.	15, s. 24(4), sch. 3 Pt. II.
c. 68	Restrictive Trade Practices Act 1956.	Pts. I (ss. 1–23), certain functions in III (ss. 28–31) Transfer of functions.	S.I. No. 1534.
c. 69	Sexual Offences Act 1956	S. 18 rep.	46, s. 11.
		S. 37(7) am. (*prosp.*) ...	54, s. 72(3), sch. 5 para. 27.
		S. 38 am.	46, s. 1(3), sch. 1 Pt. I.
		Sch. 2 para. 5 rep. ...	46, s. 11.
c. 76	Medical Act 1956 ...	Expld.	40, ss. 8(2), 11(4), 20, sch. 1 para. 8.
		S. 4(8) rep. (1.5.1970) ...	40, s. 23(1), sch. 2.
		S. 6(3) am.	40, s. 18(3).
		S. 6(4) rep. in pt. ...	40, s. 23(1), sch. 2.
		Pt. II (ss. 7–17) ext. ...	40, ss. 7, 8.
		S. 7 mod. (1.5.1970) ...	40, s. 6(1)(*b*).
		S. 8(1)–(3) subst. ...	40, s. 11(1).

Session and Chap. or No. of Measure	Short title or Subject	How affected	Chapter of 1969 Act or number of Measure or Statutory Instrument
4 & 5 Eliz. 2: c. 76—*cont.*	Medical Act 1956—*cont.*	S. 9(5) rep. in pt. ...	40, ss. 20, 23(1), sch. 1 para. 1, sch. 2.
		S. 10(2)(4) expld. ...	40, s. 11(3).
		S. 10(7) rep. in pt. ...	40, ss. 20, 23(1), sch. 1 para. 1, sch. 2.
		S. 11 Power to am. ...	40, s. 18(2).
		S. 11 expld.	40, s. 11(3).
		Ss. 11(4)(*a*), 12(1), 13(1) rep. in pt.	40, s. 23(1), sch. 2.
		S. 15(9) am.	40, s. 20, sch. 1 para. 2.
		Ss. 16(4), 17(4) expld. ...	40, s. 11(3).
		S. 17 mod. (1.5.1970) ...	40, s. 6(1)(*a*).
		Pt. III (ss. 18–26) ext. ...	40, ss. 7, 8.
		S. 18(1)(*c*)(3)(4) rep. ...	40, ss. 20, 23(1), sch. 1 para. 3, sch. 2.
		S. 18(5)(6) rep.	40, s. 23(1), sch. 2.
		S. 21(2) proviso added ...	40, s. 20, sch. 1 para. 4.
		S. 21(2)(3) am.	40, s. 11(2).
		S. 24(1)(*b*) rep. in pt. ...	40, s. 23(1), sch. 2.
		S. 25 subst.	40, s. 12.
		S. 25 as subst. ext. (1.5.1970).	40, s. 6(3).
		S. 28(3) rep. in pt. ...	40, s. 23(1), sch. 2.
		S. 33 ext.	40, s. 16(1)(2).
		S. 33(1) replaced ...	40, s. 13(1).
		S. 33(1A) expld. ...	40, s. 13(3).
		S. 33(2) am.	40, s. 13(2)(*a*).
		S. 33(3) am.	40, s. 11(3).
		S. 33(3)(*b*) am. ...	40, s. 13(2)(*a*).
		S. 34 restr.	40, s. 16(2).
		S. 34(1) am.	40, s. 20, sch. 1 para. 5.
		S. 36 ext.	40, s. 15(2).
		S. 36(1)(2) subst. ...	40, s. 14(1).
		appl.	40, s. 15(3).
		S. 36(5)(6) replaced ...	40, s. 14(2).
		S. 37(1)(*f*) am.	40, s. 13(2)(*a*)(*b*).
		S. 38(4) rep. in pt. ...	40, ss. 20, 23(1), sch. 1 para. 1, sch. 2.
		S. 39(2) am.	40, s. 13(4).
		Ss. 41–46 rep. and superseded.	40, ss. 2–9, 23(1), sch. 2.
		Ss. 48(2) rep. 49(1) proviso rep. in pt. (1.5.1970).	40, s. 23(1), sch 2.
		S. 49(1) proviso am. ...	40, s. 20, sch. 1 para. 6.
		S. 51 appl.	40, s. 20, sch. 1 para. 7.
		rep. in pt. ...	40, s. 23(1), sch. 2.

Session and Chap. or No. of Measure	Short title or Subject	How affected	Chapter of 1969 Act or number of Measure or Statutory Instrument
4 & 5 Eliz. 2: c. 76—*cont.*	Medical Act 1956—*cont.*	S. 54(1) definitions of " additional qualification " rep. in pt., " registered ", " the register " rep.	40, s. 23(1), sch. 2.
		S. 56(2) ext.	40, s. 22.
		S. 57 restr.	40, s. 21(4).
		S. 57(7)(8) rep.	40, s. 23, sch. 2.
		Sch. 1 para. 1(1A) added	40, s. 20, sch. 1 para. 9.
		para. 6(1) am. ...	40, s. 18(3).
		para. 7(1) am. ...	40, s. 20, sch. 1 para. 10.
		para. 7(1) rep. in pt.	40, ss. 20, 23(1), sch. 1 para. 10 sch. 2.
		para. 9 rep. ...	40, ss. 20, 23(1) sch. 1 para. 11, sch. 2.
		para. 11 am. ...	40, s. 20, sch. 1 para. 12.
		para. 11 rep. in pt.	40, s. 23(1), sch. 2.
		paras. 12, 13 rep. and superseded.	40, ss. 10, 23(1), sch. 2.
		Sch. 2 rep. (1.5.1970) ...	40, ss. 17(1), 23(1), sch. 2.
		Sch. 3 column 1 am. ...	40, s. 20, sch. 1 para. 13.
C.A.M.		column 3 rep. ...	40, s. 23(1), sch. 2.
No. 2 ...	Representation of the Laity Measure 1956.	Rep. (saving)	C.A.M. No. 2 s.7(3).
No. 3 ...	Parochial Church Councils (Powers) Measure 1956.	S. 2 subst.	C.A.M. No. 2, s. 6.
5 & 6 Eliz. 2: c. 6	Ghana Independence Act 1957.	S. 4(4) rep. in pt. ...	52, S.L. (Repeals).
		Sch. 2 para. 1 rep. ...	32, s. 61(6), sch. 21 Pt. IX.
c. 15	Nurses Act 1957 ...	S. 2(1) subst.	47, s. 1(1).
		S. 2(2) am.	47, 2. 10(1), sch. 1 para. 6.
		S. 3(1) am.	47, s. 7(1).
		S. 4(1) am.	47, s. 7(2).
		rep. in pt. ...	47, ss. 7(2), 10(2), sch. 2.
		S. 7(4) am.	47, s. 10(1), sch. 1 para. 7.
		S. 7(5) rep. in pt. ...	47, s. 10(2), sch. 2.
		S. 8 am.	47, s. 10(1), sch. 1 para. 8.
		S. 9(2) rep.	47, ss. 8, 10(2), sch. 2.
		S. 18(1)(2) subst. (22.9.1970).	47, s. 4(1).
		S. 18(3)(*a*)(*b*) subst. (22.9.1970).	47, s. 4(2).

Session and Chap. or No. of Measure	Short title or Subject	How affected	Chapter of 1969 Act or number of Measure or Statutory Instrument
5 & 6 Eliz. 2:			
c. 15—*cont.*	Nurses Act 1957—*cont.*	S. 19 rep.	47, s. 10(2), sch. 2.
		S. 27(1)(*b*) subst., (2)(*aa*) added.	47, s. 1(2).
		S. 31 am.	47, s. 10(1), sch. 1 para. 9.
		S. 33 appl.	47, s. 9(1).
		S. 33(1) definitions of— " registered mental nurse " am., " enrolled general nurse ", " enrolled mental nurse ", " enrolled nurse for the mentally subnormal ", " registered general nurse ", " registered nurse for the mentally subnormal ", " severe subnormality ", " subnormality " added.	47, s. 10(1), sch. 1 para. 10.
		S. 33(3) am.	47, s. 10(1), sch. 1 para. 11.
		Sch. 1 para. 1(*a*)–(*c*) am. (22.9.1970), (*e*) (*f*) added (22.9. 1970).	47, s. 2(1).
		para. 2(1) subst. (22.9.1970).	47, s. 2(2).
		para. 2(2) subst. (22.9.1970).	47, s. 2(3).
		para. 3 subst. (22.9.1970).	47, s. 2(4).
		paras. 5, 6 excl. ...	47, s. 11(4).
		para. 6(1) am. (22.9.1970).	47, s. 2(5).
		Sch. 2 para. 2(*c*) rep. ...	47, ss. 6, 10(2), sch. 2.
		Schs. 3, 4 rep.	47, s. 10(2), sch. 2.
c. 18	Customs Duties (Dumping and Subsidies) Act 1957.	Rep. (saving)	16, s. 18.
c. 20	House of Commons Disqualification Act 1957.	Sch. 1 Pt. II am. (*prosp.*)	21, s. 1(2), sch. 1 para. 10.
		am. ...	30, ss. 61(5), 64(5).
		rep. in pt. ...	35, s. 47(2), sch. 6.
		Pt. III am {	48, s. 14(20). 51, s. 1(4).
		am. (*prosp.*)	21, s. 1(2), sch. 1 para. 4.
		Sch. 2 am.	48, s. 2(7)(*a*).
		rep. in pt. {	48, s. 141, sch. 11 Pt. II. S.I. No. 1498.
		Sch. 3 am. (*prosp.*) ...	21, s. 1(2), sch. 1 paras. 4, 10.
		rep. in pt. ...	35, s. 47(2), sch. 6.
c. 22	White Fish and Herring Industries Act 1957.	S.3 Transfer of functions	S.I. No. 388.
c. 25	Rent Act 1957	Sch. 2 appl. (S.)... ...	62, s. 5(1), sch. para. 3(2).

Session and Chap. or No. of Measure	Short title or Subject	How affected	Chapter of 1969 Act or number of Measure or Statutory Instrument
5 & 6 Eliz. 2: —*cont.*			
c. 27	Solicitors Act 1957 ...	S.73(2) am. (*prosp.*) ...	58, s. 35(1), sch. 1.
		S. 73(2) Power to am. (*prosp.*)	58, s. 10(2).
		S.74(*b*) rep.	52, S.L. (Repeals)
		Sch. 1 para. 8 expld. ...	48, s. 76, sch. 4 para. 57.
c. 28	Dentists Act 1957 ...	Sch. 1 para. 14(3) am. ...	S.I. No. 388.
c. 38	Housing and Town Development (Scotland) Act 1957.	S. 14(1)(*c*) added ...	30, s. 98.
c. 43	Representation of the People (Amendment) Act 1957.	Rep.	15, s. 24(4), sch. 3 Pt. I.
c. 48	Electricity Act 1957 ...	S. 21(2)(*c*) subst. ...	32, s. 60, sch. 20 para. 28(2).
		S. 24 appl.	32, s. 60, sch. 20 para. 28(1).
		S. 28(8) expld.	48, s. 76, sch. 4 para. 8.
		S. 36 rep. (S.) ...	30, s. 107, sch. 11.
c. 49	Finance Act 1957 ...	S. 2 rep.	48, s. 137(1), sch. 8 Pt. I.
		S. 5 excl.	16, s. 10(2).
		S. 13 am.	32, s. 10(6).
		S. 38(1)(5)(8) am. ...	32, s. 40(1), sch. 17 Pt. III para. 22.
		S. 38(10) rep., (11)(12) rep. in pt.	32, s. 61(6), sch. 21 Pt. V.
		S. 38(12)(13) expld. ...	32, s. 40(1), sch. 17 Pt. II para. 12.
		S. 38(12), (13)(*b*), (16) am.	32 s. 40(1), sch. 17 Pt. III para. 22.
		Ss. 38(16) rep. in pt., 39(1) rep.	32, s. 61(6), sch. 21 Pt. V.
		S. 39(2) am.	32, s. 40(1), sch. 17 Pt. III para. 23.
c. 53	Naval Discipline Act 1957.	Ss. 42(1)(*b*), 48(2) am. ...	12, s. 1(7).
c. 55	Affiliation Proceedings Act 1957.	S. 5(2)(*a*) am. (*prosp.*) ...	54 s. 72(3), sch. 5 para. 28(1).
		S. 5(2)(*d*) rep. in pt. (*prosp.*)	54, s. 72(4), sch. 6.
		S. 7(2)(3) ext.	46, s. 5(2).
		S. 7(4)(*a*) subst. (*prosp.*)	54, s. 72(3), sch. 5 para. 28(2).
		S. 7(5) rep. in pt. (*prosp.*)	54, s. 72(4), sch. 6.
		S. 7(6) am. (*prosp.*) ...	54, s. 72(3), sch. 5 para. 28(3).
c. 56	Housing Act 1957 ...	S.3 rep.	33, s. 89(3), sch. 10.
		Pt. II (ss. 4–41) expld. ...	33, s. 40(2)(*a*).
		ext. ...	33, s. 60(6).
		S.4 appl.	33, s. 86(3).
		S.4(1) para. (cc) added ...	33, s. 71.
		para. (*h*) rep. in pt.	33, ss. 71, 89(3), sch. 10.

Session and Chap. or No. of Measure	Short title or Subject	How affected	Chapter of 1969 Act or number of Measure or Statutory Instrument
5 & 6 Eliz. 2: c. 56—*cont.*	Housing Act 1957—*cont.*	S. 9(1A) added ...	33, s. 72.
		S. 11(3) am.	33, s. 89(1), sch. 8 para. 6.
		S. 15(6) rep. in pt. (*prosp.*)	59, s. 16(2), sch. 2 Pt. I.
		S. 30 appl.	33, s. 67(3).
		ext.	33, s. 67.
		S. 30(2) rep. in pt. ...	33, ss. 65(1), 89(3), sch. 10.
		am.	33, s. 65(1).
		S. 30(3)(*a*) am.	33, s. 65(2).
		S. 30(7) am.	33, s. 89(1), sch. 8 para. 7.
		Pt. III (ss. 42–75) excl. ...	33, s. 29(3).
		ext. ...	33, s. 68(1), sch. 5 para. 3(2).
		Ss. 55–57 rep.	33, ss. 42, 89(3), sch. 10.
		S. 59(3) rep., (4) rep. in pt.	33, s. 89(3), sch. 10.
		S. 60 ext.	33, s. 67.
		Ss. 61, 63(1) rep. in pt., (*c*) rep.	33, s. 89(3), sch. 10.
		S. 64(3) proviso expld. ...	48, s. 76, sch. 4 para. 58(3).
		Ss. 67(1)(2), 70(1)(2) rep. in pt.	33, s. 89(3), sch. 10.
		Pt. IV (ss. 76–90) mod. ...	33, s. 40(2)(*b*).
		S. 90(1) am.	33, ss. 58(3), 89(1), sch. 8 para. 1.
		S. 91 am.	33, s. 89(1) sch. 8 para. 8.
		S. 98 am.	33, s. 89(1), sch. 8 para. 10.
		S. 101 am.	33, s. 89(1), sch. 8 para. 11.
		S. 121(3) subst.	33, s. 89(1), sch. 8 para. 9.
		S. 144 excl.	33, s. 32(4).
		S. 159 am.	33, s. 89(1), sch. 8 para. 11.
		appl. (mod.) ...	33, s. 61(5).
		Ss. 160, 169 am. ...	33, s. 89(1), sch. 8 para. 11.
		S. 170 am.	33, ss. 73, 89(1), sch. 8 para. 11.
		Ss. 171–176 am. ...	33, s. 89(1), sch. 8 para. 12.
		S. 179 am.	33, s. 89(1), sch. 8 para. 13.
		S. 181(1) am.	33, s. 89(1), sch. 8 para. 14.
		S. 187(1) am.	33, s. 89(1), sch. 8 para. 15.
		Sch. 2 Pt. I mod. ...	33, s. 67(4).
		Sch. 2 Pt. I ext. (mod.)...	33, s. 66, sch. 4.
		appl. ...	33, s. 67(3).
		Pt. II ext. (mod.)	33, s. 68, sch. 6.

Session and Chap. or No. of Measure	Short title or Subject	How affected	Chapter of 1969 Act or number of Measure or Statutory Instrument
5 & 6 Eliz. 2: c. 56—*cont.*	Housing Act 1957—*cont.*	Sch. 2 —*cont.*	
		para. 4 excl. ...	33, s. 68(1).
		para. 4(1)(*b*) rep. in pt.	33, ss. 68, 89(3), sch. 6 para. 1, sch. 10.
		para. 4(6)(*b*) rep.	33, s. 89(3), sch. 10.
		para. 4(7) subst....	33, s. 68, sch. 6 para. 2.
		para. 5 ext. ...	33, s. 68, sch. 5 para. 4.
		para. 6(2) proviso am.	33, s. 68, sch. 6 para. 3.
		para. 7(2) rep. in pt.	33, s. 89(3), sch. 10.
		para. 7(3) am. ...	33, s. 68, sch. 6 para. 4.
		Sch. 3 Pt I para. 2(1) proviso rep.	33, s. 89(3), sch. 10.
		Pt. I paras. 5, 6 rep.	33, s. 89(3), sch. 10.
		Pt. III para. 4 rep. in pt.	33, s. 89(3), sch. 10.
		Pt. III para. 5 rep.	33, s. 89(3), sch. 10.
		Sch. 4 para. 2 rep. in pt.	33, s. 89(3), sch. 10.
		para. 3 rep. in pt.	33, s. 89(3), sch. 10.
c. 57	Agriculture Act 1957 ...	Pt. I (ss. 1–11) Transfer of functions.	S.I. No. 388.
c. 59	Coal-Mining (Subsidence) Act 1957.	S.9 Transfer of functions	S.I. No. 383, 388.
c. 60	Federation of Malaya Independence Act 1957.	Sch. 1 para. 5 rep. ...	32, s. 61(6), sch. 21 Pt. IX.
c. 62	Governors' Pensions Act 1957.	Pensions increase ...	7, s. 1(1), sch. 1 Pt. I para. 33.
		Ss. 3(1), 9(1) am. ...	S.I. No. 1211.
6 & 7 Eliz. 2: c. 6	Import Duties Act 1958	S. 3(1) am.	16, s. 10(5).
		S. 6 am.	32, s. 54.
		S. 7(4) subst.	16, s. 12(3).
		S. 13(6) rep.	16, s. 18(1).
c. 8	Trustee Savings Banks Act 1958.	Rep.	50, s. 96(1), sch. 3 Pt. 1.
c. 23	Milford Haven Conservancy Act 1958.	S. 5(1)(4) expld. ...	48, s. 76, sch. 4 para. 61.
c. 24	Land Drainage (Scotland) Act 1958.	S. 16 ext.	10, s. 34(3).
		Sch. 2 para. 3 expld. ...	48, s. 76, sch. 4 para. 62.
c. 30	Land Powers (Defence) Act 1958.	S. 8(4) rep. (S)	30, s. 107, sch. 11.
		S. 19 rep., sch. 2 paras. 1, 12, 13, 15 rep. in pt.	48, s. 137(1), sch. 8 Pt. II.
c. 39	Maintenance Orders Act 1958.	S. 13(3) am. (15.2.1971)...	19, s. 10(3), sch. 2 para. 13.
		S. 21(1) am. (" maintenance orders ").	46, ss. 4(5)(*b*), 6 (7).

Session and Chap. or No. of Measure	Short title or Subject	How affected	Chapter of 1969 Act or number of Measure or Statutory Instrument
6 & 7 Eliz. 2: —*cont.*			
c. 42	Housing (Financial Provision) Act 1958.	S. 9 rep.	33, s. 89(3), sch. 10.
		S. 12 rep.	33, ss. 21, 89(3), sch. 10.
		S. 18 rep. in pt. ...	33, s. 89(3), sch. 10.
		S. 25 am.	33, s. 89(1), sch. 8 para. 16.
		S. 28 ext.	33, s. 89(1), sch. 8 para. 17.
		Ss. 30–42 rep.	33, s. 89(3), sch. 10.
		S. 50 restr.	33, s. 38.
		S. 50(1)(*f*) am.	33, s. 89(1), sch. 8 para. 18.
		S. 54 am.	33, s. 89(1), sch. 8 para. 19.
		S. 58(2) am.	33, s. 89(1), sch. 8 para. 20.
		Sch. 4 rep.	33, s. 89(3), sch. 10.
c. 45	Prevention of Fraud (Investments) Act 1958.	S. 28(7) rep. in pt. ...	52, S.L. (Repeals).
c. 47	Agricultural Marketing Act 1958.	Transfer of functions ...	S.I. No. 388.
c. 50	Local Government (Omnibus Shelters and Queue Barriers) (Scotland) Act 1958.	S. 3 am.	48, s. 76, sch. 4 para. 63.
c. 51	Public Records Act 1958	S. 8(3) rep.	58, ss. 27(2), 35 (2), sch. 2.
		Sch. 1 para. 3, Pt. II table am.	48, s. 75(1).
c. 55	Local Government Act 1958.	S. 60(2) Pensions increase	7, s. 1(1), sch. 1 Pt. I para. 28, Pt. II paras. 6, 9.
		S. 60(2) am.	54, s. 46(2), sch. 3 para. 2(2).
		Sch. 8 para. 2(3) rep. (*prosp.*), (4) rep. in pt. (*prosp.*), (5) rep. (*prosp.*)	54, s. 72(4), sch. 6.
c. 56	Finance Act 1958 ...	S. 28 rep.	32, s. 61(6), sch. 21 Pt. V.
		S. 29(2) am.	32, s. 40(1), sch. 17 Pt. III para. 24
		S. 30 expld.	32, s. 40(1), sch. 17 Pt. II para. 7(1).
		Sch. 8 para. 3(3), (4), (6) am.	32, s. 40(1), sch. 17 Pt. III para. 25.
c. 63	Park Lane Improvement Act 1958.	S. 22 rep.	48, s. 137(1), sch. 8 Pt. I.
c. 65	Children Act 1958 ...	Ss. 1–6 reprinted as am. (E.).	54, s. 72(5), sch. 7.
		S. 1 subst. (E.)	54, s. 51.
		S. 2(1) rep. in pt. (E.) ...	54, ss. 52(1), 72 (4), sch. 6.

Session and Chap. or No. of Measure	Short title or Subject	How affected	Chapter of 1969 Act or number of Measure or Statutory Instrument
6 & 7 Eliz. 2: c. 65—*cont.*	Children Act 1958—*cont.*	S. 2(2) rep. in pt. (E.) ...	54, s. 72(4), sch. 6.
		S. 2(3)(*c*) am. (E.) ...	54, s. 52(2).
		S. 2(3A) added (E.) ...	54, s. 52(3).
		S. 2(4) rep. in pt. (E.) (*prosp.*).	54, s. 72(4), sch. 6.
		am. (E.) (*prosp.*)	54, s. 72(3), sch. 5 para. 29.
		S. 2(4A) added (E.) ...	54, s. 52(5).
		S. 2(6)(7) rep. (E.) ...	54, s. 72(4), sch. 6.
		S. 3(1) am. (E.)	54, s. 53(2).
		S. 3(2) am. (E.)	54, s. 53(3).
		S. 3(2A) added (E.) ...	54, s. 53(4).
		S. 3(3) am. (E.)	54, s. 53(5).
		S. 3(4)(5) am. (E.) ...	54, s. 53(6).
		rep. in pt. (E.)	54, ss. 53(6), 72 (4), sch. 6.
		S. 3(5A)(5B) added (E.)...	54, s. 53(7).
		S. 3(6) rep. (E.)	54, s. 72(4), sch. 6.
		S. 4(1) am. (E.)	54, s. 54(1).
		S. 4(1A) added (E.) ...	54, s. 54(2).
		S. 4(2) am. (E.)	54, s. 55(1)(3).
		S. 4(2)(*g*)(*h*) added (E.)...	54, s. 55(2).
		S. 4(3) replaced (E.) ...	54, s. 55(4).
		S. 5(1) am. (E.)	54, s. 55(5).
		S. 6(*b*) am. (*prosp.*), (*c*)(*e*) am., (*f*) added.	54, ss. 56(1), 73(4)(*a*).
		S. 6(2) added ...	54, ss. 56(2), 73(4)(*a*).
		S. 7(2) rep. inpt. ...	52, S.L. (Repeals).
		S. 9 am. (E.) ...	54, s. 72(3), sch. 5 para. 30.
		S. 12(1) am. (E.) ...	54, s. 72(3), sch. 5 para. 31.
		S. 14 reprinted as am. (E.)	54, s. 72(5), sch. 7.
		S. 14(1)(*b*) am. (E.) ...	54, s. 54(3).
		S. 14(1A) added ...	54, ss. 57(1), 73(4)(*a*).
		S. 14(2A) added (E.) ...	54, s. 57(2).
		S. 17 definitions of— "approved school" added (E.) (*prosp.*), "place of safety" am. (E.) (*prosp.*).	54, s. 72(3), sch. 5 para. 32.
		"fit person order" rep. in pt. (*prosp.*).	54, s. 72(4), sch. 6.
		Ss. 38, 40(2) rep. ...	52, S.L. (Repeals).
		Sch. 2 rep. in pt. ...	54, s. 72(4), sch. 6.
		Sch. 3 rep.	52, S.L. (Repeals).
c. 66	Tribunals and Inquiries Act 1958.	Appl. (S.) (*prosp.*) ...	30, ss. 8(1), 63(5).
		Expld.	30, s. 64(7), sch. 6 para. 14.
		Appl. (mod.) (S.) (*prosp.*)	30, s. 27(1).
		S. 9(1) appl. (G.L.C.) ...	35, s. 36, sch. 5 para. 18(2).

Session and Chap. or No. of Measure	Short title or Subject	How affected	Chapter of 1969 Act or number of Measure or Statutory Instrument
6 & 7 Eliz. 2; c. 66—*cont.*	Tribunals and Inquiries Act 1958—*cont.*	S. 9(1)(3) appl. (mod.) (G.L.C.).	35, s. 36, sch. 5 para. 18(2).
		Sch. 1 pt. I rep. in pt. ...	48, s. 137(1), sch. 8 Pt. I.
c. 69	Opencast Coal Act 1958	S. 39(6)(*b*) ext.	48, s. 76, sch. 4 para. 93(1).
		am.	48, s. 76, sch. 4 para. 93(2).
		S. 45(1)(2) expld. ...	48, s. 76, sch. 4 para. 64(1).
		S. 45(3) am.	48, s. 76, sch. 4 para. 64(2).
c. 72	Insurance Companies Act 1958.	S. 35 rep.	48, s. 137(1), sch. 8 Pt. I.
		Sch. 3 para. 5 am. ...	48, s. 94(2)(*c*), sch. 6 Pt. III.
7 & 8 Eliz. 2: c. 5	Adoption Act 1958 ...	S. 4(3)(*a*) subst. (*prosp.*)	54, ss. 72(3), 73 (4)(*c*) sch. 5 para. 33.
		S. 15(3) am. (E.) (*prosp.*)	54, s. 72(3), sch. 5 para. 34.
		rep. in pt. (E.) (*prosp.*)	54, s. 72(4), sch. 6.
		Ss. 16, 17 saved ...	46, s. 15(6).
		S. 37(1) rep. in pt. (E.) ...	54, ss. 52(4)(*b*), 72(4), sch. 6.
		S. 37(1)(*a*) am.	54, s. 52(4)(*a*).
		S. 37(2) rep. in pt. ...	54, ss. 52(4)(*c*), 72(4), sch. 6.
		S. 37(2) am.	54, ss. 72(3), 73 (4)(*c*), sch. 5 para. 35.
		S. 37(3) rep. in pt. (E.) ...	54, s. 72(4), sch. 6.
		S. 43(2) rep. in pt. ...	52, S.L. (Repeals).
		S. 57(1) definition of— "infant" am. (S.) ...	39, s. 1(1), sch. 1 Pt. I.
		am. (E.) ...	46, s. 1(3), sch. 1 Pt. I.
		"place of safety" am. (E.) (*prosp.*)	54, s. 72(3), sch. 5 para. 36.
c. 6	National Debt Act 1958	S. 1(1) rep. in pt. ...	48, s. 141, sch. 11 Pt. II.
		S. 1(1) am.	48, s. 108(1).
		S. 2 expld.	48, s. 108(1)(*g*).
		am.	48, s. 108(2)(5).
		Ss. 4, 5 am.	48, s. 108(3).
		S. 6(3) am.	48, s. 108(4).
		S. 12(1) am.	48, s. 110(1)(3).
		S. 12(2)(*a*) am.	48, s. 110(2).
		S. 13 superseded ...	48, s. 111(2).
		rep.	48, s. 141, sch. 11 Pt. II.
		S. 16 rep.	48, s. 137(1), sch. 8 Pt. I.
		Ss. 17(4), 19 am. ...	48, s. 108(1)(*e*).
c. 9	Representation of the People (Amendment) Act 1958.	Rep.	15, s. 24(4), sch. 3 Pt. I.

Session and Chap. or No. of Measure	Short title or Subject	How affected	Chapter of 1969 Act or number of Measure or Statutory Instrument
7 & 8 Eliz. 2: —*cont.*			
c. 12	Agriculture (Small Farmers) Act 1959.	Transfer of functions ...	S.I. *No.* 388.
c. 22	County Courts Act 1959	S. 31(3) am.	58, s. 11(3).
		S. 36(1) rep. in pt. ...	58, ss. 11(1), 35(2), sch. 2.
		Ss. 39, 40 am. (*prosp.*) ...	58, s. 1.
		S. 39 expld.	58, s. 22.
		S. 40(1)(*b*) ext. ...	10, s. 28(3)(4).
		S. 41 am. (*prosp.*) ...	58, s. 2.
		S. 42 expld.	58, s. 22.
		S. 44 am. (*prosp.*) ...	58, s. 3.
		S. 45(2) am. (*prosp.*) ...	58, s. 2.
		S. 46 rep.	58, ss. 11(2), 35(2), sch. 2.
		S. 47(1) am. (*prosp.*) ...	58, ss. 4(1), 35(1), sch. 1.
		rep. in pt. (*prosp.*)	58, ss. 4(1), 35(2), sch. 2.
		S. 47(1A) added (*prosp.*)	58, s. 4(1).
		S. 47(4) rep. (*prosp.*) ...	58, ss. 4(2), 35(2), sch. 2.
		Ss. 48, 51 expld. ...	58, s. 22.
		S. 52(1) am. (*prosp.*) ...	58, s. 5.
		S. 53 expld.	58, s. 22.
		S. 60(3) am. (*prosp.*) ...	58, s. 4(3).
		S. 65 expld.	58, s. 22.
		S. 68 am. (*prosp.*) ...	58, s. 2.
		S. 74 rep. in pt. ...	58, ss. 6, 35(2), sch. 2.
		S. 74(2) added	58, s. 6.
		S. 80 am. (*prosp.*) ...	58, s. 2.
		S. 80 am.	46, s. 1(3), sch. 1 Pt. I.
		S. 84(1) am.	58, s. 11(3).
		S. 89(*c*) am.	58, s. 7(1).
		S. 89 proviso (1) rep. ...	58, ss. 7(1), 35(2), sch. 2.
		S. 89(2)(3) added ...	58, s. 7(2).
		S. 91(2) am. (2A) added,	58, s. 8.
		S. 95(4) am.	58, s. 11(4).
		S. 102 am.	58, s. 20, 21(3).
		S. 102(3)(*c*)(iii) am. (*prosp.*).	58, s. 9(1).
		S. 102(3)(*d*) subst. ...	58, s. 9(2).
		S. 102(3)(*f*) added ...	58, s. 9(3).
		S. 143(2) am.	48, s. 94(2)(*c*), sch. 6 Pt. III.
		S. 146 am. (*prosp.*) ...	58, s. 2.
		S. 192 expld.	58, s. 22.
		S. 192(1) subst. (*prosp.*)...	58, s. 10(1).
		S. 192(2) subst. (*prosp.*)...	58, s. 10(2).
		S. 203(2) expld.	58, s. 22.
		Sch. 1 am. (*prosp.*) ...	58, ss. 2, 5.
		Sch. 1 rep. in pt. ...	52, S.L. (Repeals).
c. 23	Overseas Resources Development Act 1959.	Ext. (mod.)	36, s. 2.
		S. 1(3) saved	36, s. 2(3).
		S. 2(4)(*a*) subst. ...	36, s. 2(4).

Session and Chap. or No. of Measure	Short title or Subject	How affected	Chapter of 1969 Act or number of Measure or Statutory Instrument
7 & 8 Eliz. 2: c. 23—*cont.*	Overseas Resources Development Act 1959 —*cont.*	Ss. 4, 6 saved ... ... S. 7 rep. ... ... S. 8 excl. ... ... S. 8(3) rep. in pt. ... S. 9(2)(*b*) excl. ... Ss. 12(3), 13(1) am. ...	36, s. 2(3). 36, s. 3(3)(*a*). 36, s. 2(3). 36, s. 3(3)(*a*). 36, s. 2(3). 36, s. 1.
c. 24	Building (Scotland) Act 1959.	S. 17(2) am. (*prosp.*) ... S. 25(2)(3) ext.	30, s. 105, sch. 9 para. 37. 10, s. 34(3).
c. 25	Highways Act 1959 ...	S. 64(4) added ... ... Ss. 137–139 expld. ... S. 139 excl. (London) ... S. 139(1) am. ... ... S. 152 ext. ... ... S. 152(4) rep. in pt. ... S. 223 ext. ... ... S. 236(1)(*c*) rep. in pt. ... S. 254(6) ext. ... ... expld. ... ... S. 295(1) definition of " metropolitan road " rep. S. 300(1) expld. ... S. 300(2)(3) am. ... S. 300(4) expld. ... S. 300(5) am. ... Sch. 7 ext.	35, s. 34(1). 48, s. 76, sch. 4 para. 65(2). 35, s. 31. 35, s. 31(6). 48, s. 76, sch. 4 para. 93(1). 48, s. 141, sch. 11 Pt. II. 48, s. 76, sch. 4 para. 93(1). 48, s. 141, sch. 11 Pt. II. 48, s. 76, sch. 4 para. 93(1). 48, s. 76, sch. 4 para. 93(2). 35, s. 47(2), sch. 6. 48, s. 76, sch. 4 para. 65(3). 48, s. 76, sch. 4 para. 65(4)(5). 48, s. 76, sch. 4 para. 65(6). 48, s. 76, sch. 4 para. 65(7). 48, s. 76, sch. 4 para. 93(1).
c. 31	Agricultural Improvements Grants Act 1959.	Transfer of functions ...	S.I. No. 388.
c. 33	House Purchase and Housing Act 1959.	Pt. II (ss. 4–18), ss. 28(2) rep., 29(1) definitions of " improvement grant ", " standard amenities " rep. in pt. (E.), sch. 1 paras. 1, 2, 9 rep.	33, s. 89(3), sch. 10
c. 43	Post Office Works Act 1959.	Am.	48, s. 22(1).
c. 48	Cotton Industry Act 1959	Transfer of functions ...	S.I. No. 1498.
c. 50	Pensions (Increase) Act 1959.	S. 1(2)–(6) appl.... ... S. 7(1)(*b*) Pensions increase. Sch. Pts. I, II ext. ...	7, s. 1(4), sch. 2 para. 4. 7, s. 1(1), (3) sch. 1 Pt. I para. 29, Pt. II para. 14. 7, s. 2(1), sch. 3 paras. 2, 3, 5.

Session and Chap. or No. of Measure	Short title or Subject	How affected	Chapter of 1969 Act or number of Measure or Statutory Instrument
7 & 8 Eliz. 2: c. 50—*cont.*	Pensions (Increase) Act 1959—*cont.*	Sch. Pt. I para. 22 rep. ...	48, s. 141, sch. 11 Pt. II.
c. 51	Licensing (Scotland) Act 1959.	S. 31(1)(*d*) am.	13, s. 1(2).
		S. 31(2) am.	13, s. 1(3).
		S. 31(2A)(2B) added ...	13, s. 1(4).
		S. 120 definition of " elector " rep. in pt.	15, s. 24(4), sch. 3 Pt. II.
		Sch. 1 Pt. II am. ...	S.I. No. 1019.
c. 53	Town and Country Planning Act 1959.	S. 27(3)(*b*) am. (15.2.1971)	19, s. 10(3), sch. 3 para. 14.
		S. 29 appl.	33, s. 35(7).
c. 54	Weeds Act 1959 ...	Transfer of functions ...	S.I. No. 388.
c. 55	Dog Licences Act 1959 ...	S. 7(3)–(8) rep.	48, s. 141, sch. 11 Pt. II.
c. 58	Finance Act 1959 ...	S. 23(1) rep. in pt. ...	32, s. 61(6), sch. 21, Pt. X.
		S. 34(3) rep. in pt. ...	32, s. 61(6), sch. 21 Pt. V.
c. 70	Town and Country Planning (Scotland) Act 1959.	S. 27(1) excl.	30, s. 39.
		S. 31 ext.... ...	$\left\{\begin{array}{l}\text{30, s. 13(4).}\\ \text{48, s. 76, sch. 4}\\ \text{para. 93(1).}\end{array}\right.$
		S. 31(3)(*d*) rep. (*prosp.*)...	30, s. 107, sch. 11.
		S. 31(3)(*f*)–(*l*) added (*prosp.*).	30, s. 105, sch. 9 para. 38(*a*).
		S. 31(4)(*d*) rep. in pt. (*prosp.*).	30, s. 107, sch. 11.
		S. 31(4)(*f*)–(*n*) added (*prosp.*), (5)(*b*) am. (*prosp.*).	30, s. 105, sch. 9 para. 38(*b*)(*c*).
		S. 31(5) proviso rep. in pt. (*prosp.*), (9) proviso rep., (10) rep. in pt. (*prosp.*).	30, s. 107, sch. 11.
		S. 35 ext. (*prosp.*) ...	30, s. 77(1).
		S. 35(1)(*b*) am.	30, s. 105, sch. 9 para. 39.
		S. 35(4) appl. (mod.) ...	30, s. 64(7), sch. 6 para. 8(2).
		S. 36(1)(*c*)(*d*) am. ...	30, s. 105, sch. 9 para. 40.
		S. 36(4) appl. (mod.) ...	30, s. 64(7), sch. 6 para. 8(2).
		S. 36(6) am.	30, s. 100, sch. 8.
		Pt. IV (ss. 38–42) ext. ...	30, ss. 34–36.
		S. 38 ext.	48, s. 76, sch. 4 para. 93(1).
		S. 38(1) am. (*prosp.*) ...	30, ss. 34, 35(9), sch. 3.
		S.38(1)(*a*)(*b*) rep. ...	30, ss. 35(9), 107, sch. 3, 11.
		S. 38(2) expld.	30, s. 34(3).
		S. 38(6) am. (*prosp.*), (7) added (*prosp.*).	30, s. 35(9), sch. 3.
		S. 39(1) am. (*prosp.*) ...	30, ss. 38(4), 35 (9), sch. 3.
		S. 39(2)(*c*) appl. (mod.)...	30, s. 36(6).
		Ss. 39(3) subst. (*prosp.*), 40(1) am. (*prosp.*).	30, s. 35(9), sch. 3.

Session and Chap. or No. of Measure	Short title or Subject	How affected	Chapter of 1969 Act or number of Measure or Statutory Instrument
7 & 8 Eliz. 2: c. 70—*cont.*	Town and Country Planning (Scotland) Act 1959—*cont.*	S. 40(5) appl. (mod.) ...	30, s. 36(6).
		S. 41 mod.	30, s. 37.
		S. 41(1), (2)(*b*) am. (*prosp.*).	30, s. 35(9), sch. 3.
		S. 41(3) appl. (mod.) ...	30, s. 36(6).
		am. (*prosp.*). ...	30, s. 35(9), sch. 3.
		S. 42(2) am.	30, s. 38(2).
		S. 42(2)(*a*) am. (*prosp.*)...	30, s.35(9), sch. 3.
		S. 42(2)(*b*), (3)(*b*) am. (*prosp.*).	30, ss. 35(9), 38 (3)(4), sch. 3.
		S. 42(4) am.	30, s. 38(2).
		S.42(4)(*a*) am. (*prosp.*) ...	30, s. 35(9), sch.3.
		S. 42(4)(*b*) am. (*prosp.*) ...	30, ss. 35(9), 38 (3)(4), sch. 3.
		S. 42(5) definitions of—	
		" the relevant date " am. and rep. in pt.	30, ss. 35(9), 107, schs. 3, 11.
		" the specified descriptions " subst. (*prosp.*).	30, s. 35(9), sch. 3.
		S. 42(6) rep. (*prosp.*) ...	30, s. 107, sch.11.
		S. 54(1) definition of " the Act of 1969 " added (*prosp.*).	30, s. 35(9), sch. 3.
		Sch. 5 para. 2(6) ext. ...	48, s. 76, sch. 4 para. 93(1).
		para. 2(6) am. ...	48, s. 76, sch. 4 para. 93(2).
		paras. 6, 7 rep. ...	30, ss. 38(1), 107, sch. 11.
		para. 8 am. (*prosp.*)	30, s.35(9), sch.3.
		para. 11(1)(2) appl.	30, s. 36(4).
		para. 11(3) rep. ...	30, ss. 35(9), 107, schs. 3, 11.
		para. 12(1)(2) appl. (mod.).	30, s. 36(6).
		para. 12(3) rep. ...	30, ss. 35(9), 107, schs. 3, 11.
		para. 13 am. (*prosp.*).	30, s.35(9), sch.3.
c. 72	Mental Health Act 1959	S. 9(1)(2) am.	54, s. 72(3), sch. 5 para. 37.
		S. 10(1)(*a*)(i) subst. (*prosp.*).	54, ss. 72(3), 73 (4)(*c*), sch. 5 para. 38.
		S. 36(2)(4) expld. ...	48, s. 76, sch. 4 para. 66.
		S. 49(4)(*c*) am. ...	46, s. 1(3), sch. 1 Pt. I.
		S. 50(*a*) subst. (*prosp.*) ...	54, s. 72(3), sch. 5 para. 39.
		S. 51(1) am.	46, s. 1(3), sch. 1 Pt. I.
		S. 60 appl. (*prosp.*) ...	54, ss. 1(5), 2.
		S. 60(6) am. (*prosp.*) ...	54, s. 72(3), sch. 5 para. 40.
		Ss. 60(6), 61 rep. in pt. (*prosp.*).	54, s. 72(4), sch. 6.
		S. 62(4) am. (*prosp.*) ...	54, s. 72(3), sch. 5 para. 41.

Session and Chap. or No. of Measure	Short title or Subject	How affected	Chapter of 1969 Act or number of Measure or Statutory Instrument
7 & 8 Eliz. 2: c. 72—*cont.*	Mental Health Act 1959 —*cont.*	Ss. 70(2) rep. (*prosp.*), 72(6)(*a*), 75(1)(2) rep. in pt. (*prosp.*), 79 definitions of " approved school ", " remand home " rep. (*prosp.*).	54, s. 72(4), sch. 6.
		S. 103(1)(*dd*) added ...	58, s. 17(1).
		S. 103(3) am.	58, s. 17(2).
		S. 103A added	58, s. 18.
		S. 107(1) rep. in pt. ...	58, s. 35(2), sch. 2.
		S. 107(3) am.	58, s. 19(1).
		S. 117(2A) added ...	58, s. 19(2).
		S. 119(1) definition of " will " added.	58, s. 19(3).
		S. 127(2) am.	46, s. 1(3), sch. 1 Pt. I.
		Sch. 5 rep. in pt. ...	52, S.L. (Repeals).
		Sch. 7 Pt. I rep. in pt. ... $\left\{ \begin{array}{l} \\ \\ \\ \end{array} \right.$	47, s. 10(2), sch. 2. 52, S.L. (Repeals).
8 & 9 Eliz. 2: c. 1	Mr. Speaker Morrison's Retirement Act 1959.	Pensions increase ...	7, s. 1(1), sch. 1 Pt. I para. 39.
c. 9	Judicial Pensions Act 1959.	Pensions Increase ...	7, s. 1(1), sch. 1 Pt. I para. 8.
c. 16	Road Traffic Act 1960 ...	Ss. 65(6), 66(6)(*a*) am. (*prosp.*).	27, s. 18(1).
		Pt. II (ss. 97–116) expld. (*prosp.*).	27, s. 2(8), sch. 1 para. 2.
		Functions of local authorities transfd. to Min. of Transport (*prosp.*).	27, ss. 1, 2.
		S. 98(5)(6) added (*prosp.*)	27, s. 16(1).
		S. 99(2)(*b*) Power to am. (*prosp.*).	27, s. 23(1).
		S. 99(3) saved (*prosp.*) ...	27, s. 31.
		S. 99(4) rep. (saving) (*prosp.*).	27, ss. 16(2), 37, sch. 2 para. 1, sch. 3.
		S. 99(5) subst. (*prosp.*)...	27, s. 16(2), sch. 2 para. 2.
		S. 100 subst. (*prosp.*) ...	27, s. 13.
		ext. (*prosp.*) ...	27, s. 35.
		Ss. 101, 102 subst. (saving) (*prosp.*).	27, s. 14.
		Ss. 101, 102 Power to am. (*prosp.*).	27, s. 23(1).
		Ss. 102(2) ext. (*prosp.*) ...	27, s. 35.
		S. 103 subst. (*prosp.*) ...	27, s. 15.
		S. 109(3) rep. in pt. (*prosp.*).	27, ss. 2(8), 37, sch. 1 para. 3, sch. 3.
		S. 110(*a*) rep. in pt. (*prosp.*).	27, ss. 16(2), 37, sch. 2 para. 3, sch. 3.
		S. 112 ext. (*prosp.*) ...	27, s. 16(7).

Session and Chap. or No. of Measure	Short title or Subject	How affected	Chapter of 1969 Act or number of Measure or Statutory Instrument
8 & 9 Eliz. 2: c. 16—*cont.*	Road Traffic Act 1960 —*cont.*	S. 112(1) am. (*prosp.*) ...	27, s. 16(2), sch. 2 para. 4.
		S. 112(1)(2) rep. in pt. (*prosp.*).	27, ss. 2(8), 37, sch. 1 para. 3, sch. 3.
		S. 112(3) rep. in pt. (*prosp.*).	27, ss. 16(2), 37, sch. 2 para. 4, sch. 3.
		S. 113 am.	27, s. 34(2).
		S. 113(*b*)(*c*) rep. (*prosp.*)	27, ss. 2(8), 37, sch. 1 para. 3, sch. 3.
		S. 113(*g*) power to am. (*prosp.*).	27, s. 23(1).
		rep. in pt. (*prosp.*).	27, ss. 23(2), 37, sch. 3.
		S. 114(1) rep. in pt. (*prosp.*).	27, ss. 2(8), 37, sch. 1 para. 3, sch. 3.
		S. 115 definitions of—	
		" provisional licence " am. (*prosp.*).	27, s. 16(2), sch. 2 para. 5.
		" text of fitness to drive " rep. (*prosp.*).	27, s. 37, sch. 3.
		S. 115(2) added (*prosp.*)	27, s. 2(8), sch. 1 para. 1.
		Pt. III (ss. 117–163) ext. (mod.) (L.T.E.).	35, s. 23(2).
		Ss. 119–127 ext. (mod.) (London).	35, s. 24.
		Ss. 120(1) rep. in pt., (2) rep., (4), 121 rep. in pt.	35, s. 47(2), sch. 6.
		S. 121(4) expld.	35, s. 24(3).
		S. 122 rep.	35, ss. 24(1), 47(2), sch. 6.
		Ss. 123(2) rep. in pt. (3) rep. in pt. (London), 125, 126 rep. in pt.	35, s. 47(2), sch. 6.
		S. 135–143 excl. (L.T.E.)	35, s. 23(1), sch. 4 para. 1.
		S. 135(2) am.	35, s. 24(4)(*a*).
		rep. in pt. ...	35, s. 47(2), sch. 6.
		S. 135(7) am.	35, s. 24(4)(*b*).
		rep. in pt. ...	35, s. 47(2), sch. 6.
		S. 135(8) am.	35, s. 24(4)(*c*).
		Ss. 136(2) rep. in pt., 141, 142 rep.	35, s. 47(2), sch. 6.
		S. 143(2)(*a*) am. ...	35, s. 24(4)(*d*).
		Ss. 153(5), 161(2) rep. ...	35, s. 47(2), sch. 6.
		S. 163 saved	35, s. 24(2).
		S. 163(1) am.	35, s. 24(4)(*c*).
		Ss. 165(3) rep., 193(1) rep. in pt.	35, s. 47(2), sch. 6.
		S. 202(2)(*e*) added ...	35, s. 9(2).
		S. 225(1) am. (*prosp.*) ...	27, s. 22(5).
		S. 225(1)(*d*) am. ...	27, s. 16(2), sch. 2 para. 6.
		rep. in pt. (*prosp.*) ...	27, s. 37, sch. 3.

Session and Chap. or No. of Measure	Short title or Subject	How affected	Chapter of 1969 Act or number of Measure or Statutory Instrument
8 & 9 Eliz. 2: c. 16—*cont.*	Road Traffic Act 1960 —*cont.*	S. 225(2) am. (*prosp.*) ...	27, s. 16(2), sch. 2 para. 7.
		rep. in pt. (*prosp.*)	27, ss. 16(2), 37, sch. 2 para. 7, sch. 3.
		S. 225(4) am. (*prosp.*) ...	27, s. 22(5).
		S. 226(2) am. (*prosp.*) ...	27, s. 16(2), sch. 2 para. 6.
		rep. in pt. (*prosp.*) ...	27, s. 37, sch. 3.
		S. 232(2)(*a*) am. ...	27, s. 16(2), sch. 2 para. 8.
		S. 233(1)(*h*) added ...	27, s. 16(2), sch. 2 para. 9.
		S. 241(2)(*c*)(ii), (4)(*a*) am.	27, s. 16(2), sch. 2 para. 10.
		S. 244 am.	27, s. 16(2), sch. 2 para. 11.
		S. 247(1)(2) am. ...	27, s. 16(2), sch. 2 para. 12.
		S. 247(2) rep. in pt. (*prosp.*).	27, s. 37, sch. 3.
		S. 252(1)(2) rep. in pt. ...	35, s. 47(2), sch. 6.
		Sch. 15 para. 1 am. ...	27, s. 16(2), sch. 2 para. 13.
		Sch. 17 rep. in pt. ...	35, s. 47(2), sch. 6.
c. 18	Local Employment Act	Pts. I (ss. 1–15), II (ss. 16–20), ss. 26(2), 27, 28(2) (3)(*a*). Transfer of functions.	S.I. No. 1498.
c. 22	Horticulture Act 1960 ...	Pt. I (ss. 1–8). Transfer of functions.	S.I. No. 388.
c. 24	Pawnbrokers Act 1960 ...	S. 6(1)(*c*) rep. (15.2.1971)	19, s. 17(2), sch. 4.
		Sch. am. (15.2.1971) ...	19, s. 10(3), sch 2. para. 2(3)(*b*).
c. 37	Payment of Wages Act 1960.	S. 7(1) definitions of " money order ", " postal order " subst.	48, s. 76, sch. 4 para. 67.
c. 44	Finance Act 1960 ...	S. 17(2) am.	32, s. 10(8).
		S. 17(2)(*b*) rep. in pt. ...	32, s. 61(6), sch. 21 Pt. IX.
		Ss. 21–24, 25(1)–(3)(5)(6), 26 restr.	32, s. 32(15).
		S. 27(4)(5) rep. in pt. ...	32, ss. 60, 61(6), sch. 20 para. 19(1), sch. 21 Pt. IX.
		S. 28(6)(8) am.	32, s. 60, sch. 20 para. 19(2).
		S. 28(8) rep. in pt. (6.4.1970).	32, s. 61(6), sch. 21 Pt. VIII.
		S. 28(11) proviso rep. ...	32, s. 61(6), sch. 21 Pt. IV.
		S. 33(3) am.	32, s. 60, sch. 20 para. 4(2).
		S. 33(4)(5) rep.	32, s. 61(6), sch. 21 Pt. X.

Session and Chap. or No. of Measure	Short title or Subject	How affected	Chapter of 1969 Act or number of Measure or Statutory Instrument
8 & 9 Eliz. 2: c. 44—*cont.*	Finance Act 1960—*cont.*	S. 37(7) am.	32, s. 60, sch. 20 para. 19(3).
		S. 39(2) am.	32, s. 60, sch. 20 para. 8(4)(*a*).
		S. 51 appl.	32, s. 60, sch. 20 para. 19(4).
		Ss. 51(7), 58(6) rep. in pt. (6.4.1970).	32, s. 61(6), sch. 21 Pt. VIII.
		S. 58 ext.	32, s. 60, sch. 20 para. 14.
		S. 60 appl.	32, s. 60, sch. 20 para. 19(5).
		S. 63(1) definitions of "assessment", "Summary Jurisdiction Acts (Northern Ireland)" rep.	32, s. 61(6), sch. 21 Pt. X.
		S. 64(2)(*b*)–(*d*), (4) rep. in pt.	32, s. 61(6), sch. 21 Pt. V.
		S. 69(1) rep. in pt. ...	32, s. 61(6), sch. 21 Pt. X.
		S. 69(2)(*a*) am.	32, s. 60, sch. 20 para. 19(6).
		S. 72(1) proviso, (10) rep.	32, s. 61(6), sch. 21 Pt. X.
		Sch. 6 ext.	32, ss. 18(7), 30(5), 32(13), sch. 13 para. 13(4), sch. 15 para. 10, sch. 16 para. 8(4).
		Sch. 10 para. 6(1) am. ...	32, s. 60, sch. 20 para. 4(2).
c. 52	Cyprus Act 1960 ...	Sch. para. 7 rep. ...	32, s. 61(6), sch. 21 Pt. IX.
c. 55	Nigeria Independence Act 1960.	S. 3(4) rep. in pt. ...	52, S.L. (Repeals).
		Sch. 2 para. 1 rep. ...	32, s. 61(6), sch. 21 Pt. IX.
c. 58	Charities Act 1960 ...	Saved	38, s. 8(1).
		S. 18 ext.	22, s. 4(3).
		S. 18 (exc. subs. (6), (13)) appl.	22, s. 4(4).
		S. 18(4) excl.	22, s. 4(3).
		S. 21 appl.	22, s. 4(4).
		S. 29 excl.	38, s. 8(3).
		S. 45(2) saved	38, s. 8(2).
		Sch. 6 rep. in pt. ...	52, S.L. (Repeals).
c. 61	Mental Health (Scotland) Act 1960.	S. 10(1)(*a*)(ii) subst. (*prosp.*).	54, ss. 72(3), 73(4)(*c*), sch. 5 para. 42.
		S. 45(4)(*c*) am. ...	39, s. 1(3), sch. 1 Pt. I.
		S. 46(*b*) subst. (*prosp.*) ...	54, ss. 72(3), 73(4)(*c*), sch. 5 para. 43.
		S. 47(1) am.	39, s. 1(3), sch. 2 Pt. I.
		Sch. 4 rep. in pt. ...	47, s. 10(2), sch. 1.

Session and Chap. or No. of Measure	Short title or Subject	How affected	Chapter of 1969 Act or number of Measure or Statutory Instrument
8 & 9 Eliz. 2: —*cont.*			
c. 63	Road Traffic and Roads Improvement Act 1960.	S. 2 Pensions increase ...	7, s. 1(1)(3), sch. 1 Pt. II para. 10(*b*).
c. 64	Building Societies Act 1960.	S. 63 rep., sch. 5 rep. in pt.	52, S.L. (Repeals).
c. 66	Professions Supplementary to Medicine Act 1960.	Sch. 1 para. 1(1)(*b*) am....	S.I. No. 388.
c. 68	Noise Abatement Act 1960.	S. 1(1) expld. (E.) ...	25, s. 4(3).
9 & 10 Eliz. 2:			
c. 14	Nurses (Amendment) Act 1961.	S. 1 rep. in pt.	47, s. 10(2), sch. 2.
		S. 4(1) am.	47, s. 10(1), sch. 1 para. 12.
		S. 4(2)(3) rep.	47, s. 10(2), sch. 2.
		S. 6 am.	47, s. 10(1), sch. 1 para. 13.
		rep. in pt.	47, s. 10, sch. 1 para. 13, sch. 2.
		S. 7(2)(*b*)(*c*), sch. 1 paras. 1, 3–6, 8, 9, 11 rep., 13 rep. in pt., 14 rep., 15 rep. in pt., 16 rep.	47, s. 10(2), sch. 2.
c. 15	Post Office Act 1961 ...	Ss. 1, 2(1)(2) rep. ...	48, s. 141, sch. 11 Pt. II.
		S. 2(3)(4) am.	48, s. 131(1), sch. 7 para. 1(2).
		S. 3 rep.	48, s. 141, sch. 11 Pt. II.
		S. 4 rep.	48, ss. 137(1), 141, sch. 8 Pt. I, sch. 11 Pt. II.
		Ss. 5–7, 8(1)(3), 9–11 rep.	48, s. 141, sch. 11 Pt. II.
		S. 12 ext.	48, s. 85.
		S. 13 rep.	48, s. 141, sch. 11 Pt. II.
		S. 14(1) rep. in pt., (2) rep.	48, s. 137(1), sch. 8 Pt. I.
		Ss. 15(2)(3), 16, 17 rep. ...	48, s. 141, sch. 11 Pt. II.
		S. 18 rep.	48, s. 137(1), sch. 8 Pt. I.
		S. 19 rep.	48, s. 141, sch. 11 Pt. II.
		S. 20 rep.	48, s. 137(1), sch. 8 Pt. I.
		Ss. 21, 22, 23(3) rep. ...	48, s. 141, sch. 11 Pt. II.
		S. 24(1) rep.	48, s. 137(1), sch. 8 Pt. I.
		Ss. 25, 26(1), 27(3)(4), 28(2), 29 rep.	48, s. 141, sch. 11 Pt. II.
		Sch. rep. in pt.	48, ss. 137(1), 141, sch. 8, sch. 11 Pt. II.
		rep. in pt. (S.) ...	30, s. 107, sch. 11.

Session and Chap. or No. of Measure	Short title or Subject	How affected	Chapter of 1969 Act or number of Measure or Statutory Instrument
9 & 10 Eliz. 2: —*cont.*			
c. 16	Sierra Leone Independence Act 1961.	S. 3(3) rep. in pt. ...	52, S.L. (Repeals).
		Sch. 3 para. 1 rep. ...	32, s. 61(6), sch. 21 Pt. IX.
c. 33	Land Compensation Act 1961.	Ss. 2, 4 appl. (mod.) ...	35, s. 36, sch. 5 para. 22(4).
		S. 11 ext.	48, s. 76, sch. 4 para. 93(1).
		Sch. 2 para. 1(2)(*b*) rep. in pt.	33, s. 89(3), sch. 10.
		para. 2(1)(*h*) added.	33, s. 89(1), sch. 8 para. 21.
		para. 2(2) am. ...	33, s. 89(1), sch. 8 para. 22.
		para. 3(2) am. ...	33, s. 89(1), sch. 8 para. 23.
		para. 6(2)(*c*) subst.	33, s. 89(1), sch. 8 para. 24.
		para. 1(2)(*b*) rep. in pt.	33, s. 89(3), sch. 10.
c. 36	Finance Act 1961 ...	S. 9 cont.	32, s. 1(1)(*b*).
		S. 28(2) rep. in pt. ...	32, s. 61(6), sch. 21 Pt. X.
		S. 35(1) am.	48, s. 112.
		S. 35(2) rep.	48, s. 141, sch. 11 Pt. II.
		S. 35(5) am.	48, s. 112.
c. 39	Criminal Justice Act 1961	S. 1(1), (2) proviso rep. (*prosp.*).	54, s. 72(4), sch. 6.
		S. 4 am. (*prosp.*) ...	54, s. 7(3).
		S. 4(1), (2)(*a*) rep. in pt. (*prosp.*).	54, s. 72(4), sch. 6.
		S. 5 excl. (*prosp.*) ...	54, s. 7(4).
		S. 5(1) subst. (*prosp.*) ...	54, s. 72(3), sch. 5 para. 44.
		Ss. 5(2) rep. in pt. (*prosp.*), (3), 6(1)(2) rep.(*prosp.*), (3) rep. in pt. (*prosp.*).	54, s. 72(4), sch. 6.
		S. 6(3) now s. 5(6) ...	54, s. 72(3), sch. 5 para. 44.
		Ss. 7(2) rep. (*prosp.*), (3) rep. in pt. (*prosp.*), 8 (1)(2) rep. (*prosp.*).	54, s. 72(4), sch. 6.
		S. 9 am. (*prosp.*) ...	54, s. 72(3), sch. 5 para. 45.
		Ss. 9(*a*) rep. (*prosp.*), 10 (2)(*a*) rep. in pt.(*prosp.*), 14–19, 22(4), 25 rep. (*prosp.*), 29(1)(3) rep. in pt. (*prosp.*).	54, s. 72(4), sch. 6.
		S. 29(3)(*a*) am. (*prosp.*) ...	54, s. 72(3), sch. 5 para. 46.
		Schs. 2 rep. (*prosp.*), 4 rep. in pt. (*prosp.*).	54, s. 72(4), sch. 6.
c. 41	Flood Prevention (Scotland) Act 1961.	S. 3(4) ext.	48, s. 76, sch. 4 para. 93(1).
		Sch. 1 para. 2, Sch. 2 para. 3(1)(*e*) expld.	48, s. 76, sch. 4 para. 68.

Session and Chap. or No. of Measure	Short title or Subject	How affected	Chapter of 1969 Act or number of Measure or Statutory Instrument
9 & 10 Eliz. 2: —*cont.*			
c. 42	Sheriffs' Pensions (Scotland) Act 1961.	S. 1 Pensions increase ...	7, s. 1(1), sch. 1 Pt. I para. 6.
c. 49	Covent Garden Market Act 1961.	S. 18(2) am. ... ... S. 34(1)(2) am. ...	ii, s. 8(1). ii, s. 8(2).
c. 57	Trusts (Scotland) Act 1961.	S. 1(2) am.	39, s. 1(3), sch. 1 Pt. I.
c. 62	Trustee Investments Act 1961.	S. 17(3), sch. 1 Pt. I para. 2 am. Sch. 1 Pt. II appl. (mod.) Sch. 1 Pt. II para. 9 ext. Sch. 4 paras. 4(1) rep. in pt., (2) rep., (3), 5 rep. in pt.	48, s. 94(2)(*c*), sch. 6 Pt. III. 50, s. 46(1)(2). 48, ss. 41, 88(1) sch. 2 paras. 4, 15. 50, s. 96(1), sch. 3 Pt. I.
c. 63	Highways (Miscellaneous Provisions) Act 1961.	S. 14(6) expld.	48, s. 76, sch. 4 para. 69.
c. 64	Public Health Act 1961	Sch. 4 am.	48, s. 76, sch. 4 para. 70.
c. 65	Housing Act 1961 ...	Pt. II (ss. 12–28) mod. ... S. 12(1) am. ... ... S. 12(2) rep. ... ... S. 12(4) am. ... ... S. 12(5) am. ... ... S. 13(1)(2) am. ... S. 15(1) am. ... ... S. 16 ext. ... ... S. 16(1) am. ... ... S. 18 saved ... ... S. 19(1) am. ... ... S. 19(2)(*a*)(*b*) am. ... S. 19(11)(*a*) am. ... S. 20(1)(*a*) am. ... S. 21(1) am. ... ... S. 22 am. ... ... S. 22(1)(*a*) subst. ... S. 22(5) rep. ... ... S. 22(10) am. ... ... S. 24(5) rep. in pt. ... Sch. 1 para. 3 am. (15.2.1971). Sch. 2 para. 9, sch. 3 para. 6(2) rep.	33, s. 40(2)(*b*). 33, ss. 58(3), 89(1), sch. 8 para. 2. 33, ss. 59(1), 89(3), sch. 10. 33, s. 59(2). 33, s. 59(3). 33, ss. 58(3), 89(1), sch. 8 para. 2. 33, ss. 58(3), 89(1), sch. 8 para. 2. 33, s. 60(1). 33, ss. 58(3), 89(1), sch. 8 para. 2. 33, s. 61(4). 33, s. 62(1)(*a*). 33, s. 62(1)(*b*). 33, s. 61(6). 33, s. 61(6). 33, ss. 58(3), 89(1), sch. 8 paras. 2, 3. 33, s. 64. 33, ss. 58(3), 89(1), sch. 8 para. 4. 33, s. 89(3), sch. 10. 33, s. 64(8). 33, s. 89(3), sch. 10. 19, s. 10(3), sch. 2 para. 15. 33, s. 89(3), sch. 10.

Session and Chap. or No. of Measure	Short title or Subject	How affected	Chapter of 1969 Act or number of Measure or Statutory Instrument
9 & 10 Eliz. 2: *—cont.* C.A.M. No. 3... ...	Clergy Pensions Measure 1961.	S. 1(1)(*c*), sch. 1 Pt. III am.	C.A.M. No. 1, s. 1.
10 & 11 Eliz. 2: c. 1	Tanganyika Independence Act 1961.	Power to rep. (exc. s. 1)... S. 3(4) rep. in pt. ... Sch. 2 para. 1 rep. ...	29, s. 5. 52, S.L. (Repeals). 32, s. 61(6), sch. 21 Pt. IX.
c. 13	Vehicles (Excise) Act 1962	Functions of local authorities transfd. to Min. of Transport. Ext. (Isles of Scilly) ... Power to am. (*prosp.*) ... Am. (*prosp.*)	27, ss. 1, 2. 27, s. 2(6). 27, s. 4(8). 27, s. 2(8), sch. 1 para. 4.
		S.1 am. (*prosp.*) ... S. 2(1)(2) rep. in pt. (*prosp.*).	27, ss. 11, 12. 27, ss. 4(4), 37, sch. 1 para. 13, sch. 3.
		S. 2(1)(*d*) ext. (*prosp.*) ... S.3 rep. (*prosp.*) ...	27, s. 11(2) (*f*). 27, ss. 4(5), 37, sch. 3.
		S.4 am. ... ... ext. (*prosp.*) ... S. 5(1) rep. in pt. (*prosp.*)	27, s. 9. 27, s. 16(7). 27, ss. 2(8), 37, sch. 1 para. 8, sch. 3.
		S. 5(2) am. (*prosp.*) ...	27, s. 2(8), sch. 1 para. 5.
		S. 5(3)(4) rep. in pt. (*prosp.*)(5)(6) rep. (*prosp.*) S. 6 am. (*prosp.*) ... S. 6(2A)–(2C) added ... S. 6(5) am. ... ... S. 6(6) rep. in pt. (*prosp.*)	27, ss. 2(8), 37, sch. 1 para. 8, sch. 3. 27, ss. 11, 12. 32, s. 6(1). 27, s. 10. 27, ss. 2(8), 37, sch. 1 para. 8, sch. 3.
		S. 7 am. ... ... S. 7(4) am. (*prosp.*) ... S. 7(7) am. (*prosp.*) ... S. 8(3) am. (*prosp.*) ... S. 8(4) Power to am. (*prosp.*). rep. in pt. (*prosp.*)	27, s. 9. 27, s. 16(3). 27, s. 16(4). 27, s. 29(1). 27, s. 23(1). 27, ss. 23(2), 37, sch. 3.
		S. 9 rep. (*prosp.*) ...	27, ss. 2(8), 37, sch. 1 para. 8, sch. 3.
		S. 9(1)(2)(*a*) rep. in pt. ...	32, s. 61(6), sch. 21 Pt. I.
		S. 10(3) am. (*prosp.*) ...	27, s. 4(4), sch. 1 para. 14.
		Ss. 11(1)(*a*) rep. (*prosp.*), 12(1) rep. in pt. (*prosp.*)	27, ss. 2(8), 37, sch. 1 para. 8, sch. 3.

Session and Chap. or No. of Measure	Short title or Subject	How affected	Chapter of 1969 Act or number of Measure or Statutory Instrument
10 & 11 Eliz. 2: c. 13—*cont.*	Vehicles (Excise) Act 1962 —*cont.*	S. 12 ext. (*prosp.*) ...	27, s. 11(2)(*e*).
		S. 12(1)–(5) subst. ...	32, s. 6(2), sch. 12 Pt. I.
		S. 12(1) ext. (*prosp.*) ...	27, ss. 11(2)(*g*), 12(4).
		S. 12(4) rep. (*prosp.*) ...	27, ss. 4(4), 37, sch. 1 para. 13, sch. 3.
		S. 12(5) am. (*prosp.*) ...	27, s. 4(4), sch. 1 para. 15.
		S. 12(7)(8) rep. (*prosp.*) ...	27, ss. 4(4), 37, sch. 1 para. 13, sch. 3.
		S. 12(9) subst.	32, s. 6(2), sch. 12 Pt. II para. 1.
		S. 12(10) am.	32, s. 6(2), sch. 12 Pt. II para. 2.
		S. 13 ext. (*prosp.*) ...	27, s. 20(4)(5).
		S. 13(1) am. (*prosp.*) ...	27, ss. 2(8), 7(5), sch. 1 para. 6.
		rep. in pt. (*prosp.*) ...	27, ss. 2(8), 37, sch. 1 para. 8, sch. 3.
		S. 16 subst. (*prosp.*) ...	27, s. 17.
		S. 16(*e*)(*f*) Power to am. (*prosp.*).	27, s. 23(1).
		S. 16(2) am. (*temp.*) ...	32, s. 6(2), sch. 12, Pt. II para. 3.
		S. 17(1)(2) am. (*prosp.*) ...	27, s. 28(1)(2).
		S. 17(1)(*aa*) added ...	32, s. 6(2), sch. 12 Pt. II para. 4.
		S. 17(3) subst. (*prosp.*) ...	27, s. 28(3).
		S. 18 am.	27, s. 28(4).
		S. 19(1) rep.	27, ss. 25, 37, sch. 3.
		S. 19(2) excl. (S.) ...	27, s. 26(7).
		am. (*prosp.*) ...	27, s. 2(8), sch. 1 para. 7.
		S. 19(3) rep.	27, ss. 26, 37, sch. 3.
		S. 21 am.	27, s. 28(6).
		Ss. 21(2) rep. in pt. (*prosp.*), 22 rep. (*prosp.*).	27, ss. 2(8), 37, sch. 1 para. 8, sch. 3.
		S. 22(1)(*b*) rep. in pt. ...	48, s. 141, sch. 11 Pt. II.
		S. 23 am.	27, s. 34(2).
		S. 23(1) ext. (*prosp.*) ...	27, s. 34(5).
		S. 23(2) am. (*prosp.*) ...	27, s. 23(2).
		S. 23(4) rep. (*prosp.*) ...	27, ss. 2(8), 37, sch. 1 para. 8, sch. 3.
		S. 24(1) definitions of— " county " rep. (*prosp.*).	27, ss. 2(8), 37, sch. 1 para. 8, sch. 3.
		" general trade licence ", " limited trade licence " rep.	32, s. 61(6), sch. 21 Pt. I.

3 P

Session and Chap. or No. of Measure	Short title or Subject	How affected	Chapter of 1969 Act or number of Measure or Statutory Instrument
10 & 11 Eliz. 2: c. 13—*cont.*	Vehicles (Excise) Act 1962 —*cont.*	S. 24(5) rep. (*prosp.*) ...	27, ss. 2(8), 37, sch. 1 para. 8, sch. 3.
		Sch. 7 rep. in pt. (*prosp.*)	27, s. 37, sch. 3.
c. 14	Telegraph Act 1962 ...	Rep.	48, s. 141, sch. 11 Pt. II.
c. 21	Commonwealth Immigrants Act 1962.	Pt. I (ss. 1–5) cont. until 31.12.1970.	61, s. 2(1).
		S. 2(1) am. (*prosp.*) ...	21, s. 2, sch. 2.
		ext. (*prosp.*) ...	21, ss. 13(2), 16.
		S. 2(1)(*a*) am. (*prosp.*) ...	21, s. 3(1).
		S. 2(2)(*b*) am.	21, s. 20(1).
		S. 2 (2A) am.	21, s. 20(2).
		S. 2(5) am. (*prosp.*) ...	21, s. 17(1).
		S. 4A(1) ext. (*prosp.*) ...	21, s. 2(2).
		S. 6(3)(4) ext. (*prosp.*) ...	21, s. 16.
		S. 9(3) ext. (*prosp.*) ...	21, ss. 4(1), 17.
		S. 10 ext. (*prosp.*) ...	21, s. 17.
		appl. (mod.) (*prosp.*)	21, s. 19(5).
		S. 11(1) ext. (*prosp.*) ...	21, s. 17.
		S. 11(2) am. (*prosp.*) ...	21, s. 17(4).
		S. 11(3)(4) ext. (*prosp.*)...	21, s. 17.
		S. 13 ext. (*prosp.*) ...	21, s. 17(4).
		S. 13(1)(4) ext. (*prosp.*)...	21, s. 13(1).
		S. 15(3) am. (*prosp.*) ...	21, s. 22(3).
		S. 16 am.	S.I. No. 388.
		Sch. 1 cont. until 31.12. 1970.	61, s. 2(1).
		para. 2 ext.(*prosp.*)	21, s. 16.
		para. 2(5) am. (*prosp.*).	21, s. 3(1).
		para. 3 am.(*prosp.*)	21, s. 21(1).
		para. 3(3) am. (*prosp.*).	21, ss. 2, 5, sch. 2 para. 6.
		para. 4 am.(*prosp.*)	21, ss. 2, 5, 12, sch. 2 para. 5, sch. 3 para. 1.
		para. 8(1) am. (*prosp.*).	21, s. 2, sch. 2.
		paras. 8(2), 9 am. (*prosp.*).	21, s. 5(1).
		Sch. 2 (exc. para. 2(1)) ext. (*prosp.*).	21, s. 17(1).
		Sch. 2 appl. (mod.) (*prosp.*).	21, s. 19(5).
		Sch. 3 para. 2 ext.(*prosp.*)	21, s. 3(4).
		am.(*prosp.*)	21, s. 19(1).
c. 27	Recorded Delivery Service Act 1962.	S. 1(3)(4) expld.... ...	48, s. 5.
c. 30	Northern Ireland Act 1962.	S. 1(8) saved	58, s. 16(2).
		S. 2(1)(*j*) added... ...	58, s. 35(1), sch. 1.
		S. 2(3) saved	58, s. 16(2).
		S. 7 am.	58, ss. 20, 21(4).
		Sch. 1 rep. in pt.... ...	58, s. 35(2), sch. 2.
c. 33	Health Visiting and Social Work (Training) Act 1962.	S. 7(2) am.	S.I. No. 388.

Session and Chap. or No. of Measure	Short title or Subject	How affected	Chapter of 1969 Act or number of Measure or Statutory Instrument
10 & 11 Eliz. 2: —*cont.* c. 36	Local Authorities (Historic Buildings) Act 1962.	S. 1(1)(*b*) am. (S.)(*prosp.*)	30, s. 58.
c. 37	Building Societies Act 1962.	Ss. 9, 47 am. (S) ...	39, s. 1(3), sch 1. Pt. I.
		am. (E.) ...	46, s. 1(3), sch. 1 Pt. I.
		Ss. 125(2)(4), 133(2)(5) rep.	52, S.L. (Repeals).
c. 38	Town and Country Planning Act 1962.	S. 12 ext....	48, s. 76, sch. 4 para. 93(1).
		S. 17(2)(3) ext. ...	30, s. 64(7), sch. 6 para. 10(*c*).
		Ss. 17(2)(3), 22 appl.(mod.)	30, s. 64(7), sch. 6 para. 8(2).
		S. 22(5) excl.	30, s. 64(7), sch. 6 para. 11(2).
		S. 23 appl. (mod.) ...	30, s. 64(7), sch. 6 para. 8(2).
		S. 23(5) excl.	30, s. 64(7), sch. 6 para. 11(2).
		Ss. 38, 39 Transfer of functions.	S.I. No. 1498.
		S. 41 appl. (mod.) ...	30, s. 64(7), sch. 6 para. 8(3).
		Ss. 41, 70(2), 81–83, 103 ext.	48, s. 76, sch. 4 para. 93(1).
		S. 103(3) expld. (" operational land ").	48, s. 76, sch. 4 para. 93(4).
		S. 127 appl.	35, s. 36, sch. 5 para. 22(4).
		S. 128 appl.	48, s. 57(4).
		Ss. 130–133, 138, 148(6) ext.	48, s. 76, sch. 4 para. 93(1).
		Ss. 139–151 ext. (mod.)...	33, s. 34.
		S. 148(6) expld.	48, s. 76, sch. 4 para. 93(2).
		S. 152 ext.	33, s. 34.
		S. 158(1)–(3) am. ...	48, s. 76, sch. 4 para. 71(2)–(5).
		Pt. X (Ss. 159–175) ext....	48, s. 76, sch. 4 para. 93(1).
		expld.	48, s. 76, sch. 4 para. 93(2).
		expld. (" operational land ").	48, s. 76, sch. 4 para. 93(4).
		Ss. 179(7)(*b*), 189 ext. ...	48, s. 76, sch. 4 para. 93(1).
		S. 193(3) proviso rep. ...	48, s. 141, sch. 11 Pt. II.
		Ss. 211(6), 212(1)–(3)(6) appl. (mod.).	48, s. 57(2).
		S. 212(6)(*b*) ext.	48, s. 76, sch. 4 para. 93(1).
		expld. ...	48, s. 76, sch. 4 para. 93(2).
		Sch. 14 para. 50 expld. ...	48, s. 76, sch. 4 para. 71(6).

Session and Chap. or No. of Measure	Short title or Subject	How affected	Chapter of 1969 Act or number of Measure or Statutory Instrument
10 & 11 Eliz. 2 *—cont.*			
c. 40	Jamaica Independence Act 1962.	S. 3(5) rep. in pt. ...	52, S.L. (Repeals).
		Sch. 2 para 1 rep. ...	32, s. 61(6), sch. 21 Pt. IX.
c. 44	Finance Act 1962 ...	S. 5(1) appl.	32, s. 6(2), sch. 12 pt II para. 1.
		Pt. II Ch. II (ss. 10–16) expld. ...	32, s. 42, sch. 19 para. 9.
		excl.	32, s. 42, sch. 19 para. 22(1).
		am.	32, s. 60, sch. 20 para. 9(3).
		ext.	32, s. 42, sch. 19 para. 15(1).
		S. 10(1) proviso rep. ...	32, ss. 60, 61(6), sch. 20 para. 3 (*a*), sch. 21 Pt. IX.
		S. 12(6) proviso am. ...	32, s. 42, sch. 19 para. 8(3).
		S. 12(9) rep. in pt. ...	32, s. 61(6), sch. 21 Pt. X.
		S. 16(1) definitions of " company " rep.	32, s. 61(6), sch. 21 Pt. IX.
		" legatee " am. ...	32, s. 42, sch. 19 para. 6(1).
		Ss. 16(4) rep. in pt., 17 rep.	32, s. 61(6), sch. 21 Pt. X.
		S. 22(4) rep.	32, s. 61(6), sch. 21 Pt. IX.
		Ss. 23, 24, 25(1)(2) restr.	32, s. 32(15).
		Sch. 9 para. 8 appl. ...	32, s. 41(7), sch. 18 Pt. III para. 4(3).
		para. 14 rep. ...	32, ss. 42, 61(6), sch. 19 para. 15(6), sch. 21 Pt. VI.
		para. 15A added...	32, s. 42, sch. 19 para. 3(2).
		para. 20 rep. ...	32, s. 61(6), sch. 21 Pt. IX.
c. 46	Transport Act 1962 ...	Ss. 1(1) rep. in pt., (4), 3(2), 7, 8 rep.	35, s. 47(2), sch. 6.
		Ss. 11, 12 ext. (mod.) (L.T.E.).	35, s. 6(2).
		S. 13(3) rep. in pt. ...	35, s. 47(2), sch. 6.
		S. 14(1)–(4) ext. (mod.) (L.T.E.).	35, s. 6(2).
		S. 14(3)(4) excl. (L.T.E.)	35, s. 6(3).
		S. 15 ext. (L.T.E.) ...	35, s. 6(2)(6).
		Ss. 16, 17(1)(2) ext. (mod.) (L.T.E.).	35, s. 6(2).
		S. 19(3)(ii) rep.	35, s. 47(2), sch. 6.
		S. 20 am. (L.T.E.) ...	35, s. 19(1)(*a*).
		Ss. 25(1)(2), 43 ext. (mod.) (L.T.E.).	35, s. 6(2).

Session and Chap. or No. of Measure	Short title or Subject	How affected	Chapter of 1969 Act or number of Measure or Statutory Instrument
10 & 11 Eliz. 2: c. 46—*cont.*	Transport Act 1962—*cont.*	S. 39 am. (L.T.E.) ... S. 43 mod. (London) ... S. 43(1)(*b*) am.	35, s. 19(1)(*a*). 35, s. 28. 35, s. 17(1), sch. 3 para. 4.
		Ss. 44–49 rep.	35, ss. 27(1), 47 (2), sch. 6.
		Ss. 52(4), 54(1) am. (L.T.E.). S. 56(7)–(9), (13) am. (L.T.E.).	35, s. 17(1), sch. 3 para. 1(1)(2). 35, s. 25(1).
		S. 57(2) am. ... ... Ss. 57(3)(*a*) rep., 58, 59 rep.	35, s. 27(5). 35, s. 47(2), sch. 6.
		S. 60 am. (L.T.E.) ...	35, s. 17(1), sch. 3 para. 1(1)(2).
		S. 65 am. (L.T.E.) ...	35, s. 17(1), sch. 3 para. 3.
		S. 67 am. (L.T.E.) ...	35, s. 17(1), sch. 3 para. 5(1).
		S. 67(2) ext. (L.T.E.) ...	35, s. 17(1), sch.3 para. 5(2).
		S. 68 expld.	35, s. 17(1), sch. 3 para. 6(1).
		S. 70 am. (L.T.E.) ...	35, s. 17(1), sch. 3 para. 7(3).
		S. 74 ext. (L.T.E.) ... Ss. 82, 83(7) am. (L.T.E.)	35, s. 18. 35, s. 17(1), sch. 3 para. 1(1)(2).
		S. 85(1) rep. in pt. ... S. 86 am. (L.T.E.) ...	35, s. 47(2), sch. 6. 35, s. 17(1), sch. 3 para. 1(1)(2).
		S. 92(1) definitions of " the London Passenger Transport Area ", " the London Special Area " rep.	35, s. 47(2), sch. 6.
		Sch. 2 am. (L.T.E.) ...	35, s. 17(1), sch. 3 para. 1(1)(2).
		Sch. 2 Pt. I rep. in pt. ... Sch. 6 (exc. para. 2(3)) am. (L.T.E.). Sch. 7 Pt. II rep., sch. 10 para. 9 rep. in pt.	35, s. 47(2), sch. 6. 35, s. 17(1), sch. 3 para. 1(1)(2). 35, s. 47(2), sch. 6.
c. 47	Education (Scotland) Act 1962.	Ss. 1–3 replaced S. 2 power to appl. (mod.) S. 4(*a*) am., (*c*) subst. ...	49, s. 1. 49, s. 21. 49, s. 27(1), sch. 2 Pt. I para. 1.
		S. 5 subst.	49, s. 27(1), sch. 2 Pt. I para. 2
		S. 6 subst.	49, s. 27(1), sch. 2 Pt. I para. 3.
		S. 7(1)(*c*), (4), (6), (8) am.	49 s. 27(1), sch. 2 Pt. I para. 4.
		S. 9(2) rep.	49, s. 27, sch. 2 Pt. I para. 5, sch. 3.
		S. 10(2) am.	49, s. 27(1), sch. 2 Pt. I para. 6.

Session and Chap. or No. of Measure	Short title or Subject	How affected	Chapter of 1969 Act or number of Measure or Statutory Instrument
10 & 11 Eliz. 2: c. 47—_cont._	Education (Scotland) Act 1962—_cont._	S. 11(1) am. (_temp._) ...	49, s. 27(1), sch. 2 Pt. I para. 7(1).
		am. (1.8.1970) ...	49, s. 27(1), sch. 2 Pt. I para. 7(2) (_a_).
		S. 11(2) rep. (1.8.1970) ...	49, s. 27, sch. 2 Pt. I para. 7(2) (_b_), sch. 3.
		S. 11(3)(_b_), am. (1.8.1970)	49, s. 27(1), sch. 2 Pt. I para. 7(2) (_c_).
		S. 12 am.	49, s. 27(1), sch. 2 Pt. I para. 8.
		S. 14 rep. in pt.	49, s. 27, sch. 2 Pt. I para. 9, sch. 3.
		S. 15(1) rep. in pt., (2) rep.	49, s. 27, sch. 2 Pt. I para. 10, sch. 3.
		S. 18(1) rep. in pt. ...	49, s. 27, sch. 2 Pt. I para. 11 (_a_), sch. 3.
		S. 18(3) proviso am. ...	49 s. 27(1), sch. 2, Pt. I para. 11 (_b_).
		S. 19(1) subst.	49, s. 3.
		Power to appl. (mod.).	49, s. 21.
		S. 19(2) rep.	49, s. 27, sch. 2 Pt. I para. 12 (_a_), sch. 3.
		S. 19(3)(4) subst. ...	49, s. 27(1), sch. 2 Pt. I para. 12 (_b_)(_c_).
		S. 19(5) rep.	49, s. 27, sch. 2 Pt. I para. 12 sch. 3.
		S. 20(1) am.	49, s. 27(1), sch. 2 Pt. I para. 13.
		S. 20(1A) added ...	49, s. 4.
		S. 22(1A)(1B) added ...	49, s. 5(1).
		S. 24(1)–(4) am. ...	49, s. 27(1), sch. 2 Pt. I para. 14 (_a_)–(_c_).
		S. 24(5) rep.	49, s. 27, sch. 2 Pt. I para. 14 (_d_), sch. 3.
		Ss. 25, 26 replaced ...	49, s. 6.
		S. 28 rep. in pt.	49, s. 27, sch. 2 Pt. I para. 15, sch. 3.
		S. 30 subst.	49, s. 7.
		S. 32(4) am.	49, s. 27(1), sch. 2 Pt. I para. 16.
		S. 33(1) proviso subst. ...	49, s. 8.
		S. 35(2) rep.	49, s. 27, sch. 2 Pt. I para. 17, sch. 3.
		S. 38(1), (2), (_b_) am. ...	49, s. 27, sch. 2 Pt. I para. 18.

Session and Chap. or No. of Measure	Short title or Subject	How affected	Chapter of 1969 Act or number of Measure or Statutory Instrument
10 & 11 Eliz. 2: c. 47—*cont.*	Education (Scotland) Act 1962—*cont.*	S. 40 proviso am. ...	49, s. 27(1), sch. 2 Pt. I para. 19.
		S. 49 am.	49, s. 27(1), sch. 2 Pt. I para. 20.
		S. 50(1) am.	49, s. 27(1), sch. 2 Pt. I para. 21.
		S. 54(4)(*b*) am.	49, s. 27(1), sch. 2 Pt. I para. 22.
		S. 57 subst.	49, s. 27(1), sch. 2 Pt. I para. 23.
		S. 58(1) rep. in pt. ...	49, s. 27, sch. 2 Pt. I para. 24 (*a*), sch. 3.
		S. 58(1)(2) am.	49, s. 27(1), sch. 2 Pt. I para. 24.
		S. 58A added	49, s. 9.
		S. 60(2) rep. in pt. ...	49, s. 27, sch. 2 Pt. I, para. 25 (*a*), sch. 3.
		S. 60(2)–(4) am.... ...	49, s. 27(1), sch. 2 Pt. I para. 25.
		Ss. 62–66 replaced ...	49, s. 10.
		S. 67(1) am.	49, s. 11.
		S. 75 subst. (saving) ...	49, s. 12(1)(2).
		S. 76(1) Power to appl. (mod.).	49, s. 21.
		S. 76(3) rep. (1.8.1972)...	49, s. 27, sch. 2 Pt. I para. 26, sch. 3.
		S. 77 rep.	49, ss. 13(1), 27 (2), sch. 3.
		S. 78 rep.	49, ss. 14, 28(2), sch. 3.
		S. 79 am.	49, s. 27(1), sch. 2 Pt. I para. 27.
		S. 80 rep.	49, ss. 14, 27(2), sch. 3.
		S. 81 subst.	49, s. 15.
		S. 84 rep.	49, ss. 17, 27(2), sch. 3.
		S. 85 am. (saving) ...	49, s. 18.
		S. 85(1) am.	49, s. 27(1), sch. 2 Pt. I para. 28 (*a*).
		S. 85(5)(*b*) rep.	49, s. 27, sch. 2 Pt. I para. 29 (*b*), sch. 3.
		S. 87 rep.	49, ss. 17, 27(2), sch. 3.
		S. 91(1), am., (2)(*d*) added	49, s. 27(1), sch. 2 Pt. I para. 29.
		S. 94 rep.	49, s. 27, sch. 2 Pt. I para. 30, sch. 3.
		S. 97(1) am.	49, s. 27(1), sch. 2 Pt. I para. 31 (*a*).
		S. 97(2) rep.	49, s. 27, sch. 2 Pt. I para. 31 (*b*), sch. 3.

Session and Chap. or No. of Measure	Short title or Subject	How affected	Chapter of 1969 Act or number of Measure or Statutory Instrument
10 & 11 Eliz. 2: c. 47—*cont.*	Education (Scotland) Act 1962—*cont.*	S. 98 rep.	49, s. 27, sch. 2 Pt. I para. 32, sch. 3.
		S. 118(5) am.	49, s. 27(1), sch. 2 Pt. I para. 33.
		S. 119(3) rep. in pt. ...	49, ss. 5(2), 27(2), sch. 3.
		S. 123(2) am.	49, s. 27(1), sch. 2 Pt. I para. 34.
		S. 124(3) rep. in pt. ...	49, s. 27, sch. 2 Pt. I para. 35 (*a*), sch. 3.
		S. 124(3)–(5) am. ...	49, s. 27(1), sch. 2 Pt. I para. 35 (*a*)(*b*).
		S. 124(6) rep. ...	49, s. 27, sch. 2 Pt. I para. 35 (*c*), sch. 3.
		S. 124(7) am.	49, s. 27(1), sch. 2 Pt. I para. 35 (*d*).
		Ss. 125–127 subst. ...	49, s. 19.
		S. 128 am.	49, ss. 20, 27(1), sch. 2 Pt. I para. 36.
		S. 129 am.	49, s. 27(1), sch. 2 Pt. I para. 37.
		S. 133 am.	49, s. 27(1), sch. 2 Pt. I para. 38.
		S. 135(1)(*aa*) added, (1) (*c*) subst., (3) added.	49, s. 27(1), sch. 2 Pt. 1 para. 39.
		S. 137(3) am.	49, s. 22.
		S. 141(2)(*b*) subst. ...	49, s. 27(1), sch. 2 Pt. I para. 40.
		S. 144(2)(3) rep.... ...	49, ss. 23, 27(2), sch. 3.
		S. 145 para. (1) rep. ...	49, s. 27, sch. 2 Pt. I para. 41 (*a*), sch. 3.
		paras. (11) am., (14)subst., (15A)–(15C) added (17) am., (19A) added.	4 9, s. 27(1), sch. 2 Pt. I para. 41 (*b*)–(*f*).
		para. (21) rep. in pt.	49, s. 27, sch. 2 Pt. I para. 41 (*g*), sch. 3.
		para. (22) am. ...	49, s. 27(1), sch. 2 Pt. I para. 41 (*h*).
		para. (28) rep. in pt.	49, s. 27, sch. 2 Pt. I para. 41 (*i*), sch. 3.
		paras. (30) (31) am.	49, s. 27(1), sch. 2 Pt. I para. 41 (*j*)(*k*).
		para. (35) rep. in pt.	49, s. 27, sch. 2 Pt. I para. 41 (*l*), sch. 3.
		paras. (36) am., (38A)(41A)(43A)added, (44)(45) am., (48) subst.	49, s. 27(1), sch. 2 Pt. I para. 41 (*m*)–(*s*).

Session and Chap. or No. of Measure	Short title or Subject	How affected	Chapter of 1969 Act or number of Measure or Statutory Instrument
10 & 11 Eliz. 2:			
c. 47—*cont.*	Education (Scotland) Act 1962—*cont.*	Sch. 2 rep.	49, ss. 13(1), 27 (2), sch. 3.
c. 52	Penalties for Drunkenness Act 1962.	S. 1(2)(*a*) rep. in pt. ...	53, s. 14 sch.
c. 54	Trinidad and Tobago Independence Act 1962.	S. 3(4) rep. in pt. ...	52, S.L. (Repeals).
		Sch. 2 para. 1 rep. ...	32, s. 61(6), sch. 21 Pt. IX.
c. 57	Uganda Independence Act 1962.	S. 3(4) rep. in pt. ...	52, S.L. (Repeals).
		Sch. 3 para. 1 rep. ...	32, s. 61(6), sch. 21 Pt. IX.
c. 58	Pipe-lines Act 1962 ...	Ext.	48, s. 76, sch. 4 para. 93(1).
		Expld. ...	48, s. 76, sch. 4 para. 93(2).
		S. 13 expld. (" operational land ").	48, s. 76, sch. 4 para. 93(4).
		S. 40(1) expld. ...	48, s. 76, sch. 4 para. 72.
		S. 68(2) rep. in pt. ...	48, s. 141, sch. 11 Pt. II.
c. 59	Road Traffic Act 1962 ...	S. 4(1) rep. in pt. (*prosp.*)	27, s. 37, sch. 3.
		S. 46 rep. (*prosp.*) ...	27, s. 37, sch. 3.
		Sch. 4 rep. in pt. ...	35, s. 47(2), sch. 6.
11 & 12 Eliz. 2:			
c. 1	Tanganyika Republic Act 1962.	Power to rep.	29, s. 5.
		S. 1(1) rep. in pt., (2)(3) rep.	52, S.L. (Repeals).
c. 2	Pensions (Increase) Act 1962.	S. 1 ext.	7, s. 2(1), sch. 3 paras. 1–5.
		S. 3 am.	7, s. 2(2).
		S. 3(3) am.	7, s. 1(4), sch. 2 para. 9.
		S. 3(4) rep.	7, s. 2(3).
		S. 3(5)(*b*) am.	7, s. 1(4), sch. 2 para. 9.
		Sch. 3 am.	7, s. 2(2).
1963:			
c. 2	Betting, Gaming and Lotteries Act 1963.	S. 22(1)(3) am. (S.) ...	39, s. 1(3), sch. 1 Pt. I.
		am. (E.) ...	46, s. 1(3), sch. 1 Pt. I.
		S. 24 am.	14, s. 6.
		S. 25(2)(*a*) am.	14, s. 7(3).
		S. 27 am.	14, s. 1(2)–(8).
		S. 27(5) rep. and superseded (1.4.1970).	14, ss. 1(1), 7(4).
		S. 28(1)–(4) rep.... ...	14, ss. 2(1), 7(4).
		S. 28(10) am.	14, s. 2(5).
		S. 29 ext.	14, s. 3(1).
		S. 30(1) am. (1.4.1970) ...	14, s. 5(1).
		S. 30(2) rep. (1.4.1970) ...	14, s. 7(4).
		S. 32(1)(*b*) am.	32, s. 3(8).
		S. 40 rep. in pt.	53, s. 14, sch.
		S. 54(1)(3) appl. ...	32, ss. 3(7), 5(10), sch. 9 paras. 3, 4, sch. 11 para. 9(3).

Session and Chap. or No. of Measure	Short title or Subject	How affected	Chapter of 1969 Act or number of Measure or Statutory Instrument
1963:			
c. 2—*cont.*	Betting, Gaming and Lotteries Act 1963—*cont.*	Sch. 1 para. 15(*ee*) added	14, s. 4(4).
		para. 16(1) expld.	32, s. 2(9), sch. 8 para. 15.
		para. 16(2) saved	14, s. 4(5).
		paras. 17(*b*), 27(4) (*a*) expld.	32, s. 2(9), sch. 8 para. 15.
		Sch. 5 para. 3 am. ...	17, s. 1.
		para. 5 subst. (15.2.1971).	19, s. 10(3), sch. 2 para. 17.
c. 9	Purchase Tax Act 1963 ...	S. 21(1)(3)(4) am. ...	32, s. 55(1)–(3).
		Sch. 1 Pt. I am.	32, s. 1(4), sch. 6.
		Pt. I am. ...	S.I. No. 1736.
		rep. in pt. ...	32, ss. 1(4), 61(6), sch. 6, sch. 21 Pt. I.
c. 11	Agriculture (Miscellaneous Provisions) Act 1963.	Ss. 5, 10, 11 Transfer of functions.	S.I. No. 388.
		S. 27(2) rep. in pt. ...	48, s. 141, sch. 11 Pt. II.
c. 12	Local Government (Financial Provisions) (Scotland) Act 1963.	Ss. 7(1), 9(1) am. (16.5.1971).	19, s. 10(3), sch. 2 para. 18.
c. 15	Fort William Pulp and Paper Mills Act 1963.	Transfer of functions ...	S.I. No. 1498.
c. 18	Stock Transfer Act 1963	S. 1(4)(*c*) am.	38, s. 108(1)(*f*).
c. 25	Finance Act 1963 ...	S. 12(2)(5) rep.	32, s. 61(6), sch. 21 Pt. IV.
		Ss. 14(1)(*b*), 15(1)(2) am.	32, s. 60, sch. 20 para. 1(1).
		S. 15(4) am.	32, s. 60, sch. 20 para. 20(1).
		S. 16(4)(5) appl. ...	32, s. 60, sch. 20 para. 20(2).
		S. 16(6) rep. in pt. ...	32, ss. 60, 61(6), sch. 20 para. 17(14)(*a*), sch. 21 Pt. IX.
		am.	32, s. 60, sch. 20 para. 17(14).
		S. 17 ext.	32, s. 60, sch. 20 para. 20(3).
		S. 18 appl.	32, s. 60, sch. 20 para. 20(4).
		S. 22(4) am. (*retrosp.*) ...	32, s. 34(5).
		S. 22(6) am.	32, s. 60, sch. 20 para. 20(5).
		S. 25(5) proviso rep. ...	32, s. 34(2).
		S. 25(5)(*a*) rep. in pt. and am.	32, s. 34(1).
		S. 25(5)(*b*) am.	32, s. 34(2).
		S. 25(5)(*c*) added ...	32, s. 34(4).
		S. 28(2) rep.	32, s. 61(6), sch. 21 Pt. IX.
		S. 28(3) am.	32, s. 60, sch. 20 para. 2(5).
		S. 29(1) rep. in pt. ...	32, s. 61(6), sch. 21 Pt. X.
		S. 29(5)–(7) ext. ...	32, s. 32(6).
		S. 30 appl.	32, s. 60, sch. 20 para. 20(4).

Session and Chap. or No. of Measure	Short title or Subject	How affected	Chapter of 1969 Act or number of Measure or Statutory Instrument
1963: c. 25—*cont.*	Finance Act 1963—*cont.*	S. 31(2) appl.	32, s. 18(7), sch. 13 para. 6(2).
		S. 32(1) am.	32, s. 60, sch. 20 para. 10.
		S. 43(1)(*c*) added ...	32, s. 18(7), sch. 13 para. 16.
		S. 43(4)(*a*) rep. ...	32, s. 61(6), sch. 21 Pt. II.
		S. 47(3) am.	32, s. 60, sch. 20 para. 10.
		S. 50 appl.	32, s. 26(4).
		S. 53(2) am.	32, s. 40(1), sch. 17 Pt. III para. 26.
		Sch. 4 para. 1 expld. ...	32, s. 19(5).
		para. 1 am. (*retrosp.*).	32, s. 34(6).
		para. 1 proviso added.	32, s. 18(7), sch. 13 para. 26.
		para. 7(2) am. ...	32, s. 60, sch. 20 para. 20(1).
		para. 17 excl. ...	32, s. 34(7).
		para. 19 ext. and restr.	32, s. 60, sch. 20 para. 20(6).
c. 31	Weights and Measures Act 1963.	S. 10(7) am.	S.I. No. 388.
		S. 64(1)(*a*) rep. in pt. ...	48, s. 141, sch. 11 Pt. II.
c. 33	London Government Act 1963.	S. 14(6)(*d*) rep. in pt. ...	35, s. 47(2), sch. 6.
		S. 17(1)–(3) rep. (*prosp.*)	35, ss. 29(1), 47(2), sch. 6.
		S. 17(4) rep. in pt. (*prosp.*) (6) rep. (*prosp.*).	35, s. 47(2), sch. 6.
		S. 18(1A) added (*prosp.*)	35, s. 29(4).
		S. 20 rep. (*prosp.*) ...	27, s. 37, sch. 3.
		S. 24(6) Power to am. (*prosp.*).	35, s. 30(1).
		S. 47(1)(3) rep. in pt. (*prosp.*)	54, s. 72(4), sch. 6.
		S. 72(2)(*h*) added ...	35, s. 6(4).
		S. 84 ext. (*prosp.*) ...	35, s. 29(6).
		S. 85(4) Pensions increase	7, s. 1(1), sch. 1 Pt. I paras. 28, 40, Pt. II paras. 6, 9.
		S. 89(1) definition of " metropolitan road " rep. (*prosp.*).	35, s. 47(2), sch. 6.
		Sch. 2 paras. 25–29 excl.	35, s. 8(4).
		para. 27(2)(*bb*) added	35, s. 8(4).
		Sch. 3 paras. 2(1) rep. in pt., (2) rep., 3(1) rep. in pt., (2) rep., 4–12 rep. (saving).	15, s. 24(4), sch. 3 Pt. I.
		paras. 13, 14 ext.	15, s. 26(2).
		paras. 13(2), 14(2), 21 rep. in pt.	15, s. 24(4), sch. 3 Pt. I.

Session and Chap. or No. of Measure	Short title or Subject	How affected	Chapter of 1969 Act or number of Measure or Statutory Instrument
1963: c. 33—*cont.*	London Government Act 1963—*cont.*	Sch. 3—*cont.*	
		para. 25 rep. ...	15, s. 24(4), sch. 3 Pt. II.
		paras. 26, 31, 32 rep. in pt., 36 rep.	15, s. 24(4), sch. 3 Pt. I.
		Sch. 5 Pt. I para. 24 rep. (*prosp.*).	27, s. 37, sch. 3.
		Sch. 5 Pt. I para. 26 rep., sch. 6 para. 68 rep. (*prosp.*), sch. 7, sch. 17 para. 7 rep.	35, s. 47(2), sch. 6.
		Sch. 17 para. 18(*c*) rep. (*prosp.*)	54, s. 72(4), sch. 6.
		para. 26(*a*)(*c*) rep.	35, s. 47(2), sch. 6.
c. 37	Children and Young Persons Act 1963.	S. 1 appl. (E.)	54, s. 68(1).
		Ss. 1(4) rep., 2 rep. (*prosp.*).	54, s. 72(4), sch. 6.
		S. 3(1) am. (*prosp.*) ...	54, s. 72(3), sch. 5 para. 47.
		Ss. 4–9 rep. (*prosp.*) ...	54, s. 72(4), sch. 6.
		S. 10 rep. (*prosp.*) ...	54, ss. 72(4), 73(4)(*d*), sch. 6.
		Ss. 11–15, 22 rep. (*prosp.*), 23(1) rep. in pt. (*prosp.*)	54, s. 72(4), sch. 6.
		S. 23(1)(*b*) am. (*prosp.*) ...	54, s. 72(3), sch. 5 para. 48.
		S. 23(2) rep. (*prosp.*), (3) rep. in pt. (*prosp.*)	54, s. 72(4), sch. 6.
		S. 23(5) am. (*prosp.*) ...	54, s. 72(3), sch. 5 para. 48.
		Ss. 24 rep. (*prosp*), 25(1) rep. in pt. (*prosp.*), (2) rep. (*prosp.*), 29(1) rep. in pt. (*prosp.*)	54, s. 72(4), sch. 6.
		S. 29(1) am. (*prosp.*) ...	54, s. 72(3), sch. 5 para. 49.
		S. 29(2) rep. (*prosp.*) ...	54, s. 72(3)(4), sch. 5 para. 49, sch. 6.
		S. 30(1)(3)–(5) am. (*prosp.*)	54, s. 72(3), sch. 5 para. 50.
		S. 33 rep. (*prosp.*) ...	54, s. 72(4), sch. 6.
		S. 45(1) am.	54, s. 72(3), sch. 5 para. 51.
		S. 49(1) am.	54, s. 72(3), sch. 5 para. 52.
		Ss. 53(1)(2) rep. (*prosp.*), 55 rep. in pt. (*prosp.*)	54, ss. 72(4), 73(4)(*d*), sch. 6.
		S. 57(3) subst. (*prosp.*) ...	54, ss. 72(3), 73(4)(*c*), sch. 5 para. 53.
		S. 59 rep. (*prosp.*) ...	54, ss. 72(4), 73(4)(*d*), sch. 6.

Session and Chap. or No. of Measure	Short title or Subject	How affected	Chapter of 1969 Act or number of Measure or Statutory Instrument
1963: c. 37—*cont.*	Children and Young Persons Act 1963—*cont.*	Ss. 61 rep. (*prosp.*), 65(5) rep. in pt. (*prosp.*), sch. 1 rep. (*prosp.*), sch. 3 paras. 10, 15–23, 25–27, 33–36, 44, 46, 48, 49 rep. (*prosp.*), 50 rep. in pt. (*prosp.*)	54, s. 72(4), sch. 6.
c. 38	Water Resources Act 1963	Ss. 6(3), 8(4) Transfer of functions.	S.I. No. 388.
		S. 67 am.	48, s. 76, sch. 4 para. 74(1).
		Ss. 87(6)(7)(9), 121(2)(3) am. (1.4.1971).	19, s. 10(3), sch. 2 para. 19.
		S. 130 expld.	48, s. 76, sch. 4 para. 74(2).
		S. 130(2) rep.	48, s. 76, sch. 4 para. 74(2).
		Sch. 4 para. 6, sch. 12 Transfer of functions.	S.I. No. 388.
c. 39	Criminal Justice (Scotland) Act 1963.	Sch. 5 rep. in pt. (*prosp.*)	54, s. 72(4) sch. 6.
c. 40	Commonwealth Development Act 1963.	S. 1(1)(3)(5) rep. ...	36, s. 3(3)(*b*).
c. 46	Local Government (Financial Provisions) Act 1963.	S. 6(2)(5)(6) am. (15.2.1971).	19, s. 10(3), sch. 2 para. 20.
c. 49	Contracts of Employment Act 1963.	Sch. 1 para. 10(3) saved (L.T.E.).	35, s. 16(3), sch. 2 para. 6.
c. 51	Land Compensation (Scotland) Act 1963.	Appl. (mod.)	34, s. 10.
		Ext.	34, s. 14(4).
		Excl. (*prosp.*)	30, s. 53(4).
		Appl.	30, s. 31, sch. 2 para. 6.
		Expld. (*prosp.*) ...	30, s. 105, sch. 9 para. 6.
		S. 3 appl.	30, s. 31, sch. 2 para. 13.
		Ss. 3, 5 appl. (mod.) (temp.).	30, s. 102(3).
		S. 16 rep. in pt. ...	30, s. 107, sch. 11.
		S. 18 ext.	48, s. 76, sch. 4 para. 93(1).
		S. 45(1) rep. in pt. ...	30, s. 107, sch. 11.
		Sch. 2 paras. 1(1)(2) am., (5) subst., (6), 2(1)(3), 3(1) am.	34, s. 69(2), sch. 6 para. 2.
		Sch. 2 para. 5(2) rep. ...	34, s. 69(3), sch. 7.
		Sch. 2 para. 1(2) mod. ...	34, s. 18(1).
c. 54	Kenya Independence Act 1963.	S. 4(4)(5) rep. in pt. ...	52, S.L. (Repeals).
		Sch. 2 para. 1 rep. ...	32, s. 61(6), sch. 21 Pt. IX.
c. 55	Zanzibar Act 1963 ...	Power to rep.	29, s. 5.
		Ss. 4 rep., 5(1)(2) rep. in pt.	52, S.L. (Repeals).
		Sch. 1 Pt. I para. 1 rep. ...	32, s. 61(6), sch. 21 Pt. IX.
c. 57	Nigeria Republic Act 1963	S. 2(1) rep., (2) rep. in pt., (3) rep.	52, S.L. (Repeals).

Session and Chap. or No. of Measure	Short title or Subject	How affected	Chapter of 1969 Act or number of Measure or Statutory Instrument
1963—*cont.*			
c. 59	Electricity and Gas Act 1963.	S. 1(3) rep. ... ... S. 2(2) am. ... ... Sch. 3 am.	1, s. 1(4)(*a*). 1, s. 1(4)(*b*). 1, s. 1(1).
C.A.M. No. 1... ...	Ecclesiastical Jurisdiction Measure 1963.	Expld. (*prosp.*)	C.A.M. No. 2, s. 3(6).
1964 c. 4	Trustee Savings Banks Act 1964.	Rep.	50, s. 96(1), sch. 3 Pt. I.
c. 11	Navy, Army and Air Force Reserves Act 1964.	S. 1 rep.	23, s. 1(2).
c. 20	Uganda Act 1964 ...	S. 2(1) rep., (2) rep. in pt., (3) rep.	52, S.L. (Repeals).
c. 21	Television Act 1964 ...	Expld. ... ... S. 2(6) rep. in pt. ... S. 13(4) Table subst. ... S. 29(2) rep.	48, s. 3(1). 48, s. 141, sch. 11 Pt. II. S.I. No. 875. 48, s. 141, sch. 11 Pt. II.
c. 24	Trade Union (Amalgamations, etc.) Act 1964.	S. 11(2)(3), sch. 3 rep. ...	52, S.L. (Repeals).
c. 26	Licensing Act 1964 ...	S. 30(5) am. (15.2.1971)... S. 100(2) appl. ... ... S. 100(2)(*a*) am. ... S. 101 appl. ... ... Pt. VII (ss. 118–131) cont. until 31.3.1971. Sch. 8 paras. 4, 5(1)(*c*), appx. Form D am. (16.2.1970).	19, s. 10(3), sch. 2 para. 21. 53, s. 11(4). 53, s. 13(3). 53, s. 11(4). 61, s. 2(2). 15, s. 24(2).
c. 28	Agriculture and Horticulture Act 1964.	Ss. 2, 3 Transfer of functions.	S.I. No. 388.
c. 37	Income Tax Management Act 1964.	S. 4(3)(4) excl. ... ... S. 5(8) rep. (6.4.1970) ... S. 7(8) expld. ... ... S. 9 appl. ... ... S. 9(4)(*a*) am. ... ... Ss. 9(12) rep. (6.4.1970), 12(1) rep. in pt. (6.4.1970). S. 12(2) ext. ... ... S. 12(6) rep. in pt. (6.4.1970). S. 15(2)(*a*) am. ... ... Sch. 4 rep. in pt. (6.4.1970).	32, s. 58(3). 32, s. 61(6), sch. 21 Pt. VIII. 32, s. 60, sch. 20 para. 21(1). 32, s. 25(5). 32, s. 60, sch. 20 para. 21(2). 32, s. 61(6), sch. 21 Pt. VIII. 32, s. 60, sch. 20 para. 12(4). 32, s. 61(6), sch. 21 Pt. VIII. 32, s. 60, sch. 20 para. 21(5). 32, ss. 60, 61(6), sch. 20 para. 21 (5), sch. 21 Pt. VIII.
c. 40	Harbours Act 1964 ...	Ss. 14–16, 31, 33, sch. 3 para. 6 Transfer of functions.	S.I. No. 388.

Session and Chap. or No. of Measure	Short title or Subject	How affected	Chapter of 1969 Act or number of Measure or Statutory Instrument
1964: c. 40—*cont.*	Harbours Act 1964—*cont.*	Schs. 3, 5 ext.	48, s. 76, sch. 4 para. 93(1).
		expld. ...	48, s. 76, sch. 4 para. 93(2).
c. 42	Administration of Justice Act 1964.	S. 12(2)(3) Power to am.	54, s. 61(4).
c. 44	Nurses Act 1964 ...	S. 3 definition of " the roll " am.	47, s. 10(1), sch. 1 para. 14.
c. 46	Malawi Independence Act 1964.	S. 4(4) rep. in pt., (5) rep., (6) rep. in pt.	52, S.L. (Repeals).
		Sch. 2 para. 1 rep. ...	32, s. 61(6), sch. 21 Pt. IX.
c. 48	Police Act 1964 ...	Pensions increase ...	7, ss. 1(1)(3)(4), 2(1), sch. 1 Pt. I para. 20, Pt. II paras. 8, 10, sch. 2 para. 6, sch. 3 para. 4.
		S. 5(1) excl. (*prosp.*) ...	63, s. 1(3).
		S. 45 rep. (*prosp.*) ...	63, s. 4(8).
		S. 46(3) am. (*prosp.*) ...	63, s. 4(6).
		Sch. 4 para. 2(*c*) added...	63, s. 2(4).
c. 49	Finance Act 1964 ...	S. 4(3) rep. in pt. ...	32, ss. 1(5), 61(6), sch. 7 para 3,. sch. 21 Pt. I.
		am.	32, s. 1(5), sch. 7 para. 3.
		S. 6(1) rep. and replaced	32, ss. 1(7), 61(6), sch. 7 para. 4, sch. 21 Pt. I.
		S. 6(2) am.	32, s. 1(5), sch. 7 para. 5(2).
		S. 6(4) am.	32, s. 1(3)(*c*).
		S. 6(5)(6) expld. ...	32, s. 1(5), sch. 7 para. 5(3).
		S. 11 ext. (*prosp.*) ...	27, s. 11(2)(*d*).
		S. 16 am.	32, s. 60, sch. 20 para. 9(2).
		Sch. 1 Table 1 subst. ...	32, s. 1(2), sch. 1.
		Sch. 2 subst.	32, s. 1(2), sch. 2.
		Sch. 3 subst.	32, s. 1(2), sch. 3.
		Sch. 4 subst.	32, s. 1(2), sch. 4.
		Sch. 5 subst.	32, s. 1(2), sch. 5
		Sch. 6 paras. 1, 2 expld.	32, s. 1(5), sch.7. para. 5(3).
		para. 25 subst. ...	32, s. 1(5), sch. 7 para. 5(4).
		para. 26(1) am. ...	32, s. 1(5), sch. 7 para. 5(5).
		para. 28(*a*) subst.	32, s. 1(5), sch. 7 para. 5(6).
c. 56	Housing Act 1964 ...	S. 9(2) am.	S.I. No. 518.
		S. 13(1)–(3) rep. (E.) ...	33, s. 89(3), sch. 10.
		S. 13(4) excl. (E.) ...	33, s. 41.
		S. 13(5) rep. (E.) ...	33, s. 89(3), sch. 10.
		Ss. 19–21 mod.	33, s. 40(2)(*b*).
		S. 20(4) rep.	33, s. 89(3), sch. 10.

Session and Chap. or No. of Measure	Short title or Subject	How affected	Chapter of 1969 Act or number of Measure or Statutory Instrument
1964:			
c. 56—*cont.*	Housing Act 1964—*cont.*	S. 34(3) am.	33, s. 89(1), sch. 8 para. 25.
		S. 43(1)(*g*) subst. ...	33, s. 89(1), sch. 8 para. 26.
		S. 43(3) am.	33, s. 76.
		S. 43(7) am.	33, s. 89(1), sch. 8 para. 27.
		Pt. III (ss. 45–63) (except ss. 57, 59) rep. (E.).	33, s. 89(3), sch. 10.
		S. 57(4) am.	33, s. 89(1), sch. 8 para. 28.
		Pt. IV (ss. 64–91) mod....	33, s. 40(2)(*b*).
		S. 67(1) am.	33, ss. 58(3), 89 (1), sch. 8 para. 5.
		S. 67(3) rep. in pt. (E.)...	33, ss. 62(2), 89(3), sch. 10.
		S. 68(1)(*b*) ext.	33, s. 61(5).
		S. 69 am.	33, ss. 58(3), 89 (1), sch. 8 paras. 5, 29.
		Ss. 72(1)(a), 73 am. ...	33, ss. 58(3), 89 (1), sch. 8 para. 5.
		S. 78(6) ext.	33, s. 63(9).
		S. 79 mod.	33, s. 63(2).
		S. 91 ext.	33, s. 63(11).
c. 60	Emergency Laws (Re-enactments and Repeals) Act 1964.	S. 3 cont. until 31.12.1974 S. 6 cont. until 31.12.1974 S. 16 cont. until 31.12.1974 S. 17(2) Transfer of functions.	S.I. No. 1836. S.I. No. 1058. S.I. No. 1836. S.I. No. 1498.
c. 65	Zambia Independence Act 1964.	Ss. 9 rep., 10 rep. in pt. ... Sch. 1 para. 1 rep. ...	52, S.L. (Repeals). 32, s. 61(6), sch. 21 Pt. IX.
c. 71	Trading Stamps Act 1964	S. 3(3) am. (15.2.1971) ...	19, s. 10(3), sch. 2 para. 22.
c. 75	Public Libraries and Museums Act 1964.	Sch. 2 para. 2(1) am. (15.2.1971).	19, s. 10(3), sch. 2 para. 23.
c. 81	Diplomatic Privileges Act 1964.	Sch. 1 arts. 34, 37 ext. ...	32, s. 60, sch. 20 para. 8(1)(2).
c. 86	Malta Independence Act 1964.	S. 4(4) rep. in pt., (5) rep., (7) rep. in pt. Sch. 2 para. 1 rep. ...	52, S.L. (Repeals). 32, s. 61(6), sch. 21 Pt. IX.
c. 87	Shipping Contracts and Commercial Documents Act 1964.	S. 2(2) rep. in pt. ...	S.I. No. 1498.
c. 88	Refreshment Houses Act 1964.	Ss. 1–4, sch. para. 1 rep., 2 rep. in pt.	53, s. 14, sch.
c. 92	Finance (No. 2) Act 1964	S. 1(2) rep. in pt. ...	32, s. 61(6), sch. 21 Pt. IV.
		S. 2 am.	32, s. 1(3).
		S. 9(6) rep. in pt. (*prosp.*)	27, s. 37, sch. 3.
c. 93	Gambia Independence Act 1964.	S. 4(4) rep. in pt. (5) rep., (6) rep. in pt. Sch. 2 para. 1 rep. ...	52, S.L. (Repeals). 32, s. 61(6), sch. 21 Pt. IX.

Session and Chap. or No. of Measure	Short title or Subject	How affected	Chapter of 1969 Act or number of Measure or Statutory Instrument
1964—*cont.*			
c. 98 ...	Ministers of the Crown Act 1964.	Excl.	48, s. 136.
		Sch. 1 appl. and expld....	48, s. 2(2).
		restr.	48, s. 2(4).
		Sch. 2 Pt. II rep. in pt. {	48, s. 141, sch. 11 Pt. II. S.I. No. 1498.
C.A.M. No. 3 ...	Churchwardens (Appointment and Resignation) Measure 1964.	S. 2(1) am. ... S. 3(6) restr. ... Ss. 4–6, 11(3) rep.	C.A.M. No. 2, s. 4(1), sch. 3 para. 11(2).
1965:			
c. 2	Administration of Justice Act 1965.	Sch. 1 rep. in pt. ...	48, s. 137(1) sch. 8 Pt. I.
c. 4	Science and Technology Act 1965.	S. 5(2) rep.	S.I. No. 1498.
c. 5	Kenya Republic Act 1965	S. 2(1) rep., (2) rep. in pt., (3) rep.	52, S.L. (Repeals).
c. 11	Ministerial Salaries and Members' Pensions Act 1965.	Sch. 4 rep. in pt. ...	S.I. No. 1498.
c. 12	Industrial and Provident Societies Act 1965.	S. 20 am. (S.) ...	39, s. 1(3), sch. 1 Pt. I.
		am. (E.) ...	46, s. 1(3), sch. 1 Pt. I.
		S. 25(2) am. ...	46, ss. 19(2), 28 (4)(*g*).
		S. 31 appl. (mod.) ...	50, s. 31(1).
c. 14	Cereals Marketing Act 1965.	Transfer of functions ...	S.I. No. 388.
c. 15	Dangerous Drugs Act 1965.	Sch. Pt. I para. 1 am. ...	S.I. No. 738.
c. 16	Airports Authority Act 1965.	S. 20(1)(3) expld. ...	48, s. 76, sch. 4 para. 76.
c. 19	Teaching Council (Scotland) Act 1965.	S. 7(5)(7)(8) am., (8A) added.	49, s. 27(1), sch. 2 Pt. II para. 2.
		S. 16 rep.	49, s. 27, sch. 2 Pt. II para. 3, sch. 3.
		Sch. 1 paras. 4(1), 5(3) am.	S.I. No. 586.
c. 20	Criminal Evidence Act 1965.	Ext.	48, s. 93(4).
		S. 1(4) expld.	48, s. 76, sch. 4 para. 77.
c. 25	Finance Act 1965 ...	S. 1 rep.	32, s. 61(6), sch. 21 Pt. 1.
		S. 10(5) rep.	32, s. 61(6), sch. 21 Pt. IV.
		S. 17(3) rep.	32, ss. 60, 61(6), sch. 20 para. 22(1), sch. 21 Pt. IX.
		S. 17(9) rep. in pt. ...	32, ss. 60, 61(6), sch. 20 para. 3 (*b*), sch. 21 Pt. IX.
		S. 17(12) rep.	32, s. 61(6), sch. 21 Pt. X.

Session and Chap. or No. of Measure	Short title or Subject	How affected	Chapter of 1969 Act or number of Measure or Statutory Instrument
1965: c. 25—*cont.*	Finance Act 1965—*cont.*	Ss. 17(14), 18(6) rep. ...	32, ss. 60, 61(6), sch. 20 para. 3 (*b*), sch. 21 Pt. IX.
		Pt. III (ss. 19–45) expld.	32, s. 42, sch. 19 para. 9.
		ext.	32, s. 42, sch. 19 para. 15(1). 48, s. 74(2).
		S. 22(3) excl.	32, s. 40(1), sch. 19 para. 10(2).
		S. 24(8) rep.	32, ss. 42, 61(6), sch. 19 para. 5 (4), sch. 21 Pt. VI.
		S. 24A added	32, s. 42, sch. 19 para. 5(1).
		S. 25(1) proviso am. ...	32, s. 42, sch. 19 para. 8.
		S. 25(5) am.	32, s. 42, sch. 19 para. 5(2).
		S. 25(5)(*b*) rep.	32, ss. 42, 61(6), sch. 19 para. 8, sch. 21 Pt. VI.
		S. 25(5A) added, (5)(*d*) am.	32, s. 42, sch. 19 para. 8.
		S. 26 ext.	32, s. 40(1), sch. 17 Pt. II para. 13.
		S. 29(8)(*bb*) added ...	32, s. 42, sch. 19 para. 7(1).
		S. 31(8) excl.	32, s. 39(2).
		S. 33 ext.	32, s. 42, sch. 19 para. 16.
		S. 33(6) class 5 added ...	32, s. 42, sch. 19 para. 17(1).
		S. 35(3) am.	32, s. 60, sch. 20 para. 8(4)(*b*).
		S. 41(5)(*bb*) added ...	32, s. 42, sch. 19 para. 4.
		S. 44(8) am.	32, s. 60, sch. 20 para. 22(2).
		S. 45(1) definition of " legatee " am. ...	32, s. 42, sch. 19 para. 6(1).
		Pt. IV (ss. 46–89) expld.	32, s. 42, sch. 19 paras. 18(7), 19(3).
		ext....	32, s. 30(6).
		S. 47(1) am.	32, s. 60, sch. 20 para. 22(3).
		S. 47(5) rep. in pt. ...	32, ss. 60, 61(6), sch. 20 para. 22(4), sch. 21 Pt. IX.
		S. 49(7) rep. in pt. ...	32, s. 61(6), sch. 21 Pt. X.
		S. 50(3) mod. (*retrosp.*)...	32, s. 29, sch. 14 para. 9(2).
		S. 52(3) am.	32, s. 18(5).

Session and Chap. or No. of Measure	Short title or Subject	How affected	Chapter of 1969 Act or number of Measure or Statutory Instrument
1965: c. 25—*cont.*	Finance Act 1965—*cont.*	S. 52(3)(*a*) am.	32, s. 60, sch. 20 para. 17(14).
		S. 52(5)(*a*) am.	32, s. 18(7), sch. 13 para. 27.
		S. 52(5)(*b*) am. ...	32, s. 60, sch. 20 para. 17(14).
		S. 54(3) rep. in pt. ...	32, s. 61(6), sch. 21 Pt. II.
		S. 54(5)(7) rep. ...	32, s. 61(6), sch. 21 Pt. IX.
		S. 55(1) ext.	45, s. 10.
		S. 55(4) rep.	32, s. 61(6), sch. 21 Pt. X.
		S. 58 excl.	32, s. 30(1).
		S. 61 appl.	48, s. 74(1).
		expld.	32, s. 30(4).
		S. 61(3) mod.	45, s. 9.
		S. 62(4) am. ...	32, s. 60, sch. 20 para. 22(5), (6).
		S. 62(7)(*b*) rep. in pt. ...	32, s. 61(6), sch. 21 Pt. IX.
		S. 65 rep.	32, ss. 42, 61(6), sch. 19 para. 21(7), sch. 21 Pt. IV.
		Ss. 67, 68 am.	32, s. 60, sch. 20 para. 22(7).
		S. 69(1) mod.	32, s. 29, sch. 14 para. 8(6).
		S. 69(4) rep.	32, s. 61(6), sch. 21 Pt. X.
		S. 70(7) am.	32, s. 60, sch. 20 para. 22(8).
		S. 70(9) Transfer of functions.	S.I. No. 388.
		S. 71 am.	32, s. 60, sch. 20 para. 22(9).
		S. 71(1)(*b*) rep. ...	32, s. 61(6), sch. 21 Pt. II.
		S. 71(2) appl. (mod.) ...	32, s. 60, sch. 20 para. 22(10).
		S. 71(2)(*a*) appl. ...	32, s. 53(4).
		S. 71(5) appl.	32, s. 60, sch. 20 para. 22(10).
		S. 74 rep.	32, ss. 28(1), 61(6), sch. 21 Pt. III.
		S. 75 excl.	32, s. 29, sch. 14 para. 1.
		expld.	32, s. 29, sch. 14 para. 5(1).
		S. 75(6)(*a*) subst. ...	32, s. 29, sch. 14 para. 2(3).
		S. 76 expld.	32, s. 29, sch. 14 para. 5(1).
		S. 77(2) mod.	32, s. 29, sch. 14 para. 3(1)(2).

Session and Chap. or No. of Measure	Short title or Subject	How affected	Chapter of 1969 Act or number of Measure or Statutory Instrument
1965: c. 25—*cont.*	Finance Act 1965—*cont.*	S. 77(3)(*a*) restr. ...	32, s. 60, sch. 20 para. 22(11).
		S. 77(3)(*c*) mod. ...	32, s. 29, sch. 14 para. 3(1)(2).
		S. 77(3)(*d*) rep.	32, ss. 29, 61(6), sch. 14 para. 3 (6), sch. 21 Pt. III.
		S. 77(6) proviso rep. in pt.	32, s. 61(6), sch. 21 Pt. III.
		S. 78 ext.	32, s. 27.
		S. 78(2) excl.	32, s. 27(5).
		S. 78(3) rep. in pt. ...	32, s. 61(6), sch. 21, Pt. III.
		S. 78(5)(*a*) saved ...	32, s. 60, sch. 20 para. 6(2).
		rep. in pt. ...	32, s. 61(6), sch. 21 Pt. IX.
		S. 78(7)(*c*) rep.	32, s. 61(6), sch. 21 Pt. X.
		S. 80(5) rep.	32, s. 61(6), sch. 21 Pt. X.
		S. 89(2) definition of " recognised stock ex-change " am.	32, s. 29, sch. 14 para. 6(1).
		S. 89(5) rep.	32, s. 61(6), sch. 21 Pt. III.
		S. 92(8) subst. (London)	35, s. 17(1), sch. 3 para. 8.
		Sch. 6 para. 2 ext. ...	32, s. 32(13), sch. 16 para. 10(2).
		para. 4 ext. ...	32, s. 42, sch. 19 para. 19(1).
		restr. ...	32, s. 18(7), sch. 13 para. 18(1).
		para. 4(1)(*a*) am.	32, s. 42, sch. 19 paras. 1(2), 2 (1).
		para. 5 ext. ...	32, s. 32(13), sch. 16 para. 10(2).
		para. 16(1) am. ...	32, s. 42, sch. 19 para. 5(3).
		Sch. 7 para. 1 ext. ...	32, s. 32(13), sch. 16 para. 10(1).
		am. ...	32, s. 42, sch. 19 para. 14.
		para. 2 excl. ...	32, s. 41(7), sch. 18 Pt. III, para. 4(3).
		appl. ...	32, s. 42, sch. 19 para. 1(3).
		ara. 7(2) expld....	32, s. 42, sch. 19 para. 22(1).
		excl. ...	32, s. 42, sch. 19 para. 22(2).
		para. 8 rep. ...	32, ss. 42, 61(6), sch. 19, para. 15(6), sch. 21 Pt. VI.

Session and Chap. or No. of Measure	Short title or Subject	How affected	Chapter of 1969 Act or number of Measure or Statutory Instrument
1965: c. 25—*cont.*	Finance Act 1965 —*cont.*	Sch. 7—*cont.*	
		para. 11A added	32, s. 42, sch. 19 para. 3(1).
		para. 17(3) proviso added.	32, s. 42, sch. 19 para. 12.
		para. 21 ext. ..	32, ss. 18(7), 32 (12), 39(4), sch. 13 para. 12(8).
		mod. ...	32, s. 29, sch. 14 para. 10(4).
		Sch. 9 rep. in pt. ...	32, ss. 41(8), 61 (6), sch. 21 Pt. IV.
		para. 1 appl. ...	32, s. 60, sch. 20. para. 21(4).
		Sch. 10 para. 1(2) rep. in pt. (6.4.1970).	32, s. 61(6), sch. 21 Pt. VIII.
		para. 7(4A) added	32, s. 42, sch. 19 para. 13.
		para. 8(1) rep. in pt. (6.4.1970).	32, s. 61(6), sch. 21 Pt. VIII.
		para. 12(2) am....	32, s. 42, sch. 19 para. 5(5).
		Sch. 11 para. 9 expld. ...	32, s. 29, sch. 14 paras. 4(6), 5 (1).
		para. 9(1) rep. ...	32, ss. 29, 61(6), sch. 14 para. 4(6), sch. 21 Pt. III.
		Sch. 12 para. 5(2) rep in. pt. (6.4.1970).	32, s. 61(6), sch. 21 Pt. VIII.
		para. 9 appl. ...	32, ss. 20(9), 27 (8).
		Sch. 13 Pt. I ext. ...	32, s. 42, sch. 19 para. 16(6).
		para. 2 appl. ...	32, s. 42, sch. 19 para. 21(4).
		Sch. 15 para. 3 ext. ...	32, s. 60, sch. 20 para. 17(17).
		para. 6 expld. ...	32, s. 60, sch. 20 para. 28(1).
		para. 12 rep. in pt.	32, s. 61(6), sch. 21 Pt. IX.
		para. 15(*b*) rep....	32, s. 61(6), sch. 21 Pt. IV.
		para. 16 rep. ...	32, s. 61(6), sch. 21 Pt. X.
		Sch. 16 para. 2(2) ext. ...	32, s. 60, sch. 20 para. 7(2).
		para. 4(3) expld.	32, s. 60, sch. 20 para. 22(12).
		Sch. 17 rep.	32, s. 61(6), sch. 21 Pt. IV.
		Sch. 18 para. 2 superseded	32, s. 29, sch. 14 para. 3(4).
		para. 4(1)(*c*) am.	32, s. 60, sch. 20 para. 22(13).
		para. 6(1) rep. in pt., (3) rep.	32, s. 61(6), sch. 21 Pt. III.

Session and Chap. or No. of Measure	Short title or Subject	How affected	Chapter of 1969 Act or number of Measure or Statutory Instrument
1965:			
c. 25—*cont.*	Finance Act 1965 —*cont.*	Sch. 18—*cont.*	
		para. 8(1) am. ...	32, s. 60, sch. 20 para. 22(14).
		para. 9(1)(*b*) rep.	32, s. 61(6), sch. 21 Pt. III.
c. 32	Administration of Estates (Small Payments) Act 1965.	Ss. 5(1), 6(3) am. ...	50, s. 96(10).
		Sch. 1 Pt. II rep. in pt. ...	50, s. 96(1), sch. 3 Pt. I.
c. 33	Control of Office and Industrial Development Act 1965.	Pt. I (ss. 1–18) Transfer of functions.	S.I. No. 1498.
		Pt. I (ss. 1–18) mod. (S.)	30, ss. 86–88.
		S. 1(3) excl. (S.)...	30, ss. 84(2), 88.
		appl. (S.) ...	30, s. 87(6).
		S. 2 excl. (S.) ...	30, ss. 84(4), 88.
		S. 5(1) excl. (S.)...	30, ss. 84(2), 88.
		S. 7 excl. (S.) ...	30, ss. 85, 88.
		S. 17 am.	30, s. 105, sch. 9 para. 41.
		Pt. II (ss. 19–22) Transfer of functions.	S.I. No. 1498.
c. 36	Gas Act 1965	Sch. 6 ext.	48, s. 76, sch. 4 para. 93(1).
		expld.	48, s. 76, sch. 4 para. 93(2).
c. 45	Backing of Warrants (Republic of Ireland) Act 1965.	S. 2(2) expld. (genocide)	12, s. 2(2).
		S. 12 ext.	12, s. 3(1).
c. 46	Highlands and Islands Development (Scotland) Act 1965.	S. 10(4) ext.	48, s. 76, sch. 4 para. 93(1).
		expld. ...	48, s. 76, sch. 4 para. 93(2).
c. 49	Registration of Births, Deaths and Marriages (Scotland) Act 1965.	S. 43(5)–(7) am.... ...	39, s. 1(3), sch. 1 Pt. I.
c. 50	Monopolies and Mergers Act 1965.	Transfer of functions Sch. 1 para. 6 rep. in pt.	S.I. No. 1534.
c. 51	National Insurance Act 1965.	Power to am.	44, s. 8.
		S. 4(1)(*c*)(*d*) replaced ...	44, s. 1(2).
		S. 5(1) rep. in pt., (2) am.	44, s. 1(3).
		S. 7 ext.	44, s. 1(1).
		S. 7(1) rep. in pt. ...	44, s. 11(2), sch. 7.
		S. 14(2) subst.	48, s. 121(1).
		S. 30(7) am.	44, s. 3(1).
		am. (14.2.1971)	44, s. 3(2).
		S. 39(1) ext.	44, s. 4(1).
		S. 44(*a*)(ii) am. (14.2.1971)	44, s. 3(2).
		S. 49(4) am.	S.I. No. 289.
		S. 52(1) rep. in pt. ...	48, s. 141, sch. 11 Pt. II.
		S. 52(2)(*b*) am.	4, s. 2(1)(4).
		appl.... ...	4, s. 2(3).
		S. 58 am.	44, s. 1(2).
		S. 79 Pensions increase...	7, s. 1(1), sch. 1 Pt. I para. 32.
		S. 85 ext.	44, s. 9.
		S. 85(1) rep. in pt.	48, s. 141, sch. 11 Pt. II.
		S. 86(1)(*a*) am.	44, s. 10(3).
		S. 108(9)(*d*) am. ...	4, s. 3(3).

Session and Chap. or No. of Measure	Short title or Subject	How affected	Chapter of 1969 Act or number of Measure or Statutory Instrument
1965:			
c. 51—*cont.*	National Insurance Act 1965—*cont.*	Sch. 1 subst.	44, s. 1(1), sch. 1.
		Sch. 3 subst.	44, s. 2(1), sch. 2.
		Sch. 4 subst.	44, s. 2(2), sch. 3.
c. 52	National Insurance (Industrial Injuries) Act 1965.	Power to am.	44, s. 8.
		S. 27(1) rep. in pt. ...	48, s. 141, sch. 11 Pt. II.
		S .27(2)(*b*) am.	4, s. 2(1)(4).
		S .60(1)(*a*) am.	44, s. 10(3).
		S. 61 ext.	44, s. 9.
		S. 61(1) rep. in pt. ...	48, s. 141, sch. 11 Pt. II.
		S. 67(2) expld.	48, s. 121(1).
		Sch. 2 Pt. I table subst. ...	44, s. 5(1), sch. 4.
		Sch. 3 subst.	44, s. 6(1), sch. 5.
		Sch. 4 para. 1(*a*) am., (*aa*) added.	44, s. 7.
		Para. 1(*b*) rep. ...	44, ss. 7, 11(2), sch. 7.
c. 53	Family Allowances Act 1965.	Power to am.	44, s. 8.
		S. 7(1) rep. in pt. ...	48, s. 141, sch. 11 Pt. II.
		S. 7(2) rep.	4, ss. 2(3), 4(4)(*a*).
		S. 11(1) rep. in pt. (*prosp.*)	54, ss. 72(4), 73(4)(*d*), sch. 6.
		S. 11(1)(*b*)(2)(3) am. (*prosp.*).	54, ss. 72(3), 73(4)(*c*), sch. 5 para. 54.
		S. 13(1) rep. in pt. ...	48, s. 141, sch. 11 Pt. II.
		S. 13(1)(*e*) rep. in pt. ...	4, s. 4(4)(*b*).
		S. 16(1)(*b*) rep. in pt. (2) (*b*) rep.	48, s. 141, sch. 11 Pt. II.
c. 54	National Health Service Contributions Act 1965.	S. 1 Power to am. ...	44, s. 8.
		S. 1(4)(5) am.	S.I. No. 388.
		Ss. 3(1), 4 rep. in pt. ...	48, s. 141, sch. 11 Pt. II.
c. 56	Compulsory Purchase Act 1965.	Pt. I (ss. 1–32) (exc. ss. 4–8, 27, 31) appl.	48, s. 60(1).
c. 57	Nuclear Installations Act 1965.	S. 12 (3A) added, (4) am.	18, s. 1.
		S. 13(5)(*b*) am.	18, s. 3.
		S. 17(3)(*b*)(ii) am. ...	18, s. 2(1)
		S. 18(1)(4)(*b*) am. ...	18, s. 2(2).
		S. 21(1) am.	18, s. 2(1).
c. 58	Ministerial Salaries Consolidation Act 1965.	S. 2(2) am.	S.I. No. 1498.
		S. 3 pensions increase ...	7, s. 1(1), sch. 1 Pt. I para. 1.
		S. 8(1) definition of " Parliamentary Secretary " rep. in pt.	48, s. 141, sch. 11 Pt. II.
		Sch. 1 am.	48, s. 2(7)(*b*).
		rep. in pt.	48, s. 141, sch. 11 Pt. II. / S.I. No. 1498.

Session and Chap. or No. of Measure	Short title or Subject	How affected	Chapter of 1969 Act or number of Measure or Statutory Instrument
1965—*cont.*			
c. 59	New Towns Act 1965 ...	Ext.	48, s. 76, sch. 4 para. 93(1).
		Expld.	48, s. 76, sch. 4 para. 93(2).
		Expld. (" operational land ").	48, s. 76, sch. 4 para. 93(4).
		S. 23 am.	48, s. 76, sch. 4 para. 78(1).
		S. 26 mod.	48, s. 76, sch. 4 para. 78(3).
		S. 43 am.	5, s. 1(1).
c. 62	Redundancy Payments Act 1965.	S. 8(2) saved (L.T.E.) ...	35, s. 16(3), sch. 2 para. 6.
		S. 27 Power to am. ...	44, s. 8.
		Ss. 29(1)(3) rep. in pt., 41(6)(*b*) rep., 55(1)(2)(*a*) rep. in pt., (4) rep., (6) rep. in pt.	48, s. 141, sch. 11 Pt. II.
		Sch. 5 paras. 2, 3, 9, 12 am.	8, s. 1(1).
		Sch. 7 para. 12 rep. in pt.	48, s. 137(1), sch. 8 Pt. I.
c. 64	Commons Registration Act 1965.	S. 13 rep. in pt. (*prosp.*)...	59, s. 16(2), sch. 2 Pt. I.
c. 72	Matrimonial Causes Act 1965.	Saved (1.1.1971) ...	55, s. 9(3).
		S. 1 rep. (1.1.1971) ...	55, s. 9(2), sch. 2.
		S. 3(1) am. (1.1.1971) ...	55, s. 9(1), sch. 1 para. 1.
		S. 4(1)(2) am. (1.1.1971)	55, s. 9(1), sch. 1 para. 2.
		S. 5(1)–(4) rep. (1.1.1971)	55, s. 9(2), sch. 2.
		S. 5(5) saved (1.1.1971)	55, s. 2(3),
		S. 5(6) am. (1.1.1971) ...	55, s. 9(1), sch. 1 para. 3.
		Ss. 6(1)(*c*) rep. (saving) (1.1.1971), 7(1) rep. in pt. (saving) (1.1.1971)	55, s. 9(2). sch. 2.
		S. 12(1) subst. (1.1.1971)	55, s. 8(2).
		S. 15(*b*) am. (1.1.1971) ...	55, s. 9(1), sch. 1 para. 4.
		S. 16(3) am. (1.1.1971) ...	55, s. 9(1), sch. para. 5.
		S. 17(2) am. (1.1.1971) ...	55, s. 9(1), sch. 1 para. 6.
		S. 20(1)(*b*) am. (1.1.1971)	55, s. 9(1), sch. 1 para. 7.
		S. 22(2) am.	46, s. 5(3).
		S. 26(6) definitions of—	
		" court " am. (1.1.1971)	55, s. 9(1), sch. 1 para. 8.
		" dependant " am. ...	46, s. 18(2).
		S. 30(2)(*a*) am. (1.1.1971) (*aa*) added (1.1.1971)...	55, s. 9(1), sch. 1 para. 9.
		S. 30(2)(*b*) rep. in pt. (1.1.1971).	55, s. 9(1)(2), sch. 1 para. 9, sch. 2.
		S. 33 saved (1.1.1971) ...	55, s. 8(3).

Session and Chap. or No. of Measure	Short title or Subject	How affected	Chapter of 1969 Act or number of Measure or Statutory Instrument
1965: c. 72—*cont.*	Matrimonial Causes Act 1965—*cont.*	S. 34(3) am. (1.1.1971) ...	55, s. 9(1), sch. 1 para. 10.
		S. 35(1) am.	46, s. 5(3).
		S. 36(2)–(6) ext. ...	46, s. 7(3).
		S. 37(2)(3) ext.	46, s. 7(4).
		S. 42 rep. in pt. (1.1.1971).	55, s. 9(2), sch. 2.
		S. 46(2) definition of " the court " added (1.1.1971).	55, s. 9(1), sch. 1 para. 11.
		Sch. 1 para. 2 am. (1.1.1971).	55, s. 9(1), sch. 1 para. 12.
c. 74	Superannuation Act 1965	Pensions increase ...	7, ss. 1(1), 5(3)(*a*), sch. 1 Pt. I paras. 2, 37.
		S. 12 ext.	48, s. 45(1).
		S. 13 expld.	48, s. 45(2).
		S. 39A added	58, s. 30.
		S. 97(1)(*a*) am. ...	58, s. 35(1), sch. 1.
c. 75	Rent Act 1965	S. 3(3)(*a*) mod.	34, s. 52(2).
		S. 4(5) excl.	34, ss. 52(2), 54.
		Ss. 5–7 mod.	34, s. 52(2).
		S. 6(6) excl.	34, ss. 52(2), 54.
		S. 6(7)(*a*) rep. in pt. ...	34, s. 69(3), sch. 7.
		S. 7 restr.	62, s. 6(2).
		S. 7(*b*) excl. ...	34, s. 53, sch. 4 paras. 1, 6(2). 62, s. 5(1), sch. para. 7.
		S. 11(5)(6) excl.	34, s. 53, sch. 4 para. 9.
		S. 17(2) rep. in pt. ...	34, s. 69(3), sch. 7.
		Ss. 22, 24 Pensions increase.	7, s. 1(1), sch. 1 Pt. II para. 18.
		S. 27 appl. (mod.) ...	34, s. 44(3).
		S. 27(3)(*b*) am. ...	34, s. 61.
		S. 28(2) ext. ...	34, s. 53, sch. 4 para. 7.
		appl.	62, s. 5(2).
		S. 28(3) appl. ...	62, s. 5(1), sch. para. 4(1).
		Ss. 29, 44 excl.	34, s. 48(2).
		S. 46 ext. ...	34, s. 56(1). 62, s. 6(4).
		Sch. 3 ext.	34, s. 53, sch. 4 para. 12.
		Sch. 3 paras. 4–12, 16(2)–(6) excl.	34, s. 48(2).
		para. 17 rep. ...	34, s. 69(3), sch. 7.
		Sch. 4 appl. (mod.) ...	34, s. 47(1), sch. 3 para. 4.
		ext.	34, s. 53, sch. 4 para. 12.
c. 76	Southern Rhodesia Act 1965.	S. 2 cont. until 16.11.1970	S.I. No. 1504.
c. 78	Pensions (Increase) Act 1965.	S. 2(1)(*b*)(2) am. ...	7, ss. 1(4), 2(4), sch. 2 para. 8.
		S. 3 am.	7, s. 1(4), sch. 2 para. 10.

Session and Chap. or No. of Measure	Short title or Subject	How affected	Chapter of 1969 Act or number of Measure or Statutory Instrument
1965: c. 78—*cont.*	Pensions (Increase) Act 1965—*cont.*	S. 3(2)(*a*) am.	7, s. 2(5).
		Sch. 1 Pts. I, II ext. ...	7, s. 2(1), sch. 3 paras. 1–5.
		Sch. 1 Pt. I para. 22 rep.	48, s. 141, sch. 11 Pt. II.
C.A.M. No. 1... ...	Prayer Book (Alternative and Other Services) Measure 1965.	S. 1 am. (*prosp.*) ...	C.A.M. No. 2, s. 3(1).
		S. 2 am. (*prosp.*) ...	C.A.M. No. 2, s. 3(2).
No. 3... ...	Prayer Book (Miscellaneous Provisions) Measure 1965.	S. 1(2) expld. (*prosp.*) ...	C.A.M. No. 2, s. 3(3).
No. 4... ...	Prayer Book (Versions of the Bible) Measure 1965.	Am. (*prosp.*)	C.A.M. No. 2, s. 3(4).
1966: c. 2	Church of England Convocations Act 1966.	Appl.	C.A.M. No. 2, s. 1(4).
c. 4	Mines (Working Facilities and Support) Act 1966.	S. 7(8) am.	S.I. No. 383, 388.
c. 6	National Insurance Act 1966.	S. 1(2) rep.	44, s. 11(2), sch. 7.
		S. 3(1) am.	4, s. 1.
		S. 14(4) am.	4, s. 1(3).
		S. 14(6) excl.	4, s. 1(3).
c. 8	National Health Service Act 1966.	S. 4(2)(4) am.	S.I. No. 388.
c. 9	Rating Act 1966 ...	S. 10(1) am. (15.2.1971)...	19, s. 10(3), sch. 2 para. 25.
c. 12	Post Office Savings Bank Act 1966.	Expld.	48, s. 94(2).
		S. 1(1) am., (2) rep. in pt., (3) am.	48, s. 94(2)(*b*), sch. 6 Pt. II.
		S. 1(3)(*c*) rep. ...	48, s. 141, sch. 11 Pt. II.
		S. 2(1) am., (2) rep. in pt., (4) am.	48, s. 94(2)(*b*), sch. 6 Pt. II.
		S. 3(1)(2) subst.	48, s. 96.
		S. 3(3)(*a*) rep.	48, s. 141, sch. 11 Pt. II.
		S. 3(3)(*b*) am. ...	48, s. 96.
		S. 3(3)(*c*) rep.	48, s. 141, sch. 11 Pt. II.
		S. 3(4) rep.	48, s. 141, sch. 11 Pt. I.
		Ss. 4(1)–(3) am. ...	48, s. 94(2)(*b*), sch. 6 Pt. II.
		S. 5 am.	48, s. 100(2).
		S. 6 am.	48, s. 94(2)(*b*), sch. 6 Pt. II.
		S. 7(1) am.	48, s. 105.
		S. 7(3) rep. in pt. ...	48, s. 137(1), sch. 8 Pt. I.
		Ss. 7(4)(5), 8(1)(3) rep. ...	48, s. 141, sch. 11 Pt. II.
c. 14	Guyana Independence Act 1966.	Sch. 2 para. 1 rep. ...	32, s. 61(6), sch. 21 Pt. IX.
c. 17	Transport Finances Act 1966.	S. 1(3) rep.	35, s. 47(2), sch. 6.

Session and Chap. or No. of Measure	Short title or Subject	How affected	Chapter of 1969 Act or number of Measure or Statutory Instrument
1966—*cont.* c. 18	Finance Act 1966 ...	S. 1(1) am.	16, s. 12(3).
		S. 2(13)(*a*) rep. in pt. (*prosp.*).	27, s. 37, sch. 3.
		S. 13(1)(*a*)(*b*) am. ...	32, s. 4(3), sch. 10 Pt. II para. 1.
		S. 13(2) Table subst. ...	32, s. 4(1), sch. 10 Pt. I.
		S. 13(4)(*c*)(*d*) rep., (5) rep. in pt.	32, ss. 4(2)(3), 61(6), sch. 10 Pt. II para. 1, sch. 21 Pt. I.
		S. 14 rep.	32, ss. 5(16)(1 , 61(6), sch. Pt. I.
		S. 15(4)(6) am.	32, s. 5(16).
		S. 15(6) definition of " gaming machine ", " supplier " rep.	32, s. 61(6), sch. 21 Pt. I.
		S. 20 am.	48, s. 94(2)(*c*), sch. 6 Pt. III.
		S. 25(10)(*b*) am. ...	32, s. 60, sch. 20 para. 10.
		S. 29(12)(*d*) rep.... ...	32, s. 61(6), sch. 21 Pt. X.
		S. 30(2) am.	32, s. 60, sch. 20 para. 9(2).
		S. 31(4)(*a*) am.	32, s. 29, sch. 14 para. 10(6).
		S. 35(3)(*d*) added ...	35, s. 3(2).
		S. 40 rep.	32, s. 61(6), sch. 21 Pt. V.
		S. 41(1) ext.	32, s. 40(1), sch. 17 Pt. II para. 8.
		S. 41(2)(*b*) rep. in pt. ...	32, s. 61(6), sch. 21 Pt. V.
		S. 42(1)(2)(3)(*a*) am. ...	32, s. 40(1), sch. 17 Pt. III para. 27.
		S. 44(1)(*a*)–(*d*) subst. ...	32, s. 50(1).
		Ss. 44(4) rep. in pt., (5), 48 rep.	48, s. 141, sch. 11 Pt. II.
		Sch. 3 para. 7 rep. in pt.	32, s. 61(6), sch. 21 Pt. I.
		para. 7(*b*) am. ...	32, s. 4(3), sch. 10 Pt. II para. 2.
		paras. 9 rep. in pt. 10(*b*) rep.	32, s. 61(6), sch. 21 Pt. I.
		para. 11 rep. in pt.	32, ss. 4(3), 61(6), sch. 10 Pt. II para. 3, sch. 21 Pt. I.
		paras. 13, 14 rep. in pt. 15, 16 rep., 17(1), 18(1), 19 rep. in pt.	32, s. 61(6), sch. 21 Pt. I.
		para. 20(1) appl....	32, s. 2(9), sch. 8 para. 16.

Session and Chap. or No. of Measure	Short title or Subject	How affected	Chapter of 1969 Act or number of Measure or Statutory Instrument
1966:			
c. 18—*cont.*	Finance Act 1966 —*cont.*	Sch. 3—*cont.* paras. 22 rep., 23(1) rep. in pt.	32, s. 61(6), sch. 21 Pt. I.
		Sch. 5 para. 3(1) rep. in pt.	32, s. 61(6), sch. 21 Pt. IX.
		para. 11(1) am. ...	32, s. 60, sch. 20 para. 6(1).
		para. 11(2) rep. ...	32, s. 61(6), sch. 21 Pt. IX.
		para. 17 rep. ...	32, s. 61(6), sch. 21 Pt. IV.
		para. 18(1)(*b*) rep. in pt., (3) definition of " remuneration " rep.	32, s. 61(6), sch. 21 Pt. III.
		Sch. 6 paras. 6(2)(4) rep. (6.4.1970), 9(7) rep. in pt. (6.4.1970), 11(7), 17(2) rep. (6.4.1970).	32, s. 61(6), sch. 21 Pt. VIII.
		para. 18(1) am. ...	32, s. 60, sch. 20 para. 23(1).
		para. 20(4) rep. in pt. (6.4.1970).	32, s. 61(6), sch 21 Pt. VIII.
		para. 21(2)(*a*) am.	32, s. 60, sch. 20 para. 23(2).
		para. 24(1) appl....	32, s. 60, sch. 20 para. 23(3).
		Sch. 8 para. 5 expld. ...	19, s. 7(1).
		Sch. 10 para. 9 ext. ...	32, s. 42, sch. 19 para. 10(5).
c. 20	Ministry of Social Security Act 1966.	Pt. II (ss. 4–21) Power to am.	44, s. 8.
		S. 17(1)(*e*) am.	4, s. 2(2)(4).
		S. 17(2), sch. 6 para. 17 rep.	48, s. 141, sch. 11 Pt. II.
c. 21	Overseas Aid Act 1966 ...	S. 1(1) ext. ... {	48, s. 8. 51, s. 5(4).
c. 23	Botswana Independence Act 1966.	Sch. Pt. I para. 1 rep. ...	32, s. 61(6), sch. 21 Pt. IX.
c. 24	Lesotho Independence Act 1966.	Sch. Pt. I para. 1 rep. ...	32, s. 61(6), sch. 21 Pt. IX.
c. 25	Post Office (Subway) Act 1966.	Am.	48, s. 22(1).
c. 27	Building Control Act 1966	Sch. am.	48, s. 76, sch. 4 para. 80.
		rep. in pt.	35, ss. 17(1), 47(2), sch. 3 para. 9, sch. 6.
c. 28	Docks and Harbours Act 1966.	Sch. 1 am.	S.I. No. 1209.
c. 29	Singapore Act 1966 ...	S. 4(1) rep., (2) rep. in pt., (3) rep.	52, S.L. (Repeals).
		Sch. para. 6 rep. ...	32, s. 61(6), sch. 21 Pt. IX.
c. 30	Reserve Forces Act 1966	S. 5(1) ext.	65, s. 2(4).
		S. 9 appl.	65, s. 2(3)(4).

Session and Chap. or No. of Measure	Short title or Subject	How affected	Chapter of 1969 Act or number of Measure or Statutory Instrument
1966—*cont.*			
c. 32	Selective Employment Payments Act 1966.	S. 1(2)(*a*)(i) am. ...	32, s. 51(4)(*a*).
		S. 1(2)(*a*)(vii)–(x) added	S.I. No. 867.
		S. 2(3)(*a*)(iv) am. ...	32, s. 51(4)(*b*).
		S. 2(3)(*a*)(v) added ...	S.I. No. 867.
		S. 3 am. (London) ...	35, s. 39(6).
		S. 3(1)(*b*) rep.	48, s. 141, sch. 11 Pt. II.
		S. 4(1)(i) added.... ...	32, s. 51(10).
		S. 10(1) definitions of " non-qualifying activities " am.	32, s. 51(2), (4)(*c*).
		saved	32, s. 51(5).
		" Standard Industrial Classification " am.	32, s. 51(3).
		Sch. 1 Pt. I para. 14A added.	48, s. 76, sch. 4 para. 81(1).
		para. 10 rep.	35, s. 47(2), sch. 6.
		Pt. II am. ...	S.I. No. 1255.
		rep. in pt. ...	48, s. 141, sch. 11 Pt. II.
		Pt. III rep. in pt.	35, s. 47(2), sch. 6.
c. 33	Prices and Incomes Act 1966.	Ss. 7–22 cont. until 31.12.1970.	S.I. No. 1830.
		Sch. 3 para. 2(1)(*g*) rep.	35, s. 47(2), sch. 6.
c. 34	Industrial Development Act 1966.	Pt. I (ss. 1–14) Transfer of functions.	S.I. No. 1498.
		S. 8 am.	45, s. 11(2).
		S. 13(2) rep.	48, s. 141, sch. 11 Pt. II.
		S. 15(2)(6) appl. ...	51, s. 11(3).
		S. 18(3) rep., Pt. III (ss. 22–27) Transfer of functions.	S.I. No. 1498.
		S. 23 am. (S.)	30, ss. 84(1), 88.
		S. 24(9)(*b*) am. ...	30, s. 105, sch. 9 para. 42.
		S. 30(2) rep.	48, s. 141, sch. 11 Pt. II.
		Sch. 2 rep. in pt. ...	35, ss. 17(1), 47 (2), sch. 3 para. 9, sch. 6.
		am.	48, s. 76, sch. 4 para. 82.
c. 37	Barbados Independence Act 1966.	Sch. 2 para. 1 rep. ...	32, s. 61(6), sch. 21 Pt. IX.
c. 38	Sea Fisheries Regulation Act 1966.	Ss. 1, 2. 7, 8, 13(1)(2), 18(2) Transfer of functions.	S.I. No. 388.
c. 42	Local Government Act 1966.	S. 1 excl.	35, s. 3(1).
		S. 3(1) am.	54, s. 66.
		S. 3(4) saved	54, s. 66(2).
		S. 33 am. (*prosp.*) ...	27, s. 2(8), sch. 1 para. 9.

Session and Chap. or No. of Measure	Short title or Subject	How affected	Chapter of 1969 Act or number of Measure or Statutory Instrument
1966: c. 42—*cont.*	Local Government Act 1966—*cont.*	S. 35(3)(4) rep.	48, s. 141, sch. 11 Pt. II.
		Sch. 1 Pt. II paras. 1, 3(1) am. (1.4.1971).	19, s. 10(3), sch. 2 para. 26.
		Sch. 3 Pt. II para. 2 rep.	53, s. 14, sch.
c. 44	New Towns Act 1966 ...	S. 1 rep.	5, s. 1(2).
c. 49	Housing (Scotland) Act 1966.	Ss. 1, 2 ext.	34, s. 66.
		Ss. 3, 4 rep.	34, ss. 1(4), 69(3), sch. 7.
		S. 5 rep.	34, ss. 2(5), 69(3), sch. 7.
		S. 6(1) am., (3A), (4)(*c*) added.	34, s. 69(2), sch. 6 para. 3.
		S. 11 rep.	34, ss. 24(5), 69(3), sch. 7.
		Ss. 12–14 rep.	34, s. 69(3), sch. 7.
		S. 15 am.	34, s. 17.
		mod.	34, s. 18(1).
		S. 15(1)–(4) am. ...	34, s. 69(2), sch. 6 para. 4.
		S. 15(3) am.	34, s. 23.
		S. 16 rep.	34, s. 69(3), sch. 7.
		S. 17 saved	34, s. 2(3).
		am.	34, s. 69(2), sch. 6 para. 5.
		S. 18 mod.	34, s. 18(1).
		S. 18(1)(2) am.	34, s. 69(2), sch. 6 para. 6.
		S. 18(1)(*a*)(*b*), (2)(*a*)(*b*) subst. (*prosp.*).	30, s. 105, sch. 9 para. 43.
		S. 19(1)(*b*) subst., (1A) added, (2) am., (3)–(5) replaced, (6) am.	34, s. 69(2), sch. 6 para. 7.
		S. 20 mod.	34, s. 18(1).
		S. 20(1)(*a*) am.	34, s. 69(2), sch. 6 para. 8.
		S. 20(1)(*a*) rep. in pt., (2)(*b*) rep.	34, s. 69(3), sch. 7.
		S. 20(4) am., (5)–(7) replaced.	34, s. 69(2), sch. 6 para. 8.
		S. 23(4) am.	34, s. 69(2), sch. 6 para. 9.
		S. 24 rep.	34, s. 69(2)(3), sch. 6 para. 10, sch. 7.
		S. 25 expld.	34, s. 21.
		am.	34, s. 23.
		S. 25(1) am.	34, s. 69(2), sch. 6 para. 11.
		Ss. 25(1)(*a*), 26(1) rep. in pt., (2)(3) rep., 27 rep. in pt., 28, 29 rep.	34, s. 69(3), sch. 7.
		S. 30(1) am.	34, s. 69(2), sch. 6 para. 12.
		Ss. 30(1)(2), 31(2) rep. in pt., 32 rep., 33(1) rep. in pt.	34, s. 69(3), sch. 7.
		S. 33(1)(*a*) rep.	34, s. 69(2)(3), sch. 6 para. 13, sch. 7.

Session and Chap. or No. of Measure	Short title or Subject	How affected	Chapter of 1969 Act or number of Measure or Statutory Instrument
1966: c. 49—*cont.*	Housing (Scotland) Act 1966—*cont.*	Ss. 34–55, Pt. IV (ss. 58–87) rep.	34, ss. 3, 69(3), sch. 7.
		S. 109(3)–(5) am. ...	34, s. 69(2), sch. 6 para. 14.
		S. 114(4) subst.	34, s. 69(2), sch. 6 para. 15.
		S. 127(3)(5)–(7) am. ...	34, s. 69(2), sch. 6 para. 16.
		S. 130(10) am.	34, s. 69(2), sch. 6 para. 17.
		Pt. VII (ss. 137–159) ext.	34, s. 8(3).
		S. 137 am.	34, s. 69(2), sch. 6 para. 18.
		rep. in pt. ...	34, s. 69(3), sch. 7.
		S. 144 appl.	34, s. 12.
		S. 151(2) am.	34, s. 69(2), sch. 6 para. 19.
		S. 155(4) subst.	34, s. 69(2), sch. 6 para. 20.
		S. 160(1)(*a*)(i) am. ...	34, s. 69(2), sch. 6 para. 21.
		S. 160(1)(*a*)(ii) rep. in pt.	34, s. 69(3), sch. 7.
		S. 160(1)(*a*)(v) added ...	34, s. 63.
		S. 160(4) am.	34, s. 69(2), sch. 6 para. 21.
		S. 168 excl.	34, s. 64.
		S. 169(2)(3) am. ...	34, s. 69(2), sch. 6 para. 22.
		S. 176 rep.	30, s. 107, sch. 11.
		Ss. 177–179 ext. ...	34, s. 66.
		S. 180 am.	34, s. 69(2), sch. 6 para. 23.
		S. 180(2) rep. in pt. ...	34, s. 69(3), sch. 7.
		S. 180(3) rep.	34, s. 69(2)(3), sch. 6 para. 23, sch. 7.
		Ss. 180(4) rep., 181(1)(3) (4), 182 rep. in pt.	34, s. 69(3), sch. 7.
		S. 182 am.	34, s. 69(2), sch. 6 para. 24.
		Ss. 183–184 ext. ...	34, s. 66.
		S. 183(1)(*b*) am. ...	34, s. 69(2), sch. 6 para. 25.
		S. 183(1)(*b*) rep. in pt., (*d*) rep.	34, s. 69(3), sch. 7.
		S. 185(1)(*a*) am. ...	34, s. 69(2), sch. 6 para. 26.
		Ss. 185(1)(*a*), 187(1) rep. in pt.	34, s. 69(3), sch. 7.
		S. 188 ext.	34, s. 66.
		S. 190(1) am.	34, s. 69(2), sch. 6 para. 27.
		S. 190(2)–(5) ext. ...	34, s. 66.
		S. 190(5) rep. in pt. ...	34, s. 69(3), sch. 7.
		S. 191 ext.	34, s. 66.
		S. 192(1) rep., (2) rep. in pt.	34, s. 69(3), sch. 7.
		S. 192(4)(*b*)(6)(7) am. ...	34, s. 69(2), sch. 6 para. 28.

Session and Chap. or No. of Measure	Short title or Subject	How affected	Chapter of 1969 Act or number of Measure or Statutory Instrument
1966: c. 49—*cont.*	Housing (Scotland) Act 1966—*cont.*	S. 192(7) rep. in pt. ...	34, s. 69(3), sch. 7.
		Ss. 193(1), 196–199, 200–203 ext.	34, s. 66.
		S. 202(2) rep.	34, s. 69(3), sch. 7.
		S. 205 ext.	34, s. 66.
		S. 208(1) definitions of—" clearance area ", " clearance order ", " clearance resolution ", rep., " flat " rep. in pt.	34, s. 69(3), sch. 7.
		S. 208(1A) added ...	34, s. 69(2), sch. 6 para. 29.
		S. 208(2) rep. in pt. ...	34, s. 69(3), sch. 7.
		S. 209(1) ext.	34, s. 66.
		S. 209(2) am.	34, s. 69(2), sch. 6 para. 30.
		S. 210(2) am.	34, s. 69(2), sch. 6 para. 31.
		Schs. 1–3 rep.	34, s. 69(3), sch. 7.
		Sch. 4 appl.	34, s. 10(4).
		Sch. 9 rep. in pt. ...	34, s. 69(3), sch. 7.
c. 50	Industrial Reorganisation Corporation Act 1966.	Transfer of functions ...	S.I. No. 1498.
c. 51	Local Government (Scotland) Act 1966.	Ss. 12, 14(1) am. (16.5.1971).	19, s. 10(3), sch. 2 para. 27.
		S. 25(3)(*c*) am. (*prosp.*) ...	30, s. 105, sch. 9 para. 44.
		S. 35(1) am. (*prosp.*) (1A) added (*prosp.*) (2) am. (*prosp.*).	27, s. 2(8), sch. 1 para. 10.
		S. 35(3) rep. in pt. (*prosp.*).	27, ss. 2(8), 37, sch. 1 para. 10, sch. 3.
		Ss. 43(1)(*b*) rep. in pt., (2), 44(2)(*b*)(*c*) rep.	48, s. 141, sch. 11 Pt. II.
		S. 46(1) am. (16.5.1971)...	19, s. 10(3), sch. 2 para. 27.
		Sch. 1 Pt. I para. 2 am. (16.5.1971).	19, s. 10(3), sch. 2 para. 27.
		Pt. I para. 4 rep. (1.8.1972).	49, s. 27, sch. 2 Pt. II para. 4, sch. 3.
		Pt. II para. 1, Pt. III para. 3 am. (16.5.1971).	19, s. 10(3), sch. 2 para. 27.
1967: c. 1	Land Commission Act 1967.	Excl.	32, s. 47(3).
		Ss. 2(3), 4(4) rep. in pt. ...	48, s. 141, sch. 11 Pt. II.
		S.6(3) am. (S.) (*prosp.*) ...	30, s. 105, sch. 9 para. 45.
		S. 6(3)(*c*) rep. (S.) ...	30, s. 107, sch. 11.
		S. 6(3)(*e*) rep. in pt. ...	34, s. 69(3), sch. 7.
		S. 10(5) appl. (mod.) ...	30, s. 31, sch. 2 para. 9.
		Ss. 14(2), 15(2), 35(3) ext.	48, s. 76, sch. 4 para. 93(1).

Session and Chap. or No. of Measure	Short title or Subject	How affected	Chapter of 1969 Act or number of Measure or Statutory Instrument
1967: c. 1—*cont.*	Land Commission Act 1967—*cont.*	S. 47(5) added	32, s. 49(1).
		S. 51 expld.	32, s. 18(7), sch. 12 para. 15.
		S. 51(2) proviso added ...	32, s. 49(2).
		S. 55 am.	32, s. 48(1).
		S. 58 ext.	48, s. 76, sch. 4 para. 93(1).
		expld. (" operational land ").	48, s. 76, sch. 4 para. 93(4).
		S. 58(3) am.	48, s. 76, sch. 4 para. 93(3).
		S. 59A added	32, s. 43.
		S. 60A added (*retrosp.*)...	32, s. 44(1)(2).
		S. 64(3) ext. (London) ...	35, s. 36, sch. 5 para. 12(2).
		S. 84 rep.	48, s. 141, sch. 11 Pt. II.
		S. 89(6) ext.	48, s. 76, sch. 4 para. 93(1).
		am.	48, s. 76, sch. 4 para. 93(3).
		Sch. 3 appl. (mod.) (S.) ...	30, s. 31, sch. 2 para. 9.
		Sch. 4 para. 4 subst. ...	32, s. 48(3).
		para. 5A added ...	32, s. 45(1).
		para. 15A added...	32, s. 45(2).
		para. 19(2A) added	32, s. 46.
		para. 45(*e*) am. ...	48, s. 76, sch. 4 para. 84.
		Sch. 5 paras. 10A, 10B added (*retrosp.*).	32, s. 47(1)(3).
		para. 10(1) am. (*retrosp.*).	32, s. 47(2).
		para. 18 am. ...	32, s. 48(1).
		para. 19 rep. and superseded.	32, s. 48(5).
		Sch. 6 para. 1A added ...	32, s. 49(3).
		para. 8(1) subst., (2)(*b*) am.	32, s. 48(2).
		Sch. 11 para. 2 proviso added.	32, s. 48(4).
		Sch. 13 para. 3A added ...	32, s. 49(4).
c. 4	West Indies Act 1967 ...	S. 3(3) appl.	29, s. 1(4).
c. 9	General Rate Act 1967 ...	S. 12(4) am. (1.4.1971) ...	19, s. 10(3), sch. 2 para. 28.
		S. 32 am. (L.T.E.) ...	35, s. 17(1), sch. 3 para. 1(1)(2).
		S. 48(1)(*b*) rep. in pt. (1.4.1971).	19, ss. 10(3), 17 (2), sch. 2 para. 28, sch. 4.
		S. 48(1A) added (1.4.1971)	19, s. 10(3), sch. 2 para. 28.
		S. 69 excl.	48, s. 52(4).
		S. 92 Pensions increase ...	7, ss. 1(1), 2(1), sch. 1 Pt. II para. 17, sch. 3 para. 5.
		S. 113(1)(*c*), sch. 5 para. 4(1) am. (1.4.1971).	19, s. 10(3), sch. 2 para. 28.

Session and Chap. or No. of Measure	Short title or Subject	How affected	Chapter of 1969 Act or number of Measure or Statutory Instrument
1967:			
c. 9—*cont.*	General Rate Act 1967 —*cont.*	Sch. 13 para. 2 am. ...	33, s. 89(1), sch. 8 para. 30.
c. 12	Teachers' Superannuation Act 1967.	Ss. 1, 7 Pensions increase	7, s. 1(1), sch. 1 Pt. I para. 16.
c. 13	Parliamentary Commissioner Act 1967.	Sch. 2 ext. (S.) (*prosp.*)... am. ... ... rep. in pt.	30, s. 27(2). 48, ss. 2(5), 93(3). 48, s. 141, sch. 11 Pt. II. S.I. No. 1498.
c. 15	Post Office (Borrowing Powers) Act 1967.	Rep.	48, s. 141, sch. 11 Pt. II.
c. 17	Iron and Steel Act 1967	S. 16(1) restr. ... ... S. 18(1) subst. (*retrosp.*) S. 19 restr. ... ... S. 19(1)(2) am., (2A) added S. 19(3) subst. ... S. 19(4)(5) rep. ... ... S. 20(1) am. ... ... S. 21 ext. ... ... Sch. 3 rep. in pt. ...	45, s. 5(3). 45, s. 1. 45, s. 3(1). 45, s. 7(1). 45, s. 7(2). 45, s. 16(3), sch. 45, s. 7(1). 45, s. 2(5). 45, s. 16(3), sch.
c. 20	Housing (Financial Provisions, &c.) (Scotland) Act 1967.	S. 18 appl. ... ... S. 18(1)(2)(*b*) am. ... S. 18(3)(*a*)(iii), (4) rep. ... S. 18(7) am.	34, s. 19. 34, s. 69(2), sch. 6 para. 32. 34, s. 69(3), sch. 7. 34, s. 69(2), sch. 6 para. 32.
c. 22	Agriculture Act 1967 ...	Transfer of functions ... S. 9(11) am.	S.I. No. 388. S.I. No. 1534.
c. 24	Slaughter of Poultry Act 1967.	Apptd. day for whole Act (1.1.1970).	S.I. No. 1096.
c. 28	Superannuation (Miscellaneous Provisions) Act 1967.	Pensions increase ... S. 3(4)(*aa*) added ... S. 3(4)(*a*)(v)(ix)(xi)(xii), (*b*) rep.	7, s. 1(1), sch. 1 Pt. I paras. 2, 21. 58, s. 31(2). 58, s. 35(2), sch. 2.
c. 29	Housing (Subsidies) Act 1967.	S. 12 rep. ... ... S. 14(5)(*a*) am. ... ... S. 14(5)(*b*) ext. ... ... S. 24(3)(vii) added ... S. 26A added ... S. 28(1)(*b*) am. ... S. 28(3)–(5) added ... Sch. 2 am.	33, ss. 21, 89(3), sch. 10. 33, s. 89(1), sch. 8 para. 31. 33, s. 77(3). 33, s. 79(1). 33, s. 79(2). S.I. No. 1626. 33, s. 78. 33, s. 77.
c. 30	Road Safety Act 1967 ...	Apptd. day for S. 17(1) and sch. 1 para. 9 in pt. (8.7.1969). S. 14(9) am. ... ... S. 19(2)(7) am. ... ... S. 27 am.	S.I. No. 826. 27, s. 18(2). 27, s. 16(5). 27, s. 10.
c. 32	Development of Inventions Act 1967.	S. 11(1) rep. in pt. ...	48, s. 141, sch. 11 Pt. II.
c. 33 ...	Air Corporations Act 1967.	S. 8(5)(6) appl. ... ... S. 8(7) rep. ... ... S. 14 saved (B.E.A.) ... Ss. 17, 18 saved (B.E.A.) S. 18(1) am. (*prosp.*) ...	43, s. 1(5). 43, s. 1(5). 43, s. 3(3). 43, s. 3(3) 43, s. 3(1).

Session and Chap. or No. of Measure	Short title or Subject	How affected	Chapter of 1969 Act or number of Measure or Statutory Instrument
1967: c. 33—*cont.*	Air Corporations Act 1967—*cont.*	S.19 expld.	43, s. 3(3).
		Ss. 20, 21 excl. (*prosp.*) ...	43, s. 2(2)(4).
		saved	43, s. 3(4).
		S. 22 ext. (*prosp.*)	43, s. 2(2)(4).
		S. 22(1) am.	43, s. 3(5).
		Sch. 1 para. 6A added ...	43, s. 4, sch. 2.
c. 34	Industrial Injuries and Diseases (Old Cases) Act 1967.	Power to am.	44, s. 8.
		Ss. 2(6)(*c*), 7(2)(*b*) am. ...	44, s. 6(2).
c. 38	Refreshment Houses Act 1967.	Rep.	53, s. 14, sch.
c. 40	Shipbuilding Industry Act 1967.	S. 7(5) am.	6, s. 1.
c. 43	Legal Aid (Scotland) Act 1967.	Sch. 1 Pt. II para. 1 excl.	S.I. No. 955.
c. 47	Decimal Currency Act 1967.	S. 2 ext. and expld. (15.2.1971).	19, s. 1(6).
		Ss. 2(3) rep. in pt. (1.2.1971), (4) rep. (15.2.1971), 3(3) rep. in pt. (15.2.1971).	19, s. 17(2), sch. 4.
		S. 5(1)(*d*) rep.	19, s. 17(1).
		Sch. 2 rep. in pt. (15.2.1971).	19, s. 17(2), sch. 4.
c. 52	Tokyo Convention Act 1967.	Apptd. day for s. 2 (4.12.1969).	S.I. No. 1688.
c. 54	Finance Act 1967 ...	S. 1(1)–(4) rep.	32, s. 61(6), sch. 21 Pt. I.
		S.3 Transfer of functions	S.I. No. 1498.
		S. 8(2) am.	32, s. 55(4).
		S. 11(1)(*c*) rep. ...	32, s. 61(6), sch. 21 Pt. I.
		S. 11(2) excl. (*prosp.*) ...	27, s. 5(3).
		S. 12 saved	32, s. 6(1).
		expld. (*prosp.*) ...	27, s. 30.
		S. 12(1) ext. (*prosp.*) ...	27, ss. 11(2)(*g*), 12(4).
		S. 12(2) am. (*prosp.*) ...	27, s. 4(4), sch. 1 para. 16.
		S. 12(2)(*a*) am. (*prosp.*) ...	27, s. 2(8), sch. 1 para. 11.
		S. 12(3)(4) am. (*prosp.*) ...	27, s. 4(4), sch. 1 para. 17.
		S. 12(4) am. (*prosp.*) ...	27, s. 4(4), sch. 1 para. 18.
		S. 12(8) am.	27, s. 28(4).
		S. 16(2) rep., (3) rep. in pt. (5) rep. (saving).	32, s. 61(6), sch. 21 Pt. IV.
		S. 16(3)(*b*) am. ...	32, s. 10(5).
		S. 25 am.	48, s. 106.
		S. 31 expld.	48, s. 125.
		S. 33 appl.	32, s. 42, sch. 19 para. 15(5).
		S. 33(1) mod. ...	32, s. 42, sch. 19 para. 10(5).
		S. 33 (3A) added ...	32, s. 42, sch. 19 para. 23(1).
		S. 39(2) rep. in pt. ...	32, s. 61(6), sch. 21 Pt. X.

Session and Chap. or No. of Measure	Short title or Subject	How affected	Chapter of 1969 Act or number of Measure or Statutory Instrument
1967: c. 54—*cont.*	Finance Act 1967 —*cont.*	S. 40(1)(*a*)(*c*) am. ...	S.I. No. 535.
		Sch. 2 rep.	32, s. 61(6), sch. 21 Pt. I.
		Sch. 7 para. 4 am. (15.2.1971).	19, s. 10(3), sch. 3 para. 21.
		Sch. 11 paras. 3(4)(5), 4 rep.	32, s. 61(6), sch. 21 Pt. IV.
		para. 5(7) rep. in pt.	32, s. 61(6) sch. 21 Pt. X.
		para. 6 expld. ...	32, s. 60, sch. 20 para. 24(1).
		para. 8(3) am. ...	32, s. 60, sch. 20 para. 24(2).
		para. 9 rep. in pt.	32, s. 61(6), sch. 21 Pt. III.
		Sch. 12 expld.	32, s. 50(2).
		Sch. 13 para. 11 rep. ...	32, ss. 42, 61(6), sch. 19 para. 3 (3), sch. 21 Pt. VI.
		Sch. 14 appl.	32, s. 42, sch. 19 para. 15(5).
		para. 2(3) added	32, s. 42, sch. 19 para. 23(2).
		para. 3 excl. ...	32, s. 42, sch. 19 para. 19(2).
		para. 5(4) ext. ...	32, s. 42 sch. 19 para. 11(4).
		para. 11 rep. ...	32, s. 61(6) sch. 21 Pt. VI.
		para. 12 ext. ...	32, s. 32(13), sch. 16 para. 10(1).
		Sch. 15 para. 2(1)(2) am.	32, s. 40(1), sch. 17 Pt. III, para. 28.
c. 56	Matrimonial Causes Act 1967.	S. 3 am. (1.1.1971) ...	55, s. 7(2).
c. 58	Criminal Law Act 1967...	Sch. 1 List B para. 20 added.	12, s. 1(4).
c. 62	Post Office (Data Processing Service) Act 1967.	Ss. 1, 3(2) rep.	48, s. 141, sch. 11 Pt. II.
c. 68	Fugitive Offenders Act 1967.	S. 16 ext.	12, s. 3(1).
		S. 16(2) expld.	54, s. 60(2).
		S. 17 ext.	12, s. 3(1).
		Sch. 1 am. ... {	12, s. 2(1). 54, s. 60(1).
c. 69	Civic Amenities Act 1967	S. 1(5)(*b*) am. (S.) ...	30, s. 105, sch. 9 para. 46.
		S. 1(6) am. (S) (*prosp.*) ...	30, ss. 56(1), 57.
		S. 1(6)(*b*)(*c*) rep. (S.) (*prosp.*)	30, ss. 57(4), 107, sch. 11.
		S. 2 rep. (S.) (*prosp.*) ...	30, s. 107, sch. 11.
		S. 3(4) subst. (*prosp.*) ...	30, s. 105, sch. 9 para. 47.
		S. 6(2) rep. in pt. (S.) (*prosp.*).	30, s. 107, sch. 11.
		am (S.) (*prosp.*) ...	30, s. 105, sch. 9 para. 48.

Session and Chap. or No. of Measure	Short title or Subject	How affected	Chapter of 1969 Act or number of Measure or Statutory Instrument
1967: c. 69—*cont.*	Civic Amenities Act 1967 —*cont.*	S. 7 rep. (S.) (*prosp.*) ...	30, s. 107, sch. 11.
		S. 8(3)(*b*) am. (*prosp.*) ...	30, s. 105, sch. 9 para. 49.
		Ss. 9, 10 rep. (S.) (*prosp.*)	30, s. 107, sch. 11.
		S. 14 Power to mod. (S.) (*prosp.*).	30, s. 22.
		appl. (mod.) (S.) (*prosp.*).	30, s. 23(3).
		S. 14(5)(*b*) subst. ...	30, s. 105, sch. 9 para. 50.
		S. 16(1) rep. in pt. (S.) (*prosp.*).	30, ss. 105, 107, sch. 9 para. 51(*a*), sch. 11.
		S. 16(2)(3) subst. (S.) (*prosp.*).	30, s. 105, sch. 9 para. 51(*b*).
		S. 21(1) am. (*prosp.*) ...	27, s. 29(3).
		S. 30(1) definition of " the Scottish Planning Act of 1969 " added.	30, s. 105, sch. 9 para. 52.
c. 70	Road Traffic (Amendment) Act 1967.	Apptd. day for S. 4 (1.5.1969).	S.I. No. 434.
		S. 4(1) expld. (*prosp.*) ...	27, s. 20(5).
c. 72	Wireless Telegraphy Act 1967.	Expld.	48, s. 3(1).
		S. 14(1) rep.	48, s. 141, sch. 11 Pt. II.
c. 73	National Insurance Act 1967.	Ss. 1(1)(*c*), 2(1)(*a*), (*b*), 3(1), schs. 3, 5, 6 rep.	44, s. 11(2), sch. 7.
c. 74	Superannuation Act 1965	Sch. 8 am. (*retrosp.*) ...	S.I. No. 349, 665.
c. 75	Matrimonial Homes Act 1967.	Sch. para. 1 rep. (*prosp.*)	59, ss.16(2), 17(1), sch. 2 Pt. II.
c. 76	Road Traffic Regulation Act 1967.	Ss. 6(8)(*b*) rep., (12) rep. in pt. 9(8)(*b*) rep.	35, s. 47(2), sch. 6.
		S. 21(6)(*c*) added (*prosp.*), (8) subst. (*prosp.*).	35, s. 32(1).
		S. 24(6A) added ...	35, s. 33.
		S. 35(5A) added ...	35, s. 35.
		S. 55(4) added	35, s. 34(2).
		S. 56(1) am.	35, s. 34(3).
		S. 56(2) rep.	35, ss. 34(2), 47(2), sch. 6.
		S. 56(4) added	35, s. 34(4).
		S. 81(9) Pensions increase	7, s. 1(1), sch. 1 Pt. II para. 10.
		S. 84(1) saved	35, s. 1.
		S. 85(2)(*a*) am.	27, s. 16(6).
		S. 104(1) definition of— " highway authority " am.	35, s. 34(5).
		" metropolitan road " rep. (*prosp.*).	35, s. 47(2), sch. 6.
c. 77	Police (Scotland) Act 1967.	Apptd. day for S. 39 (1.1.1970).	S.I. No. 1796.
		S. 17(2) excl. (*prosp.*) ...	63, s. 1(3).
		S. 24(1)(*c*) added ...	63, s. 2(4).
		S. 26 Pensions increase ...	7, s. 1(1)(3)(4), sch. 1 Pt. II para. 8, sch. 2 para. 6.

Session and Chap. or No. of Measure	Short title or Subject	How affected	Chapter of 1969 Act or number of Measure or Statutory Instrument
1967:			
c. 77—*cont.*	Police (Scotland) Act 1967—*cont.*	S. 26(8) rep. (*prosp.*) ...	63, s. 4(8).
		S. 26(9) am. (*prosp.*) ...	63, s. 4(6).
		S. 27(3), sch. 4 rep. in pt. (*prosp.*).	63, s. 4(8).
		S. 38 Pensions increase ...	7, s. 1(1), sch. 1 Pt. I para. 20.
c. 79	Road Traffic (Driving Instruction) Act 1967.	Apptd. day for certain specified provisions (17.3.1969).	S.I. No. 84.
c. 80	Criminal Justice Act 1967.	S. 2(3A) added (*prosp.*)...	54, s. 72(3), sch. 5 para. 55.
		S. 3(3) am. (*prosp.*) ...	54, s. 72(3), sch. 5 para. 56.
		S. 4(*a*) am. (*prosp.*) ...	54, s. 10(3).
		S. 9(3A) added (*prosp.*)...	54, s. 72(3), sch. 5 para. 55.
		S. 55 rep. in pt. (*prosp.*)...	54, s. 72(4), sch. 6.
		S. 56(5) excl. (*prosp.*) ...	27, s. 22(3).
		S. 56(10) ext. (*prosp.*) ...	27, s. 16(7).
		am. (*prosp.*) ...	27, s. 2(8), sch. 1 para. 12.
		S. 73(1)(2) am. (*prosp.*), (3A), (3B) added (*prosp.*).	54, s. 33(1), sch. 1 para. 1.
		S. 74(2)(3)(5)(6) am. (*prosp.*).	54, s. 33(1), sch. 1 para. 2.
		S. 75(4A) added (*prosp.*)	54, s. 33(1), sch. 1 para. 3.
		S. 76(1A) added (*prosp.*), (4)(*a*) am. (*prosp.*), (5) added (*prosp.*).	54, s. 33(1), sch. 1 para. 4.
		S. 77(1) am. (*prosp.*) ...	54, s. 33(1), sch. 1 para. 5.
		S. 77(1) rep. in pt. (*prosp.*)	54, ss. 33(1), 72(4), sch. 1 para. 5, sch. 6.
		S. 78(1) am.	54, s. 33(1), sch. 1 para. 6.
		S. 79(2)(3)(6) am. (*prosp.*)	54, s. 33(1), sch. 1 para. 7.
		S. 84 definitions of— " appropriate author-ity " para. (*aa*), " appropriate con-tributor " added (*prosp.*).	54, s. 33(1), sch. 1 para. 8.
		S. 84(2)(3) added (*prosp.*)	54, s. 33(1), sch. 1 para. 8.
		Sch. 3 Pt. I rep. in pt. ...	48, s. 141, sch. 11 Pt. II.
		rep. in pt. (*prosp.*).	54, s. 72(4), sch. 6.
c. 83	Sea Fisheries (Shellfish) Act 1967.	Ss. 1, 4(5)(7), 5 Transfer of functions.	S.I. No. 388.
c. 86	Countryside (Scotland) Act 1967.	S. 11(1) rep. in pt. ...	52, S.L. (Repeals).
		S. 11(5)(*f*) ext.	48, s. 76, sch. 4 para. 13(1).

Session and Chap. or No. of Measure	Short title or Subject	How affected	Chapter of 1969 Act or number of Measure or Statutory Instrument
1967:			
c. 86—*cont.*	Countryside (Scotland) Act 1967—*cont.*	S. 38(7) am.	48, s. 76, sch. 4 para. 85.
		Ss. 54(6), 75(4) ext. ...	48, s. 76, sch. 4 para. 93(1).
		S. 75(4) expld.	48, s. 76, sch. 4 para. 93(2).
		Sch. 3 ext.	48, s. 76, sch. 4 para. 93(1).
c. 87	Abortion Act 1967 ...	S. 2(2) am.	S.I. No. 388.
c. 88	Leasehold Reform Act	Pt. I (ss. 1–37) ext. ...	33, s. 81(2)(*b*).
		S. 9(1) am., (*retrosp.*) ...	33, s. 82.
1968:			
c. 3	Capital Allowances Act 1968.	S. 28 appl.	32, ss. 18(7), 22 (3), sch. 13 para. 7(3).
		S. 83(4)(*d*) added ...	35, s. 3(2).
		S. 87(3) excl.	32, s. 30(5), sch. 15 para. 8.
		Sch. 12 para. 3(4) rep. ...	32, s. 61(6), sch. 21 Pt. X.
c. 5	Administration of Justice Act 1968.	S. 1(1)(*b*)(iii) am. ...	S.I. No. 862.
c. 6	Trustee Savings Banks Act 1968.	Rep.	50, s. 96(1), sch. 3 Pt. I.
c. 7	London Cab Act 1968 ...	S. 3(3) am.	35, s. 17(1), sch. 3 para. 1(1)(2).
c. 12	Teachers Superannuation (Scotland) Act 1968.	Pensions increase ...	7, s. 1(1), sch. 1 Pt. I para. 17.
c. 13	National Loans Act 1968	S. 12 am.	32, s. 52.
		S. 12 ext. ...	43, s. 1(8), sch. 1 para. 3. 48, s. 109.
		S. 16(7) rep. in pt. ...	48, s. 141, sch. 11 Pt. II.
		S. 22(2) am.	48, s. 131(2).
		Schs. 1, 5 rep. in pt. ...	48, s. 141, sch. 11 Pt. II.
c. 14	Public Expenditure and Receipts Act 1968.	Ss. 1(1)(5) rep., 7(2) rep. in pt., sch. 1 rep.	44, s. 11(2), sch. 7.
c. 16	New Towns (Scotland) Act 1968.	Expld. (" Operational land ").	48, s. 76, sch. 4 para. 93(4).
		Expld.	48, s. 76, sch. 4 para. 93(2).
		Ext.	48, s. 76, sch. 4 para. 93(1).
		Ss. 15–17 rep.	30, s. 107, sch. 11.
		Ss. 23, 24(1) am. ...	48, s. 76, sch. 4 para. 86(1)(2).
		S. 26 restr.	48, s. 76, sch. 4 para. 86(3).
		Ss. 37(1), 38(1) am., (2) rep., (3) am., (4) rep., 39(5) am. and rep. in pt.	S.I. No. 453.
		Sch. 7 rep.	30, s. 107, sch. 11.
c. 18	Consular Relations Act 1968.	S. 9 rep.	48, s. 141, sch. 11 Pt. II.
c. 23	Rent Act 1968	Excl.	33, s. 60(7).
		Pt. I (ss. 1–9) appl. ...	33, s. 50(1).
		S. 16 rep.	33, s. 89(3), sch. 10.

Session and Chap. or No. of Measure	Short title or Subject	How affected	Chapter of 1969 Act or number of Measure or Statutory Instrument
1968: c. 23—*cont.*	Rent Act 1968—*cont.*	S. 20(3)(*a*) mod. ...	33, s. 51(2)(*a*).
		S. 21(5) excl.	33, ss. 51(2)(*c*), 53.
		S. 22 mod.	33, s. 51(2)(*b*).
		S.22(2) restr. ... {	33, s. 52, sch. 3 paras. 1, 6(2). 62, s. 5(1).
		S. 22(3) excl. ... {	33, s. 52, sch. 3 para. 13. 62, s. 5(1), sch. para. 7.
		S. 23 mod.	33, s. 51(2)(*b*).
		S. 24 mod.	33, s. 51(2)(*b*).
		S. 25(1) excl.	33, ss. 51(2)(*c*), 53.
		S. 25(4)(*a*) rep. in pt. ...	33, s. 89(3), sch. 10.
		S. 27 excl.	33, s. 52, sch. 3 para. 9.
		S. 31(*a*) rep. in pt. ...	33, s. 89(3), sch. 10.
		Pt. IV (ss. 39–51) mod. ...	33, s. 47(1).
		S. 40 Pensions increase ...	7, s. 1(1), sch. 1 Pt. II para. 18.
		S. 46 appl.	33, s. 43(4).
		S. 46(4) added	33, s. 83.
		S. 47(3) ext.	33, s. 52, sch. 3 para. 7(*a*).
		appl.	62, s. 5(2).
		S. 47(4) appl.	62, s. 5(1), sch. para. 4(1).
		S. 49 rep.	33, s. 89(3), sch. 10.
		S. 50 ext. ... {	33, s. 56(1). 62, s. 6(3).
		S. 50(2) rep. in pt. ...	33, s. 89(3), sch. 10.
		Pt. V (ss. 52–67) saved ...	33, s. 51(1).
		S. 57(1)(*a*) am.	33, s. 89(1), sch. 8 para. 32.
		S. 57(2)(*b*) am.	33, s. 89(1), sch. 8 para. 32.
		Pt. VII (ss. 85–92) excl.	33, s. 81(1)(*a*).
		S. 86 excl.	33, s. 81, sch. 7 para. 1.
		S. 106 ext.	33, s. 56(2).
		S. 115 am.	33, s. 87.
		Sch. 4 appl.	62, s. 5(1), sch. para. 3(2).
		Sch. 6 excl.	33, s. 47(2).
		Sch. 7 appl. (mod.) ...	33, ss. 46, 47, sch. 2 Pt. I para. 4.
		Sch. 16 para. 26(2) am. ...	33, s. 89(1), sch. 8 para. 33.
c. 24	Commonwealth Tele-communications Act 1968.	Apptd. day for whole Act (1.4.1969).	S.I. 143.
c. 27	Firearms Act 1968 ...	Sch. 4 para. 4 subst. (E)...	S.I. No. 1219.

Session and Chap. or No. of Measure	Short title or Subject	How affected	Chapter of 1969 Act or number of Measure or Statutory Instrument
1968—*cont.*			
c. 30	Air Corporations Act 1968.	Rep.	43, s. 3(6).
c. 31	Housing (Financial Provisions) (Scotland) Act 1968.	S. 2(6) added ...	34, s. 65.
		S. 13(1A) added ...	34, s. 31.
		S. 13(2) rep.	34, ss. 31, 69(3), sch. 7.
		S. 14 (2) proviso added, (3) am.	34, s. 32.
		S. 18(2) subst.	34, s. 33.
		S. 19(1)(*a*) rep.	34, s. 69(3), sch. 7.
		S. 19(1)(*c*) am.	34, s. 69(2), sch. 6 para. 33.
		S. 26 am.	34, s. 69(2), sch. 6 para. 34.
		S. 27(1) rep. in pt. ...	34, ss. 34, 69(3), sch. 7.
		S. 27(1A) added ...	34, s. 34.
		S. 27(2) am.	34, s. 69(2), sch. 6 para. 35.
		S.27(5) rep., (6) rep. in pt.	34, s. 69(3), sch. 7.
		S. 27(6A) added ...	34, s. 34.
		S. 27(8) am.	34, s. 69(2), sch. 6 para. 35.
		S. 27A added ...	34, s. 35.
		S. 28 subst.	34, s. 36.
		S. 29(1)(*bb*) added ...	34, s. 37.
		S. 30(2) rep. in pt. ...	34, s. 69(3), sch. 7.
		S. 31(11) am.	34, s. 69(2), sch. 6 para. 36.
		Ss. 32, 33, 36(2) proviso rep.	34, s. 69(3), sch. 7.
		S. 38(1) am.	34, s. 69(2), sch. 6 para. 37.
		S. 38(2) subst.	34, s. 38.
		S. 38(3) rep.	34, s. 69(3), sch. 7.
		S. 39(1)(*dd*) added ...	34, s. 39.
		S. 39(1)(*g*) rep.	34, ss. 39, 69(3), sch. 7.
		S. 39(3) rep. in pt. ...	34, s. 69(3), sch. 7.
		S. 40(1) rep. in pt. ...	34, ss. 40, 69(3), sch. 7.
		S. 40(2)(3) am.	34, s. 69(2), sch. 6 para. 38.
		S. 40(4)(5) rep.	34, s. 69(3), sch. 7.
		S. 41 subst.	34, s. 41.
		S. 42(3) am., (4) proviso added.	34, s. 42.
		S. 49(2) am.	34, s. 69(2), sch. 6 para. 39.
		S. 54 rep. in pt. ...	34, s. 69(3), sch. 7.
		S. 58(3)(*a*) am.	34, s. 69(2), sch. 6 para. 40.
		S. 59(4)(5) added ...	34, s. 69(2), sch. 6 para. 41.
		S. 64 am.	34, s. 69(2), sch. 6 para. 42.
		S. 66 rep. in pt. ...	34, s. 69(3), sch. 7.
		S. 67(2) am.	34, s. 69(2), sch. 6 para. 43.

Session and Chap. or No. of Measure	Short title or Subject	How affected	Chapter of 1969 Act or number of Measure or Statutory Instrument
1968:			
c. 31—*cont.*	Housing (Financial Provisions) (Scotland) Act 1968—*cont.*	Sch. 3 para. 2 subst. ...	34, s. 43.
		para. 4 rep. ...	34, ss. 43, 69(3), sch. 7.
		para. 5 am. ...	34, s. 69(2), sch. 6 para. 44.
		para. 6 rep. ...	34, ss. 43, 69(3), sch. 7.
		Sch. 5 am.	34, s. 69(2), sch. 6 para. 45.
		Sch. 6 am.	34, s. 69(2), sch. 6 para. 46.
		Sch. 9 paras. 1–4 rep. ...	34, s. 69(3), sch. 7.
c. 32	Industrial Expansion Act 1968.	S. 1 Transfer of functions, 1(3) rep. in Pt.	S.I. No. 1498.
		Sch. 1 am.	48, s. 76, sch. 4 para. 87.
		rep. in pt. ...	35, ss. 17(1), 47 (2), sch. 3 para. 9, sch. 6.
c. 33	Customs Duties (Dumping and Subsidies) Amendment Act 1968.	Rep. (saving)	16, s. 18.
c. 34	Agriculture (Miscellaneous Provisions) Act 1968.	S. 22(2) am. (1.4.1971) ...	19, s. 10(3), sch. 2 para. 30.
		S. 22(3) rep. (1.4.1971) ...	19, ss. 10(3), 17 (3), sch. 2 para. 30, sch. 4.
		Ss. 40, 44(2), 45 Transfer of functions.	S.I. No. 388.
		S. 53(*a*) rep. in pt. ...	48, s. 141, sch. 11 Pt. II.
c. 37	Education (No. 2) Act 1968.	Apptd. day for the purposes of colleges of education (1.7.1969).	S.I. No. 709.
		Apptd. day for special schools (1.10.1969).	S.I. No. 1106.
c. 40	Family Allowances and National Insurance Act 1968.	Ss. 1(2)(3), 2(2) schs. 1, 2 rep.	44, s. 11(2), sch. 7.
c. 41	Countryside Act 1968 ...	Sch. 2 para. 6 ext. ...	48, s. 76, sch. 4 para. 93(1).
c. 42	Prices and Incomes Act 1968.	S. 12 rep. (S) ...	34, ss. 62(7), 69 (3), sch. 7.
c. 44	Finance Act 1968 ...	Ss. 1(1)(2)(4), 2(1), 3(1) (*c*), 4(3), 8(2), 9(*a*), 10 (1) rep.	32, s. 61(6), sch. 21 Pt. I.
		S. 14(1) rep.	32, s. 61(6), sch. 21 Pt. IV.
		S. 14(4) am.	32, s. 11(6).
		S. 14(5)–(7) ext. ...	32, s. 11(6).
		S. 15 am. (*retrosp.*) ...	32, s. 16(4).
		S. 15(2)(*b*) am., (*c*) added	32, s. 17.
		S. 15(3) saved	32, s. 16(5).
		S. 15(7) am.	32, s. 60, sch. 20 para. 17(31).
		S. 17(6) rep. in pt. ...	32, s. 61(6), sch. 21 Pt. IX.

Session and Chap. or No. of Measure	Short title or Subject	How affected	Chapter of 1969 Act or number of Measure or Statutory Instrument
1968: c. 44—*cont.*	Finance Act 1968 —*cont.*	S. 18(6) expld.	32, s. 60, sch. 20 para. 4(4)(*a*).
		S. 27 rep.	32, s. 61(6), sch. 21 Pt. IV.
		S. 30 am.	32, s. 60, sch. 20 para. 9(2).
		S. 33(5) rep.	32, ss. 60, 61(6), sch. 20 para. 3 (*c*), Sch. 21 Pt. IX.
		S. 35(2) am.	32, s. 40(1), sch. 17 Pt. III para. 29.
		S. 36(8) am.	32, s. 40(1), sch. 17 Pt. III para. 30.
		Ss. 38, 39 rep.	32, s. 61(6), sch. 21 Pt. V.
		S. 51(1)(3) rep., (4) rep. in pt.	32, s. 61(6), sch. 21 Pt. VII.
		S. 52(3) am.	48, s. 106.
		S. 55(6) am.	32, s. 60, sch. 20 para. 25(1).
		Schs. 1–4 rep., 5 para. 1 rep. in pt., 6 paras. 1–3 rep.	32, s. 61(6), sch. 21 Pt. I.
		Sch. 8 am. (*retrosp.*) ...	32, s. 16(4).
		para. 4(1) expld.	32, s. 60, sch. 20 para. 4(4)(*b*).
		Sch. 10 para. 6(1) rep. in pt.	32, s. 61(6), sch. 21 Pt. IX.
		para. 7 rep. ...	32, s. 61(6), sch. 21 Pt. X.
		Sch. 12 para. 15(2) am.	32, s. 42, sch. 19 para. 22(5).
		paras. 16, 17 rep.	32, s. 61(6), sch. 21 Pt. IV.
		paras. 18, 19 mod.	32, s. 42, sch. 19 para. 20.
		para. 20 mod. ...	32, s. 42, sch. 19 para. 21.
		para. 20(1) proviso rep.	32, s. 61(6), sch. 21 Pt. VI.
		para. 23(2)(3) appl.	32, s. 60, sch. 20 para. 25(2).
		Sch. 13 paras. 1(4), 5(1) rep.	32, ss. 60, 61(6), sch. 20 para. 3(*c*) sch. 21 Pt. IX.
		Sch. 14 paras. 1 rep. in pt., 2(2)(3) rep.	32, s. 61(6), sch. 21 Pt. V.
		Sch. 17 para. (1)(*b*) am.	32, s. 51(1).
c. 46	Health Services and Public Health Act 1968.	Apptd. days for certain specified provisions (E.)	S.I. Nos. 158, 296.
		(S.)	S.I. Nos. 225, 364.
		Ss. 59(1), 61(1) am. ...	S.I. No. 388.

Session and Chap. or No. of Measure	Short title or Subject	How affected	Chapter of 1969 Act or number of Measure or Statutory Instrument
1968: —*cont*			
c. 47	Sewerage (Scotland) Act 1968.	S. 22 ext.	48, s. 76, sch. 4 para. 93(1).
		S. 55(3) rep. in pt. ...	48, s. 141, sch. 11 Pt. II.
c. 49	Social Work (Scotland) Act 1968.	Apptd. days for certain specified provisions.	S.I. No. 430.
		Apptd. day for certain specified provisions (17.11.1969).	S.I. No. 1274.
		S. 30(1) am.	49, s. 27(1), sch. 2 Pt. II para. 5.
		S. 44(1A) added (*prosp.*)	54, ss. 72(3), 73 (4)(*c*), sch. 5 para. 57.
		S. 72(1A) added (*prosp.*), (2) am. (*prosp.*).	54, ss. 72(3), 73 (4)(*c*), sch. 5 para. 58(1)(2).
		S. 72(2) rep. in pt. (*prosp.*)	54, ss. 72(3), 73 (4)(*d*), sch. 6.
		S. 72(4) am. (*prosp.*) ...	54, ss. 72(3), 73 (4)(*c*), sch. 5 para. 58(3).
		S. 73(1) ext. (*prosp.*) ...	54, s. 72(3), sch. 5 para. 26.
		S. 73(1) am. (*prosp.*), (1A) added (*prosp.*), (2) am. (*prosp.*).	54, ss. 72(3), 73 (4)(*c*), sch. 5 para. 59.
		Ss. 73(2), 74(3)–(5) rep. in pt. (*prosp.*).	54, ss. 72(4), 73 (4)(*d*), sch. 6.
		S. 74(6) added (*prosp.*) ...	54, ss. 72(3), 73 (4)(*c*), sch. 5 para. 60.
		S. 75 am. (*prosp.*) ...	54, ss. 72(3), 73 (4)(*c*), sch. 5 para. 61.
		S. 75(1)(3) rep. in pt. (*prosp.*).	54, ss. 72(4), 73 (4)(*d*), sch. 6.
		S. 76(1)(2)(4) rep. in pt. (*prosp.*).	54, ss. 72(4), 73 (4)(*d*), sch. 6.
		S. 76(4) am. (*prosp.*) ...	54, ss. 72(3), 73 (4)(*c*), sch. 5 para. 62.
		S. 77(1)(*b*) rep. (*prosp.*) ...	54, ss. 72(4), 73 (4)(*d*), sch. 6.
		S. 90(1) rep. in pt. (*prosp.*)	54, ss. 72(3)(4), 73(4)(*c*)(*d*), sch. 5 para. 63, sch. 6.
		S. 94(1) definitions of "prescribed" added (*prosp.*), "supervision order" am. (*prosp.*).	54, ss. 72(3), 73 (4)(*c*), sch. 5 para. 64.
		S. 97(1) am. (*prosp.*) ...	54, ss. 72(3), 73 (4)(*c*), sch. 5 para. 65.
		S. 98(3) added	54, ss. 72(3), 73 (4)(*c*), sch. 5 para. 66.

Session and Chap. or No. of Measure	Short title or Subject	How affected	Chapter of 1969 Act or number of Measure or Statutory Instrument
1968: c. 49—*cont.*	Social Work (Scotland) Act 1968—*cont.*	Sch. 2 para. 10 rep. in pt. (*prosp.*).	54, ss. 72(4), 73 (4)(*d*), sch. 6.
		para. 10(2) added (*prosp.*).	54, ss. 72(3), 73 (4)(*c*), sch. 5 para. 67.
		para. 19 am. (*prosp.*).	54, ss. 72(3), 73 (4)(*c*), sch. 5 para. 68.
		Sch. 7 para. 1(1)(*a*) am.	54, ss. 72(3), 73 (4)(*c*), sch. 5 para. 69.
		Sch. 8 paras. 2–5 rep. (*prosp.*).	54, ss. 72(4), 73 (4)(*d*), sch. 6.
		para. 7(1) subst. (*prosp.*), (2) am. (*prosp.*), (3) rep. in pt. (*prosp.*), (4)(5) added (*prosp.*).	54, ss. 72(3), 73 (4)(*c*), sch. 5 para. 70.
		para. 9(2) am. (*prosp.*).	54, ss. 72(3), 73 (4)(*c*), sch. 5 para. 71.
		para. 10 am. (*prosp.*).	54, ss. 72(3), 73 (4)(*c*), sch. 5 para. 72.
		para. 17(1) am. ...	54, ss. 72(3), 73 (4)(*c*), sch. 5 para. 73.
		paras. 18 rep., 21, 35 rep. (*prosp.*).	54, ss. 72(4), 73 (4)(*d*), sch. 6.
		Sch. 8 para. 38 am. (*prosp.*).	54, ss. 72(3), 73(4)(*c*), sch. 5 para. 74.
		para. 51(1) am., (*e*) rep.	54, ss. 72(3), 73(4)(*c*), sch. 5 para. 75.
		para. 54 am. ...	54, ss. 72(3), 73(4)(*c*), sch. 5 para. 76.
		para. 59A added (*prosp.*).	54, ss. 72(3), 73(4)(*c*), sch. 5 para. 77.
		para. 61 subst. ...	49, s. 27(1), sch. 2 Pt. II para. 6.
		para. 62(1) subst.	49, s. 27(1), sch. 2 Pt. II para. 7.
		paras. 63, 64 rep.	49, s. 27, sch. 2 Pt. II para. 8, sch. 3.
		para. 65 subst. ...	49, s. 27(1), sch. 2 Pt. II para. 9.
		para. 67 am. ...	49, s. 27(1), sch. 2 Pt. II para. 10.
		para. 74(1) subst. (*prosp.*).	54, ss. 72(3), 73(4)(*c*,) sch. 5 para. 78.
		Sch. 9 Pt. I am. (*prosp.*)	54, ss. 72(3), 73(4)(*c*), sch. 5 paras. 79–81.

Session and Chap. or No. of Measrue	Short title or Subject	How affected	Chapter of 1969 Act or number of Measure or Statutory Instrument
1968:			
c. 49—*cont.*	Social Work (Scotland) Act 1968—*cont.*	Sch. 9 Pt. II rep. in pt. (*prosp.*).	54, ss. 72(3), 73(4)(*c*), sch. 5 para. 82.
		Sch. 9 Pt. II am. (*prosp.*)	54, ss. 72(3), 73(4)(*c*), sch. 5 para. 83.
c. 50	Hearing Aid Council Act 1968.	Apptd. day for whole Act (29.12.1969).	S.I. No. 1598.
c. 56	Swaziland Independence Act 1968.	Sch. para. 1 rep. ...	32, s. 61(6), sch. 21 Pt. IX.
c. 59	Hovercraft Act 1968 ...	S. 6(1) rep. in pt. ...	48, s. 141, sch. 11 Pt. II.
c. 61	Civil Aviation Act 1968	S. 27(3) rep.	48, s. 141, sch. 11 Pt. II.
c. 62	Clean Air Act 1968 ...	Apptd. day for remaining provisions (1.10.1969).	S.I. Nos. 995, 1006.
c. 64	Civil Evidence Act 1968	Apptd. day for Pt. I (ss. 1–10), s. 20(2) in relation to heresay evidence admissible in civil proceedings (1.10.1969).	S.I. No. 1104.
c. 65	Gaming Act 1968 ...	Apptd. days for certain specified provisions.	S.I. No. 488.
		Apptd. day for certain specified provisions (1.5.1969).	S.I. No. 549.
		Apptd. day for residue of Act (exc. ss. 19, 20(7), 23(6), sch. 5) (1.7.1970).	S.I. No. 1108.
		Sch. 2 para. 20(1)(*e*) rep. in pt.	32, s. 61(6), sch. 21 Pt. I.
		para. 20(1)(*f*), (3) added.	32, s. 3(9), sch. 9 para. 22.
		para. 48(1) am. ...	32, s. 5(13), sch. 11 para. 30.
		para. 60(*c*) am. ...	32, s. 3(9), sch. 9 para. 22.
		rep. in pt.	32, s. 61(6), sch. 21 Pt. I.
		Sch. 3 para. 9 am. ...	32, s. 3(9), sch. 9 para. 23.
		para. 9(*e*) rep. in pt.	32, s. 61(6), sch. 21 Pt. I.
		para. 17(1) am. ...	32, s. 5(13), sch. 11 para. 30.
		Sch. 4 para. 11 am. ...	32, s. 3(9), sch. 9 para. 24.
		para. 11(*e*) rep. in pt.	32, s. 61(6), sch. 21 Pt. I.
		para. 15(1) am. ...	32, s. 5(13), sch. 11 para. 30.
		Sch. 11 Pt. III rep. in pt.	32, s. 61(6), sch. 21 Pt. I.
c. 66	Restrictive Trade Practices Act 1968.	Transfer of functions ...	S.I. No. 1534.
		S. 2(7) rep. in pt.	S.I. No. 1498.
		Ss. 3(3)(4)(6) am.	S.I. No. 1534.
c. 67	Medicines Act 1968 ...	Ss. 1(1)(*a*), 5(2) am. ...	S.I. No. 388.

Session and Chap. or No. of Measure	Short title or Subject	How affected	Chapter of 1969 Act or number of Measure or Statutory Instrument
1968—*cont.*			
c. 69	Justices of the Peace Act 1968.	Apptd. days for s. 1(8), Sch. 3 Pts. II, III and sch. 5 in pt.	S.I. No. 376.
		Apptd. day in respect of the City of London (10.11.1969).	S.I. No. 1373.
c. 70	Law Reform (Miscellaneous Provisions) (Scotland) Act 1968.	Apptd. day for ss. 13–15 (1.12.1969).	S.I. No. 1609.
c. 72	Town and Country Planning Act 1968.	Apptd. day for s. 81, sch. 9 paras. 49(*a*), 73, sch. 11 in pt. (10.2.1969).	S.I. No. 16.
		Apptd. days for certain specified provisions.	S.I. No. 275.
		Ss. 21(6), 22(4) excl. ...	30, s. 64(7), sch. 6 para. 11(2).
		S. 29(2) rep., (4) rep. in pt.	48, s. 141, sch. 11 Pt. II.
		S. 33(1) ext.	48, s. 76, sch. 4 para. 93(1).
		S. 34 appl.	33, s. 34.
		S. 40 excl.	22, s. 2.
		Ss. 41(1)(*c*), 48(2)(*c*), 50(3)(*c*) am.	S.I. No. 388.
		S. 62 ext. ... {	30, s. 64(1). 48, s. 76, sch. 4 para. 93(1).
		S. 62(1)(*a*)–(*c*) ext. ...	30, s. 64(7), sch. 6 para. 10.
		Ss. 63, 69–73 ext. ...	48, s. 76, sch. 4 para. 93(1).
		S. 69 excl.	48, s. 76, sch. 4 para. 89(2).
		S. 69(1) mod.	48, s. 76, sch. 4 para. 89(1).
		S. 69(2)(*b*) am.	35, s. 17(1), sch. 3 para. 1(1)(2).
		S. 71(3) expld. (" operational land ").	48, s. 76, sch. 4 para. 93(4).
		S. 73(5) expld.	48, s. 76, sch. 4 para. 93(2).
		Ss. 83(1), 88(2) Transfer of functions.	S.I. No. 1498.
		S. 90 ext.	48, s. 76, sch. 4 para. 93(1).
		S. 92(1) ext. (mod.) ...	33, s. 33(1).
		S. 92(5) mod.	33, s. 33(2)(*a*).
		S. 93 ext. (mod.) ...	33, s. 33(2)(*b*).
		Ss. 93(3), 94(3), sch. 5 paras. 13–15 ext.	48, s. 76, sch. 4 para. 93(1).
		Sch. 6 ext.	48, s. 76, sch. 4 para. 93(1).
		expld.	48, s. 76, sch. 4 para. 93(2).
		expld. (" operational land ").	48, s. 76, sch. 4 para. 93(4).

Session and Chap. or No. of Measure	Short title or Subject	How affected	Chapter of 1969 Act or number of Measure or Statutory Instrument
1968: c. 72—*cont.*	Town and Country Planning Act—1968 *cont.*		
		Sch. 7 ext.	48, s. 76, sch. 4 para. 93(2).
		para. 4 expld. ...	48, s. 76, sch. 4 para. 93(1).
		Sch. 9 para. 6 am. ...	48, s. 76, sch. 4 para. 89(3).
		ext. ...	48, s. 76, sch. 4 para. 93(1).
		paras. 66(*b*), 71(*c*) rep. (S.) (*prosp.*).	30, s. 107, sch. 11.
c. 73	Transport Act 1968 ...	Apptd. day for Ss. 126–129, 130 and sch. 14 (residue), sch. 18 Pts. II (exc. ref. to s. 80(1)(*a*)), III in pt. (21.4.1969).	S.I. No. 507.
		Apptd. days for certain specified provisions.	S.I. No. 1613.
		S. 6(1) am., (2) rep. in pt.	48, s. 76, sch. 4 para. 88.
		S. 9(1) appl. (L.T.E.) ...	35, s. 13.
		S. 13(2) am. (15.2.1971)...	19, s. 10(3), sch. 2 para. 31.
		S. 21 ext. (mod.) (L.T.E.)	35, s. 23(6).
		Ss. 24(3)(*a*) rep., 33(2) rep. (London), 41(6) rep.	35, s. 47(2), sch. 6.
		Ss. 49(1)–(3), 50(7)–(10), 51(2)(4)–(6) ext. (mod.) (L.T.E.).	35, s. 6(2).
		S. 51(5), excl. (L.T.E.) ...	35, s. 7(7).
		S. 54(1) am. (L.T.E.) ...	35, s. 25(1).
		Ss. 54(5)(*d*) rep. in pt., 59(4) rep.	35, s. 47(2), sch. 6.
		S. 94(10) excl. in pt. ...	48, s. 81(3).
		Ss. 116–120, 125 am. (L.T.E.).	35, s. 17(1), sch. 3 para. 1(1)(2).
		S. 137 ext. (L.T.E.). ...	35, s. 13.
		S. 138(3) rep. in pt. ...	35, s. 47(2), sch. 6.
		Ss. 141, 144 am. (L.T.E.).	35, 17(1) sch. 3 para. 1(1)(2).
		Ss. 145(2), 159(1) definitions of " the Boards " rep. in pt., " the London Transport Board " rep.	35, s. 47(2), sch. 6.
		S. 161(2) am.	32, s. 60, sch. 20 para. 25(1).
		S. 162 am. (L.T.E.) ...	35, s. 17(1), sch. 3 para. 1(1)(2).
		Sch. 4 ext. (mod.) ...	35, ss. 21(4), 22 (3).
		Sch. 4 paras. 7–12 ext. (L.T.E.).	35, s. 16(3), sch. 2 para. 8.
		Sch. 5 Pt. I para. 2 am. (15.2.1971).	19, s. 10(3), sch. 2 para. 31.
		Sch. 16 para. 4(5) am. (L.T.E.).	35, s. 17(1), sch. 3 para. 5(1).
		para. 5 ext. (L.T.E.).	35, s. 17(1), sch. 3 para. 7(1).
		para. 7(1) am (L.T.E.).	35, s. 17(1), sch. 3 para. 1(1)(2).

Session and Chap. or No. of Measure	Short title or Subject	How affected	Chapter of 1969 Act or number of Measure or Statutory Instrument
1968—*cont.*			
c. 74	Customs (Import Deposits) Act 1968.	Ss. 1(1), 3(4) am. ...	64, s. 1(1).
		Sch. 1 am.	S.I. No. 240.
		Sch. 2 para. 7(1) expld. (*retrosp.*).	64, s. 1(2).
c. 77	Sea Fisheries Act 1968 ...	Apptd. day for Ss. 5–14, sch. 1 Pt. II, sch. 2 Pt. II in pt. (24.11.1969).	S.I. No. 1551.
		S. 15 Transfer of functions.	S.I. No. 388.
C.A.M.			
No. 1... ...	Pastoral Measure 1968 ...	S. 29 saved	38, s. 5(4).
		S. 45 ext.	22, s. 1(1).
		S. 66 am.	22, s. 3.
		S. 91 proviso rep. ...	22, s. 7(3).
No. 2... ...	Prayer Book (Further Provisions) Measure 1968.	Ss. 2(1), 4 am. (*prosp.*) ...	C.A.M. No. 2, s. 3(5).
1969:			
c. 10	Mines and Quarries (Tips) Act 1969.	Apptd. day for Pts. I, II (30.6.1969).	S.I. Nos. 804, 805, 870.
c. 15	Representation of the People Act 1969.	Apptd. days for whole Act (exc. s. 18(1), sch. 1 Pt. II para. 4) not later than 16.2.1970.	S.I. No. 630.
c. 19	Decimal Currency Act 1969.	S. 10 excl.	44, s. 8(4).
c. 27	Vehicle and Driving Licences Act 1969.	Apptd. day for Ss. 16(5), 33, 34, 38, sch. 2 para. 16(5) (30.6.1969).	S.I. No. 866.
		Apptd. day for s. 18(2) (14.7.1969).	S.I. No. 913.
		Apptd. day for s. 2(3)(4) (19.11.1969).	S.I. No. 1579.
		Apptd. day for Ss. 9, 10, 16(6), 22, 25, 26, 28(1) (2)(*a*)(*c*) (4) (5) (6), 30, 31, 32, 35 in pt., 37 in pt., sch. 2 paras. 6, 8, 9, 10, 11, 12 (1.2.1970).	S.I. No. 1637.
		S. 2(5) expld.	48, s. 76, sch. 4 para. 71.
		S. 4(2) subst.	32, s. 6(2), sch. 12 Pt. II para. 5.
		S. 4(8) rep. (*prosp.*) ...	27, s. 4(9).
		S. 17(*bb*) subst. ...	32, s. 6(2), sch. 12 Pt. II para. 6.
		S. 33(1) rep. in pt. ...	32, s. 61(6), sch. 21 Pt. I.
c. 30	Town and Country Planning (Scotland) Act 1969.	Apptd. day for certain specified provisions (8.12.1969).	S.I. No. 1569.
		S. 30(2) rep., (4) rep. in pt.	48, s. 141, sch. 11 Pt. II.
		S. 34(1) ext.	48, s. 76, sch. 4 para. 93(1).
		S. 37 am.	34, s. 69(2), sch. 6 para. 47.

Session and Chap. or No. of Measure	Short title or Subject	How affected	Chapter of 1969 Act or number of Measure or Statutory Instrument
1969: c. 30—*cont.*	Town and Country Planning (Scotland) Act 1969—*cont.*	Ss. 62, 63, 70–74 ext. ...	48, s. 76, sch. 4 para. 93(1).
		S. 70 excl.	48, s. 76, sch. 4 para. 92(2).
		S. 70(1) mod.	48, s. 76, sch. 4 para. 92(1).
		S. 72(3) expld. ("operational land").	48, s. 76, sch. 4 para. 93(4).
		S. 74(5) expld.	48, s. 76, sch. 4 para. 93(2).
		S. 84(1) Transfer of functions.	S.I. No. 1498.
		Ss. 89, 92(3), 93(2) ext. ...	48, s. 76, sch. 4 para. 93(1).
		S. 164 excl.	48, s. 76, sch. 4 para. 93(1).
		Sch. 4 paras. 13–15 schs. 5–7 ext.	48, s. 76, sch. 4 para. 93(1).
		Sch. 5 expld. ("operational land").	48, s. 76, sch. 4 para. 93(4).
		Sch. 5, sch. 7 para. 4 expld.	48, s. 76, sch. 4 para. 93(2).
		Sch. 9 para. 5 am. ...	48, s. 76, sch. 4 para. 92(3).
		ext. ...	48, s. 76, sch. 4 para. 93(1).
c. 32	Finance Act 1969 ...	Sch. 7 para. 4(1) rep. ...	32, s. 61(6), sch. 21 Pt. I.
c. 35	Transport (London) Act 1969.	Apptd. day for ss. 19(8), 27, 28, 29(4), 41(2)(3) in pt., 43, 45, 46, 47(1) (3)–(5) (8.8.1969).	S.I. No. 1130.
		Apptd. days for remaining provisions except ss. 19(1)–(7), 29, 30, 32 not later than 1.1.1970.	S.I. No. 1510.
		Apptd. day for S.19(1) (*a*) (19.11.1969).	S.I. 1588.
		S. 19(1)(*b*)–(*d*), (2)–(7) rep.	60, s. 1.
c. 39	Age of Majority (Scotland) Act 1969.	Apptd. day for whole Act (1.1.1970).	S.I. No. 1243.
		S. 1 appl.	32, s. 16.
		Sch. 2 para. 3 rep. ...	32, ss. 16(1), 61 (6), sch. 21 Pt. IV.
c. 40	Medical Act 1969 ...	Apptd. days for whole Act not later than 1.1.1971.	S.I. No. 1492.
c. 44	National Insurance Act 1969.	Apptd. days for whole Act.	S.I. No. 1018.
c. 45	Iron and Steel Act 1969	S. 2(1) Power to cont. ...	45, s. 6(1)(2).
		S. 3(1)(*b*) rep. (*prosp.*) ...	45, s. 6(3).
		Ss. 4, 5 Power to cont. ...	45, s. 6(1)(2).
		S. 11(1) Transfer of functions.	S.I. No. 1498.

Session and Chap. or No. of Measure	Short title or Subject	How affected	Chapter of 1969 Act or number of Measure or Statutory Instrument
1969—*cont.*			
c. 46	Family Law Reform Act 1969.	Apptd. day for Pts. I (ss. 1–13), II (ss. 14–19), IV (ss. 26–28), schs. 1–3 (1.1.1970).	S.I. No. 1140.
		S. 1 appl.	32, s. 16.
		S. 9 excl.	32, s. 11(4).
		S. 13 am.	32, s. 16(2).
		Sch. 2 para. 3 rep. ...	32, ss. 16(1), 61 (6), sch. 21 Pt. IV.
c. 48	Post Office Act 1969 ...	Apptd. day for whole Act (1.10.1969).	S.I. No. 1066.
		Sch. 4 para. 83(1)–(3) am.	34, s. 69(2), sch. 6 para. 48.
		Sch. 9 para. 36 Transfer of functions.	S.I. No. 1498.
c. 49	Education (Scotland) Act 1969.	Sch. 2 Pt. 1 para. 7(1) rep. (1.8.1970).	49, s. 27(1).
c. 50	Trustee Savings Banks Act 1969.	Apptd. day for whole Act (1.10.1969).	S.I. No. 1285.
c. 54	Children and Young Persons Act 1969.	Apptd. day for ss. 69, 70, 72(3)(4) in pt., 73, sch. 5 paras. 63, 64(1), 69, 73, 75, 76, sch. 6 (16.11.1969).	S.I. No. 1552.
		Apptd. days for certain specified provisions.	S.I. No. 1565.
c. 58	Administration of Justice Act 1969.	Apptd. days for whole Act (exc. ss. 1–5, 9(1), 10) not later than (1.1.1970).	S.I. No. 1607.
c. 63	Police Act 1969 ...	Apptd. day for ss. 1(4), 2, 5–7 (17.12.1969).	S.I. No. 1775.
c. 65	Ulster Defence Regiment Act 1969.	Apptd. day for whole Act (1.1.1970).	S.I. No. 1860.

INDEX

TO THE

Public General Acts

AND

CHURCH ASSEMBLY MEASURES, 1969

A

C

PART I.—CARE AND OTHER TREATMENT OF JUVENILES
THROUGH COURT PROCEEDINGS
Care of children and young persons through juvenile courts
§ 1. Care proceedings in juvenile courts, II, p. 1477.
2. Provisions supplementary to s. 1, II, p. 1479.
3. Further supplementary provisions relating to s. 1(2)(*f*), II, p. 1482.

Consequential changes in criminal proceedings etc.
4. Prohibition of criminal proceedings for offences by children, II, p. 1485.
5. Restrictions on criminal proceedings for offences by young persons, II, p. 1485.
6. Summary trial of young persons, II, p. 1487.
7. Alterations in treatment of young offenders etc., II, p. 1488.
8. Finger-printing of suspected young persons, II, p. 1489.
9. Investigations by local authorities, II, p. 1490.
10. Further limitations on publication of particulars of children and young persons etc., II, p. 1490.

Supervision
11. Supervision orders, II, p. 1491.
12. Power to include requirements in supervision orders, II, p. 1491.
13. Selection of supervisor, II, p. 1493.
14. Duty of supervisor, II, p. 1494.
15. Variation and discharge of supervision orders, II, p. 1494.
16. Provisions supplementary to s. 15, II, p. 1496.
17. Termination of supervision, II, p. 1499.
18. Supplementary provisions relating to supervision orders, II, p. 1499.
19. Facilities for the carrying out of supervisors' directions, II, p. 1501.

E

F

3 R* 4

G

H

PART I.—FINANCIAL ASSISTANCE TOWARDS COST OF IMPROVEMENTS AND
CONVERSIONS

Grants by local authorities

§ 1. Improvement grants, standard grants and special grants, I, p. 684.

Improvement grants

2. Improvement grants, I, p. 684.
3. Conditions for approval of application for improvement grants, I, p. 685.
4. Approval of application for improvement grant, I, p. 685.
5. Amount of improvement grant, I, p. 686.
6. Payment of improvement grant, I, p. 686.

Standard grants

7, and schedule 1. Standard amenities, I, p. 687.
8. Standard grants, I, p. 687.
9. Conditions for approval of application for standard grant, I, p. 688.
10. Approval of application for standard grant, I, p. 689.
11, and schedule 1. Amount of standard grant, I, pp. 690, 733.

Effect of standard grant on amount of improvement grant

12. Effect of standard grant on amount of improvement grant, I, p. 690.

Special grants

13. Special grants, I, p. 690.
14. Approval of application for special grant, I, p. 691.
15. Amount of special grant, I, p. 691.

Contributions towards grants

16. Contributions towards grants, I, p. 691.

*Contributions towards cost of improvements and
conversions carried out by or under arrangements
with housing authorities*

17. Contributions to local authorities and other bodies for dwellings improved by them or provided by them by conversion, I, p. 692.
18. Improvement contributions, I, p. 692.
19, and schedule 1. Standard contributions, I, pp. 693, 733.
20. Effect of standard contribution on amount of improvement contribution, I, p. 693.
21. Contributions for dwellings provided or improved by housing associations under arrangements with local authorities, I, p. 694.

Power to vary contributions

22. Power to vary contributions, I, p. 695.

Supplemental

23. Statement of reasons for not approving application for grant or fixing less than maximum for improvement grant, I, p. 696.
24. Assistance for works specified in applications for grants under former enactments, I, p. 696.
25. Special provisions as to parsonages, almshouses, etc., I, p. 696.
26. Local authorities for purposes of Part I, I, p. 697.
27. Interpretation, I, p. 697.

*Alteration of the British Steel Corporation's financial
Structure and Provisions consequential thereon*

§ 1. Reduction of the Corporation's commencing capital debt, I, p. 987.
2. Public investment in the Corporation otherwise than by way of loan, I, p. 988.
3. Limit on borrowing by, and investment in, the Corporation, I, p. 989.
4. Power of the Minister to effect, for purposes of section 2(1), notional capitalisation of reserves of the Corporation and the publicly-owned companies, I, p. 989.
5. The Corporation's financial duty, I, p. 989.
6. Duration of certain of the foregoing provisions, I, p. 990.

*Miscellaneous Provisions relating to the British Steel Corporation
and the publicly-owned Companies*

7. Power of the Corporation and the publicly-owned companies to borrow money in foreign currency, I, p. 991.
8. Power of the Minister to vest in the Corporation property, rights, liabilities and obligations of certain publicly-owned companies and to dissolve certain such companies, I, p. 992.
9. Modification of provisions of the Finance Act 1965 as to company reconstructions without change of ownership in their application, in certain circumstances, to the Corporation, I, p. 992.

J

L

N

O

P

3 S

S

T

U

V

STATUTORY PUBLICATIONS OFFICE

THE INDEX TO
THE STATUTES IN FORCE

These two volumes (A–K, L–Z) index by subject-matter all the existing public general statute law under well-established headings linked by numerous cross-references. The index entries have against them references to the enactment or enactments which support the subject matter.

Since the references are to enactments (and not to pages of any book), the usefulness of the volumes is not limited to any particular set of statutes.

There is a chronological table showing the headings under which each Act or section is indexed in volumes, and a similar table for Church Assembly Measures.

The INDEX provides a service which is of the utmost value and which for its adaptability is unique.

A free list of Statutory Publications Office titles is obtainable from Her Majesty's Stationery Office, P6A, Atlantic House, Holborn Viaduct, London E.C.1

HMSO

HER MAJESTY'S STATIONERY OFFICE

Government Bookshops

49 High Holborn, London WC1
13a Castle Street, Edinburgh EH2 3AR
109 St. Mary Street, Cardiff CF1 1JW
Brazennose Street, Manchester M60 8AS
50 Fairfax Street, Bristol BS1 3DE
258 Broad Street, Birmingham 1
7 Linenhall Street, Belfast BT2 8AY

Government publications are also available
through any bookseller